Features for Students

MyStatLab provides students with a personalized, interactive environment where they can learn at their own pace and measure their progress.

Interactive tutorial exercises

MyStatLab's homework and practice exercises, correlated to the exercises in the textbook, are generated algorithmically, giving students unlimited opportunity for practice and mastery. Exercises include guided solutions, sample problems, and learning aids for extra help at point-of-use, and they offer helpful feedback when students enter incorrect answers.

StatCrunch

StatCrunch offers both numerical and data analysis and uses interactive graphics to illustrate the connection between objects selected in a graph and the underlying data. In most MyStatLab courses, all data sets from the textbook are pre-loaded in StatCrunch, and StatCrunch is also available as a tool from all online homework and practice exercises.

Student Purchasing Options

There are many ways for students to sign up for MyStatLab:
- Use the access kit bundled with a new textbook
- Purchase a stand-alone access kit from the bookstore
- Register online through www.coursecompass.com

PEARSON

www.pearsonhighered.com

A ROADMAP FOR SELECTING A STATISTICAL METHOD

TYPE OF DATA

Type of Analysis	Numerical	Categorical
Describing a group or several groups	Ordered array, stem-and-leaf display, frequency distribution, relative frequency distribution, percentage distribution, cumulative percentage distribution, histogram, polygon, cumulative percentage polygon **(Sections 2.4, 2.6)** Mean, median, mode, geometric mean, quartiles, range, interquartile range, standard deviation, variance, coefficient of variation, boxplot **(Sections 3.1, 3.2, 3.3)** Index numbers **(Online Section 16.8)**	Summary table, bar chart, pie chart, Pareto chart **(Sections 2.3, 2.5)**
Inference about one group	Confidence interval estimate of the mean **(Sections 8.1 and 8.2)** t test for the mean **(Section 9.2)** Chi-square test for a variance **(Online Section 12.7)**	Confidence interval estimate of the proportion **(Section 8.3)** Z test for the proportion **(Section 9.4)**
Comparing two groups	Tests for the difference in the means of two independent populations **(Section 10.1)** Wilcoxon rank sum test **(Section 12.5)** Paired t test **(Section 10.2)** F test for the difference between two variances **(Section 10.4)**	Z test for the difference between two proportions **(Section 10.3)** Chi-square test for the difference between two proportions **(Section 12.1)** McNemar test for two related samples **(Section 12.4)**
Comparing more than two groups	One-way analysis of variance for comparing several means **(Section 11.1)** Kruskal-Wallis test **(Section 12.6)** Two-way analysis of variance **(Section 11.2)** Randomized block design **(Online Section 11.3)**	Chi-square test for differences among more than two proportions **(Section 12.2)**
Analyzing the relationship between two variables	Scatter plot, time series plot **(Section 2.7)** Covariance, coefficient of correlation **(Section 3.5)** Simple linear regression **(Chapter 13)** t test of correlation **(Section 13.7)** Time series forecasting **(Chapter 16)**	Contingency table, side-by-side bar chart, PivotTables **(Sections 2.3, 2.5, 2.8)** Chi-square test of independence **(Section 12.3)**
Analyzing the relationship between two or more variables	Multiple regression **(Chapters 14 and 15)**	

Statistics for Managers

Using Microsoft Excel

SIXTH EDITION

Statistics for Managers

Using Microsoft Excel

SIXTH EDITION

David M. Levine

Department of Statistics and Computer Information Systems

Zicklin School of Business, Baruch College, City University of New York

David F. Stephan

Department of Statistics and Computer Information Systems

Zicklin School of Business, Baruch College, City University of New York

Timothy C. Krehbiel

Department of Management

Richard T. Farmer School of Business, Miami University

Mark L. Berenson

Department of Management and Information Systems

School of Business, Montclair State University

Prentice Hall

Boston   Columbus   Indianapolis   New York   San Francisco   Upper Saddle River
Amsterdam   Cape Town   Dubai   London   Madrid   Milan   Munich   Paris   Montreal   Toronto
Delhi   Mexico City   Sao Paulo   Sydney   Hong Kong   Seoul   Singapore   Taipei   Tokyo

Editorial Director: Sally Yagan
Editor in Chief: Eric Svendsen
Senior Acquisitions Editor: Chuck Synovec
Editorial Project Manager: Mary Kate Murray
Editorial Assistant: Jason Calcano
Director of Marketing: Patrice Lumumba Jones
Senior Marketing Manager: Anne Fahlgren
Marketing Assistant: Melinda Jensen
Senior Managing Editor: Judy Leale
Senior Operations Supervisor: Arnold Vila
Senior Art Director: Kenny Beck
Text Designers: Dina Curro/Suzanne Behnke
Cover Designer: LCI Design
Manager, Visual Research: Beth Brenzel
Photo Researcher: Kathy Ringrose AV

Manager, Rights and Permissions: Zina Arabia
Image Permission Coordinator: Angelique Sharps
Manager, Cover Visual Research & Permissions: Karen Sanatar
Cover Art: Red shopping carts/Pierre Desrosiers/ Getty Images
Media Editor: Allison Longley
Media Project Manager: Lisa Rinaldi
Full-Service Project Manager: Heidi Allgair
Composition: GGS Higher Education Resources, a Division of PreMedia Global, Inc.
Printer/Binder: Courier/Kendallville
Cover Printer: Lehigh-Phoenix Color/Hagerstown
Text Font: 10.5/12.5 Times New RomanPS

Photo Credits: p. viii: Rudy Krehbiel; pp. 2–3: Photos.com; pp. 3, 7: Maga, Shutterstock; pp. 14–15: Don Farrall, PhotoDisc/Getty Images; pp. 15, 59: Steve Coleccs, iStockphoto; pp. 84–85: Don Farrall, PhotoDisc/Getty Images; pp. 85, 121: Steve Coleccs, iStockphoto; pp. 132–133: Ljupco Smokovski, Shutterstock; pp. 133, 154: © Alan Levenson/Corbis, all rights reserved; pp. 160–161: Sebastian Kaulitzki, Shutterstock; pp. 161, 183: Monkey Business Images, Shutterstock; pp. 192–193: Alexander Kalina, Shutterstock; pp. 193, 215: Lee Morris, Shutterstock; pp. 222–223: R. Mackay Photography, Shutterstock; pp. 223, 243: © Corbis, all rights reserved; pp. 250–251: Kristy Pargeter, Shutterstock; pp. 251, 283: Marcin Balcerzak, Shutterstock; pp. 296–297: Peter Close, Shutterstock; pp. 297, 326: Maja Schon, Shutterstock; pp. 334–335: Travis Manley, Shutterstock; pp. 335, 366: Michael Bradley, Getty Images; p. 381: Joggie Botma, Shutterstock; pp. 381, 408: Alexey U, Shutterstock; p. 423: KzlKurt, Shutterstock; pp. 423, 458: Zastol'skiy' victor Leonidovich, Shutterstock; p. 471: crystalfoto, Shutterstock; pp. 471, 511: Dmitriy Shironosov, Shutterstock; p. 527: Courtesy of Sharon Rosenberg; pp. 527, 558: George Bailey, Shutterstock; pp. 570–571: Giedrius Dagys, iStockphoto.com; pp. 571, 596: Rob Crandall, Stock Boston; p. 604: Rudyanto Wijaya, iStockphoto.com; pp. 604, 643: Cathy Melloan/PhotoEdit Inc.; pp. 654–655: Ian Logan/Taxi/Getty Images; pp. 655, 684: Kim Steele/Image Bank/Getty; pp. 701, 706: Stepan Popov, iStockphoto.com; Ch. 19 Photos: Jupiter Unlimited.

Credits and acknowledgments borrowed from other sources and reproduced, with permission, in this textbook appear on appropriate page within text.

Library of Congress Cataloging-in-Publication Data

Statistics for managers using Microsoft Excel / David M. Levine . . . [et al.].—6th ed.
   p. cm.
Includes bibliographical references and index.
ISBN-13: 978-0-13-703519-9
ISBN-10: 0-13-703519-5
   1. Microsoft Excel (Computer file) 2. Management—Statistical methods.   3. Commercial statistics.
4. Electronic spreadsheets. 5. Management—Statistical methods—Computer programs.   6. Commercial statistics—Computer programs.   I. Levine, David M., 1946–
   HD30.215.S73 2011
   519.50285'554—dc22

                                                          2009052398

To our wives,
Marilyn L., Mary N., Patti K., and Rhoda B.,

---

and to our children,
Sharyn, Mark, Ed, Rudy, Rhonda, Kathy, and Lori

About the Authors

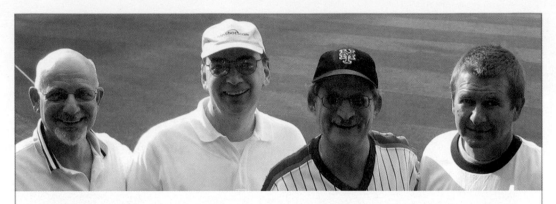

The textbook authors meet to discuss statistics at a Mets baseball game. Shown left to right: Mark Berenson, David Stephan, David Levine, and Tim Krehbiel.

David M. Levine is Professor Emeritus of Statistics and Computer Information Systems at Baruch College (City University of New York). He received B.B.A. and M.B.A. degrees in Statistics from City College of New York and a Ph.D. degree from New York University in Industrial Engineering and Operations Research. He is nationally recognized as a leading innovator in statistics education and is the co-author of 14 books, including such best-selling statistics textbooks as *Statistics for Managers Using Microsoft Excel*, *Basic Business Statistics: Concepts and Applications*, *Business Statistics: A First Course*, and *Applied Statistics for Engineers and Scientists Using Microsoft Excel and Minitab*.

He also is the co-author of *Even You Can Learn Statistics: A Guide for Everyone Who Has Ever Been Afraid of Statistics,* currently in its second edition, *Six Sigma for Green Belts and Champions* and *Design for Six Sigma for Green Belts and Champions*, and the author of *Statistics for Six Sigma Green Belts*, all published by FT Press, a Pearson imprint, and *Quality Management*, 3rd edition, McGraw-Hill/Irwin (2005). He is also the author of *Video Review of Statistics* and *Video Review of Probability*, both published by Video Aided Instruction, and the statistics module of the MBA primer published by Cengage Learning. He has published articles in various journals, including *Psychometrika*, *The American Statistician*, *Communications in Statistics*, *Multivariate Behavioral Research*, *Journal of Systems Management*, *Quality Progress*, and *The American Anthropologist*, and given numerous talks at Decision Sciences, American Statistical Association, and Making Statistics More Effective in Schools of Business conferences. Levine has also received several awards for outstanding teaching and curriculum development from Baruch College.

David F. Stephan is an independent instructional technologist. An Instructor/Lecturer of Computer Information Systems at Baruch College (City University of New York) for over 20 years, he also was an Assistant to the Dean (Business & Public Administration) & Provost for computing. He pioneered the use of computer classrooms for business teaching, devised interdisciplinary multimedia tools, and created techniques for teaching computer applications in a business context. Stephan is also the developer of PHStat2, the Pearson Education statistics add-in system for Microsoft Excel and the co-author of *Even You Can Learn Statistics: A Guide for Everyone Who Has Ever Been Afraid of Statistics*.

Timothy C. Krehbiel is Professor of Management and the Endres Faculty

Fellow at the Farmer School of Business at Miami University in Oxford, Ohio. He teaches undergraduate and graduate courses in business statistics. In 1996, he received the prestigious Instructional Innovation Award from the Decision Sciences Institute. He has also received the Farmer School of Business Administration Effective Educator Award and the MBA Teaching Excellence Award and has twice been named MBA professor of the year.

Krehbiel's research interests span many areas of business and applied statistics. His work appears in numerous journals, including *Quality Management Journal, Ecological Economics, International Journal of Production Research, Journal of Purchasing and Supply Management, Journal of Applied Business Research, Journal of Marketing Management, Communications in Statistics, Decision Sciences Journal of Innovative Education, Journal of Education for Business, Marketing Education Review, Journal of Accounting Education*, and *Teaching Statistics*. He is a co-author of three statistics text-books published by Prentice Hall: *Business Statistics: A First Course, Basic Business Statistics*, and *Statistics for Managers Using Microsoft Excel*. Krehbiel is also a co-author of the book *Sustainability Perspectives in Business and Resources*.

Krehbiel graduated *summa cum laude* with a B.A. in history from McPherson College and earned an M.S. and a Ph.D. in statistics from the University of Wyoming.

Mark L. Berenson is Professor of Management and Information Systems at

Montclair State University (Montclair, New Jersey) and also Professor Emeritus of Statistics and Computer Information Systems at Bernard M. Baruch College (City University of New York). He currently teaches graduate and undergraduate courses in statistics and in operations management in the School of Business and an undergraduate course in international justice and human rights that he co-developed in the College of Humanities and Social Sciences.

Berenson received a B.A. in economic statistics and an M.B.A. in business statistics from City College of New York and a Ph.D. in business from the City University of New York.

Berenson's research has been published in *Decision Sciences Journal of Innovative Education, Review of Business Research, The American Statistician, Communications in Statistics, Psychometrika, Educational and Psychological Measurement, Journal of Management Sciences and Applied Cybernetics, Research Quarterly, Stats Magazine, The New York Statistician, Journal of Health Administration Education, Journal of Behavioral Medicine*, and *Journal of Surgical Oncology*. His invited articles have appeared in *The Encyclopedia of Measurement & Statistics* and *Encyclopedia of Statistical Sciences*. He is co-author of 11 statistics texts published by Prentice Hall, including *Statistics for Managers using Microsoft Excel, Basic Business Statistics: Concepts and Applications*, and *Business Statistics: A First Course*.

Over the years, Berenson has received several awards for teaching and for innovative contributions to statistics education. In 2005, he was the first recipient of The Catherine A. Becker Service for Educational Excellence Award at Montclair State University.

Brief Contents

Contents

4 Basic Probability   132

5 Discrete Probability Distributions   160

6 The Normal Distribution and Other Continuous Distributions   192

9 Fundamentals of Hypothesis Testing: One-Sample Tests 296

10 Two-Sample Tests 334

11 Analysis of Variance 380

17 Statistical Applications in Quality Management 654

18 Data Analysis Overview 700

🌐 *Online Chapter:* 19 Decision Making

Appendices 709

Preface

Educational Philosophy

In our many years of teaching business statistics, we have continually searched for ways to improve the teaching of these courses. Our active participation in a series of Making Statistics More Effective in Schools and Business (MSMESB), Decision Sciences Institute (DSI), and American Statistical Association (ASA) conferences as well as the reality of serving a diverse group of students at large universities have shaped our vision for teaching these courses. Over the years, our vision has come to include these key principles:

1. **Show students the relevance of statistics.** Students need a frame of reference when learning statistics, especially when statistics is not their major. That frame of reference for business students should be the functional areas of business, such as accounting, finance, information systems, management, and marketing. Each statistics topic needs to be presented in an applied context related to at least one of these functional areas. The focus in teaching each topic should be on its application in business, the interpretation of results, the evaluation of the assumptions, and the discussion of what should be done if the assumptions are violated.

2. **Familiarize students with the statistical programs used in the business world.** Integrating these programs into all aspects of an introductory statistics course allows the course to focus on interpretation of results instead of computations. Introductory business statistics courses should recognize that programs with statistical functions are commonly found on a business decision maker's desktop computer, therefore making the *interpretation* of results more important than the tedious hand calculations required to produce them.

3. **Provide guidance to students for using statistical programs.** Books should contain clear instructions to help students effectively use the programs that are integrated with the study of statistics, without having those instructions dominate the book or the course in which they are used.

4. **Give students ample practice in understanding how to apply statistics to business.** Both classroom examples and homework exercises should involve actual or realistic data as much as possible. Students should work with data sets, both small and large, and be encouraged to look beyond the statistical analysis of data to the interpretation of results in a managerial context.

New to This Edition

MyStatLab.com This online homework, tutorial, and assessment system provides book-specific sets of course materials, including free-response exercises that are algorithmically generated for unlimited practice and mastery. Students use MyStatLab to independently improve their understanding and performance in the course. Instructors use MyStatLab as part of a complete course management system that allows them to create their own homework assignments and assessments (or use those already created for use with this book) as well as to import and work with TestGen tests that were created previously.

This sixth edition of *Statistics for Managers Using Microsoft Excel* enhances the statistical content of previous editions in these ways:

- A revised and simplified notation for test statistics in hypothesis testing.
- New chapter-ending "Using Statistics Revisited" sections that reinforce the statistical methods and applications discussed in each chapter.
- The use of the DCOVA framework (**D**efine, **C**ollect, **O**rganize, **V**isualize, and **A**nalyze) as an integrated approach for applying statistics to help solve business problems.
- A new chapter (Chapter 18) that helps students apply the statistics learned in the previous 17 chapters to future real-world situations that require the analysis of data.

- An expanded discussion of using PivotTables to summarize and explore multidimensional data.
- Many new applied examples and exercises, with data from *The Wall Street Journal, USA Today*, and other sources.
- Additional "Think About This" essays that provide greater insight into what has just been learned and raise important issues about the application of statistical knowledge.
- Even more illustrated and annotated worksheet results that are directly linked to specific step-by-step instructions.

In this sixth edition of *Statistics for Managers Using Microsoft Excel*, the instructions for using Excel have been revised, reorganized, and enhanced in new end-of-chapter Excel Guides and back-of-the book Appendices. These sections support students by:

- Providing a readiness checklist and orientation that help guide students through the process of getting ready to use Excel (the Chapter 1 Excel Guide and Appendix B "Basic Excel Knowledge").
- Giving students the option to avoid using instructions that require the use of the Analysis ToolPak, the Excel component not included in Mac Excel 2008 and OpenOffice.org Calc 3, the freely available, open-source, Excel work-alike program.
- Incorporating Excel Guide Workbooks that serve as models and templates for using Excel for statistical problem-solving. These free and reusable workbooks, annotated examples of which appear throughout the chapters of this book, can be used by students in their other courses or in their jobs.
- Allowing students to choose to either maximize their in-depth learning of Excel specifics or minimize their time spent using Excel. Students can use *In-Depth Excel* instructions to discover low-level details such as the specifics of Excel worksheet functions and formulas **or** use *PHStat2* instructions to directly create, through an automated process, completed results containing the low-level details discussed in the *In-Depth Ex*cel instructions. ***Using either way, students end up with results that are consistent with the annotated Excel Guide Workbook results used as in-chapter illustrations!***
- Discussing a number of common operations, such as opening, saving, and printing workbooks as well as handy advanced features, such as Paste Special, that facilitate the use of Excel (the new Appendix C "Useful Excel Commands").
- Presenting in one place all the technical instructions that a student may need, from how to use and download files from the book's companion Web site to how to configure Excel for use with this book (the newAppendix D).
- Answering frequently-asked questions about using Excel and PHStat2, the Pearson statistical add-in for Microsoft Windows-based Excel versions (the new Appendix G).

These in-book resources are complemented by the following electronic media:

- Downloadable data workbooks used by in-chapter examples and problems. (See Appendix F for a complete dictionary list of these files.)
- The latest version of PHStat2 (free to students using this book), that comes with simplified setup instructions that no longer require the use of Excel Analysis ToolPak and Analysis ToolPak-VBA add-ins.
- Downloadable self-documenting Excel Guide Workbooks that illustrate solutions for over 60 statistical topics and that serve as freely reusable templates for future problem-solving.
- Electronic learning aids, including the end-of-chapter Web Cases, the optional Online Topics and Chapter 19 PDF files, and a guide for using Excel 2010 with this book.
- A complete companion Web site for the book that provides access to all electronic media and a link to MyStatLab (see "Student Resources" on page xxiv).

Chapter-by-Chapter Changes in the Sixth Edition

Chapters begin with a redesigned opening page that displays the chapter sections and subsections and conclude with the new Excel Guides that discuss how to apply Excel to the statistical methods discussed in a chapter. The individual chapters contain these changes:

Chapter 1 has a completely new Section 1.4. The fifth edition's Sections 1.4 and 1.5 have been moved to Chapter 2.

Chapter 2 has been completely reorganized. Sections 1.4 and 1.5 of the previous edition, concerning data collection and types of variables, have been moved to this chapter. The Define, Collect, Organize, Visualize, and Analyze approach to solving business problems has been incorporated. The material on tables and charts has been reorganized so that the sections on organizing data into tables is presented first, in Sections 2.3 and 2.4, followed by sections on visualizing data in graphs in Sections 2.5–2.8. There is a new section on using PivotTables to explore multidimensional data and drilling down (Section 2.8). In addition, there are new examples throughout the chapter, and a new data set of bond funds has been created.

Chapter 3 has moved quartiles to the section on boxplots (which represents a name change from *box-and-whisker plots*), and a new bond fund data set has been created.

Chapter 4 has new problems throughout the chapter.

Chapter 5 has revised notation in the binomial, Poisson, and hypergeometric distributions, including p changed to π and *successes* changed to *items of interest*.

Chapter 6 has a revised normal distribution table, with additional header lines, and a "Think About This" essay on the importance of the normal distribution.

Chapter 7 has a "Think About This" essay on the pros and cons of Web-based surveys.

Chapter 8 has a greatly reduced focus on the confidence interval estimate for the mean with sigma known, revised notation that uses a subscript for distributions that indicates the α level (such as $Z_{\alpha/2}$ or $t_{\alpha/2}$), and revised normal distribution and t distribution tables with additional header lines.

Chapter 9 has combined previous Sections 9.1 and 9.2 to reduce the emphasis on testing the population mean with sigma known, has moved the t test for the mean ahead of the one-tail test, changed notation to use a subscript for distributions to indicate the α level (such as $Z_{\alpha/2}$ or $t_{\alpha/2}$), revised notation that uses the subscript $STAT$ with the test statistic (such as Z_{STAT} and t_{STAT}), and revised normal distribution and t distribution tables with additional header lines.

Chapter 10 has revised notation that uses a subscript for distributions to indicate the α level (such as $Z_{\alpha/2}$, $t_{\alpha/2}$, or F_{α}); revised notation that uses the subscript $STAT$ with the test statistic (such as Z_{STAT}, t_{STAT}, and F_{STAT}); revised normal distribution, t, and F distribution tables with additional header lines; revised F test for the difference between variances that consists of the larger variance divided by smaller variance, and a new "Think About This" essay that presents a business application of the differences between two means.

Chapter 11 has revised notation that uses a subscript for distributions to indicate the α level (such as F_{α}), revised notation that uses the subscript $STAT$ with the test statistic such as F_{STAT}, and revised F distribution tables with additional header lines.

Chapter 12 has revised notation that uses a subscript for distributions to indicate the α level and revised notation that uses the subscript $STAT$ with the test statistic and has revised χ^2 distribution tables with additional header lines.

Chapter 13 has revised notation that uses the subscript $STAT$ with the test statistic (such as t_{STAT}).

Chapter 14 has revised notation that uses the subscript $STAT$ with the test statistic (such as t_{STAT}).

Chapter 15 has revised notation that uses the subscript $STAT$ with the test statistic (such as t_{STAT}).

Chapter 16 has updated examples throughout the chapter and has moved the information on index numbers to the text Web site, where it can be downloaded.

Chapter 17 (formerly Chapter 18) has control charts preceding the discussion of total quality management and Six Sigma, has revised sections on total quality management and Six Sigma, and now includes the c chart.

Chapter 18 is a new chapter that discusses real-world data analysis and provides a roadmap so that students can apply what they have learned in the previous 17 chapters.

Chapter 19 (formerly Chapter 17) has become an electronic-only chapter (in PDF format) that can be downloaded from this book's companion Web site. This chapter includes additional decision-making criteria, a new marketing example, and a "Think About This" essay that discusses how individual investors are classified by their personal risk tolerance.

Hallmark Features

We have continued many of the traditions of past editions and have highlighted some of these features below:

Using Statistics business scenarios—Each chapter begins with a Using Statistics example that shows how statistics is used in the functional areas of business—accounting, finance, information systems, management, or marketing. Each scenario is used throughout the chapter to provide an applied context for the concepts.

Emphasis on data analysis and interpretation of software results—We believe that the use of computer software is an integral part of learning statistics. Our focus emphasizes analyzing data by interpreting worksheet results while reducing emphasis on doing computations. For example, in the coverage of tables and charts in Chapter 2, the focus is on the interpretation of various charts and on when to use each chart. In our coverage of hypothesis testing in Chapters 9 through 12, extensive computer results have been included so that the *p*-value approach can be emphasized.

Pedagogical aides—An active writing style is used, boxed numbered equations, set-off examples to provide reinforcement for learning concepts, problems divided into "Learning the Basics" and "Applying the Concepts," key equations, and key terms are included.

Answers—Most answers to the even-numbered exercises are provided in an appendix at the end of the book.

Flexibility in the use of Excel—For almost every statistical method discussed, this book presents more than one way of using Excel. Students can use *In-Depth Excel* instructions to directly work with the worksheet cell-level details **or** use the *PHStat2* instructions **or** the *Analysis ToolPak* to automate the creation of those same details.

Web Cases—An end-of-chapter Web Case is included for each of the first 16 chapters. Each Web Case extends a Using Statistics business scenario by posing additional questions and raising issues about the scenario. Students visit Web pages to sift through claims and assorted information in order to discover the data most relevant to a scenario. Students then determine whether the conclusions and claims are supported by the data. In doing so, students discover and learn how to identify common misuses of statistical information. (Instructional tips for using the Web Cases and solutions to the Web Cases are included in the Instructor's Solutions Manual.)

Case studies and team projects—Detailed case studies are included in numerous chapters. A "Managing the *Springville Herald*" continuing case and a team project related to bond funds are included at the end of most chapters, and both serve to integrate learning across the chapters.

Visual Explorations—The Excel add-in workbook allows students to interactively explore important statistical concepts in descriptive statistics, the normal distribution, sampling distributions, and regression analysis. For example, in descriptive statistics, students observe the effect of changes in the data on the mean, median, quartiles, and standard deviation. With the normal distribution, students see the effect of changes in the mean and standard deviation on the areas under the normal curve. In sampling distributions, students use simulation to explore the effect of sample size on a sampling distribution. In regression analysis, students have the opportunity to fit a line and observe how changes in the slope and intercept affect the goodness of fit.

Student Resources

Student Solutions Manual—Created by Professor Pin Tian Ng of Northern Arizona University, this manual provides detailed solutions to virtually all the even-numbered exercises and worked-out solutions to the self-test problems.

 MyStatLab—MyStatLab provides students with the following online features and tools:

- **Interactive tutorial exercises**—A comprehensive set of exercises written especially for use with this book that are algorithmically generated for unlimited practice and mastery. Most exercises are free-response exercises and provide guided solutions, sample problems, and learning aids for extra help at point of use.

- **Personalized study plan**—A plan that indicates which topics have been mastered and creates direct links to tutorial exercises for topics that have not been mastered. MyStatLab manages the study plan, updating its content based on the results of future online assessments.
- **Multimedia learning aids**—Students can use online learning aids, such as video lectures, animations, and a complete multimedia textbook, to help them independently improve their understanding and performance.
- **Statistics tools**—MyStatLab includes access to statistics animations and applets that illustrate key ideas for the course.
- **Pearson Tutor Center (www.pearsontutorservices.com)**—The MyStatlab student access code also grants access to this online resource, staffed by qualified instructors who provide book-specific tutoring via phone, fax, e-mail, and interactive Web sessions.

Companion Web site—This book's companion Web site, reached through a link at **www.pearsonhighered.com/levine**, as explained in Appendix Section D.1 on page 730, contains the online resources for this book that includes:

- The electronic-only **Chapter 19: Decision Making,** available for download (PDF format).
- The **Online Topics** that discuss additional topics for Chapters 4, 6, 7, 8, 9, 11, 12, and 16. Available for download (PDF format).
- The **Using Excel 2010 Guide** that documents the differences between Excel 2010 and Excel 2007 and explains the effect of those differences on the *In-Depth Excel* instructions presented in this book.
- Access to the supporting files for **Web Cases** and the **Managing the *Springville Herald* Case**. Available for download (ZIP file format).
- Links to download the **data workbooks** used by in-chapter examples and problems and the self-documenting **Excel Companion Workbooks** that illustrate solutions for over 60 statistical topics and that serve as freely reusable templates. (ZIP file format; individual workbooks are stored in .xls format).
- Links to download the **Visual Explorations** add-in workbook and **PHStat2,** the Pearson statistical add-in for Microsoft Windows-based Excel versions. (Self-extracting .EXE files)

Instructor Resources

Instructor's Resource Center—Reached through a link at **www.pearsonhighered.com/levine**, the Instructor's Resource Center contains the electronic files for the complete Instructor's Solutions Manual, the Test Item File, and Lecture PowerPoint presentations.

- **Register, Redeem, Log In**—At **www.pearsonhighered.com/irc**, instructors can access a variety of print, media, and presentation resources that are available with this book in downloadable digital format. Resources are also available for course management platforms such as Blackboard, WebCT, and CourseCompass.
- **It gets better**—As a registered faculty member, you can log in directly to download resource files and receive immediate access and instructions for installing course management content to your campus server.
- **Need help?**—Pearson Education's dedicated technical support team is ready to assist instructors with questions about the media supplements that accompany this text. Visit **http://247.prenhall.com** for answers to frequently asked questions and toll-free user support phone numbers. The supplements are available to adopting instructors. Detailed descriptions are provided on the Instructor's Resource Center.

Instructor's Solutions Manual—Created by Professor Pin Tian Ng of Northern Arizona University, this manual includes solutions for end-of-section and end-of-chapter problems, answers to case questions, where applicable, and teaching tips for each chapter. Electronic solutions are provided in PDF and Word formats.

Lecture PowerPoint presentations—A PowerPoint presentation, created by Professor Patrick Schur of Miami University, is available for each chapter. The PowerPoint slides provide the instructor with individual lecture outlines to accompany the text. The slides include many of the figures and tables from the text. Instructors can use these lecture notes as is or can easily modify the notes to reflect specific presentation needs.

Test Item File—Created by Professor Pin Tian Ng of Northern Arizona University, the Test Item File contains true/false, multiple-choice, fill-in, and problem-solving questions based on the definitions, concepts, and ideas developed in each chapter of the text.

TestGen—The computerized TestGen package allows instructors to customize, save, and generate classroom tests. The test program permits instructors to edit, add, or delete questions from the test bank; edit existing graphics and create new graphics; analyze test results; and organize a database of test and student results. This software provides ease of use and extensive flexibility, and it provides many options for organizing and displaying tests, along with search and sort features. The software and the test banks can be downloaded from the Instructor's Resource Center, at **www.pearsonhighered.com/levine**.

MyStatLab

MathXL for Statistics is a powerful online homework, tutorial, and assessment system that accompanies Pearson Education statistics textbooks. With MathXL for Statistics, instructors can create, edit, and assign online homework and tests using algorithmically generated exercises correlated at the objective level to the textbook. They can also create and assign their own online exercises and import TestGen tests for added flexibility. All student work is tracked in MathXL's online grade book. Students can take chapter tests in MathXL and receive personalized study plans based on their test results. Each study plan diagnoses weaknesses and links the student directly to tutorial exercises for the objectives he or she needs to study and retest. Students can also access supplemental animations and video clips directly from selected exercises. MathXL for Statistics is available to qualified adopters. For more information, visit **www.mathxl.com** or contact your sales representative.

MyStatLab—Part of the MyMathLab and MathXL product family, MyStatLab is a text-specific, easily customizable online course that integrates interactive multimedia instruction with textbook content. MyStatLab gives you the tools you need to deliver all or a portion of your course online, whether your students are in a lab setting or working from home.

- **Assessment manager**—An easy-to-use assessment manager lets instructors create online homework, quizzes, and tests that are automatically graded and correlated directly to your textbook. Assignments can be created using a mix of questions from the MyStatLab exercise bank, instructor-created custom exercises, and/or TestGen test items.
- **Grade book**—Designed specifically for mathematics and statistics, the MyStatLab grade book automatically tracks students' results and gives you control over how to calculate final grades. You can also add offline (paper-and-pencil) grades to the grade book.
- **MathXL Exercise Builder**—you can use the MathXL Exercise Builder to create static and algorithmic exercises for your online assignments. A library of sample exercises provides an easy starting point for creating questions, and you can also create questions from scratch.

Acknowledgments

We are extremely grateful to the Biometrika Trustees, American Cyanamid Company, the RAND Corporation, and the American Society for Testing and Materials for their kind permission to publish various tables in Appendix E, and the American Statistical Association for its permission to publish diagrams from the *American Statistician*. Also, we are grateful to Professors George A. Johnson and Joanne Tokle of Idaho State University and Ed Conn, Mountain States Potato Company, for their kind permission to incorporate parts of their work as our Mountain States Potato Company case in Chapter 15.

A Note of Thanks

We would like to thank Harold Beck, Southern Illinois University–Edwardsville; Margaretha Hsu, Shippensburg University; Kimberly Killmer Hollister, Montclair State University; Ram Misra, Montclair State University; Glen Miller, Piedmont College; Kumar Muthuraman, University of Texas at Austin; Dane Peterson, Missouri State University; Jan Stallert, University of Connecticut; Patrick Thompson, University of Florida; and Ross S. VanWassenhove, University of Houston, for their comments, which have made this a better book.

We would especially like to thank Chuck Synovec, Mary Kate Murray, Jason Calcano, Judy Leale, Anne Fahlgren, Melinda Jensen, and Kerri Tomasso of the editorial, marketing, and production teams at Prentice Hall. We would like to thank our statistical reader and accuracy checker Annie Puciloski for his diligence in checking our work; Kitty Wilson for her copyediting; Dorothy Pychevicz for her proofreading; and Heidi Allgair of GGS Higher Education for her work in the production of this text.

Finally, we would like to thank our families for their patience, understanding, love, and assistance in making this book a reality. It is to them that we dedicate this book.

Concluding Remarks

We have gone to great lengths to make this text both pedagogically sound and error free. If you have any suggestions or require clarification about any of the material, or if you find any errors, please contact us at **davidlevine@davidlevinestatistics.com**. Include the phrase "SMUME edition 6" in the subject line of your e-mail. For technical support for PHStat2 beyond what is presented in Appendix G and in the PHStat2 readme file that accompanies PHStat2, visit the official PHStat2 Web site, **www.pearsonhighered.com/phstat**, and click on the **Contact Pearson Technical Support** link.

David M. Levine

David F. Stephan

Timothy C. Krehbiel

Mark L. Berenson

Statistics for Managers

Using Microsoft Excel

SIXTH EDITION

1

Introduction

Learning Objectives

In this chapter, you learn:

- How businesses use statistics
- The basic vocabulary of statistics
- How to use Microsoft Excel with this book

@ Good Tunes & More

Managers at Good Tunes & More, a consumer electronics retailer, look to expand their chain to take advantage of recent store closings by their competitors. These managers have decided to approach local banks for the funding needed to underwrite the expansion. The managers know that they will have to present information about Good Tunes & More that will convince the bankers that the retailer is a good candidate for expansion.

The managers ask you to help prepare the supporting documents to be submitted to the bankers. To this end, they give you access to the retailer's sales transactions for the past five years. What should you do with this data? To help find a starting point for the task, you decide to learn more about statistics.

1.1 Why Learn Statistics

Statistics is the branch of mathematics that transforms numbers into useful information for decision makers. Statistics lets you know about the risks associated with making a business decision and allows you to understand and reduce the variation in the decision-making process.

Statistics provides you with methods for making better sense of the numbers used every day to describe or analyze the world we live in. For example, consider these news stories:

- **"Cellphones Come Back to Life"** (*USA Today,* **March 13, 2009, p. 1A**) Recycling breathes new life into cell phones. The largest recycler reported that the number of cell phones recycled increased from 2 million in 2004 to 5.5 million in 2008.
- **"Green Power Purchases Targeted to Wind, Solar"** (**P. Davidson,** *USA Today,* **April 1, 2009, p. 3B**) Approximately 55% of green power sales was for wind energy.
- **"Reducing Prices Has a Different Result at Barnes & Noble Than at Amazon"—A Study (V. Postrel, "Economic Scene,"** *The New York Times,* **September 11, 2003, p. C2)** In this study, raising book prices by 1% reduced sales by 4% at BN.com but reduced sales by only 0.5% at Amazon.com.

Do these numbers represent useful information? How can you decide? Statistical methods help you understand the information contained in "the numbers" and determine whether differences in "the numbers" are meaningful or just due to chance.

Why learn statistics? First and foremost, statistics helps you make better sense of the world. Second, statistics helps you make better business decisions.

1.2 Statistics in Business

In the business world, statistics has these important specific uses:

- To summarize business data
- To draw conclusions from those data
- To make reliable forecasts about business activities
- To improve business processes

The statistical methods you use for these tasks come from one of the two branches of statistics: descriptive statistics and inferential statistics.

DESCRIPTIVE STATISTICS

Descriptive statistics are the methods that help collect, summarize, present, and analyze a set of data.

INFERENTIAL STATISTICS

Inferential statistics are the methods that use the data collected from a small group to draw conclusions about a larger group.

Many of the tables and charts found in a typical presentation are the products of descriptive methods, as are statistics such as the mean or median of a group, an introduction to which you may have had in prior schooling. (The mean and median are among the concepts discussed in Chapter 3.) When you use statistical methods to help choose which investment from a set of investments might lead to a higher return or which marketing strategy might lead to increased sales, you are using inferential methods.

There are four important uses of statistics in business:

- Using descriptive methods **to visualize and summarize your data**.
- Using inferential methods **to reach conclusions about a large group based on data collected from a small group**.
- **Making reliable forecasts** involves developing statistical models for prediction. These models use inferential methods to increase the accuracy of predictions made about future activities.
- **Improving business processes** involves using managerial approaches such as Six Sigma that focus on quality improvement.

To use descriptive and inferential methods correctly, you must also learn the conditions and assumptions required for using those methods. And because many of the statistical methods used in business must be computerized in order to be of practical benefit, you also need to know how computers can help you apply statistics in the business world.

To help you develop and integrate these skills, which will give you the basis for making better decisions, every chapter of *Statistics for Managers Using Microsoft Excel* begins with a Using Statistics scenario. Each scenario describes a realistic business situation in which you will be asked to make decisions that can be enhanced by applying the methods of statistics. For example, in one chapter you will be asked to decide the location in a supermarket that best enhances sales of a cola drink, while in another chapter, you will be asked to forecast sales for a clothing store.

In the scenario on page 3, you need to answer the following questions: What data should you include that will convince bankers to extend the credit that Good Tunes & More needs? How should you present those data?

Because Good Tunes & More is a retailer, collecting data about the company's sales would be a reasonable starting point. You could present the details of every sales transaction for the past few years as a way of demonstrating that the business is thriving. However, presenting the bankers with the thousands of transactions would overwhelm them and not be very useful. You need to summarize the details of each transaction in some useful way that will give the bankers the information to (perhaps) uncover a favorable pattern about the sales over time.

One piece of information that the bankers would presumably want to see is the yearly dollar sales totals. Tallying and totaling sales is a common summary task. When you tally sales—or any other relevant data about Good Tunes & More that you choose to use—you follow normal business practice and tally by a business period, such as by month, quarter, or year. When you do so, you end up with multiple values: sales for this year, sales for last year, sales for the year before that, and so on.

Knowing more about statistics will definitely help you prepare a better presentation for the bankers! And the best way to begin knowing more about statistics is to learn the basic vocabulary of statistics.

1.3 Basic Vocabulary of Statistics

Seven terms—*variable, data, operational definition, population, sample, parameter, and statistic* (singular)—identify the fundamental concepts of statistics. Learning about and making sense of the statistical methods discussed in later chapters is nearly impossible if you do not first understand the meaning of these words.

Variables are characteristics of items or individuals and are what you analyze when you use a statistical method. For the Good Tunes & More scenario, sales, expenses by year, and net profit by year are variables that the bankers would want to analyze. When used in everyday speech, *variable* suggests that something changes or varies, and you would expect sales, expenses, and net profit to have different values from year to year. These different values are the *data* associated with a variable or, more simply, the "data to be analyzed."

VARIABLE

A **variable** is a characteristic of an item or individual.

DATA

Data are the different values associated with a variable.

Variables can differ for reasons other than time. For example, if you conducted an analysis of the composition of a large lecture class, you would probably want to include the variables class standing, gender, and major field of study. These variables would vary, too, because each student in the class is different. One student might be a sophomore, a male, and an accounting major, while another might be a junior, a female, and a finance major.

Variable values are meaningless unless their corresponding variables have **operational definitions**. These definitions are universally accepted meanings that are clear to all associated with an analysis. Even though the operational definition for sales per year might seem clear, miscommunication could occur if one person were to refer to sales per year for the entire chain of stores and another to sales per year per store. Even individual values for variables sometimes need definition. For the class standing variable, for example, what *exactly* is meant by the words *sophomore* and *junior*? (Perhaps the most famous examples of vague definitions have been election disputes, such as the one that occurred in Florida during the 2000 U.S. presidential election that involved the definitions for "valid" and "invalid" ballots.)

The subject of statistics creates useful information from either populations or samples.

POPULATION

A **population** consists of all the items or individuals about which you want to draw a conclusion.

SAMPLE

A **sample** is the portion of a population selected for analysis.

A *population* consists of all the items or individuals about which you want to draw a conclusion. All the Good Tunes & More sales transactions for a specific year, all the customers who shopped at Good Tunes & More this weekend, all the full-time students enrolled in a college, and all the registered voters in Ohio are examples of populations.

A *sample* is the portion of a population selected for analysis. From the four examples of populations given above, you could create a sample of 200 Good Tunes & More sales transactions randomly selected by an auditor for study, a sample of 30 Good Tunes & More customers asked to complete a customer satisfaction survey, a sample of 50 full-time students selected for a marketing study, and a sample of 500 registered voters in Ohio contacted via telephone for a political poll. In each of these examples, the transactions or people in the sample represent a portion of the items or individuals that make up the population.

Parameter and *statistic* complete the basic vocabulary of statistics.

PARAMETER

A **parameter** is a measure that describes a characteristic of a population.

STATISTIC

A **statistic** is a measure that describes a characteristic of a sample.

The average amount spent by all customers who shopped at Good Tunes & More this weekend is an example of a parameter because this amount refers to the amount spent in the entire population. In contrast, the average amount spent by the 30 customers completing the customer satisfaction survey is an example of a statistic because it refers only to the amount spent by the sample of 30 customers.

1.4 How to Use This Book

This book organizes its material according to the four important uses of statistics in business. (1) Chapters 2 and 3 present methods that summarize business data. (2) Chapters 4 through 12 discuss methods that use sample data to draw conclusions about populations. (3) Chapters 13 though 16 review methods for making reliable forecasts. (4) Chapter 17 introduces methods you can use to improve business processes. Then, Chapter 18 explains how you can go about applying your statistical knowledge in the business world and summarizes the methods discussed in earlier chapters.

As already discussed in Section 1.2, each chapter begins with a scenario that establishes a business situation that requires decision-making that can be enhanced by applying statistical methods. At the end of each chapter, you revisit the scenario to review how the methods discussed in the chapter can be applied to the business situation. At the end of each chapter, you also find sections such as Summary, Key Terms, Key Formulas, and Chapter Review Problems that help you review what you have learned.

Most chapters also include a continuing case study that allows you to apply statistics to problems faced by the management of the *Springville Herald*, a daily newspaper, as well as a "Web Case" that extends the Using Statistics scenario of the chapter. (To better understand how you can benefit from these cases, see "Learning with the Web Cases" on page 9.) Finally, each chapter, except for the last chapter, includes an Excel Guide that presents ways of applying Microsoft Excel to the statistical methods discussed in the chapter. Read the Excel Guide to this chapter (which begins on page 11) to learn more about how to use the Excel Guides and how to prepare yourself for using Excel with this book.

Don't worry if your instructor does not cover every section of every chapter, Introductory business statistics courses vary in scope, length, and number of college credits. Your chosen functional area of specialization (accounting, management, finance, marketing, etc.) may also affect what you learn in class or what you are assigned to read in this book.

And don't worry if the thought of using Microsoft Excel worries you. This book contains several appendices that will assist you in getting started with Excel. Appendix B "Basic Excel Knowledge," explains the concepts fundamental to using Excel and reviews the basic computing operations you need to operate Excel. This appendix will be especially helpful if you are new to using Excel. Appendix C, "Useful Excel Operations," discusses frequently-used operations such as opening and saving of files as well as some of the intermediate-level "tricks" that will help facilitate your use of Excel. Challenged by some of the technical issues when using Excel? Appendix D, "Technical Tips," walks you through such technical operations as checking for Excel updates and making sure your copy of Excel is properly configured for use with this book. (See the Chapter 1 Excel Guide for more information about these appendices.)

USING STATISTICS @ Good Tunes & More Revisited

In the Using Statistics scenario at the beginning of this chapter, you were asked to help prepare documents to support the Good Tunes & More expansion. The managers had decided to approach local banks for funding the expansion of their company, and you needed to determine what type of data to present and how to present it. As a first step, you decided to summarize the details of thousands of transactions into useful information in the form of yearly dollar sales totals.

SUMMARY

In this chapter, you have been introduced to the basic vocabulary of statistics and the role of statistics in turning data into information. You learned that businesses use statistics to summarize and reach conclusions from data, to make reliable forecasts, and to improve business processes. In the next two chapters, you will study data collection, the various types of data used in business, and a variety of tables and charts and descriptive measures that are used to analyze data.

KEY TERMS

data 6
descriptive statistics 4
inferential statistics 4
operational definition 6

parameter 6
population 6
sample 6
statistic 6

statistics 4
variable 6

CHAPTER REVIEW PROBLEMS

CHECKING YOUR UNDERSTANDING

1.1 What is the difference between a sample and a population?

1.2 What is the difference between a statistic and a parameter?

1.3 What is the difference between descriptive statistics and inferential statistics?

1.4 What is an operational definition, and why are operational definitions so important?

APPLYING THE CONCEPTS

1.5 Go to the official Microsoft Excel Web site, **www.office.microsoft.com/excel**. Explain how you think Microsoft Excel could be useful in the field of statistics.

1.6 In 2008, a university in the midwestern United States surveyed its full-time first-year students after they completed their first semester. Surveys were electronically distributed to all 3,727 students, and responses were obtained from 2,821 students. Of the students surveyed, 90.1% indicated that they had studied with other students, and 57.1% indicated that they had tutored another student. The report also noted that 61.3% of the students surveyed came late to class at least once, and 45.8% admitted to being bored in class at least once.
a. Describe the population of interest.
b. Describe the sample that was collected.
c. Describe a parameter of interest.
d. Describe the statistic used to estimate the parameter in (c).

1.7 The Gallup organization releases the results of recent polls at its Web site, **www.gallup.com**. Go to this site and read an article of interest.
a. Describe the population of interest.
b. Describe the sample that was collected.

1.8 A Gallup Poll indicated that 80% of Americans favored higher fuel efficiency standards for automobiles (data extracted from L. Morales, "Americans Green-Light Higher Fuel Efficiency Standards," **www.gallup.com**, May 19, 2009). The results are based on telephone interviews conducted March 5–8, 2009, with 1,012 adults living in the United States, aged 18 and older.
a. Describe the population of interest.
b. Describe the sample that was collected.
c. Is 80% a parameter or a statistic? Explain.

1.9 Three professors at Northern Kentucky University compared two different approaches to teaching courses in the school of business (M. W. Ford, D. W. Kent, and S. Devoto, "Learning from the Pros: Influence of Web-Based Expert Commentary on Vicarious Learning About Financial Markets," *Decision Sciences Journal of Innovative Education*, January 2007, 5(1), 43–63). At the time of the study, there were 2,100 students in the business school, and 96 students were involved in the study. Demographic data collected on these 96 students included class (freshman, sophomore, junior, senior), age, gender, and major.
a. Describe the population of interest.
b. Describe the sample that was collected.

END-OF-CHAPTER CASES

At the end of most chapters, you will find a continuing case study that allows you to apply statistics to problems faced by the management of the *Springville Herald*, a daily newspaper. You will also find a series of Web Cases that extend many of the Using Statistics scenarios that begin each chapter.

LEARNING WITH THE WEB CASES

People use statistical techniques to help communicate and present important information to others both inside and outside their businesses. Every day, as in these examples, people misuse these techniques. Identifying and preventing misuses of statistics, whether intentional or not, is an important responsibility for all managers. The Web Cases help you develop the skills necessary for this important task.

A Web Case asks you to review online information related to a company or statistical issue mentioned in a Using Statistics scenario found in the same chapter as the Web Case. Using a Web browser, you examine internal documents as well as publicly stated claims, seeking to identify and correct the misuses of statistics. Unlike a traditional case study, but much like real-world situations, not all of the information you encounter will be relevant to your task, and you may occasionally discover conflicting information that you need to resolve before continuing with the case.

To assist your learning, each Web Case begins with a learning objective and a summary of the problem or issue at hand. Each case directs you to one or more Web pages where you can discover the information necessary to reach your own conclusions and to answer the case questions. (You can examine these Web pages online, by using the companion Web site for this book, or view them offline, after downloading the pages from the companion Web site. See Appendix Sections D.1 and D.2 for complete instructions.)

WEB CASE EXAMPLE

To illustrate learning with a Web Case, using a Web browser, open to the Web page for the Chapter 1 Web Case or open **GTM.htm**, if you have downloaded the Web Case files. **GTM.htm** shows the home page of Good Tunes & More, the subject of the Using Statistics scenario in this chapter. Recall that the privately held Good Tunes & More is seeking financing to expand its business by opening retail locations. Because the managers are eager to show that Good Tunes & More is a thriving business, it is not surprising to discover the "our best sales year ever" claim in the "Good Times at Good Tunes & More" entry at the top of the home page.

Click the **our best sales year ever** link to display the page that supports this claim. How would you support such a claim? With a table of numbers? A chart? Remarks attributed to a knowledgeable source? Good Tunes & More has used a chart to present "two years ago" and "latest twelve months" sales data by category. Are there any problems with the choices made on this Web page? *Absolutely!*

First, note that there are no scales for the symbols used, so it is impossible to know what the actual sales volumes are. In fact, as you will learn in Section 2.9, charts that incorporate symbols in this way are considered examples of *chartjunk* and would never be used by people seeking to properly use graphs.

This important point aside, another question that arises is whether the sales data represent the number of units sold or something else. The use of the symbols creates the impression that unit sales data are being presented. If the data are unit sales, does such data best support the claim being made, or would something else, such as dollar volumes, be a better indicator of sales at the retailer?

Then there are those curious chart labels. "Latest twelve months" is ambiguous; it could include months from the current year as well as months from one year ago and therefore may not be an equivalent time period to "two years ago." But the business was established in 1997, and the claim being made is "best sales year ever," so why hasn't management included sales figures for *every* year?

Is Good Tunes & More management hiding something, or are they just unaware of the proper use of statistics? Either way, they have failed to properly communicate a vital aspect of their story.

In subsequent Web Cases, you will be asked to provide this type of analysis, using the open-ended questions in the case as your guide. Not all the cases are as straightforward as this example, and some cases include perfectly appropriate applications of statistics.

REFERENCES

1. McCullough, B. D., and D. Heiser, "On the Accuracy of Statistical Procedures in Microsoft Excel 2007," *Computational Statistics and Data Analysis*, 52 (2008), 4568–4606.
2. McCullough, B. D., and B. Wilson, "On the Accuracy of Statistical Procedures in Microsoft Excel 97," *Computational Statistics and Data Analysis*, 31 (1999), 27–37.
3. McCullough, B. D., and B. Wilson, "On the Accuracy of Statistical Procedures in Microsoft Excel 2003," *Computational Statistics and Data Analysis*, 49 (2005), 1244–52.
4. *Microsoft Excel 2007* (Redmond, WA: Microsoft Corporation, 2007).
5. Nash, J. C., "Spreadsheets in Statistical Practice— Another Look," *The American Statistician*, 60 (2006), 287–89.

EG1.1 GETTING STARTED with EXCEL and the EXCEL GUIDES

As you learn business statistics in this book, you will use Microsoft Excel to illustrate and understand statistical methods and to solve end-of-section and end-of-chapter problems.

Beginning to use Excel is not as easy as it might first seem. If Excel or Office has not come pre-installed on your system, you need to properly install Excel, specifying the correct optional components. Pre-installed or not, your version of Excel then needs to be updated by installing the Microsoft-supplied updates for Excel and Office that you can download from **office.microsoft.com/officeupdate**. And to update your Excel properly, you need to know which Excel version you are using. (If you need to know how to do these things, read Appendix Section D.3)

After you get past these start-up issues, you need to identify your Excel learning goals. This book allows you to customize how you learn Excel. For almost every statistical method discussed, this book presents more than one way of learning to use Excel—a unique feature of this book.

Table EG1.1 summarizes the ways that this book presents Excel instructions. If you want to develop a mastery of Excel and gain practice building solutions from the bottom-up, you will want to use the *In-Depth Excel* instructions. If you are more of a top-down person, who first wants quick results and then, later, looks at the details of a solution, you will want to maximize your use of the *PHStat2* instructions.

You need not choose one way over another—this book has been written to allow you to switch among the different ways as you see fit. If you do choose to use the *In-Depth Excel* instructions, you will find many of those instructions use an already-created "Excel Guide workbook." Such workbooks serve as templates, giving you a foundation for understanding how to apply Excel for a specific statistical method. When these workbooks are used in this book, *In-Depth Excel* instructions will walk you through the workbook and explain how you can modify the workbook to solve other problems. This mimics the real-world business usage of Excel in which you are more likely to be modifying a pre-existing workbook than developing one completely from scratch. (And the Excel Guide workbooks are yours to keep and reuse in other courses or on the job.)

If you are a very technically-minded person who wants to deeply learn Excel, you should note that every "Excel Guide" workbook supplements the in-book material by containing worksheets that present all formulas used in the workbook. By studying these documenting features, you will discover how to build a solution from scratch, without ever having to actually do so.

Likewise, because PHStat2 uses the same techniques that were used in creating the Excel Guide workbooks, you can use PHStat2 and still be able to study and understand the techniques necessary to apply Excel to a statistical method. This eliminates the "I used an add-in and learned nothing about Excel" phenomenon that can occur when you use other add-ins that create undocumented and unexplained results.

The rest of this Excel Guide walks you through the steps necessary to prepare you to get ready to use Excel with this book. In other chapters, the Excel Guide presents instructions arranged by chapter section numbers. For a given statistical topic, one or more ways of using Excel are presented. A few topics have only one way of applying Excel, due to the limitations of Excel, and many in-depth charting instructions have separate Excel 2007 and Excel 2003 instructions, due to differences in those versions.

This book has been written primarily for the Windows Excel versions 2003 and 2007 and their successors, including Excel 2010. If you use Mac Excel and OpenOffice.org 3 Calc (an Excel work-alike), you should be able to use almost all of the Excel Guide workbooks and most of the *In-Depth Excel* instructions. (You will not be able to use PHStat2 and only users of Mac Excel *2004* will be able to use the Analysis ToolPak.)

EG1.2 CHECKLIST for USING EXCEL with THIS BOOK

To minimize problems you may face when using Excel with this book, complete the Table EG1.2 checklist before continuing.

When you have completed the checklist, proceed by reading the next two sections of this Excel Guide. If your Excel background is limited, also read Appendix Sections C.1 through C.6 and practice the operations discussed in those sections. there. If you have not used Excel in a long time and now find yourself using Excel 2007, review Appendix Section B.2 to learn about the changes to the Excel user interface.

TABLE EG1.1

Types of Excel Guide
Instructions

***In-Depth Excel* Instructions**

Provides step-by-step instructions for applying Excel to the statistical methods of the chapter.

Advantages Applicable to all Excel versions. Creates "live" worksheets and chart sheets that automatically update when the underlying data change. Avoids some of the technological issues involved in setting up PHStat2 or the Analysis ToolPak.

Disadvantages Can be time-consuming, frustrating, and error prone, especially for novices. May force you to focus on low-level Excel details, thereby distracting you from learning statistics.

***PHStat2* Instructions**

Provides step-by-step instructions for using the free PHStat2 add-in. PHStat2 works inside Microsoft Excel and adds statistical functionality to Excel while simplifying the user experience of operating Excel. (To learn more about PHStat2, see Appendix Section F.1)

Advantages Creates live worksheets and chart sheets that are the same or similar to the ones created by the *In-Depth Excel* instructions. Frees you from having to focus on low-level Excel details. Can be used to quickly double-check results created by the *In-Depth Excel* instructions.

Disadvantages Must be installed separately (see Appendix Sections D.4 and D.5). Not compatible with Mac Excel or OpenOffice.org Calc 3. Designed for academic use; unlikely to be found in business settings.

***Analysis ToolPak* Instructions**

Provides step-by-step instructions for using the Analysis ToolPak, the statistical component packaged with many Excel versions.

Advantages Widely found in business settings.

Disadvantages Creates dead worksheets and charts that do not automatically update when the underlying data changes. Limited functionality—not available for many of the statistical methods discussed in this book. Requires separate installation or configuration (see Appendix Section D.6). Not available for Mac Excel 2008 or OpenOffice.org Calc 3.

TABLE EG1.2

Checklist for Using Excel

❏ Checked for and applied all Excel updates (see Appendix Section D.3)
❏ Downloaded Excel data workbooks and Excel Guide workbooks (see Appendix Section D.2)

If using PHStat2:

   ❏ Downloaded PHStat2 setup files (see Appendix Section D.2).
   ❏ Read the PHStat2 readme file for the latest information about PHStat2
   ❏ Installed PHStat2 (see Appendix Section D.4)
   ❏ Configured Excel to use PHStat2 (see Appendix Section D.5).

If using the Analysis ToolPak:

   ❏ Verified the presence and installation of the Analysis ToolPak (see Appendix Section D.6).
❏ Reviewed Appendix B "Basic Excel Knowledge"

EG1.3 HOW to PREPARE and USE DATA

To use any set of Excel instructions in this book successfully, you must properly prepare your data. To begin, organize your data by variable. Using a new worksheet, place the data for each variable in its own column, starting with column A. Enter the name of each variable in the cells of the first row of each column. Never skip any rows as you enter values into a column, and as a general rule, also avoid skipping columns. Pay attention to any special instructions that occur throughout the book for the order of the entry of your data. For some statistical methods, entering your data in a "wrong" column order, an order that Excel does not expect, will lead to incorrect results.

As a model for entering data, you can inspect the **DATA worksheet** of any of the Excel data workbooks you can download from this book's companion Web site (Appendix Section D.1). If you use one of these files, save the file under a unique, self-descriptive name. This will help you keep track of your own work as well as preserve the contents of the original file.

EG1.4 COMPUTING CONVENTIONS USED in THIS BOOK

The Excel instructions in this book use the conventions presented in Table EG1.3 to describe common keyboard and mousing operations.

TABLE EG1.3

Computing Conventions

Operation	Examples	Interpretation
Keyboard keys	**Enter** **Ctrl** **Shift** **Delete**	Names of keys are always the object of the verb *press*, as in "press **Enter**."
Keystroke combination	**Crtl+C** **Crtl+Shift+Enter**	A keyboarding action that requires you to press more than one key at the same time. **Crtl+C** means press the **C** key while holding down the **Ctrl** key. **Crtl+Shift+Enter** means press the **Enter** key while holding down the **Ctrl** and **Shift** keys.
Click target	Click **OK**. Click **All** in the **Page Range** section.	A target of a mouse click. Click **OK** means click the **OK** button. When click targets are part of a window that contains more than one section, tab, or panel, the section, tab, or panel name is also given. For example, "in the **Line Color** panel, click **Solid line**."
Menu or ribbon selection	**File → New** **Office Ribbon → New**	A sequence of menu bar or ribbon selections. **File → New** means first select **File** and then, from the list of choices that appears, select **New**. In Excel 2007, the equivalent sequence would be to first click the **Office Button** and then select **New**.
Placeholder object	Select *variablename*	An italicized object means that the actual object varies, depending on the context of the instruction. "Select *variablename*" might, for one problem, mean "select the **Yearly Sales** variable" and might mean "select the **Monthly Sales** variable" for another.

2 Organizing and Visualizing Data

Learning Objectives

In this chapter, you learn:

- The sources of data used in business
- The types of data used in business
- To construct tables and charts for numerical data
- To construct tables and charts for categorical data
- The principles of properly presenting graphs

@ Choice Is Yours, Part I

The Choice Is Yours investment service helps clients with their investment choices. Choice Is Yours evaluates investments as diverse as real estate, direct private equity investments, derivatives, and various specialized types of mutual funds. You've been hired to assist clients who seek to invest in mutual funds, which pool the money of many individual clients and invest the money in a mix of securities and other investments. (To learn more about mutual funds, visit **investopedia.com/university/mutualfunds**).

Because mutual funds that are highly invested in common stocks have had poor returns recently, Choice Is Yours wants to examine mutual funds that focus on investing in certain types of bonds. Company analysts have selected a sample of 180 such funds that they believe might interest clients. You have been asked to present data about these funds in a way that will help customers make good investment choices. What facts about each bond mutual fund would you collect to help customers compare and contrast the many funds?

A good starting point would be to collect data that would help customers classify mutual funds into various categories. You could research such things as the amount of risk involved in a fund's investment strategy and the type of bonds in which the mutual fund primarily invests.

Of course, you would want to learn how well the fund performed in the past, and you would want to supply the customer with several measures of each fund's past performance. (Although past performance is no assurance of future performance, past data could give customers insight into how well each mutual fund has been managed.)

As you further think about your task, you realize that the data for all 180 mutual funds would be a lot for anyone to review. You have been asked to present data about these funds in a way that will help customers make good investment choices. How can you review and explore such data in a comprehensible manner? What facts about each fund would you collect to help customers compare and contrast the many funds?

Thc challenge you face in Part I of the Choice Is Yours scenario is to examine a large amount of data and reach conclusions based on those data. You can make this business task more manageable by breaking it into the following five steps (abbreviated with the acronym **DCOVA**) of **D**efine, **C**ollect, **O**rganize, **V**isualize, and **A**nalyze:

- **Define** the variables that you want to study in order to solve a business problem or meet a business objective
- **Collect** the data from appropriate sources
- **Organize** the data collected by developing tables
- **Visualize** the data by developing charts
- **Analyze** the data by examining the appropriate tables and charts (and in later chapters by using other statistical methods) to reach conclusions.

You learned in Chapter 1 that defining a variable means selecting a characteristic of an item or individual for study and developing an operational definition for that variable. In this chapter, you will learn that identifying the type of variable you have is another part of the defining step before continuing and learning the basics of the other four steps. Having an operational definition for each variable and knowing each variable's type are necessary prerequisites for solving a business problem or meeting a business objective.

To help illustrate the five steps, this chapter often uses a sample of 180 mutual funds as the basis for its examples. (Open `Bond Funds`, one of the downloadable Excel data workbook files, to examine the sample.) By the end of the chapter, you will be able to get started with the task you face in Part I of the Choice Is Yours scenario. For example, you will be able to answer questions that compare two categories of bond funds, such as "Do intermediate government bond funds have higher returns than short-term corporate bond funds?" or "Do intermediate government bond funds tend to be less risky investments than short-term corporate bond funds?"

2.1 Types of Variables

Defining a variable includes establishing its type. You classify variables as either being categorical or numerical and further classify numerical variables as having either discrete or continuous values. Figure 2.1 demonstrates a question and response that each type of variable represents.

FIGURE 2.1
Types of variables

Data Type	Question	Responses
Categorical	Do you currently own any stocks or bonds?	Yes ☐ No ☐
Numerical — Discrete	To how many magazines do you currently subscribe?	_____ Number
Numerical — Continuous	How tall are you?	_____ Inches

Categorical variables (also known as **qualitative variables**) have values that can only be placed into categories such as yes and no. "Do you currently own bonds?" and the level of risk of a bond fund (below average, average, or above average) are examples of categorical variables.

Numerical variables (also known as **quantitative variables**) have values that represent quantities. Numerical variables are further subdivided as discrete or continuous variables.

Discrete variables have numerical values that arise from a counting process. "The number of magazines subscribed to" is an example of a discrete numerical variable because the response is one of a finite number of integers. You subscribe to zero, one, two, and so on magazines. The number of items that a customer purchases is also a discrete numerical variable because you are counting the number of items purchased.

Continuous variables produce numerical responses that arise from a measuring process. The time you wait for teller service at a bank is an example of a continuous numerical variable because the response takes on any value within a *continuum*, or interval, depending on the precision of the measuring instrument. For example, your waiting time could be 1 minute, 1.1 minutes, 1.11 minutes, or 1.113 minutes, depending on the precision of the measuring device used.

Theoretically, with sufficient precision of measurement, no two continuous values are identical. As a practical matter, however, most measuring devices are not precise enough to detect small differences, and tied values for a continuous variable (two or more items or individuals with the same value) are sometimes present in experimental or survey data.

Levels of Measurement and Measurement Scales

Using levels of measurement is another way of classifying data. There are four widely recognized levels of measurement: nominal, ordinal, interval, and ratio scales.

Nominal and Ordinal Scales Data from a categorical variable are measured on a nominal scale or on an ordinal scale. A **nominal scale** (see Figure 2.2) classifies data into distinct categories in which no ranking is implied. In the bond fund data, the type of bond fund (intermediate government or short-term corporate) is an example of a nominal scaled variable, as are your favorite soft drink, your political party affiliation, and your gender. Nominal scaling is the weakest form of measurement because you cannot specify any ranking across the various categories.

FIGURE 2.2

Examples of nominal scales

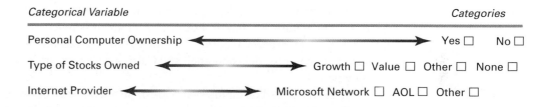

An **ordinal scale** classifies data into distinct categories in which ranking is implied. With the bond fund data, degree of risk represent an ordinal scaled variable because the categories below average, average, and above average are ranked in order of risk. Figure 2.3 lists other examples of ordinal scaled variables.

FIGURE 2.3

Examples of ordinal scales

Ordinal scaling is a stronger form of measurement than nominal scaling because an observed value classified into one category possesses more of a property than does an observed value classified into another category. However, ordinal scaling is still a relatively weak form of measurement because the scale does not account for the amount of the differences *between*

the categories. The ordering implies only *which* category is "greater," "better," or "more preferred"—not by *how much.*

Interval and Ratio Scales Data from a numerical variable are measured on an interval or a ratio scale. An **interval scale** (see Figure 2.4) is an ordered scale in which the difference between measurements is a meaningful quantity but does not involve a true zero point. For example, a noontime temperature reading of 67 degrees Fahrenheit is 2 degrees warmer than a noontime reading of 65 degrees. In addition, the 2 degrees Fahrenheit difference in the noontime temperature readings is the same as if the two noontime temperature readings were 74 and 76 degrees Fahrenheit because the difference has the same meaning anywhere on the scale.

FIGURE 2.4

Examples of interval and ratio scales

Numerical Variable	Level of Measurement
Temperature (in degrees Celsius or Fahrenheit)	Interval
Standardized exam score (e.g., ACT or SAT)	Interval
Height (in inches or centimeters)	Ratio
Weight (in pounds or kilograms)	Ratio
Age (in years or days)	Ratio
Salary (in American dollars or Japanese yen)	Ratio

A **ratio scale** is an ordered scale in which the difference between the measurements involves a true zero point, as in height, weight, age, or salary measurements. In the bond fund data, the amount of money (in U.S. dollars) in fees is an example of a ratio scaled variable. As another example, a person who weighs 240 pounds is twice as heavy as someone who weighs 120 pounds. Temperature is a trickier case: Fahrenheit and Celsius (centigrade) scales are interval but not ratio scales; the "zero" value is arbitrary, not real. You cannot say that a noontime temperature reading of 4 degrees Fahrenheit is twice as hot as 2 degrees Fahrenheit. But a Kelvin temperature reading, in which zero degrees means no molecular motion, is ratio scaled. In contrast, the Fahrenheit and Celsius scales use arbitrarily selected zero-degree beginning points.

Data measured on an interval scale or on a ratio scale constitute the highest levels of measurement. They are stronger forms of measurement than an ordinal scale because you can determine not only which observed value is the largest but also by how much.

Problems for Section 2.1

LEARNING THE BASICS

2.1 Three different beverages are sold at a fast-food restaurant—soft drinks, tea, and coffee.
a. Explain why the type of beverage sold is an example of a categorical variable.
b. Explain why the type of beverage sold is an example of a nominal scaled variable.

2.2 Soft drinks are sold in three sizes at a fast-food restaurant—small, medium, and large. Explain why the size of the soft drink is an example of an ordinal scaled variable.

2.3 Suppose that you measure the time it takes to download a video from the Internet.

a. Explain why the download time is a continuous numerical variable.
b. Explain why the download time is a ratio scaled variable.

APPLYING THE CONCEPTS

✓ **SELF Test** **2.4** For each of the following variables, determine whether the variable is categorical or numerical. If the variable is numerical, determine whether the variable is discrete or continuous. In addition, determine the level of measurement for each of the following.
a. Number of telephones per household
b. Length (in minutes) of the longest long-distance call made per month

c. Whether someone in the household owns a cell phone

d. Whether there is a high-speed Internet connection in the household

2.5 The following information is collected from students upon exiting the campus bookstore during the first week of classes:

a. Amount of time spent shopping in the bookstore

b. Number of textbooks purchased

c. Academic major

d. Gender

Classify each of these variables as categorical or numerical. If the variable is numerical, determine whether the variable is discrete or continuous. In addition, determine the level of measurement for each of these variables.

2.6 For each of the following variables, determine whether the variable is categorical or numerical. If the variable is numerical, determine whether the variable is discrete or continuous. In addition, determine the level of measurement.

a. Name of Internet provider

b. Amount of time spent surfing the Internet per week

c. Number of e-mails received in a week

d. Number of online purchases made in a month

2.7 For each of the following variables, determine whether the variable is categorical or numerical. If the variable is numerical, determine whether the variable is discrete or continuous. In addition, determine the level of measurement.

a. Amount of money spent on clothing in the past month

b. Favorite department store

c. Most likely time period during which shopping for clothing takes place (weekday, weeknight, or weekend)

d. Number of pairs of shoes owned

2.8 Suppose the following information is collected from Robert Keeler on his application for a home mortgage loan at the Metro County Savings and Loan Association:

a. Monthly payments: $1,427

b. Number of jobs in past 10 years: 1

c. Annual family income: $86,000

d. Marital status: Married

Classify each of the responses by type of data and level of measurement.

2.9 One of the variables most often included in surveys is income. Sometimes the question is phrased "What is your income (in thousands of dollars)?" In other surveys, the respondent is asked to "Select the circle corresponding to your income level" and is given a number of income ranges to choose from.

a. In the first format, explain why income might be considered either discrete or continuous.

b. Which of these two formats would you prefer to use if you were conducting a survey? Why?

2.10 If two students score a 90 on the same examination, what arguments could be used to show that the underlying variable—test score—is continuous?

2.11 The director of market research at a large department store chain wanted to conduct a survey throughout a metropolitan area to determine the amount of time working women spend shopping for clothing in a typical month.

a. Describe both the population and the sample of interest, and indicate the type of data the director might want to collect.

b. Develop a first draft of the questionnaire needed in (a) by writing three categorical questions and three numerical questions that you feel would be appropriate for this survey.

2.12 A manufacturer of cat food was planning to survey households in the United States to determine purchasing habits of cat owners. Among the variables to be collected are:

 i. The primary place of purchase for cat food

 ii. Whether dry or moist cat food is purchased

 iii. The number of cats living in the household

 iv. Whether the cat is pedigreed

a. For each of the four items listed, indicate whether the variable is categorical or numerical. If it is numerical, is it discrete or continuous?

b. Develop five categorical questions for the survey.

c. Develop five numerical questions for the survey.

2.13 The U.S. Census Bureau conducted a nationwide survey concerning education levels and earnings. Survey questions included:

 i. What is your age at your last birthday?

 ii. Did you complete high school?

 iii. Did you complete college?

 iv. What is your annual income?

The study found that among adults 75 and over, 73% had completed high school and 17% had completed college, while among adults age 25 to 29, 88% had completed high school and 31% had completed college. The study reported that workers with a high school degree earned an average of $31,286, while those with a bachelor's degree earned an average of $57,181 ("Census Bureau Releases Data Showing Relationship Between Education and Earnings," *U.S. Census Bureau News*, **www.census.gov**, April 27, 2009).

a. For each of the four questions, classify the responses as categorical or numerical.

b. For the numerical responses, determine whether they are discrete or continuous.

2.14 According to its home page, "Swivel is a place where curious people explore data—all kinds of data." Go to **www.swivel.com** and explore a data set of interest to you.

a. Describe a variable in the data set you selected.

b. Is the variable categorical or numerical?

c. If the variable is numerical, is it discrete or continuous?

2.2 Data Collection

In many situations, you need to collect the data for the variables you have defined. Examples of such **data collection** include:

- A marketing research analyst who needs to assess the effectiveness of a new television advertisement.
- A pharmaceutical manufacturer that needs to determine whether a new drug is more effective than those currently in use.
- An operations manager who wants to improve a manufacturing or service process.
- An auditor who wants to review the financial transactions of a company in order to determine whether the company is in compliance with generally accepted accounting principles.

Data collection almost always involves collecting data from a sample because collecting data from every item or individual in a population is typically too difficult or too time-consuming. (See Chapter 7 to learn more about sample selection methods.)

When you collect data, you use either a **primary data source** or a **secondary data source**. When you are collecting your own data for your own analysis, the data source is a primary one. When the data collector and analyst are not the same, the source is secondary.

Organizations and individuals that collect and publish data often use their data as a primary source and may let others use those data as a secondary source. For example, the U.S. federal government collects and distributes data in this way for both public and private purposes. The Bureau of Labor Statistics collects data on employment and also distributes the monthly consumer price index. The Census Bureau oversees a variety of ongoing surveys regarding population, housing, and manufacturing and undertakes special studies on topics such as crime, travel, and health care.

Data sources are created in one of four ways:

- As data distributed by an organization or individual
- As outcomes of a designed experiment
- As responses from a survey
- As a result of conducting an observational study

Market research firms and trade associations distribute data pertaining to specific industries or markets. Investment services such as Mergent (**www.mergent.com**) provide financial data on a company-by-company basis. Syndicated services such as Nielsen provide clients with data that enables the comparison of client products with those of their competitors. On the other hand, daily newspapers are secondary sources that are filled with numerical information regarding stock prices, weather conditions, and sports statistics obtained from primary sources.

Conducting a designed experiment is another source of data. For example, one such experiment might test several laundry detergents to compare how well each detergent removes a certain type of stain. Developing proper experimental designs is a subject mostly beyond the scope of this book because such designs often involve sophisticated statistical procedures. However, some of the fundamental experimental design concepts are discussed in Chapters 10 and 11.

Conducting a survey is a third type of data source. People being surveyed are asked questions about their beliefs, attitudes, behaviors, and other characteristics. For example, people could be asked their opinion about which laundry detergent best removes a certain type of stain. (This could lead to a result different from a designed experiment seeking the same answer.) One good way to avoid data-collection flaws when using such a survey is to distribute the questionnaire to a random sample of customers. (Chapter 7 explains how to collect a random sample.) A poor way would be to rely on a business-rating Web site that allows online visitors to rate a merchant. Such Web sites cannot provide assurance that those who do the ratings are representative of the population of customers—or that they even *are* customers.

Conducting an observational study is the fourth data source. A researcher collects data by directly observing a behavior, usually in a natural or neutral setting. Observational studies are a common tool for data collection in business. For example, market researchers use focus groups to elicit unstructured responses to open-ended questions posed by a moderator to a target audience. You can also use observational study techniques to enhance teamwork or improve the quality of products and services.

Problems for Section 2.2

APPLYING THE CONCEPTS

2.15 According to its home page, "Swivel is a place where curious people explore data—all kinds of data." Go to **www.swivel.com** and explore a data set of interest to you. Which of the four sources of data best describes the sources of the data set you selected?

2.16 Go to the Web site of the Gallup organization, at **www.galluppoll.com**. Read today's top story. What type of data source is the top story based on?

2.17 A supermarket chain wants to determine the best placement for the supermarket brand of soft drink. What type of data collection source do you think that the supermarket chain should use?

2.18 At the U.S. Census Bureau site, **www.census.gov**, click **Local Employment Dynamics** and, on the Web page to which you are directed, examine the "Did You Know" panel. What type of data source is the information presented here based on?

ORGANIZING DATA

After you define your variables and collect your data, you organize your data to help prepare for the later steps of visualizing and analyzing your data. The techniques you use to organize your data depend on the type of variable (categorical or numerical) associated with your data.

2.3 Organizing Categorical Data

You organize categorical data by tallying responses by categories and placing the results in tables. Summary tables, which are for a single categorical variable, and contingency tables which are developed for two or more categorical variables, are the most frequently used to display the results of the tallying of responses.

The Summary Table

A summary table presents tallied responses as frequencies or percentages for each category. A **summary table** helps you see the differences among the categories by displaying the frequency, amount, or percentage of items in a set of categories in separate columns. Table 2.1 illustrates a summary table (Bill Payment) that tallies the responses to a recent survey that asked adults how they pay their monthly bills:

TABLE 2.1
Types of Bill Payment

Form of Payment	Percentage (%)
Cash	15
Check	54
Electronic/online	28
Other/don't know	3

Source: *Data extracted from "How Adults Pay Monthly Bills," USA Today, October 4, 2007, p. 1.*

From Table 2.1, you can conclude that more than half the people pay by check and almost 82% pay by either check or by electronic/online forms of payment.

EXAMPLE 2.1

Summary Table of
Levels of Risk of
Bond Funds

TABLE 2.2

Frequency and
Percentage Summary
Table Pertaining to Risk
Level for 180 Bond Funds

*The SUMMARY_PIVOT
worksheet of the Chapter 2
workbook contains a
PivotTable version of Table
2.2. Create this worksheet
using the instructions in
Section EG2.3.*

The 180 bond funds involved in Part I of the Choice Is Yours scenario (see page 15) are classified according to their risk level, categorized as below average, average, and above average. Construct a summary table of the bond funds, categorized by risk.

SOLUTION From Table 2.2, you can see that about the same number of funds are below average, average, and above average in risk. This means that about 66% of the bond funds are classified as having an average or above-average level of risk.

Fund Risk Level	Number of Funds	Percentage of Funds (%)
Below average	62	34.44%
Average	60	33.33%
Above average	58	32.22%
Total	180	99.99%*

* Error due to rounding.

The Contingency Table

When you want to study patterns that may exist between the responses of two or more categorical variables, you use a *contingency table*. A **contingency table** cross-tabulates, or tallies jointly, the responses of the categorical variables. In the simplest case of two categorical variables, the joint responses appear in a table such that the category tallies of one variable are located in the rows and the category tallies of the other variable are located in the columns. Intersections of the rows and columns are called **cells**, and each cell contains a value associated with a unique pair of responses for the two variables (for example, Fee: Yes and Type: Intermediate Government in Table 2.3). Cells can contain the frequency, the percentage of the overall total, the percentage of the row total, or the percentage of the column total, depending on the type of contingency table being used.

In Part I of the Choice Is Yours scenario, you could create a contingency table to examine whether there is any pattern between the type of bond fund (intermediate government or short-term corporate) and whether the fund charges a fee (yes or no). You would begin by tallying the joint responses for each of the mutual funds in the sample of 180 bond mutual funds (found in `BondFunds`). You tally a response into one of the four possible cells in the table, depending on the type of bond fund and whether the fund charges a fee. For example, the first fund listed in the sample is classified as an intermediate government fund that does not charge a fee. Therefore, you tally this joint response into the cell that is the intersection of the Intermediate Government row and the No column. Table 2.3 shows the completed contingency table after all 180 bond funds have been tallied.

TABLE 2.3

Contingency Table
Displaying Type of Fund
and Whether a Fee Is
Charged

*The CONTINGENCY_PIVOT
worksheet of the Chapter 2
workbook contains a
PivotTable version of Table
2.3. Create this worksheet
using the instructions in
Section EG2.3.*

	FEE		
TYPE	Yes	No	Total
Intermediate Government	35	55	90
Short-Term Corporate	17	73	90
Total	52	128	180

To further explore any possible pattern between the type of bond fund and whether the fund charges a fee, you can create contingency tables based on percentages. You first convert cell tallies into percentages, using the following three totals:

- The overall total (the 180 mutual funds)
- The row totals (the 90 intermediate government funds and the 90 short-term corporate bond funds)
- The column totals (the 52 funds that charge a fee and the 128 funds that do not charge a fee)

Tables 2.4, 2.5, and 2.6 summarize these percentages.

TABLE 2.4
Contingency Table Displaying Type of Fund and Whether a Fee Is Charged, Based on Percentage of Overall Total

| | FEE | | |
TYPE	Yes	No	Total
Intermediate Government	19.44	30.56	50.00
Short-Term Corporate	9.44	40.56	50.00
Total	28.88	71.12	100.00

TABLE 2.5
Contingency Table Displaying Type of Fund and Whether a Fee Is Charged, Based on Percentage of Row Total

| | FEE | | |
TYPE	Yes	No	Total
Intermediate Government	38.89	61.11	100.00
Short-Term Corporate	18.89	81.11	100.00
Total	28.89	71.11	100.00

TABLE 2.6
Contingency Table Displaying Type of Fund and Whether a Fee Is Charged, Based on Percentage of Column Total

| | FEE | | |
TYPE	Yes	No	Total
Intermediate Government	67.31	42.97	50.00
Short-Term Corporate	32.69	57.03	50.00
Total	100.00	100.00	100.00

Table 2.4 shows that 50% of the bond funds sampled are intermediate government funds, 50% are short-term corporate bond funds, and 19.44% are intermediate government funds that charge a fee. Table 2.5 shows that 38.89% of the intermediate government funds charge a fee, while 18.89% of the short-term corporate bond funds charge a fee. Table 2.6 shows that of the funds that charge a fee, 67.31% are intermediate government funds. From the tables, you see that intermediate government funds are much more likely to charge a fee.

Problems for Section 2.3

LEARNING THE BASICS

2.19 A categorical variable has three categories, with the following frequencies of occurrence:

Category	Frequency
A	13
B	28
C	9

a. Compute the percentage of values in each category.
b. What conclusions can you reach concerning the categories?

2.20 The data at the top of page 24 represent the responses to two questions asked in a survey of 40 college students majoring in business: What is your gender? (male = M; female = F) and What is your major? (accounting = A; computer information systems = C; marketing = M):
a. Tally the data into a contingency table where the two rows represent the gender categories and the three columns represent the academic major categories.
b. Construct contingency tables based on percentages of all 40 student responses, based on row percentages and based on column percentages.

Gender:	M	M	M	F	M	F	F	M	F	M	F	M	M	M	M	F	F	M	F	F
Major:	A	C	C	M	A	C	A	A	C	C	A	A	A	M	C	M	A	A	A	C
Gender:	M	M	M	M	F	M	F	F	M	M	F	M	M	M	M	F	M	F	M	M
Major:	C	C	A	A	M	M	C	A	A	A	C	C	A	A	A	A	C	C	A	C

APPLYING THE CONCEPTS

2.21 The Transportation Security Administration reported that from January 1, 2008, to February 18, 2009, more than 14,000 banned items were collected at Palm Beach International Airport. The categories were as follows:

Category	Frequency
Flammables/irritants	8,350
Knives and blades	4,134
Prohibited tools	753
Sharp objects	497
Other	357

a. Compute the percentage of values in each category.
b. What conclusions can you reach concerning the banned items?

✓SELF **2.22** The Energy Information Administration
Test reported the following sources of electricity in the United States in 2008:

Source of Electricity	Net Electricity Generation (millions of megawatt-hours)
Coal	1,994.4
Hydroelectric	248.1
Natural gas	876.9
Nuclear	806.2
Other	184.7

Source: *Energy Information Administration, 2008.*

a. Compute the percentage of values in each category.
b. What conclusions can you reach concerning the sources of electricity in the United States in 2008?

2.23 Federal obligations for benefit programs and the national debt were $63.8 trillion in 2008. The cost per household ($) for various categories was as follows:

Category	Cost per Household ($)
Civil servant retirement	15,851
Federal debt	54,537
Medicare	284,288
Military retirement	29,694
Social Security	160,216
Other	2,172

Source: *Data extracted from "What We Owe," USA Today, May 29, 2009, p. 1A.*

a. Compute the percentage of values in each category.
b. What conclusions can you reach concerning the benefit programs?

2.24 A sample of 500 shoppers was selected in a large metropolitan area to determine various information concerning consumer behavior. Among the questions asked was "Do you enjoy shopping for clothing?" The results are summarized in the following table:

ENJOY SHOPPING FOR CLOTHING	GENDER		Total
	Male	Female	
Yes	136	224	360
No	104	36	140
Total	240	260	500

a. Construct contingency tables based on total percentages, row percentages, and column percentages.
b. What conclusions do you draw from these analyses?

2.25 Each day at a large hospital, several hundred laboratory tests are performed. The rate at which these tests are done improperly (and therefore need to be redone) seems steady, at about 4%. In an effort to get to the root cause of these nonconformances, tests that need to be redone, the director of the lab decided to keep records over a period of one week. The laboratory tests were subdivided by the shift of workers who performed the lab tests. The results are as follows:

LAB TESTS PERFORMED	SHIFT		Total
	Day	Evening	
Nonconforming	16	24	40
Conforming	654	306	960
Total	670	330	1,000

a. Construct contingency tables based on total percentages, row percentages, and column percentages.
b. Which type of percentage—row, column, or total—do you think is most informative for these data? Explain.
c. What conclusions concerning the pattern of nonconforming laboratory tests can the laboratory director reach?

2.26 An experiment was conducted by James Choi, David Laibson, and Brigitte Madrian to study the choices made in fund selection. When presented with four S&P 500 Index

	STUDENT GROUP	
FUND	Undergraduate	MBA
Lowest fee	19	19
Second-lowest fee	37	40
Third-lowest fee	17	23
Highest fee	27	18

Source: *Data extracted from J. Choi, D. Laibson, and B. Madrian, "Why Does the Law of One Practice Fail? An Experiment on Mutual Funds,"* **www.som.yale.edu/faculty/jjc83/fees.pdf**.

funds that were identical except for their fees, undergraduate and MBA students chose the funds in the percentages shown in the table at the left. Note that because the funds are identical, the best choice is the fund with the lowest fee.

What do these results tell you about the differences between undergraduate and MBA students in their ability to choose S&P 500 Index funds?

2.4 Organizing Numerical Data

You organize numerical data by using ordered arrays or creating distributions. The amount of data you have and what you seek to discover about the data influences your choices. When using Excel, your choice in organizing your numerical data may also limit your choices later on when you visualize your data.

The Ordered Array

Particularly useful when you have more than a few values, an **ordered array** arranges the values of a numerical variable in rank order, from the smallest value to the largest value.

An ordered array helps you get a better sense of the range of values in your data. For example, Table 2.7A shows the data collected for a study of the cost of meals at 50 restaurants located in a major city and at 50 restaurants located in that city's suburbs. (Open RestCost to examine the data collected.) The unordered data in Table 2.7A prevents you from reaching any quick conclusions about the meal data.

TABLE 2.7A

Cost per Person at 50 City Restaurants and 50 Suburban Restaurants

City Restaurant Meal Cost

40	26	35	25	34	51	55	13	42	62
22	26	33	35	21	61	53	26	30	41
57	41	53	39	26	62	34	75	32	35
50	41	22	53	37	45	37	68	24	66
51	35	36	39	39	44	50	43	46	62

Suburban Restaurant Meal Cost

62	27	47	42	25	36	39	32	41	50
50	37	50	47	52	31	38	44	32	47
51	26	37	26	38	22	53	40	43	35
25	65	67	28	29	35	27	28	58	38
41	50	28	41	21	40	42	50	48	37

In contrast, Table 2.7B, the ordered array version of the same data, enables you to quickly see that the cost of a meal at the city restaurants is between $13 and $75 and that the cost of a meal at the suburban restaurants is between $21 and $67.

When you have a data set that contains a large number of values, reaching conclusions from an ordered array can be difficult. In such circumstances, you can develop a frequency or percentage distribution and a cumulative percentage distribution.

TABLE 2.7B
Ordered Arrays of Cost
per Person at 50 City
Restaurants and 50
Suburban Restaurants

City Restaurant Meal Cost									
13	21	22	22	24	25	26	26	26	26
30	32	33	34	34	35	35	35	35	36
37	37	39	39	39	40	41	41	41	42
43	44	45	46	50	50	51	51	53	53
53	55	57	61	62	62	62	66	68	75

Suburban Restaurant Meal Cost									
21	22	25	25	26	26	27	27	28	28
28	29	31	32	32	35	35	36	37	37
37	38	38	38	39	40	40	41	41	41
42	42	43	44	47	47	47	48	50	50
50	50	50	51	52	53	58	62	65	67

The Frequency Distribution

A **frequency distribution** summarizes numerical values by tallying them into a set of numerically ordered **classes**. Classes are groups that represent a range of values, called a **class interval**. Each value can be in only one class and every value must be contained in one of the classes.

To create a useful frequency distribution, you must think about how many classes are appropriate for your data and also determine a suitable *width* for each class interval.

In general, a frequency distribution should have at least 5 classes but no more than 15 classes because having too few or too many classes provides little new information. To determine the **class interval width** (see Equation 2.1), you subtract the lowest value from the highest value and divide that result by the number of classes you want your frequency distribution to have.

DETERMINING THE CLASS INTERVAL WIDTH

$$\text{Interval width} = \frac{\text{highest value} - \text{lowest value}}{\text{number of classes}} \tag{2.1}$$

Because the city restaurant data consist of a sample of only 50 restaurants, between 5 and 10 classes are acceptable. From the ordered city cost array in Table 2.7B, the difference between the highest value of $75 and the lowest value of $13 is $62. Using Equation (2.1), you approximate the class interval width as follows:

$$\text{Interval width} = \frac{62}{10} = 6.2$$

This result suggests that you should choose an interval width of $6.20. However, your width should always be an amount that simplifies the reading and interpretation of the frequency distribution. In this example, an interval width of $10 would be much better than an interval width of $6.20.

Because each value can appear in only one class, you must establish proper and clearly defined **class boundaries** for each class. For example, if you chose $10 as the class interval for the restaurant data, you would need to establish boundaries that would include all the values and simplify the reading and interpretation of the frequency distribution. Because the cost of a city restaurant meal varies from $13 to $75, establishing the first class interval as from $10 to less than $20, the second from $20 to less than $30, and so on, until the last class interval is from $70 to less than $80, would meet the requirements. Table 2.8 is a frequency distribution of the cost per meal for the 50 city restaurants and the 50 suburban restaurants that uses these class intervals.

TABLE 2.8

Frequency Distributions of the Cost per Meal for 50 City Restaurants and 50 Suburban Restaurants

Cost per Meal ($)	City Frequency	Suburban Frequency
10 but less than 20	1	0
20 but less than 30	9	12
30 but less than 40	15	13
40 but less than 50	9	13
50 but less than 60	9	9
60 but less than 70	6	3
70 but less than 80	1	0
Total	50	50

The frequency distribution allows you to reach conclusions about the major characteristics of the data. For example, Table 2.8 shows that the cost of meals at both city restaurants and suburban restaurants is concentrated between $20 and $60.

For some charts discussed later in this chapter, class intervals are identified by their **class midpoints**, the values that are halfway between the lower and upper boundaries of each class. For the frequency distributions shown in Table 2.8, the class midpoints are $15, $25, $35, $45, $55, $65, and $75 (amounts that are simple to read and interpret).

If the data set does not contain a large number of values, different sets of class intervals can create different impressions of the data. Such perceived changes will diminish as you collect more data. Likewise, choosing different lower and upper class boundaries can also affect impressions.

EXAMPLE 2.2

Frequency Distributions of the 2008 Return for Intermediate Government and Short-Term Corporate Bond Mutual Funds

TABLE 2.9

Frequency Distributions of the 2008 Return for Intermediate Government and Short-Term Corporate Bond Funds

The **FD_COMBINED** worksheet of the **Chapter 2 workbook** contains frequency distributions similar to Table 2.9. Create this worksheet using the instructions in Section EG2.4.

In the Using Statistics scenario, you are interested in comparing the 2008 return of intermediate government and short-term corporate bond mutual funds. Construct frequency distributions for the intermediate government funds and the short-term corporate bond funds.

SOLUTION The 2008 returns of the intermediate government bond funds are highly concentrated between 5 and 10, whereas the 2008 returns of the short-term corporate bond funds are highly concentrated between −5 and 5 (see Table 2.9).

2008 Return	Intermediate Government Frequency	Short-Term Corporate Frequency
−35 but less than −30	0	1
−30 but less than −25	0	0
−25 but less than −20	0	1
−20 but less than −15	0	7
−15 but less than −10	0	5
−10 but less than −5	2	10
−5 but less than 0	12	33
0 but less than 5	14	30
5 but less than 10	46	3
10 but less than 15	15	0
15 but less than 20	1	0
Total	90	90

Although, for the bond fund data, the number of frequencies is the same in the two groups, that is not usually the case. When the number of frequencies in the two groups is not the same, you need to use proportions or relative frequencies and percentages in order to compare the groups.

The Relative Frequency Distribution and the Percentage Distribution

When you are comparing two or more groups, as is done in Table 2.10, knowing the proportion or percentage of the total that is in each group is more useful than knowing the frequency count of each group. For such situations, you create a relative frequency distribution or a percentage distribution instead of a frequency distribution. (If your two or more groups have different sample sizes, you *must* use either a relative frequency distribution or a percentage distribution.)

TABLE 2.10

Relative Frequency Distributions and Percentage Distributions of the Cost of Meals at City and Suburban Restaurants

	CITY		SUBURBAN	
COST PER MEAL ($)	Relative Frequency	Percentage (%)	Relative Frequency	Percentage (%)
10 but less than 20	0.02	2.0	0.00	0.0
20 but less than 30	0.18	18.0	0.24	24.0
30 but less than 40	0.30	30.0	0.26	26.0
40 but less than 50	0.18	18.0	0.26	26.0
50 but less than 60	0.18	18.0	0.18	18.0
60 but less than 70	0.12	12.0	0.06	6.0
70 but less than 80	0.02	2.0	0.00	0.0
Total	1.00	100.0	1.00	100.0

The **proportion**, or **relative frequency**, in each group is equal to the number of frequencies in each class divided by the total number of values. The percentage in each group is its proportion multiplied by 100%.

COMPUTING THE PROPORTION OR RELATIVE FREQUENCY

The proportion, or relative frequency, is the number of frequencies in each class divided by the total number of values.

$$\text{Proportion} = \text{Relative Frequency} = \frac{\text{frequency in each class}}{\text{total number of values}} \qquad (2.2)$$

Thus, if there are 80 values and the frequency in a certain class is 20, the proportion of values in that class is

$$\frac{20}{80} = 0.25$$

and the percentage is

$$0.25 \times 100\% = 25\%$$

You form the **relative frequency distribution** by first determining the relative frequency in each class. For example, in Table 2.8 on page 27, there are 50 city restaurants, and the cost per meal at 9 of these restaurants is between $20 and $30. Therefore, as shown in Table 2.10, the proportion (or relative frequency) of meals that cost between $20 and $30 at city restaurants is

$$\frac{9}{50} = 0.18$$

You form the **percentage distribution** by multiplying each proportion (or relative frequency) by 100%. Thus, the proportion of meals at city restaurants that cost between $20 and $30 is 9 divided by 50, or 0.18, and the percentage is 18%. Table 2.10 presents the relative frequency distribution and percentage distribution of the cost of meals at city and suburban restaurants.

From Table 2.10, you conclude that meals cost slightly more at city restaurants than at suburban restaurants. Also, 12% of the meals cost between $60 and $70 at city restaurants as compared to 6% of the meals at suburban restaurants; and 18% of the meals cost between $20 and $30 at city restaurants as compared to 24% of the meals at suburban restaurants.

EXAMPLE 2.3

Relative Frequency Distributions and Percentage Distributions of the 2008 Return for Intermediate Government and Short-Term Corporate Bond Mutual Funds

The FD_ENHANCED worksheet of the Chapter 2 workbook contains a frequency distribution that include the percentages shown in Table 2.11. The instructions in Section EG2.4 explain how to add a column of percentages to a frequency distribution.

In the Using Statistics scenario, you are interested in comparing the 2008 return of intermediate government and short-term corporate bond mutual funds. Construct relative frequency distributions and percentage distributions for these funds.

SOLUTION You conclude (see Table 2.11) that the 2008 return for the corporate bond funds is much lower than for the intermediate government funds. For example, 36.67% of the corporate bond funds have returns between −5 and 0, while 13.33% of the intermediate government funds have returns between −5 and 0. Of the intermediate government funds, 51.11% have returns between 5 and 10 as compared to only 3.33% of the corporate bond funds.

TABLE 2.11

Relative Frequency Distributions and Percentage Distributions of the 2008 Return for Intermediate Government and Short-Term Corporate Bond Mutual Funds

2008 RETURN	INTERMEDIATE GOVERNMENT		SHORT-TERM CORPORATE	
	Proportion	**Percentage**	**Proportion**	**Percentage**
−35 but less than −30	0.0000	0.00	0.0111	1.11
−30 but less than −25	0.0000	0.00	0.0000	0.00
−25 but less than −20	0.0000	0.00	0.0111	1.11
−20 but less than −15	0.0000	0.00	0.0778	7.78
−15 but less than −10	0.0000	0.00	0.0556	5.56
−10 but less than −5	0.0222	2.22	0.1111	11.11
−5 but less than 0	0.1333	13.33	0.3667	36.67
0 but less than 5	0.1556	15.56	0.3333	33.33
5 but less than 10	0.5111	51.11	0.0333	3.33
10 but less than 15	0.1667	16.67	0.0000	0.00
15 but less than 20	0.0111	1.11	0.0000	0.00
Total	1.0000	100.00	1.0000	100.00

The Cumulative Distribution

The **cumulative percentage distribution** provides a way of presenting information about the percentage of values that are less than a specific amount. For example, you might want to know what percentage of the city restaurant meals cost less than $20 or what percentage cost less than $50. You use the percentage distribution to form the cumulative percentage distribution. Table 2.12 shows how percentages of individual class intervals are combined to form the cumulative percentage distribution for the cost of meals at city restaurants. From this table, you see that none (0%) of the meals cost less than $10, 2% of meals cost less than $20, 20% of meals cost less than $30 (because 18% of the meals cost between $20 and $30), and so on, until all 100% of the meals cost less than $80.

Table 2.13 summarizes the cumulative percentages of the cost of city and suburban restaurant meals. The cumulative distribution shows that the cost of meals is slightly lower in suburban restaurants than in city restaurants. Table 2.13 shows that 24% of the meals at suburban restaurants cost less than $30 as compared to 20% of the meals at city restaurants; 76% of the meals at suburban restaurants cost less than $50 as compared to 68% of the meals at city restaurants; and 94% of the meals at suburban restaurants cost less than $60 as compared to 86% of the meals at city restaurants.

TABLE 2.12

Developing the Cumulative Percentage Distribution for the Cost of Meals at City Restaurants

Cost per Meal ($)	Percentage (%)	Percentage of Meals Less Than Lower Boundary of Class Interval (%)
10 but less than 20	2	0
20 but less than 30	18	2
30 but less than 40	30	$20 = 2 + 18$
40 but less than 50	18	$50 = 2 + 18 + 30$
50 but less than 60	18	$68 = 2 + 18 + 30 + 18$
60 but less than 70	12	$86 = 2 + 18 + 30 + 18 + 18$
70 but less than 80	2	$98 = 2 + 18 + 30 + 18 + 18 + 12$
80 but less than 90	0	$100 = 2 + 18 + 30 + 18 + 18 + 12 + 2$

TABLE 2.13

Cumulative Percentage Distributions of the Cost of City and Suburban Restaurant Meals

Cost ($)	Percentage of City Restaurants with Meals Less Than Indicated Amount	Percentage of Suburban Restaurants with Meals Less Than Indicated Amount
10	0	0
20	2	0
30	20	24
40	50	50
50	68	76
60	86	94
70	98	100
80	100	100

EXAMPLE 2.4

Cumulative Percentage Distributions of the 2008 Return for Intermediate Government and Short-Term Corporate Bond Mutual Funds

The FD_ENHANCED worksheet of the Chapter 2 workbook contains a frequency distribution that include the cumulative percentages shown in Table 2.14. The instructions in Section EG2.4 explain how to add a column of cumulative percentage frequencies to a frequency distribution.

In the Using Statistics scenario, you are interested in comparing the 2008 return for intermediate government and short-term corporate bond mutual funds. Construct cumulative percentage distributions for the intermediate government and short-term corporate bond mutual funds.

SOLUTION The cumulative distribution in Table 2.14 indicates that returns are much lower for the short-term corporate bond funds than for the intermediate government funds. The table shows that 15.55% of the intermediate government funds have negative returns as compared to 63.34% of the short-term corporate bond funds; 2.22% of the intermediate government funds have returns below -5 as compared to 26.67% of the short-term corporate bond funds; and 31.11% of the intermediate government funds have returns below 5 as compared to 96.67% of the short-term corporate bond funds.

TABLE 2.14

Cumulative Percentage Distributions of the 2008 Return for Intermediate Government and Short-Term Corporate Bond Funds

2008 Return	Intermediate Government Percentage Less Than Indicated Value	Short-Term Corporate Percentage Less Than Indicated Value
-35	0.00	0.00
-30	0.00	1.11
-25	0.00	1.11
-20	0.00	2.22
-15	0.00	10.00
-10	0.00	15.56
-5	2.22	26.67
0	15.55	63.34
5	31.11	96.67
10	82.22	100.00
15	98.89	100.00
20	100.00	100.00

Problems for Section 2.4

LEARNING THE BASICS

2.27 Form an ordered array, given the following data from a sample of $n = 7$ midterm exam scores in accounting:

$$68 \quad 94 \quad 63 \quad 75 \quad 71 \quad 88 \quad 64$$

2.28 Form an ordered array, given the following data from a sample of $n = 7$ midterm exam scores in marketing:

$$88 \quad 78 \quad 78 \quad 73 \quad 91 \quad 78 \quad 85$$

2.29 The GMAT scores from a sample of 50 applicants to an MBA program indicate that none of the applicants scored below 450. A frequency distribution was formed by choosing class intervals 450 to 499, 500 to 549, and so on, with the last class having an interval from 700 to 749. Two applicants scored in the interval 450 to 499, and 16 applicants scored in the interval 500 to 549.
a. What percentage of applicants scored below 500?
b. What percentage of applicants scored between 500 and 549?
c. What percentage of applicants scored below 550?
d. What percentage of applicants scored below 750?

2.30 A set of data has values that vary from 11.6 to 97.8.
a. If these values are grouped into nine classes, indicate the class boundaries.
b. What class interval width did you choose?
c. What are the nine class midpoints?

APPLYING THE CONCEPTS

2.31 As player salaries have increased, the cost of attending baseball games has increased dramatically. The file BBCost contains the following 2009 data concerning the total cost at each of the 30 Major League Baseball parks for four tickets, two beers, four soft drinks, four hot dogs, two game programs, two baseball caps, and parking for one vehicle:

164 326 224 180 205 162 141 170 411 187 185 165 151 166 114
158 305 145 161 170 210 222 146 259 220 135 215 172 223 216

Source: *Data extracted from **teammarketing.com**, April 1, 2009.*

a. Place the data into an ordered array.
b. Construct a frequency distribution and a percentage distribution.
c. Around which class grouping, if any, are the costs of attending a baseball game concentrated? Explain.

✓SELF Test **2.32** The file Utility contains the following data about the cost of electricity during July 2009 for a random sample of 50 one-bedroom apartments in a large city:

Raw Data on Utility Charges ($)

96	171	202	178	147	102	153	197	127	82
157	185	90	116	172	111	148	213	130	165
141	149	206	175	123	128	144	168	109	167
95	163	150	154	130	143	187	166	139	149
108	119	183	151	114	135	191	137	129	158

a. Construct a frequency distribution and a percentage distribution that have class intervals with the upper class boundaries $99, $119, and so on.
b. Construct a cumulative percentage distribution.
c. Around what amount does the monthly electricity cost seem to be concentrated?

2.33 One operation of a mill is to cut pieces of steel into parts that will later be used as the frame for front seats in an automobile. The steel is cut with a diamond saw and requires the resulting parts to be within ±0.005 inch of the length specified by the automobile company. Data are collected from a sample of 100 steel parts and stored in Steel. The measurement reported is the difference in inches between the actual length of the steel part, as measured by a laser measurement device, and the specified length of the steel part. For example, the first value, −0.002, represents a steel part that is 0.002 inch shorter than the specified length.
a. Construct a frequency distribution and a percentage distribution.
b. Construct a cumulative percentage distribution.
c. Is the steel mill doing a good job meeting the requirements set by the automobile company? Explain.

2.34 A manufacturing company produces steel housings for electrical equipment. The main component part of the housing is a steel trough that is made out of a 14-gauge steel coil. It is produced using a 250-ton progressive punch press with a wipe-down operation that puts two 90-degree forms in the flat steel to make the trough. The distance from one side of the form to the other is critical because of weatherproofing in outdoor applications. The company requires that the width of the trough be between 8.31 inches and 8.61 inches. Data are collected from a sample of 49 troughs and stored in Trough, which contains the widths of the troughs, in inches.

8.312	8.343	8.317	8.383	8.348	8.410	8.351	8.373
8.481	8.422	8.476	8.382	8.484	8.403	8.414	8.419
8.385	8.465	8.498	8.447	8.436	8.413	8.489	8.414
8.481	8.415	8.479	8.429	8.458	8.462	8.460	8.444
8.429	8.460	8.412	8.420	8.410	8.405	8.323	8.420
8.396	8.447	8.405	8.439	8.411	8.427	8.420	8.498
8.409							

a. Construct a frequency distribution and a percentage distribution.

b. Construct a cumulative percentage distribution.

c. What can you conclude about the number of troughs that will meet the company's requirements of troughs being between 8.31 and 8.61 inches wide?

2.35 The manufacturing company in Problem 2.34 also produces electric insulators. If the insulators break when in use, a short circuit is likely to occur. To test the strength of the insulators, destructive testing in high-powered labs is carried out to determine how much *force* is required to break the insulators. Force is measured by observing how many pounds must be applied to the insulator before it breaks. Data are collected from a sample of 30 insulators. The file `Force` contains the strengths as follows:

1,870	1,728	1,656	1,610	1,634	1,784	1,522	1,696
1,592	1,662	1,866	1,764	1,734	1,662	1,734	1,774
1,550	1,756	1,762	1,866	1,820	1,744	1,788	1,688
1,810	1,752	1,680	1,810	1,652	1,736		

a. Construct a frequency distribution and a percentage distribution.

b. Construct a cumulative percentage distribution.

c. What can you conclude about the strength of the insulators if the company requires a force measurement of at least 1,500 pounds before the insulator breaks?

2.36 The ordered arrays in the following table (found in `Bulbs`) show the life (in hours) of a sample of 40 100-watt light bulbs produced by Manufacturer A and a sample of 40 100-watt light bulbs produced by Manufacturer B:

Manufacturer A					Manufacturer B				
684	697	720	773	821	819	836	888	897	903
831	835	848	852	852	907	912	918	942	943
859	860	868	870	876	952	959	962	986	992
893	899	905	909	911	994	1,004	1,005	1,007	1,015
922	924	926	926	938	1,016	1,018	1,020	1,022	1,034
939	943	946	954	971	1,038	1,072	1,077	1,077	1,082
972	977	984	1,005	1,014	1,096	1,100	1,113	1,113	1,116
1,016	1,041	1,052	1,080	1,093	1,153	1,154	1,174	1,188	1,230

a. Construct a frequency distribution and a percentage distribution for each manufacturer, using the following class interval widths for each distribution:
Manufacturer A: 650 but less than 750, 750 but less than 850, and so on.
Manufacturer B: 750 but less than 850, 850 but less than 950, and so on.

b. Construct cumulative percentage distributions.

c. Which bulbs have a longer life—those from Manufacturer A or Manufacturer B? Explain.

2.37 The following data (found in `Drink`) represent the amount of soft drink in a sample of 50 2-liter bottles:

2.109 2.086 2.066 2.075 2.065 2.057 2.052 2.044 2.036 2.038
2.031 2.029 2.025 2.029 2.023 2.020 2.015 2.014 2.013 2.014
2.012 2.012 2.012 2.010 2.005 2.003 1.999 1.996 1.997 1.992
1.994 1.986 1.984 1.981 1.973 1.975 1.971 1.969 1.966 1.967
1.963 1.957 1.951 1.951 1.947 1.941 1.941 1.938 1.908 1.894

a. Construct a cumulative percentage distribution.

b. On the basis of the results of (a) and (b), does the amount of soft drink filled in the bottles concentrate around specific values?

VISUALIZING DATA

When you organize your data, you sometimes begin to discover patterns or relationships in your data, as examples in Sections 2.3 and 2.4 illustrate. To better explore and discover patterns and relationships, you can visualize your data using various charts and special "displays." As is the case with the organizing step, the techniques you use to visualize your data depend on the variable type (categorical or numerical) of your data.

2.5 Visualizing Categorical Data

To visualize the data for a single categorical variable, you choose a chart, depending on whether you seek to emphasize how categories directly compare to each other (bar chart), show how categories form parts of a whole (pie chart), or have data in which most of the data are in a few categories (Pareto chart). To visualize the data for two categorical variables, you use a side-by-side bar chart.

The Bar Chart

A **bar chart** compares different categories by using individual bars to represent the tallies for each category. The length of a bar represents the amount, frequency, or percentage of values falling into a category. Unlike with a histogram, discussed in Section 2.6, with a bar chart there is a separation of the bars between the categories. Figure 2.5 displays the bar chart for the data of Table 2.1 on page 21, which is based on a recent survey that asked adults how they pay their monthly bills ("How Adults Pay Monthly Bills," *USA Today*, October 4, 2007, p. 1).

FIGURE 2.5

Bar chart for how adults pay their monthly bills

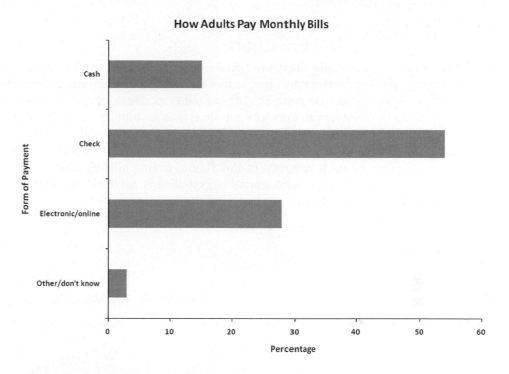

Reviewing Figure 2.5, you see that respondents are most likely to pay by check or electronically/online, followed by paying by cash. Very few respondents mentioned other or did not know.

EXAMPLE 2.5

Bar Chart of Levels of Risk of Bond Mutual Funds

FIGURE 2.6

Bar chart of the levels of risk of bond mutual funds

The BAR_RISK chart sheet of the Chapter 2 workbook contains the Figure 2.6 bar chart. Create this worksheet using the instructions in Section EG2.5.

In Part I of the Choice Is Yours scenario, you are interested in examining the risk of the bond funds. You have already defined the variables and collected the data from a sample of 180 bond funds. Now, you need to construct a bar chart of the risk of the bond funds (based on Table 2.2 on page 22) and interpret the results.

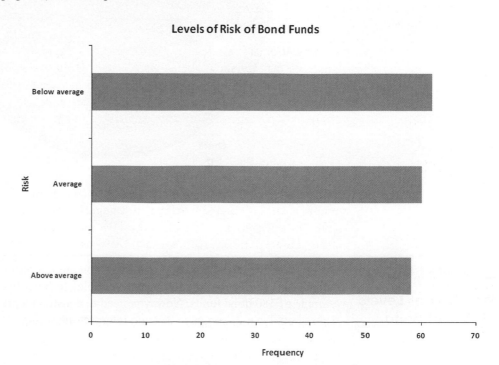

SOLUTION Reviewing Figure 2.6, you see that below average is the largest category, closely followed by average, and above average.

The Pie Chart

A **pie chart** uses parts of a circle to represent the tallies of each category. The size of each part, or pie slice, varies according to the percentage in each category. For example, in Table 2.1 on page 21, 54% of the respondents stated that they paid bills by check. To represent this category as a pie slice, you multiply 54% by the 360 degrees that makes up a circle to get a pie slice that takes up 194.4 degrees of the 360 degrees of the circle. From Figure 2.7, you can see that the pie chart lets you visualize the portion of the entire pie that is in each category. In this figure, paying bills by check is the largest slice, containing 54% of the pie. The second largest slice is paying bills electronically/online, which contains 28% of the pie.

FIGURE 2.7

Pie chart for how people pay their bills

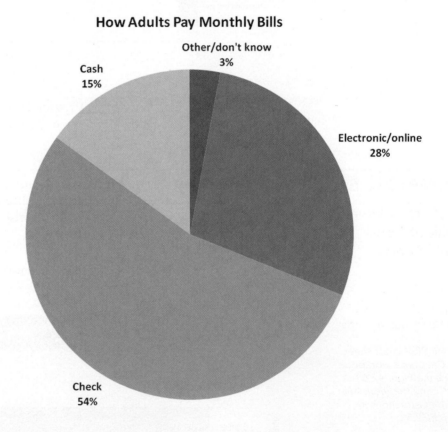

How Adults Pay Monthly Bills

Other/don't know 3%

Cash 15%

Electronic/online 28%

Check 54%

EXAMPLE 2.6

Pie Chart of Levels of Risk of Bond Mutual Funds

In Part I of the Choice Is Yours scenario, you are interested in examining the risk of the bond funds. You have already defined the variables to be collected and collected the data from a sample of 180 bond funds. Now, you need to construct a pie chart of the risk of the bond funds (based on Table 2.2 on page 22) and interpret the results.

FIGURE 2.8
Pie chart of the levels of
risk of bond mutual funds

*The PIE_RISK chart sheet of
the Chapter 2 workbook
contains the Figure 2.8
chart. Create this worksheet
using the instructions in
Section EG2.5.*

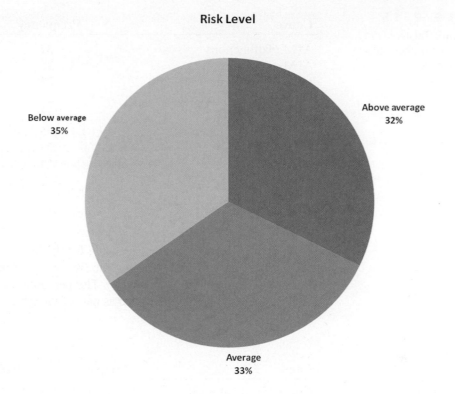

SOLUTION Reviewing Figure 2.8, you see that approximately one-third of the funds are below average risk, one-third are average risk, and one-third are above-average risk.

The Pareto Chart

In a **Pareto chart**, the tallies for each category are plotted as vertical bars in descending order, according to their frequencies, and are combined with a cumulative percentage line on the same chart. A Pareto chart can reveal situations in which the Pareto principle occurs.

> PARETO PRINCIPLE
>
> The **Pareto principle** exists when the majority of items in a set of data occur in a small number of categories and the few remaining items are spread out over a large number of categories. These two groups are often referred to as the "vital few" and the "trivial many."

A Pareto chart has the capability to separate the "vital few" from the "trivial many," enabling you to focus on the important categories. In situations in which the data involved consist of defective or nonconforming items, a Pareto chart is a powerful tool for prioritizing improvement efforts.

To study a situation in which the Pareto chart proved to be especially appropriate, consider the problem faced by a bank. The bank defined the problem of interest to be the incomplete automated teller machine (ATM) transactions. Data concerning the causes of incomplete ATM transactions were collected (see ATM Transactions). Table 2.15 shows the causes of incomplete ATM transactions, the frequency for each cause, and the percentage of incomplete ATM transactions due to each cause.

TABLE 2.15

Summary Table of
Causes of Incomplete
ATM Transactions

Cause	Frequency	Percentage (%)
ATM malfunctions	32	4.42
ATM out of cash	28	3.87
Invalid amount requested	23	3.18
Lack of funds in account	19	2.62
Magnetic strip unreadable	234	32.32
Warped card jammed	365	50.41
Wrong key stroke	23	3.18
Total	724	100.00

Source: *Data extracted from A. Bhalla, "Don't Misuse the Pareto Principle,"* Six Sigma Forum Magazine, *May 2009, pp. 15–18.*

Table 2.16 presents a summary table for the incomplete ATM transactions data in which the categories are ordered based on the frequency of incomplete ATM transactions present (rather than arranged alphabetically). The percentages and cumulative percentages for the ordered categories are also included as part of the table.

TABLE 2.16

Ordered Summary Table
of Causes of Incomplete
ATM Transactions

Cause	Frequency	Percentage (%)	Cumulative Percentage (%)
Warped card jammed	365	50.41%	50.41%
Magnetic strip unreadable	234	32.32%	82.73%
ATM malfunctions	32	4.42%	87.15%
ATM out of cash	28	3.87%	91.02%
Invalid amount requested	23	3.18%	94.20%
Wrong key stroke	23	3.18%	97.38%
Lack of funds in account	19	2.62%	100.00%
Total	724	100.00%	

Figure 2.9 shows a Pareto chart based on the results displayed in Table 2.16.

FIGURE 2.9

Pareto chart for the
incomplete ATM
transactions data

*The PARETO_ATM chart
sheet of the Chapter 2
workbook contains the Figure
2.9 chart. Create this chart
using the instructions in
Section EG2.5.*

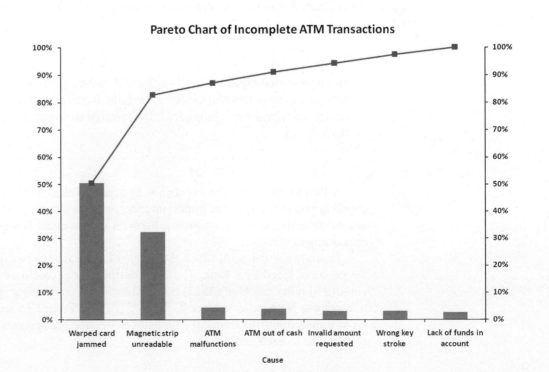

A Pareto chart presents the bars vertically, along with a cumulative percentage line. The cumulative line is plotted at the midpoint of each category, at a height equal to the cumulative percentage. In order for a Pareto chart to include all categories, even those with few defects, in some situations, you need to include a category labeled *Other* or *Miscellaneous*. In these situations, the bar representing these categories should be placed to the right of the other bars.

Because the categories in a Pareto chart are ordered by the frequency of occurrence, you can see where to concentrate efforts to improve the process. Analyzing the Pareto chart in Figure 2.9, if you follow the line, you see that these first two categories account for 82.73% of the incomplete ATM transactions. The first category listed is warped card jammed (with 50.41% of the defects), followed by magnetic strip unreadable (with 32.32%). Attempts to reduce incomplete ATM transactions due to warped card jammed and magnetic strip unreadable should produce the greatest payoff. The team should focus on finding why these errors occurred.

The Side-by-Side Bar Chart

A **side-by-side bar chart** uses sets of bars to show the joint responses from two categorical variables. Figure 2.10 uses the data of Table 2.3 on page 22, which shows the frequency of bond funds that charge a fee for the intermediate government bond funds and short-term corporate bond funds.

FIGURE 2.10

Side-by-side bar chart of fund type and whether a fee is charged

The SIDE_BY_SIDE chart sheet of the Chapter 2 workbook contains the Figure 2.10 chart. Create this chart using the instructions in Section EG2.5.

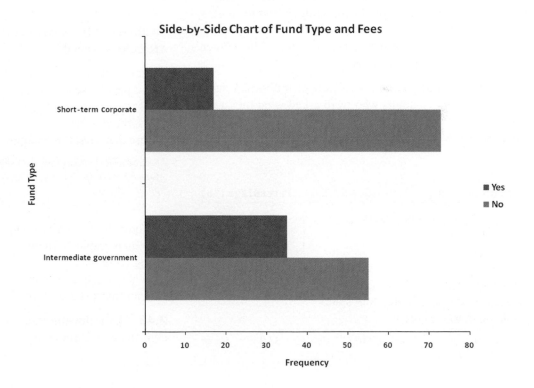

Reviewing Figure 2.10, you see that a much higher percentage of the intermediate government bond funds charge a fee than the short-term corporate bond funds.

Problems for Section 2.5

APPLYING THE CONCEPTS

✓ **SELF Test** **2.38** A survey of 1,264 women asked who their most trusted shopping advisers were. The survey results were as follows:

Shopping Advisers	Percentage (%)
Advertising	7
Friends/family	45
Manufacturer Web sites	5
News media	11
Online user reviews	13
Retail Web sites	4
Salespeople	1
Other	14

Source: *Data extracted from "Snapshots," USA Today, October 19, 2006, p. 1B.*

a. Construct a bar chart, a pie chart, and a Pareto chart.
b. Which graphical method do you think is best for portraying these data?
c. What conclusions can you reach concerning women's most trusted shopping advisers?

2.39 What would you do if you won $1 million? A survey was taken of 1,078 adults who were asked what they would spend money on first if they won $1 million in a March Madness NCAA pool. The results were as follows:

Spending Choice	Percentage (%)
Buy 2010 Final Four tickets	4
Charity	4
Pay off debt	59
Save it	16
Take a cruise	8
Take money, never enter pool again	4
Take luck to Las Vegas	5

Source: *Data extracted from "If I Win $1 Million," USA Today, March 19, 2009, p. 1A.*

a. Construct a bar chart, a pie chart, and a Pareto chart.
b. Which graphical method do you think is best for portraying these data?
c. What conclusions can you reach concerning what adults would do with $1 million?

2.40 The Energy Information Administration reported the following sources of electricity in the United States in 2008:

Source of Electricity	Net Electricity Generation (millions of megawatt-hours)
Coal	1,994.4
Hydroelectric	248.1
Natural gas	876.9
Nuclear	806.2
Other	184.7

Source: *Energy Information Administration, 2008.*

a. Construct a Pareto chart.
b. What percentage of power is derived from coal, nuclear, or natural gas?
c. Construct a pie chart.
d. For these data, do you prefer using a Pareto chart or the pie chart? Why?

2.41 An article discussed the number of Internet search results that Web surfers typically scan before selecting one. The following table represents the results for a sample of 2,369 people:

Number of Internet Search Results Scanned	Percentage (%)
A few search results	23
First page of search results	39
First two pages	19
First three pages	9
More than first three pages	10

Source: *Data extracted from K. Delaney, "How Search Engine Rules Cause Sites to Go Missing," The Wall Street Journal, March 13, 2007, pp. B1, B4.*

a. Construct a bar chart and a pie chart.
b. Which graphical method do you think is best for portraying these data?
c. What conclusions can you reach concerning how people scan Internet search results?

2.42 The following table indicates the percentage of foreign students enrolled in U.S. colleges in 2004–2005:

Region of Origin	Percentage (%)
Africa	6
Asia	58
Canada	5
Europe	13
Latin America	12
Middle East	6

Source: *U.S. Department of Education, 2008.*

a. Construct a bar chart, a pie chart, and a Pareto chart.

b. Which graphical method do you think is best for portraying these data?

c. What conclusions can you reach concerning the region of origin of foreign students studying at U.S. colleges in 2004–2005?

2.43 A study of 1,000 people asked what respondents wanted to grill during barbecue season. The results were as follows:

Type of Food	Percentage (%)
Beef	38
Chicken	23
Fruit	1
Hot dogs	6
Pork	8
Seafood	19
Vegetables	5

Source: *Data extracted from "What Folks Want Sizzling on the Grill During Barbecue Season," USA Today, March 29, 2009, p. 1A.*

a. Construct a bar chart, a pie chart, and a Pareto chart.

b. Which graphical method do you think is best for portraying these data?

c. What conclusions can you reach concerning what folks want sizzling on the grill during barbecue season?

2.44 A sample of 500 shoppers was selected in a large metropolitan area to determine various information concerning consumer behavior. Among the questions asked was "Do you enjoy shopping for clothing?" The results are summarized in the following table:

ENJOY SHOPPING FOR CLOTHING	GENDER		
	Male	Female	Total
Yes	136	224	360
No	104	36	140
Total	240	260	500

a. Construct a side-by-side bar chart of enjoying shopping and gender.

b. What conclusions do you reach from this chart?

2.45 Each day at a large hospital, several hundred laboratory tests are performed. The rate at which these tests are done improperly (and therefore need to be redone) seems steady, at about 4%. In an effort to get to the root cause of these nonconformances, tests that need to be redone, the director of the lab decided to keep records over a period of one week. The laboratory tests were subdivided by the shift of workers who performed the lab tests. The results are as follows:

LAB TESTS PERFORMED	SHIFT		
	Day	Evening	Total
Nonconforming	16	24	40
Conforming	654	306	960
Total	670	330	1,000

a. Construct a side-by-side bar chart of nonconformances and shift.

b. What conclusions concerning the pattern of nonconforming laboratory tests can the laboratory director reach?

2.46 An experiment was conducted by James Choi, David Laibson, and Brigitte Madrian to study the choices made in fund selection. When presented with four S&P 500 Index funds that were identical except for their fees, undergraduate and MBA students chose the funds as follows (in percentages). Note that because the funds are identical, the best choice is the fund with the lowest fee.

FUND	STUDENT GROUP	
	Undergraduate	MBA
Lowest fee	19	19
Second-lowest fee	37	40
Third-lowest fee	17	23
Highest fee	27	18

Source: *Data extracted from J. Choi, D. Laibson, and B. Madrian, "Why Does the Law of One Practice Fail? An Experiment on Mutual Funds,"* **www.som.yale.edu/faculty/jjc83/fees.pdf**.

a. Construct a side-by-side bar chart of fund and student group.

b. What do these results tell you about the differences between undergraduate and MBA students in terms of ability to choose S&P 500 Index funds?

2.6 Visualizing Numerical Data

Among the charts you use to visualize numerical data are the stem-and-leaf display, the histogram, the percentage polygon, and the cumulative percentage polygon (ogive).

The Stem-and-Leaf Display

A **stem-and-leaf display** organizes data into groups (called stems) so that the values within each group (the leaves) branch out to the right of the stems on each row. The resulting display allows you to see how the data are distributed and where concentrations of data exist. To learn how to construct a stem-and-leaf display, suppose that 15 students from your class eat lunch at a fast-food restaurant. The following data are the amounts ($) spent for lunch:

5.40   4.30   4.80   5.50   7.30   8.50   6.10   4.80   4.90   4.90   5.50   3.50   5.90   6.30   6.60

To construct the stem-and-leaf display, you use the units as the stems and round the decimals (the leaves) to one decimal place. For example, the first value is 5.40. Its stem (row) is 5, and its leaf is 4. The second value is 4.30. Its stem (row) is 4, and its leaf is 3. You continue with the remainder of the 15 values and then reorder the leaves within each stem as follows:

```
3 | 5
4 | 38899
5 | 4559
6 | 136
7 | 3
8 | 5
```

EXAMPLE 2.7

Stem-and-Leaf Display of the 2008 Return of the Intermediate Government Bond Funds

FIGURE 2.11

Stem-and-leaf display of the return in 2008 of intermediate government bond funds

The STEM_LEAF worksheet of the Chapter 2 workbook is shown in Figure 2.11. Create this worksheet using the instructions in Section EG2.6.

In Part I of the Choice Is Yours scenario, you are interested in studying the past performance of the intermediate government bond funds. One measure of past performance is the return in 2008. You have already defined the variables to be collected and collected the data from a sample of 90 intermediate government bond funds. Now, you need to construct a stem-and-leaf display of the return in 2008.

SOLUTION Figure 2.11 illustrates the stem-and-leaf display of the return in 2008 for intermediate government bond funds.

	A	B	C
1	Stem-and-Leaf Display of 2008 Return		
2	for Intermediate Government Bond Funds		
3	Stem unit: 1		
4			
5	-8	6	
6	-7		
7	-6	9	
8	-5		
9	-4	9	
10	-3	7 0	
11	-2	5 4 3 0	
12	-1	9 6 4	
13	-0	8 6	
14	0	1 8	
15	1	1	
16	2		
17	3	3 3 4 4 6 7	
18	4	0 2 6 9 9	
19	5	0 2 6 7 7 9	
20	6	0 0 2 3 4 5 8 9 9 9 9	
21	7	1 1 1 2 2 3 3 6 6 6 7 7 9 9	
22	8	2 2 3 3 4 4 4 5 7 7 8 9	
23	9	1 4 5	
24	10	1 4 6	
25	11	0 1 2 4 5 6	
26	12	4 9	
27	13	5 8 9	
28	14	1	
29	15	0	

Analyzing Figure 2.11, you conclude that:

- The lowest return in 2008 was -8.6.
- The highest return in 2008 was 15.0.
- The returns in 2008 were concentrated between 6 and 9.
- There were 14 funds that had negative 2008 returns and 16 funds that had 2008 returns above 10.

The Histogram

A **histogram** is a bar chart for grouped numerical data in which you use vertical bars to represent the frequencies or percentages in each group. In a histogram, there are no gaps between adjacent bars. You display the variable of interest along the horizontal (X) axis. The vertical (Y) axis represents either the frequency or the percentage of values per class interval.

Figure 2.12 displays frequency histograms for the cost of meals at city restaurants and suburban restaurants.

FIGURE 2.12

Histograms for the cost of restaurant meals at city and suburban restaurants

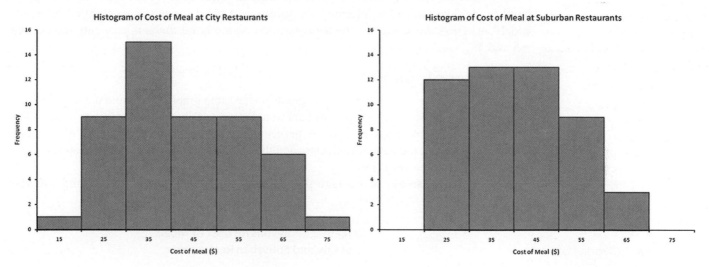

The histogram for city restaurants shows that the cost of meals is concentrated between approximately $20 and $60, with the highest concentration between $30 and $40. Very few meals at city restaurants cost less than $20 or more than $70. The histogram for suburban restaurants shows that the cost of meals is concentrated between $20 and $50. Very few meals at suburban restaurants cost more than $60.

EXAMPLE 2.8

Histograms of the 2008 Return for the Intermediate Government and Short-Term Corporate Bond Funds

In Part I of the Choice Is Yours scenario, you are interested in comparing the past performance of the intermediate government bond funds and the short-term corporate bond funds. One measure of past performance is the return in 2008. You have already defined the variables to be collected and collected the data from a sample of 180 bond funds. Now, you need to construct histograms for the intermediate government and the short-term corporate bond funds.

SOLUTION Figure 2.13 displays frequency histograms for the 2008 return for the intermediate government and the short-term corporate bond funds.

FIGURE 2.13

FIGURE 2.13

Frequency histograms of the 2008 return for the intermediate government and short-term corporate bond funds

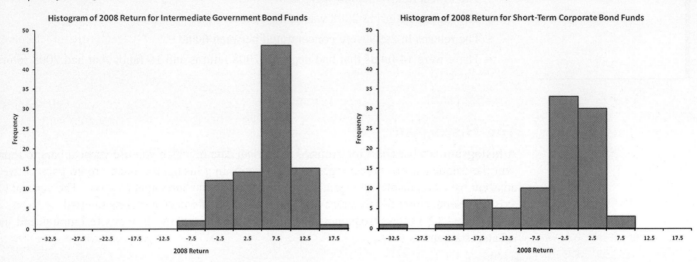

The IG_HISTOGRAM and STC_HISTOGRAM chart sheets of the Chapter 2 workbook are shown in Figure 2.13. Create these charts using the instructions in Section EG2.6.

Reviewing the histograms in Figure 2.13 leads you to conclude that the returns were much higher for the intermediate government bond funds than for the short-term corporate bond funds. The return for intermediate government bond funds is concentrated between 5 and 10, whereas the return for the short-term corporate bond funds is concentrated between −5 and 5.

The Percentage Polygon

If you tried to construct two or more histograms on the same graph, you would not be able to easily interpret each histogram because the bars would overlap. When there are two or more groups, you should use a percentage polygon. A **percentage polygon** uses the midpoints of each class interval to represent the data of each class and then plots the midpoints, at their respective class percentages, as points on a line.

Figure 2.14 displays percentage polygons for the cost of meals at city and suburban restaurants.

FIGURE 2.14

Percentage polygons of the cost of restaurant meals for city and suburban restaurants

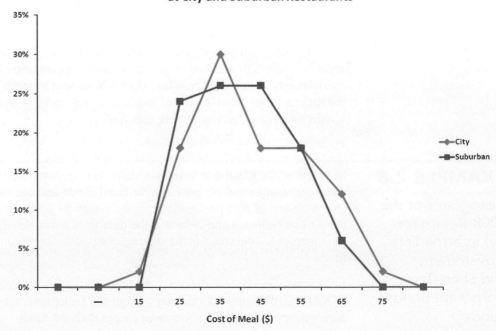

Reviewing the two polygons in Figure 2.14 leads you to conclude that the highest concentration of the cost of meals at city restaurants is between $30 and $40, while the cost of meals at suburban restaurants is evenly concentrated between $20 and $50. However, city restaurants have a higher percentage of meals that cost $60 or more than suburban restaurants.

The polygons in Figure 2.14 have points whose values on the X axis represent the midpoint of the class interval. For example, look at the points plotted at $X = 65$ ($65). The point for the cost of meals at city restaurants (the higher one) represents the fact that 12% of the meals at these restaurants cost between $60 and $70. The point for the cost of meals at suburban restaurants (the lower one) represents the fact that 6% of meals at these restaurants cost between $60 and $70.

When you construct polygons or histograms, the vertical (Y) axis should show the true zero, or "origin," so as not to distort the character of the data. The horizontal (X) axis does not need to show the zero point for the variable of interest, although the range of the variable should include the major portion of the axis.

EXAMPLE 2.9

Percentage Polygons of the 2008 Return for the Intermediate Government and Short-Term Corporate Bond Funds

FIGURE 2.15

Percentage polygons of the 2008 return for the intermediate government bond and short-term corporate bond funds

The *PCTAGE_POLYGON* chart sheet of the *Chapter 2 workbook* contains Figure 2.15. Create this chart using the instructions in Section EG2.6.

In Part I of the Choice Is Yours scenario, you are interested in comparing the past performance of the intermediate government bond funds and the short-term corporate bond funds. One measure of past performance is the return in 2008. You have already defined the variables and collected the data from a sample of 180 bond funds. Now, you need to construct percentage polygons for the intermediate government bond and short-term corporate bond funds.

SOLUTION Figure 2.15 displays percentage polygons of the 2008 returns for the intermediate government bond and short-term corporate bond funds.

Analyzing Figure 2.15 leads you to conclude that the distribution of the 2008 return of intermediate government funds is much higher than for short-term corporate bond funds. The polygon for the intermediate government funds is to the right (the returns are higher than) of the polygon for the short-term corporate bond funds. The return for intermediate government funds is concentrated between 5 and 10, whereas the return for the short-term corporate bond funds is concentrated between −5 and 5.

The Cumulative Percentage Polygon (Ogive)

The **cumulative percentage polygon**, or **ogive**, uses the cumulative percentage distribution discussed in Section 2.4 to display the variable of interest along the X axis and the cumulative percentages along the Y axis.

Figure 2.16 shows cumulative percentage polygons for the cost of meals at city and suburban restaurants.

FIGURE 2.16
Cumulative percentage polygons of the cost of restaurant meals at city and suburban restaurants

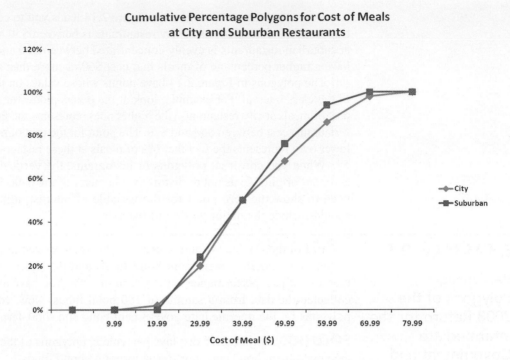

Cumulative Percentage Polygons for Cost of Meals at City and Suburban Restaurants

Reviewing the curves leads you to conclude that most of the curve of the cost of meals at the city restaurants is located slightly to the right of the curve for the suburban restaurants. This indicates that the city restaurants have slightly fewer meals that cost less than a particular value. For example, 68% of the meals at city restaurants cost less than $50 as compared to 76% of the meals at suburban restaurants.

EXAMPLE 2.10

Cumulative Percentage Polygons of the 2008 Return for the Intermediate Government and Short-Term Corporate Bond Funds

In Part I of the Choice Is Yours scenario, you are interested in comparing the past performance of the intermediate government bond funds and the short-term corporate bond funds. One measure of past performance is the return in 2008. You have already defined the variables and collected the data from a sample of 180 bond funds. Now, you need to construct cumulative percentage polygons for the intermediate government bond and the short-term corporate bond funds.

SOLUTION   Figure 2.17 displays cumulative percentage polygons for the 2008 return for the intermediate government bond and short-term corporate bond funds.

FIGURE 2.17

Cumulative percentage polygons of the 2008 return of intermediate government bonds and short-term corporate bond funds

The CPCTAGE_POLYGON chart sheet of the Chapter 2 workbook contains Figure 2.17. Create this chart using the instructions in Section EG2.6.

Cumulative Percentage Polygons for the Intermediate Government and Short-Term Corporate Bond Funds

Reviewing the cumulative percentage polygons in Figure 2.17 leads you to conclude that the 2008 return of intermediate government bond funds is located far to the right of the curve for the short-term corporate bond funds. This indicates that the intermediate government bond funds have many more 2008 returns that are higher than a particular value (and that the short-term corporate bond funds have many more funds whose return is less than a particular value). For example, 15.55% of the intermediate government bond funds had negative (returns below 0) 2008 returns as compared to 63.34% of the short-term corporate bond funds. You can conclude that, in general, the intermediate government bond funds outperformed the short-term corporate bond funds in 2008.

Problems for Section 2.6

LEARNING THE BASICS

2.47 Construct a stem-and-leaf display, given the following data from a sample of $n = 7$ midterm exam scores in finance:

$$80 \quad 54 \quad 69 \quad 98 \quad 93 \quad 53 \quad 74$$

2.48 Form an ordered array, given the following stem-and-leaf display from a sample of $n = 7$ midterm exam scores in information systems:

```
5 | 0
6 |
7 | 446
8 | 19
9 | 2
```

APPLYING THE CONCEPTS

2.49 The following is a stem-and-leaf display representing the amount of gasoline purchased, in gallons (with leaves in tenths of gallons), for a sample of 25 cars that use a particular service station on the New Jersey Turnpike:

```
 9 | 147
10 | 02238
11 | 125566777
12 | 223489
13 | 02
```

a. Place the data into an ordered array.
b. Which of these two displays seems to provide more information? Discuss.
c. What amount of gasoline (in gallons) is most likely to be purchased?
d. Is there a concentration of the purchase amounts in the center of the distribution?

✓SELF **2.50** As player salaries have increased, the cost **Test** of attending baseball games has increased dramatically. The file **BBCost** contains the following 2009 data concerning the total cost at each of the 30 Major League

Baseball parks for four tickets, two beers, four soft drinks, four hot dogs, two game programs, two baseball caps, and parking for one vehicle:

164 326 224 180 205 162 141 170 411 187 185 165 151 166 114
158 305 145 161 170 210 222 146 259 220 135 215 172 223 216

Source: *Data extracted from* **teammarketing.com**, *April 1, 2009.*

a. Construct a stem-and-leaf display for these data.
b. Around what value, if any, are the costs of attending a baseball game concentrated? Explain.

2.51 The file **DarkChocolate** contains the cost per ounce ($), for a sample of 14 dark chocolate bars.

0.68   0.72   0.92   1.14   1.42   0.94   0.77
0.57   1.51   0.57   0.55   0.86   1.41   0.90

Source: *Data extracted from "Dark Chocolate: Which Bars Are Best?"* Consumer Reports, *September 2007, p. 8.*

a. Place the data into an ordered array.
b. Construct a stem-and-leaf display.
c. Does the ordered array or the stem-and-leaf display provide more information? Discuss.
d. Around what value, if any, is the cost of dark chocolate bars concentrated? Explain.

2.52 The file **Utility** contains the cost of electricity during July 2009 for a random sample of 50 one-bedroom apartments in a large city:

Raw Data on Utility Charges ($)

96	171	202	178	147	102	153	197	127	82
157	185	90	116	172	111	148	213	130	165
141	149	206	175	123	128	144	168	109	167
95	163	150	154	130	143	187	166	139	149
108	119	183	151	114	135	191	137	129	158

a. Construct a histogram and a percentage polygon.
b. Construct a cumulative percentage polygon.
c. Around what amount does the monthly electricity cost seem to be concentrated?

2.53 As player salaries have increased, the cost of attending baseball games has increased dramatically. The following histogram visualizes the 2009 data about the total cost at each of the 30 Major League Baseball parks for four tickets, two beers, four soft drinks, four hot dogs, two game programs, two baseball caps, and parking for one vehicle, found in BBCost.

What conclusions can you reach concerning the cost of attending a baseball game at different ballparks?

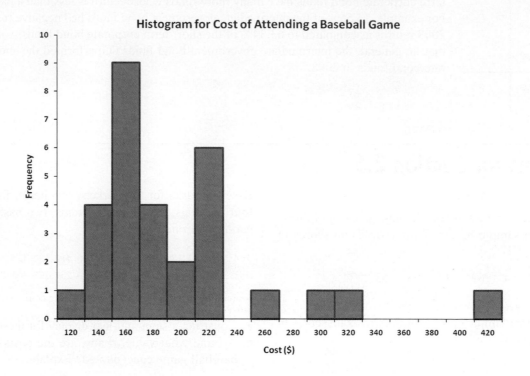

2.54 The following histogram and cumulative percentage polygon visualizes the data about the property taxes per capita for the 50 states and the District of Columbia, found in PropertyTaxes.

What conclusions can you reach concerning the property taxes per capita?

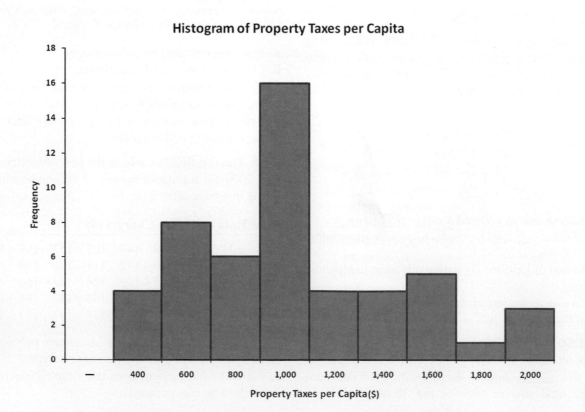

Cumulative Percentage Polygon of Property Taxes per Capita

2.55 One operation of a mill is to cut pieces of steel into parts that will later be used as the frame for front seats in an automobile. The steel is cut with a diamond saw and requires the resulting parts to be within ±0.005 inch of the length specified by the automobile company. The data are collected from a sample of 100 steel parts and stored in Steel . The measurement reported is the difference in inches between the actual length of the steel part, as measured by a laser measurement device, and the specified length of the steel part. For example, the first value, −0.002, represents a steel part that is 0.002 inch shorter than the specified length.

a. Construct a percentage histogram.
b. Is the steel mill doing a good job meeting the requirements set by the automobile company? Explain.

2.56 A manufacturing company produces steel housings for electrical equipment. The main component part of the housing is a steel trough that is made out of a 14-gauge steel coil. It is produced using a 250-ton progressive punch press with a wipe-down operation that puts two 90-degree forms in the flat steel to make the trough. The distance from one side of the form to the other is critical because of weatherproofing in outdoor applications. The company requires that the width of the trough be between 8.31 inches and 8.61 inches. Data are collected from a sample of 49 troughs and stored in Trough , which contains the following widths of the troughs.

8.312	8.343	8.317	8.383	8.348	8.410	8.351	8.373
8.481	8.422	8.476	8.382	8.484	8.403	8.414	8.419
8.385	8.465	8.498	8.447	8.436	8.413	8.489	8.414
8.481	8.415	8.479	8.429	8.458	8.462	8.460	8.444
8.429	8.460	8.412	8.420	8.410	8.405	8.323	8.420
8.396	8.447	8.405	8.439	8.411	8.427	8.420	8.498
8.409							

a. Construct a percentage histogram and a percentage polygon.
b. Plot a cumulative percentage polygon.
c. What can you conclude about the number of troughs that will meet the company's requirements of troughs being between 8.31 and 8.61 inches wide?

2.57 The manufacturing company in Problem 2.56 also produces electric insulators. If the insulators break when in use, a short circuit is likely to occur. To test the strength of the insulators, destructive testing in high-powered labs is carried out to determine how much *force* is required to break the insulators. Force is measured by observing how many pounds must be applied to the insulator before it breaks. Data are collected from a sample of 30 insulators. The file Force contains the strengths as follows:

1,870	1,728	1,656	1,610	1,634	1,784	1,522	1,696
1,592	1,662	1,866	1,764	1,734	1,662	1,734	1,774
1,550	1,756	1,762	1,866	1,820	1,744	1,788	1,688
1,810	1,752	1,680	1,810	1,652	1,736		

a. Construct a percentage histogram and a percentage polygon.

b. Construct a cumulative percentage polygon.

c. What can you conclude about the strengths of the insulators if the company requires a force measurement of at least 1,500 pounds before the insulator breaks?

2.58 The ordered arrays in the following table (and stored in **Bulbs**) show the life (in hours) of a sample of 40 100-watt light bulbs produced by Manufacturer A and a sample of 40 100-watt light bulbs produced by Manufacturer B:

Manufacturer A					Manufacturer B				
684	697	720	773	821	819	836	888	897	903
831	835	848	852	852	907	912	918	942	943
859	860	868	870	876	952	959	962	986	992
893	899	905	909	911	994	1,004	1,005	1,007	1,015
922	924	926	926	938	1,016	1,018	1,020	1,022	1,034
939	943	946	954	971	1,038	1,072	1,077	1,077	1,082
972	977	984	1,005	1,014	1,096	1,100	1,113	1,113	1,116
1,016	1,041	1,052	1,080	1,093	1,153	1,154	1,174	1,188	1,230

Use the following class interval widths for each distribution:

Manufacturer A: 650 but less than 750, 750 but less than 850, and so on.

Manufacturer B: 750 but less than 850, 850 but less than 950, and so on.

a. Construct percentage histograms on separate graphs and plot the percentage polygons on one graph.

b. Plot cumulative percentage polygons on one graph.

c. Which manufacturer has bulbs with a longer life—Manufacturer A or Manufacturer B? Explain.

2.59 The file **Drink** contains the amount of soft drink in a sample of 50 2-liter bottles:

2.109 2.086 2.066 2.075 2.065 2.057 2.052 2.044 2.036 2.038
2.031 2.029 2.025 2.029 2.023 2.020 2.015 2.014 2.013 2.014
2.012 2.012 2.012 2.010 2.005 2.003 1.999 1.996 1.997 1.992
1.994 1.986 1.984 1.981 1.973 1.975 1.971 1.969 1.966 1.967
1.963 1.957 1.951 1.951 1.947 1.941 1.941 1.938 1.908 1.894

a. Construct a histogram and a percentage polygon.

b. Construct a cumulative percentage polygon.

c. On the basis of the results in (a) and (b), does the amount of soft drink filled in the bottles concentrate around specific values?

2.7 Visualizing Two Numerical Variables

Often you will want to explore possible relationships between two numerical variables. You use a scatter plot as a first step to visualize such relationships. In the special case where one of your variables represents the passage of time, you use a time-series plot.

The Scatter Plot

Often, you have two numerical measurements about the same item or individual. A **scatter plot** can explore the possible relationship between those measurements by plotting the data of one numerical variable on the horizontal, or X, axis and the data of a second numerical variable on the vertical, or Y, axis. For example, a marketing analyst could study the effectiveness of advertising by comparing advertising expenses and sales revenues of 50 stores. Using a scatter plot, a point is plotted on the two-dimensional graph for each store, using the X axis to represent advertising expenses and the Y axis to represent sales revenues.

Table 2.17 presents revenues and valuations (both in millions of dollars) for all 30 NBA professional basketball teams and stored in the file **NBAValues**. To explore the possible relationship between the revenues generated by a team and the value of a team, you can create a scatter plot.

TABLE 2.17

Values and Revenues for NBA Teams

Team	Value ($millions)	Revenue ($millions)	Team	Value ($millions)	Revenue ($millions)
Atlanta	306	102	Milwaukee	278	94
Boston	447	149	Minnesota	301	100
Charlotte	284	95	New Jersey	295	98
Chicago	504	165	New Orleans	285	95
Cleveland	477	159	New York	613	208
Dallas	466	153	Orlando	300	82
Denver	329	112	Philadelphia	349	100
Detroit	480	160	Phoenix	360	116
Golden State	335	112	Portland	452	148
Houston	469	156	Sacramento	307	114
Indiana	303	101	San Antonio	350	117
Los Angeles Clippers	297	99	Seattle	415	138
Los Angeles Lakers	584	191	Toronto	400	138
Memphis	294	95	Utah	358	119
Miami	393	131	Washington	353	118

Source: *Data extracted from* **www.forbes.com/lists/2008/32/nba08_NBA-Team-Valuations_MetroArea.html**.

For each team, you plot the revenues on the X axis and the valuations on the Y axis. Figure 2.18 presents a scatter plot for these two variables.

FIGURE 2.18

Scatter plot of value and revenues

The SCATTER chart sheet of the Chapter 2 workbook contains Figure 2.18. Create this chart using the instructions in Section EG2.7.

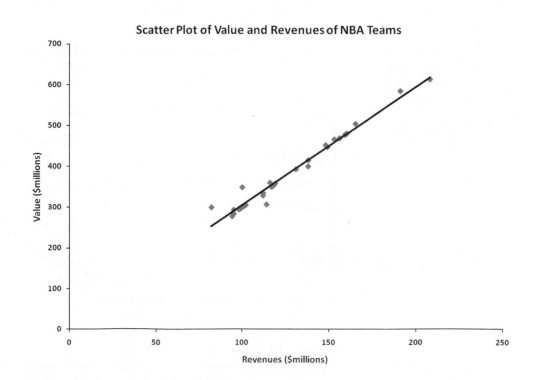

Reviewing Figure 2.18, you see that there appears to be a very strong increasing (positive) relationship between revenues and the value of a team. In other words, teams that generate a smaller amount of revenues have a lower valuation, while teams that generate higher revenues have a higher valuation. Notice the straight line that has been superimposed on the plotted data in Figure 2.18. For these data, this line is very close to the points in the scatter plot. This line is a linear regression prediction line that will be discussed in Chapter 13. (In Section 3.5, you will return to this example when you learn about the covariance and the coefficient of correlation.)

Other pairs of variables may have a decreasing (negative) relationship in which one variable decreases as the other increases. In other situations, there may be a weak or no relationship between the variables.

The Time-Series Plot

A **time-series plot** plots the values of a numerical variable on the Y axis and plots the time period associated with each numerical value on the X axis. A time-series plot can help explore trends in data that occur over time.

For example, consider the amount of solar power installed (in megawatts) in the United States per year during 2000 through 2008 that is shown in Table 2.18, and stored in Solar Power. To better visualize this data, you create the time-series plot shown in Figure 2.19.

TABLE 2.18

Amount of Solar Power Installed in the United States

Year	Amount of Solar Power Installed (megawatts)
2000	18
2001	27
2002	44
2003	68
2004	83
2005	100
2006	140
2007	210
2008	250

Source: *Data extracted from P. Davidson, "Glut of Rooftop Solar Systems Sinks Price,"* USA Today, *January 13, 2009, p. 1B.*

FIGURE 2.19

Time-series plot of amount of solar power installed per year from 2000 to 2008

The TIME_SERIES chart sheet of the Chapter 2 workbook contains Figure 2.19. Create this chart using the instructions in Section EG2.7.

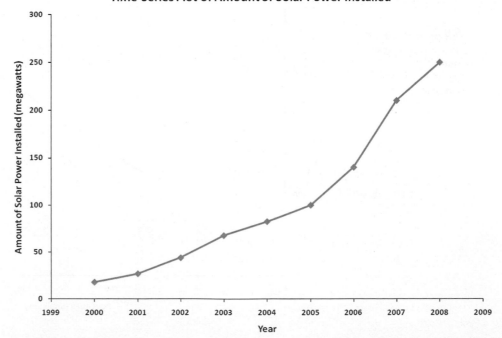

From Figure 2.19, you see that there was a steady increase in the amount of solar power installed in the United States between 2000 and 2008. During that time, the amount of solar power installed annually increased from 44 megawatts to 250 megawatts. The annual rate of increase appears to have accelerated after 2005.

Problems for Section 2.7

LEARNING THE BASICS

2.60 The following is a set of data from a sample of $n = 11$ items:

X	7	5	8	3	6	10	12	4	9	15	18
Y	21	15	24	9	18	30	36	12	27	45	54

a. Construct a scatter plot.
b. Is there a relationship between X and Y? Explain.

2.61 The following is a series of annual sales (in millions of dollars) over an 11-year period (1998 to 2008):

Year:	1998	1999	2000	2001	2002	2003	2004	2005	2006	2007	2008
Sales:	13.0	17.0	19.0	20.0	20.5	20.5	20.5	20.0	19.0	17.0	13.0

a. Construct a time-series plot.
b. Does there appear to be any change in annual sales over time? Explain.

APPLYING THE CONCEPTS

✓SELF Test **2.62** There are several methods for calculating fuel economy. The following table (in the file **Mileage**) indicates the mileage, as calculated by owners and by current government standards, for nine car models:

Car	Owner	Government
2005 Ford F-150	14.3	16.8
2005 Chevrolet Silverado	15.0	17.8
2002 Honda Accord LX	27.8	26.2
2002 Honda Civic	27.9	34.2
2004 Honda Civic Hybrid	48.8	47.6
2002 Ford Explorer	16.8	18.3
2005 Toyota Camry	23.7	28.5
2003 Toyota Corolla	32.8	33.1
2005 Toyota Prius	37.3	56.0

Source: *Data extracted from J. Healey, "Fuel Economy Calculations to be Altered," USA Today, January 11, 2006, p. 1B.*

a. Construct a scatter plot with owner mileage on the X axis and current government standards mileage on the Y axis.
b. Does there appear to be a relationship between owner and current government standards mileage? If so, is the relationship positive or negative?

2.63 The file **VeggieBurger** contains data on the calories and total fat (in grams per serving) for a sample of 12 veggie burgers:

Source: *Data extracted from "Healthful Burgers That Taste Good," Consumer Reports, June 2008, p 8.*

a. Construct a scatter plot with calories on the X axis and total fat on the Y axis.
b. What conclusions can you reach about the relationship between the calories and total fat in veggie burgers?

2.64 College basketball is big business, with coaches' salaries, revenues, and expenses in millions of dollars. The file **Colleges-Basketball** contains the coaches' salary and revenue for college basketball at selected schools in a recent year (data extracted from R. Adams, "Pay for Playoffs," *The Wall Street Journal*, March 11–12, 2006, pp. P1, P8).
a. Do you think schools with higher revenues also have higher coaches' salaries?
b. Construct a scatter plot with revenue on the X axis and coaches' salaries on the Y axis.
c. Does the scatter plot confirm or contradict your answer to (a)?

2.65 College football players trying out for the NFL are given the Wonderlic standardized intelligence test. The file **Wonderlic** contains the average Wonderlic scores of football players trying out for the NFL and the graduation rate for football players at selected schools (data extracted from S. Walker, "The NFL's Smartest Team," *The Wall Street Journal*, September 30, 2005, pp. W1, W10).
a. Construct a scatter plot with average Wonderlic score on the X axis and graduation rate on the Y axis.
b. What conclusions can you reach about the relationship between the average Wonderlic score and graduation rate?

2.66 The U.S. Bureau of Labor Statistics compiles data on a wide variety of workforce issues. The following table (stored in **Unemployment**) gives the monthly seasonally adjusted civilian unemployment rate for the United States from 2001 to 2008:
a. Construct a time-series plot of the U.S. unemployment rate.
b. Does there appear to be any pattern in the data?

Month	2001	2002	2003	2004	2005	2006	2007	2008
January	4.2	5.7	5.8	5.7	5.2	4.7	4.6	4.9
February	4.2	5.7	5.9	5.6	5.4	4.8	4.5	4.8
March	4.3	5.7	5.9	5.7	5.1	4.7	4.4	5.1
April	4.4	5.9	6.0	5.5	5.1	4.7	4.5	5.0
May	4.3	5.8	6.1	5.6	5.1	4.6	4.5	5.5
June	4.5	5.8	6.3	5.6	5.0	4.6	4.6	5.6
July	4.6	5.8	6.2	5.5	5.0	4.8	4.7	5.8
August	4.9	5.7	6.1	5.4	4.9	4.7	4.7	6.2
September	5.0	5.7	6.1	5.4	5.1	4.6	4.7	6.2
October	5.3	5.7	6.0	5.4	4.9	4.4	4.8	6.6
November	5.5	5.9	5.9	5.4	5.0	4.5	4.7	6.8
December	5.7	6.0	5.7	5.4	4.9	4.5	4.9	7.2

Source: *"U.S. Bureau of Labor Statistics"* **www.bls.gov**, *January 13, 2009.*

2.67 According to the U.S. Census Bureau, in November 2008, the average price of a new home was $287,500 (extracted from **www.census.gov**, January 21, 2009). The file New Home Prices contains the average price paid for a new home from January 1, 2004, through November 2008.
a. Construct a time-series plot of new home prices.
b. What pattern, if any, is present in the data?

2.68 The following table, stored in Cellphones , shows the number of cell phones (in millions) collected by the largest recycler from 2004 to 2008.

Year	Cellphones Collected (millions)
2004	2.0
2005	2.1
2006	3.3
2007	4.0
2008	5.5

Source: *Data extracted from "Cellphones Come Back to Life," "Snapshots,"* USA Today, *March 13, 2009, p. 1A.*

a. Construct a time-series plot for the number of cell phones collected by the largest recycler from 2004 to 2008.
b. What pattern, if any, is present in the data?
c. If you had to make a prediction about the number of cell phones collected by the largest recycler in 2009, what would you predict?

2.69 The following data, stored in Hotels , provide the average hotel room rate from 1996 to 2006 (data extracted from "*Snapshots,*" USA Today, February 13, 2008, p. 1A):

Year	Rates ($)	Year	Rates ($)
1996	70.63	2002	83.54
1997	75.31	2003	82.52
1998	78.62	2004	86.23
1999	81.33	2005	90.88
2000	85.89	2006	97.78
2001	88.27		

a. Construct a time-series plot.
b. What pattern, if any, is present in the data?
c. If you had to make a prediction about the average room rate in 2007, what would you predict?

2.8 Using PivotTables to Explore Multidimensional Data

In this chapter you have learned methods for organizing and visualizing a single variable and methods for jointly organizing and visualizing two variables. More and more, businesses need to organize and visualize **multidimensional data**, to discover possible patterns and relationships that simpler explorations might miss. While the full complexities of working with multidimensional data exceed the capabilities of Microsoft Excel, you can explore the basics of multidimensional data by using Excel **PivotTables**.

A PivotTable is an Excel tool for creating tables that summarize data. In their simplest applications, PivotTables help you create the summary tables and contingency tables discussed in Section 2.3. For example, Figure 2.20 shows the PivotTable version of the Table 2.3 contingency table (see page 22) that can be created using the instructions in Section EG2.3.

FIGURE 2.20

PivotTable version of the Table 2.3 contingency table

	A	B	C	D
1	**PivotTable of Type and Fees**			
2				
3	Count of Type	Fees ▼		
4	Type ▼	Yes	No	Grand Total
5	Intermediate Government	35	55	90
6	Short Term Corporate	17	73	90
7	Grand Total	52	128	180

As discussed in Section 2.3, using contingency tables based on percentages permits further exploration of possible patterns in the data. PivotTables allow you to easily convert the contents of cells from tallies (called **Count of** *variable* in PivotTables) to any type of contingency table percentage. Figure 2.21 shows the PivotTable version of Table 2.4, the contingency table that shows percentages of the overall total. From this table, you see that intermediate government funds are much more likely to charge a fee.

	A	B	C	D
1	**PivotTable of Type and Fees**			
2				
3	Count of Type	Fees ▼		
4	Type ▼	Yes	No	Grand Total
5	Intermediate Government	19.44%	30.56%	50.00%
6	Short Term Corporate	9.44%	40.56%	50.00%
7	Grand Total	28.89%	71.11%	100.00%

More importantly, PivotTables let you can change or add variables to a table. For example, suppose that you want to know whether the pattern of risk is the same for all combinations of fund type and fee charge. If you add the risk variable to the existing PivotTable, the new multidimensional PivotTable (see Figure 2.22) reveals several patterns that cannot be seen in the original Table 2.3 contingency table:

	A	B	C	D	E
1	**PivotTable of Type, Risk, and Fees**				
2					
3	Count of Type		Fees ▼		
4	Type ▼	Risk ▼	No	Yes	Grand Total
5	⊟Intermediate Government	Above Average	9.44%	8.89%	18.33%
6		Average	10.56%	5.56%	16.11%
7		Below Average	10.56%	5.00%	15.56%
8	Intermediate Government Total		30.56%	19.44%	50.00%
9	⊟Short Term Corporate	Above Average	11.11%	2.78%	13.89%
10		Average	12.78%	4.44%	17.22%
11		Below Average	16.67%	2.22%	18.89%
12	Short Term Corporate Total		40.56%	9.44%	50.00%
13	Grand Total		71.11%	28.89%	100.00%

- Although the ratio of fee-yes to fee-no bond funds for intermediate government category seems to be about 2 to 3 (19% to 31%), the ratio for above-average-risk intermediate government bond funds is closer to 1 to 1 (8.9% to 9.4%).
- While the group "intermediate government funds that do not charge a fee" has nearly equal numbers of above-average-risk, average-risk, and below-average-risk funds, the group "short-term corporate bond funds that do not charge a fee" contains about 50% more below-average-risk funds than above-average ones.
- The pattern of risk percentages differs between the fee-yes and fee-no funds in each of bond fund categories.

(Using methods presented in later chapters, you can confirm whether these first impressions are statistically significant.)

For any PivotTable, you can also change the statistic displayed. For example, Figure 2.23 shows a PivotTable in which the percentage of assets held by the four groupings of type of fund and whether a fee is charged has replaced the percentage counts of Figure 2.21. One of the patterns this PivotTable reveals is that although there are an equal number of intermediate government and short-term corporate bond funds (see Table 2.3 on page 22), the intermediate government bond funds hold a disproportionate percentage (61%) of the total assets.

	A	B	C	D
1	**PivotTable of Type and Fees,**			
2	**showing percentage of overall assets**			
3	Sum of Assets	Fees ▼		
4	Type ▼	Yes	No	Grand Total
5	Intermediate Government	20.69%	40.66%	61.34%
6	Short Term Corporate	6.41%	32.25%	38.66%
7	Grand Total	27.10%	72.90%	100.00%

The Figure 2.23 PivotTable computes the sum of a numerical variable (Assets) for each of the four groupings and then divides each of those sums by the overall sum of Assets to get the percentages displayed. For numerical variables, PivotTables can do much more, including computing some of the descriptive statistics discussed in Sections 3.1 and 3.2. For example, Figure 2.24 modifies the Figure 2.22 PivotTable to show the average, or mean, three-year rates of return in each cell. (See Section 3.1 to learn more about the mean.) This PivotTable reveals differences in the patterns of the three-year rates of return for the two categories of bond funds.

FIGURE 2.24

PivotTable of fund type, risk, and fees, showing averages of the three-year return

	A	B	C	D	E
1	**PivotTable of Type, Risk, and Fees**				
2	**showing averages of 3-year return**				
3	Average of 3-Year Return		Fees ▼		
4	Type ▼	Risk ▼	Yes	No	Grand Total
5	⊟ Intermediate Government	Above Average	4.44	6.79	5.65
6		Average	5.59	5.89	5.79
7		Below Average	4.90	4.78	4.82
8	Intermediate Government Total		4.89	5.79	5.44
9	⊟ Short Term Corporate	Above Average	-1.14	0.23	-0.04
10		Average	2.49	2.69	2.64
11		Below Average	3.10	3.25	3.23
12	Short Term Corporate Total		1.56	2.24	2.12
13	Grand Total		3.80	3.77	3.78

As Figure 2.23 and Figure 2.24 illustrate, you can mix categorical and numerical variables (such as assets and three-year return) in a PivotTable, making the PivotTable unique among the techniques described in this chapter. All four PivotTables shown in this section use categorical variables as the row and column variables and use either categorical or numerical variables for the individual cells that display the results. Generally, you should use categorical variables or variables that represent units of time for your rows and columns and never use a continuous numerical variable for the rows and columns. If you use a continuous numerical variable as the row or column variable, Excel will create rows or columns for each unique value, possibly creating a table with a very large number of rows or columns, a situation you definitely want to avoid.

While Excel imposes no limits (aside from your system's hardware resources) on the number of variables you can use in a PivotTable, three variables, as used in Figure 2.24, is a practical limit. A PivotTable with four or more variables can create cluttered displays that are hard to review without using advanced Excel techniques that are beyond the scope of this book.

Be aware that sometimes Excel automatically creates a matching PivotChart when you create a PivotTable. Be wary of such charts, as often Excel will use an inappropriate chart type or create a chart that violates at least one of the rules of good charting discussed in Section 2.9. For example, the PivotChart created from the Figure 2.20 PivotTable will be a column chart and not the side-by-side bar chart you would want.

Drill-down

Double-clicking a cell in a PivotTable causes Excel to **drill down** and display the data underlying the cell value in a new worksheet. For example, in the PivotTable shown in Figure 2.21 on page 53, double-clicking cell B6, which tallies the joint response "short-term corporate bond fund and fee-yes," creates the new worksheet shown in Figure 2.25. For this new worksheet, you see that bond funds numbered 100, 102, 103, 112, 119, 130, 139, 143, 145, 146, 151, 152, 153, 160, 175, 176, and 177 share the joint response.

Worksheets created using drill-down can be used like any other worksheets. You can use statistical methods for the data of such a worksheet without affecting the source PivotTable.

FIGURE 2.25

Drill-down worksheet

	A	B	C	D	E	F	G	H	I
1	Fund Number	Type	Assets	Fees	Expense Ratio	Return 2008	3-Year Return	5-Year Return	Risk
2	FN-177	Short Term Corporate	1070.8	Yes	0.7	-14	-2.2	-0.1	Above Average
3	FN-176	Short Term Corporate	49.6	Yes	0.89	-15.4	-3.4	-1.6	Above Average
4	FN-175	Short Term Corporate	60.9	Yes	0.98	-16.9	-4.7	-1.3	Above Average
5	FN-160	Short Term Corporate	129.2	Yes	0.99	-3.6	1.9	1.9	Above Average
6	FN-153	Short Term Corporate	346.4	Yes	0.64	-4.2	1.4	1.5	Average
7	FN-152	Short Term Corporate	213.8	Yes	0.87	-1.1	2.7	2.1	Above Average
8	FN-151	Short Term Corporate	118.5	Yes	1.01	-4.5	0.5	0.6	Below Average
9	FN-146	Short Term Corporate	132.8	Yes	0.7	-9.7	-0.4	0.5	Average
10	FN-145	Short Term Corporate	226	Yes	0.94	0.8	3.6	2.7	Average
11	FN-143	Short Term Corporate	248.2	Yes	1.04	-7.1	-0.1	0.5	Average
12	FN-139	Short Term Corporate	3924.1	Yes	0.67	-1.4	2.5	2.2	Average
13	FN-130	Short Term Corporate	50.8	Yes	0.98	2.6	3.9	2.4	Below Average
14	FN-119	Short Term Corporate	252.6	Yes	0.84	2.2	4.1	3.3	Average
15	FN-112	Short Term Corporate	17.1	Yes	0.8	3.4	4.3	3.1	Below Average
16	FN-103	Short Term Corporate	242.1	Yes	1.12	7.4	5.5	3.8	Average
17	FN-102	Short Term Corporate	86.7	Yes	1	1.4	3.7	3	Below Average
18	FN-100	Short Term Corporate	1237.4	Yes	1.08	-1	3.3	3.4	Average

Problems for Section 2.8

APPLYING THE CONCEPTS

✓SELF Test 2.70 For this problem, use the data in Mutual Funds.
a. Construct a PivotTable of category, objective, and risk.
b. What conclusions can you reach concerning differences among the categories of mutual funds (large cap, medium cap, and small cap), based on objective (growth and value) and the risk factor (low, average, and high)?
c. Drill down to select the cell large cap, value, and low risk. Construct a histogram of the 2006 return.
d. What conclusions can you reach from the histogram you constructed in (c)?

2.71 For this problem, use the data in Mutual Funds.
a. Construct a PivotTable of category, objective, and fees.
b. What conclusions can you reach concerning differences among the categories of mutual funds (large cap, medium cap, and small cap), based on objective (growth and value) and fees (yes and no)?
c. Drill down to select the cell large cap, value, and no fee. Construct a histogram of the 2006 return.
d. What conclusions can you reach from the histogram you constructed in (c)?

2.72 For this problem, use the data in Mutual Funds.
a. Construct a PivotTable of category, fees, and risk.

b. What conclusions can you reach concerning differences among the categories of mutual funds (large cap, medium cap, and small cap), based on fees (yes and no) and the risk factor (low, average, and high)?
c. Drill down to select the cell large cap, no fee, and low risk. Construct a histogram of the 2006 return.
d. What conclusions can you reach from the histogram you constructed in (c)?

2.73 For this problem, use the data in Mutual Funds.
a. Construct a PivotTable of category, objective, fees, and risk.
b. What conclusions can you reach concerning differences among the categories of mutual funds (large cap, medium cap, and small cap), based on objective (growth and value), the risk factor (low, average, and high), and fees (yes and no)?
c. Which PivotTable do you think is easier to interpret, the one in this problem or the ones in Problems 2.70–2.72? Explain.
d. Drill down to select the cell large cap, value, no fee, and low risk. Construct a histogram of the 2006 return.
e. What conclusions can you reach from the histogram you constructed in (d)?

2.9 Misuses and Common Errors in Visualizing Data

Good graphical displays clearly and unambiguously reveal what the data convey. Unfortunately, many graphs presented in the media (broadcast, print, and online) are incorrect, misleading, or so unnecessarily complicated that they should never be used. To illustrate the misuse of graphs, the chart presented in Figure 2.26 is similar to one that was printed in *Time* magazine as part of an article on increasing exports of wine from Australia to the United States.

FIGURE 2.26

"Improper" display of Australian wine exports to the United States, in millions of gallons

Source: *Based on S. Watterson, "Liquid Gold—Australians Are Changing the World of Wine. Even the French Seem Grateful," Time, November 22, 1999, p. 68.*

We're drinking more . . .
Australian wine exports to the U.S. in millions of gallons

1.04 — 1989
2.25 — 1992
3.67 — 1995
6.77 — 1997

In Figure 2.26, the wineglass icon representing the 6.77 million gallons for 1997 does not appear to be almost twice the size of the wineglass icon representing the 3.67 million gallons for 1995, nor does the wineglass icon representing the 2.25 million gallons for 1992 appear to be twice the size of the wineglass icon representing the 1.04 million gallons for 1989. Part of the reason for this is that the three-dimensional wineglass icon is used to represent the two dimensions of exports and time. Although the wineglass presentation may catch the eye, the data should instead be presented in a summary table or a time-series plot.

In addition to the type of distortion created by the wineglass icons in the *Time* magazine graph displayed in Figure 2.26, improper use of the vertical and horizontal axes leads to distortions. Figure 2.27 presents another graph used in the same *Time* magazine article.

FIGURE 2.27

"Improper" display of amount of land planted with grapes for the wine industry

Source: *Based on S. Watterson, "Liquid Gold—Australians Are Changing the World of Wine. Even the French Seem Grateful," Time, November 22, 1999, pp. 68–69.*

...they're growing more...
Amount of land planted with grapes for the wine industry

1997–1998 243,644 acres
1979–1980 172,075 acres
1949–1950 135,326 acres
1969–1970 150,300 acres
1989–1990 146,204 acres
1959–1960 130,201 acres

There are several problems in this graph. First, there is no zero point on the vertical axis. Second, the acreage of 135,326 for 1949–1950 is plotted above the acreage of 150,300 for 1969–1970. Third, it is not obvious that the difference between 1979–1980 and 1997–1998 (71,569 acres) is approximately 3.5 times the difference between 1979–1980 and 1969–1970 (21,775 acres). Fourth, there are no scale values on the horizontal axis. Years are plotted next to the acreage totals, not on the horizontal axis. Fifth, the values for the time dimension are not properly spaced along the horizontal axis. For example, the value for 1979–1980 is much closer to 1989–1990 than it is to 1969–1970.

Other types of eye-catching displays that you typically see in magazines and newspapers often include information that is not necessary and just adds excessive clutter. Figure 2.28 represents one such display.

FIGURE 2.28

"Improper" plot of market share of soft drinks

Source: *Based on Anne B. Carey and Sam Ward, "Coke Still Has Most Fizz," USA Today, May 10, 2000, p. 1B.*

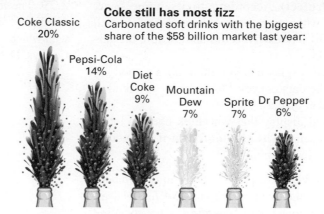

Coke still has most fizz
Carbonated soft drinks with the biggest share of the $58 billion market last year:

Coke Classic 20%
Pepsi-Cola 14%
Diet Coke 9%
Mountain Dew 7%
Sprite 7%
Dr Pepper 6%

The graph in Figure 2.28 shows those products with the largest market share for soft drinks. The graph suffers from too much clutter, although it is designed to show the differences in market share among the soft drinks. The display of the fizz for each soft drink takes up too much of the graph relative to the data. The same information could be better conveyed with a bar chart or pie chart.

Some guidelines for developing good graphs are as follows:

- A graph should not distort the data.
- A graph should not contain **chartjunk**, unnecessary adornments that convey no useful information.
- Any two-dimensional graph should contain a scale for each axis.
- The scale on the vertical axis should begin at zero.
- All axes should be properly labeled.
- The graph should contain a title.
- The simplest possible graph should be used for a given set of data.

Often these guidelines are unknowingly violated by individuals unaware of how to construct appropriate graphs. Programs such as Microsoft Excel tempt you to create "pretty" charts that may be fancy in their designs but that represent unwise choices. For example, making a simple pie chart more fancy by adding exploded 3D slices is unwise as this can complicate a viewer's interpretation of the data. Uncommon chart choices such as doughnut, radar, surface, bubble, cone, and pyramid charts may look visually striking, but in most cases they obscure the data.

Problems for Section 2.9

APPLYING THE CONCEPTS

2.74 (Student Project) Bring to class a chart from a Web site, newspaper, or magazine that you believe to be a poorly drawn representation of a numerical variable. Be prepared to submit the chart to the instructor with comments about why you believe it is inappropriate. Do you believe that the intent of the chart is to purposely mislead the reader? Also, be prepared to present and comment on this in class.

2.75 (Student Project) Bring to class a chart from a Web site, newspaper, or magazine that you believe to be a poorly drawn representation of a categorical variable. Be prepared to submit the chart to the instructor with comments about why you consider it inappropriate. Do you believe that the intent of the chart is to purposely mislead the reader? Also, be prepared to present and comment on this in class.

2.76 (Student Project) According to its home page, Swivel is "a place where curious people explore data—all kinds of data." Go to **www.swivel.com** and explore the various graphical displays.

a. Select a graphical display that you think does a good job revealing what the data convey. Discuss why you think it is a good graphical display.

b. Select a graphical display that you think needs a lot of improvement. Discuss why you think that it is a poorly constructed graphical display.

2.77 The following visual display contains an overembellished chart similar to one that appeared in *USA Today*, dealing with the average consumer's Valentine's Day spending ("USA Today Snapshots: The Price of Romance," *USA Today*, February 14, 2007, p. 1B).

Valentine's Day Average Consumer Spending

a. Describe at least one good feature of this visual display.
b. Describe at least one bad feature of this visual display.
c. Redraw the graph, using the guidelines given on page 57.

2.78 The following visual display contains an overembellished chart similar to one that appeared in *USA Today*, dealing with the estimated number of hours the typical American will spend using various media ("USA Today Snapshots: Minding Their Media," *USA Today*, March 2, 2007, p. 1B).

Media Usage
Estimated number of hours the typical American will spend using various media this year.

Listening to music 175
Reading newspapers 175
Using Internet 195
Listening to Radio 974
Watching TV 1555

a. Describe at least one good feature of this visual display.
b. Describe at least one bad feature of this visual display.
c. Redraw the graph, using the guidelines given on page 57.

2.79 The following visual display contains an overembellished chart similar to one that appeared in *USA Today*, dealing with which card is safer to use ("USA Today Snapshots: Credit Card vs. Debit Card," *USA Today*, March 14, 2007, p. 1B).

Credit Card vs. Debit Card:
Which one is safer to use?

a. Describe at least one good feature of this visual display.
b. Describe at least one bad feature of this visual display.
c. Redraw the graph, using the guidelines given on page 57.

2.80 An article in *The New York Times* (D. Rosato, "Worried About the Numbers? How About the Charts?" *The New York Times*, September 15, 2002, p. B7) reported on research done on annual reports of corporations by Professor Deanna Oxender Burgess of Florida Gulf Coast University. Professor Burgess found that even slight distortions in a chart changed readers' perception of the information. The article displayed sales information from the annual report of Zale Corporation and showed how results were exaggerated.

Using Internet or library sources, study the most recent annual report of a selected corporation. Find at least one chart in the report that you think needs improvement and develop an improved version of the chart. Explain why you believe the improved chart is better than the one included in the annual report.

2.81 Figures 2.5 and 2.7 show a bar chart and a pie chart for how adults pay their monthly bills (see pages 33 and 34).

a. Create an exploded pie chart, a doughnut chart, a cone chart, and a pyramid chart that show where people pay their monthly bills.

b. Which graphs do you prefer—the bar chart or pie chart or the exploded pie chart, doughnut chart, cone chart, and pyramid chart? Explain.

2.82 Figures 2.6 and 2.8 show a bar chart and a pie chart for the risk level for the bond fund data (see pages 33 and 35).

a. Create an exploded pie chart, a doughnut chart, a cone chart, and a pyramid chart for the risk level.

b. Which graphs do you prefer—the bar chart or pie chart or the exploded pie chart, doughnut chart, cone chart, and pyramid chart? Explain.

USING STATISTICS @ Choice Is Yours, Part I Revisited

In the Using Statistics scenario, you were hired by the Choice Is Yours Investment company to assist clients who seek to invest in mutual funds. A sample of 180 bond mutual funds was selected, and information on the funds and past performance history was recorded. For each of the 180 funds, data were collected on eight variables. With so much information, visualizing all these numbers required the use of properly selected graphical displays.

From bar charts and pie charts, you were able to illustrate that about one-third of the funds were classified as having below-average risk, about one-third had average risk, and about one-third had above-average risk. Cross tabulations of the funds by whether the fund charged a fee and whether the fund invested in intermediate government bonds or short-term corporate bonds revealed that intermediate government bond funds are more likely to charge fees. After constructing histograms on the 2008 return, you were able to conclude that the returns were much higher for the intermediate government bond funds then for the short-term corporate bonds. The return for intermediate government funds is concentrated between 5 and 10, whereas the return for the short-term corporate bond funds is concentrated between −5 and 5. With these insights, you can inform your clients about how the different funds performed. Of course, past performance history does not guarantee future performance.

Using graphical methods such as these is an important first step in summarizing and interpreting data. Although the proper display of data (as discussed in Section 2.9) helps to avoid ambiguity, graphical methods always contain a certain degree of subjectivity. Next, you will need descriptive statistics to further analyze the past performance of the mutual funds. Chapter 3 presents descriptive statistics (for example, mean, median, and mode).

SUMMARY

As you can see in Table 2.19, this chapter discusses how to organize and visualize data. You have used various tables and charts to draw conclusions about how people prefer to pay their bills, about the cost of restaurant meals in a city and its suburbs, and about the set of bond mutual funds in the Using Statistics scenario. Now that you have studied tables and charts, in Chapter 3 you will learn about a variety of descriptive statistics useful for data analysis and interpretation.

TABLE 2.19
Roadmap for Selecting Tables and Charts

	Type of Data	
Type of Analysis	**Numerical**	**Categorical**
Organizing data	Ordered array, frequency distribution, relative frequency distribution, percentage distribution, cumulative percentage distribution (Section 2.4)	Summary table, contingency table (Section 2.3)
Visualizing one variable	Stem-and-leaf display, histogram, percentage polygon, cumulative percentage polygon (ogive) (Section 2.6)	Bar chart, pie chart, Pareto chart (Section 2.5)
Visualizing two variables	Scatter plot, time-series plot (Section 2.7)	Side-by-side bar chart (Section 2.5)
Exploring multidimensional data	PivotTables (Section 2.8)	PivotTables (Section 2.8)

KEY EQUATIONS

Determining the Class Interval Width

$$\text{Interval width} = \frac{\text{highest value} - \text{lowest value}}{\text{number of classes}} \qquad (2.1)$$

Computing the Proportion or Relative Frequency

$$\text{Proportion} = \text{relative frequency} = \frac{\text{frequency in each class}}{\text{total number of values}} \qquad (2.2)$$

KEY TERMS

Analyze 16
bar chart 32
categorical variable 16
cell 22
chartjunk 57
class boundaries 26
class interval 26
class interval width 26
class midpoint 27
class 26
Collect 16
contingency table 22
continuous variable 17
cumulative percentage distribution 29
cumulative percentage polygon (ogive) 43
data collection 20
DCOVA 16

Define 16
discrete variable 16
drill down 54
frequency distribution 26
histogram 41
interval scale 18
multidimensional data 52
nominal scale 17
numerical variable 16
ogive (cumulative percentage polygon) 43
ordered array 25
ordinal scale 17
Organize 16
Pareto chart 35
Pareto principle 35
percentage distribution 28
percentage polygon 42

pie chart 34
PivotTable 52
primary data source 20
proportion 28
qualitative variable 16
quantitative variable 16
ratio scale 18
relative frequency 28
relative frequency distribution 28
scatter plot 48
secondary data source 20
side-by-side bar chart 37
stem-and-leaf display 40
summary table 21
time-series plot 50
Visualize 16

CHAPTER REVIEW PROBLEMS

CHECKING YOUR UNDERSTANDING

2.83 How do histograms and polygons differ in their construction and use?

2.84 Why would you construct a summary table?

2.85 What are the advantages and disadvantages of using a bar chart, a pie chart, or a Pareto chart?

2.86 Compare and contrast the bar chart for categorical data with the histogram for numerical data.

2.87 What is the difference between a time-series plot and a scatter plot?

2.88 Why is it said that the main feature of a Pareto chart is its ability to separate the "vital few" from the "trivial many"?

2.89 What are the three different ways to break down the percentages in a contingency table?

2.90 What is the difference between a PivotTable and a contingency table?

2.91 What insights can you gain from a three-way table that are not available in a two-way table?

APPLYING THE CONCEPTS

2.92 The summary table on the next page presents the breakdown of the price of a new college textbook:
a. Using the four categories, publisher, bookstore, author, and freight, construct a bar chart, a pie chart, and a Pareto chart.
b. Using the four subcategories of publisher and three subcategories of bookstore, along with the author and freight categories, construct a Pareto chart.
c. Based on the results of (a) and (b), what conclusions can you reach concerning who gets the revenue from the sales of new college textbooks? Do any of these results surprise you? Explain.

Revenue Category	Percentage (%)	
Publisher	64.8	
Manufacturing costs		32.3
Marketing and promotion		15.4
Administrative costs and taxes		10.0
After-tax profit		7.1
Bookstore	22.4	
Employee salaries and benefits		11.3
Operations		6.6
Pretax profit		4.5
Author	11.6	
Freight	1.2	

Source: *Data extracted from T. Lewin, "When Books Break the Bank,"* The New York Times, *September 16, 2003, pp. B1, B4.*

2.93 The following table represents the estimated green power sales by renewable energy source in 2008:

Source	Percentage (%)
Geothermal	2.8
Hydro	11.3
Landfill mass and biomass	28.1
Solar	0.2
Unreported	2.5
Wind	55.1

Source: *National Renewable Energy Laboratory, 2008.*

a. Construct a bar chart, a pie chart, and a Pareto chart.
b. What conclusions can you reach about the sources of green power?

2.94 People conduct hundreds of millions of search queries every day. In response, businesses are estimated to spend almost $20 billion annually on online ad spending. The following represents the categories of online ad spending and the results of a Yahoo! keyword tool for searches related to "sneakers":

Categories of Online Ad Spending

Type	Spending ($billions)
Classified	3.32
Display ads	3.90
Paid search	8.29
Rich media/video	2.15
Other	1.85
Total	19.51

Source: *Data extracted from K. J. Delaney, "The New Benefits of Web-Search Queries,"* The Wall Street Journal, *February 6, 2007, p. B3.*

Results of a Yahoo! Keyword Tool for Searches Related to "Sneakers"

Search Result	Number of Occurrences
Jordan sneaker	13,240
Nike sneaker	8,139
Puma sneaker	6,768
Sneaker	58,995
Sneaker pimps*	15,357

* Sneaker pimps is a British electropop band.

Source: *Data extracted from K. J. Delaney, "The New Benefits of Web-Search Queries,"* The Wall Street Journal, *February 6, 2007, p. B3.*

a. For categories of online ad spending, construct a bar chart, a pie chart, and a Pareto chart.
b. Which graphical method do you think is best for portraying these data?
c. For the results of "sneakers" searches, construct a bar chart, a pie chart, and a Pareto chart.
d. Which graphical method do you think is best for portraying these data?
e. What conclusions can you reach concerning online ad spending and the results of "sneakers" searches?

2.95 The owner of a restaurant serving Continental-style entrées has the business objective of learning more about the patterns of patron demand during the Friday-to-Sunday weekend time period. Data were collected from 630 customers on the type of entrée ordered and organized in the following table:

Type of Entrée	Number Served
Beef	187
Chicken	103
Mixed	30
Duck	25
Fish	122
Pasta	63
Shellfish	74
Veal	26
Total	630

a. Construct a percentage summary table for the types of entrées ordered.
b. Construct a bar chart, a pie chart, and a Pareto chart for the types of entrées ordered.
c. Do you prefer using a Pareto chart or a pie chart for these data? Why?
d. What conclusions can the restaurant owner reach concerning demand for different types of entrées?

2.96 Suppose that the owner of the restaurant in Problem 2.95 also wanted to study the demand for dessert during the same time period. She decided that in addition to studying whether a dessert was ordered, she would also study the gender of the individual and whether a beef entrée was ordered.

Data were collected from 600 customers and organized in the following contingency tables:

DESSERT ORDERED	GENDER		
	Male	Female	Total
Yes	40	96	136
No	240	224	464
Total	280	320	600

DESSERT ORDERED	BEEF ENTRÉE		
	Yes	No	Total
Yes	71	65	136
No	116	348	464
Total	187	413	600

a. For each of the two contingency tables, construct contingency tables of row percentages, column percentages, and total percentages.

b. Which type of percentage (row, column, or total) do you think is most informative for each gender? For beef entrée? Explain.

c. What conclusions concerning the pattern of dessert ordering can the restaurant owner reach?

2.97 The following data represent the method for recording votes in the November 2006 election, broken down by percentage of counties in the United States, using each method and the number of counties using each method in 2000 and 2006.

Method	Percentage of Counties Using Method in 2006 (%)
Electronic	36.6
Hand-counted paper ballots	1.8
Lever	2.0
Mixed	3.0
Optically scanned paper ballots	56.2
Punch card	0.4

Source: *Data extracted from R. Wolf, "Paper-Trail Voting Gets Organized Opposition," USA Today, April 24, 2007, p. 2A.*

Method	Number of Counties	
	2000	2006
Electronic	309	1,142
Hand-counted paper ballots	370	57
Lever	434	62
Mixed	149	92
Optically scanned paper ballots	1,279	1,752
Punch card	572	13

Source: *Data extracted from R. Wolf, "Paper-Trail Voting Gets Organized Opposition," USA Today, April 24, 2007, p. 2A.*

a. Construct a pie chart and a Pareto chart for the percentage of counties using the various methods.

b. What conclusions can you reach concerning the type of voting method used in November 2006?

c. What differences are there between the methods used in 2000 and 2006?

2.98 In summer 2000, a growing number of warranty claims on Firestone tires sold on Ford SUVs prompted Firestone and Ford to issue a major recall. An analysis of warranty claims data helped identify which models to recall. A breakdown of 2,504 warranty claims based on tire size is given in the following table:

Tire Size	Number of Warranty Claims
23575R15	2,030
311050R15	137
30950R15	82
23570R16	81
331250R15	58
25570R16	54
Others	62

Source: *Data extracted from Robert L. Simison, "Ford Steps Up Recall Without Firestone," The Wall Street Journal, August 14, 2000, p. A3.*

The 2,030 warranty claims for the 23575R15 tires can be categorized into ATX models and Wilderness models. The type of incident leading to a warranty claim, by model type, is summarized in the following table:

Incident Type	ATX Model Warranty Claims	Wilderness Warranty Claims
Tread separation	1,365	59
Blowout	77	41
Other/unknown	422	66
Total	1,864	166

Source: *Data extracted from Robert L. Simison, "Ford Steps Up Recall Without Firestone," The Wall Street Journal, August 14, 2000, p. A3.*

a. Construct a Pareto chart for the number of warranty claims by tire size. What tire size accounts for most of the claims?

b. Construct a pie chart to display the percentage of the total number of warranty claims for the 23575R15 tires that come from the ATX model and Wilderness model. Interpret the chart.

c. Construct a Pareto chart for the type of incident causing the warranty claim for the ATX model. Does a certain type of incident account for most of the claims?

d. Construct a Pareto chart for the type of incident causing the warranty claim for the Wilderness model. Does a certain type of incident account for most of the claims?

2.99 One of the major measures of the quality of service provided by an organization is the speed with which the organization responds to customer complaints. A large family-held department store selling furniture and flooring, including carpet, had undergone a major expansion in the past several years. In particular, the flooring department had expanded from 2 installation crews to an installation supervisor, a measurer, and 15 installation crews. A business objective of the company was to reduce the time between when the complaint is received and when it is resolved. During a recent year, the company received 50 complaints concerning carpet installation. The data from the 50 complaints, organized in Furniture, represent the number of days between the receipt of the complaint and the resolution of the complaint:

54	5	35	137	31	27	152	2	123	81	74	27
11	19	126	110	110	29	61	35	94	31	26	5
12	4	165	32	29	28	29	26	25	1	14	13
13	10	5	27	4	52	30	22	36	26	20	23
33	68										

a. Construct a frequency distribution and a percentage distribution.
b. Construct a histogram and a percentage polygon.
c. Construct a cumulative percentage distribution and plot a cumulative percentage polygon (ogive).
d. On the basis of the results of (a) through (c), if you had to tell the president of the company how long a customer should expect to wait to have a complaint resolved, what would you say? Explain.

2.100 Data concerning 128 of the best-selling domestic beers in the United States are contained in DomesticBeer. The values for three variables are included: percentage alcohol, number of calories per 12 ounces, and number of carbohydrates (in grams) per 12 ounces.
Source: *Data extracted from* **www.Beer100.com**, *June 15, 2009.*
a. Construct a percentage histogram for each of the three variables.
b. Construct three scatter plots: percentage alcohol versus calories, percentage alcohol versus carbohydrates, and calories versus carbohydrates.
c. Discuss what you learn from studying the graphs in (a) and (b).

2.101 The file CigaretteTax contains the state cigarette tax, in dollars, for each state as of April 1, 2009.
a. Develop an ordered array.
b. Plot a percentage histogram.
c. What conclusions can you reach about the differences in the state cigarette tax between the states?

2.102 The file SavingsRate contains the yields for a money market account, a one-year certificate of deposit (CD), and a five-year CD, for 23 banks in the metropolitan New York area, as of May 28, 2009.
Source: *Data extracted from* **www.Bankrate.com**, *May 28, 2009.*

a. Construct a stem-and-leaf display for each of the three variables.
b. Construct three scatter plots: money market account versus one-year CD, money market account versus five-year CD, and one-year CD versus five-year CD.
c. Discuss what you learn from studying the graphs in (a) and (b).

2.103 The file Compensation includes the total compensation (in $) of CEOs of large public companies in 2008.
Source: *Data extracted from D. Jones and B. Hansen, "CEO Pay Dives in a Rough 2008,"* **www.usatoday.com**, *May 1, 2009.*
a. Construct a frequency distribution and a percentage distribution.
b. Construct a histogram and a percentage polygon.
c. Construct a cumulative percentage distribution and plot a cumulative percentage polygon (ogive).
d. Based on (a) through (c), what conclusions can you reach concerning CEO compensation in 2008?

2.104 Studies conducted by a manufacturer of "Boston" and "Vermont" asphalt shingles have shown product weight to be a major factor in customers' perception of quality. Moreover, the weight represents the amount of raw materials being used and is therefore very important to the company from a cost standpoint. The last stage of the assembly line packages the shingles before the packages are placed on wooden pallets. The variable of interest is the weight in pounds of the pallet which for most brands holds 16 squares of shingles. The company expects pallets of its "Boston" brand-name shingles to weigh at least 3,050 pounds but less than 3,260 pounds. For the company's "Vermont" brand-name shingles, pallets should weigh at least 3,600 pounds but less than 3,800. Data are collected from a sample of 368 pallets of "Boston" shingles and 330 pallets of "Vermont" shingles and stored in Pallet.
a. For the "Boston" shingles, construct a frequency distribution and a percentage distribution having eight class intervals, using 3,015, 3,050, 3,085, 3,120, 3,155, 3,190, 3,225, 3,260, and 3,295 as the class boundaries.
b. For the "Vermont" shingles, construct a frequency distribution and a percentage distribution having seven class intervals, using 3,550, 3,600, 3,650, 3,700, 3,750, 3,800, 3,850, and 3,900 as the class boundaries.
c. Construct percentage histograms for the "Boston" shingles and for the "Vermont" shingles.
d. Comment on the distribution of pallet weights for the "Boston" and "Vermont" shingles. Be sure to identify the percentage of pallets that are underweight and overweight.

2.105 The file Cost of Living includes the overall cost index, the monthly rent for a two-bedroom apartment, the cost of a cup of coffee with service, the cost of a fast-food hamburger meal, the cost of dry-cleaning a men's blazer, the cost of toothpaste, and the cost of movie tickets in 10 different cities.

a. Construct six separate scatter plots. For each, use the overall cost index as the *Y* axis. Use the monthly rent for a two-bedroom apartment, the costs of a cup of coffee with service, a fast-food hamburger meal, dry-cleaning a men's blazer, toothpaste, and movie tickets as the *X* axis.

b. What conclusions can you reach about the relationship of the overall cost index to these six variables?

2.106 The file `Protein` contains calorie and cholesterol information concerning popular protein foods (fresh red meats, poultry, and fish).

Source: *U.S. Department of Agriculture.*

a. Construct a percentage histogram for the number of calories.

b. Construct a percentage histogram for the amount of cholesterol.

c. What conclusions can you reach from your analyses in (a) and (b)?

2.107 The file `Gas Prices` contains the weekly average price of gasoline in the United States from January 1, 2007, to January 12, 2009. Prices are in dollars per gallon.

Source: *U.S. Department of Energy,* **www.eia.doe.gov***, January 14, 2009.*

a. Construct a time-series plot.

b. What pattern, if any, is present in the data?

2.108 The file `Drink` contains data for the amount of soft drink filled in a sample of 50 consecutive 2-liter bottles. The results are listed horizontally in the order of being filled:

```
2.109 2.086 2.066 2.075 2.065 2.057 2.052 2.044 2.036 2.038
2.031 2.029 2.025 2.029 2.023 2.020 2.015 2.014 2.013 2.014
2.012 2.012 2.012 2.010 2.005 2.003 1.999 1.996 1.997 1.992
1.994 1.986 1.984 1.981 1.973 1.975 1.971 1.969 1.966 1.967
1.963 1.957 1.951 1.951 1.947 1.941 1.941 1.938 1.908 1.894
```

a. Construct a time-series plot for the amount of soft drink on the *Y* axis and the bottle number (going consecutively from 1 to 50) on the *X* axis.

b. What pattern, if any, is present in these data?

c. If you had to make a prediction about the amount of soft drink filled in the next bottle, what would you predict?

d. Based on the results of (a) through (c), explain why it is important to construct a time-series plot and not just a histogram, as was done in Problem 2.59 on page 48.

2.109 The S&P 500 Index tracks the overall movement of the stock market by considering the stock prices of 500 large corporations. The file `Stock Prices` contains weekly data for this index as well as the daily closing stock prices for three companies from January 2, 2008, to January 12, 2009. The following variables are included:

WEEK—Week ending on date given
S&P—Weekly closing value for the S&P 500 Index
GE—Weekly closing stock price for General Electric

IBM—Weekly closing stock price for IBM
AAPL—Weekly closing stock price for Apple

Source: *Data extracted from* **finance.yahoo.com***, January 13, 2009.*

a. Construct a time-series plot for the weekly closing values of the S&P 500 Index, General Electric, IBM, and Apple.

b. Explain any patterns present in the plots.

c. Write a short summary of your findings.

2.110 (Class Project) Have each student in the class respond to the question "Which carbonated soft drink do you most prefer?" so that the teacher can tally the results into a summary table.

a. Convert the data to percentages and construct a Pareto chart.

b. Analyze the findings.

2.111 (Class Project) Let each student in the class be cross-classified on the basis of gender (male, female) and current employment status (yes, no) so that the teacher can tally the results.

a. Construct a table with either row or column percentages, depending on which you think is more informative.

b. What would you conclude from this study?

c. What other variables would you want to know regarding employment in order to enhance your findings?

REPORT WRITING EXERCISES

2.112 Referring to the results from Problem 2.104 on page 63 concerning the weight of "Boston" and "Vermont" shingles, write a report that evaluates whether the weight of the pallets of the two types of shingles are what the company expects. Be sure to incorporate tables and charts into the report.

2.113 Referring to the results from Problem 2.98 on page 62 concerning the warranty claims on Firestone tires, write a report that evaluates warranty claims on Firestone tires sold on Ford SUVs. Be sure to incorporate tables and charts into the report.

TEAM PROJECT

The file `Bond Funds` contains information regarding nine variables from a sample of 180 mutual funds:

Fund number—Identification number for each bond fund
Type—Bond fund type (intermediate government or short-term corporate)
Assets—In millions of dollars
Fees—Sales charges (no or yes)
Expense ratio—Ratio of expenses to net assets in percentage
Return 2008—Twelve-month return in 2008
Three-year return—Annualized return, 2006–2008
Five-year return—Annualized return, 2004–2008
Risk—Risk-of-loss factor of the mutual fund (below average, average, or above average)

2.114 For this problem, consider the expense ratio.

a. Construct a percentage histogram.

b. Using a single graph, plot percentage polygons of the expense ratio for bond funds that have fees and bond funds that do not have fees.

c. What conclusions about the expense ratio can you reach, based on the results of (a) and (b)?

2.115 For this problem, consider the three-year annualized return from 2006 to 2008.

a. Construct a percentage histogram.

b. Using a single graph, plot percentage polygons of the three-year annualized return from 2006 to 2008 for intermediate government funds and short-term corporate funds.

c. What conclusions about the three-year annualized return from 2006 to 2008 can you reach, based on the results of (a) and (b)?

2.116 For this problem, consider the five-year annualized return from 2004 to 2008.

a. Construct a percentage histogram.

b. Using a single graph, plot percentage polygons of the five-year annualized return from 2004 to 2008 for intermediate government funds and short-term corporate funds.

c. What conclusions about the five-year annualized return from 2004 to 2008 can you reach, based on the results of (a) and (b)?

STUDENT SURVEY DATABASE

2.117 A sample of 50 undergraduate students answered the following survey:

1. What is your gender? Female _____ Male _____
2. What is your age (*as of last birthday*)? _____
3. What is your height (*in inches*)? _____
4. What is your current registered class designation?
   Freshman _____ Sophomore _____
   Junior _____ Senior _____
5. What is your major area of study?
   Accounting _____ Economics/Finance _____
   Information Systems _____ International
   Business _____ Management _____
   Marketing/Retailing _____ Other _____
   Undecided _____
6. At the present time, do you plan to attend graduate school?
   Yes _____ No _____ Not sure _____
7. What is your current cumulative grade point average? _____
8. What would you expect your starting annual salary (*in $000*) to be if you were to seek employment immediately after obtaining your bachelor's degree? _____
9. What do you anticipate your salary to be (*in $000*) after five years of full-time work experience? _____
10. What is your current employment status?
    Full-time _____ Part-time _____
    Unemployed _____

11. How many clubs, groups, organizations, or teams are you currently affiliated with on campus?
12. How satisfied are you with the student advisement services on campus? _____

1	2	3	4	5	6	7
Extremely unsatisfied			Neutral			Extremely satisfied

13. About how much money did you spend this semester on textbooks and supplies? _____

The results of the survey are stored in `UndergradSurvey`.

a. Which variables in the survey are categorical?

b. Which variables in the survey are numerical?

c. Which variables are discrete numerical variables?

d. For these data, construct all the appropriate tables and charts and write a report summarizing your conclusions.

2.118 Problem 2.117 describes a survey of 50 undergraduate students (stored in `UndergradSurvey`).

a. Select a sample of 50 undergraduate students at your school and conduct a similar survey for those students.

b. For the data collected in (a), construct all the appropriate tables and charts and write a report summarizing your conclusions.

c. Compare the results of (b) to those of Problem 2.117.

2.119 A sample of 40 MBA students answered the following survey:

1. What is your gender? Female _____ Male _____
2. What is your age (*as of last birthday*)? _____
3. What is your height (*in inches*)? _____
4. What is your current major area of study?
   Accounting _____ Economics/Finance _____
   Information Systems _____ International
   Business _____ Management _____
   Marketing/Retailing _____ Other _____
   Undecided _____
5. What is your graduate cumulative grade point average? _____
6. What was your undergraduate major?
   Biological Sciences _____ Business
   Administration _____ Computers or Math _____
   Education _____ Engineering _____
   Humanities _____ Performing Arts _____
   Physical Sciences _____ Social Sciences _____
   Other _____
7. What was your undergraduate cumulative grade point average? _____
8. What was your GMAT score? _____
9. What is your current employment status?
   Full-time _____ Part-time _____
   Unemployed _____
10. How many full-time jobs have you held in the past 10 years? _____

11. What do you expect your annual salary (*in $000*) to be immediately after completion of the MBA program? _____

12. What do you anticipate your salary to be (*in $000*) after five years of full-time work experience following the completion of the MBA program? _____

13. How satisfied are you with the student advisement services on campus?

1	2	3	4	5	6	7
Extremely unsatisfied			Neutral			Extremely satisfied

14. About how much money did you spend this semester on textbooks and supplies? _____

The results of the survey are stored in GradSurvey .

a. Which variables in the survey are categorical?

b. Which variables in the survey are numerical?

c. Which variables are discrete numerical variables?

d. For these data, construct all appropriate tables and charts and write a report summarizing your conclusions.

2.120 Problem 2.119 describes a survey of 40 MBA students (stored in GradSurvey).

a. Select a sample of 40 MBA students in your MBA program and conduct a similar survey for those students.

b. For the data collected in (a), construct all the appropriate tables and charts and write a report summarizing your conclusions.

c. Compare the results of (b) to those of Problem 2.119.

MANAGING THE *SPRINGVILLE HERALD*

Advertising fees are an important source of revenue for any newspaper. In an attempt to boost these revenues and to minimize costly errors, the management of the *Herald* has established a task force charged with the business objective of improving customer service in the advertising department. Using a Web browser, visit this book's companion Web site and open to the Web page for the Chapter 2 *Herald* Case (see Appendix Section D.1) or open **Ad_Errors.htm**, if you have downloaded the Herald Case files. Review the

task force's data collection. Identify the variables that are important in describing the customer service problems. For each variable you identify, construct the graphical representation you think is most appropriate and explain your choice. Also, suggest what other information concerning the different types of errors would be useful to examine. Offer possible courses of action for either the task force or management to take that would support the goal of improving customer service.

WEB CASE

In the Using Statistics scenario, you were asked to gather information to help make wise investment choices. Sources for such information include brokerage firms and investment counselors. Apply your knowledge about the proper use of tables and charts in this Web Case about the claims of foresight and excellence by a Springville financial services firm.

Visit this book's companion Web site and open to the Web page for the Chapter 2 Web Case (see Appendix Section D.1) or open **EndRun.htm**, if you have downloaded the Web Case files, to examine the EndRun Financial Services Web site. Review the company's investment claims and supporting data and then answer the following.

1. How does the presentation of the general information about EndRun on its home page affect your perception of the business?

2. Is EndRun's claim about having more winners than losers a fair and accurate reflection of the quality of its investment service? If you do not think that the claim is a fair and accurate one, provide an alternate presentation that you think is fair and accurate.

3. EndRun's "Big Eight" mutual funds are part of the sample found in the Mutual Funds worksheet. Is there any other relevant data from that file that could have been included in the Big Eight table? How would that new data alter your perception of EndRun's claims?

4. EndRun is proud that all Big Eight funds have gained in value over the past five years. Do you agree that EndRun should be proud of its selections? Why or why not?

REFERENCES

1. Huff, D., *How to Lie with Statistics* (New York: Norton, 1954).
2. *Microsoft Excel 2007* (Redmond, WA: Microsoft Corporation, 2007).
3. Tufte, E. R., *Beautiful Evidence* (Cheshire, CT: Graphics Press, 2006).
4. Tufte, E. R., *Envisioning Information* (Cheshire, CT: Graphics Press, 1990).
5. Tufte, E. R., *The Visual Display of Quantitative Information*, 2nd ed. (Cheshire, CT: Graphics Press, 2002).
6. Tufte, E. R., *Visual Explanations* (Cheshire, CT: Graphics Press, 1997).
7. Wainer, H., *Visual Revelations: Graphical Tales of Fate and Deception from Napoleon Bonaparte to Ross Perot* (New York: Copernicus/Springer-Verlag, 1997).

EG2.1 TYPES of VARIABLES

Excel infers the variable type from the data it finds in a column. If Excel discovers a column containing numbers, it will treat the column as a numerical variable. If Excel discovers a column containing words or alphanumeric entries, it will treat the column as non-numerical data. This imperfect method works most of the time in Excel, especially if you make sure that the categories for your categorical variables are words or phrases such as "yes" and "no" and are not coded values that could be mistaken for numerical values, such as "1," "2," and "3."

Because you cannot explicitly define the variable type, Excel will occasionally make "mistakes" by either offering or allowing you to do nonsensical things such as using a statistical method that is designed for numerical variables on categorical variables.

EG2.2 DATA COLLECTION

Regardless of the method of data collection you use, you place the data you collect in a worksheet for use in Excel. Place the data for each variable in a separate column, starting with Column A, and enter the names of each variable into the cells of the first row of each column, as first discussed in section EG1.3 on page 12 and shown below.

	A	B	C	D	E	F	G	H	I
1	Fund Number	Type	Assets	Fees	Expense Ratio	Return 2008	3-Year Return	5-Year Return	Risk
2	FN-1	Intermediate Government	158.2	No	0.61	7.6	6.3	5.0	Average
3	FN-2	Intermediate Government	420.6	No	0.61	8.9	6.7	5.3	Average
4	FN-3	Intermediate Government	243.1	No	0.93	11.1	7.4	5.0	Above Average
5	FN-4	Intermediate Government	24.7	No	0.49	7.3	6.5	5.4	Above Average

EG2.3 ORGANIZING CATEGORICAL DATA

The Summary Table

PHStat2 Use the **One-Way Tables & Charts** procedure to create a summary table. For example, to create a summary table similar to Table 2.2 on page 22, open to the **DATA worksheet** of the **Bond Funds workbook**. Select **PHStat → Descriptive Statistics → One-Way Tables & Charts**. In the procedure's dialog box (shown below):

1. Click **Raw Categorical Data**. (The **DATA worksheet** contains unsummarized data. For data that have already been tallied into categories, click **Table of Frequencies**.)

2. Enter **I1:I181** as the **Raw Data Cell Range** and check **First cell contains label**.

3. Enter a **Title**, check **Percentage Column**, and click **OK**.

In-Depth Excel 2007 For data that need to be tallied, use the PivotTable feature to create a summary table. (For the case in which data have already been tallied, use the **SUMMARY_SIMPLE worksheet** of the **Chapter 2 workbook** as a model for creating a summary table.)

For example, to create a summary table similar to Table 2.2 on page 22, open to the **DATA worksheet** of the **Bond Funds workbook** and select **Insert → PivotTable**. In the Create PivotTable dialog box (shown below):

1. Click **Select a table or range** and enter **I1:I181** as the **Table/Range** cell range.

2. Select the **New Worksheet** option and click **OK**.

In the PivotTable Field List task pane:

3. Check **Risk** in the **Choose fields to add to report** box.

4. Drag the checked **Risk** label and drop it in the **Row Labels** box. Drag a second copy of this checked **Risk**

label and drop it in the Σ **Values** box. This second label changes to **Count of Risk** to indicate that a count, or tally, of the occurrences of each risk category will be displayed in the PivotTable.

In the PivotTable being created:

5. Right-click and then click **PivotTable Options** in the shortcut menu that appears.

In the PivotTable Options dialog box:

6. Click the **Layout & Format** tab.
7. Check **For empty cells, show** and enter **0** as its value. Leave all other settings unchanged.
8. Click **OK** to complete the PivotTable.

To add a column for the percentage frequency:

9. Enter **Percentage** in cell C4. Enter the formula = **B5/B$8** in cell **C5** and copy it down through row 7.
10. Select cell range **C5:E5**, right-click, and select **Format Cells** in the shortcut menu.
11. In the **Number** tab of the Format Cells dialog box, select **Percentage** as the **Category** and click **OK**.

In-Depth Excel 2003 For data that need to be tallied, use the PivotTable feature to create a summary table. (For the case in which data have already been tallied, use the **SUMMARY_SIMPLE worksheet** of the **Chapter 2 workbook** as a model for creating a summary table.)

For example, to create the Table 2.2 summary table on page 22, open to the **DATA worksheet** of the **Bond Funds workbook**. Select **Data → PivotTable and PivotChart Report**. In the PivotTable Wizard Step 1 dialog box:

1. Click **Microsoft Excel list or database** as the data to analyze and **PivotTable** as the report type.
2. Click **Next**.

In the Wizard Step 2 dialog box:

3. Enter **I1:I181** as the **Range** and click **Next**.

In the Wizard Step 3 dialog box:

4. Click **New worksheet** and then click **Layout**.

In the Layout dialog box (shown at left in Figure EG2.1 below):

5. Drag the **Risk** label (on the right edge of the dialog box) and drop it in the **ROW area**.
6. Drag a second copy of the **Risk** label and drop it in the **DATA area**. (Note: The second label changes to **Count of Risk** to indicate that a count, or tally, of each risk category will be displayed in the **DATA area**.)
7. Click **OK**.

FIGURE EG2.1   PivotTable Layout and Options dialog boxes

Back in the Wizard Step 3 dialog box:

8. Click **Options**.

In the PivotTable Options dialog box (shown in Figure EG2.1):

9. Check **For empty cells, show** and enter **0** as its value. Leave all other settings unchanged.

10. Click **OK**.

Back in the Wizard Step 3 dialog box:

11. Click **Finish** to create the PivotTable.

To add a column for the percentage frequency:

12. Enter **Percentage** in cell C4. Enter the formula =B5/B$8 in cell C5 and copy it down through row 7.

13. Select cell range **C5:E5**, right-click, and select **Format Cells** in the shortcut menu.

14. In the **Number** tab of the Format Cells dialog box, select **Percentage** as the **Category** and click **OK**.

The Contingency Table

PHStat2 Use the **Two-Way Tables & Charts** procedure to create a contingency table for data that need to be tallied. For example, to create the Table 2.3 contingency table on page 22, open to the **DATA worksheet** of the **Bond Funds workbook**. Select **PHStat → Descriptive Statistics → Two-Way Tables & Charts**. In the procedure's dialog box (shown below):

1. Enter **B1:B181** as the **Row Variable Cell Range**.

2. Enter **D1:D181** as the **Column Variable Cell Range**.

3. Check **First cell in each range contains label**.

4. Enter a **Title** and click **OK**.

After the procedure creates the PivotTable, rearrange the order of the "No" and "Yes" columns:

5. In Excel 2007, click the **Fees** drop-down list in cell B3 and select **Sort Z to A**. In Excel 2003, right-click the **No** label in cell B4, then select **Order → Move Right** in the shortcut menu.

In-Depth Excel 2007 For data that need to be tallied, use the PivotTable feature to create a contingency table. (For the case in which data have already been tallied, use the **CONTINGENCY_SIMPLE worksheet** of the **Chapter 2 workbook** as a model for creating a contingency table.)

For example, to create the Table 2.3 contingency table on page 22, open to the **DATA worksheet** of the **Bond Funds workbook**. Select **Insert → PivotTable**. In the Create PivotTable dialog box:

1. Click **Select a table or range** and enter **B1:D181** as the **Table/Range** cell range. (Although **Type** is in column B and **Fees** is in column D, Excel does not allow you to enter a range comprised of nonadjacent columns.)

2. Select the **New Worksheet** option and click **OK**. In the PivotTable Field List task pane:

3. Check **Type** and **Fees** in the **Choose fields to add to report** box.

4. Drag the checked **Type** label and drop it in the **Row Labels** box.

5. Drag a second copy of the check **Type** label and drop it in the Σ **Values** box. (This label changes to **Count of Type**.) Then drag the checked **Fees** label and drop it in the **Column Labels** area.

In the PivotTable being created:

6. Click the **Fees** drop-down list in cell B3 and select **Sort Z to A** to rearrange the order of the "No" and "Yes" columns.

7. Right-click and then click **PivotTable Options** in the shortcut menu that appears.

In the PivotTable Options dialog box (a reorganized version of the Excel 2003 PivotTable Options dialog box shown in Figure EG2.1):

8. Click the **Layout & Format** tab.

9. Check **For empty cells, show** and enter **0** as its value. Leave all other settings unchanged.

10. Click the **Total & Filters** tab.

11. Check **Show grand totals for columns** and **Show grand totals for rows**.

12. Click **OK** to complete the table.

In-Depth Excel 2003 For data that need to be tallied, use the PivotTable feature to create a contingency table. (For the case in which data have already been tallied, use the **CONTINGENCY_SIMPLE worksheet** of the **Chapter 2 workbook** as a model for creating a contingency table.)

For example, to create the Table 2.3 contingency table on page 22, open to the **DATA worksheet** of the **Bond Funds workbook**. Select **Data → PivotTable and PivotChart Report**. In the PivotTable Wizard Step 1 dialog box:

1. Click **Microsoft Excel list or database** as the source data and **PivotTable** as the report type.

2. Click **Next**.

In the Wizard Step 2 dialog box:

3. Enter **B1:D181** as the **Range**. (Although **Type** is in column B and **Fees** is in column D, Excel does not

allow you to enter a range comprised of nonadjacent columns.)

  4. Click **Next**.

In the Wizard Step 3 dialog box:

  5. Click **New worksheet** and then click **Layout**.

In the Layout dialog box:

  6. Drag the **Type** label and drop it in the **ROW area**.

  7. Drag a second copy of the **Type** label and drop it in the **DATA area**. (The label changes to **Count of Type**.)

  8. Drag the **Fees** label and drop it in the **COLUMN area**.

  9. Click **OK**.

Back in the Wizard Step 3 dialog box:

  10. Click **Options**.

In the PivotTable Options dialog box:

  11. Check **Grand total for columns** and **Grand totals for rows**.

  12. Check **For empty cells, show** and enter **0** as its value. Leave all other settings unchanged.

Back in the Wizard Step 3 dialog box:

  13. Click **Finish** to create the PivotTable.

In the PivotTable:

  14. Right-click the **No** label in cell **B4** and then select **Order → Move Right** in the shortcut menu to make the "No" column appear to the right of the "Yes" column.

EG2.4 ORGANIZING NUMERICAL DATA

The Ordered Array

In-Depth Excel 2007 To create an ordered array, first select the data to be sorted. Then select **Home → Sort & Filter** (in the **Editing group**) → **Sort Smallest to Largest**.

In-Depth Excel 2003 To create an ordered array, first select the data to be sorted. Then select **Data → Sort**. In the Sort dialog box, select the column to sort from the **Sort by** drop-down list. Click the first **Ascending** option button and **Header row**. Then click **OK** to complete the sort.

The Frequency Distribution, Part I

To create a frequency distribution, you must first translate your classes into what Excel calls *bins*. Bins approximate the classes of a frequency distribution. Unlike classes, bins do not have precise lower and upper boundary values. You establish bins by entering, in ascending order, a list of "bin numbers" into a column cell range. Each bin number, in turn, defines a bin: A bin is all the values that are less than or equal to its bin number and that are greater than the previous bin number.

Because the first bin number does not have a "previous" bin number, the first bin can never have a precise lower boundary value, as a first class always has. A common

workaround to this problem, used in the examples throughout this book, is to define an extra bin, using a bin number that is slightly lower than the lower boundary value of the first class. This extra bin number, appearing first, will allow the now-second bin number to better approximate the first class, though at the cost of adding an unwanted bin to the results.

In this chapter, Tables 2.8 through 2.11 on pages 27–29 use class groupings in the form "*valueA* but less than *valueB*." You can translate class groupings in this form into nearly equivalent bins by creating a list of bin numbers that are slightly lower than each *valueB* that appears in the class groupings. For example, the Table 2.9 classes on page 27 could be translated into nearly equivalent bins by using this bin number list: −35.01 (the extra bin number), −30.01 ("slightly less" than −30), −25.01, −20.01, −15.01, −10.01, −5.01, −0.01, 4.99 (slightly less than 5), 9.99, 14.99, and 19.99.

For class groupings in the form "all values from *valueA* to *valueB*," such as the set 0.0 through 4.9, 5.0 through 9.9, 10.0 through 14.9, and 15.0 through 19.9, you can approximate each class grouping by choosing a bin number slightly more than each *valueB*, as in this list of bin numbers: −0.01 (the extra bin number), 4.99 (slightly more than 4.9), 9.99, 14.99, and 19.99.

Use an empty column in the worksheet that contains your untallied data to enter your bin numbers (in ascending order). Enter **Bins** in the row 1 cell of that column as the column heading. Enter your bin numbers before you use the Part II instructions to create frequency distributions.

Before you continue with Part II, note that you can include frequency, percentage, and/or cumulative percentages as columns of one distribution, unlike what is shown in Tables 2.8 through 2.11. Also, when you use Excel, you create frequency distributions for individual categories separately (for example, a frequency distribution for intermediate government bond funds, followed by one for short-term corporate bond funds). To form worksheets that look like two-category Tables 2.8 through 2.11, you cut and paste parts of separately created frequency distributions. (Examine the **FD_IG** and **FD_STC worksheets** of the **Chapter 2 workbook** and then examine the **FD_COMBINED worksheet** to see how frequency distributions for an individual category can be cut and pasted to form one table.)

The Frequency Distribution, Part II

PHStat2 Use the **Frequency Distribution** procedure or **Histogram & Polygons** procedure (discussed in Section EG2.6) to create a frequency distribution. For example, to create the Table 2.9 frequency distribution on page 27, open to the **DATA worksheet** of the **Bond Funds workbook**. Select **PHStat → Descriptive Statistics → Frequency Distribution**. In the procedure's dialog box:

  1. Enter **F1:F181** as the **Variable Cell Range**, enter **J1:J13** as the **Bins Cell Range**, and check **First cell in each range contains label**.

2. Click **Multiple Groups – Stacked** and enter **B1:B181** as the **Grouping Variable Cell Range**. (In the DATA worksheet, the 2008 returns for both types of bond funds are stacked, or placed in a single column. The column B values allow PHStat2 to separate the returns for intermediate government funds from the returns for the short-term corporate funds.)

3. Enter a **Title** and click **OK**.

When creating other frequency distributions, if you use a worksheet that contains data for a single group, such as the **IGDATA** or **STCDATA worksheets**, click **Single Group Variable** in step 2.

In-Depth Excel Use the **FREQUENCY** worksheet function and a bin number list (see "The Frequency Distribution, Part I" on page 71) to create a frequency distribution. For example, to create the Table 2.9 frequency distribution on page 27, open to and review the **IGDATA** and **STCDATA worksheets** of the **Bond Funds workbook**. Note that the worksheets divide the bond funds sample by fund type and that the two worksheets contain identical bin number lists in column J. With the workbook open to the IGDATA worksheet:

1. Right-click the **IGDATA worksheet** tab and click **Insert** in the shortcut menu to insert a new worksheet.

2. In the new worksheet, enter a worksheet title in cell **A1**, enter **Bins** in cell **A3**, and **Frequency** in cell **B3**.

3. Copy the **bin number list** that is in the cell range **J2:J13** of the IGDATA worksheet and paste this list into column A of the new worksheet, starting with cell **A4**.

4. Select the cell range **B4:B15** that will contain the frequency function.

5. Type, but do not press the **Enter** or **Tab** key, the formula **=FREQUENCY(IGDATA!$F$1:$F$91, $A$4:$A$15)**. Then, while holding down the **Ctrl** and **Shift** keys (or the **Apple** key on a Mac), press the

Enter key. [This combination keystroke enters the formula as an "array formula" in the cell range **B4:B15**. If you make a mistake entering this formula, you must re-select the range **B4:B15** first, make your corrections, and, again, press **Enter** while holding down **Ctrl** and **Shift** (or **Apple**).]

To create the frequency distribution for short-term corporate bonds, repeat steps 1 through 5, but enter the formula **=FREQUENCY(STCDATA!$F$1:$F$91, $A$4:$A$15** in step 5. Then cut and paste the results from the two frequency distributions to create a table similar to Table 2.9.

Note that in step 5, you entered the cell range as **IGDATA!$F$1:$F$91** (or **STCDATA!$F$1:$F$91**) and not as **F1:F91** because the data to be summarized is located on another worksheet and you wanted to use absolute cell references to facilitate the copying of the frequency column to create a table similar to Table 2.9.

Analysis ToolPak Use the **Histogram** procedure and a bin number list (see "The Frequency Distribution, Part I" on page 26) to create a frequency distribution. For example, to create the Table 2.9 frequency distribution on page 27, open to the **IGDATA worksheet** of the **Bond Funds workbook** and:

1. Select **Data → Data Analysis** (Excel 2007) or **Tools → Data Analysis** (Excel 2003).

2. In the Data Analysis dialog box, select **Histogram** from the **Analysis Tools** list and then click **OK**.

In the Histogram dialog box (see below):

3. Enter **F1:F91** as the **Input Range** and enter **J1:J13** as the **Bin Range**. (If you leave **Bin Range** blank, the procedure creates a set of bins that will not be as well-formed as the ones you can specify.)

4. Check **Labels** and click **New Worksheet Ply**.

5. Click **OK** to create the frequency distribution (and histogram) on a new worksheet.

In the new worksheet:

6. Select row 1. Right-click row 1 and click the **Insert** shortcut menu. Repeat. (This creates two blank rows at the top of the worksheet.)

7. Enter a title for the frequency distribution in cell A1.

The ToolPak creates a frequency distribution that contains an improper bin labeled **More**. Correct this error as follows:

8. Manually add the frequency count of the **More** row to the count of the preceding bin.

9. Click the worksheet row number for the **More** row (to select the entire worksheet row), right-click on the row, and click **Delete** in the shortcut menu that appears.

Open to the **STCDATA worksheet** and repeat steps 1 through 9. Then cut and paste the results from the two frequency distributions to create a table similar to Table 2.9.

The Relative Frequency, Percentage, or Cumulative Percentage Distribution

PHStat2 To create these other distributions, first use the *PHStat2* instructions in "The Frequency Distribution, Part II" to create a frequency distribution that contains a column of percentages and cumulative percentages. To create a column of relative frequencies, reformat the percentage column. Select the cells containing the percentages, right-click, and then select **Format Cells** from the shortcut menu. In the **Number** tab of the Format Cells dialog box, select **Number** as the **Category** and click **OK**.

In-Depth Excel To create these other distributions, modify a frequency distribution created using the "The Frequency Distribution, Part II" *In-Depth Excel* instructions by adding a column for percentages (or relative frequencies) and a column for cumulative percentages. For example, open to the **FD_IG worksheet** of the **Chapter 2 workbook**. This worksheet contains the frequency distribution for the intermediate government bond funds. To modify this worksheet to include percentage and cumulative percentage distributions:

1. Enter **Total** in cell **A16** and enter **=SUM(B4:B15)** in cell **B15**.

2. Enter **Percentage** in cell **C3** and **Cumulative Pctage** in cell **D3**.

3. Enter **=B4/B$16** in cell **C4** and copy this formula down through all the rows of the frequency distribution.

4. Enter **=C4** in cell **D4**. Enter **=D4+C5** in cell **D5** and copy this formula down through all the rows of the frequency distribution.

5. Select the cell range **C4:D15**, right-click, and click **Format Cells** in the shortcut menu.

6. In the **Number** tab of the Format Cells dialog box, select **Percentage** as the **Category** and click **OK**.

If you want a column of relative frequencies instead of percentages, change the cell **C4** column heading to **Rel. Frequencies**. Then select the cell range **C4:C15**, right-click, and click **Format Cells** in the shortcut menu. In the **Number** tab of the Format Cells dialog box, select **Number** as the **Category** and click **OK**.

Analysis ToolPak Use the preceding *In-Depth Excel* instructions to modify a frequency distribution created using the "The Frequency Distribution, Part II" instructions.

EG2.5 VISUALIZING CATEGORICAL DATA

The Bar Chart and The Pie Chart

PHStat2 Modify the Section EG2.3 *PHStat2* instructions (page 68) to create a bar or pie chart. In step 3 of those instructions, check either **Bar Chart** and/or **Pie Chart** in addition to entering a **Title** and clicking **OK**.

In-Depth Excel 2007 Create charts from a summary table. For example, to create the Figure 2.6 bar chart on page 33 or the Figure 2.8 pie chart on page 35, open to the **SUMMARY_PIVOT worksheet** of the **Chapter 2 workbook** and:

1. Select cell range cell **A4:B7** (Begin your selection at cell B7 and not at cell A4 as you would normally do).

2. Select **Insert**. For a bar chart, click **Bar** in the **Charts group** and then select the first **2-D Bar** gallery choice (**Clustered Bar**). For a pie chart, click **Pie** in the **Charts group** and then select the first **2-D Pie** gallery choice (**Pie**).

3. Relocate the chart to a chart sheet and adjust chart formatting by using the instructions in Appendix Section C.7 on page 726.

For a pie chart, select **Layout → Data Labels → More Data Label Options**. In the Format Data Labels dialog box, click **Label Options** in the left pane. In the Label Options right pane, check **Category Name** and **Percentage** and clear the other check boxes. Click **Outside End** and then click **Close**.

For a bar chart, if the horizontal axis scale does not begin with 0, right-click the horizontal (value) axis and click **Format Axis** in the shortcut menu. In the Format Axis dialog box, click **Axis Options** in the left pane. In the Axis Options right pane, click the first **Fixed** option button (for Minimum) and enter **0** in its box. Click **Close**.

In-Depth Excel 2003 Create charts from a summary table. For example, to create the Figure 2.6 bar chart on page 33 or the Figure 2.8 pie chart on page 35, open to the **SUMMARY_PIVOT worksheet** of the **Chapter 2 workbook**. Click an empty cell outside the table to prevent Excel from automatically selecting a (wrong) chart type. Select **Insert → Chart** and:

In the Chart Wizard Step 1 dialog box:

1. Click the **Standard Types** tab. For a bar chart, click **Bar** as the **Chart type** and then click the first **Chart sub-type** choice, labeled **Clustered Bar** when selected. For a pie chart, click **Pie** as the **Chart type** and then click the first **Chart sub-type** choice, labeled **Pie** when selected.

2. Click **Next**.

In the Chart Wizard Step 2 dialog box:

3. Click the **Data Range** tab and enter **A4:B7** as the **Data range**. Click **Columns** if this option is visible

4. Click **Next**.

In the Chart Wizard Step 3 dialog box:

5. Click the **Titles** tab and enter a **Chart title**. For a bar chart, enter appropriate values for the **Category (X) axis** and **Value (Y) axis** titles and use the formatting settings discussed in Appendix Section C.8 on page 727 for the **Axes**, **Gridlines**, **Legend**, **Data Labels**, and **Data Table** tabs.

   For a pie chart, click the **Legend** tab and clear **Show legend**. Then click the **Data Labels** tab and click **Category name** and **Percentage**.

6. Click **Next**.

In the Chart Wizard Step 4 dialog box:

7. Click **As new sheet** and then click **Finish** to complete the chart.

If you see a boxed label such as "Count of Risk," right-click the boxed label and click **Hide PivotChart Field Buttons** from the shortcut menu. If the horizontal axis scale on the bar chart does not begin with 0, right-click the horizontal (value) axis and click **Format Axis** in the shortcut menu. In the Format Axis dialog box, click the **Scale** tab and in that tab, change the value in the **Minimum** box to **0**, and click **OK**.

The Pareto Chart

PHStat2 Modify the Section EG2.2 *PHStat2* instructions for creating a summary table on page 68 to create a Pareto chart. In step 3 of those instructions, check **Pareto Chart** in addition to entering a **Title** and clicking **OK**.

In-Depth Excel 2007 Create a chart based on a modified summary table that was originally created using the instructions in Section EG2.3 to create a Pareto chart. In the original table, first sort the table in order of decreasing frequencies and then add a column for cumulative percentage. Use the sorted, modified table to create the Pareto chart.

   For example, to create the Figure 2.9 Pareto chart, open to the **ATMTable worksheet** of the **ATM Transactions workbook**. Begin by sorting the modified table by decreasing order of frequency:

1. Select row **11** (the Total row), right-click, and click **Hide** in the shortcut menu. (This prevents the total row from getting sorted.)

2. Select cell **B4** (the first frequency), right-click, and select **Sort → Sort Largest to Smallest**.

3. Select rows **10** and **12** (there is no row 11), right-click, and click **Unhide** in the shortcut menu.

Next, add a column for cumulative percentage:

4. Enter **Cumulative Pctage** in cell **D3**. Enter **=C4** in cell **D4**. Enter **=D4+C5** in cell **D5** and copy this formula down through row 10.

5. Select the cell range **C4:D10**, right-click, and click **Format Cells** in the shortcut menu.

6. In the **Number** tab of the Format Cells dialog box, select **Percentage** as the **Category** and click **OK**.

Next, create the Pareto chart:

7. Select the cell range **A3:A10** and while holding down the **Ctrl** key additionally select the cell range **C3:D10**.

8. Select **Insert → Column** (in the Charts group) and select the first **2-D Column** gallery choice (**Clustered Column**).

9. Select **Format** (under **Chart Tools**). In the Current Selection group, select the entry for the cumulative percentage series from the drop-down list and then click **Format Selection**.

10. In the Format Data Series dialog box, click **Series Options** in the left pane and in the **Series Options** right pane, click **Secondary Axis**. Click **Close**.

11. With the cumulative percentage series still selected in the Current Selection group, select **Design → Change Chart Type**, and in the **Change Chart Type** gallery, select the fourth **Line** gallery choice (**Line with Markers**). Click **OK**.

Next, set the maximum value of the primary and secondary (left and right) *Y* axes scales to 100%. For each *Y* axis:

12. Right-click on the axis and click **Format Axis** in the shortcut menu.

13. In the Format Axis dialog box, click **Axis Options** in the left pane and in the **Axis Options** right pane, click the second **Fixed** option button (for Maximum) and enter **1** in its box. Click **Close**.

Relocate the chart to a chart sheet and adjust chart formatting by using the instructions in Appendix Section C.7 on page 726.

   When using a PivotTable as a summary table, table sorting is simpler: Right-click the cell that contains the first frequency (cell B5 in the sample worksheet) and select **Sort → Sort Largest to Smallest**. However, creating a Pareto chart from a PivotTable and additional columns for percentage and cumulative percentage is much more difficult than creating a chart from a simple summary table. The best workaround is to convert the PivotTable to a simple summary table by copying the category names and frequencies in the PivotTable, along with the additional columns, to an empty worksheet area.

In-Depth Excel 2003 Create a chart based on a modified summary table that was originally created using the instructions of Section EG2.3 to create a Pareto chart. To the original table, first sort the table in order of decreasing frequencies and then add a column for cumulative percentage. Use the sorted, modified table to create the Pareto chart.

For example, to create the Figure 2.9 Pareto chart, open to the **ATMTable worksheet** of the **ATM Transactions workbook**. Begin by sorting the modified table by decreasing order of frequency:

1. Select row 11 (the Total row), right-click, and select **Hide** in the shortcut menu. (This prevents the Total row from getting sorted.)

2. Select **Data → Sort**. In the Sort dialog box, select **Frequency** from the **Sort by** drop-down list, click the Sort by **Descending** option button, click **Header row**, and click **OK**.

3. Select rows 10 and 12 (there is no row 11), right-click, and select **Unhide** in the shortcut menu.

Next, use steps 4 through 6 of the *In-Depth Excel 2007* instructions to add a column for cumulative percentage. Then, create the Pareto chart:

7. Select **Insert → Chart**.

In the Chart Wizard Step 1 dialog box:

8. Click the **Custom Types** tab. Click **Built-in** (near the bottom of the dialog box) and then click **Line - Column on 2 Axes** as the **Chart type**.

9. Click **Next**.

In the Chart Wizard Step 2 dialog box:

10. Click the **Data Range** tab. Enter **A3:A10,C3:D10** as the **Data range**. (Be sure to include the comma in the range you type.)

11. Click **Columns** and then click **Next**.

In the Chart Wizard Step 3 dialog box:

12. Click the **Titles** tab. Enter a **Chart title**, **Cause** for the **Category (X) axis** title, and **Percentage** as the **Value (Y) axis** title. Use the formatting settings discussed in Appendix Section C.8 on page 727 for the **Axes**, **Gridlines**, **Legend**, **Data Labels**, and **Data Table** tabs.

13. Click **Next**.

In the Chart Wizard Step 4 dialog box:

14. Click **As new sheet** and then click **Finish** to complete the chart.

Finally, set the maximum value of the primary and secondary (left and right) *Y* axes scales to 100%. For each *Y* axis:

15. Right-click the axis and click **Format Axis** in the shortcut menu.

16. In the **Scale** tab of the Format Axis dialog box, change the **Maximum** value to **1** and click **OK**.

When using a PivotTable as a summary table, replace steps 1 through 3, 7, and 10, with these instructions:

1. Select the cell containing the first frequency.

2. Select **Data → Sort**.

3. In the Sort dialog box, click **Descending** and then click **OK**.

7. Select the cell range of the percentage and cumulative percentage columns. Then, select **Insert → Chart**.

10. Click the **Series** tab. Enter the cell range of the categories, exclusive of the column heading cell, as a formula in the form *=SheetName!CellRange* for the **Category (X)** axis labels.

The Side-by-Side Chart

PHStat2 Modify the Section EG2.3 PHStat2 instructions for creating a contingency table on page 70 to create a side-by-side chart. In step 4 of those instructions, check **Side-by-Side Bar Chart** in addition to entering a **Title** and clicking **OK**.

In-Depth Excel 2007 Create a chart based on a contingency table to create a side-by-side chart. For example, to create the Figure 2.10 side-by-side bar chart on page 37, open to the **CONTINGENCY_PIVOT worksheet** of the **Chapter 2 workbook**. Select cell **A4** (or any other cell inside the PivotTable). Select **Insert → Bar** and click the first **2-D Bar** gallery choice (**Clustered Bar**). Relocate the chart to a chart sheet and adjust the chart formatting by using the instructions in Appendix Section C.7 on page 726, but with this exception: When you click **Legend**, select **Show Legend at Right**.

When creating a chart from a contingency table that is not a PivotTable, select the cell range of the contingency table, including row and column headings, but excluding the total row and total column, before selecting **Insert → Bar**.

Occasionally when you create a side-by-side chart, the row and column variables need to be swapped. If your chart uses a PivotTable, rearrange the PivotTable by making the row variable, the column variable and vice versa. If your chart does not use a PivotTable, right-click the chart and click **Select Data** in the shortcut menu. In the Select Data Source dialog box (see below), click **Switch Row/Column** and then click **OK**.

In-Depth Excel 2003 Create a chart based on a contingency table to create a side-by-side chart. For example, to create the Figure 2.10 side-by-side bar chart on page 29, open to the **CONTINGENCY_PIVOT worksheet** of the **Chapter 2 workbook**. Select a cell that is outside the contingency table. Select **Insert → Chart** and:

In the Chart Wizard Step 1 dialog box:

1. Click the **Standard Types** tab. Click **Bar** as the **Chart type** and then click the first **Chart sub-type** choice, labeled **Clustered Bar** when selected.

2. Click **Next**.

In the Chart Wizard Step 2 dialog box:

3. Enter **A4:C6** as the **Data range**.

4. Click **Columns** and then click **Next**.

In the Chart Wizard Step 3 dialog box:

5. Click the **Titles** tab. Enter a **Chart title**, **Fund Type** for the **Category (X) axis** title, and **Percentage** for the **Value (Y) axis** title. (Unlike what you might expect, Excel considers the horizontal axis to be the *Value (Y) axis* and the vertical axis of this chart to be the *Category (X) axis*.) Relocate the chart and use the formatting settings discussed in Appendix Section C.8 on page 727 for the **Axes**, **Gridlines**, **Data Labels**, and **Data Table** tabs. Click the **Legend** tab and check **Show legend**.

6. Click **Next**.

In the Chart Wizard Step 4 dialog box:

7. Click **As new sheet** and then click **Finish** to complete the chart.

If field buttons appear on the chart, right-click any button and click **Hide PivotChart Field Buttons** in the shortcut menu.

EG2.6 VISUALIZING NUMERICAL DATA

The Stem-and-Leaf Display

PHStat2 Use the **Stem-and-Leaf Display** procedure to create a stem-and-leaf display. For example, to create the Figure 2.11 stem-and-leaf display, open to the **IGDATA worksheet** of the **Chapter 2 workbook**. Select **PHStat → Descriptive Statistics → Stem-and-Leaf Display**. In the procedure's dialog box (shown below):

1. Enter **F1:F91** as the **Variable Cell Range** and check **First cell contains label**.

2. Leave **Autocalculate stem unit** selected.

3. Enter a **Title** and click **OK**.

For other displays you create, the **Set stem unit as** option should be used sparingly and only if **Autocalculate stem unit** creates a display that has too few or too many stems. (Any stem unit you specify must be a power of 10.)

In-Depth Excel Manually construct the stems and leaves on a new worksheet to create a stem-and-leaf display. Use the **STEM_LEAF worksheet** of the **Chapter 2 workbook** as a guide to formatting your display.

The Histogram

PHStat2 Use the **Histogram & Polygons** procedure to create a histogram from unsummarized data. For example, to create the pair of histograms shown in Figure 2.13 on page 42, open to the **DATA worksheet** of the **Bond Funds workbook**. Select **PHStat → Descriptive Statistics → Histogram & Polygons**. In the procedure's dialog box (shown below):

1. Enter **F1:F181** as the **Variable Cell Range**, **J1:J13** as the **Bins Cell Range**, **K1:K12** as the **Midpoints Cell Range**, and check **First cell in each range contains label**.

2. Click **Multiple Groups - Stacked** and enter **B1:B181** as the **Grouping Variable Cell Range**. (In the DATA worksheet, the 2008 returns for both types of bond funds are stacked, or placed in a single column. The column B values allow PHStat2 to separate the returns for intermediate government funds from the returns for the short-term corporate funds.)

3. Enter a **Title**, check **Histogram**, and click **OK**.

The **Bins Cell Range** and the **Midpoints Cell Range** should appear in the same worksheet as the unsummarized data, as the **DATA worksheet** of the **Bond Funds** workbook illustrates. Because a first bin can never have a midpoint (because that bin does not have a lower boundary value defined), the procedure assigns the first midpoint to the second bin and uses "---" as the label for the first bin. Therefore, the **Midpoints Cell Range** you enter must be one cell smaller in size than the **Bins Cell Range**. Read "The Histogram: Follow-up" on page 78 for a possible change that you can make to the histograms created by this procedure.

In-Depth Excel Create a chart from a frequency distribution. For example, to create the Figure 2.13 pair of histograms on page 42, first use the Section EG2.4 "The Frequency Distribution, Part II" *In-Depth Excel* instructions.

Follow those instructions to create a pair of frequency distributions, one for the intermediate government bond funds, and the other for the short-term corporate bond funds, on separate worksheets. In each worksheet, add a column of midpoints by entering the column heading **Midpoints** in cell **C3**, **'---** in cell **C4**, and starting in cell **C5**, the midpoints $-32.5, -27.5, -22.5, -17.5, -12.5, -7.5, -2.5,$ $2.5, 7.5, 12.5,$ and $17.5.$ Continue with either the *In-Depth Excel 2007* or *In-Depth Excel 2003* instructions.

In-Depth Excel 2007 *Continued from In-Depth Excel . . .*
In each worksheet:

1. Select the cell range **B3:B15** (the cell range of the frequencies).
2. Select **Insert ➔ Column** and select the first **2-D Column** gallery choice (**Clustered Column**).
3. Right-click the chart background and click **Select Data**.

In the Select Data Source dialog box:

4. Click **Edit** under the **Horizontal (Categories) Axis Labels** heading.
5. In the Axis Labels dialog box (see below), enter the cell range *formula* in the form **=*SheetName*!C4:C15** (where *SheetName* is the name of the current worksheet) and then click **OK** to return to the Select Data Source dialog box.
6. Click **OK**.

In the chart:

7. Right-click inside a bar and click **Format Data Series** in the shortcut menu.

In the Format Data Series dialog box:

8. Click **Series Options** in the left pane. In the Series Options right pane, change the **Gap Width** slider to **No Gap**. Click **Close**.

Relocate the chart to a chart sheet and adjust the chart formatting by using the instructions in Appendix Section C.7 on page 726. Read "The Histogram: Follow-up" on page 78 for an additional possible change that you can make to the histograms created.

In-Depth Excel 2003 *Continued from In-Depth Excel in the left column . . .*
In each worksheet:

1. Select the cell range **B3:B15** (the cell range of the frequencies).
2. Select **Insert ➔ Chart** and:

In the Chart Wizard Step 1 dialog box:

3. Click the **Standard Types** tab. Click **Column** as the **Chart type** and then click the first **Chart sub-type** choice, labeled **Clustered Column** when selected.
4. Click **Next**.

In the Chart Wizard Step 2 dialog box:

5. Click the **Data Range** tab. Click **Columns**.
6. Click the **Series tab**. Enter the cell range *formula* in the form **=*SheetName*!C4:C15** (where *SheetName* is the name of the current worksheet) as the **Category (X) axis labels**.
7. Click **Next**.

In the Chart Wizard Step 3 dialog box:

8. Click the **Titles** tab. Enter a **Chart title**, **2008 Return** as the **Category (X) axis** title, and **Frequency** as the **Value (Y) axis** title. Use the formatting settings discussed in Appendix Section C.8 on page 727 for the **Axes**, **Gridlines**, **Legend**, **Data Labels**, and **Data Table** tabs.

In the Chart Wizard Step 4 dialog box:

9. Click **As new sheet** and then click **Finish** to create a chart.

In the chart, right-click inside a bar and click **Format Data Series** in the shortcut menu. In the Format Data Series dialog box, click the **Options tab**, set the **Gap width** to **0**, and click **OK**.

Read "The Histogram: Follow-up" on page 78 for an additional possible change that you can make to the histograms created.

Analysis ToolPak Modify the Section EG2.4 Analysis ToolPak instructions for "The Frequency Distribution, Part II" on page 71 to create a histogram. In step 5 of those instructions, check **Chart Output** before clicking **OK**.

For example, to create the pair of histograms in Figure 2.13 on page 42, use the modified step 5 with both the **IGDATA** and **STCDATA** worksheets of the **Chapter 2 workbook** (as discussed on page 42) to create a pair of worksheets that contain a frequency distribution and a histogram. Each histogram will have (the same) two formatting errors that you can correct:

To eliminate the gaps between bars:

1. Right-click inside one of the histogram bars and click **Format Data Series** in the shortcut menu that appears.

2. In Excel 2007, In the **Series Options pane** of the Format Data Series dialog box (partially shown below), move the **Gap Width** slider to **No Gap** and click **Close**. In Excel 2003, click the **Options tab** of the Format Data Series dialog box, change the value of **Gap width** to **0**, and click **OK**.

To change the histogram bin labels:

1. Enter the column heading **Midpoints** in cell **C3** and enter '--- in cell **C4** (the first bin has no midpoint). Starting in cell **C5**, enter the midpoints $-32.5, -27.5, -22.5, -17.5, -12.5, -7.5, -2.5, 2.5, 7.5, 12.5,$ and 17.5, in column C. (The midpoints will serve as the new bin labels in step 3.)

2. Right-click the chart background and click **Select Data** (Excel 2007) or **Source Data** (Excel 2003).

3. For Excel 2007, in the Select Data Source dialog box, click **Edit** under the **Horizontal (Categories) Axis Labels** heading. In the Axis Labels dialog box, enter the cell range *formula* in the form **=SheetName!C4:C15** as the **Axis label range** and click **OK**. Back in the Select Data Source dialog box, click **OK** to complete the task.

    For Excel 2003, select the **Series** tab in the Source Data dialog box and enter the cell range of the midpoints as a formula, in the form **=SheetName!C4:C15** as the **Category (X) axis labels** and click **OK**.

In step 3, substitute the name of the worksheet that contains the frequency distribution and histogram for *SheetName* and note that the cell range **C4:C15** does not include the column heading cell. Read the next section for an additional possible change that you can make to the histograms created.

The Histogram: Follow-up

In Section EG2.4, "The Frequency Distribution, Part I" discusses a workaround that uses an extra bin that appears first as a method to better translate classes into bins. Because the example used throughout "The Histogram" uses this workaround, the histogram you create using those instructions will have the extra—meaningless for your analysis—bin. If you would like to remove this extra bin, as was done for charts shown in Figures 2.12 and 2.13 on pages 41 and 42, apply the *In-Depth Excel* instructions that follow. These instructions will work even if you used PHStat2 or the Analysis ToolPak to create your histogram.

In-Depth Excel 2007 To remove the extra bin, right-click the histogram background and click **Select Data**. In the Select Data Source Data dialog box, first click **Edit** under the **Legend Entries (Series)** heading. In the Edit Series dialog box, edit the **Series values** cell range formula. Then click **Edit** under the **Horizontal (Categories) Axis Labels** heading. In the Axis Labels dialog box, edit the **Axis label range**. For the example used in the previous section, change the starting cell for the **Series values** cell range formula from B4 to B5 and change the starting cell for the **Axis label range** cell range formula from C4 to C5.

In-Depth Excel 2003 To remove the extra bin, right-click the histogram background and click **Source Data**. In the Source Data dialog box, click the **Series** tab. Edit the cell range formulas for **Values** and **Category (X) axis labels**. For the example used in the previous section, change the starting cell for the **Values** cell range formula from B4 to B5 and change the starting cell for the **Category (X) axis labels** cell range formula from C4 to C5.

The Percentage Polygon

PHStat2 Modify the *PHStat2* instructions for creating a histogram on page 76 to create a percentage polygon. In step 3 of those instructions, click **Percentage Polygon** before clicking **OK**.

In-Depth Excel 2007 Create a chart based on a modified percentage distribution to create a percentage polygon. For example, to create the Figure 2.15 percentage polygons on page 43, open to the **CPD_IG worksheet** of the **Bond Funds workbook**. (This worksheet contains a frequency distribution for the intermediate government bond funds and includes columns for the percentages and cumulative percentages in column C and D.) Begin by modifying the distribution:

1. Enter the column heading **Midpoints** in cell **E3** and enter '--- in cell **E4** (the first bin has no midpoint). Starting in cell **E5**, enter $-32.5, -27.5, -22.5, -17.5, -12.5, -7.5, -2.5, 2.5, 7.5, 12.5,$ and 17.5, in column E.

2. Select row 4 (the first bins row), right-click, and select **Insert** in the shortcut menu.

3. Select row 17 (the total row), right-click, and select **Insert** in the shortcut menu.

4. Select the cell range **C3:C17**.

Next, create the chart:

5. Select **Insert → Line** and select the fourth **2-D Line** gallery choice (**Line with Markers**).

6. Right-click the chart and click **Select Data** in the shortcut menu.

In the Select Data Source dialog box:

7. Click **Edit** under the **Legend Entries (Series)** heading. In the Edit Series dialog box (shown below), enter the formula **="Intermediate Government"** for the **Series name** and click **OK**.

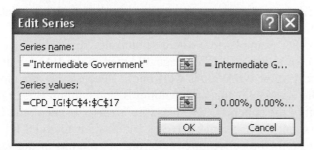

8. Click **Edit** under the **Horizontal (Categories) Axis Labels** heading. In the Axis Labels dialog box, enter the cell range formula **=CPD_IG!E4:E17** for the **Axis label range** and click **OK**.

9. Back in the Select Data Source dialog box, click **OK**.

Back in the chart sheet:

10. Right-click the vertical axis and click **Format Axis** in the shortcut menu.

11. In the Format Axis dialog box, click **Number** in left pane and then select **Percentage** from the **Category** list in the Number right pane. Enter **0** as the **Decimal places** and click **OK**.

Relocate the chart to a chart sheet and adjust chart formatting by using the instructions in Appendix Section C.7 on page 726.

Figure 2.15 on page 43 also contains the polygon for the short-term corporate bond funds. To add this polygon to the chart just created, open to the **CPD_STC worksheet**. Repeat steps 1 through 5 to modify this distribution. Then open to the chart sheet that contains the intermediate government polygon. Select **Layout → Legend → Show Legend at Right**. Right-click the chart and click **Select Data** in the shortcut menu. In the Select Data Source dialog box, click **Add**. In the Edit Series dialog box, enter the formula **="Short Term Corporate"** as the **Series name**, and enter the cell range formula **=CPD_STC!C4:C17** as the **Series values**. Click **OK**. Back in the Select Data Source dialog box, click **OK**.

In-Depth Excel 2003 Create a chart based on a modified percentage distribution to create a percentage polygon. For example, to create the Figure 2.15 percentage polygons on page 43, open to the **CPD_IG worksheet** of the **Bond Funds workbook**. (This worksheet contains a frequency distribution for the intermediate government bond funds and includes columns for the percentages and cumulative percentages in column C and D.) Begin by using steps 1

through 4 of the *In-Depth Excel 2007* instructions to modify the distribution. Then select **Insert → Chart** and:

In the Chart Wizard Step 1 dialog box:

1. Click the **Standard Types** tab and then click **Line** as the **Chart type**. Click the first choice in the second row of **Chart sub-type** choices, labeled **Line with markers displayed at each data value** when selected.

2. Click **Next**.

In the Chart Wizard Step 2 dialog box:

3. Click the **Data Range** tab. Enter **C3:C17** as the **Data range** and click **Columns.**

4. Click the **Series** tab. Enter the formula **="Intermediate Government"** as the **Name** and enter the cell range formula **=CPD_IG!E4:E17** for the **Category (X) axis labels**.

5. Click **Next**.

In the Chart Wizard Step 3 dialog box:

6. Click the **Titles** tab. Enter a **Chart title** and **2008 Return** as the **Category (X) axis** title.

7. Adjust chart formatting by using the instructions in Appendix Section C.7 on page 726 for the **Axes, Gridlines, Legend, Data Labels,** and **Data Table** tabs.

8. Click **Next**.

In the Chart Wizard Step 4 dialog box:

9. Click **As new sheet** and then click **Finish** to complete the chart.

Back in the chart sheet:

10. Right-click the vertical axis and click **Format Axis** in the shortcut menu.

11. In the Format Axis dialog box, click the **Number** tab and select **Percentage** from the **Category** list. Enter **0** as the **Decimal places** and click **OK**.

Figure 2.15 also contains the percentage polygon for the short-term corporate bond funds. To add this polygon to the chart just created, open to the **CPD_STC worksheet**. Repeat steps 1 through 4 of the *In-Depth Excel 2007* instructions to modify this distribution. Then open to the chart sheet that contains the intermediate government polygon. Right-click the chart and click **Chart Options** in the shortcut menu. In the Chart Options dialog box, click the **Legend** tab, check **Show legend**, and click **OK**. Then select **Chart → Add Data**. In the Add Data dialog box, enter the cell range formula **= CPD_STC!C4:C17** as the **Range** and click **OK**. If the Paste Special dialog box appears, click **New series** and **Columns**, clear all check boxes, and click **OK**. Right-click the chart and select **Source Data** from the shortcut menu. Click the **Series** tab. Click the new series name in the **Series** box. Enter the formula **="Short Term Corporate"** as the **Name** and click **OK**.

The Cumulative Percentage Polygon (Ogive)

PHStat2 Modify the *PHStat2* instructions for creating a histogram on page 76 to create a cumulative percentage polygon, In step 3 of those instructions, click **Cumulative Percentage Polygon (Ogive)** before clicking **OK**.

In-Depth Excel 2007 Create a cumulative percentage polygon by modifying the *In-Depth Excel 2007* instructions for creating a percentage polygon. For example, to create the Figure 2.17 cumulative percentage polygons on page 44, use the instructions for creating percentage polygons, replacing steps 4 and 8 with the following:

4. Select the cell range **D3:D16**.

8. Click **Edit** under the **Horizontal (Categories) Axis Labels** heading. In the Axis Labels dialog box, enter the cell range formula **=CPD_IG!A4:A16** for the **Axis label range** and click **OK**.

Later, when adding the second polygon for the short-term corporate bond funds, enter the cell range formula **=CPD_STC!D4:D16** (replacing **=CPD_STC!C4:C17**) as the **Series values** in the Edit Series dialog box.

In-Depth Excel 2003 Create a cumulative percentage polygon by modifying the *In-Depth Excel 2003* instructions for creating a percentage polygon. For example, to create the Figure 2.17 cumulative percentage polygons on page 44, use the instructions for creating percentage polygons, but enter **D3:D16** as the **Data range** in step 3 and enter the cell range formula **=CPD_IG!A4:A16** for the **Category (X) axis labels** in step 4. Later, when adding the second polygon, enter the cell range formula **=CPD_STC!D4:D16** (replacing **=CPD_STC!C4:C17**) as the **Range** in the Add Data dialog box.

EG2.7 VISUALIZING TWO NUMERICAL VARIABLES

The Scatter Plot

PHStat2 Use the **Scatter Plot** procedure to create a scatter plot. For example, to create a sctter plot similar to the one shown in Figure 2.18 on page 49, open to the **DATA worksheet** of the **NBAValues workbook**. Select **PHStat2 → Descriptive Statistics → Scatter Plot**. In the procedure's dialog below (shown below):

1. Enter **B1:B31** as the **Y Variable Cell Range**.
2. Enter **C1:C31** as the **X Variable Cell Range**.
3. Check **First cells in each range contains label**.
4. Enter a **Title** and click **OK**.

You can also use the **Scatter Plot** Output Option of **Simple Linear Regression** procedure to create a scatter plot. Scatter plots created using this alternative will contain a superimposed line like the one seen in Figure 2.18. To learn more about using the **Simple Linear Regression** procedure, see the Section EG13.2 *PHStat2* instructions that begin on page 521.

In-Depth Excel 2007 Create a chart from a worksheet in which the column for the X variable data is to the left of the column for the Y variable data to create a scatter plot. (If the worksheet is arranged Y then X, cut and paste the Y variable column to the right of the X variable column.)

For example, to create a scatter plot similar to the one shown in Figure 2.18 on page 49, open to the **DATA worksheet** of the **NBAValues workbook**. Because the valuations (the Y variable) appear in column B, and column B is to the left of the column C revenues (the *X variable* in column C), first cut the cell range B1:B31 and paste it into cell D1 to create the proper required ordering of columns of the variables. Select the cell range **C1:D31**. Then select **Insert → Scatter** and select the first **Scatter** gallery choice (**Scatter with only Markers**). Then select **Layout → Trendline→ Linear Trendline**. Relocate the chart to a chart sheet and adjust chart formatting by using the instructions in Appendix Section C.7 on page 726.

In-Depth Excel 2003 Create a chart from a worksheet in which the column for the X variable data is to the left of the column for the Y variable data to create a scatter plot. (If the worksheet is arranged Y then X, cut and paste the Y variable column to the right of the X variable column.)

For example, to create the Figure 2.18 scatter plot on page 49, open to the **DATA worksheet** of the **NBAValues workbook**. Because the valuations (the Y variable) appear in column B, to the left of the column C revenues (the X variable), first cut the cell range B1:B31 and paste it into cell D1 to create the required ordering of columns. Select the cell range **C1:D31**. Select **Insert → Chart** and:

In the Chart Wizard Step 1 dialog box:

1. Click the **Standard Types** tab and then click **XY (Scatter)** as the **Chart type**. Click the first **Chart subtype**, labeled as **Scatter**.
2. Click **Next**.

In the Chart Wizard Step 2 dialog box:

3. Click **Next**. (Entries and selections in this dialog box are correct as is.)

In the Chart Wizard Step 3 dialog box:

4. Click the **Titles** tab. Enter a **Chart title**, **Revenues ($millions)** as the **Value (X) axis** title, and **Value ($millions)** as the **Value (Y) axis** title. Adjust chart formatting by using the instructions in Appendix Section

C.8 on page 727 for the **Axes**, **Gridlines**, **Legend**, and **Data Labels** tabs.

   5. Click **Next**.

In the Chart Wizard Step 4 dialog box:

   6. Click **As new sheet** and then click **Finish** to create the chart.

With the workbook opened to the new chart sheet, select **Chart → Add Trendline**. In the Add Trendline dialog box, click **Linear** and then click **OK**.

The Time-Series Plot

In-Depth Excel 2007 Create a chart from a worksheet in which the column for the time variable data appears to the immediate left of the column for the numerical variable data. (Use cut and paste to rearrange columns, if necessary.)

   For example, to create the Figure 2.19 time-series plot on page 50, open to the **DATA worksheet** of the **Solar Power workbook**. Select the cell range **A1:B10** (containing the year and amount of solar power installed data) and then select **Insert → Scatter** and select the fourth **Scatter** gallery choice (**Scatter with Straight Lines and Markers**). Relocate the chart to a chart sheet and adjust chart formatting by using the instructions in Appendix Section C.8 on page 727.

In-Depth Excel 2003 Create a chart from a worksheet in which the column for the time variable data appears to the immediate left of the column for the numerical variable data. (Use cut and paste to rearrange columns, if necessary.)

   For example, to create the Figure 2.19 time-series plot on page 50, open to the **DATA worksheet** of the **Solar Power workbook**. Select the cell range **A1:B10** and select **Insert → Chart** and:

In the Chart Wizard Step 1 dialog box:

   1. Click the **Standard Types** tab and then click **XY (Scatter)** as the **Chart type**. Click the first **Chart sub-type**, labeled **Scatter**. Click the first **Chart sub-type** in the third row, identified as **Scatter with data points connected by lines**.

   2. Click **Next**.

In the Chart Wizard Step 2 dialog box:

   3. Click **Next**. (Entries and selections in this dialog box are correct as is.)

In the Chart Wizard Step 3 dialog box:

   4. Click the **Titles** tab. Enter a **Chart title**, **Year** as the **Value (X) axis** title, and **Amount of Solar Power Installed (megawatts)** as the **Value (Y) axis** title.

   5. Adjust the chart formatting by using the instructions in Appendix Section C.8 on page 727 for the **Axes**, **Gridlines**, **Legend**, **Data Labels**, and **Data Table** tabs.

In the Chart Wizard Step 4 dialog box:

   6. Click **As new sheet** and then click **Finish** to complete the chart.

EG2.8 USING PIVOTTABLES to EXPLORE MULTIDIMENSIONAL DATA

Converting Cell Tallies into Percentages

Section 2.3 discusses how the overall total, the row totals, and the column totals can be used to convert the contents of the contingency table cells from tallies to either percentages of the overall total, percentages of a row total, or percentages of a column total. Section 2.8 discusses how PivotTables automate the calculations necessary for the conversion and presents Figure 2.21 (see page 53) as the PivotTable version of the Table 2.4 contingency table that displays percentages of the overall total.

   PivotTables created using the Section EG2.3 "The Contingency Table" instructions display cell tallies. To change these tallies into percentages, use the *In-Depth Excel* instructions that follow.

In-Depth Excel 2007 Change the value field setting for the cells. For example, to create the Figure 2.21 PivotTable that displays percentages of the overall total, open to the **FIGURE_2.20 worksheet** of the **PivotTable Examples workbook**. Select cell **B5**, right-click, and click **Value Field Settings** in the shortcut menu. In the Value Field Settings dialog box (see below), click the **Show values as** tab and in the **Show values as** drop-down list, select **% of total**, and then click **OK**.

   To convert cells in other PivotTables to either percentages of a row or percentages of a column, select either **% of row** or **% of column** from the **Show values as** drop-down list in the Value Field Settings dialog box.

In-Depth Excel 2003 Change the PivotTable value field setting for the cells. For example, to create the Figure 2.21 PivotTable that displays percentages of the overall total, open to the **FIGURE_2.20 worksheet** of the **PivotTable Examples workbook**. Select cell **B5**, right-click, and click **Field Settings** in the shortcut menu. In the PivotTable Field dialog box (see below), click **Options** to reveal the lower half of the dialog box. Select **% of total** from the **Show data as** drop-down list (you may have to scroll down the drop-down list to see this choice), and then click **OK**.

Adding a Variable to a PivotTable

Adding a variable to a PivotTable requires some planning. When you initially create a PivotTable, you need to include, as part of the cell range you enter into the Excel 2007 Create PivotTable dialog box or the Excel 2003 PivotTable Wizard Step 2 dialog box, the columns containing the variables you might want to use later. For example, substituting **A1:I181** for the cell range **B1:D181** (of the **DATA worksheet** of the **Bond Funds workbook**) used in the Section EG2.3 "The Contingency Table" instructions would allow you to add any variable from the bond funds data later on.

To experiment with adding a variable, open to the **FIGURE_2.21 worksheet** of the **PivotTable Examples workbook**. (The PivotTable in this worksheet was created using the data of all the variables in the **DATA worksheet**.) Click the PivotTable. In the **PivotTable Field List** pane, drag the **Risk** label and drop it near the right edge of cell **A4** (the Type column heading). If you drag the label as these instructions intended, you will end up with the Figure 2.22 PivotTable (contained in the **FIGURE_2.22 worksheet**). If you make a mistake, press **Ctrl+Z** to undo the drag-and-drop or select the improperly positioned **Risk** label and drag it somewhere else.

If the PivotTable Field List pane does not appear when you click the PivotTable, right-click the PivotTable and click **Show Field List** in the shortcut menu.

Changing a Statistic in a PivotTable

To change a statistic, drag the label for the current statistic outside the PivotTable and then drag-and-drop the label

for the replacement statistic. For example, to change the Figure 2.20 PivotTable into the Figure 2.23 PivotTable that displays percentages of overall assets, open to the **FIGURE_2.21 worksheet** of the **PivotTable Examples workbook**. Drag the **Count of Type** label in cell **A3** and drop it on a cell outside the PivotTable such as cell **F1**. (The label disappears.) If the PivotTable Field List pane is not onscreen, right-click the PivotTable and click **Show Field List** in the shortcut menu. Then drag the **Assets** label from the PivotTable Field List pane and drop it on cell **A3**.

When you drop the **Assets** label on cell **A3**, the PivotTable displays the sum of assets in its cell. Use the "Converting Cell Tallies into Percentages" instructions in this section to change the sums into percentages of the overall total, as is shown in Figure 2.23 (contained in the **FIGURE_2.23 worksheet**).

Including Descriptive Statistics in a PivotTable

To include a descriptive statistic, change the value field setting (Excel 2007) or the PivotTable field setting (Excel 2003). For example, to create the Figure 2.24 PivotTable that displays the average three-year returns, open to the **FIGURE_2.22 worksheet** of the **PivotTable Examples workbook**. First drag the **Count of Type** label in cell **A3** and drop it on a cell outside the PivotTable, such as cell **F1**. If the PivotTable Field List pane is not onscreen, right-click the PivotTable and click **Show Field List** in the shortcut menu. Then drag the **3-Year Return** label from the PivotTable Field List pane and drop it on cell **A3**. Note that the label changes to **Sum of 3-Year Return**, a meaningless calculation for this problem.

In Excel 2007, select cell **C5**, right-click, and click **Value Field Settings** in the shortcut menu. In the Value Field Settings dialog box, click the **Summarize by** tab, select **Average** in the **Summarize value field by** list, and click **OK**. Note that when you select **Average**, the **Custom Name** changes from **Sum of 3-Year Return** to **Average of 3-Year Return**, as shown below.

In Excel 2003, select cell **C5**, right-click, and click **Field Settings** in the shortcut menu. In the PivotTable Field dialog box, select **Average** in the **Summarize by** list and then click **OK**.

3 Numerical Descriptive Measures

Learning Objectives

In this chapter, you learn:

- To describe the properties of central tendency, variation, and shape in numerical data
- To construct and interpret a boxplot
- To compute descriptive summary measures for a population
- To compute the covariance and the coefficient of correlation

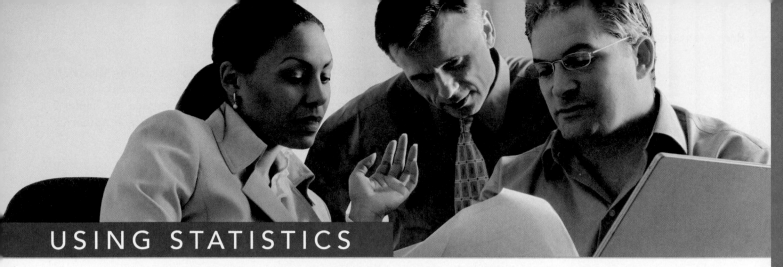

@ Choice Is Yours, Part II

T he tables and charts you prepared for the sample of 180 bond mutual funds has proved useful to the customers of the Choice Is Yours service. However, customers have become frustrated trying to evaluate mutual fund performance. Although they know how the 2008 returns are distributed, they have no idea what a typical 2008 rate of return is for a particular category of mutual funds, such as intermediate government and short-term corporate bond funds. They also have no idea of the extent of the variability in the 2008 rate of return. Are all the values relatively similar, or do they include very small and very large values? Are there a lot of small values and a few large ones, or vice versa, or are there a similar number of small and large values?

How could you help the customers get answers to these questions so that they could better evaluate the mutual funds?

Tax-Exempt Funds

Investment Perspectus

The customers in Part II of the Choice Is Yours scenario are asking questions about numerical variables. When summarizing and describing numerical variables, you need to do more than just prepare the tables and charts discussed in Chapter 2. You also need to consider the central tendency, variation, and shape of each numerical variable.

> ### CENTRAL TENDENCY
> The **central tendency** is the extent to which the data values group around a typical or central value.
>
> ### VARIATION
> The **variation** is the amount of dispersion, or scattering, of values away from a central value.
>
> ### SHAPE
> The **shape** is the pattern of the distribution of values from the lowest value to the highest value.

This chapter discusses ways you can measure the central tendency, variation, and shape of a variable. You will also learn about the covariance and the coefficient of correlation, which help measure the strength of the association between two numerical variables. Using these measures would give the customers of the Choice Is Yours service the answers they seek.

3.1 Measures of Central Tendency

Most sets of data show a distinct tendency to group around a central value. When people talk about an "average value" or the "middle value" or the "most frequent value," they are talking informally about the mean, median, and mode—three measures of central tendency.

The Mean

The **arithmetic mean** (typically referred to as the **mean**) is the most common measure of central tendency. The mean is the only common measure in which all the values play an equal role. The mean serves as a "balance point" in a set of data (like the fulcrum on a seesaw). You calculate the mean by adding together all the values in a data set and then dividing that sum by the number of values in the data set.

The symbol $\overline{X}$, called X-bar, is used to represent the mean of a sample. For a sample containing n values, the equation for the mean of a sample is written as

$$\overline{X} = \frac{\text{sum of the values}}{\text{number of values}}$$

Using the series $X_1, X_2, \ldots, X_n$ to represent the set of n values and n to represent the number of values in the sample, the equation becomes

$$\overline{X} = \frac{X_1 + X_2 + \cdots + X_n}{n}$$

By using summation notation (discussed fully in Appendix A), you replace the numerator $X_1 + X_2 + \cdots + X_n$ with the term $\sum_{i=1}^{n} X_i$, which means sum all the X_i values from the first X value, X_1, to the last X value, X_n, to form Equation (3.1), a formal definition of the sample mean.

SAMPLE MEAN

The **sample mean** is the sum of the values in a sample divided by the number of values in the sample.

$$\overline{X} = \frac{\sum\limits_{i=1}^{n} X_i}{n} \qquad\qquad (3.1)$$

where

$$\overline{X} = \text{sample mean}$$
$$n = \text{number of values or sample size}$$
$$X_i = i\text{th value of the variable } X$$
$$\sum_{i=1}^{n} X_i = \text{summation of all } X_i \text{ values in the sample}$$

Because all the values play an equal role, a mean is greatly affected by any value that is greatly different from the others. When you have such extreme values, you should avoid using the mean as a measure of central tendency.

The mean can suggest a typical or central value for a data set. For example, if you knew the typical time it takes you to get ready in the morning, you might be able to better plan your morning and minimize any excessive lateness (or earliness) going to your destination. Following the Define, Collect, Organize, Visualize, and Analyze approach, you first define the time to get ready as the time (rounded to the nearest minute) from when you get out of bed to when you leave your home. Then, you collect the times shown below for 10 consecutive workdays (stored in Times):

Day:	1	2	3	4	5	6	7	8	9	10
Time (minutes):	39	29	43	52	39	44	40	31	44	35

The first statistic that you compute to analyze these data is the mean. For these data, the mean time is 39.6 minutes, computed as follows:

$$\overline{X} = \frac{\text{sum of the values}}{\text{number of values}}$$

$$\overline{X} = \frac{\sum\limits_{i=1}^{n} X_i}{n}$$

$$\overline{X} = \frac{39 + 29 + 43 + 52 + 39 + 44 + 40 + 31 + 44 + 35}{10}$$

$$= \frac{396}{10} = 39.6$$

Even though no individual day in the sample actually had the value 39.6 minutes, allotting about 40 minutes to get ready would be a good rule for planning your mornings. The mean is a good measure of central tendency here because the data set does not contain any exceptionally small or large values.

Consider a case in which the value on Day 4 is 102 minutes instead of 52 minutes. This extreme value causes the mean to rise to 44.6 minutes, as follows:

$$\overline{X} = \frac{\text{sum of the values}}{\text{number of values}}$$

$$\overline{X} = \frac{\sum\limits_{i=1}^{n} X_i}{n}$$

$$\overline{X} = \frac{446}{10} = 44.6$$

The one extreme value has increased the mean from 39.6 to 44.6 minutes. In contrast to the original mean that was in the "middle" (i.e., greater than 5 of the getting-ready times and less than the 5 other times), the new mean is greater than 9 of the 10 getting-ready times. Because of the extreme value, now the mean is not a good measure of central tendency.

EXAMPLE 3.1

The Mean Calories for Coffee Drinks

The file **CoffeeDrink** contains the calories of 16-ounce iced coffee drinks at Dunkin' Donuts and Starbucks:

Product	Calories
Dunkin' Donuts Iced Mocha Swirl latte (whole milk)	240
Starbucks Coffee Frappuccino blended coffee	260
Dunkin' Donuts Coffee Coolatta (cream)	350
Starbucks Iced Coffee Mocha Espresso (whole milk and whipped cream)	350
Starbucks Mocha Frappuccino blended coffee (whipped cream)	420
Starbucks Chocolate Brownie Frappuccino blended coffee (whipped cream)	510
Starbucks Chocolate Frappuccino blended crème (whipped cream)	530

Source: *Data extracted from "Coffee as Candy at Dunkin' Donuts and Starbucks,"* Consumer Reports, *June 2004, p. 9.*

Compute the mean number of calories for the iced coffee drinks.

SOLUTION The mean number of calories is 380, calculated as follows:

$$\overline{X} = \frac{\text{sum of the values}}{\text{number of values}}$$

$$\overline{X} = \frac{\sum_{i=1}^{n} X_i}{n}$$

$$= \frac{2,660}{7} = 380$$

The Median

The **median** is the middle value in an ordered array of data that has been ranked from smallest to largest. Half the values are smaller than or equal to the median, and half the values are larger than or equal to the median. The median is not affected by extreme values, so you can use the median when extreme values are present.

To calculate the median for a set of data, you first rank the values from smallest to largest and then use Equation (3.2) to compute the rank of the value that is the median.

MEDIAN

$$\text{Median} = \frac{n+1}{2} \text{ ranked value} \qquad (3.2)$$

You compute the median by following one of two rules:

- **Rule 1** If the data set contains an *odd* number of values, the median is the measurement associated with the middle-ranked value.
- **Rule 2** If the data set contains an *even* number of values, the median is the measurement associated with the *average* of the two middle-ranked values.

To further analyze the sample of 10 times to get ready in the morning, you can compute the median. To do so, you rank the daily times as follows:

Ranked values:	29	31	35	39	39	40	43	44	44	52
Ranks:	1	2	3	4	5	6	7	8	9	10

$$\uparrow$$
$$\text{Median} = 39.5$$

Because the result of dividing $n + 1$ by 2 is $(10 + 1)/2 = 5.5$ for this sample of 10, you must use Rule 2 and average the measurements associated with the fifth and sixth ranked values, 39 and 40. Therefore, the median is 39.5. The median of 39.5 means that for half the days, the time to get ready is less than or equal to 39.5 minutes, and for half the days, the time to get ready is greater than or equal to 39.5 minutes. In this case, the median time to get ready of 39.5 minutes is very close to the mean time to get ready of 39.6 minutes.

EXAMPLE 3.2

Computing the Median From an Odd-Sized Sample

The file **CoffeeDrink** (see Example 3.1 on page 88) contains the calories of 16-ounce iced coffee drinks at Dunkin' Donuts and Starbucks. Compute the median number of calories for the iced coffee drinks at Dunkin' Donuts and Starbucks.

SOLUTION Because the result of dividing $n + 1$ by 2 is $(7 + 1)/2 = 4$ for this sample of seven, using Rule 1, the median is the measurement associated with fourth ranked value. The number of calories in 16-ounce iced coffee drinks at Dunkin' Donuts and Starbucks are ranked from the smallest to the largest:

Ranked values:	240	260	350	350	420	510	530
Ranks:	1	2	3	4	5	6	7

$$\uparrow$$
$$\text{Median} = 350$$

The median number of calories is 350. Half the iced coffee drinks have equal to or less than 350 calories, and half the iced coffee drinks have equal to or more than 350 calories.

The Mode

The **mode** is the value in a set of data that appears most frequently. Like the median and unlike the mean, extreme values do not affect the mode. Often, there is no mode or there are several modes in a set of data. For example, consider the time-to-get-ready data shown as follows:

29   31   35   39   39   40   43   44   44   52

There are two modes, 39 minutes and 44 minutes, because each of these values occurs twice.

EXAMPLE 3.3

Determining the Mode

A systems manager in charge of a company's network keeps track of the number of server failures that occur in a day. Determine the mode for the following data, which represents the number of server failures in a day for the past two weeks:

1   3   0   3   26   2   7   4   0   2   3   3   6   3

SOLUTION The ordered array for these data is

0   0   1   2   2   3   3   3   3   3   4   6   7   26

Because 3 occurs five times, more times than any other value, the mode is 3. Thus, the systems manager can say that the most common occurrence is having three server failures in a day. For this data set, the median is also equal to 3, and the mean is equal to 4.5. The value 26 is an extreme value. For these data, the median and the mode are better measures of central tendency than the mean.

A set of data has no mode if none of the values is "most typical." Example 3.4 presents a data set with no mode.

EXAMPLE 3.4

Data with No Mode

The bounced check fees ($) for a sample of 10 banks is

$$26 \quad 28 \quad 20 \quad 21 \quad 22 \quad 25 \quad 18 \quad 23 \quad 15 \quad 30$$

Compute the mode.

SOLUTION These data have no mode. None of the values is most typical because each value appears once.

The Geometric Mean

When you want to measure the rate of change of a variable over time, you need to use the geometric mean instead of the arithmetic mean. Equation (3.3) defines the geometric mean.

> **GEOMETRIC MEAN**
> The **geometric mean** is the nth root of the product of n values.
>
> $$\overline{X}_G = (X_1 \times X_2 \times \cdots \times X_n)^{1/n} \tag{3.3}$$

The **geometric mean rate of return** measures the average percentage return of an investment over time. Equation (3.4) defines the geometric mean rate of return.

> **GEOMETRIC MEAN RATE OF RETURN**
>
> $$\overline{R}_G = [(1 + R_1) \times (1 + R_2) \times \cdots \times (1 + R_n)]^{1/n} - 1 \tag{3.4}$$
>
> where
>
> $$R_i \text{ is the rate of return in time period } i$$

To illustrate these measures, consider an investment of $100,000 that declined to a value of $50,000 at the end of Year 1 and then rebounded back to its original $100,000 value at the end of Year 2. The rate of return for this investment for the two-year period is 0 because the starting and ending value of the investment is unchanged. However, the arithmetic mean of the yearly rates of return of this investment is

$$\overline{X} = \frac{(-0.50) + (1.00)}{2} = 0.25 \text{ or } 25\%$$

because the rate of return for Year 1 is

$$R_1 = \left(\frac{50{,}000 - 100{,}000}{100{,}000} \right) = -0.50 \text{ or } -50\%$$

and the rate of return for Year 2 is

$$R_2 = \left(\frac{100{,}000 - 50{,}000}{50{,}000} \right) = 1.00 \text{ or } 100\%$$

Using Equation (3.4), the geometric mean rate of return for the two years is

$$\begin{aligned}
\bar{R}_G &= [(1 + R_1) \times (1 + R_2)]^{1/n} - 1 \\
&= [(1 + (-0.50)) \times (1 + (1.0))]^{1/2} - 1 \\
&= [(0.50) \times (2.0)]^{1/2} - 1 \\
&= [1.0]^{1/2} - 1 \\
&= 1 - 1 = 0
\end{aligned}$$

Thus, the geometric mean rate of return more accurately reflects the (zero) change in the value of the investment for the two-year period than does the arithmetic mean.

EXAMPLE 3.5

Computing the Geometric Mean Rate of Return

The percentage change in the Russell 2000 Index of the stock prices of 2,000 small companies was −2.75% in 2007 and −34.80% in 2008. Compute the geometric rate of return.

SOLUTION Using Equation (3.4), the geometric mean rate of return in the Russell 2000 Index for the two years is

$$\begin{aligned}
\bar{R}_G &= [(1 + R_1) \times (1 + R_2)]^{1/n} - 1 \\
&= [(1 + (-0.0275)) \times (1 + (-0.3480))]^{1/2} - 1 \\
&= [(0.9725) \times (0.6520)]^{1/2} - 1 \\
&= [0.63407]^{1/2} - 1 \\
&= 0.7963 - 1 = -0.2037
\end{aligned}$$

The geometric mean rate of return in the Russell 2000 Index for the two years is −20.37%.

3.2 Variation and Shape

In addition to central tendency, every data set can be characterized by its variation and shape. Variation measures the **spread**, or **dispersion**, of values in a data set. One simple measure of variation is the range, the difference between the largest and smallest values. More commonly used in statistics are the standard deviation and variance, two measures explained later in this section. The shape of a data set represents a pattern of all the values, from the lowest to highest value. As you will learn later in this section, many data sets have a pattern that looks approximately like a bell, with a peak of values somewhere in the middle.

The Range

The **range** is the simplest numerical descriptive measure of variation in a set of data.

RANGE

The range is equal to the largest value minus the smallest value.

$$\text{Range} = X_{\text{largest}} - X_{\text{smallest}} \tag{3.5}$$

To further analyze the sample of 10 times to get ready in the morning, you can compute the range. To do so, you rank the data from smallest to largest:

$$29 \quad 31 \quad 35 \quad 39 \quad 39 \quad 40 \quad 43 \quad 44 \quad 44 \quad 52$$

Using Equation (3.5), the range is $52 - 29 = 23$ minutes. The range of 23 minutes indicates that the largest difference between any two days in the time to get ready in the morning is 23 minutes.

EXAMPLE 3.6

Computing the Range in the Calories in Iced Coffee Drinks

The file **CoffeeDrink** (see Example 3.1 on page 88) contains the calories of 16-ounce iced coffee drinks at Dunkin' Donuts and Starbucks. Compute the range in the number of calories for the iced coffee drinks at Dunkin' Donuts and Starbucks.

SOLUTION Ranked from smallest to largest, the calories for the seven iced coffee drinks are

$$240 \quad 260 \quad 350 \quad 350 \quad 420 \quad 510 \quad 530$$

Therefore, using Equation (3.5), the range $= 530 - 240 = 290$. The largest difference in the number of calories between any two iced coffee drinks is 290.

The range measures the *total spread* in the set of data. Although the range is a simple measure of the total variation in the data, it does not take into account *how* the data are distributed between the smallest and largest values. In other words, the range does not indicate whether the values are evenly distributed throughout the data set, clustered near the middle, or clustered near one or both extremes. Thus, using the range as a measure of variation when at least one value is an extreme value is misleading.

The Variance and the Standard Deviation

Being a simple measure of variation, the range does not consider how the values distribute or cluster between the extremes. Two commonly used measures of variation that take into account how all the data values are distributed are the **variance** and the **standard deviation**. These statistics measure the "average" scatter around the mean—how larger values fluctuate above it and how smaller values fluctuate below it.

A simple measure of variation around the mean might take the difference between each value and the mean and then sum these differences. However, if you did that, you would find that because the mean is the balance point in a set of data, for *every* set of data, these differences sum to zero. One measure of variation that differs from data set to data set *squares* the difference between each value and the mean and then sums these squared differences. In statistics, this quantity is called a **sum of squares (SS)**. This sum is then divided by the number of values minus 1 (for sample data), to get the sample variance (S^2). The square root of the sample variance is the sample standard deviation (S).

Because this sum of squares will always be nonnegative according to the rules of algebra, *neither the variance nor the standard deviation can ever be negative.* For virtually all sets of data, the variance and standard deviation will be a positive value. Both of these statistics will be zero only if there is no variation in a set of data which happens only when each value in the sample is the same.

For a sample containing n values, $X_1, X_2, X_3, \ldots, X_n$, the sample variance (given by the symbol S^2) is

$$S^2 = \frac{(X_1 - \overline{X})^2 + (X_2 - \overline{X})^2 + \cdots + (X_n - \overline{X})^2}{n - 1}$$

Equation (3.6) expresses the sample variance using summation notation, and Equation (3.7) expresses the sample standard deviation.

SAMPLE VARIANCE

The **sample variance** is the sum of the squared differences around the mean divided by the sample size minus 1.

$$S^2 = \frac{\sum_{i=1}^{n}(X_i - \bar{X})^2}{n-1} \tag{3.6}$$

where

$$\bar{X} = \text{sample mean}$$
$$n = \text{sample size}$$
$$X_i = i\text{th value of the variable } X$$

$$\sum_{i=1}^{n}(X_i - \bar{X})^2 = \text{summation of all the squared differences between the } X_i \text{ values and } \bar{X}$$

SAMPLE STANDARD DEVIATION

The **sample standard deviation** is the square root of the sum of the squared differences around the mean divided by the sample size minus 1.

$$S = \sqrt{S^2} = \sqrt{\frac{\sum_{i=1}^{n}(X_i - \bar{X})^2}{n-1}} \tag{3.7}$$

If the denominator were n instead of $n-1$, Equation (3.6) [and the inner term in Equation (3.7)] would calculate the average of the squared differences around the mean. However, $n-1$ is used because the statistic S^2 has certain mathematical properties that make it desirable for statistical inference (see Section 7.4 on page 232). As the sample size increases, the difference between dividing by n and by $n-1$ becomes smaller and smaller.

You will most likely use the sample standard deviation as the measure of variation [defined in Equation (3.7)]. Unlike the sample variance, which is a squared quantity, the standard deviation is always a number that is in the same units as the original sample data. The standard deviation helps you see how a set of data clusters or distributes around its mean. For almost all sets of data, the majority of the observed values lie within an interval of plus and minus one standard deviation above and below the mean. Therefore, knowledge of the mean and the standard deviation usually helps define where at least the majority of the data values are clustering.

To hand-calculate the sample variance, S^2, and the sample standard deviation, S, do the following:

1. Compute the difference between each value and the mean.
2. Square each difference.
3. Add the squared differences.
4. Divide this total by $n-1$ to get the sample variance.
5. Take the square root of the sample variance to get the sample standard deviation.

To further analyze the sample of 10 times to get ready in the morning, Table 3.1 shows the first four steps for calculating the variance and standard deviation with a mean ($\bar{X}$) equal to 39.6. (See page 87 for the calculation of the mean.) The second column of Table 3.1 shows step 1. The third column of Table 3.1 shows step 2. The sum of the squared differences (step 3) is shown at the bottom of Table 3.1. This total is then divided by $10-1=9$ to compute the variance (step 4).

TABLE 3.1

Computing the Variance of the Getting-Ready Times

Time (X)	Step 1: $(X_i - \bar{X})$	Step 2: $(X_i - \bar{X})^2$
	$\bar{X} = 39.6$	
39	−0.60	0.36
29	−10.60	112.36
43	3.40	11.56
52	12.40	153.76
39	−0.60	0.36
44	4.40	19.36
40	0.40	0.16
31	−8.60	73.96
44	4.40	19.36
35	−4.60	21.16
	Step 3: Sum:	Step 4: Divide by $(n-1)$:
	412.40	45.82

You can also calculate the variance by substituting values for the terms in Equation (3.6):

$$S^2 = \frac{\sum_{i=1}^{n}(X_i - \bar{X})^2}{n - 1}$$

$$= \frac{(39 - 39.6)^2 + (29 - 39.6)^2 + \cdots + (35 - 39.6)^2}{10 - 1}$$

$$= \frac{412.4}{9}$$

$$= 45.82$$

Because the variance is in squared units (in squared minutes, for these data), to compute the standard deviation, you take the square root of the variance. Using Equation (3.7) on page 93, the sample standard deviation, S, is

$$S = \sqrt{S^2} = \sqrt{\frac{\sum_{i=1}^{n}(X_i - \bar{X})^2}{n - 1}} = \sqrt{45.82} = 6.77$$

This indicates that the getting-ready times in this sample are clustering within 6.77 minutes around the mean of 39.6 minutes (i.e., clustering between $\bar{X} - 1S = 32.83$ and $\bar{X} + 1S = 46.37$). In fact, 7 out of 10 getting-ready times lie within this interval.

Using the second column of Table 3.1, you can also calculate the sum of the differences between each value and the mean to be zero. For any set of data, this sum will always be zero:

$$\sum_{i=1}^{n}(X_i - \bar{X}) = 0 \text{ for all sets of data}$$

This property is one of the reasons that the mean is used as the most common measure of central tendency.

EXAMPLE 3.7

Computing the Variance and Standard Deviation of the Number of Calories in Iced Coffee Drinks

The file **CoffeeDrink** (see Example 3.1 on page 88) contains the calories of 16-ounce iced coffee drinks at Dunkin' Donuts and Starbucks. Compute the variance and standard deviation of the calories in 16-ounce iced coffee drinks.

SOLUTION Table 3.2 illustrates the computation of the variance and standard deviation for the calories in 16-ounce iced coffee drinks.

TABLE 3.2

Computing the Variance of the Calories in 16-Ounce Iced Coffee Drinks

$\bar{X} = 380$		
Calories	Step 1: $(X_i - \bar{X})$	Step 2: $(X_i - \bar{X})^2$
240	−140	19,600
260	−120	14,400
350	−30	900
350	−30	900
420	40	1,600
510	130	16,900
530	150	22,500
	Step 3: Sum:	Step 4: Divide by $(n - 1)$:
	76,800	12,800

Using Equation (3.6) on page 93:

$$S^2 = \frac{\sum_{i=1}^{n}(X_i - \bar{X})^2}{n - 1}$$

$$= \frac{(240 - 380)^2 + (260 - 380)^2 + \cdots + (530 - 380)^2}{7 - 1}$$

$$= \frac{76,800}{6}$$

$$= 12,800$$

Using Equation (3.7) on page 93, the sample standard deviation, S, is

$$S = \sqrt{S^2} = \sqrt{\frac{\sum_{i=1}^{n}(X_i - \bar{X})^2}{n - 1}} = \sqrt{12,800} = 113.1371$$

The standard deviation of 113.1371 indicates that the calories in the iced coffee drinks are clustering within 113.1371 around the mean of 380 (i.e., clustering between $\bar{X} - 1S = 266.8629$ and $\bar{X} + 1S = 493.1371$). In fact, 42.9% (3 out of 7) of the calories lie within this interval.

The characteristics of the range, variance, and standard deviation can be summarized as follows:

- The greater the spread or dispersion of the data, the larger the range, variance, and standard deviation.
- The greater the concentration of the data around a central value, the smaller the range, variance, and standard deviation.
- If the values are all the same (so that there is no variation in the data), the range, variance, and standard deviation will all equal zero.
- None of the measures of variation (the range, variance, and standard deviation) can *ever* be negative.

The Coefficient of Variation

Unlike the measures of variation presented previously, the **coefficient of variation** is a *relative measure* of variation that is always expressed as a percentage rather than in terms of the units of the particular data. The coefficient of variation, denoted by the symbol *CV*, measures the scatter in the data relative to the mean.

COEFFICIENT OF VARIATION

The coefficient of variation is equal to the standard deviation divided by the mean, multiplied by 100%.

$$CV = \left(\frac{S}{\overline{X}}\right)100\%$$

(3.8)

where

$$S = \text{sample standard deviation}$$

$$\overline{X} = \text{sample mean}$$

For the sample of 10 getting-ready times, because $\overline{X} = 39.6$ and $S = 6.77$, the coefficient of variation is

$$CV = \left(\frac{S}{\overline{X}}\right)100\% = \left(\frac{6.77}{39.6}\right)100\% = 17.10\%$$

For the getting-ready times, the standard deviation is 17.1% of the size of the mean.

The coefficient of variation is especially useful when comparing two or more sets of data that are measured in different units, as Example 3.8 illustrates.

EXAMPLE 3.8

Comparing Two Coefficients of Variation When The Two Variables Have Different Units of Measurement

The operations manager of a package delivery service is deciding whether to purchase a new fleet of trucks. When packages are stored in the trucks in preparation for delivery, the manager needs to consider two major constraints—the weight (in pounds) and the volume (in cubic feet) for each item.

The operations manager samples 200 packages and finds that the mean weight is 26.0 pounds, with a standard deviation of 3.9 pounds, and the mean volume is 8.8 cubic feet, with a standard deviation of 2.2 cubic feet. How can the operations manager compare the variation of the weight and the volume?

SOLUTION Because weight and volume have different units of measurement, the operations manager should compare the relative variability in the two measurements.

For weight, the coefficient of variation is

$$CV_W = \left(\frac{3.9}{26.0}\right)100\% = 15\%$$

For volume, the coefficient of variation is

$$CV_V = \left(\frac{2.2}{8.8}\right)100\% = 25\%$$

Thus, relative to the mean, the package volume is much more variable than the package weight.

Z Scores

An **extreme value** or **outlier** is a value located far away from the mean. The **Z score**, which is the difference between the value and the mean, divided by the standard deviation, is useful in identifying outliers. The larger the Z score, the greater the distance from the value to the mean.

Z SCORE

$$Z = \frac{X - \overline{X}}{S} \qquad \qquad \textbf{(3.9)}$$

To further analyze the sample of 10 times to get ready in the morning, you can compute the Z scores. Because the mean is 39.6 minutes, the standard deviation is 6.77 minutes, and the time to get ready on the first day is 39.0 minutes, you compute the Z score for Day 1 by using Equation (3.9):

$$Z = \frac{X - \overline{X}}{S}$$
$$= \frac{39.0 - 39.6}{6.77}$$
$$= -0.09$$

Table 3.3 shows the Z scores for all 10 days.

TABLE 3.3

Z Scores for the 10 Getting-Ready Times

	Time (X)	Z Score
	39	-0.90
	29	-1.57
	43	0.50
	52	1.83
	39	-0.09
	44	0.65
	40	0.06
	31	-1.27
	44	0.65
	35	-0.68
Mean	39.6	
Standard deviation	6.77	

The largest Z score is 1.83 for Day 4, on which the time to get ready was 52 minutes. The lowest Z score is -1.57 for Day 2, on which the time to get ready was 29 minutes. As a general rule, a Z score is considered an outlier if it is less than -3.0 or greater than +3.0. None of the times in this case meet that criterion to be considered outliers.

EXAMPLE 3.9

Computing the Z Scores of the Number of Calories in Iced Coffee Drinks

The file CoffeeDrink (see Example 3.1 on page 88) contains the calories of 16-ounce iced coffee drinks at Dunkin' Donuts and Starbucks. Compute the Z scores of the calories of 16-ounce iced coffee drinks.

SOLUTION Table 3.4 illustrates the Z scores of the calories of 16-ounce iced coffee drinks. The largest Z score is 1.33, for an iced coffee drink with 530 calories. The lowest Z score is -1.24 for an iced coffee drink with 240 calories. There are no apparent outliers in these data because none of the Z scores are less than -3.0 or greater than +3.0.

TABLE 3.4

Z Scores of the Number of Calories in Iced Coffee Drinks

	Calories	Z Scores
	240	-1.24
	260	-1.06
	350	-0.27
	350	-0.27
	420	0.35
	510	1.15
	530	1.33
Mean	380	
Standard deviation	113.1371	

Shape

Shape is the pattern of the distribution of data values throughout the entire range of all the values. A distribution is either symmetrical or skewed. In a **symmetrical** distribution, the values below the mean are distributed exactly the same way as the values above the mean. In this case, the low and high values balance each other out. In a **skewed** distribution, the values are not symmetrical around the mean. This skewness results in an imbalance of low values or high values.

Shape influences the relationship of the mean to the median in the following ways:

- Mean < median: negative, or left-skewed
- Mean = median: symmetric, or zero skewness
- Mean > median: positive, or right-skewed

Figure 3.1 depicts three data sets, each with a different shape.

FIGURE 3.1

A comparison of three data sets that differ in shape

Panel A
Negative, or left-skewed

Panel B
Symmetrical

Panel C
Positive, or right-skewed

The data in Panel A are negative, or **left-skewed**. In this panel, most of the values are in the upper portion of the distribution. A long tail and distortion to the left is caused by some extremely small values. These extremely small values pull the mean downward so that the mean is less than the median.

The data in Panel B are symmetrical. Each half of the curve is a mirror image of the other half of the curve. The low and high values on the scale balance, and the mean equals the median.

The data in Panel C are positive, or **right-skewed**. In this panel, most of the values are in the lower portion of the distribution. A long tail on the right is caused by some extremely large values. These extremely large values pull the mean upward so that the mean is greater than the median.

Skewness and **kurtosis** are two shape-related statistics. The skewness statistic measures the extent to which a set of data is not symmetric. The kurtosis statistic measures the relative concentration of values in the center of the distribution of a data set, as compared with the tails.

A symmetric distribution has a skewness value of zero. A right-skewed distribution has a positive skewness value, and a left-skewed distribution has a negative skewness value.

A bell-shaped distribution has a kurtosis value of zero. A distribution that is flatter than a bell-shaped distribution has a negative kurtosis value. A distribution with a sharper peak (one that has a higher concentration of values in the center of the distribution) than a bell-shaped distribution has a positive kurtosis value.

EXAMPLE 3.10

Descriptive Statistics for Intermediate Government and Short-Term Corporate Bond Mutual Funds

In Part II of the Choice Is Yours scenario, you are interested in comparing the past performance of the intermediate government bond and short-term corporate bond funds. One measure of past performance is the return in 2008. You have already defined the variables to be collected and collected the data from a sample of 180 bond funds. Compute descriptive statistics for the intermediate government and short-term corporate bond funds.

SOLUTION Figure 3.2 presents a table of descriptive summary measures for the two types of bond funds, calculated by Excel. The table includes the mean, standard error, median, mode, standard deviation, variance, kurtosis, skewness, range, minimum, maximum, sum (which is meaningless for this example), and count (the sample size). The standard error, discussed in Section 7.4, is the standard deviation divided by the square root of the sample size.

FIGURE 3.2

Descriptive statistics for the 2008 return for the intermediate government and short-term corporate bond funds

Figure 3.2 displays the COMPUTE worksheet of the Descriptive workbook. Create this worksheet using the instructions in Section EG3.2.

	A	B	C
1	Descriptive Statistics for Return 2008		
2		Intermediate Government	Short Term Corporate
3	Mean	5.9576	-3.3237
4	Standard Error	0.5165	0.7471
5	Median	7.0000	-1.4500
6	Mode	6.9000	0.4000
7	Standard Deviation	4.8999	7.0874
8	Sample Variance	24.0090	50.2307
9	Kurtosis	0.4418	2.2169
10	Skewness	-0.7824	-1.3676
11	Range	23.6200	39.3000
12	Minimum	-8.6200	-31.9000
13	Maximum	15.0000	7.4000
14	Sum	536.1800	-299.1300
15	Count	90	90

In examining the results, you see that there are large differences in the 2008 return for the intermediate government bond and short-term corporate bond funds. The intermediate government bond funds had a mean 2008 return of 5.9576 and a median return of 7.0. This compares to a mean of −3.3237 and a median of −1.45 for the short-term corporate bond funds. The medians indicate that half of the intermediate government bond funds had returns of 7.0 or better, and half the short-term corporate bond funds had returns below −1.45. You conclude that the intermediate government bond funds had a much higher return than the short-term corporate bond funds.

The intermediate government corporate bond funds had a smaller standard deviation than the short-term corporate bond funds (4.899 as compared to 7.0874). While both the intermediate government bond funds and the short-term corporate bond funds showed left or negative skewness, the intermediate government bond funds had less skewness. The kurtosis of the short-term corporate bond funds was very positive, indicating a much more peaked distribution than a bell-shaped distribution.

VISUAL EXPLORATIONS Exploring Descriptive Statistics

Use the Visual Explorations Descriptive Statistics procedure to see the effect of changing data values on measures of central tendency, variation, and shape. Open the **Visual Explorations add-in workbook (Visual Explorations.xla)** and:

1. In Excel 2007, select **Add-ins → VisualExplorations → Descriptive Statistics**. In Excel 2003, select **VisualExplorations → Descriptive Statistics**.
2. Read the instructions in the Descriptive Statistics dialog box and then click **OK** (see the illustration at right).
3. Experiment by entering an extreme value such as 5 into one of the tinted column A cells.

Which measures are affected by this change? Which ones are not? You can switch between the "before" and "after" diagrams by repeatedly pressing **Ctrl+Z** (undo) followed by **Ctrl+Y** (redo) to better see the changes the extreme value has caused in the diagram. (To learn more about Visual Explorations, see Appendix Section D.7.)

Problems for Sections 3.1 and 3.2

LEARNING THE BASICS

3.1 The following is a set of data from a sample of $n = 5$:

  7 4 9 8 2

a. Compute the mean, median, and mode.
b. Compute the range, variance, standard deviation, and coefficient of variation.
c. Compute the Z scores. Are there any outliers?
d. Describe the shape of the data set.

3.2 The following is a set of data from a sample of $n = 6$:

  7 4 9 7 3 12

a. Compute the mean, median, and mode.
b. Compute the range, variance, standard deviation, and coefficient of variation.
c. Compute the Z scores. Are there any outliers?
d. Describe the shape of the data set.

3.3 The following set of data is from a sample of $n = 7$:

  12 7 4 9 0 7 3

a. Compute the mean, median, and mode.
b. Compute the range, variance, standard deviation, and coefficient of variation.
c. Compute the Z scores. Are there any outliers?
d. Describe the shape of the data set.

3.4 The following is a set of data from a sample of $n = 5$:

  7 −5 −8 7 9

a. Compute the mean, median, and mode.
b. Compute the range, variance, standard deviation, and coefficient of variation.
c. Compute the Z scores. Are there any outliers?
d. Describe the shape of the data set.

3.5 Suppose that the rate of return for a particular stock during the past two years was 10% and 30%. Compute the geometric rate of return. (*Note:* A rate of return of 10% is recorded as 0.10, and a rate of return of 30% is recorded as 0.30.)

3.6 Suppose that the rate of return for a particular stock during the past two years was 20% and −30%. Compute the geometric rate of return.

APPLYING THE CONCEPTS

3.7 A business school reported its findings from a study of recent graduates. A sample of $n = 10$ finance majors had a mean starting salary of $45,000, a median starting salary of $45,000, and a standard deviation of $10,000. A sample of $n = 10$ information systems majors had a mean starting salary of $56,000, a median of $45,000, and a standard deviation of $37,000. Discuss the central tendency, variation, and shape of starting salaries for the two majors.

3.8 The operations manager of a plant that manufactures tires wants to compare the actual inner diameters of two grades of tires, each of which is expected to be 575 millimeters. A sample of five tires of each grade was selected, and the results representing the inner diameters of the tires, ranked from smallest to largest, are as follows:

Grade X	Grade Y
568 570 575 578 584	573 574 575 577 578

a. For each of the two grades of tires, compute the mean, median, and standard deviation.
b. Which grade of tire is providing better quality? Explain.
c. What would be the effect on your answers in (a) and (b) if the last value for grade Y were 588 instead of 578? Explain.

3.9 According to the U.S. Census Bureau, in November 2008 the median sales price of new houses was $220,400, and the mean sales price was $287,500 (extracted from **www.census.gov**, January 21, 2009).

a. Interpret the median sales price.
b. Interpret the mean sales price.
c. Discuss the shape of the distribution of the price of new houses.

3.10 The file **MoviePrices** contains the prices for two tickets, with online service charges, large popcorn, and two medium soft drinks, at a sample of six theater chains:

  $36.15 $31.00 $35.05 $40.25 $33.75 $43.00

Source: *Data extracted from K. Kelly, "The Multiplex Under Siege,"* The Wall Street Journal, *December 24–25, 2005, pp. P1, P5.*

a. Compute the mean and median.
b. Compute the variance, standard deviation, range, and coefficient of variation.
c. Are the data skewed? If so, how?
d. Based on the results of (a) through (c), what conclusions can you reach concerning the cost of going to the movies?

3.11 The file **Sedans** contains the overall miles per gallon (MPG) of 2009 sedans priced under $20,000.

  27 31 30 28 27 24 29 32
  32 27 26 26 25 26 25 24

Source: *Data extracted from "Vehicle Ratings,"* Consumer Reports, *April 2009, p. 27.*

a. Compute the mean, median, and mode.
b. Compute the variance, standard deviation, range, coefficient of variation, and Z scores.
c. Are the data skewed? If so, how?
d. Compare the results of (a) through (c) to those of Problem 3.12 (a) through (c) that refer to the miles per gallon of SUVs priced under $30,000.

3.12 The file **SUV** contains the overall miles per gallon (MPG) of 2009 small SUVs priced under $30,000.

24 23 22 21 22 22 18 19 19 19 21 21

21 18 19 21 17 22 18 18 22 16 16

Source: *Data extracted from "Vehicle Ratings," Consumer Reports, April 2009, pp. 33–34.*

a. Compute the mean, median, and mode.
b. Compute the variance, standard deviation, range, coefficient of variation, and Z scores.
c. Are the data skewed? If so, how?
d. Compare the results of (a) through (c) to those of Problem 3.11 (a) through (c) that refer to the miles per gallon of sedans priced under $20,000.

3.13 The file **ChocolateChip** contains the cost (in cents) per 1-ounce serving for a sample of 13 chocolate chip cookies. The data are as follows:

54 22 25 23 36 43 7 43 25 47 24 45 44

Source: *Data extracted from "Chip, Chip, Hooray," Consumer Reports, June 2009, p. 7.*

a. Compute the mean, median, and mode.
b. Compute the variance, standard deviation, range, coefficient of variation, and Z scores. Are there any outliers? Explain.
c. Are the data skewed? If so, how?
d. Based on the results of (a) through (c), what conclusions can you reach concerning the cost of chocolate chip cookies?

3.14 The file **DarkChocolate** contains the cost per ounce ($) for a sample of 14 dark chocolate bars.

0.68 0.72 0.92 1.14 1.42 0.94 0.77

0.57 1.51 0.57 0.55 0.86 1.41 0.90

Source: *Data extracted from "Dark Chocolate: Which Bars Are Best?" Consumer Reports, September 2007, p. 8.*

a. Compute the mean, median, and mode.
b. Compute the variance, standard deviation, range, coefficient of variation, and Z scores. Are there any outliers? Explain.
c. Are the data skewed? If so, how?
d. Based on the results of (a) through (c), what conclusions can you reach concerning the cost of dark chocolate bars?

3.15 Is there a difference in the variation of the yields of different types of investments? The file **Bankyield** contains the nationwide highest yields of money market accounts and five-year CDs as of May 17, 2009:

Money Market	Five-Year CD
2.25	3.70
2.20	3.66
2.12	3.65
2.03	3.50
2.02	3.50

Source: *Data extracted from* **www.Bankrate.com**, *May 17, 2009.*

a. For money market accounts and five-year CDs, separately compute the variance, standard deviation, range, and coefficient of variation.
b. Based on the results of (a), do money market accounts or five-year CDs have more variation in the highest yields offered? Explain.

3.16 The file **ThemeParks** contains the starting admission price (in $) for one-day tickets to 10 theme parks in the United States:

58 63 41 42 29 50 62 43 40 40

Source: *Data extracted from C. Jackson and E. Gamerman, "Rethinking the Thrill Factor," The Wall Street Journal, April 15–16, 2006, pp. P1, P4.*

a. Compute the mean, median, and mode.
b. Compute the range, variance, and standard deviation.
c. Based on the results of (a) and (b), what conclusions can you reach concerning the starting admission price for one-day tickets.
d. Suppose that the first value was 98 instead of 58. Repeat (a) through (c), using this value. Comment on the difference in the results.

3.17 A bank branch located in a commercial district of a city has the business objective of developing an improved process for serving customers during the noon-to-1:00 P.M. lunch period. The waiting time, in minutes, is defined as the time the customer enters the line to when he or she reaches the teller window. Data are collected from a sample of 15 customers during this hour. The file **Bank1** contains the results, which are listed below:

4.21 5.55 3.02 5.13 4.77 2.34 3.54 3.20

4.50 6.10 0.38 5.12 6.46 6.19 3.79

a. Compute the mean and median.
b. Compute the variance, standard deviation, range, coefficient of variation, and Z scores. Are there any outliers? Explain.
c. Are the data skewed? If so, how?
d. As a customer walks into the branch office during the lunch hour, she asks the branch manager how long she can expect to wait. The branch manager replies, "Almost certainly less than five minutes." On the basis of the results of (a) through (c), evaluate the accuracy of this statement.

3.18 Suppose that another bank branch, located in a residential area, is also concerned with the noon-to-1 P.M. lunch hour. The waiting time, in minutes, collected from a sample of 15 customers during this hour, is contained in the file **Bank2** and listed below:

9.66 5.90 8.02 5.79 8.73 3.82 8.01 8.35

10.49 6.68 5.64 4.08 6.17 9.91 5.47

a. Compute the mean and median.
b. Compute the variance, standard deviation, range, coefficient of variation, and Z scores. Are there any outliers? Explain.

c. Are the data skewed? If so, how?

d. As a customer walks into the branch office during the lunch hour, he asks the branch manager how long he can expect to wait. The branch manager replies, "Almost certainly less than five minutes." On the basis of the results of (a) through (c), evaluate the accuracy of this statement.

3.19 General Electric (GE) is one of the world's largest companies; it develops, manufactures, and markets a wide range of products, including medical diagnostic imaging devices, jet engines, lighting products, and chemicals. Through its affiliate, NBC Universal, GE produces and delivers network television and motion pictures. In 2007, GE's stock price rose 2.67%, but in 2008, the price dropped 53.94%.

Source: *Data extracted from* **finance.yahoo.com**, *June 18, 2009.*

a. Compute the geometric mean rate of increase for the two-year period 2007–2008. (*Hint:* Denote an increase of 2.67% as $R_1 = 0.0267$.)

b. If you purchased $1,000 of GE stock at the start of 2007, what was its value at the end of 2008?

c. Compare the result of (b) to that of Problem 3.20 (b).

☑ SELF
Test **3.20** TASER International, Inc., develops, manufactures, and sells nonlethal self-defense devices known as tasers. Marketing primarily to law enforcement, corrections institutions, and the military, TASER's popularity has enjoyed a roller-coaster ride. The stock price in 2007 increased 89.09%, but in 2008, it decreased 63.31%.

Source: *Data extracted from* **finance.yahoo.com**, *June 18, 2009.*

a. Compute the geometric mean rate of increase for the two-year period 2007–2008. (*Hint:* Denote an increase of 89.09% as $R_1 = 0.8909$.)

b. If you purchased $1,000 of TASER stock at the start of 2007, what was its value at the end of 2008?

c. Compare the result of (b) to that of Problem 3.19 (b).

3.21 In 2008, all the major stock market indices decreased dramatically due to the world financial crisis. This followed two years in which the indices had increased. The data in the following table (stored in **Indices**) represent the total rate of return (in percentage) for the Dow Jones Industrial Average (DJIA), the Standard & Poor's 500 (S&P 500), and the technology-heavy NASDAQ Composite (NASDAQ) from 2006 through 2008.

Year	DJIA	S&P 500	NASDAQ
2008	−33.8	−38.5	−40.5
2007	6.4	3.5	9.8
2006	16.3	13.6	9.5

Source: *Data extracted from* **finance.yahoo.com**, *June 18, 2009.*

a. Calculate the geometric mean rate of return for the DJIA, S&P 500, and NASDAQ from 2006 through 2008.

b. What conclusions can you reach concerning the geometric mean rates of return of the three market indices?

c. Compare the results of (b) to those of Problem 3.22 (b).

3.22 In 2006–2008, precious metals changed rapidly in value. The data in the following table (contained in the file **Metals**) represent the total rate of return (in percentage) for platinum, gold, and silver from 2006 through 2008:

Year	Platinum	Gold	Silver
2008	−41.3	4.3	−26.9
2007	36.9	31.9	14.4
2006	15.9	23.2	46.1

Source: *Data extracted from* **www.kitco.com**, *June 18, 2009.*

a. Calculate the geometric mean rate of return for platinum, gold, and silver from 2006 through 2008.

b. What conclusions can you reach concerning the geometric mean rates of return of the three precious metals?

c. Compare the results of (b) to those of Problem 3.21 (b).

3.3 Exploring Numerical Data

Sections 3.1 and 3.2 discuss measures of central tendency, variation, and shape. Another way of describing numerical data is through an exploratory data analysis that includes the quartiles, the five-number summary, and the boxplot. In Excel, you can also develop complex tables that display descriptive statistics by using PivotTables as discussed in Section 2.8. (This enables you to explore these descriptive statistics across several categorical variables in a single table.)

Quartiles

[1]The Q_1, median, and Q_3 are also the 25th, 50th, and 75th percentiles, respectively. Equations (3.2), (3.10), and (3.11) can be expressed generally in terms of finding percentiles: $(p \times 100)$th percentile = $p \times (n + 1)$ ranked value where p = the proportion.

Quartiles split a set of data into four equal parts—the **first quartile, Q_1**, divides the smallest 25.0% of the values from the other 75.0% that are larger. The **second quartile, Q_2**, is the median—50.0% of the values are smaller than the median and 50.0% are larger. The **third quartile, Q_3**, divides the smallest 75.0% of the values from the largest 25.0%. Equations (3.10) and (3.11) define the first and third quartiles.[1]

FIRST QUARTILE, Q_1

25.0% of the values are smaller than or equal to Q_1, the first quartile, and 75.0% are larger than or equal to the first quartile, Q_1.

$$Q_1 = \frac{n+1}{4} \text{ ranked value} \qquad (3.10)$$

THIRD QUARTILE, Q_3

75.0% of the values are smaller than or equal to the third quartile, Q_3, and 25.0% are larger than or equal to the third quartile, Q_3.

$$Q_3 = \frac{3(n+1)}{4} \text{ ranked value} \qquad (3.11)$$

Use the following rules to compute the quartiles from a set of ranked values:

- **Rule 1** If the ranked value is a whole number, the quartile is equal to the measurement that corresponds to that ranked value. For example, if the sample size $n = 7$, the first quartile, Q_1, is equal to the measurement associated with the $(7+1)/4 =$ second ranked value.

The Excel QUARTILE function uses different rules to compute quartiles. Use the QUARTILES workbook, as explained in Section EG3.3, to compute quartiles using these rules.

- **Rule 2** If the ranked value is a fractional half (2.5, 4.5, etc.), the quartile is equal to the measurement that corresponds to the average of the measurements corresponding to the two ranked values involved. For example, if the sample size $n = 9$, the first quartile, Q_1, is equal to the $(9+1)/4 = 2.5$ ranked value, halfway between the second ranked value and the third ranked value.
- **Rule 3** If the ranked value is neither a whole number nor a fractional half, you round the result to the nearest integer and select the measurement corresponding to that ranked value. For example, if the sample size $n = 10$, the first quartile, Q_1, is equal to the $(10+1)/4 = 2.75$ ranked value. Round 2.75 to 3 and use the third ranked value.

To further analyze the sample of 10 times to get ready in the morning, you can compute the quartiles. To do so, you rank the data from smallest to largest:

Ranked values:	29	31	35	39	39	40	43	44	44	52
Ranks:	1	2	3	4	5	6	7	8	9	10

The first quartile is the $(n+1)/4 = (10+1)/4 = 2.75$ ranked value. Using Rule 3, you round up to the third ranked value. The third ranked value for the time-to-get-ready data is 35 minutes. You interpret the first quartile of 35 to mean that on 25% of the days, the time to get ready is less than or equal to 35 minutes, and on 75% of the days, the time to get ready is greater than or equal to 35 minutes.

The third quartile is the $3(n+1)/4 = 3(10+1)/4 = 8.25$ ranked value. Using Rule 3 for quartiles, you round this down to the eighth ranked value. The eighth ranked value is 44 minutes. Thus, on 75% of the days, the time to get ready is less than or equal to 44 minutes, and on 25% of the days, the time to get ready is greater than or equal to 44 minutes.

EXAMPLE 3.11

Computing the Quartiles

The file **CoffeeDrink** (see Example 3.1 on page 88) contains the calories of 16-ounce iced coffee drinks at Dunkin' Donuts and Starbucks. Compute the first quartile (Q_1) and third quartile (Q_3) number of calories for the iced coffee drinks at Dunkin' Donuts and Starbucks.

SOLUTION Ranked from smallest to largest, the number of calories for the seven iced coffee drinks are as follows:

Ranked values:	240	260	350	350	420	510	530
Ranks:	1	2	3	4	5	6	7

For these data

$$Q_1 = \frac{(n+1)}{4} \text{ ranked value}$$

$$= \frac{7+1}{4} \text{ ranked value} = 2\text{nd ranked value}$$

Therefore, using Rule 1, Q_1 is the second ranked value. Because the second ranked value is 260, the first quartile, Q_1, is 260.

To compute the third quartile, Q_3,

$$Q_3 = \frac{3(n+1)}{4} \text{ ranked value}$$

$$= \frac{3(7+1)}{4} \text{ ranked value} = 6\text{th ranked value}$$

Therefore, using Rule 1, Q_3 is the sixth ranked value. Because the sixth ranked value is 510, Q_3 is 510.

The first quartile of 260 indicates that 25% of the iced coffee drinks have calories that are below or equal to 260 and 75% are greater than or equal to 260. The third quartile of 510 indicates that 75% of the iced coffee drinks have calories that are below or equal to 510 and 25% are greater than or equal to 510.

The Interquartile Range

The **interquartile range** (also called **midspread**) is the difference between the third and first quartiles in a set of data.

> INTERQUARTILE RANGE
> The interquartile range is the difference between the third quartile and the first quartile.
> $$\text{Interquartile range} = Q_3 - Q_1 \qquad (3.12)$$

The interquartile range measures the spread in the middle 50% of the data. Therefore, it is not influenced by extreme values. To further analyze the sample of 10 times to get ready in the morning, you can compute the interquartile range. You first order the data as follows:

29 31 35 39 39 40 43 44 44 52

You use Equation (3.12) and the earlier results above, $Q_1 = 35$ and $Q_3 = 44$:

Interquartile range = 44 − 35 = 9 minutes

Therefore, the interquartile range in the time to get ready is 9 minutes. The interval 35 to 44 is often referred to as the *middle fifty*.

EXAMPLE 3.12

Computing the Interquartile Range for the Number of Calories in Iced Coffee Drinks

The file **CoffeeDrink** (see Example 3.1 on page 88) contains the calories of 16-ounce iced coffee drinks at Dunkin' Donuts and Starbucks. Compute the interquartile range of the number of calories of 16-ounce iced coffee drinks.

SOLUTION Ranked from smallest to largest, the number of calories for the seven iced coffee drinks are as follows:

240 260 350 350 420 510 530

Using Equation (3.12) and the earlier results from Example 3.10 on page 104, $Q_1 = 260$ and $Q_3 = 510$:

$$\text{Interquartile range} = 510 - 260 = 250$$

Therefore, the interquartile range of the number of calories of 16-ounce iced coffee drinks is 250 calories.

Because the interquartile range does not consider any value smaller than Q_1 or larger than Q_3, it cannot be affected by extreme values. Descriptive statistics such as the median, Q_1, Q_3, and the interquartile range, which are not influenced by extreme values, are called **resistant measures**.

The Five-Number Summary

A **five-number summary**, which consists of the following, provides a way to determine the shape of a distribution:

$$X_{\text{smallest}} \quad Q_1 \quad \text{Median} \quad Q_3 \quad X_{\text{largest}}$$

Table 3.5 explains how the relationships among these five numbers allows you to recognize the shape of a data set.

TABLE 3.5

Relationships Among the Five-Number Summary and the Type of Distribution

| Comparison | Type of Distribution | | |
	Left-Skewed	Symmetric	Right-Skewed
The distance from X_{smallest} to the median versus the distance from the median to X_{largest}.	The distance from X_{smallest} to the median is greater than the distance from the median to X_{largest}.	The two distances are the same.	The distance from X_{smallest} to the median is less than the distance from the median to X_{largest}.
The distance from X_{smallest} to Q_1 versus the distance from Q_3 to X_{largest}.	The distance from X_{smallest} to Q_1 is greater than the distance from Q_3 to X_{largest}.	The two distances are the same.	The distance from X_{smallest} to Q_1 is less than the distance from Q_3 to X_{largest}.
The distance from Q_1 to the median versus the distance from the median to Q_3.	The distance from Q_1 to the median is greater than the distance from the median to Q_3.	The two distances are the same.	The distance from Q_1 to the median is less than the distance from the median to Q_3.

To further analyze the sample of 10 times to get ready in the morning, you can compute the five-number summary. For these data, the smallest value is 29 minutes, and the largest value is 52 minutes (see page 104). Calculations done on pages 89 and 103 show that the median $= 39.5, Q_1 = 35$, and $Q_3 = 44$. Therefore, the five-number summary is as follows:

$$29 \quad 35 \quad 39.5 \quad 44 \quad 52$$

The distance from X_{smallest} to the median $(39.5 - 29 = 10.5)$ is slightly less than the distance from the median to X_{largest} $(52 - 39.5 = 12.5)$. The distance from X_{smallest} to Q_1 $(35 - 29 = 6)$ is slightly less than the distance from Q_3 to X_{largest} $(52 - 44 = 8)$. The distance from Q_1 to the median $(39.5 - 35 = 4.5)$ is the same as the distance from the median to Q_3 $(44 - 39.5 = 4.5)$. Therefore, the getting-ready times are slightly right-skewed.

EXAMPLE 3.13

Computing the Five-Number Summary of the Number of Calories in Iced Coffee Drinks

The file **CoffeeDrink** (see Example 3.1 on page 88) contains the calories of 16-ounce iced coffee drinks at Dunkin' Donuts and Starbucks. Compute the five-number summary of the number of calories of 16-ounce iced coffee drinks.

SOLUTION From previous computations for the calories of 16-ounce iced coffee drinks (see pages 89 and 104), you know that the median $= 350, Q_1 = 260$, and $Q_3 = 510$. In addition, the smallest value in the data set is 240, and the largest value is 530. Therefore, the five-number summary is as follows:

$$240 \quad 260 \quad 350 \quad 510 \quad 530$$

The three comparisons listed in Table 3.5 are used to evaluate skewness. The distance from $X_{smallest}$ to the median $(350 - 240 = 110)$ is less than the distance $(530 - 350 = 180)$ from the median to $X_{largest}$. The distance from $X_{smallest}$ to $Q_1 (260 - 240 = 20)$ is the same as the distance from Q_3 to $X_{largest} (530 - 510 = 20)$. The distance from Q_1 to the median $(350 - 260 = 90)$ is less than the distance from the median to $Q_3 (510 - 350 = 160)$. Two comparisons indicate a right-skewed distribution, whereas the other indicates a symmetric distribution. Therefore, you can conclude that the number of calories in iced coffee drinks is slightly right-skewed.

The Boxplot

A **boxplot** provides a graphical representation of the data based on the five-number summary. To further analyze the sample of 10 times to get ready in the morning, you can construct a boxplot, as displayed in Figure 3.3.

FIGURE 3.3
Boxplot for the getting ready times

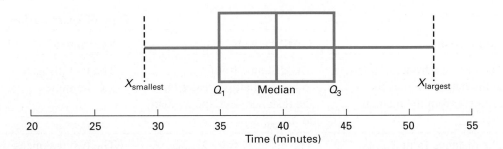

The vertical line drawn within the box represents the median. The vertical line at the left side of the box represents the location of Q_1, and the vertical line at the right side of the box represents the location of Q_3. Thus, the box contains the middle 50% of the values. The lower 25% of the data are represented by a line connecting the left side of the box to the location of the smallest value, $X_{smallest}$. Similarly, the upper 25% of the data are represented by a line connecting the right side of the box to $X_{largest}$.

The boxplot of the getting-ready times in Figure 3.3 indicates slight right-skewness because the distance between the median and the highest value is slightly greater than the distance between the lowest value and the median. Also, the right tail is slightly longer than the left tail.

EXAMPLE 3.14

Boxplots of the 2008 Returns of Intermediate Government Bond and Short-Term Corporate Bond Funds

In Part II of the Choice Is Yours scenario, you are interested in comparing the past performance of the intermediate government bond and short-term corporate bond funds. One measure of past performance is the return in 2008. You have already defined the variables to be collected and collected the data from a sample of 180 bond funds. Construct the boxplot of the 2008 returns for the intermediate government bond and short-term corporate bond funds.

SOLUTION Figure 3.4 shows a five-number summary (Panel A) and boxplots of the 2008 return (Panel B) for the intermediate government bond and short-term corporate bond funds.

FIGURE 3.4

Boxplots of the 2008
return for intermediate
government bond and
short-term corporate bond
funds

*Create boxplots using the
instructions in Section
EG3.3.*

Panel A

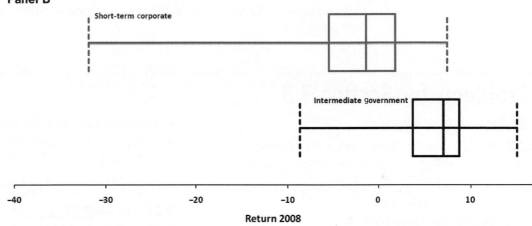

	A	B	C
1	Five-Number Summary for Bond Funds		
2			
3		Intermediate Government	Short Term Corporate
4	Minimum	-8.62	-31.90
5	First Quartile	3.70	-5.50
6	Median	7.00	-1.45
7	Third Quartile	8.70	1.80
8	Maximum	15.00	7.40

Panel B

The median return, the quartiles, and the minimum and maximum return are much higher for the intermediate government bond funds than for the short-term corporate bond funds. The median return for the intermediate government bond funds is almost as high as the maximum return for the short-term corporate bond funds. The first quartile return (3.70) for the intermediate government bond funds is more than twice the third quartile return (1.80) for the short-term corporate bond funds. Both the intermediate government bond and short-term corporate bond funds are left-skewed, but the short-term corporate bond funds are much more skewed, with a very long tail in the lower part of the range. These results are consistent with the statistics computed in Figure 3.2 on page 99.

Figure 3.5 demonstrates the relationship between the boxplot and the density curve for four different types of distributions. (*Note:* The area under each density curve is split into quartiles corresponding to the five-number summary for the boxplot.)

FIGURE 3.5

Boxplots and
corresponding density
curves for four
distributions

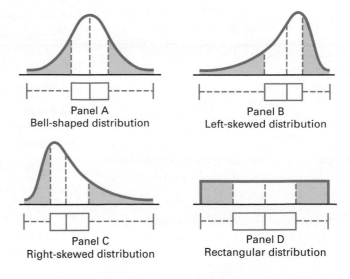

The distributions in Panels A and D of Figure 3.5 are symmetric. In these distributions, the mean and median are equal. In addition, the length of the left tail is equal to the length of the right tail, and the median line divides the box in half.

The distribution in Panel B of Figure 3.5 is left-skewed. The few small values distort the mean toward the left tail. For this left-skewed distribution, there is a heavy clustering of values at the high end of the scale (i.e., the right side); 75% of all values are found between the left edge of the box (Q_1) and the end of the right tail $(X_{largest})$. There is a long left tail that contains the smallest 25% of the values, demonstrating the lack of symmetry in this data set.

The distribution in Panel C of Figure 3.5 is right-skewed. The concentration of values is on the low end of the scale (i.e., the left side of the boxplot). Here, 75% of all values are found between the beginning of the left tail and the right edge of the box (Q_3) There is a long right tail that contains the largest 25% of the values, demonstrating the lack of symmetry in this data set.

Problems for Section 3.3

LEARNING THE BASICS

3.23 The following is a set of data from a sample of $n = 7$:

> 12   7   4   9   0   7   3

a. Compute the first quartile (Q_1), the third quartile (Q_3), and the interquartile range.
b. List the five-number summary.
c. Construct a boxplot and describe its shape.
d. Compare your answer in (c) with that from Problem 3.3(d) on page 100. Discuss.

3.24 The following is a set of data from a sample of $n = 6$:

> 7   4   9   7   3   12

a. Compute the first quartile (Q_1), the third quartile (Q_3), and the interquartile range.
b. List the five-number summary.
c. Construct a boxplot and describe its shape.
d. Compare your answer in (c) with that from Problem 3.2(d) on page 100. Discuss.

3.25 The following is a set of data from a sample of $n = 5$:

> 7   4   9   8   2

a. Compute the first quartile (Q_1), the third quartile (Q_3), and the interquartile range.
b. List the five-number summary.
c. Construct a boxplot and describe its shape.
d. Compare your answer in (c) with that from Problem 3.1(d) on page 100. Discuss.

3.26 The following is a set of data from a sample of $n = 5$:

> 7   −5   −8   7   9

a. Compute the first quartile (Q_1), the third quartile (Q_3), and the interquartile range.
b. List the five-number summary.

c. Construct a boxplot and describe its shape.
d. Compare your answer in (c) with that from Problem 3.4(d) on page 100. Discuss.

APPLYING THE CONCEPTS

3.27 The file **ChocolateChip** contains the cost (in cents) per 1-ounce serving, for a sample of 13 chocolate chip cookies. The data are as follows:

> 54   22   25   23   36   43   7   43   25   47   24   45   44

Source: *Data extracted from "Chip, Chip, Hooray,"* Consumer Reports, *June 2009, p. 7.*

a. Compute the first quartile (Q_1), the third quartile (Q_3), and the interquartile range.
b. List the five-number summary.
c. Construct a boxplot and describe its shape.

 3.28 The file **Dark Chocolate** represent the cost ($) per ounce for a sample of 14 dark chocolate bars:

> 0.68   0.72   0.92   1.14   1.42   0.94   0.77   0.57   1.51
> 0.57   0.55   0.86   1.41   0.90

Source: *Data extracted from "Dark Chocolate Which Bars are Best?"* Consumer Reports, *September 2007, pp. 1–8.*

a. Compute the first quartile (Q_1), the third quartile (Q_3), and the interquartile range.
b. List the five-number summary.
c. Construct a boxplot and describe its shape.

3.29 The file **ThemeParks** contains data on the starting admission price ($) for one-day tickets to 10 theme parks in the United States:

> 58   63   41   42   29   50   62   43   40   40

Source: *Data extracted from C. Jackson and E. Gamerman, "Rethinking the Thrill Factor,"* The Wall Street Journal, *April 15–16, 2006, pp. P1, P4.*

a. Compute the first quartile (Q_1), the third quartile (Q_3), and the interquartile range.

b. List the five-number summary.

c. Construct a boxplot and describe its shape.

3.30 The file SUV contains the overall miles per gallon (MPG) of 2009 small SUVs priced under $30,000:

24 23 22 21 22 22 18 19 19 19 21 21
21 18 19 21 17 22 18 18 22 16 16

Source: *Data extracted from "Vehicle Ratings," Consumer Reports, April 2009, p. 33–34.*

a. Compute the first quartile (Q_1), the third quartile (Q_3), and the interquartile range.

b. List the five-number summary.

c. Construct a boxplot and describe its shape.

3.31 The file SavingsRate contains the yields for a money market account, a one-year certificate of deposit (CD), and a five-year CD for 23 banks in the metropolitan New York area, as of May 28, 2009. For each type of account:

Source: *Data extracted from* **www.Bankrate.com**, *May 28, 2009.*

a. Compute the first quartile (Q_1), the third quartile (Q_3), and the interquartile range.

b. List the five-number summary.

c. Construct a boxplot and describe its shape.

3.32 A bank branch located in a commercial district of a city has the business objective of developing an improved process for serving customers during the noon-to-1:00 P.M. lunch period. The waiting time, in minutes, is defined as the time the customer enters the line to when he or she reaches the teller window. Data is collected from a sample of 15 customers during this hour. The file Bank1 contains the results, which are listed below:

4.21 5.55 3.02 5.13 4.77 2.34 3.54 3.20
4.50 6.10 0.38 5.12 6.46 6.19 3.79

Another bank branch, located in a residential area, is also concerned with the noon-to-1 P.M. lunch hour. The waiting time, in minutes, collected from a sample of 15 customers during this hour, is contained in the file Bank2 and listed below:

9.66 5.90 8.02 5.79 8.73 3.82 8.01 8.35
10.49 6.68 5.64 4.08 6.17 9.91 5.47

a. List the five-number summaries of the waiting times at the two bank branches.

b. Construct boxplots and describe the shapes of the distributions for the two bank branches.

c. What similarities and differences are there in the distributions of the waiting times at the two bank branches?

3.33 Using the data in Mutual Funds,

a. Construct a PivotTable of the mean 2006 return by category and risk.

b. Construct a PivotTable of the standard deviation of the 2006 return by category and risk.

c. What conclusions can you reach concerning differences between the categories of mutual funds (large cap, medium cap, and small cap) based on risk factor (low, average, and high)?

3.34 Using the data in Mutual Funds,

a. Construct a PivotTable of the mean three-year return by category and risk.

b. Construct a PivotTable of the standard deviation of the three-year return by category and risk.

c. What conclusions can you reach concerning differences between the categories of mutual funds (large cap, medium cap, and small cap) based on risk factor (low, average, and high)?

3.35 Using the data in Mutual Funds,

a. Construct a PivotTable of the mean five-year return by category and risk.

b. Construct a PivotTable of the standard deviation of the five-year return by category and risk.

c. What conclusions can you reach concerning differences between the categories of mutual funds (large cap, medium cap, and small cap) based on risk factor (low, average, and high)?

3.36 Using the data in Mutual Funds,

a. Construct a PivotTable of the mean 2006 return by category, objective, and risk.

b. Construct a PivotTable of the standard deviation of the 2006 return by category, objective, and risk.

c. What conclusions can you reach concerning differences between the categories of mutual funds (large cap, medium cap, and small cap) based on objective (growth or value) and risk factor (low, average, and high)?

3.4 Numerical Descriptive Measures for a Population

Sections 3.1 and 3.2 present various statistics that described the properties of central tendency and variation for a sample. If your data set represents numerical measurements for an entire population, you need to calculate and interpret parameters and summary measures for a population. In this section, you will learn about three population parameters: the population mean, population variance, and population standard deviation.

To help illustrate these parameters, first review Table 3.6, which contains the one-year returns for the five largest bond funds (in terms of total assets) as of May 20, 2009 (stored in LargestBonds).

Bond Fund	One-Year Return
Pimco:Total Rtn;Inst	5.90
American Funds Bond;A	−9.00
Vanguard Tot Bd;Inv	4.30
Vanguard GNMA;Adm	7.80
Vanguard Int-TmTx;Adm	4.40

Source: *Data extracted from* The Wall Street Journal, *May 20, 2009, p. C4.*

The Population Mean

The **population mean** is represented by the symbol μ, the Greek lowercase letter mu. Equation (3.13) defines the population mean.

POPULATION MEAN

The population mean is the sum of the values in the population divided by the population size, N.

$$\mu = \frac{\sum_{i=1}^{N} X_i}{N} \tag{3.13}$$

where

$$\mu = \text{population mean}$$

$$X_i = i\text{th value of the variable } X$$

$$\sum_{i=1}^{N} X_i = \text{summation of all } X_i \text{ values in the population}$$

To compute the mean one-year return for the population of bond funds given in Table 3.6, use Equation (3.13):

$$\mu = \frac{\sum_{i=1}^{N} X_i}{N} = \frac{5.90 - 9.00 + 4.30 + 7.80 + 4.40}{5} = \frac{13.4}{5} = 2.68$$

Thus, the mean percentage return for these bond funds is 2.68.

The Population Variance and Standard Deviation

*Section EG3.4 describes
the VARP and STDEVP
functions, which compute
the population variance and
population standard
deviation.*

The **population variance** and the **population standard deviation** measure variation in a population. As was the case for the sample statistics, the population standard deviation is the square root of the population variance. The symbol σ^2, the Greek lowercase letter sigma squared, represents the population variance, and the symbol σ, the Greek lowercase letter sigma, represents the population standard deviation. Equations (3.14) and (3.15) define these parameters. The denominators for the right-side terms in these equations use N and not the $(n - 1)$ term that is used in the equations for the sample variance and standard deviation [see Equations (3.6) and (3.7) on page 93].

POPULATION VARIANCE

The population variance is the sum of the squared differences around the population mean divided by the population size, N.

$$\sigma^2 = \frac{\sum_{i=1}^{N} (X_i - \mu)^2}{N} \tag{3.14}$$

where

$$\mu = \text{population mean}$$

$$X_i = i\text{th value of the variable } X$$

$$\sum_{i=1}^{N}(X_i - \mu)^2 = \text{summation of all the squared differences between the } X_i \text{ values and } \mu$$

POPULATION STANDARD DEVIATION

$$\sigma = \sqrt{\frac{\sum_{i=1}^{N}(X_i - \mu)^2}{N}} \tag{3.15}$$

To compute the population variance for the data of Table 3.6 on page 110, you use Equation (3.14):

$$
\begin{aligned}
\sigma^2 &= \frac{\sum_{i=1}^{N}(X_i - \mu)^2}{N} \\
&= \frac{(5.9 - 2.68)^2 + (-9.0 - 2.68)^2 + (4.3 - 2.68)^2 + (7.8 - 2.68)^2 + (4.4 - 2.68)^2}{5} \\
&= \frac{10.3684 + 136.4224 + 2.6244 + 26.2144 + 2.9584}{5} \\
&= \frac{178.5880}{5} = 35.7176
\end{aligned}
$$

Thus, the variance of the one-year returns is 35.7176 squared percentage return. The squared units make the variance difficult to interpret. You should use the standard deviation that is expressed in the original units of the data (percentage return). From Equation (3.15),

$$\sigma = \sqrt{\sigma^2} = \sqrt{\frac{\sum_{i=1}^{N}(X_i - \mu)^2}{N}} = \sqrt{\frac{178.5880}{5}} = 5.9764$$

Therefore, the typical percentage return differs from the mean of 2.68 by approximately 5.9764. This large amount of variation suggests that these large bond funds produce results that differ greatly.

The Empirical Rule

In most data sets, a large portion of the values tend to cluster somewhere near the median. In right-skewed data sets, this clustering occurs to the left of the mean—that is, at a value less than the mean. In left-skewed data sets, the values tend to cluster to the right of the mean—that is, greater than the mean. In symmetric data sets, where the median and mean are the same, the values often tend to cluster around the median and mean, producing a bell-shaped distribution. You can use the **empirical rule** to examine the variability in such distributions:

- Approximately 68% of the values are within a distance of ±1 standard deviation from the mean.
- Approximately 95% of the values are within a distance of ±2 standard deviations from the mean.
- Approximately 99.7% of the values are within a distance of ±3 standard deviations from the mean.

The empirical rule helps you measure how the values distribute above and below the mean and can help you identify outliers. The empirical rule implies that for bell-shaped distributions, only about 1 out of 20 values will be beyond two standard deviations from the mean in either direction. As a general rule, you can consider values not found in the interval $\mu \pm 2\sigma$ as potential outliers. The rule also implies that only about 3 in 1,000 will be beyond three standard deviations from the mean. Therefore, values not found in the interval $\mu \pm 3\sigma$ are almost always considered outliers.

EXAMPLE 3.15

Using the Empirical Rule

A population of 12-ounce cans of cola is known to have a mean fill-weight of 12.06 ounces and a standard deviation of 0.02. The population is known to be bell-shaped. Describe the distribution of fill-weights. Is it very likely that a can will contain less than 12 ounces of cola?

SOLUTION

$$\mu \pm \sigma = 12.06 \pm 0.02 = (12.04, 12.08)$$

$$\mu \pm 2\sigma = 12.06 \pm 2(0.02) = (12.02, 12.10)$$

$$\mu \pm 3\sigma = 12.06 \pm 3(0.02) = (12.00, 12.12)$$

Using the empirical rule, you can see that approximately 68% of the cans will contain between 12.04 and 12.08 ounces, approximately 95% will contain between 12.02 and 12.10 ounces, and approximately 99.7% will contain between 12.00 and 12.12 ounces. Therefore, it is highly unlikely that a can will contain less than 12 ounces.

For heavily skewed data sets and those not appearing bell-shaped, you should use the Chebyshev rule, discussed next, instead of the empirical rule.

The Chebyshev Rule

The **Chebyshev rule** (see reference 1 at the end of this chapter) states that for any data set, regardless of shape, the percentage of values that are found within distances of k standard deviations from the mean must be at least

$$\left(1 - \frac{1}{k^2}\right) \times 100\%$$

You can use this rule for any value of k greater than 1. For example, consider $k = 2$. The Chebyshev rule states that at least $[1 - (1/2)^2] \times 100\% = 75\%$ of the values must be found within ± 2 standard deviations of the mean.

The Chebyshev rule is very general and applies to any distribution. The rule indicates *at least* what percentage of the values fall within a given distance from the mean. However, if the data set is approximately bell-shaped, the empirical rule will more accurately reflect the greater concentration of data close to the mean. Table 3.7 compares the Chebyshev and empirical rules.

TABLE 3.7

How Data Vary Around the Mean

	% of Values Found in Intervals Around the Mean	
Interval	Chebyshev (any distribution)	Empirical Rule (bell-shaped distribution)
$(\mu - \sigma, \mu + \sigma)$	At least 0%	Approximately 68%
$(\mu - 2\sigma, \mu + 2\sigma)$	At least 75%	Approximately 95%
$(\mu - 3\sigma, \mu + 3\sigma)$	At least 88.89%	Approximately 99.7%

EXAMPLE 3.16	As in Example 3.15, a population of 12-ounce cans of cola is known to have a mean fill-weight of 12.06 ounces and a standard deviation of 0.02. However, the shape of the population is unknown, and you cannot assume that it is bell-shaped. Describe the distribution of fill-weights. Is it very likely that a can will contain less than 12 ounces of cola?
Using the Chebyshev Rule	

SOLUTION

$$\mu \pm \sigma = 12.06 \pm 0.02 = (12.04, 12.08)$$

$$\mu \pm 2\sigma = 12.06 \pm 2(0.02) = (12.02, 12.10)$$

$$\mu \pm 3\sigma = 12.06 \pm 3(0.02) = (12.00, 12.12)$$

Because the distribution may be skewed, you cannot use the empirical rule. Using the Chebyshev rule, you cannot say anything about the percentage of cans containing between 12.04 and 12.08 ounces. You can state that at least 75% of the cans will contain between 12.02 and 12.10 ounces and at least 88.89% will contain between 12.00 and 12.12 ounces. Therefore, between 0 and 11.11% of the cans will contain less than 12 ounces.

You can use these two rules to understand how data are distributed around the mean when you have sample data. With each rule, you use the value you calculated for $\overline{X}$ in place of μ and the value you calculated for S in place of σ. The results you compute using the sample statistics are *approximations* because you used sample statistics $(\overline{X}, S)$ and not population parameters (μ, σ).

Problems for Section 3.4

LEARNING THE BASICS

3.37 The following is a set of data for a population with $N = 10$:

7 5 11 8 3 6 2 1 9 8

a. Compute the population mean.
b. Compute the population standard deviation.

3.38 The following is a set of data for a population with $N = 10$:

7 5 6 6 6 4 8 6 9 3

a. Compute the population mean.
b. Compute the population standard deviation.

APPLYING THE CONCEPTS

3.39 The file Tax contains the quarterly sales tax receipts (in thousands of dollars) submitted to the comptroller of the Village of Fair Lake for the period ending March 2009 by all 50 business establishments in that locale:

10.3	11.1	9.6	9.0	14.5
13.0	6.7	11.0	8.4	10.3
13.0	11.2	7.3	5.3	12.5
8.0	11.8	8.7	10.6	9.5
11.1	10.2	11.1	9.9	9.8
11.6	15.1	12.5	6.5	7.5
10.0	12.9	9.2	10.0	12.8
12.5	9.3	10.4	12.7	10.5
9.3	11.5	10.7	11.6	7.8
10.5	7.6	10.1	8.9	8.6

a. Compute the mean, variance, and standard deviation for this population.
b. What percentage of these businesses have quarterly sales tax receipts within ±1, ±2, or ±3 standard deviations of the mean?
c. Compare your findings with what would be expected on the basis of the empirical rule. Are you surprised at the results in (b)?

3.40 Consider a population of 1,024 mutual funds that primarily invest in large companies. You have determined that μ, the mean one-year total percentage return achieved by all the funds, is 8.20 and that σ, the standard deviation, is 2.75.

a. According to the empirical rule, what percentage of these funds are expected to be within ±1 standard deviation of the mean?
b. According to the empirical rule, what percentage of these funds are expected to be within ±2 standard deviations of the mean?
c. According to the Chebyshev rule, what percentage of these funds are expected to be within ±1, ±2, or ±3 standard deviations of the mean?
d. According to the Chebyshev rule, at least 93.75% of these funds are expected to have one-year total returns between what two amounts?

3.41 The file CigaretteTax contains the state cigarette tax, in dollars, for each of the 50 states as of April 1, 2009.
a. Compute the population mean and population standard deviation for the state cigarette tax.
b. Interpret the parameters in (a).

SELF **3.42** The file Energy contains the per capita
Test energy consumption, in kilowatt-hours, for each of
the 50 states and the District of Columbia during a recent year.
a. Compute the mean, variance, and standard deviation for
   the population.
b. What proportion of these states has per capita energy
   consumption within ± 1 standard deviation of the mean,
   within ± 2 standard deviations of the mean, and within
   ± 3 standard deviations of the mean?
c. Compare your findings with what would be expected
   based on the empirical rule. Are you surprised at the
   results in (b)?
d. Repeat (a) through (c) with the District of Columbia
   removed. How have the results changed?

3.43 Thirty companies comprise the DJIA. Just how big
are these companies? One common method for measuring
the size of a company is to use its market capitalization,
which is computed by multiplying the number of stock
shares by the price of a share of stock. On June 19, 2009, the
market capitalization of these companies ranged from
Caterpillar's \$20.5 billion to ExxonMobil's \$347.4 billion.
The entire population of market capitalization values is
stored in DowMarketCap.
Source: *Data extracted from* **money.cnn.com**, *June 19, 2009.*

a. Calculate the mean and standard deviation of the market
   capitalization for this population of 30 companies.
b. Interpret the parameters calculated in (a).

3.5 The Covariance and the Coefficient of Correlation

In Section 2.7, you used scatter plots to visually examine the relationship between two numerical variables. This section presents two measures of the relationship between two numerical variables: the covariance and the coefficient of correlation.

The Covariance

The **covariance** measures the strength of the linear relationship between two numerical variables (X and Y). Equation (3.16) defines the **sample covariance**, and Example 3.17 illustrates its use.

SAMPLE COVARIANCE

$$\mathrm{cov}(X, Y) = \frac{\sum_{i=1}^{n} (X_i - \bar{X})(Y_i - \bar{Y})}{n - 1}$$ (3.16)

EXAMPLE 3.17

Computing the
Sample Covariance

In Figure 2.18 on page 49, you constructed a scatter plot that showed the relationship
between the value and the annual revenue of the 30 teams that make up the National
Basketball Association (NBA) (extracted from **www.forbes.com/lists/2008/32/nba08_NBA-
Team-Valuations_MetroArea.html**; stored in NBAValues). Now, you want to measure the
association between the value of a franchise and annual revenue by computing the sample
covariance.

SOLUTION Table 3.8 provides the value and the annual revenue of the 30 teams.
   Figure 3.6 contains a worksheet that calculates the covariance for these data. The
Calculations Area section of Figure 3.6 breaks down Equation (3.16) into a set of smaller calculations. From cell F9, or by using Equation (3.16) directly, you find that the covariance is
2,836.2069:

$$\mathrm{cov}(X, Y) = \frac{82,250}{30 - 1}$$

$$= 2,836.2069$$

TABLE 3.8

Values and Annual Revenues of the 30 NBA Teams (in millions of dollars)

Team	Value	Revenue
Atlanta	306	102
Boston	447	149
Charlotte	284	95
Chicago	504	165
Cleveland	477	159
Dallas	466	153
Denver	329	112
Detroit	480	160
Golden State	335	112
Houston	469	156
Indiana	303	101
Los Angeles Clippers	297	99
Los Angeles Lakers	584	191
Memphis	294	95
Miami	393	131
Milwaukee	278	94
Minnesota	301	100
New Jersey	295	98
New Orleans	285	95
New York	613	208
Orlando	300	82
Philadelphia	349	100
Phoenix	360	116
Portland	452	148
Sacramento	307	114
San Antonio	350	117
Seattle	415	138
Toronto	400	138
Utah	358	119
Washington	353	118

FIGURE 3.6

Microsoft Excel worksheet for the covariance between the value and the annual revenue of the 30 NBA teams

The *FIGURE_3.6 worksheet* of the *Chapter 3 workbook* contains the Figure 3.6 worksheet. Compute the covariance using the instructions in Section EG3.5.

	A	B	C	D	E	F
1	Covariance Analysis					
2						
3	Value	Revenue	(X-XBar)(Y-YBar)			
4	306	102	1726.4667		Calculations Area	
5	447	149	1587.0333		XBar	379.4667
6	284	95	2911.7333		YBar	125.5
7	504	165	4919.0667		n -1	29
8	477	159	3267.3667		Sum	82250.0000
9	466	153	2379.6667		Covariance	2836.2069
10	329	112	681.3000			
11	480	160	3468.4000			
12	335	112	600.3000			
13	469	156	2730.7667			
14	303	101	1873.4333			
15	297	99	2185.3667			
16	584	191	13396.9333			
17	294	95	2606.7333			
18	393	131	74.4333			
19	278	94	3196.2000			
20	301	100	2000.9000			
21	295	98	2322.8333			
22	285	95	2881.2333			
23	613	208	19266.5000			
24	300	82	3456.8000			
25	349	100	776.9000			
26	360	116	184.9333			
27	452	148	1632.0000			
28	307	114	833.3667			
29	350	117	250.4667			
30	415	138	444.1667			
31	400	138	256.6667			
32	358	119	139.5333			
33	353	118	198.5000			

The covariance has a major flaw as a measure of the linear relationship between two numerical variables. Because the covariance can have any value, you are unable to use it to determine the relative strength of the relationship. In other words, you cannot tell whether the value 2,836.2069 indicates a strong relationship or a weak relationship. To better determine the relative strength of the relationship, you need to compute the coefficient of correlation.

The Coefficient of Correlation

The **coefficient of correlation** measures the relative strength of a linear relationship between two numerical variables. The values of the coefficient of correlation range from -1 for a perfect negative correlation to $+1$ for a perfect positive correlation. *Perfect* in this case means that if the points were plotted on a scatter plot, all the points could be connected with a straight line. When dealing with population data for two numerical variables, the Greek letter ρ *(rho)* is used as the symbol for the coefficient of correlation. Figure 3.7 illustrates three different types of association between two variables.

FIGURE 3.7

Types of association between variables

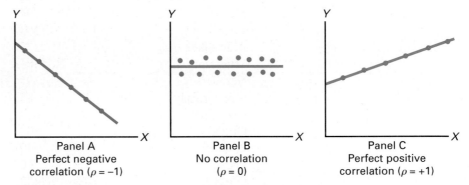

Panel A	Panel B	Panel C
Perfect negative correlation ($\rho = -1$)	No correlation ($\rho = 0$)	Perfect positive correlation ($\rho = +1$)

In Panel A of Figure 3.7, there is a perfect negative linear relationship between X and Y. Thus, the coefficient of correlation, ρ, equals -1, and when X increases, Y decreases in a perfectly predictable manner. Panel B shows a situation in which there is no relationship between X and Y. In this case, the coefficient of correlation, ρ, equals 0, and as X increases, there is no tendency for Y to increase or decrease. Panel C illustrates a perfect positive relationship where ρ equals $+1$. In this case, Y increases in a perfectly predictable manner when X increases.

Correlation alone cannot prove that there is a causation effect—that is, that the change in the value of one variable caused the change in the other variable. A strong correlation can be produced simply by chance, by the effect of a third variable not considered in the calculation of the correlation, or by a cause-and-effect relationship. You would need to perform additional analysis to determine which of these three situations actually produced the correlation. Therefore, you can say that *causation implies correlation, but correlation alone does not imply causation.*

Equation (3.17) defines the **sample coefficient of correlation (r)**.

SAMPLE COEFFICIENT OF CORRELATION

$$r = \frac{\text{cov}(X, Y)}{S_X S_Y} \qquad (3.17)$$

where

$$\text{cov}(X, Y) = \frac{\sum_{i=1}^{n}(X_i - \bar{X})(Y_i - \bar{Y})}{n - 1}$$

$$S_X = \sqrt{\frac{\sum_{i=1}^{n}(X_i - \bar{X})^2}{n - 1}}$$

$$S_Y = \sqrt{\frac{\sum_{i=1}^{n}(Y_i - \bar{Y})^2}{n - 1}}$$

When you have sample data, you can compute the sample coefficient of correlation, r. When using sample data, you are unlikely to have a sample coefficient of exactly $+1$, 0, or -1. Figure 3.8 presents scatter plots along with their respective sample coefficients of correlation, r, for six data sets, each of which contains 100 values of X and Y.

FIGURE 3.8

Six Microsoft Excel scatter plots and their sample coefficients of correlation, r

In Panel A, the coefficient of correlation, r, is -0.9. You can see that for small values of X, there is a very strong tendency for Y to be large. Likewise, the large values of X tend to be paired with small values of Y. The data do not all fall on a straight line, so the association between X and Y cannot be described as perfect. The data in Panel B have a coefficient of correlation equal to -0.6, and the small values of X tend to be paired with large values of Y. The linear relationship between X and Y in Panel B is not as strong as that in Panel A. Thus, the coefficient of correlation in Panel B is not as negative as that in Panel A. In Panel C, the linear relationship between X and Y is very weak, $r = -0.3$, and there is only a slight tendency for the small values of X to be paired with the large values of Y. Panels D through F depict data sets that have positive coefficients of correlation because small values of X tend to be paired with small values of Y and large values of X tend to be associated with large values of Y. Panel D shows weak positive correlation, with $r = 0.3$. Panel E shows stronger positive correlation with $r = 0.6$. Panel F shows very strong positive correlation, with $r = 0.9$.

EXAMPLE 3.18

Computing the Sample Coefficient of Correlation

In Example 3.17 on page 114, you computed the covariance of the values and revenues of 30 NBA basketball teams. Using Figure 3.6 and Equation (3.17) on page 116, compute the sample coefficient of correlation.

SOLUTION

$$r = \frac{\text{cov}(X, Y)}{S_X S_Y}$$

$$= \frac{2{,}836.2069}{(91.9324)(31.2948)}$$

$$= 0.9858$$

FIGURE 3.9

Microsoft Excel worksheet for the sample coefficient of correlation, r, between the cost values and revenues of 30 NBA basketball teams

FIGURE_3.9 displays the COMPUTE worksheet of the Correlation workbook. Compute the coefficient of correlation using the instructions in Section EG3.5.

	A	B	C	D	E	F	G	H
1	Coefficient of Correlation Calculations							
2								
3	Value	Revenue	(X-XBar)²	(Y-YBar)²	(X-XBar)(Y-YBar)		Calculations Area	
4	306	102	5397.3511	552.2500	1726.4667		XBar	379.4667
5	447	149	4560.7511	552.2500	1587.0333		YBar	125.5
6	284	95	9113.8844	930.2500	2911.7333		n -1	29
7	504	165	15508.5511	1560.2500	4919.0667		Covariance	2836.2069
8	477	159	9512.7511	1122.2500	3267.3667		S_X	91.9324
9	466	153	7488.0178	756.2500	2379.6667		S_Y	31.2948
10	329	112	2546.8844	182.2500	681.3000		r	0.9858
11	480	160	10106.9511	1190.2500	3468.4000			
12	335	112	1977.2844	182.2500	600.3000			
13	469	156	8016.2178	930.2500	2730.7667			
14	303	101	5847.1511	600.2500	1873.4333			
15	297	99	6800.7511	702.2500	2185.3667			
16	584	191	41833.8844	4290.2500	13396.9333			
17	294	95	7304.5511	930.2500	2606.7333			
18	393	131	183.1511	30.2500	74.4333			
19	278	94	10295.4844	992.2500	3196.2000			
20	301	100	6157.0178	650.2500	2000.9000			
21	295	98	7134.6178	756.2500	2322.8333			
22	285	95	8923.9511	930.2500	2881.2333			
23	613	208	54537.8178	6806.2500	19266.5000			
24	300	82	6314.9511	1892.2500	3456.8000			
25	349	100	928.2178	650.2500	776.9000			
26	360	116	378.9511	90.2500	184.9333			
27	452	148	5261.0844	506.2500	1632.0000			
28	307	114	5251.4178	132.2500	833.3667			
29	350	117	868.2844	72.2500	250.4667			
30	415	138	1262.6178	156.2500	444.1667			
31	400	138	421.6178	156.2500	256.6667			
32	358	119	460.8178	42.2500	139.5333			
33	353	118	700.4844	56.2500	198.5000			
34		Sums:	245095.4667	28401.5	82250.0000			

The value and revenues of the NBA teams are very highly correlated. The teams with the lowest revenues have the lowest values. The teams with the highest revenues have the highest values. This relationship is very strong, as indicated by the coefficient of correlation, $r = 0.9848$.

Although in general you cannot assume that just because two variables are correlated that changes in one variable caused changes in the other variable, for this example, it makes sense to conclude that changes in revenue will cause changes in the value of a team.

In summary, the coefficient of correlation indicates the linear relationship, or association, between two numerical variables. When the coefficient of correlation gets closer to $+1$ or -1, the linear relationship between the two variables is stronger. When the coefficient of correlation is near 0, little or no linear relationship exists. The sign of the coefficient of correlation indicates whether the data are positively correlated (i.e., the larger values of X are typically paired with the larger values of Y) or negatively correlated (i.e., the larger values of X are typically paired with the smaller values of Y). The existence of a strong correlation does not imply a causation effect. It only indicates the tendencies present in the data.

Problems for Section 3.5

LEARNING THE BASICS

3.44 The following is a set of data from a sample of $n = 11$ items:

| X | 7 | 5 | 8 | 3 | 6 | 10 | 12 | 4 | 9 | 15 | 18 |
| Y | 21 | 15 | 24 | 9 | 18 | 30 | 36 | 12 | 27 | 45 | 54 |

a. Compute the covariance.
b. Compute the coefficient of correlation.
c. How strong is the relationship between X and Y? Explain.

APPLYING THE CONCEPTS

3.45 A study of 218 students at Ohio State University suggests a link between time spent on the social networking site Facebook and grade point average. Students who rarely or never used Facebook had higher grade point averages than the students who use Facebook.

Source: *Data extracted from M. B. Marklein, "Facebook Use Linked to Less Textbook Time,"* www.usatoday.com, *April 14, 2009.*

a. Does the study suggest that time spent on Facebook and grade point average are positively correlated or negatively correlated?
b. Do you think that there might be a cause-and-effect relationship between time spent on Facebook and grade point average? Explain.

✓ SELF Test 3.46 The file **CoffeeDrink** contains the calories and fat, in grams, of 16-ounce iced coffee drinks at Dunkin' Donuts and Starbucks:

Product	Calories	Fat
Dunkin' Donuts Iced Mocha Swirl latte (whole milk)	240	8.0
Starbucks Coffee Frappuccino blended coffee	260	3.5
Dunkin' Donuts Coffee Coolatta (cream)	350	22.0
Starbucks Iced Coffee Mocha Espresso (whole milk and whipped cream)	350	20.0
Starbucks Mocha Frappuccino blended coffee (whipped cream)	420	16.0
Starbucks Chocolate Brownie Frappuccino blended coffee (whipped cream)	510	22.0
Starbucks Chocolate Frappuccino blended crème (whipped cream)	530	19.0

Source: *Data extracted from "Coffee as Candy at Dunkin' Donuts and Starbucks,"* Consumer Reports, *June 2004, p. 9.*

a. Compute the covariance.
b. Compute the coefficient of correlation.
c. Which do you think is more valuable in expressing the relationship between calories and fat—the covariance or the coefficient of correlation? Explain.
d. Based on (a) and (b), what conclusions can you reach about the relationship between calories and fat?

3.47 There are several methods for calculating fuel efficiency. The following table (stored in **Mileage**) indicates mileage (in miles per gallon), as calculated by owners and by current government standards:

Car	Owner	Government
2005 Ford F-150	14.3	16.8
2005 Chevrolet Silverado	15.0	17.8
2002 Honda Accord LX	27.8	26.2
2002 Honda Civic	27.9	34.2
2004 Honda Civic Hybrid	48.8	47.6
2002 Ford Explorer	16.8	18.3
2005 Toyota Camry	23.7	28.5
2003 Toyota Corolla	32.8	33.1
2005 Toyota Prius	37.3	56.0

Source: *Data extracted from J. Healey, "Fuel Economy Calculations to Be Altered," USA Today, January 11, 2006, p. 1B.*

a. Compute the covariance.
b. Compute the coefficient of correlation.
c. Which do you think is more valuable in expressing the relationship between owner-calculated and current government standards mileage—the covariance or the coefficient of correlation? Explain.
d. Based on (a) and (b), what conclusions can you reach about the relationship between owner-calculated and current government standards mileage?

3.48 College basketball is big business, with coaches' salaries, revenues, and expenses in the millions of dollars. The file Colleges-Basketball contains the coaches' salaries and revenue for college basketball at selected schools in a recent year.

Source: *Data extracted from R. Adams, "Pay for Playoffs," The Wall Street Journal, March 11–12, 2006, pp. P1, P8.*

a. Compute the covariance.
b. Compute the coefficient of correlation.
c. Based on (a) and (b), what conclusions can you reach about the relationship between a coaches' salaries and revenues?

3.49 College football players trying out for the NFL are given the Wonderlic standardized intelligence test. The file Wonderlic contains the average Wonderlic score of football players trying out for the NFL and the graduation rate for football players at selected schools.

Source: *Data extracted from S. Walker, "The NFL's Smartest Team," The Wall Street Journal, September 30, 2005, pp. W1, W10.*

a. Compute the covariance.
b. Compute the coefficient of correlation.
c. Based on (a) and (b), what conclusions can you reach about the relationship between the average Wonderlic score and graduation rate?

3.6 Descriptive Statistics: Pitfalls and Ethical Issues

This chapter describes how a set of numerical data can be characterized by the statistics that measure the properties of central tendency, variation, and shape. In business, descriptive statistics such as the ones you have learned about are frequently included in summary reports that are prepared periodically.

The volume of information available on the Internet, in newspapers, and in magazines has produced much skepticism about the objectivity of data. When you are reading information that contains descriptive statistics, you should keep in mind the quip often attributed to the famous nineteenth-century British statesman Benjamin Disraeli: "There are three kinds of lies: lies, damned lies, and statistics."

For example, in examining statistics, you need to compare the mean and the median. Are they similar or are they very different? Or, is only the mean provided? The answers to these questions will enable you to determine whether the data are skewed or symmetrical and whether the median might be a better measure of central tendency than the mean. In addition, you should look to see whether the standard deviation has been included in the statistics provided. Without the standard deviation, it is difficult to determine the amount of variation that exists in the data.

Ethical considerations arise when you are deciding what results to include in a report. You should document both good and bad results. In addition, when making oral presentations and presenting written reports, you need to give results in a fair, objective, and neutral manner. Unethical behavior occurs when you selectively fail to report pertinent findings that are detrimental to the support of a particular position.

USING STATISTICS @ Choice Is Yours, Part II Revisited

In Part II of the Choice Is Yours scenario, you were hired by the Choice Is Yours investment company to assist investors interested in bond mutual funds. A sample of 180 bond mutual funds included 90 intermediate government funds and 90 short-term corporate bond funds. By comparing these two categories, you were able to provide investors with valuable insights.

The 2008 returns for both the intermediate government funds and the short-term corporate bond funds were left-skewed. The returns for the short-term corporate bond funds were especially left-skewed, as indicated by the boxplots (see Figure 3.4 on page 107). The descriptive statistics (see Figure 3.2 on page 99) allowed you to compare the central tendency and variability of returns of the intermediate government funds and the short-term corporate bond funds. The mean indicated that the intermediate government funds returned an average of 5.96, and the median indicated that half of the funds had returns of 7.0 or more. The short-term corporate bond funds' central tendencies were much lower than those of the intermediate government funds—they had an average of -3.32, and half the funds had returns below -1.45. In addition, the intermediate government funds showed less variability in their returns than the short-term corporate bond funds—they had a range of 23.62 as compared to 39.3; an interquartile range of 5.00 as compared to 7.30; and a standard deviation of 4.9 as compared to 7.09. Thus, not only did a typical intermediate government fund have a much higher return in 2008 than did a short-term corporate bond fund, the sample of 90 intermediate government funds had returns that were much more closely clustered near the center. An interesting insight is that while 75% of the intermediate government funds had returns of 3.70 or higher ($Q_1 = 3.70$), only 25% of the short-term corporate bond funds had returns of 1.8 or higher ($Q_3 = 1.80$). Although past performance is no assurance of future performance, in 2008, the intermediate government funds greatly outperformed the short-term corporate funds.

SUMMARY

In this chapter and the previous chapter, you studied descriptive statistics—how you can visualize data through tables and charts, and then how you can use different statistics to help you analyze the data and reach conclusions. In Chapter 2, you were able to visualize data through the use of bar and pie charts, histograms, and other graphical methods. In this chapter, you learned how descriptive statistics such as the mean, median, quartiles, range, and standard deviation are used to describe the characteristics of central tendency, variability, and shape. In addition, you constructed boxplots to visualize the distribution of the data. You also learned how the coefficient of correlation is used to describe the relationship between two numerical variables. Table 3.9 provides a list of the descriptive statistics covered in this chapter.

In the next chapter, the basic principles of probability are presented in order to bridge the gap between the subject of descriptive statistics and the subject of inferential statistics.

TABLE 3.9

Summary of Descriptive Statistics

Type of Analysis	Numerical Data
Describing central tendency, variation, and shape of a numerical variable	Mean, median, mode, quartiles, range, interquartile range, variance, standard deviation, coefficient of variation, Z scores, boxplot (Sections 3.1 through 3.4)
Describing the relationship between two numerical variables	Covariance, coefficient of correlation (Section 3.5)

KEY EQUATIONS

Sample Mean

$$\bar{X} = \frac{\sum_{i=1}^{n} X_i}{n} \tag{3.1}$$

Median

$$\text{Median} = \frac{n+1}{2} \text{ ranked value} \tag{3.2}$$

Geometric Mean

$$\bar{X}_G = (X_1 \times X_2 \times \cdots \times X_n)^{1/n} \tag{3.3}$$

Geometric Mean Rate of Return

$$\bar{R}_G = [(1 + R_1) \times (1 + R_2) \times \cdots \times (1 + R_n)]^{1/n} - 1 \tag{3.4}$$

Range

$$\text{Range} = X_{\text{largest}} - X_{\text{smallest}} \tag{3.5}$$

Sample Variance

$$S^2 = \frac{\sum_{i=1}^{n} (X_i - \bar{X})^2}{n-1} \tag{3.6}$$

Sample Standard Deviation

$$S = \sqrt{S^2} = \sqrt{\frac{\sum_{i=1}^{n} (X_i - \bar{X})^2}{n-1}} \tag{3.7}$$

Coefficient of Variation

$$CV = \left(\frac{S}{\bar{X}}\right) 100\% \tag{3.8}$$

Z Score

$$Z = \frac{X - \bar{X}}{S} \tag{3.9}$$

First Quartile Q_1

$$Q_1 = \frac{n+1}{4} \text{ ranked value} \tag{3.10}$$

Third Quartile Q_3

$$Q_3 = \frac{3(n+1)}{4} \text{ ranked value} \tag{3.11}$$

Interquartile Range

$$\text{Interquartile range} = Q_3 - Q_1 \tag{3.12}$$

Population Mean

$$\mu = \frac{\sum_{i=1}^{N} X_i}{N} \tag{3.13}$$

Population Variance

$$\sigma^2 = \frac{\sum_{i=1}^{N} (X_i - \mu)^2}{N} \tag{3.14}$$

Population Standard Deviation

$$\sigma = \sqrt{\frac{\sum_{i=1}^{N} (X_i - \mu)^2}{N}} \tag{3.15}$$

Sample Covariance

$$\text{cov}(X, Y) = \frac{\sum_{i=1}^{n} (X_i - \bar{X})(Y_i - \bar{Y})}{n-1} \tag{3.16}$$

Sample Coefficient of Correlation

$$r = \frac{\text{cov}(X, Y)}{S_X S_Y} \tag{3.17}$$

KEY TERMS

arithmetic mean 86	mean 86	sample coefficient of
boxplot 106	median 88	correlation (r) 116
central tendency 86	midspread 104	sample covariance 114
Chebyshev rule 112	mode 89	sample mean 87
coefficient of correlation 116	outlier 96	sample standard deviation 93
coefficient of variation 96	population mean 110	sample variance 93
covariance 114	population standard	shape 86
dispersion 91	deviation 110	skewed 98
empirical rule 111	population variance 110	skewness 98
extreme value 96	Q_1: first quartile 102	spread 91
five-number summary 105	Q_2: second quartile 102	standard deviation 92
geometric mean 90	Q_3: third quartile 102	sum of squares (SS) 92
geometric mean rate of return 90	quartile 102	symmetrical 98
interquartile range 104	range 91	variance 92
kurtosis 98	resistant measure 105	variation 86
left-skewed 98	right-skewed 98	Z score 96

CHAPTER REVIEW PROBLEMS

CHECKING YOUR UNDERSTANDING

3.50 What are the properties of a set of numerical data?

3.51 What is meant by the property of central tendency?

3.52 What are the differences among the mean, median, and mode, and what are the advantages and disadvantages of each?

3.53 How do you interpret the first quartile, median, and third quartile?

3.54 What is meant by the property of variation?

3.55 What does the Z score measure?

3.56 What are the differences among the various measures of variation, such as the range, interquartile range, variance, standard deviation, and coefficient of variation, and what are the advantages and disadvantages of each?

3.57 How does the empirical rule help explain the ways in which the values in a set of numerical data cluster and distribute?

3.58 How do the empirical rule and the Chebyshev rule differ?

3.59 What is meant by the property of shape?

3.60 How do the covariance and the coefficient of correlation differ?

APPLYING THE CONCEPTS

3.61 The American Society for Quality (ASQ) conducted a salary survey of all its members. ASQ members work in all areas of manufacturing and service-related institutions, with a common theme of an interest in quality. For the U.S. survey, e-mails were sent to 70,227 members, and 9,449 valid responses were received. The two most common job titles were manager and quality engineer. Another title is Master Black Belt, who is a person who takes a leadership role as the keeper of the Six Sigma process (see Section 17.8). An additional title is Inspector. Descriptive statistics concerning salaries for these four titles are given below. Compare the salaries of inspectors, managers, quality engineers, and Master Black Belts.

Title	Sample Size	Minimum	Maximum	Standard Deviation	Mean	Median
Inspector	154	21,000	110,000	17,197	45,949	41,800
Manager	2,228	27,000	202,516	24,109	85,551	83,500
Quality engineer	1,387	20,000	174,000	18,796	72,824	70,000
Master Black Belt	134	33,000	185,250	24,738	113,385	114,100

Source: *Data extracted from I. E. Allen, "Salary Survey: Seeing Green,"* Quality Progress, *December 2008, pp. 20–53.*

3.62 In New York State, savings banks are permitted to sell a form of life insurance called savings bank life insurance (SBLI). The approval process consists of underwriting, which includes a review of the application, a medical information bureau check, possible requests for additional medical information and medical exams, and a policy compilation stage, during which the policy pages are generated and sent to the bank for delivery. The ability to deliver approved policies to customers in a timely manner is critical to the profitability of this service to the bank. During a period of one month, a random sample of 27 approved policies was selected, and the following were the total processing times (stored in `Insurance`):

73 19 16 64 28 28 31 90 60 56 31 56 22 18
45 48 17 17 17 91 92 63 50 51 69 16 17

a. Compute the mean, median, first quartile, and third quartile.
b. Compute the range, interquartile range, variance, standard deviation, and coefficient of variation.
c. Construct a boxplot. Are the data skewed? If so, how?
d. What would you tell a customer who enters the bank to purchase this type of insurance policy and asks how long the approval process takes?

3.63 One of the major measures of the quality of service provided by an organization is the speed with which it responds to customer complaints. A large family-held department store selling furniture and flooring, including carpet, had undergone a major expansion in the past several years. In particular, the flooring department had expanded from 2 installation crews to an installation supervisor, a measurer, and 15 installation crews. The business objective of the company was to reduce the time between when the complaint is received and when it is resolved. During a recent year, the company got 50 complaints concerning carpet installation. The data from the 50 complaints, organized in `Furniture` represent the number of days between the receipt of a complaint and the resolution of the complaint:

54   5   35 137 31 27 152   2 123 81 74 27 11
19 126 110 110 29 61   35 94   31 26   5 12   4
165   32   29   28 29 26   25   1   14 13 13 10   5
27   4   52   30 22 36   26 20   23 33 68

a. Compute the mean, median, first quartile, and third quartile.
b. Compute the range, interquartile range, variance, standard deviation, and coefficient of variation.
c. Construct a boxplot. Are the data skewed? If so, how?
d. On the basis of the results of (a) through (c), if you had to tell the president of the company how long a customer should expect to wait to have a complaint resolved, what would you say? Explain.

3.64 A manufacturing company produces steel housings for electrical equipment. The main component part of the housing is a steel trough that is made of a 14-gauge steel coil. It is produced using a 250-ton progressive punch press with a wipe-down operation and two 90-degree forms placed in the flat steel to make the trough. The distance from one side of the form to the other is critical because of weatherproofing in outdoor applications. The company requires that the width of the trough be between 8.31 inches and 8.61 inches. Data are collected from a sample of 49 troughs and

stored in `Trough`, which contains the widths of the troughs in inches as shown below.

8.312 8.343 8.317 8.383 8.348 8.410 8.351 8.373 8.481 8.422
8.476 8.382 8.484 8.403 8.414 8.419 8.385 8.465 8.498 8.447
8.436 8.413 8.489 8.414 8.481 8.415 8.479 8.429 8.458 8.462
8.460 8.444 8.429 8.460 8.412 8.420 8.410 8.405 8.323 8.420
8.396 8.447 8.405 8.439 8.411 8.427 8.420 8.498 8.409

a. Calculate the mean, median, range, and standard deviation for the width. Interpret these measures of central tendency and variability.
b. List the five-number summary.
c. Construct a boxplot and describe its shape.
d. What can you conclude about the number of troughs that will meet the company's requirement of troughs being between 8.31 and 8.61 inches wide?

3.65 The manufacturing company in Problem 3.64 also produces electric insulators. If the insulators break when in use, a short circuit is likely to occur. To test the strength of the insulators, destructive testing is carried out to determine how much force is required to break the insulators. Force is measured by observing how many pounds must be applied to an insulator before it breaks. Data are collected from a sample of 30 insulators. The file `Force` contains the strengths as follows:

1,870 1,728 1,656 1,610 1,634 1,784 1,522 1,696 1,592 1,662
1,866 1,764 1,734 1,662 1,734 1,774 1,550 1,756 1,762 1,866
1,820 1,744 1,788 1,688 1,810 1,752 1,680 1,810 1,652 1,736

a. Calculate the mean, median, range, and standard deviation for the force needed to break the insulator.
b. Interpret the measures of central tendency and variability in (a).
c. Construct a boxplot and describe its shape.
d. What can you conclude about the strength of the insulators if the company requires a force measurement of at least 1,500 pounds before breakage?

3.66 The file `VeggieBurger` contains data on the calories and total fat (in grams per serving) for a sample of 12 veggie burgers.
Source: *Data extracted from "Healthful Burgers That Taste Good,"* Consumer Reports, *June 2008, p 8.*

a. For each variable, compute the mean, median, first quartile, and third quartile.
b. For each variable, compute the range, interquartile range, variance, standard deviation, and coefficient of variation.
c. For each variable, construct a boxplot. Are the data skewed? If so, how?
d. Compute the coefficient of correlation between calories and total fat.
e. What conclusions can you reach concerning calories and total fat?

3.67 A quality characteristic of interest for a tea-bag-filling process is the weight of the tea in the individual bags. If the bags are underfilled, two problems arise. First, customers may not be able to brew the tea to be as strong as they wish. Second, the company may be in violation of the truth-in-labeling laws. For this product, the label weight on the package indicates that, on average, there are 5.5 grams of tea in a bag. If the mean amount of tea in a bag exceeds the label weight, the company is giving away product. Getting an exact amount of tea in a bag is problematic because of variation in the temperature and humidity inside the factory, differences in the density of the tea, and the extremely fast filling operation of the machine (approximately 170 bags per minute). The file Teabags, as shown below, contains the weights, in grams, of a sample of 50 tea bags produced in one hour by a single machine:

5.65	5.44	5.42	5.40	5.53	5.34	5.54	5.45	5.52	5.41
5.57	5.40	5.53	5.54	5.55	5.62	5.56	5.46	5.44	5.51
5.47	5.40	5.47	5.61	5.53	5.32	5.67	5.29	5.49	5.55
5.77	5.57	5.42	5.58	5.58	5.50	5.32	5.50	5.53	5.58
5.61	5.45	5.44	5.25	5.56	5.63	5.50	5.57	5.67	5.36

a. Compute the mean, median, first quartile, and third quartile.
b. Compute the range, interquartile range, variance, standard deviation, and coefficient of variation.
c. Interpret the measures of central tendency and variation within the context of this problem. Why should the company producing the tea bags be concerned about the central tendency and variation?
d. Construct a boxplot. Are the data skewed? If so, how?
e. Is the company meeting the requirement set forth on the label that, on average, there are 5.5 grams of tea in a bag? If you were in charge of this process, what changes, if any, would you try to make concerning the distribution of weights in the individual bags?

3.68 The manufacturer of Boston and Vermont asphalt shingles provides its customers with a 20-year warranty on most of its products. To determine whether a shingle will last as long as the warranty period, accelerated-life testing is conducted at the manufacturing plant. Accelerated-life testing exposes a shingle to the stresses it would be subject to in a lifetime of normal use via an experiment in a laboratory setting that takes only a few minutes to conduct. In this test, a shingle is repeatedly scraped with a brush for a short period of time, and the shingle granules removed by the brushing are weighed (in grams). Shingles that experience low amounts of granule loss are expected to last longer in normal use than shingles that experience high amounts of granule loss. In this situation, a shingle should experience no more than 0.8 gram of granule loss if it is expected to last the length of the warranty period. The file Granule contains a sample of 170 measurements made on the company's

Boston shingles and 140 measurements made on Vermont shingles.
a. List the five-number summaries for the Boston shingles and for the Vermont shingles.
b. Construct side-by-side boxplots for the two brands of shingles and describe the shapes of the distributions.
c. Comment on the ability of each type of shingles to achieve a granule loss of 0.8 gram or less.

3.69 A study conducted by Zagat Survey concluded that many first-rate restaurants are located in hotels across the United States. Travelers can find quality food, service, and décor without leaving their hotels. The top-rated hotel restaurant is The French Room, located in The Adolphus Hotel in Dallas, Texas. The estimated price for dinner, including one drink and tip, at The French Room is $80. The highest price reported is $179 at Alain Ducasse, located in the Jumeirah Essex House in New York City. The file BestRest contains the top 100 hotel restaurants in the United States and the variables state, city, restaurant, hotel, cost (estimated price of dinner including one drink and tip), and rating (1 to 100, with 1 the top-rated restaurant).
Source: *Data extracted from Gary Stoller, "Top Restaurants Check into Luxury Hotels," USA Today, April 11, 2006, p. 5B.*
a. Construct the five-number summary of dinner price.
b. Construct a boxplot of dinner price and interpret the distribution of dinner prices.
c. Calculate and interpret the correlation coefficient of the rating and dinner price.

3.70 The file Protein contains calories, protein, and cholesterol of popular protein foods (fresh red meats, poultry, and fish).
Source: *U.S. Department of Agriculture.*
a. Compute the correlation coefficient between calories and protein.
b. Compute the correlation coefficient between calories and cholesterol.
c. Compute the correlation coefficient between protein and cholesterol.
d. Based on the results of (a) through (c), what conclusions can you reach concerning calories, protein, and cholesterol?

3.71 The file Cost of Living contains the overall cost index, the monthly rent for a two-bedroom apartment, the cost of a cup of coffee with service, the cost of a fast-food hamburger meal, the cost of dry-cleaning a men's blazer, the cost of toothpaste, and the cost of movie tickets in 10 different cities.
a. Compute the correlation coefficient between the overall cost index and the monthly rent for a two-bedroom apartment, the cost of a cup of coffee with service, the cost of a fast-food hamburger meal, the cost of dry-cleaning a men's blazer, the cost of toothpaste, and the cost of movie tickets. (There will be six separate correlation coefficients.)
b. What conclusions can you reach about the relationship of the overall cost index to each of these six variables?

3.72 The file `PropertyTaxes` contains the property taxes per capita for the 50 states and the District of Columbia.
a. Compute the mean, median, first quartile, and third quartile.
b. Compute the range, interquartile range, variance, standard deviation, and coefficient of variation.
c. Construct a boxplot. Are the data skewed? If so, how?
d. Based on the results of (a) through (c), what conclusions can you reach concerning property taxes per capita, in thousands of dollars, for each state and the District of Columbia?

3.73 The file `Compensation` includes the total compensation (in $) of CEOs of the large public companies in 2008.
Source: *Data extracted from D. Jones and B. Hansen, "CEO Pay Dives in a Rough 2008,"* **www.usatoday.com**, *May 1, 2009.*
a. Compute the mean, median, first quartile, and third quartile.
b. Compute the range, interquartile range, variance, standard deviation, and coefficient of variation.
c. Construct a boxplot. Are the data skewed? If so, how?
d. Based on the results of (a) through (c), what conclusions can you reach concerning the total compensation (in $millions) of CEOs?
e. Compute the correlation coefficient between compensation and the amount of bonus.
f. Compute the correlation coefficient between compensation and the change in stock price in 2008.
g. What conclusions can you reach from the results of (e) and (f)?

3.74 You are planning to study for your statistics examination with a group of classmates, one of whom you particularly want to impress. This individual has volunteered to use Microsoft Excel to get the needed summary information, tables, and charts for a data set containing several numerical and categorical variables assigned by the instructor for study purposes. This person comes over to you with the printout and exclaims, "I've got it all—the means, the medians, the standard deviations, the boxplots, the pie charts—for all our variables. The problem is, some of the output looks weird—like the boxplots for gender and for major and the pie charts for grade point index and for height. Also, I can't understand why Professor Krehbiel said we can't get the descriptive stats for some of the variables; I got them for everything! See, the mean for height is 68.23, the mean for grade point index is 2.76, the mean for gender is 1.50, the mean for major is 4.33." What is your reply?

REPORT WRITING EXERCISES

3.75 The file `DomesticBeer` contains the percentage of alcohol, number of calories per 12 ounces, and number of carbohydrates (in grams) per 12 ounces for 128 of the best-selling domestic beers in the United States.
Your task is to write a report based on a complete descriptive evaluation of each of the numerical variables—percentage of alcohol, number of calories per 12 ounces, and number of carbohydrates (in grams) per 12 ounces.

Appended to your report should be all appropriate tables, charts, and numerical descriptive measures.
Source: *Data extracted from* **www.Beer100.com**, *June 15, 2009.*

TEAM PROJECTS
The file `Bond Funds` contains information regarding nine variables from a sample of 180 mutual funds:
Fund number—Identification number for each bond fund
Type—Type of bonds comprising the bond fund (intermediate government or short-term corporate)
Assets—In millions of dollars
Fees—Sales charges (no or yes)
Expense ratio—Ratio of expenses to net assets in percentage
Return 2008—Twelve-month return in 2008
Three-year return—Annualized return, 2006–2008
Five-year return—Annualized return, 2004–2008
Risk—Risk-of-loss factor of the mutual fund (low, average, or high)

3.76 For expense ratio in percentage, three-year return, and five-year return,
a. Compute the mean, median, first quartile, and third quartile.
b. Compute the range, interquartile range, variance, standard deviation, and coefficient of variation.
c. Construct a boxplot. Are the data skewed? If so, how?
d. Based on the results of (a) through (c), what conclusions can you reach concerning these variables?

3.77 You want to compare bond funds that have fees to those that do not have fees. For each of these two groups, for the variables expense ratio in percentage, return 2008, three-year return, and five-year return,
a. Compute the mean, median, first quartile, and third quartile.
b. Compute the range, interquartile range, variance, standard deviation, and coefficient of variation.
c. Construct a boxplot. Are the data skewed? If so, how?
d. Based on the results of (a) through (c), what conclusions can you reach about differences between mutual funds that have fees and those that do not have fees?

3.78 You want to compare intermediate government to the short-term corporate bond funds. For each of these two groups, for the variables expense ratio in percentage, three-year return, and five-year return,
a. Compute the mean, median, first quartile, and third quartile.
b. Compute the range, interquartile range, variance, standard deviation, and coefficient of variation.
c. Construct a boxplot. Are the data skewed? If so, how?
d. Based on the results of (a) through (c), what conclusions can you reach about differences between intermediate government and short-term corporate bond funds?

3.79 You want to compare bond funds based on risk. For each of these three levels of risk (below average, average, above average), for the variables expense ratio in percentage, return 2008, three-year return, and five-year return,

a. Compute the mean, median, first quartile, and third quartile.

b. Compute the range, interquartile range, variance, standard deviation, and coefficient of variation.

c. Construct a boxplot. Are the data skewed? If so, how?

d. Based on the results of (a) through (c), what conclusions can you reach about differences between bond funds based on risk?

STUDENT SURVEY DATA BASE

3.80 Problem 2.117 on page 65 describes a survey of 50 undergraduate students (stored in `UndergradSurvey`). For these data, for each numerical variable,

a. Compute the mean, median, first quartile, and third quartile.

b. Compute the range, interquartile range, variance, standard deviation, and coefficient of variation.

c. Construct a boxplot. Are the data skewed? If so, how?

d. Write a report summarizing your conclusions.

3.81 Problem 2.117 on page 65 describes a survey of 50 undergraduate students (stored in `UndergradSurvey`).

a. Select a sample of 50 undergraduate students at your school and conduct a similar survey for those students.

b. For the data collected in (a), repeat (a) through (d) of Problem 3.80.

c. Compare the results of (b) to those of Problem 3.80.

3.82 Problem 2.119 on page 65 describes a survey of 40 MBA students (stored in `GradSurvey`). For these data, for each numerical variable,

a. Compute the mean, median, first quartile, and third quartile.

b. Compute the range, interquartile range, variance, standard deviation, and coefficient of variation.

c. Construct a boxplot. Are the data skewed? If so, how?

d. Write a report summarizing your conclusions.

3.83 Problem 2.119 on page 65 describes a survey of 40 MBA students (stored in `GradSurvey`).

a. Select a sample of 40 graduate students from your MBA program and conduct a similar survey for those students.

b. For the data collected in (a), repeat (a) through (d) of Problem 3.82.

c. Compare the results of (b) to those of Problem 3.82.

MANAGING THE *SPRINGVILLE HERALD*

For what variable in the Chapter 2 "Managing the *Springville Herald*" case (see page 66) are numerical descriptive measures needed?

1. For the variable you identify, compute the appropriate numerical descriptive measures and construct a boxplot.

2. For the variable you identify, identify another graphical display that might be useful and construct it. What conclusions can you reach from this other plot that cannot be made from the boxplot?

3. Summarize your findings in a report that can be included with the task force's study.

WEB CASE

Apply your knowledge about the proper use of numerical descriptive measures in this continuing Web Case from Chapter 2.

Using a Web browser, open to the Web page for the Chapter 3 Web Case (or open **EndRun.htm** if you have downloaded the Web Case files) to visit EndRun Financial Services a second time. Reexamine EndRun's supporting data and then answer the following:

1. Can descriptive measures be computed for any variables? How would such summary statistics support EndRun's

claims? How would those summary statistics affect your perception of EndRun's record?

2. Evaluate the methods EndRun used to summarize the results of its customer survey (click the **Show me the survey results** link on the page or open **ER_Survey.htm**). Is there anything you would do differently to summarize these results?

3. Note that the last question of the survey has fewer responses than the other questions. What factors may have limited the number of responses to that question?

REFERENCES

1. Kendall, M. G., A. Stuart, and J. K. Ord, *Kendall's Advanced Theory of Statistics*, *Volume 1: Distribution Theory*, 6th ed. (New York: Oxford University Press, 1994).

2. *Microsoft Excel 2007* (Redmond, WA: Microsoft Corporation, 2007).

EG3.1 MEASURES of CENTRAL TENDENCY

The Mean, Median, and Mode

In-Depth Excel Use the **AVERAGE** (for the mean), **MEDIAN**, or **MODE** functions in worksheet formulas to calculate measures of central tendency. Enter these functions in the form *FUNCTION(cell range of the data values)*. See Section EG3.2 for an example of their use.

Analysis ToolPak Use the **Descriptive Statistics** procedure to create a list that includes measures of central tendency. (Section EG3.2 fully explains this procedure.)

EG3.2 VARIATION and SHAPE

The Range, Variance, Standard Deviation, Coefficient of Variation, and Shape

In-Depth Excel Use the **VAR** (sample variance), **STDEV** (sample standard deviation), **KURT** (kurtosis), **SKEW** (skewness), **MIN** (minimum value), and **MAX** (maximum value) functions to calculate measures of variation. Enter these functions in the form *FUNCTION(cell range of the data values)*.

Use the difference between **MAX** and **MIN** to calculate the range. Use the **COUNT** function to determine the sample size and divide the sample standard deviation by the square root (**SQRT**) of the sample size to compute the standard error.

For example, to create the Figure 3.2 worksheet that presents descriptive statistics (including measures of central tendency) for the 2008 return for the intermediate government and short-term corporate bond funds (see page 99), open to the **RETURN2008 worksheet** of the **Bond Funds workbook** and:

Right-click the **RETURN2008** sheet tab and click **Insert** in the shortcut menu. In the Insert dialog box, click the **Worksheet** icon and then click **OK**. In the new worksheet:

1. Enter the row 1 and row 2 titles and column headings and the column A row labels, using Figure 3.2 as your guide.
2. Enter the formulas in the cell range **B3:B15** shown in Figure EG3.1.
3. Select cell range **B3:B15** and copy the cell range to cell **C3**. (Excel adjusts the cell ranges in all functions to **RETURN2008!B2:B91**, the cell range for the short-term corporate return 2008 values.)

Although not part of the Figure 3.2 worksheet, to add the coefficient of variation, first enter **Coefficient of variation** in cell **A16**. Then, enter the formula **=B7/B3** in cell **B16** and then copy it to cell **C16**. Finally, format cells B16 and C16 for percentage display.

	A	B
1	*Descriptive Statistics for Return 2008*	
2		Intermediate Government
3	Mean	=AVERAGE(RETURN2008!A2:A91)
4	Standard Error	=B7/SQRT(B15)
5	Median	=MEDIAN(RETURN2008!A2:A91)
6	Mode	=MODE(RETURN2008!A2:A91)
7	Standard Deviation	=STDEV(RETURN2008!A2:A91)
8	Sample Variance	=VAR(RETURN2008!A2:A91)
9	Kurtosis	=KURT(RETURN2008!A2:A91)
10	Skewness	=SKEW(RETURN2008!A2:A91)
11	Range	=B13-B12
12	Minimum	=MIN(RETURN2008!A2:A91)
13	Maximum	=MAX(RETURN2008!A2:A91)
14	Sum	=SUM(RETURN2008!A2:A91)
15	Count	=COUNT(RETURN2008!A2:A91)

FIGURE EG3.1 Column B formulas for the DESCRIPTIVE worksheet.

Analysis ToolPak Use the **Descriptive Statistics** procedure to create a list that contains measures of variation and shape along with central tendency.

For example, to create the Figure 3.2 worksheet that presents descriptive statistics for the 2008 return for the intermediate government and short-term corporate bond funds (see page 99), open to the **RETURN2008 worksheet** of the **Bond Funds workbook** and:

1. Select **Data → Data Analysis** (Excel 2007) or **Tools → Data Analysis** (Excel 2003).
2. In the Data Analysis dialog box, select **Descriptive Statistics** from the **Analysis Tools** list and then click **OK**.

In the Descriptive Statistics dialog box (shown below):

3. Enter **A1:B91** as the **Input Range**. Click **Columns** and check **Labels in first row**.
4. Click **New Worksheet Ply**, check **Summary statistics**, top of pg 130 dialog box needs to appear here after step 4 and then click **OK**.

In the new worksheet:

5. Select column C, right-click and click **Delete** in the shortcut menu (to eliminate the duplicate row labels).
6. Edit the row 1 cell entry as **Return 2008**. Enter **Intermediate Government** in cell B2 and **Short Term Corporate** in cell C2.
7. Adjust column headings and adjust cell formatting, using Figure 3.2 as a guide. (See Appendix Section C.5 for help with these adjustments.)

The procedure creates a worksheet that is similar to the **DESCRIPTIVE_ATP worksheet** of the **Descriptive workbook.** While visually identical to the **DESCRIPTIVE worksheet**, **DESCRIPTIVE_ATP** contains no formulas in its cells.

To add the coefficient of variation to this worksheet, first enter **Coefficient of variation** in cell **A16**. Then, enter the formula **=B7/B3** in cell **B16** and then copy it to cell **C16**. Finally, format cells B16 and C16 for percentage display.

Computing Z Scores

In-Depth Excel Use the **STANDARDIZE** function to compute Z scores. Enter the function in the form **STANDARDIZE***(value, mean, standard deviation),* where *value* is an X value. Open to the **TABLE_3.3 worksheet** of the **Descriptive workbook** to see an example of using the **STANDARDIZE** function to compute the Z Scores shown in Table 3.3 on page 97.

EG3.3 EXPLORING NUMERICAL DATA

Quartiles

In-Depth Excel As noted on page 102, the Excel **QUARTILE** function, entered as **QUARTILE***(cell range of data to be summarized, quartile number)*, uses rules that differ from the rules listed in Section 3.3 to compute quartiles. To compute quartiles using the Section 3.3 rules, open to the **COMPUTE worksheet** of the **QUARTILES workbook** and enter a set of data values in column A. (The worksheet contains the values for Example 3.11. Overwrite these values when you enter another set of data values.)

Quartiles results using the Section 3.3 rules are shown in the column **D** (the **Book Rules** column). The column D results rely on a series of advanced formulas in columns G through I to implement the Section 3.3 rules. Open to the **COMPUTE_FORMULAS worksheet** to examine these formulas and to see how the **IF** function selects which rule applies to the computation. (A full explanation of the other functions used in columns G through I is beyond the scope of this book.)

The Boxplot

PHStat2 Use the **Boxplot** procedure to create a boxplot. For example, to create the Figure 3.4 boxplot, open to the **DATA worksheet** of the **Bond Funds workbook**. Select **PHStat → Descriptive Statistics → Boxplot**. In the procedure's dialog box (shown below):

1. Enter **F1:F181** as the **Raw Data Cell Range** and check **First cell contains label**.
2. Click **Multiple Groups-Stacked** and enter **B1:B181** as the **Grouping Variable Cell Range**.
3. Enter a **Title**, check **Five-Number Summary**, and click **OK**.

The boxplot appears on its own chart sheet, separate from the worksheet that contains the five-number summary.

In-Depth Excel Use the **PLOT worksheet** of the **Boxplot workbook** as a template for creating a boxplot. Because Excel does not include a boxplot as one of its chart types, creating a boxplot requires the advanced and creative "misuse" of Excel charting features. Open to the **PLOT_FORMULAS worksheet** to examine this "misuse" (beyond the scope of this book to fully explain). Explore the boxplot chart to discover the 8(!) separate line graphs that are "misused" to create the boxplot image. (Use the **PLOT_DATA worksheet** in the same workbook as a template for computing a five-number summary and a boxplot in one worksheet.)

EG3.4 NUMERICAL DESCRIPTIVE MEASURES for a POPULATION

The Population Variance and Standard Deviation

In-Depth Excel Use the **VARP** and **STDEVP** functions to compute the population variance and standard deviation, respectively. Enter these functions in the form **VARP***(cell range of the population)* and **STDEVP***(cell range of the population)*.

EG3.5 THE COVARIANCE and the COEFFICIENT of CORRELATION

The Covariance

In-Depth Excel Use the **COMPUTE worksheet** of the **Covariance workbook** as a template for covariance analysis. (The worksheet contains the set of 30 values for Example 3.17. Overwrite these values when you enter the set of data values.) Follow the instructions in the worksheet for modifying the worksheet when you have less than or more than 30 values.

Open to the **COMPUTE_FORMULAS worksheet** to examine the formulas used in the worksheet. Take special note of the Calculations Area (see Figure EG3.2 below) that computes the values for $\overline{X}$ and $\overline{Y}$ and the values used to compute the covariance.

	E	F
4	**Calculations Area**	
5	XBar	=AVERAGE(A4:A33)
6	YBar	=AVERAGE(B4:B33)
7	*n* -1	=COUNT(A4:A33)-1
8	Sum	=SUM(C4:C33)
9	Covariance	=F8/F7

FIGURE EG3.2
Calculations Area for covariance.

The Coefficient of Correlation

In-Depth Excel Use the **CORREL** function to compute the coefficient of correlation. Enter this function in the form **CORREL(*cell range of the* X *values, cell range of the* Y *values*)**.

Use the **COMPUTE worksheet** of the **Correlation workbook** as a template for correlation analysis shown in Figure 3.9 on page 118. In this worksheet, the cell H10 formula **=CORREL(A4:A33,B4:B33)** computes the coefficient of correlation.

4

Basic Probability

Learning Objectives

In this chapter, you learn:

- Basic probability concepts
- Conditional probability
- Bayes' theorem to revise probabilities

USING STATISTICS

@ M&R Electronics World

As the marketing manager for M&R Electronics World, you are analyzing the survey results of an intent-to-purchase study. This study asked the heads of 1,000 households about their intentions to purchase a big-screen television (defined as 36 inches or larger) sometime during the next 12 months. As a follow-up, you plan to survey the same people 12 months later to see whether they purchased televisions. In addition, for households purchasing big-screen televisions, you would like to know whether the television they purchased was a plasma screen, whether they also purchased a digital video recorder (DVR) in the past 12 months, and whether they were satisfied with their purchase of the big-screen television.

You are expected to use the results of this survey to plan a new marketing strategy that will enhance sales and better target those households likely to purchase multiple or more expensive products. What questions can you ask in this survey? How can you express the relationships among the various intent-to-purchase responses of individual households?

In previous chapters, you learned descriptive methods to summarize categorical and numerical variables. In this chapter, you will learn about probability to answer questions such as the following:

- What is the probability that a household is planning to purchase a big-screen television in the next year?
- What is the probability that a household will actually purchase a big-screen television?
- What is the probability that a household is planning to purchase a big-screen television and actually purchases the television?
- Given that the household is planning to purchase a big-screen television, what is the probability that the purchase is made?
- Does knowledge of whether a household *plans* to purchase the television change the likelihood of predicting whether the household *will* purchase the television?
- What is the probability that a household that purchases a big-screen television will purchase a plasma-screen television?
- What is the probability that a household that purchases a big-screen television with a plasma screen will also purchase a DVR?
- What is the probability that a household that purchases a big-screen television will be satisfied with the purchase?

With answers to questions such as these, you can begin to make decisions about your marketing strategy. Should your strategy for selling more big-screen televisions target those households that have indicated an intent to purchase? Should you concentrate on selling plasma screens? Is it likely that households that purchase big-screen televisions with plasma screens can be easily persuaded to also purchase DVRs?

The principles of probability help bridge the worlds of descriptive statistics and inferential statistics. Reading this chapter will help you learn about different types of probabilities, how to compute probabilities, and how to revise probabilities in light of new information. Probability principles are the foundation for the probability distribution, the concept of mathematical expectation, and the binomial, Poisson, and hypergeometric distributions, topics that are discussed in Chapter 5.

4.1 Basic Probability Concepts

What is meant by the word *probability*? A **probability** is the numeric value representing the chance, likelihood, or possibility that a particular event will occur, such as the price of a stock increasing, a rainy day, a defective product, or the outcome five in a single toss of a die. In all these instances, the probability involved is a proportion or fraction whose value ranges between 0 and 1, inclusive. An event that has no chance of occurring (the **impossible event**) has a probability of 0. An event that is sure to occur (the **certain event**) has a probability of 1.

There are three types of probability:

- *A priori*
- Empirical
- Subjective

In *a priori* **probability**, the probability of success is based on prior knowledge of the process involved. In the simplest case, where each outcome is equally likely, the chance of occurrence of the event is defined in Equation (4.1).

PROBABILITY OF OCCURRENCE

$$\text{Probability of occurrence} = \frac{X}{T} \qquad \textbf{(4.1)}$$

where

X = number of ways in which the event occurs

T = total number of possible outcomes

Consider a standard deck of cards that has 26 red cards and 26 black cards. The probability of selecting a black card is 26/52 = 0.50 because there are X = 26 black cards and T = 52 total cards. What does this probability mean? If each card is replaced after it is selected, does it mean that 1 out of the next 2 cards selected will be black? No, because you cannot say for certain what will happen on the next several selections. However, you can say that in the long run, if this selection process is continually repeated, the proportion of black cards selected will approach 0.50. Example 4.1 shows another example of computing an *a priori* probability.

EXAMPLE 4.1	A standard six-sided die has six faces. Each face of the die contains either one, two, three, four,
Finding *A Priori* Probabilities	five, or six dots. If you roll a die, what is the probability that you will get a face with five dots?

EXAMPLE 4.1

Finding *A Priori* Probabilities

A standard six-sided die has six faces. Each face of the die contains either one, two, three, four, five, or six dots. If you roll a die, what is the probability that you will get a face with five dots?

SOLUTION Each face is equally likely to occur. Because there are six faces, the probability of getting a face with five dots is 1/6.

The preceding examples use the *a priori* probability approach because the number of ways the event occurs and the total number of possible outcomes are known from the composition of the deck of cards or the faces of the die.

In the **empirical probability** approach, the probabilities are based on observed data, not on prior knowledge of a process. Surveys are often used to generate empirical probabilities.

Examples of this type of probability are the proportion of individuals in the Using Statistics scenario who actually purchase big-screen televisions, the proportion of registered voters who prefer a certain political candidate, and the proportion of students who have part-time jobs. For example, if you take a survey of students, and 60% state that they have part-time jobs, then there is a 0.60 probability that an individual student has a part-time job.

The third approach to probability, **subjective probability**, differs from the other two approaches because subjective probability differs from person to person. For example, the development team for a new product may assign a probability of 0.6 to the chance of success for the product, while the president of the company may be less optimistic and assign a probability of 0.3. The assignment of subjective probabilities to various outcomes is usually based on a combination of an individual's past experience, personal opinion, and analysis of a particular situation. Subjective probability is especially useful in making decisions in situations in which you cannot use *a priori* probability or empirical probability.

Events and Sample Spaces

The basic elements of probability theory are the individual outcomes of a variable under study. You need the following definitions to understand probabilities.

> ### EVENT
> Each possible outcome of a variable is referred to as an **event**.
> A **simple event** is described by a single characteristic.

For example, when you toss a coin, the two possible outcomes are heads and tails. Each of these represents a simple event. When you roll a standard six-sided die in which the six faces of the die contain either one, two, three, four, five, or six dots, there are six possible simple events. An event can be any one of these simple events, a set of them, or a subset of all of them. For example, the event of an *even number of dots* consists of three simple events (i.e., two, four, or six dots).

> ### JOINT EVENT
> A **joint event** is an event that has two or more characteristics.

Getting two heads when you toss a coin twice is an example of a joint event because it consists of heads on the first toss and heads on the second toss.

> ### COMPLEMENT
> The **complement** of event A (represented by the symbol A') includes all events that are not part of A.

The complement of a head is a tail because that is the only event that is not a head. The complement of face five on a die is not getting face five. Not getting face five consists of getting face one, two, three, four, or six.

> ### SAMPLE SPACE
> The collection of all the possible events is called the **sample space**.

The sample space for tossing a coin consists of heads and tails. The sample space when rolling a die consists of one, two, three, four, five, and six dots. Example 4.2 demonstrates events and sample spaces.

EXAMPLE 4.2

Events and Sample Spaces

The Using Statistics scenario on page 133 concerns M&R Electronics World. Table 4.1 presents the results of the sample of 1,000 households in terms of purchase behavior for big-screen televisions.

TABLE 4.1

Purchase Behavior for Big-Screen Televisions

PLANNED TO PURCHASE	ACTUALLY PURCHASED		
	Yes	No	Total
Yes	200	50	250
No	100	650	750
Total	300	700	1,000

What is the sample space? Give examples of simple events and joint events.

SOLUTION The sample space consists of the 1,000 respondents. Simple events are "planned to purchase," "did not plan to purchase," "purchased," and "did not purchase." The complement of the event "planned to purchase" is "did not plan to purchase." The event "planned to purchase and actually purchased" is a joint event because in this joint event the respondent must plan to purchase the television *and* actually purchase it.

Contingency Tables

There are several ways in which you can view a particular sample space. The method used in this textbook involves using a **contingency table** (see Section 2.3) such as the one displayed in Table 4.1. You get the values in the cells of the table by subdividing the sample space of 1,000 households according to whether someone planned to purchase and actually purchased a big-screen television set. For example, 200 of the respondents planned to purchase a big-screen television set and subsequently did purchase the big-screen television set.

Simple Probability

Now you can answer some of the questions posed in the Using Statistics scenario. Because the results are based on data collected in a survey (refer to Table 4.1), you can use the empirical probability approach.

As stated previously, the most fundamental rule for probabilities is that they range in value from 0 to 1. An impossible event has a probability of 0, and an event that is certain to occur has a probability of 1.

Compute simple probabilities using the instructions in Section EG4.1.

Simple probability refers to the probability of occurrence of a simple event, $P(A)$. A simple probability in the Using Statistics scenario is the probability of planning to purchase a big-screen television. How can you determine the probability of selecting a household that planned to purchase a big-screen television? Using Equation (4.1) on page 134:

$$\text{Probability of occurrence} = \frac{X}{T}$$

$$P(\text{Planned to purchase}) = \frac{\text{Number who planned to purchase}}{\text{Total number of households}}$$

$$= \frac{250}{1,000} = 0.25$$

Thus, there is a 0.25 (or 25%) chance that a household planned to purchase a big-screen television.

Example 4.3 illustrates another application of simple probability.

EXAMPLE 4.3

Computing the Probability That the Big-Screen Television Purchased Is a Plasma Screen

TABLE 4.2

Purchase Behavior Regarding Purchasing a Plasma-Screen Television and DVR

In the Using Statistics follow-up survey, additional questions were asked of the 300 households that actually purchased big-screen televisions. Table 4.2 indicates the consumers' responses to whether the television purchased was a plasma screen and whether they also purchased a DVR in the past 12 months.

Find the probability that if a household that purchased a big-screen television is randomly selected, the television purchased is a plasma screen.

| | **PURCHASED DVR** | | |
PURCHASED PLASMA SCREEN	Yes	No	Total
Plasma screen	38	42	80
Not plasma screen	70	150	220
Total	108	192	300

SOLUTION Using the following definitions:

$$A = \text{purchased a plasma screen} \qquad B = \text{purchased a DVR}$$
$$A' = \text{did not purchase a plasma screen} \quad B' = \text{did not purchase a DVR}$$

$$P(\text{Plasma screen}) = \frac{\text{Number of plasma screen televisions}}{\text{Total number of televisions}}$$

$$= \frac{80}{300} = 0.267$$

There is a 26.7% chance that a randomly selected big-screen television purchase is a purchase of a plasma-screen television.

Joint Probability

Compute joint probabilities using the instructions in Section EG4.1.

Whereas simple or marginal probability refers to the probability of occurrence of simple events, **joint probability** refers to the probability of an occurrence involving two or more events. An example of joint probability is the probability that you will get heads on the first toss of a coin and heads on the second toss of a coin.

In Table 4.1 on page 136, the group of individuals who planned to purchase and actually purchased a big-screen television consist only of the outcomes in the single cell "yes—planned to purchase *and* yes—actually purchased." Because this group consists of 200 households, the probability of picking a household that planned to purchase *and* actually purchased a big-screen television is

$$P(\text{Planned to purchase } and \text{ actually purchased}) = \frac{\text{Planned to purchase } and \text{ actually purchased}}{\text{Total number of respondents}}$$

$$= \frac{200}{1,000} = 0.20$$

Example 4.4 also demonstrates how to determine joint probability.

EXAMPLE 4.4

Determining the Joint Probability That a Big-Screen Television Customer Purchased a Plasma-Screen Television and a DVR

In Table 4.2, the purchases are cross-classified as plasma screen or not plasma screen and whether or not the household purchased a DVR. Find the probability that a randomly selected household that purchased a big-screen television also purchased a plasma-screen television and a DVR.

SOLUTION Using Equation (4.1) on page 134,

$$P(\text{Plasma screen } and \text{ DVR}) = \frac{\text{Number that purchased a plasma screen } and \text{ a DVR}}{\text{Total number of big-screen television purchasers}}$$

$$= \frac{38}{300} = 0.127$$

Therefore, there is a 12.7% chance that a randomly selected household that purchased a big-screen television purchased a plasma-screen television and a DVR.

Marginal Probability

The **marginal probability** of an event consists of a set of joint probabilities. You can determine the marginal probability of a particular event by using the concept of joint probability just discussed. For example, if B consists of two events, B_1 and B_2, then $P(A)$, the probability of event A, consists of the joint probability of event A occurring with event B_1 and the joint probability of event A occurring with event B_2. You use Equation (4.2) to compute marginal probabilities.

MARGINAL PROBABILITY

$$P(A) = P(A \text{ and } B_1) + P(A \text{ and } B_2) + \cdots + P(A \text{ and } B_k) \qquad \textbf{(4.2)}$$

where $B_1, B_2, \ldots, B_k$ are k mutually exclusive and collectively exhaustive events, defined as follows:

Two events are **mutually exclusive** if both the events cannot occur simultaneously. A set of events is **collectively exhaustive** if one of the events must occur.

Heads and tails in a coin toss are mutually exclusive events. The result of a coin toss cannot simultaneously be a head and a tail. Heads and tails in a coin toss are also collectively exhaustive events. One of them must occur. If heads does not occur, tails must occur. If tails does not occur, heads must occur. Being male and being female are mutually exclusive and collectively exhaustive events. No person is both (the two are mutually exclusive), and everyone is one or the other (the two are collectively exhaustive).

You can use Equation (4.2) to compute the marginal probability of "planned to purchase" a big-screen television:

$$P(\text{Planned to purchase}) = P(\text{Planned to purchase } and \text{ purchased})$$
$$+ P(\text{Planned to purchase } and \text{ did not purchase})$$

$$= \frac{200}{1,000} + \frac{50}{1,000}$$

$$= \frac{250}{1,000} = 0.25$$

You get the same result if you add the number of outcomes that make up the simple event "planned to purchase."

General Addition Rule

How do you find the probability of event "*A or B*"? You need to consider the occurrence of either event A or event B or both A and B. For example, how can you determine the probability that a household planned to purchase *or* actually purchased a big-screen television? The event "planned to purchase *or* actually purchased" includes all households that planned to purchase and all households that actually purchased a big-screen television. You examine each cell of the contingency table (Table 4.1 on page 136) to determine whether it is part of this event. From Table 4.1, the cell "planned to purchase *and* did not actually purchase" is part of the event because it includes respondents who planned to purchase. The cell "did not plan to purchase *and* actually purchased" is included because it contains respondents who actually purchased. Finally, the cell "planned to purchase *and* actually purchased" has both characteristics of interest. Therefore, one way to calculate the probability of "planned to purchase *or* actually purchased" is

P(Planned to purchase *or* actually purchased) $=$ P(Planned to purchase *and* did not actually purchase) $+$ P(Did not plan to purchase *and* actually purchase) $+$ P(Planned to purchase *and* actually purchased)

$$= \frac{50}{1,000} + \frac{100}{1,000} + \frac{200}{1,000}$$

$$= \frac{350}{1,000} = 0.35$$

Often, it is easier to determine $P(A\ or\ B)$, the probability of the event $A\ or\ B$, by using the **general addition rule**, defined in Equation (4.3).

GENERAL ADDITION RULE

The probability of $A\ or\ B$ is equal to the probability of A plus the probability of B minus the probability of $A\ and\ B$.

$$P(A\ or\ B) = P(A) + P(B) - P(A\ and\ B) \qquad \textbf{(4.3)}$$

Applying Equation (4.3) to the previous example produces the following result:

P(Planned to purchase *or* actually purchased) $=$ P(Planned to purchase) $+$ P(Actually purchased) $-$ P(Planned to purchase *and* actually purchased)

$$= \frac{250}{1,000} + \frac{300}{1,000} - \frac{200}{1,000}$$

$$= \frac{350}{1,000} = 0.35$$

Apply the general addition rule using the instructions in Section EG4.1.

The general addition rule consists of taking the probability of A and adding it to the probability of B and then subtracting the probability of the joint event $A\ and\ B$ from this total because the joint event has already been included in computing both the probability of A and the probability of B. Referring to Table 4.1 on page 136, if the outcomes of the event "planned to purchase" are added to those of the event "actually purchased," the joint event "planned to purchase *and* actually purchased" has been included in each of these simple events. Therefore, because this joint event has been double-counted, you must subtract it to provide the correct result. Example 4.5 illustrates another application of the general addition rule.

EXAMPLE 4.5

Using the General Addition Rule for the Households That Purchased Big-Screen Televisions

In Example 4.3 on page 137, the purchases were cross-classified in Table 4.2 as a plasma screen or not a plasma screen and whether or not the household purchased a DVR. Find the probability that among households that purchased a big-screen television, they purchased a plasma-screen television or a DVR.

SOLUTION Using Equation (4.3),

P(Plasma screen *or* DVR) $=$ P(Plasma screen) $+$ P(DVR) $-$ P(Plasma screen *and* DVR)

$$= \frac{80}{300} + \frac{108}{300} - \frac{38}{300}$$

$$= \frac{150}{300} = 0.50$$

Therefore, of those households that purchased a big-screen television , there is a 50.0% chance that a randomly selected household purchased a plasma-screen television or a DVR.

Problems for Section 4.1

LEARNING THE BASICS

4.1 Two coins are tossed.
a. Give an example of a simple event.
b. Give an example of a joint event.
c. What is the complement of a head on the first toss?

4.2 An urn contains 12 red balls and 8 white balls. One ball is to be selected from the urn.
a. Give an example of a simple event.
b. What is the complement of a red ball?

4.3 Given the following contingency table:

	B	B'
A	10	20
A'	20	40

What is the probability of
a. event A?
b. event A'?
c. event A and B?
d. event A or B?

4.4 Given the following contingency table:

	B	B'
A	10	30
A'	25	35

What is the probability of
a. event A'?
b. event A and B?
c. event A' and B'?
d. event A' or B'?

APPLYING THE CONCEPTS

4.5 For each of the following, indicate whether the type of probability involved is an example of *a priori* probability, empirical probability, or subjective probability.
a. The next toss of a fair coin will land on heads.
b. Italy will win soccer's World Cup the next time the competition is held.
c. The sum of the faces of two dice will be seven.
d. The train taking a commuter to work will be more than 10 minutes late.

4.6 For each of the following, state whether the events created are mutually exclusive and collectively exhaustive. If they are not mutually exclusive and collectively exhaustive, either reword the categories to make them mutually exclusive and collectively exhaustive or explain why that would not be useful.
a. Registered voters in the United States were asked whether they are registered as Republicans or Democrats.
b. Each respondent was classified by the origin of the car he or she drives: American, European, Japanese, or none.
c. People were asked, "Do you currently live in (i) an apartment or (ii) a house?"
d. A product was classified as defective or not defective.

4.7 Which of the following events occur with a probability of zero? For each, state why or why not.
a. A voter in the United States is registered as a Republican and as a Democrat.
b. A voter in the United States is female and registered as a Republican.
c. An automobile is a Ford and a Toyota.
d. An automobile is a Toyota and was manufactured in the United States.

4.8 According to an Ipsos poll, the perception of unfairness in the U.S. tax code is spread fairly evenly across income groups, age groups, and education levels. In an April 2006 survey of 1,005 adults, Ipsos reported that almost 60% of all people said the code is unfair, whereas slightly more than 60% of those making more than $50,000 viewed the code as unfair ("People Cry Unfairness," *The Cincinnati Enquirer*, April 16, 2006, p. A8). Suppose that the following contingency table represents the specific breakdown of responses:

U.S. TAX CODE	INCOME LEVEL		
	Less Than $50,000	More Than $50,000	Total
Fair	225	180	405
Unfair	280	320	600
Total	505	500	1,005

a. Give an example of a simple event.
b. Give an example of a joint event.
c. What is the complement of "tax code is fair"?
d. Why is "tax code is fair *and* makes less than $50,000" a joint event?

4.9 Referring to the contingency table in Problem 4.8, if a respondent is selected at random, what is the probability that he or she
a. thinks the tax code is unfair?
b. thinks the tax code is unfair *and* makes less than $50,000?
c. thinks the tax code is unfair *or* makes less than $50,000?
d. Explain the difference in the results in (b) and (c).

4.10 Do people of different age groups differ in their response to e-mail messages? A survey by the Center for the Digital Future of the University of Southern California (data extracted from A. Mindlin, "Older E-mail Users Favor Fast Replies," *The New York Times*, July 14, 2008, p. B3) reported that 70.7% of users over 70 years of age believe that e-mail messages should be answered quickly, as compared to 53.6% of users 12 to 50 years old. Suppose that the survey was based on 1,000 users over 70 years of age and 1,000 users 12 to 50 years old. The following table summarizes the results:

ANSWERS QUICKLY	AGE OF RESPONDENTS		
	12–50	Over 70	Total
Yes	536	707	1,243
No	464	293	757
Total	1,000	1,000	2,000

a. Give an example of a simple event.
b. Give an example of a joint event.
c. What is the complement of a respondent who answers quickly?
d. Why is a respondent who answers quickly and is over 70 years old a joint event?

4.11 Referring to the contingency table in Problem 4.10, if a respondent is selected at random, what is the probability that
a. he or she answers quickly?
b. is over 70 years old?
c. he or she answers quickly *or* is over 70 years old?
d. Explain the difference in the results in (b) and (c).

SELF Test **4.12** According to a Gallup Poll, the extent to which employees are engaged with their workplace varies from country to country. Gallup reports that the percentage of U.S. workers engaged with their workplace is more than twice as high as the percentage of German workers. The study also shows that having more engaged workers leads to increased innovation, productivity, and profitability, as well as reduced employee turnover. The results of the poll are summarized in the following table:

ENGAGEMENT	COUNTRY		
	United States	Germany	Total
Engaged	550	246	796
Not engaged	1,345	1,649	2,994
Total	1,895	1,895	3,790

Source: *Data extracted from M. Nink, "Employee Disengagement Plagues Germany,"* Gallup Management Journal, **gmj.gallup.com**, *April 9, 2009.*

If an employee is selected at random, what is the probability that he or she
a. is engaged with his or her workplace?
b. is a U.S. worker?
c. is engaged with his or her workplace *or* is a U.S. worker?
d. Explain the difference in the results in (b) and (c).

4.13 Where people turn for news is different for various age groups. A study conducted on this issue (data extracted from P. Johnson, "Young People Turn to the Web for News," *USA Today*, March 23, 2006, p. 9D) was based on 200 respondents who were between ages 36 and 50 and 200 respondents who were over age 50. Of the 200 respondents who were between ages 36 and 50, 82 got their news primarily from newspapers. Of the 200 respondents who were over age 50, 104 got their news primarily from newspapers. Construct a contingency table to evaluate the probabilities. If a respondent is selected at random, what is the probability that he or she
a. got news primarily from newspapers?
b. got news primarily from newspapers *and* is over 50 years old?
c. got news primarily from newspapers *or* is over 50 years old?
d. Explain the difference in the results in (b) and (c).

4.14 A sample of 500 respondents in a large metropolitan area was selected to study consumer behavior. Among the questions asked was "Do you enjoy shopping for clothing?" Of 240 males, 136 answered yes. Of 260 females, 224 answered yes. Construct a contingency table to evaluate the probabilities. What is the probability that a respondent chosen at random
a. enjoys shopping for clothing?
b. is a female *and* enjoys shopping for clothing?
c. is a female *or* enjoys shopping for clothing?
d. is a male *or* a female?

4.15 Each year, ratings are compiled concerning the performance of new cars during the first 90 days of use. Suppose that the cars have been categorized according to whether a car needs warranty-related repair (yes or no) and the country in which the company manufacturing a car is based (United States or not United States). Based on the data collected, the probability that the new car needs a warranty repair is 0.04, the probability that the car was manufactured by a U.S.-based company is 0.60, and the probability that the new car needs a warranty repair *and* was manufactured by a U.S.-based company is 0.025. Construct a contingency table to evaluate the probabilities of a warranty-related repair. What is the probability that a new car selected at random
a. needs a warranty repair?
b. needs a warranty repair *and* was manufactured by a U.S.-based company?
c. needs a warranty repair *or* was manufactured by a U.S.-based company?
d. needs a warranty repair *or* was not manufactured by a U.S.-based company?

4.2 Conditional Probability

Each example in Section 4.1 involves finding the probability of an event when sampling from the entire sample space. How do you determine the probability of an event if you know certain information about the events involved?

Computing Conditional Probabilities

Conditional probability refers to the probability of event A, given information about the occurrence of another event, B.

> ### CONDITIONAL PROBABILITY
>
> The probability of A given B is equal to the probability of A *and* B divided by the probability of B.
>
> $$P(A \mid B) = \frac{P(A \text{ and } B)}{P(B)} \tag{4.4a}$$
>
> The probability of B given A is equal to the probability of A *and* B divided by the probability of A.
>
> $$P(B \mid A) = \frac{P(A \text{ and } B)}{P(A)} \tag{4.4b}$$
>
> where
>
> $$P(A \text{ and } B) = \text{joint probability of } A \text{ and } B$$
>
> $$P(A) = \text{marginal probability of } A$$
>
> $$P(B) = \text{marginal probability of } B$$

Referring to the Using Statistics scenario involving the purchase of big-screen televisions, suppose you were told that a household planned to purchase a big-screen television. Now, what is the probability that the household actually purchased the television? In this example, the objective is to find P(Actually purchased | Planned to purchase). Here you are given the information that the household planned to purchase the big-screen television. Therefore, the sample space does not consist of all 1,000 households in the survey. It consists of only those households that planned to purchase the big-screen television. Of 250 such households, 200 actually purchased the big-screen television. Therefore, based on Table 4.1 on page 136, the probability that a household actually purchased the big-screen television given that he or she planned to purchase is

$$P(\text{Actually purchased} \mid \text{Planned to purchase}) = \frac{\text{Planned to purchase } and \text{ actually purchased}}{\text{Planned to purchase}}$$

$$= \frac{200}{250} = 0.80$$

You can also use Equation (4.4b) to compute this result:

$$P(B \mid A) = \frac{P(A \text{ and } B)}{P(A)}$$

where

A = planned to purchase

B = actually purchased

then

$$P(\text{Actually purchased} \mid \text{Planned to purchase}) = \frac{200/1{,}000}{250/1{,}000}$$

$$= \frac{200}{250} = 0.80$$

Example 4.6 further illustrates conditional probability.

EXAMPLE 4.6

Finding the Conditional Probability of Purchasing a DVR

Table 4.2 on page 137 is a contingency table for whether the household purchased a plasma-screen television and whether the household purchased a DVR. If a household purchased a plasma-screen television, what is the probability that it also purchased a DVR?

SOLUTION Because you know that the household purchased a plasma-screen television, the sample space is reduced to 80 households. Of these 80 households, 38 also purchased a DVR. Therefore, the probability that a household purchased a DVR, given that the household purchased a plasma-screen television, is

$$P(\text{Purchased DVR} \mid \text{Purchased plasma screen}) = \frac{\text{Number purchasing plasma screen \textit{and} DVR}}{\text{Number purchasing plasma screen}}$$

$$= \frac{38}{80} = 0.475$$

If you use Equation (4.4b) on page 142:

$$A = \text{Purchased plasma-screen television} \quad B = \text{Purchased DVR}$$

then

$$P(B \mid A) = \frac{P(A \text{ and } B)}{P(A)} = \frac{38/300}{80/300} = 0.475$$

Therefore, given that the household purchased a plasma-screen television, there is a 47.5% chance that the household also purchased a DVR. You can compare this conditional probability to the marginal probability of purchasing a DVR, which is $108/300 = 0.36$, or 36%. These results tell you that households that purchased plasma-screen televisions are more likely to purchase DVRs than are households that purchased big-screen televisions that are not plasma-screen televisions.

Decision Trees

In Table 4.1 on page 136, households are classified according to whether they planned to purchase and whether they actually purchased big-screen televisions. A **decision tree** is an alternative to the contingency table. Figure 4.1 represents the decision tree for this example.

FIGURE 4.1

Decision tree for M&R Electronics World example

$P(A) = \frac{250}{1{,}000}$ Actually Purchased $P(A \text{ and } B) = \frac{200}{1{,}000}$

Planned to Purchase

Entire Set of Households

Did Not Actually Purchase $P(A \text{ and } B') = \frac{50}{1{,}000}$

Did Not Plan to Purchase

Actually Purchased $P(A' \text{ and } B) = \frac{100}{1{,}000}$

$P(A') = \frac{750}{1{,}000}$

Did Not Actually Purchase $P(A' \text{ and } B') = \frac{650}{1{,}000}$

In Figure 4.1, beginning at the left with the entire set of households, there are two "branches" for whether or not the household planned to purchase a big-screen television. Each of these branches has two subbranches, corresponding to whether the household actually purchased or did not actually purchase the big-screen television. The probabilities at the end of the initial branches represent the marginal probabilities of A and A'. The probabilities at the end of each of the four subbranches represent the joint probability for each combination of events A and B. You compute the conditional probability by dividing the joint probability by the appropriate marginal probability.

For example, to compute the probability that the household actually purchased, given that the household planned to purchase the big-screen television, you take P(Planned to purchase *and* actually purchased) and divide by P(Planned to purchase). From Figure 4.1,

$$P(\text{Actually purchased /Planned to purchase}) = \frac{200/1{,}000}{250/1{,}000}$$

$$= \frac{200}{250} = 0.80$$

Example 4.7 illustrates how to construct a decision tree.

EXAMPLE 4.7

Forming the Decision Tree for the Households That Purchased Big-Screen Televisions

Using the cross-classified data in Table 4.2 on page 137, construct the decision tree. Use the decision tree to find the probability that a household purchased a DVR, given that the household purchased a plasma-screen television.

SOLUTION The decision tree for purchased a DVR and a plasma-screen television is displayed in Figure 4.2. Using Equation (4.4b) on page 142 and the following definitions,

$$A = \text{Purchased plasma-screen television}$$
$$B = \text{Purchased DVR}$$

$$P(B\,|\,A) = \frac{P(A \text{ and } B)}{P(A)} = \frac{38/300}{80/300} = 0.475$$

FIGURE 4.2

Decision tree for purchased a DVR and a plasma-screen television

Independence

In the example concerning the purchase of big-screen televisions, the conditional probability is $200/250 = 0.80$ that the selected household actually purchased the big-screen television, given that the household planned to purchase. The simple probability of selecting a household that actually purchased is $300/1{,}000 = 0.30$. This result shows that the prior knowledge that the household planned to purchase affected the probability that the household actually purchased the television. In other words, the outcome of one event is *dependent* on the outcome of a second event.

When the outcome of one event does *not* affect the probability of occurrence of another event, the events are said to be independent. **Independence** can be determined by using Equation (4.5).

INDEPENDENCE

Two events, A and B, are independent if and only if

$$P(A \mid B) = P(A) \qquad (4.5)$$

where

$$P(A \mid B) = \text{conditional probability of } A \text{ given } B$$
$$P(A) = \text{marginal probability of } A$$

Example 4.8 demonstrates the use of Equation (4.5).

EXAMPLE 4.8

Determining Independence

In the follow-up survey of the 300 households that actually purchased big-screen televisions, the households were asked if they were satisfied with their purchases. Table 4.3 cross-classifies the responses to the satisfaction question with the responses to whether the television was a plasma-screen television.

TABLE 4.3

Satisfaction with Purchase of Big-Screen Televisions

	SATISFIED WITH PURCHASE?		
TYPE OF TELEVISION	**Yes**	**No**	**Total**
Plasma screen	64	16	80
Not plasma screen	176	44	220
Total	240	60	300

Determine whether being satisfied with the purchase and type of television purchased are independent.

SOLUTION For these data,

$$P(\text{Satisfied} \mid \text{Plasma screen}) = \frac{64/300}{80/300} = \frac{64}{80} = 0.80$$

which is equal to

$$P(\text{Satisfied}) = \frac{240}{300} = 0.80$$

Thus, being satisfied with the purchase and type of television purchased are independent. Knowledge of one event does not affect the probability of the other event.

Multiplication Rules

The **general multiplication rule** is derived using Equation (4.4a) on page 142:

$$P(A \mid B) = \frac{P(A \text{ and } B)}{P(B)}$$

and solving for the joint probability $P(A \text{ and } B)$.

GENERAL MULTIPLICATION RULE

The probability of A and B is equal to the probability of A given B times the probability of B.

$$P(A \text{ and } B) = P(A \mid B)P(B) \qquad (4.6)$$

Example 4.9 demonstrates the use of the general multiplication rule.

EXAMPLE 4.9

Using the General Multiplication Rule

Consider the 80 households that purchased plasma-screen televisions. In Table 4.3 on page 145 you see that 64 households are satisfied with their purchase, and 16 households are dissatisfied. Suppose 2 households are randomly selected from the 80 households. Find the probability that both households are satisfied with their purchase.

SOLUTION Here you can use the multiplication rule in the following way. If

$$A = \text{second household selected is satisfied}$$
$$B = \text{first household selected is satisfied}$$

then, using Equation (4.6),

$$P(A \text{ and } B) = P(A \mid B)P(B)$$

The probability that the first household is satisfied with the purchase is 64/80. However, the probability that the second household is also satisfied with the purchase depends on the result of the first selection. If the first household is not returned to the sample after the satisfaction level is determined (i.e., sampling without replacement), the number of households remaining is 79. If the first household is satisfied, the probability that the second is also satisfied is 63/79 because 63 satisfied households remain in the sample. Therefore,

$$P(A \text{ and } B) = \left(\frac{63}{79}\right)\left(\frac{64}{80}\right) = 0.6380$$

There is a 63.80% chance that both of the households sampled will be satisfied with their purchase.

The **multiplication rule for independent events** is derived by substituting $P(A)$ for $P(A \mid B)$ in Equation (4.6).

MULTIPLICATION RULE FOR INDEPENDENT EVENTS

If A and B are independent, the probability of A and B is equal to the probability of A times the probability of B.

$$P(A \text{ and } B) = P(A)P(B) \tag{4.7}$$

If this rule holds for two events, A and B, then A and B are independent. Therefore, there are two ways to determine independence:

1. Events A and B are independent if, and only if, $P(A \mid B) = P(A)$.
2. Events A and B are independent if, and only if, $P(A \text{ and } B) = P(A)P(B)$.

Marginal Probability Using the General Multiplication Rule

In Section 4.1, marginal probability was defined using Equation (4.2) on page 138. You can state the equation for marginal probability by using the general multiplication rule. If

$$P(A) = P(A \text{ and } B_1) + P(A \text{ and } B_2) + \cdots + P(A \text{ and } B_k)$$

then, using the general multiplication rule, Equation (4.8) defines the marginal probability.

MARGINAL PROBABILITY USING THE GENERAL MULTIPLICATION RULE

$$P(A) = P(A \mid B_1)P(B_1) + P(A \mid B_2)P(B_2) + \cdots + P(A \mid B_k)P(B_k) \tag{4.8}$$

where $B_1, B_2, \ldots, B_k$ are k mutually exclusive and collectively exhaustive events.

To illustrate Equation (4.8), refer to Table 4.1 on page 136. Let

$$P(A) = \text{probability of "planned to purchase"}$$
$$P(B_1) = \text{probability of "actually purchased"}$$
$$P(B_2) = \text{probability of "did not actually purchase"}$$

Then, using Equation (4.8), the probability of planned to purchase is

$$P(A) = P(A \mid B_1)P(B_1) + P(A \mid B_2)P(B_2)$$
$$= \left(\frac{200}{300}\right)\left(\frac{300}{1{,}000}\right) + \left(\frac{50}{700}\right)\left(\frac{700}{1{,}000}\right)$$
$$= \frac{200}{1{,}000} + \frac{50}{1{,}000} = \frac{250}{1{,}000} = 0.25$$

Problems for Section 4.2

LEARNING THE BASICS

4.16 Given the following contingency table:

	B	B'
A	10	20
A'	20	40

What is the probability of
a. $A \mid B$?
b. $A \mid B'$?
c. $A' \mid B'$?
d. Are events A and B independent?

4.17 Given the following contingency table:

	B	B'
A	10	30
A'	25	35

What is the probability of
a. $A \mid B$?
b. $A' \mid B'$?
c. $A \mid B'$?
d. Are events A and B independent?

4.18 If $P(A \text{ and } B) = 0.4$ and $P(B) = 0.8$, find $P(A \mid B)$.

4.19 If $P(A) = 0.7, P(B) = 0.6$, and A and B are independent, find $P(A \text{ and } B)$.

4.20 If $P(A) = 0.3, P(B) = 0.4$, and $P(A \text{ and } B) = 0.2$, are A and B independent?

APPLYING THE CONCEPTS

4.21 Where people turn for news is different for various age groups. Suppose that a study conducted on this issue (data extracted from P. Johnson, "Young People Turn to the Web for News," *USA Today*, March 23, 2006, p. 9D) was based on 200 respondents who were between ages 36 and 50 and

200 respondents who were over age 50. Of the 200 respondents who were between ages 36 and 50, 82 got their news primarily from newspapers. Of the 200 respondents who were over age 50, 104 got their news primarily from newspapers.
a. Given that a respondent is over age 50, what is the probability that he or she gets news primarily from newspapers?
b. Given that a respondent gets news primarily from newspapers, what is the probability that he or she is over age 50?
c. Explain the difference in the results in (a) and (b).
d. Are the two events whether the respondent is over age 50 and whether he or she gets news primarily from newspapers independent?

4.22 Do people of different age groups differ in their response to e-mail messages? A survey by the Center for the Digital Future of the University of Southern California (data extracted from A. Mindlin, "Older E-mail Users Favor Fast Replies," *The New York Times*, July 14, 2008, p. B3) reported that 70.7% of users over 70 years of age believe that e-mail messages should be answered quickly, as compared to 53.6% of users 12 to 50 years old. Suppose that the survey was based on 1,000 users over 70 years of age and 1,000 users 12 to 50 years old. The following table summarizes the results:

	AGE OF RESPONDENTS		
ANSWERS QUICKLY	12–50	Over 70	Total
Yes	536	707	1,243
No	464	293	757
Total	1,000	1,000	2,000

a. Suppose you know that the respondent is between 12 and 50 years old. What is the probability that he or she answers quickly?
b. Suppose you know that the respondent is over 70 years old. What is the probability that he or she answers quickly?
c. Are the two events, answers quickly and age, independent? Explain.

4.23 According to an Ipsos poll, the perception of unfairness in the U.S. tax code is spread fairly evenly across income groups, age groups, and education levels. In an April 2006 survey of 1,005 adults, Ipsos reported that almost 60% of all people said the code is unfair, whereas slightly more than 60% of those making more than $50,000 viewed the code as unfair ("People Cry Unfairness," *The Cincinnati Enquirer*, April 16, 2006, p. A8). Suppose that the following contingency table represents the specific breakdown of responses:

	INCOME LEVEL		
	---	---	---
TAX CODE	**Less Than $50,000**	**More Than $50,000**	**Total**
Fair	225	180	405
Unfair	280	320	600
Total	505	500	1,005

a. Given that a respondent earns less than $50,000, what is the probability that he or she said that the tax code is fair?
b. Given that a respondent earns more than $50,000, what is the probability that he or she said that the tax code is fair?
c. Is income level independent of attitude about whether the tax code is fair? Explain.

✓ SELF Test **4.24** According to a Gallup Poll, the extent to which employees are engaged with their workplace varies from country to country. Gallup reports that the percentage of U.S. workers engaged with their workplace is more than twice as high as the percentage of German workers. The study also shows that having more engaged workers leads to increased innovation, productivity, and profitability, as well as reduced employee turnover. The results of the poll are summarized in the following table:

	COUNTRY		
	---	---	---
ENGAGEMENT	**United States**	**Germany**	**Total**
Engaged	550	246	796
Not Engaged	1,345	1,649	2,994
Total	1,895	1,895	3,790

Source: *Data extracted from M. Nink, "Employee Disengagement Plagues Germany,"* Gallup Management Journal, **gmj.gallup.com**, *April 9, 2009.*

a. Given that a worker is from the United States, what is the probability that the worker is engaged?
b. Given that a worker is from the United States, what is the probability that the worker is not engaged?
c. Given that a worker is from Germany, what is the probability that the worker is engaged?
d. Given that a worker is from Germany, what is the probability that the worker is not engaged?

4.25 A sample of 500 respondents in a large metropolitan area was selected to study consumer behavior, with the following results:

ENJOYS SHOPPING FOR CLOTHING	GENDER		
	---	---	---
	Male	**Female**	**Total**
Yes	136	224	360
No	104	36	140
Total	240	260	500

a. Suppose the respondent chosen is a female. What is the probability that she does not enjoy shopping for clothing?
b. Suppose the respondent chosen enjoys shopping for clothing. What is the probability that the individual is a male?
c. Are enjoying shopping for clothing and the gender of the individual independent? Explain.

4.26 Each year, ratings are compiled concerning the performance of new cars during the first 90 days of use. Suppose that the cars have been categorized according to whether a car needs warranty-related repair (yes or no) and the country in which the company manufacturing a car is based (United States or not United States). Based on the data collected, the probability that the new car needs a warranty repair is 0.04, the probability that the car is manufactured by a U.S.-based company is 0.60, and the probability that the new car needs a warranty repair *and* was manufactured by a U.S.-based company is 0.025.
a. Suppose you know that a company based in the United States manufactured a particular car. What is the probability that the car needs warranty repair?
b. Suppose you know that a company based in the United States did not manufacture a particular car. What is the probability that the car needs warranty repair?
c. Are need for warranty repair and location of the company manufacturing the car independent?

4.27 In 37 of the 59 years from 1950 through 2008, the S&P 500 finished higher after the first 5 days of trading. In 32 of those 37 years, the S&P 500 finished higher for the year. Is a good first week a good omen for the upcoming year? The following table gives the first-week and annual performance over this 59-year period:

	S&P 500'S ANNUAL PERFORMANCE	
	---	---
FIRST WEEK	**Higher**	**Lower**
Higher	32	5
Lower	11	11

a. If a year is selected at random, what is the probability that the S&P 500 finished higher for the year?
b. Given that the S&P 500 finished higher after the first 5 days of trading, what is the probability that it finished higher for the year?

c. Are the two events "first-week performance" and "annual performance" independent? Explain.

d. Look up the performance after the first 5 days of 2009 and the 2009 annual performance of the S&P 500 at **finance.yahoo.com**. Comment on the results.

4.28 A standard deck of cards is being used to play a game. There are four suits (hearts, diamonds, clubs, and spades), each having 13 faces (ace, 2, 3, 4, 5, 6, 7, 8, 9, 10, jack, queen, and king), making a total of 52 cards. This complete deck is thoroughly mixed, and you will receive the first 2 cards from the deck, without replacement (the first card is not returned to the deck after it is selected).

a. What is the probability that both cards are queens?

b. What is the probability that the first card is a 10 and the second card is a 5 or 6?

c. If you were sampling with replacement (the first card is returned to the deck after it is selected), what would be the answer in (a)?

d. In the game of blackjack, the picture cards (jack, queen, king) count as 10 points, and the ace counts as either 1 or 11 points. All other cards are counted at their face value. Blackjack is achieved if 2 cards total 21 points. What is the probability of getting blackjack in this problem?

4.29 A box of nine gloves contains two left-handed gloves and seven right-handed gloves.

a. If two gloves are randomly selected from the box, without replacement (the first glove is not returned to the box after it is selected), what is the probability that both gloves selected will be right-handed?

b. If two gloves are randomly selected from the box, without replacement (the first glove is not returned to the box after it is selected), what is the probability that there will be one right-handed glove and one left-handed glove selected?

c. If three gloves are selected, with replacement (the gloves are returned to the box after they are selected), what is the probability that all three will be left-handed?

d. If you were sampling with replacement (the first glove is returned to the box after it is selected), what would be the answers to (a) and (b)?

4.3 Bayes' Theorem

Bayes' theorem is used to revise previously calculated probabilities based on new information. Developed by Thomas Bayes in the eighteenth century (see references 1, 2, and 5), Bayes' theorem is an extension of what you previously learned about conditional probability.

Apply Bayes' theorem using the instructions in Section EG4.3.

You can apply Bayes' theorem to the situation in which M&R Electronics World is considering marketing a new model of television. In the past, 40% of the new model televisions have been successful, and 60% have been unsuccessful. Before introducing the new model television, the marketing research department conducts an extensive study and releases a report, either favorable or unfavorable. In the past, 80% of the successful new model televisions had received favorable market research reports, and 30% of the unsuccessful new model televisions had received favorable reports. For the new model of television under consideration, the marketing research department has issued a favorable report. What is the probability that the television will be successful?

Bayes' theorem is developed from the definition of conditional probability. To find the conditional probability of B given A, consider Equation (4.4b) (originally presented on page 142 and shown below):

$$P(B|A) = \frac{P(A \text{ and } B)}{P(A)} = \frac{P(A|B)P(B)}{P(A)}$$

Bayes' theorem is derived by substituting Equation (4.8) on page 146 for $P(A)$ in the denominator of Equation (4.4b).

BAYES' THEOREM

$$P(B_i|A) = \frac{P(A|B_i)P(B_i)}{P(A|B_1)P(B_1) + P(A|B_2)P(B_2) + \cdots + P(A|B_k)P(B_k)} \quad (4.9)$$

where B_i is the ith event out of k mutually exclusive and collectively exhaustive events.

To use Equation (4.9) for the television-marketing example, let

$$\text{event } S = \text{successful television} \qquad \text{event } F = \text{favorable report}$$
$$\text{event } S' = \text{unsuccessful television} \quad \text{event } F' = \text{unfavorable report}$$

and

$$P(S) = 0.40 \quad P(F \mid S) = 0.80$$
$$P(S') = 0.60 \quad P(F \mid S') = 0.30$$

Then, using Equation (4.9),

$$P(S \mid F) = \frac{P(F \mid S)P(S)}{P(F \mid S)P(S) + P(F \mid S')P(S')}$$

$$= \frac{(0.80)(0.40)}{(0.80)(0.40) + (0.30)(0.60)}$$

$$= \frac{0.32}{0.32 + 0.18} = \frac{0.32}{0.50}$$

$$= 0.64$$

The probability of a successful television, given that a favorable report was received, is 0.64. Thus, the probability of an unsuccessful television, given that a favorable report was received, is $1 - 0.64 = 0.36$. Table 4.4 summarizes the computation of the probabilities, and Figure 4.3 presents the decision tree.

TABLE 4.4

Bayes' Theorem Calculations for the Television-Marketing Example

Event S_i	Prior Probability $P(S_i)$	Conditional Probability $P(F \mid S_i)$	Joint Probability $P(F \mid S_i)P(S_i)$	Revised Probability $P(S_i \mid F)$
S = successful television	0.40	0.80	0.32	$P(S \mid F) = 0.32/0.50$ $= 0.64$
S' = unsuccessful television	0.60	0.30	$\dfrac{0.18}{0.50}$	$P(S' \mid F) = 0.18/0.50$ $= 0.36$

FIGURE 4.3

Decision tree for marketing a new television

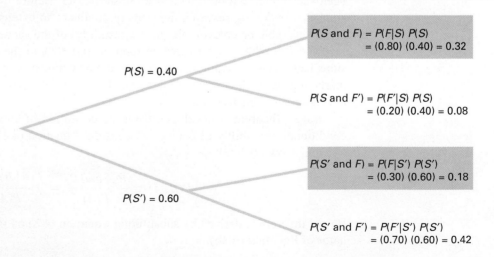

Example 4.10 applies Bayes' theorem to a medical diagnosis problem.

EXAMPLE 4.10

Using Bayes' Theorem in a Medical Diagnosis Problem

The probability that a person has a certain disease is 0.03. Medical diagnostic tests are available to determine whether the person actually has the disease. If the disease is actually present, the probability that the medical diagnostic test will give a positive result (indicating that the disease is present) is 0.90. If the disease is not actually present, the probability of a positive test result (indicating that the disease is present) is 0.02. Suppose that the medical diagnostic test has given a positive result (indicating that the disease is present). What is the probability that the disease is actually present? What is the probability of a positive test result?

SOLUTION Let

$$\text{event } D = \text{has disease} \qquad \text{event } T = \text{test is positive}$$
$$\text{event } D' = \text{does not have disease} \quad \text{event } T' = \text{test is negative}$$

and

$$P(D) = 0.03 \quad P(T|D) = 0.90$$
$$P(D') = 0.97 \quad P(T|D') = 0.02$$

Using Equation (4.9) on page 149,

$$P(D\,|\,T) = \frac{P(T\,|\,D)P(D)}{P(T\,|\,D)P(D) + P(T\,|\,D')P(D')}$$

$$= \frac{(0.90)(0.03)}{(0.90)(0.03) + (0.02)(0.97)}$$

$$= \frac{0.0270}{0.0270 + 0.0194} = \frac{0.0270}{0.0464}$$

$$= 0.582$$

The probability that the disease is actually present, given that a positive result has occurred (indicating that the disease is present), is 0.582. Table 4.5 summarizes the computation of the probabilities, and Figure 4.4 presents the decision tree.

TABLE 4.5

Bayes' Theorem Calculations for the Medical Diagnosis Problem

Event D_i	Prior Probability $P(D_i)$	Conditional Probability $P(T\,|\,D_i)$	Joint Probability $P(T\,|\,D_i)P(D_i)$	Revised Probability $P(D_i\,|\,T)$
D = has disease	0.03	0.90	0.0270	$P(D\,|\,T) = 0.0270/0.0464$ = 0.582
D' = does not have disease	0.97	0.02	$\dfrac{0.0194}{0.0464}$	$P(D'\,|\,T) = 0.0194/0.0464$ = 0.418

FIGURE 4.4

Decision tree for the medical diagnosis problem

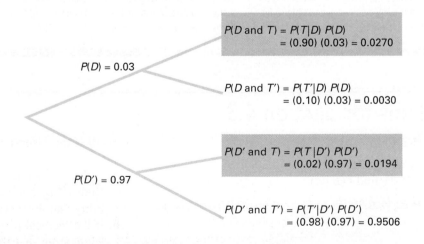

$P(D \text{ and } T) = P(T|D)\ P(D)$
$= (0.90)\ (0.03) = 0.0270$

$P(D) = 0.03$

$P(D \text{ and } T') = P(T'|D)\ P(D)$
$= (0.10)\ (0.03) = 0.0030$

$P(D' \text{ and } T) = P(T\,|D')\ P(D')$
$= (0.02)\ (0.97) = 0.0194$

$P(D') = 0.97$

$P(D' \text{ and } T') = P(T'|D')\ P(D')$
$= (0.98)\ (0.97) = 0.9506$

The denominator in Bayes' theorem represents $P(T)$, the probability of a positive test result, which in this case is 0.0464, or 4.64%.

THINK ABOUT THIS   Divine Providence and Spam

Would you ever guess that the essays *Divine Benevolence: Or, An Attempt to Prove That the Principal End of the Divine Providence and Government Is the Happiness of His Creatures* and *An Essay Towards Solving a Problem in the Doctrine of Chances* were written by the same person? Probably not, and in doing so you illustrate a modern-day application of Bayesian statistics: spam, or junk mail, filters.

In not guessing correctly, you probably looked at the words in the titles of the essays and concluded that they were talking about two different things. An implicit rule you used was that word frequencies vary by subject matter. A statistics essay would very likely contain the word *statistics* as well as words such as *chance, problem,* and *solving.* An eighteenth-century essay about theology and religion would be more likely to contain the uppercase forms of *Divine* and *Providence.*

Likewise, there are words you would guess to be very unlikely to appear in either book, such as technical terms from finance and words that are most likely to appear in both—common words such as *a, and,* and *the.* That words would either be likely or unlikely suggests an application of probability theory. Of course, likely and unlikely are fuzzy concepts, and we might occasionally misclassify an essay if we kept things too simple, such as relying solely on the occurrence of the words *Divine* and *Providence.*

For example, a profile of the late Harris Milstead, better known as *Divine,* the star of *Hairspray* and other films, visiting Providence (Rhode Island), would most certainly not be an essay about theology. But if we widened the number of words we examined and found such words as *movie* or the name John Waters (Divine's director in many films), we probably would quickly realize the essay had something to do with twentieth-century cinema and little to do with theology and religion.

We can use a similar process to try to classify a new e-mail message in your in-box as either spam or a legitimate message (called "ham," in this context). We would first need to add to your e-mail program a "spam filter" that has the ability to track word frequencies associated with spam and ham messages as you identify them on a day-to-day basis. This would allow the filter to constantly update the prior probabilities necessary to use Bayes' theorem. With these probabilities, the filter can ask, "What is the probability that an e-mail is spam, given the presence of a certain word?"

Applying the terms of Equation (4.9) on page 149, such a Bayesian spam filter would multiply the probability of finding the word in a spam e-mail, $P(A|B)$, by the probability that the e-mail is spam, $P(B)$, and then divide by the probability of finding the word in an e-mail, the denominator in Equation (4.9). Bayesian spam filters also use shortcuts by focusing on a small set of words that have a high probability of being found in a spam message as well as on a small set of other words that have a low probability of being found in a spam message.

As spammers (people who send junk e-mail) learned of such new filters, they tried to outfox them. Having learned that Bayesian filters might be assigning a high $P(A|B)$ value to words commonly found in spam, such as Viagra, spammers thought they could fool the filter by misspelling the word as Vi@gr@ or V1agra. What they overlooked was that the misspelled variants were even *more likely* to be found in a spam message than the original word. Thus, the misspelled variants made the job of spotting spam *easier* for the Bayesian filters.

Other spammers tried to fool the filters by adding "good" words, words that would have a low probability of being found in a spam message, or "rare" words, words not frequently encountered in any message. But these spammers overlooked the fact that the conditional probabilities are constantly updated and that words once considered "good" would be soon discarded from the good list by the filter as their $P(A|B)$ value increased. Likewise, as "rare" words grew more common in spam and yet stayed rare in ham, such words acted like the misspelled variants that others had tried earlier.

Even then, and perhaps after reading about Bayesian statistics, spammers thought that they could "break" Bayesian filters by inserting random words in their messages. Those random words would affect the filter by causing it to see many words whose $P(A|B)$ value would be low. The Bayesian filter would begin to label many spam messages as ham and end up being of no practical use. Because the Internet still contains some Web pages and posts that triumph this approach, we will leave it to you to figure out why this method of attack cannot succeed in the long run and why this method is not as initially successful as some would claim.

Today, spammers are still trying to outwit Bayesian filters. Some spammers have decided to eliminate all or most of the words in their messages and replace them with graphics so that Bayesian filters will have very few words to work with. But this approach will fail, too, as Bayesian filters are rewritten to consider things other than words in a message. After all, Bayes' theorem concerns *events,* and "graphics present with no text" is as valid an event as "some word, *X,* present in a message." Other future tricks will ultimately fail for the same reason. (By the way, spam filters use non-Bayesian techniques as well, which make spammers' lives even more difficult.)

Bayesian spam filters are an example of the unexpected way that applications of statistics can show up in your daily life. You will discover more examples as you read the rest of this book.

Problems for Section 4.3

LEARNING THE BASICS

4.30 If $P(B) = 0.05, P(A|B) = 0.80, P(B') = 0.95,$ and $P(A|B') = 0.40,$ find $P(B|A).$

4.31 If $P(B) = 0.30, P(A|B) = 0.60, P(B') = 0.70,$ and $P(A|B') = 0.50,$ find $P(B|A).$

APPLYING THE CONCEPTS

4.32 In Example 4.10 on page 150, suppose that the probability that a medical diagnostic test will give a positive result if the disease is not present is reduced from 0.02 to 0.01. Given this information,

a. if the medical diagnostic test has given a positive result (indicating that the disease is present), what is the probability that the disease is actually present?

b. if the medical diagnostic test has given a negative result (indicating that the disease is not present), what is the probability that the disease is not present?

4.33 An advertising executive is studying television viewing habits of married men and women during prime-time

hours. Based on past viewing records, the executive has determined that during prime time, husbands are watching television 60% of the time. When the husband is watching television, 40% of the time the wife is also watching. When the husband is not watching television, 30% of the time the wife is watching television. Find the probability that
a. if the wife is watching television, the husband is also watching television.
b. the wife is watching television during prime time.

✓ SELF Test **4.34** Olive Construction Company is determining whether it should submit a bid for a new shopping center. In the past, Olive's main competitor, Base Construction Company, has submitted bids 70% of the time. If Base Construction Company does not bid on a job, the probability that Olive Construction Company will get the job is 0.50. If Base Construction Company bids on a job, the probability that Olive Construction Company will get the job is 0.25.
a. If Olive Construction Company gets the job, what is the probability that Base Construction Company did not bid?
b. What is the probability that Olive Construction Company will get the job?

4.35 Laid-off workers who become entrepreneurs because they cannot find meaningful employment with another company are known as *entrepreneurs by necessity*. The Wall Street Journal reports that these entrepreneurs by necessity are less likely to grow into large businesses than are *entrepreneurs by choice* (J. Bailey, "Desire—More Than Need—Builds a Business," *The Wall Street Journal*, May 21, 2001, p. B4). This article states that 89% of the entrepreneurs in the United States are entrepreneurs by choice and 11% are entrepreneurs by necessity. Only 2% of entrepreneurs by necessity expect their new business to employ 20 or more people within five years, whereas 14% of entrepreneurs by choice expect to employ at least 20 people within five years.

a. If an entrepreneur is selected at random, and that individual expects that his or her new business will employ 20 or more people within five years, what is the probability that this individual is an entrepreneur by choice?
b. Discuss several possible reasons why entrepreneurs by choice are more likely than entrepreneurs by necessity to believe that they will grow their businesses.

4.36 The editor of a textbook publishing company is trying to decide whether to publish a proposed business statistics textbook. Information on previous textbooks published indicates that 10% are huge successes, 20% are modest successes, 40% break even, and 30% are losers. However, before a publishing decision is made, the book will be reviewed. In the past, 99% of the huge successes received favorable reviews, 70% of the moderate successes received favorable reviews, 40% of the break-even books received favorable reviews, and 20% of the losers received favorable reviews.
a. If the proposed textbook receives a favorable review, how should the editor revise the probabilities of the various outcomes to take this information into account?
b. What proportion of textbooks receives favorable reviews?

4.37 A municipal bond service has three rating categories (A, B, and C). Suppose that in the past year, of the municipal bonds issued throughout the United States, 70% were rated A, 20% were rated B, and 10% were rated C. Of the municipal bonds rated A, 50% were issued by cities, 40% by suburbs, and 10% by rural areas. Of the municipal bonds rated B, 60% were issued by cities, 20% by suburbs, and 20% by rural areas. Of the municipal bonds rated C, 90% were issued by cities, 5% by suburbs, and 5% by rural areas.
a. If a new municipal bond is to be issued by a city, what is the probability that it will receive an A rating?
b. What proportion of municipal bonds are issued by cities?
c. What proportion of municipal bonds are issued by suburbs?

4.4 Ethical Issues and Probability

Ethical issues can arise when any statements related to probability are presented to the public, particularly when these statements are part of an advertising campaign for a product or service. Unfortunately, many people are not comfortable with numerical concepts (see reference 4) and tend to misinterpret the meaning of the probability. In some instances, the misinterpretation is not intentional, but in other cases, advertisements may unethically try to mislead potential customers.

One example of a potentially unethical application of probability relates to advertisements for state lotteries. When purchasing a lottery ticket, the customer selects a set of numbers (such as 6) from a larger list of numbers (such as 54). Although virtually all participants know that they are unlikely to win the lottery, they also have very little idea of how unlikely it is for them to select all 6 winning numbers from the list of 54 numbers. They have even less idea of the probability of winning a consolation prize by selecting either 4 or 5 winning numbers.

Given this background, you might consider a recent commercial for a state lottery that stated, "We won't stop until we have made everyone a millionaire" to be deceptive and possibly unethical. Do you think the state has any intention of ever stopping the lottery, given the fact that the state relies on it to bring millions of dollars into its treasury? Is it possible that the lottery can make everyone a millionaire? Is it ethical to suggest that the purpose of the lottery is to make everyone a millionaire?

Another example of a potentially unethical application of probability relates to an investment newsletter promising a 90% probability of a 20% annual return on investment. To make the claim in the newsletter an ethical one, the investment service needs to (a) explain the basis on which this probability estimate rests, (b) provide the probability statement in another format, such as 9 chances in 10, and (c) explain what happens to the investment in the 10% of the cases in which a 20% return is not achieved (e.g., is the entire investment lost?).

These are serious ethical issues. If you were going to write an advertisement for the state lottery that ethically describes the probability of winning a certain prize, what would you say? If you were going to write an advertisement for the investment newsletter that ethically states the probability of a 20% return on an investment, what would you say?

4.5 Online Topic: Counting Rules

In many cases, there are a large number of possible outcomes, and determining the exact number of outcomes can be difficult. In these situations, rules have been developed for counting exactly the number of possible outcomes. To study this topic, read the **Section 4.5** online topic file that is available on this book's companion Web site. (See Appendix Section D.8 to learn how to access the online topic files.)

USING STATISTICS @ M&R Electronics World Revisited

As the marketing manager for M&R Electronics World, you analyzed the survey results of an intent-to-purchase study. This study asked the heads of 1,000 households about their intentions to purchase a big-screen television sometime during the next 12 months, and as a follow-up, M&R surveyed the same people 12 months later to see whether such a television was purchased. In addition, for households purchasing big-screen televisions, the survey asked whether the television they purchased was a plasma-screen television, whether they also purchased a digital video recorder (DVR) in the past 12 months, and whether they were satisfied with their purchase of the big-screen television.

By analyzing the results of these surveys, you were able to uncover many pieces of valuable information that will help you plan a marketing strategy to enhance sales and better target those households likely to purchase multiple or more expensive products. Whereas only 30% of the households actually purchased a big-screen television, if a household indicated that it planned to purchase a big-screen television in the next 12 months, there was an 80% chance that the household actually made the purchase. Thus the marketing strategy should target those households that have indicated an intention to purchase.

You determined that for households that purchased a plasma-screen television, there was a 47.5% chance that the household also purchased a DVR. You then compared this conditional probability to the marginal probability of purchasing a DVR, which was 36%. Thus, households that purchased plasma-screen televisions are more likely to purchase DVRs than are households that purchased big-screen televisions that are not plasma-screen televisions.

You were also able to apply Bayes' theorem to M&R Electronics World's market research reports. The reports investigate a potential new television model prior to its scheduled release. If a favorable report was received, then there was a 64% chance that the new television model would be successful. However, if an unfavorable report was received, there is only a 16% chance that the model would be successful. Therefore, the marketing strategy of M&R needs to pay close attention to whether a report's conclusion is favorable or unfavorable.

SUMMARY

This chapter began by developing the basic concepts of probability. You learned that probability is a numeric value from 0 to 1 that represents the chance, likelihood, or possibility that a particular event will occur. In addition to simple probability, you learned about conditional probabilities and independent events. Bayes' theorem was used to revise previously calculated probabilities based on new information. Throughout the chapter, contingency tables and decision trees were used to display information. In the next chapter, important discrete probability distributions such as the binomial, Poisson, and hypergeometric distributions are developed.

KEY EQUATIONS

Probability of Occurrence

$$\text{Probability of occurrence} = \frac{X}{T} \qquad (4.1)$$

Marginal Probability

$$P(A) = P(A \text{ and } B_1) + P(A \text{ and } B_2)$$
$$+ \cdots + P(A \text{ and } B_k) \qquad (4.2)$$

General Addition Rule

$$P(A \text{ or } B) = P(A) + P(B) - P(A \text{ and } B) \qquad (4.3)$$

Conditional Probability

$$P(A \mid B) = \frac{P(A \text{ and } B)}{P(B)} \qquad (4.4a)$$

$$P(B \mid A) = \frac{P(A \text{ and } B)}{P(A)} \qquad (4.4b)$$

Independence

$$P(A \mid B) = P(A) \qquad (4.5)$$

General Multiplication Rule

$$P(A \text{ and } B) = P(A \mid B)P(B) \qquad (4.6)$$

Multiplication Rule for Independent Events

$$P(A \text{ and } B) = P(A)P(B) \qquad (4.7)$$

Marginal Probability Using the General Multiplication Rule

$$P(A) = P(A \mid B_1)P(B_1) + P(A \mid B_2)P(B_2)$$
$$+ \cdots + P(A \mid B_k)P(B_k) \qquad (4.8)$$

Bayes' Theorem

$$P(B_i \mid A) =$$
$$\frac{P(A \mid B_i)P(B_i)}{P(A \mid B_1)P(B_1) + P(A \mid B_2)P(B_2) + \cdots + P(A \mid B_k)P(B_k)}$$
$$(4.9)$$

KEY TERMS

a priori probability   134
Bayes' theorem   149
certain event   134
collectively exhaustive   138
complement   135
conditional probability   142
contingency table   136
decision tree   143
empirical probability   134

event   135
general addition rule   139
general multiplication rule   145
impossible event   134
independence   145
joint event   135
joint probability   137
marginal probability   138

multiplication rule for independent events   146
mutually exclusive   138
probability   134
sample space   135
simple event   135
simple probability   136
subjective probability   135

CHAPTER REVIEW PROBLEMS

CHECKING YOUR UNDERSTANDING

4.38 What are the differences between *a priori* probability, empirical probability, and subjective probability?

4.39 What is the difference between a simple event and a joint event?

4.40 How can you use the general addition rule to find the probability of occurrence of event *A* or *B*?

4.41 What is the difference between mutually exclusive events and collectively exhaustive events?

4.42 How does conditional probability relate to the concept of independence?

4.43 How does the multiplication rule differ for events that are and are not independent?

4.44 How can you use Bayes' theorem to revise probabilities in light of new information?

4.45 In Bayes' theorem, how does the prior probability differ from the revised probability?

APPLYING THE CONCEPTS

4.46 A survey by the Pew Research Center ("Snapshots: Goals of 'Gen Next' vs. 'Gen X,'" *USA Today*, March 27, 2007, p. 1A) indicated that 81% of 18- to 25-year-olds had getting rich as a goal, as compared to 62% of 26- to 40-year-olds. Suppose that the survey was based on 500 respondents from each of the two groups.
a. Form a contingency table.
b. Give an example of a simple event and a joint event.
c. What is the probability that a randomly selected respondent has a goal of getting rich?
d. What is the probability that a randomly selected respondent has a goal of getting rich *and* is in the 26- to 40-year-old group?
e. Are the events "age group" and "has getting rich as a goal" independent? Explain.

4.47 The owner of a restaurant serving Continental-style entrées was interested in studying ordering patterns of patrons for the Friday-to-Sunday weekend time period. Records were maintained that indicated the demand for dessert during the same time period. The owner decided to study two other variables, along with whether a dessert was ordered: the gender of the individual and whether a beef entrée was ordered. The results are as follows:

DESSERT ORDERED	GENDER		
	Male	Female	Total
Yes	96	40	136
No	224	240	464
Total	320	280	600

DESSERT ORDERED	BEEF ENTRÉE		
	Yes	No	Total
Yes	71	65	136
No	116	348	464
Total	187	413	600

A waiter approaches a table to take an order for dessert. What is the probability that the first customer to order at the table
a. orders a dessert?
b. orders a dessert *or* has ordered a beef entrée?
c. is a female *and* does not order a dessert?
d. is a female *or* does not order a dessert?
e. Suppose the first person from whom the waiter takes the dessert order is a female. What is the probability that she does not order dessert?
f. Are gender and ordering dessert independent?
g. Is ordering a beef entrée independent of whether the person orders dessert?

4.48 James Choi, David Laibson, and Brigitte Madrian conducted an experiment to study the choices made in fund selection. Suppose 100 undergraduate students and 100 MBA students were selected. When presented with four S&P 500 Index funds that were identical except for their fees, undergraduate and MBA students chose the funds as follows:

FUND	STUDENT GROUP	
	Undergraduate	MBA
Lowest-cost fund	19	19
Second-lowest-cost fund	37	40
Third-lowest-cost fund	17	23
Highest-cost fund	27	18

Source: *Data extracted from J. J. Choi, D. Laibson, and B. C. Madrian, Why Does the Law of One Price Fail: An Experiment on Mutual Funds?* **www.som.yale.edu/faculty/jjc83/fees.pdf**.

If a student is selected at random, what is the probability that he or she
a. selected the lowest- *or* second-lowest-cost fund?
b. selected the lowest-cost fund *and* is an undergraduate?
c. selected the lowest-cost fund *or* is an undergraduate?
d. Given that a student is an undergraduate, what is the probability that he or she selected the highest-cost fund?
e. Do you think undergraduate students and graduate students differ in their fund selection? Explain.

4.49 According to a Gallup Poll, companies with employees who are engaged with their workplace have greater innovation, productivity, and profitability, as well as less employee turnover. A survey of 1,795 workers in Germany found that 13% of the workers were engaged, 67% were not engaged, and 20% were actively disengaged. The survey also noted that 48% of engaged workers strongly agreed with the statement "My current job brings out my most creative ideas." Only 20% of the not engaged workers and 3% of the actively disengaged workers agreed with this statement (data extracted from M. Nink, "Employee Disengagement Plagues Germany," *Gallup Management Journal*, **gmj.gallup.com**, April 9, 2009). If a worker is known to strongly agree with the statement "My current job brings out my most creative ideas," what is the probability that the worker is engaged?

4.50 Sport utility vehicles (SUVs), vans, and pickups are generally considered to be more prone to roll over than cars. In 1997, 24.0% of all highway fatalities involved rollovers; 15.8% of all fatalities in 1997 involved SUVs, vans, and pickups, given that the fatality involved a rollover. Given that a rollover was not involved, 5.6% of all fatalities involved SUVs, vans, and pickups (data extracted from A. Wilde Mathews, "Ford Ranger, Chevy Tracker Tilt in Test," *The Wall Street Journal*, July 14, 1999, p. A2). Consider the following definitions:

A = fatality involved an SUV, van, or pickup
B = fatality involved a rollover

a. Use Bayes' theorem to find the probability that a fatality involved a rollover, given that the fatality involved an SUV, a van, or a pickup.
b. Compare the result in (a) to the probability that a fatality involved a rollover and comment on whether SUVs, vans, and pickups are generally more prone to rollover accidents than other vehicles.

4.51 Enzyme-linked immunosorbent assay (ELISA) is the most common type of screening test for detecting the HIV virus. A positive result from an ELISA indicates that the HIV virus is present. For most populations, ELISA has a high degree of sensitivity (to detect infection) and specificity (to detect noninfection). (See HIVInSite, at **HIVInsite.ucsf.edu**.) Suppose the probability that a person is infected with the HIV virus for a certain population is 0.015. If the HIV virus is actually present, the probability that the ELISA test will give a positive result is 0.995. If the HIV virus is not actually present, the probability of a positive result from an ELISA is 0.01. If the ELISA has given a positive result, use Bayes' theorem to find the probability that the HIV virus is actually present.

TEAM PROJECT

The file **Bond Funds** contains information regarding three categorical variables from a sample of 180 mutual funds. The variables include

Type—Bond fund type (intermediate government or short term corporate)
Fees—Sales charges (no or yes)
Risk—Risk-of-loss factor of the mutual fund (below average, average, or above average)

4.52 Construct contingency tables of type and fees, type and risk, and fees and risk.

a. For each of these contingency tables, compute all the conditional and marginal probabilities.
b. Based on (a), what conclusions can you reach about whether these variables are independent?

STUDENT SURVEY DATABASE

4.53 Problem 2.117 on page 65 describes a survey of 50 undergraduate students (see the file **UndergradSurvey**). For these data, construct contingency tables of gender and major, gender and graduate school intention, gender and employment status, class and graduate school intention, class and employment status, major and graduate school intention, and major and employment status.

a. For each of these contingency tables, compute all the conditional and marginal probabilities.
b. Based on (a), what conclusions can you reach about whether these variables are independent?

4.54 Problem 2.117 on page 65 describes a survey of 50 undergraduate students (stored in **UndergradSurvey**).

a. Select a sample of 50 undergraduate students at your school and conduct a similar survey for those students.
b. For your data, construct contingency tables of gender and major, gender and graduate school intention, gender and employment status, class and graduate school intention, class and employment status, major and graduate school intention, and major and employment status. For each of these contingency tables, compute all the conditional and marginal probabilities.
c. Based on (b), what conclusions can you reach about whether these variables are independent?
d. Compare the results of (c) to those of Problem 4.53 (b).

4.55 Problem 2.119 on page 65 describes a survey of 40 MBA students (stored in **GradSurvey**). For these data, construct contingency tables of gender and graduate major, gender and undergraduate major, gender and employment status, graduate major and undergraduate major, and graduate major and employment status.

a. For each of these contingency tables, compute all the conditional and marginal probabilities.
b. Based on (b), what conclusions can you reach about whether these variables are independent?

4.56 Problem 2.119 on page 65 describes a survey of 40 MBA students (stored in **GradSurvey**).

a. Select a sample of 40 MBA students from your MBA program and conduct a similar survey for those students.
b. For your data, construct contingency tables of gender and graduate major, gender and undergraduate major, gender and employment status, graduate major and undergraduate major, and graduate major and employment status. For each of these contingency tables, compute all the conditional and marginal probabilities.
c. Based on (b), what conclusions can you reach about whether these variables are independent?
d. Compare the results of (c) to those of Problem 4.55 (b).

WEB CASE

Apply your knowledge about contingency tables and the proper application of simple and joint probabilities in this continuing Web Case from Chapter 3.

Using a Web browser, open to the Web page for the Chapter 4 Web Case (or open **ER_Guaranteed.htm** if you have downloaded the Web Case files) to visit the EndRun Guaranteed Investment Package (GIP) Web page. Read the claims and examine the supporting data. Then answer the following questions:

1. How accurate is the claim of the probability of success for EndRun's GIP? In what ways is the claim misleading?

How would you calculate and state the probability of having an annual rate of return not less than 15%?

2. Click the **Show me the Winning Probabilities!** link (or open **ER_Guaranteed3.htm**). Using the table found on the "Winning Probabilities" Web page, compute the proper probabilities for the group of investors. What mistake was made in reporting the 7% probability claim?

3. Are there any probability calculations that would be appropriate for rating an investment service? Why or why not?

REFERENCES

1. Bellhouse, D. R., "The Reverend Thomas Bayes, FRS: A Biography to Celebrate the Tercentenary of His Birth," *Statistical Science* 19 (2004), 3–43.
2. Lowd, D., and C. Meek, "Good Word Attacks on Statistical Spam Filters," presented at the Second Conference on Email and Anti-Spam, CEAS 2005.
3. *Microsoft Excel 2007* (Redmond, WA: Microsoft Corp., 2007).
4. Paulos, J. A., *Innumeracy* (New York: Hill and Wang, 1988).
5. Silberman, S., "The Quest for Meaning," *Wired 8.02*, February 2000.
6. T. Zeller, "The Fight Against V1@gra (and Other Spam)," *The New York Times*, May 21, 2006, pp. B1, B6.

EG4.1 BASIC PROBABILITY CONCEPTS

Simple and Joint Probability and the General Addition Rule

PHStat2 Use the **Simple & Joint Probabilities** procedure to compute basic probabilities. Select **PHStat → Probability & Prob. Distributions → Simple & Joint Probabilities**. Unlike with other procedures, with this procedure, no dialog appears. Instead, the procedure inserts a worksheet similar to Figure EG4.1 into the current workbook. To use the worksheet, fill in the Sample Space area with your data.

In-Depth Excel Use the **COMPUTE worksheet** of the **Probabilities workbook** as a template for computing basic probabilities (see Figure EG4.1, below). (The worksheet contains the Table 4.1 purchase behavior data shown on page 136. Overwrite these values when you enter the set of data values.)

Open to the **COMPUTE_FORMULAS worksheet** to examine the formulas used in the worksheet. Take special note of the column A formulas that use the concatenation operator (**&**) to form row labels from the event names you enter in cells B5, B6, C4, and D4.

	A	B	C	D	E
1	**Probabilities**				
2					
3	**Sample Space**		**ACTUALLY PURCHASED**		
4			Yes	No	Totals
5	**PLANNED TO PURCHASE**	Yes	200	50	250
6		No	100	650	750
7		Totals	300	700	1000
8					
9	**Simple Probabilities**		**Simple Probabilities**		
10	P(Yes)	0.25	="P(" & B5 & ")"	=E5/E7	
11	P(No)	0.75	="P(" & B6 & ")"	=E6/E7	
12	P(Yes)	0.30	="P(" & C4 & ")"	=C7/E7	
13	P(No)	0.70	="P(" & D4 & ")"	=D7/E7	
14					
15	**Joint Probabilities**		**Joint Probabilities**		
16	P(Yes and Yes)	0.20	="P(" & B5 & " and " & C4 & ")"	=C5/E7	
17	P(Yes and No)	0.05	="P(" & B5 & " and " & D4 & ")"	=D5/E7	
18	P(No and Yes)	0.10	="P(" & B6 & " and " & C4 & ")"	=C6/E7	
19	P(No and No)	0.65	="P(" & B6 & " and " & D4 & ")"	=D6/E7	
20					
21	**Addition Rule**		**Addition Rule**		
22	P(Yes or Yes)	0.35	="P(" & B5 & " or " & C4 & ")"	=B10 + B12 - B16	
23	P(Yes or No)	0.90	="P(" & B5 & " or " & D4 & ")"	=B10 + B13 - B17	
24	P(No or Yes)	0.95	="P(" & B6 & " or " & C4 & ")"	=B11 + B12 - B18	
25	P(No or No)	0.80	="P(" & B6 & " or " & D4 & ")"	=B11 + B13 - B19	

FIGURE EG4.1 COMPUTE worksheet of the Probabilities workbook

EG4.2 CONDITIONAL PROBABILITY

There is no Excel material for this section.

EG4.3 BAYES' THEOREM

In-Depth Excel Use the **COMPUTE worksheet** of the **Bayes workbook** as a template for computing basic probabilities (see Figure EG4.2, at right). The worksheet contains television-marketing example of Table 4.4 on page 150. Overwrite these values when you enter the set of data values.

Open to the **COMPUTE_FORMULAS worksheet** to examine the simple arithmetic formulas that compute the probabilities. These formulas are also shown in Figure EG4.2.

	A	B	C	D	E
1	**Bayes Theorem Calculations**				
2					
3			**Probabilities**		
4	**Event**	Prior	Conditional	Joint	Revised
5	S	0.4	0.8	0.32	0.64
6	S'	0.6	0.3	0.18	0.36
7			Total:	0.5	

Joint	Revised
=B5 * C5	=D5/$D$7
=B6 * C6	=D6/$D$7
=D5 + D6	

FIGURE EG4.2 Bayes Theorem Calculations

5

Discrete Probability Distributions

Learning Objectives

In this chapter, you learn:

- The properties of a probability distribution
- To compute the expected value and variance of a probability distribution
- To calculate the covariance and understand its use in finance
- To compute probabilities from the binomial, Poisson, and hypergeometric distributions
- How the binomial, Poisson, and hypergeometric distributions can be used to solve business problems

USING STATISTICS

@ Saxon Home Improvement

You are an accountant for the Saxon Home Improvement Company, which uses a state-of-the-art accounting information system to manage its accounting and financial operations.

Accounting information systems collect, process, store, transform, and distribute financial information to decision makers both internal and external to a business organization (see reference 6). These systems continuously audit accounting information, looking for errors or incomplete or improbable information. For example, when customers of the Saxon Home Improvement Company submit online orders, the company's accounting information system reviews the order forms for possible mistakes. Any questionable invoices are tagged and included in a daily *exceptions report*. Recent data collected by the company show that the likelihood is 0.10 that an order form will be tagged. Saxon would like to determine the likelihood of finding a certain number of tagged forms in a sample of a specific size. For example, what would be the likelihood that none of the order forms are tagged in a sample of four forms? That one of the order forms is tagged?

H ow could the Saxon Home Improvement Company determine the solution to this type of probability problem? One way is to use a model, or small-scale representation, that approximates the process. By using such an approximation, Saxon managers could make inferences about the actual order process. In this case, the Saxon managers can use *probability distributions*, mathematical models suited for solving the type of probability problems the managers are facing.

This chapter introduces you to the concept and characteristics of probability distributions. You will learn how the knowledge about a probability distribution can help you choose between alternative investment strategies. You will also learn how the binomial, Poisson, and hypergeometric distributions can be applied to help solve business problems.

5.1 The Probability Distribution for a Discrete Random Variable

In Section 2.1, a *numerical variable* was defined as a variable that yields numerical responses, such as the number of magazines you subscribe to or your height. Numerical variables are either *discrete* or *continuous*. Continuous numerical variables produce outcomes that come from a measuring process (e.g., your height). Discrete numerical variables produce outcomes that come from a counting process (e.g., the number of magazines you subscribe to). This chapter deals with probability distributions that represent discrete numerical variables.

> **PROBABILITY DISTRIBUTION FOR A DISCRETE RANDOM VARIABLE**
>
> A **probability distribution for a discrete random variable** is a mutually exclusive list of all the possible numerical outcomes along with the probability of occurrence of each outcome.

For example, Table 5.1 gives the distribution of the number of interruptions per day in a large computer network. The list in Table 5.1 is collectively exhaustive because all possible outcomes are included. Thus, the probabilities sum to 1. Figure 5.1 is a graphical representation of Table 5.1.

TABLE 5.1

Probability Distribution of the Number of Interruptions per Day

Interruptions per Day	Probability
0	0.35
1	0.25
2	0.20
3	0.10
4	0.05
5	0.05

FIGURE 5.1

Probability distribution of the number of interruptions per day

Expected Value of a Discrete Random Variable

Compute the expected value of a discrete random variable using the instructions in Section EG5.1.

The mean, μ, of a probability distribution is the **expected value** of its random variable. To calculate the expected value, you multiply each possible outcome, X, by its corresponding probability, $P(X)$, and then sum these products.

EXPECTED VALUE, μ, OF A DISCRETE RANDOM VARIABLE

$$\mu = E(X) = \sum_{i=1}^{N} X_i P(X_i)$$ **(5.1)**

where

X_i = the ith outcome of the discrete random variable X

$P(X_i)$ = probability of occurrence of the ith outcome of X

For the probability distribution of the number of interruptions per day in a large computer network (Table 5.1), the expected value is computed as follows, using Equation (5.1), and is also shown in Table 5.2:

$$\mu = E(X) = \sum_{i=1}^{N} X_i P(X_i)$$

$$= (0)(0.35) + (1)(0.25) + (2)(0.20) + (3)(0.10) + (4)(0.05) + (5)(0.05)$$

$$= 0 + 0.25 + 0.40 + 0.30 + 0.20 + 0.25$$

$$= 1.40$$

TABLE 5.2

Computing the Expected Value of the Number of Interruptions per Day

Interruptions per Day (X_i)	$P(X_i)$	$X_i P(X_i)$
0	0.35	$(0)(0.35) = 0.00$
1	0.25	$(1)(0.25) = 0.25$
2	0.20	$(2)(0.20) = 0.40$
3	0.10	$(3)(0.10) = 0.30$
4	0.05	$(4)(0.05) = 0.20$
5	0.05	$(5)(0.05) = 0.25$
	1.00	$\mu = E(X) = 1.4$

The expected value is 1.40. The expected value of 1.4 for the number of interruptions per day is not a possible outcome because the actual number of interruptions in a given day must be an integer value. The expected value represents the *mean* number of interruptions in a given day.

Variance and Standard Deviation of a Discrete Random Variable

You compute the variance of a probability distribution by multiplying each possible squared difference $[X_i - E(X)]^2$ by its corresponding probability, $P(X_i)$, and then summing the resulting products. Equation (5.2) defines the **variance of a discrete random variable**.

VARIANCE OF A DISCRETE RANDOM VARIABLE

$$\sigma^2 = \sum_{i=1}^{N} [X_i - E(X)]^2 P(X_i)$$ **(5.2)**

where

X_i = the ith outcome of the discrete random variable X

$P(X_i)$ = probability of occurrence of the ith outcome of X

Equation (5.3) defines the **standard deviation of a discrete random variable**.

Compute the variance and standard deviation of a discrete random variable using the instructions in Section EG5.1.

STANDARD DEVIATION OF A DISCRETE RANDOM VARIABLE

$$\sigma = \sqrt{\sigma^2} = \sqrt{\sum_{i=1}^{N}[X_i - E(X)]^2 P(X_i)} \tag{5.3}$$

The variance and the standard deviation of the number of interruptions per day are computed as follows and in Table 5.3, using Equations (5.2) and (5.3):

$$\sigma^2 = \sum_{i=1}^{N}[X_i - E(X)]^2 P(X_i)$$

$$= (0 - 1.4)^2(0.35) + (1 - 1.4)^2(0.25) + (2 - 1.4)^2(0.20) + (3 - 1.4)^2(0.10)$$

$$+ (4 - 1.4)^2(0.05) + (5 - 1.4)^2(0.05)$$

$$= 0.686 + 0.040 + 0.072 + 0.256 + 0.338 + 0.648$$

$$= 2.04$$

TABLE 5.3

Computing the Variance and Standard Deviation of the Number of Interruptions per Day

Interruptions per Day (X_i)	$P(X_i)$	$X_i P(X_i)$	$[X_i - E(X)]^2 P(X_i)$
0	0.35	$(0)(0.35) = 0.00$	$(0 - 1.4)^2(0.35) = 0.686$
1	0.25	$(1)(0.25) = 0.25$	$(1 - 1.4)^2(0.25) = 0.040$
2	0.20	$(2)(0.20) = 0.40$	$(2 - 1.4)^2(0.20) = 0.072$
3	0.10	$(3)(0.10) = 0.30$	$(3 - 1.4)^2(0.10) = 0.256$
4	0.05	$(4)(0.05) = 0.20$	$(4 - 1.4)^2(0.05) = 0.338$
5	0.05	$(5)(0.05) = 0.25$	$(5 - 1.4)^2(0.05) = 0.648$
	1.00	$\mu = E(X) = 1.4$	$\sigma^2 = 2.04$

and

$$\sigma = \sqrt{\sigma^2} = \sqrt{2.04} = 1.4283$$

Thus, the mean number of interruptions per day is 1.4, the variance is 2.04, and the standard deviation is approximately 1.43 interruptions per day.

Problems for Section 5.1

LEARNING THE BASICS

5.1 Given the following probability distributions:

Distribution *A*		Distribution *B*	
X	**P(X)**	**X**	**P(X)**
0	0.50	0	0.05
1	0.20	1	0.10
2	0.15	2	0.15
3	0.10	3	0.20
4	0.05	4	0.50

a. Compute the expected value for each distribution.
b. Compute the standard deviation for each distribution.
c. Compare the results of distributions *A* and *B*.

APPLYING THE CONCEPTS

✓SELF Test **5.2** The following table contains the probability distribution for the number of traffic accidents daily in a small city:

Number of Accidents Daily (*X*)	*P(X)*
0	0.10
1	0.20
2	0.45
3	0.15
4	0.05
5	0.05

a. Compute the mean number of accidents per day.
b. Compute the standard deviation.

5.3 Recently, a regional automobile dealership sent out fliers to perspective customers, indicating that they had already won one of three different prizes: a 2008 Kia Optima valued at $15,000, a $500 gas card, or a $5 Wal-Mart shopping card. To claim his or her prize, a prospective customer needed to present the flier at the dealership's showroom. The fine print on the back of the flier listed the probabilities of winning. The chance of winning the car was 1 out of 31,478, the chance of winning the gas card was 1 out of 31,478, and the chance of winning the shopping card was 31,476 out 31,478.

a. How many fliers do you think the automobile dealership sent out?
b. Using your answer to (a) and the probabilities listed on the flier, what is the expected value of the prize won by a prospective customer receiving a flier?
c. Using your answer to (a) and the probabilities listed on the flier, what is the standard deviation of the value of the prize won by a prospective customer receiving a flier?
d. Do you think this is an effective promotion? Why or why not?

5.4 In the carnival game Under-or-Over-Seven, a pair of fair dice is rolled once, and the resulting sum determines whether the player wins or loses his or her bet. For example, the player can bet $1 that the sum will be under 7—that is, 2, 3, 4, 5, or 6. For this bet, the player wins $1 if the result is under 7 and loses $1 if the outcome equals or is greater than 7. Similarly, the player can bet $1 that the sum will be over 7—that is, 8, 9, 10, 11, or 12. Here, the player wins $1 if the result is over 7 but loses $1 if the result is 7 or under. A third method of play is to bet $1 on the outcome 7. For this bet, the player wins $4 if the result of the roll is 7 and loses $1 otherwise.

a. Construct the probability distribution representing the different outcomes that are possible for a $1 bet on under 7.
b. Construct the probability distribution representing the different outcomes that are possible for a $1 bet on over 7.
c. Construct the probability distribution representing the different outcomes that are possible for a $1 bet on 7.
d. Show that the expected long-run profit (or loss) to the player is the same, no matter which method of play is used.

5.5 The number of arrivals per minute at a bank located in the central business district of a large city was recorded over a period of 200 minutes, with the following results:

Arrivals	Frequency
0	14
1	31
2	47
3	41
4	29
5	21
6	10
7	5
8	2

a. Compute the expected number of arrivals per minute.
b. Compute the standard deviation.

5.6 The manager of the commercial mortgage department of a large bank has collected data during the past two years concerning the number of commercial mortgages approved per week. The results from these two years (104 weeks) indicated the following:

Number of Commercial Mortgages Approved	Frequency
0	13
1	25
2	32
3	17
4	9
5	6
6	1
7	1

a. Compute the expected number of mortgages approved per week.
b. Compute the standard deviation.

5.2 Covariance and Its Application in Finance

In Section 5.1, the expected value, variance, and standard deviation of a discrete random variable of a probability distribution are discussed. In this section, the covariance between two variables is introduced and applied to portfolio management, a topic of great interest to financial analysts.

Covariance

The **covariance,** σ_{XY}, measures the strength of the relationship between two numerical random variables, X and Y. A positive covariance indicates a positive relationship. A negative covariance indicates a negative relationship. A covariance of 0 indicates that the two variables are independent. Equation (5.4) defines the covariance for a discrete probability distribution.

COVARIANCE

$$\sigma_{XY} = \sum_{i=1}^{N}[X_i - E(X)][Y_i - E(Y)]P(X_iY_i) \qquad (5.4)$$

where

X = discrete random variable X

X_i = ith outcome of X

Y = discrete random variable Y

Y_i = ith outcome of Y

$P(X_iY_i)$ = probability of occurrence of the ith outcome of X and the ith outcome of Y

$i = 1, 2, \ldots, N$ for X and Y

To illustrate the covariance, suppose that you are deciding between two alternative investments for the coming year. The first investment is a mutual fund that consists of the stocks that comprise the Dow Jones Industrial Average. The second investment is a mutual fund that is expected to perform best when economic conditions are weak. Table 5.4 summarizes your estimate of the returns (per $1,000 investment) under three economic conditions, each with a given probability of occurrence.

TABLE 5.4

Estimated Returns for Each Investment Under Three Economic Conditions

		Investment	
$P(X_iY_i)$	**Economic Condition**	**Dow Jones Fund**	**Weak-Economy Fund**
0.2	Recession	−$300	+$200
0.5	Stable economy	+$100	+$50
0.3	Expanding economy	+$250	−$100

The expected value and standard deviation for each investment and the covariance of the two investments are computed as follows:

Let X = Dow Jones fund, and Y = weak-economy fund

$E(X) = \mu_X = (-300)(0.2) + (100)(0.5) + (250)(0.3) = \$65$

$E(Y) = \mu_Y = (+200)(0.2) + (50)(0.5) + (-100)(0.3) = \$35$

$Var(X) = \sigma_X^2 = (-300 - 65)^2(0.2) + (100 - 65)^2(0.5) + (250 - 65)^2(0.3)$

$\qquad = 37,525$

$\sigma_X = \$193.71$

$Var(Y) = \sigma_Y^2 = (200 - 35)^2(0.2) + (50 - 35)^2(0.5) + (-100 - 35)^2(0.3)$

$\qquad = 11,025$

$\sigma_Y = \$105.00$

$\sigma_{XY} = (-300 - 65)(200 - 35)(0.2) + (100 - 65)(50 - 35)(0.5)$

$\qquad + (250 - 65)(-100 - 35)(0.3)$

$\qquad = -12,045 + 262.5 - 7,492.5$

$\qquad = -19,275$

Thus, the Dow Jones fund has a higher expected value (i.e., larger expected return) than the weak-economy fund but also has a higher standard deviation (i.e., more risk). The covariance of $-19,275$ between the two investments indicates a negative relationship in which the two investments are varying in the *opposite* direction. Therefore, when the return on one investment is high, typically, the return on the other is low.

Expected Value, Variance, and Standard Deviation of the Sum of Two Random Variables

Equations (5.1) through (5.3) define the expected value, variance, and standard deviation of a probability distribution, and Equation (5.4) defines the covariance between two variables, X and Y. The **expected value of the sum of two random variables** is equal to the sum of the expected values. The **variance of the sum of two random variables** is equal to the sum of the variances plus twice the covariance. The **standard deviation of the sum of two random variables** is the square root of the variance of the sum of two random variables.

EXPECTED VALUE OF THE SUM OF TWO RANDOM VARIABLES

$$E(X + Y) = E(X) + E(Y) \tag{5.5}$$

VARIANCE OF THE SUM OF TWO RANDOM VARIABLES

$$Var(X + Y) = \sigma_{X+Y}^2 = \sigma_X^2 + \sigma_Y^2 + 2\sigma_{XY} \tag{5.6}$$

STANDARD DEVIATION OF THE SUM OF TWO RANDOM VARIABLES

$$\sigma_{X+Y} = \sqrt{\sigma_{X+Y}^2} \tag{5.7}$$

To illustrate the expected value, variance, and standard deviation of the sum of two random variables, consider the two investments previously discussed. If X = Dow Jones fund and Y = weak-economy fund, using Equations (5.5), (5.6), and (5.7),

$$E(X + Y) = E(X) + E(Y) = 65 + 35 = \$100$$

$$\sigma_{X+Y}^2 = \sigma_X^2 + \sigma_Y^2 + 2\sigma_{XY}$$

$$= 37,525 + 11,025 + (2)(-19,275)$$

$$= 10,000$$

$$\sigma_{X+Y} = \$100$$

The expected value of the sum of the Dow Jones fund and the weak-economy fund is $100, with a standard deviation of $100. The standard deviation of the sum of the two investments is less than the standard deviation of either single investment because there is a large negative covariance between the investments.

Portfolio Expected Return and Portfolio Risk

Perform portfolio analysis using the instructions in Section EG5.2

Now that the covariance and the expected value and standard deviation of the sum of two random variables have been defined, these concepts can be applied to the study of a group of assets referred to as a **portfolio**. Investors combine assets into portfolios to reduce their risk (see references 1 and 2). Often, the objective is to maximize the return while minimizing the risk. For such portfolios, rather than study the sum of two random variables, the investor weights each investment by the proportion of assets assigned to that investment. Equations (5.8) and (5.9) define the **portfolio expected return** and **portfolio risk**.

PORTFOLIO EXPECTED RETURN

The portfolio expected return for a two-asset investment is equal to the weight assigned to asset X multiplied by the expected return of asset X plus the weight assigned to asset Y multiplied by the expected return of asset Y.

$$E(P) = wE(X) + (1 - w)E(Y) \qquad (5.8)$$

where

$$E(P) = \text{portfolio expected return}$$
$$w = \text{portion of the portfolio value assigned to asset } X$$
$$(1 - w) = \text{portion of the portfolio value assigned to asset } Y$$
$$E(X) = \text{expected return of asset } X$$
$$E(Y) = \text{expected return of asset } Y$$

PORTFOLIO RISK

$$\sigma_p = \sqrt{w^2\sigma_X^2 + (1 - w)^2\sigma_Y^2 + 2w(1 - w)\sigma_{XY}} \qquad (5.9)$$

In the previous section, you evaluated the expected return and risk of two different investments, a Dow Jones fund and a weak-economy fund. You also computed the covariance of the two investments. Now, suppose that you want to form a portfolio of these two investments that consists of an equal investment in each of these two funds. To compute the portfolio expected return and the portfolio risk, using Equations (5.8) and (5.9), with $w = 0.50, E(X) = \$65, E(Y) = \$35, \sigma_X^2 = 37{,}525, \sigma_Y^2 = 11{,}025,$ and $\sigma_{XY} = -19{,}275,$

$$E(P) = (0.5)(65) + (1 - 0.5)(35) = \$50$$
$$\sigma_p = \sqrt{(0.5)^2(37{,}525) + (1 - 0.5)^2(11{,}025) + 2(0.5)(1 - 0.5)(-19{,}275)}$$
$$= \sqrt{2{,}500} = \$50$$

Thus, the portfolio has an expected return of $50 for each $1,000 invested (a return of 5%) and has a portfolio risk of $50. The portfolio risk here is smaller than the standard deviation of either investment because there is a large negative covariance between the two investments. The fact that each investment performs best under different circumstances reduces the overall risk of the portfolio.

Problems for Section 5.2

LEARNING THE BASICS

5.7 Given the following probability distributions for variables X and Y:

$P(X_iY_i)$	X	Y
0.4	100	200
0.6	200	100

Compute
a. $E(X)$ and $E(Y)$.
b. σ_X and σ_Y.
c. σ_{XY}.
d. $E(X + Y)$.

5.8 Given the following probability distributions for variables X and Y:

$P(X_iY_i)$	X	Y
0.2	-100	50
0.4	50	30
0.3	200	20
0.1	300	20

Compute
a. $E(X)$ and $E(Y)$.
b. σ_X and σ_Y.
c. σ_{XY}.
d. $E(X + Y)$.

5.9 Two investments, X and Y, have the following characteristics:

$$E(X) = \$50, E(Y) = \$100, \sigma_X^2 = 9,000,$$

$$\sigma_Y^2 = 15,000, \text{ and } \sigma_{XY} = 7,500.$$

If the weight of portfolio assets assigned to investment X is 0.4, compute the
a. portfolio expected return.
b. portfolio risk.

APPLYING THE CONCEPTS

5.10 The process of being served at a bank consists of two independent parts—the time waiting in line and the time it takes to be served by the teller. Suppose that the time waiting in line has an expected value of 4 minutes, with a standard deviation of 1.2 minutes, and the time it takes to be served by the teller has an expected value of 5.5 minutes, with a standard deviation of 1.5 minutes. Compute the
a. expected value of the total time it takes to be served at the bank.
b. standard deviation of the total time it takes to be served at the bank.

5.11 In the portfolio example in this section (see page 168), half the portfolio assets are invested in the Dow Jones fund and half in a weak-economy fund. Recalculate the portfolio expected return and the portfolio risk if
a. 30% of the portfolio assets are invested in the Dow Jones fund and 70% in a weak-economy fund.
b. 70% of the portfolio assets are invested in the Dow Jones fund and 30% in a weak-economy fund.
c. Which of the three investment strategies (30%, 50%, or 70% in the Dow Jones fund) would you recommend? Why?

SELF Test **5.12** You are trying to develop a strategy for investing in two different stocks. The anticipated annual return for a $1,000 investment in each stock under four different economic conditions has the following probability distribution:

		Returns	
Probability	Economic Condition	Stock X	Stock Y
0.1	Recession	−100	50
0.3	Slow growth	0	150
0.3	Moderate growth	80	−20
0.3	Fast growth	150	−100

Compute the
a. expected return for stock X and for stock Y.
b. standard deviation for stock X and for stock Y.
c. covariance of stock X and stock Y.
d. Would you invest in stock X or stock Y? Explain.

5.13 Suppose that in Problem 5.12 you wanted to create a portfolio that consists of stock X and stock Y. Compute the portfolio expected return and portfolio risk for each of the following percentages invested in stock X:
a. 30%
b. 50%
c. 70%
d. On the basis of the results of (a) through (c), which portfolio would you recommend? Explain.

5.14 You are trying to develop a strategy for investing in two different stocks. The anticipated annual return for a $1,000 investment in each stock under four different economic conditions has the following probability distribution:

		Returns	
Probability	Economic Condition	Stock X	Stock Y
0.1	Recession	−50	−100
0.3	Slow growth	20	50
0.4	Moderate growth	100	130
0.2	Fast growth	150	200

Compute the
a. expected return for stock X and for stock Y.
b. standard deviation for stock X and for stock Y.
c. covariance of stock X and stock Y.
d. Would you invest in stock X or stock Y? Explain.

5.15 Suppose that in Problem 5.14 you wanted to create a portfolio that consists of stock X and stock Y. Compute the portfolio expected return and portfolio risk for each of the following percentages invested in stock X:
a. 30%
b. 50%
c. 70%
d. On the basis of the results of (a) through (c), which portfolio would you recommend? Explain.

5.16 You plan to invest $1,000 in a corporate bond fund or in a common stock fund. The following information about the annual return (per $1,000) of each of these investments under different economic conditions is available, along with the probability that each of these economic conditions will occur:

Probability	Economic Condition	Corporate Bond Fund	Common Stock Fund
0.10	Recession	−70	−300
0.15	Stagnation	30	−100
0.35	Slow growth	80	100
0.30	Moderate growth	100	150
0.10	High growth	120	350

Compute the
a. expected return for the corporate bond fund and for the common stock fund.

b. standard deviation for the corporate bond fund and for the common stock fund.

c. covariance of the corporate bond fund and the common stock fund.

d. Would you invest in the corporate bond fund or the common stock fund? Explain.

5.17 Suppose that in Problem 5.16 you wanted to create a portfolio that consists of the corporate bond fund and the common stock fund. Compute the portfolio expected return and portfolio risk for each of the following situations:

a. $300 in the corporate bond fund and $700 in the common stock fund.

b. $500 in each fund.

c. $700 in the corporate bond fund and $300 in the common stock fund.

d. On the basis of the results of (a) through (c), which portfolio would you recommend? Explain.

5.3 Binomial Distribution

The next three sections use mathematical models to solve business problems.

> **MATHEMATICAL MODEL**
> A **mathematical model** is a mathematical expression that represents a variable of interest.

When a mathematical expression is available, you can compute the exact probability of occurrence of any particular outcome of the variable.

The **binomial distribution** is one of the most useful mathematical models. You use the binomial distribution when the discrete random variable is the number of events of interest in a sample of n observations. The binomial distribution has four basic properties:

- The sample consists of a fixed number of observations, n.
- Each observation is classified into one of two mutually exclusive and collectively exhaustive categories.
- The probability of an observation being classified as the event of interest, π, is constant from observation to observation. Thus, the probability of an observation being classified as not being the event of interest, $1-\pi$, is constant over all observations.
- The outcome of any observation is independent of the outcome of any other observation. To ensure independence, the observations can be randomly selected either from an *infinite population with or without replacement* or from a *finite population with replacement*.

Returning to the Saxon Home Improvement scenario presented on page 161 concerning the accounting information system, suppose the event of interest is defined as a tagged order form. You are interested in the number of tagged order forms in a given sample of orders.

What results can occur? If the sample contains four orders, there could be none, one, two, three, or four tagged order forms. No other value can occur because the number of tagged order forms cannot be more than the sample size, n, and cannot be less than zero. Therefore, the range of the binomial random variable is from 0 to n.

Suppose that you observe the following result in a sample of four orders:

First Order	Second Order	Third Order	Fourth Order
Tagged	Tagged	Not tagged	Tagged

What is the probability of having three tagged order forms in a sample of four orders in this particular sequence? Because the historical probability of a tagged order is 0.10, the probability that each order occurs in the sequence is

First Order	Second Order	Third Order	Fourth Order
$\pi = 0.10$	$\pi = 0.10$	$1 - \pi = 0.90$	$\pi = 0.10$

Each outcome is independent of the others because the order forms were selected from an extremely large or practically infinite population without replacement. Therefore, the probability of having this particular sequence is

$$\pi\pi(1 - \pi)\pi = \pi^3(1 - \pi)^1$$
$$= (0.10)^3(0.90)^1$$
$$= (0.10)(0.10)(0.10)(0.90)$$
$$= 0.0009$$

This result indicates only the probability of three tagged order forms (events of interest) from a sample of four order forms in a *specific sequence*. To find the number of ways of selecting X objects from n objects, *irrespective of sequence*, you use the **rule of combinations** given in Equation (5.10).

COMBINATIONS

The number of combinations of selecting x objects[1] out of n objects is given by

$$_nC_x = \frac{n!}{x!(n - x)!} \qquad \textbf{(5.10)}$$

where

$n! = (n)(n - 1)\cdots(1)$ is called n factorial. By definition, $0! = 1$.

With $n = 4$ and $x = 3$, there are

$$_nC_x = \frac{n!}{x!(n - x)!} = \frac{4!}{3!(4 - 3)!} = \frac{4 \times 3 \times 2 \times 1}{(3 \times 2 \times 1)(1)} = 4$$

such sequences. The four possible sequences are

Sequence 1 = *tagged, tagged, tagged, not tagged*, with probability
$$\pi\pi\pi(1 - \pi) = \pi^3(1 - \pi)^1 = 0.0009$$

Sequence 2 = *tagged, tagged, not tagged, tagged*, with probability
$$\pi\pi(1 - \pi)\pi = \pi^3(1 - \pi)^1 = 0.0009$$

Sequence 3 = *tagged, not tagged, tagged, tagged*, with probability
$$\pi(1 - \pi)\pi\pi = \pi^3(1 - \pi)^1 = 0.0009$$

Sequence 4 = *not tagged, tagged, tagged, tagged*, with probability
$$(1 - \pi)\pi\pi\pi = \pi^3(1 - \pi)^1 = 0.0009$$

Therefore, the probability of three tagged order forms is equal to

(Number of possible sequences) $\times$ (Probability of a particular sequence)

$$= (4) \times (0.0009) = 0.0036$$

You can make a similar, intuitive derivation for the other possible outcomes of the random variable—zero, one, two, and four tagged order forms. However, as n, the sample size, gets large, the computations involved in using this intuitive approach become time-consuming. Equation (5.11) is the mathematical model that provides a general formula for computing any probability from the binomial distribution with the number of events of interest, x, given n and π.

BINOMIAL DISTRIBUTION

$$P(X = x \mid n, \pi) = \frac{n!}{x!(n - x)!} \pi^x (1 - \pi)^{n-x} \qquad \textbf{(5.11)}$$

where

$P(X = x \mid n, \pi) = $ probability that $X = x$ events of interest, given n and π

$n = $ number of observations

$\pi = $ probability of an event of interest

$1 - \pi = $ probability of not having an event of interest

$x = $ number of events of interest in the sample $(X = 0, 1, 2, \cdots, n)$

$\dfrac{n!}{x!(n - x)!} = $ the number of combinations of x events of interest out of n observations

Equation (5.11) restates what was intuitively derived previously. The binomial variable X can have any integer value x from 0 through n. In Equation (5.11), the product

$$\pi^x (1 - \pi)^{n-x}$$

represents the probability of exactly x events of interest from n observations in a *particular sequence*.

The term

$$\frac{n!}{x!(n - x)!}$$

is the number of *combinations* of the x events of interest from the n observations possible. Hence, given the number of observations, n, and the probability of an event of interest, π, the probability of x events of interest is

$$P(X = x \mid n, \pi) = (\text{Number of combinations}) \times (\text{Probability of a particular combination})$$

$$= \frac{n!}{x!(n - x)!} \pi^x (1 - \pi)^{n-x}$$

Example 5.1 illustrates the use of Equation (5.11).

EXAMPLE 5.1

Determining $P(X = 3)$, Given $n = 4$ and $\pi = 0.1$

If the likelihood of a tagged order form is 0.1, what is the probability that there are three tagged order forms in the sample of four?

SOLUTION Using Equation (5.11) above, the probability of three tagged orders from a sample of four is

$$P(X = 3 \mid n = 4, \pi = 0.1) = \frac{4!}{3!(4 - 3)!} (0.1)^3 (1 - 0.1)^{4-3}$$

$$= \frac{4!}{3!(1)!} (0.1)^3 (0.9)^1$$

$$= 4(0.1)(0.1)(0.1)(0.9) = 0.0036$$

Examples 5.2 and 5.3 show the computations for other values of X.

EXAMPLE 5.2

Determining $P(X \geq 3)$, Given $n = 4$ and $\pi = 0.1$

If the likelihood of a tagged order form is 0.1, what is the probability that there are three or more (i.e., at least three) tagged order forms in the sample of four?

SOLUTION In Example 5.1, you found that the probability of *exactly* three tagged order forms from a sample of four is 0.0036. To compute the probability of *at least* three tagged order forms, you need to add the probability of three tagged order forms to the probability of four tagged order forms. The probability of four tagged order forms is

$$P(X = 4 \mid n = 4, \pi = 0.1) = \frac{4!}{4!(4-4)!} (0.1)^4 (1 - 0.1)^{4-4}$$

$$= \frac{4!}{4!(0)!} (0.1)^4 (0.9)^0$$

$$= 1(0.1)(0.1)(0.1)(0.1) = 0.0001$$

Thus, the probability of at least three tagged order forms is

$$P(X \geq 3) = P(X = 3) + P(X = 4)$$

$$= 0.0036 + 0.0001$$

$$= 0.0037$$

There is a 0.37% chance that there will be at least three tagged order forms in a sample of four.

EXAMPLE 5.3

Determining $P(X < 3)$, Given $n = 4$ and $\pi = 0.1$

If the likelihood of a tagged order form is 0.1, what is the probability that there are fewer than three tagged order forms in the sample of four?

SOLUTION The probability that there are fewer than three tagged order forms is

$$P(X < 3) = P(X = 0) + P(X = 1) + P(X = 2)$$

Using Equation (5.11) on page 172, these probabilities are

$$P(X = 0 \mid n = 4, \pi = 0.1) = \frac{4!}{0!(4-0)!} (0.1)^0 (1 - 0.1)^{4-0} = 0.6561$$

$$P(X = 1 \mid n = 4, \pi = 0.1) = \frac{4!}{1!(4-1)!} (0.1)^1 (1 - 0.1)^{4-1} = 0.2916$$

$$P(X = 2 \mid n = 4, \pi = 0.1) = \frac{4!}{2!(4-2)!} (0.1)^2 (1 - 0.1)^{4-2} = 0.0486$$

Therefore, $P(X < 3) = 0.6561 + 0.2916 + 0.0486 = 0.9963$. $P(X < 3)$ could also be calculated from its complement, $P(X \geq 3)$, as follows:

$$P(X < 3) = 1 - P(X \geq 3)$$

$$= 1 - 0.0037 = 0.9963$$

Computing binomial probabilities become tedious as n gets large. Figure 5.2 shows how the worksheet **BINOMDIST** function simplifies the computation of binomial probabilities. Binomial probabilities can also be looked up in a table of probabilities, as shown in the **Binomial** online topic available on this book's companion Web site (see Appendix Section D.8 to learn how to access online topics).

FIGURE 5.2

Worksheet for computing
binomial probabilities

*Figure 5.2 displays the
COMPUTE worksheet of the
Binomial workbook and
reveals the formulas the
worksheet uses. See
Section EG5.3 to learn
how to compute binomial
probabilities and how to use
the Binomial workbook as a
template for other problems.*

	A	B	
1	Binomial Probabilities		
2			
3	Data		
4	Sample size	4	
5	Probability of an event of interest	0.1	
6			
7	Statistics		
8	Mean	0.4	=B4 * B5
9	Variance	0.36	=B8 * (1 - B5)
10	Standard deviation	0.6	=SQRT(B9)
11			
12	Binomial Probabilities Table		
13	X	P(X)	
14	0	0.6561	=BINOMDIST(A14, $B$4, $B$5, FALSE)
15	1	0.2916	=BINOMDIST(A15, $B$4, $B$5, FALSE)
16	2	0.0486	=BINOMDIST(A16, $B$4, $B$5, FALSE)
17	3	0.0036	=BINOMDIST(A17, $B$4, $B$5, FALSE)
18	4	0.0001	=BINOMDIST(A18, $B$4, $B$5, FALSE)

The shape of a binomial probability distribution depends on the values of n and π. Whenever $\pi = 0.5$, the binomial distribution is symmetrical, regardless of how large or small the value of n. When $\pi \neq 0.5$, the distribution is skewed. The closer π is to 0.5 and the larger the number of observations, n, the less skewed the distribution becomes. For example, the distribution of the number of tagged order forms is highly skewed to the right because $\pi = 0.1$ and $n = 4$ (see Figure 5.3).

FIGURE 5.3

Histogram of the binomial
probability distribution
with $n = 4$ and $\pi = 0.1$

*Create this chart sheet using
the instructions in Section
EG5.3.*

Binomial Probability Histogram

Observe from Figure 5.3 that unlike the histogram for continuous variables in Section 2.6, the bars for the values are very thin, and there is a large gap between each pair of values. That is because the histogram represents a discrete variable. (Theoretically, the bars should have no width. They should be vertical lines.)

The mean (or expected value) of the binomial distribution is equal to the product of n and π. Instead of using Equation (5.1) on page 163 to compute the mean of the probability distribution, you use Equation (5.12) to compute the mean for variables that follow the binomial distribution.

MEAN OF THE BINOMIAL DISTRIBUTION

The mean, μ, of the binomial distribution is equal to the sample size, n, multiplied by the probability of an event of interest, π.

$$\mu = E(X) = n\pi \qquad (5.12)$$

On the average, over the long run, you theoretically expect $\mu = E(X) = n\pi = (4)(0.1) = 0.4$ tagged order form in a sample of four orders.

The standard deviation of the binomial distribution is calculated using Equation (5.13).

STANDARD DEVIATION OF THE BINOMIAL DISTRIBUTION

$$\sigma = \sqrt{\sigma^2} = \sqrt{Var(X)} = \sqrt{n\pi(1-\pi)} \qquad (5.13)$$

The standard deviation of the number of tagged order forms is

$$\sigma = \sqrt{4(0.1)(0.9)} = 0.60$$

You get the same result if you use Equation (5.3) on page 164.

Example 5.4 applies the binomial distribution to service at a fast-food restaurant.

EXAMPLE 5.4

Computing Binomial Probabilities

Accuracy in taking orders at a drive-through window is important for fast-food chains. Periodically, *QSR Magazine* (data extracted from **www.qsrmagazine.com/reports/drive-thru_time_study/2008/chart-accuracy_breakdown.phtml**) publishes the results of its surveys. Accuracy is measured as the percentage of orders that are filled correctly. Recently, the percentage of orders filled correctly at Wendy's was approximately 92%. If a sample of three orders is taken, what are the mean and standard deviation of the binomial distribution for the number of orders filled correctly? Suppose that you go to the drive-through window at Wendy's and place an order. Two friends of yours independently place orders at the drive-through window at the same Wendy's. What are the probabilities that all three, that none of the three, and that at least two of the three orders will be filled correctly?

SOLUTION Because there are three orders and the probability of a correct order is 0.92, $n = 3$ and $\pi = 0.92$. Using Equations (5.12) and (5.13),

$$\mu = E(X) = n\pi = 3(0.92) = 2.76$$
$$\sigma = \sqrt{\sigma^2} = \sqrt{Var(X)} = \sqrt{n\pi(1-\pi)}$$
$$= \sqrt{3(0.92)(0.08)}$$
$$= \sqrt{0.2208} = 0.4699$$

Using Equation (5.11) on page 172,

$$P(X = 3 \mid n = 3, \pi = 0.92) = \frac{3!}{3!(3-3)!}(0.92)^3(1-0.92)^{3-3}$$
$$= \frac{3!}{3!(3-3)!}(0.92)^3(0.08)^0$$
$$= 1(0.92)(0.92)(0.92)(1) = 0.7787$$

$$P(X = 0 \mid n = 3, \pi = 0.92) = \frac{3!}{0!(3-0)!}(0.92)^0(1-0.92)^{3-0}$$

$$= \frac{3!}{0!(3-0)!}(0.92)^0(0.08)^3$$

$$= 1(1)(0.08)(0.08)(0.08) = 0.0005$$

$$P(X = 2 \mid n = 3, \pi = 0.92) = \frac{3!}{2!(3-2)!}(0.92)^2(1-0.92)^{3-2}$$

$$= \frac{3!}{2!(3-2)!}(0.92)^2(0.08)^1$$

$$= 3(0.92)(0.92)(0.08) = 0.2031$$

$$P(X \geq 2) = P(X = 2) + P(X = 3)$$

$$= 0.2031 + 0.7787$$

$$= 0.9818$$

The mean number of orders filled correctly in a sample of three orders is 2.76, and the standard deviation is 0.4699. The probability that all three orders are filled correctly is 0.7787, or 77.87%. The probability that none of the orders are filled correctly is 0.0005, or 0.05%. The probability that at least two orders are filled correctly is 0.9818, or 98.18%.

In this section, you have been introduced to the binomial distribution. The binomial distribution is an important mathematical model in many business situations.

Problems for Section 5.3

LEARNING THE BASICS

5.18 If $n = 5$ and $\pi = 0.40$, what is the probability that
a. $X = 4$?
b. $X \leq 3$?
c. $X < 2$?
d. $X > 1$?

5.19 Determine the following:
a. For $n = 4$ and $\pi = 0.12$, what is $P(X = 0)$?
b. For $n = 10$ and $\pi = 0.40$, what is $P(X = 9)$?
c. For $n = 10$ and $\pi = 0.50$, what is $P(X = 8)$?
d. For $n = 6$ and $\pi = 0.83$, what is $P(X = 5)$?

5.20 Determine the mean and standard deviation of the random variable X in each of the following binomial distributions:
a. $n = 4$ and $\pi = 0.10$
b. $n = 4$ and $\pi = 0.40$
c. $n = 5$ and $\pi = 0.80$
d. $n = 3$ and $\pi = 0.50$

APPLYING THE CONCEPTS

5.21 The increase or decrease in the price of a stock between the beginning and the end of a trading day is assumed to be an equally likely random event. What is the probability that a stock will show an increase in its closing price on five consecutive days?

5.22 A recent article (Dennis R. Owens, "The Probability of Reoccurrence: $P(r)$," *Quality Progress*, April 2007, 40, p. 88) discusses a manufacturing company assessing the chance that its product will fail. The article identifies six independent events that can cause a failure. The probability of each of these events failing is quite low, 0.05, but for a product to ultimately be a success, it must not experience a failure in any of the six events.
a. Use the binomial probability distribution to calculate the probability that a product will ultimately be successful (i.e., that a product will not fail).
b. If the probabilities of the six events are not all equal, how could you calculate the probability in (a)?

5.23 A student is taking a multiple-choice exam in which each question has four choices. Assuming that she has no knowledge of the correct answers to any of the questions, she has decided on a strategy in which she will place four balls (marked A, B, C, and D) into a box. She randomly selects one ball for each question and replaces the ball in the box. The marking on the ball will determine her answer to the question. There are five multiple-choice questions on the exam. What is the probability that she will get
a. five questions correct?
b. at least four questions correct?
c. no questions correct?
d. no more than two questions correct?

5.24 Investment advisors agree that near-retirees, defined as people aged 55 to 65, should have balanced portfolios. Most advisors suggest that the near-retirees have no more than 50% of their investments in stocks. However, during the huge decline in the stock market in 2008, 22% of near-retirees had 90% or more of their investments in stocks (P. Regnier, "What I Learned from the Crash," *Money*, May 2009, p. 114). Suppose you have a random sample of 10 people who would have been labeled as near-retirees in 2008. What is the probability that during 2008
a. zero had 90% or more of their investment in stocks?
b. exactly one had 90% or more of his or her investment in stocks?
c. two or fewer had 90% or more of their investment in stocks?
d. three or more had 90% or more of their investment in stocks?

5.25 When a customer places an order with Rudy's On-Line Office Supplies, a computerized accounting information system (AIS) automatically checks to see if the customer has exceeded his or her credit limit. Past records indicate that the probability of customers exceeding their credit limit is 0.05. Suppose that, on a given day, 20 customers place orders. Assume that the number of customers that the AIS detects as having exceeded their credit limit is distributed as a binomial random variable.
a. What are the mean and standard deviation of the number of customers exceeding their credit limits?

b. What is the probability that zero customers will exceed their limits?
c. What is the probability that one customer will exceed his or her limit?
d. What is the probability that two or more customers will exceed their limits?

SELF Test **5.26** In Example 5.4 on page 175, you and two friends decided to go to Wendy's. Now, suppose that instead you go to Popeye's, which last month filled approximately 84% of orders correctly. What is the probability that
a. all three orders will be filled correctly?
b. none of the three will be filled correctly?
c. at least two of the three will be filled correctly?
d. What are the mean and standard deviation of the binomial distribution used in (a) through (c)? Interpret these values.

5.27 In Example 5.4 on page 175, you and two friends decided to go to Wendy's. Now, suppose that instead you go to McDonald's, which last month filled approximately 94.5% of the orders correctly. What is the probability that
a. all three orders will be filled correctly?
b. none of the three will be filled correctly?
c. at least two of the three will be filled correctly?
d. What are the mean and standard deviation of the binomial distribution used in (a) through (c)? Interpret these values.
e. Compare the result of (a)–(d) with those of Popeye's in Problem 5.26 and Wendy's in Example 5.4 on page 175.

5.4 Poisson Distribution

Many studies are based on counts of the times a particular event occurs in a given *area of opportunity*. An **area of opportunity** is a continuous unit or interval of time, volume, or any physical area in which there can be more than one occurrence of an event. Examples of variables that follow the Poisson distribution are the surface defects on a new refrigerator, the number of network failures in a day, the number of people arriving at a bank, and the number of fleas on the body of a dog. You can use the **Poisson distribution** to calculate probabilities in situations such as these if the following properties hold:

- You are interested in counting the number of times a particular event occurs in a given area of opportunity. The area of opportunity is defined by time, length, surface area, and so forth.
- The probability that an event occurs in a given area of opportunity is the same for all the areas of opportunity.
- The number of events that occur in one area of opportunity is independent of the number of events that occur in any other area of opportunity.
- The probability that two or more events will occur in an area of opportunity approaches zero as the area of opportunity becomes smaller.

Consider the number of customers arriving during the lunch hour at a bank located in the central business district in a large city. You are interested in the number of customers that arrive each minute. Does this situation match the four properties of the Poisson distribution given earlier? First, the *event* of interest is a customer arriving, and the *given area of opportunity* is defined as a 1-minute interval. Will zero customers arrive, one customer arrive, two customers arrive, and so on? Second, it is reasonable to assume that the probability that a customer arrives during a particular 1-minute interval is the same as the probability for all the other 1-minute intervals. Third, the arrival of one customer in any 1-minute interval has no effect on (i.e., is independent of) the arrival of any other customer in any other 1-minute interval. Finally, the probability that two or more customers will arrive in a given time period approaches zero as the time interval becomes small. For example, the probability is virtually zero that two customers will arrive in a time interval of 0.01 second. Thus, you can use the Poisson distribution to determine probabilities involving the number of customers arriving at the bank in a 1-minute time interval during the lunch hour.

The Poisson distribution has one parameter, called λ (the Greek lowercase letter *lambda*), which is the mean or expected number of events per unit. The variance of a Poisson distribution is also equal to λ, and the standard deviation is equal to $\sqrt{\lambda}$. The number of events, X, of the Poisson random variable ranges from 0 to infinity (∞).

Equation (5.14) is the mathematical expression for the Poisson distribution for computing the probability of X events, given that λ events are expected.

POISSON DISTRIBUTION

$$P(X = x \mid \lambda) = \frac{e^{-\lambda}\lambda^x}{x!} \tag{5.14}$$

where

$P(X = x \mid \lambda)$ = the probability that $X = x$ events in an area of opportunity given λ

λ = expected number of events

e = mathematical constant approximated by 2.71828

x = number of events ($x = 0, 1, 2, \ldots, \infty$)

To illustrate an application of the Poisson distribution, suppose that the mean number of customers who arrive per minute at the bank during the noon-to-1 P.M. hour is equal to 3.0. What is the probability that in a given minute, exactly two customers will arrive? And what is the probability that more than two customers will arrive in a given minute?

Using Equation (5.14) and $\lambda = 3$, the probability that in a given minute exactly two customers will arrive is

$$P(X = 2 \mid \lambda = 3) = \frac{e^{-3.0}(3.0)^2}{2!} = \frac{9}{(2.71828)^3(2)} = 0.2240$$

To determine the probability that in any given minute more than two customers will arrive,

$$P(X > 2) = P(X = 3) + P(X = 4) + \cdots + P(X = \infty)$$

Because in a probability distribution, all the probabilities must sum to 1, the terms on the right side of the equation $P(X > 2)$ also represent the complement of the probability that X is less than or equal to 2 [i.e., $1 - P(X \leq 2)$]. Thus,

$$P(X > 2) = 1 - P(X \leq 2) = 1 - [P(X = 0) + P(X = 1) + P(X = 2)]$$

Now, using Equation (5.14),

$$P(X > 2) = 1 - \left[\frac{e^{-3.0}(3.0)^0}{0!} + \frac{e^{-3.0}(3.0)^1}{1!} + \frac{e^{-3.0}(3.0)^2}{2!} \right]$$

$$= 1 - [0.0498 + 0.1494 + 0.2240]$$

$$= 1 - 0.4232 = 0.5768$$

Thus, there is a 57.68% chance that more than two customers will arrive in the same minute.

Computing Poisson probabilities can be tedious. Figure 5.4 shows how the worksheet **POISSON** function simplifies the computation of Poisson probabilities. Poisson probabilities can also be looked up in a table of probabilities, as shown in the **Poisson** online topic available on this book's companion Web site (see Appendix Section D.8 to learn how to access online topics).

FIGURE 5.4

Worksheet for computing Poisson probabilities with $\lambda = 3$

Figure 5.4 displays the **COMPUTE worksheet** *of the* **Poisson workbook** *and reveals the formulas the worksheet uses. See Section EG5.4 to learn how to compute Poisson probabilities and how to use the Poisson workbook as a template for other problems.*

	A	B	C D E
1	Poisson Probabilities		
2			
3		Data	
4	Mean/Expected number of events of interest:		3
5			
6	Poisson Probabilities Table		
7	X	P(X)	
8	0	0.0498	=POISSON(A8, $E$4, FALSE)
9	1	0.1494	=POISSON(A9, $E$4, FALSE)
10	2	0.2240	=POISSON(A10, $E$4, FALSE)
11	3	0.2240	=POISSON(A11, $E$4, FALSE)
12	4	0.1680	=POISSON(A12, $E$4, FALSE)
13	5	0.1008	=POISSON(A13, $E$4, FALSE)
14	6	0.0504	=POISSON(A14, $E$4, FALSE)
15	7	0.0216	=POISSON(A15, $E$4, FALSE)
16	8	0.0081	=POISSON(A16, $E$4, FALSE)
17	9	0.0027	=POISSON(A17, $E$4, FALSE)
18	10	0.0008	=POISSON(A18, $E$4, FALSE)
19	11	0.0002	=POISSON(A19, $E$4, FALSE)
20	12	0.0001	=POISSON(A20, $E$4, FALSE)
21	13	0.0000	=POISSON(A21, $E$4, FALSE)
22	14	0.0000	=POISSON(A22, $E$4, FALSE)
23	15	0.0000	=POISSON(A23, $E$4, FALSE)
24	16	0.0000	=POISSON(A24, $E$4, FALSE)
25	17	0.0000	=POISSON(A25, $E$4, FALSE)
26	18	0.0000	=POISSON(A26, $E$4, FALSE)
27	19	0.0000	=POISSON(A27, $E$4, FALSE)
28	20	0.0000	=POISSON(A28, $E$4, FALSE)

EXAMPLE 5.5

Computing Poisson Probabilities

The number of work-related injuries per month in a manufacturing plant is known to follow a Poisson distribution with a mean of 2.5 work-related injuries a month. What is the probability that in a given month no work-related injuries occur? That at least one work-related injury occurs?

SOLUTION Using Equation (5.14) on page 178 with $\lambda = 2.5$ (or Excel or a Poisson table lookup), the probability that in a given month no work-related injuries occur is

$$P(X = 0 \mid \lambda = 2.5) = \frac{e^{-2.5}(2.5)^0}{0!} = \frac{1}{(2.71828)^{2.5}(1)} = 0.0821$$

The probability that there will be no work-related injuries in a given month is 0.0821, or 8.21%. Thus,

$$P(X \geq 1) = 1 - P(X = 0)$$
$$= 1 - 0.0821$$
$$= 0.9179$$

The probability that there will be at least one work-related injury is 0.9179, or 91.79%.

Problems for Section 5.4

LEARNING THE BASICS

5.28 Assume a Poisson distribution.
a. If $\lambda = 2.5$, find $P(X = 2)$.
b. If $\lambda = 8.0$, find $P(X = 8)$.
c. If $\lambda = 0.5$, find $P(X = 1)$.
d. If $\lambda = 3.7$, find $P(X = 0)$.

5.29 Assume a Poisson distribution.
a. If $\lambda = 2.0$, find $P(X \geq 2)$.
b. If $\lambda = 8.0$, find $P(X \geq 3)$.
c. If $\lambda = 0.5$, find $P(X \leq 1)$.
d. If $\lambda = 4.0$, find $P(X \geq 1)$.
e. If $\lambda = 5.0$, find $P(X \leq 3)$.

5.30 Assume a Poisson distribution with $\lambda = 5.0$. What is the probability that
a. $X = 1$?
b. $X < 1$?
c. $X > 1$?
d. $X \leq 1$?

APPLYING THE CONCEPTS

5.31 Assume that the number of network errors experienced in a day on a local area network (LAN) is distributed as a Poisson random variable. The mean number of network errors experienced in a day is 2.4. What is the probability that in any given day
a. zero network errors will occur?
b. exactly one network error will occur?
c. two or more network errors will occur?
d. fewer than three network errors will occur?

✓ SELF Test **5.32** The quality control manager of Marilyn's Cookies is inspecting a batch of chocolate-chip cookies that has just been baked. If the production process is in control, the mean number of chip parts per cookie is 6.0. What is the probability that in any particular cookie being inspected
a. fewer than five chip parts will be found?
b. exactly five chip parts will be found?
c. five or more chip parts will be found?
d. either four or five chip parts will be found?

5.33 Refer to Problem 5.32. How many cookies in a batch of 100 should the manager expect to discard if company policy requires that all chocolate-chip cookies sold have at least four chocolate-chip parts?

5.34 The U.S. Department of Transportation maintains statistics for mishandled bags per 1,000 airline passengers. In 2007, airlines had mishandled 7 bags per 1,000 passengers (data extracted from R. Yu, "Airline Performance Nears 20 Year Low," *USA Today*, April 8, 2008, p. B1). What is the probability that in the next 1,000 passengers, airlines will have
a. no mishandled bags?
b. at least one mishandled bag?
c. at least two mishandled bags?

5.35 The U.S. Department of Transportation maintains statistics for consumer complaints per 100,000 airline passengers. In 2007, consumer complaints were 1.42 per 100,000 passengers (data extracted from R. Yu, "Airline Performance Nears 20 Year Low," *USA Today*, April 8, 2008, p. B1). What is the probability that in the next 100,000 passengers, there will be
a. no complaints?
b. at least one complaint?
c. at least two complaints?

5.36 Based on past experience, it is assumed that the number of flaws per foot in rolls of grade 2 paper follows a Poisson distribution with a mean of 1 flaw per 5 feet of paper (0.2 flaw per foot). What is the probability that in a
a. 1-foot roll, there will be at least 2 flaws?
b. 12-foot roll, there will be at least 1 flaw?
c. 50-foot roll, there will be more than or equal to 5 flaws and fewer than or equal to 15 flaws?

5.37 J.D. Power and Associates calculates and publishes various statistics concerning car quality. The initial quality score measures the number of problems per new car sold. For 2009 model cars, Ford had 1.02 problems per car and Dodge had 1.34 problems per car (S. Carty, "U.S. Autos Power Forward with Gains in Quality Survey," *USA Today*, June 23, 2009, p. 3B). Let the random variable X be equal to the number of problems with a newly purchased 2009 Ford.
a. What assumptions must be made in order for X to be distributed as a Poisson random variable? Are these assumptions reasonable?
Making the assumptions as in (a), if you purchased a 2009 Ford, what is the probability that the new car will have
b. zero problems?
c. two or fewer problems?
d. Give an operational definition for *problem*. Why is the operational definition important in interpreting the initial quality score?

5.38 Refer to Problem 5.37. If you purchased a 2009 Dodge, what is the probability that the new car will have
a. zero problems?
b. two or fewer problems?
c. Compare your answers in (a) and (b) to those for the Ford in Problem 5.37 (b) and (c).

5.39 Refer to Problem 5.37. Another article (S. Carty, "Ford Moves Up in Quality Survey," *USA Today*, June 5, 2008, p. 3B) reported that in 2008, Ford had 1.12 problems per car and Dodge had 1.41 problems per car. If you purchased a 2008 Ford, what is the probability that the new car will have
a. zero problems?
b. two or fewer problems?
c. Compare your answers in (a) and (b) to those for the 2009 Ford in Problem 5.37 (b) and (c).

5.40 Refer to Problem 5.39. If you purchased a 2008 Dodge, what is the probability that the new car will have
a. zero problems?
b. two or fewer problems?
c. Compare your answers in (a) and (b) to those for the 2009 Dodge in Problem 5.38 (a) and (b).

5.41 A toll-free phone number is available from 9 a.m. to 9 p.m. for your customers to register complaints about a product purchased from your company. Past history indicates that an average of 0.4 calls are received per minute.

a. What properties must be true about the situation described here in order to use the Poisson distribution to calculate probabilities concerning the number of phone calls received in a 1-minute period?

Assuming that this situation matches the properties discussed in (a), what is the probability that during a 1-minute period
b. zero phone calls will be received?
c. three or more phone calls will be received?
d. What is the maximum number of phone calls that will be received in a 1-minute period 99.99% of the time?

5.5 Hypergeometric Distribution

Both the binomial distribution and the **hypergeometric distribution** are concerned with the number of events of interest in a sample containing n observations. One of the differences in these two probability distributions is in the way the samples are selected. For the binomial distribution, the sample data are selected *with* replacement from a *finite* population or *without* replacement from an *infinite* population. Thus, the probability of an event of interest, π, is constant over all observations, and the outcome of any particular observation is independent of any other. For the hypergeometric distribution, the sample data are selected *without* replacement from a *finite* population. Thus, the outcome of one observation is dependent on the outcomes of the previous observations.

Consider a population of size N. Let A represent the total number of events of interest in the population. The hypergeometric distribution is then used to find the probability of X events of interest in a sample of size n, selected without replacement. Equation (5.15) represents the mathematical expression of the hypergeometric distribution for finding X events of interest, given a knowledge of n, N, and A.

HYPERGEOMETRIC DISTRIBUTION

$$P(X = x \mid n, N, A) = \frac{\binom{A}{x}\binom{N-A}{n-x}}{\binom{N}{n}} \tag{5.15}$$

where

$P(X = x \mid n, N, A) =$ the probability of x events of interest, given knowledge of n, N, and A

$n =$ sample size

$N =$ population size

$A =$ number of events of interest in the population

$N - A =$ number of events that are not of interest in the population

$x =$ number of events of interest in the sample

$\binom{A}{x} = {}_A C_x$ [see Equation (5.10) on p. 171]

$x \leq A$
$x \leq n$
$A \leq n$

Because the number of events of interest in the sample, represented by x, cannot be greater than the number of events of interest in the population, A, nor can A be greater than the sample size, n, the range of the hypergeometric random variable is limited to the sample size or to the number of events of interest in the population, whichever is smaller.

Equation (5.16) defines the mean of the hypergeometric distribution, and Equation (5.17) defines the standard deviation.

MEAN OF THE HYPERGEOMETRIC DISTRIBUTION

$$\mu = E(X) = \frac{nA}{N} \tag{5.16}$$

STANDARD DEVIATION OF THE HYPERGEOMETRIC DISTRIBUTION

$$\sigma = \sqrt{\frac{nA(N-A)}{N^2}}\sqrt{\frac{N-n}{N-1}} \tag{5.17}$$

In Equation (5.17), the expression $\sqrt{\frac{N-n}{N-1}}$ is a **finite population correction factor** that results from sampling without replacement from a finite population.

To illustrate the hypergeometric distribution, suppose that you are forming a team of 8 managers from different departments within your company. Your company has a total of 30 managers, and 10 of these people are from the finance department. If you are to randomly select members of the team, what is the probability that the team will contain 2 managers from the finance department? Here, the population of $N = 30$ managers within the company is finite. In addition, $A = 10$ are from the finance department. A team of $n = 8$ members is to be selected.

Using Equation (5.15),

$$P(X = 2 \mid n = 8, N = 30, A = 10) = \frac{\binom{10}{2}\binom{20}{6}}{\binom{30}{8}}$$

$$= \frac{\left(\dfrac{10!}{2!(8)!}\right)\left(\dfrac{(20)!}{(6)!(14)!}\right)}{\left(\dfrac{30!}{8!(22)!}\right)}$$

$$= 0.298$$

Thus, the probability that the team will contain two members from the finance department is 0.298, or 29.8%.

Computing hypergeometric probabilities can be tedious, especially as N gets large. Figure 5.5 shows how the worksheet **HYPGEOMDIST** function simplifies the computation of hypergeometric probabilities for the team-formation example.

FIGURE 5.5

Worksheet for the team member example

*Figure 5.5 displays the **COMPUTE worksheet** of the **Hypergeometric workbook** and reveals the formulas the worksheet uses. See Section EG5.5 to learn how to compute hypergeometric probabilities and how to use the Hypergeometric workbook as a template for other problems.*

	A	B	
1	Hypergeometric Probabilities		
2			
3	**Data**		
4	Sample size	8	
5	No. of events of interest in population	10	
6	Population size	30	
7			
8	**Hypergeometric Probabilities Table**		
9	X	P(X)	
10	0	0.0215	=HYPGEOMDIST(A10, $B$4, $B$5, $B$6)
11	1	0.1324	=HYPGEOMDIST(A11, $B$4, $B$5, $B$6)
12	2	0.2980	=HYPGEOMDIST(A12, $B$4, $B$5, $B$6)
13	3	0.3179	=HYPGEOMDIST(A13, $B$4, $B$5, $B$6)
14	4	0.1738	=HYPGEOMDIST(A14, $B$4, $B$5, $B$6)
15	5	0.0491	=HYPGEOMDIST(A15, $B$4, $B$5, $B$6)
16	6	0.0068	=HYPGEOMDIST(A16, $B$4, $B$5, $B$6)
17	7	0.0004	=HYPGEOMDIST(A17, $B$4, $B$5, $B$6)
18	8	0.0000	=HYPGEOMDIST(A18, $B$4, $B$5, $B$6)

Problems for Section 5.5

LEARNING THE BASICS

5.42 Determine the following:
a. If $n = 4, N = 10$, and $A = 5$, find $P(X = 3)$.
b. If $n = 4, N = 6$, and $A = 3$, find $P(X = 1)$.
c. If $n = 5, N = 12$, and $A = 3$, find $P(X = 0)$.
d. If $n = 3, N = 10$, and $A = 3$, find $P(X = 3)$.

5.43 Referring to Problem 5.42, compute the mean and standard deviation for the hypergeometric distributions described in (a) through (d).

APPLYING THE CONCEPTS

✓ SELF **5.44** An auditor for the Internal Revenue Service
Test is selecting a sample of 6 tax returns for an audit. If 2 or more of these returns are "improper," the entire population of 100 tax returns will be audited. What is the probability that the entire population will be audited if the true number of improper returns in the population is
a. 25?
b. 30?
c. 5?
d. 10?
e. Discuss the differences in your results, depending on the true number of improper returns in the population.

5.45 The dean of a business school wishes to form an executive committee of 5 from among the 40 tenured faculty members at the school. The selection is to be random, and at the school there are 8 tenured faculty members in accounting. What is the probability that the committee will contain
a. none of them?

b. at least 1 of them?
c. not more than 1 of them?
d. What is your answer to (a) if the committee consists of 7 members?

5.46 From an inventory of 30 cars being shipped to a local automobile dealer, 4 are SUVs. What is the probability that if 4 cars arrive at a particular dealership,
a. all 4 are SUVs?
b. none are SUVs?
c. at least 1 is an SUV?
d. What are your answers to (a) through (c) if 6 cars being shipped are SUVs?

5.47 A state lottery is conducted in which 6 winning numbers are selected from a total of 54 numbers. What is the probability that if 6 numbers are randomly selected,
a. all 6 numbers will be winning numbers?
b. 5 numbers will be winning numbers?
c. none of the numbers will be winning numbers?
d. What are your answers to (a) through (c) if the 6 winning numbers are selected from a total of 40 numbers?

5.48 In a shipment of 15 sets of golf clubs, 3 are left-handed. If 4 sets of golf clubs are selected, what is the probability that
a. exactly 1 is left-handed?
b. at least 1 is left-handed?
c. no more than 2 are left-handed?
d. What is the mean number of left-handed sets of golf clubs that you would expect to find in the sample of 4 sets of golf clubs?

USING STATISTICS @ Saxon Home Improvement Revisited

I n the Saxon Home Improvement scenario, you were an accountant for the Saxon Home Improvement Company. The company's accounting information system automatically reviews order forms from online customers for possible mistakes. Any questionable invoices are tagged and included in a daily exceptions report. Knowing that the probability that an order will be tagged is 0.10, you were able to use the binomial distribution to determine the chance of finding a certain number of tagged forms in a sample of size 4. There was a 65.6% chance that none of the forms would be tagged, a 29.2% chance that one would be tagged, and a 5.2% chance that two or more would be tagged. You were also able to determine that, on average, you would expect 0.4 forms to be tagged, and the standard deviation of the number of tagged order forms would be 0.6. Now that you have learned the mechanics of using the binomial distribution for a known probability of 0.10 and a sample size of four, you will be able to apply the same approach to any given probability and sample size. Thus, you will be able to make inferences about the online ordering process and, more importantly, evaluate any changes or proposed changes to the process.

SUMMARY

In this chapter, you have studied mathematical expectation and three important discrete probability distributions: the binomial, Poisson, and hypergeometric distributions. In the following chapter, you will study several important continuous distributions including the normal distribution.

To help decide what probability distribution to use for a particular situation, you need to ask the following questions:

- Is there a fixed number of observations, n, each of which is classified as an event of interest or not an event of interest? Or is there an area of opportunity? If

there is a fixed number of observations, n, each of which is classified as an event of interest or not an event of interest, you use the binomial or hypergeometric distribution. If there is an area of opportunity, you use the Poisson distribution.

- In deciding whether to use the binomial or hypergeometric distribution, is the probability of an event of interest constant over all trials? If yes, you can use the binomial distribution. If no, you can use the hypergeometric distribution.

KEY EQUATIONS

Expected Value, μ, of a Discrete Random Variable

$$\mu = E(X) = \sum_{i=1}^{N} X_i P(X_i) \tag{5.1}$$

Variance of a Discrete Random Variable

$$\sigma^2 = \sum_{i=1}^{N} [X_i - E(X)]^2 P(X_i) \tag{5.2}$$

Standard Deviation of a Discrete Random Variable

$$\sigma = \sqrt{\sigma^2} = \sqrt{\sum_{i=1}^{N} [X_i - E(X)]^2 P(X_i)} \tag{5.3}$$

Covariance

$$\sigma_{XY} = \sum_{i=1}^{N} [X_i - E(X)][Y_i - E(Y)]P(X_iY_i) \tag{5.4}$$

Expected Value of the Sum of Two Random Variables

$$E(X + Y) = E(X) + E(Y) \tag{5.5}$$

Variance of the Sum of Two Random Variables

$$Var(X + Y) = \sigma_{X+Y}^2 = \sigma_X^2 + \sigma_Y^2 + 2\sigma_{XY} \tag{5.6}$$

Standard Deviation of the Sum of Two Random Variables

$$\sigma_{X+Y} = \sqrt{\sigma_{X+Y}^2} \tag{5.7}$$

Portfolio Expected Return

$$E(P) = wE(X) + (1 - w)E(Y) \tag{5.8}$$

Portfolio Risk

$$\sigma_p = \sqrt{w^2\sigma_X^2 + (1 - w)^2\sigma_Y^2 + 2w(1 - w)\sigma_{XY}} \tag{5.9}$$

Combinations

$$_nC_x = \frac{n!}{x!(n - x)!} \tag{5.10}$$

Binomial Distribution

$$P(X = x \mid n,\pi) = \frac{n!}{x!(n - x)!} \pi^x(1 - \pi)^{n-x} \tag{5.11}$$

Mean of the Binomial Distribution

$$\mu = E(X) = n\pi \tag{5.12}$$

Standard Deviation of the Binomial Distribution

$$\sigma = \sqrt{\sigma^2} = \sqrt{Var(X)} = \sqrt{n\pi(1 - \pi)} \tag{5.13}$$

Poisson Distribution

$$P(X = x \mid \lambda) = \frac{e^{-\lambda}\lambda^x}{x!} \tag{5.14}$$

Hypergeometric Distribution

$$P(X = x \mid n, N, A) = \frac{\binom{A}{x}\binom{N - A}{n - x}}{\binom{N}{n}} \tag{5.15}$$

Mean of the Hypergeometric Distribution

$$\mu = E(X) = \frac{nA}{N} \tag{5.16}$$

Standard Deviation of the Hypergeometric Distribution

$$\sigma = \sqrt{\frac{nA(N - A)}{N^2}} \sqrt{\frac{N - n}{N - 1}} \tag{5.17}$$

KEY TERMS

area of opportunity   177
binomial distribution   170
covariance, σ_{XY} 165
expected value   162
expected value, μ, of a discrete
   random variable   162
expected value of the sum of two
   random variables   167
finite population correction
   factor   182

hypergeometric distribution   181
mathematical model   170
Poisson distribution   177
portfolio   167
portfolio expected return   167
portfolio risk   167
probability distribution for a discrete
   random variable   162
rule of combinations   171

standard deviation of a discrete
   random variable   164
standard deviation of the sum of two
   random variables   167
variance of a discrete random
   variable   163
variance of the sum of two random
   variables   167

CHAPTER REVIEW PROBLEMS

CHECKING YOUR UNDERSTANDING

5.49 What is the meaning of the expected value of a probability distribution?

5.50 What are the four properties that must be present in order to use the binomial distribution?

5.51 What are the four properties that must be present in order to use the Poisson distribution?

5.52 When do you use the hypergeometric distribution instead of the binomial distribution?

APPLYING THE CONCEPTS

5.53 Darwin Head, a 35-year-old sawmill worker, won $1 million and a Chevrolet Malibu Hybrid by scoring 15 goals within 24 seconds at the Vancouver Canucks National Hockey League game (B. Ziemer, "Darwin Evolves into an Instant Millionaire," *Vancouver Sun*, February 28, 2008, p.1). Head said he would use the money to pay off his mortgage and provide for his children, and he had no plans to quit his job. The contest was part of the Chevrolet Malibu Million Dollar Shootout, sponsored by General Motors Canadian Division. Did GM-Canada risk the $1 million? No! GM-Canada purchased event insurance from a company specializing in promotions at sporting events such as a half-court basketball shot or a hole-in-one giveaway at the local charity golf outing. The event insurance company estimates the probability of a contestant winning the contest, and for a modest charge, insures the event. The promoters pay the insurance premium but take on no added risk as the insurance company will make the large payout in the unlikely event that a contestant wins. To see how it works, suppose that the insurance company estimates that the probability a contestant would win a Million Dollar Shootout is 0.001, and that the insurance company charges $4,000.
a. Calculate the expected value of the profit made by the insurance company.

b. Many call this kind of situation a win–win opportunity for the insurance company and the promoter. Do you agree? Explain.

5.54 Between 1872 and 2000, stock prices rose in 74% of the years (M. Hulbert, "The Stock Market Must Rise in 2002? Think Again," *The New York Times*, December 6, 2001, Business, p. 6). Based on this information, and assuming a binomial distribution, what do you think is the probability that the stock market will rise
a. next year?
b. the year after next?
c. in four of the next five years?
d. in none of the next five years?
e. For this situation, what assumption of the binomial distribution might not be valid?

5.55 The mean cost of a phone call handled by an automated customer-service system is $0.45. The mean cost of a phone call passed on to a "live" operator is $5.50. However, as more and more companies have implemented automated systems, customer annoyance with such systems has grown. Many customers are quick to leave an automated system when given an option such as "Press zero to talk to a customer-service representative." According to the Center for Client Retention, 40% of all callers to automated customer-service systems automatically opt to go to a live operator when given the chance (J. Spencer, "In Search of the Operator," *The Wall Street Journal*, May 8, 2002, p. D1).

If 10 independent callers contact an automated customer-service system, what is the probability that
a. 0 will automatically opt to talk to a live operator?
b. exactly 1 will automatically opt to talk to a live operator?
c. 2 or fewer will automatically opt to talk to a live operator?
d. all 10 will automatically opt to talk to a live operator?
e. If all 10 automatically opt to talk to a live operator, do you think that the 40% value given in the article applies to this particular system? Explain.

5.56 One theory concerning the Dow Jones Industrial Average is that it is likely to increase during U.S. presidential election years. From 1964 through 2008, the Dow Jones Industrial Average increased in 9 of the 12 U.S. presidential election years. Assuming that this indicator is a random event with no predictive value, you would expect that the indicator would be correct 50% of the time.

a. What is the probability of the Dow Jones Industrial Average increasing in 9 or more of the 12 U.S. presidential election years if the true probability of an increase in the Dow Jones Industrial Average is 0.50?

b. From 1964 to 2008, the Dow Jones Industrial Average increased in 75% of the years. What is the probability that the Dow Jones Industrial Average will increase in 9 or more of the 12 U.S. presidential election years if the probability of an increase in the Dow Jones Industrial Average in any year is 0.75?

5.57 Errors in a billing process often lead to customer dissatisfaction and ultimately hurt bottom-line profits. An article in *Quality Progress* (L. Tatikonda, "A Less Costly Billing Process," *Quality Progress*, January 2008, pp. 30–38) discussed a company where 40% of the bills prepared contained errors. If 10 bills are processed, what is the probability that

a. 0 bills will contain errors?

b. exactly 1 bill will contain an error?

c. 2 or more bills will contain errors?

d. What are the mean and the standard deviation of the probability distribution?

5.58 Refer to Problem 5.57. Suppose that a quality improvement initiative has reduced the percentage of bills containing errors to 20%. If 10 bills are processed, what is the probability that

a. 0 bills will contain errors?

b. exactly 1 bill will contain an error?

c. 2 or more bills will contain errors?

d. What are the mean and the standard deviation of the probability distribution?

e. Compare the results of (a) through (c) to those of Problem 5.57 (a) through (c).

5.59 A study by the Center for Financial Services Innovation showed that only 64% of U.S. income earners aged 15 and older had bank accounts (A. Carrns, "Banks Court a New Client," *The Wall Street Journal*, March 16, 2007, p. D1).

If a random sample of 20 U.S. income earners aged 15 and older is selected, what is the probability that

a. all 20 have bank accounts?

b. no more than 15 have bank accounts?

c. more than 10 have bank accounts?

d. What assumptions did you have to make to answer (a) through (c)?

5.60 One of the biggest frustrations for the consumer electronics industry is that customers are accustomed to return goods for any reason (C. Lawton, "The War on Returns," *The Wall Street Journal*, May 8, 2008, pp. D1, D6). Recently, it was reported that returns for "no trouble found" were 68% of all the returns. Consider a sample of 20 customers who returned consumer electronics purchases. Use the binomial model to answer the following questions:

a. What is the expected value, or mean, of the binomial distribution?

b. What is the standard deviation of the binomial distribution?

c. What is the probability that 15 of the 20 customers made a return for "no trouble found"?

d. What is the probability that no more than 10 of the customers made a return for "no trouble found"?

e. What is the probability that 10 or more of the customers made a return for "no trouble found"?

5.61 Refer to Problem 5.60. In the same time period, 27% of the returns were for "buyer's remorse."

a. What is the expected value, or mean, of the binomial distribution?

b. What is the standard deviation of the binomial distribution?

c. What is the probability that none of the 20 customers made a return for "buyer's remorse"?

d. What is the probability that no more than 2 of the customers made a return for "buyer's remorse"?

e. What is the probability that 3 or more of the customers made a return for "buyer's remorse"?

5.62 One theory concerning the S&P 500 Index is that if it increases during the first five trading days of the year, it is likely to increase during the entire year. From 1950 through 2008, the S&P 500 Index had these early gains in 38 years. In 32 of these 38 years, the S&P 500 Index increased for the entire year. Assuming that this indicator is a random event with no predictive value, you would expect that the indicator would be correct 50% of the time. What is the probability of the S&P 500 Index increasing in 32 or more years if the true probability of an increase in the S&P 500 Index is

a. 0.50?

b. 0.70?

c. 0.90?

d. Based on the results of (a) through (c), what do you think is the probability that the S&P 500 Index will increase if there is an early gain in the first five trading days of the year? Explain.

5.63 *Spurious correlation* refers to the apparent relationship between variables that either have no true relationship or are related to other variables that have not been measured. One widely publicized stock market indicator in the United States that is an example of spurious correlation is the relationship between the winner of the National Football League Super Bowl and the performance of the Dow Jones Industrial Average in that year. The indicator states that when a team representing the National Football Conference wins the Super Bowl, the Dow Jones Industrial Average will increase in that year. When a team representing the American Football Conference wins the Super Bowl, the Dow Jones Industrial Average will decline in that year. Since the first Super Bowl was held in 1967 through 2008, the indicator has been correct 33 out of 42 times. Assuming that this indicator is a random event with no predictive value, you would expect that the indicator would be correct 50% of the time.

a. What is the probability that the indicator would be correct 33 or more times in 42 years?

b. What does this tell you about the usefulness of this indicator?

5.64 Worldwide golf ball sales total more than $1 billion annually. One reason for such a large number of golf ball purchases is that golfers lose them at a rate of 4.5 per 18-hole round ("Snapshots," **www.usatoday.com**, January 29, 2004). Assume that the number of golf balls lost in an 18-hole round is distributed as a Poisson random variable.

a. What assumptions need to be made so that the number of golf balls lost in an 18-hole round is distributed as a Poisson random variable?

Making the assumptions given in (a), what is the probability that

b. 0 balls will be lost in an 18-hole round?

c. 5 or fewer balls will be lost in an 18-hole round?

d. 6 or more balls will be lost in an 18-hole round?

5.65 According to a Virginia Tech survey, college students make an average of 11 calls per day on their cell phone. Moreover, 80% of the students surveyed indicated that their parents pay their cell phone expenses (J. Elliot, "Professor Researches Cell Phone Usage Among Students," **www.physorg.com**, February 26, 2007).

a. What distribution can you use to model the number of calls a student makes in a day?

b. If you select a student at random, what is the probability that he or she makes more than 10 calls in a day? More than 15? More than 20?

c. If you select a random sample of 10 students, what distribution can you use to model the proportion of students who have parents who pay their cell phone expenses?

d. Using the distribution selected in (c), what is the probability that all 10 have parents who pay their cell phone expenses? At least 9? At least 8?

5.66 Mega Millions is one of the most popular lottery games in the United States. States participating in Mega Millions are Georgia, Illinois, Maryland, Massachusetts, Michigan, New Jersey, New York, Ohio, and Virginia. Rules for playing and the list of prizes are given below ("Win Megamoney Playing Ohio's Biggest Jackpot Game," Ohio Lottery Headquarters, 2002):

Rules:
- Select five numbers from a pool of numbers from 1 to 52 and one Mega Ball number from a second pool of numbers from 1 to 52.
- Each wager costs $1.

Prizes:
- Match all five numbers + Mega Ball—win jackpot (minimum of $10,000,000)
- Match all five numbers—win $175,000
- Match four numbers + Mega Ball—win $5,000
- Match four numbers—win $150
- Match three numbers + Mega Ball—win $150
- Match two numbers + Mega Ball—win $10
- Match three numbers—win $7
- Match one number + Mega Ball—win $3
- Match Mega Ball—win $2

Find the probability of winning

a. the jackpot.

b. the $175,000 prize. (Note that this requires matching all five numbers but not matching the Mega Ball.)

c. $5,000.

d. $150.

e. $10.

f. $7.

g. $3.

h. $2.

i. nothing.

j. All stores selling Mega Millions tickets are required to have a brochure that gives complete game rules and probabilities of winning each prize (the probability of having a losing ticket is not given). The slogan for all lottery games in the state of Ohio is "Play Responsibly. Odds Are, You'll Have Fun." Do you think Ohio's slogan and the requirement of making available complete game rules and probabilities of winning is an ethical approach to running the lottery system?

MANAGING THE *SPRINGVILLE HERALD*

The *Herald* marketing department is seeking to increase home-delivery sales through an aggressive direct-marketing campaign that includes mailings, discount coupons, and telephone solicitations. Feedback from these efforts indicates that getting their newspapers delivered early in the morning is a very important factor for both prospective and existing subscribers. After several brainstorming sessions, a team consisting of members from the marketing and circulation departments decided that guaranteeing newspaper delivery by a specific time could be an important selling point in retaining and getting new subscribers. The team concluded that the *Herald* should offer a guarantee that customers will receive their newspapers by a certain time or else that day's issue is free.

To assist the team in setting a guaranteed delivery time, Al Leslie, the research director, determined that the circulation department had data that showed the percentage of newspapers yet undelivered every quarter hour from 6 A.M. to 8 A.M. Jan Shapiro remembered that customers were asked on their subscription forms at what time they would be looking for their copy of the *Herald* to be delivered. These data were subsequently combined and posted on an internal *Herald* Web page. Using a Web browser, open to the Web page for the Chapter 5 *Springville Herald* Case or open **Circulation_Data.htm** if you have downloaded the Herald Case files.

EXERCISES

Review the internal data and propose a reasonable time (to the nearest quarter hour) to guarantee delivery. To help explore the effects of your choice, calculate the following probabilities:

SH5.1 If a sample of 50 customers is selected on a given day, what is the probability, given your selected delivery time, that
   a. fewer than 3 customers will receive a free newspaper?
   b. 2, 3, or 4 customers will receive a free newspaper?
   c. more than 5 customers will receive a free newspaper?

SH5.2 Consider the effects of improving the newspaper delivery process so that the percentage of newspapers that go undelivered by your guaranteed delivery time decreases by 2%. If a sample of 50 customers is selected on a given day, what is the probability, given your selected delivery time (and the delivery improvement), that
   a. fewer than 3 customers will receive a free newspaper?
   b. 2, 3, or 4 customers will receive a free newspaper?
   c. more than 5 customers will receive a free newspaper?

WEB CASE

Apply your knowledge about expected value and the covariance in this continuing Web Case from Chapters 3 and 4.

Using a Web browser, open to the Web page for the Chapter 5 Web Case or open **ER_BullsandBears.htm**, if you have downloaded the Web Case files, to visit the EndRun Bulls and Bears Web page. Read the claims and examine the supporting data. Then answer the following:

1. Are there any "catches" about the claims the Web site makes for the rate of return of Happy Bull and Worried Bear Funds?

2. What subjective data influence the rate-of-return analyses of these funds? Could EndRun be accused of making false and misleading statements? Why or why not?

3. The expected-return analysis seems to show that the Worried Bear Fund has a greater expected return than the Happy Bull Fund. Should a rational investor never invest in the Happy Bull Fund? Why or why not?

REFERENCES

1. Bernstein, P. L., *Against the Gods: The Remarkable Story of Risk* (New York: Wiley, 1996).
2. Emery, D. R., J. D. Finnerty, and J. D. Stowe, *Corporate Financial Management*, 3rd ed. (Upper Saddle River, NJ: Prentice Hall, 2007).
3. Kirk, R. L., ed., *Statistical Issues: A Reader for the Behavioral Sciences* (Belmont, CA: Wadsworth, 1972).
4. Levine, D. M., P. Ramsey, and R. Smidt, *Applied Statistics for Engineers and Scientists Using Microsoft Excel and Minitab* (Upper Saddle River, NJ: Prentice Hall, 2001).
5. *Microsoft Excel 2007* (Redmond, WA: Microsoft Corp., 2007).
6. Moscove, S. A., M. G. Simkin, and N. A. Bagranoff, *Core Concepts of Accounting Information Systems*, 10th ed. (New York: Wiley, 2007).

CHAPTER 5 EXCEL GUIDE

EG5.1 THE PROBABILITY DISTRIBUTION for a DISCRETE RANDOM VARIABLE

In-Depth Excel Use the **COMPUTE worksheet** of the **Discrete Random Variable workbook** as a template for computing the expected value, variance, and standard deviation of a discrete random variable (see Figure EG5.1). The worksheet contains the data for the Section 5.1 example involving the number of interruptions per day in a large computer network. Overwrite the X and $P(X)$ values when you enter data for other problems. If a problem has more or fewer than six outcomes, first select the cell range **A5:E5** and:

To increase the number of outcomes:

1. Right-click and click **Insert** from the shortcut menu.
2. If a dialog box appears, click **Shift cells down** and then click **OK**.
3. Repeat steps 1 and 2 as many times as necessary.
4. Select the formulas in cell range **C4:E4** and copy them down through the new table rows.
5. Enter the new X and $P(X)$ values in columns **A** and **B**.

To decrease the number of outcomes:

1. Right-click and click **Delete** from the shortcut menu.
2. If a dialog box appears, click **Shift cells up** and then click **OK**.
3. Repeat steps 1 and 2 as many times as necessary.
4. Enter the new X and $P(X)$ values in columns **A** and **B**.

	A	B	C	D	E	F	G	H	
1	Discrete Random Variable Probability Distribution								
2							Statistics		
3	X	P(X)	X*P(X)	[X-E(X)]^2	[X-E(X)]^2*P(X)		Expected value	1.4	=SUM(C:C)
4	0	0.35	0	1.96	0.686		Variance	2.04	=SUM(E:E)
5	1	0.25	0.25	0.16	0.04		Standard deviation	1.43	=SQRT(H4)
6	2	0.20	0.4	0.36	0.072				
7	3	0.10	0.3	2.56	0.256		X*P(X)	[X-E[X]]^2	[X-E[X]]^2*P(X)
8	4	0.05	0.2	6.76	0.338		=A4 * B4	=(A4 - $H$3)^2	=D4 * B4
9	5	0.05	0.25	12.96	0.648		=A5 * B5	=(A5 - $H$3)^2	=D5 * B5
							=A6 * B6	=(A6 - $H$3)^2	=D6 * B6
							=A7 * B7	=(A7 - $H$3)^2	=D7 * B7
							=A8 * B8	=(A8 - $H$3)^2	=D8 * B8
							=A9 * B9	=(A9 - $H$3)^2	=D9 * B9

FIGURE EG5.1 Discrete random variable probability worksheet

EG5.2 COVARIANCE and ITS APPLICATION in FINANCE

PHStat2 Use the **Covariance and Portfolio Analysis** procedure to perform portfolio analysis. For example, to create the portfolio analysis for the Section 5.2 investment example,

select **PHStat → Decision-Making → Covariance and Portfolio Analysis**. In the procedure's dialog box:

1. Enter **5** as the **Number of Outcomes**.
2. Enter a **Title**, check **Portfolio Management Analysis**, and click **OK**.

In the new worksheet:

3. Enter the probabilities and outcomes in the table that begins in cell **B3** (see Figure EG5.2 below).
4. Enter **0.5** as the **Weight assigned to X**.

In-Depth Excel Use the **COMPUTE worksheet** of the **Portfolio workbook** as a template for performing portfolio analysis (see Figure EG5.2). The worksheet contains the data for the Section 5.2 investment example. Overwrite the

	A	B	C	D
1	Portfolio Expected Return and Risk			
2				
3	Probabilities & Outcomes:	P	X	Y
4		0.2	-300	200
5		0.5	100	50
6		0.3	250	-100
7				
8	Weight Assigned to X	0.5		
9				
10	Statistics			
11	E(X)	65	=SUMPRODUCT(B4:B6, C4:C6)	
12	E(Y)	35	=SUMPRODUCT(B4:B6, D4:D6)	
13	Variance(X)	37525	=SUMPRODUCT(B4:B6, H4:H6)	
14	Standard Deviation(X)	193.71	=SQRT(B13)	
15	Variance(Y)	11025	=SUMPRODUCT(B4:B6, I4:I6)	
16	Standard Deviation(Y)	105	=SQRT(B15)	
17	Covariance(XY)	-19275	=SUMPRODUCT(B4:B6, J4:J6)	
18	Variance(X+Y)	10000	=B13 + B15 + 2 * B17	
19	Standard Deviation(X+Y)	100	=SQRT(B18)	
20				
21	Portfolio Management			
22	Weight Assigned to X	0.5	=B8	
23	Weight Assigned to Y	0.5	=1-B22	
24	Portfolio Expected Return	50	=B22 * B11 + B23 * B12	
25	Portfolio Risk	50	=SQRT(B22^2 * B13 + B23^2 * B15	
			+ 2 * B22 * B23 * B17)	

FIGURE EG5.2 Portfolio analysis worksheet

X and $P(X)$ values and the weight assigned to the X value when you enter data for other problems. If a problem has more or fewer than three outcomes, first select row **5**, right-click, and click **Insert** (or **Delete**) in the shortcut menu to insert (or delete) rows one at a time. If you insert rows, select the cell range **B5:J5** and copy the contents of this range down through the new table rows.

Figure EG5.2 also reveals the column B formulas. In that column, the **SUMPRODUCT** function computes the sum of the products of corresponding elements of two cell ranges (each of which is treated as an array). The function multiplies the set of $P(X_i Y_i)$ probabilities (in B4:B6) by their corresponding values in column C to compute $E(X)$ and by the corresponding values in column D to compute $E(Y)$.

Figure EG5.3 shows the Calculations Area of the COMPUTE worksheet. **SUMPRODUCT** also multiplies the set of $P(X_i Y_i)$ probabilities by the set of values computed in columns H through J to compute the variances and the covariance.

	E	F	G	H	I	J
1			Calculations Area			
2		For variance and standard deviation:				For covariance:
3		X-mu	Y-mu	(X-mu)^2	(Y-mu)^2	(X-mu)(Y-mu)
4		=C4 - $B$11	=D4 - $B$12	=F4^2	=G4^2	=F4 * G4
5		=C5 - $B$11	=D5 - $B$12	=F5^2	=G5^2	=F5 * G5
6		=C6 - $B$11	=D6 - $B$12	=F6^2	=G6^2	=F6 * G6

FIGURE EG5.3   Calculations Area of the portfolio analysis worksheet

EG5.3 BINOMIAL DISTRIBUTION

PHStat2 Use the **Binomial** procedure to compute binomial probabilities. For example, to create a binomial probabilities table and histogram for Example 5.3, similar to those in Figures 5.2 and 5.3, select **PHStat → Probability & Prob. Distributions → Binomial**. In the procedure's dialog box (see below):

1. Enter **4** as the **Sample Size**.
2. Enter **0.1** as the **Prob. of an Event of Interest**.
3. Enter **0** as the **Outcomes From** value and enter **4** as the (Outcomes) **To** value.
4. Enter a **Title**, check **Histogram**, and click **OK**.

To add columns to the binomial probabilities table for $P(<=X), P(<X), P(>X)$, and $P(\geq)$, check **Cumulative Probabilities** before clicking **OK** in step 4.

In-Depth Excel Use the **BINOMDIST** function to compute binomial probabilities. Enter the function as **BINOMDIST** (*X, sample size, π, cumulative*), where X is the number of events of interest, π is the probability of an event of interest, and *cumulative* is a **True** or **False** value. (When *cumulative* is **True**, the function computes the probability of X or fewer events of interest; when *cumulative* is **False**, the function computes the probability of exactly X events of interest.)

Use the **COMPUTE worksheet** of the **Binomial workbook**, shown in Figure 5.2 on page 174, as a template for computing binomial probabilities. The worksheet contains the data for the Section 5.2 tagged orders example. Overwrite these values when you enter data for other problems. If a problem has a sample size other than 4, select row **15**, right-click, and click either **Insert** (or **Delete**) in the shortcut menu to insert (or delete) rows one at a time. Then edit the X values in column A and if you inserted rows, select the cell **B14** formula and copy it down through the new table rows.

To create a histogram of the probability distribution, use the instructions in Section C.9 (for Excel 2007) or Section C.10 (for Excel 2003) in Appendix C.

EG5.4 POISSON DISTRIBUTION

PHStat2 Use the **Poisson** procedure to compute Poisson probabilities. For example, to create a Poisson probabilities table similar to Figure 5.4 on page 179, select **PHStat → Probability & Prob. Distributions → Poisson**. In this procedure's dialog box:

1. Enter **3** as the **Mean/Expected No. of Events of Interest**.
2. Enter a **Title** and click **OK**.

To add columns to the Poisson probabilities table for $P(<=X), P(<X), P(>X)$, and $P(\geq)$, check **Cumulative Probabilities** before clicking **OK** in step 2. To create a histogram of the probability distribution on a separate chart sheet, check **Histogram** before clicking **OK** in step 2.

In-Depth Excel Use the **POISSON** function to compute Poisson probabilities. Enter the function as **POISSON(X, lambda, cumulative)**, where *X* is the number of events of interest, *lambda* is the average or expected number of events of interest, and *cumulative* is a **True** or **False** value. (When *cumulative* is **True**, the function computes the probability of *X* or fewer events of interest; when *cumulative* is **False**, the function computes the probability of exactly *X* events of interest.)

Use the **COMPUTE worksheet** of the **Poisson workbook**, shown in Figure 5.4 on page 179, as a template for computing Poisson probabilities. The worksheet contains the entries for the bank customer arrivals problem of Section 5.4. To adapt this worksheet to other problems, change the **Mean/Expected number of events of interest value** in cell **E4**.

To create a histogram of the probability distribution, use the instructions in Section C.9 (for Excel 2007) or Section C.10 (for Excel 2003) in Appendix C.

EG5.5 HYPERGEOMETRIC DISTRIBUTION

PHStat2 Use the **Hypergeometric** procedure to compute hypergeometric probabilities. For example, to create a hypergeometric probabilities table similar to Figure 5.5 on page 182, select **PHStat → Probability & Prob. Distributions → Hypergeometric**. In this procedure's dialog box:

1. Enter **8** as the **Sample Size**.
2. Enter **10** as the **No. of Events of Interest in Pop.** (population).
3. Enter **30** as the **Population Size**.
4. Enter a **Title** and click **OK**.

To create a histogram of the probability distribution on a separate chart sheet, check **Histogram** before clicking **OK** in step 4.

In-Depth Excel Use the **HYPGEOMDIST** function to compute hypergeometric probabilities. Enter the function as **HYPGEOMDIST(X, sample size, A, population size)**, where *X* is the number of events of interest and *A* is the number of events of interest in the population.

Use the **COMPUTE worksheet** of the **Hypergeometric workbook**, shown in Figure 5.5 on page 182, as a template for computing hypergeometric probabilities. The worksheet contains the data for the Section 5.5 team-formation example. To adapt this worksheet to other problems, change the sample size, the number of events of interest, and population size values in cells **B4**, **B5**, and **B6**, respectively.

If a problem has a sample size other than 8, select row **11**, right-click, and click **Insert** (or **Delete**) in the shortcut menu to insert (or delete) rows one at a time. Then edit the *X* values in column A and if you inserted rows, select the cell **B10** formula, and copy it down through the new table rows.

To create a histogram of the probability distribution, use the instructions in Section C.9 (for Excel 2007) or Section C.10 (for Excel 2003) in Appendix C.

6

The Normal Distribution and Other Continuous Distributions

Learning Objectives

In this chapter, you learn:

- To compute probabilities from the normal distribution
- How to use the normal distribution to solve business problems
- To use the normal probability plot to determine whether a set of data is approximately normally distributed
- To compute probabilities from the uniform distribution
- To compute probabilities from the exponential distribution

USING STATISTICS

@ OurCampus!

You are a designer for the *OurCampus!* Web site, a social networking site that targets college students. To attract and retain visitors to the site, you need to make sure that the exclusive-content daily videos can be quickly downloaded and played in a user's browser. Download time, the amount of time, in seconds, that passes from the first linking to the Web site home page until the first video is ready to play, is both a function of the design of the home page and the number of simultaneous users of the Web site. To check how fast a video downloads, you open a Web browser on a PC at the corporate offices of OurCampus! and measure the download time. Past data indicate that the mean download time is 7 seconds and that the standard deviation is 2 seconds. Approximately two-thirds of the download times are between 5 and 9 seconds, and about 95% of the download times are between 3 and 11 seconds. In other words, the download times are distributed as a bell-shaped curve, with a clustering around the mean of 7 seconds. How could you use this information to answer questions about the download times of the first video?

193

I n Chapter 5, Saxon Home Improvement Company managers wanted to be able to solve problems about the number of tagged items in a given sample size. As an OurCampus! Web designer, you face a different task, one that involves a continuous measurement because a download time could be any value and not just a whole number. How can you answer questions, such as the following, about this *continuous numerical variable*:

- What proportion of the video downloads take more than 9 seconds?
- How many seconds elapse before 10% of the downloads are complete?
- How many seconds elapse before 99% of the downloads are complete?
- How would redesigning the home page to download faster affect the answers to these questions?

As in Chapter 5, you can use a probability distribution as a model. Reading this chapter will help you learn about characteristics of continuous probability distributions and how to use the normal, uniform, and exponential distributions to solve business problems.

6.1 Continuous Probability Distributions

A **probability density function** is a mathematical expression that defines the distribution of the values for a continuous random variable. Figure 6.1 graphically displays three probability density functions.

FIGURE 6.1

Three continuous probability distributions

Values of *X*	Values of *X*	Values of *X*
Panel A	Panel B	Panel C
Normal Distribution	Uniform Distribution	Exponential Distribution

Panel A depicts a normal distribution. The normal distribution is symmetrical and bell-shaped, implying that most values tend to cluster around the mean, which, due to the distribution's symmetrical shape, is equal to the median. Although the values in a normal distribution can range from negative infinity to positive infinity, the shape of the distribution makes it very unlikely that extremely large or extremely small values will occur.

Panel B shows a *uniform distribution* where each value has an equal probability of occurrence anywhere in the range between the smallest value and the largest value. Sometimes referred to as the *rectangular distribution*, the uniform distribution is symmetrical, and therefore the mean equals the median.

Panel C illustrates an *exponential distribution*. This distribution is skewed to the right, making the mean larger than the median. The range for an exponential distribution is zero to positive infinity, but the distribution's shape makes the occurrence of extremely large values unlikely.

6.2 The Normal Distribution

The **normal distribution** (sometimes referred to as the *Gaussian distribution*) is the most common continuous distribution used in statistics. The normal distribution is vitally important in statistics for three main reasons:

- Numerous continuous variables common in business have distributions that closely resemble the normal distribution.
- The normal distribution can be used to approximate various discrete probability distributions.
- The normal distribution provides the basis for *classical statistical inference* because of its relationship to the *central limit theorem* (which is discussed in Section 7.4).

The normal distribution is represented by the classic bell shape shown in Panel A of Figure 6.1. In the normal distribution, you can calculate the probability that values occur within certain ranges or intervals. However, the *exact* probability of a *particular value* from a continuous distribution such as the normal distribution is zero. This property distinguishes continuous variables, which are measured, from discrete variables, which are counted. As an example, time (in seconds) is measured and not counted. Therefore, you can determine the probability that the download time for a video on a Web browser is between 7 and 10 seconds, or the probability that the download time is between 8 and 9 seconds, or the probability that the download time is between 7.99 and 8.01 seconds. However, the probability that the download time is *exactly* 8 seconds is zero.

The normal distribution has several important theoretical properties:

- It is symmetrical, and its mean and median are therefore equal.
- It is bell-shaped in its appearance.
- Its interquartile range is equal to 1.33 standard deviations. Thus, the middle 50% of the values are contained within an interval of two-thirds of a standard deviation below the mean and two-thirds of a standard deviation above the mean.
- It has an infinite range ($-\infty < X < \infty$).

In practice, many variables have distributions that closely resemble the theoretical properties of the normal distribution. The data in Table 6.1 represent the amount of soft drink in 10,000 1-liter bottles filled on a recent day. The continuous variable of interest, the amount of soft drink filled, can be approximated by the normal distribution. The measurements of the amount of soft drink in the 10,000 bottles cluster in the interval 1.05 to 1.055 liters and distribute symmetrically around that grouping, forming a bell-shaped pattern.

TABLE 6.1

Amount of Fill in 10,000 Bottles of a Soft Drink

Amount of Fill (liters)	Relative Frequency
< 1.025	48/10,000 = 0.0048
1.025 < 1.030	122/10,000 = 0.0122
1.030 < 1.035	325/10,000 = 0.0325
1.035 < 1.040	695/10,000 = 0.0695
1.040 < 1.045	1,198/10,000 = 0.1198
1.045 < 1.050	1,664/10,000 = 0.1664
1.050 < 1.055	1,896/10,000 = 0.1896
1.055 < 1.060	1,664/10,000 = 0.1664
1.060 < 1.065	1,198/10,000 = 0.1198
1.065 < 1.070	695/10,000 = 0.0695
1.070 < 1.075	325/10,000 = 0.0325
1.075 < 1.080	122/10,000 = 0.0122
1.080 or above	48/10,000 = 0.0048
Total	1.0000

Figure 6.2 shows the relative frequency histogram and polygon for the distribution of the amount filled in 10,000 bottles.

FIGURE 6.2

Relative frequency histogram and polygon of the amount filled in 10,000 bottles of a soft drink

Source: Data are taken from Table 6.1.

For these data, the first three theoretical properties of the normal distribution are approximately satisfied. However, the fourth one, having an infinite range, is not. The amount filled in a bottle cannot possibly be zero or below, nor can a bottle be filled beyond its capacity. From Table 6.1, you see that only 48 out of every 10,000 bottles filled are expected to contain 1.08 liters or more, and an equal number are expected to contain less than 1.025 liters.

The mathematical expression representing a probability density function is denoted by the symbol $f(X)$. For the normal distribution, the **normal probability density function** is given in Equation (6.1).

NORMAL PROBABILITY DENSITY FUNCTION

$$f(X) = \frac{1}{\sqrt{2\pi}\sigma} e^{-(1/2)[(X-\mu)/\sigma]^2} \qquad \textbf{(6.1)}$$

where

e = the mathematical constant approximated by 2.71828

π = the mathematical constant approximated by 3.14159

μ = the mean

σ = the standard deviation

X = any value of the continuous variable, where $-\infty < X < \infty$

Because e and π are mathematical constants, the probabilities of the random variable X are dependent only on the two parameters of the normal distribution—the mean, μ, and the standard deviation, σ. Every time you specify particular values of μ and σ, a *different* normal probability distribution is generated. Figure 6.3 illustrates three different normal distributions.

FIGURE 6.3

Three normal distributions

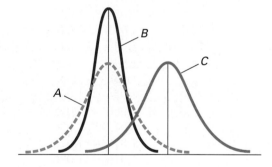

Distributions A and B have the same mean (μ) but have different standard deviations. Distributions A and C have the same standard deviation (σ) but have different means. Distributions B and C have different values for both μ and σ.

Finding probabilities using the mathematical expression in Equation (6.1) is computationally tedious and requires integral calculus. Because normal probability tables are available, you *never* need to use Equation (6.1) to make computations of normal distribution probabilities. The first step in finding normal probabilities is to use the **transformation formula**, given in Equation (6.2), to convert any normally distributed random variable, X, to a **standardized normal random variable**, Z. The Z value expresses the difference of the X value from the mean, μ, in standard deviation units (see Section 3.2 on p. 97).

TRANSFORMATION FORMULA

The Z value is equal to the difference between X and the mean, μ, divided by the standard deviation, σ.

$$Z = \frac{X - \mu}{\sigma} \qquad \textbf{(6.2)}$$

Although the random variable, X, has mean μ and standard deviation σ, the standardized random variable, Z, always has mean $\mu = 0$ and standard deviation $\sigma = 1$.

Any set of normally distributed values can be converted to its standardized form. Then you can determine the probabilities by using Table E.2, the **cumulative standardized normal distribution**. To see how the transformation formula is applied and how the results are used to find probabilities from Table E.2, recall from the Using Statistics scenario on page 193 that past data indicate that the time to download a video is normally distributed, with a mean $\mu = 7$ seconds and a standard deviation $\sigma = 2$ seconds. From Figure 6.4, you see that every measurement X has a corresponding standardized measurement Z, computed from the transformation formula [Equation (6.2)]. Therefore, a download time of 9 seconds is equivalent to 1 standardized unit (i.e., 1 standard deviation) above the mean because

$$Z = \frac{9 - 7}{2} = +1$$

FIGURE 6.4

Transformation of scales

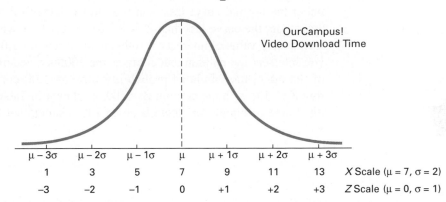

A download time of 1 second is equivalent to 3 standardized units (3 standard deviations) below the mean because

$$Z = \frac{1 - 7}{2} = -3$$

Thus, the standard deviation is the unit of measurement. In other words, a time of 9 seconds is 2 seconds (i.e., 1 standard deviation) higher, or *slower*, than the mean time of 7 seconds. Similarly, a time of 1 second is 6 seconds (i.e., 3 standard deviations) lower, or *faster*, than the mean time.

To further illustrate the transformation formula, suppose that another Web site has a download time for a video that is normally distributed, with a mean $\mu = 4$ seconds and a standard deviation $\sigma = 1$ second. This distribution is illustrated in Figure 6.5.

FIGURE 6.5

A different transformation of scales

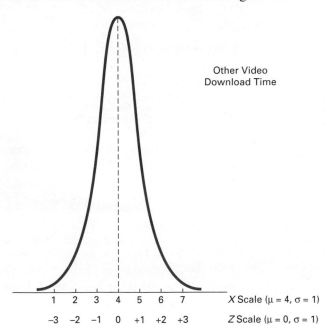

Comparing these results with those of the OurCampus! Web site, you see that a download time of 5 seconds is 1 standard deviation above the mean download time because

$$Z = \frac{5 - 4}{1} = +1$$

A time of 1 second is 3 standard deviations below the mean download time because

$$Z = \frac{1 - 4}{1} = -3$$

Suppose you wanted to find the probability that the download time for the OurCampus! site is less than 9 seconds. First, you use Equation (6.2) on page 196 to transform $X = 9$ to standardized Z units. Because $X = 9$ is one standard deviation above the mean, $Z = +1.00$. Next, you use Table E.2, a portion of which is shown in Table 6.2, to find the cumulative area under the normal curve less than (i.e., to the left of) $Z = +1.00$. To read the probability or area under the curve less than $Z = +1.00$, you scan down the Z column in Table E.2 until you locate the Z value of interest (in 10ths) in the Z row for 1.0. Next, you read across this row until you intersect the column that contains the 100ths place of the Z value. Therefore, in the body of the table, the tabulated probability for $Z = 1.00$ corresponds to the intersection of the row $Z = 1.0$ with the column $Z = .00$, as shown in Table 6.2. This probability is 0.8413. As illustrated in Figure 6.6, there is an 84.13% chance that the download time will be less than 9 seconds.

TABLE 6.2

Finding a Cumulative Area Under the Normal Curve

				Cumulative Probabilities					
Z	.00	.01	.02	.03	.04	.05	.06	.07	.08	.09
0.0	.5000	.5040	.5080	.5120	.5160	.5199	.5239	.5279	.5319	.5359
0.1	.5398	.5438	.5478	.5517	.5557	.5596	.5636	.5675	.5714	.5753
0.2	.5793	.5832	.5871	.5910	.5948	.5987	.6026	.6064	.6103	.6141
0.3	.6179	.6217	.6255	.6293	.6331	.6368	.6406	.6443	.6480	.6517
0.4	.6554	.6591	.6628	.6664	.6700	.6736	.6772	.6808	.6844	.6879
0.5	.6915	.6950	.6985	.7019	.7054	.7088	.7123	.7157	.7190	.7224
0.6	.7257	.7291	.7324	.7357	.7389	.7422	.7454	.7486	.7518	.7549
0.7	.7580	.7612	.7642	.7673	.7704	.7734	.7764	.7794	.7823	.7852
0.8	.7881	.7910	.7939	.7967	.7995	.8023	.8051	.8078	.8106	.8133
0.9	.8159	.8186	.8212	.8238	.8264	.8289	.8315	.8340	.8365	.8389
1.0	.8413	.8438	.8461	.8485	.8508	.8531	.8554	.8577	.8599	.8621

Source: *Extracted from Table E.2.*

FIGURE 6.6

Determining the area less than Z from a cumulative standardized normal distribution

OurCampus! Download Time

Area 0.8413

| X Scale | 1 | 3 | 5 | 7 | 9 | 11 | 13 |
| Z Scale | −3.00 | −2.00 | −1.00 | 0 | +1.00 | +2.00 | +3.00 |

However, for the other Web site, you see that a time of 5 seconds is 1 standardized unit above the mean time of 4 seconds. Thus, the probability that the download time will be less than 5 seconds is also 0.8413. Figure 6.7 shows that regardless of the value of the mean, μ, and standard deviation, σ, of a normally distributed variable, Equation (6.2) can transform the X value to a Z value.

FIGURE 6.7

Demonstrating a transformation of scales for corresponding cumulative portions under two normal curves

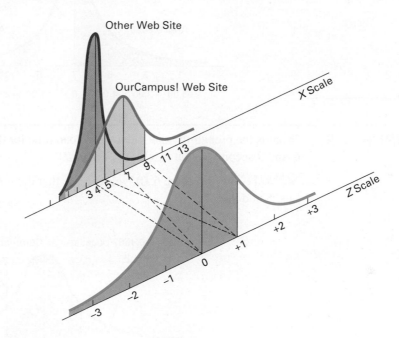

Now that you have learned to use Table E.2 with Equation (6.2), you can answer many questions related to the OurCampus! home page, using the normal distribution.

EXAMPLE 6.1

Finding $P(X > 9)$

What is the probability that the video download time for the OurCampus! Web site will be more than 9 seconds?

SOLUTION The probability that the download time will be less than 9 seconds is 0.8413 (see Figure 6.6 on page 198). Thus, the probability that the download time will be at least 9 seconds is the *complement* of less than 9 seconds, $1 - 0.8413 = 0.1587$. Figure 6.8 illustrates this result.

FIGURE 6.8

Finding $P(X > 9)$

EXAMPLE 6.2

Finding
$P(X < 7 \text{ or } X > 9)$

What is the probability that the video download time for the OurCampus! Web site will be under 7 seconds or over 9 seconds?

SOLUTION To find this probability, you separately calculate the probability of a download time less than 7 seconds and the probability of a download time greater than 9 seconds and then add these two probabilities together. Figure 6.9 on page 200 illustrates this result. Because the mean is 7 seconds, 50% of download times are under 7 seconds. From Example 6.1, you know that the probability that the download time is greater than 9 seconds is 0.1587. Therefore, the probability that a download time is under 7 or over 9 seconds, $P(X < 7 \text{ or } X > 9)$, is $0.5000 + 0.1587 = 0.6587$.

FIGURE 6.9

Finding
$P(X < 7 \text{ or } X > 9)$

EXAMPLE 6.3

Finding
$P(5 < X < 9)$

What is the probability that video download time for the OurCampus! Web site will be between 5 and 9 seconds—that is, $P(5 < X < 9)$?

SOLUTION In Figure 6.10, you can see that the area of interest is located between two values, 5 and 9.

FIGURE 6.10

Finding $P(5 < X < 9)$

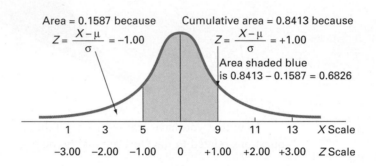

In Example 6.1 on page 199, you already found that the area under the normal curve less than 9 seconds is 0.8413. To find the area under the normal curve less than 5 seconds,

$$Z = \frac{5 - 7}{2} = -1.00$$

Using Table E.2, you look up $Z = -1.00$ and find 0.1587. Therefore, the probability that the download time will be between 5 and 9 seconds is $0.8413 - 0.1587 = 0.6826$, as displayed in Figure 6.10.

The result of Example 6.3 enables you to state that for any normal distribution, 68.26% of the values will fall within ± 1 standard deviation of the mean. From Figure 6.11, you know that 95.44% of the values will fall within ± 2 standard deviations of the mean. Thus, 95.44% of the download times are between 3 and 11 seconds. From Figure 6.12, you know that 99.73% of the values are within ± 3 standard deviations above or below the mean. Thus, 99.73% of the download times are between 1 and 13 seconds. Therefore, it is unlikely (0.0027, or only 27 in 10,000) that a download time will be so fast or so slow that it will take under 1 second or more than 13 seconds. In general, you can use 6σ (that is, 3 standard deviations below the mean to 3 standard deviations above the mean) as a practical approximation of the range for normally distributed data.

FIGURE 6.11

Finding $P(3 < X < 11)$

FIGURE 6.12
Finding $P(1 < X < 13)$

Figures 6.10, 6.11, and 6.12 illustrate how the values of a normal distribution cluster near the mean. For any normal distribution,

- Approximately 68.26% of the values fall within ±1 standard deviation of the mean.
- Approximately 95.44% of the values fall within ±2 standard deviations of the mean.
- Approximately 99.73% of the values fall within ±3 standard deviations of the mean.

This result is the justification for the empirical rule presented on page 111. The accuracy of the empirical rule improves as a data set follows the normal distribution more closely.

Examples 6.1 through 6.3 require you to use the normal distribution Table E.2 to find an area under the normal curve that corresponds to a specific X value. There are many circumstances in which you want to find the X value that corresponds to a specific area. Examples 6.4 and 6.5 illustrate such situations.

EXAMPLE 6.4

Finding the X Value for a Cumulative Probability of 0.10

How much time (in seconds) will elapse before 10% of the downloads of a OurCampus! video are complete?

SOLUTION Because 10% of the videos are expected to download in under X seconds, the area under the normal curve less than this value is 0.1000. Using the body of Table E.2, you search for the area or probability of 0.1000. The closest result is 0.1003, as shown in Table 6.3 (which is extracted from Table E.2).

TABLE 6.3

Finding a Z Value Corresponding to a Particular Cumulative Area (0.10) Under the Normal Curve

Z					Cumulative Probabilities					
	.00	.01	.02	.03	.04	.05	.06	.07	.08	.09
.	.	.	.	.	.	.	.	.	.	.
.	.	.	.	.	.	.	.	.	.	.
.	.	.	.	.	.	.	.	.	.	.
−1.5	.0668	.0655	.0643	.0630	.0618	.0606	.0594	.0582	.0571	.0559
−1.4	.0808	.0793	.0778	.0764	.0749	.0735	.0721	.0708	.0694	.0681
−1.3	.0968	.0951	.0934	.0918	.0901	.0885	.0869	.0853	.0838	.0823
−1.2	.1151	.1131	.1112	.1093	.1075	.0156	.0138	.1020	.1003	.0985

Source: *Extracted from Table E.2.*

Working from this area to the margins of the table, you find that the Z value corresponding to the particular Z row (−1.2) and Z column (.08) is −1.28 (see Figure 6.13).

FIGURE 6.13

Finding Z to determine X

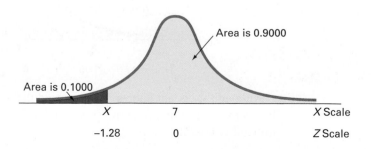

Once you find Z, you use the transformation formula Equation (6.2) on page 196 to determine the X value. Because

$$Z = \frac{X - \mu}{\sigma}$$

then

$$X = \mu + Z\sigma$$

Substituting $\mu = 7$, $\sigma = 2$, and $Z = -1.28$,

$$X = 7 + (-1.28)(2) = 4.44 \text{ seconds}$$

Thus, 10% of the download times are 4.44 seconds or less.

In general, you use Equation (6.3) for finding an X value.

FINDING AN X VALUE ASSOCIATED WITH A KNOWN PROBABILITY

The X value is equal to the mean, μ, plus the product of the Z value and the standard deviation, σ.

$$X = \mu + Z\sigma \qquad (6.3)$$

To find a *particular* value associated with a known probability, follow these steps:

1. Sketch the normal curve and then place the values for the mean and X on the X and Z scales.
2. Find the cumulative area less than X.
3. Shade the area of interest.
4. Using Table E.2, determine the Z value corresponding to the area under the normal curve less than X.
5. Using Equation (6.3), solve for X:

$$X = \mu + Z\sigma$$

EXAMPLE 6.5

Finding the X Values That Include 95% of the Download Times

What are the lower and upper values of X, symmetrically distributed around the mean, that include 95% of the download times for a video at the OurCampus! Web site?

SOLUTION First, you need to find the lower value of X (called X_L). Then, you find the upper value of X (called X_U). Because 95% of the values are between X_L and X_U, and because X_L and X_U are equally distant from the mean, 2.5% of the values are below X_L (see Figure 6.14).

FIGURE 6.14

Finding Z to determine X_L

Although X_L is not known, you can find the corresponding Z value because the area under the normal curve less than this Z is 0.0250. Using the body of Table 6.4, you search for the probability 0.0250.

TABLE 6.4

Finding a Z Value Corresponding to a Cumulative Area of 0.025 Under the Normal Curve

					Cumulative Area				
Z	.00	.01	.02	.03	.04	.05	.06	.07	.08	.09
.	.	.	.	.	.	.	.	.	.
.	.	.	.	.	.	.	.	.	.
.	.	.	.	.	.	.	.	.	.
−2.0	.0228	.0222	.0217	.0212	.0207	.0202	.0197	.0192	.0188	.0183
−1.9	.0287	.0281	.0274	.0268	.0262	.0256	.0250	.0244	.0239	.0233
−1.8	.0359	.0351	.0344	.0336	.0329	.0232	.0314	.0307	.0301	.0294

Source: *Extracted from Table E.2.*

Working from the body of the table to the margins of the table, you see that the Z value corresponding to the particular Z row (-1.9) and Z column $(.06)$ is -1.96.

Once you find Z, the final step is to use Equation (6.3) on page 202 as follows:

$$X = \mu + Z\sigma$$
$$= 7 + (-1.96)(2)$$
$$= 7 - 3.92$$
$$= 3.08 \text{ seconds}$$

You use a similar process to find X_U. Because only 2.5% of the video downloads take longer than X_U seconds, 97.5% of the video downloads take less than X_U seconds. From the symmetry of the normal distribution, you find that the desired Z value, as shown in Figure 6.15, is $+1.96$ (because Z lies to the right of the standardized mean of 0). You can also extract this Z value from Table 6.5. You can see that 0.975 is the area under the normal curve less than the Z value of $+1.96$.

FIGURE 6.15

Finding Z to determine X_U

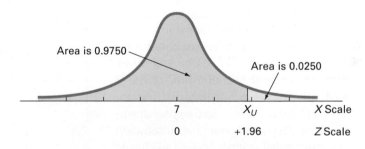

TABLE 6.5

Finding a Z Value Corresponding to a Cumulative Area of 0.975 Under the Normal Curve

					Cumulative Area				
Z	.00	.01	.02	.03	.04	.05	.06	.07	.08	.09
.	.	.	.	.	.	.	.	.	.
.	.	.	.	.	.	.	.	.	.
.	.	.	.	.	.	.	.	.	.
+1.8	.9641	.9649	.9656	.9664	.9671	.9678	.9686	.9693	.9699	.9706
+1.9	.9713	.9719	.9726	.9732	.9738	.9744	.9750	.9756	.9761	.9767
+2.0	.9772	.9778	.9783	.9788	.9793	.9798	.9803	.9808	.9812	.9817

Source: *Extracted from Table E.2.*

Using Equation (6.3) on page 202,

$$X = \mu + Z\sigma$$
$$= 7 + (+1.96)(2)$$
$$= 7 + 3.92$$
$$= 10.92 \text{ seconds}$$

Therefore, 95% of the download times are between 3.08 and 10.92 seconds.

Figure 6.16 illustrates using the worksheet **NORMDIST** function to compute normal probabilities for problems similar to Examples 6.1 through 6.3. This worksheet also uses the worksheet **NORMINV** function in cell E18 to compute probabilities for problems similar to Examples 6.4 and 6.5.

FIGURE 6.16

Worksheet for computing normal probabilities.

Figure 6.16 displays the **COMPUTE worksheet** *of the* **Normal workbook** *and reveals the formulas the worksheet uses. (The figure divides the worksheet in two areas, columns A and B and columns D and E. Column C is blank in the worksheet and is not shown in the figure.)*

See Section EG6.1 to learn how to compute normal probabilities and how to use the Normal workbook as a template for other problems.

	A	B	
1	**Normal Probabilities**		
2			
3	**Common Data**		
4	Mean	7	
5	Standard Deviation	2	
6			
7	**Probability for X <=**		
8	X Value	7	
9	Z Value	0	=STANDARDIZE(B8,B4,B5)
10	P(X<=7)	0.5000	=NORMDIST(B8,B4,B5,TRUE)
11			
12	**Probability for X >**		
13	X Value	9	
14	Z Value	1	=STANDARDIZE(B13,B4,B5)
15	P(X>9)	0.1587	=1-NORMDIST(B13,B4,B5,TRUE)
16			
17	**Probability for X<7 or X >9**		
18	P(X<7 or X >9)	0.6587	=B10+B15

	D	E	
1			
2			
3			
4			
5			
6	**Probability for a Range**		
7	From X Value	5	
8	To X Value	9	
9	Z Value for 5	-1	=STANDARDIZE(E7,B4,B5)
10	Z Value for 9	1	=STANDARDIZE(E8,B4,B5)
11	P(X<=5)	0.1587	=NORMDIST(E7,B4,B5,TRUE)
12	P(X<=9)	0.8413	=NORMDIST(E8,B4,B5,TRUE)
13	P(5<=X<=9)	0.6827	=ABS(E12-E11)
14			
15	**Find X and Z Given Cum. Pctage.**		
16	Cumulative Percentage	10.00%	
17	Z Value	-1.2816	=NORMSINV(E16)
18	X Value	4.4369	=NORMINV(E16,B4,B5)

VISUAL EXPLORATIONS   Exploring the Normal Distribution

Use the Visual Explorations Normal Distribution procedure to see the effects of changes in the mean and standard deviation on the area under a normal distribution curve. Open the **Visual Explorations add-in workbook** (see Appendix Section D.7). In Excel 2007, select **Add-ins → VisualExplorations → Normal Distribution.** In Excel 2003, select **VisualExplorations → Normal Distribution.**

You will see a normal curve for the *OurCampus!* download example and a floating control panel (see illustration at right). Use the control panel spinner buttons to change the values for the mean, standard deviation, and *X* value and note the effects of these changes on the probability of *X <=* value and the corresponding shaded area under the curve (see illustration at right). If you prefer to see the normal curve labeled with *Z* values, click **Z Values.**

Click the **Reset** button to reset the control panel values or click **Help** for additional information about the problem. Click **Finish** when you are done exploring.

THINK ABOUT THIS   What Is Normal?

Ironically, the statistician who popularized the use of "normal" to describe the distribution discussed in Section 6.2 was someone who saw the distribution as anything but the everyday, anticipated occurrence that the adjective *normal* usually suggests.

Starting with an 1894 paper, Karl Pearson argued that measurements of phenomena do not naturally, or "normally," conform to the classic bell shape. Pearson believed that individuals in populations could show true variability and that variability in the measurement of individuals in

populations reflected true variability and not errors made in measurement. While this principle underlies statistics today, Pearson's point of view was radical to contemporaries who saw the world as standardized and normal. Pearson changed minds by showing that some populations are naturally *skewed* (coining that term in passing), and he helped put to rest the notion that the normal distribution underlies all phenomena.

Today, unfortunately, people still make the type of mistake that Pearson refuted. Maybe you have heard about the small class of three students in which a professor announced that one student would get an A, one would get a B, and one would get a C "because grades need to be normally distributed." (That the professor was describing a uniform distribution was a double irony.) As a student, you are probably familiar with discussions about grade inflation (undoubtedly a phenomena at many schools). But, have you ever realized that a "proof" of this inflation—that there are "too few" low grades because grades are skewed toward A's and B's—wrongly implies that grades should be "normally" distributed. By the time you finish reading this book, you may realize that because college students represent small nonrandom samples, there are plenty of reasons to suspect that the distribution of grades would not be "normal."

Misunderstandings about the normal distribution have occurred both in business and in the public sector through the years. These misunderstandings have caused a number of business blunders and have sparked some famous public policy debates. As you study this chapter, make sure you understand the "normal" distribution and the assumptions that must hold for its proper use. Not verifying whether these assumptions hold is another common error made by decision makers using this distribution. And, most importantly, always remember that the name *normal* distribution does not mean to suggest normal in the everyday (dare we say "normal"?) sense of the word!

Problems for Section 6.2

LEARNING THE BASICS

6.1 Given a standardized normal distribution (with a mean of 0 and a standard deviation of 1, as in Table E.2), what is the probability that
a. Z is less than 1.57?
b. Z is greater than 1.84?
c. Z is between 1.57 and 1.84?
d. Z is less than 1.57 or greater than 1.84?

6.2 Given a standardized normal distribution (with a mean of 0 and a standard deviation of 1, as in Table E.2), what is the probability that
a. Z is between -1.57 and 1.84?
b. Z is less than -1.57 or greater than 1.84?
c. What is the value of Z if only 2.5% of all possible Z values are larger?
d. Between what two values of Z (symmetrically distributed around the mean) will 68.26% of all possible Z values be contained?

6.3 Given a standardized normal distribution (with a mean of 0 and a standard deviation of 1, as in Table E.2), what is the probability that
a. Z is less than 1.08?
b. Z is greater than -0.21?
c. Z is less than -0.21 or greater than the mean?
d. Z is less than -0.21 or greater than 1.08?

6.4 Given a standardized normal distribution (with a mean of 0 and a standard deviation of 1, as in Table E.2), determine the following probabilities:
a. $P(Z > 1.08)$
b. $P(Z < -0.21)$
c. $P(-1.96 < Z < -0.21)$
d. What is the value of Z if only 15.87% of all possible Z values are larger?

6.5 Given a normal distribution with $\mu = 100$ and $\sigma = 10$, what is the probability that
a. $X > 75$?
b. $X < 70$?
c. $X < 80$ or $X > 110$?
d. Between what two X values (symmetrically distributed around the mean) are 80% of the values?

6.6 Given a normal distribution with $\mu = 50$ and $\sigma = 4$, what is the probability that
a. $X > 43$?
b. $X < 42$?
c. 5% of the values are less than what X value?
d. Between what two X values (symmetrically distributed around the mean) are 60% of the values?

APPLYING THE CONCEPTS

6.7 In a recent year, about two-thirds of U.S. households purchased ground coffee. Consider the annual ground coffee expenditures for households purchasing ground coffee, assuming that these expenditures are approximately distributed as a normal random variable with a mean of $65.16 and a standard deviation of $10.00.
a. Find the probability that a household spent less than $35.00.
b. Find the probability that a household spent more than $60.00.
c. What proportion of the households spent between $40.00 and $50.00?
d. 99% of the households spent less than what amount?

✓ SELF Test **6.8** Toby's Trucking Company determined that the distance traveled per truck per year is normally distributed, with a mean of 50.0 thousand miles and a standard deviation of 12.0 thousand miles.
a. What proportion of trucks can be expected to travel between 34.0 and 50.0 thousand miles in a year?
b. What percentage of trucks can be expected to travel either below 30.0 or above 60.0 thousand miles in a year?
c. How many miles will be traveled by at least 80% of the trucks?
d. What are your answers to (a) through (c) if the standard deviation is 10.0 thousand miles?

6.9 The owner of a fish market determined that the mean weight for salmon is 12.3 pounds, with a standard deviation of 2 pounds. Assuming that the weights of salmon are normally distributed, what is the probability that a randomly selected salmon will weigh

a. between 12 and 15 pounds?
b. less than 10 pounds?
c. Between what two values will 95% of the salmon weights fall?

6.10 A set of final examination grades in an introductory statistics course is normally distributed, with a mean of 73 and a standard deviation of 8.

a. What is the probability of getting a grade below 91 on this exam?
b. What is the probability that a student scored between 65 and 89?
c. The probability is 5% that a student taking the test scores higher than what grade?
d. If the professor grades on a curve (i.e., gives A's to the top 10% of the class, regardless of the score), are you better off with a grade of 81 on this exam or a grade of 68 on a different exam, where the mean is 62 and the standard deviation is 3? Show your answer statistically and explain.

6.11 A statistical analysis of 1,000 long-distance telephone calls made from the headquarters of the Bricks and Clicks Computer Corporation indicates that the length of these calls is normally distributed, with $\mu = 240$ seconds and $\sigma = 40$ seconds.

a. What is the probability that a call lasted less than 180 seconds?
b. What is the probability that a call lasted between 180 and 300 seconds?

c. What is the probability that a call lasted between 110 and 180 seconds?
d. 1% of all calls will last less than how many seconds?

6.12 According to the American Society for Quality, a certified quality engineer (CQE) is a professional who understands the principles of product and service quality evaluation and control. In a 2008 survey, the mean salary of 1,387 CQEs was $72,824, with a standard deviation of $18,796 (I. Elaine Allen, "Salary Survey: Seeing Green," *Quality Progress*, December 2008, pp. 20–53). Assume that the salaries of CQEs is approximately normally distributed. For a randomly selected CQE, what is the probability that he or she has a salary

a. below $50,000?
b. above $75,000?
c. above $100,000?

6.13 Many manufacturing problems involve the matching of machine parts, such as shafts that fit into a valve hole. A particular design requires a shaft with a diameter of 22.000 mm, but shafts with diameters between 21.990 mm and 22.010 mm are acceptable. Suppose that the manufacturing process yields shafts with diameters normally distributed, with a mean of 22.002 mm and a standard deviation of 0.005 mm. For this process, what is

a. the proportion of shafts with a diameter between 21.99 mm and 22.00 mm?
b. the probability that a shaft is acceptable?
c. the diameter that will be exceeded by only 2% of the shafts?
d. What would be your answers in (a) through (c) if the standard deviation of the shaft diameters were 0.004 mm?

6.3 Evaluating Normality

As discussed in Section 6.2, many continuous variables used in business closely follow a normal distribution. This section presents two approaches for determining whether a set of data can be approximated by the normal distribution:

1. Comparing the characteristics of the data with the theoretical properties of the normal distribution
2. Constructing a normal probability plot

Comparing Data Characteristics to Theoretical Properties

The normal distribution has several important theoretical properties:

- It is symmetrical; thus, the mean and median are equal.
- It is bell-shaped; thus, the empirical rule applies.
- The interquartile range equals 1.33 standard deviations.
- The range is approximately equal to 6 standard deviations.

In actual practice, a continuous variable may have characteristics that approximate these theoretical properties. However, many continuous variables are neither normally distributed nor approximately normally distributed. For such variables, the descriptive characteristics of the data do not match well with the properties of a normal distribution. One approach to determining whether a data set follows a normal distribution is to compare the characteristics of the data with what would be expected if the data followed a normal distribution:

- Construct charts and observe their appearance. For small- or moderate-sized data sets, create a stem-and-leaf display or a boxplot. For large data sets, in addition, plot a histogram or polygon.
- Compute descriptive statistics and compare these statistics with the theoretical properties of the normal distribution. Compare the mean and median. Is the interquartile range approximately 1.33 times the standard deviation? Is the range approximately 6 times the standard deviation?
- Evaluate how the values are distributed. Determine whether approximately two-thirds of the values lie between the mean and ±1 standard deviation. Determine whether approximately four-fifths of the values lie between the mean and ±1.28 standard deviations. Determine whether approximately 19 out of every 20 values lie between the mean and ±2 standard deviations.

Do the returns in 2008 discussed in Chapters 2 and 3 (see the **Bond Funds** file) have the properties of the normal distribution? Figure 6.17 displays descriptive statistics for these data, and Figure 6.18 presents a five-number summary and a boxplot.

FIGURE 6.17

Descriptive statistics for the 2008 returns

Section EG3.2 on page 129 discusses how to create a list of descriptive statistics similar to that shown in Figure 6.17.

	A	B
1	**Return 2008**	
2		
3	Mean	1.3169
4	Standard Error	0.5704
5	Median	2.6000
6	Mode	6.9000
7	Standard Deviation	7.6530
8	Sample Variance	58.5680
9	Kurtosis	1.7690
10	Skewness	-1.0445
11	Range	46.9000
12	Minimum	-31.9000
13	Maximum	15.0000
14	Sum	237.0500
15	Count	180.0000

FIGURE 6.18

Five-number summary and boxplot for the 2008 returns

Figure 6.18 was created using the PHStat2 Boxplot procedure. As Section EG3.3 on page 130 explains, PHStat2 offers the only practical way to create boxplots in Excel.

	A	B
1	Bond Funds 2008 Returns	
2	Five-Number Summary	
3		
4	Minimum	-31.9
5	First Quartile	-2.5
6	Median	2.6
7	Third Quartile	7.1
8	Maximum	15.0

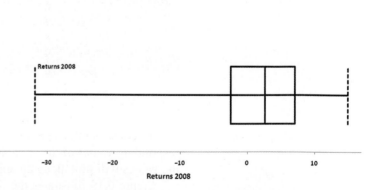

From Figures 6.17 and 6.18 and from an ordered array of the returns (not shown here), you can make the following statements:

- The mean of 1.3169 is less than the median of 2.6. (In a normal distribution, the mean and median are equal.)

- The boxplot is very left-skewed, with a long tail on the left. (The normal distribution is symmetrical.)
- The interquartile range of 9.6 is approximately 1.25 standard deviations. (In a normal distribution, the interquartile range is 1.33 standard deviations.)
- The range of 46.9 is equal to 6.13 standard deviations. (In a normal distribution, the range is approximately six standard deviations.)
- 76.69% of the returns are within ±1 standard deviation of the mean. (In a normal distribution, 68.26% of the values lie within ±1 standard deviation of the mean.)
- 82.78% of the returns are within ±1.28 standard deviations of the mean. (In a normal distribution, 80% of the values lie within ±1.28 standard deviations of the mean.)
- 93.89% of the returns are within ±2 standard deviations of the mean. (In a normal distribution, 95.44% of the values lie within ±2 standard deviations of the mean.)

Based on these statements and the criteria given on page 207, the 2008 returns are highly left-skewed and have somewhat more values within ±1 standard deviation of the mean than expected. The range is approximately what would be expected in a normal distribution, but this is mostly due to the single outlier at −31.9. Primarily because of the skewness, you can conclude that the data characteristics of the 2008 returns differ from the theoretical properties of a normal distribution.

Constructing the Normal Probability Plot

A **normal probability plot** is a visual display that helps you evaluate whether the data are normally distributed. One common plot is called the **quantile–quantile plot**. To create this plot, you first transform each ordered value to a Z value. For example, if you have a sample of $n = 19$, the Z value for the smallest value corresponds to a cumulative area of $\dfrac{1}{n+1} = \dfrac{1}{19+1} = \dfrac{1}{20} = 0.05$. The Z value for a cumulative area of 0.05 (from Table E.2) is −1.65. Table 6.6 illustrates the entire set of Z values for a sample of $n = 19$.

TABLE 6.6

Ordered Values and Corresponding Z Values for a Sample of $n = 19$

Ordered Value	Z Value	Ordered Value	Z Value
1	−1.65	11	0.13
2	−1.28	12	0.25
3	−1.04	13	0.39
4	−0.84	14	0.52
5	−0.67	15	0.67
6	−0.52	16	0.84
7	−0.39	17	1.04
8	−0.25	18	1.28
9	−0.13	19	1.65
10	−0.00		

To construct the quantile–quantile plot, the Z values are plotted on the X axis, and the corresponding values of the variable are plotted on the Y axis. If the data are normally distributed, the values will plot along an approximately straight line.

Figure 6.19 illustrates the typical shape of normal probability plots for a left-skewed distribution (Panel A), a normal distribution (Panel B), and a right-skewed distribution (Panel C). If the data are left-skewed, the curve will rise more rapidly at first and then level off. If the data are normally distributed, the points will plot along an approximately straight line. If the data are right-skewed, the data will rise more slowly at first and then rise at a faster rate for higher values of the variable being plotted.

FIGURE 6.19

Normal probability plots for a left-skewed distribution, a normal distribution, and a right-skewed distribution

Left-skewed
Panel A

Normal
Panel B

Right-skewed
Panel C

Figure 6.20 shows a quantile–quantile normal probability plot for the 2008 returns.

FIGURE 6.20

Normal probability plot for 2008 returns

Figure 6.20 displays the NORMAL PLOT chart sheet of the NPP workbook. Create this chart sheet using the instructions in Section EG6.3.

Figures 6.20 shows that the 2008 returns rise more rapidly at first and then level off. Thus, you can conclude that the 2008 returns are left-skewed.

Problems for Section 6.3

LEARNING THE BASICS

6.14 Show that for a sample of $n = 39$, the smallest and largest Z values are -1.96 and $+1.96$, and the middle (i.e., 20th) Z value is 0.00.

6.15 For a sample of $n = 6$, list the six Z values.

APPLYING THE CONCEPTS

6.16 The file **SUV** contains the overall miles per gallon (MPG) of 2009 small SUVs priced under $30,000.

24, 23, 22, 21, 22, 22, 18, 19, 19, 19, 21, 21,
21, 18, 19, 21, 17, 22, 18, 18, 22, 16, 16

Source: *Data extracted from "Vehicle Ratings,"* Consumer Reports, *April 2009, p. 33–34.*

Decide whether the data appear to be approximately normally distributed by
a. comparing data characteristics to theoretical properties.
b. constructing a normal probability plot.

6.17 As player salaries have increased, the cost of attending baseball games has increased dramatically. The file **BBCost** contains the cost of four tickets, two beers, four soft drinks, four hot dogs, two game programs, two baseball caps, and the parking fee for one car for each of the 30 Major League Baseball teams in 2009.

164, 326, 224, 180, 205, 162, 141, 170,
411, 187, 185, 165, 151, 166, 114, 158,
305, 145, 161, 170, 210, 222, 146, 259,
220, 135, 215, 172, 223, 216

Source: *Data extracted from* **teammarketing.com,** *April 1, 2009.*

Decide whether the data appear to be approximately normally distributed by
a. comparing data characteristics to theoretical properties.
b. constructing a normal probability plot.

6.18 The file **PropertyTaxes** contains the property taxes per capita for the 50 states and the District of Columbia.

Decide whether the data appear to be approximately normally distributed by

a. comparing data characteristics to theoretical properties.

b. constructing a normal probability plot.

6.19 Thirty companies comprise the DJIA. Just how big are these companies? One common method for measuring the size of a company is to use its market capitalization, which is computed by multiplying the number of stock shares by the price of a share of stock. On June 19, 2009, the market capitalization of these companies ranged from Caterpillar's $20.5 billion to ExxonMobil's $347.4 billion. The market capitalization values for the 30 companies that comprise the DJIA are stored in DowMarketCap .

Source: *Data extracted from* **money.cnn.com**, *June 19, 2009.*

Decide whether the market capitalization of companies in the DJIA appears to be approximately normally distributed by

a. comparing data characteristics to theoretical properties.

b. constructing a normal probability plot.

c. constructing a histogram.

6.20 One operation of a mill is to cut pieces of steel into parts that will later be used as the frame for front seats in an automotive plant. The steel is cut with a diamond saw, and the resulting parts must be within ±0.005 inch of the length specified by the automobile company. The data come from a sample of 100 steel parts and are stored in Steel . The measurement reported is the difference, in inches, between the actual length of the steel part, as measured by a laser measurement device, and the specified length of the steel part.

Determine whether the data appear to be approximately normally distributed by

a. comparing data characteristics to theoretical properties.

b. constructing a normal probability plot.

6.21 The file SavingsRate contains the yields for a money market account, a one-year certificate of deposit (CD), and a five-year CD for 23 banks in the metropolitan New York area, as of May 28, 2009 (extracted from **www.bankrate.com**, May 28, 2009). For each of the three types of investments, decide whether the data appear to be approximately normally distributed by

a. comparing data characteristics to theoretical properties.

b. constructing a normal probability plot.

6.22 The file Utility contains the electricity costs, in dollars, during July 2009 for a random sample of 50 two-bedroom apartments in a large city:

96	171	202	178	147	102	153	197	127	82
157	185	90	116	172	111	148	213	130	165
141	149	206	175	123	128	144	168	109	167
95	163	150	154	130	143	187	166	139	149
108	119	183	151	114	135	191	137	129	158

Decide whether the data appear to be approximately normally distributed by

a. comparing data characteristics to theoretical properties.

b. constructing a normal probability plot.

6.4 The Uniform Distribution

In the **uniform distribution**, a value has the same probability of occurrence anywhere in the range between the smallest value, *a*, and the largest value, *b*. Because of its shape, the uniform distribution is sometimes called the **rectangular distribution** (see Panel B of Figure 6.1 on page 194). Equation (6.4) defines the probability density function for the uniform distribution.

UNIFORM PROBABILITY DENSITY FUNCTION

$$f(X) = \frac{1}{b - a} \text{ if } a \leq X \leq b \text{ and } 0 \text{ elsewhere} \tag{6.4}$$

where

$$a = \text{the minimum value of } X$$

$$b = \text{the maximum value of } X$$

Equation (6.5) defines the mean of the uniform distribution.

MEAN OF THE UNIFORM DISTRIBUTION

$$\mu = \frac{a + b}{2} \tag{6.5}$$

Equation (6.6) defines the variance and standard deviation of the uniform distribution.

VARIANCE AND STANDARD DEVIATION OF THE UNIFORM DISTRIBUTION

$$\sigma^2 = \frac{(b-a)^2}{12} \qquad \qquad \textbf{(6.6a)}$$

$$\sigma = \sqrt{\frac{(b-a)^2}{12}} \qquad \qquad \textbf{(6.6b)}$$

One of the most common uses of the uniform distribution is in the selection of random numbers. When you use simple random sampling (see Section 7.1), you assume that each random number comes from a uniform distribution that has a minimum value of 0 and a maximum value of 1.

Figure 6.21 illustrates the uniform distribution with $a = 0$ and $b = 1$. The total area inside the rectangle is equal to the base (1.0) times the height (1.0). Thus, the resulting area of 1.0 satisfies the requirement that the area under any probability density function equals 1.0.

FIGURE 6.21

Probability density function for a uniform distribution with $a = 0$ and $b = 1$

In this distribution, what is the probability of getting a random number between 0.10 and 0.30? The area between 0.10 and 0.30, depicted in Figure 6.22, is equal to the base (which is $0.30 - 0.10 = 0.20$) times the height (1.0). Therefore,

$$P(0.10 < X < 0.30) = (\text{Base})(\text{Height}) = (0.20)(1.0) = 0.20$$

FIGURE 6.22

Finding $P(0.10 < X < 0.30)$ for a uniform distribution with $a = 0$ and $b = 1$

From Equations (6.5) and (6.6), the mean and standard deviation of the uniform distribution for $a = 0$ and $b = 1$ are computed as follows:

$$\mu = \frac{a+b}{2}$$

$$= \frac{0+1}{2} = 0.5$$

and

$$\sigma^2 = \frac{(b-a)^2}{12}$$

$$= \frac{(1-0)^2}{12}$$

$$= \frac{1}{12} = 0.0833$$

$$\sigma = \sqrt{0.0833} = 0.2887$$

Thus, the mean is 0.5, and the standard deviation is 0.2887.

Problems for Section 6.4

LEARNING THE BASICS

6.23 Suppose you sample one value from a uniform distribution with $a = 0$ and $b = 10$. What is the probability that the value will be
a. between 5 and 7?
b. between 2 and 3?
c. What is the mean?
d. What is the standard deviation?

APPLYING THE CONCEPTS

✓ SELF Test **6.24** The time between arrivals of customers at a bank during the noon-to-1 P.M. hour has a uniform distribution between 0 to 120 seconds. What is the probability that the time between the arrival of two customers will be
a. less than 20 seconds?
b. between 10 and 30 seconds?
c. more than 35 seconds?
d. What are the mean and standard deviation of the time between arrivals?

6.25 A study of the time spent shopping in a supermarket for a market basket of 20 specific items showed an approximately uniform distribution between 20 minutes and 40 minutes. What is the probability that the shopping time will be
a. between 25 and 30 minutes?
b. less than 35 minutes?

c. What are the mean and standard deviation of the shopping time?

6.26 How long does it take you to download a game for your iPod? According to Apple's technical support site, **www.apple.com/support/itunes**, downloading an iPod game using a broadband connection should take 3 to 6 minutes. Assume that the download times are uniformly distributed between 3 and 6 minutes. If you download a game, what is the probability that the download time will be
a. less than 3.3 minutes?
b. less than 4 minutes?
c. between 4 and 5 minutes?
d. What are the mean and standard deviation of the download times?

6.27 The scheduled commuting time on the Long Island Railroad from Glen Cove to New York City is 65 minutes. Suppose that the actual commuting time is uniformly distributed between 64 and 74 minutes. What is the probability that the commuting time will be
a. less than 70 minutes?
b. between 65 and 70 minutes?
c. greater than 65 minutes?
d. What are the mean and standard deviation of the commuting time?

6.5 The Exponential Distribution

The **exponential distribution** is a continuous distribution that is right-skewed and ranges from zero to positive infinity (see Panel C of Figure 6.1 on page 194). The exponential distribution is widely used in waiting-line (i.e., queuing) theory to model the length of time between arrivals in processes such as customers at a bank's ATM, patients entering a hospital emergency room, and hits on a Web site.

The exponential distribution is defined by a single parameter, λ, the mean number of arrivals per unit of time. The probability density function for the length of time between arrivals is given by Equation (6.7).

EXPONENTIAL PROBABILITY DENSITY FUNCTION

$$f(X) = \lambda e^{-\lambda x} \text{ for } X > 0 \qquad \textbf{(6.7)}$$

where

e = the mathematical constant approximated by 2.71828

λ = the mean number of arrivals per unit

X = any value of the continuous variable where $0 < X < \infty$

The mean time between arrivals, μ, is given by Equation (6.8),

MEAN TIME BETWEEN ARRIVALS

$$\mu = \frac{1}{\lambda} \qquad \textbf{(6.8)}$$

and the standard deviation of the time between arrivals, σ, is given by Equation (6.9).

STANDARD DEVIATION OF THE TIME BETWEEN ARRIVALS

$$\sigma = \frac{1}{\lambda} \qquad \textbf{(6.9)}$$

The value $1/\lambda$ is equal to the mean time between arrivals. For example, if the mean number of arrivals in a minute is $\lambda = 4$, then the mean time between arrivals is $1/\lambda = 0.25$ minutes, or 15 seconds. Equation (6.10) defines the cumulative probability that the length of time before the next arrival is less than or equal to X.

CUMULATIVE EXPONENTIAL PROBABILITY

$$P(\text{arrival time} \leq X) = 1 - e^{-\lambda x} \qquad \textbf{(6.10)}$$

To illustrate the exponential distribution, suppose that customers arrive at a bank's ATM at a rate of 20 per hour. If a customer has just arrived, what is the probability that the next customer will arrive within 6 minutes (i.e., 0.1 hour)? For this example, $\lambda = 20$ and $X = 0.1$. Using Equation (6.10),

$$P(\text{Arrival time} \leq 0.1) = 1 - e^{-20(0.1)}$$
$$= 1 - e^{-2}$$
$$= 1 - 0.1353 = 0.8647$$

Thus, the probability that a customer will arrive within 6 minutes is 0.8647, or 86.47%. You can also use worksheet **EXPONDIST** function to compute this probability (see Figure 6.23).

FIGURE 6.23

Worksheet for finding exponential probabilities

Figure 6.23 displays the **COMPUTE worksheet** *of the* **Exponential workbook** *and reveals the formula the worksheet uses. See Section EG6.5 to learn how to use the Exponential workbook as a template for other problems.*

	A	B
1	**Exponential Probability**	
2		
3	Data	
4	Mean	20
5	X Value	0.1
6		
7	Results	
8	P(<=X)	0.8647 =EXPONDIST(B5, B4, TRUE)

EXAMPLE 6.6

Computing
Exponential
Probabilities

In the ATM example, what is the probability that the next customer will arrive within 3 minutes (i.e., 0.05 hour)?

SOLUTION For this example, $\lambda = 20$ and $X = 0.05$. Using Equation (6.10),

$$P(\text{Arrival time} \leq 0.05) = 1 - e^{-20(0.05)}$$
$$= 1 - e^{-1}$$
$$= 1 - 0.3679 = 0.6321$$

Thus, the probability that a customer will arrive within 3 minutes is 0.6321, or 63.21%.

Problems for Section 6.5

LEARNING THE BASICS

6.28 Given an exponential distribution with $\lambda = 10$, what is the probability that the arrival time is
a. less than $X = 0.1$?
b. greater than $X = 0.1$?
c. between $X = 0.1$ and $X = 0.2$?
d. less than $X = 0.1$ or greater than $X = 0.2$?

6.29 Given an exponential distribution with $\lambda = 30$, what is the probability that the arrival time is
a. less than $X = 0.1$?
b. greater than $X = 0.1$?
c. between $X = 0.1$ and $X = 0.2$?
d. less than $X = 0.1$ or greater than $X = 0.2$?

6.30 Given an exponential distribution with $\lambda = 5$, what is the probability that the arrival time is
a. less than $X = 0.3$?
b. greater than $X = 0.3$?
c. between $X = 0.3$ and $X = 0.5$?
d. less than $X = 0.3$ or greater than $X = 0.5$?

APPLYING THE CONCEPTS

6.31 Autos arrive at a toll plaza located at the entrance to a bridge at a rate of 50 per minute during the 5:00-to-6:00 P.M. hour. If an auto has just arrived,
a. what is the probability that the next auto will arrive within 3 seconds (0.05 minute)?
b. what is the probability that the next auto will arrive within 1 second (0.0167 minute)?
c. What are your answers to (a) and (b) if the rate of arrival of autos is 60 per minute?
d. What are your answers to (a) and (b) if the rate of arrival of autos is 30 per minute?

✓SELF **6.32** Customers arrive at the drive-up window of
Test a fast-food restaurant at a rate of 2 per minute during the lunch hour.
a. What is the probability that the next customer will arrive within 1 minute?

b. What is the probability that the next customer will arrive within 5 minutes?
c. During the dinner time period, the arrival rate is 1 per minute. What are your answers to (a) and (b) for this period?

6.33 Telephone calls arrive at the information desk of a large computer software company at a rate of 15 per hour.
a. What is the probability that the next call will arrive within 3 minutes (0.05 hour)?
b. What is the probability that the next call will arrive within 15 minutes (0.25 hour)?
c. Suppose the company has just introduced an updated version of one of its software programs, and telephone calls are now arriving at a rate of 25 per hour. Given this information, what are your answers to (a) and (b)?

6.34 An on-the-job injury occurs once every 10 days on average at an automobile plant. What is the probability that the next on-the-job injury will occur within
a. 10 days?
b. 5 days?
c. 1 day?

6.35 The time between unplanned shutdowns of a power plant has an exponential distribution with a mean of 20 days. Find the probability that the time between two unplanned shutdowns is
a. less than 14 days.
b. more than 21 days.
c. less than 7 days.

6.36 Golfers arrive at the starter's booth of a public golf course at a rate of 8 per hour during the Monday-to-Friday midweek period. If a golfer has just arrived,
a. what is the probability that the next golfer will arrive within 15 minutes (0.25 hour)?
b. what is the probability that the next golfer will arrive within 3 minutes (0.05 hour)?
c. The actual arrival rate on Fridays is 15 per hour. What are your answers to (a) and (b) for Fridays?

6.37 TrafficWeb.org claims that it can deliver 10,000 hits to a Web site in the next 60 days for only $21.50 (**www.trafficweb.org**, July 1, 2009). If this amount of Web site traffic is experienced, then the time between hits has a mean of 8.64 minutes (or 0.116 per minute). Assume that your Web site does get 10,000 hits in the next 60 days and that the time between hits has an exponential distribution. What is the probability that the time between two hits is

a. less than 5 minutes?
b. less than 10 minutes?
c. more than 15 minutes?
d. Do you think it is reasonable to assume that the time between hits has an exponential distribution?

6.6 🌐 *Online Topic:* The Normal Approximation to the Binomial Distribution

In many circumstances, you can use the normal distribution to approximate the binomial distribution. To study this topic, read the **Section 6.6** online topic file that is available on this book's companion Web site. (See Appendix Section D.8 to learn how to access the online topic files.)

USING STATISTICS @ OurCampus! Revisited

In the OurCampus! scenario, you were a designer for a social networking Web site. You sought to ensure that a video could be downloaded quickly for playback in the Web browsers of site visitors. (Quick playback of videos would help attract and retain those visitors.) By running experiments in the corporate offices, you determined that the amount of time, in seconds, that passes from first linking to the Web site until a video is fully displayed is a bell-shaped distribution with a mean download time of 7 seconds and standard deviation of 2 seconds. Using the normal distribution, you were able to calculate that approximately 84% of the download times are 9 seconds or less, and 95% of the download times are between 3.08 and 10.92 seconds.

Now that you understand how to calculate probabilities from the normal distribution, you can evaluate download times of a video using different Web page designs. For example, if the standard deviation remained at 2 seconds, lowering the mean to 6 seconds would shift the entire distribution lower by 1 second. Thus, approximately 84% of the download times would be 8 seconds or less, and 95% of the download times would be between 2.08 and 9.92 seconds. Another change that could reduce long download times would be reducing the variation. For example, consider the case where the mean remained at the original 7 seconds but the standard deviation was reduced to 1 second. Again, approximately 84% of the download times would be 8 seconds or less, and 95% of the download times would be between 5.04 and 8.96 seconds.

SUMMARY

In this and the previous chapter, you have learned about mathematical models called probability distributions and how they can be used to solve business problems. In Chapter 5, you used discrete probability distributions in situations where the outcomes come from a counting process (e.g., the number of courses you are enrolled in, the number of tagged order forms in a report generated by an accounting informa-

tion system). In this chapter, you learned about continuous probability distributions where the outcomes come from a measuring process (e.g., your height, the download time of a video). Continuous probability distributions come in various shapes, but the most common and most important in business is the normal distribution. The normal distribution is symmetrical; thus, its mean and median are equal. It is also bell-shaped, and approximately 68.26% of its observations are within one standard deviation of the mean, approximately 95.44% of its observations are within two standard deviations of the mean, and approximately 99.73% of its observations are within three standard deviations of the mean. Although many data sets in business are closely approximated by the normal distribution, do not think that all data can be approximated using the normal distribution.

In Section 6.3, you learned about various methods for evaluating normality in order to determine whether the normal distribution is a reasonable mathematical model to use in specific situations. In Sections 6.4 and 6.5, you studied continuous distributions that were not normally distributed—in particular, the uniform and exponential distributions. In Chapter 7, the normal distribution is used in developing the subject of statistical inference.

KEY EQUATIONS

Normal Probability Density Function

$$f(X) = \frac{1}{\sqrt{2\pi}\sigma} e^{-(1/2)[(X-\mu)/\sigma]^2} \quad (6.1)$$

Transformation Formula

$$Z = \frac{X - \mu}{\sigma} \quad (6.2)$$

Finding an X Value Associated with a Known Probability

$$X = \mu + Z\sigma \quad (6.3)$$

Uniform Probability Density Function

$$f(X) = \frac{1}{b - a} \quad (6.4)$$

Mean of the Uniform Distribution

$$\mu = \frac{a + b}{2} \quad (6.5)$$

Variance and Standard Deviation of the Uniform Distribution

$$\sigma^2 = \frac{(b - a)^2}{12} \quad (6.6a)$$

$$\sigma = \sqrt{\frac{(b - a)^2}{12}} \quad (6.6b)$$

Exponential Probability Density Function

$$f(X) = \lambda e^{-\lambda x} \text{ for } X > 0 \quad (6.7)$$

Mean Time Between Arrivals

$$\mu = \frac{1}{\lambda} \quad (6.8)$$

Standard Deviation of the Time Between Arrivals

$$\sigma = \frac{1}{\lambda} \quad (6.9)$$

Cumulative Exponential Probability

$$P(\text{arrival time} \leq X) = 1 - e^{-\lambda x} \quad (6.10)$$

KEY TERMS

cumulative standardized normal distribution 197
exponential distribution 212
normal distribution 194
normal probability density function 196

normal probability plot 208
probability density function 194
quantile–quantile plot 208
rectangular distribution 210
standardized normal random variable 196

transformation formula 196
uniform distribution 210

CHAPTER REVIEW PROBLEMS

CHECKING YOUR UNDERSTANDING

6.38 Why is it that only one normal distribution table such as Table E.2 is needed to find any probability under the normal curve?

6.39 How do you find the area between two values under the normal curve?

6.40 How do you find the X value that corresponds to a given percentile of the normal distribution?

6.41 What are some of the distinguishing properties of a normal distribution?

6.42 How does the shape of the normal distribution differ from the shapes of the uniform and exponential distributions?

6.43 How can you use the normal probability plot to evaluate whether a set of data is normally distributed?

6.44 Under what circumstances can you use the exponential distribution?

APPLYING THE CONCEPTS

6.45 An industrial sewing machine uses ball bearings that are targeted to have a diameter of 0.75 inch. The lower and upper specification limits under which the ball bearings can operate are 0.74 inch and 0.76 inch, respectively. Past experience has indicated that the actual diameter of the ball bearings is approximately normally distributed, with a mean of 0.753 inch and a standard deviation of 0.004 inch. What is the probability that a ball bearing is
a. between the target and the actual mean?
b. between the lower specification limit and the target?
c. above the upper specification limit?
d. below the lower specification limit?
e. Of all the ball bearings, 93% of the diameters are greater than what value?

6.46 The fill amount in soft drink bottles is normally distributed, with a mean of 2.0 liters and a standard deviation of 0.05 liter. If bottles contain less than 95% of the listed net content (1.90 liters, in this case), the manufacturer may be subject to penalty by the state office of consumer affairs. Bottles that have a net content above 2.10 liters may cause excess spillage upon opening. What proportion of the bottles will contain
a. between 1.90 and 2.0 liters?
b. between 1.90 and 2.10 liters?
c. below 1.90 liters or above 2.10 liters?
d. At least how much soft drink is contained in 99% of the bottles?
e. 99% of the bottles contain an amount that is between which two values (symmetrically distributed) around the mean?

6.47 In an effort to reduce the number of bottles that contain less than 1.90 liters, the bottler in Problem 6.46 sets the filling machine so that the mean is 2.02 liters. Under these

circumstances, what are your answers in Problem 6.46 (a) through (e)?

6.48 An orange juice producer buys all his oranges from a large orange grove. The amount of juice squeezed from each of these oranges is approximately normally distributed, with a mean of 4.70 ounces and a standard deviation of 0.40 ounce.
a. What is the probability that a randomly selected orange will contain between 4.70 and 5.00 ounces of juice?
b. What is the probability that a randomly selected orange will contain between 5.00 and 5.50 ounces of juice?
c. At least how many ounces of juice will 77% of the oranges contain?
d. 80% of the oranges contain between what two values (in ounces of juice), symmetrically distributed around the population mean?

6.49 The file **DomesticBeer** contains the percentage alcohol, number of calories per 12 ounces, and number of carbohydrates (in grams) per 12 ounces for 128 of the best-selling domestic beers in the United States. For each of the three variables, decide whether the data appear to be approximately normally distributed. Support your decision through the use of appropriate statistics and graphs.
Source: *Data extracted from* **www.Beer100.com**, *June 15, 2009.*

6.50 The evening manager of a restaurant was very concerned about the length of time some customers were waiting in line to be seated. She also had some concern about the seating times—that is, the length of time between when a customer is seated and the time he or she leaves the restaurant. Over the course of one week, 100 customers (no more than 1 per party) were randomly selected, and their waiting and seating times (in minutes) were recorded in **Wait**.
a. Think about your favorite restaurant. Do you think waiting times more closely resemble a uniform, an exponential, or a normal distribution?
b. Again, think about your favorite restaurant. Do you think seating times more closely resemble a uniform, an exponential, or a normal distribution?
c. Construct a histogram and a normal probability plot of the waiting times. Do you think these waiting times more closely resemble a uniform, an exponential, or a normal distribution?
d. Construct a histogram and a normal probability plot of the seating times. Do you think these seating times more closely resemble a uniform, an exponential, or a normal distribution?

6.51 All the major stock market indexes posted heavy losses in 2008. The mean one-year return for stocks in the S&P 500, a group of 500 very large companies, was -38.5%. The mean one-year return for the NASDAQ, a group of 3,200 small and medium-sized companies, was -40.5%. Historically, the one-year returns are approximately normal, the standard deviation in the S&P 500 is approximately 20%, and the standard deviation in the NASDAQ is approximately 30%.

a. What is the probability that a stock in the S&P 500 gained value in 2008?

b. What is the probability that a stock in the S&P 500 gained 10% or more?

c. What is the probability that a stock in the S&P 500 lost 50% or more in 2008?

d. What is the probability that a stock in the S&P 500 lost 60% or more?

e. Repeat (a) through (d) for a stock in the NASDAQ.

f. Write a short summary on your findings. Be sure to include a discussion of the risks associated with a large standard deviation.

6.52 An article reported (L. J. Flynn, "Tax Surfing," *The New York Times*, March 25, 2002, p. C10) that the mean time to download the home page for the Internal Revenue Service, **www.irs.gov**, is 0.8 second. Suppose that the download time is normally distributed, with a standard deviation of 0.2 second. What is the probability that a download time is

a. less than 1 second?

b. between 0.5 and 1.5 seconds?

c. above 0.5 second?

d. Above how many seconds are 99% of the download times?

e. 95% of the download times are between what two values, symmetrically distributed around the mean?

6.53 The same article mentioned in Problem 6.52 also reported that the mean download time for the H&R Block Web site, **www.hrblock.com**, is 2.5 seconds. Suppose that the download time is normally distributed, with a standard deviation of 0.5 second. What is the probability that a download time is

a. less than 1 second?

b. between 0.5 and 1.5 seconds?

c. above 0.5 second?

d. Above how many seconds are 99% of the download times?

e. Compare the results for the IRS site computed in Problem 6.52 to those of the H&R Block site.

6.54 (Class Project) According to Burton G. Malkiel, the daily changes in the closing price of stock follow a *random walk*—that is, these daily events are independent of each other and move upward or downward in a random manner—and can be approximated by a normal distribution. To test this theory, use either a newspaper or the Internet to select one company traded on the NYSE, one company traded on the American Stock Exchange, and one company traded on the NASDAQ and then do the following:

1. Record the daily closing stock price of each of these companies for six consecutive weeks (so that you have 30 values per company).

2. Record the daily changes in the closing stock price of each of these companies for six consecutive weeks (so that you have 30 values per company).

For each of your six data sets, decide whether the data are approximately normally distributed by

a. constructing the stem-and-leaf display, histogram or polygon, and boxplot.

b. comparing data characteristics to theoretical properties.

c. constructing a normal probability plot.

d. Discuss the results of (a) through (c). What can you say about your three stocks with respect to daily closing prices and daily changes in closing prices? Which, if any, of the data sets are approximately normally distributed?

Note: *The random-walk theory pertains to the daily changes in the closing stock price, not the daily closing stock price.*

TEAM PROJECTS

The file **Bond Funds** contains information regarding eight variables from a sample of 180 mutual funds:

Type—Type of bonds comprising the bond fund (intermediate government or short-term corporate)

Assets—In millions of dollars

Fees—Sales charges (no or yes)

Expense ratio—Ratio of expenses to net assets in percentage

Return 2008—Twelve-month return in 2008

Three-year return—Annualized return, 2006–2008

Five-year return—Annualized return, 2004–2008

Risk—Risk-of-loss factor of the mutual fund (below average, average, or above average)

6.55 For the expense ratio, three-year return, and five-year return, decide whether the data are approximately normally distributed by

a. comparing data characteristics to theoretical properties.

b. constructing a normal probability plot.

STUDENT SURVEY DATABASE

6.56 Problem 2.117 on page 65 describes a survey of 50 undergraduate students (stored in **UndergradSurvey**). For these data, for each numerical variable, decide whether the data are approximately normally distributed by

a. comparing data characteristics to theoretical properties.

b. constructing a normal probability plot.

6.57 Problem 2.117 on page 65 describes a survey of 50 undergraduate students (stored in **UndergradSurvey**).

a. Select a sample of 50 undergraduate students and conduct a similar survey for those students.

b. For the data collected in (a), repeat (a) and (b) of Problem 6.56.

c. Compare the results of (b) to those of Problem 6.56.

6.58 Problem 2.119 on page 65 describes a survey of 40 MBA students (stored in **GradSurvey**). For these data, for each numerical variable, decide whether the data are approximately normally distributed by

a. comparing data characteristics to theoretical properties.

b. constructing a normal probability plot.

6.59 Problem 2.119 on page 65 describes a survey of 40 MBA students (stored in GradSurvey).
a. Select a sample of 40 graduate students and conduct a similar survey for those students.

b. For the data collected in (a), repeat (a) and (b) of Problem 6.58.
c. Compare the results of (b) to those of Problem 6.58.

MANAGING THE *SPRINGVILLE HERALD*

The *Springville Herald* production department has embarked on a quality improvement effort. Its first project relates to the blackness of the newspaper print. Each day, a determination needs to be made concerning how black the newspaper is printed. Blackness is measured on a standard scale in which the target value is 1.0. Data collected over the past year indicate that the blackness is approximately normally distributed, with a mean of 1.005 and a standard deviation of 0.10. Each day, one spot on the first newspaper printed is chosen, and the blackness of the spot is measured. The blackness of the newspaper is considered acceptable if the blackness of a spot is between 0.95 and 1.05.

EXERCISES

SH6.1 Assuming that the distribution has not changed from what it was in the past year, what is the probability that the blackness of the spot is

a. less than 1.0?
b. between 0.95 and 1.0?
c. between 1.0 and 1.05?
d. less than 0.95 or greater than 1.05?

SH6.2 The objective of the production team is to reduce the probability that the blackness is below 0.95 or above 1.05. Should the team focus on process improvement that lowers the mean to the target value of 1.0 or on process improvement that reduces the standard deviation to 0.075? Explain.

WEB CASE

Apply your knowledge about the normal distribution in this Web Case, which extends the Using Statistics scenario from this chapter.

To satisfy concerns of potential advertisers, the management of OurCampus! has undertaken a research project to learn the amount of time it takes users to download a complex video features page. The marketing department has collected data and has made some claims based on the assertion that the data follow a normal distribution.

Using a Web browser, open to the Web page for the Chapter 6 Web Case or open **Our_DownloadResearch.htm**,

if you have downloaded the Web Case files, and read the internal marketing report that reviews these data and conclusions. Then answer the following:

1. Can the collected data be approximated by the normal distribution?

2. Review and evaluate the conclusions made by the OurCampus! marketing department. Which conclusions are correct? Which ones are incorrect?

3. If OurCampus! could improve the mean time by five minutes, how would the probabilities change?

REFERENCES

1. Gunter, B., "Q-Q Plots," *Quality Progress* (February 1994), 81–86.
2. Levine, D. M., P. Ramsey, and R. Smidt, *Applied Statistics for Engineers and Scientists Using Microsoft Excel and Minitab* (Upper Saddle River, NJ: Prentice Hall, 2001).
3. *Microsoft Excel 2007* (Redmond, WA: Microsoft Corp., 2007).
4. Miller, J., "Earliest Known Uses of Some of the Words of Mathematics," **http://jeff560.tripod.com/mathword.html**.
5. Pearl, R., "Karl Pearson, 1857–1936," *Journal of the American Statistical Association*, 31 (1936), 653–664.
6. Pearson, E. S., "Some Incidents in the Early History of Biometry and Statistics, 1890–94," *Biometrika*, 52 (1965), 3–18.
7. Walker, H., "The Contributions of Karl Pearson," *Journal of the American Statistical Association*, 53 (1958), 11–22.

EG6.1 CONTINUOUS PROBABILITY DISTRIBUTIONS

There are no Excel Guide instructions for this section.

EG6.2 THE NORMAL DISTRIBUTION

Computing Normal Probabilities

PHStat2 Use the **Normal** procedure to compute normal probabilities. For example, to create the Figure 6.16 worksheet (see page 204) that computes probabilities for a number of Chapter 6 examples, select **PHStat → Probability & Prob. Distributions → Normal.** In this procedure's dialog box (shown below):

1. Enter **7** as the **Mean** and **2** as the **Standard Deviation.**
2. Check **Probability for: X <=** and enter **7** in its box.
3. Check **Probability for: X >** and enter **9** in its box.
4. Check **X for Cumulative Percentage** and enter **10** in its box.
5. Enter a **Title** and click **OK.**

In-Depth Excel Use the **NORMDIST** function to compute normal probabilities. Enter the function as **NORMDIST** (*X value, mean, standard deviation*, **True**) to return the cumulative probability for less than or equal to the specified *X* value.

Use the **COMPUTE worksheet** of the **Normal workbook**, shown in Figure 6.16 on page 204, as a template for computing normal probabilities. The worksheet contains the data for solving the problems in Examples 6.1 through 6.4. Change the values for the **Mean**, **Standard Deviation**, **X Value**, **From X Value**, **To X Value**, and/or **Cumulative Percentage** to solve similar problems. To solve a problem that is similar to Example 6.5 on page 202, change the **Cumulative**

Percentage cell twice, once to determine the lower value of *X* and the other time to determine the upper value of *X*.

The COMPUTE worksheet also uses these four statistical functions to compute results:

STANDARDIZE(*X value, mean, standard deviation*) computes *Z* values in cells B9, B14, E9, and E10.

NORMDIST(*X value, mean, standard deviation*, True) computes the probability of less than or equal to the *X* value in cells B10, B15, E11, and E12.

NORMSINV(*cumulative percentage*) computes the *Z* value for the cumulative percentage in cell E17.

NORMINV(*cumulative percentage, mean, standard deviation*) computes the *X* value for the given cumulative probability, mean, and standard deviation in cell E18.

Not shown in Figure 6.16 are the formulas in cells A10, A15, A17, A18, D11, D12, and D13 that update probability labels when you change an *X* value in either cells B8, B13, E7, or E8. Open to the **COMPUTE_FORMULAS** worksheet in the **Normal workbook** to examine these formulas.

EG6.3 EVALUATING NORMALITY

Constructing the Normal Probability Plot

PHStat2 Use the **Normal Probability Plot** procedure to create a normal probability plot. For example, to create the Figure 6.20 normal probability plot on page 209, open to the **DATA worksheet** of the **Bond Funds workbook**. Select **PHStat2 → Probability & Prob. Distributions → Normal Probability Plot.** In the procedure's dialog box (shown below):

1. Enter **F1:F181** as the **Variable Cell Range.**
2. Check **First cell contains label.**
3. Enter a **Title** and click **OK.**

In addition to the chart sheet containing the normal probability plot, the procedure creates a worksheet that uses the **NORMSINV** function to compute the *Z* values used in the plot. To learn more about the worksheet, see the following *In-Depth Excel* section.

In-Depth Excel Create a normal probability plot by first creating a worksheet that computes *Z* values and then creating a chart from that worksheet.

For example, to create the Figure 6.20 normal probability plot on page 209, open to the **DATA worksheet** of the **Bond Funds workbook.** Right-click the **DATA worksheet** tab and click **Insert** in the shortcut menu to insert a new worksheet. In the new worksheet:

1. Enter the column headings **Rank**, **Proportion**, and **Z Value** in cells A1 through A3, respectively.

2. Open to the **DATA worksheet** and copy the cell range **F1:F181** (the range of the **Return 2008** variable, including its column heading). Paste this range into cell **D1** of the **new worksheet** to place all the **Return 2008** values in column D through cell D181.

3. Enter **1** in cell **A2**, the formula **=A2/181** in cell **B2**, and the formula **=NORMSINV(B2)** in cell **C2**. (The cell B2 formula uses 181 as the divisor because for this example *n* + 1 equals 181.)

4. Select cell range **A1:C1** and copy the range down through row 181. (This operation increments the rank number for each row.)

The first three and last three data rows of the completed worksheet are shown in Figure EG6.1. The column C formulas use the **NORMSINV** function to compute the *Z* values for the cumulative percentages that are computed in column B. (Open to the **PLOT_FORMULAS worksheet** of the **NPP workbook** to examine the formulas for all rows.)

With the Z values worksheet complete, continue with either the In-Depth Excel 2007 or In-Depth Excel 2003 instructions to create the normal probability plot.

	A	B	C	D
1	Rank	Proportion	Z Value	Return 2008
2	1	=A2/181	=NORMSINV(B2)	-31.9
3	2	=A3/181	=NORMSINV(B3)	-21
4	3	=A4/181	=NORMSINV(B4)	-18.9
179	178	=A179/181	=NORMSINV(B179)	13.9
180	179	=A180/181	=NORMSINV(B180)	14.1
181	180	=A181/181	=NORMSINV(B181)	15

FIGURE EG6.1 Worksheet to compute Z values

In-Depth Excel 2007 Open to the completed worksheet that computes *Z* values. Select the cell range **C1:D181.** Then select **Insert → Scatter** and select the first **Scatter** gallery choice (**Scatter with only Markers**). Relocate the chart to a chart sheet and adjust the chart formatting by using the instructions in Appendix Section C.7.

In-Depth Excel 2003 Open to the completed worksheet that computes *Z* values. Select the cell range **C1:D181.** Select **Insert → Chart** and:

In the Chart Wizard Step 1 dialog box:

1. Click the **Standard Types** tab and then click **XY (Scatter)** as the **Chart type.** Click the first **Chart subtype**, labeled **Scatter.**

2. Click **Next.**

In the Chart Wizard Step 2 dialog box:

3. Click **Next.** (Entries and selections in this dialog box are correct as is.)

In the Chart Wizard Step 3 dialog box:

4. Click the **Titles** tab. Enter a **Chart title**, **Z Value** as the **Value (X) axis** title, and **Return 2008** as the **Value (Y) axis** title. Adjust chart formatting by using the instructions in Appendix Section C.8 for the **Axes, Gridlines, Legend**, and **Data Labels** tabs.

5. Click **Next.**

In the Chart Wizard Step 4 dialog box:

6. Click **As new sheet** and then click **Finish** to create the chart.

EG6.4 THE UNIFORM DISTRIBUTION

There are no Excel Guide instructions for this section.

EG6.5 THE EXPONENTIAL DISTRIBUTION

Computing Exponential Probabilities

PHStat2 Use the **Exponential** procedure to compute an exponential probability. For example, to create the Figure 6.23 worksheet that computes the exponential probability for the bank ATM example (see page 213), select **PHStat → Probability & Prob. Distributions → Exponential.** In the procedure's dialog box (shown below):

1. Enter **20** as the **Mean per unit (Lambda)** and **0.1** as the **X Value.**

2. Enter a **Title** and click **OK.**

In-Depth Excel Use the **EXPONDIST** function to compute an exponential probability. Enter the function as **EXPONDIST(*X Value, mean,* True).**

Use the **COMPUTE worksheet** of the **Exponential workbook**, shown in Figure 6.23 on page 213, as a template for computing exponential probabilities. The worksheet contains the probability for the bank ATM problem of Section 6.5. To adapt this worksheet for other problems, change the **Mean** and **X Value** values in cells B4 and B5.

7

Sampling and Sampling Distributions

Learning Objectives

In this chapter, you learn:

- About different sampling methods
- The concept of the sampling distribution
- To compute probabilities related to the sample mean and the sample proportion
- The importance of the Central Limit Theorem

@ Oxford Cereals

Oxford Cereals fills thousands of boxes of cereal during an eight-hour shift. As the plant operations manager, you are responsible for monitoring the amount of cereal placed in each box. To be consistent with package labeling, boxes should contain a mean of 368 grams of cereal. Because of the speed of the process, the cereal weight varies from box to box, causing some boxes to be underfilled and others overfilled. If the process is not working properly, the mean weight in the boxes could vary too much from the label weight of 368 grams to be acceptable.

Because weighing every single box is too time-consuming, costly, and inefficient, you must take a sample of boxes. For each sample you select, you plan to weigh the individual boxes and calculate a sample mean. You need to determine the probability that such a sample mean could have been randomly selected from a population whose mean is 368 grams. Based on your analysis, you will have to decide whether to maintain, alter, or shut down the cereal-filling process.

I n Chapter 6, you used the normal distribution to study the distribution of video download times from the OurCampus! Web site. In this chapter, you need to make a decision about the cereal-filling process, based on the weights of a sample of cereal boxes packaged at Oxford Cereals. You will learn different methods of sampling and about sampling distributions and how to use them to solve business problems.

7.1 Types of Sampling Methods

In Section 1.3, a sample was defined as the portion of a population that has been selected for analysis. Rather than selecting every item in the population, statistical sampling procedures focus on collecting a small representative group of the larger population. The results of the sample are then used to estimate characteristics of the entire population. There are three main reasons for selecting a sample:

- Selecting a sample is less time-consuming than selecting every item in the population.
- Selecting a sample is less costly than selecting every item in the population.
- An analysis of a sample is less cumbersome and more practical than an analysis of the entire population.

The sampling process begins by defining the **frame**, a listing of items that make up the population. Frames are data sources such as population lists, directories, or maps. Samples are drawn from frames. Inaccurate or biased results can occur if a frame excludes certain portions of the population. Using different frames to generate data can lead to dissimilar conclusions.

After you select a frame, you draw a sample from the frame. As illustrated in Figure 7.1, there are two types of samples: nonprobability samples and probability samples.

FIGURE 7.1
Types of samples

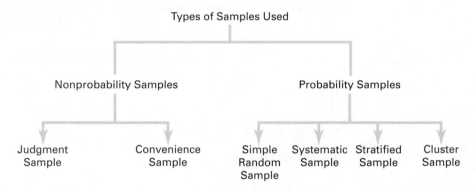

In a **nonprobability sample**, you select the items or individuals without knowing their probabilities of selection. Because of this, the theory of statistical inference that has been developed for probability sampling cannot be applied to nonprobability samples. A common type of nonprobability sampling is **convenience sampling**. In convenience sampling, items selected are easy, inexpensive, or convenient to sample. For example, if you were sampling tires stacked in a warehouse, it would be much more convenient to sample tires at the top of a stack than tires at the bottom of a stack. In many cases, participants in the sample select themselves. For example, many companies conduct surveys by giving visitors to their Web site the opportunity to complete survey forms and submit them electronically. The responses to these surveys can provide large amounts of data quickly and inexpensively, but the sample consists of self-selected Web users. For many studies, only a nonprobability sample such as a judgment sample is available. In a **judgment sample**, you get the opinions of preselected experts in the subject matter. Although the experts may be well informed, you cannot generalize their results to the population.

Nonprobability samples can have certain advantages, such as convenience, speed, and low cost. However, their lack of accuracy due to selection bias and the fact that the results cannot be used for statistical inference more than offset these advantages.

In a **probability sample**, you select items based on known probabilities. Whenever possible, you should use probability sampling methods. Probability samples allow you to make inferences about the population of interest. The four types of probability samples most commonly used are simple random, systematic, stratified, and cluster samples. These sampling methods vary in their cost, accuracy, and complexity.

Simple Random Samples

In a **simple random sample**, every item from a frame has the same chance of selection as every other item. In addition, every sample of a fixed size has the same chance of selection as every other sample of that size. Simple random sampling is the most elementary random sampling technique. It forms the basis for the other random sampling techniques.

With simple random sampling, you use n to represent the sample size and N to represent the frame size. You number every item in the frame from 1 to N. The chance that you will select any particular member of the frame on the first selection is $1/N$.

You select samples with replacement or without replacement. **Sampling with replacement** means that after you select an item, you return it to the frame, where it has the same probability of being selected again. Imagine that you have a fishbowl containing N business cards, one card for each person. On the first selection, you select the card for Judy Craven. You record pertinent information and replace the business card in the bowl. You then mix up the cards in the bowl and select a second card. On the second selection, Judy Craven has the same probability of being selected again, $1/N$. You repeat this process until you have selected the desired sample size, n.

Section EG7.1 discusses how to carry out sampling (with or without replacement) in Excel.

However, usually you do not want the same item to be selected again. **Sampling without replacement** means that once you select an item, you cannot select it again. The chance that you will select any particular item in the frame—for example, the business card for Judy Craven—on the first draw is $1/N$. The chance that you will select any card not previously selected on the second draw is now 1 out of $N - 1$. This process continues until you have selected the desired sample of size n.

Regardless of whether you have sampled with or without replacement, "fishbowl" methods of sample selection have a major drawback—the ability to thoroughly mix the cards and randomly select the sample. As a result, fishbowl methods are not very useful. You need to use less cumbersome and more scientific methods of selection.

One such method uses a **table of random numbers** (see Table E.1 in Appendix E) for selecting the sample. A table of random numbers consists of a series of digits listed in a randomly generated sequence (see reference 6). Because the numeric system uses 10 digits $(0, 1, 2, \ldots, 9)$, the chance that you will randomly generate any particular digit is equal to the probability of generating any other digit. This probability is 1 out of 10. Hence, if you generate a sequence of 800 digits, you would expect about 80 to be the digit 0, 80 to be the digit 1, and so on. Because every digit or sequence of digits in the table is random, the table can be read either horizontally or vertically. The margins of the table designate row numbers and column numbers. The digits themselves are grouped into sequences of five in order to make reading the table easier.

To use Table E.1 instead of a fishbowl for selecting the sample, you first need to assign code numbers to the individual items of the frame. Then you generate the random sample by reading the table of random numbers and selecting those individuals from the frame whose assigned code numbers match the digits found in the table. You can better understand the process of sample selection by studying Example 7.1.

EXAMPLE 7.1 Selecting a Simple Random Sample by Using a Table of Random Numbers	A company wants to select a sample of 32 full-time workers from a population of 800 full-time employees in order to collect information on expenditures concerning a company-sponsored dental plan. How do you select a simple random sample?

SOLUTION The company decides to conduct an e-mail survey. Assuming that not everyone will respond to the survey, you need to send more than 32 surveys to get the necessary 32 responses. Assuming that 8 out of 10 full-time workers will respond to such a survey (i.e., a response rate of 80%), you decide to send 40 surveys. Because you want to send the 40 surveys to 40 different individuals, you should sample without replacement.

The frame consists of a listing of the names and e-mail addresses of all $N = 800$ full-time employees taken from the company personnel files. Thus, the frame is a complete listing of the population. To select the random sample of 40 employees from this frame, you use a table of random numbers. Because the frame size (800) is a three-digit number, each assigned code number must also be three digits so that every full-time worker has an equal chance of selection. You assign a code of 001 to the first full-time employee in the population listing, a code of 002 to the second full-time employee in the population listing, and so on, until a code of 800 is assigned to the Nth full-time worker in the listing. Because $N = 800$ is the largest possible coded value, you discard all three-digit code sequences greater than 800 (i.e., 801 through 999 and 000).

To select the simple random sample, you choose an arbitrary starting point from the table of random numbers. One method you can use is to close your eyes and strike the table of random numbers with a pencil. Suppose you used this procedure and you selected row 06, column 05 of Table 7.1 (which is extracted from Table E.1) as the starting point. Although you can go in any direction, in this example you read the table from left to right, in sequences of three digits, without skipping.

See Section EG7.1 for ways of using Excel to select this sample.

TABLE 7.1
Using a Table of Random Numbers

	Row	00000 12345	00001 67890	11111 12345	11112 67890	22222 12345	22223 67890	33333 12345	33334 67890
					Column				
	01	49280	88924	35779	00283	81163	07275	89863	02348
	02	61870	41657	07468	08612	98083	97349	20775	45091
	03	43898	65923	25078	86129	78496	97653	91550	08078
	04	62993	93912	30454	84598	56095	20664	12872	64647
	05	33850	58555	51438	85507	71865	79488	76783	31708
Begin	06	97340	03364	88472	04334	63919	36394	11095	92470
selection	07	70543	29776	10087	10072	55980	64688	68239	20461
(row 06,	08	89382	93809	00796	95945	34101	81277	66090	88872
column 05)	09	37818	72142	67140	50785	22380	16703	53362	44940
	10	60430	22834	14130	96593	23298	56203	92671	15925
	11	82975	66158	84731	19436	55790	69229	28661	13675
	12	39087	71938	40355	54324	08401	26299	49420	59208
	13	55700	24586	93247	32596	11865	63397	44251	43189
	14	14756	23997	78643	75912	83832	32768	18928	57070
	15	32166	53251	70654	92827	63491	04233	33825	69662
	16	23236	73751	31888	81718	06546	83246	47651	04877
	17	45794	26926	15130	82455	78305	55058	52551	47182
	18	09893	20505	14225	68514	46427	56788	96297	78822
	19	54382	74598	91499	14523	68479	27686	46162	83554
	20	94750	89923	37089	20048	80336	94598	26940	36858
	21	70297	34135	53140	33340	42050	82341	44104	82949
	22	85157	47954	32979	26575	57600	40881	12250	73742
	23	11100	02340	12860	74697	96644	89439	28707	25815
	24	36871	50775	30592	57143	17381	68856	25853	35041
	25	23913	48357	63308	16090	51690	54607	72407	55538

Source: *Data extracted from The Rand Corporation,* A Million Random Digits with 100,000 Normal Deviates *(Glencoe, IL: The Free Press, 1955) and displayed in Table E.1 in Appendix E.*

The individual with code number 003 is the first full-time employee in the sample (row 06 and columns 05–07), the second individual has code number 364 (row 06 and columns 08–10), and the third individual has code number 884. Because the highest code for any employee is 800, you discard the number 884. Individuals with code numbers 720, 433, 463, 363, 109, 592, 470, and 705 are selected third through tenth, respectively.

You continue the selection process until you get the required sample size of 40 full-time employees. If any three-digit sequence repeats during the selection process, you discard the repeating sequence because you are sampling without replacement.

Systematic Samples

In a **systematic sample**, you partition the N items in the frame into n groups of k items, where

$$k = \frac{N}{n}$$

You round k to the nearest integer. To select a systematic sample, you choose the first item to be selected at random from the first k items in the frame. Then, you select the remaining $n - 1$ items by taking every kth item thereafter from the entire frame.

If the frame consists of a listing of prenumbered checks, sales receipts, or invoices, a systematic sample is faster and easier to take than a simple random sample. A systematic sample is also a convenient mechanism for collecting data from telephone books, class rosters, and consecutive items coming off an assembly line.

To take a systematic sample of $n = 40$ from the population of $N = 800$ full-time employees, you partition the frame of 800 into 40 groups, each of which contains 20 employees. You then select a random number from the first 20 individuals and include every twentieth individual after the first selection in the sample. For example, if the first random number you select is 008, your subsequent selections are 028, 048, 068, 088, 108, ..., 768, and 788.

Simple random sampling and systematic sampling are simpler than other, more sophisticated probability sampling methods, but generally require a larger sample size. In addition, systematic sampling is prone to selection bias. When using systematic sampling, if there is a pattern in the frame, you could have severe selection biases. To overcome the inefficiency of simple random sampling and the potential selection bias involved with systematic sampling, you can use either stratified sampling methods or cluster sampling methods.

Stratified Samples

In a **stratified sample**, you first subdivide the N items in the frame into separate subpopulations, or **strata**. A stratum is defined by some common characteristic, such as gender or year in school. You select a simple random sample within each of the strata and combine the results from the separate simple random samples. Stratified sampling is more efficient than either simple random sampling or systematic sampling because you are ensured of the representation of items across the entire population. The homogeneity of items within each stratum provides greater precision in the estimates of underlying population parameters.

EXAMPLE 7.2

Selecting a Stratified Sample

A company wants to select a sample of 32 full-time workers from a population of 800 full-time employees in order to estimate expenditures from a company-sponsored dental plan. Of the full-time employees, 25% are managers and 75% are nonmanagerial workers. How do you select the stratified sample in order for the sample to represent the correct percentage of managers and nonmanagerial workers?

SOLUTION If you assume an 80% response rate, you need to send 40 surveys to get the necessary 32 responses. The frame consists of a listing of the names and e-mail addresses of all $N = 800$ full-time employees included in the company personnel files. Because 25% of the full-time employees are managers, you first separate the frame into two strata: a subpopulation listing of all 200 managerial-level personnel and a separate subpopulation listing of all 600 full-time nonmanagerial workers. Because the first stratum consists of a listing of 200 managers, you assign three-digit code numbers from 001 to 200. Because the second stratum contains a listing of 600 nonmanagerial workers, you assign three-digit code numbers from 001 to 600.

To collect a stratified sample proportional to the sizes of the strata, you select 25% of the overall sample from the first stratum and 75% of the overall sample from the second stratum. You take two separate simple random samples, each of which is based on a distinct random starting point from a table of random numbers (Table E.1). In the first sample, you select 10 managers from the listing of 200 in the first stratum, and in the second sample, you select 30 nonmanagerial workers from the listing of 600 in the second stratum. You then combine the results to reflect the composition of the entire company.

Cluster Samples

In a **cluster sample**, you divide the N items in the frame into several clusters so that each cluster is representative of the entire population. **Clusters** are naturally occurring designations, such as counties, election districts, city blocks, households, or sales territories. You then take a random sample of one or more clusters and study all items in each selected cluster. If clusters are large, a probability-based sample taken from a single cluster is all that is needed.

Cluster sampling is often more cost-effective than simple random sampling, particularly if the population is spread over a wide geographic region. However, cluster sampling often requires a larger sample size to produce results as precise as those from simple random sampling or stratified sampling. A detailed discussion of systematic sampling, stratified sampling, and cluster sampling procedures can be found in reference 1.

Problems for Section 7.1

LEARNING THE BASICS

7.1 For a population containing $N = 902$ individuals, what code number would you assign for
a. the first person on the list?
b. the fortieth person on the list?
c. the last person on the list?

7.2 For a population of $N = 902$, verify that by starting in row 05, column 01 of the table of random numbers (Table E.1), you need only six rows to select a sample of $N = 60$ *without* replacement.

7.3 Given a population of $N = 93$, starting in row 29, column 01 of the table of random numbers (Table E.1), and reading across the row, select a sample of $N = 15$
a. *without* replacement.
b. *with* replacement.

APPLYING THE CONCEPTS

7.4 For a study that consists of personal interviews with participants (rather than mail or phone surveys), explain why simple random sampling might be less practical than some other sampling methods.

7.5 You want to select a random sample of $n = 1$ from a population of three items (which are called $A, B,$ and C). The rule for selecting the sample is as follows: Flip a coin; if it is heads, pick item A; if it is tails, flip the coin again; this time, if it is heads, choose B; if it is tails, choose C. Explain why this is a probability sample but not a simple random sample.

7.6 A population has four members (called $A, B, C,$ and D). You would like to select a random sample of $n = 2$, which you decide to do in the following way: Flip a coin; if it is heads, the sample will be items A and B; if it is tails, the sample will be items C and D. Although this is a random sample, it is not a simple random sample. Explain why. (Compare the procedure described in Problem 7.5 with the procedure described in this problem.)

7.7 The registrar of a college with a population of $N = 4,000$ full-time students is asked by the president to conduct a survey to measure satisfaction with the quality of life on campus. The following table contains a breakdown of the 4,000 registered full-time students, by gender and class designation:

Gender	Class Designation				
	Fr.	So.	Jr.	Sr.	Total
Female	700	520	500	480	2,200
Male	560	460	400	380	1,800
Total	1,260	980	900	860	4,000

The registrar intends to take a probability sample of $n = 200$ students and project the results from the sample to the entire population of full-time students.
a. If the frame available from the registrar's files is an alphabetical listing of the names of all $N = 4,000$ registered full-time students, what type of sample could you take? Discuss.
b. What is the advantage of selecting a simple random sample in (a)?
c. What is the advantage of selecting a systematic sample in (a)?
d. If the frame available from the registrar's files is a listing of the names of all $N = 4,000$ registered full-time students compiled from eight separate alphabetical lists, based on the gender and class designation breakdowns shown in the class designation table, what type of sample should you take? Discuss.
e. Suppose that each of the $N = 4,000$ registered full-time students lived in one of the 10 campus dormitories. Each dormitory accommodates 400 students. It is college policy to fully integrate students by gender and class designation in each dormitory. If the registrar is able to compile a listing of all students by dormitory, explain how you could take a cluster sample.

7.8 Prenumbered sales invoices are kept in a sales journal. The invoices are numbered from 0001 to 5000.
a. Beginning in row 16, column 01, and proceeding horizontally in Table E.1, select a simple random sample of 50 invoice numbers.
b. Select a systematic sample of 50 invoice numbers. Use the random numbers in row 20, columns 05–07, as the starting point for your selection.
c. Are the invoices selected in (a) the same as those selected in (b)? Why or why not?

7.9 Suppose that 5,000 sales invoices are separated into four strata. Stratum 1 contains 50 invoices, stratum 2 contains 500 invoices, stratum 3 contains 1,000 invoices, and stratum 4 contains 3,450 invoices. A sample of 500 sales invoices is needed.
a. What type of sampling should you do? Why?
b. Explain how you would carry out the sampling according to the method stated in (a).
c. Why is the sampling in (a) not simple random sampling?

7.2 Evaluating Survey Worthiness

Surveys are used to collect data. Nearly every day, you read or hear about survey or opinion poll results in newspapers, on the Internet, or on radio or television. To identify surveys that lack objectivity or credibility, you must critically evaluate what you read and hear by examining the worthiness of the survey. First, you must evaluate the purpose of the survey, why it was conducted, and for whom it was conducted.

The second step in evaluating the worthiness of a survey is to determine whether it was based on a probability or nonprobability sample (as discussed in Section 7.1). You need to remember that the only way to make valid statistical inferences from a sample to a population is through the use of a probability sample. Surveys that use nonprobability sampling methods are subject to serious, perhaps unintentional, biases that may make the results meaningless.

Survey Error

Even when surveys use random probability sampling methods, they are subject to potential errors. There are four types of survey errors:

- Coverage error
- Nonresponse error
- Sampling error
- Measurement error

Well-designed surveys reduce or minimize these four types of errors, often at considerable cost.

Coverage Error The key to proper sample selection is having an adequate frame. Remember, a frame is an up-to-date list of all the items from which you will select the sample. **Coverage error** occurs if certain groups of items are excluded from the frame so that they have no chance of being selected in the sample. Coverage error results in a **selection bias**. If the frame is inadequate because certain groups of items in the population were not properly included, any random probability sample selected will provide only an estimate of the characteristics of the frame, not the *actual* population.

Nonresponse Error Not everyone is willing to respond to a survey. In fact, research has shown that individuals in the upper and lower economic classes tend to respond less frequently to surveys than do people in the middle class. **Nonresponse error** arises from failure to collect data on all items in the sample and results in a **nonresponse bias**. Because you cannot always assume that persons who do not respond to surveys are similar to those who do, you need to follow up on the nonresponses after a specified period of time. You should make several attempts to convince such individuals to complete the survey. The follow-up responses are then compared to the initial responses in order to make valid inferences from the survey (reference 1). The mode of response you use affects the rate of response. Personal interview and telephone interview usually produce a higher response rate than does mail survey—but at a higher cost.

Sampling Error As discussed earlier, a sample is selected because it is simpler, less costly, and more efficient to examine than an entire population. However, chance dictates which individuals or items will or will not be included in the sample. **Sampling error** reflects the variation, or "chance differences," from sample to sample, based on the probability of particular individuals or items being selected in the particular samples.

When you read about the results of surveys or polls in newspapers or magazines, there is often a statement regarding a margin of error, such as "the results of this poll are expected to be within ±4 percentage points of the actual value." This **margin of error** is the sampling error. You can reduce sampling error by using larger sample sizes, although doing so increases the cost of conducting the survey.

Measurement Error In the practice of good survey research, you design a questionnaire with the intention of gathering meaningful information. But you have a dilemma here: Getting meaningful measurements is often easier said than done. Consider the following proverb:

A person with one watch always knows what time it is;

A person with two watches always searches to identify the correct one;

A person with ten watches is always reminded of the difficulty in measuring time.

Unfortunately, the process of measurement is often governed by what is convenient, not what is needed. The measurements you get are often only a proxy for the ones you really desire. Much attention has been given to measurement error that occurs because of a weakness in question wording (reference 2). A question should be clear, not ambiguous. Furthermore, in order to avoid *leading questions*, you need to present questions in a neutral manner.

Three sources of **measurement error** are ambiguous wording of questions, the Hawthorne effect, and respondent error. As an example of ambiguous wording, several years ago, the U.S. Department of Labor reported that the unemployment rate in the United States had been underestimated for more than a decade because of poor questionnaire wording in the Current Population Survey. In particular, the wording had led to a significant undercount of women in the labor force. Because unemployment rates are tied to benefit programs such as state unemployment compensation, survey researchers had to rectify the situation by adjusting the questionnaire wording.

The *Hawthorne effect* occurs when a respondent feels obligated to please the interviewer. Proper interviewer training can minimize the Hawthorne effect.

Respondent error occurs as a result of an overzealous or underzealous effort by the respondent. You can minimize this error in two ways: (1) by carefully scrutinizing the data and then recontacting those individuals whose responses seem unusual and (2) by establishing a program of recontacting a small number of randomly chosen individuals in order to determine the reliability of the responses.

Ethical Issues

Ethical considerations arise with respect to the four types of potential errors that can occur when designing surveys: coverage error, nonresponse error, sampling error, and measurement error. Coverage error can result in selection bias and becomes an ethical issue if particular groups or individuals are *purposely* excluded from the frame so that the survey results are more favorable to the survey's sponsor. Nonresponse error can lead to nonresponse bias and becomes an ethical issue if the sponsor knowingly designs the survey so that particular groups or individuals are less likely than others to respond. Sampling error becomes an ethical issue if the findings are purposely presented without reference to sample size and margin of error so that the sponsor can promote a viewpoint that might otherwise be truly insignificant. Measurement error becomes an ethical issue in one of three ways: (1) a survey sponsor chooses leading questions that guide the responses in a particular direction; (2) an interviewer, through mannerisms and tone, purposely creates a Hawthorne effect or otherwise guides the responses in a particular direction; or (3) a respondent willfully provides false information.

Ethical issues also arise when the results of nonprobability samples are used to form conclusions about the entire population. When you use a nonprobability sampling method, you need to explain the sampling procedures and state that the results cannot be generalized beyond the sample.

THINK ABOUT THIS | Probability Sampling Versus Web-Based Surveys

In Sections 7.1 and 7.2, you learned that statistical inferences about populations can be made only by analyzing data collected from probability samples. This type of sampling has been the "gold standard" in survey research for more than 50 years. Companies using surveys based on probability sampling typically make a great effort (and spend large sums) to deal with coverage error, nonresponse error, sampling error, and measurement error.

Some survey companies are now offering an Internet alternative to traditional surveys based on random sampling. YouGov, a British company, introduced Internet-based polling in the United States for the 2008 presidential election (**www.yougov.com** and T. Crampton, "About Online Surveys, Traditional Pollsters Are Somewhat Disappointed," *The New York Times,* May 31, 2007).

YouGov uses a large panel of respondents who answer questions online. These panelists supposedly come from a diverse group, and special efforts are made to include people who are less likely to use the Internet. In addition, panelists are paid to participate. This method of sampling (and the fact that respondents are paid and are not volunteers) makes Web-based sampling scientifically unacceptable to traditional pollsters.

Despite these concerns, YouGov's American affiliate, Polimetrix, conducts online surveys in the United States through its PollingPoint Web site. The founder of Polimetrix, Professor Douglas Rivers of Stanford University, claims that the margin of error of Polimetrix polls is similar to that of telephone polls. YouGov's chief executive, Nadhim Zahawi, points out that modern technology, such as cell phones, has made old-fashioned polls more unreliable due to the increased difficulty of contacting people at home.

However, Leendert de Voogd, managing director of TSN Opinion in Brussels, believes that "Internet polling is like the Wild West, with no rules, no sheriff, and no reference points." He believes that only polling with probability sampling will deliver valid results. On the other hand, Professor Anthony King of the University of Essex does not believe that Internet polling fails to reflect a nation's population. According to Professor King, "There is no evidence to suggest that people who use the Internet are fundamentally different from those without it. One mad, awful lady living in a poor neighborhood without Internet does not differ much from her mad, awful friend next door who goes online." Perhaps only time will tell who is right.

Postscript: A recent survey found that 79.8% of U.S. households had at least one cellular telephone and that about one-quarter of that group (20.2% of all U.S. households) were cell phone-only households. (S. Blumberg and J. Lake, "Wireless Substitution," **www.cdc.gov/nchs/data/nhis/earlyrelease/wireless200905.htm**)

Problems for Section 7.2

APPLYING THE CONCEPTS

7.10 A survey indicates that the vast majority of college students own their own personal computers. What information would you want to know before you accepted the results of this survey?

7.11 A simple random sample of $n = 300$ full-time employees is selected from a company list containing the names of all $N = 5,000$ full-time employees in order to evaluate job satisfaction.
a. Give an example of possible coverage error.
b. Give an example of possible nonresponse error.
c. Give an example of possible sampling error.
d. Give an example of possible measurement error.

SELF Test **7.12** Business Professor Thomas Callarman traveled to China more than a dozen times from 2000 to 2005. He warns people about believing everything they read about surveys conducted in China and gives two specific reasons: "First, things are changing so rapidly that what you hear today may not be true tomorrow. Second, the people who answer the surveys may tell you what they think you want to hear, rather than what they really believe" (T. E. Callarman, "Some Thoughts on China," *Decision Line,* March 2006, pp. 1, 43–44).
a. List the four types of survey error discussed in this section.
b. Which of the types of survey error in (a) are the basis for Professor Callarman's two reasons to question the surveys being conducted in China?

7.13 A recent survey of college freshmen investigated the amount of involvement their parents have with decisions concerning their education. When asked about the decision to go to college, 84% said their parents' involvement was about right, 10.3% said it was too much, and 5.7% said too little. When it came to selecting individual courses, 72.5% said their parents' involvement was about right, 3.5% said it was too much, and 24.0% said too little (M. B. Marklein, "Study: Colleges Shouldn't Fret Over Hands-On Parents," **www.usatoday.com**, January 23, 2008). What additional information would you want to know about the survey before you accepted the results of the study?

7.14 Recruiters are finding a wealth of unfiltered information about candidates on Internet sites such as MySpace. A recent survey found that 83% of recruiters use search engines to learn more about candidates, and 43% eliminated candidates based on information they found (I. Phaneuf, "Who's Googling You?" *Job Postings,* Spring 2009, pp.12–13). What additional information would you want to know about a survey before you accepted the results of the study?

7.3 Sampling Distributions

In many applications, you want to make inferences that are based on statistics calculated from samples to estimate the values of population parameters. In the next two sections, you will learn about how the sample mean (a statistic) is used to estimate the population mean (a parameter) and how the sample proportion (a statistic) is used to estimate the population proportion (a parameter). Your main concern when making a statistical inference is drawing conclusions about a population, *not* about a sample. For example, a political pollster is interested in the sample results only as a way of estimating the actual proportion of the votes that each candidate will receive from the population of voters. Likewise, as plant operations manager for Oxford Cereals, you are only interested in using the sample mean weight calculated from a sample of cereal boxes for estimating the mean weight of a population of boxes.

See Section EG7.4 for ways to create simulated sampling distributions using Excel.

In practice, you select a single random sample of a predetermined size from the population. Hypothetically, to use the sample statistic to estimate the population parameter, you could examine *every* possible sample of a given size that could occur. A **sampling distribution** is the distribution of the results if you actually selected all possible samples. The single result you obtain in practice is just one of the results in the sampling distribution.

7.4 Sampling Distribution of the Mean

In Chapter 3, several measures of central tendency, including the mean, median, and mode, were discussed. Undoubtedly, the mean is the most widely used measure of central tendency. The sample mean is often used to estimate the population mean. The **sampling distribution of the mean** is the distribution of all possible sample means if you select all possible samples of a given size.

The Unbiased Property of the Sample Mean

The sample mean is **unbiased** because the mean of all the possible sample means (of a given sample size, n) is equal to the population mean, μ. A simple example concerning a population of four administrative assistants demonstrates this property. Each assistant is asked to type the same page of a manuscript. Table 7.2 presents the number of errors. This population distribution is shown in Figure 7.2.

TABLE 7.2

Number of Errors Made by Each of Four Administrative Assistants

Administrative Assistant	Number of Errors
Ann	$X_1 = 3$
Bob	$X_2 = 2$
Carla	$X_3 = 1$
Dave	$X_4 = 4$

FIGURE 7.2

Number of errors made by a population of four administrative assistants

When you have the data from a population, you compute the mean by using Equation (7.1).

POPULATION MEAN

The population mean is the sum of the values in the population divided by the population size, N.

$$\mu = \frac{\sum_{i=1}^{N} X_i}{N} \qquad (7.1)$$

You compute the population standard deviation, σ, by using Equation (7.2).

POPULATION STANDARD DEVIATION

$$\sigma = \sqrt{\frac{\sum_{i=1}^{N} (X_i - \mu)^2}{N}} \qquad (7.2)$$

Thus, for the data of Table 7.2,

Excel can compute the population mean and the population standard deviation. See Section EG7.4 for details.

$$\mu = \frac{3 + 2 + 1 + 4}{4} = 2.5 \text{ errors}$$

and

$$\sigma = \sqrt{\frac{(3 - 2.5)^2 + (2 - 2.5)^2 + (1 - 2.5)^2 + (4 - 2.5)^2}{4}} = 1.12 \text{ errors}$$

If you select samples of two administrative assistants *with* replacement from this population, there are 16 possible samples ($N^n = 4^2 = 16$). Table 7.3 lists the 16 possible sample outcomes. If you average all 16 of these sample means, the mean of these values, $\mu_{\overline{X}}$, is equal to 2.5, which is also the mean of the population, μ.

TABLE 7.3

All 16 Samples of $n = 2$ Administrative Assistants from a Population of $N = 4$ Administrative Assistants When Sampling with Replacement

Sample	Administrative Assistants	Sample Outcomes	Sample Mean
1	Ann, Ann	3, 3	$\overline{X}_1 = 3$
2	Ann, Bob	3, 2	$\overline{X}_2 = 2.5$
3	Ann, Carla	3, 1	$\overline{X}_3 = 2$
4	Ann, Dave	3, 4	$\overline{X}_4 = 3.5$
5	Bob, Ann	2, 3	$\overline{X}_5 = 2.5$
6	Bob, Bob	2, 2	$\overline{X}_6 = 2$
7	Bob, Carla	2, 1	$\overline{X}_7 = 1.5$
8	Bob, Dave	2, 4	$\overline{X}_8 = 3$
9	Carla, Ann	1, 3	$\overline{X}_9 = 2$
10	Carla, Bob	1, 2	$\overline{X}_{10} = 1.5$
11	Carla, Carla	1, 1	$\overline{X}_{11} = 1$
12	Carla, Dave	1, 4	$\overline{X}_{12} = 2.5$
13	Dave, Ann	4, 3	$\overline{X}_{13} = 3.5$
14	Dave, Bob	4, 2	$\overline{X}_{14} = 3$
15	Dave, Carla	4, 1	$\overline{X}_{15} = 2.5$
16	Dave, Dave	4, 4	$\overline{X}_{16} = 4$
			$\mu_{\overline{X}} = 2.5$

Because the mean of the 16 sample means is equal to the population mean, the sample mean is an unbiased estimator of the population mean. Therefore, although you do not know how close the sample mean of any particular sample selected comes to the population mean, you are at least assured that the mean of all the possible sample means that could have been selected is equal to the population mean.

Standard Error of the Mean

Figure 7.3 illustrates the variation in the sample means when selecting all 16 possible samples.

FIGURE 7.3

Sampling distribution of the mean, based on all possible samples containing two administrative assistants

Source: *Data are from Table 7.3.*

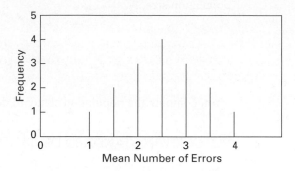

In this small example, although the sample means vary from sample to sample, depending on which two administrative assistants are selected, the sample means do not vary as much as the individual values in the population. That the sample means are less variable than the individual values in the population follows directly from the fact that each sample mean averages together all the values in the sample. A population consists of individual outcomes that can take on a wide range of values, from extremely small to extremely large. However, if a sample contains an extreme value, although this value will have an effect on the sample mean, the effect is reduced because the value is averaged with all the other values in the sample. As the sample size increases, the effect of a single extreme value becomes smaller because it is averaged with more values.

The value of the standard deviation of all possible sample means, called the **standard error of the mean**, expresses how the sample means vary from sample to sample. Equation (7.3) defines the standard error of the mean when sampling *with* replacement or sampling *without* replacement from large or infinite populations.

STANDARD ERROR OF THE MEAN

The standard error of the mean, $\sigma_{\bar{X}}$, is equal to the standard deviation in the population, σ, divided by the square root of the sample size, n.

$$\sigma_{\bar{X}} = \frac{\sigma}{\sqrt{n}} \qquad\qquad (7.3)$$

Therefore, as the sample size increases, the standard error of the mean decreases by a factor equal to the square root of the sample size.

You can also use Equation (7.3) as an approximation of the standard error of the mean when the sample is selected without replacement if the sample contains less than 5% of the entire population. Example 7.3 computes the standard error of the mean for such a situation.

EXAMPLE 7.3

Computing the Standard Error of the Mean

Returning to the cereal-filling process described in the Using Statistics scenario on page 223, if you randomly select a sample of 25 boxes without replacement from the thousands of boxes filled during a shift, the sample contains far less than 5% of the population. Given that the standard deviation of the cereal-filling process is 15 grams, compute the standard error of the mean.

SOLUTION Using Equation (7.3) with $n = 25$ and $\sigma = 15$, the standard error of the mean is

$$\sigma_{\bar{X}} = \frac{\sigma}{\sqrt{n}} = \frac{15}{\sqrt{25}} = \frac{15}{5} = 3$$

The variation in the sample means for samples of $n = 25$ is much less than the variation in the individual boxes of cereal (i.e., $\sigma_{\bar{X}} = 3$ while $\sigma = 15$).

Sampling from Normally Distributed Populations

Now that the concept of a sampling distribution has been introduced and the standard error of the mean has been defined, what distribution will the sample mean, $\bar{X}$, follow? If you are sampling from a population that is normally distributed with mean, μ, and standard deviation, σ, then regardless of the sample size, n, the sampling distribution of the mean is normally distributed, with mean, $\mu_{\bar{X}} = \mu$, and standard error of the mean, $\sigma_{\bar{X}} = \sigma/\sqrt{n}$.

In the simplest case, if you take samples of size $n = 1$, each possible sample mean is a single value from the population because

$$\bar{X} = \frac{\sum_{i=1}^{n} X_i}{n} = \frac{X_1}{1} = X_1$$

Therefore, if the population is normally distributed, with mean, μ, and standard deviation, σ, the sampling distribution of $\bar{X}$, for samples of $n = 1$ must also follow the normal distribution, with mean $\mu_{\bar{X}} = \mu$ and standard error of the mean $\sigma_{\bar{X}} = \sigma/\sqrt{1} = \sigma$. In addition, as the sample size increases, the sampling distribution of the mean still follows a normal distribution, with $\mu_{\bar{X}} = \mu$, but the standard error of the mean decreases, so that a larger proportion of sample means are closer to the population mean. Figure 7.4 illustrates this reduction in variability. Note that 500 samples of 1, 2, 4, 8, 16, and 32 were randomly selected from a normally distributed population. From the polygons in Figure 7.4, you can see that, although the sampling distribution of the mean is approximately[1] normal for each sample size, the sample means are distributed more tightly around the population mean as the sample size increases.

[1]Remember that "only" 500 samples out of an infinite number of samples have been selected, so that the sampling distributions shown are only approximations of the true population distributions.

FIGURE 7.4

Sampling distributions of the mean from 500 samples of sizes $n = 1, 2, 4, 8, 16,$ and 32 selected from a normal population

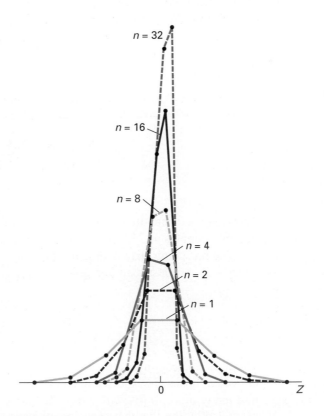

To further examine the concept of the sampling distribution of the mean, consider the Using Statistics scenario described on page 223. The packaging equipment that is filling 368-gram boxes of cereal is set so that the amount of cereal in a box is normally distributed, with a mean of 368 grams. From past experience, you know the population standard deviation for this filling process is 15 grams.

If you randomly select a sample of 25 boxes from the many thousands that are filled in a day and the mean weight is computed for this sample, what type of result could you expect? For example, do you think that the sample mean could be 368 grams? 200 grams? 365 grams?

The sample acts as a miniature representation of the population, so if the values in the population are normally distributed, the values in the sample should be approximately normally distributed. Thus, if the population mean is 368 grams, the sample mean has a good chance of being close to 368 grams.

How can you determine the probability that the sample of 25 boxes will have a mean below 365 grams? From the normal distribution (Section 6.2), you know that you can find the area below any value X by converting to standardized Z values:

$$Z = \frac{X - \mu}{\sigma}$$

In the examples in Section 6.2, you studied how any single value, X, differs from the population mean. Now, in this example, you want to study how a sample mean, $\overline{X}$, differs from the population mean. Substituting $\overline{X}$ for X, $\mu_{\overline{X}}$ for μ, and $\sigma_{\overline{X}}$ for σ in the equation above results in Equation (7.4).

FINDING Z FOR THE SAMPLING DISTRIBUTION OF THE MEAN

The Z value is equal to the difference between the sample mean, $\overline{X}$, and the population mean, μ, divided by the standard error of the mean, $\sigma_{\overline{X}}$.

$$Z = \frac{\overline{X} - \mu_{\overline{X}}}{\sigma_{\overline{X}}} = \frac{\overline{X} - \mu}{\dfrac{\sigma}{\sqrt{n}}} \tag{7.4}$$

To find the area below 365 grams, from Equation (7.4),

$$Z = \frac{\overline{X} - \mu_{\overline{X}}}{\sigma_{\overline{X}}} = \frac{365 - 368}{\dfrac{15}{\sqrt{25}}} = \frac{-3}{3} = -1.00$$

The area corresponding to $Z = -1.00$ in Table E.2 is 0.1587. Therefore, 15.87% of all the possible samples of 25 boxes have a sample mean below 365 grams.

The preceding statement is not the same as saying that a certain percentage of *individual* boxes will have less than 365 grams of cereal. You compute that percentage as follows:

$$Z = \frac{X - \mu}{\sigma} = \frac{365 - 368}{15} = \frac{-3}{15} = -0.20$$

The area corresponding to $Z = -0.20$ in Table E.2 is 0.4207. Therefore, 42.07% of the *individual* boxes are expected to contain less than 365 grams. Comparing these results, you see that many more *individual boxes* than *sample means* are below 365 grams. This result is explained by the fact that each sample consists of 25 different values, some small and some large. The averaging process dilutes the importance of any individual value, particularly when the sample size is large. Thus, the chance that the sample mean of 25 boxes is far away from the population mean is less than the chance that a *single* box is far away.

Examples 7.4 and 7.5 show how these results are affected by using different sample sizes.

EXAMPLE 7.4

The Effect of Sample Size, *n*, on the Computation of $\sigma_{\bar{X}}$

How is the standard error of the mean affected by increasing the sample size from 25 to 100 boxes?

SOLUTION If $n = 100$ boxes, then using Equation (7.3) on page 234:

$$\sigma_{\bar{X}} = \frac{\sigma}{\sqrt{n}} = \frac{15}{\sqrt{100}} = \frac{15}{10} = 1.5$$

The fourfold increase in the sample size from 25 to 100 reduces the standard error of the mean by half—from 3 grams to 1.5 grams. This demonstrates that taking a larger sample results in less variability in the sample means from sample to sample.

EXAMPLE 7.5

The Effect of Sample Size, *n*, on the Clustering of Means in the Sampling Distribution

If you select a sample of 100 boxes, what is the probability that the sample mean is below 365 grams?

SOLUTION Using Equation (7.4) on page 236,

$$Z = \frac{\bar{X} - \mu_{\bar{X}}}{\sigma_{\bar{X}}} = \frac{365 - 368}{\frac{15}{\sqrt{100}}} = \frac{-3}{1.5} = -2.00$$

From Table E.2, the area less than $Z = -2.00$ is 0.0228. Therefore, 2.28% of the samples of 100 boxes have means below 365 grams, as compared with 15.87% for samples of 25 boxes.

Sometimes you need to find the interval that contains a fixed proportion of the sample means. You need to determine a distance below and above the population mean containing a specific area of the normal curve. From Equation (7.4) on page 236,

$$Z = \frac{\bar{X} - \mu}{\frac{\sigma}{\sqrt{n}}}$$

Solving for $\bar{X}$ results in Equation (7.5).

FINDING $\bar{X}$ FOR THE SAMPLING DISTRIBUTION OF THE MEAN

$$\bar{X} = \mu + Z\frac{\sigma}{\sqrt{n}} \tag{7.5}$$

Example 7.6 illustrates the use of Equation (7.5).

EXAMPLE 7.6

Determining the Interval That Includes a Fixed Proportion of the Sample Means

In the cereal-filling example, find an interval symmetrically distributed around the population mean that will include 95% of the sample means, based on samples of 25 boxes.

SOLUTION If 95% of the sample means are in the interval, then 5% are outside the interval. Divide the 5% into two equal parts of 2.5%. The value of Z in Table E.2 corresponding to an area of 0.0250 in the lower tail of the normal curve is -1.96, and the value of Z corresponding to a cumulative area of 0.9750 (i.e., 0.0250 in the upper tail of the normal curve) is $+1.96$. The lower value of $\bar{X}$ (called $\bar{X}_L$) and the upper value of $\bar{X}$ (called $\bar{X}_U$) are found by using Equation (7.5):

$$\bar{X}_L = 368 + (-1.96)\frac{15}{\sqrt{25}} = 368 - 5.88 = 362.12$$

$$\bar{X}_U = 368 + (1.96)\frac{15}{\sqrt{25}} = 368 + 5.88 = 373.88$$

Therefore, 95% of all sample means, based on samples of 25 boxes, are between 362.12 and 373.88 grams.

Sampling from Non-Normally Distributed Populations—The Central Limit Theorem

Thus far in this section, only the sampling distribution of the mean for a normally distributed population has been considered. However, in many instances, either you know that the population is not normally distributed or it is unrealistic to assume that the population is normally distributed. An important theorem in statistics, the Central Limit Theorem, deals with this situation.

> ### THE CENTRAL LIMIT THEOREM
>
> The **Central Limit Theorem** states that as the sample size (i.e., the number of values in each sample) gets *large enough*, the sampling distribution of the mean is approximately normally distributed. This is true regardless of the shape of the distribution of the individual values in the population.

What sample size is large enough? A great deal of statistical research has gone into this issue. As a general rule, statisticians have found that for many population distributions, when the sample size is at least 30, the sampling distribution of the mean is approximately normal. However, you can apply the Central Limit Theorem for even smaller sample sizes if the population distribution is approximately bell-shaped. In the case in which the distribution of a variable is extremely skewed or has more than one mode, you may need sample sizes larger than 30 to ensure normality in the sampling distribution of the mean.

Figure 7.5 illustrates the application of the Central Limit Theorem to different populations. The sampling distributions from three different continuous distributions (normal, uniform, and exponential) for varying sample sizes ($n = 2, 5, 30$) are displayed.

FIGURE 7.5

Sampling distribution of the mean for different populations for samples of $n = 2, 5,$ and 30

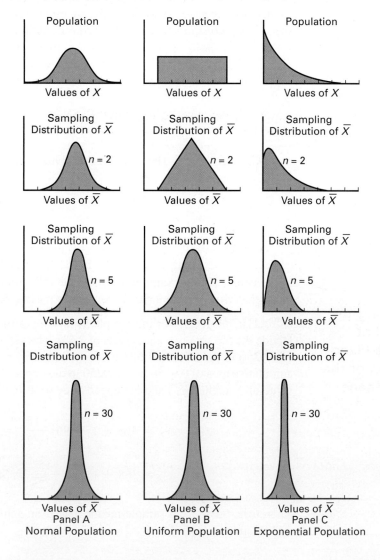

In each of the panels, because the sample mean has the property of being unbiased, the mean of any sampling distribution is always equal to the mean of the population.

Panel A of Figure 7.5 shows the sampling distribution of the mean selected from a normal population. As mentioned earlier in this section, when the population is normally distributed, the sampling distribution of the mean is normally distributed for any sample size. [You can measure the variability by using the standard error of the mean, Equation (7.3), on page 234.]

Panel B of Figure 7.5 depicts the sampling distribution from a population with a uniform (or rectangular) distribution (see Section 6.4). When samples of size $n = 2$ are selected, there is a peaking, or *central limiting*, effect already working. For $n = 5$, the sampling distribution is bell-shaped and approximately normal. When $n = 30$, the sampling distribution looks very similar to a normal distribution. In general, the larger the sample size, the more closely the sampling distribution will follow a normal distribution. As with all other cases, the mean of each sampling distribution is equal to the mean of the population, and the variability decreases as the sample size increases.

Panel C of Figure 7.5 presents an exponential distribution (see Section 6.5). This population is extremely right-skewed. When $n = 2$, the sampling distribution is still highly right-skewed but less so than the distribution of the population. For $n = 5$, the sampling distribution is slightly right-skewed. When $n = 30$, the sampling distribution looks approximately normal. Again, the mean of each sampling distribution is equal to the mean of the population, and the variability decreases as the sample size increases.

Using the results from the normal, uniform, and exponential distributions, you can reach the following conclusions regarding the Central Limit Theorem:

- For most population distributions, regardless of shape, the sampling distribution of the mean is approximately normally distributed if samples of at least size 30 are selected.
- If the population distribution is fairly symmetric, the sampling distribution of the mean is approximately normal for samples as small as size 5.
- If the population is normally distributed, the sampling distribution of the mean is normally distributed, regardless of the sample size.

The Central Limit Theorem is of crucial importance in using statistical inference to draw conclusions about a population. It allows you to make inferences about the population mean without having to know the specific shape of the population distribution.

VISUAL EXPLORATIONS   Exploring Sampling Distributions

Use the Visual Explorations **Two Dice Probability** procedure to observe the effects of simulated throws on the frequency distribution of the sum of the two dice. Open the **Visual Explorations add-in workbook** (see Appendix D.7) and:

1. In Excel 2007, select **Add-Ins → VisualExplorations → Two Dice Probability**. In Excel 2003, select **VisualExplorations → Two Dice Probability**.
2. Click the **Tally** button to tally a set of throws in the frequency distribution table and histogram. Optionally, click the spinner buttons to adjust the number of throws per tally (round).
3. Repeat step 2 as many times as necessary.
4. Click **Finish** to end this exploration.

Problems for Section 7.4

LEARNING THE BASICS

7.15 Given a normal distribution with $\mu = 100$ and $\sigma = 10$, if you select a sample of $n = 25$, what is the probability that $\bar{X}$ is
a. less than 95?
b. between 95 and 97.5?
c. above 102.2?
d. There is a 65% chance that $\bar{X}$ is above what value?

7.16 Given a normal distribution with $\mu = 50$ and $\sigma = 5$, if you select a sample of $n = 100$, what is the probability that $\bar{X}$ is
a. less than 47?
b. between 47 and 49.5?
c. above 51.1?
d. There is a 35% chance that $\bar{X}$ is above what value?

APPLYING THE CONCEPTS

7.17 For each of the following three populations, indicate what the sampling distribution for samples of 25 would consist of:
a. Travel expense vouchers for a university in an academic year.
b. Absentee records (days absent per year) in 2009 for employees of a large manufacturing company.
c. Yearly sales (in gallons) of unleaded gasoline at service stations located in a particular state.

7.18 The following data represent the number of days absent per year in a population of six employees of a small company:

$$1 \quad 3 \quad 6 \quad 7 \quad 9 \quad 10$$

a. Assuming that you sample without replacement, select all possible samples of $n = 2$ and construct the sampling distribution of the mean. Compute the mean of all the sample means and also compute the population mean. Are they equal? What is this property called?
b. Repeat (a) for all possible samples of $n = 3$.
c. Compare the shape of the sampling distribution of the mean in (a) and (b). Which sampling distribution has less variability? Why?
d. Assuming that you sample with replacement, repeat (a) through (c) and compare the results. Which sampling distributions have the least variability—those in (a) or (b)? Why?

7.19 The diameter of a brand of Ping-Pong balls is approximately normally distributed, with a mean of 1.30 inches and a standard deviation of 0.04 inch. If you select a random sample of 16 Ping-Pong balls,
a. what is the sampling distribution of the mean?

b. what is the probability that the sample mean is less than 1.28 inches?
c. what is the probability that the sample mean is between 1.31 and 1.33 inches?
d. The probability is 60% that the sample mean will be between what two values, symmetrically distributed around the population mean?

7.20 The U.S. Census Bureau announced that the median sales price of new houses sold in April 2009 was $221,600, and the mean sales price was $274,300 (**www.census.gov/ newhomesales**, July 20, 2009). Assume that the standard deviation of the prices is $90,000.
a. If you select samples of $n = 2$, describe the shape of the sampling distribution of $\bar{X}$.
b. If you select samples of $n = 100$, describe the shape of the sampling distribution of $\bar{X}$.
c. If you select a random sample of $n = 100$, what is the probability that the sample mean will be less than $300,000?
d. If you select a random sample of $n = 100$, what is the probability that the sample mean will be between $275,000 and $290,000?

7.21 Time spent using e-mail per session is normally distributed, with $\mu = 8$ minutes and $\sigma = 2$ minutes. If you select a random sample of 25 sessions,
a. what is the probability that the sample mean is between 7.8 and 8.2 minutes?
b. what is the probability that the sample mean is between 7.5 and 8 minutes?
c. If you select a random sample of 100 sessions, what is the probability that the sample mean is between 7.8 and 8.2 minutes?
d. Explain the difference in the results of (a) and (c).

 7.22 The amount of time a bank teller spends with each customer has a population mean, μ, of 3.10 minutes and standard deviation, σ, of 0.40 minute. If you select a random sample of 16 customers,
a. what is the probability that the mean time spent per customer is at least 3 minutes?
b. there is an 85% chance that the sample mean is less than how many minutes?
c. What assumption must you make in order to solve (a) and (b)?
d. If you select a random sample of 64 customers, there is an 85% chance that the sample mean is less than how many minutes?

7.5 Sampling Distribution of the Proportion

Consider a categorical variable that has only two categories, such as the customer prefers your brand or the customer prefers the competitor's brand. You are interested in the proportion of items belonging to one of the categories—for example, the proportion of customers that prefer your brand. The population proportion, represented by π, is the proportion of items in the entire population with the characteristic of interest. The sample proportion, represented by p, is the proportion of items in the sample with the characteristic of interest. The sample proportion, a statistic, is used to estimate the population proportion, a parameter. To calculate the sample proportion, you assign one of two possible values, 1 or 0, to represent the presence or absence of the characteristic. You then sum all the 1 and 0 values and divide by n, the sample size. For example, if, in a sample of five customers, three preferred your brand and two did not, you have three 1s and two 0s. Summing the three 1s and two 0s and dividing by the sample size of 5 results in a sample proportion of 0.60.

SAMPLE PROPORTION

$$p = \frac{X}{n} = \frac{\text{Number of items having the characteristic of interest}}{\text{Sample size}} \tag{7.6}$$

The sample proportion, p, takes on values between 0 and 1. If all items have the characteristic, you assign each a score of 1, and p is equal to 1. If half the items have the characteristic, you assign half a score of 1 and assign the other half a score of 0, and p is equal to 0.5. If none of the items have the characteristic, you assign each a score of 0, and p is equal to 0.

In Section 7.4, you learned that the sample mean, $\overline{X}$, is an unbiased estimator of the population mean, μ. Similarly, the statistic p is an unbiased estimator of the population proportion, π.

By analogy to the sampling distribution of the mean, whose standard error is $\sigma_{\overline{X}} = \dfrac{\sigma}{\sqrt{n}}$, the **standard error of the proportion**, σ_p, is given in Equation (7.7).

STANDARD ERROR OF THE PROPORTION

$$\sigma_p = \sqrt{\frac{\pi(1 - \pi)}{n}} \tag{7.7}$$

The **sampling distribution of the proportion** follows the binomial distribution, as discussed in Section 5.3. However, you can use the normal distribution to approximate the binomial distribution when $n\pi$ and $n(1 - \pi)$ are each at least 5. In most cases in which inferences are made about the proportion, the sample size is substantial enough to meet the conditions for using the normal approximation (see reference 1). Therefore, in many instances, you can use the normal distribution to estimate the sampling distribution of the proportion.

Substituting p for $\overline{X}$, π for μ, and $\sqrt{\dfrac{\pi(1 - \pi)}{n}}$ for $\dfrac{\sigma}{\sqrt{n}}$ in Equation (7.4) on page 236 results in Equation (7.8).

FINDING Z FOR THE SAMPLING DISTRIBUTION OF THE PROPORTION

$$Z = \frac{p - \pi}{\sqrt{\dfrac{\pi(1 - \pi)}{n}}} \tag{7.8}$$

To illustrate the sampling distribution of the proportion, suppose that the manager of the local branch of a bank determines that 40% of all depositors have multiple accounts at the bank. If you select a random sample of 200 depositors, because $n\pi = 200(0.40) = 80 \geq 5$ and $n(1 - \pi) = 200(0.60) = 120 \geq 5$, the sample size is large enough to assume that the sampling distribution of the proportion is approximately normally distributed. Then, you can calculate the probability that the sample proportion of depositors with multiple accounts is less than 0.30 by using Equation (7.8):

$$Z = \frac{p - \pi}{\sqrt{\dfrac{\pi(1 - \pi)}{n}}}$$

$$= \frac{0.30 - 0.40}{\sqrt{\frac{(0.40)(0.60)}{200}}} = \frac{-0.10}{\sqrt{\frac{0.24}{200}}} = \frac{-0.10}{0.0346}$$

$$= -2.89$$

Using Table E.2, the area under the normal curve less than -2.89 is 0.0019. Therefore, if the true proportion of items of interest in the population is 0.40, then only 0.19% of the samples of $n = 200$ would be expected to have sample proportions less than 0.30.

Problems for Section 7.5

LEARNING THE BASICS

7.23 In a random sample of 64 people, 48 are classified as "successful."
a. Determine the sample proportion, p, of "successful" people.
b. If the population proportion is 0.70, determine the standard error of the proportion.

7.24 A random sample of 50 households was selected for a telephone survey. The key question asked was, "Do you or any member of your household own a cellular telephone that you can use to access the Internet?" Of the 50 respondents, 15 said yes and 35 said no.
a. Determine the sample proportion, p, of households with cellular telephones that can be used to access the Internet.
b. If the population proportion is 0.40, determine the standard error of the proportion.

7.25 The following data represent the responses (Y for yes and N for no) from a sample of 40 college students to the question "Do you currently own shares in any stocks?"

N N Y N N Y N Y N Y N N Y N Y Y N N N Y
N Y N N N N Y N N Y Y N N N Y N N Y N N

a. Determine the sample proportion, p, of college students who own shares of stock.
b. If the population proportion is 0.30, determine the standard error of the proportion.

APPLYING THE CONCEPTS

✓SELF Test **7.26** A political pollster is conducting an analysis of sample results in order to make predictions on election night. Assuming a two-candidate election, if a specific candidate receives at least 55% of the vote in the sample, that candidate will be forecast as the winner of the election. If you select a random sample of 100 voters, what is the probability that a candidate will be forecast as the winner when
a. the true percentage of her vote is 50.1%?
b. the true percentage of her vote is 60%?
c. the true percentage of her vote is 49% (and she will actually lose the election)?
d. If the sample size is increased to 400, what are your answers to (a) through (c)? Discuss.

7.27 You plan to conduct a marketing experiment in which students are to taste one of two different brands of soft drink. Their task is to correctly identify the brand tasted. You select a random sample of 200 students and assume that the students have no ability to distinguish between the two brands. (Hint: If an individual has no ability to distinguish between the two soft drinks, then the two brands are equally likely to be selected.)
a. What is the probability that the sample will have between 50% and 60% of the identifications correct?
b. The probability is 90% that the sample percentage is contained within what symmetrical limits of the population percentage?
c. What is the probability that the sample percentage of correct identifications is greater than 65%?
d. Which is more likely to occur—more than 60% correct identifications in the sample of 200 or more than 55% correct identifications in a sample of 1,000? Explain.

7.28 In an online survey of 4,001 respondents, 8% were classified as productivity enhancers who are comfortable with technology and use the Internet for its practical value (data extracted from M. Himowitz, "How to Tell What Kind of Tech User You Are," *Newsday*, May 27, 2007, p. F6). Suppose you select a sample of 400 students at your school, and the population proportion of productivity enhancers is 0.08.
a. What is the probability that in the sample, fewer than 10% of the students will be productivity enhancers?
b. What is the probability that in the sample, between 6% and 10% of the students will be productivity enhancers?
c. What is the probability that in the sample, more than 5% of the students will be productivity enhancers?
d. If a sample of 100 is taken, how does this change your answers to (a) through (c)?

7.29 Companies often make flextime scheduling available to help recruit and keep women employees who have children. Other workers sometimes view these flextime schedules as unfair. An article in *USA Today* indicates that 25% of male employees state that they have to pick up the slack for moms working flextime schedules (data extracted from D. Jones, "Poll Finds Resentment of Flextime," **www.usatoday.com**,

May 11, 2007). Suppose you select a random sample of 100 male employees working for companies offering flextime.

a. What is the probability that 25% or fewer male employees will indicate that they have to pick up the slack for moms working flextime?

b. What is the probability that 20% or fewer will indicate that they have to pick up the slack for moms working flextime?

c. If a random sample of 500 is taken, how does this change your answers to (a) and (b)?

7.30 According to Gallup's poll on personal finances, 46% of U.S. workers say they feel that they will have enough money to live comfortably when they retire. (Data extracted from *The Gallup Poll*, **www.gallup.com**, May 6, 2008.) If you select a random sample of 200 U.S. workers,

a. what is the probability that the sample will have between 45% and 55% who say they feel they will have enough money to live comfortably when they retire?

b. the probability is 90% that the sample percentage will be contained within what symmetrical limits of the population percentage?

c. the probability is 95% that the sample percentage will be contained within what symmetrical limits of the population percentage?

7.31 The Agency for Healthcare Research and Quality reports that medical errors are responsible for injury in 1 out of every 25 hospital patients in the United States (data extracted from M. Ozan-Rafferty, "Hospitals: Never Have a Never Event," *The Gallup Management Journal*, **gmj.gallup.com**, May 7, 2009). These errors are tragic and expensive. Preventable health care-related errors cost the U.S. economy an estimated $29 billion each year. Suppose that you select a sample of 100 U.S. hospital patients.

a. What is the probability that the sample percentage will be between 5% and 10%?

b. The probability is 90% that the sample percentage will be within what symmetrical limits of the population percentage?

c. The probability is 95% that the sample percentage will be within what symmetrical limits of the population percentage?

d. Suppose you selected a sample of 400 U.S. hospital patients. How does this change your answers in (a) through (c)?

7.32 Yahoo HotJobs reported that 56% of full-time office workers believe that dressing down can affect jobs, salaries, or promotions (data extracted from J. Yang and K. Carter, "Dress Can Affect Size of Paycheck," **www.usatoday.com**, May 9, 2007).

a. Suppose that you take a sample of 100 full-time workers. If the true population proportion of workers who believe that dressing down can affect jobs, salaries, or promotions is 0.56, what is the probability that fewer than half in your sample hold that same belief?

b. Suppose that you take a sample of 500 full-time workers. If the true population proportion of workers who believe that dressing down can affect jobs, salaries, or promotions is 0.56, what is the probability that fewer than half in your sample hold that same belief?

c. Discuss the effect of sample size on the sampling distribution of the proportion in general and the effect on the probabilities in (a) and (b).

7.6 ✥*Online Topic:* Sampling from Finite Populations

In this section, sampling without replacement from finite populations is discussed. To study this topic, read the **Section 7.6** online topic file that is available on this book's companion Web site. (See Appendix Section D.8 to learn how to access the online topic files.)

USING STATISTICS @ Oxford Cereals Revisited

As the plant operations manager for Oxfords Cereals, you were responsible for monitoring the amount of cereal placed in each box. To be consistent with package labeling, boxes should contain a mean of 368 grams of cereal. Thousands of boxes are produced during a shift, and weighing every single box was determined to be too time-consuming, costly, and inefficient. Instead, a sample of boxes was selected. Based on your analysis of the sample, you had to decide whether to maintain, alter, or shut down the process.

Using the concept of the sampling distribution of the mean, you were able to determine probabilities that such a sample mean could have been randomly selected from a population with a mean of 368 grams. Specifically, if a sample of size $n = 25$ is selected from a population with a mean of 368 and standard deviation of 15, you calculated the probability of selecting a sample with a mean of 365 grams or less to be 15.87%. If a larger sample size is selected, the sample mean should be closer to the population mean. This result was illustrated when you calculated the probability if the sample size were increased to $n = 100$. Using the larger sample size, you determined the probability of selecting a sample with a mean of 365 grams or less to be 2.28%.

SUMMARY

You have learned that in many business situations, the population is so large that you cannot gather information on every item. Instead, statistical sampling procedures focus on collecting a small representative group of the larger population. The results of the sample are then used to estimate characteristics of the entire population. Selecting a sample is less time-consuming, less costly, and more practical than analyzing the entire population.

In this chapter, you studied four common sampling methods—simple random, systematic, stratified, and cluster sampling. You also studied the sampling distribution of the sample mean and the sampling distribution of the sample proportion and their relationship to the Central Limit Theorem. You learned that the sample mean is an unbiased estimator of the population mean, and the sample proportion is an unbiased estimator of the population proportion. In the next five chapters, the techniques of confidence intervals and tests of hypotheses commonly used for statistical inference are discussed.

KEY EQUATIONS

Population Mean

$$\mu = \frac{\sum_{i=1}^{N} X_i}{N} \tag{7.1}$$

Population Standard Deviation

$$\sigma = \sqrt{\frac{\sum_{i=1}^{N}(X_i - \mu)^2}{N}} \tag{7.2}$$

Standard Error of the Mean

$$\sigma_{\overline{X}} = \frac{\sigma}{\sqrt{n}} \tag{7.3}$$

Finding Z for the Sampling Distribution of the Mean

$$Z = \frac{\overline{X} - \mu_{\overline{X}}}{\sigma_{\overline{X}}} = \frac{\overline{X} - \mu}{\dfrac{\sigma}{\sqrt{n}}} \tag{7.4}$$

Finding $\overline{X}$ for the Sampling Distribution of the Mean

$$\overline{X} = \mu + Z\frac{\sigma}{\sqrt{n}} \tag{7.5}$$

Sample Proportion

$$p = \frac{X}{n} \tag{7.6}$$

Standard Error of the Proportion

$$\sigma_p = \sqrt{\frac{\pi(1 - \pi)}{n}} \tag{7.7}$$

Finding Z for the Sampling Distribution of the Proportion

$$Z = \frac{p - \pi}{\sqrt{\dfrac{\pi(1 - \pi)}{n}}} \tag{7.8}$$

KEY TERMS

Central Limit Theorem   238
cluster   228
cluster sample   228
convenience sampling   224
coverage error   229
frame   224
judgment sample   224
margin of error   230
measurement error   230
nonprobability sample   224

nonresponse bias   229
nonresponse error   229
probability sample   224
sampling distribution   232
sampling distribution of the mean   232
sampling distribution of the
   proportion   241
sampling error   230
sampling with replacement   225
sampling without replacement   225

selection bias   229
simple random sample   225
standard error of the mean   234
standard error of the proportion   241
strata   227
stratified sample   227
systematic sample   227
table of random numbers   225
unbiased   232

CHAPTER REVIEW PROBLEMS

CHECKING YOUR UNDERSTANDING

7.33 Why is the sample mean an unbiased estimator of the population mean?

7.34 Why does the standard error of the mean decrease as the sample size, n, increases?

7.35 Why does the sampling distribution of the mean follow a normal distribution for a large enough sample size, even though the population may not be normally distributed?

7.36 What is the difference between a population distribution and a sampling distribution?

7.37 Under what circumstances does the sampling distribution of the proportion approximately follow the normal distribution?

7.38 What is the difference between probability sampling and nonprobability sampling?

7.39 What are some potential problems with using "fishbowl" methods to select a simple random sample?

7.40 What is the difference between sampling *with* replacement versus sampling *without* replacement?

7.41 What is the difference between a simple random sample and a systematic sample?

7.42 What is the difference between a simple random sample and a stratified sample?

7.43 What is the difference between a stratified sample and a cluster sample?

APPLYING THE CONCEPTS

7.44 An industrial sewing machine uses ball bearings that are targeted to have a diameter of 0.75 inch. The lower and upper specification limits under which the ball bearing can operate are 0.74 inch (lower) and 0.76 inch (upper). Past experience has indicated that the actual diameter of the ball bearings is approximately normally distributed, with a mean of 0.753 inch and a standard deviation of 0.004 inch. If you select a random sample of 25 ball bearings, what is the probability that the sample mean is
a. between the target and the population mean of 0.753?
b. between the lower specification limit and the target?
c. greater than the upper specification limit?
d. less than the lower specification limit?
e. The probability is 93% that the sample mean diameter will be greater than what value?

7.45 The fill amount of bottles of a soft drink is normally distributed, with a mean of 2.0 liters and a standard deviation of 0.05 liter. If you select a random sample of 25 bottles, what is the probability that the sample mean will be
a. between 1.99 and 2.0 liters?
b. below 1.98 liters?
c. greater than 2.01 liters?

d. The probability is 99% that the sample mean amount of soft drink will be at least how much?
e. The probability is 99% that the sample mean amount of soft drink will be between which two values (symmetrically distributed around the mean)?

7.46 An orange juice producer buys all his oranges from a large orange grove that has one variety of orange. The amount of juice squeezed from these oranges is approximately normally distributed, with a mean of 4.70 ounces and a standard deviation of 0.40 ounce. Suppose that you select a sample of 25 oranges.
a. What is the probability that the sample mean amount of juice will be at least 4.60 ounces?
b. The probability is 70% that the sample mean amount of juice will be contained between what two values symmetrically distributed around the population mean?
c. The probability is 77% that the sample mean amount of juice will be greater than what value?

7.47 In his management information systems textbook, Professor David Kroenke raises an interesting point: "If 98% of our market has Internet access, do we have a responsibility to provide non-Internet materials to that other 2%?" (D. M. Kroenke, *Using MIS*, Upper Saddle River, NJ: Prentice Hall, 2007, p. 29a). Suppose that 98% of the customers in your market have Internet access, and you select a random sample of 500 customers. What is the probability that the sample has
a. greater than 99% of the customers with Internet access?
b. between 97% and 99% of the customers with Internet access?
c. fewer than 97% of the customers with Internet access?

7.48 International mutual funds reported weak returns in 2008. The population of international mutual funds earned a mean return of −43.95% in 2008 (data extracted from *The Wall Street Journal*, January 2, 2009, p. R6). Assume that the returns for international mutual funds were distributed as a normal random variable, with a mean of −43.95 and a standard deviation of 20. If you selected a random sample of 10 funds from this population, what is the probability that the sample would have a mean return
a. less than −10?
b. between 0 and −20?
c. greater than −30?

7.49 The article mentioned in Problem 7.48 reported that long-term Treasury bonds had a mean return of 24.03% in 2008. Assume that the returns for the long-term Treasury bonds were distributed as a normal random variable, with a mean of 24.03 and a standard deviation of 10. If you select an individual Treasury bond from this population, what is the probability that it would have a return
a. less than 0—that is, a loss?
b. between 10 and 20?
c. greater than 10?

If you selected a random sample of 4 Treasury bonds from this population, what is the probability that the sample would have a mean return

d. less than 0—that is, a loss?
e. between 10 and 20?
f. greater than 10?
g. Compare your results in parts (d) through (f) to those in (a) through (c).

7.50 Telephone interviews have traditionally been the number-one tool in political polling. Recently, many people have argued that compared to other polling methods Internet polling is faster and less expensive and produces a higher response rate. Dr. Doug Usher, a leading authority on political polling, agrees that the telephone poll is still the gold standard in political polls due to its superior statistical reliability, even though it is getting harder to reach people via the telephone with the growing use of caller ID and the fact that many younger people no longer have landlines (D. Usher, "The Internet's Unfulfilled Promise for Political Polling," **www.mysterypollster.com**, June 30, 2005). What concerns, if any, do you have about Internet polling?

7.51 A survey sponsored by the American Dietetic Association and the agribusiness giant ConAgra found that 53% of office workers take 30 minutes or less for lunch each day. Approximately 37% take 30 to 60 minutes, and 10% take more than an hour (data extracted from "Snapshots," **www.usatoday.com**, April 26, 2006).
a. What additional information would you want to know before you accepted the results of the survey?
b. Discuss the four types of survey error in the context of this survey.
c. One of the types of survey error discussed in part (b) should have been measurement error. Explain how the root cause of measurement error in this survey could be the Hawthorne effect.

7.52 A survey conducted by AOL and the Associated Press found that fewer than 25% of adults use instant messaging (IM), and almost 75% of adults who use IM use e-mail more often than IM. The survey also showed that almost 50% of teens use IM, and almost 75% of teens who use IM use IM more often than e-mail (data extracted from M. Levitt, "Bridging the Collaboration Age Gap with Unified Communications and Web 2.0," *KM World*, June 2007, p. 10).
a. What other information would you want to know before you used the results of this survey?
b. Suppose you work for AOL and want to investigate IM and e-mail usage by AOL users. Define the population, frame, and sampling method you would use.

7.53 (Class Project) The table of random numbers is an example of a uniform distribution because each digit is equally likely to occur. Starting in the row corresponding to the day of the month in which you were born, use the table of random numbers (Table E.1) to take one digit at a time.

Select five different samples each of $n = 2, n = 5$, and $n = 10$. Compute the sample mean of each sample. Develop a frequency distribution of the sample means for the results of the entire class, based on samples of sizes $n = 2, n = 5$, and $n = 10$.

What can be said about the shape of the sampling distribution for each of these sample sizes?

7.54 (Class Project) Toss a coin 10 times and record the number of heads. If each student performs this experiment five times, a frequency distribution of the number of heads can be developed from the results of the entire class. Does this distribution seem to approximate the normal distribution?

7.55 (Class Project) The number of cars waiting in line at a car wash is distributed as follows:

Number of Cars	Probability
0	0.25
1	0.40
2	0.20
3	0.10
4	0.04
5	0.01

You can use the table of random numbers (Table E.1) to select samples from this distribution by assigning numbers as follows:
1. Start in the row corresponding to the day of the month in which you were born.
2. Select a two-digit random number.
3. If you select a random number from 00 to 24, record a length of 0; if from 25 to 64, record a length of 1; if from 65 to 84, record a length of 2; if from 85 to 94, record a length of 3; if from 95 to 98, record a length of 4; if 99, record a length of 5.

Select samples of $n = 2, n = 5$, and $n = 10$. Compute the mean for each sample. For example, if a sample of size 2 results in the random numbers 18 and 46, these would correspond to lengths 0 and 1, respectively, producing a sample mean of 0.5. If each student selects five different samples for each sample size, a frequency distribution of the sample means (for each sample size) can be developed from the results of the entire class. What conclusions can you reach concerning the sampling distribution of the mean as the sample size is increased?

7.56 (Class Project) Using Table E.1, simulate the selection of different-colored balls from a bowl, as follows:
1. Start in the row corresponding to the day of the month in which you were born.
2. Select one-digit numbers.
3. If a random digit between 0 and 6 is selected, consider the ball white; if a random digit is a 7, 8, or 9, consider the ball red.

Select samples of $n = 10, n = 25$, and $n = 50$ digits. In each sample, count the number of white balls and compute the proportion of white balls in the sample. If each student in the class selects five different samples for each sample size, a frequency distribution of the proportion of white balls (for each sample size) can be developed from the results of the entire class. What conclusions can you reach about the sampling distribution of the proportion as the sample size is increased?

7.57 (Class Project) Suppose that step 3 of Problem 7.56 uses the following rule: "If a random digit between 0 and 8 is selected, consider the ball to be white; if a random digit of 9 is selected, consider the ball to be red." Compare and contrast the results in this problem and those in Problem 7.56.

MANAGING THE *SPRINGVILLE HERALD*

Continuing its quality improvement effort first described in the Chapter 6 "Managing the *Springville Herald*" case, the production department of the newspaper has been monitoring the blackness of the newspaper print. As before, blackness is measured on a standard scale in which the target value is 1.0. Data collected over the past year indicate that the blackness is approximately normally distributed, with a mean of 1.005 and a standard deviation of 0.10.

EXERCISE

SH7.1 Each day, 25 spots on the first newspaper printed are chosen, and the blackness of the spots is measured.

Assuming that the distribution has not changed from what it was in the past year, what is the probability that the mean blackness of the spots is
a. less than 1.0?
b. between 0.95 and 1.0?
c. between 1.0 and 1.05?
d. less than 0.95 or greater than 1.05?
e. Suppose that the mean blackness of today's sample of 25 spots is 0.952. What conclusion can you reach about the blackness of today's newspaper based on this result? Explain.

WEB CASE

Apply your knowledge about sampling distributions in this Web Case, which reconsiders the Oxford Cereals Using Statistics scenario.

The advocacy group Consumers Concerned About Cereal Cheaters (CCACC) suspects that cereal companies, including Oxford Cereals, are cheating consumers by packaging cereals at less than labeled weights. Using a Web browser, open to the Web page for the Chapter 7 Web Case or open **ConsumersConcerned.htm**, if you have downloaded the Web Case files, to visit the organization's home page. Examine the group's claims and supporting data, and then answer the following questions:
1. Are the data collection procedures that the CCACC uses to form its conclusions flawed? What procedures could the group follow to make its analysis more rigorous?
2. Assume that the two samples of five cereal boxes (one sample for each of two cereal varieties) listed on the CCACC Web site were collected randomly by organization members. For each sample, do the following:

a. Calculate the sample mean.
b. Assume that the standard deviation of the process is 15 grams and the population mean is 368 grams. Calculate the percentage of all samples for each process that have a sample mean less than the value you calculated in (a).
c. Again, assuming that the standard deviation is 15 grams, calculate the percentage of individual boxes of cereal that have a weight less than the value you calculated in (a).
3. What, if any, conclusions can you form by using your calculations about the filling processes for the two different cereals?
4. A representative from Oxford Cereals has asked that the CCACC take down its page discussing shortages in Oxford Cereals boxes. Is that request reasonable? Why or why not?
5. Can the techniques discussed in this chapter be used to prove cheating in the manner alleged by the CCACC? Why or why not?

REFERENCES

1. Cochran, W. G., *Sampling Techniques*, 3rd ed. (New York: Wiley, 1977).
2. Gallup, G. H., *The Sophisticated Poll-Watcher's Guide* (Princeton, NJ: Princeton Opinion Press, 1972).
3. Goleman, D., "Pollsters Enlist Psychologists in Quest for Unbiased Results," *The New York Times*, September 7, 1993, pp. C1, C11.
4. Hahn, G., and W. Meeker, *Statistical Intervals, A Guide for Practitioners* (New York: John Wiley and Sons, Inc., 1991).
5. *Microsoft Excel 2007* (Redmond, WA: Microsoft Corp., 2007).
6. Rand Corporation, *A Million Random Digits with 100,000 Normal Deviates* (New York: The Free Press, 1955).

EG7.1 TYPES of SAMPLING METHODS

Selecting a Simple Random Sample with Replacement

In-Depth Excel Use the RANDBETWEEN function to select a random integer that can be used to select an item from a frame. Enter the function as **RANDBETWEEN (1,** *population size***).**

Use the **COMPUTE worksheet** of the **Random workbook** as a template for creating a random sample. This worksheet contains 40 copies of the formula **=RANDBETWEEN(1, 800)** in column B and provides an alternative way to selecting the sample desired in Example 7.1 on page 225. The RANDBETWEEN function samples with replacement. To create a sample without replacement, add additional copies of the formula in new column B rows until you have the sample size you need.

In Excel 2003, this function requires that the Analysis ToolPak be installed. Also in Excel 2003, you may see the **#NAME?** error message when you first open the COMPUTE worksheet, even if the Analysis ToolPak is installed. If you see this message, reenter all the column B formulas, starting with the formula in cell B4.

Analysis ToolPak Use the **Sampling** procedure to create a random sample with replacement. For example, to select a random sample of $n = 5$, from a cell range A1:A100 that includes a column heading in cell A1:

1. Select **Data → Data Analysis** (Excel 2007) or **Tools → Data Analysis** (Excel 2003).
2. In the Data Analysis dialog box, select **Sampling** from the **Analysis Tools** list and then click **OK**.

In the procedure's dialog box (see below):

3. Enter **A1:A100** as the **Input Range** and check **Labels**.
4. Click **Random** and enter **5** as the **Number of Samples**.
5. Click **New Worksheet Ply** and then click **OK**.

Selecting a Simple Random Sample Without Replacement

PHStat2 Use the **Random Sample Generation** procedure to create a random sample without replacement. For example, to select the Example 7.1 sample of 40 workers, Select **PHStat → Sampling → Random Sample Generation**. In the procedure's dialog box (shown below):

1. Enter **40** as the **Sample Size**.
2. Click **Generate list of random numbers** and enter **800** as the **Population Size**.
3. Enter a **Title** and click **OK**.

In-Depth Excel See "Selecting a Simple Random Sample with Replacement" *In-Depth Excel* instructions in the left column, which also explains how to select without replacement.

EG7.2 EVALUATING SURVEY WORTHINESS

There are no Excel Guide instructions for this section.

EG7.3 SAMPLING DISTRIBUTIONS

There are no Excel Guide instructions for this section.

EG7.4 SAMPLING DISTRIBUTION of the MEAN

In-Depth Excel Use the **AVERAGE** and **STDEVP** functions, first discussed in Sections EG3.1 and EG3.4 of the Chapter 3 Excel Guide to compute the population mean and the population standard deviation.

Creating a Simulated Sampling Distribution

PHStat2 Use the **Sampling Distributions Simulation** procedure to create a simulated sampling distribution. For example, to create 100 samples of sample size 30 from a uniformly distributed population, select **PHStat** ➔ **Sampling** ➔ **Sampling Distributions Simulation**. In the procedure's dialog box (shown below):

1. Enter **100** as the **Number of Samples**.
2. Enter **30** as the **Sample Size**.
3. Click **Uniform**.
4. Enter a **Title** and click **OK**.

The sample means, overall mean, and standard error of the mean can be found starting in row 103 of the worksheet that the procedure creates.

Analysis ToolPak Use the **Random Number Generation** procedure to create a simulated sampling distribution. For example, to create 100 samples of sample size 30 from a uniformly distributed population, select **Data** ➔ **Data Analysis (Excel 2007) or** ➔ **Tools** ➔ **Data Analysis** (Excel 2003) and in the Data Analysis dialog box, click **Random Number Generation** and then click **OK**. In the procedure's dialog box (shown below):

1. Enter **100** as the **Number of Variables**
2. Enter **30** as the **Number of Random Numbers**.
3. Select **Uniform** from the **Distribution** drop-down list.
4. Click **New Worksheet Ply** and then click **OK**.

Use the formulas that appear in rows 104 through 108 in the **SDS_FORMULAS worksheet** of the **SDS workbook** as models if you want to compute sample means, the overall mean, and the standard error of the mean.

If, for other problems, you select **Discrete** in step 3, you must have open a worksheet that contains a cell range of X and $P(X)$ values. Enter this cell range as the **Value and Probability Input Range** (not shown when **Uniform** has been selected) in the **Parameters** section of the dialog box.

EG7.5 SAMPLING DISTRIBUTION of the PROPORTION

There are no Excel Guide instructions for this section.

8

Confidence Interval Estimation

Learning Objectives

In this chapter, you learn:

- To construct and interpret confidence interval estimates for the mean and the proportion
- How to determine the sample size necessary to develop a confidence interval estimate for the mean or proportion
- How to use confidence interval estimates in auditing

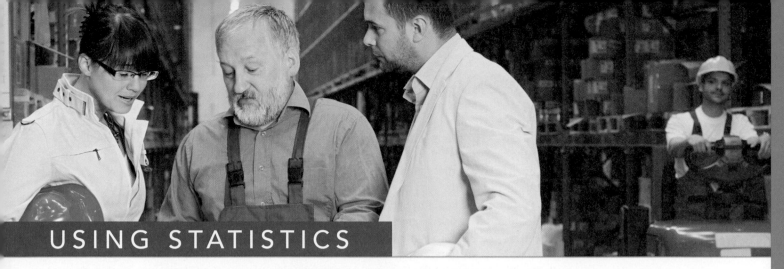

@ Saxon Home Improvement

Saxon Home Improvement distributes home improvement supplies in the northeastern United States. As a company accountant, you are responsible for the accuracy of the integrated inventory management and sales information system. You could review the contents of each and every record to check the accuracy of this system, but such a detailed review would be time-consuming and costly. A better approach is to use statistical inference techniques to draw conclusions about the population of all records from a relatively small sample collected during an audit. At the end of each month, you could select a sample of the sales invoices to estimate the following:

- The mean dollar amount listed on the sales invoices for the month
- The proportion of invoices that contain errors that violate the internal control policy of the warehouse
- The total dollar amount listed on the sales invoices for the month
- Any differences between the dollar amounts on the sales invoices and the amounts entered into the sales information system

How accurate are the results from the sample, and how do you use this information? Is the sample size large enough to give you the information you need?

In Section 7.4, you used the Central Limit Theorem and knowledge of the population distribution to determine the percentage of sample means that are within certain distances of the population mean. For instance, in the cereal-filling example used throughout Chapter 7 (see Example 7.6 on page 237), you can conclude that 95% of all sample means are between 362.12 and 373.88 grams. This is an example of *deductive* reasoning because the conclusion is based on taking something that is true in general (for the population) and applying it to something specific (the sample means).

Getting the results that Saxon Home Improvement needs requires *inductive* reasoning. Inductive reasoning lets you use some specifics to make broader generalizations. You cannot guarantee that the broader generalizations are absolutely correct, but with a careful choice of the specifics and a rigorous methodology, you can get useful conclusions. As a Saxon accountant, you need to use inferential statistics, which uses sample results (the "some specifics") to *estimate* ("the making of the broader generalization") unknown population parameters such as a population mean or a population proportion. Note that statisticians use the word *estimate* in the same sense of the everyday usage, something you are reasonably certain about but cannot flatly say is absolutely correct.

You estimate population parameters by using either point estimates or interval estimates. A **point estimate** is the value of a single sample statistic, such as a sample mean. A **confidence interval estimate** is a range of numbers, called an *interval*, constructed around the point estimate. The confidence interval is constructed such that the probability that the population parameter is located somewhere within the interval is known.

Suppose you want to estimate the mean GPA of all the students at your university. The mean GPA for all the students is an unknown population mean, denoted by μ. You select a sample of students and compute the sample mean, denoted by $\overline{X}$, to be 2.80. As a *point estimate* of the population mean, μ, you ask how accurate is the 2.80 value as an estimate of the population mean, μ? By taking into account the known variability from sample to sample (see Section 7.4, concerning the sampling distribution of the mean), you can construct a confidence interval estimate for the population mean to answer this question.

When you construct a confidence interval estimate, you indicate the confidence of correctly estimating the value of the population parameter, μ. This allows you to say that there is a specified confidence that μ is somewhere in the range of numbers defined by the interval.

After studying this chapter, you might find that a 95% confidence interval for the mean GPA at your university is $(2.75 \leq \mu \leq 2.85)$. You can interpret this interval estimate by stating that you are 95% confident that the mean GPA at your university is between 2.75 and 2.85.

In this chapter, you learn to construct a confidence interval for both the population mean and population proportion. You also learn how to determine the sample size that is necessary to construct a confidence interval of a desired width.

8.1 Confidence Interval Estimate for the Mean (σ Known)

In Section 7.4, you used the Central Limit Theorem and knowledge of the population distribution to determine the percentage of sample means that are within certain distances of the population mean. Suppose that in the cereal-filling example, you wished to estimate the population mean, using the information from a single sample. Thus, rather than take $\mu \pm (1.96)(\sigma/\sqrt{n})$ to find the upper and lower limits around μ, as in Section 7.4, you substitute the sample mean, $\overline{X}$, for the unknown μ and use $\overline{X} \pm (1.96)(\sigma/\sqrt{n})$ as an interval to estimate the unknown μ. Although in practice you select a single sample of n values and compute the mean, $\overline{X}$, in order to understand the full meaning of the interval estimate, you need to examine a hypothetical set of all possible samples of n values.

Suppose that a sample of $n = 25$ boxes has a mean of 362.3 grams. The interval developed to estimate μ is $362.3 \pm (1.96)(15)/(\sqrt{25})$ or 362.3 ± 5.88. The estimate of μ is

$$356.42 \leq \mu \leq 368.18$$

Because the population mean, μ (equal to 368), is included within the interval, this sample results in a correct statement about μ (see Figure 8.1).

FIGURE 8.1

Confidence interval estimates for five different samples of $n = 25$ taken from a population where $\mu = 368$ and $\sigma = 15$

To continue this hypothetical example, suppose that for a different sample of $n = 25$ boxes, the mean is 369.5. The interval developed from this sample is

$$369.5 \pm (1.96)(15)/(\sqrt{25})$$

or 369.5 ± 5.88. The estimate is

$$363.62 \le \mu \le 375.38$$

Because the population mean, μ (equal to 368), is also included within this interval, this statement about μ is correct.

Now, before you begin to think that correct statements about μ are always made by developing a confidence interval estimate, suppose a third hypothetical sample of $n = 25$ boxes is selected and the sample mean is equal to 360 grams. The interval developed here is $360 \pm (1.96)(15)/(\sqrt{25})$, or 360 ± 5.88. In this case, the estimate of μ is

$$354.12 \le \mu \le 365.88$$

This estimate is *not* a correct statement because the population mean, μ, is not included in the interval developed from this sample (see Figure 8.1). Thus, for some samples, the interval estimate for μ is correct, but for others it is incorrect. In practice, only one sample is selected, and because the population mean is unknown, you cannot determine whether the interval estimate is correct. To resolve this problem of sometimes having an interval that provides a correct estimate and sometimes having an interval that does not, you need to determine the proportion of samples producing intervals that result in correct statements about the population mean, μ. To do this, consider two other hypothetical samples: the case in which $\bar{X} = 362.12$ grams and the case in which $\bar{X} = 373.88$ grams. If $\bar{X} = 362.12$, the interval is $362.12 \pm (1.96)(15)/(\sqrt{25})$, or 362.12 ± 5.88. This leads to the following interval:

$$356.24 \le \mu \le 368.00$$

Because the population mean of 368 is at the upper limit of the interval, the statement is a correct one (see Figure 8.1).

When $\bar{X} = 373.88$, the interval is $373.88 \pm (1.96)(15)/(\sqrt{25})$, or 373.88 ± 5.88. The interval estimate for the mean is

$$368.00 \le \mu \le 379.76$$

In this case, because the population mean of 368 is included at the lower limit of the interval, the statement is correct.

In Figure 8.1, you see that when the sample mean falls somewhere between 362.12 and 373.88 grams, the population mean is included *somewhere* within the interval. In Example 7.6 on page 237, you found that 95% of the sample means fall between 362.12 and 373.88 grams. Therefore, 95% of all samples of $n = 25$ boxes have sample means that will result in intervals that include the population mean.

Because, in practice, you select only one sample of size n, and μ is unknown, you never know for sure whether your specific interval includes the population mean. However, if you take all possible samples of n and compute their 95% confidence intervals, 95% of the intervals will include the population mean, and only 5% of them will not. In other words, you have 95% confidence that the population mean is somewhere in your interval.

Consider once again the first sample discussed in this section. A sample of $n = 25$ boxes had a sample mean of 362.3 grams. The interval constructed to estimate μ is

$$362.3 \pm (1.96)(15)/(\sqrt{25})$$

$$362.3 \pm 5.88$$

$$356.42 \leq \mu \leq 368.18$$

The interval from 356.42 to 368.18 is referred to as a *95% confidence interval*. The following contains an interpretation of the interval that most business professionals will understand. (For a technical discussion of different ways to interpret confidence intervals, see Reference 3.)

"I am 95% confident that the mean amount of cereal in the population of boxes is somewhere between 356.42 and 368.18 grams."

To assist in your understanding of the meaning of the confidence interval, the following example concerns the order-filling process at a Web site. Filling orders consists of several steps, including receiving an order, picking the parts of the order, checking the order, packing, and shipping the order. The file Order contains the time, in minutes, to fill orders for a population of 200 on a recent day. Although in practice the population characteristics are rarely known, for this population of orders, the mean, μ, is known to be equal to 69.637 minutes, and the standard deviation, σ, is known to be equal to 10.411 minutes. To illustrate how the sample mean and sample standard deviation can vary from one sample to another, 20 different samples of $n = 10$ were selected from the population of 200 orders, and the sample mean and sample standard deviation (and other statistics) were calculated for each sample. Figure 8.2 shows these results.

FIGURE 8.2

Sample statistics and 95% confidence intervals for 20 samples of $n = 10$ selected from the population of 200 orders

Variable	Count	Mean	StDev	Minimum	Median	Maximum	Range	95% CI
Sample 1	10	74.15	13.39	56.10	76.85	97.70	41.60	(67.6973, 80.6027)
Sample 2	10	61.10	10.60	46.80	61.35	79.50	32.70	(54.6473, 67.5527)
Sample 3	10	74.36	6.50	62.50	74.50	84.00	21.50	(67.9073, 80.8127)
Sample 4	10	70.40	12.80	47.20	70.95	84.00	36.80	(63.9473, 76.8527)
Sample 5	10	62.18	10.85	47.10	59.70	84.00	36.90	(55.7273, 68.6327)
Sample 6	10	67.03	9.68	51.10	69.60	83.30	32.20	(60.5773, 73.4827)
Sample 7	10	69.03	8.81	56.60	68.85	83.70	27.10	(62.5773, 75.4827)
Sample 8	10	72.30	11.52	54.20	71.35	87.00	32.80	(65.8473, 78.7527)
Sample 9	10	68.18	14.10	50.10	69.95	86.20	36.10	(61.7273, 74.6327)
Sample 10	10	66.67	9.08	57.10	64.65	86.10	29.00	(60.2173, 73.1227)
Sample 11	10	72.42	9.76	59.60	74.65	86.10	26.50	(65.9673, 78.8727)
Sample 12	10	76.26	11.69	50.10	80.60	87.00	36.90	(69.8073, 82.7127)
Sample 13	10	65.74	12.11	47.10	62.15	86.10	39.00	(59.2873, 72.1927)
Sample 14	10	69.99	10.97	51.00	73.40	84.60	33.60	(63.5373, 76.4427)
Sample 15	10	75.76	8.60	61.10	75.05	87.80	26.70	(69.3073, 82.2127)
Sample 16	10	67.94	9.19	56.70	67.70	87.80	31.10	(61.4873, 74.3927)
Sample 17	10	71.05	10.48	50.10	71.15	86.20	36.10	(64.5973, 77.5027)
Sample 18	10	71.68	7.96	55.60	72.35	82.60	27.00	(65.2273, 78.1327)
Sample 19	10	70.97	9.83	54.40	70.05	84.60	30.20	(64.5173, 77.4227)
Sample 20	10	74.48	8.80	62.00	76.25	85.70	23.70	(68.0273, 80.9327)

From Figure 8.2, you can see the following:

- The sample statistics differ from sample to sample. The sample means vary from 61.10 to 76.26 minutes, the sample standard deviations vary from 6.50 to 14.10 minutes, the sample medians vary from 59.70 to 80.60 minutes, and the sample ranges vary from 21.50 to 41.60 minutes.
- Some of the sample means are greater than the population mean of 69.637 minutes, and some of the sample means are less than the population mean.
- Some of the sample standard deviations are greater than the population standard deviation of 10.411 minutes, and some of the sample standard deviations are less than the population standard deviation.
- The variation in the sample ranges is much more than the variation in the sample standard deviations.

The variation of sample statistics from sample to sample is called *sampling error*. Sampling error is the variation that occurs due to selecting a single sample from the population. The size of the sampling error is primarily based on the amount of variation in the population and on the sample size. Large samples have less sampling error than small samples, but large samples cost more to select.

The last column of Figure 8.2 contains 95% confidence interval estimates of the population mean order-filling time, based on the results of those 20 samples of $n = 10$. Begin by examining the first sample selected. The sample mean is 74.15 minutes, and the interval estimate for the population mean is 67.6973 to 80.6027 minutes. In a typical study, you would not know for sure whether this interval estimate is correct because you rarely know the value of the population mean. However, for this example *concerning the order-filling times*, the population mean is known to be 69.637 minutes. If you examine the interval 67.6973 to 80.6027 minutes, you see that the population mean of 69.637 minutes is located *between* these lower and upper limits. Thus, the first sample provides a correct estimate of the population mean in the form of an interval estimate. Looking over the other 19 samples, you see that similar results occur for all the other samples *except* for samples 2, 5, and 12. For each of the intervals generated (other than samples 2, 5, and 12), the population mean of 69.637 minutes is located *somewhere* within the interval.

For sample 2, the sample mean is 61.10 minutes, and the interval is 54.6473 to 67.5527 minutes; for sample 5, the sample mean is 62.18, and the interval is between 55.7273 and 68.6327; for sample 12, the sample mean is 76.26, and the interval is between 69.8073 and 82.7127 minutes. The population mean of 69.637 minutes is *not* located within any of these intervals, and the estimate of the population mean made using these intervals is incorrect. Although 3 of the 20 intervals did not include the population mean, if you had selected all the possible samples of $n = 10$, 95% of the intervals would include the population mean.

In some situations, you might want a higher degree of confidence of including the population mean within the interval (such as 99%). In other cases, you might accept less confidence (such as 90%) of correctly estimating the population mean. In general, the **level of confidence** is symbolized by $(1 - \alpha) \times 100\%$, where α is the proportion in the tails of the distribution that is outside the confidence interval. The proportion in the upper tail of the distribution is $\alpha/2$, and the proportion in the lower tail of the distribution is $\alpha/2$. You use Equation (8.1) to construct a $(1 - \alpha) \times 100\%$ confidence interval estimate for the mean with σ known.

CONFIDENCE INTERVAL FOR THE MEAN (σ KNOWN)

$$\bar{X} \pm Z_{\alpha/2} \frac{\sigma}{\sqrt{n}}$$

or

$$\bar{X} - Z_{\alpha/2} \frac{\sigma}{\sqrt{n}} \leq \mu \leq \bar{X} + Z_{\alpha/2} \frac{\sigma}{\sqrt{n}} \tag{8.1}$$

where $Z_{\alpha/2}$ is the value corresponding to an upper-tail probability of $\alpha/2$ from the standardized normal distribution (i.e., a cumulative area of $1 - \alpha/2$).

Section EG8.1 discusses how to construct this confidence interval estimate using the worksheet function CONFIDENCE.

The value of $Z_{\alpha/2}$ needed for constructing a confidence interval is called the **critical value** for the distribution. 95% confidence corresponds to an α value of 0.05. The critical Z value corresponding to a cumulative area of 0.975 is 1.96 because there is 0.025 in the upper tail of the distribution, and the cumulative area less than $Z = 1.96$ is 0.975.

There is a different critical value for each level of confidence, $1 - \alpha$. A level of confidence of 95% leads to a Z value of 1.96 (see Figure 8.3). 99% confidence corresponds to an α value of 0.01. The Z value is approximately 2.58 because the upper-tail area is 0.005 and the cumulative area less than $Z = 2.58$ is 0.995 (see Figure 8.4).

FIGURE 8.3

Normal curve for determining the Z value needed for 95% confidence

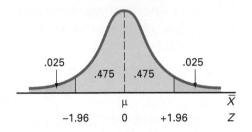

FIGURE 8.4

Normal curve for determining the Z value needed for 99% confidence

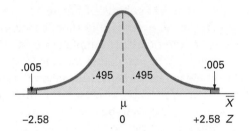

Now that various levels of confidence have been considered, why not make the confidence level as close to 100% as possible? Before doing so, you need to realize that any increase in the level of confidence is achieved only by widening (and making less precise) the confidence interval. There is no "free lunch" here. You would have more confidence that the population mean is within a broader range of values; however, this might make the interpretation of the confidence interval less useful. The trade-off between the width of the confidence interval and the level of confidence is discussed in greater depth in the context of determining the sample size in Section 8.4. Example 8.1 illustrates the application of the confidence interval estimate.

EXAMPLE 8.1

Estimating the Mean Paper Length with 95% Confidence

A paper manufacturer has a production process that operates continuously throughout an entire production shift. The paper is expected to have a mean length of 11 inches, and the standard deviation of the length is 0.02 inch. At periodic intervals, a sample is selected to determine whether the mean paper length is still equal to 11 inches or whether something has gone wrong in the production process to change the length of the paper produced. You select a random sample of 100 sheets, and the mean paper length is 10.998 inches. Construct a 95% confidence interval estimate for the population mean paper length.

SOLUTION Using Equation (8.1) on page 255, with $Z_{\alpha/2} = 1.96$ for 95% confidence,

$$\bar{X} \pm Z_{\alpha/2} \frac{\sigma}{\sqrt{n}} = 10.998 \pm (1.96)\frac{0.02}{\sqrt{100}}$$

$$= 10.998 \pm 0.00392$$

$$10.99408 \leq \mu \leq 11.00192$$

Thus, with 95% confidence, you conclude that the population mean is between 10.99408 and 11.00192 inches. Because the interval includes 11, the value indicating that the production process is working properly, you have no reason to believe that anything is wrong with the production process.

To see the effect of using a 99% confidence interval, examine Example 8.2.

EXAMPLE 8.2

Estimating the Mean Paper Length with 99% Confidence

Construct a 99% confidence interval estimate for the population mean paper length.

SOLUTION Using Equation (8.1) on page 255, with $Z_{\alpha/2} = 2.58$ for 99% confidence,

$$\overline{X} \pm Z_{\alpha/2}\frac{\sigma}{\sqrt{n}} = 10.998 \pm (2.58)\frac{0.02}{\sqrt{100}}$$

$$= 10.998 \pm 0.00516$$

$$10.99284 \leq \mu \leq 11.00316$$

Once again, because 11 is included within this wider interval, you have no reason to believe that anything is wrong with the production process.

As discussed in Section 7.4, the sampling distribution of the sample mean, $\overline{X}$, is normally distributed if the population for your characteristic of interest, X, follows a normal distribution. And, if the population of X does not follow a normal distribution, the Central Limit Theorem almost always ensures that $\overline{X}$ is approximately normally distributed when n is large. However, when dealing with a small sample size and a population that does not follow a normal distribution, the sampling distribution of $\overline{X}$ is not normally distributed, and therefore the confidence interval discussed in this section is inappropriate. In practice, however, as long as the sample size is large enough and the population is not very skewed, you can use the confidence interval defined in Equation (8.1) to estimate the population mean when σ is known. To assess the assumption of normality, you can evaluate the shape of the sample data by constructing a histogram, stem-and-leaf display, boxplot, or normal probability plot.

Can You Ever Know the Population Standard Deviation?

To solve Equation 8.1, you must know the value for σ, the population standard deviation. To know σ implies that you know all the values in the entire population. (How else would you know the value of this population parameter?) If you knew all the values in the entire population, you could directly compute the population mean. There would be no need to use the *inductive* reasoning of inferential statistics to *estimate* the population mean. In other words, if you knew σ, you really do not have a need to use Equation 8.1 to construct a "confidence interval estimate of the mean (σ known)."

More significantly, in virtually all real-world business situations, you would never know the standard deviation of the population. In business situations, populations are often too large to examine all the values. So why study the confidence interval estimate of the mean (σ known) at all? This method serves as an effective introduction to the concept of a confidence interval because it uses the normal distribution, which has already been much discussed in Chapters 6 and 7. In the next section, you will see that constructing a confidence interval estimate when σ is not known requires another distribution (the t distribution) not previously mentioned in this book.

Because the confidence interval concept is a very important concept to understand when reading the rest of this book, review this section carefully to understand the underlying concept—even if you never have a practical reason to use the confidence interval estimate of the mean (σ known).

Problems for Section 8.1

LEARNING THE BASICS

8.1 If $\overline{X} = 85, \sigma = 8$, and $n = 64$, construct a 95% confidence interval estimate for the population mean, μ.

8.2 If $\overline{X} = 125, \sigma = 24$, and $n = 36$, construct a 99% confidence interval estimate for the population mean, μ.

8.3 Why is it not possible in Example 8.1 on page 256 to have 100% confidence? Explain.

8.4 Is it true in Example 8.1 on page 256 that you do not know for sure whether the population mean is between 10.99408 and 11.00192 inches? Explain.

APPLYING THE CONCEPTS

8.5 A market researcher selects a simple random sample of $n = 100$ customers from a population of 2 million customers. After analyzing the sample, she states that she has

95% confidence that the mean annual income of the 2 million customers is between $70,000 and $85,000. Explain the meaning of this statement.

8.6 Suppose that you are going to collect a set of data, either from an entire population or from a random sample taken from that population.
a. Which statistical measure would you compute first: the mean or the standard deviation? Explain.
b. What does your answer to (a) tell you about the "practicality" of using the confidence interval estimate formula given in Equation (8.1)?

8.7 Consider the confidence interval estimate discussed in Problem 8.5. Suppose that the population mean annual income is $71,000. Is the confidence interval estimate stated in Problem 8.5 correct? Explain.

8.8 You are working as an assistant to the dean of institutional research at your university. She wants to survey members of the alumni association who obtained their baccalaureate degrees 5 years ago to learn what their starting salaries were in their first full-time job after receiving their degrees. A sample of 100 alumni is to be randomly selected from the list of 2,500 graduates in that class. If her goal is to construct a 95% confidence interval estimate for the population mean starting salary, why is it unlikely that you will be able to use Equation (8.1) on page 255 for this purpose? Explain.

8.9 The manager of a paint supply store wants to estimate the actual amount of paint contained in 1-gallon cans purchased from a nationally known manufacturer. The manufacturer's specifications state that the standard deviation of the amount of paint is equal to 0.02 gallon. A random sample of 50 cans is selected, and the sample mean amount of paint per 1-gallon can is 0.995 gallon.
a. Construct a 99% confidence interval estimate for the population mean amount of paint included in a 1-gallon can.
b. On the basis of these results, do you think that the manager has a right to complain to the manufacturer? Why?
c. Must you assume that the population amount of paint per can is normally distributed here? Explain.
d. Construct a 95% confidence interval estimate. How does this change your answer to (b)?

✓**SELF Test** **8.10** The quality control manager at a light bulb factory needs to estimate the mean life of a large shipment of light bulbs. The standard deviation is 100 hours. A random sample of 64 light bulbs indicated a sample mean life of 350 hours.
a. Construct a 95% confidence interval estimate for the population mean life of light bulbs in this shipment.
b. Do you think that the manufacturer has the right to state that the light bulbs have a mean life of 400 hours? Explain.
c. Must you assume that the population light bulb life is normally distributed? Explain.
d. Suppose that the standard deviation changes to 80 hours. What are your answers in (a) and (b)?

8.2 Confidence Interval Estimate for the Mean (σ Unknown)

In the previous section, you learned that in most business situations, you do not know σ, the population standard deviation. This section discusses a method of constructing a confidence interval estimate of μ that uses the sample statistic S as an estimate of the population parameter σ.

Student's t Distribution

At the start of the twentieth century, William S. Gosset was working at Guinness, trying to help the Irish brewer brew better beer less expensively (see reference 4). As he had only small samples to study, he needed to find a way to make inferences about means without having to know σ. Writing under the pen name "Student,"[1] Gosset solved this problem by developing what today is known as the **Student's t distribution**, or the t distribution, for short.

If the random variable X is normally distributed, then the following statistic

$$t = \frac{\bar{X} - \mu}{\frac{S}{\sqrt{n}}}$$

[1]Guinness considered all research conducted to be proprietary and a trade secret. The firm prohibited its employees from publishing their results. Gosset circumvented this ban by using the pen name "Student" to publish his findings.

has a t distribution with $n - 1$ **degrees of freedom**. This expression has the same form as the Z statistic in Equation (7.4) on page 236, except that S is used to estimate the unknown σ.

Properties of the t Distribution

The t distribution is very similar in appearance to the standardized normal distribution. Both distributions are symmetrical and bell-shaped, with the mean and the median equal to zero. However, the t distribution has more area in the tails and less in the center than does the standardized normal distribution (see Figure 8.5). This is due to the fact that because S is used to estimate the unknown σ, the values of t are more variable than those for Z.

The degrees of freedom, $n - 1$, are directly related to the sample size, n. The concept of *degrees of freedom* is discussed further on page 260. As the sample size and degrees of freedom increase, S becomes a better estimate of σ, and the t distribution gradually approaches the standardized normal distribution, until the two are virtually identical. With a sample size of about 120 or more, S estimates σ precisely enough so that there is little difference between the t and Z distributions.

As stated earlier, the t distribution assumes that the random variable X is normally distributed. In practice, however, when the sample size is large enough and the population is not very skewed, in most cases you can use the t distribution to estimate the population mean when σ is unknown. When dealing with a small sample size and a skewed population distribution, the confidence interval estimate may not provide a valid estimate of the population mean. To assess the assumption of normality, you can evaluate the shape of the sample data by constructing a histogram, stem-and-leaf display, boxplot, or normal probability plot. However, the ability of any of these graphs to help you evaluate normality is limited when you have a small sample size.

You find the critical values of t for the appropriate degrees of freedom from the table of the t distribution (see Table E.3). The columns of the table present the most commonly used cumulative probabilities and corresponding upper-tail areas. The rows of the table represent the degrees of freedom. The critical t values are found in the cells of the table. For example, with 99 degrees of freedom, if you want 95% confidence, you find the appropriate value of t, as shown in Table 8.1. The 95% confidence level means that 2.5% of the values (an area of 0.025) are in each tail of the distribution. Looking in the column for a cumulative probability of 0.975 and an upper-tail area of 0.025 in the row corresponding to 99 degrees of freedom gives you

TABLE 8.1

Determining the Critical Value from the t Table for an Area of 0.025 in Each Tail with 99 Degrees of Freedom

	Cumulative Probabilities					
	.75	.90	.95	.975	.99	.995
	Upper-Tail Areas					
Degrees of Freedom	.25	.10	.05	.025	.01	.005
1	1.0000	3.0777	6.3138	12.7062	31.8207	63.6574
2	0.8165	1.8856	2.9200	4.3027	6.9646	9.9248
3	0.7649	1.6377	2.3534	3.1824	4.5407	5.8409
4	0.7407	1.5332	2.1318	2.7764	3.7469	4.6041
5	0.7267	1.4759	2.0150	2.5706	3.3649	4.0322
⋮	⋮	⋮	⋮	⋮	⋮	⋮
96	0.6771	1.2904	1.6609	1.9850	2.3658	2.6280
97	0.6770	1.2903	1.6607	1.9847	2.3654	2.6275
98	0.6770	1.2902	1.6606	1.9845	2.3650	2.6269
99	0.6770	1.2902	1.6604	1.9842	2.3646	2.6264
100	0.6770	1.2901	1.6602	1.9840	2.3642	2.6259

Source: *Extracted from Table E.3.*

a critical value for t of 1.9842 (see Figure 8.6). Because t is a symmetrical distribution with a mean of 0, if the upper-tail value is $+1.9842$, the value for the lower-tail area (lower 0.025) is -1.9842. A t value of -1.9842 means that the probability that t is less than -1.9842 is 0.025, or 2.5%.

FIGURE 8.6

t distribution with 99 degrees of freedom

Note that for a 95% confidence interval, you will always have a cumulative probability of 0.975 and an upper-tail area of 0.025. Similarly, for a 99% confidence interval, you will have 0.995 and 0.005, and for a 90% confidence interval you will have 0.95 and 0.05.

The Concept of Degrees of Freedom

In Chapter 3, you learned that the numerator of the sample variance, S^2 [see Equation (3.6) on page 93], requires the computation

$$\sum_{i=1}^{n}(X_i - \bar{X})^2$$

In order to compute S^2, you first need to know $\bar{X}$. Therefore, only $n - 1$ of the sample values are free to vary. This means that you have $n - 1$ degrees of freedom. For example, suppose a sample of five values has a mean of 20. How many values do you need to know before you can determine the remainder of the values? The fact that $n = 5$ and $\bar{X} = 20$ also tells you that

$$\sum_{i=1}^{n}X_i = 100$$

because

$$\frac{\sum_{i=1}^{n}X_i}{n} = \bar{X}$$

Thus, when you know four of the values, the fifth one is *not* free to vary because the sum must add to 100. For example, if four of the values are 18, 24, 19, and 16, the fifth value must be 23 so that the sum equals 100.

The Confidence Interval Statement

Equation (8.2) defines the $(1 - \alpha) \times 100\%$ confidence interval estimate for the mean with σ unknown.

CONFIDENCE INTERVAL FOR THE MEAN (σ UNKNOWN)

$$\bar{X} \pm t_{\alpha/2}\frac{S}{\sqrt{n}}$$

or

$$\bar{X} - t_{\alpha/2}\frac{S}{\sqrt{n}} \leq \mu \leq \bar{X} + t_{\alpha/2}\frac{S}{\sqrt{n}} \tag{8.2}$$

where $t_{\alpha/2}$ is the critical value corresponding to an upper-tail probability of $\alpha/2$ (i.e., a cumulative area of $1 - \alpha/2$) from the t distribution with $n - 1$ degrees of freedom.

To illustrate the application of the confidence interval estimate for the mean when the standard deviation is unknown, recall the Saxon Home Improvement scenario presented on page 251. Using the Define, Collect, Organize, Visualize, and Analyze steps first discussed in Chapter 2, you define the variable of interest as the dollar amount listed on the sales invoices for the month. Your business objective is to estimate the mean dollar amount. Then, you collect the data by selecting a sample of 100 sales invoices from the population of sales invoices during the month. Once you have collected the data, you organize the data in a worksheet. You can construct various graphs (not shown here) to better visualize the distribution of the dollar amounts. To analyze the data, you compute the sample mean of the 100 sales invoices to be equal to $110.27 and the sample standard deviation to be equal to $28.95. For 95% confidence, the critical value from the t distribution (as shown in Table 8.1 on page 259) is 1.9842. Using Equation (8.2),

$$\overline{X} \pm t_{\alpha/2}\frac{S}{\sqrt{n}}$$

$$= 110.27 \pm (1.9842)\frac{28.95}{\sqrt{100}}$$

$$= 110.27 \pm 5.74$$

$$\$104.53 \le \mu \le \$116.01$$

Figure 8.7 shows a worksheet solution that uses the **TINV** function to compute the critical value from the t distribution.

FIGURE 8.7

Worksheet to compute a confidence interval estimate for the mean sales invoice amount for the Saxon Home Improvement Company

Figure 8.7 displays the **COMPUTE worksheet** *of the* **CIE sigma unknown workbook** *and reveals the formulas the worksheet uses. See Section EG8.2 to learn how to construct a confidence interval estimate and how to use the CIE sigma unknown workbook as a template for other problems.*

	A	B
1	Estimate for the Mean Sales Invoice Amount	
2		
3	**Data**	
4	Sample Standard Deviation	28.95
5	Sample Mean	110.27
6	Sample Size	100
7	Confidence Level	95%
8		
9	**Intermediate Calculations**	
10	Standard Error of the Mean	2.8950 =B4/SQRT(B6)
11	Degrees of Freedom	99 =B6 - 1
12	t Value	1.9842 =TINV(1 - B7, B11)
13	Interval Half Width	5.7443 =B12 * B10
14		
15	**Confidence Interval**	
16	Interval Lower Limit	104.53 =B5 - B13
17	Interval Upper Limit	116.01 =B5 + B13

Thus, with 95% confidence, you conclude that the mean amount of all the sales invoices is between $104.53 and $116.01. The 95% confidence level indicates that if you selected all possible samples of 100 (something that is never done in practice), 95% of the intervals developed would include the population mean somewhere within the interval. The validity of this confidence interval estimate depends on the assumption of normality for the distribution of the amount of the sales invoices. With a sample of 100, the normality assumption is not overly restrictive (see the Central Limit Theorem on page 238), and the use of the t distribution is likely appropriate. Example 8.3 further illustrates how you construct the confidence interval for a mean when the population standard deviation is unknown.

EXAMPLE 8.3

Estimating the Mean Force Required to Break Electric Insulators

A manufacturing company produces electric insulators. Using the Define, Collect, Organize, Visualize, and Analyze steps first discussed in Chapter 2, you define the variable of interest as the strength of the insulators. If the insulators break when in use, a short circuit is likely. To test the strength of the insulators, you carry out destructive testing to determine how much *force* is required to break the insulators. You measure force by observing how many pounds are applied to the insulator before it breaks. You collect the data by selecting 30 insulators to be used in the experiment. You organize the data collected in a worksheet. Table 8.2 lists 30 values from this experiment, which are stored in Force. To analyze the data, you need to construct a 95% confidence interval estimate for the population mean force required to break the insulator.

TABLE 8.2

Force (in Pounds) Required to Break Insulators

1,870	1,728	1,656	1,610	1,634	1,784	1,522	1,696	1,592	1,662
1,866	1,764	1,734	1,662	1,734	1,774	1,550	1,756	1,762	1,866
1,820	1,744	1,788	1,688	1,810	1,752	1,680	1,810	1,652	1,736

SOLUTION To visualize the data, you construct a boxplot of the force, as displayed in Figure 8.8, and a normal probability plot, as shown in Figure 8.9. To analyze the data, you construct the confidence interval estimate shown in Figure 8.10.

FIGURE 8.8

Boxplot for the amount of force required to break electric insulators

Create boxplots using the instructions in Section EG3.3.

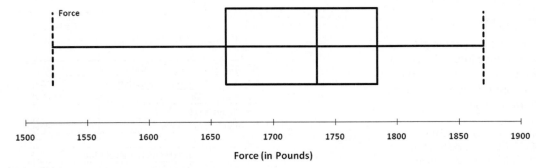

FIGURE 8.9

Normal probability plot for the amount of force required to break electric insulators

Create normal probability plots using the instructions in Section EG6.3.

FIGURE 8.10

Worksheet to construct a confidence interval estimate for the mean amount of force required to break electric insulators

*See Section EG8.2 to learn how to construct a confidence interval estimate and how to use the **CIE sigma unknown workbook** as a template for this problem.*

	A	B	
1	Estimate for the Mean Amount of Force Required		
2			
3	**Data**		
4	Sample Standard Deviation	89.55	
5	Sample Mean	1723.4	
6	Sample Size	30	
7	Confidence Level	95%	
8			
9	**Intermediate Calculations**		
10	Standard Error of the Mean	16.3495	=B4/SQRT(B6)
11	Degrees of Freedom	29	=B6 - 1
12	t Value	2.0452	=TINV(1 - B7, B11)
13	Interval Half Width	33.4385	=B12 * B10
14			
15	**Confidence Interval**		
16	Interval Lower Limit	1689.96	=B5 - B13
17	Interval Upper Limit	1756.84	=B5 + B13

Figure 8.10 shows that the sample mean is $\overline{X} = 1{,}723.4$ pounds and the sample standard deviation is $S = 89.55$ pounds. Using Equation (8.2) on page 260 to construct the confidence interval, you need to determine the critical value from the t table, using the row for 29 degrees of freedom. For 95% confidence, you use the column corresponding to an upper-tail area of 0.025 and a cumulative probability of 0.975. From Table E.3, you see that $t_{\alpha/2} = 2.0452$. Thus, using $\overline{X} = 1{,}723.4$, $S = 89.55$, $n = 30$, and $t_{\alpha/2} = 2.0452$,

$$\overline{X} \pm t_{\alpha/2}\frac{S}{\sqrt{n}}$$

$$= 1{,}723.4 \pm (2.0452)\frac{89.55}{\sqrt{30}}$$

$$= 1{,}723.4 \pm 33.44$$

$$1{,}689.96 \le \mu \le 1{,}756.84$$

You conclude with 95% confidence that the mean breaking force required for the population of insulators is between 1,689.96 and 1,756.84 pounds. The validity of this confidence interval estimate depends on the assumption that the force required is normally distributed. Remember, however, that you can slightly relax this assumption for large sample sizes. Thus, with a sample of 30, you can use the t distribution even if the amount of force required is only slightly left-skewed. From the boxplot displayed in Figure 8.8 and the normal probability plot shown in Figure 8.9, the amount of force required appears only slightly left-skewed. Thus, the t distribution is appropriate for these data.

The interpretation of the confidence interval when σ is unknown is the same as when σ is known. To illustrate the fact that the confidence interval for the mean varies more when σ is unknown, return to the example concerning the order-filling times discussed in Section 8.1 on pages 254–255. Suppose that, in this case, you do *not* know the population standard deviation and instead use the sample standard deviation to construct the confidence interval estimate of the mean. Figure 8.11 on page 264 shows the results for each of 20 samples of $n = 10$ orders.

In Figure 8.11, observe that the standard deviation of the samples varies from 6.25 (sample 17) to 14.83 (sample 3). Thus, the width of the confidence interval developed varies from 8.94 in sample 17 to 21.22 in sample 3. Because you know that the population mean order time $\mu = 69.637$ minutes, you can see that the interval for sample 8(69.68 − 85.48) and the interval for sample 10(56.41 − 68.69) do not correctly estimate the population mean. All the other intervals correctly estimate the population mean. Once again, remember that in practice you select only one sample, and you have no way of knowing for sure whether this one sample provides a confidence interval that includes the population mean.

FIGURE 8.11

Confidence interval estimates of the mean for 20 samples of $n = 10$, selected from the population of 200 orders with σ unknown

Variable	N	Mean	StDev	SE Mean	95% CI
Sample 1	10	71.64	7.58	2.40	(66.22, 77.06)
Sample 2	10	67.22	10.95	3.46	(59.39, 75.05)
Sample 3	10	67.97	14.83	4.69	(57.36, 78.58)
Sample 4	10	73.90	10.59	3.35	(66.33, 81.47)
Sample 5	10	67.11	11.12	3.52	(59.15, 75.07)
Sample 6	10	68.12	10.83	3.43	(60.37, 75.87)
Sample 7	10	65.80	10.85	3.43	(58.03, 73.57)
Sample 8	10	77.58	11.04	3.49	(69.68, 85.48)
Sample 9	10	66.69	11.45	3.62	(58.50, 74.88)
Sample 10	10	62.55	8.58	2.71	(56.41, 68.69)
Sample 11	10	71.12	12.82	4.05	(61.95, 80.29)
Sample 12	10	70.55	10.52	3.33	(63.02, 78.08)
Sample 13	10	65.51	8.16	2.58	(59.67, 71.35)
Sample 14	10	64.90	7.55	2.39	(59.50, 70.30)
Sample 15	10	66.22	11.21	3.54	(58.20, 74.24)
Sample 16	10	70.43	10.21	3.23	(63.12, 77.74)
Sample 17	10	72.04	6.25	1.98	(67.57, 76.51)
Sample 18	10	73.91	11.29	3.57	(65.83, 81.99)
Sample 19	10	71.49	9.76	3.09	(64.51, 78.47)
Sample 20	10	70.15	10.84	3.43	(62.39, 77.91)

Problems for Section 8.2

LEARNING THE BASICS

8.11 If $\bar{X} = 75, S = 24$, and $n = 36$, and assuming that the population is normally distributed, construct a 95% confidence interval estimate for the population mean, μ.

8.12 Determine the critical value of t in each of the following circumstances:
a. $1 - \alpha = 0.95, n = 10$
b. $1 - \alpha = 0.99, n = 10$
c. $1 - \alpha = 0.95, n = 32$
d. $1 - \alpha = 0.95, n = 65$
e. $1 - \alpha = 0.90, n = 16$

8.13 Assuming that the population is normally distributed, construct a 95% confidence interval estimate for the population mean for each of the following samples:

Sample A: 1 1 1 1 8 8 8 8
Sample B: 1 2 3 4 5 6 7 8

Explain why these two samples produce different confidence intervals even though they have the same mean and range.

8.14 Assuming that the population is normally distributed, construct a 95% confidence interval for the population mean, based on the following sample of size $n = 7$: 1, 2, 3, 4, 5, 6, and 20. Change the number 20 to 7 and recalculate the confidence interval. Using these results, describe the effect of an outlier (i.e., an extreme value) on the confidence interval.

APPLYING THE CONCEPTS

8.15 A stationery store wants to estimate the mean retail value of greeting cards that it has in its inventory. A random sample of 100 greeting cards indicates a mean value of $2.55 and a standard deviation of $0.44.

a. Assuming a normal distribution, construct a 95% confidence interval estimate for the mean value of all greeting cards in the store's inventory.
b. Suppose there were 2,500 greeting cards in the store's inventory. How are the results in (a) useful in assisting the store owner to estimate the total value of the inventory?

8.16 ✓ SELF Test Southside Hospital in Bay Shore, New York, commonly conducts stress tests to study the heart muscle after a person has a heart attack. Members of the diagnostic imaging department conducted a quality improvement project with the objective of reducing the turnaround time for stress tests. Turnaround time is defined as the time from when a test is ordered to when the radiologist signs off on the test results. Initially, the mean turnaround time for a stress test was 68 hours. After incorporating changes into the stress-test process, the quality improvement team collected a sample of 50 turnaround times. In this sample, the mean turnaround time was 32 hours, with a standard deviation of 9 hours (data extracted from E. Godin, D. Raven, C. Sweetapple, and F. R. Del Guidice, "Faster Test Results," *Quality Progress*, January 2004, 37(1), pp. 33–39).
a. Construct a 95% confidence interval estimate for the population mean turnaround time.
b. Interpret the interval constructed in (a).
c. Do you think the quality improvement project was a success?

8.17 The U.S. Department of Transportation requires tire manufacturers to provide tire performance information on the sidewall of a tire to better inform prospective customers as they make purchasing decisions. One very important measure of tire performance is the tread wear index, which indicates the tire's resistance to tread wear compared with a tire graded with a base of 100. A tire with a grade of 200 should last twice as long, on average, as a tire graded with a base of 100. A consumer organization wants to estimate the actual tread wear index of a brand name of tires that claims "graded 200" on the sidewall of the tire. A random sample of $n = 18$ indicates a sample mean tread wear index of 195.3 and a sample standard deviation of 21.4.

a. Assuming that the population of tread wear indexes is normally distributed, construct a 95% confidence interval estimate for the population mean tread wear index for tires produced by this manufacturer under this brand name.

b. Do you think that the consumer organization should accuse the manufacturer of producing tires that do not meet the performance information provided on the sidewall of the tire? Explain.

c. Explain why an observed tread wear index of 210 for a particular tire is not unusual, even though it is outside the confidence interval developed in (a).

8.18 The file **MoviePrices** contains the price for two movie tickets, with online service charges, large popcorn, and two medium soft drinks at a sample of six theater chains:

$36.15 $31.00 $35.05 $40.25 $33.75 $43.00

Source: *Data extracted from K. Kelly, "The Multiplex Under Siege,"* The Wall Street Journal, *December 24–25, 2005, pp. P1, P5.*

a. Construct a 95% confidence interval estimate for the population mean price for two movie tickets, with online service charges, large popcorn, and two medium soft drinks, assuming a normal distribution.

b. Interpret the interval constructed in (a).

8.19 The file **Sedans** contains the overall miles per gallon (MPG) of 2009 sedans priced under $20,000.

27 31 30 28 27 24 29 32 32 27 26 26 25 26 25 24

Source: *Data extracted from "Vehicle Ratings,"* Consumer Reports, *April 2009, p. 27.*

a. Construct a 95% confidence interval estimate for the population mean MPG of 2009 sedans (4 cylinder) priced under $20,000, assuming a normal distribution.

b. Interpret the interval constructed in (a).

c. Compare the results in (a) to those in Problem 8.20(a).

8.20 The file **SUV** contains the overall miles per gallon (MPG) of 2009 small SUVs priced under $30,000.

24 23 22 21 22 22 18 19 19 19 21 21 21 18 19 21 17 22 18 18 22 16 16

Source: *Data extracted from "Vehicle Ratings,"* Consumer Reports, *April 2009, p. 33–34.*

a. Construct a 95% confidence interval estimate for the population mean MPG of 2009 SUVs priced under $30,000, assuming a normal distribution.

b. Interpret the interval constructed in (a).

c. Compare the results in (a) to those in Problem 8.19(a).

8.21 The stocks included in the S&P 500 are those of large publicly held companies that trade on either the New York

Stock Exchange or the NASDAQ. In 2008, the S&P 500 was down 38.5%, but what about financial compensation (salary, bonuses, stock options, etc.) to the 500 CEOs that run the companies? To learn more about the mean CEO compensation, an alphabetical list of the 500 companies was obtained and ordered from 1 (3M) to 500 (Zions Bancorp). Next, the random number table was used to select a random number from 1 to 50. The number selected was 10. Then, the companies numbered 10, 60, 110, 160, 210, 260, 310, 360, 410, and 460 were investigated and the total CEO compensation recorded. The data, stored in **CEO**, are as follows:

Number	Company	Compensation
10	Aflac	10,783,232
60	Big Lots	9,862,262
110	Comerica	4,108,245
160	EMC	13,874,262
210	Harley-Davidson	6,048,027
260	Kohl's	11,638,049
310	Molson Coors Brewing	5,558,499
360	Pfizer	6,629,955
410	Sigma-Aldrich	3,983,596
460	United Parcel Service	5,168,664

Source: *Data extracted from D. Jones and B. Hansen, "CEO Pay Dives in a Rough 2008,"* **www.usatoday.com**, *May 1, 2009.*

a. Construct a 95% confidence interval estimate for the mean 2008 compensation for CEOs of S&P 500 companies.

b. Construct a 99% confidence interval estimate for the mean 2008 compensation for CEOs of S&P 500 companies.

c. Comment on the effect that changing the level of confidence had on your answers in (a) and (b).

8.22 One of the major measures of the quality of service provided by any organization is the speed with which it responds to customer complaints. A large family-held department store selling furniture and flooring, including carpet, had undergone a major expansion in the past several years. In particular, the flooring department had expanded from 2 installation crews to an installation supervisor, a measurer, and 15 installation crews. The store had the business objective of improving its response to complaints. The variable of interest was defined as the number of days between when the complaint was made and when it was resolved. Data were collected from 50 complaints that were made in the last year. The data were stored in **Furniture**, and are as follows:

54	5	35	137	31	27	152	2	123	81	74	27
11	19	126	110	110	29	61	35	94	31	26	5
12	4	165	32	29	28	29	26	25	1	14	13
13	10	5	27	4	52	30	22	36	26	20	23
33	68										

a. Construct a 95% confidence interval estimate for the population mean number of days between the receipt of a complaint and the resolution of the complaint.

b. What assumption must you make about the population distribution in order to construct the confidence interval estimate in (a)?

c. Do you think that the assumption needed in order to construct the confidence interval estimate in (a) is valid? Explain.

d. What effect might your conclusion in (c) have on the validity of the results in (a)?

8.23 In New York State, savings banks are permitted to sell a form of life insurance called savings bank life insurance (SBLI). The approval process consists of underwriting, which includes a review of the application, a medical information bureau check, possible requests for additional medical information and medical exams, and a policy compilation stage in which the policy pages are generated and sent to the bank for delivery. The ability to deliver approved policies to customers in a timely manner is critical to the profitability of this service to the bank. During a period of one month, a random sample of 27 approved policies was selected, and the total processing time, in days, was as shown below and stored in **Insurance**:

73 19 16 64 28 28 31 90 60 56 31 56 22 18
45 48 17 17 17 91 92 63 50 51 69 16 17

a. Construct a 95% confidence interval estimate for the population mean processing time.

b. What assumption must you make about the population distribution in order to construct the confidence interval estimate in (a)?

c. Do you think that the assumption needed in order to construct the confidence interval estimate in (a) is valid? Explain.

8.24 The file **DarkChocolate** contains the cost per ounce ($) for a sample of 14 dark chocolate bars.

0.68 0.72 0.92 1.14 1.42 0.94 0.77
0.57 1.51 0.57 0.55 0.86 1.41 0.90

Source: *Data extracted from "Dark Chocolate: Which Bars Are Best?" Consumer Reports, September 2007, p. 8.*

a. Construct a 95% confidence interval estimate for the population cost per ounce ($) of dark chocolate bars.

b. What assumption do you need to make about the population distribution to construct the interval in (a)?

c. Given the data presented, do you think the assumption needed in (a) is valid? Explain.

8.25 One operation of a mill is to cut pieces of steel into parts that are used in the frame for front seats in an automobile. The steel is cut with a diamond saw, and the resulting parts must be cut to be within ±0.005 inch of the length specified by the automobile company. The measurement reported from a sample of 100 steel parts (stored in **Steel**) is the difference, in inches, between the actual length of the steel part, as measured by a laser measurement device, and the specified length of the steel part. For example, the first observation, -0.002, represents a steel part that is 0.002 inch shorter than the specified length.

a. Construct a 95% confidence interval estimate for the population mean difference between the actual length of the steel part and the specified length of the steel part.

b. What assumption must you make about the population distribution in order to construct the confidence interval estimate in (a)?

c. Do you think that the assumption needed in order to construct the confidence interval estimate in (a) is valid? Explain.

d. Compare the conclusions reached in (a) with those of Problem 2.33 on page 31.

8.3 Confidence Interval Estimation for the Proportion

The concept of a confidence interval also applies to categorical data. With categorical data, you want to estimate the proportion of items in a population having a certain characteristic of interest. The unknown population proportion is represented by the Greek letter π. The point estimate for π is the sample proportion, $p = X/n$, where n is the sample size and X is the number of items in the sample having the characteristic of interest. Equation (8.3) defines the confidence interval estimate for the population proportion.

CONFIDENCE INTERVAL ESTIMATE FOR THE PROPORTION

$$p \pm Z_{\alpha/2}\sqrt{\frac{p(1-p)}{n}}$$

or

$$p - Z_{\alpha/2}\sqrt{\frac{p(1-p)}{n}} \le \pi \le p + Z_{\alpha/2}\sqrt{\frac{p(1-p)}{n}} \tag{8.3}$$

where

$$p = \text{sample proportion} = \frac{X}{n} = \frac{\text{Number of items having the characteristic}}{\text{sample size}}$$

π = population proportion

$Z_{\alpha/2}$ = critical value from the standardized normal distribution

n = sample size

Note: To use this interval, the sample size n must be large enough to ensure that both X and $n - X$ are greater than 5.

You can use the confidence interval estimate for the proportion defined in Equation (8.3) to estimate the proportion of sales invoices that contain errors (see the Saxon Home Improvement scenario on page 251). Using the Define, Collect, Organize, Visualize, and Analyze steps, you define the variable of interest as whether the invoice contains errors (Yes or No). Then, you collect the data from a sample of 100 sales invoices. The results, which you organize and store in a worksheet, show that 10 invoices contain errors. To analyze the data, you compute, for these data, $p = X/n = 10/100 = 0.10$. Using Equation (8.3) and $Z_{\alpha/2} = 1.96$, for 95% confidence,

$$p \pm Z_{\alpha/2}\sqrt{\frac{p(1 - p)}{n}}$$

$$= 0.10 \pm (1.96)\sqrt{\frac{(0.10)(0.90)}{100}}$$

$$= 0.10 \pm (1.96)(0.03)$$

$$= 0.10 \pm 0.0588$$

$$0.0412 \leq \pi \leq 0.1588$$

Therefore, you have 95% confidence that the population proportion of all sales invoices is between 0.0412 and 0.1588. This means that between 4.12% and 15.88% of all the sales invoices contain errors. Figure 8.12 shows a worksheet solution for this example.

FIGURE 8.12

Worksheet to construct a confidence interval estimate for the proportion of sales invoices that contain errors

Figure 8.12 displays the **COMPUTE worksheet** *of the* **CIE Proportion workbook** *and reveals the formulas the worksheet uses. See Section EG8.3 to learn how to construct a confidence interval estimate and how to use the CIE Proportion workbook as a template for other problems.*

	A	B	
1	Proportion of In-Error Sales Invoices		
2			
3	**Data**		
4	Sample Size	100	
5	Number of Successes	10	
6	Confidence Level	95%	
7			
8	**Intermediate Calculations**		
9	Sample Proportion	0.1	=B5/B4
10	Z Value	-1.9600	=NORMSINV((1 - B6)/2)
11	Standard Error of the Proportion	0.03	=SQRT(B9 * (1 - B9)/B4)
12	Interval Half Width	0.0588	=ABS(B10 * B11)
13			
14	**Confidence Interval**		
15	Interval Lower Limit	0.0412	=B9 - B12
16	Interval Upper Limit	0.1588	=B9 + B12

Example 8.4 illustrates another application of a confidence interval estimate for the proportion.

EXAMPLE 8.4

Estimating the Proportion of Nonconforming Newspapers Printed

The operations manager at a large newspaper wants to estimate the proportion of newspapers printed that have a nonconforming attribute. Using the Define, Collect, Organize, Visualize, and Analyze steps, you define the variable of interest as whether the newspaper has excessive ruboff, improper page setup, missing pages, or duplicate pages. You collect the data by selecting a random sample of $n = 200$ newspapers from all the newspapers printed during a single day. You organize the results, which show that 35 newspapers contain some type of nonconformance, into a workbook. To analyze the data, you need to construct and interpret a 90% confidence interval for the proportion of newspapers printed during the day that have a nonconforming attribute.

SOLUTION Using Equation (8.3),

$$p = \frac{X}{n} = \frac{35}{200} = 0.175, \text{ and with a 90\% level of confidence } Z_{\alpha/2} = 1.645$$

$$p \pm Z_{\alpha/2}\sqrt{\frac{p(1-p)}{n}}$$

$$= 0.175 \pm (1.645)\sqrt{\frac{(0.175)(0.825)}{200}}$$

$$= 0.175 \pm (1.645)(0.0269)$$

$$= 0.175 \pm 0.0442$$

$$0.1308 \leq \pi \leq 0.2192$$

You conclude with 90% confidence that the population proportion of all newspapers printed that day with nonconformities is between 0.1308 and 0.2192. This means that between 13.08% and 21.92% of the newspapers printed on that day have some type of nonconformance.

Equation (8.3) contains a Z statistic because you can use the normal distribution to approximate the binomial distribution when the sample size is sufficiently large. In Example 8.4, the confidence interval using Z provides an excellent approximation for the population proportion because both X and $n - X$ are greater than 5. However, if you do not have a sufficiently large sample size, you should use the binomial distribution rather than Equation (8.3) (see references 1 and 2). The exact confidence intervals for various sample sizes and proportions of successes have been tabulated by Fisher and Yates (reference 2).

Problems for Section 8.3

LEARNING THE BASICS

8.26 If $n = 200$ and $X = 50$, construct a 95% confidence interval estimate for the population proportion.

8.27 If $n = 400$ and $X = 25$, construct a 99% confidence interval estimate for the population proportion.

APPLYING THE CONCEPTS

✓ SELF Test **8.28** The telephone company wants to estimate the proportion of households that would purchase an additional telephone line if it were made available at a substantially reduced installation cost. A random sample of 500 households is selected. The results indicate that 135 of the households would purchase the additional telephone line at a reduced installation cost.

a. Construct a 99% confidence interval estimate for the population proportion of households that would purchase the additional telephone line.

b. How would the manager in charge of promotional programs concerning residential customers use the results in (a)?

8.29 CareerBuilder.com surveyed 1,124 mothers who were currently employed full time. Of the women surveyed, 281 said that they were dissatisfied with their work–life balance, and 495 said that they would take a pay cut to spend more time with their kids (data extracted from D. Jones, "Poll Finds Resentment of Flextime," www.usatoday.com May 11, 2007).

a. Construct a 95% confidence interval estimate for the population proportion of mothers employed full time who are dissatisfied with their work–life balance.

b. Construct a 95% confidence interval estimate for the population proportion of mothers employed full time who would take a pay cut to spend more time with their kids.

c. Write a short summary of the information derived from (a) and (b).

8.30 Have you ever negotiated a pay raise? According to an Accenture survey, 52% of U.S. workers have (J. Yang and K. Carter, "Have You Ever Negotiated a Pay Raise?", "Snapshots," **www.usatoday.com**, May 22, 2009).

a. Suppose that the survey had a sample size of n = 500. Construct a 95% confidence interval for the proportion of all U.S. workers who have negotiated a pay raise.

b. Based on (a), can you claim that more than half of all U.S. workers have negotiated a pay raise?

c. Repeat parts (a) and (b), assuming that the survey had a sample size of n = 5,000.

d. Discuss the effect of sample size on confidence interval estimation.

8.31 In a survey of 1,000 airline travelers, 760 responded that the airline fee that is most unreasonable is additional charges to redeem points/miles (extracted from "Which Airline Fee Is Most Unreasonable?" *USA Today*, December 2, 2008, p. B1). Construct a 95% confidence interval estimate for the population proportion of airline travelers who think that the airline fee that is most unreasonable is additional charges to redeem points/miles.

8.32 In a survey of 2,395 adults, 1,916 reported that e-mails are easy to misinterpret, but only 1,269 reported that telephone conversations are easy to misinterpret (extracted from "Open to Misinterpretation," *USA Today*, July 17, 2007, p. 1D).

a. Construct a 95% confidence interval estimate for the population proportion of adults who report that e-mails are easy to misinterpret.

b. Construct a 95% confidence interval estimate for the population proportion of adults who report that telephone conversations are easy to misinterpret.

c. Compare the results of (a) and (b).

8.33 The utility of mobile devices raises new questions about the intrusion of work into personal life. In a survey by **CareerJournal.com** (data extracted from P. Kitchen, "Can't Turn It Off," *Newsday*, October 20, 2006, pp. F4–F5), 158 of 473 employees responded that they typically took work with them on vacation, and 85 responded that there are unwritten and unspoken expectations that they stay connected during vacation.

a. Construct a 95% confidence interval estimate for the population proportion of employees who typically take work with them on vacation.

b. Construct a 95% confidence interval estimate for the population proportion of employees who said that there are unwritten and unspoken expectations that they stay connected during vacation.

c. Interpret the intervals in (a) and (b).

d. Explain the difference in the results in (a) and (b).

8.4 Determining Sample Size

In each confidence interval developed so far in this chapter, the sample size was reported along with the results, with little discussion of the width of the resulting confidence interval. In the business world, sample sizes are determined prior to data collection to ensure that the confidence interval is narrow enough to be useful in making decisions. Determining the proper sample size is a complicated procedure, subject to the constraints of budget, time, and the amount of acceptable sampling error. In the Saxon Home Improvement example, if you want to estimate the mean dollar amount of the sales invoices, you must determine in advance how large a sampling error to allow in estimating the population mean. You must also determine, in advance, the level of confidence (i.e., 90%, 95%, or 99%) to use in estimating the population parameter.

Sample Size Determination for the Mean

To develop an equation for determining the appropriate sample size needed when constructing a confidence interval estimate for the mean, recall Equation (8.1) on page 255:

$$\bar{X} \pm Z_{\alpha/2}\frac{\sigma}{\sqrt{n}}$$

The amount added to or subtracted from $\bar{X}$ is equal to half the width of the interval. This quantity represents the amount of imprecision in the estimate that results from sampling error.[2] The **sampling error**, e, is defined as

$$e = Z_{\alpha/2}\frac{\sigma}{\sqrt{n}}$$

[2] In this context, some statisticians refer to e as the **margin of error**.

Solving for n gives the sample size needed to construct the appropriate confidence interval estimate for the mean. "Appropriate" means that the resulting interval will have an acceptable amount of sampling error.

SAMPLE SIZE DETERMINATION FOR THE MEAN

The sample size, n, is equal to the product of the $Z_{\sigma/2}$ value squared and the standard deviation, σ, squared, divided by the square of the sampling error, e.

$$n = \frac{Z_{\alpha/2}^2 \sigma^2}{e^2} \tag{8.4}$$

To compute the sample size, you must know three factors:

[3]You use Z instead of t because, to determine the critical value of t, you need to know the sample size, but you do not know it yet. For most studies, the sample size needed is large enough that the standardized normal distribution is a good approximation of the t distribution.

1. The desired confidence level, which determines the value of $Z_{\alpha/2}$, the critical value from the standardized normal distribution[3]
2. The acceptable sampling error, e
3. The standard deviation, σ

In some business-to-business relationships that require estimation of important parameters, legal contracts specify acceptable levels of sampling error and the confidence level required. For companies in the food and drug sectors, government regulations often specify sampling errors and confidence levels. In general, however, it is usually not easy to specify the three factors needed to determine the sample size. How can you determine the level of confidence and sampling error? Typically, these questions are answered only by a subject matter expert (i.e., an individual very familiar with the variables under study). Although 95% is the most common confidence level used, if more confidence is desired, then 99% might be more appropriate; if less confidence is deemed acceptable, then 90% might be used. For the sampling error, you should think not of how much sampling error you would like to have (you really do not want any error) but of how much you can tolerate when reaching conclusions from the confidence interval.

In addition to specifying the confidence level and the sampling error, you need an estimate of the standard deviation. Unfortunately, you rarely know the population standard deviation, σ. In some instances, you can estimate the standard deviation from past data. In other situations, you can make an educated guess by taking into account the range and distribution of the variable. For example, if you assume a normal distribution, the range is approximately equal to 6σ (i.e., $\pm 3\sigma$ around the mean) so that you estimate σ as the range divided by 6. If you cannot estimate σ in this way, you can conduct a small-scale study and estimate the standard deviation from the resulting data.

To explore how to determine the sample size needed for estimating the population mean, consider again the audit at Saxon Home Improvement. In Section 8.2, you selected a sample of 100 sales invoices and constructed a 95% confidence interval estimate for the population mean sales invoice amount. How was this sample size determined? Should you have selected a different sample size?

Suppose that, after consultation with company officials, you determine that a sampling error of no more than $\pm\$5$ is desired, along with 95% confidence. Past data indicate that the standard deviation of the sales amount is approximately \$25. Thus, $e = \$5, \sigma = \$25$, and $Z_{\alpha/2} = 1.96$ (for 95% confidence). Using Equation (8.4),

$$n = \frac{Z_{\alpha/2}^2 \sigma^2}{e^2} = \frac{(1.96)^2 (25)^2}{(5)^2}$$

$$= 96.04$$

Because the general rule is to slightly oversatisfy the criteria by rounding the sample size up to the next whole integer, you should select a sample of size 97. Thus, the sample of size $n = 100$ used on page 271 is slightly more than what is necessary to satisfy the needs of the company, based on the estimated standard deviation, desired confidence level, and sampling error. Because the calculated sample standard deviation is slightly higher than expected, $28.95 compared to $25.00, the confidence interval is slightly wider than desired. Figure 8.13 shows a worksheet solution for determining the sample size.

FIGURE 8.13

Worksheet for determining sample size for estimating the mean sales invoice amount for the Saxon Home Improvement Company

Figure 8.13 displays the **COMPUTE worksheet** *of the* **Sample Size Mean workbook** *and reveals the formulas that the worksheet uses. See Section EG8.4 to learn how to determine sample size and how to use the Sample Size Mean workbook as a template for other problems.*

	A	B
1	**For the Mean Sales Invoice Amount**	
2		
3	**Data**	
4	Population Standard Deviation	25
5	Sampling Error	5
6	Confidence Level	95%
7		
8	**Intemediate Calculations**	
9	Z Value	-1.9600 =NORMSINV((1 - B6)/2)
10	Calculated Sample Size	96.0365 =((B9 * B4)/B5)^2
11		
12	**Result**	
13	Sample Size Needed	97 =ROUNDUP(B10, 0)

Example 8.5 illustrates another application of determining the sample size needed to develop a confidence interval estimate for the mean.

EXAMPLE 8.5

Determining the Sample Size for the Mean

Returning to Example 8.3 on page 261, suppose you want to estimate, with 95% confidence, the population mean force required to break the insulator to within ±25 pounds. On the basis of a study conducted the previous year, you believe that the standard deviation is 100 pounds. Determine the sample size needed.

SOLUTION Using Equation (8.4) on page 270 and $e = 25, \sigma = 100$, and $Z_{\alpha/2} = 1.96$ for 95% confidence,

$$n = \frac{Z_{\alpha/2}^2\sigma^2}{e^2} = \frac{(1.96)^2(100)^2}{(25)^2}$$

$$= 61.47$$

Therefore, you should select a sample of 62 insulators because the general rule for determining sample size is to always round up to the next integer value in order to slightly oversatisfy the criteria desired. An actual sampling error slightly larger than 25 will result if the sample standard deviation calculated in this sample of 62 is greater than 100 and slightly smaller if the sample standard deviation is less than 100.

Sample Size Determination for the Proportion

So far in this section, you have learned how to determine the sample size needed for estimating the population mean. Now suppose that you want to determine the sample size necessary for estimating a population proportion.

To determine the sample size needed to estimate a population proportion, π, you use a method similar to the method for a population mean. Recall that in developing the sample size for a confidence interval for the mean, the sampling error is defined by

$$e = Z_{\alpha/2}\frac{\sigma}{\sqrt{n}}$$

When estimating a proportion, you replace σ with $\sqrt{\pi(1 - \pi)}$. Thus, the sampling error is

$$e = Z_{\alpha/2}\sqrt{\frac{\pi(1 - \pi)}{n}}$$

Solving for n, you have the sample size necessary to develop a confidence interval estimate for a proportion.

SAMPLE SIZE DETERMINATION FOR THE PROPORTION

The sample size n is equal to the product of $Z_{\alpha/2}$ squared, the population proportion, π, and 1 minus the population proportion, π, divided by the square of the sampling error, e.

$$n = \frac{Z_{\alpha/2}^2 \pi(1-\pi)}{e^2} \qquad (8.5)$$

To determine the sample size, you must know three factors:

1. The desired confidence level, which determines the value of $Z_{\alpha/2}$, the critical value from the standardized normal distribution
2. The acceptable sampling error (or margin of error), e
3. The population proportion, π

In practice, selecting these quantities requires some planning. Once you determine the desired level of confidence, you can find the appropriate $Z_{\alpha/2}$ value from the standardized normal distribution. The sampling error, e, indicates the amount of error that you are willing to tolerate in estimating the population proportion. The third quantity, π, is actually the population parameter that you want to estimate! Thus, how do you state a value for what you are trying to determine?

Here you have two alternatives. In many situations, you may have past information or relevant experience that provides an educated estimate of π. Or, if you do not have past information or relevant experience, you can try to provide a value for π that would never *underestimate* the sample size needed. Referring to Equation (8.5), you can see that the quantity $\pi(1-\pi)$ appears in the numerator. Thus, you need to determine the value of π that will make the quantity $\pi(1-\pi)$ as large as possible. When $\pi = 0.5$, the product $\pi(1-\pi)$ achieves its maximum value. To show this result, consider the following values of π, along with the accompanying products of $\pi(1-\pi)$:

When $\pi = 0.9$, then $\pi(1-\pi) = (0.9)(0.1) = 0.09$
When $\pi = 0.7$, then $\pi(1-\pi) = (0.7)(0.3) = 0.21$
When $\pi = 0.5$, then $\pi(1-\pi) = (0.5)(0.5) = 0.25$
When $\pi = 0.3$, then $\pi(1-\pi) = (0.3)(0.7) = 0.21$
When $\pi = 0.1$, then $\pi(1-\pi) = (0.1)(0.9) = 0.09$

Therefore, when you have no prior knowledge or estimate for the population proportion, π, you should use $\pi = 0.5$ for determining the sample size. Using $\pi = 0.5$ produces the largest possible sample size and results in the narrowest and most precise confidence interval. This increased precision comes at the cost of spending more time and money for an increased sample size. Also, note that if you use $\pi = 0.5$ and the proportion is different from 0.5, you will overestimate the sample size needed, because you will get a confidence interval narrower than originally intended.

Returning to the Saxon Home Improvement scenario on page 251, suppose that the auditing procedures require you to have 95% confidence in estimating the population proportion of sales invoices with errors to within ±0.07. The results from past months indicate that the largest proportion has been no more than 0.15. Thus, using Equation (8.5) with $e = 0.07, \pi = 0.15$, and $Z_{\alpha/2} = 1.96$ for 95% confidence,

$$n = \frac{Z_{\alpha/2}^2 \pi(1-\pi)}{e^2}$$
$$= \frac{(1.96)^2(0.15)(0.85)}{(0.07)^2}$$
$$= 99.96$$

Because the general rule is to round the sample size up to the next whole integer to slightly oversatisfy the criteria, a sample size of 100 is needed. Thus, the sample size needed to satisfy the requirements of the company, based on the estimated proportion, desired confidence level, and sampling error, is equal to the sample size taken on page 267. The actual confidence interval is narrower than required because the sample proportion is 0.10, whereas 0.15 was used for π in Equation (8.5). Figure 8.14 shows a worksheet solution for determining the sample size.

FIGURE 8.14

Worksheet for determining sample size for estimating the proportion of sales invoices with errors for the Saxon Home Improvement Company

Figure 8.14 displays the **COMPUTE worksheet** *of the* **Sample Size Proportion workbook** *and reveals the formulas the worksheet uses. See Section EG8.4 to learn how to determine sample size and how to use the Sample Size Proportion workbook as a template for other problems.*

	A	B	
1	**For the Proportion of In-Error Sales Invoices**		
2			
3	**Data**		
4	Estimate of True Proportion	0.15	
5	Sampling Error	0.07	
6	Confidence Level	95%	
7			
8	**Intermediate Calculations**		
9	Z Value	-1.9600	=NORMSINV((1 - B6)/2)
10	Calculated Sample Size	99.9563	=(B9^2 * B4 * (1 - B4))/B5^2
11			
12	**Result**		
13	Sample Size Needed	100	=ROUNDUP(B10, 0)

Example 8.6 provides another application of determining the sample size for estimating the population proportion.

EXAMPLE 8.6

Determining the Sample Size for the Population Proportion

You want to have 90% confidence of estimating the proportion of office workers who respond to e-mail within an hour to within ±0.05. Because you have not previously undertaken such a study, there is no information available from past data. Determine the sample size needed.

SOLUTION Because no information is available from past data, assume that $\pi = 0.50$. Using Equation (8.5) on page 272 and $e = 0.05$, $\pi = 0.50$, and $Z_{a/2} = 1.645$ for 90% confidence,

$$n = \frac{Z_{\alpha/2}^2 \pi(1 - \pi)}{e^2}$$

$$= \frac{(1.645)^2(0.50)(0.50)}{(0.05)^2}$$

$$= 270.6$$

Therefore, you need a sample of 271 office workers to estimate the population proportion to within ±0.05 with 90% confidence.

Problems for Section 8.4

LEARNING THE BASICS

8.34 If you want to be 95% confident of estimating the population mean to within a sampling error of ±5 and the standard deviation is assumed to be 15, what sample size is required?

8.35 If you want to be 99% confident of estimating the population mean to within a sampling error of ±20 and the standard deviation is assumed to be 100, what sample size is required?

8.36 If you want to be 99% confident of estimating the population proportion to within a sampling error of ±0.04, what sample size is needed?

8.37 If you want to be 95% confident of estimating the population proportion to within a sampling error of ±0.02 and there is historical evidence that the population proportion is approximately 0.40, what sample size is needed?

APPLYING THE CONCEPTS

√SELF **8.38** A survey is planned to determine the mean **Test** annual family medical expenses of employees of a large company. The management of the company wishes to be 95% confident that the sample mean is correct to within ±$50 of the population mean annual family medical expenses.

A previous study indicates that the standard deviation is approximately $400.

a. How large a sample is necessary?

b. If management wants to be correct to within ±$25, how many employees need to be selected?

8.39 If the manager of a paint supply store wants to estimate, with 95% confidence, the mean amount of paint in a 1-gallon can to within ±0.004 gallon and also assumes that the standard deviation is 0.02 gallon, what sample size is needed?

8.40 If a quality control manager wants to estimate, with 95% confidence, the mean life of light bulbs to within ±20 hours and also assumes that the population standard deviation is 100 hours, how many light bulbs need to be selected?

8.41 If the inspection division of a county weights and measures department wants to estimate the mean amount of soft-drink fill in 2-liter bottles to within ±0.01 liter with 95% confidence and also assumes that the standard deviation is 0.05 liter, what sample size is needed?

8.42 A consumer group wants to estimate the mean electric bill for the month of July for single-family homes in a large city. Based on studies conducted in other cities, the standard deviation is assumed to be $25. The group wants to estimate, with 99% confidence, the mean bill for July to within ±$5.

a. What sample size is needed?

b. If 95% confidence is desired, how many homes need to be selected?

8.43 An advertising agency that serves a major radio station wants to estimate the mean amount of time that the station's audience spends listening to the radio daily. From past studies, the standard deviation is estimated as 45 minutes.

a. What sample size is needed if the agency wants to be 90% confident of being correct to within ±5 minutes?

b. If 99% confidence is desired, how many listeners need to be selected?

8.44 A growing niche in the restaurant business is gourmet-casual breakfast, lunch, and brunch. Chains in this group include Le Peep, Good Egg, Eggs & I, First Watch, and Eggs Up Grill. The mean per-person check for First Watch is approximately $7, and the mean per-person check for Eggs Up Grill is $6.50 (data extracted from J. Hayes, "Competition Heats Up as Breakfast Concepts Eye Growth," *Nation's Restaurant News*, April 24, 2006, pp. 8, 66).

a. Assuming a standard deviation of $2.00, what sample size is needed to estimate, with 95% confidence, the mean per-person check for Good Egg to within ±$0.25?

b. Assuming a standard deviation of $2.50, what sample size is needed to estimate, with 95% confidence, the mean per-person check for Good Egg to within ±$0.25?

c. Assuming a standard deviation of $3.00, what sample size is needed to estimate, with 95% confidence, the mean per-person check for Good Egg to within ±$0.25?

d. Discuss the effect of variation on the sample size needed.

8.45 What proportion of Americans get most of their news from the Internet? According to a poll conducted by Pew Research Center, 40% get most of their news from the Internet (data extracted from "Drill Down," *The New York Times*, January 5, 2009, p. B3).

a. To conduct a follow-up study that would provide 95% confidence that the point estimate is correct to within ±0.04 of the population proportion, how large a sample size is required?

b. To conduct a follow-up study that would provide 99% confidence that the point estimate is correct to within ±0.04 of the population proportion, how many people need to be sampled?

c. To conduct a follow-up study that would provide 95% confidence that the point estimate is correct to within ±0.02 of the population proportion, how large a sample size is required?

d. To conduct a follow-up study that would provide 99% confidence that the point estimate is correct to within ±0.02 of the population proportion, how many people need to be sampled?

e. Discuss the effects on sample size requirements of changing the desired confidence level and the acceptable sampling error.

8.46 A survey of 1,000 adults was conducted in March 2009 concerning "green practices." In response to the question of what was the most beneficial thing to do for the environment, 28% said buying renewable energy, 19% said using greener transportation, and 7% said selecting minimal or reduced packaging (data extracted from "Environmentally Friendly Choices," *USA Today*, March 31, 2009, p. D1). Construct a 95% confidence interval estimate of the population proportion of who said that the most beneficial thing to do for the environment was

a. buy renewable energy.

b. use greener transportation.

c. select minimal or reduced packaging.

d. You have been asked to update the results of this study. Determine the sample size necessary to estimate, with 95% confidence, the population proportions in (a) through (c) to within ±0.02.

8.47 In a study of 500 executives, 315 stated that their company informally monitored social networking sites to stay on top of information related to their company (data extracted from "Checking Out the Buzz," *USA Today*, June 26, 2009, p. 1B).

a. Construct a 95% confidence interval for the proportion of companies that informally monitored social networking sites to stay on top of information related to their company.

b. Interpret the interval constructed in (a).

c. If you wanted to conduct a follow-up study to estimate the population proportion of companies that informally monitored social networking sites to stay on top of information related to their company to within ±0.01 with 95% confidence, how many executives would you survey?

8.48 In response to the question "How do you judge a company?"(data extracted from "How Do You Judge a Company?" *USA Today*, December 22, 2008, p. 1B), 84% said the most important way was how a company responded to a crisis.

a. If you conduct a follow-up study to estimate the population proportion of individuals who said that the most important way to judge a company was how the company responded to a crisis, would you use a π of 0.84 or 0.50 in the sample size formula? Discuss.

b. Using your answer to (a), find the sample size necessary to estimate, with 95% certainty, the population proportion to within ±0.03.

8.49 There are many reasons adults use credit cards. A recent survey ("Why Adults Use Credit Cards," *USA Today*, October 18, 2007, p. 1D) found that 66% of adults used credit cards for convenience.

a. To conduct a follow-up study that would provide 99% confidence that the point estimate is correct to within ±0.03 of the population proportion, how many people need to be sampled?

b. To conduct a follow-up study that would provide 99% confidence that the point estimate is correct to within ±0.05 of the population proportion, how many people need to be sampled?

c. Compare the results of (a) and (b).

8.5 Applications of Confidence Interval Estimation in Auditing

Auditing is one of the areas in business that makes widespread use of probability sampling methods in order to construct confidence interval estimates.

AUDITING

Auditing is the collection and evaluation of evidence about information related to an economic entity, such as a sole business proprietor, a partnership, a corporation, or a government agency, in order to determine and report on how well the information corresponds to established criteria.

Auditors rarely examine a complete population of information. Instead, they rely on estimation techniques based on the probability sampling methods you have studied in this text. The following list contains some of the reasons sampling is used in auditing:

- Sampling is less time-consuming.
- Sampling is less costly.
- Sampling provides an objective way of estimating the sample size in advance.
- Sampling provides results that are objective and defensible. Because the sample size is based on demonstrable statistical principles, the audit is defensible before one's superiors and in a court of law.
- Sampling provides an estimate of the sampling error and therefore allows auditors to generalize their findings to the population with a known sampling error.
- Sampling is often more accurate than other methods for drawing conclusions about large populations. Examining every item in large populations is time-consuming and therefore often subject to more nonsampling error than is statistical sampling.
- Sampling allows auditors to combine, and then evaluate collectively, samples from different individuals.

Estimating the Population Total Amount

In auditing applications, you are often more interested in developing estimates of the population **total amount** than in the population mean. Equation (8.6) shows how to estimate a population total amount.

ESTIMATING THE POPULATION TOTAL

The point estimate for the population total is equal to the population size, N, times the sample mean.

$$\text{Total} = N\bar{X} \qquad (8.6)$$

Equation (8.7) defines the confidence interval estimate for the population total.

CONFIDENCE INTERVAL ESTIMATE FOR THE TOTAL

$$N\bar{X} \pm N(t_{\alpha/2})\frac{S}{\sqrt{n}}\sqrt{\frac{N - n}{N - 1}} \qquad (8.7)$$

where $t_{\alpha/2}$ is the critical value corresponding to an upper-tail probability of $\alpha/2$ from the t distribution with $n - 1$ degrees of freedom (i.e., a cumulative area of $1 - \alpha/2$).

To demonstrate the application of the confidence interval estimate for the population total amount, return to the Saxon Home Improvement scenario on page 251. In addition to estimating the mean dollar amount in Section 8.2 on page 261, one of the auditing tasks defined in the business problem is to estimate the total dollar amount of all sales invoices for the month. If there are 5,000 invoices for that month and $\bar{X} = \$110.27$, then using Equation (8.6),

$$N\bar{X} = (5,000)(\$110.27) = \$551,350$$

Since $n = 100$ and $S = \$28.95$, then using Equation (8.7) with $t_{\alpha/2} = 1.9842$ for 95% confidence and 99 degrees of freedom,

$$N\bar{X} \pm N(t_{\alpha/2})\frac{S}{\sqrt{n}}\sqrt{\frac{N - n}{N - 1}} = 551,350 \pm (5,000)(1.9842)\frac{28.95}{\sqrt{100}}\sqrt{\frac{5,000 - 100}{5,000 - 1}}$$

$$= 551,350 \pm 28,721.295(0.99005)$$

$$= 551,350 \pm 28,435.72$$

$$\$522,914.28 \leq \text{Population total} \leq \$579,785.72$$

Therefore, with 95% confidence, you estimate that the total amount of sales invoices is between $522,914.28 and $579,785.72. Figure 8.15 shows a worksheet solution for constructing this confidence interval estimate.

FIGURE 8.15

Worksheet for the confidence interval estimate of the total amount of all invoices for the Saxon Home Improvement Company

Figure 8.15 displays the COMPUTE worksheet of the CIE Total workbook and reveals the column B formulas the worksheet uses. See Section EG8.5 to learn how to construct a confidence interval estimate and how to use the CIE Total workbook as a template for other problems.

	A	B	
1	**Total Amount of All Sales Invoices**		
2			
3	**Data**		
4	Population Size	5000	
5	Sample Mean	110.27	
6	Sample Size	100	
7	Sample Standard Deviation	28.95	
8	Confidence Level	95%	
9			
10	**Intermediate Calculations**		
11	Population Total	551350.00	=B4 * B5
12	FPC Factor	0.9900	=SQRT((B4 - B6)/(B4 - 1))
13	Standard Error of the Total	14330.9521	=(B4 * B7 * B12)/SQRT(B6)
14	Degrees of Freedom	99	=B6 - 1
15	t Value	1.9842	=TINV(1 - B8, B14)
16	Interval Half Width	28435.72	=B15 * B13
17			
18	**Confidence Interval**		
19	Interval Lower Limit	522914.28	=B11 - B16
20	Interval Upper Limit	579785.72	=B11 + B16

Example 8.7 further illustrates the population total.

EXAMPLE 8.7

Developing a Confidence Interval Estimate for the Population Total

An auditor is faced with a population of 1,000 vouchers and wants to estimate the total value of the population of vouchers. A sample of 50 vouchers is selected, with the following results:

$$\text{Mean voucher amount } (\overline{X}) = \$1,076.39$$
$$\text{Standard deviation } (S) = \$273.62$$

Construct a 95% confidence interval estimate of the total amount for the population of vouchers.

SOLUTION Using Equation (8.6) on page 275, the point estimate of the population total is

$$N\overline{X} = (1,000)(1,076.39) = \$1,076,390$$

From Equation (8.7) on page 276, a 95% confidence interval estimate of the population total amount is

$$(1,000)(1,076.39) \pm (1,000)(2.0096)\frac{273.62}{\sqrt{50}}\sqrt{\frac{1,000 - 50}{1,000 - 1}}$$

$$= 1,076,390 \pm 77,762.878\,(0.97517)$$

$$= 1,076,390 \pm 75,832$$

$$\$1,000,558 \leq \text{Population total} \leq \$1,152,222$$

Therefore, with 95% confidence, you estimate that the total amount of the vouchers is between $1,000,558 and $1,152,222.

Difference Estimation

An auditor uses **difference estimation** when he or she believes that errors exist in a set of items and he or she wants to estimate the magnitude of the errors based only on a sample. The following steps are used in difference estimation:

1. Determine the sample size required.
2. Calculate the differences between the values reached during the audit and the original values recorded. The difference in value i, denoted D_i, is equal to 0 if the auditor finds that the original value is correct, is a positive value when the audited value is larger than the original value, and is negative when the audited value is smaller than the original value.
3. Compute the mean difference in the sample, $\overline{D}$, by dividing the total difference by the sample size, as shown in Equation (8.8).

MEAN DIFFERENCE

$$\overline{D} = \frac{\sum_{i=1}^{n} D_i}{n} \tag{8.8}$$

where D_i = Audited value − Original value

4. Compute the standard deviation of the differences, S_D, as shown in Equation (8.9). *Remember that any item that is not in error has a difference value of 0.*

STANDARD DEVIATION OF THE DIFFERENCE

$$S_D = \sqrt{\frac{\sum_{i=1}^{n}(D_i - \overline{D})^2}{n - 1}} \tag{8.9}$$

5. Use Equation (8.10) to construct a confidence interval estimate of the total difference in the population.

CONFIDENCE INTERVAL ESTIMATE FOR THE TOTAL DIFFERENCE

$$N\overline{D} \pm N(t_{\alpha/2})\frac{S_D}{\sqrt{n}}\sqrt{\frac{N-n}{N-1}} \qquad (8.10)$$

where $t_{\alpha/2}$ is the critical value corresponding to an upper-tail probability of $\alpha/2$ from the t distribution with $n-1$ degrees of freedom (i.e., a cumulative area of $1-\alpha/2$).

The auditing procedures for Saxon Home Improvement require a 95% confidence interval estimate of the difference between the audited dollar amounts on the sales invoices and the amounts originally entered into the integrated inventory and sales information system. The data are collected by taking a sample of 100 sales invoices. The results of the sample are organized and stored in the PlumbInv workbook. There are 12 invoices in which the audited dollar amount on the sales invoice and the amount originally entered into the integrated inventory management and sales information system are different. These 12 differences are

$9.03 $7.47 $17.32 $8.30 $5.21 $10.80 $6.22 $5.63 $4.97 $7.43 $2.99 $4.63

The other 88 invoices are not in error. Their *differences* are each 0. Thus, to analyze the data, you compute

$$\overline{D} = \frac{\sum_{i=1}^{n} D_i}{n} = \frac{90}{100} = 0.90$$

[4]In the numerator, there are 100 differences. Each of the last 88 are equal to $(0-0.9)^2$.

and[4]

$$S_D = \sqrt{\frac{\sum_{i=1}^{n}(D_i - \overline{D})^2}{n-1}}$$

$$= \sqrt{\frac{(9.03 - 0.9)^2 + (7.47 - 0.9)^2 + \cdots + (0 - 0.9)^2}{100 - 1}}$$

$$S_D = 2.752$$

Using Equation (8.10), you construct the 95% confidence interval estimate for the total difference in the population of 5,000 sales invoices, as follows:

$$(5,000)(0.90) \pm (5,000)(1.9842)\frac{2.752}{\sqrt{100}}\sqrt{\frac{5,000 - 100}{5,000 - 1}}$$

$$= 4,500 \pm 2,702.91$$

$$\$1,797.09 \le \text{Total difference} \le \$7,202.91$$

Thus, the auditor estimates with 95% confidence that the total difference between the sales invoices, as determined during the audit, and the amount originally entered into the accounting system is between $1,797.09 and $7,202.91. Figure 8.16 shows the worksheet results for these data.

In the previous example, all 12 differences are positive because the audited amount on the sales invoice is more than the amount originally entered into the accounting system. In some circumstances, you could have negative errors. Example 8.8 illustrates such a situation.

FIGURE 8.16

Worksheet for the total difference between the invoice amounts found during audit and the amounts entered into the accounting system for the Saxon Home Improvement Company

Figure 8.16 displays the COMPUTE worksheet of the CIE Total Difference workbook and reveals the formulas the worksheet uses.

See Section EG8.5 to learn how to construct a confidence interval estimate and how to use the CIE Total Difference workbook as a template for other problems.

	A	B	
1	Total Difference In Actual and Entered		
2			
3	Data		
4	Population Size	5000	
5	Sample Size	100	
6	Confidence Level	95%	
7			
8	Intermediate Calculations		
9	Sum of Differences	90	=SUM(DIFFERENCES!A:A)
10	Average Difference in Sample	0.9	=B9/B5
11	Total Difference	4500	=B4 * B10
12	Standard Deviation of Differences	2.7518	=SQRT(E15)
13	FPC Factor	0.9900	=SQRT((B4 - B5)/(B4 - 1))
14	Standard Error of the Total Diff.	1362.2064	=(B4 * B12 * B13)/SQRT(B5)
15	Degrees of Freedom	99	=B5 - 1
16	t Value	1.9842	=TINV(1 - B6, B15)
17	Interval Half Width	2702.9129	=B16 * B14
18			
19	Confidence Interval		
20	Interval Lower Limit	1797.09	=B11 - B17
21	Interval Upper Limit	7202.91	=B11 + B17

	D	E	
1			
2			
3			
4			
5			
6			
7			
8	Additional Calculations		
9	For standard deviation of differences:		
10	Number of Differences Not =0	12	=COUNT(DIFFERENCES!A:A)
11	Number of Differences =0	88	=B5 - E10
12	SS for Differences Not =0	678.3864	=SUM(DIFFERENCES!B:B)
13	SS for Differences =0	71.28	=E11 * (-B10)^2
14	Sum of Squares	749.6664	=E12 + E13
15	Variance of Differences	7.5724	=E14/B15

EXAMPLE 8.8

Difference Estimation

Returning to Example 8.7 on page 277, suppose that 14 vouchers in the sample of 50 vouchers contain errors. The values of the 14 errors are listed below and stored in `DiffTest`. Observe that two differences are negative:

$75.41	$38.97	$108.54	−$37.18	$62.75	$118.32	−$88.84
$127.74	$55.42	$39.03	$29.41	$47.99	$28.73	$84.05

Construct a 95% confidence interval estimate for the total difference in the population of 1,000 vouchers.

SOLUTION For these data,

$$\overline{D} = \frac{\sum_{i=1}^{n} D_i}{n} = \frac{690.34}{50} = 13.8068$$

and

$$S_D = \sqrt{\frac{\sum_{i=1}^{n} (D_i - \overline{D})^2}{n - 1}}$$

$$= \sqrt{\frac{(75.41 - 13.8068)^2 + (38.97 - 13.8068)^2 + \cdots + (0 - 13.8068)^2}{50 - 1}}$$

$$= 37.427$$

Using Equation (8.10) on page 278, construct the confidence interval estimate for the total difference in the population, as follows:

$$(1,000)(13.8068) \pm (1,000)(2.0096)\frac{37.427}{\sqrt{50}}\sqrt{\frac{1,000 - 50}{1,000 - 1}}$$

$$= 13,806.8 \pm 10,372.4$$

$$\$3,434.40 \le \text{Total difference} \le \$24,179.20$$

Therefore, with 95% confidence, you estimate that the total difference in the population of vouchers is between $3,434.40 and $24,179.20.

One-Sided Confidence Interval Estimation of the Rate of Noncompliance with Internal Controls

Organizations use internal control mechanisms to ensure that individuals act in accordance with company guidelines. For example, Saxon Home Improvement requires that an authorized warehouse-removal slip be completed before goods are removed from the warehouse. During the monthly audit of the company, the auditing team is charged with the task of estimating the proportion of times goods were removed without proper authorization. This is referred to as the *rate of noncompliance with the internal control*. To estimate the rate of noncompliance, auditors take a random sample of sales invoices and determine how often merchandise was shipped without an authorized warehouse-removal slip. The auditors then compare their results with a previously established tolerable exception rate, which is the maximum allowable proportion of items in the population not in compliance. When estimating the rate of noncompliance, it is commonplace to use a **one-sided confidence interval**. That is, the auditors estimate an upper bound on the rate of noncompliance. Equation (8.11) defines a one-sided confidence interval for a proportion.

ONE-SIDED CONFIDENCE INTERVAL FOR A PROPORTION

$$\text{Upper bound} = p + Z_\alpha\sqrt{\frac{p(1 - p)}{n}}\sqrt{\frac{N - n}{N - 1}} \qquad \textbf{(8.11)}$$

where Z_a = the value corresponding to a cumulative area of $(1 - \alpha)$ from the standardized normal distribution (i.e., a right-hand-tail probability of α).

If the tolerable exception rate is higher than the upper bound, the auditor concludes that the company is in compliance with the internal control. If the upper bound is higher than the tolerable exception rate, the auditor has failed to prove that the company is in compliance. The auditor may then request a larger sample.

Suppose that in the monthly audit, you select 400 sales invoices from a population of 10,000 invoices. In the sample of 400 sales invoices, 20 are in violation of the internal control. If the tolerable exception rate for this internal control is 6%, what should you conclude? Use a 95% level of confidence.

The one-sided confidence interval is computed using $p = 20/400 = 0.05$ and $Z_\alpha = 1.645$. Using Equation (8.11),

$$\text{Upper bound} = p + Z_\alpha\sqrt{\frac{p(1 - p)}{n}}\sqrt{\frac{N - n}{N - 1}} = 0.05 + 1.645\sqrt{\frac{0.05(1 - 0.05)}{400}}\sqrt{\frac{10,000 - 400}{10,000 - 1}}$$

$$= 0.05 + 1.645(0.0109)(0.98) = 0.05 + 0.0176 = 0.0676$$

Thus, you have 95% confidence that the rate of noncompliance is less than 6.76%. Because the tolerable exception rate is 6%, the rate of noncompliance may be too high for this internal control. In other words, it is possible that the noncompliance rate for the population is higher than the rate deemed tolerable. Therefore, you should request a larger sample.

In many cases, the auditor is able to conclude that the rate of noncompliance with the company's internal controls is acceptable. Example 8.9 illustrates such an occurrence.

EXAMPLE 8.9

Estimating the Rate of Noncompliance

A large electronics firm writes 1 million checks a year. An internal control policy for the company is that the authorization to sign each check is granted only after an invoice has been initialed by an accounts payable supervisor. The company's tolerable exception rate for this control is 4%. If control deviations are found in 8 of the 400 invoices sampled, what should the auditor do? To solve this, use a 95% level of confidence.

SOLUTION The auditor constructs a 95% one-sided confidence interval for the proportion of invoices in noncompliance and compares this to the tolerable exception rate. Using Equation (8.11) on page 280, $p = 8/400 = 0.02$, and $Z_\alpha = 1.645$ for 95% confidence,

$$\text{Upper bound} = p + Z_\alpha \sqrt{\frac{p(1-p)}{n}} \sqrt{\frac{N-n}{N-1}} = 0.02 + 1.645 \sqrt{\frac{0.02(1-0.02)}{400}} \sqrt{\frac{1,000,000-400}{1,000,000-1}}$$
$$= 0.02 + 1.645(0.007)(0.9998) = 0.02 + 0.0115 = 0.0315$$

The auditor concludes with 95% confidence that the rate of noncompliance is less than 3.15%. Because this is less than the tolerable exception rate, the auditor concludes that the internal control compliance is adequate. In other words, the auditor is more than 95% confident that the rate of noncompliance is less than 4%.

Problems for Section 8.5

LEARNING THE BASICS

8.50 A sample of 25 is selected from a population of 500 items. The sample mean is 25.7, and the sample standard deviation is 7.8. Construct a 99% confidence interval estimate for the population total.

8.51 Suppose that a sample of 200 (stored in ItemErr) is selected from a population of 10,000 items. Of these, 10 items are found to have errors of the following amounts:

13.76	42.87	34.65	11.09	14.54
22.87	25.52	9.81	10.03	15.49

Construct a 95% confidence interval estimate for the total difference in the population.

8.52 If $p = 0.04, n = 300$, and $N = 5,000$, calculate the upper bound for a one-sided confidence interval estimate for the population proportion, π, using the following levels of confidence:
a. 90%
b. 95%
c. 99%

APPLYING THE CONCEPTS

8.53 A stationery store wants to estimate the total retail value of the 1,000 greeting cards it has in its inventory. Construct a 95% confidence interval estimate for the population total value of all greeting cards that are in inventory if a random sample of 100 greeting cards indicates a mean value of $2.55 and a standard deviation of $0.44.

SELF Test **8.54** The personnel department of a large corporation employing 3,000 workers wants to estimate the family dental expenses of its employees to determine the feasibility of providing a dental insurance plan. A random sample of 10 employees (stored in the file Dental) reveals the following family dental expenses (in dollars) for the preceding year:

110	362	246	85	510	208	173	425	316	179

Construct a 90% confidence interval estimate for the total family dental expenses for all employees in the preceding year.

8.55 A branch of a chain of large electronics stores is conducting an end-of-month inventory of the merchandise in stock. There were 1,546 items in inventory at that time. A sample of 50 items was randomly selected, and an audit was conducted, with the following results:

Value of Merchandise
$$\bar{X} = \$252.28 \qquad S = \$93.67$$

Construct a 95% confidence interval estimate for the total value of the merchandise in inventory at the end of the month.

8.56 A customer in the wholesale garment trade is often entitled to a discount for a cash payment for goods. The amount of discount varies by vendor. A sample of 150 items selected from a population of 4,000 invoices at the end of a period of time (stored in Discount) revealed that in 13 cases, the customer failed to take the discount to which he or she was entitled. The amounts (in dollars) of the 13 discounts that were not taken were as follows:

6.45	15.32	97.36	230.63	104.18	84.92	132.76
66.12	26.55	129.43	88.32	47.81	89.01	

Construct a 99% confidence interval estimate for the population total amount of discounts not taken.

8.57 Econe Dresses is a small company that manufactures women's dresses for sale to specialty stores. It has 1,200 inventory items, and the historical cost is recorded on a first-in, first-out (FIFO) basis. In the past, approximately 15% of the inventory items were incorrectly priced. However, any misstatements were usually not significant. A sample of 120 items was selected (see the **Fifo** file), and the historical cost of each item was compared with the audited value. The results indicated that 15 items differed in their historical costs and audited values. These values were as follows:

Sample Number	Historical Cost ($)	Audited Value ($)	Sample Number	Historical Cost ($)	Audited Value ($)
5	261	240	60	21	210
9	87	105	73	140	152
17	201	276	86	129	112
18	121	110	95	340	216
28	315	298	96	341	402
35	411	356	107	135	97
43	249	211	119	228	220
51	216	305			

Construct a 95% confidence interval estimate for the total population difference in the historical cost and audited value.

8.58 Tom and Brent's Alpine Outfitters conducts an annual audit of its financial records. An internal control policy for the company is that a check can be issued only after the accounts payable manager initials the invoice. The tolerable exception rate for this internal control is 0.04. During an audit, a sample of 300 invoices is examined from a population of 10,000 invoices, and 11 invoices are found to violate the internal control.

a. Calculate the upper bound for a 95% one-sided confidence interval estimate for the rate of noncompliance.

b. Based on (a), what should the auditor conclude?

8.59 An internal control policy for Rhonda's Online Fashion Accessories requires a quality assurance check before a shipment is made. The tolerable exception rate for this internal control is 0.05. During an audit, 500 shipping records were sampled from a population of 5,000 shipping records, and 12 were found that violated the internal control.

a. Calculate the upper bound for a 95% one-sided confidence interval estimate for the rate of noncompliance.

b. Based on (a), what should the auditor conclude?

8.6 Confidence Interval Estimation and Ethical Issues

Ethical issues related to the selection of samples and the inferences that accompany them can occur in several ways. The major ethical issue relates to whether confidence interval estimates are provided along with the point estimates. Providing a point estimate without also including the confidence interval limits (typically set at 95%), the sample size used, and an interpretation of the meaning of the confidence interval in terms that a person untrained in statistics can understand raises ethical issues. Failure to include a confidence interval estimate might mislead the user of the results into thinking that the point estimate is all that is needed to predict the population characteristic with certainty.

When media outlets publicize the results of a political poll, they often overlook including this information. Sometimes, the results of a poll include the sampling error, but the sampling error is often presented in fine print or as an afterthought to the story being reported. A fully ethical presentation of poll results would give equal prominence to the confidence levels, sample size, sampling error, and confidence limits of the poll.

When you prepare your own point estimates, always state the interval estimate in a prominent place and include a brief explanation of the meaning of the confidence interval. In addition, make sure you highlight the sample size and sampling error.

8.7 🌐 *Online Topic*: Estimation and Sample Size Determination for Finite Populations

In this section, confidence intervals are developed and the sample size is determined for situations in which sampling is done without replacement from a finite population. To study this topic, read the **Section 8.7** online topic file that is available on this book's companion Web site. (See Appendix Section D.8 to learn how to access the online topic files.)

@ Saxon Home Improvement Revisited

I n the Saxon Home Improvement scenario, you were an accountant for a distributor of home improvement supplies in the northeastern United States. You were responsible for the accuracy of the integrated inventory management and sales information system. You used confidence interval estimation techniques to draw conclusions about the population of all records from a relatively small sample collected during an audit.

At the end of the month, you collected a random sample of 100 sales invoices and made the following inferences:

- With 95% confidence, you concluded that the mean amount of all the sales invoices is between $104.53 and $116.01.
- With 95% confidence, you concluded that between 4.12% and 15.88% of all the sales invoices contain errors.
- With 95% confidence, you concluded that the total amount of all the sales invoices is between $522,914 and $579,786.
- With 95% confidence, you concluded that the total difference between the actual and audited amounts of sales invoices was between $1,797.09 and $7,202.91.

These estimates provide an interval of values that you believe contain the true population parameters. If these intervals are too wide (i.e., the sampling error is too large) for the types of decisions Saxon Home Improvement needs to make, you will need to take a larger sample. You can use the sample size formulas in Section 8.4 to determine the number of sales invoices to sample to ensure that the size of the sampling error is acceptable.

SUMMARY

This chapter discusses confidence intervals for estimating the characteristics of a population, along with how you can determine the necessary sample size. You learned how to apply these methods to numerical and categorical data. Table 8.3 provides a list of topics covered in this chapter.

To determine what equation to use for a particular situation, you need to answer two questions:

- Are you constructing a confidence interval, or are you determining sample size?
- Do you have a numerical variable, or do you have a categorical variable?

The next four chapters develop a hypothesis-testing approach to making decisions about population parameters.

TABLE 8.3

Summary of Topics in Chapter 8

Type of Analysis	Type of Data	
	Numerical	**Categorical**
Confidence interval for a population parameter	Confidence interval estimate for the mean (Sections 8.1 and 8.2) Confidence interval estimate for the total and mean difference (Section 8.5)	Confidence interval estimate for the proportion (Section 8.3) One-sided confidence interval estimate for the proportion (Section 8.5)
Determining sample size	Sample size determination for the mean (Section 8.4)	Sample size determination for the proportion (Section 8.4)

KEY EQUATIONS

Confidence Interval for the Mean (σ Known)

$$\bar{X} \pm Z_{\alpha/2}\frac{\sigma}{\sqrt{n}}$$

or

$$\bar{X} - Z_{\alpha/2}\frac{\sigma}{\sqrt{n}} \leq \mu \leq \bar{X} + Z_{\alpha/2}\frac{\sigma}{\sqrt{n}} \qquad (8.1)$$

Confidence Interval for the Mean (σ Unknown)

$$\bar{X} \pm t_{\alpha/2}\frac{S}{\sqrt{n}}$$

or

$$\bar{X} - t_{\alpha/2}\frac{S}{\sqrt{n}} \leq \mu \leq \bar{X} + t_{\alpha/2}\frac{S}{\sqrt{n}} \qquad (8.2)$$

Confidence Interval Estimate for the Proportion

$$p \pm Z_{\alpha/2}\sqrt{\frac{p(1-p)}{n}}$$

or

$$p - Z_{\alpha/2}\sqrt{\frac{p(1-p)}{n}} \leq \pi \leq p + Z_{\alpha/2}\sqrt{\frac{p(1-p)}{n}} \qquad (8.3)$$

Sample Size Determination for the Mean

$$n = \frac{Z_{\alpha/2}^2\sigma^2}{e^2} \qquad (8.4)$$

Sample Size Determination for the Proportion

$$n = \frac{Z_{\alpha/2}^2\pi(1-\pi)}{e^2} \qquad (8.5)$$

Estimating the Population Total

$$\text{Total} = N\bar{X} \qquad (8.6)$$

Confidence Interval Estimate for the Total

$$N\bar{X} \pm N(t_{\alpha/2})\frac{S}{\sqrt{n}}\sqrt{\frac{N-n}{N-1}} \qquad (8.7)$$

Mean Difference

$$\bar{D} = \frac{\sum\limits_{i=1}^{n}D_i}{n} \qquad (8.8)$$

Standard Deviation of the Difference

$$S_D = \sqrt{\frac{\sum\limits_{i=1}^{n}(D_i - \bar{D})^2}{n-1}} \qquad (8.9)$$

Confidence Interval Estimate for the Total Difference

$$N\bar{D} \pm N(t_{\alpha/2})\frac{S_D}{\sqrt{n}}\sqrt{\frac{N-n}{N-1}} \qquad (8.10)$$

One-Sided Confidence Interval for a Proportion

$$\text{Upper bound} = p + Z_{\alpha}\sqrt{\frac{p(1-p)}{n}}\sqrt{\frac{N-n}{N-1}} \qquad (8.11)$$

KEY TERMS

auditing   275
confidence interval estimate   252
critical value   256
degrees of freedom   258

difference estimation   277
level of confidence   255
margin of error   269
one-sided confidence interval   280

point estimate   252
sampling error   269
Student's t distribution   258
total amount   275

CHAPTER REVIEW PROBLEMS

CHECKING YOUR UNDERSTANDING

8.60 Why can you never really have 100% confidence of correctly estimating the population characteristic of interest?

8.61 When are you able to use the *t* distribution to develop the confidence interval estimate for the mean?

8.62 Why is it true that for a given sample size, *n*, an increase in confidence is achieved by widening (and making less precise) the confidence interval?

8.63 Under what circumstances do you use a one-sided confidence interval instead of a two-sided confidence interval?

8.64 When would you want to estimate the population total instead of the population mean?

8.65 How does difference estimation differ from estimation of the mean?

APPLYING THE CONCEPTS

8.66 You work in the corporate office for a nationwide convenience store franchise that operates nearly 10,000 stores. The per-store daily customer count has been steady, at 900, for some time (i.e., the mean number of customers in a store in one day is 900). To increase the customer count, the franchise is considering cutting coffee prices by approximately half. The 12-ounce size will now be $0.59 instead of $0.99, and the 16-ounce size will be $0.69 instead of $1.19. Even with this reduction in price, the franchise will have a 40% gross margin on coffee. To test the new initiative, the franchise has reduced coffee prices in a sample of 34 stores, where customer counts have been running almost exactly at the national average of 900. After four weeks, the sample stores stabilize at a mean customer count of 974 and a standard deviation of 96. This increase seems like a substantial amount to you, but it also seems like a pretty small sample. Is there some way to get a feel for what the mean per-store count in all the stores will be if you cut coffee prices nationwide? Do you think reducing coffee prices is a good strategy for increasing the mean customer count?

8.67 What do Americans do to conserve energy? A survey of 500 adults (data extracted from "Going on an Energy Diet," *USA Today*, April 16, 2009, p. 1A) found the following percentages:

Turn off lights, power strips, unplug things: 73%
Recycle aluminum, plastic, newspapers, cardboard: 47%
Recycle harder-to-recycle products: 36%
Buy products with least packaging: 34%
Ride a bike or walk: 23%

a. Construct 95% confidence interval estimates for the population proportion of what adults do to conserve energy.

b. What conclusions can you reach concerning what adults do to conserve energy?

8.68 A market researcher for a consumer electronics company wants to study the television viewing habits of residents of a particular area. A random sample of 40 respondents is selected, and each respondent is instructed to keep a detailed record of all television viewing in a particular week. The results are as follows:
- Viewing time per week: $\bar{X} = 15.3$ hours, $S = 3.8$ hours.
- 27 respondents watch the evening news on at least three weeknights.

a. Construct a 95% confidence interval estimate for the mean amount of television watched per week in this area.

b. Construct a 95% confidence interval estimate for the population proportion who watch the evening news on at least 3 weeknights per week.

Suppose that the market researcher wants to take another survey in a different location. Answer these questions:

c. What sample size is required to be 95% confident of estimating the population mean to within ±2 hours and assumes that the population standard deviation is equal to 5 hours?

d. How many respondents need to be selected to be 95% confident of being within ±0.035 of the population proportion who watch the evening news on at least three weeknights if no previous estimate is available?

e. Based on (c) and (d), how many respondents should the market researcher select if a single survey is being conducted?

8.69 The real estate assessor for a county government wants to study various characteristics of single-family houses in the county. A random sample of 70 houses reveals the following:
- Heated area of the houses (in square feet): $\bar{X} = 1{,}759$, $S = 380$.
- 42 houses have central air-conditioning.

a. Construct a 99% confidence interval estimate for the population mean heated area of the houses.

b. Construct a 95% confidence interval estimate for the population proportion of houses that have central air-conditioning.

8.70 The personnel director of a large corporation wishes to study absenteeism among clerical workers at the corporation's central office during the year. A random sample of 25 clerical workers reveals the following:
- Absenteeism: $\bar{X} = 9.7$ days, $S = 4.0$ days.
- 12 clerical workers were absent more than 10 days.

a. Construct a 95% confidence interval estimate for the mean number of absences for clerical workers during the year.

b. Construct a 95% confidence interval estimate for the population proportion of clerical workers absent more than 10 days during the year.

Suppose that the personnel director also wishes to take a survey in a branch office. Answer these questions:

c. What sample size is needed to have 95% confidence in estimating the population mean absenteeism to within ±1.5 days if the population standard deviation is estimated to be 4.5 days?

d. How many clerical workers need to be selected to have 90% confidence in estimating the population proportion to within ±0.075 if no previous estimate is available?

e. Based on (c) and (d), what sample size is needed if a single survey is being conducted?

8.71 The market research director for Dotty's Department Store wants to study women's spending on cosmetics. A survey of the store's customers is designed in order to estimate the proportion of women who purchase their cosmetics primarily from Dotty's Department Store and the mean yearly amount that women spend on cosmetics. A previous survey found that the standard deviation of the amount women spend on cosmetics in a year is approximately $18.

a. What sample size is needed to have 99% confidence of estimating the population mean to within ±$5?

b. How many of the store's credit card holders need to be selected to have 90% confidence of estimating the population proportion to within ±0.045?

8.72 The branch manager of a nationwide bookstore chain (located near a college campus) wants to study characteristics of her store's customers. She decides to focus on two variables: the amount of money spent by customers and whether the customers would consider purchasing educational DVDs related to graduate preparation exams, such as the GMAT, GRE, or LSAT. The results from a sample of 70 customers are as follows:

- Amount spent: $\overline{X} = \$28.52, S = \$11.39$.
- 28 customers stated that they would consider purchasing the educational DVDs.

a. Construct a 95% confidence interval estimate for the population mean amount spent in the bookstore.

b. Construct a 90% confidence interval estimate for the population proportion of customers who would consider purchasing educational DVDs.

Assume that the branch manager of another store in the chain (also located close to a college campus) wants to conduct a similar survey in his store. Answer the following questions:

c. What sample size is needed to have 95% confidence of estimating the population mean amount spent in this store to within ±$2 if the standard deviation is assumed to be $10?

d. How many customers need to be selected to have 90% confidence of estimating the population proportion who would consider purchasing the educational DVDs to within ±0.04?

e. Based on your answers to (c) and (d), how large a sample should the manager take?

8.73 The branch manager of an outlet (Store 1) of a nationwide chain of pet supply stores wants to study characteristics of her customers. In particular, she decides to focus on two variables: the amount of money spent by customers and whether the customers own only one dog, only one cat, or more than one dog and/or cat. The results from a sample of 70 customers are as follows:

- Amount of money spent: $\overline{X} = \$21.34, S = \$9.22$.
- 37 customers own only a dog.
- 26 customers own only a cat.
- 7 customers own more than one dog and/or cat.

a. Construct a 95% confidence interval estimate for the population mean amount spent in the pet supply store.

b. Construct a 90% confidence interval estimate for the population proportion of customers who own only a cat.

The branch manager of another outlet (Store 2) wishes to conduct a similar survey in his store. The manager does not have access to the information generated by the manager of Store 1. Answer the following questions:

c. What sample size is needed to have 95% confidence of estimating the population mean amount spent in this store to within ±$1.50 if the standard deviation is estimated to be $10?

d. How many customers need to be selected to have 90% confidence of estimating the population proportion of customers who own only a cat to within ±0.045?

e. Based on your answers to (c) and (d), how large a sample should the manager take?

8.74 Scarlett and Heather, the owners of an upscale restaurant in Dayton, Ohio, want to study the dining characteristics of their customers. They decide to focus on two variables: the amount of money spent by customers and whether customers order dessert. The results from a sample of 60 customers are as follows:

- Amount spent: $\overline{X} = \$38.54, S = \$7.26$.
- 18 customers purchased dessert.

a. Construct a 95% confidence interval estimate for the population mean amount spent per customer in the restaurant.

b. Construct a 90% confidence interval estimate for the population proportion of customers who purchase dessert.

Jeanine, the owner of a competing restaurant, wants to conduct a similar survey in her restaurant. Jeanine does not have access to the information that Scarlett and Heather have obtained from the survey they conducted. Answer the following questions:

c. What sample size is needed to have 95% confidence of estimating the population mean amount spent in her restaurant to within ±$1.50, assuming that the standard deviation is estimated to be $8?

d. How many customers need to be selected to have 90% confidence of estimating the population proportion of customers who purchase dessert to within ±0.04?

e. Based on your answers to (c) and (d), how large a sample should Jeanine take?

8.75 The manufacturer of "Ice Melt" claims its product will melt snow and ice at temperatures as low as 0° Fahrenheit.

A representative for a large chain of hardware stores is interested in testing this claim. The chain purchases a large shipment of 5-pound bags for distribution. The representative wants to know, with 95% confidence and within ±0.05, what proportion of bags of Ice Melt perform the job as claimed by the manufacturer.

a. How many bags does the representative need to test? What assumption should be made concerning the population proportion? (This is called *destructive testing*; i.e., the product being tested is destroyed by the test and is then unavailable to be sold.)

b. Suppose that the representative tests 50 bags, and 42 of them do the job as claimed. Construct a 95% confidence interval estimate for the population proportion that will do the job as claimed.

c. How can the representative use the results of (b) to determine whether to sell the Ice Melt product?

8.76 An auditor needs to estimate the percentage of times a company fails to follow an internal control procedure. A sample of 50 from a population of 1,000 items is selected, and in 7 instances, the internal control procedure was not followed.

a. Construct a 90% one-sided confidence interval estimate for the population proportion of items in which the internal control procedure was not followed.

b. If the tolerable exception rate is 0.15, what should the auditor conclude?

8.77 An auditor for a government agency needs to evaluate payments for doctors' office visits paid by Medicare in a particular zip code during the month of June. A total of 25,056 visits occurred during June in this area. The auditor wants to estimate the total amount paid by Medicare to within ±$5 with 95% confidence. On the basis of past experience, she believes that the standard deviation is approximately $30.

a. What sample size should she select?

Using the sample size selected in (a), an audit is conducted, with the following results.

Amount of Reimbursement
$\bar{X} = \$93.70 \qquad S = \$34.55$

In 12 of the office visits, an incorrect amount of reimbursement was provided. For the 12 office visits in which there was an incorrect reimbursement, the differences between the amount reimbursed and the amount that the auditor determined should have been reimbursed were as follows (and stored in Medicare):

$17 $25 $14 −$10 $20 $40 $35 $30 $28 $22 $15 $5

b. Construct a 90% confidence interval estimate for the population proportion of reimbursements that contain errors.

c. Construct a 95% confidence interval estimate for the population mean reimbursement per office visit.

d. Construct a 95% confidence interval estimate for the population total amount of reimbursements for this geographic area in June.

e. Construct a 95% confidence interval estimate for the total difference between the amount reimbursed and the amount that the auditor determined should have been reimbursed.

8.78 A home furnishings store that sells bedroom furniture is conducting an end-of-month inventory of the beds (mattress, bed spring, and frame) in stock. An auditor for the store wants to estimate the mean value of the beds in stock at that time. She wants to have 99% confidence that her estimate of the mean value is correct to within ±$100. On the basis of past experience, she estimates that the standard deviation of the value of a bed is $200.

a. How many beds should she select?

b. Using the sample size selected in (a), an audit was conducted, with the following results:

$$\bar{X} = \$1,654.27 \qquad S = \$184.62$$

Construct a 99% confidence interval estimate for the total value of the beds in stock at the end of the month if there were 258 beds in stock.

8.79 A quality characteristic of interest for a tea-bag-filling process is the weight of the tea in the individual bags. In this example, the label weight on the package indicates that the mean amount is 5.5 grams of tea in a bag. If the bags are underfilled, two problems arise. First, customers may not be able to brew the tea to be as strong as they wish. Second, the company may be in violation of the truth-in-labeling laws. On the other hand, if the mean amount of tea in a bag exceeds the label weight, the company is giving away product. Getting an exact amount of tea in a bag is problematic because of variation in the temperature and humidity inside the factory, differences in the density of the tea, and the extremely fast filling operation of the machine (approximately 170 bags per minute). The following data (stored in Teabags) are the weights, in grams, of a sample of 50 tea bags produced in one hour by a single machine:

5.65 5.44 5.42 5.40 5.53 5.34 5.54 5.45 5.52 5.41
5.57 5.40 5.53 5.54 5.55 5.62 5.56 5.46 5.44 5.51
5.47 5.40 5.47 5.61 5.53 5.32 5.67 5.29 5.49 5.55
5.77 5.57 5.42 5.58 5.58 5.50 5.32 5.50 5.53 5.58
5.61 5.45 5.44 5.25 5.56 5.63 5.50 5.57 5.67 5.36

a. Construct a 99% confidence interval estimate for the population mean weight of the tea bags.

b. Is the company meeting the requirement set forth on the label that the mean amount of tea in a bag is 5.5 grams?

c. Do you think the assumption needed to construct the confidence interval estimate in (a) is valid?

8.80 A manufacturing company produces steel housings for electrical equipment. The main component part of the housing is a steel trough that is made from a 14-gauge steel coil. It is produced using a 250-ton progressive punch press with a wipe-down operation that puts two 90-degree forms in the flat steel to make the trough. The distance from one side of the form to the other is critical because of weatherproofing in outdoor applications. The widths (in inches), shown below and stored in Trough, are from a sample of 49 troughs:

```
8.312  8.343  8.317  8.383  8.348  8.410  8.351  8.373  8.481  8.422
8.476  8.382  8.484  8.403  8.414  8.419  8.385  8.465  8.498  8.447
8.436  8.413  8.489  8.414  8.481  8.415  8.479  8.429  8.458  8.462
8.460  8.444  8.429  8.460  8.412  8.420  8.410  8.405  8.323  8.420
8.396  8.447  8.405  8.439  8.411  8.427  8.420  8.498  8.409
```

a. Construct a 95% confidence interval estimate for the mean width of the troughs.
b. Interpret the interval developed in (a).
c. Do you think the assumption needed to construct the confidence interval estimate in (a) in valid?

8.81 The manufacturer of Boston and Vermont asphalt shingles knows that product weight is a major factor in a customer's perception of quality. The last stage of the assembly line packages the shingles before they are placed on wooden pallets. Once a pallet is full (a pallet for most brands holds 16 squares of shingles), it is weighed, and the measurement is recorded. The file Pallet contains the weight (in pounds) from a sample of 368 pallets of Boston shingles and 330 pallets of Vermont shingles.
a. For the Boston shingles, construct a 95% confidence interval estimate for the mean weight.
b. For the Vermont shingles, construct a 95% confidence interval estimate for the mean weight.
c. Do you think the assumption needed to construct the confidence interval estimates in (a) and (b) is valid?
d. Based on the results of (a) and (b), what conclusions can you reach concerning the mean weight of the Boston and Vermont shingles?

8.82 The manufacturer of Boston and Vermont asphalt shingles provides its customers with a 20-year warranty on most of its products. To determine whether a shingle will last as long as the warranty period, accelerated-life testing is conducted at the manufacturing plant. Accelerated-life testing exposes the shingle to the stresses it would be subject to in a lifetime of normal use via a laboratory experiment that takes only a few minutes to conduct. In this test, a shingle is repeatedly scraped with a brush for a short period of time, and the shingle granules removed by the brushing are weighed (in grams). Shingles that experience low amounts of granule loss are expected to last longer in normal use than shingles that experience high amounts of granule loss. In this situation, a shingle should experience no more than 0.8 grams of granule loss if it is expected to last the length of the warranty period. The file Granule contains a sample of 170 measurements made on the company's Boston shingles and 140 measurements made on Vermont shingles.

a. For the Boston shingles, construct a 95% confidence interval estimate for the mean granule loss.
b. For the Vermont shingles, construct a 95% confidence interval estimate for the mean granule loss.
c. Do you think the assumption needed to construct the confidence interval estimates in (a) and (b) is valid?
d. Based on the results of (a) and (b), what conclusions can you reach concerning the mean granule loss of the Boston and Vermont shingles?

REPORT WRITING EXERCISES

8.83 Referring to the results in Problem 8.80 concerning the width of a steel trough, write a report that summarizes your conclusions.

TEAM PROJECT

8.84 Refer to the team project on page 64 that uses the data in Bond Funds. Construct all appropriate confidence interval estimates of the population characteristics of below-average-risk, average-risk, and above-average-risk mutual funds. Include these estimates in a report to the vice president for research at the financial investment service.

STUDENT SURVEY DATABASE

8.85 Problem 2.117 on page 65 describes a survey of 50 undergraduate students (stored in UndergradSurvey).
a. For these data, for each variable, construct a 95% confidence interval estimate for the population characteristic.
b. Write a report that summarizes your conclusions.

8.86 Problem 2.117 on page 65 describes a survey of 50 undergraduate students (stored in UndergradSurvey).
a. Select a sample of 50 undergraduate students at your school and conduct a similar survey for those students.
b. For the data collected in (a), repeat (a) and (b) of Problem 8.85.
c. Compare the results of (b) to those of Problem 8.85.

8.87 Problem 2.119 on page 65 describes a survey of 40 MBA students (stored in GradSurvey).
a. For these data, for each variable, construct a 95% confidence interval estimate for the population characteristic.
b. Write a report that summarizes your conclusions.

8.88 Problem 2.119 on page 65 describes a survey of 40 MBA students (stored in GradSurvey).
a. Select a sample of 40 graduate students in your MBA program and conduct a similar survey for those students.
b. For the data collected in (a), repeat (a) and (b) of Problem 8.87.
c. Compare the results of (b) to those of Problem 8.87.

MANAGING THE *SPRINGVILLE HERALD*

The marketing department has been considering ways to increase the number of new subscriptions and increase the rate of retention among customers who agreed to a trial subscription. Following the suggestion of Assistant Manager Lauren Adler, the department staff designed a survey to help determine various characteristics of readers of the newspaper who were not home-delivery subscribers. The survey consists of the following 10 questions:

1. Do you or a member of your household ever purchase the *Springville Herald*?
   (1) Yes   (2) No
   [If the respondent answers no, the interview is terminated.]

2. Do you receive the *Springville Herald* via home delivery?
   (1) Yes   (2) No
   [If no, skip to question 4.]

3. Do you receive the *Springville Herald*:
   (1) Monday–Saturday
   (2) Sunday only
   (3) Every day
   [Skip to question 9.]

4. How often during the Monday–Saturday period do you purchase the *Springville Herald*?
   (1) Every day
   (2) Most days
   (3) Occasionally or never

5. How often do you purchase the *Springville Herald* on Sundays?
   (1) Every Sunday
   (2) 2–3 Sundays per month
   (3) No more than once a month

6. Where are you most likely to purchase the *Springville Herald*?
   (1) Convenience store
   (2) Newsstand/candy store
   (3) Vending machine
   (4) Supermarket
   (5) Other

7. Would you consider subscribing to the *Springville Herald* for a trial period if a discount were offered?
   (1) Yes   (2) No
   [If no, skip to question 9.]

8. The *Springville Herald* currently costs $0.50 Monday–Saturday and $1.50 on Sunday, for a total of $4.50 per week. How much would you be willing to pay per week to get home delivery for a 90-day trial period?

9. Do you read a daily newspaper other than the *Springville Herald*?
   (1) Yes   (2) No

10. As an incentive for long-term subscribers, the newspaper is considering the possibility of offering a card that would provide discounts at certain restaurants in the Springville area to all subscribers who pay in advance for six months of home delivery. Would you want to get such a card under the terms of this offer?
    (1) Yes   (2) No

The marketing department agreed to use a random-digit dialing method to poll 500 local households by telephone. Using this approach, the last four digits of a telephone number are randomly selected to go with an area code and exchange (the first 6 digits of a 10-digit telephone number). Only those pairs of area codes and exchanges that were for the Springville city area were used for this survey.

Of the 500 households selected, 94 households either refused to participate, could not be contacted after repeated attempts, or had telephone numbers that were not in service. The summary results are as follows:

Households That Purchase the *Springville Herald*	Frequency
Yes	352
No	54

Households with Home Delivery	Frequency
Yes	136
No	216

Type of Home Delivery Subscription	Frequency
Monday–Saturday	18
Sunday only	25
7 days a week	93

Purchase Behavior of Nonsubscribers for Monday–Saturday Editions	Frequency
Every day	78
Most days	95
Occasionally or never	43

Purchase Behavior of Nonsubscribers for Sunday Editions	Frequency
Every Sunday	138
2–3 Sundays a month	54
No more than once a month	24

Nonsubscribers' Purchase Location	Frequency
Convenience store	74
Newsstand/candy store	95
Vending machine	21
Supermarket	13
Other locations	13

Would Consider Trial Subscription if Offered a Discount	Frequency
Yes	46
No	170

Rate ($) Willing to Pay per Week for a 90-Day Home-Delivery Trial Subscription (stored in SH8)

4.15	3.60	4.10	3.60	3.60	3.60	4.40	3.15	4.00	3.75	4.00
3.25	3.75	3.30	3.75	3.65	4.00	4.10	3.90	3.50	3.75	3.00
3.40	4.00	3.80	3.50	4.10	4.25	3.50	3.90	3.95	4.30	4.20
3.50	3.75	3.30	3.85	3.20	4.40	3.80	3.40	3.50	2.85	3.75
3.80	3.90									

Read a Daily Newspaper Other Than the *Springville Herald*

	Frequency
Yes	138
No	214

Would Prepay Six Months to Receive a Restaurant Discount Card

	Frequency
Yes	66
No	286

EXERCISES

SH8.1 Some members of the marketing department are concerned about the random-digit dialing method used to collect survey responses. Prepare a memorandum that examines the following issues:
- The advantages and disadvantages of using the random-digit dialing method.
- Possible alternative approaches for conducting the survey and their advantages and disadvantages.

SH8.2 Analyze the results of the survey of Springville households. Write a report that discusses the marketing implications of the survey results for the *Springville Herald*.

WEB CASE

Apply your knowledge about confidence interval estimation in this Web Case, which extends the OurCampus! Web Case from Chapter 6.

Among its other features, the OurCampus! Web site allows customers to purchase OurCampus! LifeStyles merchandise online. To handle payment processing, the management of OurCampus! has contracted with the following firms:

- **PayAFriend (PAF)** This is an online payment system with which customers and businesses such as OurCampus! register in order to exchange payments in a secure and convenient manner, without the need for a credit card.
- **Continental Banking Company (Conbanco)** This processing services provider allows OurCampus! customers to pay for merchandise using nationally recognized credit cards issued by a financial institution.

To reduce costs, the management is considering eliminating one of these two payment systems. However, Virginia Duffy of the sales department suspects that customers use the two forms of payment in unequal numbers and that customers display different buying behaviors when using the two forms of payment. Therefore, she would like to first determine:

a. The proportion of customers using PAF and the proportion of customers using a credit card to pay for their purchases.

b. The mean purchase amount when using PAF and the mean purchase amount when using a credit card.

Assist Ms. Duffy by preparing an appropriate analysis, based on a random sample of 50 transactions that she has prepared. Using a Web browser, open to the Web page for the Chapter 8 Web Case or open **OurCampus_PymtSample.htm**, if you have downloaded the Web Case files, to review her data. Summarize your findings to determine whether Ms. Duffy's conjectures about OurCampus! customer purchasing behaviors are correct. If you want the sampling error to be no more than $3 when estimating the mean purchase amount, is Ms. Duffy's sample large enough to perform a valid analysis?

REFERENCES

1. Cochran, W. G., *Sampling Techniques*, 3rd ed. (New York: Wiley, 1977).
2. Fisher, R. A., and F. Yates, *Statistical Tables for Biological, Agricultural and Medical Research*, 5th ed. (Edinburgh: Oliver & Boyd, 1957).
3. Hahn, G., and W. Meeker, *Statistical Intervals, A Guide for Practitioners* (New York: John Wiley and Sons, Inc., 1991).
4. Kirk, R. E., ed., *Statistical Issues: A Reader for the Behavioral Sciences* (Belmont, CA: Wadsworth, 1972).

5. Larsen, R. L., and M. L. Marx, *An Introduction to Mathematical Statistics and Its Applications*, 4th ed. (Upper Saddle River, NJ: Prentice Hall, 2006).

6. *Microsoft Excel 2007* (Redmond, WA: Microsoft Corp., 2007).

7. Snedecor, G. W., and W. G. Cochran, *Statistical Methods*, 7th ed. (Ames, IA: Iowa State University Press, 1980).

CHAPTER 8 EXCEL GUIDE

EG8.1 CONFIDENCE INTERVAL ESTIMATION for the MEAN (σ KNOWN)

PHStat2 Use the **Estimate for the Mean, sigma known** procedure to compute the confidence interval estimate for the mean when σ is known. For example, to compute the estimate for the Example 8.1 mean paper length problem on page 256, select **PHStat → Confidence Intervals → Estimate for the Mean, sigma known**. In the procedure's dialog box (shown below):

1. Enter **0.02** as the **Population Standard Deviation**.

2. Enter **95** as the **Confidence Level** percentage.

3. Click **Sample Statistics Known** and enter **100** as the **Sample Size** and **10.998** as the **Sample Mean**.

4. Enter a **Title** and click **OK**.

For problems that use unsummarized data, in step 3, click **Sample Statistics Unknown** and enter the **Sample Cell Range**.

In-Depth Excel Use the **CONFIDENCE** function to compute the half-width of a confidence interval. Enter the function as **CONFIDENCE(1 – *confidence level, population standard deviation, sample size*)**.

Use the **COMPUTE worksheet** of the **CIE sigma known workbook**, shown in Figure EG8.1, as a template

for computing confidence interval estimates when σ is known. The worksheet contains the data for the Example 8.1 mean paper length problem. To compute confidence interval estimates for other problems, change the **Population Standard Deviation, Sample Mean, Sample Size**, and **Confidence Level** values in cells B4 through B7, respectively.

	A	B	
1	**Estimate for the Mean Paper Length**		
2			
3	**Data**		
4	Population Standard Deviation	0.02	
5	Sample Mean	10.998	
6	Sample Size	100	
7	Confidence Level	95%	
8			
9	**Intermediate Calculations**		
10	Standard Error of the Mean	0.002	=B4/SQRT(B6)
11	Z Value	-1.9600	=NORMSINV((1 - B7)/2)
12	Interval Half Width	0.0039	=CONFIDENCE(1 - B7, B4, B6)
13			
14	**Confidence Interval**		
15	Interval Lower Limit	10.9941	=B5 - B12
16	Interval Upper Limit	11.0019	=B5 + B12

FIGURE EG8.1 Worksheet to compute a confidence interval estimate when σ is known.

The COMPUTE worksheet also uses the **NORMSINV** (*cumulative percentage*) function to compute the Z value in cell B11 for one-half of the $(1 - \alpha)$ value.

EG8.2 CONFIDENCE INTERVAL ESTIMATION for the mean (σ UNKNOWN)

PHStat2 Use the **Estimate for the Mean, sigma unknown** procedure to compute the confidence interval estimate for the mean when σ is unknown. For example, to compute the Figure 8.7 estimate for the mean sales invoice amount (see page 261), select **PHStat → Confidence Intervals → Estimate for the Mean, sigma unknown**. In the procedure's dialog box (shown on page 293):

1. Enter **95** as the **Confidence Level** percentage.

2. Click **Sample Statistics Known** and enter **100** as the **Sample Size, 110.27** as the **Sample Mean**, and **28.95** as the **Sample Std. Deviation**.

3. Enter a **Title** and click **OK**.

3. Enter **95** as the **Confidence Level** percentage.

4. Enter a **Title** and click **OK**.

For problems that use unsummarized data, in step 3, click **Sample Statistics Unknown** and enter the **Sample Cell Range**.

In-Depth Excel Use the **TINV** function to determine the critical value from the *t* distribution in order to compute a confidence interval estimates when σ is unknown. Enter the function as **TINV(1 – *confidence level, degrees of freedom*)**.

Use the **COMPUTE worksheet** of the **CIE sigma unknown workbook**, shown in Figure 8.7 on page 261, as a template for computing confidence interval estimates when σ is unknown. The worksheet contains the data for the Section 8.2 example for estimating the mean sales invoice amount and uses the TINV function in cell B12. To compute confidence interval estimates for other problems, change the **Sample Standard Deviation, Sample Mean, Sample Size,** and **Confidence Level** values in cells B4 through B7, respectively.

EG8.3 CONFIDENCE INTERVAL ESTIMATION for the PROPORTION

PHStat2 Use the **Estimate for the Proportion** procedure to compute the confidence interval estimate for the proportion. For example, to compute the Figure 8.12 estimate for the proportion of in-error sales invoices (see page 267), select **PHStat → Confidence Intervals → Estimate for the Proportion**. In the procedure's dialog box (shown in the right column):

1. Enter **100** as the **Sample Size**.

2. Enter **10** as the **Number of Successes**.

In-Depth Excel Use the **NORMSINV** and **SQRT** functions to help compute a confidence interval estimate for the proportion. Enter the functions as **NORMSINV((1 – *confidence level*)/2)** and **SQRT(*sample proportion * (1 – sample proportion)/ sample size*)** to compute the *Z* value and the standard error of the proportion, respectively.

Use the **COMPUTE worksheet** of the **CIE Proportion workbook**, shown in Figure 8.12 on page 267, as a template for computing confidence interval estimates for the proportion. The worksheet contains the data for the Figure 8.12 estimate for the proportion of in-error sales invoices and uses the **NORMSINV** function to determine the *Z* value in cell B10 and uses the **SQRT** function to compute the standard error of the proportion in cell B11. To compute confidence interval estimates for other problems, change the **Sample Size, Number of Successes,** and **Confidence Level** values in cells B4 through B6.

EG8.4 DETERMINING SAMPLE SIZE

Sample Size Determination for the Mean

PHStat2 Use the **Determination for the Mean** procedure to compute the sample size needed for estimating the mean. For example, to determine the sample size for the mean sales invoice amount, shown in Figure 8.13 on page 271, select **PHStat → Sample Size → Determination for the Mean**. In the procedure's dialog box shown on page 294:

1. Enter **25** as the **Population Standard Deviation**.

2. Enter **5** as the **Sampling Error**.

3. Enter **95** as the **Confidence Level** percentage.

4. Enter a **Title** and click **OK**.

In-Depth Excel Use the **NORMSINV** and **ROUNDUP** functions to help determine the sample size needed for estimating the mean. Enter **NORMSINV((1 – *confidence level*)/2)** to compute the Z value and enter **ROUNDUP** (*calculated sample size*, **0**) to round up the calculated sample size to the next higher integer.

Use the **COMPUTE worksheet** of the **Sample Size Mean workbook**, shown in Figure 8.13 on page 271, as a template for determining the sample size needed for estimating the mean. The worksheet contains the data for the Section 8.4 mean sales invoice amount problem and uses the NORMSINV and ROUNDUP functions in cells B9 and B13, respectively. To compute confidence interval estimates for other problems, change the **Population Standard Deviation**, **Sampling Error**, and **Confidence Level** values in cells B4 through B6.

Sample Size Determination for the Proportion

PHStat2 Use the **Determination for the Proportion** procedure to compute the sample size needed for estimating the proportion. For example, to determine the sample size for the proportion of in-error sales invoices, shown in Figure 8.14 on page 273, select **PHStat → Sample Size → Determination for the Proportion**. In the procedure's dialog box (shown below):

1. Enter **0.15** as the **Estimate of True Proportion**.
2. Enter **0.07** as the **Sampling Error**.
3. Enter **95** as the **Confidence Level** percentage.
4. Enter a **Title** and click **OK**.

In-Depth Excel Use the **NORMSINV** and **ROUNDUP** functions to help determine the sample size needed for estimating the proportion. Enter **NORMSINV((1 – *confidence level*)/2)** to compute the Z value and enter **ROUNDUP(*calculated sample size*, 0)** to round up the calculated sample size to the next higher integer.

Use the **COMPUTE worksheet** of the **Sample Size Proportion workbook**, shown in Figure 8.14 on page 273, as a template for determining the sample size needed for estimating the proportion. The worksheet contains the data for the Section 8.4 in-error sales invoice problem and uses the NORMSINV and ROUNDUP functions in cells B9 and B13, respectively. To compute confidence interval estimates for other problems, change the **Estimate of True Proportion**, **Sampling Error**, and **Confidence Level** in cells B4 through B6.

EG8.5 APPLICATIONS of CONFIDENCE INTERVAL ESTIMATION in AUDITING

Estimating the Population Total Amount

PHStat2 Use the **Estimate for the Population Total** procedure to compute the confidence interval estimate for the population total. For example, to compute the Figure 8.15 estimate for the total of all sales invoices (see page 276), select **PHStat → Confidence Intervals → Estimate for the Population Total.** In the procedure's dialog box (shown below):

1. Enter **5000** as the **Population Size**.
2. Enter **95** as the **Confidence Level** percentage.
3. Click **Sample Statistics Known** and enter **100** as the **Sample Size**, **110.27** as the **Sample Mean**, and **28.95** as the **Sample Std. Deviation**.
4. Enter a **Title** and click **OK**.

In-Depth Excel Use the **TINV** function to determine the critical value from the *t* distribution in order to help compute a confidence interval estimate for the population total. Enter the function as **TINV(1 – *confidence level*, *degrees of freedom*)**.

Use the **COMPUTE worksheet** of the **CIE Total workbook**, shown in Figure 8.15 on page 276, as a template for computing confidence interval estimates for the population total. The worksheet contains the data for the Figure 8.15 estimate for the total amount of all sales invoices and uses the **TINV** function to determine the *Z* value in cell B15. To compute confidence interval estimates for other problems, change the **Population Size**, **Sample Mean**, **Sample Size**, **Sample Standard Deviation**, and **Confidence Level** values in cells B4 through B8.

Difference Estimation

PHStat2 Use the **Estimate for the Total Difference** procedure to compute the confidence interval estimate for the total difference. For example, to compute the Figure 8.16 estimate for the total difference in the Saxon Home Improvement invoice auditing example (see page 279), open to the **DATA worksheet** of the **PlumbInv workbook**. Select **PHStat → Confidence Intervals → Estimate for the Total Difference**. In the procedure's dialog box (shown below):

1. Enter **100** as the **Sample Size**.
2. Enter **5000** as the **Population Size**.
3. Enter **95** as the **Confidence Level** percentage.
4. Enter **A1:A13** as the **Differences Cell Range** and check **First cell contains label**.
5. Enter a **Title** and click **OK**.

This procedure creates a worksheet containing the results and a second worksheet that contains computations that help to calculate the standard deviation of the differences. (See the following *In-Depth Excel* section for an explanation of the second worksheet.)

In-Depth Excel Use the **COMPUTE worksheet** of the **CIE Total Difference workbook**, shown in Figure 8.16 on page 279, as a template for computing confidence interval estimates for the total difference. The worksheet contains the data for the Figure 8.16 Saxon Home Improvement invoice auditing example, including the difference data in PlumbInv.

In the COMPUTE worksheet, the **Sum of Differences** in cell B9 and the **Standard Deviation of Differences** in cell B12 rely on computations found in a **DIFFERENCES worksheet**.

Figure EG8.2 shows this worksheet and reveals the column B formulas that are summed to compute the **SS for Differences Not = 0** in cell E12 of the COMPUTE worksheet. (Note that the column B formulas use **COMPUTE!B10**, the cell that computes the **Average Difference in Sample**.)

Computing the total difference confidence interval estimate for other problems requires changes to both the COMPUTE and DIFFERENCES worksheets. First, in the COMPUTE worksheet, change the **Populations Size**, **Sample Size**, and **Confidence Level** in cells B4 through B6, respectively. Then, in the DIFFERENCES worksheet, enter the differences in column A and adjust the column B formulas so that there is a column B formula for each difference listed. If there are more than 12 differences, select cell B13 and copy down through all the rows. If there are fewer than 12 differences, delete formulas in column B from the bottom up, starting with cell B13, until there are as many formulas as there are difference values.

	A	B	
1	Differences	(D-DBar)^2)	
2	9.03	66.0969	=(A2 - COMPUTE!$B$10)^2
3	7.47	43.1649	=(A3 - COMPUTE!$B$10)^2
4	17.32	269.6164	=(A4 - COMPUTE!$B$10)^2
5	8.3	54.76	=(A5 - COMPUTE!$B$10)^2
6	5.21	18.5761	=(A6 - COMPUTE!$B$10)^2
7	10.8	98.01	=(A7 - COMPUTE!$B$10)^2
8	6.22	28.3024	=(A8 - COMPUTE!$B$10)^2
9	5.63	22.3729	=(A9 - COMPUTE!$B$10)^2
10	4.97	16.5649	=(A10 - COMPUTE!$B$10)^2
11	7.43	42.6409	=(A11 - COMPUTE!$B$10)^2
12	2.99	4.3681	=(A12 - COMPUTE!$B$10)^2
13	4.63	13.9129	=(A13 - COMPUTE!$B$10)^2

FIGURE EG8.2 DIFFERENCES worksheet

9 Fundamentals of Hypothesis Testing: One-Sample Tests

Learning Objectives

In this chapter, you learn:

- The basic principles of hypothesis testing
- How to use hypothesis testing to test a mean or proportion
- The assumptions of each hypothesis-testing procedure, how to evaluate them, and the consequences if they are seriously violated
- How to avoid the pitfalls involved in hypothesis testing
- Ethical issues involved in hypothesis testing

@ Oxford Cereals, Part II

A s in Chapter 7, you again find yourself as plant operations manager for Oxford Cereals. You are responsible for monitoring the amount in each cereal box filled. Company specifications require a mean weight of 368 grams per box. It is your responsibility to adjust the process when the mean fill weight in the population of boxes differs from 368 grams. How can you make the decision whether to adjust the process when you are unable to weigh every single box as it is being filled? You begin by selecting and weighing a random sample of 25 cereal boxes. After computing the sample mean, how do you proceed?

In Chapter 7, you learned methods to determine whether the value of a sample mean is consistent with a known population mean. In this Oxford Cereals scenario, you want to use a sample mean to validate a claim about the population mean, a somewhat different problem. For this type of problem, you use an inferential method called **hypothesis testing**. Hypothesis testing requires that you state a claim unambiguously. In this scenario, the claim is that the population mean is 368 grams. You examine a sample statistic to see if it better supports the stated claim, called the *null hypothesis*, or the mutually exclusive alternative (for this scenario, that the population mean is not 368 grams).

In this chapter, you will learn several applications of hypothesis testing. You will learn how to make inferences about a population parameter by *analyzing differences* between the results observed, the sample statistic, and the results you would expect to get if an underlying hypothesis were actually true. For the Oxford Cereals scenario, hypothesis testing allows you to infer one of the following:

- The mean weight of the cereal boxes in the sample is a value consistent with what you would expect if the mean of the entire population of cereal boxes is 368 grams.
- The population mean is not equal to 368 grams because the sample mean is significantly different from 368 grams.

9.1 Fundamentals of Hypothesis-Testing Methodology

Hypothesis testing typically begins with some theory, claim, or assertion about a particular parameter of a population. For example, your initial hypothesis in the cereal example is that the process is working properly, so the mean fill is 368 grams, and no corrective action is needed.

The Null and Alternative Hypotheses

The hypothesis that the population parameter is equal to the company specification is referred to as the null hypothesis. A **null hypothesis** is always one of status quo and is identified by the symbol H_0. Here the null hypothesis is that the filling process is working properly, and therefore the mean fill is the 368-gram specification provided by Oxford Cereals. This is stated as

$$H_0: \mu = 368$$

Even though information is available only from the sample, the null hypothesis is stated in terms of the population parameter because your focus is on the population of all cereal boxes. You use the sample statistic to make inferences about the entire filling process. One inference may be that the results observed from the sample data indicate that the null hypothesis is false. If the null hypothesis is considered false, something else must be true.

Whenever a null hypothesis is specified, an alternative hypothesis is also specified, and it must be true if the null hypothesis is false. The **alternative hypothesis**, H_1, is the opposite of the null hypothesis, H_0. This is stated in the cereal example as

$$H_1: \mu \neq 368$$

The alternative hypothesis represents the conclusion reached by rejecting the null hypothesis. The null hypothesis is rejected when there is sufficient evidence from the sample data that the null hypothesis is false. In the cereal example, if the weights of the sampled boxes are sufficiently above or below the expected 368-gram mean specified by Oxford Cereals, you reject the null hypothesis in favor of the alternative hypothesis that the mean fill is different from 368 grams. You stop production and take whatever action is necessary to correct the problem. If the null hypothesis is not rejected, you should continue to believe in the status quo, that the process is working correctly and therefore no corrective action is necessary. In this second circumstance, you have not proven that the process is working correctly. Rather, you have failed to prove that it is working incorrectly, and therefore you continue your belief (although unproven) in the null hypothesis.

In hypothesis testing, you reject the null hypothesis when the sample evidence suggests that it is far more likely that the alternative hypothesis is true. However, failure to reject the null hypothesis is not proof that it is true. You can never prove that the null hypothesis is correct because the decision is based only on the sample information, not on the entire population. Therefore, if you fail to reject the null hypothesis, you can only conclude that there is insufficient evidence to warrant its rejection. The following key points summarize the null and alternative hypotheses:

- The null hypothesis, H_0, represents the status quo or the current belief in a situation.
- The alternative hypothesis, H_1, is the opposite of the null hypothesis and represents a research claim or specific inference you would like to prove.
- If you reject the null hypothesis, you have statistical proof that the alternative hypothesis is correct.
- If you do not reject the null hypothesis, you have failed to prove the alternative hypothesis. The failure to prove the alternative hypothesis, however, does not mean that you have proven the null hypothesis.
- The null hypothesis, H_0, always refers to a specified value of the population parameter (such as μ), not a sample statistic (such as $\overline{X}$).
- The statement of the null hypothesis always contains an equal sign regarding the specified value of the population parameter (e.g., $H_0: \mu = 368$ grams).
- The statement of the alternative hypothesis never contains an equal sign regarding the specified value of the population parameter (e.g., $H_1: \mu \neq 368$ grams).

EXAMPLE 9.1

The Null and Alternative Hypotheses

You are the manager of a fast-food restaurant. You want to determine whether the waiting time to place an order has changed in the past month from its previous population mean value of 4.5 minutes. State the null and alternative hypotheses.

SOLUTION The null hypothesis is that the population mean has not changed from its previous value of 4.5 minutes. This is stated as

$$H_0: \mu = 4.5$$

The alternative hypothesis is the opposite of the null hypothesis. Because the null hypothesis is that the population mean is 4.5 minutes, the alternative hypothesis is that the population mean is not 4.5 minutes. This is stated as

$$H_1: \mu \neq 4.5$$

The Critical Value of the Test Statistic

The logic of hypothesis testing involves determining how likely the null hypothesis is to be true by considering the data collected in a sample. In the Oxford Cereal Company scenario, the null hypothesis is that the mean amount of cereal per box in the entire filling process is 368 grams (the population parameter specified by the company). You select a sample of boxes from the filling process, weigh each box, and compute the sample mean. This statistic is an estimate of the corresponding parameter (the population mean, μ). Even if the null hypothesis is true, the statistic (the sample mean, $\overline{X}$) is likely to differ from the value of the parameter (the population mean, μ) because of variation due to sampling. However, you expect the sample statistic to be close to the population parameter if the null hypothesis is true. If the sample statistic is close to the population parameter, you have insufficient evidence to reject the null hypothesis. For example, if the sample mean is 367.9, you might conclude that the population mean has not changed (i.e., $\mu = 368$) because a sample mean of 367.9 is very close to the hypothesized value of 368. Intuitively, you think that it is likely that you could get a sample mean of 367.9 from a population whose mean is 368.

However, if there is a large difference between the value of the statistic and the hypothesized value of the population parameter, you might conclude that the null hypothesis is false. For example, if the sample mean is 320, you might conclude that the population mean is not 368 (i.e., $\mu \neq 368$), because the sample mean is very far from the hypothesized value of 368.

In such a case, you conclude that it is very unlikely to get a sample mean of 320 if the population mean is really 368. Therefore, it is more logical to conclude that the population mean is not equal to 368. Here you reject the null hypothesis.

However, the decision-making process is not always so clear-cut. Determining what is "very close" and what is "very different" is arbitrary without clear definitions. Hypothesis-testing methodology provides clear definitions for evaluating differences. Furthermore, it enables you to quantify the decision-making process by computing the probability of getting a certain sample result if the null hypothesis is true. You calculate this probability by determining the sampling distribution for the sample statistic of interest (e.g., the sample mean) and then computing the particular **test statistic** based on the given sample result. Because the sampling distribution for the test statistic often follows a well-known statistical distribution, such as the standardized normal distribution or t distribution, you can use these distributions to help determine whether the null hypothesis is true.

Regions of Rejection and Nonrejection

The sampling distribution of the test statistic is divided into two regions, a **region of rejection** (sometimes called the critical region) and a **region of nonrejection** (see Figure 9.1). If the test statistic falls into the region of nonrejection, you do not reject the null hypothesis. In the Oxford Cereals scenario, you conclude that there is insufficient evidence that the population mean fill is different from 368 grams. If the test statistic falls into the rejection region, you reject the null hypothesis. In this case, you conclude that the population mean is not 368 grams.

FIGURE 9.1

Regions of rejection and nonrejection in hypothesis testing

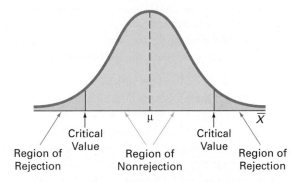

The region of rejection consists of the values of the test statistic that are unlikely to occur if the null hypothesis is true. These values are much more likely to occur if the null hypothesis is false. Therefore, if a value of the test statistic falls into this *rejection region*, you reject the null hypothesis because that value is unlikely if the null hypothesis is true.

To make a decision concerning the null hypothesis, you first determine the **critical value** of the test statistic. The critical value divides the nonrejection region from the rejection region. Determining the critical value depends on the size of the rejection region. The size of the rejection region is directly related to the risks involved in using only sample evidence to make decisions about a population parameter.

Risks in Decision Making Using Hypothesis Testing

When using a sample statistic to make decisions about a population parameter, there is a risk that you will reach an incorrect conclusion. You can make two different types of errors when applying hypothesis testing, Type I and Type II errors.

TYPE I AND TYPE II ERRORS

A **Type I error** occurs if you reject the null hypothesis, H_0, when it is true and should not be rejected. The probability of a Type I error occurring is α.

A **Type II error** occurs if you do not reject the null hypothesis, H_0, when it is false and should be rejected. The probability of a Type II error occurring is β.

In the Oxford Cereals scenario, you make a Type I error if you conclude that the population mean fill is *not* 368 when it *is* 368. This error causes you to adjust the filling process even though the process is working properly. Thus, a Type I error is a "false alarm." You make a Type II error if you conclude that the population mean fill *is* 368 when it is *not* 368. Here, you would allow the process to continue without adjustment, even though adjustments are needed. Thus, a Type II error represents a "missed opportunity."

The Level of Significance (α) The probability of committing a Type I error, denoted by α (the lowercase Greek letter *alpha*), is referred to as the **level of significance** of the statistical test. Traditionally, you control the Type I error by determining the risk level, α, that you are willing to have of rejecting the null hypothesis when it is true. Because you specify the level of significance before the hypothesis test is performed, the risk of committing a Type I error, α, is directly under your control. Traditionally, you select levels of 0.01, 0.05, or 0.10. The choice of a particular risk level for making a Type I error depends on the cost of making a Type I error. After you specify the value for α, you can then determine the critical values that divide the rejection and nonrejection regions. You know the size of the rejection region because α is the probability of rejection when the null hypothesis is true. From this, you can then determine the critical value or values that divide the rejection and nonrejection regions.

The Confidence Coefficient The complement of the probability of a Type I error, $(1 - \alpha)$, is called the confidence coefficient. When multiplied by 100%, the confidence coefficient yields the confidence level that was studied when constructing confidence intervals (see Section 8.1).

> The **confidence coefficient**, $(1 - \alpha)$, is the probability that you will not reject the null hypothesis, H_0, when it is true and should not be rejected. The **confidence level** of a hypothesis test is $(1 - \alpha) \times 100\%$.

In terms of hypothesis testing, the confidence coefficient represents the probability of concluding that the value of the parameter as specified in the null hypothesis is plausible when it is true. In the Oxford Cereals scenario, the confidence coefficient measures the probability of concluding that the population mean fill is 368 grams when it is actually 368 grams.

The β Risk The β risk is the probability of committing a Type II error. Unlike a Type I error, which you control by the selection of α, the probability of making a Type II error depends on the difference between the hypothesized and actual value of the population parameter. Because large differences are easier to find than small ones, if the difference between the hypothesized and actual value of the population parameter is large, β is small. For example, if the population mean is 330 grams, there is a small chance (β) that you will conclude that the mean has not changed from 368. However, if the difference between the hypothesized and actual value of the parameter is small, β is large. For example, if the population mean is actually 367 grams, there is a large chance (β) that you will conclude that the mean is still 368 grams.

The Power of a Test The complement of the probability of a Type II error, $(1 - \beta)$, is called the power of a statistical test.

> The **power of a statistical test**, $(1 - \beta)$, is the probability that you will reject the null hypothesis when it is false and should be rejected.

In the Oxford Cereals scenario, the power of the test is the probability that you will correctly conclude that the mean fill amount is not 368 grams when it actually is not 368 grams. For an in-depth discussion of the power of a statistical test, read the **Section 9.6** online topic file that is available on this book's companion Web site. (See Appendix Section D.8 to learn how to access the online topic files.)

Risks in Decision Making: A Delicate Balance Table 9.1 illustrates the results of the two possible decisions (do not reject H_0 or reject H_0) that you can make in any hypothesis test. You can make a correct decision or make one of two types of errors.

TABLE 9.1

Hypothesis Testing and Decision Making

	Actual Situation	
Statistical Decision	**H_0 True**	**H_0 False**
Do not reject H_0	Correct decision Confidence $= (1 - \alpha)$	Type II error P(Type II error) $= \beta$
Reject H_0	Type I error P(Type I error) $= \alpha$	Correct decision Power $= (1 - \beta)$

One way to reduce the probability of making a Type II error is by increasing the sample size. Large samples generally permit you to detect even very small differences between the hypothesized values and the actual population parameters. For a given level of α, increasing the sample size decreases β and therefore increases the power of the test to detect that the null hypothesis, H_0, is false. However, there is always a limit to your resources, and this affects the decision of how large a sample you can select. Thus, for a given sample size, you must consider the trade-offs between the two possible types of errors. Because you can directly control the risk of Type I error, you can reduce this risk by selecting a smaller value for α. For example, if the negative consequences associated with making a Type I error are substantial, you could select $\alpha = 0.01$ instead of 0.05. However, when you decrease α, you increase β, so reducing the risk of a Type I error results in an increased risk of a Type II error. However, to reduce β, you could select a larger value for α. Therefore, if it is important to try to avoid a Type II error, you can select α of 0.05 or 0.10 instead of 0.01.

In the Oxford Cereals scenario, the risk of a Type I error occurring involves concluding that the mean fill amount has changed from the hypothesized 368 grams when it actually has not changed. The risk of a Type II error occurring involves concluding that the mean fill amount has not changed from the hypothesized 368 grams when it actually has changed. The choice of reasonable values for α and β depends on the costs inherent in each type of error. For example, if it is very costly to change the cereal-filling process, you would want to be very confident that a change is needed before making any changes. In this case, the risk of a Type I error occurring is more important, and you would choose a small α. However, if you want to be very certain of detecting changes from a mean of 368 grams, the risk of a Type II error occurring is more important, and you would choose a higher level of α.

Now that you have been introduced to hypothesis testing, recall that in the Using Statistics scenario on page 297, the business problem facing Oxford Cereals is to determine whether the cereal-filling process is working properly (i.e., whether the mean fill throughout the entire packaging process remains at the specified 368 grams, and no corrective action is needed). To evaluate the 368-gram requirement, you select a random sample of 25 boxes, weigh each box, compute the sample mean, $\bar{X}$, and then evaluate the difference between this sample statistic and the hypothesized population parameter by comparing the sample mean weight (in grams) to the expected population mean of 368 grams specified by the company. The null and alternative hypotheses are

$$H_0: \mu = 368$$

$$H_1: \mu \neq 368$$

When the standard deviation, σ, is known (which rarely occurs), you use the **Z test for the mean** if the population is normally distributed. If the population is not normally distributed, you can still use the Z test if the sample size is large enough for the Central Limit Theorem to take effect (see Section 7.4). Equation (9.1) defines the Z_{STAT} test statistic for determining the difference between the sample mean, $\bar{X}$ and the population mean, μ, when the standard deviation, σ, is known.

Z TEST FOR THE MEAN (σ KNOWN)

$$Z_{STAT} = \frac{\bar{X} - \mu}{\dfrac{\sigma}{\sqrt{n}}} \tag{9.1}$$

In Equation (9.1), the numerator measures the difference between the observed sample mean, $\overline{X}$, and the hypothesized mean, μ. The denominator is the standard error of the mean, so Z_{STAT} represents the difference between $\overline{X}$ and μ in standard error units.

Hypothesis Testing Using the Critical Value Approach

The critical value approach compares the computed Z_{STAT} test statistic value from Equation (9.1) to critical values that divide the normal distribution into regions of rejection and nonrejection. The critical values are expressed as standardized Z values that are determined by the level of significance.

For example, if you use a level of significance of 0.05, the size of the rejection region is 0.05. Because the rejection region is divided into the two tails of the distribution, you divide the 0.05 into two equal parts of 0.025 each. For this **two-tail test**, a rejection region of 0.025 in each tail of the normal distribution results in a cumulative area of 0.025 below the lower critical value and a cumulative area of 0.975 ($1 - 0.025$) below the upper critical value (which leaves an area of 0.025 in the upper tail). According to the cumulative standardized normal distribution table (Table E.2), the critical values that divide the rejection and nonrejection regions are -1.96 and $+1.96$. Figure 9.2 illustrates that if the mean is actually 368 grams, as H_0 claims, the values of the Z_{STAT} test statistic have a standardized normal distribution centered at $Z = 0$ (which corresponds to an $\overline{X}$ value of 368 grams). Values of Z_{STAT} greater than $+1.96$ or less than -1.96 indicate that $\overline{X}$ is sufficiently different from the hypothesized $\mu = 368$ that it is unlikely that such a $\overline{X}$ value would occur if H_0 were true.

FIGURE 9.2

Testing a hypothesis about the mean (σ known) at the 0.05 level of significance

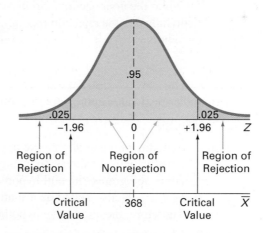

Therefore, the decision rule is

$$\text{Reject } H_0 \text{ if } Z_{STAT} > +1.96$$

$$\text{or if } Z_{STAT} < -1.96;$$

$$\text{otherwise, do not reject } H_0.$$

Suppose that the sample of 25 cereal boxes indicates a sample mean, $\overline{X}$, of 372.5 grams, and the population standard deviation, σ, is 15 grams. Using Equation (9.1) on page 302,

$$Z_{STAT} = \frac{\overline{X} - \mu}{\dfrac{\sigma}{\sqrt{n}}} = \frac{372.5 - 368}{\dfrac{15}{\sqrt{25}}} = +1.50$$

Because $Z_{STAT} = +1.50$ is between -1.96 and $+1.96$, you do not reject H_0 (see Figure 9.3 on page 304). You continue to believe that the mean fill amount is 368 grams. To take into account the possibility of a Type II error, you state the conclusion as "there is insufficient evidence that the mean fill is different from 368 grams."

Exhibit 9.1 summarizes the critical value approach to hypothesis testing. Steps 1 though 4 correspond to the Define task, step 5 combines the Collect and Organize tasks, and step 6 corresponds to the Visualize and Analyze tasks of the business problem-solving methodology first introduced in Chapter 2.

FIGURE 9.3

Testing a hypothesis about the mean cereal weight (σ known) at the 0.05 level of significance

EXHIBIT 9.1 THE CRITICAL VALUE APPROACH TO HYPOTHESIS TESTING

1. State the null hypothesis, H_0, and the alternative hypothesis, H_1.
2. Choose the level of significance, α, and the sample size, n. The level of significance is based on the relative importance of the risks of committing Type I and Type II errors in the problem.
3. Determine the appropriate test statistic and sampling distribution.
4. Determine the critical values that divide the rejection and nonrejection regions.
5. Collect the sample data, organize the results, and compute the value of the test statistic.
6. Make the statistical decision and state the managerial conclusion. If the test statistic falls into the nonrejection region, you do not reject the null hypothesis. If the test statistic falls into the rejection region, you reject the null hypothesis. The managerial conclusion is written in the context of the real-world problem.

EXAMPLE 9.2

Applying the Critical Value Approach to Hypothesis Testing at Oxford Cereals

State the critical value approach to hypothesis testing at Oxford Cereals.

SOLUTION

Step 1: State the null and alternative hypotheses. The null hypothesis, H_0, is always stated as a mathematical expression, using population parameters. In testing whether the mean fill is 368 grams, the null hypothesis states that μ equals 368. The alternative hypothesis, H_1, is also stated as a mathematical expression, using population parameters. Therefore, the alternative hypothesis states that μ is not equal to 368 grams.

Step 2: Choose the level of significance and the sample size. You choose the level of significance, α, according to the relative importance of the risks of committing Type I and Type II errors in the problem. The smaller the value of α, the less risk there is of making a Type I error. In this example, making a Type I error means that you conclude that the population mean is not 368 grams when it is 368 grams. Thus, you will take corrective action on the filling process even though the process is working properly. Here, $\alpha = 0.05$ is selected. The sample size, n, is 25.

Step 3: Select the appropriate test statistic. Because σ is known from information about the filling process, you use the normal distribution and the Z_{STAT} test statistic.

Step 4: Determine the rejection region. Critical values for the appropriate test statistic are selected so that the rejection region contains a total area of α when H_0 is true and the nonrejection region contains a total area of $1 - \alpha$ when H_0 is true. Because $\alpha = 0.05$ in the cereal example, the critical values of the Z_{STAT} test statistic are -1.96 and $+1.96$. The rejection region is therefore $Z_{STAT} < -1.96$ or $Z_{STAT} > +1.96$. The nonrejection region is $-1.96 \leq Z_{STAT} \leq +1.96$.

Step 5: Collect the sample data and compute the value of the test statistic. In the cereal example, $\bar{X} = 372.5$, and the value of the test statistic is $Z_{STAT} = +1.50$.

Step 6: State the statistical decision and the managerial conclusion. First, determine whether the test statistic has fallen into the rejection region or the nonrejection region. For the cereal example, $Z_{STAT} = +1.50$ is in the region of nonrejection because

$-1.96 \leq Z_{STAT} = +1.50 \leq +1.96$. Because the test statistic falls into the nonrejection region, the statistical decision is to not reject the null hypothesis, H_0. The managerial conclusion is that insufficient evidence exists to prove that the mean fill is different from 368 grams. No corrective action on the filling process is needed.

EXAMPLE 9.3

Testing and Rejecting a Null Hypothesis

You are the manager of a fast-food restaurant. The business problem is to determine whether the population mean waiting time to place an order has changed in the past month from its previous population mean value of 4.5 minutes. From past experience, you can assume that the population is normally distributed, with a population standard deviation of 1.2 minutes. You select a sample of 25 orders during a one-hour period. The sample mean is 5.1 minutes. Use the six-step approach listed in Exhibit 9.1 on page 304 to determine whether there is evidence at the 0.05 level of significance that the population mean waiting time to place an order has changed in the past month from its previous population mean value of 4.5 minutes.

SOLUTION

Step 1: The null hypothesis is that the population mean has not changed from its previous value of 4.5 minutes:

$$H_0: \mu = 4.5$$

The alternative hypothesis is the opposite of the null hypothesis. Because the null hypothesis is that the population mean is 4.5 minutes, the alternative hypothesis is that the population mean is not 4.5 minutes:

$$H_1: \mu \neq 4.5$$

Step 2: You have selected a sample of $n = 25$. The level of significance is 0.05 (i.e., $\alpha = 0.05$).

Step 3: Because σ is assumed known, you use the normal distribution and the Z_{STAT} test statistic.

Step 4: Because $\alpha = 0.05$, the critical values of the Z_{STAT} test statistic are -1.96 and $+1.96$. The rejection region is $Z_{STAT} < -1.96$ or $Z_{STAT} > +1.96$. The nonrejection region is $-1.96 \leq Z_{STAT} \leq +1.96$

Step 5: You collect the sample data and compute $\overline{X} = 5.1$. Using Equation (9.1) on page 302, you compute the test statistic:

$$Z_{STAT} = \frac{\overline{X} - \mu}{\frac{\sigma}{\sqrt{n}}} = \frac{5.1 - 4.5}{\frac{1.2}{\sqrt{25}}} = +2.50$$

Step 6: Because $Z_{STAT} = +2.50 > +1.96$, you reject the null hypothesis. You conclude that there is evidence that the population mean waiting time to place an order has changed from its previous value of 4.5 minutes. The mean waiting time for customers is longer now than it was last month. As manager, you would now want to determine how waiting time could be reduced to improve service.

Hypothesis Testing Using the *p*-Value Approach

Using a *p*-value to determine rejection and nonrejection is another approach to hypothesis testing.

> **p-VALUE**
>
> The **p-value** is the probability of getting a test statistic equal to or more extreme than the sample result, given that the null hypothesis, H_0, is true. (The *p*-value is also known as the *observed level of significance*.)

The decision rules for rejecting H_0 in the *p*-value approach are

- If the *p*-value is greater than or equal to α, do not reject the null hypothesis.
- If the *p*-value is less than α, reject the null hypothesis.

Many people confuse these rules, mistakenly believing that a high p-value is reason for rejection. You can avoid this confusion by remembering the following mantra:

If the p-value is low, then H_0 must go.

To understand the p-value approach, consider the Oxford Cereals scenario. You tested whether the mean fill was equal to 368 grams. The test statistic resulted in a Z_{STAT} value of +1.50, and you did not reject the null hypothesis because +1.50 was less than the upper critical value of +1.96 and greater than the lower critical value of −1.96.

To use the p-value approach for the *two-tail test*, you find the probability of getting a test statistic Z_{STAT} that is equal to or *more extreme than* 1.50 standard error units from the center of a standardized normal distribution. In other words, you need to compute the probability of a Z_{STAT} value greater than +1.50, along with the probability of a Z_{STAT} value less than −1.50. Table E.2 shows that the probability of a Z_{STAT} value below −1.50 is 0.0668. The probability of a value below +1.50 is 0.9332, and the probability of a value above +1.50 is $1 − 0.9332 = 0.0668$. Therefore, the p-value for this two-tail test is $0.0668 + 0.0668 = 0.1336$ (see Figure 9.4). Thus, the probability of a test statistic equal to or more extreme than the sample result is 0.1336. Because 0.1336 is greater than $\alpha = 0.05$, you do not reject the null hypothesis.

FIGURE 9.4

Finding a p-value for a two-tail test

In this example, the observed sample mean is 372.5 grams, 4.5 grams above the hypothesized value, and the p-value is 0.1336. Thus, if the population mean is 368 grams, there is a 13.36% chance that the sample mean differs from 368 grams by at least 4.5 grams (i.e., is ≥372.5 grams or ≤363.5 grams). Therefore, even though 372.5 is above the hypothesized value of 368, a result as extreme as or more extreme than 372.5 is not highly unlikely when the population mean is 368.

Unless you are dealing with a test statistic that follows the normal distribution, you will only be able to approximate the p-value from the tables of the distribution. However, programs such as Microsoft Excel can compute the p-value for any hypothesis test. If you have access to a program that computes p-values, you can substitute the p-value approach for the critical value approach when you do hypothesis testing.

Figure 9.5 shows a worksheet solution for the cereal-filling example discussed in this section. Although the worksheet uses the p-value approach in cell A18 to determine rejection or nonrejection, the worksheet also includes the Z_{STAT} test statistic and critical values.

FIGURE 9.5

Worksheet for the Z test for the mean (σ known) for the cereal-filling example

Figure 9.5 displays the **COMPUTE worksheet** *of the* **Z Mean workbook**. *Create this worksheet using the instructions in Section EG9.1.*

	A	B	
1	Z Test for the Mean		
2			
3	**Data**		
4	Null Hypothesis μ=	368	
5	Level of Significance	0.05	
6	Population Standard Deviation	15	
7	Sample Size	25	
8	Sample Mean	372.5	
9			
10	**Intermediate Calculations**		
11	Standard Error of the Mean	3	=B6/SQRT(B7)
12	Z Test Statistic	1.5	=(B8 - B4)/B11
13			
14	**Two-Tail Test**		
15	Lower Critical Value	-1.9600	=NORMSINV(B5/2)
16	Upper Critical Value	1.9600	=NORMSINV(1 - B5/2)
17	p-Value	0.1336	=2 * (1 - NORMSDIST(ABS(B12)))
18	Do not reject the null hypothesis		=IF(B17 < B5, "Reject the null hypothesis",
			"Do not reject the null hypothesis")

Exhibit 9.2 summarizes the *p*-value approach to hypothesis testing.

> **EXHIBIT 9.2 THE *p*-VALUE APPROACH TO HYPOTHESIS TESTING**
> 1. State the null hypothesis, H_0, and the alternative hypothesis, H_1.
> 2. Choose the level of significance, α, and the sample size, n. The level of significance is based on the relative importance of the risks of committing Type I and Type II errors in the problem.
> 3. Determine the appropriate test statistic and the sampling distribution.
> 4. Collect the sample data, compute the value of the test statistic, and compute the *p*-value.
> 5. Make the statistical decision and state the managerial conclusion. If the *p*-value is greater than or equal to α, you do not reject the null hypothesis. If the *p*-value is less than α, you reject the null hypothesis. Remember the mantra: If the *p*-value is low, then H_0 must go. The managerial conclusion is written in the context of the real-world problem.

EXAMPLE 9.4

Testing and Rejecting a Null Hypothesis Using the *p*-Value Approach

You are the manager of a fast-food restaurant. The business problem is to determine whether the population mean waiting time to place an order has changed in the past month from its previous value of 4.5 minutes. From past experience, you can assume that the population standard deviation is 1.2 minutes. You select a sample of 25 orders during a one-hour period. The sample mean is 5.1 minutes. Use the five-step *p*-value approach of Exhibit 9.2 to determine whether there is evidence that the population mean waiting time to place an order has changed in the past month from its previous population mean value of 4.5 minutes.

SOLUTION

Step 1: The null hypothesis is that the population mean has not changed from its previous value of 4.5 minutes:

$$H_0: \mu = 4.5$$

The alternative hypothesis is the opposite of the null hypothesis. Because the null hypothesis is that the population mean is 4.5 minutes, the alternative hypothesis is that the population mean is not 4.5 minutes:

$$H_1: \mu \neq 4.5$$

Step 2: You have selected a sample of $n = 25$, and you have chosen a 0.05 level of significance (i.e., $\alpha = 0.05$).

Step 3: Select the appropriate test statistic. Because σ is assumed known, you use the normal distribution and the Z_{STAT} test statistic.

Step 4: You collect the sample data and compute $\bar{X} = 5.1$ Using Equation (9.1) on page 302, you compute the test statistic as follows:

$$Z_{STAT} = \frac{\bar{X} - \mu}{\dfrac{\sigma}{\sqrt{n}}} = \frac{5.1 - 4.5}{\dfrac{1.2}{\sqrt{25}}} = +2.50$$

To find the probability of getting a Z_{STAT} test statistic that is equal to or more extreme than 2.50 standard error units from the center of a standardized normal distribution, you compute the probability of a Z_{STAT} value greater than $+2.50$ along with the probability of a Z_{STAT} value less than -2.50. From Table E.2, the probability of a Z_{STAT} value below -2.50 is 0.0062. The probability of a value below $+2.50$ is 0.9938. Therefore, the probability of a value above $+2.50$ is $1 - 0.9938 = 0.0062$. Thus, the *p*-value for this two-tail test is $0.0062 + 0.0062 = 0.0124$.

Step 5: Because the *p*-value $= 0.0124 < \alpha = 0.05$, you reject the null hypothesis. You conclude that there is evidence that the population mean waiting time to place an order has changed from its previous population mean value of 4.5 minutes. The mean waiting time for customers is longer now than it was last month.

A Connection Between Confidence Interval Estimation and Hypothesis Testing

This chapter and Chapter 8 discuss confidence interval estimation and hypothesis testing, the two major elements of statistical inference. Although confidence interval estimation and hypothesis testing share the same conceptual foundation, they are used for different purposes. In Chapter 8, confidence intervals estimated parameters. In this chapter, hypothesis testing makes decisions about specified values of population parameters. Hypothesis tests are used when trying to prove that a parameter is less than, more than, or not equal to a specified value. Proper interpretation of a confidence interval, however, can also indicate whether a parameter is less than, more than, or not equal to a specified value. For example, in this section, you tested whether the population mean fill amount was different from 368 grams by using Equation (9.1) on page 302:

$$Z_{STAT} = \frac{\overline{X} - \mu}{\dfrac{\sigma}{\sqrt{n}}}$$

Instead of testing the null hypothesis that $\mu = 368$ grams, you can reach the same conclusion by constructing a confidence interval estimate of μ. If the hypothesized value of $\mu = 368$ is contained within the interval, you do not reject the null hypothesis because 368 would not be considered an unusual value. However, if the hypothesized value does not fall into the interval, you reject the null hypothesis because "$\mu = 368$ grams" is then considered an unusual value. Using Equation (8.1) on page 255 and the following data:

$$n = 25, \overline{X} = 372.5 \text{ grams}, \sigma = 15 \text{ grams}$$

for a confidence level of 95% (i.e., $\alpha = 0.05$),

$$\overline{X} \pm Z_{\alpha/2} \frac{\sigma}{\sqrt{n}}$$

$$372.5 \pm (1.96)\frac{15}{\sqrt{25}}$$

$$372.5 \pm 5.88$$

so that

$$366.62 \leq \mu \leq 378.38$$

Because the interval includes the hypothesized value of 368 grams, you do not reject the null hypothesis. There is insufficient evidence that the mean fill amount over the entire filling process is not 368 grams. You reached the same decision by using two-tail hypothesis testing.

Can You Ever Know the Population Standard Deviation?

The end of Section 8.1 discussed how learning a confidence interval estimation method that required knowing σ, the population standard deviation, served as an effective introduction to the concept of a confidence interval. That passage then revealed you would be unlikely to use that procedure for most practical application for several reasons.

Likewise, for most practical applications, you are unlikely to use a hypothesis-testing method that requires knowing σ. If you knew the population standard deviation, you would also know the population mean and would not need to form a hypothesis about the mean and then test that hypothesis. So why study a hypothesis testing of the mean that requires that σ is known? Using such a test makes it much easier to explain the fundamentals of hypothesis testing. With a known population standard deviation, you can use the normal distribution and compute p-values using the tables of the normal distribution.

Because it is important that you understand the test of hypothesis concept when reading the rest of this book, review this section carefully to understand the underlying concept—even if you anticipate never having a practical reason to use the test represented by Equation (9.1).

Problems for Section 9.1

LEARNING THE BASICS

9.1 If you use a 0.05 level of significance in a (two-tail) hypothesis test, what will you decide if $Z_{STAT} = -0.76$?

9.2 If you use a 0.05 level of significance in a (two-tail) hypothesis test, what will you decide if $Z_{STAT} = +2.21$?

9.3 If you use a 0.10 level of significance in a (two-tail) hypothesis test, what is your decision rule for rejecting a null hypothesis that the population mean is 500 if you use the Z test?

9.4 If you use a 0.01 level of significance in a (two-tail) hypothesis test, what is your decision rule for rejecting $H_0: \mu = 12.5$ if you use the Z test?

9.5 What is your decision in Problem 9.4 if $Z_{STAT} = -2.61$?

9.6 What is the p-value if, in a two-tail hypothesis test, $Z_{STAT} = +2.00$?

9.7 In Problem 9.6, what is your statistical decision if you test the null hypothesis at the 0.10 level of significance?

9.8 What is the p-value if, in a two-tail hypothesis test, $Z_{STAT} = -1.38$?

APPLYING THE CONCEPTS

9.9 In the U.S. legal system, a defendant is presumed innocent until proven guilty. Consider a null hypothesis, H_0, that the defendant is innocent, and an alternative hypothesis, H_1, that the defendant is guilty. A jury has two possible decisions: Convict the defendant (i.e., reject the null hypothesis) or do not convict the defendant (i.e., do not reject the null hypothesis). Explain the meaning of the risks of committing either a Type I or Type II error in this example.

9.10 Suppose the defendant in Problem 9.9 is presumed guilty until proven innocent, as in some other judicial systems. How do the null and alternative hypotheses differ from those in Problem 9.9? What are the meanings of the risks of committing either a Type I or Type II error here?

9.11 The U.S. Food and Drug Administration (FDA) is responsible for approving new drugs. Many consumer groups feel that the approval process is too easy and, therefore, too many drugs are approved that are later found to be unsafe. On the other hand, a number of industry lobbyists have pushed for a more lenient approval process so that pharmaceutical companies can get new drugs approved more easily and quickly (data extracted from R. Sharpe, "FDA Tries to Find Right Balance on Drug Approvals," *The Wall Street Journal*, April 20, 1999, p. A24). Consider a null hypothesis that a new, unapproved drug is unsafe and an alternative hypothesis that a new, unapproved drug is safe.
a. Explain the risks of committing a Type I or Type II error.

b. Which type of error are the consumer groups trying to avoid? Explain.
c. Which type of error are the industry lobbyists trying to avoid? Explain.
d. How would it be possible to lower the chances of both Type I and Type II errors?

9.12 As a result of complaints from both students and faculty about lateness, the registrar at a large university wants to adjust the scheduled class times to allow for adequate travel time between classes and is ready to undertake a study. Until now, the registrar has believed that there should be 20 minutes between scheduled classes. State the null hypothesis, H_0, and the alternative hypothesis, H_1.

9.13 Do students at your school study more than, less than, or about the same as students at other business schools? *BusinessWeek* reported that at the top 50 business schools, students studied an average of 14.6 hours per week (data extracted from "Cracking the Books," Special Report/Online Extra, **www.businessweek.com**, March 19, 2007). Set up a hypothesis test to try to prove that the mean number of hours studied at your school is different from the 14.6-hour per week benchmark reported by *BusinessWeek*.
a. State the null and alternative hypotheses.
b. What is a Type I error for your test?
c. What is a Type II error for your test?

☑SELF **9.14** The quality-control manager at a light bulb
Test factory needs to determine whether the mean life of a large shipment of light bulbs is equal to 375 hours. The population standard deviation is 100 hours. A random sample of 64 light bulbs indicates a sample mean life of 350 hours.
a. At the 0.05 level of significance, is there evidence that the mean life is different from 375 hours?
b. Compute the p-value and interpret its meaning.
c. Construct a 95% confidence interval estimate of the population mean life of the light bulbs.
d. Compare the results of (a) and (c). What conclusions do you reach?

9.15 The manager of a paint supply store wants to determine whether the mean amount of paint contained in 1-gallon cans purchased from a nationally known manufacturer is actually 1 gallon. You know from the manufacturer's specifications that the standard deviation of the amount of paint is 0.02 gallon. You select a random sample of 50 cans, and the mean amount of paint per 1-gallon can is 0.995 gallon.
a. Is there evidence that the mean amount is different from 1.0 gallon (use $\alpha = 0.01$)?
b. Compute the p-value and interpret its meaning.
c. Construct a 99% confidence interval estimate of the population mean amount of paint.
d. Compare the results of (a) and (c). What conclusions do you reach?

9.2 t Test of Hypothesis for the Mean (σ Unknown)

In virtually all hypothesis-testing situations concerning the population mean, μ, you do not know the population standard deviation, σ. Instead, you use the sample standard deviation, S. If you assume that the population is normally distributed, the sampling distribution of the mean follows a t distribution with $n - 1$ degrees of freedom, and you use the **t test for the mean**. If the population is not normally distributed, you can still use the t test if the sample size is large enough for the Central Limit Theorem to take effect (see Section 7.4). Equation (9.2) defines the test statistic for determining the difference between the sample mean, $\overline{X}$, and the population mean, μ, when using the sample standard deviation, S.

> ### t TEST OF HYPOTHESIS FOR THE MEAN (σ UNKNOWN)
>
> $$t_{STAT} = \frac{\overline{X} - \mu}{\dfrac{S}{\sqrt{n}}} \qquad (9.2)$$
>
> where the t_{STAT} test statistic follows a t distribution having $n - 1$ degrees of freedom.

To illustrate the use of the t test for the mean, return to the Chapter 8 Saxon Home Improvement scenario on page 251. The business objective is to determine whether the mean amount per sales invoice is unchanged from the $120 of the last five years. As an accountant for the company, you need to determine if this amount changes. In other words, the hypothesis test is used to try to prove that the mean amount per sales invoice is increasing or decreasing.

The Critical Value Approach

To perform this two-tail hypothesis test, you use the six-step method listed in Exhibit 9.1 on page 304.

Step 1: You define the following hypotheses:

$H_0: \mu = \$120$

$H_1: \mu \neq \$120$

The alternative hypothesis contains the statement you are trying to prove. If the null hypothesis is rejected, then there is statistical proof that the population mean amount per sales invoice is no longer $120. If the statistical conclusion is "do not reject H_0," then you will conclude that there is insufficient evidence to prove that the mean amount differs from the long-term mean of $120.

Step 2: You collect the data from a sample of $n = 12$ sales invoices. You decide to use $\alpha = 0.05$.

Step 3: Because σ is unknown, you use the t distribution and the t_{STAT} test statistic. You must assume that the population of sales invoices is normally distributed since the sample size of 12 is too small for the Central Limit Theorem to take effect. This assumption is discussed on page 312.

Step 4: For a given sample size, n, the test statistic t_{STAT} follows a t distribution with $n - 1$ degrees of freedom. The critical values of the t distribution with $12 - 1 = 11$ degrees of freedom are found in Table E.3, as illustrated in Table 9.2 and Figure 9.6. The alternative hypothesis, $H_1: \mu \neq \$120$, has two tails. The area in the rejection region of the t distribution's left (lower) tail is 0.025, and the area in the rejection region of the t distribution's right (upper) tail is also 0.025.

From the t table as given in Table E.3, a portion of which is shown in Table 9.2, the critical values are ± 2.2010. The decision rule is

$$\text{Reject } H_0 \text{ if } t_{STAT} < -t_{\alpha/2} = -2.2010$$

$$\text{or if } t_{STAT} > t_{\alpha/2} = +2.2010;$$

$$\text{otherwise, do not reject } H_0.$$

TABLE 9.2

Determining the Critical Value from the *t* Table for an Area of 0.025 in Each Tail, with 11 Degrees of Freedom

	Cumulative Probabilities					
	.75	.90	.95	.975	.99	.995
	Upper-Tail Areas					
Degrees of Freedom	.25	.10	.05	.025	.01	.005
1	1.0000	3.0777	6.3138	12.7062	31.8207	63.6574
2	0.8165	1.8856	2.9200	4.3027	6.9646	9.9248
3	0.7649	1.6377	2.3534	3.1824	4.5407	5.8409
4	0.7407	1.5332	2.1318	2.7764	3.7469	4.6041
5	0.7267	1.4759	2.0150	2.5706	3.3649	4.0322
6	0.7176	1.4398	1.9432	2.4469	3.1427	3.7074
7	0.7111	1.4149	1.8946	2.3646	2.9980	3.4995
8	0.7064	1.3968	1.8595	2.3060	2.8965	3.3554
9	0.7027	1.3830	1.8331	2.2622	2.8214	3.2498
10	0.6998	1.3722	1.8125	2.2281	2.7638	3.1693
11	0.6974	1.3634	1.7959	2.2010	2.7181	3.1058

Source: *Extracted from Table E.3.*

FIGURE 9.6

Testing a hypothesis about the mean (σ unknown) at the 0.05 level of significance with 11 degrees of freedom

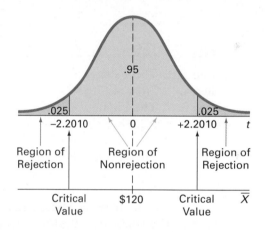

Step 5: You organize and store the data from a random sample of 12 sales invoices in **Invoices**:

108.98 152.22 111.45 110.59 127.46 107.26
93.32 91.97 111.56 75.71 128.58 135.11

Using Equations (3.1) and (3.7) on pages 87 and 93,

$$\bar{X} = \frac{\sum_{i=1}^{n} X_i}{n} = \$112.85 \quad \text{and} \quad S = \sqrt{\frac{\sum_{i=1}^{n}(X_i - \bar{X})^2}{n-1}} = \$20.80$$

From Equation (9.2) on page 310,

$$t_{STAT} = \frac{\bar{X} - \mu}{\frac{S}{\sqrt{n}}} = \frac{112.85 - 120}{\frac{20.80}{\sqrt{12}}} = -1.1908$$

Figure 9.7 shows a worksheet solution for this test of hypothesis.

Step 6: To analyze the results, because $-2.2010 < t_{STAT} = -1.1908 < 2.2010$, you do not reject H_0. You have insufficient evidence to conclude that the mean amount per sales invoice differs from $120. The audit suggests that the mean amount per invoice has not changed.

FIGURE 9.7

Worksheet for the *t* test of sales invoices

Figure 9.7 displays the COMPUTE worksheet of the T Mean workbook. Create this worksheet using the instructions in Section EG9.2.

	A	B	
1	t Test for the Hypothesis of the Mean		
2			
3	**Data**		
4	Null Hypothesis μ=	120	
5	Level of Significance	0.05	
6	Sample Size	12	
7	Sample Mean	112.85	
8	Sample Standard Deviation	20.8	
9			
10	**Intermediate Calculations**		
11	Standard Error of the Mean	6.0044	=B8/SQRT(B6)
12	Degrees of Freedom	11	=B6 - 1
13	t Test Statistic	-1.1908	=(B7 - B4)/B11
14			
15	**Two-Tail Test**		
16	Lower Critical Value	-2.2010	=-TINV(B5, B12)
17	Upper Critical Value	2.2010	=TINV(B5, B12)
18	p -Value	0.2588	=TDIST(ABS(B13), B12, 2)
19	Do not reject the null hypothesis		=IF(B18 < B5, "Reject the null hypothesis", "Do not reject the null hypothesis")

The *p*-Value Approach

Step 1–3. These steps are the same as in the critical value approach.

Step 4. From the Figure 9.7 worksheet, $t_{STAT} = -1.19$ and the *p*-value = 0.2588.

Step 5. The Figure 9.7 worksheet results show that the *p*-value for this two-tail test is 0.2588. Because the *p*-value of 0.2588 is greater than $\alpha = 0.05$, you do not reject H_0. The data provide insufficient evidence to conclude that the mean amount per sales invoice differs from $120. The audit suggests that the mean amount per invoice has not changed. The *p*-value indicates that if the null hypothesis is true, the probability that a sample of 12 invoices could have a sample mean that differs by $7.15 or more from the stated $120 is 0.2588. In other words, if the mean amount per sales invoice is truly $120, then there is a 25.88% chance of observing a sample mean below $112.85 or above $127.15.

In the preceding example, it is incorrect to state that there is a 25.88% chance that the null hypothesis is true. Remember that the *p*-value is a conditional probability, calculated by *assuming* that the null hypothesis is true. In general, it is proper to state the following:

If the null hypothesis is true, there is a (*p*-value) × 100% chance of observing a test statistic at least as contradictory to the null hypothesis as the sample result.

Checking the Normality Assumption

You use the *t* test when the population standard deviation, σ, is not known and is estimated using the sample standard deviation, *S*. To use the *t* test, you assume that the data represent a random sample from a population that is normally distributed. In practice, as long as the sample size is not very small and the population is not very skewed, the *t* distribution provides a good approximation to the sampling distribution of the mean when σ is unknown.

There are several ways to evaluate the normality assumption necessary for using the *t* test. You can examine how closely the sample statistics match the normal distribution's theoretical properties. You can also construct a histogram, stem-and-leaf display, boxplot, or normal probability plot to visualize the distribution of the sales invoice amounts. For details on evaluating normality, see Section 6.3 on pages 206–209.

Descriptive statistics, a boxplot, and a normal probability plot for the sales invoice data are shown in Figures 9.8 through 9.10.

FIGURE 9.8

Worksheet for the sales invoice data descriptive statistics

Compute descriptive statistics using the instructions of Section EG3.2.

	A	B
1	**Invoice Amount**	
2		
3	Mean	112.8508
4	Standard Error	6.0039
5	Median	111.02
6	Mode	#N/A
7	Standard Deviation	20.7980
8	Sample Variance	432.5565
9	Kurtosis	0.1727
10	Skewness	0.1336
11	Range	76.51
12	Minimum	75.71
13	Maximum	152.22
14	Sum	1354.21
15	Count	12

FIGURE 9.9

Boxplot for the sales invoice data

Create boxplots using the instructions in Section EG3.3.

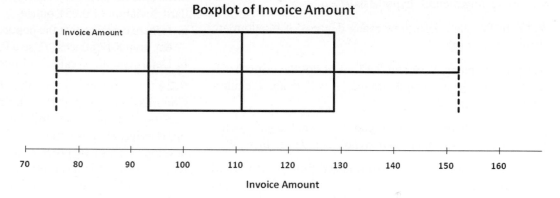

FIGURE 9.10

Normal probability plot for the sales invoice data

Create normal probability plots using the instructions in Section EG6.3.

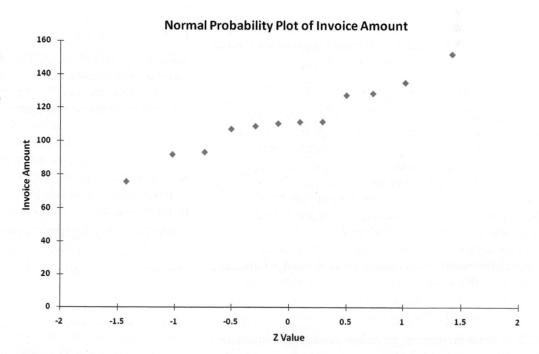

The mean is very close to the median, and the points on the normal probability plot appear to be increasing approximately in a straight line. The boxplot appears approximately symmetrical. Thus, you can assume that the population of sales invoices is approximately normally distributed. The normality assumption is valid, and therefore the auditor's results are valid.

The t test is a **robust** test. It does not lose power if the shape of the population departs somewhat from a normal distribution, particularly when the sample size is large enough to enable the test statistic t to be influenced by the Central Limit Theorem (see Section 7.4). However, you can reach erroneous conclusions and can lose statistical power if you use the t test incorrectly. If the sample size, n, is small (i.e., less than 30) and you cannot easily make the assumption that the underlying population is at least approximately normally distributed, then *nonparametric* testing procedures are more appropriate (see references 1 and 2).

Problems for Section 9.2

LEARNING THE BASICS

9.16 If, in a sample of $n = 16$ selected from a normal population, $\bar{X} = 56$ and $S = 12$, what is the value of t_{STAT} if you are testing the null hypothesis $H_0: \mu = 50$?

9.17 In Problem 9.16, how many degrees of freedom are there in the t test?

9.18 In Problems 9.16 and 9.17, what are the critical values of t if the level of significance, α, is 0.05 and the alternative hypothesis, H_1, is $\mu \neq 50$?

9.19 In Problems 9.16, 9.17, and 9.18, what is your statistical decision if the alternative hypothesis, H_1, is $\mu \neq 50$?

9.20 If, in a sample of $n = 16$ selected from a left-skewed population, $\bar{X} = 65$, and $S = 21$, would you use the t test to test the null hypothesis $H_0: \mu = 60$? Discuss.

9.21 If, in a sample of $n = 160$ selected from a left-skewed population, $\bar{X} = 65$, and $S = 21$, would you use the t test to test the null hypothesis $H_0: \mu = 60$? Discuss.

APPLYING THE CONCEPTS

SELF Test **9.22** You are the manager of a restaurant for a fast-food franchise. Last month, the mean waiting time at the drive-through window for branches in your geographical region, as measured from the time a customer places an order until the time the customer receives the order, was 3.7 minutes. You select a random sample of 64 orders. The sample mean waiting time is 3.57 minutes, with a sample standard deviation of 0.8 minute.
a. At the 0.05 level of significance, is there evidence that the population mean waiting time is different from 3.7 minutes?
b. Because the sample size is 64, do you need to be concerned about the shape of the population distribution when conducting the t test in (a)? Explain.

9.23 A manufacturer of chocolate candies uses machines to package candies as they move along a filling line. Although the packages are labeled as 8 ounces, the company wants the packages to contain a mean of 8.17 ounces so that virtually none of the packages contain less than 8 ounces. A sample of 50 packages is selected periodically, and the packaging process is stopped if there is evidence that the mean amount packaged is different from 8.17 ounces. Suppose that in a particular sample of 50 packages, the mean amount dispensed is 8.159 ounces, with a sample standard deviation of 0.051 ounce.
a. Is there evidence that the population mean amount is different from 8.17 ounces? (Use a 0.05 level of significance.)
b. Determine the p-value and interpret its meaning.

9.24 In a recent year, the Federal Communications Commission reported that the mean wait for repairs for Verizon customers was 36.5 hours. In an effort to improve this service, suppose that a new repair service process was developed. This new process, when used for a sample of 100 repairs, resulted in a sample mean of 34.5 hours and a sample standard deviation of 11.7 hours.
a. Is there evidence that the population mean amount is different from 36.5 hours? (Use a 0.05 level of significance.)
b. Determine the p-value and interpret its meaning.

9.25 In a recent year, the Federal Communications Commission reported that the mean wait for repairs for AT&T customers was 25.3 hours. In an effort to improve this service, suppose that a new repair service process was developed. This new process, when used for a sample of 100 repairs, resulted in a sample mean of 22.3 hours and a sample standard deviation of 8.3 hours.
a. Is there evidence that the population mean amount is different from 25.3 hours? (Use a 0.05 level of significance.)
b. Determine the p-value and interpret its meaning.

9.26 The file MoviePrices contains prices (in dollars) for two tickets, with online service charges, large popcorn, and two medium soft drinks at a sample of six theater chains:

36.15 31.00 35.05 40.25 33.75 43.00

Source: *Data extracted from K. Kelly, "The Multiplex Under Siege," The Wall Street Journal, December 24–25, 2005, pp. P1, P5.*

a. At the 0.05 level of significance, is there evidence that the mean price for two movie tickets, with online service charges, large popcorn, and two medium soft drinks, is different from $35?
b. Determine the p-value in (a) and interpret its meaning.

c. What assumption must you make about the population distribution in order to conduct the *t* test in (a) and (b)?

d. Because the sample size is 6, do you need to be concerned about the shape of the population distribution when conducting the *t* test in (a)? Explain.

9.27 In New York State, savings banks are permitted to sell a form of life insurance called savings bank life insurance (SBLI). The approval process consists of underwriting, which includes a review of the application, a medical information bureau check, possible requests for additional medical information and medical exams, and a policy compilation stage in which the policy pages are generated and sent to the bank for delivery. The ability to deliver approved policies to customers in a timely manner is critical to the profitability of this service. During a period of one month, a random sample of 27 approved policies is selected, and the total processing time, in days, is recorded (and stored in Insurance):

73 19 16 64 28 28 31 90 60 56 31 56 22 18
45 48 17 17 17 91 92 63 50 51 69 16 17

a. In the past, the mean processing time was 45 days. At the 0.05 level of significance, is there evidence that the mean processing time has changed from 45 days?

b. What assumption about the population distribution is needed in order to conduct the *t* test in (a)?

c. Construct a boxplot or a normal probability plot to evaluate the assumption made in (b).

d. Do you think that the assumption needed in order to conduct the *t* test in (a) is valid? Explain.

9.28 The following data (in Drink) represent the amount of soft-drink filled in a sample of 50 consecutive 2-liter bottles. The results, listed horizontally in the order of being filled, were

2.109 2.086 2.066 2.075 2.065 2.057 2.052 2.044 2.036 2.038

2.031 2.029 2.025 2.029 2.023 2.020 2.015 2.014 2.013 2.014

2.012 2.012 2.012 2.010 2.005 2.003 1.999 1.996 1.997 1.992

1.994 1.986 1.984 1.981 1.973 1.975 1.971 1.969 1.966 1.967

1.963 1.957 1.951 1.951 1.947 1.941 1.941 1.938 1.908 1.894

a. At the 0.05 level of significance, is there evidence that the mean amount of soft drink filled is different from 2.0 liters?

b. Determine the *p*-value in (a) and interpret its meaning.

c. In (a), you assumed that the distribution of the amount of soft drink filled was normally distributed. Evaluate this assumption by constructing a boxplot or a normal probability plot.

d. Do you think that the assumption needed in order to conduct the *t* test in (a) is valid? Explain.

e. Examine the values of the 50 bottles in their sequential order, as given in the problem. Is there a pattern to the results? If so, what impact might this pattern have on the validity of the results in (a)?

9.29 One of the major measures of the quality of service provided by any organization is the speed with which it responds to customer complaints. A large family-held department store selling furniture and flooring, including carpet, had undergone a major expansion in the past several years. In particular, the flooring department had expanded from 2 installation crews to an installation supervisor, a measurer, and 15 installation crews. The store had the business objective of improving its response to complaints. The variable of interest was defined as the number of days between when the complaint was made and when it was resolved. Data were collected from 50 complaints that were made in the last year. The data were stored in Furniture, and are as follows:

54   5 35 137 31 27 152   2 123 81 74 27
11 19 126 110 110 29 61 35 94 31 26   5
12   4 165 32 29 28 29 26 25   1 14 13
13 10   5 27   4 52 30 22 36 26 20 23
33 68

a. The installation supervisor claims that the mean number of days between the receipt of a complaint and the resolution of the complaint is 20 days. At the 0.05 level of significance, is there evidence that the claim is not true (i.e., that the mean number of days is different from 20)?

b. What assumption about the population distribution is needed in order to conduct the *t* test in (a)?

c. Construct a boxplot or a normal probability plot to evaluate the assumption made in (b).

d. Do you think that the assumption needed in order to conduct the *t* test in (a) is valid? Explain.

9.30 A manufacturing company produces steel housings for electrical equipment. The main component part of the housing is a steel trough that is made out of a 14-gauge steel coil. It is produced using a 250-ton progressive punch press with a wipe-down operation that puts two 90-degree forms in the flat steel to make the trough. The distance from one side of the form to the other is critical because of weatherproofing in outdoor applications. The company requires that the width of the trough be between 8.31 inches and 8.61 inches. The file Trough contains the widths of the troughs, in inches, for a sample of *n* = 49:

8.312 8.343 8.317 8.383 8.348 8.410 8.351 8.373 8.481 8.422

8.476 8.382 8.484 8.403 8.414 8.419 8.385 8.465 8.498 8.447

8.436 8.413 8.489 8.414 8.481 8.415 8.479 8.429 8.458 8.462

8.460 8.444 8.429 8.460 8.412 8.420 8.410 8.405 8.323 8.420

8.396 8.447 8.405 8.439 8.411 8.427 8.420 8.498 8.409

a. At the 0.05 level of significance, is there evidence that the mean width of the troughs is different from 8.46 inches?

b. What assumption about the population distribution is needed in order to conduct the *t* test in (a)?

c. Evaluate the assumption made in (b).

d. Do you think that the assumption needed in order to conduct the *t* test in (a) is valid? Explain.

9.31 One operation of a steel mill is to cut pieces of steel into parts that are used in the frame for front seats in an automobile. The steel is cut with a diamond saw and requires the resulting parts must be cut to be within ±0.005 inch of the length specified by the automobile company. The file **Steel** contains a sample of 100 steel parts. The measurement reported is the difference, in inches, between the actual length of the steel part, as measured by a laser measurement device, and the specified length of the steel part. For example, a value of −0.002 represents a steel part that is 0.002 inch shorter than the specified length.

a. At the 0.05 level of significance, is there evidence that the mean difference is not equal to 0.0 inches?

b. Construct a 95% confidence interval estimate of the population mean. Interpret this interval.

c. Compare the conclusions reached in (a) and (b).

d. Because $n = 100$, do you have to be concerned about the normality assumption needed for the t test and t interval?

9.32 In Problem 3.67 on page 125, you were introduced to a tea-bag-filling operation. An important quality characteristic of interest for this process is the weight of the tea in the individual bags. The file **Teabags** contains an ordered array of the weight, in grams, of a sample of 50 tea bags produced during an eight-hour shift.

a. Is there evidence that the mean amount of tea per bag is different from 5.5 grams (use $\alpha = 0.01$)?

b. Construct a 99% confidence interval estimate of the population mean amount of tea per bag. Interpret this interval.

c. Compare the conclusions reached in (a) and (b).

9.33 Although many people think they can put a meal on the table in a short period of time, an article reported that they end up spending about 40 minutes doing so (data extracted from N. Hellmich, "Americans Go for the Quick Fix for Dinner," *USA Today*, February 14, 2006). Suppose another study is conducted to test the validity of this statement. A sample of 25 people is selected, and the length of time to prepare and cook dinner (in minutes) is recorded, with the following results (in **Dinner**):

44.0 51.9 49.7 40.0 55.5 33.0 43.4 41.3 45.2 40.7 41.1 49.1 30.9

45.2 55.3 52.1 55.1 38.8 43.1 39.2 58.6 49.8 43.2 47.9 46.6

a. Is there evidence that the population mean time to prepare and cook dinner is different from 40 minutes? Use the p-value approach and a level of significance of 0.05.

b. What assumption about the population distribution is needed in order to conduct the t test in (a)?

c. Make a list of the various ways you could evaluate the assumption noted in (b).

d. Evaluate the assumption noted in (b) and determine whether the t test in (a) is valid.

9.3 One-Tail Tests

In Section 9.1, hypothesis testing was used to examine the question of whether the population mean amount of cereal filled is 368 grams. The alternative hypothesis ($H_1: \mu \neq 368$) contains two possibilities: Either the mean is less than 368 grams, or the mean is more than 368 grams. For this reason, the rejection region is divided into the two tails of the sampling distribution of the mean. In Section 9.2, a two-tail test was used to determine whether the mean amount per invoice had changed from $120.

In contrast to these two examples, many situations require an alternative hypothesis that focuses on a *particular direction*. For example, the population mean is *less than* a specified value. One such situation involves the business problem concerning the service time at the drive-through window of a fast-food restaurant. The speed with which customers are served is of critical importance to the success of the service (see **www.qsrmagazine.com/reports/drive-thru_time_study**). In a recent study, McDonald's had a mean service time of 158.77 seconds, which was the fifth best in the industry. Suppose that McDonald's has embarked on a quality improvement effort to reduce the service time and has developed improvements to the service process at the drive-through. Data from the new process will be collected from a test in a sample of 25 stores. Because McDonald's would only want to institute the new process in all of its stores if it resulted in *decreased* drive-through time, the entire rejection region is located in the lower tail of the distribution.

The Critical Value Approach

You wish to determine whether the new drive-through process has a mean that is less than 158.77 seconds. To perform this one-tail hypothesis test, you use the six-step method listed in Exhibit 9.1 on page 304.

Step 1: You define the null and alternative hypotheses.

$$H_0: \mu \geq 158.77$$

$$H_1: \mu < 158.77$$

The alternative hypothesis contains the statement you are trying to prove. If the conclusion of the test is "reject H_0," there is statistical proof that the mean drive-through time is less than the drive-through time in the old process. This would be reason to change the drive-through process for the entire population of stores. If the conclusion of the test is "do not reject H_0," then there is insufficient evidence to prove that the mean drive-through time in the new process is significantly less than the drive-through time in the old process. If this occurs, there would be insufficient reason to institute the new drive-through process in the population of stores.

Step 2: You collect the data by selecting a sample of $n = 25$ stores. You decide to use $\alpha = 0.05$.

Step 3: Because σ is unknown, you use the t distribution and the t_{STAT} test statistic. You must assume that the service time is normally distributed.

Step 4: The rejection region is entirely contained in the lower tail of the sampling distribution of the mean because you want to reject H_0 only when the sample mean is significantly less than 158.77 seconds. When the entire rejection region is contained in one tail of the sampling distribution of the test statistic, the test is called a **one-tail test**, or **directional test**. If the alternative hypothesis includes the *less than* sign, the critical value of t is negative. As shown in Table 9.3 and Figure 9.11, because the entire rejection region is in the lower tail of the t distribution and contains an area of 0.05, due to the symmetry of the t distribution, the critical value of the t test statistic with $25 - 1 = 24$ degrees of freedom is -1.7109.

The decision rule is

$$\text{Reject } H_0 \text{ if } t_{STAT} < -1.7109;$$

$$\text{otherwise, do not reject } H_0.$$

TABLE 9.3

Determining the Critical Value from the t Table for an Area of 0.05 in the Lower Tail, with 24 Degrees of Freedom

	Cumulative Probabilities					
	.75	.90	.95	.975	.99	.995
	Upper-Tail Areas					
Degrees of Freedom	.25	.10	.05	.025	.01	.005
1	1.0000	3.0777	6.3138	12.7062	31.8207	63.6574
2	0.8165	1.8856	2.9200	4.3027	6.9646	9.9248
3	0.7649	1.6377	2.3534	3.1824	4.5407	5.8409
.	.	.	.	.	.	.
.	.	.	.	.	.	.
.	.	.	.	.	.	.
23	0.6853	1.3195	1.7139	2.0687	2.4999	2.8073
24	0.6848	1.3178	1.7109	2.0639	2.4922	2.7969
25	0.6844	1.3163	1.7081	2.0595	2.4851	2.7874

Source: *Extracted from Table E.3.*

FIGURE 9.11

One-tail test of hypothesis for a mean (σ unknown) at the 0.05 level of significance

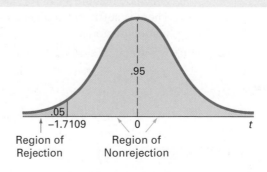

Step 5: From the sample of 25 stores you selected, you find that the sample mean service time at the drive-through equals 147.5 seconds and the sample standard deviation equals 20 seconds. Using $n = 25, \overline{X} = 147.5, S = 20$, and Equation (9.2) on page 310,

$$t_{STAT} = \frac{\overline{X} - \mu}{\frac{S}{\sqrt{n}}} = \frac{147.5 - 158.77}{\frac{20}{\sqrt{25}}} = -2.82$$

Step 6: Because $t_{STAT} = -2.82 < -1.7109$, you reject the null hypothesis (see Figure 9.11). You conclude that the mean service time at the drive-through is less than 158.77 seconds. There is sufficient evidence to change the drive-through process for the entire population of stores.

The p-Value Approach

Use the five steps listed in Exhibit 9.2 on page 307 to illustrate the t test for the drive-through time study using the p-value approach.

Step 1–3. These steps are the same as in the critical value approach on page 317.

Step 4. $t_{STAT} = -2.82$ (see step 5 of the critical value approach). Because the alternative hypothesis indicates a rejection region entirely in the *lower* tail of the sampling distribution, to compute the p-value you need to find the probability that the t_{STAT} test statistic will be less than –2.82. From Figure 9.12, the p-value is 0.0048.

FIGURE 9.12

Worksheet for the t test for the drive-through time study

Figure 9.12 displays the **COMPUTE_LOWER** *worksheet of the* **T Mean** *workbook. Create this worksheet using the instructions in Section EG9.3.*

	A	B	
1	t Test for the Hypothesis of the Mean		
2			
3	**Data**		
4	Null Hypothesis μ=	158.77	
5	Level of Significance	0.05	
6	Sample Size	25	
7	Sample Mean	147.5	
8	Sample Standard Deviation	20	
9			
10	**Intermediate Calculations**		
11	Standard Error of the Mean	4.0000	=B8/SQRT(B6)
12	Degrees of Freedom	24	=B6 - 1
13	t Test Statistic	-2.8175	=(B7 - B4)/B11
14			
15	**Lower-Tail Test**		
16	Lower Critical Value	-1.7109	=-TINV(2 * B5, B12)
17	p -Value	0.0048	=IF(B13 < 0, E22, E23)
18	Reject the null hypothesis		=IF(B17 < B5, "Reject the null hypothesis", "Do not reject the null hypothesis")

Not shown
Cell E22: =TDIST(ABS(B13), B12, 1)
Cell E23: =1 - E22

Step 5. The p-value of 0.0048 is less than $\alpha = 0.05$ (see Figure 9.13). You reject H_0, and conclude that the mean service time at the drive-through is less than 158.77 seconds. There is sufficient evidence to change the drive-through process for the entire population of stores.

FIGURE 9.13

Determining the p-value for a one-tail test

0.0048

.9952

–2.82 t

EXAMPLE 9.5

A One-Tail Test for the Mean

A company that manufactures chocolate bars is particularly concerned that the mean weight of a chocolate bar is not greater than 6.03 ounces. A sample of 50 chocolate bars is selected; the sample mean is 6.034 ounces, and the sample standard deviation is 0.02 ounces. Using the $\alpha = 0.01$ level of significance, is there evidence that the population mean weight of the chocolate bars is greater than 6.03 ounces?

SOLUTION Using the critical value approach,

Step 1: First, you define your hypotheses:

$$H_0: \mu \leq 6.03$$
$$H_1: \mu > 6.03$$

Step 2: You collect the data from a sample of $n = 50$. You decide to use $\alpha = 0.01$.

Step 3: Because σ is unknown, you use the t distribution and the t_{STAT} test statistic.

Step 4: The rejection region is entirely contained in the upper tail of the sampling distribution of the mean because you want to reject H_0 only when the sample mean is significantly greater than 6.03 ounces. Because the entire rejection region is in the upper tail of the t distribution and contains an area of 0.01, the critical value of the t distribution with $50 - 1 = 49$ degrees of freedom is 2.4049 (see Table E.3).

The decision rule is

Reject H_0 if $t_{STAT} > 2.4049$;

otherwise, do not reject H_0.

Step 5: From your sample of 50 chocolate bars, you find that the sample mean weight is 6.034 ounces, and the sample standard deviation is 0.02 ounces. Using $n = 50, \bar{X} = 6.034, S = 0.02$, and Equation (9.2) on page 310,

$$t_{STAT} = \frac{\bar{X} - \mu}{\frac{S}{\sqrt{n}}} = \frac{6.034 - 6.03}{\frac{0.02}{\sqrt{50}}} = 1.414$$

Step 6: Because $t_{STAT} = 1.414 < 2.4049$, or using Microsoft Excel, the p-value is $0.0818 > 0.01$, you do not reject the null hypothesis. There is insufficient evidence to conclude that the population mean weight is greater than 6.03 ounces.

To perform one-tail tests of hypotheses, you must properly formulate H_0 and H_1. A summary of the null and alternative hypotheses for one-tail tests is as follows:

- The null hypothesis, H_0, represents the status quo or the current belief in a situation.
- The alternative hypothesis, H_1, is the opposite of the null hypothesis and represents a research claim or specific inference you would like to prove.
- If you reject the null hypothesis, you have statistical proof that the alternative hypothesis is correct.
- If you do not reject the null hypothesis, then you have failed to prove the alternative hypothesis. The failure to prove the alternative hypothesis, however, does not mean that you have proven the null hypothesis.
- The null hypothesis always refers to a specified value of the *population parameter* (such as μ), not to a *sample statistic* (such as $\bar{X}$).
- The statement of the null hypothesis *always* contains an equal sign regarding the specified value of the parameter (e.g., $H_0: \mu \geq 158.77$).
- The statement of the alternative hypothesis *never* contains an equal sign regarding the specified value of the parameter (e.g., $H_1: \mu < 158.77$).

Problems for Section 9.3

LEARNING THE BASICS

9.34 In a one-tail hypothesis test where you reject H_0 only in the *upper* tail, what is the *p*-value if $Z_{STAT} = +2.00$?

9.35 In Problem 9.34, what is your statistical decision if you test the null hypothesis at the 0.05 level of significance?

9.36 In a one-tail hypothesis test where you reject H_0 only in the *lower* tail, what is the *p*-value if $Z_{STAT} = -1.38$?

9.37 In Problem 9.36, what is your statistical decision if you test the null hypothesis at the 0.01 level of significance?

9.38 In a one-tail hypothesis test where you reject H_0 only in the *lower* tail, what is the *p*-value if $Z_{STAT} = +1.38$?

9.39 In Problem 9.38, what is the statistical decision if you test the null hypothesis at the 0.01 level of significance?

9.40 In a one-tail hypothesis test where you reject H_0 only in the *upper* tail, what is the critical value of the *t*-test statistic with 10 degrees of freedom at the 0.01 level of significance?

9.41 In Problem 9.40, what is your statistical decision if $t_{STAT} = +2.39$?

9.42 In a one-tail hypothesis test where you reject H_0 only in the *lower* tail, what is the critical value of the t_{STAT} test statistic with 20 degrees of freedom at the 0.01 level of significance?

9.43 In Problem 9.42, what is your statistical decision if $t_{STAT} = -1.15$?

APPLYING THE CONCEPTS

9.44 In a recent year, the Federal Communications Commission reported that the mean wait for repairs for Verizon customers was 36.5 hours. In an effort to improve this service, suppose that a new repair service process was developed. This new process, used for a sample of 100 repairs, resulted in a sample mean of 34.5 hours and a sample standard deviation of 11.7 hours.
a. Is there evidence that the population mean amount is less than 36.5 hours? (Use a 0.05 level of significance.)
b. Determine the *p*-value and interpret its meaning.
c. Compare the results in (a) and (b) to those of Problem 9.24 (a) and (b) on page 314.

9.45 In a recent year, the Federal Communications Commission reported that the mean wait for repairs for AT&T customers was 25.3 hours. In an effort to improve this service, suppose that a new repair service process was developed. This new process, used for a sample of 100 repairs, resulted in a sample mean of 22.3 hours and a sample standard deviation of 8.3 hours.
a. Is there evidence that the population mean amount is less than 25.3 hours? (Use a 0.05 level of significance.)

b. Determine the *p*-value and interpret its meaning.
c. Compare the results in (a) and (b) to those of Problem 9.25 (a) and (b) on page 314.

 9.46 The Glen Valley Steel Company manufactures steel bars. If the production process is working properly, it turns out steel bars that are normally distributed with mean length of *at least* 2.8 feet. Longer steel bars can be used or altered, but shorter bars must be scrapped. You select a sample of 25 bars; the mean length is 2.73 feet, and the sample standard deviation is 0.20 foot.
a. If you test the null hypothesis at the 0.05 level of significance, what decision do you make using the critical value approach to hypothesis testing?
b. If you test the null hypothesis at the 0.05 level of significance, what decision do you make using the *p*-value approach to hypothesis testing?
c. Interpret the meaning of the *p*-value in this problem.
d. Compare your conclusions in (a) and (b).

9.47 You are the manager of a restaurant that delivers pizza to college dormitory rooms. You have just changed your delivery process in an effort to reduce the mean time between the order and completion of delivery from the current 25 minutes. A sample of 36 orders using the new delivery process yields a sample mean of 22.4 minutes and a sample standard deviation of 6 minutes.
a. Using the six-step critical value approach, at the 0.05 level of significance, is there evidence that the population mean delivery time has been reduced below the previous population mean value of 25 minutes?
b. At the 0.05 level of significance, use the five-step *p*-value approach.
c. Interpret the meaning of the *p*-value in (b).
d. Compare your conclusions in (a) and (b).

9.48 Children in the United States account directly for $36 billion in sales annually. When their indirect influence over product decisions from stereos to vacations is considered, the total economic spending affected by children in the United States is $290 billion. It is estimated that by age 10, a child makes an average of more than five trips a week to a store (data extracted from M. E. Goldberg, G. J. Gorn, L. A. Peracchio, and G. Bamossy, "Understanding Materialism Among Youth," *Journal of Consumer Psychology*, 2003, 13(3), pp. 278–288). Suppose that you want to prove that children in your city average more than five trips a week to a store. Let μ represent the population mean number of times children in your city make trips to a store.
a. State the null and alternative hypotheses.
b. Explain the meaning of the Type I and Type II errors in the context of this scenario.
c. Suppose that you carry out a similar study in the city in which you live. You take a sample of 100 children and

find that the mean number of trips to the store is 5.47 and the sample standard deviation of the number of trips to the store is 1.6. At the 0.01 level of significance, is there evidence that the population mean number of trips to the store is greater than 5 per week?

d. Interpret the meaning of the *p*-value in (c).

9.49 The population mean waiting time to check out of a supermarket has been 10.73 minutes. Recently, in an effort to reduce the waiting time, the supermarket has experimented with a system in which there is a single waiting line with multiple checkout servers. A sample of 100 customers was selected, and their mean waiting time to check out was 9.52 minutes, with a sample standard deviation of 5.8 minutes.

a. At the 0.05 level of significance, using the critical value approach to hypothesis testing, is there evidence that the population mean waiting time to check out is less than 10.73 minutes?

b. At the 0.05 level of significance, using the *p*-value approach to hypothesis testing, is there evidence that the population mean waiting time to check out is less than 10.73 minutes?

c. Interpret the meaning of the *p*-value in this problem.

d. Compare your conclusions in (a) and (b).

9.4 *Z* Test of Hypothesis for the Proportion

In some situations, you want to test a hypothesis about the proportion of events of interest in the population, π, rather than test the population mean. To begin, you select a random sample and compute the **sample proportion**, $p = X/n$. You then compare the value of this statistic to the hypothesized value of the parameter, π, in order to decide whether to reject the null hypothesis. If the number of events of interest (X) and the number of events that are not of interest ($n - X$) are each at least five, the sampling distribution of a proportion approximately follows a normal distribution. You use the **Z test for the proportion** given in Equation (9.3) to perform the hypothesis test for the difference between the sample proportion, p, and the hypothesized population proportion, π.

Z TEST FOR THE PROPORTION

$$Z_{STAT} = \frac{p - \pi}{\sqrt{\dfrac{\pi(1 - \pi)}{n}}} \tag{9.3}$$

where

$$p = \text{Sample proportion} = \frac{X}{n} = \frac{\text{Number of events of interest in the sample}}{\text{Sample size}}$$

$$\pi = \text{Hypothesized proportion of events of interest in the population}$$

The Z_{STAT} test statistic approximately follows a standardized normal distribution when X and $(n - X)$ are each at least 5.

Alternatively, by multiplying the numerator and denominator by n, you can write the Z_{STAT} test statistic in terms of the number of events of interest, X, as shown in Equation (9.4).

Z TEST FOR THE PROPORTION IN TERMS OF THE NUMBER OF EVENTS OF INTEREST

$$Z_{STAT} = \frac{X - n\pi}{\sqrt{n\pi(1 - \pi)}} \tag{9.4}$$

The Critical Value Approach

To illustrate the Z test for a proportion, consider a survey that sought to determine whether customer service is better or worse at e-commerce sites than it is at physical stores (data extracted from "Consumers Happier with E-Commerce," *USA Today*, March 13, 2007, p. 1B). Of 1,100 respondents, 561 stated that customer service was better at e-commerce sites than at physical stores. For this survey, the null and alternative hypotheses are stated as follows:

H_0: $\pi = 0.50$ (i.e., half of all consumers believe that customer service is better at e-commerce sites than at physical stores)

H_1: $\pi \neq 0.50$ (i.e., either less than half or more than half of all consumers believe that customer service is better at e-commerce sites than at physical stores)

Because you are interested in determining whether the population proportion of consumers who believe that customer service is better at e-commerce sites than at physical stores is less than or more than 0.50, you use a two-tail test. If you select the $\alpha = 0.05$ level of significance, the rejection and nonrejection regions are set up as in Figure 9.14, and the decision rule is

$$\text{Reject } H_0 \text{ if } Z_{STAT} < -1.96 \text{ or if } Z_{STAT} > +1.96;$$

otherwise, do not reject H_0.

FIGURE 9.14

Two-tail test of hypothesis for the proportion at the 0.05 level of significance

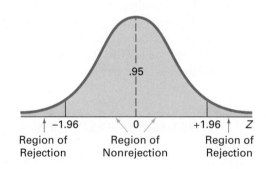

Because 561 of the 1,100 respondents stated that customer service was better at e-commerce sites than at physical stores,

$$p = \frac{561}{1,100} = 0.51$$

Using Equation (9.3),

$$Z_{STAT} = \frac{p - \pi}{\sqrt{\dfrac{\pi(1 - \pi)}{n}}} = \frac{0.51 - 0.50}{\sqrt{\dfrac{0.50(1 - 0.50)}{1,100}}} = \frac{0.01}{0.0151} = 0.6633$$

or, using Equation (9.4),

$$Z_{STAT} = \frac{X - n\pi}{\sqrt{n\pi(1 - \pi)}} = \frac{561 - (1,100)(0.50)}{\sqrt{1,100(0.50)(0.50)}} = \frac{11}{16.5831} = 0.6633$$

Because $-1.96 < Z_{STAT} = 0.6633 < 1.96$, you do not reject H_0. There is insufficient evidence to prove that the population proportion of all consumers who believe that customer service is better at e-commerce sites than at physical stores is not 0.50. Figure 9.15 presents the worksheet results for these data.

FIGURE 9.15

Worksheet for the *Z* test for the survey of whether customer service is better or worse at e-commerce sites than at physical stores

Figure 9.15 displays the COMPUTE worksheet of the Z Proportion workbook. Create this worksheet using the instructions in Section EG9.4.

	A	B	
1	Z Test of Hypothesis for the Proportion		
2			
3	**Data**		
4	Null Hypothesis *p* =	0.5	
5	Level of Significance	0.05	
6	Number of Items of Interest	561	
7	Sample Size	1100	
8			
9	**Intermediate Calculations**		
10	Sample Proportion	0.5100	=B6/B7
11	Standard Error	0.0151	=SQRT(B4*(1 - B4)/B7)
12	Z Test Statistic	0.6633	=(B10 - B4)/B11
13			
14	**Two-Tail Test**		
15	Lower Critical Value	-1.9600	=NORMSINV(B5/2)
16	Upper Critical Value	1.9600	=NORMSINV(1 - B5/2)
17	*p*-Value	0.5071	=2 * (1 - NORMSDIST(ABS(B12)))
18	Do not reject the null hypothesis		=IF(B17 < B5, "Reject the null hypothesis", "Do not reject the null hypothesis")

The *p*-Value Approach

As an alternative to the critical value approach, you can compute the *p*-value. For this two-tail test in which the rejection region is located in the lower tail and the upper tail, you need to find the area below a *Z* value of -0.6633 and above a *Z* value of $+0.6633$. Figure 9.15 reports a *p*-value of 0.5071. Because this value is greater than the selected level of significance ($\alpha = 0.05$), you do not reject the null hypothesis.

EXAMPLE 9.6

Testing a Hypothesis for a Proportion

A fast-food chain has developed a new process to ensure that orders at the drive-through are filled correctly. The business problem is defined as determining whether the new process can increase the percentage of orders processed correctly. The previous process filled orders correctly 85% of the time. Data are collected from a sample of 100 orders using the new process. The results indicate that 94 orders were filled correctly. At the 0.01 level of significance, can you conclude that the new process has increased the proportion of orders filled correctly?

SOLUTION The null and alternative hypotheses are

$H_0: \pi \leq 0.85$ (i.e., the population proportion of orders filled correctly using the new process is less than or equal to 0.85)
$H_1: \pi > 0.85$ (i.e., the population proportion of orders filled correctly using the new process is greater than 0.85)

Using Equation (9.3) on page 321,

$$p = \frac{X}{n} = \frac{94}{100} = 0.94$$

$$Z_{STAT} = \frac{p - \pi}{\sqrt{\dfrac{\pi(1 - \pi)}{n}}} = \frac{0.94 - 0.85}{\sqrt{\dfrac{0.85(1 - 0.85)}{100}}} = \frac{0.09}{0.0357} = 2.52$$

The *p*-value for $Z_{STAT} > 2.52$ is 0.0059.

Using the critical value approach, you reject H_0 if $Z_{STAT} > 2.33$. Using the *p*-value approach, you reject H_0 if *p*-value < 0.01. Because $Z_{STAT} = 2.52 > 2.33$ or the *p*-value $= 0.0059 < 0.01$, you reject H_0. You have evidence that the new process has increased the proportion of correct orders above 0.85.

Problems for Section 9.4

LEARNING THE BASICS

9.50 If, in a random sample of 400 items, 88 are defective, what is the sample proportion of defective items?

9.51 In Problem 9.50, if the null hypothesis is that 20% of the items in the population are defective, what is the value of Z_{STAT}?

9.52 In Problems 9.50 and 9.51, suppose you are testing the null hypothesis $H_0: \pi = 0.20$ against the two-tail alternative hypothesis $H_1: \pi \neq 0.20$ and you choose the level of significance $\alpha = 0.05$. What is your statistical decision?

APPLYING THE CONCEPTS

9.53 The U.S. Department of Education reports that 46% of full-time college students are employed while attending college (data extracted from "The Condition of Education 2009," *National Center for Education Statistics*, **nces.ed.gov**). A recent survey of 60 full-time students at Miami University found that 29 were employed.

a. Use the five-step *p*-value approach to hypothesis testing and a 0.05 level of significance to determine whether the proportion of full-time students at Miami University is different than the national norm of 0.46.

b. Assume that the study found that 36 of the 60 full-time students were employed and repeat (a). Are the conclusions the same?

9.54 Online magazines make it easy for readers to link to an advertiser's Web site directly from an advertisement placed in the digital magazine. A recent survey indicated that 56% of online magazine readers have clicked on an advertisement and linked directly to the advertiser's Web site. The survey was based on a sample size of $n = 6,403$ (data extracted from "Metrics," *EContent*, January/February, 2007, p. 20).

a. Use the five-step *p*-value approach to try to determine whether there is evidence that more than half of all the readers of online magazines have linked to an advertiser's Web site. (Use the 0.05 level of significance.)

b. Suppose that the sample size was only $n = 100$, and as before, 56% of the online magazine readers indicated that they had clicked on an advertisement to link directly to the advertiser's Web site. Use the five-step *p*-value approach to try to determine whether there is evidence that more than half of all the readers of online magazines have linked to an advertiser's Web site. (Use the 0.05 level of significance.)

c. Discuss the effect that sample size has on hypothesis testing.

d. What do you think are your chances of rejecting any null hypothesis concerning a population proportion if a sample size of $n = 20$ is used?

9.55 One of the issues facing organizations is increasing diversity throughout the organization. One of the ways to evaluate an organization's success at increasing diversity is to compare the percentage of employees in the organization in a particular position with a specific background to the percentage in a particular position with that specific background in the general workforce. Recently, a large academic medical center determined that 9 of 17 employees in a particular position were female, whereas 55% of the employees for this position in the general workforce were female. At the 0.05 level of significance, is there evidence that the proportion of females in this position at this medical center is different from what would be expected in the general workforce?

9.56 Of 1,000 respondents aged 24 to 35, 65% reported that they preferred to "look for a job in a place where I would like to live" rather than "look for the best job I can find, the place where I live is secondary" (data extracted from L. Belkin, "What Do Young Jobseekers Want? (Something Other Than a Job)," *The New York Times*, September 6, 2007, p. G2). At the 0.05 level of significance, is there evidence that the proportion of all young jobseekers aged 24 to 35 who preferred to "look for a job in a place where I would like to live" rather than "look for the best job I can find, the place where I live is secondary" is different from 60%?

9.57 One of the biggest issues facing e-retailers is the ability to reduce the proportion of customers who cancel their transactions after they have selected their products. It has been estimated that about half of prospective customers cancel their transactions after they have selected their products (data extracted from B. Tedeschi, "E-Commerce, a Cure for Abandoned Shopping Carts: A Web Checkout System That Eliminates the Need for Multiple Screens," *The New York Times*, February 14, 2005, p. C3). Suppose that a company changed its Web site so that customers could use a single-page checkout process rather than multiple pages. A sample of 500 customers who had selected their products were provided with the new checkout system. Of these 500 customers, 210 cancelled their transactions after they had selected their products.

a. At the 0.01 level of significance, is there evidence that the population proportion of customers who select products and then cancel their transaction is less than 0.50 with the new system?

b. Suppose that a sample of $n = 100$ customers (instead of $n = 500$ customers) were provided with the new checkout system and that 42 of those customers cancelled their transactions after they had selected their products. At the 0.01 level of significance, is there evidence that the population proportion of customers who select products and then cancel their transaction is less than 0.50 with the new system?

c. Compare the results of (a) and (b) and discuss the effect that sample size has on the outcome, and, in general, in hypothesis testing.

9.58 A recent study by the Pew Internet and American Life Project (**pewinternet.org**) found that Americans had a complex and ambivalent attitude toward technology (data extracted from M. Himowitz, "How to Tell What Kind of Tech User You Are," *Newsday*, May 27, 2007, p. F6). The study reported that 8% of the respondents were "Omnivores" who are gadget lovers, text messengers, and online gamers (often with their own blogs or Web pages), video makers, and YouTube posters. You believe that the percentage of students at your school who are Omnivores is greater than 8%, and you plan to carry out a study to prove that this is so.

a. State the null and alternative hypotheses.
You select a sample of 200 students at your school and find that 30 students can be classified as Omnivores.

b. Use either the six-step critical value hypothesis-testing approach or the five-step *p*-value approach to determine at the 0.05 level of significance whether there is evidence that the percentage of Omnivores at your school is greater than 8%.

9.5 Potential Hypothesis-Testing Pitfalls and Ethical Issues

To this point, you have studied the fundamental concepts of hypothesis testing. You have used hypothesis testing to analyze differences between sample statistics and hypothesized population parameters in order to make business decisions concerning the underlying population characteristics. You have also learned how to evaluate the risks involved in making these decisions.

When planning to carry out a hypothesis test based on a survey, research study, or designed experiment, you must ask several questions to ensure that you use proper methodology. You need to raise and answer questions such as the following in the planning stage:

1. What is the goal of the survey, study, or experiment? How can you translate the goal into a null hypothesis and an alternative hypothesis?
2. Is the hypothesis test a two-tail test or one-tail test?
3. Can you select a random sample from the underlying population of interest?
4. What types of data will you collect in the sample? Are the variables numerical or categorical?
5. At what level of significance should you conduct the hypothesis test?
6. Is the intended sample size large enough to achieve the desired power of the test for the level of significance chosen?
7. What statistical test procedure should you use and why?
8. What conclusions and interpretations can you reach from the results of the hypothesis test?

Failing to consider these questions early in the planning process can lead to biased or incomplete results. Proper planning can help ensure that the statistical study will provide objective information needed to make good business decisions.

Statistical Significance Versus Practical Significance You need to make a distinction between the existence of a statistically significant result and its practical significance in the context within a field of application. Sometimes, due to a very large sample size, you may get a result that is statistically significant but has little practical significance. For example, suppose that prior to a national marketing campaign focusing on a series of expensive television commercials, you believe that the proportion of people who recognize your brand is 0.30. At the completion of the campaign, a survey of 20,000 people indicates that 6,168 recognized your brand. A one-tail test trying to prove that the proportion is now greater than 0.30 results in a *p*-value of 0.0047, and the correct statistical conclusion is that the proportion of consumers recognizing your brand name has now increased. Was the campaign successful? The result of the hypothesis test indicates a statistically significant increase in brand awareness, but is this increase practically important? The population proportion is now estimated at $6,168/20,000 = 0.3084$, or 30.84%. This increase is less than 1% more than the hypothesized value of 30%. Did the large expenses associated with the marketing campaign produce a result with a meaningful increase in brand awareness? Because of the minimal real-world impact an increase of less than 1% has on the overall marketing strategy and the huge expenses associated with the marketing campaign, you should conclude that the campaign was not successful. On the other hand, if the campaign increased brand awareness from 30% to 50%, you could conclude that the campaign was successful.

Reporting of Findings In conducting research, you should document both good and bad results. You should not just report the results of hypothesis tests that show statistical significance but omit those for which there is insufficient evidence in the findings. In instances in which there is insufficient evidence to reject H_0, you must make it clear that this does not prove that the null hypothesis is true. What the result does indicate is that with the sample size used, there is not enough information to *disprove* the null hypothesis.

Ethical Issues You also need to distinguish between poor research methodology and unethical behavior. Ethical considerations arise when the hypothesis-testing process is manipulated. Some of the areas where ethical issues can arise include the use of human subjects in experiments, the data collection method, the type of test (one-tail or two-tail test), the choice of the level of significance, the cleansing and discarding of data, and the failure to report pertinent findings.

9.6 🖱 *Online Topic:* The Power of a Test

Section 9.1 defines Type I and Type II errors and the power of a test. To examine the power of a test in greater depth, read the **Section 9.6** online topic file that is available on this book's companion Web site. (See Appendix Section D.8 to learn how to access the online topic files.)

USING STATISTICS @ Oxford Cereals, Part II Revisited

As the plant operations manager for Oxford Cereals, you were responsible for the cereal-filling process. It was your responsibility to adjust the process when the mean fill weight in the population of boxes deviated from the company specifications of 368 grams. Because weighing all the cereal boxes would be too time-consuming and impractical, you needed to select and weigh a sample of boxes and conduct a hypothesis test.

You determined that the null hypothesis should be that the population mean fill was 368 grams. If the weights of the sampled boxes were sufficiently above or below the expected 368-gram mean specified by Oxford Cereals, you would reject the null hypothesis in favor of the alternative hypothesis that the mean fill was different from 368 grams. If this happened, you would stop production and take whatever action is necessary to correct the problem. If the null hypothesis was not rejected, you would continue to believe in the status quo, that the process was working correctly, and therefore take no corrective action.

Before proceeding, you considered the risks involved with hypothesis tests. If you rejected a true null hypothesis, then you would make a Type I error and conclude that the population mean fill was not 368 when it actually was 368. This error would result in adjusting the filling process even though the process was working properly. If you did not reject a false null hypothesis, then you would make a Type II error and conclude that the population mean fill was 368 when it actually was not 368. Here, you would allow the process to continue without adjustment even though the process was not working properly.

After collecting a random sample of 25 cereal boxes, you used the six-step critical value approach to hypothesis testing. Because the test statistic fell into the nonrejection region, you did not reject the null hypothesis. You concluded that there was insufficient evidence to prove that the mean fill differed from 368 grams. No corrective action on the filling process was needed.

SUMMARY

This chapter presented the foundation of hypothesis testing. You learned how to perform tests on the population mean and on the population proportion. The chapter developed both the critical value approach and the *p*-value approach to hypothesis testing.

In deciding which test to use, you should ask the following question: Does the test involve a numerical variable or a categorical variable? If the test involves a categorical variable, use the *Z* test for the proportion. If the test involves a numerical variable, use the *t* test for the mean. Table 9.4 provides a list of hypothesis tests covered in the chapter.

TABLE 9.4
Summary of Topics in Chapter 9

Type of Analysis	Type of Data	
	Numerical	Categorical
Hypothesis test concerning a single parameter	*t* test of hypothesis for the mean (Section 9.2)	*Z* test of hypothesis for the proportion (Section 9.4)

KEY EQUATIONS

Z Test for the Mean (σ Known)

$$Z_{STAT} = \frac{\overline{X} - \mu}{\frac{\sigma}{\sqrt{n}}} \tag{9.1}$$

t Test for the Mean (σ Unknown)

$$t_{STAT} = \frac{\overline{X} - \mu}{\frac{S}{\sqrt{n}}} \tag{9.2}$$

Z Test for the Proportion

$$Z_{STAT} = \frac{p - \pi}{\sqrt{\frac{\pi(1 - \pi)}{n}}} \tag{9.3}$$

Z Test for the Proportion in Terms of the Number of Events of Interest

$$Z_{STAT} = \frac{X - n\pi}{\sqrt{n\pi(1 - \pi)}} \tag{9.4}$$

KEY TERMS

alternative hypothesis (H_1)   298
β risk   301
confidence coefficient   301
confidence level   301
critical value   300
directional test   317
hypothesis testing   298
level of significance (α)   301

null hypothesis (H_0)   298
one-tail test   317
p-value   305
power of a statistical test   301
region of nonrejection   300
region of rejection   300
robust   314
sample proportion   321

t test for the mean   310
test statistic   300
two-tail test   303
Type I error   300
Type II error   300
Z test for the mean   302
Z test for the proportion   321

CHAPTER REVIEW PROBLEMS

CHECKING YOUR UNDERSTANDING

9.59 What is the difference between a null hypothesis, H_0, and an alternative hypothesis, H_1?

9.60 What is the difference between a Type I error and a Type II error?

9.61 What is meant by the power of a test?

9.62 What is the difference between a one-tail test and a two-tail test?

9.63 What is meant by a *p*-value?

9.64 How can a confidence interval estimate for the population mean provide conclusions to the corresponding two-tail hypothesis test for the population mean?

9.65 What is the six-step critical value approach to hypothesis testing?

9.66 What is the five-step p-value approach to hypothesis testing?

APPLYING THE CONCEPTS

9.67 An article in *Marketing News* (T. T. Semon, "Consider a Statistical Insignificance Test," *Marketing News*, February 1, 1999) argued that the level of significance used when comparing two products is often too low—that is, sometimes you should be using an α value greater than 0.05. Specifically, the article recounted testing the proportion of potential customers with a preference for product 1 over product 2. The null hypothesis was that the population proportion of potential customers preferring product 1 was 0.50, and the alternative hypothesis was that it was not equal to 0.50. The p-value for the test was 0.22. The article suggested that, in some cases, this should be enough evidence to reject the null hypothesis.
a. State, in statistical terms, the null and alternative hypotheses for this example.
b. Explain the risks associated with Type I and Type II errors in this case.
c. What would be the consequences if you rejected the null hypothesis for a p-value of 0.22?
d. Why do you think the article suggested raising the value of α?
e. What would you do in this situation?
f. What is your answer in (e) if the p-value equals 0.12? What if it equals 0.06?

9.68 La Quinta Motor Inns developed a computer model to help predict the profitability of sites that are being considered as locations for new hotels. If the computer model predicts large profits, La Quinta buys the proposed site and builds a new hotel. If the computer model predicts small or moderate profits, La Quinta chooses not to proceed with that site (data extracted from S. E. Kimes and J. A. Fitzsimmons, "Selecting Profitable Hotel Sites at La Quinta Motor Inns," *Interfaces*, Vol. 20, March–April 1990, pp. 12–20). This decision-making procedure can be expressed in the hypothesis-testing framework. The null hypothesis is that the site is not a profitable location. The alternative hypothesis is that the site is a profitable location.
a. Explain the risks associated with committing a Type I error in this case.
b. Explain the risks associated with committing a Type II error in this case.
c. Which type of error do you think the executives at La Quinta Motor Inns want to avoid? Explain.
d. How do changes in the rejection criterion affect the probabilities of committing Type I and Type II errors?

9.69 Webcredible, a UK-based consulting firm specializing in Web sites, intranets, mobile devices, and applications, conducted a survey of 1,132 mobile phone users between February and April 2009. The survey found that 52% of mobile phone users are now using the mobile Internet (data extracted from "Email and Social Networking Most Popular Mobile Internet Activities," **www.webcredible.co.uk**, May 13, 2009). The authors of the article imply that the survey proves that more than half of all mobile phone users are now using the mobile Internet.
a. Use the five-step p-value approach to hypothesis testing and a 0.05 level of significance to try to prove that more than half of all mobile phone users are now using the mobile Internet.
b. Based on your result in (a), is the claim implied by the authors valid?
c. Suppose the survey found that 53% of mobile phone users are now using the mobile Internet. Repeat parts (a) and (b).
d. Compare the results of (b) and (c).

9.70 The owner of a gasoline station wants to study gasoline purchasing habits by motorists at his station. He selects a random sample of 60 motorists during a certain week, with the following results:
• The amount purchased was $\bar{X} = 11.3$ gallons, $S = 3.1$ gallons.
• Eleven motorists purchased premium-grade gasoline.
a. At the 0.05 level of significance, is there evidence that the population mean purchase was different from 10 gallons?
b. Determine the p-value in (a).
c. At the 0.05 level of significance, is there evidence that less than 20% of all the motorists at the station purchased premium-grade gasoline?
d. What is your answer to (a) if the sample mean equals 10.3 gallons?
e. What is your answer to (c) if 7 motorists purchased premium-grade gasoline?

9.71 An auditor for a government agency is assigned the task of evaluating reimbursement for office visits to physicians paid by Medicare. The audit was conducted on a sample of 75 of the reimbursements, with the following results:
• In 12 of the office visits, an incorrect amount of reimbursement was provided.
• The amount of reimbursement was $\bar{X} = \$93.70$, $S = \$34.55$.
a. At the 0.05 level of significance, is there evidence that the population mean reimbursement was less than $100?
b. At the 0.05 level of significance, is there evidence that the proportion of incorrect reimbursements in the population was greater than 0.10?
c. Discuss the underlying assumptions of the test used in (a).
d. What is your answer to (a) if the sample mean equals $90?
e. What is your answer to (b) if 15 office visits had incorrect reimbursements?

9.72 A bank branch located in a commercial district of a city has developed an improved process for serving customers during the noon-to-1:00 P.M. lunch period. The waiting time (defined as the time the customer enters the line until he or she reaches the teller window) of all customers during this hour is recorded over a period of a week. A random sample of 15 customers is selected, and the results (stored in Bank1) are as follows:

4.21	5.55	3.02	5.13	4.77	2.34	3.54	3.20
4.50	6.10	0.38	5.12	6.46	6.19	3.79	

a. At the 0.05 level of significance, is there evidence that the population mean waiting time is less than 5 minutes?
b. What assumption about the population distribution is needed in order to conduct the t test in (a)?
c. Construct a boxplot or a normal probability plot to evaluate the assumption made in (b).
d. Do you think that the assumption needed in order to conduct the t test in (a) is valid? Explain.
e. As a customer walks into the branch office during the lunch hour, she asks the branch manager how long she can expect to wait. The branch manager replies, "Almost certainly not longer than 5 minutes." On the basis of the results of (a), evaluate this statement.

9.73 A manufacturing company produces electrical insulators. If the insulators break when in use, a short circuit is likely to occur. To test the strength of the insulators, destructive testing is carried out to determine how much force is required to break the insulators. Force is measured by observing the number of pounds of force applied to the insulator before it breaks. The following data (stored in Force) are from 30 insulators subjected to this testing:

1,870	1,728	1,656	1,610	1,634	1,784	1,522	1,696	1,592	1,662
1,866	1,764	1,734	1,662	1,734	1,774	1,550	1,756	1,762	1,866
1,820	1,744	1,788	1,688	1,810	1,752	1,680	1,810	1,652	1,736

a. At the 0.05 level of significance, is there evidence that the population mean force is greater than 1,500 pounds?
b. What assumption about the population distribution is needed in order to conduct the t test in (a)?
c. Construct a histogram, boxplot, or normal probability plot to evaluate the assumption made in (b).
d. Do you think that the assumption needed in order to conduct the t test in (a) is valid? Explain.

9.74 An important quality characteristic used by the manufacturer of Boston and Vermont asphalt shingles is the amount of moisture the shingles contain when they are packaged. Customers may feel that they have purchased a product lacking in quality if they find moisture and wet shingles inside the packaging. In some cases, excessive moisture can cause the granules attached to the shingle for texture and coloring purposes to fall off the shingle, resulting in appearance problems. To monitor the amount of moisture present, the company conducts moisture tests. A shingle is weighed and then dried. The shingle is then reweighed, and, based on the amount of moisture taken out of the product, the pounds of moisture per 100 square feet are calculated. The company would like to show that the mean moisture content is less than 0.35 pound per 100 square feet. The file Moisture includes 36 measurements (in pounds per 100 square feet) for Boston shingles and 31 for Vermont shingles.
a. For the Boston shingles, is there evidence at the 0.05 level of significance that the population mean moisture content is less than 0.35 pound per 100 square feet?
b. Interpret the meaning of the p-value in (a).
c. For the Vermont shingles, is there evidence at the 0.05 level of significance that the population mean moisture content is less than 0.35 pound per 100 square feet?
d. Interpret the meaning of the p-value in (c).
e. What assumption about the population distribution is needed in order to conduct the t tests in (a) and (c)?
f. Construct a histogram, boxplot, or normal probability plot to evaluate the assumption made in (a) and (c).
g. Do you think that the assumption needed in order to conduct the t tests in (a) and (c) is valid? Explain.

9.75 Studies conducted by the manufacturer of Boston and Vermont asphalt shingles have shown product weight to be a major factor in the customer's perception of quality. Moreover, the weight represents the amount of raw materials being used and is therefore very important to the company from a cost standpoint. The last stage of the assembly line packages the shingles before the packages are placed on wooden pallets. Once a pallet is full (a pallet for most brands holds 16 squares of shingles), it is weighed, and the measurement is recorded. The file Pallet contains the weight (in pounds) from a sample of 368 pallets of Boston shingles and 330 pallets of Vermont shingles.
a. For the Boston shingles, is there evidence that the population mean weight is different from 3,150 pounds?
b. Interpret the meaning of the p-value in (a).
c. For the Vermont shingles, is there evidence that the population mean weight is different from 3,700 pounds?
d. Interpret the meaning of the p-value in (c).
e. In (a) through (d), do you have to worry about the normality assumption? Explain.

9.76 The manufacturer of Boston and Vermont asphalt shingles provides its customers with a 20-year warranty on most of its products. To determine whether a shingle will last as long as the warranty period, accelerated-life testing is conducted at the manufacturing plant. Accelerated-life testing exposes the shingle to the stresses it would be subject to in a lifetime of normal use in a laboratory setting via an experiment that takes only a few minutes to conduct. In this test, a shingle is repeatedly scraped with a brush for a short period of time, and the shingle granules removed by the brushing are weighed (in grams). Shingles that experience low amounts of granule loss are expected to last longer in normal use than shingles that experience high amounts of granule loss. The file Granule contains a sample of 170 measurements made on the company's Boston shingles and 140 measurements made on Vermont shingles.

a. For the Boston shingles, is there evidence that the population mean granule loss is different from 0.50 gram?

b. Interpret the meaning of the p-value in (a).

c. For the Vermont shingles, is there evidence that the population mean granule loss is different from 0.50 gram?

d. Interpret the meaning of the p-value in (c).

e. In (a) through (d), do you have to worry about the normality assumption? Explain.

REPORT WRITING EXERCISES

9.77 Referring to the results of Problems 9.74 through 9.76 concerning Boston and Vermont shingles, write a report that evaluates the moisture level, weight, and granule loss of the two types of shingles.

MANAGING THE *SPRINGVILLE HERALD*

Continuing its monitoring of the blackness of the newspaper print, first described in the Chapter 6 "Managing the *Springville Herald*" case, the production department of the newspaper wants to ensure that the mean blackness of the print for all newspapers is at least 0.97 on a standard scale in which the target value is 1.0. A random sample of 50 newspapers was selected, and the blackness of one spot on each of the 50 newspapers is measured (and stored in SH9).

0.854	1.023	1.005	1.030	1.219	0.977	1.044	0.778	1.122	1.114
1.091	1.086	1.141	0.931	0.723	0.934	1.060	1.047	0.800	0.889
1.012	0.695	0.869	0.734	1.131	0.993	0.762	0.814	1.108	0.805
1.223	1.024	0.884	0.799	0.870	0.898	0.621	0.818	1.113	1.286
1.052	0.678	1.162	0.808	1.012	0.859	0.951	1.112	1.003	0.972

Calculate the sample statistics and determine whether there is evidence that the population mean blackness is less than 0.97. Write a memo to management that summarizes your conclusions.

WEB CASE

Apply your knowledge about hypothesis testing in this Web Case, which continues the cereal-fill-packaging dispute Web Case from Chapter 7.

In response to the negative statements made by the Consumers Concerned About Cereal Cheaters (CCACC) in the Chapter 7 Web Case, Oxford Cereals recently conducted an experiment concerning cereal packaging. The company claims that the results of the experiment refute the CCACC allegations that Oxford Cereals has been cheating consumers by packaging cereals at less than labeled weights.

Using a Web browser, open to the Web page for the Chapter 9 Web Case or open **OC_FullUp.htm**, if you have downloaded the Web Case files to review the Oxford Cereals

press release and supporting documents that describe the experiment. Then answer the following questions:

1. Are the results of the experiment valid? Why or why not? If you were conducting the experiment, is there anything you would change?

2. Do the results support the claim that Oxford Cereals is not cheating its customers?

3. Is the claim of the Oxford Cereals CEO that many cereal boxes contain *more* than 368 grams surprising? Is it true?

4. Could there ever be a circumstance in which the results of the Oxford Cereals experiment *and* the CCACC's results are both correct? Explain

REFERENCES

1. Bradley, J. V., *Distribution-Free Statistical Tests* (Upper Saddle River, NJ: Prentice Hall, 1968).
2. Daniel, W., *Applied Nonparametric Statistics*, 2nd ed. (Boston: Houghton Mifflin, 1990).
3. *Microsoft Excel 2007* (Redmond, WA: Microsoft Corp., 2007).

EG9.1 FUNDAMENTALS of HYPOTHESIS-TESTING METHODOLOGY

Using the Z Test for the Mean (σ Known)

PHStat2 Use the **Z Test for the Mean, sigma known** procedure to perform the Z test for the mean when σ is known. For example, to perform the Z test for the Figure 9.5 cereal-filling example on page 306, select **PHStat → One-Sample Tests → Z Test for the Mean, sigma known**. In the procedure's dialog box (shown below):

1. Enter **368** as the **Null Hypothesis**.
2. Enter **0.05** as the **Level of Significance**.
3. Enter **15** as the **Population Standard Deviation**.
4. Click **Sample Statistics Known** and enter **25** as the **Sample Size** and **372.5** as the **Sample Mean**.
5. Click **Two-Tail Test**.
6. Enter a **Title** and click **OK**.

For problems that use unsummarized data, click **Sample Statistics Unknown** in step 4 and enter the cell range of the unsummarized data as the **Sample Cell Range**.

In-Depth Excel Use the **NORMSINV** and **NORMSDIST** functions to help perform the Z test for the mean (σ known). For the two-tail test, enter **NORMSINV(*level of significance*/2)** and **NORMSINV(1 – *level of significance*/2)** to compute the lower and upper critical values and enter the expression **2 * (1 – NORMSDIST(*absolute value of the Z test statistic*))** to compute the *p*-value.

Use the **COMPUTE worksheet** of the **Z Mean workbook**, shown in Figure 9.5 on page 306, as a template for performing the two-tail Z test. The worksheet uses the **IF** function in the form **IF(*p-value* < *level of significance*, *display reject message*, *display do not reject message*)** to indicate the results of the test in cell A18. The worksheet contains the data for the Figure 9.5 cereal-filling example on page 306. For other problems, change the **Data** fields in cells B4 through B8 as necessary.

The Chapter 9 Excel Guide continues on page 332.

EG9.2 *t* TEST of HYPOTHESIS for the MEAN (σ UNKNOWN)

PHStat2 Use the *t* Test for the Mean, sigma unknown procedure to perform the *t* test for the mean when σ is unknown. For example, to perform the *t* test for the Figure 9.7 sales invoice example on page 312, select **PHStat → One-Sample Tests → t Test for the Mean, sigma unknown**. In the procedure's dialog box (shown below):

1. Enter **120** as the **Null Hypothesis**.
2. Enter **0.05** as the **Level of Significance**.
3. Click **Sample Statistics Known** and enter **12** as the **Sample Size**, **112.85** as the **Sample Mean**, and **20.8** as the **Sample Standard Deviation**.
4. Click **Two-Tail Test**.
5. Enter a **Title** and click **OK**.

For problems that use unsummarized data, click **Sample Statistics Unknown** in step 3 and enter the cell range of the unsummarized data as the **Sample Cell Range**.

In-Depth Excel Use the **TINV** and **TDIST** functions to help perform the *t* test for the mean when σ is unknown. For the two-tail test, enter the expression −**TINV**(*level of significance*, *degrees of freedom*) and **TINV**(*level of significance*, *degrees of freedom*) to compute the lower and upper critical values and enter **TDIST**(*absolute value of the t test statistic*, *degrees of freedom*, **2**) to compute the *p*-value.

Use the **COMPUTE** worksheet of the **T mean** workbook, shown in Figure 9.7 on page 312, as a template for performing the two-tail *t* test. The worksheet uses the **IF** function in the form **IF**(*p-value* < *level of significance*, *display reject message*, *display do not reject message*) to indicate the results of the test in cell A19. The worksheet contains the data for the Figure 9.7 sales invoice example on page 312. For other problems, change the **Data** fields in cells B4 through B8 as necessary.

EG9.3 ONE-TAIL TESTS

PHStat2 Click either **Lower-Tail Test** or **Upper-Tail Test** in the procedure dialog boxes discussed in Sections EG9.1 or 9.2 to perform a one-tail test. For example, to perform the Figure 9.12 one-tail test for the drive-through time study example on page 318, select **PHStat → One-Sample Tests → t Test for the Mean, sigma unknown**. In the procedure's dialog box:

1. Enter **158.77** as the **Null Hypothesis**.
2. Enter **0.05** as the **Level of Significance**.
3. Click **Sample Statistics Known** and enter **25** as the **Sample Size**, **147.5** as the **Sample Mean**, and **20** as the **Sample Standard Deviation**.
4. Click **Lower-Tail Test**.
5. Enter a **Title** and click **OK**.

In-Depth Excel Modify the functions discussed in Section EG9.1 and 9.2 to perform one-tail tests. For the Section EG9.1 *Z* test, enter **NORMSINV**(*level of significance*) or **NORMSINV**(1 − *level of significance*) to compute the lower-tail or upper-tail critical value. Enter **NORMSDIST** (*Z test statistic*) and 1 − **NORMSDIST**(*absolute value of the Z test statistic*) to compute the lower-tail or upper-tail *p*-value.

For the Section EG9.2 *t* test, enter −**TINV**(2 * *level of significance*, *degrees of freedom*) and **TINV**(2 * *level of significance*, *degrees of freedom*) to compute the lower-tail and upper-tail critical values. Computing *p*-values is more complex. If the *t* test statistic is less than zero, then the lower-tail *p*-value is equal to **TDIST**(*absolute value of the t test statistic*, *degrees of freedom*, **1**), and the upper-tail *p*-value is equal to 1 − **TDIST**(*absolute value of the t test statistic*, *degrees of freedom*, **1**). If the *t* test statistic is not less than zero, then the values are reversed.

Use the **COMPUTE_LOWER** worksheet or the **COMPUTE_UPPER** worksheets of the **Z Mean workbook** or the **T mean workbook** as templates for performing one-tail *t* tests. Examine the **COMPUTE_ALL_FORMULAS worksheet** of either workbook to examine how the worksheet use the **IF** function to help compute one-tail *p*-values.

EG9.4 Z TEST of HYPOTHESIS for the PROPORTION

PHStat2 Use the **Z Test for the Proportion** procedure to perform the *Z* test of hypothesis for the proportion. For example, to perform the *Z* test for the Figure 9.15 customer service study example on page 323, select **PHStat → One-Sample Tests → Z Test for the Proportion**. In the procedure's dialog box (shown below):

1. Enter **0.5** as the **Null Hypothesis**.
2. Enter **0.05** as the **Level of Significance**.
3. Enter **561** as the **Number of Items of Interest**.
4. Enter **1100** as the **Sample Size**.
5. Click **Two-Tail Test**.
6. Enter a **Title** and click **OK**.

In-Depth Excel Use the **NORMSINV** and **NORMSDIST** functions to help perform the *Z* test for the proportion. For the two-tail test, enter **NORMSINV(***level of significance*/**2)** and **NORMSINV(1 −** *level of significance*/**2)** to compute the lower and upper critical values and enter the expression **2 * (1 − NORMSDIST(***absolute value of the Z test statistic***)** to compute the *p*-value.

Use the **COMPUTE worksheet** of the **Z Proportion workbook**, shown in Figure 9.15 on page 323, as a template for performing the two-tail *Z* test. The worksheet uses the **IF** function in the form **IF(***p-value* < *level of significance*, *display reject message*, *display do not reject message***)** to indicate the results of the test in cell A18. The worksheet contains the data for the Figure 9.15 customer service study example on page 323. For other problems, change the **Data** fields in cells B4 through B7 as necessary. For one-tail tests, use either the **COMPUTE_LOWER worksheet** or **COMPUTE_UPPER worksheet** as a template for performing one-tail tests. These worksheets are similar to the pair of same-named worksheets in the **Z Mean workbook** and use **NORMSINV** and **NORMSDIST** to compute critical values and *p*-values in same way as that pair of worksheets (see Section EG9.3).

10 Two-Sample Tests

Learning Objectives

In this chapter, you learn how to use hypothesis testing for comparing the difference between:

- The means of two independent populations
- The means of two related populations
- The proportions of two independent populations
- The variances of two independent populations

USING STATISTICS

@ BLK Foods

Does the type of display used in a supermarket affect the sales of products? As the regional sales manager for BLK Foods, you want to compare the sales volume of BLK Cola when the product is placed in the normal shelf location to the sales volume when the product is featured in a special end-aisle display. To test the effectiveness of the end-aisle displays, you select 20 stores from the BLK supermarket chain that all experience similar storewide sales volumes. You then randomly assign 10 of the 20 stores to sample 1 and 10 stores to sample 2. The managers of the 10 stores in sample 1 place the BLK Cola in the normal shelf location, alongside the other cola products. The 10 stores in sample 2 use the special end-aisle promotional display. At the end of one week, the sales of BLK Cola are recorded. How can you determine whether sales of BLK Cola using the end-aisle displays are the same as those when the cola is placed in the normal shelf location? How can you decide if the variability in BLK Cola sales from store to store is the same for the two types of displays? How could you use the answers to these questions to improve sales of BLK Cola?

Hypothesis testing provides a *confirmatory* approach to data analysis. In Chapter 9, you learned a variety of commonly used hypothesis-testing procedures that relate to a single sample of data selected from a single population. In this chapter, you learn how to extend hypothesis testing to **two-sample tests** that compare statistics from samples of data selected from two populations. One such test for the BLK Foods scenario would be "Are the mean weekly sales of BLK Cola when using the normal shelf location (one population) equal to the mean weekly sales of BLK Cola when using an end-aisle display (a second population)?"

10.1 Comparing the Means of Two Independent Populations

In Sections 8.1 and 9.1, you learned that in almost all cases, you would not know the population standard deviation of the population under study. Likewise, when you take a random sample from each of two independent populations, you almost always do not know the standard deviations of either population. In addition, you need to know whether you can assume that the variances in the two populations are equal because the method you use to compare the means of each population depends on whether you can assume that the variances of the two populations are equal.

Pooled-Variance *t* Test for the Difference Between Two Means

If you assume that the random samples are independently selected from two populations and that the populations are normally distributed and have equal variances, you can use a **pooled-variance *t* test** to determine whether there is a significant difference between the means of the two populations. If the populations are not normally distributed, the pooled-variance *t* test can still be used if the sample sizes are large enough (typically ≥ 30 for each sample[1]).

[1]Review the Section 7.4 discussion about the Central Limit Theorem on page 238 to understand more about "large enough" sample sizes.

Using subscripts to distinguish between the population mean of the first population, μ_1, and the population mean of the second population, μ_2, the null hypothesis of no difference in the means of two independent populations can be stated as

$$H_0: \mu_1 = \mu_2 \quad \text{or} \quad \mu_1 - \mu_2 = 0$$

and the alternative hypothesis, that the means are not the same, can be stated as

$$H_1: \mu_1 \neq \mu_2 \quad \text{or} \quad \mu_1 - \mu_2 \neq 0$$

To test the null hypothesis, use the pooled-variance *t*-test statistic t_{STAT} shown in Equation (10.1). The pooled-variance *t* test gets its name from the fact that the test statistic pools, or combines, the two sample variances S_1^2 and S_2^2 to compute S_p^2, the best estimate of the variance common to both populations, under the assumption that the two population variances are equal.[2]

[2]When the two sample sizes are equal (i.e., $n_1 = n_2$), the equation for the pooled variance can be simplified to

$$S_p^2 = \frac{S_1^2 + S_2^2}{2}$$

POOLED-VARIANCE *t* TEST FOR THE DIFFERENCE BETWEEN TWO MEANS

$$t_{STAT} = \frac{(\overline{X}_1 - \overline{X}_2) - (\mu_1 - \mu_2)}{\sqrt{S_p^2\left(\dfrac{1}{n_1} + \dfrac{1}{n_2}\right)}} \tag{10.1}$$

where

$$S_p^2 = \frac{(n_1 - 1)S_1^2 + (n_2 - 1)S_2^2}{(n_1 - 1) + (n_2 - 1)}$$

and

S_p^2 = pooled variance

$\overline{X}_1$ = mean of the sample taken from population 1

S_1^2 = variance of the sample taken from population 1

$$n_1 = \text{size of the sample taken from population 1}$$
$$\overline{X}_2 = \text{mean of the sample taken from population 2}$$
$$S_2^2 = \text{variance of the sample taken from population 2}$$
$$n_2 = \text{size of the sample taken from population 2}$$

The t_{STAT} test statistic follows a t distribution with $n_1 + n_2 - 2$ degrees of freedom.

For a given level of significance, α, in a two-tail test, you reject the null hypothesis if the computed t_{STAT} test statistic is greater than the upper-tail critical value from the t distribution or if the computed t_{STAT} test statistic is less than the lower-tail critical value from the t distribution. Figure 10.1 displays the regions of rejection.

FIGURE 10.1

Regions of rejection and nonrejection for the pooled-variance t test for the difference between the means (two-tail test)

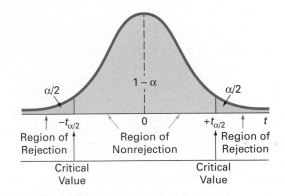

In a one-tail test in which the rejection region is in the lower tail, you reject the null hypothesis if the computed t_{STAT} test statistic is less than the lower-tail critical value from the t distribution. In a one-tail test in which the rejection region is in the upper tail, you reject the null hypothesis if the computed t_{STAT} test statistic is greater than the upper-tail critical value from the t distribution.

To demonstrate the use of the pooled-variance t test, return to the BLK Foods scenario on page 335. You define the business objective as determining whether the mean weekly sales of BLK Cola are the same when using a normal shelf location and when using an end-aisle display. There are two populations of interest. The first population is the set of all possible weekly sales of BLK Cola if all the BLK supermarkets used the normal shelf location. The second population is the set of all possible weekly sales of BLK Cola if all the BLK supermarkets used the end-aisle displays. You collect the data from a sample of 10 BLK supermarkets that have been assigned a normal shelf location and another sample of 10 BLK supermarkets that have been assigned an end-aisle display. You organize and store the results in Cola. Table 10.1 contains the BLK Cola sales (in number of cases) for the two samples.

TABLE 10.1

Comparing BLK Cola Weekly Sales from Two Different Display Locations (in Number of Cases)

Display Location									
Normal					**End-Aisle**				
22	34	52	62	30	52	71	76	54	67
40	64	84	56	59	83	66	90	77	84

The null and alternative hypotheses are

$$H_0: \mu_1 = \mu_2 \quad \text{or} \quad \mu_1 - \mu_2 = 0$$
$$H_1: \mu_1 \neq \mu_2 \quad \text{or} \quad \mu_1 - \mu_2 \neq 0$$

Assuming that the samples are from normal populations having equal variances, you can use the pooled-variance t test. The t_{STAT} test statistic follows a t distribution with

$10 + 10 - 2 = 18$ degrees of freedom. Using $\alpha = 0.05$ level of significance, you divide the rejection region into the two tails for this two-tail test (i.e., two equal parts of 0.025 each). Table E.3 shows that the critical values for this two-tail test are $+2.1009$ and -2.1009. As shown in Figure 10.2, the decision rule is

$$\text{Reject } H_0 \text{ if } t_{STAT} > +2.1009$$

$$\text{or if } t_{STAT} < -2.1009;$$

$$\text{otherwise do not reject } H_0.$$

FIGURE 10.2

Two-tail test of hypothesis for the difference between the means at the 0.05 level of significance with 18 degrees of freedom

From Figure 10.3, the computed t_{STAT} test statistic for this test is -3.0446 and the *p*-value is 0.0070.

FIGURE 10.3

Pooled-variance *t* test worksheet for the BLK Cola display locations

Figure 10.3 displays the **COMPUTE worksheet** *of the* **Pooled-Variance T workbook.** *Create this worksheet using the instructions in Section EG10.1.*

	A	B	
1	Pooled-Variance *t* Test for the Difference Between Two Means		
2	(assumes equal population variances)		
3	**Data**		
4	Hypothesized Difference	0	
5	Level of Significance	0.05	
6	**Population 1 Sample**		
7	Sample Size	10	=COUNT(DATACOPY!$A:$A)
8	Sample Mean	50.3	=AVERAGE(DATACOPY!$A:$A)
9	Sample Standard Deviation	18.7264	=STDEV(DATACOPY!$A:$A)
10	**Population 2 Sample**		
11	Sample Size	10	=COUNT(DATACOPY!$B:$B)
12	Sample Mean	72	=AVERAGE(DATACOPY!$B:$B)
13	Sample Standard Deviation	12.5433	=STDEV(DATACOPY!$B:$B)
14			
15	**Intermediate Calculations**		
16	Population 1 Sample Degrees of Freedom	9	=B7 - 1
17	Population 2 Sample Degrees of Freedom	9	=B11 - 1
18	Total Degrees of Freedom	18	=B16 + B17
19	Pooled Variance	254.0056	=((B16 * B9^2) + (B17 * B13^2))/B18
20	Standard Error	7.1275	=SQRT(B19 * (1/B7 + 1/B11))
21	Difference in Sample Means	-21.7	=B8 - B12
22	*t* Test Statistic	-3.0446	=(B21 - B4)/B20
23			
24	**Two-Tail Test**		
25	Lower Critical Value	-2.1009	=-TINV(B5, B18)
26	Upper Critical Value	2.1009	=TINV(B5, B18)
27	*p*-Value	0.0070	=TDIST(ABS(B22), B18, 2)
28	**Reject the null hypothesis**		=IF(B27 < B5, "Reject the null hypothesis", "Do not reject the null hypothesis")

Using Equation (10.1) on page 336 and the descriptive statistics provided in Figure 10.3,

$$t_{STAT} = \frac{(\bar{X}_1 - \bar{X}_2) - (\mu_1 - \mu_2)}{\sqrt{S_p^2 \left(\dfrac{1}{n_1} + \dfrac{1}{n_2} \right)}}$$

where

$$S_p^2 = \frac{(n_1 - 1)S_1^2 + (n_2 - 1)S_2^2}{(n_1 - 1) + (n_2 - 1)}$$

$$= \frac{9(18.7264)^2 + 9(12.5433)^2}{9 + 9} = 254.0056$$

Therefore,

$$t_{STAT} = \frac{(50.3 - 72.0) - 0.0}{\sqrt{254.0056\left(\dfrac{1}{10} + \dfrac{1}{10}\right)}} = \frac{-21.7}{\sqrt{50.801}} = -3.0446$$

You reject the null hypothesis because $t_{STAT} = -3.0446 < -2.1009$ and the p-value is 0.0070. In other words, the probability that $t_{STAT} > 3.0446$ or $t_{STAT} < -3.0446$ is equal to 0.0070. This p-value indicates that if the population means are equal, the probability of observing a difference this large or larger in the two sample means is only 0.0070. Because the p-value is less than $\alpha = 0.05$, there is sufficient evidence to reject the null hypothesis. You can conclude that the mean sales are different for the normal shelf location and the end-aisle location. Based on these results, the sales are lower for the normal location (i.e., higher for the end-aisle location).

In testing for the difference between the means, you assume that the populations are normally distributed, with equal variances. For situations in which the two populations have equal variances, the pooled-variance t test is **robust** (or not sensitive) to moderate departures from the assumption of normality, provided that the sample sizes are large. In such situations, you can use the pooled-variance t test without serious effects on its power. However, if you cannot assume that both populations are normally distributed, you have two choices. You can use a nonparametric procedure, such as the Wilcoxon rank sum test (see Section 12.5), that does not depend on the assumption of normality for the two populations, or you can use a normalizing transformation (see reference 5) on each of the outcomes and then use the pooled-variance t test.

To check the assumption of normality in each of the two populations, construct the boxplot of the sales for the two display locations shown in Figure 10.4. For these two small samples, there appears to be only moderate departure from normality, so the assumption of normality needed for the t test is not seriously violated.

FIGURE 10.4

Boxplot for the sales for two display locations

Create boxplots using the instructions in Section EG3.3.

Boxplot of Normal and End-Aisle Sales

Example 10.1 provides another application of the pooled-variance t test.

EXAMPLE 10.1

Testing for the Difference in the Mean Delivery Times

You and some friends have decided to test the validity of an advertisement by a local pizza restaurant, which says it delivers to the dormitories faster than a local branch of a national chain. Both the local pizza restaurant and national chain are located across the street from your college campus. You define the variable of interest as the delivery time, in minutes, from the time the pizza is ordered to when it is delivered. You collect the data by ordering 10 pizzas from the local pizza restaurant and 10 pizzas from the national chain, all at different times. You organize and store the data in **PizzaTime**. Table 10.2 shows the delivery times.

TABLE 10.2

Delivery Times (in minutes) for Local Pizza Restaurant and National Pizza Chain

Local		Chain	
16.8	18.1	22.0	19.5
11.7	14.1	15.2	17.0
15.6	21.8	18.7	19.5
16.7	13.9	15.6	16.5
17.5	20.8	20.8	24.0

At the 0.05 level of significance, is there evidence that the mean delivery time for the local pizza restaurant is less than the mean delivery time for the national pizza chain?

SOLUTION Because you want to know whether the mean is *lower* for the local pizza restaurant than for the national pizza chain, you have a one-tail test with the following null and alternative hypotheses:

$H_0: \mu_1 \geq \mu_2$ (The mean delivery time for the local pizza restaurant is equal to or greater than the mean delivery time for the national pizza chain.)

$H_1: \mu_1 < \mu_2$ (The mean delivery time for the local pizza restaurant is less than the mean delivery time for the national pizza chain.)

Figure 10.5 displays a worksheet solution for the pooled-variance t test for these data.

FIGURE 10.5

Pooled-variance t test worksheet for the pizza delivery time data

Create this worksheet using the instructions in Section EG10.1.

	A	B
1	Pooled-Variance *t* Test for the Difference Between Two Means	
2	(assumes equal population variances)	
3	**Data**	
4	Hypothesized Difference	0
5	Level of Significance	0.05
6	**Population 1 Sample**	
7	Sample Size	10
8	Sample Mean	16.7
9	Sample Standard Deviation	3.0955
10	**Population 2 Sample**	
11	Sample Size	10
12	Sample Mean	18.88
13	Sample Standard Deviation	2.8662
14		
15	**Intermediate Calculations**	
16	Population 1 Sample Degrees of Freedom	9
17	Population 2 Sample Degrees of Freedom	9
18	Total Degrees of Freedom	18
19	Pooled Variance	8.8987
20	Standard Error	1.3341
21	Difference in Sample Means	-2.18
22	*t* Test Statistic	-1.6341
23		
24	**Lower-Tail Test**	
25	Lower Critical Value	-1.7341
26	*p*-Value	0.0598
27	Do not reject the null hypothesis	

To illustrate the computations, using Equation (10.1) on page 336,

$$t_{STAT} = \frac{(\bar{X}_1 - \bar{X}_2) - (\mu_1 - \mu_2)}{\sqrt{S_p^2\left(\dfrac{1}{n_1} + \dfrac{1}{n_2}\right)}}$$

where

$$S_p^2 = \frac{(n_1 - 1)S_1^2 + (n_2 - 1)S_2^2}{(n_1 - 1) + (n_2 - 1)}$$

$$= \frac{9(3.0955)^2 + 9(2.8662)^2}{9 + 9} = 8.8987$$

Therefore,

$$t_{STAT} = \frac{(16.7 - 18.88) - 0.0}{\sqrt{8.8987\left(\dfrac{1}{10} + \dfrac{1}{10}\right)}} = \frac{-2.18}{\sqrt{1.7797}} = -1.6341$$

You do not reject the null hypothesis because $t_{STAT} = -1.6341 > -1.7341$. The p-value (as computed in the Figure 10.5 worksheet) is 0.0598. This p-value indicates that the probability that $t_{STAT} < -1.6341$ is equal to 0.0598. In other words, if the population means are equal, the probability that the sample mean delivery time for the local pizza restaurant is at least 2.18 minutes faster than the national chain is 0.0598. Because the p-value is greater than $\alpha = 0.05$, there is insufficient evidence to reject the null hypothesis. Based on these results, there is insufficient evidence for the local pizza restaurant to make the advertising claim that it has a faster delivery time.

Confidence Interval Estimate for the Difference Between Two Means

Instead of, or in addition to, testing for the difference in the means of two independent populations, you can use Equation (10.2) to develop a confidence interval estimate of the difference in the means.

The COMPUTE worksheet of the Pooled-Variance T workbook computes the confidence interval estimate for the difference between two means.

CONFIDENCE INTERVAL ESTIMATE FOR THE DIFFERENCE IN THE MEANS OF TWO INDEPENDENT POPULATIONS

$$(\bar{X}_1 - \bar{X}_2) \pm t_{\alpha/2}\sqrt{S_p^2\left(\frac{1}{n_1} + \frac{1}{n_2}\right)}$$

or

$$(\bar{X}_1 - \bar{X}_2) - t_{\alpha/2}\sqrt{S_p^2\left(\frac{1}{n_1} + \frac{1}{n_2}\right)} \leq \mu_1 - \mu_2 \leq (\bar{X}_1 - \bar{X}_2) + t_{\alpha/2}\sqrt{S_p^2\left(\frac{1}{n_1} + \frac{1}{n_2}\right)} \quad (10.2)$$

where $t_{\alpha/2}$ is the critical value of the t distribution, with $n_1 + n_2 - 2$ degrees of freedom, for an area of $\alpha/2$ in the upper tail.

For the sample statistics pertaining to the two aisle locations reported in Figure 10.3 on page 338, using 95% confidence, and Equation (10.2),

$$\bar{X}_1 = 50.3, n_1 = 10, \bar{X}_2 = 72.0, n_2 = 10, S_p^2 = 254.0056, \text{ and with } 10 + 10 - 2$$

$$= 18 \text{ degrees of freedom, } t_{0.025} = 2.1009$$

$$(50.3 - 72.0) \pm (2.1009)\sqrt{254.0056\left(\frac{1}{10} + \frac{1}{10}\right)}$$

$$-21.7 \pm (2.1009)(7.1275)$$

$$-21.7 \pm 14.97$$

$$-36.67 \leq \mu_1 - \mu_2 \leq -6.73$$

Therefore, you are 95% confident that the difference in mean sales between the normal aisle location and the end-aisle location is between -36.67 cases of cola and -6.73 cases of cola. In other words, the end-aisle location sells, on average, 6.73 to 36.67 cases more than the normal aisle location. From a hypothesis-testing perspective, because the interval does not include zero, you reject the null hypothesis of no difference between the means of the two populations.

t Test for the Difference Between Two Means Assuming Unequal Variances

If you cannot make the assumption that the two independent populations have equal variances, you cannot pool the two sample variances into the common estimate S_p^2 and therefore cannot use the pooled-variance t test. Instead, you use the **separate-variance t test** developed by Satterthwaite (see reference 4). This test procedure uses a series of computations that involves computing the two separate sample variances in order to compute degrees of freedom for the t-test statistic.

Figure 10.6 displays a worksheet solution that performs the separate-variance t test for the display location data.

FIGURE 10.6

Separate-variance t test worksheet for the display location data

	A	B		D	E	
1	Separate-Variances t Test for the Difference Between Two Means					
2	(assumes unequal population variances)					
3	**Data**					
4	Hypothesized Difference	0				
5	Level of Significance	0.05				
6	**Population 1 Sample**					
7	Sample Size	10	=COUNT(DATACOPY!$A:$A)			
8	Sample Mean	50.3	=AVERAGE(DATACOPY!$A:$A)			
9	Sample Standard Deviation	18.7264	=STDEV(DATACOPY!$A:$A)			
10	**Population 2 Sample**					
11	Sample Size	10	=COUNT(DATACOPY!$B:$B)			
12	Sample Mean	72	=AVERAGE(DATACOPY!$B:$B)			
13	Sample Standard Deviation	12.5433	=STDEV(DATACOPY!$B:$B)			
14						
15	**Intermediate Calculations**			**Calculations Area**		
16	Numerator of Degrees of Freedom	2580.7529	=(E18 + E19)^2	Pop. 1 Sample Variance	350.6778	=B9^2
17	Denominator of Degrees of Freedom	164.1430	=(E18^2)/(B7 - 1) + (E19^2)/(B11 - 1)	Pop. 2 Sample Variance	157.3333	=B13^2
18	Total Degrees of Freedom	15.7226	=B16/B17	Pop. 1 Sample Var./Sample Size	35.0678	=E16/B7
19	Degrees of Freedom	15	=INT(B18)	Pop. 2 Sample Var./Sample Size	15.7333	=E17/B11
20	Standard Error	7.1275	=SQRT(E18 + E19)	For one-tailed tests:		
21	Difference in Sample Means	-21.7	=B8 - B12	TDIST value	0.0041	=TDIST(ABS(B22), B19, 1)
22	Separate-Variance t Test Statistic	-3.0446	=B21/B20	1-TDIST value	0.9959	=1 - E21
23						
24	**Two-Tail Test**					
25	Lower Critical Value	-2.1314	=-TINV(B5, B19)			
26	Upper Critical Value	2.1314	=TINV(B5, B19)			
27	p-Value	0.0082	=TDIST(ABS(B22), B19, 2)			
28	**Reject the null hypothesis**		=IF(B27 < B5, "Reject the null hypothesis", "Do not reject the null hypothesis")			

Figure 10.6 displays the COMPUTE worksheet of the Separate-Variance T workbook.

Create this worksheet using the instructions in Section EG10.1.

In Figure 10.6, the test statistic $t_{STAT} = -3.0446$ and the p-value is $0.0082 < 0.05$. Thus, the results for the separate-variance t test are almost exactly the same as those of the pooled-variance t test. The assumption of equality of population variances had no real effect on the results. Sometimes, however, the results from the pooled-variance and separate-variance t tests conflict because the assumption of equal variances is violated. Therefore, it is important that you evaluate the assumptions and use those results as a guide in appropriately selecting a test procedure. In Section 10.4, the F test for the ratio of two variances is used to determine whether there is evidence of a difference in the two population variances. The results of that test can help you determine which of the t tests—pooled-variance or separate-variance—is more appropriate.

If you have ever used a telephone to seek customer service, at least once you've probably heard a message that begins "this call may be monitored . . ." Most of the time the message explains that the monitoring is for "quality assurance purposes," but do companies really monitor your calls to improve quality?

From one of our previous students, we've learned that a certain large financial corporation really does monitor calls for quality purposes. This student was asked to develop an improved training program for a call center that was hiring people to answer phone calls customers make about outstanding loans. For feedback and evaluation, she planned to randomly select phone calls received by each new employee and rate the employee on 10 aspects of the call, including whether the employee maintained a pleasant tone with the customer.

Who You Gonna Call?

Our previous student presented her plan to her boss for approval, but her boss, remembering the words of a famous statistician, said, "In God we trust, all others must bring data." That is, her boss wanted proof that her new training program would improve customer service. Faced with such a request, who would you call? She called one of us. "Hey, Professor, you'll never believe why I called. I work for a large company, and in the project I am currently working on, I have to put some of the statistics you taught us to work! Can you help?" The answer was "yes," and together they formulated this test:

- Randomly assign the 60 most recent hires to two training programs. Half would go through the preexisting training program, and half would be trained using the new program.

- At the end of the first month, compare the mean score for the 30 employees in the new

training program against the mean score for the 30 employees in the preexisting training program.

She listened as her professor explained, "What you are trying to prove is that the mean score from the new training program is higher than the mean score from the current program. You can make the null hypothesis that the means are equal and see if you can reject it in favor of the alternative that the mean score from the new program is higher."

"Or, as you used to say, 'if the p-value is low, H_0 must go!'—yes, I do remember!" she replied. Her professor chuckled and said, "Yes, that's correct. And if you can reject H_0, you will have the proof to present to your boss." She thanked him for his help and got back to work, with the newfound confidence that she would be able to successfully apply the t test that compares the means of two independent populations.

Problems for Section 10.1

LEARNING THE BASICS

10.1 If you have samples of $n_1 = 12$ and $n_2 = 15$, in performing the pooled-variance t test, how many degrees of freedom do you have?

10.2 Assume that you have a sample of $n_1 = 8$, with the sample mean $\bar{X}_1 = 42$, and a sample standard deviation $S_1 = 4$, and you have an independent sample of $n_2 = 15$ from another population with a sample mean of $\bar{X}_2 = 34$ and a sample standard deviation $S_2 = 5$.
a. What is the value of the pooled-variance t_{STAT} test statistic for testing $H_0: \mu_1 = \mu_2$?
b. In finding the critical value $t_{\alpha/2}$, how many degrees of freedom are there?
c. Using the level of significance $\alpha = 0.01$, what is the critical value for a one-tail test of the hypothesis $H_0: \mu_1 \le \mu_2$ against the alternative, $H_1: \mu_1 > \mu_2$?
d. What is your statistical decision?

10.3 What assumptions about the two populations are necessary in Problem 10.2?

10.4 Referring to Problem 10.2, construct a 95% confidence interval estimate of the population mean difference between μ_1 and μ_2.

10.5 Referring to Problem 10.2, if $n_1 = 5$ and $n_2 = 4$, how many degrees of freedom do you have?

10.6 Referring to Problem 10.2, if $n_1 = 5$ and $n_2 = 4$, at the 0.01 level of significance, is there evidence that $\mu_1 > \mu_2$?

APPLYING THE CONCEPTS

10.7 According to a recent study, when shopping online for luxury goods, men spend a mean of $2,401, whereas women spend a mean of $1,527 (data extracted from R. A. Smith, "Fashion Online: Retailers Tackle the Gender Gap," *The Wall Street Journal*, March 13, 2008, pp. D1, D10). Suppose that the study was based on a sample of 600 men and 700 females, and the standard deviation of the amount spent was $1,200 for men and $1,000 for women.
a. State the null and alternative hypothesis if you want to determine whether the mean amount spent is higher for men than for women.
b. In the context of this study, what is the meaning of the Type I error?
c. In the context of this study, what is the meaning of the Type II error?
d. At the 0.01 level of significance, is there evidence that the mean amount spent is higher for men than for women?

10.8 A recent study ("Snack Ads Spur Children to Eat More," *The New York Times*, July 20, 2009, p. B3) found that children who watched a cartoon with food advertising ate, on average, 28.5 grams of Goldfish crackers as compared to an average 19.7 grams of Goldfish crackers for children who watched a cartoon without food advertising. Although there were 118 children in the study, neither the sample size in each group nor the sample standard deviations were reported. Suppose that there were 59 children in each group, and the sample standard deviation for those children who watched the food ad was 8.6 grams and the sample standard deviation for those children who did not watch the food ad was 7.9 grams.

a. Assuming that the population variances are equal and $\alpha = 0.05$, is there evidence that the mean amount of Goldfish crackers eaten was significantly higher for the children who watched food ads?

b. Assuming that the population variances are equal, construct a 95% confidence interval estimate of the difference between the mean amount of Goldfish crackers eaten by the children who watched and did not watch the food ad.

c. Compare the results of (a) and (b) and discuss.

10.9 A problem with a telephone line that prevents a customer from receiving or making calls is disconcerting to both the customer and the telephone company. The file Phone contains samples of 20 problems reported to two different offices of a telephone company and the time to clear these problems (in minutes) from the customers' lines:

Central Office I Time to Clear Problems (minutes)

1.48 1.75 0.78 2.85 0.52 1.60 4.15 3.97 1.48 3.10

1.02 0.53 0.93 1.60 0.80 1.05 6.32 3.93 5.45 0.97

Central Office II Time to Clear Problems (minutes)

7.55 3.75 0.10 1.10 0.60 0.52 3.30 2.10 0.58 4.02

3.75 0.65 1.92 0.60 1.53 4.23 0.08 1.48 1.65 0.72

a. Assuming that the population variances from both offices are equal, is there evidence of a difference in the mean waiting time between the two offices? (Use $\alpha = 0.05$.)

b. Find the p-value in (a) and interpret its meaning.

c. What other assumption is necessary in (a)?

d. Assuming that the population variances from both offices are equal, construct and interpret a 95% confidence interval estimate of the difference between the population means in the two offices.

SELF ✓ **Test** **10.10** The Computer Anxiety Rating Scale (CARS) measures an individual's level of computer anxiety, on a scale from 20 (no anxiety) to 100 (highest level of anxiety). Researchers at Miami University administered CARS to 172 business students. One of the objectives of the study was to determine whether there is a difference in the level of computer anxiety experienced by female and male business students. They found the following:

	Males	Females
$\overline{X}$	40.26	36.85
S	13.35	9.42
n	100	72

Source: *Data extracted from T. Broome and D. Havelka, "Determinants of Computer Anxiety in Business Students,"* The Review of Business Information Systems, *Spring 2002, 6(2), pp. 9–16.*

a. At the 0.05 level of significance, is there evidence of a difference in the mean computer anxiety experienced by female and male business students?

b. Determine the p-value and interpret its meaning.

c. What assumptions do you have to make about the two populations in order to justify the use of the t test?

10.11 Digital cameras have taken over the majority of the point-and-shoot camera market. One of the important features of a camera is the battery life, as measured by the number of shots taken until the battery needs to be recharged. The file DigitalCameras contains the battery life of 29 subcompact cameras and 16 compact cameras (data extracted from "Digital Cameras," *Consumer Reports*, July 2009, pp. 28–29).

a. Assuming that the population variances from both types of digital cameras are equal, is there evidence of a difference in the mean battery life between the two types of digital cameras ($\alpha = 0.05$)?

b. Determine the p-value in (a) and interpret its meaning.

c. Assuming that the population variances from both types of digital cameras are equal, construct and interpret a 95% confidence interval estimate of the difference between the population mean battery life of the two types of digital cameras.

10.12 A bank with a branch located in a commercial district of a city has developed an improved process for serving customers during the noon-to-1 P.M. lunch period. The waiting time (operationally defined as the time elapsed from when the customer enters the line until he or she reaches the teller window) needs to be shortened to increase customer satisfaction. A random sample of 15 customers is selected, and the results (in minutes) are as follows (and stored in Bank1):

4.21 5.55 3.02 5.13 4.77 2.34 3.54 3.20

4.50 6.10 0.38 5.12 6.46 6.19 3.79

Suppose that another branch, located in a residential area, is also concerned with the noon-to-1 p.m. lunch period. A random sample of 15 customers is selected, and the results are as follows (and stored in Bank2):

9.66 5.90 8.02 5.79 8.73 3.82 8.01 8.35

10.49 6.68 5.64 4.08 6.17 9.91 5.47

a. Assuming that the population variances from both banks are equal, is there evidence of a difference in the mean waiting time between the two branches? (Use $\alpha = 0.05$.)

b. Determine the p-value in (a) and interpret its meaning.

c. In addition to equal variances, what other assumption is necessary in (a)?

d. Construct and interpret a 95% confidence interval estimate of the difference between the population means in the two branches.

10.13 Repeat Problem 10.12(a), assuming that the population variances in the two branches are not equal. Compare the results with those of Problem 10.12(a).

10.14 In intaglio printing, a design or figure is carved beneath the surface of hard metal or stone. Suppose that an experiment is designed to compare differences in mean surface hardness of steel plates used in intaglio printing (measured in indentation numbers), based on two different surface conditions—untreated and treated by lightly polishing with emery paper. In the experiment, 40 steel plates are randomly assigned—20 that are untreated, and 20 that are treated. The results of the experiment (in Intaglio) are as follows:

Untreated		Treated	
164.368	177.135	158.239	150.226
159.018	163.903	138.216	155.620
153.871	167.802	168.006	151.233
165.096	160.818	149.654	158.653
157.184	167.433	145.456	151.204
154.496	163.538	168.178	150.869
160.920	164.525	154.321	161.657
164.917	171.230	162.763	157.016
169.091	174.964	161.020	156.670
175.276	166.311	167.706	147.920

a. Assuming that the population variances from both conditions are equal, is there evidence of a difference in the mean surface hardness between untreated and treated steel plates? (Use $\alpha = 0.05$.)
b. Determine the *p*-value in (a) and interpret its meaning.
c. In addition to equal variances, what other assumption is necessary in (a)?
d. Construct and interpret a 95% confidence interval estimate of the difference between the population means from treated and untreated steel plates.

10.15 Repeat Problem 10.14(a), assuming that the population variances from untreated and treated steel plates are not equal. Compare the results with those of Problem 10.14(a).

10.16 Do young children use cell phones? Apparently so, according to a recent study (data extracted from A. Ross, "Message to Santa; Kids Want a Phone," *Palm Beach Post*, December 16, 2008, pp. 1A, 4A), which stated that cell phone users under 12 years of age averaged 137 calls per month as compared to 231 calls per month for cell phone users 13 to 17 years of age. No sample sizes were reported. Suppose that the results were based on samples of 50 cell phone users in each group and that the sample standard deviation for cell phone users under 12 years of age was 51.7 calls per month and the sample standard deviation for cell phone users 13 to 17 years of age was 67.6 calls per month.
a. Assuming that the variances in the populations of cell phone users are equal, is there evidence of a difference in the mean cell phone usage between cell phone users under 12 years of age and cell phone users 13 to 17 years of age? (Use a 0.05 level of significance.)
b. In addition to equal variances, what other assumption is necessary in (a)?

10.17 Nondestructive evaluation is a method that is used to describe the properties of components or materials without causing any permanent physical change to the units. It includes the determination of properties of materials and the classification of flaws by size, shape, type, and location. This method is most effective for detecting surface flaws and characterizing surface properties of electrically conductive materials. Data were collected that classified each component as having a flaw or not, based on manual inspection and operator judgment, and the data also reported the size of the crack in the material. Do the components classified as unflawed have a smaller mean crack size than components classified as flawed? The results in terms of crack size (in inches) are in Crack (data extracted from B. D. Olin and W. Q. Meeker, "Applications of Statistical Methods to Nondestructive Evaluation," *Technometrics*, 38, 1996, p. 101).
a. Assuming that the population variances are equal, is there evidence that the mean crack size is smaller for the unflawed specimens than for the flawed specimens? (Use $\alpha = 0.05$.)
b. Repeat (a), assuming that the population variances are not equal.
c. Compare the results of (a) and (b).

10.2 Comparing the Means of Two Related Populations

The hypothesis-testing procedures presented in Section 10.1 enable you to make comparisons and examine differences in the means of two *independent* populations. In this section, you will learn about a procedure for analyzing the difference between the means of two populations when you collect sample data from populations that are related—that is, when results of the first population are *not* independent of the results of the second population.

There are two situations that involve related data between populations. Either you take repeated measurements from the same set of items or individuals or you match items or individuals according to some characteristic. In either situation, you are interested in the *difference between the two related values* rather than the *individual values* themselves.

When you take **repeated measurements** on the same items or individuals, you assume that the same items or individuals will behave alike if treated alike. Your objective is to show that any differences between two measurements of the same items or individuals are due to different treatment conditions. For example, when performing a taste-testing experiment comparing two beverages, you can use each person in the sample as his or her own control so that you can have *repeated measurements* on the same individual.

The second situation that involves related data between populations is when you have **matched samples**. Here items or individuals are paired together according to some characteristic of interest. For example, in test marketing a product in two different advertising campaigns, a sample of test markets can be *matched* on the basis of the test market population size and/or demographic variables. By accounting for the differences in test market population size and/or demographic variables, you are better able to measure the effects of the two different advertising campaigns.

Regardless of whether you have matched samples or repeated measurements, the objective is to study the difference between two measurements by reducing the effect of the variability that is due to the items or individuals themselves. Table 10.3 shows the differences in the individual values for two related populations. To read this table, let $X_{11}, X_{12}, \ldots, X_{1n}$ represent the n values from a sample. And let $X_{21}, X_{22}, \ldots, X_{2n}$ represent either the corresponding n matched values from a second sample or the corresponding n repeated measurements from the initial sample. Then, $D_1, D_2, \ldots, D_n$ will represent the corresponding set of n difference *scores* such that

$$D_1 = X_{11} - X_{21}, D_2 = X_{12} - X_{22}, \ldots, \text{ and } D_n = X_{1n} - X_{2n}.$$

To test for the mean difference between two related populations, you treat the difference scores, each D_i, as values from a single sample.

TABLE 10.3

Determining the Difference Between Two Related Samples

Value	Sample 1	Sample 2	Difference
1	X_{11}	X_{21}	$D_1 = X_{11} - X_{21}$
2	X_{12}	X_{22}	$D_2 = X_{12} - X_{22}$
.	.	.	.
.	.	.	.
.	.	.	.
i	X_{1i}	X_{2i}	$D_i = X_{1i} - X_{2i}$
.	.	.	.
.	.	.	.
.	.	.	.
n	X_{1n}	X_{2n}	$D_n = X_{1n} - X_{2n}$

Paired t Test

If you assume that the difference scores are randomly and independently selected from a population that is normally distributed, you can use the **paired t test for the mean difference** in related populations to determine whether there is a significant population mean difference. Like the one-sample t test developed in Section 9.2 [see Equation (9.2) on page 310], the t-test statistic developed here follows the t distribution, with $n - 1$ degrees of freedom. Although you must assume that the population is normally distributed, as long as the sample size is not very small and the population is not highly skewed, you can use the paired t test.

To test the null hypothesis that there is no difference in the means of two related populations:

$$H_0: \mu_D = 0 \text{ (where } \mu_D = \mu_1 - \mu_2)$$

against the alternative that the means are not the same:

$$H_1: \mu_D \neq 0$$

you compute the t_{STAT} test statistic using Equation (10.3).

PAIRED t TEST FOR THE MEAN DIFFERENCE

$$t_{STAT} = \frac{\overline{D} - \mu_D}{\frac{S_D}{\sqrt{n}}}$$

(10.3)

where

μ_D = hypothesized mean difference

$$\overline{D} = \frac{\sum_{i=1}^{n} D_i}{n}$$

$$S_D = \sqrt{\frac{\sum_{i=1}^{n} (D_i - \overline{D})^2}{n - 1}}$$

The t_{STAT} test statistic follows a t distribution with $n - 1$ degrees of freedom.

For a two-tail test with a given level of significance, α, you reject the null hypothesis if the computed t_{STAT} test statistic is greater than the upper-tail critical value $t_{\alpha/2}$ from the t distribution, or if the computed t_{STAT} test statistic is less than the lower-tail critical value $-t_{\alpha/2}$ from the t distribution. The decision rule is

Reject H_0 if $t_{STAT} > t_{\alpha/2}$

or if $t_{STAT} < -t_{\alpha/2}$;

otherwise, do not reject H_0.

The following example illustrates the use of the t test for the mean difference. The Automobile Association of America (AAA) conducted a mileage test to compare the fuel economy from real-life driving done by AAA members and results of driving done according to government standards (J. Healey, "Fuel Economy Calculations to Be Altered," *USA Today*, January 11, 2006, p. 1B).

What is the best way to design an experiment to compare the mileage from real-life driving done by AAA members and results of driving done according to government standards? One approach is to take two independent samples and then use the hypothesis tests discussed in Section 10.1. In this approach, you would use one set of automobiles to test the real-life driving done by AAA members. Then you would use a second set of different automobiles to test the results of driving done according to government standards.

However, because the first set of automobiles to test the real-life driving done by AAA members may get lower or higher mileage than the second set of automobiles, this is not a good approach. A better approach is to use a repeated-measurements experiment. In this experiment, you use one set of automobiles. For each automobile, you conduct a test of real-life driving done by an AAA member and a test of driving done according to government standards. By measuring the two mileages for the same automobiles, you can reduce the variability in the mileages compared with what would occur if you used two independent sets of automobiles. This approach focuses on the differences between the real-life driving done by an AAA member and the driving done according to government standards.

You decide to collect data by conducting an experiment from a sample of $n = 9$ automobiles. You organize and store the data in AAAMileage. Table 10.4 shows the results.

TABLE 10.4

Repeated Measurements of Mileage for Real-Life Driving by AAA Members and Driving Done According to Government Standards

Model	Members	Government	Difference (D_i)
2005 Ford F-150	14.3	16.8	−2.5
2005 Chevrolet Silverado	15.0	17.8	−2.8
2002 Honda Accord LX	27.8	26.2	+1.6
2002 Honda Civic	27.9	33.2	−5.3
2004 Honda Civic Hybrid	48.8	47.6	+1.2
2002 Ford Explorer	16.8	18.3	−1.5
2005 Toyota Camry	23.7	28.5	−4.8
2003 Toyota Corolla	32.8	33.1	−0.3
2005 Toyota Prius	37.3	44.0	−6.7
			−21.1

Your objective is to determine whether there is any difference in the mean mileage between the real-life driving done by an AAA member and the driving done according to government standards. In other words, is there evidence that the mean mileage is different between the two types of driving? Thus, the null and alternative hypotheses are

H_0: $\mu_D = 0$ (There is no difference in mean mileage between the real-life driving done by an AAA member and the driving done according to government standards.)

H_1: $\mu_D \neq 0$ (There is a difference in mean mileage between the real-life driving done by an AAA member and the driving done according to government standards.)

Choosing the level of significance of $\alpha = 0.05$ and assuming that the differences are normally distributed, you use the paired t test [Equation (10.3)]. For a sample of $n = 9$ automobiles, there are $n - 1 = 8$ degrees of freedom. Using Table E.3, the decision rule is

$$\text{Reject } H_0 \text{ if } t_{STAT} > t_{0.025} = 2.3060$$

$$\text{or if } t_{STAT} < -t_{0.025} = -2.3060;$$

$$\text{otherwise, do not reject } H_0.$$

For the $n = 9$ differences (see Table 10.4), the sample mean difference is

$$\overline{D} = \frac{\sum\limits_{i=1}^{n} D_i}{n} = \frac{-21.1}{9} = -2.3444$$

and

$$S_D = \sqrt{\frac{\sum\limits_{i=1}^{n} (D_i - \overline{D})^2}{n - 1}} = 2.8936$$

From Equation (10.3) on page 347,

$$t_{STAT} = \frac{\overline{D} - \mu_D}{\dfrac{S_D}{\sqrt{n}}} = \frac{-2.3444 - 0}{\dfrac{2.8936}{\sqrt{9}}} = -2.4307$$

Because $t_{STAT} = -2.4307$ is less than -2.3060, you reject the null hypothesis, H_0 (see Figure 10.7). There is evidence of a difference in mean mileage between the real-life driving done by an AAA member and the driving done according to government standards. Real-life driving results in a lower mean mileage.

FIGURE 10.7

Two-tail paired t test at the 0.05 level of significance with 8 degrees of freedom

Figure 10.8 presents a worksheet solution for this example that computes both the test statistic and the p-value. Because the p-value $= 0.0412 < \alpha = 0.05$, you reject H_0. The p-value indicates that if the two types of driving have the same population mean mileage, the probability that one type of driving would have a sample mean 2.3444 miles per gallon less than the other type is 0.0412. Because this probability is less than $\alpha = 0.05$, you conclude that the alternative hypothesis is true.

FIGURE 10.8

Paired t test worksheet for the car mileage data

	A	B
1	Paired t Test	
2		
3	**Data**	
4	Hypothesized Mean Diff.	0
5	Level of significance	0.05
6		
7	**Intermediate Calculations**	
8	Sample Size	9 =COUNT(PtCalcs!$A:$A)
9	DBar	-2.3444 =AVERAGE(PtCalcs!$C:$C)
10	degrees of freedom	8 =B8 - 1
11	S_D	2.8936 =SQRT(SUM(PtCalcs!$D:$D)/B10)
12	Standard Error	0.9645 =B11/SQRT(B8)
13	t Test Statistic	-2.4307 =(B9 - B4)/B12
14		
15	**Two-Tail Test**	
16	Lower Critical Value	-2.3060 =-TINV(B5, B10)
17	Upper Critical Value	2.3060 =TINV(B5, B10)
18	p-Value	0.0412 =TDIST(ABS(B13), B10, 2)
19	Reject the null hypothesis	=IF(B18 <B5, D27, D28)

	A	B	C	D	E F	G
1	Members	Government	D_i	$(D_i-DBar)^2$	DBar	-2.3444
2	14.3	16.8	-2.5	0.0242		
3	15	17.8	-2.8	0.2075		
4	27.8	26.2	1.6	15.5586		
5	27.9	33.2	-5.3	8.7353		
6	48.8	47.6	1.2	12.5631		
7	16.8	18.3	-1.5	0.7131		
8	23.7	28.5	-4.8	6.0298		
9	32.8	33.1	-0.3	4.1798		
10	37.3	44	-6.7	18.9709		

Not shown
Cell D27: Reject the null hypothesis
Cell D28: Do not reject the null hypothesis

Figure 10.8 displays the **COMPUTE** (left) and **PtCalcs** (right) **worksheets** of the **Paired T workbook**. The COMPUTE worksheet uses values computed in PtCalcs.

Create these worksheets using the instructions in Section EG10.2.

To evaluate the validity of the assumption of normality, you construct a boxplot of the differences, as shown in Figure 10.9.

FIGURE 10.9
Boxplot for the car
mileage data

Boxplot for the Car Mileage Differences

The Figure 10.9 boxplot shows approximate symmetry. Thus, the data do not greatly contradict the underlying assumption of normality. If a boxplot, histogram, or normal probability plot reveals that the assumption of underlying normality in the population is severely violated, then the *t* test may be inappropriate especially if the sample size is small. If you believe that the *t* test is inappropriate, you can use either a *nonparametric* procedure that does not make the assumption of underlying normality (see references 1 and 2) or make a data transformation (see reference 5) and then recheck the assumptions to determine whether you should use the *t* test.

EXAMPLE 10.2

Paired *t* Test of Pizza Delivery Times

Recall from Example 10.1 on page 340 that a local pizza restaurant situated across the street from your college campus advertises that it delivers to the dormitories faster than the local branch of a national pizza chain. In order to determine whether this advertisement is valid, you and some friends have decided to order 10 pizzas from the local pizza restaurant and 10 pizzas from the national chain. In fact, each time you ordered a pizza from the local pizza restaurant, at the same time, your friends ordered a pizza from the national pizza chain. Thus, you have matched samples. For each of the 10 times that pizzas were ordered, you have one measurement from the local pizza restaurant and one from the national chain. At the 0.05 level of significance, is the mean delivery time for the local pizza restaurant less than the mean delivery time for the national pizza chain?

SOLUTION Use the paired *t* test to analyze the Table 10.5 data (stored in PizzaTime). Figure 10.10 shows a worksheet that presents the paired *t*-test results for the pizza delivery data.

TABLE 10.5

Delivery Times for
Local Pizza Restaurant
and National Pizza
Chain

Time	Local	Chain	Difference
1	16.8	22.0	−5.2
2	11.7	15.2	−3.5
3	15.6	18.7	−3.1
4	16.7	15.6	1.1
5	17.5	20.8	−3.3
6	18.1	19.5	−1.4
7	14.1	17.0	−2.9
8	21.8	19.5	2.3
9	13.9	16.5	−2.6
10	20.8	24.0	−3.2
			−21.8

FIGURE 10.10

Paired *t*-test worksheet for the pizza delivery data

Figure 10.10 contains a worksheet based on the COMPUTE_LOWER worksheet of the Paired T workbook. Create one-tail worksheets using the instructions in Section EG10.2.

	A	B
1	Paired *t* Test	
2		
3	**Data**	
4	Hypothesized Mean Diff.	0
5	Level of significance	0.05
6		
7	**Intermediate Calculations**	
8	Sample Size	10 =COUNT(PtCalcs!$A:$A)
9	DBar	-2.1800 =AVERAGE(PtCalcs!$C:$C)
10	degrees of freedom	9 =B8 -1
11	S_D	2.2641 =SQRT(SUM(PtCalcs!$D:$D)/B10)
12	Standard Error	0.7160 =B11/SQRT(B8)
13	*t* Test Statistic	-3.0448 =(B9 - B4)/B12
14		
15	**Lower-Tail Test**	
16	Lower Critical Value	-1.8331 =-TINV(2 * B5, B10)
17	*p*-Value	0.0070 =IF(B13, E23, E24)
18	Reject the null hypothesis	=IF(B17 < B5, D27, D28)

Not shown
Cell E23: =TDIST(ABS(B13), B10, 1)
Cell E24: =1 - E23
Cell D27: Reject the null hypothesis
Cell D28: Do not reject the null hypothesis
and the PtCalcs worksheet for this problem

The null and alternative hypotheses are

$H_0: \mu_D \geq 0$ (Mean delivery time for the local pizza restaurant is greater than or equal to the mean delivery time for the national pizza chain.)

$H_1: \mu_D < 0$ (Mean delivery time for the local pizza restaurant is less than the mean delivery time for the national pizza chain.)

Choosing the level of significance $\alpha = 0.05$ and assuming that the differences are normally distributed, you use the paired *t* test [Equation (10.3) on page 347]. For a sample of $n = 10$ delivery times, there are $n - 1 = 9$ degrees of freedom. Using Table E.3, the decision rule is

$$\text{Reject } H_0 \text{ if } t_{STAT} < -t_{0.05} = -1.8331;$$

$$\text{otherwise, do not reject } H_0.$$

To illustrate the computations, for $n = 10$ differences (see Table 10.5), the sample mean difference is

$$\overline{D} = \frac{\sum_{i=1}^{n} D_i}{n} = \frac{-21.8}{10} = -2.18$$

and the sample standard deviation of the difference is

$$S_D = \sqrt{\frac{\sum_{i=1}^{n} (D_i - \overline{D})^2}{n - 1}} = 2.2641$$

From Equation (10.3) on page 347,

$$t_{STAT} = \frac{\overline{D} - \mu_D}{\frac{S_D}{\sqrt{n}}} = \frac{-2.18 - 0}{\frac{2.2641}{\sqrt{10}}} = -3.0448$$

Because $t_{STAT} = -3.0448$ is less than -1.8331, you reject the null hypothesis, H_0 (the p-value is $0.0070 < 0.05$). There is evidence that the mean delivery time is lower for the local pizza restaurant than for the national pizza chain.

This conclusion is different from the one you reached in Example 10.1 on page 340 when you used the pooled-variance t test for these data. By pairing the delivery times, you are able to focus on the differences between the two pizza delivery services and not the variability created by ordering pizzas at different times of day. The paired t test is a more powerful statistical procedure that is better able to detect the difference between the two pizza delivery services, because you are controlling for the time of day they were ordered.

Confidence Interval Estimate for the Mean Difference

Instead of, or in addition to, testing for the difference between the means of two related populations, you can use Equation (10.4) to construct a confidence interval estimate for the mean difference.

CONFIDENCE INTERVAL ESTIMATE FOR THE MEAN DIFFERENCE

$$\overline{D} \pm t_{\alpha/2}\frac{S_D}{\sqrt{n}}$$

or

$$\overline{D} - t_{\alpha/2}\frac{S_D}{\sqrt{n}} \leq \mu_D \leq \overline{D} + t_{\alpha/2}\frac{S_D}{\sqrt{n}} \tag{10.4}$$

where $t_{\alpha/2}$ is the critical value of the t distribution, with $n - 1$ degrees of freedom, for an area of $\alpha/2$ in the upper tail.

Return to the example comparing mileage generated by real-life driving and by government standards on page 348. Using Equation (10.4), $\overline{D} = -2.3444$, $S_D = 2.8936$, $n = 9$, and $t_{\alpha/2} = 2.306$ (for 95% confidence and $n - 1 = 8$ degrees of freedom),

$$-2.3444 \pm (2.306)\frac{2.8936}{\sqrt{9}}$$

$$-2.3444 \pm 2.2242$$

$$-4.5686 \leq \mu_D \leq -0.1202$$

Thus, with 95% confidence, the mean difference in gasoline mileage between the real-life driving done by an AAA member and the driving done according to government standards is between -4.5686 and -0.1202 miles per gallon. Because the interval estimate contains only values less than zero, you can conclude that there is a difference in the population means. The mean miles per gallon for the real-life driving done by an AAA member is less than the mean miles per gallon for the driving done according to government standards.

Problems for Section 10.2

LEARNING THE BASICS

10.18 An experimental design for a paired t test has 20 pairs of identical twins. How many degrees of freedom are there in this t test?

10.19 Fifteen volunteers are recruited to participate in an experiment. A measurement is made (such as blood pressure) before each volunteer is asked to read a particularly upsetting passage from a book and after each volunteer

reads the passage from the book. In the analysis of the data collected from this experiment, how many degrees of freedom are there in the test?

APPLYING THE CONCEPTS

SELF Test **10.20** Nine experts rated two brands of Colombian coffee in a taste-testing experiment. A rating on a 7-point scale (1 = extremely unpleasing, 7 = extremely pleasing) is given for each of four characteristics: taste, aroma, richness, and acidity. The following data (stored in **Coffee**) display the summated ratings—accumulated over all four characteristics.

	BRAND	
EXPERT	A	B
C.C.	24	26
S.E.	27	27
E.G.	19	22
B.L.	24	27
C.M.	22	25
C.N.	26	27
G.N.	27	26
R.M.	25	27
P.V.	22	23

a. At the 0.05 level of significance, is there evidence of a difference in the mean summated ratings between the two brands?
b. What assumption is necessary about the population distribution in order to perform this test?
c. Determine the *p*-value in (a) and interpret its meaning.
d. Construct and interpret a 95% confidence interval estimate of the difference in the mean summated ratings between the two brands.

10.21 In industrial settings, alternative methods often exist for measuring variables of interest. The data in **Measurement** (coded to maintain confidentiality) represent measurements in-line that were collected from an analyzer during the production process and from an analytical lab (data extracted from M. Leitnaker, "Comparing Measurement Processes: In-line Versus Analytical Measurements," *Quality Engineering*, 13, 2000–2001, pp. 293–298).
a. At the 0.05 level of significance, is there evidence of a difference in the mean measurements in-line and from an analytical lab?
b. What assumption is necessary about the population distribution in order to perform this test?
c. Use a graphical method to evaluate the validity of the assumption in (a).
d. Construct and interpret a 95% confidence interval estimate of the difference in the mean measurements in-line and from an analytical lab.

10.22 Can students save money by comparison shopping for textbooks at Amazon.com? To investigate this possibility, a random sample of 19 textbooks used during the Spring 2009 semester at Miami University was selected. The prices for these textbooks at both a local bookstore and through Amazon.com were recorded. The prices for the textbooks are stored in **BookPrices**.

a. At the 0.01 level of significance, is there evidence of a difference between the mean price of textbooks at the local bookstore and Amazon.com?
b. What assumption is necessary about the population distribution in order to perform this test?
c. Construct a 99% confidence interval estimate of the mean difference in price. Interpret the interval.
d. Compare the results of (a) and (c).

10.23 In tough economic times, magazines and other media have trouble selling advertisements. Thus, one indicator of a weak economy is a reduction in the number of magazine pages devoted to advertisements. The file **Ad Pages** contains the number of pages devoted to advertisements in May 2008 and May 2009 for 12 men's magazines (extracted from W. Levith, "Magazine Monitor," *Mediaweek*, April 20, 2009, p.53).
a. At the 0.05 level of significance, is there evidence that the mean number of pages devoted to advertisements in men's magazines was higher in May 2008 than in May 2009?
b. What assumption is necessary about the population distribution in order to perform this test?
c. Use a graphical method to evaluate the validity of the assumption in (b).
d. Construct and interpret a 95% confidence interval estimate of the difference in the mean number of pages devoted to advertisements in men's magazines between May 2008 and May 2009.

10.24 Multiple myeloma, or blood plasma cancer, is characterized by increased blood vessel formulation (angiogenesis) in the bone marrow that is a predictive factor in survival. One treatment approach used for multiple myeloma is stem cell transplantation with the patient's own stem cells. The following data (stored in **Myeloma**) represent the bone marrow microvessel density for patients who had a complete response to the stem cell transplant (as measured by blood and urine tests). The measurements were taken immediately prior to the stem cell transplant and at the time the complete response was determined:

Patient	Before	After
1	158	284
2	189	214
3	202	101
4	353	227
5	416	290
6	426	176
7	441	290

Source: *Data extracted from S. V. Rajkumar, R. Fonseca, T. E. Witzig, M. A. Gertz, and P. R. Greipp, "Bone Marrow Angiogenesis in Patients Achieving Complete Response After Stem Cell Transplantation for Multiple Myeloma,"* Leukemia, *1999, 13, pp. 469–472.*

a. At the 0.05 level of significance, is there evidence that the mean bone marrow microvessel density is higher before the stem cell transplant than after the stem cell transplant?

b. Interpret the meaning of the *p*-value in (a).

c. Construct and interpret a 95% confidence interval estimate of the mean difference in bone marrow microvessel density before and after the stem cell transplant.

d. What assumption is necessary about the population distribution in order to perform the test in (a)?

10.25 Over the past year, the vice president for human resources at a large medical center has run a series of three-month workshops aimed at increasing worker motivation and performance. To check the effectiveness of the workshops, she selected a random sample of 35 employees from the personnel files. She collected the employee performance ratings recorded before and after workshop attendance and stored the paired ratings for all 35 in `Perform`. Worksheet results for this sample are shown below and at the right. State your findings and conclusions in a report to the vice president for human resources.

	A	B
1	Difference	
2		
3	Mean	-5.2571
4	Standard Error	1.9478
5	Median	-5
6	Mode	-10
7	Standard Deviation	11.5232
8	Sample Variance	132.7849
9	Kurtosis	1.1038
10	Skewness	0.1103
11	Range	61
12	Minimum	-34
13	Maximum	27
14	Sum	-184
15	Count	35

	A	B
1	Paired *t* Test	
2		
3	**Data**	
4	Hypothesized Mean Diff.	0
5	Level of significance	0.05
6		
7	**Intermediate Calculations**	
8	Sample Size	35
9	DBar	-5.2571
10	degrees of freedom	34
11	S_D	11.5232
12	Standard Error	1.9478
13	*t* Test Statistic	-2.6990
14		
15	**Two-Tail Test**	
16	Lower Critical Value	-2.0322
17	Upper Critical Value	2.0322
18	*p*-Value	0.0108
19	Reject the null hypothesis	
20		
21	**Lower-Tail Test**	
22	Lower Critical Value	-1.6909
23	*p*-Value	0.0054
24	Reject the null hypothesis	

10.26 The data in `Concrete1` represent the compressive strength, in thousands of pounds per square inch (psi), of 40 samples of concrete taken two and seven days after pouring.

Source: *Data extracted from O. Carrillo-Gamboa and R. F. Gunst, "Measurement-Error-Model Collinearities," Technometrics, 34, 1992, pp. 454–464.*

a. At the 0.01 level of significance, is there evidence that the mean strength is lower at two days than at seven days?

b. What assumption is necessary about the population distribution in order to perform this test?

c. Find the *p*-value in (a) and interpret its meaning.

10.3 Comparing the Proportions of Two Independent Populations

Often, you need to make comparisons and analyze differences between two population proportions. You can perform a test for the difference between two proportions selected from independent populations by using two different methods. This section presents a procedure whose test statistic, Z_{STAT}, is approximated by a standardized normal distribution. In Section 12.1, a procedure is developed whose test statistic, χ^2_{STAT}, is approximated by a chi-square distribution. As you will see when you read that section, the results from these two tests are equivalent.

Z Test for the Difference Between Two Proportions

In evaluating differences between two population proportions, you can use a **Z test for the difference between two proportions**. The Z_{STAT} test statistic is based on the difference between two sample proportions ($p_1 - p_2$). This test statistic, given in Equation (10.5), approximately follows a standardized normal distribution for large enough sample sizes.

Z TEST FOR THE DIFFERENCE BETWEEN TWO PROPORTIONS

$$Z_{STAT} = \frac{(p_1 - p_2) - (\pi_1 - \pi_2)}{\sqrt{\bar{p}(1 - \bar{p})\left(\frac{1}{n_1} + \frac{1}{n_2}\right)}} \qquad (10.5)$$

with

$$\bar{p} = \frac{X_1 + X_2}{n_1 + n_2} \qquad p_1 = \frac{X_1}{n_1} \qquad p_2 = \frac{X_2}{n_2}$$

where

p_1 = proportion of items of interest in sample 1

X_1 = number of items of interest in sample 1

n_1 = sample size of sample 1

π_1 = proportion of items of interest in population 1

p_2 = proportion of items of interest in sample 2

X_2 = number of items of interest in sample 2

n_2 = sample size of sample 2

π_2 = proportion of items of interest in population 2

$\bar{p}$ = pooled estimate of the population proportion of items of interest

The Z_{STAT} test statistic approximately follows a standardized normal distribution.

Under the null hypothesis, you assume that the two population proportions are equal ($\pi_1 = \pi_2$). Because the pooled estimate for the population proportion is based on the null hypothesis, you combine, or pool, the two sample proportions to compute $\bar{p}$, an overall estimate of the common population proportion. This estimate is equal to the number of items of interest in the two samples combined ($X_1 + X_2$) divided by the total sample size from the two samples combined ($n_1 + n_2$).

As shown in the following table, you can use this Z test for the difference between population proportions to determine whether there is a difference in the proportion of items of interest in the two populations (two-tail test) or whether one population has a higher proportion of items of interest than the other population (one-tail test):

Two-Tail Test	One-Tail Test	One-Tail Test
$H_0: \pi_1 = \pi_2$	$H_0: \pi_1 \geq \pi_2$	$H_0: \pi_1 \leq \pi_2$
$H_1: \pi_1 \neq \pi_2$	$H_1: \pi_1 < \pi_2$	$H_1: \pi_1 > \pi_2$

where

π_1 = proportion of items of interest in population 1

π_2 = proportion of items of interest in population 2

To test the null hypothesis that there is no difference between the proportions of two independent populations:

$$H_0: \pi_1 = \pi_2$$

against the alternative that the two population proportions are not the same:

$$H_1: \pi_1 \neq \pi_2$$

use the Z_{STAT} test statistic, given by Equation (10.5). For a given level of significance, α, you reject the null hypothesis if the computed Z_{STAT} test statistic is greater than the upper-tail critical value from the standardized normal distribution, or if the computed Z_{STAT} test statistic is less than the lower-tail critical value from the standardized normal distribution.

To illustrate the use of the Z test for the equality of two proportions, suppose that you are the manager of T.C. Resort Properties, a collection of five upscale resort hotels located on two tropical islands. On one of the islands, T.C. Resort Properties has two hotels, the Beachcomber and the Windsurfer. You have defined the business objective as improving the return rate of guests at the Beachcomber and the Windsurfer hotels. On the questionnaire completed by hotel guests upon their departure, one question asked is whether the guest is likely to return to the hotel. Responses to this and other questions were collected from 227 guests at the Beachcomber and 262 guests at the Windsurfer. The results for this question indicated that 163 of 227 guests at the Beachcomber responded yes, they were likely to return to the hotel and 154 of 262 guests at the Windsurfer responded yes, they were likely to return to the hotel. At the 0.05 level of significance, is there evidence of a significant difference in guest satisfaction (as measured by the likelihood to return to the hotel) between the two hotels?

The null and alternative hypotheses are

$$H_0: \pi_1 = \pi_2 \quad \text{or} \quad \pi_1 - \pi_2 = 0$$

$$H_1: \pi_1 \neq \pi_2 \quad \text{or} \quad \pi_1 - \pi_2 \neq 0$$

Using the 0.05 level of significance, the critical values are -1.96 and $+1.96$ (see Figure 10.11), and the decision rule is

Reject H_0 if $Z_{STAT} < -1.96$

or if $Z_{STAT} > +1.96$;

otherwise, do not reject H_0.

FIGURE 10.11

Regions of rejection and nonrejection when testing a hypothesis for the difference between two proportions at the 0.05 level of significance

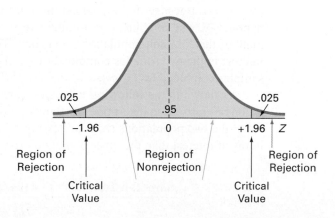

Using Equation (10.5) on page 355,

$$Z_{STAT} = \frac{(p_1 - p_2) - (\pi_1 - \pi_2)}{\sqrt{\bar{p}(1 - \bar{p})\left(\dfrac{1}{n_1} + \dfrac{1}{n_2}\right)}}$$

where

$$p_1 = \frac{X_1}{n_1} = \frac{163}{227} = 0.7181 \qquad p_2 = \frac{X_2}{n_2} = \frac{154}{262} = 0.5878$$

and

$$\bar{p} = \frac{X_1 + X_2}{n_1 + n_2} = \frac{163 + 154}{227 + 262} = \frac{317}{489} = 0.6483$$

so that

$$Z_{STAT} = \frac{(0.7181 - 0.5878) - (0)}{\sqrt{0.6483(1 - 0.6483)\left(\dfrac{1}{227} + \dfrac{1}{262}\right)}}$$

$$= \frac{0.1303}{\sqrt{(0.228)(0.0082)}}$$

$$= \frac{0.1303}{\sqrt{0.00187}}$$

$$= \frac{0.1303}{0.0432} = +3.0088$$

Using the 0.05 level of significance, you reject the null hypothesis because $Z_{STAT} = +3.0088 > +1.96$. The p-value is 0.0026 (computed using Table E.2 or from the Figure 10.12 worksheet) and indicates that if the null hypothesis is true, the probability that a Z_{STAT} test statistic is less than -3.0088 is 0.0013, and, similarly, the probability that a Z_{STAT} test statistic is greater than $+3.0088$ is 0.0013. Thus, for this two-tail test, the p-value is $0.0013 + 0.0013 = 0.0026$. Because $0.0026 < \alpha = 0.05$, you reject the null hypothesis. There is evidence to conclude that the two hotels are significantly different with respect to guest satisfaction; a greater proportion of guests are willing to return to the Beachcomber than to the Windsurfer.

FIGURE 10.12

Z test for the difference between two proportions worksheet for the hotel guest satisfaction problem

Figure 10.12 displays the **COMPUTE worksheet** of the **Z Two Proportions workbook**. Create this worksheet using the instructions in Section EG10.3

	A	B	
1	Z Test for Differences in Two Proportions		
2			
3	**Data**		
4	Hypothesized Difference	0	
5	Level of Significance	0.05	
6	**Group 1**		
7	Number of Items of Interest	163	
8	Sample Size	227	
9	**Group 2**		
10	Number of Items of Interest	154	
11	Sample Size	262	
12			
13	**Intermediate Calculations**		
14	Group 1 Proportion	0.7181	=B7/B8
15	Group 2 Proportion	0.5878	=B10/B11
16	Difference in Two Proportions	0.1303	=B14 - B15
17	Average Proportion	0.6483	=(B7 + B10)/(B8 + B11)
18	Z Test Statistic	3.0088	=(B16 - B4)/SQRT(B17 * (1 - B17) * (1/B8 + 1/B11))
19			
20	**Two-Tail Test**		
21	Lower Critical Value	-1.9600	=NORMSINV(B5/2)
22	Upper Critical Value	1.9600	=NORMSINV(1 - B5/2)
23	p-Value	0.0026	=2 * (1 - NORMSDIST(ABS(B18)))
24	Reject the null hypothesis		=IF(B23 < B5, "Reject the null hypothesis", "Do not reject the null hypothesis")

EXAMPLE 10.3

Testing for the Difference in Two Proportions

Technology has led to the rise of extreme workers who are on the job 60 hours a week or more. One of the reasons cited by employees about why they worked long hours was that they loved their job because it is stimulating/challenging/provides an adrenaline rush (data extracted from S. Armour, "Hi, I'm Joan and I'm a Workaholic," *USA Today*, May 23, 2007, pp. 1B, 2B). Suppose that the survey of 1,564 workaholics included 786 men and 778 women and that 707 men and 638 women loved their job because it is stimulating/challenging/provides an adrenaline rush. At the 0.05 level of significance, you would like to determine whether the proportion of workaholic men who love their job because it is stimulating/challenging/provides an adrenaline rush is greater than the proportion of women.

SOLUTION Because you want to know whether there is evidence that the proportion of workaholic men who love their job because it is stimulating/challenging/provides an adrenaline rush is *greater* than the proportion of women, you have a one-tail test. The null and alternative hypotheses are

$H_0: \pi_1 \le \pi_2$ (Proportion of workaholic men who love their job because it is stimulating/challenging/provides an adrenaline rush is less than or equal to the proportion of women who love their jobs.)

$H_1: \pi_1 > \pi_2$ (Proportion of workaholic men who love their job because it is stimulating/challenging/provides an adrenaline rush is greater than the proportion of women who love their jobs.)

Using the 0.05 level of significance, for the one-tail test in the upper tail, the critical value is $+1.645$. The decision rule is

$$\text{Reject } H_0 \text{ if } Z_{STAT} > +1.645;$$

$$\text{otherwise, do not reject } H_0.$$

Using Equation (10.5) on page 355,

$$Z_{STAT} = \frac{(p_1 - p_2) - (\pi_1 - \pi_2)}{\sqrt{\bar{p}(1-\bar{p})\left(\frac{1}{n_1} + \frac{1}{n_2}\right)}}$$

where

$$p_1 = \frac{X_1}{n_1} = \frac{707}{786} = 0.8995 \quad p_2 = \frac{X_2}{n_2} = \frac{638}{778} = 0.8201$$

and

$$\bar{p} = \frac{X_1 + X_2}{n_1 + n_2} = \frac{707 + 638}{786 + 778} = \frac{1,345}{1,564} = 0.8600$$

so that

$$Z_{STAT} = \frac{(0.8995 - 0.8201) - (0)}{\sqrt{0.86(1-0.86)\left(\frac{1}{786} + \frac{1}{778}\right)}}$$

$$= \frac{0.0794}{\sqrt{(0.1204)(0.0025575)}}$$

$$= \frac{0.0794}{\sqrt{0.0003079}}$$

$$= \frac{0.0794}{0.017547} = +4.53$$

Using the 0.05 level of significance, you reject the null hypothesis because $Z_{STAT} = +4.53 > +1.645$. The p-value is approximately 0.0000. Therefore, if the null hypothesis is true, the probability that a Z_{STAT} test statistic is greater than $+4.53$ is approximately 0.0000 (which is less than $\alpha = 0.05$). You conclude that there is evidence that the proportion of workaholic men who love their job because it is stimulating/challenging/provides an adrenaline rush is greater than the proportion of women who love their jobs.

Confidence Interval Estimate for the Difference Between Two Proportions

Instead of, or in addition to, testing for the difference between the proportions of two independent populations, you can construct a confidence interval estimate for the difference between the two proportions using Equation (10.6).

CONFIDENCE INTERVAL ESTIMATE FOR THE DIFFERENCE BETWEEN TWO PROPORTIONS

The **COMPUTE worksheet** of the **Z Two Proportions workbook** computes the confidence interval estimate for the difference between two proportions in columns D and E (not shown in Figure 10.12 on page 357).

or

$$(p_1 - p_2) \pm Z_{\alpha/2}\sqrt{\frac{p_1(1 - p_1)}{n_1} + \frac{p_2(1 - p_2)}{n_2}}$$

$$(p_1 - p_2) - Z_{\alpha/2}\sqrt{\frac{p_1(1 - p_1)}{n_1} + \frac{p_2(1 - p_2)}{n_2}} \le (\pi_1 - \pi_2)$$

$$\le (p_1 - p_2) + Z_{\alpha/2}\sqrt{\frac{p_1(1 - p_1)}{n_1} + \frac{p_2(1 - p_2)}{n_2}} \qquad \textbf{(10.6)}$$

To construct a 95% confidence interval estimate for the population difference between the proportion of guests who would return to the Beachcomber and who would return to the Windsurfer, you use the results on page 356 or from Figure 10.12 on page 357:

$$p_1 = \frac{X_1}{n_1} = \frac{163}{227} = 0.7181 \quad p_2 = \frac{X_2}{n_2} = \frac{154}{262} = 0.5878$$

Using Equation (10.6),

$$(0.7181 - 0.5878) \pm (1.96)\sqrt{\frac{0.7181(1 - 0.7181)}{227} + \frac{0.5878(1 - 0.5878)}{262}}$$

$$0.1303 \pm (1.96)(0.0426)$$

$$0.1303 \pm 0.0835$$

$$0.0468 \le (\pi_1 - \pi_2) \le 0.2138$$

Thus, you have 95% confidence that the difference between the population proportion of guests who would return to the Beachcomber and the Windsurfer is between 0.0468 and 0.2138. In percentages, the difference is between 4.68% and 21.38%. Guest satisfaction is higher at the Beachcomber than at the Windsurfer.

Problems for Section 10.3

LEARNING THE BASICS

10.27 Let $n_1 = 100$, $X_1 = 50$, $n_2 = 100$, and $X_2 = 30$.
a. At the 0.05 level of significance, is there evidence of a significant difference between the two population proportions?
b. Construct a 95% confidence interval estimate for the difference between the two population proportions.

10.28 Let $n_1 = 100$, $X_1 = 45$, $n_2 = 50$, and $X_2 = 25$.
a. At the 0.01 level of significance, is there evidence of a significant difference between the two population proportions?
b. Construct a 99% confidence interval estimate for the difference between the two population proportions.

APPLYING THE CONCEPTS

10.29 A survey of 500 shoppers was taken in a large metropolitan area to determine various information about consumer behavior. Among the questions asked was, "Do you enjoy shopping for clothing?" Of 240 males, 136 answered yes. Of 260 females, 224 answered yes.
a. Is there evidence of a significant difference between males and females in the proportion who enjoy shopping for clothing at the 0.01 level of significance?
b. Find the p-value in (a) and interpret its meaning.
c. Construct and interpret a 99% confidence interval estimate for the difference between the proportion of males and females who enjoy shopping for clothing.
d. What are your answers to (a) through (c) if 206 males enjoyed shopping for clothing?

10.30 A study funded by the Massachusetts Institute of Technology tested the notion that even when it comes to sugar pills, some people think a costly one works better than a cheap one. Researchers randomly divided 82 healthy paid volunteers into two groups. All the volunteers thought they would be testing a new pain reliever. One group was told the pain reliever they would be using cost $2.50 a pill, and the other group was told it cost only 10 cents a pill. In reality, the pills they were all about to take were simply sugar pills. The volunteers were given a light electric shock on the wrist. Then the volunteers were given a sugar pill, and a short time later they were shocked again. Of the volunteers who took the expensive pill, 35 of the 41 said they felt less pain afterward. Of the volunteers who took the cheap pill, 25 of the 41 said they felt less pain afterward (data extracted from R. Rubin, "Placebo Study Tests 'Costlier Is Better' Notion," **www.usatoday.com**, March 5, 2008).

a. Set up the null and alternative hypotheses to try to prove that people think an expensive pill works better than a cheap pill.
b. Conduct the hypothesis test defined in (a), using the 0.05 level of significance.
c. Does the result of your test in (b) make it appropriate to claim that people think an expensive pill works better than a cheap pill?

10.31 Some people enjoy the *anticipation* of an upcoming product or event and prefer to pay in advance and delay the actual consumption/delivery date. In other cases, people do not want a delay. An article in the *Journal of Marketing Research* reported on an experiment in which 50 individuals were told that they had just purchased a ticket to a concert and 50 were told that they had just purchased a personal digital assistant (PDA). The participants were then asked to indicate their preferences for attending the concert or receiving the PDA. Did they prefer tonight or tomorrow, or would they prefer to wait two to four weeks? The individuals were told to ignore their schedule constraints in order to better measure their willingness to delay the consumption/delivery of their purchase. The following table gives partial results of the study:

	Concert	PDA
Tonight or tomorrow	28	47
Two to four weeks	22	3
Total	50	50

Source: *Data adapted from O. Amir and D. Ariely, "Decisions by Rules: The Case of Unwillingness to Pay for Beneficial Delays,"* Journal of Marketing Research, *February 2007, Vol. XLIV, pp. 142–152.*

a. What proportion of the participants would prefer delaying the date of the concert?
b. What proportion of the participants would prefer delaying receipt of a new PDA?
c. Using the 0.05 level of significance, is there evidence of a significant difference in the proportion willing to delay the date of the concert and the proportion willing to delay receipt of a new PDA?

 10.32 Do people of different age groups differ in their response to e-mail messages? A survey by

the Center for the Digital Future of the University of Southern California (data extracted from A. Mindlin, "Older E-mail Users Favor Fast Replies," *The New York Times*, July 14, 2008, p. B3) reported that 70.7% of users over 70 years of age believe that e-mail messages should be answered quickly as compared to 53.6% of users 12 to 50 years old. Suppose that the survey was based on 1,000 users over 70 years of age and 1,000 users 12 to 50 years old.
a. At the 0.01 level of significance, is there evidence of a significant difference between the two age groups that believe that e-mail messages should be answered quickly?
b. Find the p-value in (a) and interpret its meaning.

10.33 Are women more risk averse in the stock market? A sample of men and women were asked the following question: "If both the stock market and a stock you owned dropped 25% in three months, would you buy more shares while the price is low?" (data extracted from "Women Are More Risk Averse in the Stock Market," *USA Today*, September 25, 2006, p. 1C). Of 965 women, 338 said yes. Of 1,066 men, 554 said yes.
a. At the 0.05 level of significance, is there evidence that the proportion of women who would buy more shares while the price is low is less than the proportion of men?
b. Find the p-value in (a) and interpret its meaning.

10.34 An experiment was conducted to study the choices made in mutual fund selection. Undergraduate and MBA students were presented with different S&P 500 index funds that were identical except for fees. Suppose that 100 undergraduate students and 100 MBA students were selected. Partial results are shown in the following table:

	STUDENT GROUP	
FUND	Undergraduate	MBA
Highest-cost fund	27	18
Not-highest-cost fund	73	82

Source: *Data extracted from J. Choi, D. Laibson, and B. Madrian, "Why Does the Law of One Practice Fail? An Experiment on Mutual Funds,"* **www.som.yale.edu/faculty/jjc83/fees.pdf**.

a. At the 0.05 level of significance, is there evidence of a difference between undergraduate and MBA students in the proportion who selected the highest-cost fund?
b. Find the p-value in (a) and interpret its meaning.

10.35 Where people turn for news is different for various age groups (data extracted from P. Johnson, "Young People Turn to the Web for News," *USA Today*, March 23, 2006, p. 9D). Suppose that a study conducted on this issue was based on 200 respondents who were between the ages of 36 and 50 and 200 respondents who were above age 50. Of the 200 respondents who were between the ages of 36 and 50, 82 got their news primarily from newspapers. Of the 200 respondents who were above age 50, 104 got their news primarily from newspapers.

a. Is there evidence of a significant difference in the proportion that get their news primarily from newspapers between those respondents 36 to 50 years old and those above 50 years old? (Use $\alpha = 0.05$.)

b. Determine the *p*-value in (a) and interpret its meaning.

c. Construct and interpret a 95% confidence interval estimate for the difference between the population proportion of respondents who get their news primarily from newspapers between those respondents 36 to 50 years old and those above 50 years old.

10.4 *F* Test for the Ratio of Two Variances

Often you need to determine whether two independent populations have the same variability. By testing variances, you can detect differences in the variability in two independent populations. One important reason to test for the difference between the variances of two populations is to determine whether to use the pooled-variance *t* test (which assumes equal variances) or the separate-variance *t* test (which does not assume equal variances) while comparing the means of two independent populations.

The test for the difference between the variances of two independent populations is based on the ratio of the two sample variances. If you assume that each population is normally distributed, then the ratio S_1^2/S_2^2 follows the *F* distribution (see Table E.5). The critical values of the **F distribution** in Table E.5 depend on the degrees of freedom in the two samples. The degrees of freedom in the numerator of the ratio are for the first sample, and the degrees of freedom in the denominator are for the second sample. The first sample taken from the first population is defined as the sample that has the *larger* sample variance. The second sample taken from the second population is the sample with the *smaller* sample variance. Equation (10.7) defines the **F test for the ratio of two variances**.

F-TEST STATISTIC FOR TESTING THE RATIO OF TWO VARIANCES

The F_{STAT} test statistic is equal to the variance of sample 1 (the larger sample variance) divided by the variance of sample 2 (the smaller sample variance).

$$F_{STAT} = \frac{S_1^2}{S_2^2} \tag{10.7}$$

where

S_1^2 = variance of sample 1 (the larger sample variance)

S_2^2 = variance of sample 2 (the smaller sample variance)

n_1 = size of sample 1

n_2 = size of sample 2

$n_1 - 1$ = degrees of freedom from sample 1 (i.e., the numerator degrees of freedom)

$n_2 - 1$ = degrees of freedom from sample 2 (i.e., the denominator degrees of freedom)

The F_{STAT} test statistic follows an *F* distribution with $n_1 - 1$ and $n_2 - 1$ degrees of freedom.

For a given level of significance, α, to test the null hypothesis of equality of population variances:

$$H_0: \sigma_1^2 = \sigma_2^2$$

against the alternative hypothesis that the two population variances are not equal:

$$H_1: \sigma_1^2 \neq \sigma_2^2$$

you reject the null hypothesis if the computed F_{STAT} test statistic is greater than the upper-tail critical value, $F_{\alpha/2}$, from the F distribution, with $n_1 - 1$ degrees of freedom in the numerator and $n_2 - 1$ degrees of freedom in the denominator. Thus, the decision rule is

$$\text{Reject } H_0 \text{ if } F_{STAT} > F_{\alpha/2};$$

$$\text{otherwise, do not reject } H_0.$$

To illustrate how to use the F test to determine whether the two variances are equal, return to the BLK Foods scenario on page 335 concerning the sales of BLK Cola in two different display locations. To determine whether to use the pooled-variance t test or the separate-variance t test in Section 10.1, you can test the equality of the two population variances. The null and alternative hypotheses are

$$H_0: \sigma_1^2 = \sigma_2^2$$

$$H_1: \sigma_1^2 \neq \sigma_2^2$$

Because you are defining sample 1 as having the larger sample variance, the rejection region in the upper tail of the F distribution contains $\alpha/2$. Using the level of significance $\alpha = 0.05$, the rejection region in the upper tail contains 0.025 of the distribution.

Because there are samples of 10 stores for each of the two display locations, there are $10 - 1 = 9$ degrees of freedom in the numerator (the sample with the larger variance) and also in the denominator (the sample with the smaller variance). $F_{\alpha/2}$, the upper-tail critical value of the F distribution, is found directly from Table E.5, a portion of which is presented in Table 10.6. Because there are 9 degrees of freedom in the numerator and 9 degrees of freedom in the denominator, you find the upper-tail critical value, $F_{\alpha/2}$, by looking in the column labeled 9 and the row labeled 9. Thus, the upper-tail critical value of this F distribution is 4.03. Therefore, the decision rule is

$$\text{Reject } H_0 \text{ if } F_{STAT} > F_{0.025} = 4.03;$$

$$\text{otherwise, do not reject } H_0.$$

TABLE 10.6

Finding the Upper-Tail Critical Value of F with 9 and 9 Degrees of Freedom for an Upper-Tail Area of 0.025

	Cumulative Probabilities = 0.975 Upper-Tail Area = 0.025 Numerator df_1						
Denominator df_2	1	2	3	...	7	8	9
1	647.80	799.50	864.20	...	948.20	956.70	963.30
2	38.51	39.00	39.17	...	39.36	39.37	39.39
3	17.44	16.04	15.44	...	14.62	14.54	14.47
.	.	.	.	.	.	.	.
.	.	.	.	.	.	.	.
.	.	.	.	.	.	.	.
7	8.07	6.54	5.89	...	4.99	4.90	4.82
8	7.57	6.06	5.42	...	4.53	4.43	4.36
9	7.21	5.71	5.08	...	4.20	4.10	4.03

Source: *Extracted from Table E.5.*

Using Equation (10.7) on page 361 and the cola sales data (see Table 10.1 on page 337),

$$S_1^2 = (18.7264)^2 = 350.6778 \qquad S_2^2 = (12.5433)^2 = 157.3333$$

so that

$$F_{STAT} = \frac{S_1^2}{S_2^2}$$

$$= \frac{350.6778}{157.3333} = 2.2289$$

Because $F_{STAT} = 2.2289 < 4.03$, you do not reject H_0. Figure 10.13 shows the worksheet results for this test, including the *p*-value, 0.2482. Because $0.2482 > 0.05$, you conclude that there is no significant difference in the variability of the sales of cola for the two display locations.

FIGURE 10.13

F test worksheet for the BLK Cola sales data

Figure 10.13 displays the COMPUTE worksheet of the F Two Variances workbook. Create this worksheet using the instructions in Section EG10.4.

	A	B	
1	F Test for Differences in Two Variances		
2			
3	**Data**		
4	Level of Significance	0.05	
5	**Larger-Variance Sample**		
6	Sample Size	10	=COUNT(DATACOPY!$A:$A)
7	Sample Variance	350.6778	=VAR(DATACOPY!$A:$A)
8	**Smaller-Variance Sample**		
9	Sample Size	10	=COUNT(DATACOPY!$B:$B)
10	Sample Variance	157.3333	=VAR(DATACOPY!$B:$B)
11			
12	**Intermediate Calculations**		
13	F Test Statistic	2.2289	=B7/B10
14	Population 1 Sample Degrees of Freedom	9	=B6 - 1
15	Population 2 Sample Degrees of Freedom	9	=B9 - 1
16			
17	**Two-Tail Test**		
18	Upper Critical Value	4.0260	=FINV(B4/2, B14, B15)
19	*p*-Value	0.2482	=2 * E17
20	Do not reject the null hypothesis		=IF(B19 < B4, "Reject the null hypothesis", "Do not reject the null hypothesis")

Not shown
Cell E17: =FDIST(B13, B14, B15)

In testing for a difference between two variances using the *F* test described in this section, you assume that each of the two populations is normally distributed. The *F* test is very sensitive to the normality assumption. If boxplots or normal probability plots suggest even a mild departure from normality for either of the two populations, you should not use the *F* test. If this happens, you should use the Levene test (see Section 11.1) or a nonparametric approach (see references 1 and 2).

In testing for the equality of variances as part of assessing the validity of the pooled-variance *t* test procedure, the *F* test is a two-tail test with $\alpha/2$ in the upper tail. However, when you are interested in examining the variability in situations other than the pooled-variance *t* test, the *F* test is often a one-tail test. Example 10.4 illustrates a one-tail test.

EXAMPLE 10.4

A One-Tail Test for the Difference Between Two Variances

Shipments of meat, meat by-products, and other ingredients are mixed together in several filling lines at a pet food canning factory. Operations managers suspect that, although the mean amount filled per can of pet food is usually stable, the variability of the cans filled in line *A* is greater than that of line *B*. The following data from a sample of 8-ounce cans is as follows:

	Line *A*	Line *B*
$\overline{X}$	8.005	7.997
S	0.012	0.005
n	11	16

At the 0.05 level of significance, is there evidence that the variance in line *A* is greater than the variance in line *B*? Assume that the population amounts filled are normally distributed.

SOLUTION The null and alternative hypotheses are

$$H_0: \sigma_A^2 \leq \sigma_B^2$$

$$H_1: \sigma_A^2 > \sigma_B^2$$

The F_{STAT} test statistic is given by Equation (10.7) on page 361:

$$F_{STAT} = \frac{S_1^2}{S_2^2}$$

You use Table E.5 to find the upper critical value of the F distribution. With $n_1 - 1 = 11 - 1 = 10$ degrees of freedom in the numerator, $n_2 - 1 = 16 - 1 = 15$ degrees of freedom in the denominator, and $\alpha = 0.05$, the upper critical value, $F_{0.05}$, is 2.54.

The decision rule is

Reject H_0 if $F_{STAT} > 2.54$;

otherwise, do not reject H_0.

From Equation (10.7) on page 361,

$$F_{STAT} = \frac{S_1^2}{S_2^2}$$

$$= \frac{(0.012)^2}{(0.005)^2} = 5.76$$

Because $F_{STAT} = 5.76 > 2.54$, you reject H_0. Using a 0.05 level of significance, you conclude that there is evidence that the variance of line A is greater than the variance of line B. In other words, the amount of pet food in the cans filled by line A is more variable than the amount of pet food in cans filled by line B.

Problems for Section 10.4

LEARNING THE BASICS

10.36 Determine the upper-tail critical values of F in each of the following two-tail tests:
a. $\alpha = 0.10$, $n_1 = 16$, $n_2 = 21$
b. $\alpha = 0.05$, $n_1 = 16$, $n_2 = 21$
c. $\alpha = 0.01$, $n_1 = 16$, $n_2 = 21$

10.37 Determine the upper-tail critical value of F in each of the following one-tail tests:
a. $\alpha = 0.05$, $n_1 = 16$, $n_2 = 21$
b. $\alpha = 0.01$, $n_1 = 16$, $n_2 = 21$

10.38 The following information is available for two samples selected from independent normally distributed populations:

Population A: $n_1 = 25$ $S_1^2 = 16$

Population B: $n_2 = 25$ $S_2^2 = 25$

a. Which sample variance do you place in the numerator of F_{STAT}?
b. What is the value of F_{STAT}?

10.39 The following information is available for two samples selected from independent normally distributed populations:

Population A: $n_1 = 25$ $S_1^2 = 161.9$

Population B: $n_2 = 25$ $S_2^2 = 133.7$

What is the value of F_{STAT} if you are testing the null hypothesis $H_0: \sigma_1^2 = \sigma_2^2$?

10.40 In Problem 10.39, how many degrees of freedom are there in the numerator and denominator of the F test?

10.41 In Problems 10.39 and 10.40, what is the upper critical value for F if the level of significance, α, is 0.05 and the alternative hypothesis is $H_1: \sigma_1^2 \neq \sigma_2^2$?

10.42 In Problems 10.39 through 10.41, what is your statistical decision?

10.43 The following information is available for two samples selected from independent but very right-skewed populations:

Population A: $n_1 = 16$ $S_1^2 = 47.3$

Population B: $n_2 = 13$ $S_2^2 = 36.4$

Should you use the F test to test the null hypothesis of equality of variances? Discuss.

10.44 In Problem 10.43, assume that two samples are selected from independent normally distributed populations.
a. At the 0.05 level of significance, is there evidence of a difference between σ_1^2 and σ_2^2?
b. Suppose that you want to perform a one-tail test. At the 0.05 level of significance, what is the upper-tail critical value of F to determine whether there is evidence that $\sigma_1^2 > \sigma_2^2$? What is your statistical decision?

APPLYING THE CONCEPTS

10.45 A professor in the accounting department of a business school claims that there is more variability in the final exam scores of students taking the introductory accounting course who are not majoring in accounting than for students taking the course who are majoring in accounting. Random samples of 13 non-accounting majors and 10 accounting majors are selected from the professor's class roster in his large lecture, and the following results are computed based on the final exam scores:

$$\text{Non-accounting: } n_1 = 13 \quad S_1^2 = 210.2$$
$$\text{Accounting: } n_2 = 10 \quad S_2^2 = 36.5$$

a. At the 0.05 level of significance, is there evidence to support the professor's claim?
b. Interpret the *p*-value.
c. What assumption do you need to make in (a) about the two populations in order to justify your use of the *F* test?

✓**SELF** **10.46** The Computer Anxiety Rating Scale
Test (CARS) measures an individual's level of computer anxiety, on a scale from 20 (no anxiety) to 100 (highest level of anxiety). Researchers at Miami University administered CARS to 172 business students. One of the objectives of the study was to determine whether there is a difference between the level of computer anxiety experienced by female students and male students. They found the following:

	Males	Females
$\overline{X}$	40.26	36.85
S	13.35	9.42
n	100	72

Source: *Data extracted from T. Broome and D. Havelka, "Determinants of Computer Anxiety in Business Students,"* The Review of Business Information Systems, *Spring 2002, 6(2), pp. 9–16.*

a. At the 0.05 level of significance, is there evidence of a difference in the variability of the computer anxiety experienced by males and females?
b. Interpret the *p*-value.
c. What assumption do you need to make about the two populations in order to justify the use of the *F* test?
d. Based on (a) and (b), which *t* test defined in Section 10.1 should you use to test whether there is a significant difference in mean computer anxiety for female and male students?

10.47 A bank with a branch located in a commercial district of a city has developed an improved process for serving customers during the noon-to-1 P.M. lunch period. The waiting time (defined as the time elapsed from when the customer enters the line until he or she reaches the teller window) needs to be shortened to increase customer satisfaction. A random sample of 15 customers is selected (and stored in Bank1), and the results (in minutes) are as follows:

4.21 5.55 3.02 5.13 4.77 2.34 3.54 3.20
4.50 6.10 0.38 5.12 6.46 6.19 3.79

Suppose that another branch, located in a residential area, is also concerned with the noon-to-1 P.M. lunch period. A random sample of 15 customers is selected (and stored in Bank2), and the results (in minutes) are as follows:

9.66 5.90 8.02 5.79 8.73 3.82 8.01 8.35
10.49 6.68 5.64 4.08 6.17 9.91 5.47

a. Is there evidence of a difference in the variability of the waiting time between the two branches? (Use $\alpha = 0.05$.)
b. Determine the *p*-value in (a) and interpret its meaning.
c. What assumption about the population distribution of the two banks is necessary in (a)? Is the assumption valid for these data?
d. Based on the results of (a), is it appropriate to use the pooled-variance *t* test to compare the means of the two branches?

10.48 Digital cameras have taken over the majority of the point-and-shoot camera market. One of the important features of a camera is the battery life, as measured by the number of shots taken until the battery needs to be recharged. The file DigitalCameras contains battery life information for 29 subcompact cameras and 16 compact cameras (data extracted from "Digital Cameras," *Consumer Reports*, July 2009, pp. 28–29).
a. Is there evidence of a difference in the variability of the battery life between the two types of digital cameras? (Use $\alpha = 0.05$.)
b. Determine the *p*-value in (a) and interpret its meaning.
c. What assumption about the population distribution of the two types of cameras is necessary in (a)? Is the assumption valid for these data?
d. Based on the results of (a), which *t* test defined in Section 10.1 should you use to compare the mean battery life of the two types of cameras?

10.49 Do young children use cell phones? Apparently so, according to a recent study (A. Ross, "Message to Santa; Kids Want a Phone," *Palm Beach Post*, December 16, 2008, pp. 1A, 4A), which stated that cell phone users under 12 years of age averaged 137 calls per month as compared to 231 calls per month for cell phone users 13 to 17 years of age. No sample sizes were reported. Suppose that the results were based on samples of 50 cell phone users in each group and that the sample standard deviation for cell phone users under 12 years of age was 51.7 calls per month and the sample standard deviation for cell phone users 13 to 17 years of age was 67.6 calls per month.
a. Using a 0.05 level of significance, is there evidence of a difference in the variances of cell phone usage between

cell phone users under 12 years of age and cell phone users 13 to 17 years of age?

b. On the basis of the results in (a), which *t* test defined in Section 10.1 should you use to compare the means of the two groups of cell phone users? Discuss.

10.50 Is there a difference in the variation of the yield of different types of investment between banks? The following data (in BankYield) represent the yields for a sample of money market accounts and five-year CDs as of May 17, 2009:

Money Market Accounts	Five-Year CD
2.25 2.20 2.12 2.03 2.02	3.70 3.66 3.65 3.50 3.50

Source: *Data extracted from* **www.bankrate.com**, *May 17, 2009.*

At the 0.05 level of significance, is there evidence of a difference in the variance of the yield between money market accounts and five-year CDs? Assume that the population yields are normally distributed.

USING STATISTICS @ BLK Foods Revisited

In the Using Statistics scenario, you were the regional sales manager for BLK Foods. You compared the sales volume of BLK Cola when the product is placed in the normal shelf location to the sales volume when the product is featured in a special end-aisle display. An experiment was performed where 10 stores used the normal shelf location and 10 stores used the end-aisle displays. Using a *t* test for the difference between two means, you were able to conclude that the mean sales using end-aisle location are higher than the mean sales for the normal shelf location. A confidence interval allowed you to infer with 95% confidence that the end-aisle location sells, on average, 6.73 to 36.67 cases more than the normal shelf location. You also performed the *F* test for the difference between two variances to see if the store-to-store variability in sales in stores using the end-aisle location differed from the store-to-store variability in sales in stores using the normal shelf location. You concluded that there was no significant difference in the variability of the sales of cola for the two display locations. As regional sales manager, your next step in increasing sales is to convince more stores to use the special end-aisle display.

SUMMARY

In this chapter, you were introduced to a variety of two-sample tests. For situations in which the samples are independent, you learned statistical test procedures for analyzing possible differences between means, variances, and proportions. In addition, you learned a test procedure that is frequently used when analyzing differences between the means of two related samples. Remember that you need to select the test that is most appropriate for a given set of conditions and to critically investigate the validity of the assumptions underlying each of the hypothesis-testing procedures.

Table 10.7 provides a list of topics covered in this chapter. The roadmap in Figure 10.14 illustrates the steps needed in determining which two-sample test of hypothesis to use. The following are the questions you need to consider:

1. What type of data do you have? If you are dealing with categorical variables, use the *Z* test for the difference between two proportions. (This test assumes independent samples.)
2. If you have a numerical variable, determine whether you have independent samples or related samples. If you have related samples, use the paired *t* test.
3. If you have independent samples, is your focus on variability or central tendency? If the focus is on variability, use the *F* test.
4. If your focus is central tendency, determine whether you can assume that the variances of the two populations are equal. (This assumption can be tested using the *F* test.)
5. If you can assume that the two populations have equal variances, use the pooled-variance *t* test. If you cannot assume that the two populations have equal variances, use the separate-variance *t* test.

TABLE 10.7

Summary of Topics
in Chapter 10

Type of Analysis	Types of Data		
	Numerical		**Categorical**
Comparing two populations	t tests for the difference in the means of two independent populations (Section 10.1)		Z test for the difference between two proportions (Section 10.3)
	Paired t test (Section 10.2)		
	F test for the ratio of two variances (Section 10.4)		

FIGURE 10.14

Roadmap for selecting a
two-sample test of
hypothesis

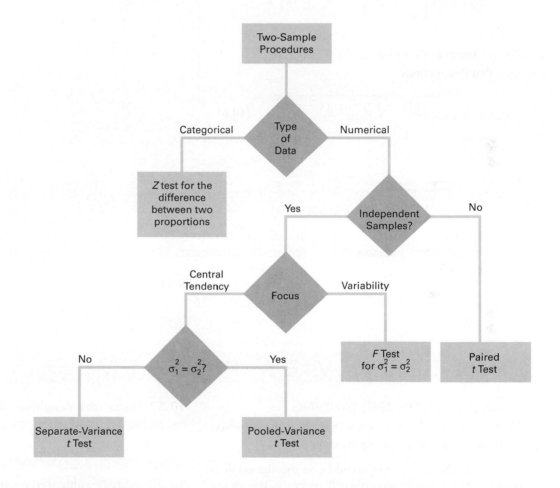

KEY EQUATIONS

Pooled-Variance t Test for the Difference Between Two Means

$$t_{STAT} = \frac{(\bar{X}_1 - \bar{X}_2) - (\mu_1 - \mu_2)}{\sqrt{S_p^2\left(\frac{1}{n_1} + \frac{1}{n_2}\right)}} \quad (10.1)$$

Confidence Interval Estimate for the Difference in the Means of Two Independent Populations

$$(\bar{X}_1 - \bar{X}_2) \pm t_{\alpha/2}\sqrt{S_p^2\left(\frac{1}{n_1} + \frac{1}{n_2}\right)} \quad (10.2)$$

or

$$(\bar{X}_1 - \bar{X}_2) - t_{\alpha/2}\sqrt{S_p^2\left(\frac{1}{n_1} + \frac{1}{n_2}\right)} \leq \mu_1 - \mu_2$$

$$\leq (\bar{X}_1 - \bar{X}_2) + t_{\alpha/2}\sqrt{S_p^2\left(\frac{1}{n_1} + \frac{1}{n_2}\right)}$$

Paired t Test for the Mean Difference

$$t_{STAT} = \frac{\bar{D} - \mu_D}{\frac{S_D}{\sqrt{n}}} \quad (10.3)$$

Confidence Interval Estimate for the Mean Difference

$$\overline{D} \pm t_{\alpha/2}\frac{S_D}{\sqrt{n}} \tag{10.4}$$

or

$$\overline{D} - t_{\alpha/2}\frac{S_D}{\sqrt{n}} \leq \mu_D \leq \overline{D} + t_{\alpha/2}\frac{S_D}{\sqrt{n}}$$

Z Test for the Difference Between Two Proportions

$$Z_{STAT} = \frac{(p_1 - p_2) - (\pi_1 - \pi_2)}{\sqrt{\overline{p}(1-\overline{p})\left(\dfrac{1}{n_1} + \dfrac{1}{n_2}\right)}} \tag{10.5}$$

Confidence Interval Estimate for the Difference Between Two Proportions

$$(p_1 - p_2) \pm Z_{\alpha/2}\sqrt{\left(\frac{p_1(1-p_1)}{n_1} + \frac{p_2(1-p_2)}{n_2}\right)} \tag{10.6}$$

or

$$(p_1 - p_2) - Z_{\alpha/2}\sqrt{\frac{p_1(1-p_1)}{n_1} + \frac{p_2(1-p_2)}{n_1}} \leq (\pi_1 - \pi_2)$$

$$\leq (p_1 - p_2) + Z_{\alpha/2}\sqrt{\frac{p_1(1-p_1)}{n_1} + \frac{p_2(1-p_2)}{n_2}}$$

F Test for the Ratio of Two Variances

$$F_{STAT} = \frac{S_1^2}{S_2^2} \tag{10.7}$$

KEY TERMS

F distribution 361
F test for the ratio of two variances 361
matched samples 346
paired t test for the mean
   difference 346

pooled-variance t test 336
repeated measurements 345
robust 339
separate-variance t test 342
two-sample test 336

Z test for the difference between two
   proportions 354

CHAPTER REVIEW PROBLEMS

CHECKING YOUR UNDERSTANDING

10.51 What are some of the criteria used in the selection of a particular hypothesis-testing procedure?

10.52 Under what conditions should you use the pooled-variance t test to examine possible differences in the means of two independent populations?

10.53 Under what conditions should you use the F test to examine possible differences in the variances of two independent populations?

10.54 What is the distinction between two independent populations and two related populations?

10.55 What is the distinction between repeated measurements and matched items?

10.56 When you have two independent populations, explain the similarities and differences between the test of hypothesis for the difference between the means and the confidence interval estimate for the difference between the means.

10.57 Under what conditions should you use the paired t test for the mean difference between two related populations?

APPLYING THE CONCEPTS

10.58 A study compared music compact disc prices for Internet-based retailers and traditional brick-and-mortar retailers [data extracted from L. Zoonky and S. Gosain, "A Longitudinal Price Comparison for Music CDs in Electronic and Brick-and-Mortar Markets: Pricing Strategies in Emergent Electronic Commerce," *Journal of Business Strategies*, Spring 2002, 19(1), pp. 55–72]. Before collecting the data, the researchers carefully defined several research hypotheses, including the following:
1. The price dispersion on the Internet is lower than the price dispersion in the brick-and-mortar market.
2. Prices in electronic markets are lower than prices in physical markets.
a. Consider research hypothesis 1. Write the null and alternative hypotheses in terms of population parameters. Carefully define the population parameters used.

b. Define a Type I and Type II error for the hypotheses in (a).
c. What type of statistical test should you use?
d. What assumptions are needed to perform the test you selected?
e. Repeat (a) through (d) for research hypothesis 2.

10.59 A study conducted in March 2009 found that about half of U.S. adults trusted the U.S. government more than U.S. business to solve the economic problems of the United States. However, when the population is subdivided by political party affiliation, the results are very different. The study showed that 72% of Democrats trusted the government more, but only 29% of Republicans trusted the government more. Suppose that you are in charge of updating the study. You will take a national sample of Democrats and a national sample of Republicans and then try to use the results to show statistical evidence that the proportion of Democrats trusting the government more than business is greater than the proportion of Republicans trusting the government more than business.
a. What are the null and alternative hypotheses?
b. What is a Type I error in the context of this study?
c. What is a Type II error in the context of this study?

10.60 The American Society for Quality (ASQ) conducted a salary survey of all its members. ASQ members work in all areas of manufacturing and service-related institutions, with a common theme of an interest in quality. Two job titles associated with high salaries are manager and master black belt. (In Section 17.8, you will learn that a master black belt is a person who takes a leadership and training role in a Six Sigma quality improvement initiative.) Descriptive statistics concerning salaries for these two job titles are given in the following table:

Job Title	Sample Size	Mean	Standard Deviation
Manager	2,228	85,551	24,109
Master black belt	134	113,385	24,738

Source: *Data extracted from I. E. Allen, "Salary Survey: Seeing Green,"* Quality Progress, *December 2008, pp. 20–53.*

a. Using a 0.05 level of significance, is there a difference in the variability of salaries between managers and master black belts?
b. Based on the result of (a), which *t* test defined in Section 10.1 is appropriate for comparing mean salaries?
c. Using a 0.05 level of significance, is there a difference between the mean salary of managers and the mean salary of master black belts?

10.61 Do male and female students study the same amount per week? In 2007, 58 sophomore business students were surveyed at a large university that has more than 1,000 sophomore business students each year. The file StudyTime contains the gender and the number of hours spent studying in a typical week for the sampled students.

a. At the 0.05 level of significance, is there a difference in the variance of the study time for male students and female students?
b. Using the results of (a), which *t* test is appropriate for comparing the mean study time for male and female students?
c. At the 0.05 level of significance, conduct the test selected in (b).
d. Write a short summary of your findings.

10.62 Two professors wanted to study how students from their two universities compared in their capabilities of using Excel spreadsheets in undergraduate information systems courses (data extracted from H. Howe and M. G. Simkin, "Factors Affecting the Ability to Detect Spreadsheet Errors," *Decision Sciences Journal of Innovative Education*, January 2006, pp. 101–122). A comparison of the student demographics was also performed. One school is a state university in the western United States, and the other school is a state university in the eastern United States. The following table contains information regarding the ages of the students:

School	Sample Size	Mean Age	Standard Deviation
Western	93	23.28	6.29
Eastern	135	21.16	1.32

a. Using a 0.01 level of significance, is there evidence of a difference in the variances of the age of students at the western school and at the eastern school?
b. Discuss the practical implications of the test performed in (a). Address, specifically, the impact equal (or unequal) variances in age has on teaching an undergraduate information systems course.
c. To test for a difference in the mean age of students, is it most appropriate to use the pooled-variance *t* test or the separate-variance *t* test?

The following table contains information regarding the years of spreadsheet usage of the students:

School	Sample Size	Mean Years	Standard Deviation
Western	93	2.6	2.4
Eastern	135	4.0	2.1

d. Using a 0.01 level of significance, is there evidence of a difference in the variances of the years of spreadsheet usage of students at the western school and at the eastern school?
e. Based on the results of (d), use the most appropriate test to determine, at the 0.01 level of significance, whether there is evidence of a difference in the mean years of spreadsheet usage of students at the western school and at the eastern school.

10.63 The file RestCost contains the ratings for food, decor, service, and the price per person for a sample of 50 restaurants located in a city and 50 restaurants located in a suburb. Completely analyze the differences between city and suburban restaurants for the variables food rating, decor rating, service rating, and cost per person, using $\alpha = 0.05$.

Source: *Data extracted from* Zagat Survey 2008: New York City Restaurants *and* Zagat Survey 2007–2008: Long Island Restaurants.

10.64 A computer information systems professor is interested in studying the amount of time it takes students enrolled in the introduction to computers course to write and run a program in Visual Basic. The professor hires you to analyze the following results (in minutes) from a random sample of nine students (the data are stored in the VB file):

$$10 \quad 13 \quad 9 \quad 15 \quad 12 \quad 13 \quad 11 \quad 13 \quad 12$$

a. At the 0.05 level of significance, is there evidence that the population mean amount is greater than 10 minutes? What will you tell the professor?

b. Suppose the computer professor, when checking her results, realizes that the fourth student needed 51 minutes rather than the recorded 15 minutes to write and run the Visual Basic program. At the 0.05 level of significance, reanalyze the question posed in (a), using the revised data. What will you tell the professor now?

c. The professor is perplexed by these paradoxical results and requests an explanation from you regarding the justification for the difference in your findings in (a) and (b). Discuss.

d. A few days later, the professor calls to tell you that the dilemma is completely resolved. The original number 15 (the fourth data value) was correct, and therefore your findings in (a) are being used in the article she is writing for a computer journal. Now she wants to hire you to compare the results from that group of introduction to computers students against those from a sample of 11 computer majors in order to determine whether there is evidence that computer majors can write a Visual Basic program in less time than introductory students. For the computer majors, the sample mean is 8.5 minutes, and the sample standard deviation is 2.0 minutes. At the 0.05 level of significance, completely analyze these data. What will you tell the professor?

e. A few days later, the professor calls again to tell you that a reviewer of her article wants her to include the p-value for the "correct" result in (a). In addition, the professor inquires about an unequal-variances problem, which the reviewer wants her to discuss in her article. In your own words, discuss the concept of p-value and also describe the unequal-variances problem. Then, determine the p-value in (a) and discuss whether the unequal-variances problem had any meaning in the professor's study.

10.65 An article (data extracted from A. Jennings, "What's Good for a Business Can be Hard on Friends," *The New York Times*, August 4, 2007, pp. C1–C2) reported that according to

a poll, the mean number of cell phone calls per month was 290 for 18- to 24-year-olds and 194 for 45- to 54-year-olds, whereas the mean number of text messages per month was 290 for 18- to 24-year-olds and 57 for 45- to 54-year-olds. Suppose that the poll was based on a sample of 100 18- to 24-year-olds and 100 45- to 54-year-olds and that the standard deviation of the number of cell phone calls per month was 100 for 18- to 24-year-olds and 90 for 45- to 54-year-olds, whereas the standard deviation of the number of text messages per month was 90 for 18- to 24-year-olds and 77 for 45- to 54-year-olds.

Using a level of significance of 0.05,

a. Is there evidence of a difference in the variances of the number of cell phone calls per month for 18- to 24-year-olds and for 45- to 54-year-olds?

b. Is there evidence of a difference in the mean number of cell phone calls per month for 18- to 24-year-olds and for 45- to 54-year-olds?

c. Construct and interpret a 95% confidence interval estimate for the difference in the mean number of cell phone calls per month for 18- to 24-year-olds and 45- to 54-year-olds.

d. Is there evidence of a difference in the variances of the number of text messages per month for 18- to 24-year-olds and 45- to 54-year-olds?

e. Is there evidence of a difference in the mean number of text messages per month for 18- to 24-year-olds and 45- to 54-year-olds?

f. Construct and interpret a 95% confidence interval estimate for the difference in the mean number of text messages per month for 18- to 24-year-olds and 45- to 54-year-olds.

g. Based on the results of (a) through (f), what conclusions can you make concerning cell phone and text message usage between 18- to 24-year-olds and 45- to 54-year-olds?

10.66 The lengths of life (in hours) of a sample of 40 100-watt light bulbs produced by manufacturer A and a sample of 40 100-watt light bulbs produced by manufacturer B are stored in Bulbs. Completely analyze the differences between the lengths of life of the bulbs produced by the two manufacturers. (Use $\alpha = 0.05$.)

10.67 A hotel manager is concerned with increasing the return rate for hotel guests. One aspect of first impressions by guests relates to the time it takes to deliver the guest's luggage to the room after check-in to the hotel. A random sample of 20 deliveries on a particular day were selected in Wing A of the hotel, and a random sample of 20 deliveries were selected in Wing B. The results are stored in Luggage. Analyze the data and determine whether there is a difference in the mean delivery time in the two wings of the hotel. (Use $\alpha = 0.05$.)

10.68 Many people are economizing due to recent economic conditions, but is there a difference between men and women in what they did to economize? A recent survey (data extracted from "He Spends, She Doesn't," *Consumer Reports*,

December 2008, p. 17) reported the following results. Suppose the survey was based on 100 men and 100 women.

What They Did	Men	Women
Spent less on entertainment and eating out	49%	62%
Reduced credit card spending	49	57
Planned to cut down on holiday spending	36	63
Put more money into savings	39	40
Postponed a home improvement project	26	43
Put off a big home purchase	24	39
Canceled or postponed a vacation	27	36
Put off buying a new car	27	34
Put off a doctor visit or a medical procedure	20	27

For *each type of spending cutback*, determine whether there is a difference between men and women in what they would do to economize at the 0.05 level of significance.

10.69 The manufacturer of Boston and Vermont asphalt shingles knows that product weight is a major factor in the customer's perception of quality. Moreover, the weight represents the amount of raw materials being used and is therefore very important to the company from a cost standpoint. The last stage of the assembly line packages the shingles before they are placed on wooden pallets. Once a pallet is full (a pallet for most brands holds 16 squares of shingles), it is weighed, and the measurement is recorded. The file **Pallet** contains the weight (in pounds) from a sample of 368 pallets of Boston shingles and 330 pallets of Vermont shingles. Completely analyze the differences in the weights of the Boston and Vermont shingles, using $\alpha = 0.05$.

10.70 The manufacturer of Boston and Vermont asphalt shingles provides its customers with a 20-year warranty on most of its products. To determine whether a shingle will last as long as the warranty period, accelerated-life testing is conducted at the manufacturing plant. Accelerated-life testing exposes the shingle to the stresses it would be subject to in a lifetime of normal use in a laboratory setting via an experiment that takes only a few minutes to conduct. In this test, a shingle is repeatedly scraped with a brush for a short period of time, and the shingle granules removed by the brushing are weighed (in grams). Shingles that experience low amounts of granule loss are expected to last longer in normal use than shingles that experience high amounts of granule loss. In this situation, a shingle should experience no more than 0.8 grams of granule loss if it is expected to last the length of the warranty period. The file **Granule** contains a sample of 170 measurements made on the company's Boston shingles and 140 measurements made on Vermont shingles. Completely analyze the differences in the granule loss of the Boston and Vermont shingles, using $\alpha = 0.05$.

REPORT WRITING EXERCISE

10.71 Referring to the results of Problems 10.69 and 10.70 concerning the weight and granule loss of Boston and Vermont shingles, write a report that summarizes your conclusions.

TEAM PROJECT

The file **Bond Funds** contains information regarding eight variables from a sample of 180 bond mutual funds:

Type—Type of bonds comprising the bond fund (intermediate government or short-term corporate)
Assets—In millions of dollars
Fees—Sales charges (no or yes)
Expense ratio—Ratio of expenses to net assets, in percentage
Return 2008—Twelve-month return in 2008
Three-year return—Annualized return, 2006–2008
Five-year return—Annualized return, 2004–2008
Risk—Risk-of-loss factor of the mutual fund (below average, average, or above average)

10.72 Completely analyze the differences between bond funds without fees and bond funds with fees in terms of 2008 return, three-year return, five-year return, and expense ratio. Write a report summarizing your findings.

10.73 Completely analyze the difference between intermediate government bond funds and short-term corporate bond funds in terms of 2008 return, three-year return, five-year return, and expense ratio. Write a report summarizing your findings.

STUDENT SURVEY DATABASE

10.74 Problem 2.117 on page 65 describes a survey of 50 undergraduate students (stored in **UndergradSurvey**). For these data,
a. at the 0.05 level of significance, is there evidence of a difference between males and females in grade point average, expected starting salary, salary expected in five years, age, and spending on textbooks and supplies?
b. at the 0.05 level of significance, is there evidence of a difference between students who plan to go to graduate school and those who do not plan to go to graduate school in grade point average, expected starting salary, salary expected in five years, age, and spending on textbooks and supplies?

10.75 Problem 2.117 on page 65 describes a survey of 50 undergraduate students (stored in **UndergradSurvey**).
a. Select a sample of 50 undergraduate students at your school and conduct a similar survey for them.
b. For the data collected in (a), repeat (a) and (b) of Problem 10.74.
c. Compare the results of (b) to those of Problem 10.74.

10.76 Problem 2.119 on page 65 describes a survey of 40 MBA students (stored in **GradSurvey**). For these data, at the 0.05 level of significance, is there evidence of a difference between males and females in age, undergraduate grade point average, graduate grade point average, GMAT score, expected salary upon graduation, salary expected in five years, and spending on textbooks and supplies?

10.77 Problem 2.119 on page 65 describes a survey of 40 MBA students (stored in GradSurvey).

a. Select a sample of 40 graduate students in your MBA program and conduct a similar survey for those students.
b. For the data collected in (a), repeat Problem 10.76.
c. Compare the results of (b) to those of Problem 10.76.

MANAGING THE *SPRINGVILLE HERALD*

A marketing department team is charged with improving the telemarketing process in order to increase the number of home-delivery subscriptions sold. After several brainstorming sessions, it was clear that the longer a caller speaks to a respondent, the greater the chance that the caller will sell a home-delivery subscription. Therefore, the team decided to find ways to increase the length of the phone calls.

Initially, the team investigated the impact that the time of a call might have on the length of the call. Under current arrangements, calls were made in the evening hours, between 5:00 P.M. and 9:00 P.M., Monday through Friday. The team wanted to compare the length of calls made early in the evening (before 7:00 P.M.) with those made later in the evening (after 7:00 P.M.) to determine whether one of these time periods leads to longer calls and, correspondingly, to increased subscription sales. The team selected a sample of 30 female callers who staff the telephone bank on Wednesday evenings and randomly assigned 15 of them to the "early" time period and 15 to the "later" time period. The callers knew that the team was observing their efforts that evening but didn't know which calls were monitored. The callers had been trained to make their telephone presentations in a structured manner. They were to read from a script, and their greeting was personal but informal ("Hi, this is Leigh Richardson from the *Springville Herald*. May I speak to Stuart Knoll?").

Measurements were taken on the length of the call (defined as the difference, in seconds, between the time the person answered the phone and the time he or she hung up). The results (stored in SH10) are presented in Table SH10.1.

TABLE SH10.1

Length of Calls, in Seconds, Based on Time of Call— Early Versus Late in the Evening

Time of Call		Time of Call	
Early	**Late**	**Early**	**Late**
41.3	37.1	40.6	40.7
37.5	38.9	33.3	38.0
39.3	42.2	39.6	43.6
37.4	45.7	35.7	43.8
33.6	42.4	31.3	34.9
38.5	39.0	36.8	35.7
32.6	40.9	36.3	47.4
37.3	40.5		

EXERCISES

SH10.1 Analyze the data in Table SH10.1 and write a report to the marketing department team that indicates your findings. Include an attached appendix in which you discuss the reason you selected a particular statistical test to compare the two independent groups of callers.

SH10.2 Suppose that instead of the research design described here, there were only 15 callers sampled, and each caller was to be monitored twice in the evening— once in the early time period and once in the later time period. Thus, in Table SH10.1, each pair of values represents a particular caller's two measurements. Reanalyze these data and write a report for presentation to the team that indicates your findings.

SH10.3 What other variables should be investigated next? Why?

WEB CASE

Apply your knowledge about hypothesis testing in this Web Case, which continues the cereal-fill packaging dispute Web Case from Chapters 7 and 9.

Even after the recent public experiment about cereal box weights, the Consumers Concerned About Cereal Cheaters (CCACC) remains convinced that Oxford Cereals has misled the public. The group has created and posted a document in which it claims that cereal boxes produced at Plant Number 2 in Springville weigh less than the claimed mean of 368

grams. Using a Web browser, open to the Web page for the Chapter 10 Web Case or open **MoreCheating.htm** if you have downloaded the Web Case files, to visit the CCACC More Cheating page. Then answer the following questions:

1. Do the CCACC's results prove that there is a statistically significant difference in the mean weights of cereal boxes produced at Plant Numbers 1 and 2?

2. Perform the appropriate analysis to test the CCACC's hypothesis. What conclusions can you reach based on the data?

REFERENCES

1. Conover, W. J., *Practical Nonparametric Statistics*, 3rd ed. (New York: Wiley, 2000).
2. Daniel, W., *Applied Nonparametric Statistics*, 2nd ed. (Boston: Houghton Mifflin, 1990).
3. *Microsoft Excel 2007* (Redmond, WA: Microsoft Corp., 2007).
4. Satterthwaite, F. E., "An Approximate Distribution of Estimates of Variance Components," *Biometrics Bulletin*, 2(1946): 110–114.
5. Snedecor, G. W., and W. G. Cochran, *Statistical Methods*, 8th ed. (Ames, IA: Iowa State University Press, 1989).
6. Winer, B. J., D. R. Brown, and K. M. Michels, *Statistical Principles in Experimental Design*, 3rd ed. (New York: McGraw-Hill, 1989).

ORGANIZING TWO-SAMPLE DATA

Data values for two-sample tests can be stored in one column per group, called *unstacked data*, or all values in a single column, called *stacked data*. Stacked data requires a second column that identifies to which one of the groups the data value for the row belongs. Examine the worksheets of the **StackedAndUnstacked workbook** to see examples of both arrangements.

All the Excel methods discussed in this guide use unstacked data. If your two-sample data has been stored as stacked data, sort your data by group and then cut and paste the data of the second group (now in contiguous rows) into an empty column, using the row 1 cell in that column to identify the second group. You can also use the **Unstack Data** PHStat2 procedure to convert stacked data into its unstacked equivalent. Open to the worksheet that contains the stacked data. Select **PHStat → Data Preparation → Unstack Data**. In the procedure's dialog box, enter the single-column cell range containing the population labels as the **Grouping Variable Cell Range**, enter the single-column cell range containing the data as **Stacked Data Cell Range**, and click **OK**.

EG10.1 COMPARING the MEANS of TWO INDEPENDENT POPULATIONS

Pooled-Variance *t* Test for the Difference Between Two Means

PHStat2 Use the **Pooled-Variance t Test procedure** to perform this *t* test. For example, to perform the Figure 10.3 pooled-variance *t* test for the BLK Cola data shown on page 338, open to the **DATA worksheet** of the **COLA workbook**. Select **PHStat → Two-Sample Tests (Unsummarized Data) → Pooled-Variance t Test**. In the procedure's dialog box (shown at the top of the next column):

1. Enter **0** as the **Hypothesized Difference**.
2. Enter **0.05** as the **Level of Significance**.
3. Enter **A1:A11** as the **Population 1 Sample Cell Range**.
4. Enter **B1:B11** as the **Population 2 Sample Cell Range**.
5. Check **First cells in both ranges contain label**.
6. Click **Two-Tail Test**.
7. Enter a **Title** and click **OK**.

For problems that use summarized data, select **PHStat → Two-Sample Tests (Summarized Data) → Pooled-Variance t Test**. In that procedure's dialog box, enter the hypothesized difference, level of significance, and the sample size, sample mean, and sample standard deviation for each sample.

In-Depth Excel Use the **TINV** and **TDIST** functions to help perform the pooled-variance *t* test. For the two-tail test shown in Figure 10.3 on page 338, enter the expressions −**TINV**(*level of significance*, *degrees of freedom*) and **TINV**(*level of significance*, *degrees of freedom*) to compute the lower and upper critical values and enter **TDIST**(*absolute value of the t test statistic*, *degrees of freedom*, **2**) to compute the *p*-value. Also, enter an IF function as **IF**(*p-value* < *level of significance*, *display reject message*, *display do not reject message*) to indicate the results of the test.

Use the **COMPUTE worksheet** of the **Pooled-Variance T workbook**, shown in Figure 10.3 on page 338, as a template for performing the two-tail *t* test. The worksheet contains data and formulas to use the unsummarized data for the BLK Cola example. For other problems, use the COMPUTE worksheet with either unsummarized or summarized data. For unsummarized data, keep the formulas that calculate the sample size, sample mean, and sample standard deviation in cell ranges B7:B9 and B11:B13 and change the data in columns A and B in the **DATACOPY worksheet**. For summarized data, replace the formulas in cell ranges B7:B9 and B11:B13 with the sample statistics and ignore the DATACOPY worksheet.

Use the similar **COMPUTE_LOWER** or **COMPUTE_ UPPER worksheets** in the same workbook as templates for performing one-tail pooled-variance *t* tests. These worksheets can use either unsummarized or summarized data; follow the instructions for using the COMPUTE worksheet in the previous paragraph.

Analysis ToolPak Use the **t-Test: Two-Sample Assuming Equal Variances** procedure to perform the pooled-variance *t* test for unsummarized data. For example, to create results equivalent to those in the Figure 10.3 pooled-variance *t* test for the BLK Cola example on page 338, open to the **DATA worksheet** of the **COLA workbook** and do the following:

1. Select **Data → Data Analysis** (Excel 2007) or **Tools → Data Analysis** (Excel 2003).
2. In the Data Analysis dialog box, select **t-Test: Two-Sample Assuming Equal Variances** from the **Analysis Tools** list and then click **OK**.

In the procedure's dialog box (shown below):

3. Enter **A1:A11** as the **Variable 1 Range** and enter **B1:B11** as the **Variable 2 Range**.
4. Enter **0** as the **Hypothesized Mean Difference**.
5. Check **Labels** and enter **0.05** as **Alpha**.
6. Click **New Worksheet Ply**.
7. Click **OK** to create the results shown in Figure EG10.1.

	A	B	C
1	t-Test: Two-Sample Assuming Equal Variances		
2			
3		*Normal*	*End-Aisle*
4	Mean	50.3	72
5	Variance	350.6778	157.3333
6	Observations	10	10
7	Pooled Variance	254.0056	
8	Hypothesized Mean Difference	0	
9	df	18	
10	t Stat	-3.0446	
11	P(T<=t) one-tail	0.0035	
12	t Critical one-tail	1.7341	
13	P(T<=t) two-tail	0.0070	
14	t Critical two-tail	2.1009	

FIGURE EG10.1

Analysis ToolPak pooled-variance *t* test results

Confidence Interval Estimate for the Difference Between Two Means

PHStat2 Use the *PHStat2* instructions for the pooled-variance *t* test. In step 7, also check **Confidence Interval Estimate** and enter a **Confidence Level** in its box, in addition to entering a **Title** and clicking **OK**.

In-Depth Excel Use the *In-Depth Excel* instructions for the pooled-variance *t* tests. The worksheets in the **Pooled-Variance T workbook** include a confidence interval estimate for the difference between two means in the cell range D3:E16.

t Test for the Difference Between Two Means Assuming Unequal Variances

PHStat2 Use the **Separate-Variance t Test** procedure to perform this *t* test. For example, to perform the Figure 10.6 separate-variance *t* test for the BLK Cola data on page 342, open to the **DATA worksheet** of the **COLA workbook**. Select **PHStat → Two-Sample Tests (Unsummarized Data) → Separate-Variance t Test**. In the procedure's dialog box (shown below):

1. Enter **0** as the **Hypothesized Difference**.
2. Enter **0.05** as the **Level of Significance**.
3. Enter **A1:A11** as the **Population 1 Sample Cell Range**.
4. Enter **B1:B11** as the **Population 2 Sample Cell Range**.
5. Check **First cells in both ranges contain label**.
6. Click **Two-Tail Test**.
7. Enter a **Title** and click **OK**.

For problems that use summarized data, select **PHStat → Two-Sample Tests (Summarized Data) → Separate-Variance t Test**. In that procedure's dialog box, enter the hypothesized difference, the level of significance, and the sample size, sample mean, and sample standard deviation for each group.

In-Depth Excel Use the **TINV** and **TDIST** functions to help perform the separate-variance *t* test. For the two-tail test shown in Figure 10.6 on page 342, enter the expressions –TINV(*level of significance*, *degrees of freedom*) and TINV(*level of significance*, *degrees of freedom*) to compute the lower and upper critical values and enter **TDIST**(*absolute value of the t test statistic*, *degrees of freedom*, **2**) to compute the *p*-value. Also, enter an IF function as **IF**(*p-value* < *level of significance*, *display reject message*, *display do not reject message*) to indicate the results of the test.

Use the **COMPUTE worksheet** of the **Separate-Variance T workbook**, shown in Figure 10.6 on page 342, as a template for performing the two-tail *t* test. The worksheet contains data and formulas to use the unsummarized data for the BLK Cola example. For other problems, use the COMPUTE worksheet with either unsummarized or summarized data. For unsummarized data, keep the formulas that calculate the sample size, sample mean, and sample standard deviation in cell ranges B7:B9 and B11:B13 and change the data in columns A and B in the **DATACOPY worksheet**. For summarized data, replace the formulas in cell ranges B7:B9 and B11:B13 with the sample statistics and ignore the DATACOPY worksheet.

Use the similar **COMPUTE_LOWER** or **COMPUTE_UPPER worksheets** in the same workbook as templates for performing one-tail separate-variance *t* tests. These worksheets can use either unsummarized or summarized data; follow the instructions for using the COMPUTE worksheet in the previous paragraph.

Analysis ToolPak Use the **t-Test: Two-Sample Assuming Unequal Variances** procedure to perform the separate-variance *t* test for unsummarized data. For example, to create results equivalent to those in the Figure 10.6 separate-variance *t* test for the BLK Cola data on page 342, open to the **DATA worksheet** of the **COLA workbook** and do the following:

1. Select **Data → Data Analysis** (Excel 2007) or **Tools → Data Analysis** (Excel 2003).
2. In the Data Analysis dialog box, select **t-Test: Two-Sample Assuming Unequal Variances** from the **Analysis Tools** list and then click **OK**.

In the procedure's dialog box:

3. Enter **A1:A11** as the **Variable 1 Range** and enter **B1:B11** as the **Variable 2 Range**.
4. Enter **0** as the **Hypothesized Mean Difference**.
5. Check **Labels** and enter **0.05** as **Alpha**.
6. Click **New Worksheet Ply**.
7. Click **OK** to create the results shown in Figure EG10.2.

Because the Analysis ToolPak uses table lookups to approximate the critical values and the *p*-value, the ToolPak reports slightly different values from those computed in the Figure 10.6 worksheet.

	A	B	C
1	t-Test: Two-Sample Assuming Unequal Variances		
2			
3		*Normal*	*End-Aisle*
4	**Mean**	50.3	72
5	**Variance**	350.6778	157.3333
6	**Observations**	10	10
7	**Hypothesized Mean Difference**	0	
8	**df**	16	
9	**t Stat**	-3.0446	
10	**P(T<=t) one-tail**	0.0039	
11	**t Critical one-tail**	1.7459	
12	**P(T<=t) two-tail**	0.0077	
13	**t Critical two-tail**	2.1199	

FIGURE EG10.2

Analysis ToolPak separate-variance *t* test results

EG10.2 COMPARING the MEANS of TWO RELATED POPULATIONS

Paired *t* Test

PHStat2 Use the **Paired t Test** procedure to perform this *t* test. For example, to perform the Figure 10.8 paired *t* test for the AAA mileage data on page 349, open to the **DATA worksheet** of the **AAAMileage workbook**. Select **PHStat → Two-Sample Tests (Unsummarized Data) → Paired t Test**. In the procedure's dialog box (shown below):

1. Enter **0** as the **Hypothesized Mean Difference**.
2. Enter **0.05** as the **Level of Significance**.
3. Enter **B1:B10** as the **Population 1 Sample Cell Range**.
4. Enter **C1:C10** as the **Population 2 Sample Cell Range**.
5. Check **First cells in both ranges contain label**.
6. Click **Two-Tail Test**.
7. Enter a **Title** and click **OK**.

For problems that use summarized data, select **PHStat → Two-Sample Tests (Summarized Data) → Paired t Test**. In that procedure's dialog box, enter the hypothesized mean difference, the level of significance, and the sample size, sample mean, and sample standard deviation for each sample.

In-Depth Excel Use the **TINV** and **TDIST** functions to help perform the paired t test. For the two-tail test shown in Figure 10.8, enter the expressions −TINV(*level of significance, degrees of freedom*) and TINV(*level of significance, degrees of freedom*) to compute the lower and upper critical values and enter **TDIST**(*absolute value of the t test statistic, degrees of freedom*, **2**) to compute the p-value. Also, enter an IF function as **IF**(*p-value < level of significance, display reject message, display do not reject message*) to indicate the results of the test.

Use the **COMPUTE** and **PtCalcs worksheets** of the **Paired T workbook**, shown in Figure 10.8 on page 349, as a template for performing the two-tail paired t test. The PtCalcs worksheet contains intermediate calculations that allow the COMPUTE worksheet to compute the sample size, $\overline{D}$, and S_D. Formulas used in the PtCalcs worksheet are shown in Figure EG10.3.

	C	D	E	F	G
1	D_i	$(D_i - DBar)^2$		DBar	=AVERAGE(C:C)
2	=A2 - B2	=(C2 - G$1)^2			
3	=A3 - B3	=(C3 - G$1)^2			
4	=A4 - B4	=(C4 - G$1)^2			
5	=A5 - B5	=(C5 - G$1)^2			
6	=A6 - B6	=(C6 - G$1)^2			
7	=A7 - B7	=(C7 - G$1)^2			
8	=A8 - B8	=(C8 - G$1)^2			
9	=A9 - B9	=(C9 - G$1)^2			
10	=A10 - B10	=(C10 - G$1)^2			

FIGURE EG10.3

PtCalcs worksheet formulas

The COMPUTE and PtCalcs worksheets contain the data and formulas for the unsummarized data for the AAA mileage data example. For other problems, paste the unsummarized data into columns A and B of the PtCalcs worksheet. For sample sizes greater than 9, select the cell range C10:D10 and copy the formulas in those cells down through the last data row. For sample sizes less than 9, delete the column C and D formulas for which there are no column A and B values.

If you know the sample size, $\overline{D}$, and S_D values, you can ignore the PtCalcs worksheets and enter the values in B8, B9, and B11 of the COMPUTE worksheet, overwriting the formulas that those cells contain.

Use the **COMPUTE_LOWER** or **COMPUTE_ UPPER worksheets** in the same workbook as templates for performing one-tail t tests. Follow the instructions for modifying the COMPUTE and PtCalcs worksheets in the previous paragraphs to use these worksheets for other problems.

Analysis ToolPak Use **the t-Test: Paired Two Sample for Means** procedure to perform the paired t test for unsummarized data. For example, to create results equivalent to those in the Figure 10.8 paired t test for the AAA mileage data on page 349, open to the **DATA worksheet** of the **AAAMileage workbook** and do the following:

1. Select **Data → Data Analysis** (Excel 2007) or **Tools → Data Analysis** (Excel 2003).
2. In the Data Analysis dialog box, select **t-Test: Paired Two Sample for Means** from the **Analysis Tools** list and then click **OK**.

In the procedure's dialog box:

3. Enter **B1:B10** as the **Variable 1 Range** and enter **C1:C10** as the **Variable 2 Range**.
4. Enter **0** as the **Hypothesized Mean Difference**.
5. Check **Labels** and enter **0.05** as **Alpha**.
6. Click **New Worksheet Ply**.
7. Click **OK** to create the results shown in Figure EG10.4.

	A	B	C
1	t-Test: Paired Two Sample for Means		
2			
3		Members	Government
4	Mean	27.1556	29.5
5	Variance	129.5528	125.0025
6	Observations	9	9
7	Pearson Correlation	0.9673	
8	Hypothesized Mean Difference	0	
9	df	8	
10	t Stat	-2.4307	
11	P(T<=t) one-tail	0.0206	
12	t Critical one-tail	1.8595	
13	P(T<=t) two-tail	0.0412	
14	t Critical two-tail	2.3060	

FIGURE EG10.4

Analysis ToolPak paired t test results

EG10.3 COMPARING the PROPORTIONS of TWO INDEPENDENT POPULATIONS

Z Test for the Difference Between Two Proportions

PHStat2 Use the **Z Test for the Differences in Two Proportions** procedure to perform this Z test. For example, to perform the Figure 10.12 Z test for the hotel guest satisfaction survey on page 357, select **PHStat → Two-Sample Tests (Summarized Data) → Z Test for the Differences in Two Proportions**. In the procedure's dialog box (at the top of page 378):

1. Enter **0** as the **Hypothesized Difference**.
2. Enter **0.05** as the **Level of Significance**.
3. For the Population 1 Sample, enter **163** as the **Number of Items of Interest** and **227** as the **Sample Size**.
4. For the Population 2 Sample, enter **154** as the **Number of Items of Interest** and **262** as the **Sample Size**.
5. Click **Two-Tail Test**.
6. Enter a **Title** and click **OK**.

confidence interval estimate for the difference between two means in the cell range D3:E16.

EG10.4 *F* TEST for the RATIO of TWO VARIANCES

PHStat2 Use the **F Test for the Differences in Two Variances** procedure to perform this *F* test. For example, to perform the Figure 10.13 *F* test for the BLK Cola sales data on page 363, open to the **DATA worksheet** of the **COLA workbook**. Select **PHStat → Two-Sample Tests (Unsummarized Data) → F Test for the Differences in Two Variances**. In the procedure's dialog box (shown below):

1. Enter **0.05** as the **Level of Significance**.
2. Enter **A1:A11** as the **Population 1 Sample Cell Range**.
3. Enter **B1:B11** as the **Population 2 Sample Cell Range**.
4. Check **First cells in both ranges contain label**.
5. Click **Two-Tail Test**.
6. Enter a **Title** and click **OK**.

In-Depth Excel Use the **NORMSINV** and **NORMSDIST** functions to help perform the *Z* test for the proportion. For the two-tail test, enter **NORMSINV(*level of significance*/2)** and **NORMSINV(1 – *level of significance*/2)** to compute the lower and upper critical values and enter the expression **2 * (1 – NORMSDIST(*absolute value of the Z test statistic*)** to compute the *p*-value. Also, enter an IF function as **IF(*p-value < level of significance*, *display reject message*, *display do not reject message*)** to indicate the results of the test.

Use the **COMPUTE worksheet** of the **Z Two Proportions workbook**, shown in Figure 10.12 on page 357, as a template for performing the two-tail *Z* test for the difference between two proportions. The worksheet contains data for the hotel guest satisfaction survey. For other problems, change the **Data** fields in cells B4, B5, B7, B8, B10, and B11 as necessary.

Use the similar **COMPUTE_LOWER** or **COMPUTE_UPPER worksheets** in the same workbook as templates for performing one-tail separate-variance *t* tests. For other problems, also change the values in cells B4, B5, B7, B8, B10, and B11 as necessary.

Confidence Interval Estimate for the Difference Between Two Proportions

PHStat2 Use the *PHStat2* instructions for the *Z* test for the difference between two proportions. In step 6, also check **Confidence Interval Estimate** and enter a **Confidence Level** in its box, in addition to entering a **Title** and clicking **OK**.

In-Depth Excel Use the *In-Depth Excel* instructions for the *Z* test for the difference between two proportions. The worksheets in the **Z Two Proportions** workbook include a

For problems that use summarized data, select **PHStat → Two-Sample Tests (Summarized Data) → F Test for the Differences in Two Variances**. In that procedure's dialog box, enter the level of significance and the sample size and sample variance for each sample.

In-Depth Excel Use the **FINV** and **FDIST** functions to help perform the *F* test for the difference between two variances. For the two-tail test, enter **FINV(*level of significance*/2, *population 1 sample degrees of freedom*, *population 2 sample degrees of freedom*)** to compute the upper critical value and enter the expression **2 * FDIST(*F test statistic*, *population 1 sample degrees of freedom*, *population 2 sample degrees of freedom*)** to compute the *p*-value. Also, enter an IF function as **IF(*p-value < level of significance*, *display reject message*, *display do not reject message*)** to indicate the results of the test.

Use the **COMPUTE worksheet** of the **F Two Variances workbook**, shown in Figure 10.13 on page 363, as a template for performing the two-tail *F* test for the ratio of two variances. The worksheet contains data and formulas for using the unsummarized data for the BLK Cola example. For other problems, use the COMPUTE worksheet with either unsummarized or summarized data. For unsummarized data, keep the formulas that calculate the sample size and sample variance in cell ranges B6:B7 and B9:B10 and change the data in columns A and B in the **DATACOPY worksheet**. For summarized data, replace the formulas in cell ranges B6:B7 and B9:B10 with the sample statistics and ignore the DATACOPY worksheet.

Use the similar **COMPUTE_UPPER worksheet** in the same workbook as a template for performing the upper-tail test. This worksheet can use either unsummarized or summarized data; follow the instructions for using the COMPUTE worksheet in the previous paragraph.

Analysis ToolPak   Use the **F-Test Two-Sample for Variances** procedure to perform the F test for the difference between two variances for unsummarized data. For example, to create results equivalent to those in the Figure 10.13 F test for the BLK Cola sales data on page 363, open to the **DATA worksheet** of the **COLA workbook** and do the following:

1. Select **Data → Data Analysis** (Excel 2007) or **Tools → Data Analysis** (Excel 2003).
2. In the Data Analysis dialog box, select **F-Test Two-Sample for Variances** from the **Analysis Tools** list and then click **OK**.

In the procedure's dialog box:

3. Enter **A1:A11** as the **Variable 1 Range** and enter **B1:B11** as the **Variable 2 Range**.
4. Check **Labels** and enter **0.05** as **Alpha**.
5. Click **New Worksheet Ply**.
6. Click **OK** to create the results shown in Figure EG10.5.

	A	B	C
1	F-Test Two-Sample for Variances		
2			
3		*Normal*	*End-Aisle*
4	Mean	50.3	72
5	Variance	350.6778	157.3333
6	Observations	10	10
7	df	9	9
8	F	2.2289	
9	P(F<=f) one-tail	0.1241	
10	F Critical one-tail	3.1789	

FIGURE EG10.5

Analysis ToolPak results for an *F* test for the difference between two variances

The Analysis ToolPak results show only the one-tail test *p*-value (0.1241), which must be doubled for the two-tail test shown in Figure 10.13 on page 363.

11 Analysis of Variance

Learning Objectives

In this chapter, you learn:

- The basic concepts of experimental design
- How to use the one-way analysis of variance to test for differences among the means of several groups
- How to use the two-way analysis of variance and interpret the interaction effect
- How to perform multiple comparisons in a one-way analysis of variance and a two-way analysis of variance

@ Perfect Parachutes

Y ou are the production manager at the Perfect Parachutes Company. Parachutes are woven in your factory using a synthetic fiber purchased from one of four different suppliers. Strength of these fibers is an important characteristic that ensures quality parachutes. You need to decide whether the synthetic fibers from each of your four suppliers result in parachutes of equal strength. Furthermore, your factory uses two types of looms to produce parachutes, the *Jetta* and the *Turk*. You need to establish that the parachutes woven on both types of looms are equally strong. You also want to know if any differences in the strength of the parachute that can be attributed to the four suppliers are dependent on the type of loom used. How would you go about finding this information?

In Chapter 10, you used hypothesis testing to reach conclusions about possible differences between two populations. As a manager at Perfect Parachutes, you need to design an experiment to test the strength of parachutes woven from the synthetic fibers from the *four* suppliers. That is, you need to evaluate differences among *more than two* populations, or groups. (Populations are called *groups* in this chapter.)

This chapter begins by examining a *completely randomized design* that has one *factor* (which supplier to use) and several groups (the four suppliers). The completely randomized design is then extended to the *factorial design*, in which more than one factor at a time is simultaneously studied in a single experiment. For example, an experiment incorporating the four suppliers and the two types of looms would help you determine which supplier and type of loom to use in order to manufacture the strongest parachutes. Throughout the chapter, emphasis is placed on the assumptions behind the use of the various testing procedures.

11.1 The Completely Randomized Design: One-Way Analysis of Variance

In many situations, you need to examine differences among more than two **groups**. The groups involved are classified according to **levels** of a **factor** of interest. For example, a factor such as baking temperature may have several groups defined by *numerical levels* such as 300°, 350°, 400°, and 450°, and a factor such as preferred supplier for a parachute manufacturer may have several groups defined by *categorical levels* such as Supplier 1, Supplier 2, Supplier 3, and Supplier 4. When there is only one factor, the experimental design is called a **completely randomized design**.

One-Way ANOVA *F* Test for Differences Among More Than Two Means

When you are analyzing a numerical variable and certain assumptions are met, you use the **analysis of variance (ANOVA)** to compare the means of the groups. The ANOVA procedure used for the completely randomized design is referred to as the **one-way ANOVA**, and it is an extension of the pooled variance *t* test for the difference between two means discussed in Section 10.1. Although ANOVA is an acronym for *analysis of variance*, the term is misleading because the objective in ANOVA is to analyze differences among the group means, *not* the variances. However, by analyzing the variation among and within the groups, you can reach conclusions about possible differences in group means. In ANOVA, the total variation is subdivided into variation that is due to differences *among* the groups and variation that is due to differences *within* the groups (see Figure 11.1). **Within-group variation** measures random variation. **Among-group variation** is due to differences from group to group. The symbol *c* is used to indicate the number of groups.

FIGURE 11.1

Partitioning the total variation in a completely randomized design

Partitioning the Total Variation
$SST = SSA + SSW$

Total Variation (SST) $df = n - 1$

Among-Group Variation (SSA) $df = c - 1$

Within-Group Variation (SSW) $df = n - c$

Assuming that the *c* groups represent populations whose values are randomly and independently selected, follow a normal distribution, and have equal variances, the null hypothesis of no differences in the population means:

$$H_0: \mu_1 = \mu_2 = \cdots = \mu_c$$

is tested against the alternative that not all the *c* population means are equal:

$$H_1: \text{Not all } \mu_j \text{ are equal (where } j = 1, 2, \ldots, c).$$

To perform an ANOVA test of equality of population means, you subdivide the total variation in the values into two parts—that which is due to variation among the groups and that which is due to variation within the groups. The **total variation** is represented by the **sum of squares total (*SST*)**. Because the population means of the c groups are assumed to be equal under the null hypothesis, you compute the total variation among all the values by summing the squared differences between each individual value and the **grand mean,** $\bar{\bar{X}}$. The grand mean is the mean of all the values in all the groups combined. Equation (11.1) shows the computation of the total variation.

TOTAL VARIATION IN ONE-WAY ANOVA

$$SST = \sum_{j=1}^{c} \sum_{i=1}^{n_j} (X_{ij} - \bar{\bar{X}})^2 \qquad (11.1)$$

where

$$\bar{\bar{X}} = \frac{\sum_{j=1}^{c} \sum_{i=1}^{n_j} X_{ij}}{n} = \text{Grand mean}$$

$X_{ij} = i$th value in group j

$n_j = $ number of values in group j

$n = $ total number of values in all groups combined
(that is, $n = n_1 + n_2 + \cdots + n_c$)

$c = $ number of groups

You compute the among-group variation, usually called the **sum of squares among groups (*SSA*)**, by summing the squared differences between the sample mean of each group, $\bar{X}_j$, and the grand mean, $\bar{\bar{X}}$, weighted by the sample size, n_j, in each group. Equation (11.2) shows the computation of the among-group variation.

AMONG-GROUP VARIATION IN ONE-WAY ANOVA

$$SSA = \sum_{j=1}^{c} n_j (\bar{X}_j - \bar{\bar{X}})^2 \qquad (11.2)$$

where

$c = $ number of groups

$n_j = $ number of values in group j

$\bar{X}_j = $ sample mean of group j

$\bar{\bar{X}} = $ grand mean

The within-group variation, usually called the **sum of squares within groups (*SSW*)**, measures the difference between each value and the mean of its own group and sums the squares of these differences over all groups. Equation (11.3) shows the computation of the within-group variation.

WITHIN-GROUP VARIATION IN ONE-WAY ANOVA

$$SSW = \sum_{j=1}^{c} \sum_{i=1}^{n_\xi} (X_{ij} - \bar{X}_j)^2 \qquad (11.3)$$

where

$$X_{ij} = i\text{th value in group } j$$

$$\overline{X}_j = \text{sample mean of group } j$$

Because you are comparing c groups, there are $c - 1$ degrees of freedom associated with the sum of squares among groups. Because each of the c groups contributes $n_j - 1$ degrees of freedom, there are $n - c$ degrees of freedom associated with the sum of squares within groups. In addition, there are $n - 1$ degrees of freedom associated with the sum of squares total because you are comparing each value, X_{ij}, to the grand mean, $\overline{\overline{X}}$, based on all n values.

If you divide each of these sums of squares by its respective degrees of freedom, you have three variances, or **mean square** terms: MSA (mean square among), MSW (mean square within), and MST (mean square total).

MEAN SQUARES IN ONE-WAY ANOVA

$$MSA = \frac{SSA}{c - 1} \tag{11.4a}$$

$$MSW = \frac{SSW}{n - c} \tag{11.4b}$$

$$MST = \frac{SST}{n - 1} \tag{11.4c}$$

Although you want to compare the means of the c groups to determine whether a difference exists among them, the name ANOVA comes from the fact that you are comparing variances. If the null hypothesis is true and there are no differences in the c group means, all three mean squares (or *variances*)—MSA, MSW, and MST—provide estimates of the overall variance in the data. Thus, to test the null hypothesis:

$$H_0: \mu_1 = \mu_2 = \cdots = \mu_c$$

against the alternative:

$$H_1: \text{Not all } \mu_j \text{ are equal (where } j = 1, 2, \ldots, c)$$

you compute the one-way ANOVA F_{STAT} test statistic as the ratio of MSA to MSW, as in Equation (11.5).

ONE-WAY ANOVA F_{STAT} TEST STATISTIC

$$F_{STAT} = \frac{MSA}{MSW} \tag{11.5}$$

The F_{STAT} test statistic follows an **F distribution**, with $c - 1$ degrees of freedom in the numerator and $n - c$ degrees of freedom in the denominator. For a given level of significance, α, you reject the null hypothesis if the F_{STAT} test statistic computed in Equation (11.5) is greater than the upper-tail critical value, F_α, from the F distribution with $c - 1$ degrees of freedom in the numerator and $n - c$ in the denominator (see Table E.5). Thus, as shown in Figure 11.2, the decision rule is

$$\text{Reject } H_0 \text{ if } F_{STAT} > F_\alpha;$$

otherwise, do not reject H_0.

FIGURE 11.2

Regions of rejection and nonrejection when using ANOVA

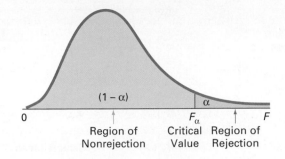

If the null hypothesis is true, the computed F_{STAT} test statistic is expected to be approximately equal to 1 because both the numerator and denominator mean square terms are estimating the overall variance in the data. If H_0 is false (and there are differences in the group means), the computed F_{STAT} test statistic is expected to be larger than 1 because the numerator, MSA, is estimating the differences among groups in addition to the overall variability in the values, while the denominator, MSW, is measuring only the overall variability in the values. Thus, when you use the ANOVA procedure, you reject the null hypothesis at a selected level of significance, α, only if the computed F_{STAT} test statistic is greater than F_α, the upper-tail critical value of the F distribution having $c - 1$ and $n - c$ degrees of freedom, as illustrated in Figure 11.2.

The results of an analysis of variance are usually displayed in an **ANOVA summary table**, as shown in Table 11.1. The entries in this table include the sources of variation (i.e., among-groups, within-groups, and total), the degrees of freedom, the sums of squares, the mean squares (i.e., the variances), and the computed F_{STAT} test statistic. The p-value, the probability of having an F_{STAT} value as large as or larger than the one computed, given that the null hypothesis is true, usually appears also. The p-value allows you to reach direct conclusions about the null hypothesis without referring to a table of critical values of the F distribution. If the p-value is less than the chosen level of significance, α, you reject the null hypothesis.

ANOVA results worksheets presented in this book include the p-value in a column F cell of the ANOVA summary table.

TABLE 11.1

Analysis-of-Variance Summary Table

Source	Degrees of Freedom	Sum of Squares	Mean Square (Variance)	F
Among groups	$c - 1$	SSA	$MSA = \dfrac{SSA}{c - 1}$	$F_{STAT} = \dfrac{MSA}{MSW}$
Within groups	$n - c$	SSW	$MSW = \dfrac{SSW}{n - c}$	
Total	$n - 1$	SST		

To illustrate the one-way ANOVA F test, return to the Perfect Parachutes scenario (see page 381). You define the business problem as whether significant differences exist in the strength of parachutes woven using synthetic fiber purchased from each of the four suppliers. The strength of the parachutes is measured by placing them in a testing device that pulls on both ends of a parachute until it tears apart. The amount of force required to tear the parachute is measured on a tensile-strength scale, where the larger the value, the stronger the parachute.

Five parachutes are woven using the fiber supplied by each group—Supplier 1, Supplier 2, Supplier 3, and Supplier 4. You perform the experiment of testing the strength of each of the 20 parachutes by collecting the tensile strength measurement of each parachute. These results are organized by group and stored, along with the sample mean and the sample standard deviation, in Parachute. Figure 11.3 shows the worksheet that holds these data.

FIGURE 11.3

Worksheet of the tensile strength for parachutes woven with synthetic fibers from four different suppliers, along with the sample mean and sample standard deviation

Figure 11.3 displays the DATA_SUMMARY worksheet of the Parachute workbook. This worksheet contains formulas that use the AVERAGE and STDEV functions to compute the sample mean and sample standard deviation in the cell range B8:E9.

	A	B	C	D	E
1		Supplier 1	Supplier 2	Supplier 3	Supplier 4
2		18.5	26.3	20.6	25.4
3		24.0	25.3	25.2	19.9
4		17.2	24.0	20.8	22.6
5		19.9	21.2	24.7	17.5
6		18.0	24.5	22.9	20.4
7					
8	Sample Mean	19.52	24.26	22.84	21.16
9	Sample Standard Deviation	2.69	1.92	2.13	2.98

In Figure 11.3, observe that there are differences in the sample means for the four suppliers. For Supplier 1, the mean tensile strength is 19.52. For Supplier 2, the mean tensile strength is 24.26. For Supplier 3, the mean tensile strength is 22.84, and for Supplier 4, the mean tensile strength is 21.16. What you need to determine is whether these sample results are sufficiently different to conclude that the *population* means are not all equal.

The scatter plot shown in Figure 11.4 enables you to visualize the data and see how the measurements of tensile strength distribute. You can also observe differences among the groups as well as within groups. If the sample sizes in each group were larger, you could construct stem-and-leaf displays, boxplots, and normal probability plots.

FIGURE 11.4

Scatter plot of tensile strengths for four different suppliers

Create scatter plots using the instructions in Section EG2.7.

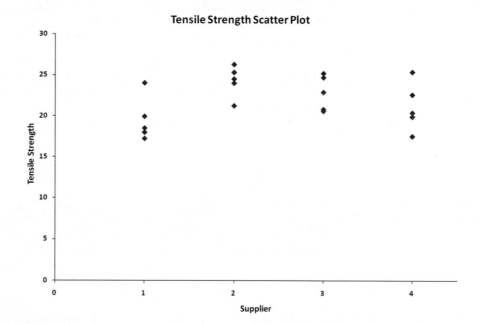

The null hypothesis states that there is no difference in mean tensile strength among the four suppliers:

$$H_0: \mu_1 = \mu_2 = \mu_3 = \mu_4$$

The alternative hypothesis states that at least one of the suppliers differs with respect to the mean tensile strength:

$$H_1: \text{Not all the means are equal.}$$

To construct the ANOVA summary table, you first compute the sample means in each group (see Figure 11.3 above). Then you compute the grand mean by summing all 20 values and dividing by the total number of values:

$$\bar{\bar{X}} = \frac{\sum_{j=1}^{c} \sum_{i=1}^{n_j} X_{ij}}{n} = \frac{438.9}{20} = 21.945$$

Then, using Equations (11.1) through (11.3) on page 383, you compute the sum of squares:

$$SSA = \sum_{j=1}^{c} n_j(\bar{X}_j - \bar{\bar{X}})^2 = (5)(19.52 - 21.945)^2 + (5)(24.26 - 21.945)^2$$

$$+ (5)(22.84 - 21.945)^2 + (5)(21.16 - 21.945)^2$$

$$= 63.2855$$

$$SSW = \sum_{j=1}^{c} \sum_{i=1}^{n_j}(X_{ij} - \bar{X}_j)^2$$

$$= (18.5 - 19.52)^2 + \cdots + (18 - 19.52)^2 + (26.3 - 24.26)^2 + \cdots + (24.5 - 24.26)^2$$

$$+ (20.6 - 22.84)^2 + \cdots + (22.9 - 22.84)^2 + (25.4 - 21.16)^2 + \cdots + (20.4 - 21.16)^2$$

$$= 97.5040$$

$$SST = \sum_{j=1}^{c} \sum_{i=1}^{n_j}(X_{ij} - \bar{\bar{X}})^2$$

$$= (18.5 - 21.945)^2 + (24 - 21.945)^2 + \cdots + (20.4 - 21.945)^2$$

$$= 160.7895$$

You compute the mean square terms by dividing the sum of squares by the corresponding degrees of freedom [see Equation (11.4) on page 384]. Because $c = 4$ and $n = 20$,

$$MSA = \frac{SSA}{c - 1} = \frac{63.2855}{4 - 1} = 21.0952$$

$$MSW = \frac{SSW}{n - c} = \frac{97.5040}{20 - 4} = 6.0940$$

so that using Equation (11.5) on page 384,

$$F_{STAT} = \frac{MSA}{MSW} = \frac{21.0952}{6.0940} = 3.4616$$

For a selected level of significance, α, you find the upper-tail critical value, F_α, from the F distribution using Table E.5. A portion of Table E.5 is presented in Table 11.2. In the parachute supplier example, there are 3 degrees of freedom in the numerator and 16 degrees of freedom in the denominator. F_α, the upper-tail critical value at the 0.05 level of significance, is 3.24.

TABLE 11.2

Finding the Critical Value of F with 3 and 16 Degrees of Freedom at the 0.05 Level of Significance

				Cumulative Probabilities = 0.95					
				Upper-Tail Area = 0.05					
				Numerator df_1					
Denominator df_2	1	2	3	4	5	6	7	8	9
.	.	.	.	.	.	.	.	.	.
.	.	.	.	.	.	.	.	.	.
.	.	.	.	.	.	.	.	.	.
11	4.84	3.98	3.59	3.36	3.20	3.09	3.01	2.95	2.90
12	4.75	3.89	3.49	3.26	3.11	3.00	2.91	2.85	2.80
13	4.67	3.81	3.41	3.18	3.03	2.92	2.83	2.77	2.71
14	4.60	3.74	3.34	3.11	2.96	2.85	2.76	2.70	2.65
15	4.54	3.68	3.29	3.06	2.90	2.79	2.71	2.64	2.59
16	4.49	3.63	3.24	3.01	2.85	2.74	2.66	2.59	2.54

Source: *Extracted from Table E.5.*

Because $F_{STAT} = 3.4616$ is greater than $F_\alpha = 3.24$, you reject the null hypothesis (see Figure 11.5). You conclude that there is a significant difference in the mean tensile strength among the four suppliers.

FIGURE 11.5

Regions of rejection and nonrejection for the one-way ANOVA at the 0.05 level of significance, with 3 and 16 degrees of freedom

Figure 11.6 shows the ANOVA results worksheet for the parachute experiment, including the p-value in cell F13. In this worksheet, the Among Groups variation of Table 11.1 (see page 385) is labeled the Between Groups variation.

FIGURE 11.6

ANOVA results worksheet for the parachute experiment

Figure 11.6 displays the **COMPUTE worksheet** *of the* **One-Way ANOVA workbook.** *Create this worksheet using the instructions in Section EG11.1. Read the In-Depth Excel instructions for this worksheet to learn about the formulas used in this worksheet.*

	A	B	C	D	E	F	G	H	I	J
1	ANOVA: Single Factor								Calculations	
2									c	4
3	SUMMARY								n	20
4	*Groups*	*Count*	*Sum*	*Average*	*Variance*					
5	Supplier 1	5	97.6	19.52	7.237					
6	Supplier 2	5	121.3	24.26	3.683					
7	Supplier 3	5	114.2	22.84	4.553					
8	Supplier 4	5	105.8	21.16	8.903					
9										
10										
11	ANOVA									
12	*Source of Variation*	*SS*	*df*	*MS*	*F*	*P-value*	*F crit*			
13	Between Groups	63.2855	3	21.0952	3.4616	0.0414	3.2389			
14	Within Groups	97.504	16	6.0940						
15										
16	Total	160.7895	19							
17						Level of significance	0.05			

The p-value, or probability of getting a computed F_{STAT} statistic of 3.4616 or larger when the null hypothesis is true, is 0.0414. Because this p-value is less than the specified α of 0.05, you reject the null hypothesis. The p-value of 0.0414 indicates that there is a 4.14% chance of observing differences this large or larger if the population means for the four suppliers are all equal. After performing the one-way ANOVA and finding a significant difference among the suppliers, you still do not know *which* suppliers differ. All you know is that there is sufficient evidence to state that the population means are not all the same. In other words, one or more population means are significantly different. To determine which suppliers differ, you can use a multiple comparisons procedure such as the Tukey-Kramer procedure.

Multiple Comparisons: The Tukey-Kramer Procedure

In the Perfect Parachutes scenario on page 381, you used the one-way ANOVA F test to determine that there was a difference among the suppliers. The next step is to construct **multiple comparisons** to determine which suppliers are different.

Although many procedures are available (see references 5, 6, and 9), this text uses the **Tukey-Kramer multiple comparisons procedure for one-way ANOVA** to determine which of the c means are significantly different. The Tukey-Kramer procedure enables you to simultaneously make comparisons between all pairs of groups. You use the following four steps to construct the comparisons.

1. Compute the absolute mean differences, $|\bar{X}_j - \bar{X}_{j'}|$ (where $j \neq j'$), among all $c(c-1)/2$ pairs of sample means.
2. Compute the **critical range** for the Tukey-Kramer procedure, using Equation (11.6).

CRITICAL RANGE FOR THE TUKEY-KRAMER PROCEDURE

$$\text{Critical range} = Q_\alpha \sqrt{\frac{MSW}{2}\left(\frac{1}{n_j} + \frac{1}{n_{j'}}\right)} \qquad \text{(11.6)}$$

where Q_α is the upper-tail critical value from a **Studentized range distribution** having c degrees of freedom in the numerator and $n - c$ degrees of freedom in the denominator. (Values for the Studentized range distribution are found in Table E.7.)

If the sample sizes differ, you compute a critical range for each pairwise comparison of sample means.

3. Compare each of the $c(c-1)/2$ pairs of means against its corresponding critical range. You declare a specific pair significantly different if the absolute difference in the sample means, $|\bar{X}_j - \bar{X}_{j'}|$, is greater than the critical range.
4. Interpret the results.

In the parachute example, there are four suppliers. Thus, there are $4(4-1)/2 = 6$ pairwise comparisons. To apply the Tukey-Kramer multiple comparisons procedure, you first compute the absolute mean differences for all six pairwise comparisons. *Multiple comparisons* refer to the fact that you are going to simultaneously make an inference about all six of these comparisons:

1. $|\bar{X}_1 - \bar{X}_2| = |19.52 - 24.26| = 4.74$
2. $|\bar{X}_1 - \bar{X}_3| = |19.52 - 22.84| = 3.32$
3. $|\bar{X}_1 - \bar{X}_4| = |19.52 - 21.16| = 1.64$
4. $|\bar{X}_2 - \bar{X}_3| = |24.26 - 22.84| = 1.42$
5. $|\bar{X}_2 - \bar{X}_4| = |24.26 - 21.16| = 3.10$
6. $|\bar{X}_3 - \bar{X}_4| = |22.84 - 21.16| = 1.68$

You need to compute only one critical range because the sample sizes in the four groups are equal. From the ANOVA summary table (Figure 11.6 on page 388), $MSW = 6.094$ and $n_j = n_{j'} = 5$. From Table E.7, for $\alpha = 0.05, c = 4$, and $n - c = 20 - 4 = 16, Q_\alpha$, the upper-tail critical value of the test statistic, is 4.05 (see Table 11.3).

TABLE 11.3

Finding the Studentized Range, Q_α, Statistic for $\alpha = 0.05$, with 4 and 16 Degrees of Freedom

	Cumulative Probabilities = 0.95 Upper-Tail Area = 0.05 Numerator df_1							
Denominator df_2	**2**	**3**	**4**	**5**	**6**	**7**	**8**	**9**
.								
.	.	.	.	.	.	.	.	.
.	.	.	.	.	.	.	.	.
11	3.11	3.82	4.26	4.57	4.82	5.03	5.20	5.35
12	3.08	3.77	4.20	4.51	4.75	4.95	5.12	5.27
13	3.06	3.73	4.15	4.45	4.69	4.88	5.05	5.19
14	3.03	3.70	4.11	4.41	4.64	4.83	4.99	5.13
15	3.01	3.67	4.08	4.37	4.60	4.78	4.94	5.08
16	3.00	3.65	4.05	4.33	4.56	4.74	4.90	5.03

Source: *Extracted from Table E.7.*

From Equation (11.6),

$$\text{Critical range} = 4.05\sqrt{\left(\frac{6.094}{2}\right)\left(\frac{1}{5} + \frac{1}{5}\right)} = 4.4712$$

Because $4.74 > 4.4712$, there is a significant difference between the means of Suppliers 1 and 2. All other pairwise differences are small enough that they may be due to chance. With 95% confidence, you can conclude that parachutes woven using fiber from Supplier 1 have a lower mean tensile strength than those from Supplier 2, but there are no statistically significant differences between Suppliers 1 and 3, Suppliers 1 and 4, Suppliers 2 and 3, Suppliers 2 and 4, and Suppliers 3 and 4. Note that by using $\alpha = 0.05$, you are able to make all six of the comparisons with an overall error rate of only 5%.

These results are shown in Figure 11.7. Figure 11.7 follows the steps used on page 389 for evaluating the comparisons. Each mean is computed, and the absolute differences are determined, the critical range is computed, and then each comparison is declared significant (means are different) or not significant (means are not different).

FIGURE 11.7

Tukey-Kramer procedure worksheet for the parachute experiment

Figure 11.7 displays the TK4 worksheet of the One-Way ANOVA workbook. Create this worksheet using the instructions in Section EG11.1. Read the In-Depth Excel instructions for this worksheet to learn about the formulas used in this worksheet.

	A	B	C	D	E	F	G	H	I
1	Tukey Kramer Multiple Comparisons								
2									
3		Sample	Sample			Absolute	Std. Error	Critical	
4	Group	Mean	Size		Comparison	Difference	of Difference	Range	Results
5	1: Supplier 1	19.52	5		Group 1 to Group 2	4.74	1.103992754	4.4712	Means are different
6	2: Supplier 2	24.26	5		Group 1 to Group 3	3.32	1.103992754	4.4712	Means are not different
7	3: Supplier 3	22.84	5		Group 1 to Group 4	1.64	1.103992754	4.4712	Means are not different
8	4: Supplier 4	21.16	5		Group 2 to Group 3	1.42	1.103992754	4.4712	Means are not different
9					Group 2 to Group 4	3.1	1.103992754	4.4712	Means are not different
10	Other Data				Group 3 to Group 4	1.68	1.103992754	4.4712	Means are not different
11	Level of significance	0.05							
12	Numerator d.f.	4							
13	Denominator d.f.	16							
14	MSW	6.094							
15	Q Statistic	4.05							

Online Topic: The Analysis of Means (ANOM)

The analysis of means (ANOM) provides an alternative approach that allows you to determine which, if any, of the c groups has a mean significantly different from the overall mean of all the group means combined. To study this topic, download the ANOM online topic file that is available on this book's companion Web site. (See Appendix Section D.8 to learn how to access the online topic files.)

ANOVA Assumptions

In Chapters 9 and 10, you learned about the assumptions required in order to use each hypothesis-testing procedure and the consequences of departures from these assumptions. To use the one-way ANOVA F test, you must make the following assumptions about the populations:

- Randomness and independence
- Normality
- Homogeneity of variance

The first assumption, **randomness and independence**, is critically important. The validity of any experiment depends on random sampling and/or the randomization process. To avoid biases in the outcomes, you need to select random samples from the c groups or randomly assign the items to the c levels of the factor. Selecting a random sample, or randomly assigning the levels, ensures that a value from one group is independent of any other value in the experiment. Departures from this assumption can seriously affect inferences from the ANOVA. These problems are discussed more thoroughly in references 5 and 9.

The second assumption, **normality**, states that the sample values in each group are from a normally distributed population. Just as in the case of the t test, the one-way ANOVA F test is fairly robust against departures from the normal distribution. As long as the distributions are not extremely different from a normal distribution, the level of significance of the ANOVA F test is usually not greatly affected, particularly for large samples. You can assess the normality of each of the c samples by constructing a normal probability plot or a boxplot.

The third assumption, **homogeneity of variance**, states that the variances of the c groups are equal (that is, $\sigma_1^2 = \sigma_2^2 = \cdots = \sigma_c^2$). If you have equal sample sizes in each group, inferences based on the F distribution are not seriously affected by unequal variances. However, if you have unequal sample sizes, unequal variances can have a serious effect on inferences from the ANOVA procedure. Thus, when possible, you should have equal sample sizes in all groups. You can use the Levene test for homogeneity of variance presented next to test whether the variances of the c groups are equal.

When only the normality assumption is violated, you can use the Kruskal-Wallis rank test, a nonparametric procedure discussed in Section 12.6. When only the homogeneity-of-variance assumption is violated, you can use procedures similar to those used in the separate-variance t test of Section 10.1 (see references 1 and 2). When both the normality and homogeneity-of-variance assumptions have been violated, you need to use an appropriate data transformation that both normalizes the data and reduces the differences in variances (see reference 6) or use a more general nonparametric procedure (see references 2 and 3).

Levene Test for Homogeneity of Variance

Although the one-way ANOVA F test is relatively robust with respect to the assumption of equal group variances, large differences in the group variances can seriously affect the level of significance and the power of the F test. One procedure for testing the equality of the variances with high statistical power is the modified **Levene test** (see references 1, 4, and 7). To test for the homogeneity of variance, you use the following null hypothesis:

$$H_0: \sigma_1^2 = \sigma_2^2 = \cdots = \sigma_c^2$$

against the alternative hypothesis:

$$H_1: \text{Not all } \sigma_j^2 \text{ are equal } (j = 1, 2, 3, \ldots, c)$$

To test the null hypothesis of equal variances, you first compute the absolute value of the difference between each value and the median of the group. Then you perform a one-way ANOVA on these *absolute differences*. Most statisticians suggest using a level of significance of $\alpha = 0.05$ when performing the ANOVA. To illustrate the modified Levene test, return to the Perfect Parachutes scenario concerning the tensile strength of parachutes first presented on page 381. Table 11.4 summarizes the absolute differences from the median of each supplier.

TABLE 11.4

Absolute Differences from the Median Tensile Strength for Four Suppliers

Supplier 1 (Median = 18.5)	Supplier 2 (Median = 24.5)	Supplier 3 (Median = 22.9)	Supplier 4 (Median = 20.4)
$\lvert 18.5 - 18.5 \rvert = 0.0$	$\lvert 26.3 - 24.5 \rvert = 1.8$	$\lvert 20.6 - 22.9 \rvert = 2.3$	$\lvert 25.4 - 20.4 \rvert = 5.0$
$\lvert 24.0 - 18.5 \rvert = 5.5$	$\lvert 25.3 - 24.5 \rvert = 0.8$	$\lvert 25.2 - 22.9 \rvert = 2.3$	$\lvert 19.9 - 20.4 \rvert = 0.5$
$\lvert 17.2 - 18.5 \rvert = 1.3$	$\lvert 24.0 - 24.5 \rvert = 0.5$	$\lvert 20.8 - 22.9 \rvert = 2.1$	$\lvert 22.6 - 20.4 \rvert = 2.2$
$\lvert 19.9 - 18.5 \rvert = 1.4$	$\lvert 21.2 - 24.5 \rvert = 3.3$	$\lvert 24.7 - 22.9 \rvert = 1.8$	$\lvert 17.5 - 20.4 \rvert = 2.9$
$\lvert 18.0 - 18.5 \rvert = 0.5$	$\lvert 24.5 - 24.5 \rvert = 0.0$	$\lvert 22.9 - 22.9 \rvert = 0.0$	$\lvert 20.4 - 20.4 \rvert = 0.0$

Using the absolute differences given in Table 11.4, you perform a one-way ANOVA (see Figure 11.8).

FIGURE 11.8

Levene test worksheet results for the absolute differences for the parachute experiment

Figure 11.8 displays the **COMPUTE worksheet** of the **Levene workbook**. COMPUTE uses the absolute differences computed in the **AbsDiffs worksheet** as the data for the Levene test. Create these worksheets using the instructions in Section EG11.1. Read the In-Depth Excel instructions for the Levene test to learn about the formulas used in the AbsDiffs worksheet.

	A	B	C	D	E	F	G	H	I	J
1	ANOVA: Levene Test								Calculations	
2									c	4
3	SUMMARY								n	20
4	Groups	Count	Sum	Average	Variance					
5	Supplier 1	5	8.7	1.74	4.753					
6	Supplier 2	5	6.4	1.28	1.707					
7	Supplier 3	5	8.5	1.7	0.945					
8	Supplier 4	5	10.6	2.12	4.007					
9										
10										
11	ANOVA									
12	Source of Variation	SS	df	MS	F	P-value	F crit			
13	Between Groups	1.77	3	0.5900	0.2068	0.8902	3.2389			
14	Within Groups	45.648	16	2.8530						
15										
16	Total	47.418	19							
17						Level of significance	0.05			

From Figure 11.8, observe that $F_{STAT} = 0.2068$. (Excel labels this value F.) Because $F_{STAT} = 0.2068 < 3.2389$ (or the p-value $= 0.8902 > 0.05$), you do not reject H_0. There is no evidence of a significant difference among the four variances. In other words, it is reasonable to assume that the materials from the four suppliers produce parachutes with an equal amount of variability. Therefore, the homogeneity-of-variance assumption for the ANOVA procedure is justified.

EXAMPLE 11.1

ANOVA of the Speed of Drive-Through Service at Fast-Food Chains

For fast-food restaurants, the drive-through window is an increasing source of revenue. The chain that offers the fastest service is likely to attract additional customers. Each month *QSR Magazine*, **www.qsrmagazine.com**, publishes its results of drive-through service times (from menu board to departure) at fast-food chains. In a recent month, the mean time was 131.08 seconds for Wendy's, 153.06 seconds for Burger King, 154.88 seconds for Taco Bell, 158.77 seconds for McDonald's, and 178.52 seconds for KFC. Suppose the study was based on 20 customers for each fast-food chain and the ANOVA table given in Table 11.5 was developed.

TABLE 11.5

ANOVA Summary Table of Drive-Through Service Times at Fast-Food Chains

Source	Degrees of Freedom	Sum of Squares	Mean Squares	F	p-Value
Among chains	4	22,860.09	5,715.02	43.76	0.0000
Within chains	95	12,407.00	130.60		

At the 0.05 level of significance, is there evidence of a difference in the mean drive-through service times of the five chains?

SOLUTION

$H_0: \mu_1 = \mu_2 = \mu_3 = \mu_4 = \mu_5$ where 1 = Wendy's, 2 = Burger King, 3 = Taco Bell, 4 = McDonald's, 5 = KFC

$H_1:$ Not all μ_j are equal where $j = 1, 2, 3, 4, 5$

Decision rule: If p-value < 0.05, reject H_0. Because the p-value is virtually 0, which is less than $\alpha = 0.05$, reject H_0.

You have sufficient evidence to conclude that the mean drive-through times of the five chains are not all equal.

To determine which of the means are significantly different from one another, use the Tukey-Kramer procedure [Equation (11.6) on page 389] to establish the critical range:

Critical value of Q with 5 and 95 degrees of freedom ≈ 3.92

$$\text{Critical range} = Q_\alpha \sqrt{\left(\frac{MSW}{2}\right)\left(\frac{1}{n_j} + \frac{1}{n_{j'}}\right)} = (3.92)\sqrt{\left(\frac{130.6}{2}\right)\left(\frac{1}{20} + \frac{1}{20}\right)}$$

$$= 10.02$$

Any observed difference greater than 10.02 is considered significant. The mean drive-through service times are different between Wendy's (mean of 131.08 seconds) and each of the other four chains. Also, the mean drive-through service time for KFC is different from those of the other four chains. Thus, with 95% confidence, you can conclude that the mean drive-through service time for Wendy's is faster than those of Burger King, Taco Bell, McDonald's, and KFC. In addition, the mean drive-through service time for KFC is slower than those of Wendy's, Burger King, Taco Bell, and McDonald's.

Problems for Section 11.1

LEARNING THE BASICS

11.1 An experiment has a single factor with five groups and seven values in each group.
a. How many degrees of freedom are there in determining the among-group variation?
b. How many degrees of freedom are there in determining the within-group variation?
c. How many degrees of freedom are there in determining the total variation?

11.2 You are working with the same experiment as in Problem 11.1.
a. If $SSA = 60$ and $SST = 210$, what is SSW?
b. What is MSA?
c. What is MSW?
d. What is the value of F_{STAT}?

11.3 You are working with the same experiment as in Problems 11.1 and 11.2.
a. Construct the ANOVA summary table and fill in all values in the table.
b. At the 0.05 level of significance, what is the upper-tail critical value from the F distribution?
c. State the decision rule for testing the null hypothesis that all five groups have equal population means.
d. What is your statistical decision?

11.4 Consider an experiment with three groups, with seven values in each.
a. How many degrees of freedom are there in determining the among-group variation?
b. How many degrees of freedom are there in determining the within-group variation?
c. How many degrees of freedom are there in determining the total variation?

11.5 Consider an experiment with four groups, with eight values in each. For the ANOVA summary table below, fill in all the missing results:

Source	Degrees of Freedom	Sum of Squares	Mean Square (Variance)	F
Among groups	$c - 1 = ?$	$SSA = ?$	$MSA = 80$	$F_{STAT} = ?$
Within groups	$n - c = ?$	$SSW = 560$	$MSW = ?$	
Total	$n - 1 = ?$	$SST = ?$		

11.6 You are working with the same experiment as in Problem 11.5.
a. At the 0.05 level of significance, state the decision rule for testing the null hypothesis that all four groups have equal population means.
b. What is your statistical decision?
c. At the 0.05 level of significance, what is the upper-tail critical value from the Studentized range distribution?
d. To perform the Tukey-Kramer procedure, what is the critical range?

APPLYING THE CONCEPTS

11.7 The Computer Anxiety Rating Scale (CARS) measures an individual's level of computer anxiety, on a scale from 20 (no anxiety) to 100 (highest level of anxiety). Researchers at Miami University administered CARS to 172 business students. One of the objectives of the study was to determine whether there are differences in the amount of computer anxiety experienced by students with different majors. They found the following:

Source	Degrees of Freedom	Sum of Squares	Mean Squares	F
Among majors	5	3,172		
Within majors	166	21,246		
Total	171	24,418		

Major	n	Mean
Marketing	19	44.37
Management	11	43.18
Other	14	42.21
Finance	45	41.80
Accountancy	36	37.56
MIS	47	32.21

Source: *Extracted from T. Broome and D. Havelka, "Determinants of Computer Anxiety in Business Students," The Review of Business Information Systems, Spring 2002, 6(2), pp. 9–16.*

a. Complete the ANOVA summary table.
b. At the 0.05 level of significance, is there evidence of a difference in the mean computer anxiety experienced by different majors?
c. If the results in (b) indicate that it is appropriate, use the Tukey-Kramer procedure to determine which majors differ in mean computer anxiety. Discuss your findings.

SELF Test **11.8** Students in a business statistics course performed a completely randomized design to test the strength of four brands of trash bags. One-pound weights were placed into a bag, one at a time, until the bag broke. A total of 40 bags, 10 for each brand, were used. The data in **Trashbags** give the weight (in pounds) required to break the trash bags.

a. At the 0.05 level of significance, is there evidence of a difference in the mean strength of the four brands of trash bags?
b. If appropriate, determine which brands differ in mean strength.
c. At the 0.05 level of significance, is there evidence of a difference in the variation in strength among the four brands of trash bags?
d. Which brand(s) should you buy, and which brand(s) should you avoid? Explain.

11.9 A hospital conducted a study of the waiting time in its emergency room. The hospital has a main campus and three satellite locations. Management had a business objective of reducing waiting time for emergency room cases that did not require immediate attention. To study this, a random sample of 15 emergency room cases that did not require immediate attention at each location were selected on a particular day, and the waiting time (measured from check-in to

when the patient was called into the clinic area) was measured. The results are stored in **ERWaiting**.

a. At the 0.05 level of significance, is there evidence of a difference in the mean waiting times in the four locations?
b. If appropriate, determine which locations differ in mean waiting time.
c. At the 0.05 level of significance, is there evidence of a difference in the variation in waiting time among the four locations?

11.10 An advertising agency has been hired by a manufacturer of pens to develop an advertising campaign for the upcoming holiday season. To prepare for this project, the research director decides to initiate a study of the effect of advertising on product perception. An experiment is designed to compare five different advertisements. Advertisement *A* greatly undersells the pen's characteristics. Advertisement *B* slightly undersells the pen's characteristics. Advertisement *C* slightly oversells the pen's characteristics. Advertisement *D* greatly oversells the pen's characteristics. Advertisement *E* attempts to correctly state the pen's characteristics. A sample of 30 adult respondents, taken from a larger focus group, is randomly assigned to the five advertisements (so that there are six respondents to each). After reading the advertisement and developing a sense of "product expectation," all respondents unknowingly receive the same pen to evaluate. The respondents are permitted to test the pen and the plausibility of the advertising copy. The respondents are then asked to rate the pen from 1 to 7 (lowest to highest) on the product characteristic scales of appearance, durability, and writing performance. The *combined* scores of three ratings (appearance, durability, and writing performance) for the 30 respondents (stored in **Pen**) are as follows:

A	B	C	D	E
15	16	8	5	12
18	17	7	6	19
17	21	10	13	18
19	16	15	11	12
19	19	14	9	17
20	17	14	10	14

a. At the 0.05 level of significance, is there evidence of a difference in the mean rating of the five advertisements?
b. If appropriate, determine which advertisements differ in mean ratings.
c. At the 0.05 level of significance, is there evidence of a difference in the variation in ratings among the five advertisements?
d. Which advertisement(s) should you use, and which advertisement(s) should you avoid? Explain.

11.11 The file **SavingsRate** contains the yields for a money market account, a one-year certificate of deposit

(CD), and a five-year CD for 23 banks in the metropolitan New York area, as of May 28, 2009 (data extracted from **www.bankrate.com**, May 28, 2009).

a. At the 0.05 level of significance, is there evidence of a difference in the mean yields of the different accounts?
b. If appropriate, determine which accounts differ in mean yields.
c. At the 0.05 level of significance, is there evidence of a difference in the variation in yields among the different accounts?
d. What effect does your result in (c) have on the validity of the results in (a) and (b)?

11.12 Integrated circuits are manufactured on silicon wafers through a process that involves a series of steps. An experiment was carried out to study the effect on the yield of using three methods in the cleansing step (coded to maintain confidentiality). The results (stored in Yield-OneWay) are as follows:

New1	New2	Standard
38	29	31
34	35	23
38	34	38
34	20	29
19	35	32
28	37	30

Source: *Extracted from J. Ramirez and W. Taam, "An Autologistic Model for Integrated Circuit Manufacturing,"* Journal of Quality Technology, *2000, 32, pp. 254–262.*

a. At the 0.05 level of significance, is there evidence of a difference in the mean yield among the methods used in the cleansing steps?
b. If appropriate, determine which methods differ in mean yields.
c. At the 0.05 level of significance, is there evidence of a difference in the variation in yields among the different methods?
d. What effect does your result in (c) have on the validity of the results in (a) and (b)?

11.13 A pet food company has a business objective of expanding its product line beyond its current kidney- and shrimp-based cat foods. The company developed two new products, one based on chicken livers and the other based on salmon. The company conducted an experiment to compare the two new products with its two existing ones, as well as a generic beef-based product sold in a supermarket chain.

For the experiment, a sample of 50 cats from the population at a local animal shelter was selected. Ten cats were randomly assigned to each of the five products being tested. Each of the cats was then presented with 3 ounces of the selected food in a dish at feeding time. The researchers defined the variable to be measured as the number of ounces of food that the cat consumed within a 10-minute time interval that began when the filled dish was presented. The results for this experiment are summarized in the following table and stored in CatFood.

Kidney	Shrimp	Chicken Liver	Salmon	Beef
2.37	2.26	2.29	1.79	2.09
2.62	2.69	2.23	2.33	1.87
2.31	2.25	2.41	1.96	1.67
2.47	2.45	2.68	2.05	1.64
2.59	2.34	2.25	2.26	2.16
2.62	2.37	2.17	2.24	1.75
2.34	2.22	2.37	1.96	1.18
2.47	2.56	2.26	1.58	1.92
2.45	2.36	2.45	2.18	1.32
2.32	2.59	2.57	1.93	1.94

a. At the 0.05 level of significance, is there evidence of a difference in the mean amount of food eaten among the various products?
b. If appropriate, which products appear to differ significantly in the mean amount of food eaten?
c. At the 0.05 level of significance, is there evidence of a significant difference in the variation in the amount of food eaten among the various products?
d. What should the pet food company conclude? Fully describe the pet food company's options with respect to the products.

11.14 A sporting goods manufacturing company wanted to compare the distance traveled by golf balls produced using each of four different designs. Ten balls were manufactured with each design and were brought to the local golf course for the club professional to test. The order in which the balls were hit with the same club from the first tee was randomized so that the pro did not know which type of ball was being hit. All 40 balls were hit in a short period of time, during which the environmental conditions were essentially the same. The results (distance traveled in yards) for the four designs are provided in the following table (and stored in Golfball):

Design			
1	2	3	4
206.32	217.08	226.77	230.55
207.94	221.43	224.79	227.95
206.19	218.04	229.75	231.84
204.45	224.13	228.51	224.87
209.65	211.82	221.44	229.49
203.81	213.90	223.85	231.10
206.75	221.28	223.97	221.53
205.68	229.43	234.30	235.45
204.49	213.54	219.50	228.35
210.86	214.51	233.00	225.09

a. At the 0.05 level of significance, is there evidence of a difference in the mean distances traveled by the golf balls with different designs?

b. If the results in (a) indicate that it is appropriate, use the Tukey-Kramer procedure to determine which designs differ in mean distances.

c. What assumptions are necessary in (a)?

d. At the 0.05 level of significance, is there evidence of a difference in the variation of the distances traveled by the golf balls with different designs?

e. What golf ball design should the manufacturing manager choose? Explain.

11.2 The Factorial Design: Two-Way Analysis of Variance

In Section 11.1, you learned about the completely randomized design. In this section, the single-factor completely randomized design is extended to the **two-factor factorial design**, in which two factors are simultaneously evaluated. Each factor is evaluated at two or more levels. For example, in the Perfect Parachutes scenario on page 381, the company faces the business problem of simultaneously evaluating four suppliers and two types of looms to determine which supplier and which loom produce the strongest parachutes. Although this section uses only two factors, factorial designs for three or more factors are also possible (see references 4, 5, 6, 7, and 9).

To analyze data from a two-factor factorial design, you use **two-way ANOVA**. The following definitions are needed to develop the two-way ANOVA procedure:

r = number of levels of factor A

c = number of levels of factor B

n' = number of values (replicates) for each cell (combination of a particular level of factor A and a particular level of factor B)

n = number of values in the entire experiment (where $n = rcn'$)

X_{ijk} = value of the kth observation for level i of factor A and level j of factor B

$$\bar{\bar{X}} = \frac{\sum_{i=1}^{r}\sum_{j=1}^{c}\sum_{k=1}^{n'} X_{ijk}}{rcn'} = \text{grand mean}$$

$$\bar{X}_{i..} = \frac{\sum_{j=1}^{c}\sum_{k=1}^{n'} X_{ijk}}{cn'} = \text{mean of the } i\text{th level of factor } A \text{ (where } i = 1, 2, \ldots, r)$$

$$\bar{X}_{.j.} = \frac{\sum_{i=1}^{r}\sum_{k=1}^{n'} X_{ijk}}{rn'} = \text{mean of the } j\text{th level of factor } B \text{ (where } j = 1, 2, \ldots, c)$$

$$\bar{X}_{ij.} = \frac{\sum_{k=1}^{n'} X_{ijk}}{n'} = \text{mean of the cell } ij, \text{ the combination of the } i\text{th level of factor } A \text{ and the } j\text{th level of factor } B$$

Because of the complexity of these computations, you should use only computerized methods when performing this analysis. However, to help explain the two-way ANOVA, the decomposition of the total variation computed using this method is illustrated. In this discussion, only cases in which there are an equal number of **replicates** (sample sizes n') for each combination of the levels of factor A with those of factor B are considered. (See references 1 and 6 for a discussion of two-factor factorial designs with unequal sample sizes.)

Testing for Factor and Interaction Effects

There is an **interaction** between factors A and B if the effect of factor A is dependent on the level of factor B. Thus, when dividing the total variation into different sources of variation, you need to account for a possible interaction effect, as well as for factor A, factor B, and random error. To accomplish this, the total variation (*SST*) is subdivided into sum of squares due to factor *A* (or *SSA*), sum of squares due to factor *B* (or *SSB*), sum of squares due to the interaction effect of *A* and *B* (or *SSAB*), and sum of squares due to random variation (or *SSE*). This decomposition of the total variation (*SST*) is displayed in Figure 11.9.

FIGURE 11.9
Partitioning the total variation in a two-factor factorial design

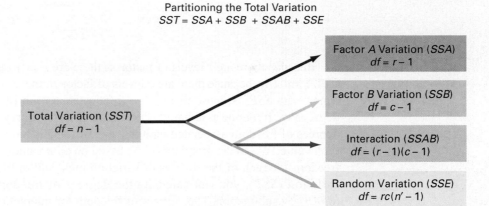

The sum of squares total (*SST*) represents the total variation among all the values around the grand mean. Equation (11.7) shows the computation for total variation.

TOTAL VARIATION IN TWO-WAY ANOVA

$$SST = \sum_{i=1}^{r}\sum_{j=1}^{c}\sum_{k=1}^{n'}(X_{ijk} - \bar{\bar{X}})^2 \tag{11.7}$$

The **sum of squares due to factor *A* (*SSA*)** represents the differences among the various levels of factor *A* and the grand mean. Equation (11.8) shows the computation for factor *A* variation.

FACTOR A VARIATION

$$SSA = cn'\sum_{i=1}^{r}(\bar{X}_{i..} - \bar{\bar{X}})^2 \tag{11.8}$$

The **sum of squares due to factor *B* (*SSB*)** represents the differences among the various levels of factor *B* and the grand mean. Equation (11.9) shows the computation for factor *B* variation.

FACTOR B VARIATION

$$SSB = rn'\sum_{j=1}^{c}(\bar{X}_{.j.} - \bar{\bar{X}})^2 \tag{11.9}$$

The **sum of squares due to interaction (*SSAB*)** represents the interacting effect of specific combinations of factor *A* and factor *B*. Equation (11.10) shows the computation for interaction variation.

INTERACTION VARIATION

$$SSAB = n'\sum_{i=1}^{r}\sum_{j=1}^{c}(\bar{X}_{ij.} - \bar{X}_{i..} - \bar{X}_{.j.} + \bar{\bar{X}})^2 \tag{11.10}$$

The **sum of squares error (SSE)** represents random variation, that is, the differences among the values within each cell and the corresponding cell mean. Equation (11.11) shows the computation for random variation.

RANDOM VARIATION IN TWO-WAY ANOVA

$$SSE = \sum_{i=1}^{r} \sum_{j=1}^{c} \sum_{k=1}^{n'} (X_{ijk} - \overline{X}_{ij.})^2 \qquad \textbf{(11.11)}$$

Because there are r levels of factor A, there are $r - 1$ degrees of freedom associated with SSA. Similarly, because there are c levels of factor B, there are $c - 1$ degrees of freedom associated with SSB. Because there are n' replicates in each of the rc cells, there are $rc(n' - 1)$ degrees of freedom associated with the SSE term. Carrying this further, there are $n - 1$ degrees of freedom associated with the sum of squares total (SST) because you are comparing each value, X_{ijk}, to the grand mean, $\overline{\overline{X}}$, based on all n values. Therefore, because the degrees of freedom for each of the sources of variation must add to the degrees of freedom for the total variation (SST), you can calculate the degrees of freedom for the interaction component ($SSAB$) by subtraction. The degrees of freedom for interaction are $(r - 1)(c - 1)$.

If you divide each sum of squares by its associated degrees of freedom, you have the four variances or mean square terms (MSA, MSB, $MSAB$, and MSE). Equations (11.12a–d) give the mean square terms needed for the two-way ANOVA table.

MEAN SQUARES IN TWO-WAY ANOVA

$$MSA = \frac{SSA}{r - 1} \qquad \textbf{(11.12a)}$$

$$MSB = \frac{SSB}{c - 1} \qquad \textbf{(11.12b)}$$

$$MSAB = \frac{SSAB}{(r - 1)(c - 1)} \qquad \textbf{(11.12c)}$$

$$MSE = \frac{SSE}{rc(n' - 1)} \qquad \textbf{(11.12d)}$$

There are three different tests to perform in a two-way ANOVA:

1. To test the hypothesis of no difference due to factor A:

$$H_0: \mu_{1..} = \mu_{2..} = \cdots = \mu_{r..}$$

against the alternative:

$$H_1: \text{Not all } \mu_{i..} \text{ are equal}$$

you use the F_{STAT} test statistic in Equation (11.13).

F TEST FOR FACTOR A EFFECT

$$F_{STAT} = \frac{MSA}{MSE} \qquad \textbf{(11.13)}$$

You reject the null hypothesis at the α level of significance if

$$F_{STAT} = \frac{MSA}{MSE} > F_\alpha$$

where F_α is the upper-tail critical value from an F distribution with $r - 1$ and $rc(n' - 1)$ degrees of freedom.

2. To test the hypothesis of no difference due to factor B:

$$H_0: \mu_{.1.} = \mu_{.2.} = \cdots = \mu_{.c.}$$

against the alternative:

$$H_1: \text{Not all } \mu_{.j.} \text{ are equal}$$

you use the F_{STAT} test statistic in Equation (11.14).

F TEST FOR FACTOR B EFFECT

$$F_{STAT} = \frac{MSB}{MSE} \tag{11.14}$$

You reject the null hypothesis at the α level of significance if

$$F_{STAT} = \frac{MSB}{MSE} > F_\alpha$$

where F_α is the upper-tail critical value from an F distribution with $c - 1$ and $rc(n' - 1)$ degrees of freedom.

3. To test the hypothesis of no interaction of factors A and B:

$$H_0: \text{The interaction of } A \text{ and } B \text{ is equal to zero}$$

against the alternative:

$$H_1: \text{The interaction of } A \text{ and } B \text{ is not equal to zero}$$

you use the F_{STAT} test statistic in Equation (11.15).

F TEST FOR INTERACTION EFFECT

$$F_{STAT} = \frac{MSAB}{MSE} \tag{11.15}$$

You reject the null hypothesis at the α level of significance if

$$F_{STAT} = \frac{MSAB}{MSE} > F_\alpha$$

where F_α is the upper-tail critical value from an F distribution with $(r - 1)(c - 1)$ and $rc(n' - 1)$ degrees of freedom.

Table 11.6 presents the entire two-way ANOVA table.

TABLE 11.6
Analysis of Variance Table for the Two-Factor Factorial Design

Source	Degrees of Freedom	Sum of Squares	Mean Square (Variance)	F
A	$r - 1$	SSA	$MSA = \dfrac{SSA}{r - 1}$	$F_{STAT} = \dfrac{MSA}{MSE}$
B	$c - 1$	SSB	$MSB = \dfrac{SSB}{c - 1}$	$F_{STAT} = \dfrac{MSB}{MSE}$
AB	$(r - 1)(c - 1)$	SSAB	$MSAB = \dfrac{SSAB}{(r - 1)(c - 1)}$	$F_{STAT} = \dfrac{MSAB}{MSE}$
Error	$rc(n' - 1)$	SSE	$MSE = \dfrac{SSE}{rc(n' - 1)}$	
Total	$n - 1$	SST		

To examine a two-way ANOVA, return to the Perfect Parachutes scenario on page 381. As production manager at Perfect Parachutes, the business problem you decided to examine involved not just the different suppliers but also whether parachutes woven on the Jetta looms are as strong as those woven on the Turk looms. In addition, you need to determine whether any differences among the four suppliers in the strength of the parachutes are dependent on the type of loom being used. Thus, you have decided to collect the data by performing an experiment in which five different parachutes from each supplier are manufactured on each of the two different looms. The results are organized in Table 11.7 and stored in Parachute2.

TABLE 11.7

Tensile Strengths of Parachutes Woven by Two Types of Looms, Using Synthetic Fibers from Four Suppliers

	SUPPLIER			
LOOM	**1**	**2**	**3**	**4**
Jetta	20.6	22.6	27.7	21.5
Jetta	18.0	24.6	18.6	20.0
Jetta	19.0	19.6	20.8	21.1
Jetta	21.3	23.8	25.1	23.9
Jetta	13.2	27.1	17.7	16.0
Turk	18.5	26.3	20.6	25.4
Turk	24.0	25.3	25.2	19.9
Turk	17.2	24.0	20.8	22.6
Turk	19.9	21.2	24.7	17.5
Turk	18.0	24.5	22.9	20.4

Figure 11.10 presents the worksheet results for this example. In this worksheet, the *A*, *B*, and Error sources of variation of Table 11.6 (see page 399) are labeled Sample, Columns, and Within, respectively, in the ANOVA table.

FIGURE 11.10

Two-way ANOVA worksheet for the parachute loom and supplier experiment

Figure 11.10 displays the COMPUTE worksheet of the Two-Way ANOVA workbook. Create this worksheet using the instructions in Section EG11.2. Read the In-Depth Excel instructions for this worksheet to learn about the formulas used in this worksheet.

	A	B	C	D	E	F	G
1	ANOVA: Two-Factor With Replication						
2							
3	SUMMARY	Supplier 1	Supplier 2	Supplier 3	Supplier 4	Total	
4	Jetta						
5	Count	5	5	5	5	20	
6	Sum	92.1	117.7	109.9	102.5	422.2	
7	Average	18.42	23.54	21.98	20.5	21.11	
8	Variance	10.2020	7.5680	18.3970	8.3550	13.1283	
9							
10	Turk						
11	Count	5	5	5	5	20	
12	Sum	97.6	121.3	114.2	105.8	438.9	
13	Average	19.52	24.26	22.84	21.16	21.945	
14	Variance	7.2370	3.6830	4.5530	8.9030	8.4626	
15							
16	Total						
17	Count	10	10	10	10		
18	Sum	189.7	239	224.1	208.3		
19	Average	18.97	23.9	22.41	20.83		
20	Variance	8.0868	5.1444	10.4054	7.7912		
21							
22							
23	ANOVA						
24	Source of Variation	SS	df	MS	F	P-value	F crit
25	Sample	6.9722	1	6.9722	0.8096	0.3750	4.1491
26	Columns	134.3488	3	44.7829	5.1999	0.0049	2.9011
27	Interaction	0.2868	3	0.0956	0.0111	0.9984	2.9011
28	Within	275.5920	32	8.6123			
29							
30	Total	417.1998	39				
31						Level of significance	0.05

To interpret the results, you start by testing whether there is an interaction effect between factor A (loom) and factor B (supplier). If the interaction effect is significant, further analysis will focus on this interaction. If the interaction effect is not significant, you can focus on the **main effects**—potential differences in looms (factor A) and potential differences in suppliers (factor B).

Using the 0.05 level of significance, to determine whether there is evidence of an interaction effect, you reject the null hypothesis of no interaction between loom and supplier if the computed F_{STAT} statistic is greater than 2.9011, the upper-tail critical value from the F distribution, with 3 and 32 degrees of freedom (see Figures 11.10 and 11.11).[1]

FIGURE 11.11

Regions of rejection and nonrejection at the 0.05 level of significance, with 3 and 32 degrees of freedom

Because $F_{STAT} = 0.0111 < F_\alpha = 2.9011$ or the p-value $= 0.9984 > 0.05$, you do not reject H_0. You conclude that there is insufficient evidence of an interaction effect between loom and supplier. You can now focus on the main effects.

Using the 0.05 level of significance and testing for a difference between the two looms (factor A), you reject the null hypothesis if the computed F_{STAT} test statistic is greater than 4.1491, the (approximate) upper-tail critical value from the F distribution with 1 and 32 degrees of freedom (see Figures 11.10 and 11.12). Because $F_{STAT} = 0.8096 < F_\alpha = 4.1491$ or the p-value $= 0.3750 > 0.05$, you do not reject H_0. You conclude that there is insufficient evidence of a difference between the two looms in terms of the mean tensile strengths of the parachutes manufactured.

FIGURE 11.12

Regions of rejection and nonrejection at the 0.05 level of significance, with 1 and 32 degrees of freedom

Using the 0.05 level of significance and testing for a difference among the suppliers (factor B), you reject the null hypothesis of no difference if the computed F_{STAT} test statistic is greater than 2.9011, the upper-tail critical value from the F distribution with 3 degrees of freedom in the numerator and 32 degrees of freedom in the denominator (see Figures 11.10 and 11.11). Because $F_{STAT} = 5.1999 > F_\alpha = 2.9011$ or the p-value $= 0.0049 < 0.05$, reject H_0. You conclude that there is evidence of a difference among the suppliers in terms of the mean tensile strength of the parachutes.

Multiple Comparisons: The Tukey Procedure

If one or both of the factor effects are significant and there is no significant interaction effect, when there are more than two levels of a factor, you can determine the particular levels that are significantly different by using the **Tukey multiple comparisons procedure for two-way ANOVA** (see references 6 and 9). Equation (11.16) gives the critical range for factor A.

CRITICAL RANGE FOR FACTOR A

$$\text{Critical range} = Q_\alpha \sqrt{\frac{MSE}{cn'}} \tag{11.16}$$

where Q_α is the upper-tail critical value from a Studentized range distribution having r and $rc(n' - 1)$ degrees of freedom. (Values for the Studentized range distribution are found in Table E.7.)

Equation (11.17) gives the critical range for factor B.

CRITICAL RANGE FOR FACTOR B

$$\text{Critical range} = Q_\alpha \sqrt{\frac{MSE}{rn'}} \tag{11.17}$$

where Q_α is the upper-tail critical value from a Studentized range distribution having c and $rc(n' - 1)$ degrees of freedom. (Values for the Studentized range distribution are found in Table E.7.)

To use the Tukey procedure, return to the parachute manufacturing data of Table 11.7 on page 400. In the ANOVA summary table in Figure 11.10 on page 400, the interaction effect is not significant. Using $\alpha = 0.05$, there is no evidence of a significant difference between the two looms (Jetta and Turk) that comprise factor A, but there is evidence of a significant difference among the four suppliers that comprise factor B. Thus, you can use the Tukey multiple comparisons procedure to determine which of the four suppliers differ.

Because there are four suppliers, there are $4(4 - 1)/2 = 6$ pairwise comparisons. Using the calculations presented in Figure 11.10, the absolute mean differences are as follows:

1. $|\bar{X}_{.1.} - \bar{X}_{.2.}| = |18.97 - 23.90| = 4.93$
2. $|\bar{X}_{.1.} - \bar{X}_{.3.}| = |18.97 - 22.41| = 3.44$
3. $|\bar{X}_{.1.} - \bar{X}_{.4.}| = |18.97 - 20.83| = 1.86$
4. $|\bar{X}_{.2.} - \bar{X}_{.3.}| = |23.90 - 22.41| = 1.49$
5. $|\bar{X}_{.2.} - \bar{X}_{.4.}| = |23.90 - 20.83| = 3.07$
6. $|\bar{X}_{.3.} - \bar{X}_{.4.}| = |22.41 - 20.83| = 1.58$

To determine the critical range, refer to Figure 11.10 to find $MSE = 8.6123, r = 2, c = 4$, and $n' = 5$. From Table E.7 [for $\alpha = 0.05, c = 4$, and $rc(n' - 1) = 32$], Q_α, the upper-tail critical value of the Studentized range distribution with 4 and 32 degrees of freedom, is approximated as 3.84. Using Equation (11.17),

$$\text{Critical range} = 3.84 \sqrt{\frac{8.6123}{10}} = 3.56$$

Because $4.93 > 3.56$, only the means of Suppliers 1 and 2 are different. You can conclude that the mean tensile strength is lower for Supplier 1 than for Supplier 2, but there are no statistically significant differences between Suppliers 1 and 3, Suppliers 1 and 4, Suppliers 2 and 3, Suppliers 2 and 4, and Suppliers 3 and 4. Note that by using $\alpha = 0.05$, you are able to make all six comparisons with an overall error rate of only 5%.

Visualizing Interaction Effects: The Cell Means Plot

You can get a better understanding of the interaction effect by plotting the **cell means**, the means of all possible factor-level combinations. Figure 11.13 presents a cell means plot that uses the cell means for the loom/supplier combinations shown in Figure 11.10 on page 400. From the plot of the mean tensile strength for each combination of loom and supplier, observe that the two lines (representing the two looms) are roughly parallel. This indicates that the *difference* between the mean tensile strengths of the two looms is virtually the same for the four suppliers. In other words, there is no *interaction* between these two factors, as was indicated by the F test.

FIGURE 11.13

Cell means plot of tensile strength based on loom and supplier

Create a cell means plot using the instructions in Section EG11.2.

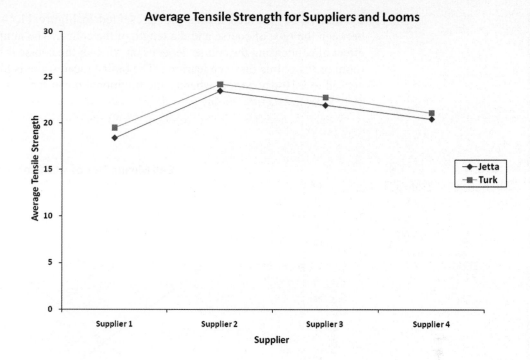

Average Tensile Strength for Suppliers and Looms

Interpreting Interaction Effects

What is the interpretation if there is an interaction? In such a situation, some levels of factor A would respond better with certain levels of factor B. For example, with respect to tensile strength, suppose that some suppliers were better for the Jetta loom and other suppliers were better for the Turk loom. If this were true, the lines of Figure 11.13 would not be nearly as parallel, and the interaction effect might be statistically significant. In such a situation, the difference between the looms is no longer the same for all suppliers. Such an outcome would also complicate the interpretation of the *main effects* because differences in one factor (the loom) would not be consistent across the other factor (the supplier).

Example 11.2 illustrates a situation with a significant interaction effect.

EXAMPLE 11.2

Interpreting Significant Interaction Effects

A nationwide company specializing in preparing students for college and graduate school entrance exams, such as the SAT, ACT, and LSAT, had the business objective of improving its ACT Preparatory Course. Two factors of interest to the company are the length of the course (a condensed 10-day period or a regular 30-day period) and the type of course (traditional classroom or online distance learning). The company collected data by randomly assigning 10 clients to each of the four cells that represent a combination of length of the course and type of course. The results are organized in the file **ACT** and presented in Table 11.8.

What are the effects of the type of course and the length of the course on ACT scores?

TABLE 11.8

ACT Scores for Different Types and Lengths of Courses

| TYPE OF COURSE | LENGTH OF COURSE | | | |
	Condensed		Regular	
Traditional	26	18	34	28
Traditional	27	24	24	21
Traditional	25	19	35	23
Traditional	21	20	31	29
Traditional	21	18	28	26
Online	27	21	24	21
Online	29	32	16	19
Online	30	20	22	19
Online	24	28	20	24
Online	30	29	23	25

SOLUTION The cell means plot presented in Figure 11.14 shows a strong interaction between the type of course and the length of the course. The nonparallel lines indicate that the effect of condensing the course depends on whether the course is taught in the traditional classroom or via online distance learning. The online mean score is higher when the course is condensed to a 10-day period, whereas the traditional mean score is higher when the course takes place over the regular 30-day period.

FIGURE 11.14

Cell means plot of ACT scores

Create a cell means plot using the instructions in Section EG11.2.

To verify the somewhat subjective analysis provided by interpreting the cell means plot, you begin by testing whether there is a statistically significant interaction between factor A (length of course) and factor B (type of course). Using a 0.05 level of significance, you reject the null hypothesis because $F_{STAT} = 24.2569 > 4.1132$ or the p-value equals $0.000 < 0.05$ (see Figure 11.15). Thus, the hypothesis test confirms the interaction evident in the cell means plot. The existence of this significant interaction effect complicates the interpretation of the hypothesis tests concerning the two main effects. You cannot directly conclude that there is no effect with respect to length of course and type of course, even though both have p-values > 0.05.

Given that the interaction is significant, you can reanalyze the data with the two factors collapsed into four groups of a single factor rather than a two-way ANOVA with two levels of each of the two factors (see ACT-OneWay). Group 1 is traditional condensed. Group 2 is traditional regular. Group 3 is online condensed. Group 4 is online regular. Figure 11.16 shows the worksheet solution for this example.

From Figure 11.16, because $F_{STAT} = 8.2239 > 2.8663$ or p-value $= 0.0003 < 0.05$, there is evidence of a significant difference in the four groups (traditional condensed, traditional regular, online condensed, and online regular). Traditional condensed is different from traditional regular and from online condensed. Traditional regular is also different from online regular, and online condensed is also different from online regular. Thus, whether condensing a course is a good idea depends on whether the course is offered in a traditional classroom or as an online distance learning course. To ensure the highest mean ACT scores, the company should use the traditional approach for courses that are given over a 30-day period but use the online approach for courses that are condensed into a 10-day period.

FIGURE 11.15

Two-way ANOVA worksheet results for ACT scores

Create this worksheet using the instructions in Section EG11.2. The In-Depth Excel portion of Section EG11.2 discusses the formulas used in this worksheet.

	A	B	C	D	E	F	G
1	ANOVA: Two-Factor With Replication						
2							
3	SUMMARY	Condensed	Regular	Total			
4	traditional						
5	Count	10	10	20			
6	Sum	219	279	498			
7	Average	21.9	27.9	24.9			
8	Variance	11.2111	20.9889	24.7263			
9							
10	online						
11	Count	10	10	20			
12	Sum	270	213	483			
13	Average	27	21.3	24.15			
14	Variance	16.2222	8.0111	20.0289			
15							
16	Total						
17	Count	20	20				
18	Sum	489	492				
19	Average	24.45	24.6				
20	Variance	19.8395	25.2000				
21							
22							
23	ANOVA						
24	Source of Variation	SS	df	MS	F	P-value	F crit
25	Sample	5.6250	1	5.6250	0.3987	0.5318	4.1132
26	Columns	0.2250	1	0.2250	0.0159	0.9002	4.1132
27	Interaction	342.2250	1	342.2250	24.2569	0.0000	4.1132
28	Within	507.9000	36	14.1083			
29							
30	Total	855.9750	39				
31						Level of significance	0.05

FIGURE 11.16

One-way ANOVA results and Tukey-Kramer worksheets for the ACT scores

Create the Tukey-Kramer results worksheet using the instructions in Section EG11.1.

	A	B	C	D	E	F	G	H	I	J
1	ANOVA: Single Factor								Calculations	
2									c	4
3	SUMMARY								n	40
4	Groups	Count	Sum	Average	Variance					
5	Group 1	10	219	21.9	11.2111					
6	Group 2	10	279	27.9	20.9889					
7	Group 3	10	270	27	16.2222					
8	Group 4	10	213	21.3	8.0111					
9										
10										
11	ANOVA									
12	Source of Variation	SS	df	MS	F	P-value	F crit			
13	Between Groups	348.075	3	116.0250	8.2239	0.0003	2.8663			
14	Within Groups	507.9	36	14.1083						
15										
16	Total	855.975	39							
17						Level of significance	0.05			

	A	B	C	D	E	F	G	H	I
1	Tukey Kramer Multiple Comparisons								
2									
3		Sample	Sample			Absolute	Std. Error	Critical	
4	Group	Mean	Size		Comparison	Difference	of Difference	Range	Results
5	1: Group 1	21.9	10		Group 1 to Group 2	6	1.187785054	4.5017	Means are different
6	2: Group 2	27.9	10		Group 1 to Group 3	5.1	1.187785054	4.5017	Means are different
7	3: Group 3	27	10		Group 1 to Group 4	0.6	1.187785054	4.5017	Means are not different
8	4: Group 4	21.3	10		Group 2 to Group 3	0.9	1.187785054	4.5017	Means are not different
9					Group 2 to Group 4	6.6	1.187785054	4.5017	Means are different
10	Other Data				Group 3 to Group 4	5.7	1.187785054	4.5017	Means are different
11	Level of significance	0.05							
12	Numerator d.f.	4							
13	Denominator d.f.	36							
14	MSW	14.10833							
15	Q Statistic	3.79							

Problems for Section 11.2

LEARNING THE BASICS

11.15 Consider a two-factor factorial design with three levels in factor A, three levels in factor B, and four replicates in each of the nine cells.
a. How many degrees of freedom are there in determining the factor A variation and the factor B variation?
b. How many degrees of freedom are there in determining the interaction variation?
c. How many degrees of freedom are there in determining the random variation?
d. How many degrees of freedom are there in determining the total variation?

11.16 Assume that you are working with the results from Problem 11.15.
a. If $SSA = 120, SSB = 110, SSE = 270$, and $SST = 540$, what is $SSAB$?
b. What are MSA and MSB?
c. What is $MSAB$?
d. What is MSE?

11.17 Assume that you are working with the results from Problems 11.15 and 11.16.
a. What is the value of the F_{STAT} test statistic for the interaction effect?
b. What is the value of the F_{STAT} test statistic for the factor A effect?
c. What is the value of the F_{STAT} test statistic for the factor B effect?
d. Form the ANOVA summary table and fill in all values in the body of the table.

11.18 Given the results from Problems 11.15 through 11.17,
a. at the 0.05 level of significance, is there an effect due to factor A?
b. at the 0.05 level of significance, is there an effect due to factor B?
c. at the 0.05 level of significance, is there an interaction effect?

11.19 Given a two-way ANOVA with two levels for factor A, five levels for factor B, and four replicates in each of the 10 cells, with $SSA = 18, SSB = 64, SSE = 60$, and $SST = 150$,
a. form the ANOVA summary table and fill in all values in the body of the table.
b. at the 0.05 level of significance, is there an effect due to factor A?
c. at the 0.05 level of significance, is there an effect due to factor B?
d. at the 0.05 level of significance, is there an interaction effect?

11.20 Given a two-factor factorial experiment and the ANOVA summary table that follows, fill in all the missing results:

Source	Degrees of Freedom	Sum of Squares	Mean Square (Variance)	F
A	$r - 1 = 2$	$SSA = ?$	$MSA = 80$	$F_{STAT} = ?$
B	$c - 1 = ?$	$SSB = 220$	$MSB = ?$	$F_{STAT} = 11.0$
AB interaction	$(r - 1)(c - 1) = 8$	$SSAB = ?$	$MSAB = 10$	$F_{STAT} = ?$
Error	$rc(n' - 1) = 30$	$SSE = ?$	$MSE = ?$	
Total	$n - 1 = ?$	$SST = ?$		

11.21 Given the results from Problem 11.20,
a. at the 0.05 level of significance, is there an effect due to factor A?
b. at the 0.05 level of significance, is there an effect due to factor B?
c. at the 0.05 level of significance, is there an interaction effect?

APPLYING THE CONCEPTS

11.22 The effects of developer strength (factor A) and development time (factor B) on the density of photographic plate film were being studied. Two strengths and two development times were used, and four replicates in each of the four cells were evaluated. The results (with larger being best) are stored in **Photo** and shown in the following table:

| DEVELOPER STRENGTH | DEVELOPMENT TIME (MINUTES) | |
	10	14
1	0	1
1	5	4
1	2	3
1	4	2
2	4	6
2	7	7
2	6	8
2	5	7

At the 0.05 level of significance,
a. is there an interaction between developer strength and development time?
b. is there an effect due to developer strength?
c. is there an effect due to development time?
d. Plot the mean density for each developer strength for each development time.
e. What can you conclude about the effect of developer strength and development time on density?

11.23 A chef in a restaurant that specializes in pasta dishes was experiencing difficulty in getting brands of pasta to be *al dente*—that is, cooked enough so as not to feel starchy or hard but still feel firm when bitten into. She decided to conduct an experiment in which two brands of pasta, one American and one Italian, were cooked for either 4 or 8 minutes. The variable of interest was weight of the pasta because cooking the pasta enables it to absorb water. A pasta with a faster rate of water absorption may provide a shorter interval in which the pasta is *al dente*, thereby increasing the chance that it might be overcooked. The experiment was conducted by using 150 grams of uncooked pasta. Each trial began by bringing a pot containing 6 quarts of cold, unsalted water to a moderate boil. The 150 grams of uncooked pasta was added and then weighed after a given period of time by lifting the pasta from the pot via a built-in strainer. The results (in terms of weight in grams) for two replicates of each type of pasta and cooking time are stored in Pasta and are as follows:

TYPE OF PASTA	COOKING TIME (MINUTES)	
	4	8
American	265	310
American	270	320
Italian	250	300
Italian	245	305

At the 0.05 level of significance,
a. is there an interaction between type of pasta and cooking time?
b. is there an effect due to type of pasta?
c. is there an effect due to cooking time?
d. Plot the mean weight for each type of pasta for each cooking time.
e. What conclusions can you reach concerning the importance of each of these two factors on the weight of the pasta?

✓ SELF Test **11.24** A student team in a business statistics course performed a factorial experiment to investigate the time required for pain-relief tablets to dissolve in a glass of water. The two factors of interest were brand name (Equate, Kroger, or Alka-Seltzer) and temperature of the water (hot or cold). The experiment consisted of four replicates for each of the six factor combinations. The following data (stored in PainRelief) show the time a tablet took to dissolve (in seconds) for the 24 tablets used in the experiment:

WATER	BRAND OF PAIN-RELIEF TABLET		
	Equate	Kroger	Alka-Seltzer
Cold	85.87	75.98	100.11
Cold	78.69	87.66	99.65
Cold	76.42	85.71	100.83
Cold	74.43	86.31	94.16
Hot	21.53	24.10	23.80
Hot	26.26	25.83	21.29
Hot	24.95	26.32	20.82
Hot	21.52	22.91	23.21

At the 0.05 level of significance,
a. is there an interaction between brand of pain reliever and water temperature?
b. is there an effect due to brand?
c. is there an effect due to water temperature?
d. Plot the mean dissolving time for each brand for each water temperature.
e. Discuss the results of (a) through (d).

11.25 Integrated circuits are manufactured on silicon wafers through a process that involves a series of steps. An experiment was carried out to study the effect of the cleansing and etching steps on the yield (coded to maintain confidentiality). The results (stored in Yield) are as follows:

CLEANSING STEP	ETCHING STEP	
	New	Standard
New 1	38	34
New 1	34	19
New 1	38	28
New 2	29	20
New 2	35	35
New 2	34	37
Standard	31	29
Standard	23	32
Standard	38	30

Source: *Extracted from J. Ramirez and W. Taam, "An Autologistic Model for Integrated Circuit Manufacturing,"* Journal of Quality Technology, *2000, 32, pp. 254–262.*

At the 0.05 level of significance,
a. is there an interaction between the cleansing step and the etching step?
b. is there an effect due to the cleansing step?
c. is there an effect due to the etching step?
d. Plot the mean yield for each cleansing step for each etching step.
e. Discuss the results of (a) through (d).

11.26 An experiment was conducted to study the distortion of drive gears in automobiles. Two factors were studied—the tooth size of the gear and the part positioning. The results (stored in Gear) are as follows:

TOOTH SIZE	PART POSITIONING	
	Low	High
Low	18.0	13.5
Low	16.5	8.5
Low	26.0	11.5
Low	22.5	16.0
Low	21.5	−4.5
Low	21.0	4.0
Low	30.0	1.0
Low	24.5	9.0

TOOTH SIZE	PART POSITIONING	
	Low	High
High	27.5	17.5
High	19.5	11.5
High	31.0	10.0
High	27.0	1.0
High	17.0	14.5
High	14.0	3.5
High	18.0	7.5
High	17.5	6.5

Source: *Extracted from D. R. Bingham and R. R. Sitter, "Design Issues in Fractional Factorial Split-Plot Experiments,"* Journal of Quality Technology, *33, 2001, pp. 2–15.*

At the 0.05 level of significance,
a. is there an interaction between the tooth size and the part positioning?
b. is there an effect due to tooth size?
c. is there an effect due to the part positioning?
d. Plot the mean yield for each tooth size for each part position.
e. Discuss the results of (a) through (d).

11.3 🌐 *Online Topic:* The Randomized Block Design

The randomized block design is an extension of the paired *t* test discussed in Section 10.2. To study this topic, read the **Section 11.3** online topic file that is available on this book's companion Web site. (See Appendix Section D.8 to learn how to access the online topic files.)

USING STATISTICS @ Perfect Parachutes Revisited

In the Using Statistics scenario, you were the production manager at the Perfect Parachute Company. You performed an experiment to determine whether there was a difference in the strength of parachutes woven from synthetic fibers from four different suppliers. Using the one-way ANOVA, you were able to determine that there was a difference in the mean strength of the parachutes from the different suppliers. You then were able to conclude that the mean strength of parachutes woven from synthetic fibers from Supplier 1 was less than for Supplier 2. Further experimentation was carried out to study the effect of the loom. You determined that there was no interaction between the supplier and loom and there was no difference in mean strength between the looms. Your next step as production manager is to investigate reasons the mean strength of parachutes woven from synthetic fibers from Supplier 1 was less than for Supplier 2 and possibly reduce the number of suppliers.

SUMMARY

In this chapter, various statistical procedures were used to analyze the effect of one or two factors of interest. The assumptions required for using these procedures were discussed in detail. Remember that you need to critically investigate the validity of the assumptions underlying the hypothesis-testing procedures. Table 11.9 summarizes the topics covered in this chapter.

TABLE 11.9
Summary of Topics in Chapter 11

Type of Analysis (Numerical Data Only)	Number of Factors
Comparing more than two groups	One-way analysis of variance (Section 11.1)
	Two-way analysis of variance (Section 11.2)

KEY EQUATIONS

Total Variation in One-Way ANOVA

$$SST = \sum_{j=1}^{c} \sum_{i=1}^{n_j} (X_{ij} - \bar{\bar{X}})^2 \tag{11.1}$$

Among-Group Variation in One-Way ANOVA

$$SSA = \sum_{j=1}^{c} n_j (\bar{X}_j - \bar{\bar{X}})^2 \tag{11.2}$$

Within-Group Variation in One-Way ANOVA

$$SSW = \sum_{j=1}^{c} \sum_{i=1}^{n_j} (X_{ij} - \bar{X}_j)^2 \tag{11.3}$$

Mean Squares in One-Way ANOVA

$$MSA = \frac{SSA}{c-1} \tag{11.4a}$$

$$MSW = \frac{SSW}{n-c} \tag{11.4b}$$

$$MST = \frac{SST}{n-1} \tag{11.4c}$$

One-Way ANOVA F_{STAT} Test Statistic

$$F_{STAT} = \frac{MSA}{MSW} \tag{11.5}$$

Critical Range for the Tukey-Kramer Procedure

$$\text{Critical range} = Q_\alpha \sqrt{\frac{MSW}{2} \left(\frac{1}{n_j} + \frac{1}{n_{j'}} \right)} \tag{11.6}$$

Total Variation in Two-Way ANOVA

$$SST = \sum_{i=1}^{r} \sum_{j=1}^{c} \sum_{k=1}^{n'} (X_{ijk} - \bar{\bar{X}})^2 \tag{11.7}$$

Factor A Variation

$$SSA = cn' \sum_{i=1}^{r} (\bar{X}_{i..} - \bar{\bar{X}})^2 \tag{11.8}$$

Factor B Variation

$$SSB = rn' \sum_{j=1}^{c} (\bar{X}_{.j.} - \bar{\bar{X}})^2 \tag{11.9}$$

Interaction Variation

$$SSAB = n' \sum_{i=1}^{r} \sum_{j=1}^{c} (\bar{X}_{ij.} - \bar{X}_{i..} - \bar{X}_{.j.} + \bar{\bar{X}})^2 \tag{11.10}$$

Random Variation in Two-Way ANOVA

$$SSE = \sum_{i=1}^{r} \sum_{j=1}^{c} \sum_{k=1}^{n'} (X_{ijk} - \bar{X}_{ij.})^2 \tag{11.11}$$

Mean Squares in Two-Way ANOVA

$$MSA = \frac{SSA}{r-1} \tag{11.12a}$$

$$MSB = \frac{SSB}{c-1} \tag{11.12b}$$

$$MSAB = \frac{SSAB}{(r-1)(c-1)} \tag{11.12c}$$

$$MSE = \frac{SSE}{rc(n'-1)} \tag{11.12d}$$

F Test for Factor A Effect

$$F_{STAT} = \frac{MSA}{MSE} \tag{11.13}$$

F Test for Factor B Effect

$$F_{STAT} = \frac{MSB}{MSE} \tag{11.14}$$

F Test for Interaction Effect

$$F_{STAT} = \frac{MSAB}{MSE} \tag{11.15}$$

Critical Range for Factor A

$$\text{Critical range} = Q_\alpha \sqrt{\frac{MSE}{cn'}} \tag{11.16}$$

Critical Range for Factor B

$$\text{Critical range} = Q_\alpha \sqrt{\frac{MSE}{rn'}} \tag{11.17}$$

KEY TERMS

CHAPTER REVIEW PROBLEMS

CHECKING YOUR UNDERSTANDING

11.27 In a one-way ANOVA, what is the difference between the among-groups variance MSA and the within-groups variance MSW?

11.28 What are the distinguishing features of the completely randomized design and two-factor factorial designs?

11.29 What are the assumptions of ANOVA?

11.30 Under what conditions should you use the one-way ANOVA F test to examine possible differences among the means of c independent populations?

11.31 When and how should you use multiple comparison procedures for evaluating pairwise combinations of the group means?

11.32 What is the difference between the one-way ANOVA F test and the Levene test?

11.33 Under what conditions should you use the two-way ANOVA F test to examine possible differences among the means of each factor in a factorial design?

11.34 What is meant by the concept of interaction in a two-factor factorial design?

11.35 How can you determine whether there is an interaction in the two-factor factorial design?

APPLYING THE CONCEPTS

11.36 The operations manager for an appliance manufacturer wants to determine the optimal length of time for the washing cycle of a household clothes washer. An experiment is designed to measure the effect of detergent brand and washing cycle time on the amount of dirt removed from standard household laundry loads. Four brands of detergent (A, B, C, D) and four levels of washing cycle (18, 20, 22, and 24 minutes) are specifically selected for analysis. In order to run the experiment, 32 standard household laundry loads (having equal weight and dirt) are randomly assigned, 2 each, to the 16 detergent/washing cycle time combinations. The results, in pounds of dirt removed (stored in Laundry), are as follows:

DETERGENT BRAND	WASHING CYCLE TIME (IN MINUTES)			
	18	20	22	24
A	0.11	0.13	0.17	0.17
A	0.09	0.13	0.19	0.18
B	0.12	0.14	0.17	0.19
B	0.10	0.15	0.18	0.17
C	0.08	0.16	0.18	0.20
C	0.09	0.13	0.17	0.16
D	0.11	0.12	0.16	0.15
D	0.13	0.13	0.17	0.17

At the 0.05 level of significance,
a. is there an interaction between detergent brand and washing cycle time?
b. is there an effect due to detergent brand?
c. is there an effect due to washing cycle time?
d. Plot the mean amount of dirt removed (in pounds) for each detergent brand for each washing cycle time.
e. If appropriate, use the Tukey procedure to determine differences between detergent brands and between washing cycle times.

f. What washing cycle time should be used for this type of household clothes washer?

g. Repeat the analysis, using washing cycle time as the only factor. Compare your results to those of (c), (e), and (f).

11.37 The quality control director for a clothing manufacturer wants to study the effect of operators and machines on the breaking strength (in pounds) of wool serge material. A batch of the material is cut into square-yard pieces, and these are randomly assigned, 3 each, to all 12 combinations of 4 operators and 3 machines chosen specifically for the experiment. The results (stored in Breakstw) are as follows:

OPERATOR	MACHINE I	II	III
A	115	111	109
A	115	108	110
A	119	114	107
B	117	105	110
B	114	102	113
B	114	106	114
C	109	100	103
C	110	103	102
C	106	101	105
D	112	105	108
D	115	107	111
D	111	107	110

At the 0.05 level of significance,

a. is there an interaction between operator and machine?

b. is there an effect due to operator?

c. is there an effect due to machine?

d. Plot the mean breaking strength for each operator for each machine.

e. If appropriate, use the Tukey procedure to examine differences among operators and among machines.

f. What can you conclude about the effects of operators and machines on breaking strength? Explain.

g. Repeat the analysis, using machines as the only factor. Compare your results to those of (c), (e), and (f).

11.38 An operations manager wants to examine the effect of air-jet pressure (in psi) on the breaking strength of yarn. Three different levels of air-jet pressure are to be considered: 30 psi, 40 psi, and 50 psi. A random sample of 18 yarns are selected from the same batch, and the yarns are randomly assigned, 6 each, to the 3 levels of air-jet pressure. The breaking strength scores are in the file Yarn .

a. Is there evidence of a significant difference in the variances of the breaking strengths for the three air-jet pressures? (Use $\alpha = 0.05$).

b. At the 0.05 level of significance, is there evidence of a difference among mean breaking strengths for the three air-jet pressures?

c. If appropriate, use the Tukey-Kramer procedure to determine which air-jet pressures significantly differ with respect to mean breaking strength. (Use $\alpha = 0.05$.)

d. What should the operations manager conclude?

11.39 Suppose that, when setting up the experiment in Problem 11.38, the operations manager is able to study the effect of side-to-side aspect in addition to air-jet pressure. Thus, instead of the one-factor completely randomized design in Problem 11.38, a two-factor factorial design was used, with the first factor, side-to-side aspects, having two levels (nozzle and opposite) and the second factor, air-jet pressure, having three levels (30 psi, 40 psi, and 50 psi). A sample of 18 yarns is randomly assigned, 3 to each of the 6 side-to-side aspect and pressure level combinations. The breaking-strength scores (stored in Yarn) are as follows:

SIDE-TO-SIDE ASPECT	AIR-JET PRESSURE 30 psi	40 psi	50 psi
Nozzle	25.5	24.8	23.2
Nozzle	24.9	23.7	23.7
Nozzle	26.1	24.4	22.7
Opposite	24.7	23.6	22.6
Opposite	24.2	23.3	22.8
Opposite	23.6	21.4	24.9

At the 0.05 level of significance,

a. is there an interaction between side-to-side aspect and air-jet pressure?

b. is there an effect due to side-to-side aspect?

c. is there an effect due to air-jet pressure?

d. Plot the mean yarn breaking strength for each level of side-to-side aspect and each level of air-jet pressure.

e. If appropriate, use the Tukey procedure to study differences among the air-jet pressures.

f. On the basis of the results of (a) through (e), what conclusions can you reach concerning yarn breaking strength? Discuss.

g. Compare your results in (a) through (f) with those from the completely randomized design in Problem 11.38. Discuss fully.

11.40 A hotel wanted to develop a new system for delivering room service breakfasts. In the current system, an order form is left on the bed in each room. If the customer wishes to receive a room service breakfast, he or she places the order form on the doorknob before 11 p.m. The current system requires customers to select a 15-minute interval for desired delivery time (6:30–6:45 A.M., 6:45–7:00 A.M., etc.). The new system is designed to allow the customer to request a specific delivery time. The hotel wants to measure the difference between the actual delivery time and the requested delivery time of room service orders for breakfast. (A negative time means that the order was delivered before the requested time. A positive time means that the order was delivered after the requested time.) The factors included were the menu choice (American or Continental) and the desired time period in which the order was to be delivered (Early Time Period [6:30–8:00 A.M.] or Late Time Period [8:00–9:30 A.M.]). Ten orders for each combination of menu choice and desired time period were studied on a particular day. The data (stored in Breakfast) are as follows:

TYPE OF BREAKFAST	DESIRED TIME	
	Early Time Period	Late Time Period
Continental	1.2	−2.5
Continental	2.1	3.0
Continental	3.3	−0.2
Continental	4.4	1.2
Continental	3.4	1.2
Continental	5.3	0.7
Continental	2.2	−1.3
Continental	1.0	0.2
Continental	5.4	−0.5
Continental	1.4	3.8
American	4.4	6.0
American	1.1	2.3
American	4.8	4.2
American	7.1	3.8
American	6.7	5.5
American	5.6	1.8
American	9.5	5.1
American	4.1	4.2
American	7.9	4.9
American	9.4	4.0

At the 0.05 level of significance,
a. is there an interaction between type of breakfast and desired time?
b. is there an effect due to type of breakfast?
c. is there an effect due to desired time?
d. Plot the mean delivery time difference for each desired time for each type of breakfast.
e. On the basis of the results of (a) through (d), what conclusions can you reach concerning delivery time difference? Discuss.

11.41 Refer to the room service experiment in Problem 11.40. Now suppose that the results are as shown at the top of the next column (and stored in Breakfast2). Repeat (a) through (e), using these data, and compare the results to those of (a) through (e) of Problem 11.40.

TYPE OF BREAKFAST	DESIRED TIME	
	Early	Late
Continental	1.2	−0.5
Continental	2.1	5.0
Continental	3.3	1.8
Continental	4.4	3.2
Continental	3.4	3.2
Continental	5.3	2.7
Continental	2.2	0.7
Continental	1.0	2.2
Continental	5.4	1.5
Continental	1.4	5.8
American	4.4	6.0
American	1.1	2.3
American	4.8	4.2
American	7.1	3.8
American	6.7	5.5
American	5.6	1.8
American	9.5	5.1
American	4.1	4.2
American	7.9	4.9
American	9.4	4.0

11.42 Modern software applications require rapid data access capabilities. An experiment was conducted to test the effect of data file size on the ability to access the files (as measured by read time, in milliseconds). Three different levels of data file size were considered: small—50,000 characters; medium—75,000 characters; and large—100,000 characters. A sample of eight files of each size was evaluated. The access read times, in milliseconds, are stored in Access.
a. Is there evidence of a significant difference in the variance of the access read times for the three file sizes? (Use $\alpha = 0.05$.)
b. At the 0.05 level of significance, is there evidence of a difference among mean access read times for the three file sizes?
c. If appropriate, use the Tukey-Kramer multiple comparisons procedure to determine which file sizes significantly differ with respect to mean access read time. (Use $\alpha = 0.05$.)
d. What conclusions can you reach?

11.43 Suppose, when designing the experiment in Problem 11.42, that the effect of the input/output buffer size was studied in addition to the effect of the data file size. Thus, instead of the one-factor completely randomized design given in Problem 11.42, the experiment used a two-factor factorial design, with the first factor, buffer size, having two levels (20 kilobytes and 40 kilobytes) and the second factor, data file size, having three levels (small, medium, and large). That is, there are two factors under consideration: buffer size and data file size. A sample of four programs (replicates) were evaluated for each buffer size and data file size combination. The access read times, in milliseconds, are stored in Access.

At the 0.05 level of significance,
a. is there an interaction between buffer size and data file size?
b. is there an effect due to buffer size?
c. is there an effect due to data file size?
d. Plot the mean access read times (in milliseconds) for each buffer size level for each data file size level. Describe the interaction and discuss why you can or cannot interpret the main effects in (b) and (c).
e. On the basis of the results of (a) through (d), what conclusions can you reach concerning access read times? Discuss.
f. Compare and contrast your results in (a) through (e) with those from the completely randomized design in Problem 11.42. Discuss fully.

11.44 When a team studying the weight of canned cat food realized that the size of the pieces of meat that were contained in the can and the can fill height could impact the weight of the can, they wondered whether the current larger chunk size produced higher can weight and more variability, so a finer cutting size was studied, along with the current size. In addition, the target for the sensing mechanism that determines the fill height was lowered slightly to determine the effect on can weight. Twenty cans were filled for each of the four combinations of piece size (fine and current) and fill height (low and current). The contents of each can were weighed, and the amount above or below the label weight of 3 ounces was recorded as the variable Coded Weight. For example, a can containing 2.90 ounces was given a Coded Weight of -0.10. The results are stored in CatFood2.

Analyze these data and write a report for presentation to the team. Indicate the importance of the piece size and the fill height on the weight of the canned cat food. Be sure to include a recommendation for the level of each factor that will come closest to meeting the target weight and the limitations of this experiment, along with recommendations for future experiments that might be undertaken.

TEAM PROJECT

The file Bond Funds contains information regarding eight variables from a sample of 180 mutual funds:

Type—Type of bonds comprising the bond fund (intermediate government or short-term corporate)
Assets—In millions of dollars
Fees—Sales charges (no or yes)
Expense ratio—Ratio of expenses to net assets in percentage
Return 2008—Twelve-month return in 2008
Three-year return—Annualized return, 2006–2008
Five-year return—Annualized return, 2004–2008
Risk—Risk-of-loss factor of the bond mutual fund (below average, average, or above average)

11.45 Completely analyze the difference between below-average-risk, average-risk, and above-average-risk bond mutual funds in terms of 2008 return, three-year return, five-year return, and expense ratio. Write a report summarizing your findings.

STUDENT SURVEY DATABASE

11.46 Problem 2.117 on page 65 describes a survey of 50 undergraduate students (stored in UnderGradsurvey). For these data,
a. at the 0.05 level of significance, is there evidence of a difference based on academic major in grade point index, expected starting salary, salary expected in five years, age, and spending on textbooks and supplies?
b. at the 0.05 level of significance, is there evidence of a difference based on graduate school intention in grade point index, expected starting salary, salary expected in five years, age, and spending on textbooks and supplies?
c. at the 0.05 level of significance, is there evidence of a difference based on employment status in grade point index, expected starting salary, salary expected in five years, age, and spending on textbooks and supplies?

11.47 Problem 2.117 on page 65 describes a survey of 50 undergraduate students (stored in UnderGradSurvey).
a. Select a sample of 50 undergraduate students at your school and conduct a similar survey for those students.
b. For the data collected in (a), repeat (a) through (c) of Problem 11.46.
c. Compare the results of (b) to those of Problem 11.46.

11.48 Problem 2.119 on page 65 describes a survey of 40 MBA students (stored in GradSurvey). For these data, at the 0.05 level of significance,
a. is there evidence of a difference, based on undergraduate major, in age, undergraduate grade point index, graduate grade point index, GMAT score, expected salary upon graduation, salary expected in five years, and spending on textbooks and supplies?
b. is there evidence of a difference, based on graduate major, in age, undergraduate grade point index, graduate grade point index, GMAT score, expected salary upon graduation, salary expected in five years, and spending on textbooks and supplies?
c. is there evidence of a difference, based on employment status, in age, undergraduate grade point index, graduate grade point index, GMAT score, expected salary upon graduation, salary expected in five years, and spending on textbooks and supplies?

11.49 Problem 2.119 on page 65 describes a survey of 40 MBA students (stored in GradSurvey).
a. Select a sample of 40 graduate students in your MBA program and conduct a similar survey for those students.
b. For the data collected in (a), repeat (a) through (c) of Problem 11.48.
c. Compare the results of (b) to those of Problem 11.48.

MANAGING THE *SPRINGVILLE HERALD*

Phase 1

In studying the home delivery solicitation process, the marketing department team determined that the so-called "later" calls made between 7:00 P.M. and 9:00 P.M. were significantly more conducive to lengthier calls than those made earlier in the evening (between 5:00 P.M. and 7:00 P.M.).

Knowing that the 7:00 P.M. to 9:00 P.M. time period is superior, the team sought to investigate the effect of the type of presentation on the length of the call. A group of 24 female callers was randomly assigned, 8 each, to one of three presentation plans—structured, semistructured, and unstructured—and trained to make the telephone presentation. All calls were made between 7:00 P.M. and 9:00 P.M., the later time period, and the callers were to provide an introductory greeting that was personal but informal ("Hi, this is Leigh Richardson from the *Springville Herald*. May I speak to Stuart Knoll?"). The callers knew that the team was observing their efforts that evening but didn't know which particular calls were monitored. Measurements were taken on the length of call (defined as the difference, in seconds, between the time the person answers the phone and the time he or she hangs up). Table SH11.1 presents the results (stored in SH11-1).

TABLE SH11.1

Length of Calls (in Seconds), Based on Presentation Plan

PRESENTATION PLAN		
Structured	**Semistructured**	**Unstructured**
38.8	41.8	32.9
42.1	36.4	36.1
45.2	39.1	39.2
34.8	28.7	29.3
48.3	36.4	41.9
37.8	36.1	31.7
41.1	35.8	35.2
43.6	33.7	38.1

EXERCISE

SH11.1 Analyze these data and write a report to the team that indicates your findings. Be sure to include your recommendations based on your findings. Also, include an appendix in which you discuss the reason you selected a particular statistical test to compare the three independent groups of callers.

DO NOT CONTINUE UNTIL THE PHASE 1 EXERCISE HAS BEEN COMPLETED.

Phase 2

In analyzing the data of Table SH11.1, the marketing department team observed that the structured presentation plan resulted in a significantly longer call than either the semistructured or unstructured plans. The team decided to tentatively recommend that all solicitations be completely structured calls made later in the evening, from 7:00 P.M. to 9:00 P.M. The team also decided to study the effect of two additional factors on the length of call:

- Gender of the caller: male versus female.
- Type of greeting: personal but formal (for example, "Hello, my name is Leigh Richardson from the *Springville Herald*. May I speak to Mr. Knoll?"), personal but informal (for example, "Hi, this is Leigh Richardson from the *Springville Herald*. May I speak to Stuart Knoll?"), or impersonal (for example, "I represent the *Springville Herald* . . .").

The team acknowledged that in its previous studies, it had controlled for these variables. Only female callers were selected to participate in the studies, and they were trained to use a personal but informal greeting style. However, the team wondered if this choice of gender and greeting type was, in fact, best.

The team designed a study in which a total of 30 callers, 15 males and 15 females, were chosen to participate. The callers were randomly assigned to one of the three greeting-type style training groups so that there were five callers in each of the six combinations of the two factors, gender and greeting style (personal but formal—PF; personal but informal—PI; and impersonal). The callers knew that the team was observing their efforts that evening but didn't know which particular calls were monitored.

Measurements were taken on the length of call (defined as the difference, in seconds, between the time the person answers and the time he or she hangs up the phone). Table SH11.2 summarizes the results (stored in SH11-2).

TABLE SH11.2

Length of Calls (in Seconds), Based on Gender and Type of Greeting

GENDER	GREETING		
	PF	**PI**	**Impersonal**
Male	45.6	41.7	35.3
Male	49.0	42.8	37.7
Male	41.8	40.0	41.0
Male	35.6	39.6	28.7
Male	43.4	36.0	31.8
Female	44.1	37.9	43.3
Female	40.8	41.1	40.0
Female	46.9	35.8	43.1
Female	51.8	45.3	39.6
Female	48.5	40.2	33.2

EXERCISES

SH11.2 Completely analyze these data and write a report to the team that indicates the importance of each of the two factors and/or the interaction between them on the length of the call. Include recommendations for future experiments to perform.

SH11.3 Do you believe the length of the telephone call is the most appropriate outcome to study? What other variables should be investigated next? Discuss.

WEB CASE

Apply your knowledge about ANOVA in this Web Case, which continues the cereal-fill packaging dispute Web Case from Chapters 7, 9, and 10.

After reviewing CCACC's latest posting (see the Web Case for Chapter 10), Oxford Cereals is complaining that CCACC is guilty of using selective data. Using a Web browser, open to the Web page for the Chapter 11 Web Case or open **OC_DataSelective.htm**, if you have downloaded the Web Case files. Review the objections of Oxford Cereals to CCACC's latest posting and then answer the following questions:

1. Does Oxford Cereals have a legitimate argument? Why or why not?

2. Assuming that the samples Oxford Cereals has posted were randomly selected, perform the appropriate analysis to resolve the ongoing weight dispute.

3. What conclusions can you reach from your results? If you were called as an expert witness, would you support the claims of the CCACC or the claims of Oxford Cereals? Explain.

REFERENCES

1. Berenson, M. L., D. M. Levine, and M. Goldstein, *Intermediate Statistical Methods and Applications: A Computer Package Approach* (Upper Saddle River, NJ: Prentice Hall, 1983).

2. Conover, W. J., *Practical Nonparametric Statistics*, 3rd ed. (New York: Wiley, 2000).

3. Daniel, W. W., *Applied Nonparametric Statistics*, 2nd ed. (Boston: PWS Kent, 1990).

4. Gitlow, H. S., and D. M. Levine, *Six Sigma for Green Belts and Champions: Foundations, DMAIC, Tools, Cases, and Certification* (Upper Saddle River, NJ: Financial Times/Prentice Hall, 2005).

5. Hicks, C. R., and K. V. Turner, *Fundamental Concepts in the Design of Experiments*, 5th ed. (New York: Oxford University Press, 1999).

6. Kutner, M. H, J. Neter, C. Nachtsheim, and W. Li, *Applied Linear Statistical Models*, 5th ed. (New York: McGraw-Hill-Irwin, 2005).

7. Levine, D. M., *Statistics for Six Sigma Green Belts* (Upper Saddle River, NJ: Financial Times/Prentice Hall, 2006).

8. *Microsoft Excel 2007* (Redmond, WA: Microsoft Corp., 2007).

9. Montgomery, D. M., *Design and Analysis of Experiments*, 6th ed. (New York: Wiley, 2005).

ORGANIZING MULTIPLE-SAMPLE DATA

Organize multiple-sample data as unstacked data, one column per group, in order to use the methods discussed in this chapter's Excel Guide. For more information about unstacked and stacked data, see the beginning of the Chapter 10 Excel Guide on page 374 and examine the worksheets of the **StackedAndUnstacked workbook**.

EG11.1 The COMPLETELY RANDOMIZED DESIGN: ONE-WAY ANALYSIS of VARIANCE

One-Way ANOVA F Test for Differences Among More Than Two Means

PHStat2 Use the **One-Way ANOVA** procedure to perform the one-way ANOVA F test. For example, to perform the Figure 11.6 one-way ANOVA for the parachute experiment on page 388, open to the **DATA worksheet** of the **Parachute workbook**. Select **PHStat → Multiple-Sample Tests → One-Way ANOVA**. In the procedure's dialog box (shown below):

1. Enter **0.05** as the **Level of Significance**.
2. Enter **A1:D6** as the **Group Data Cell Range**.
3. Check **First cells contain label**.
4. Enter a **Title**, clear the **Tukey-Kramer Procedure** check box, and click **OK**.

The one-way ANOVA F test is computed with a level of significance equal to 0.05. Change the level of significance in cell G17, if necessary. (In addition to the worksheet shown in Figure 11.6, this procedure creates an **ASFData worksheet** to hold the data used for the test. See the following *In-Depth Excel* section for a complete description of these worksheets.)

In-Depth Excel Use the **FINV**, **FDIST**, and **DEVSQ** functions to help perform the one-way ANOVA F test. (These functions will appear in the ANOVA summary table area of the worksheet.) Enter **FINV(*level of significance, degrees of freedom between groups, degrees of freedom within groups*)** to compute the F critical value and enter **FDIST(*F test statistic, degrees of freedom between groups, degrees of freedom within groups*)** to calculate the p-value. Enter **DEVSQ(*cell range of data of all groups*)** to compute *SST*, the total variation. Enter an expression in the form *SST* – **DEVSQ(*group 1 data cell range*)** – **DEVSQ(*group 2 data cell range*)** . . . – **DEVSQ(*group n data cell range*)** to compute *SSA*, the sum of squares among groups. (To compute *SSW*, enter a formula that subtracts *SSA* from *SST*.)

Use the **COMPUTE worksheet** of the **One-Way ANOVA workbook**, shown in Figure 11.6 on page 388, as a template for performing the one-way ANOVA F test. The worksheet performs the test for the Section 11.1 parachute experiment, using the data in the **ASFData worksheet**. The *SSA* in cell B13 is labeled **Between Groups** (not Among Groups) for consistency with the Analysis ToolPak results.

Modifying the One-Way ANOVA workbook for use with other problems is a bit more difficult than modifications discussed in the Excel Guide in previous chapters, but it can be done using these steps:

1. Paste the data for the problem into the **ASFData worksheet**, overwriting the parachute experiment data.

In the COMPUTE worksheet (see Figure 11.6):

2. Edit the cell B16 *SST* formula **=DEVSQ (ASFData!$A$1:$D$6)** to use the cell range of the new data just pasted into the ASFData worksheet.
3. Edit the cell B13 *SSA* formula so there are as many **– DEVSQ(*group n data cell range*)** terms as there are groups.
4. Change the level of significance in cell G17, if necessary.
5. If the problem contains three groups, select **row 8**, right-click, and select **Delete** from the shortcut menu.
6. If the problem contains more than four groups, select **row 8**, right-click, and click **Insert** from the shortcut menu. Repeat this step as many times as necessary.
7. If the problem contains more than four groups, cut and paste the formulas in columns B through E of the new last row of the summary table to the cell range **B8:E8**. (These formulas were in row 8 before you inserted new rows.) For each new row inserted, enter formulas in columns B through E that refer to the next subsequent column in the ASFData worksheet. For example, in

row 9 enter =**COUNT(ASFData!$E:$E)** in cell **B9**, =**SUM(ASFData!$E:$E)** in cell **C9**, =**AVERAGE (ASFData!$E:$E)** in cell **D9**, and =**VAR(ASFData! $E:$E)** in cell **E9**.

8. Adjust table formatting as necessary.

Open to the **COMPUTE_FORMULAS worksheet** of the **One-Way ANOVA workbook** to examine the details of other formulas used in the COMPUTE worksheet. Of note is the formula =**COUNTA(ASFData!$1:$1)** in cell J2, a tricky way to determine the number of groups by counting the number of column heading entries found in row 1 of the ASFData worksheet. See Appendix Section C.11 on page 728 for more information about formula tricks used in the ANOVA results worksheets.

Analysis ToolPak Use the **Anova: Single Factor** procedure to perform the one-way ANOVA F test. For example, to perform the Figure 11.6 one-way ANOVA for the parachute experiment on page 388, open to the **DATA worksheet** of the **Parachute workbook** and:

1. Select **Data → Data Analysis** (Excel 2007) or **Tools → Data Analysis** (Excel 2003).
2. In the Data Analysis dialog box, select **Anova: Single Factor** from the **Analysis Tools** list and then click **OK**.

In the procedure's dialog box (see below):

3. Enter **A1:D6** as the **Input Range**.
4. Click **Columns**, check **Labels in First Row**, and enter **0.05** as **Alpha**.
5. Click **New Worksheet Ply**.
6. Click **OK** to create the frequency distribution (and histogram) on a new worksheet.

The Analysis ToolPak creates a worksheet that is visually similar to Figure 11.6 on page 388 but contains only values and does not include any cell formulas. The ToolPak worksheet also does not contain the level of significance in row 17 or the columns I and J entries seen in Figure 11.6.

Multiple Comparisons: The Tukey-Kramer Procedure

PHStat2 Use the *PHStat2* instructions for the one-way ANOVA F test. In step 3, check **Tukey-Kramer Procedure** instead of clearing this check box. The procedure creates a worksheet identical to the one shown in Figure 11.7 on page 390 and discussed in the following *In-Depth Excel* section. To complete the worksheet, enter the **Studentized Range Q statistic** (look up the value using Table E.7 on page 747) for the level of significance and the numerator and denominator degrees of freedom that are given in the worksheet.

In-Depth Excel First, use the *In-Depth Excel* instructions for the one-way ANOVA F test. Then open to the appropriate "**TK**" **worksheet** in the **One-Way ANOVA workbook** and enter the **Studentized Range Q statistic** (look up the value using Table E.7 on page 747) for the level of significance and the numerator and denominator degrees of freedom that are given in the worksheet.

For example, to create the Figure 11.7 Tukey-Kramer worksheet for the parachute experiment on page 390, first follow the "One-Way ANOVA F Test for Differences Among More Than Two Means" *In-Depth Excel* instructions. Next, open to the **TK4 worksheet**. Enter the **Studentized Range Q statistic** (look up the value using Table E.7 on page 747) in cell B15 for the level of significance and the numerator and denominator degrees of freedom that are given in cells B11 through B13.

The TK worksheets use an IF function in the form **IF(*absolute difference > critical range, display means are different message, display means are not different message*)** to indicate which pair of means are different. The worksheets use formulas to compare the absolute differences to the critical range for problems using three (**TK3**), four (**TK4**), five (**TK5**), six (**TK6**), or seven (**TK7**) groups. When you use either the **TK5**, **TK6**, and **TK7** worksheets, you must also enter the name, sample mean, and sample size for the fifth and, if applicable, sixth and seventh groups.

The TK worksheets use an IF function in the form **IF(*absolute difference > critical range, display means are different message, display means are not different message*)** to indicate which pair of means are different. Critical ranges are computed by multiplying the Q statistic by the standard error of the difference. The standard error of the difference is computed by taking the square root of the following: *MSW/2 * ((1/sample size of first group) + (1/sample size of second group))*. Open to the **TK4_FORMULAS worksheet** of the **One-Way ANOVA workbook** to examine the details of all the formulas found in a TK worksheet.

Analysis ToolPak Adapt the previous *In-Depth Excel* instructions to perform the Tukey-Kramer procedure in conjunction with using the **Anova: Single Factor** procedure.

Transfer selected values from the ToolPak results worksheet to one of the TK worksheets in the **One-Way ANOVA workbook**. For example, to perform the Figure 11.7 Tukey-Kramer procedure for the parachute experiment on page 390:

1. Use the **Anova: Single Factor** procedure, as described earlier in this section to create a worksheet that contains ANOVA results for the parachute experiment.

2. Record the name, **sample size** (in the **Count** column), and **sample mean** (in the **Average** column) of each group. Also record the *MSW* value, found in the cell that is the intersection of the **MS** column and **Within Groups** row, and the **denominator degrees of freedom**, found in the cell that is the intersection of the **df** column and **Within Groups** row.

3. Open to the **TK4 worksheet** of the **One-Way ANOVA workbook**.

In the TK4 worksheet:

4. Overwrite the formulas in cell range A5:C8 by entering the name, sample mean, and sample size of each group into that range.

5. Enter **0.05** in cell B11 (the level of significance used in the Anova: Single Factor procedure).

6. Enter **4** in cell B12 as the **Numerator d.f.** (equal to the number of groups).

7. Enter **16** in cell B13 as the **Denominator d.f.**

8. Enter **6.094** in cell B14 as the **MSW**.

9. Enter **4.05** in cell B15 as the **Q Statistic**. (Look up the **Studentized Range *Q* statistic** using Table E.7 on page 747.)

Levene Test for Homogeneity of Variance

PHStat2 Use the **Levene Test** procedure to perform this test. For example, to perform the Figure 11.8 Levene test for the parachute experiment on page 392, open to the **DATA worksheet** of the **Parachute workbook**. Select **PHStat → Multiple-Sample Tests → One-Way ANOVA**. In the procedure's dialog box (shown below):

1. Enter **0.05** as the **Level of Significance**.

2. Enter **A1:D6** as the **Sample Data Cell Range**.

3. Check **First cells contain label**.

4. Enter a **Title** and click **OK**.

This procedure works only with data in which the sample sizes of each group are equal. The procedure creates a worksheet that performs the Table 11.4 absolute differences computations (see page 391) as well as the worksheet shown in Figure 11.8. (See the following *In-Depth Excel* section for a complete description of these worksheets.)

In-Depth Excel Use the *In-Depth Excel* instructions for performing the one-way ANOVA *F* test given earlier in this section using the **One-Way ANOVA workbook**. In step 1, paste the absolute differences from the median of each group into the **ASFData worksheet**, overwriting the parachute experiment data on page 392. If the absolute differences have not already been computed, compute them using the **AbsDiffs worksheet** and **Medians worksheet** in the **Levene workbook** as a guide. For example, to compute the absolute differences from the median of each group for the parachute experiment data:

1. Open to the **DATA worksheet** of the **Parachute workbook**.

2. In cell A7, the first empty cell in column A, enter the label **Medians**.

3. In cell A8, enter the formula **=MEDIAN(A2:A6)**. (Cell range A2:A6 contains the data for the first group, Supplier 1.)

4. Copy the cell A8 formula across through column D.

5. Insert a new worksheet.

In the new worksheet:

6. Enter row 1 column headings **AbsDiff1**, **AbsDiff2**, **AbsDiff3**, and **AbsDiff4** in columns A through D.

7. Enter the formula **=ABS(DATA!A2 − DATA!A$8)** in cell A2. Copy this formula down through row 6. This formula computes the absolute difference of the first data value (Data!A2) and the median of the Supplier 1 group data (DATA!A$8).

8. Copy the formulas now in cell range A2:A6 across through column D. Absolute differences now appear in the cell range A2:D6.

Continue with steps 2 through 8 of the *In-Depth Excel* instructions for performing the one-way ANOVA *F* test. At this point, the COMPUTE worksheet contains the proper organization but uses the values on the DATA worksheet instead of the new worksheet you inserted in step 5. To make this final correction, open to the **COMPUTE worksheet**. Press **Crtl+H** and in the Find and Replace dialog box, enter **DATA** as the **Find What** value and the name of the worksheet inserted in step 5 above as the **Replace With** value. Then click **Replace All**.

Use the worksheets of the **Levene workbook** (a modified version of the **One-Way ANOVA workbook**) as a guide for making the additions and modifications necessary to perform the Levene test.

Analysis ToolPak Use the **Anova: Single Factor** procedure with absolute difference data to perform the Levene test. If the absolute differences have not already been computed, use steps 1 through 7 of the preceding *In-Depth Excel* instructions to compute them.

EG11.2 The FACTORIAL DESIGN: TWO-WAY ANALYSIS of VARIANCE

PHStat2 Use the **Two-Way ANOVA with replication** procedure to perform a two-way ANOVA. This procedure requires that the labels that identify factor *A* appear stacked in column A, followed by columns for factor *B*. For example, to perform the Figure 11.10 two-way ANOVA for the supplier and loom parachute example on page 400, open to the **DATA worksheet** of the **Parachute2 workbook**. Select **PHStat → Multiple-Sample Tests → Two-Way ANOVA**. In the procedure's dialog box (shown below):

1. Enter **0.05** as the **Level of Significance**.
2. Enter **A1:E11** as the **Sample Data Cell Range**.
3. Check **First cells contain label**.
4. Enter a **Title** and click **OK**.

See the following *In-Depth Excel* section for a complete description of the worksheets.

In-Depth Excel Use the **FINV, FDIST**, and **DEVSQ** functions to help perform the two-way ANOVA. (These functions will appear in the ANOVA summary table area of the worksheet.) Enter **FINV(*level of significance, degrees of freedom for source, Error degrees of freedom*)** to compute the *F* critical value for the sources of variation *A, B*, and *AB* (see Table 11.6 on page 399). Enter **FDIST(*F test statistic for source, degrees of freedom for source, Error degrees of freedom within groups*)** to calculate the *p*-value for the three sources of variation.

Enter **DEVSQ(*cell range of all data*)** to compute *SST*. Enter a formula that subtracts the list of DEVSQs for each level of factor *A* from *SST* to compute *SSA*. Enter a formula that subtracts the list of DEVSQs for each level of factor *B* to compute *SSB*. To compute *SSE*, add the DEVSQs for each combination of levels of the two factors. To compute *SSAB*, subtract *SSA, SSB*, and *SSE* from *SST*.

Use the **COMPUTE worksheet** of the **Two-Way ANOVA workbook**, shown in Figure 11.10 on page 400, as a model for performing a two-way ANOVA. The worksheet performs the test for the supplier and loom parachute example of Section 11.2, using the data in the **TWAData worksheet**. In the ANOVA summary table of this worksheet, the source labeled *A* in Table 11.6 on page 399 is labeled **Sample**, source *B* is labeled **Columns**, source *AB* is labeled **Interaction**, and source *Error* is labeled **Within**.

Modifying the Two-Way ANOVA workbook for use with other problems is challenging, given the complexity of the computations in the ANOVA summary table. In the COMPUTE worksheet, given that Factor *A* has 2 levels ($r = 2$) and Factor B has 4 levels ($c = 4$), the formula for *SSE* in cell B28 contains 8 (r times c) different DEVSQ terms. For another problem in which $r = 4$ and $c = 4$, this formula would expand to 16 different DEVSQ terms!

While modifying the COMPUTE worksheet for other problems is discouraged, (it is better to use PHStat2 or the Analysis ToolPak for other problems), the following steps are a guideline for those who seek to try:

1. Paste the data for the problem into the **TWAData worksheet**, overwriting the parachute experiment data.

In the COMPUTE worksheet (see Figure 11.10 on page 400):

2. Select the cell range **E1:E20** (the current Supplier 4 column).

3. For problems in which $c > 4$, right-click and select **Insert** from the shortcut menu. In the Insert dialog box, click **Shift cells right** and click **OK**. Repeat this step as many times as necessary. (See Appendix Section C.12 on page 729 for more information about the Insert and Delete dialog boxes.)

4. For problems in which $c < 4$, right-click and select **Delete** from the shortcut menu. In the Delete dialog box, click **Shift cells left** and click **OK**.

5. For problems in which $c = 2$, select cell range **D1:D20**, right-click, and select **Delete** from the shortcut menu. In the Delete dialog box, again click **Shift cells left** and click **OK**.

6. For problems in which $r > 2$, select the cell range **A10:G15** (which includes the current *Turk* rows). Right-click and select **Insert** from the shortcut menu. In the Insert dialog box, click **Shift cells down** and click **OK**. Repeat the previous sentence as many times as necessary. Enter new row labels in the new column A cells as necessary.

7. Edit the formulas in the top table area. Remember that each cell range in every formula in this area refers to a cell range on the TWAData worksheet that contains the range that hold the *n'* number of cells for a unique combination of a Factor *A* level and a Factor *B* level.

8. **(Extremely difficult)** Edit the column B formulas for *SSA*, *SSB*, *SSE*, and *SST* that appear in the ANOVA summary table at the bottom of the worksheet. (The formula for *SSAB* does not need to be edited.)

Open to the **COMPUTE_FORMULAS worksheet** of the **Two-Way ANOVA workbook** to examine the details of other formulas used in the COMPUTE worksheet. Of note is the formula =**INT(COUNTA(TWAData!A:A)/COUNTIF (TWAData!A:A, TWAData!A2))** − **1** in cell C25, a tricky way of computing the expression $r - 1$. (See Appendix Section C.11 on page 728 for more information about this formula and the worksheet functions that it uses.)

Analysis ToolPak Use the **Anova: Two-Factor With Replication** procedure to perform a two-way ANOVA. This procedure requires that the labels that identify factor *A* appear stacked in column A, followed by columns for factor *B*. For example, to create a worksheet similar to Figure 11.10 on page 400 that performs the two-way ANOVA for the supplier and loom parachute example of Section 11.2, open to the **DATA worksheet** of the **Parachute2 workbook** and:

1. Select **Data → Data Analysis** (Excel 2007) or **Tools → Data Analysis** (Excel 2003).

2. In the Data Analysis dialog box, select **Anova: Two-Factor With Replication** from the **Analysis Tools** list and then click **OK**.

In the procedure's dialog box (see below):

3. Enter **A1:E11** as the **Input Range**.

4. Enter **5** as the **Rows per sample**.

5. Enter **0.05** as **Alpha**.

6. Click **New Worksheet Ply**.

7. Click **OK** to create the ANOVA worksheet.

The Analysis ToolPak creates a worksheet that is visually similar to Figure 11.10 on page 400 but contains only values and does not include any cell formulas. The ToolPak worksheet also does not contain the level of significance in row 31.

Visualizing Interaction Effects: The Cell Means Plot

PHStat2 Use the *PHStat2* instructions for the two-way ANOVA. In step 4, check **Cell Means Plot** before clicking **OK**.

In-Depth Excel Create a cell means plot from a two-way ANOVA results worksheet.

To organize the data, insert a new worksheet and first copy and paste the Factor *B* level names to row 1 of the new worksheet and then copy and use Paste Special to transfer the values in the **Average** rows data for each Factor *B* level to the new worksheet. (See Appendix Section C.12 on page 729 to learn more about the Paste Special command.)

For example, to create the Figure 11.13 cell means plot for the mean tensile strength for suppliers and looms on page 403, open to the **COMPUTE worksheet** of the **Two-Way ANOVA** workbook. (This worksheet is shown in Figure 11.10 on page 400.) Insert a new worksheet. Copy and paste the cell range **B3:E3** of the COMPUTE worksheet (the Factor *B* level names) to cell **B1** of the new worksheet. Copy the cell range **B7:E7** of the COMPUTE worksheet (the AVERAGE row for the *Jetta* level of Factor *A*) and paste to cell **B2** of the new worksheet, using the Paste Special **Values option**. Copy the cell range **B13:E13** of the COMPUTE worksheet (the AVERAGE row for the *Turk* level of Factor *A*) and paste to cell **B3** of a new worksheet, and enter **Jetta** in cell **B3** of the new worksheet, using Paste Special **Values**. **Turk** in cell **A3** of the new worksheet as labels for the Factor *A* levels.

Continue with either the *In-Depth Excel 2007* or *In-Depth Excel 2003* instructions to complete the cell means chart.

In-Depth Excel 2007 *Continued from In-Depth Excel . . .*

1. Select the cell range **A1:E3**.

2. Select **Insert → Line** and click the fourth **2-D Line** gallery choice (**Line with Markers**).

Relocate the chart to a chart sheet and adjust the chart formatting by using the instructions in Appendix Section C.7 on page 726.

In-Depth Excel 2003 *Continued from In-Depth Excel . . .*

1. Select the cell range **A1:E3**.

2. Select **Insert → Chart**.

In the Chart Wizard Step 1 dialog box:

3. Click the **Standard Types** tab. Click **Line** from the **Standard Types Chart Type** box and select the first Chart sub-type in the second row, identified as **Line with markers displayed at each value**.

4. Click **Next**.

In the Chart Wizard Step 2 dialog box:

5. Leave the entries as they are and click **Next**.

In the Chart Wizard Step 3 dialog box:

6. Click the **Titles** tab. Enter a **Chart title**, **Supplier** as the **Category (X) axis** title, and **Average Tensile Strength** as the **Value (Y) axis** title. Use the formatting settings discussed in Appendix Section C.8 on page 727 for the **Axes**, **Gridlines**, **Data Labels**, and **Data Table** tabs.

7. Click **Next**.

In the Chart Wizard Step 4 dialog box:

8. Click **As new sheet** and then click **Finish** to create a chart.

Analysis ToolPak Use the *In-Depth Excel* instructions for creating a cell means plot.

12 Chi-Square Tests and Nonparametric Tests

Learning Objectives

In this chapter, you learn:

- How and when to use the chi-square test for contingency tables
- How to use the Marascuilo procedure for determining pairwise differences when evaluating more than two proportions
- How and when to use the McNemar test
- How and when to use nonparametric tests

USING STATISTICS

@ T.C. Resort Properties

You are the manager of T.C. Resort Properties, a collection of five upscale hotels located on two tropical islands. Guests who are satisfied with the quality of services during their stay are more likely to return on a future vacation and to recommend the hotel to friends and relatives. To assess the quality of services being provided by your hotels, guests are encouraged to complete a satisfaction survey when they check out. You need to analyze the data from these surveys to determine the overall satisfaction with the services provided, the likelihood that the guests will return to the hotel, and the reasons some guests indicate that they will not return. For example, on one island, T.C. Resort Properties operates the Beachcomber and Windsurfer hotels. Is the perceived quality at the Beachcomber Hotel the same as at the Windsurfer Hotel? If there is a difference, how can you use this information to improve the overall quality of service at T.C. Resort Properties? Furthermore, if guests indicate that they are not planning to return, what are the most common reasons given for this decision? Are the reasons given unique to a certain hotel or common to all hotels operated by T.C. Resort Properties?

In the preceding three chapters, you used hypothesis-testing procedures to analyze both numerical and categorical data. Chapter 9 presented some one-sample tests, and Chapter 10 developed several two-sample tests. Chapter 11 discussed the analysis of variance (ANOVA), which you use to study one or two factors of interest. This chapter extends hypothesis testing to analyze differences between population proportions based on two or more samples, as well as the hypothesis of *independence* in the joint responses to two categorical variables. The chapter concludes with nonparametric tests as alternatives to several hypothesis tests considered in Chapters 10 and 11.

12.1 Chi-Square Test for the Difference Between Two Proportions

In Section 10.3, you studied the Z test for the difference between two proportions. In this section, the data are examined from a different perspective. The hypothesis-testing procedure uses a test statistic that is approximated by a chi-square (χ^2) distribution. The results of this χ^2 test are equivalent to those of the Z test described in Section 10.3.

If you are interested in comparing the counts of categorical responses between two independent groups, you can develop a two-way **contingency table** (see Section 2.3) to display the frequency of occurrence of items of interest and items not of interest for each group. In Chapter 4, contingency tables were used to define and study probability.

To illustrate the contingency table, return to the Using Statistics scenario concerning T.C. Resort Properties. On one of the islands, T.C. Resort Properties has two hotels (the Beachcomber and the Windsurfer). You define the business objective as improving the quality of service at T.C. Resort Properties. You collect data from customer satisfaction surveys and focus on the responses to the single question "Are you likely to choose this hotel again?" You organize the results of the survey and determine that 163 of 227 guests at the Beachcomber responded yes to "Are you likely to choose this hotel again?" and 154 of 262 guests at the Windsurfer responded yes to "Are you likely to choose this hotel again?" You wish to analyze the results to determine whether, at the 0.05 level of significance, there is evidence of a significant difference in guest satisfaction (as measured by likelihood to return to the hotel) between the two hotels.

The contingency table displayed in Table 12.1, which has two rows and two columns, is called a **2 × 2 contingency table**. The cells in the table indicate the frequency for each row and column combination.

TABLE 12.1

Layout of a 2 × 2 Contingency Table

ROW VARIABLE	COLUMN VARIABLE (GROUP)		
	1	2	Totals
Items of interest	X_1	X_2	X
Items not of interest	$n_1 - X_1$	$n_2 - X_2$	$n - X$
Totals	n_1	n_2	n

where

$$X_1 = \text{number of items of interest in group 1}$$
$$X_2 = \text{number of items of interest in group 2}$$
$$n_1 - X_1 = \text{number of items that are not of interest in group 1}$$
$$n_2 - X_2 = \text{number of items that are not of interest in group 2}$$
$$X = X_1 + X_2, \text{the total number of items of interest}$$
$$n - X = (n_1 - X_1) + (n_2 - X_2), \text{the total number of items that are not of interest}$$
$$n_1 = \text{sample size in group 1}$$
$$n_2 = \text{sample size in group 2}$$
$$n = n_1 + n_2 = \text{total sample size}$$

Table 12.2 contains the contingency table for the hotel guest satisfaction study. The contingency table has two rows, indicating whether the guests would return to the hotel or would not return to the hotel, and two columns, one for each hotel. The cells in the table indicate the frequency of each row and column combination. The row totals indicate the number of guests who would return to the hotel and those who would not return to the hotel. The column totals are the sample sizes for each hotel location.

TABLE 12.2
2 × 2 Contingency Table for the Hotel Guest Satisfaction Survey

	HOTEL		
CHOOSE HOTEL AGAIN?	**Beachcomber**	**Windsurfer**	**Total**
Yes	163	154	317
No	64	108	172
Total	227	262	489

To test whether the population proportion of guests who would return to the Beachcomber, π_1, is equal to the population proportion of guests who would return to the Windsurfer, π_2, you can use the χ^2 **test for the difference between two proportions**. To test the null hypothesis that there is no difference between the two population proportions:

$$H_0: \pi_1 = \pi_2$$

against the alternative that the two population proportions are not the same:

$$H_1: \pi_1 \neq \pi_2$$

you use the χ^2_{STAT} test statistic, shown in Equation (12.1).

χ^2 TEST FOR THE DIFFERENCE BETWEEN TWO PROPORTIONS

The χ^2_{STAT} test statistic is equal to the squared difference between the observed and expected frequencies, divided by the expected frequency in each cell of the table, summed over all cells of the table.

$$\chi^2_{STAT} = \sum_{all\ cells} \frac{(f_o - f_e)^2}{f_e} \tag{12.1}$$

where

f_o = **observed frequency** in a particular cell of a contingency table

f_e = **expected frequency** in a particular cell if the null hypothesis is true

The χ^2_{STAT} test statistic approximately follows a chi-square distribution with 1 degree of freedom.[1]

---

[1]In general, the degrees of freedom in a contingency table are equal to (number of rows −1) multiplied by (number of columns −1).

To compute the expected frequency, f_e, in any cell, you need to understand that if the null hypothesis is true, the proportion of items of interest in the two populations will be equal. Then the sample proportions you compute from each of the two groups would differ from each other only by chance. Each would provide an estimate of the common population parameter, π. A statistic that combines these two separate estimates together into one overall estimate of the population parameter provides more information than either of the two separate estimates could provide by itself. This statistic, given by the symbol $\bar{p}$, represents the estimated overall proportion of items of interest for the two groups combined (i.e., the total number of items of interest divided by the total sample size). The complement of $\bar{p}$, $1 - \bar{p}$, represents the estimated overall proportion of items that are not of interest in the two groups. Using the notation presented in Table 12.1 on page 424, Equation (12.2) defines $\bar{p}$.

COMPUTING THE ESTIMATED OVERALL PROPORTION FOR TWO GROUPS

$$\bar{p} = \frac{X_1 + X_2}{n_1 + n_2} = \frac{X}{n} \qquad\qquad (12.2)$$

To compute the expected frequency, f_e, for each cell pertaining to items of interest (i.e., the cells in the first row in the contingency table), you multiply the sample size (or column total) for a group by $\bar{p}$. To compute the expected frequency, f_e, for each cell pertaining to items that are not of interest (i.e., the cells in the second row in the contingency table), you multiply the sample size (or column total) for a group by $1 - \bar{p}$.

The χ^2_{STAT} test statistic shown in Equation (12.1) on page 425 approximately follows a **chi-square (χ^2) distribution** (see Table E.4) with 1 degree of freedom. Using a level of significance α, you reject the null hypothesis if the computed χ^2_{STAT} test statistic is greater than χ^2_α, the upper-tail critical value from the χ^2 distribution with 1 degree of freedom. Thus, the decision rule is

Reject H_0 if $\chi^2_{STAT} > \chi^2_\alpha$;

otherwise, do not reject H_0.

Figure 12.1 illustrates the decision rule.

FIGURE 12.1

Regions of rejection and nonrejection when using the chi-square test for the difference between two proportions, with level of significance α

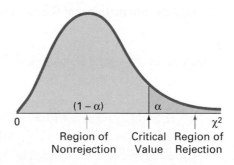

If the null hypothesis is true, the computed χ^2_{STAT} test statistic should be close to zero because the squared difference between what is actually observed in each cell, f_o, and what is theoretically expected, f_e, should be very small. If H_0 is false, then there are differences in the population proportions, and the computed χ^2_{STAT} test statistic is expected to be large. However, what is a large difference in a cell is relative. The same actual difference between f_o and f_e from a cell with a small number of expected frequencies contributes more to the χ^2_{STAT} test statistic than a cell with a large number of expected frequencies.

To illustrate the use of the chi-square test for the difference between two proportions, return to the Using Statistics scenario concerning T.C. Resort Properties on page 423 and the corresponding contingency table displayed in Table 12.2 on page 425. The null hypothesis ($H_0: \pi_1 = \pi_2$) states that there is no difference between the proportion of guests who are likely to choose either of these hotels again. To begin,

$$\bar{p} = \frac{X_1 + X_2}{n_1 + n_2} = \frac{163 + 154}{227 + 262} = \frac{317}{489} = 0.6483$$

$\bar{p}$ is the estimate of the common parameter π, the population proportion of guests who are likely to choose either of these hotels again if the null hypothesis is true. The estimated proportion of guests who are *not* likely to choose these hotels again is the complement of $\bar{p}$, $1 - 0.6483 = 0.3517$. Multiplying these two proportions by the sample size for the Beachcomber Hotel gives the number of guests expected to choose the Beachcomber again and the number not expected to choose this hotel again. In a similar manner, multiplying the two proportions by the Windsurfer Hotel's sample size yields the corresponding expected frequencies for that group.

EXAMPLE 12.1

Computing the Expected Frequencies

Compute the expected frequencies for each of the four cells of Table 12.2 on page 425.

SOLUTION

Yes—Beachcomber: $\bar{p} = 0.6483$ and $n_1 = 227$, so $f_e = 147.16$

Yes—Windsurfer: $\bar{p} = 0.6483$ and $n_2 = 262$, so $f_e = 169.84$

No—Beachcomber: $1 - \bar{p} = 0.3517$ and $n_1 = 227$, so $f_e = 79.84$

No—Windsurfer: $1 - \bar{p} = 0.3517$ and $n_2 = 262$, so $f_e = 92.16$

Table 12.3 presents these expected frequencies next to the corresponding observed frequencies.

TABLE 12.3

Comparing the Observed (f_o) and Expected (f_e) Frequencies

	HOTEL				
	BEACHCOMBER		WINDSURFER		
CHOOSE HOTEL AGAIN?	**Observed**	**Expected**	**Observed**	**Expected**	**Total**
Yes	163	147.16	154	169.84	317
No	64	79.84	108	92.16	172
Total	227	227.00	262	262.00	489

To test the null hypothesis that the population proportions are equal:

$$H_0: \pi_1 = \pi_2$$

against the alternative that the population proportions are not equal:

$$H_1: \pi_1 \neq \pi_2$$

you use the observed and expected frequencies from Table 12.3 to compute the χ^2_{STAT} test statistic given by Equation (12.1) on page 425. Table 12.4 presents the calculations.

TABLE 12.4

Computing the χ^2_{STAT} Test Statistic for the Hotel Guest Satisfaction Survey

f_o	f_e	$(f_o - f_e)$	$(f_o - f_e)^2$	$(f_o - f_e)^2/f_e$
163	147.16	15.84	250.91	1.71
154	169.84	−15.84	250.91	1.48
64	79.84	−15.84	250.91	3.14
108	92.16	15.84	250.91	2.72
				9.05

The chi-square (χ^2) distribution is a right-skewed distribution whose shape depends solely on the number of degrees of freedom. You find the critical value for the χ^2 test from Table E.4, a portion of which is presented as Table 12.5.

TABLE 12.5

Finding the Critical Value from the Chi-Square Distribution with 1 Degree of Freedom, Using the 0.05 Level of Significance

	Cumulative Probabilities						
	.005	.01	...	.95	.975	.99	.995
	Upper-Tail Area						
Degrees of Freedom	.995	.99	...	.05	.025	.01	.005
1			...	3.841	5.024	6.635	7.879
2	0.010	0.020	...	5.991	7.378	9.210	10.597
3	0.072	0.115	...	7.815	9.348	11.345	12.838
4	0.207	0.297	...	9.488	11.143	13.277	14.860
5	0.412	0.554	...	11.071	12.833	15.086	16.750

The values in Table 12.5 refer to selected upper-tail areas of the χ^2 distribution. A 2×2 contingency table has $(2 - 1)(2 - 1) = 1$ degree of freedom. Using $\alpha = 0.05$, with 1 degree of freedom, the critical value of χ^2 from Table 12.5 is 3.841. You reject H_0 if the computed χ^2_{STAT} test statistic is greater than 3.841 (see Figure 12.2). Because $\chi^2_{STAT} = 9.05 > 3.841$, you reject H_0. You conclude that the proportion of guests who would return to the Beachcomber is different from the proportion of guests who would return to the Windsurfer.

FIGURE 12.2

Regions of rejection and nonrejection when finding the χ^2 critical value with 1 degree of freedom, at the 0.05 level of significance

Figure 12.3 shows a worksheet solution for the Table 12.2 guest satisfaction contingency table on page 425.

FIGURE 12.3

Chi-square test worksheet for the two-hotel guest satisfaction data

Figure 12.3 displays the **COMPUTE worksheet** *of the* **Chi-Square workbook.** *Create this worksheet using the instructions in Section EG12.1. Read the* In-Depth Excel *instructions for this worksheet to learn about the formulas used in the observed and expected frequencies table (not shown in Figure 12.3).*

	A	B	C	D	E	F	G
1	Chi-Square Test						
2							
3		**Observed Frequencies**					
4			Hotel			Calculations	
5	Choose Again?	Beachcomber	Windsurfer	Total		fo-fe	
6	Yes	163	154	317		15.84458	-15.8446 =B6 - B13 =C6 - C13
7	No	64	108	172		-15.8446	15.8446 =B7 - B14 =C7 - C14
8	Total	227	262	489			
9							
10		**Expected Frequencies**					
11			Hotel				
12	Choose Again?	Beachcomber	Windsurfer	Total		(fo-fe)^2/fe	
13	Yes	147.1554	169.8446	317		1.7060	1.4781 =F6^2/B13 =G6^2/C13
14	No	79.8446	92.1554	172		3.1442	2.7242 =F7^2/B14 =G7^2/C14
15	Total	227	262	489			
16							
17	**Data**						
18	Level of Significance	0.05					
19	Number of Rows	2					
20	Number of Columns	2					
21	Degrees of Freedom	1	=(B19 - 1) * (B20 -1)				
22							
23	**Results**						
24	Critical Value	3.8415	=CHIINV(B18, B21)				
25	Chi-Square Test Statistic	9.0526	=SUM(F13:G14)				
26	*p* -Value	0.0026	=CHIDIST(B25, B21)				
27	**Reject the null hypothesis**		=IF(B26 < B18, "Reject the null hypothesis",				
28			"Do not reject the null hypothesis")				
29	***Expected frequency assumption***						
30	***is met.***		=IF(OR(B13 < 5, C13 < 5, B14 < 5, C14 < 5),				
			" is violated.", " is met.")				

These results include the expected frequencies, χ^2_{STAT}, degrees of freedom, and p-value. The computed χ^2_{STAT} test statistic is 9.0526, which is greater than the critical value of 3.8415 (or the p-value $= 0.0026 < 0.05$), so you reject the null hypothesis that there is no difference in guest satisfaction between the two hotels. The p-value of 0.0026 is the probability of observing sample proportions as different as or more different than the actual difference $(0.718 - 0.588 = 0.13)$ observed in the sample data, if the population proportions for the Beachcomber and Windsurfer hotels are equal. Thus, there is strong evidence to conclude that the two hotels are significantly different with respect to guest satisfaction, as measured by whether a guest is likely to return to the hotel again. From Table 12.3 on page 427 you can see that a greater proportion of guests are likely to return to the Beachcomber than to the Windsurfer.

For the χ^2 test to give accurate results for a 2 × 2 table, you must assume that each expected frequency is at least 5. If this assumption is not satisfied, you can use alternative procedures such as Fisher's exact test (see references 1, 2, and 4).

In the hotel guest satisfaction survey, both the Z test based on the standardized normal distribution (see Section 10.3) and the χ^2 test based on the chi-square distribution provide the same conclusion. You can explain this result by the interrelationship between the standardized normal distribution and a chi-square distribution with 1 degree of freedom. For such situations, the χ^2_{STAT} test statistic is the square of the Z_{STAT} test statistic. For instance, in the guest satisfaction study, the computed Z_{STAT} test statistic is $+3.0088$ and the computed χ^2_{STAT} test statistic is 9.0526. Except for rounding error, this 9.0526 value is the square of $+3.0088$ [i.e., $(+3.0088)^2 \cong 9.0526$]. Also, if you compare the critical values of the test statistics from the two distributions, at the 0.05 level of significance, the χ^2 value of 3.841 with 1 degree of freedom is the square of the Z value of ±1.96. Furthermore, the p-values for both tests are equal. Therefore, when testing the null hypothesis of equality of proportions:

$$H_0: \pi_1 = \pi_2$$

against the alternative that the population proportions are not equal:

$$H_1: \pi_1 \neq \pi_2$$

the Z test and the χ^2 test are equivalent.

If you are interested in determining whether there is evidence of a *directional* difference, such as $\pi_1 > \pi_2$, then you must use the Z test, with the entire rejection region located in one tail of the standardized normal distribution.

In Section 12.2, the χ^2 test is extended to make comparisons and evaluate differences between the proportions among more than two groups. However, you cannot use the Z test if there are more than two groups.

Problems for Section 12.1

LEARNING THE BASICS

12.1 Determine the critical value of χ^2 with 1 degree of freedom in each of the following circumstances:
a. $\alpha = 0.01$
b. $\alpha = 0.005$
c. $\alpha = 0.10$

12.2 Determine the critical value of χ^2 with 1 degree of freedom in each of the following circumstances:
a. $\alpha = 0.05$
b. $\alpha = 0.025$
c. $\alpha = 0.01$

12.3 Use the following contingency table:

	A	B	Total
1	20	30	50
2	30	45	75
Total	50	75	125

a. Compute the expected frequency for each cell.
b. Compare the observed and expected frequencies for each cell.
c. Compute χ^2_{STAT}. Is it significant at $\alpha = 0.05$?

12.4 Use the following contingency table:

	A	B	Total
1	20	30	50
2	30	20	50
Total	50	50	100

a. Compute the expected frequency for each cell.
b. Compute χ^2_{STAT}. Is it significant at $\alpha = 0.05$?

APPLYING THE CONCEPTS

12.5 A sample of 500 shoppers was selected in a large metropolitan area to determine various information concerning consumer behavior. Among the questions asked was, "Do you enjoy shopping for clothing?" The results are summarized in the following contingency table:

ENJOY SHOPPING FOR CLOTHING	GENDER		
	Male	**Female**	**Total**
Yes	136	224	360
No	104	36	140
Total	240	260	500

a. Is there evidence of a significant difference between the proportion of males and females who enjoy shopping for clothing at the 0.01 level of significance?
b. Determine the p-value in (a) and interpret its meaning.
c. What are your answers to (a) and (b) if 206 males enjoyed shopping for clothing and 34 did not?
d. Compare the results of (a) through (c) to those of Problem 10.29 (a), (b), and (d) on page 359.

12.6 A study funded by the Massachusetts Institute of Technology tested the notion that even when it comes to sugar pills, some people think a costly one works better than a cheap one. Researchers randomly divided 82 healthy paid volunteers into two groups. All the volunteers thought they would be testing a new pain reliever. One group was told the pain reliever they would be using cost $2.50 a pill, and the other group was told it cost only 10 cents a pill. In reality, the pills they were all about to take were simply sugar pills. The volunteers were given a light electric shock on the wrist. Then the volunteers were given a sugar pill, and a short time later they were shocked again. Of the volunteers who took the expensive pill, 35 of the 41 said they felt less pain afterward. Of the volunteers who took the cheap pill, 25 of the 41 said they felt less pain afterward (R. Rubin, "Placebo Study Tests 'Costlier is Better' Notion," **www.usatoday.com**, March 5, 2008).
a. Is there evidence of a difference in the proportion of people who think an expensive pill works to reduce pain and the proportion of people who think a cheap pill works to reduce pain at the 0.05 level of significance?

b. Determine the p-value in (a) and interpret its meaning.
c. Why shouldn't you compare the results in (a) to those of Problem 10.30 (b) on page 359?

12.7 Some people enjoy the *anticipation* of an upcoming product or event and prefer to pay in advance and delay the actual consumption/delivery date. In other cases, people do not want a delay. An article in the *Journal of Marketing Research* reported on an experiment in which 50 individuals were told that they had just purchased a ticket to a concert and 50 were told that they had just purchased a personal digital assistant (PDA). The participants were then asked to indicate their preferences for attending the concert or receiving the PDA. Did they prefer tonight or tomorrow, or would they prefer to wait two to four weeks? The individuals were told to ignore their schedule constraints in order to better measure their willingness to delay the consumption/delivery of their purchase. The following table gives partial results of the study:

	Concert	PDA
Tonight or tomorrow	28	47
Two to four weeks	22	3
Total	50	50

Source: *Data adapted from O. Amir and D. Ariely, "Decisions by Rules: The Case of Unwillingness to Pay for Beneficial Delays,"* Journal of Marketing Research, *February 2007, Vol. XLIV, pp. 142–152.*

a. What proportion of the participants would prefer delaying the date of the concert?
b. What proportion of the participants would prefer delaying receipt of a new PDA?
c. Using the 0.05 level of significance, is there evidence of a significance difference in the proportion willing to delay the date of the concert and the proportion willing to delay receipt of a new PDA?

✓ SELF **12.8** Do people of different age groups differ in
Test their response to e-mail messages? A survey by the Center for the Digital Future of the University of Southern California (data extracted from A. Mindlin, "Older E-mail Users Favor Fast Replies," *The New York Times*, July 14, 2008, p. B3) reported that 70.7% of users above age 70 believe that e-mail messages should be answered quickly as compared to 53.6% of users 12 to 50 years old. Suppose that the survey was based on 1,000 users above age 70 and 1,000 users 12 to 50 years old.
a. At the 0.01 level of significance, is there evidence of a significant difference between the two age groups that believe e-mail messages should be answered quickly?
b. Find the p-value in (a) and interpret its meaning.
c. Compare the results of (a) and (b) to those of Problem 10.32 on page 360.

12.9 Where people turn for news is different for various age groups. Suppose that a study conducted on this issue (data extracted from P. Johnson, "Young People Turn to the Web for News," *USA Today*, March 23, 2006, p. 9D) was based on 200 respondents who were between the ages of 36 and 50 and 200 respondents who were above age 50. Of the 200 respondents who were between the ages of 36 and 50, 82 got their news primarily from newspapers. Of the 200 respondents who were above age 50, 104 got their news primarily from newspapers.

a. Construct a 2 × 2 contingency table.

b. Is there evidence of a significant difference in the proportion who get their news primarily from newspapers between those 36 to 50 years old and those above 50 years old? (Use $\alpha = 0.05$.)

c. Determine the *p*-value in (b) and interpret its meaning.

d. Compare the results of (b) and (c) to those of Problem 10.35 (a) and (b) on page 360.

12.10 An experiment was conducted to study the choices made in mutual fund selection. Undergraduate and MBA students were presented with different S&P 500 index funds that were identical except for fees. Suppose 100 undergraduate students and 100 MBA students were selected. Partial results are as follows:

	STUDENT GROUP	
FUND	**Undergraduate**	**MBA**
Highest-cost fund	27	18
Not highest-cost fund	73	82

Source: *Data extracted from J. Choi, D. Laibson, and B. Madrian, "Why Does the Law of One Practice Fail? An Experiment on Mutual Funds," www.som.yale.edu/faculty/jjc83/fees.pdf.*

a. At the 0.05 level of significance, is there evidence of a difference between undergraduate and MBA students in the proportion who selected the highest-cost fund?

b. Determine the *p*-value in (a) and interpret its meaning.

c. Compare the results of (a) and (b) to those of Problem 10.34 on page 360.

12.2 Chi-Square Test for Differences Among More Than Two Proportions

In this section, the χ^2 test is extended to compare more than two independent populations. The letter *c* is used to represent the number of independent populations under consideration. Thus, the contingency table now has two rows and *c* columns. To test the null hypothesis that there are no differences among the *c* population proportions:

$$H_0: \pi_1 = \pi_2 = \cdots = \pi_c$$

against the alternative that not all the *c* population proportions are equal:

$$H_1: \text{Not all } \pi_j \text{ are equal (where } j = 1, 2, \ldots, c)$$

you use Equation (12.1) on page 425:

$$\chi^2_{STAT} = \sum_{\text{all cells}} \frac{(f_o - f_e)^2}{f_e}$$

where

f_o = observed frequency in a particular cell of a 2 × c contingency table
f_e = expected frequency in a particular cell if the null hypothesis is true

If the null hypothesis is true and the proportions are equal across all *c* populations, the *c* sample proportions should differ only by chance. In such a situation, a statistic that combines these *c* separate estimates into one overall estimate of the population proportion, π, provides more information than any one of the *c* separate estimates alone. To expand on Equation (12.2) on page 426, the statistic $\bar{p}$ in Equation (12.3) represents the estimated overall proportion for all *c* groups combined.

COMPUTING THE ESTIMATED OVERALL PROPORTION FOR *c* GROUPS

$$\bar{p} = \frac{X_1 + X_2 + \cdots + X_c}{n_1 + n_2 + \cdots + n_c} = \frac{X}{n} \tag{12.3}$$

To compute the expected frequency, f_e, for each cell in the first row in the contingency table, multiply each sample size (or column total) by $\bar{p}$. To compute the expected frequency, f_e, for each cell in the second row in the contingency table, multiply each sample size (or column total) by $(1 - \bar{p})$. The test statistic shown in Equation (12.1) on page 425 approximately follows a chi-square distribution, with degrees of freedom equal to the number of rows in the contingency table minus 1, multiplied by the number of columns in the table minus 1. For a **2 × c contingency table**, there are $c - 1$ degrees of freedom:

$$\text{Degrees of freedom} = (2 - 1)(c - 1) = c - 1$$

Using the level of significance α, you reject the null hypothesis if the computed χ^2_{STAT} test statistic is greater than χ^2_α, the upper-tail critical value from a chi-square distribution with $c - 1$ degrees of freedom. Therefore, the decision rule is

$$\text{Reject } H_0 \text{ if } \chi^2_{STAT} > \chi^2_\alpha;$$

otherwise, do not reject H_0.

Figure 12.4 illustrates the decision rule.

FIGURE 12.4

Regions of rejection
and nonrejection when
testing for differences
among c proportions
using the χ^2 test

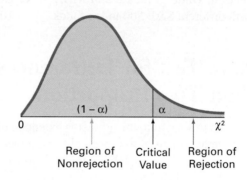

To illustrate the χ^2 test for equality of proportions when there are more than two groups, return to the Using Statistics scenario on page 423 concerning T.C. Resort Properties. Once again, you define the business objective as improving the quality of service, but this time, three hotels located on a different island are to be surveyed. Data are collected from customer satisfaction surveys at these three hotels. You organize the responses into the contingency table shown in Table 12.6.

TABLE 12.6

2 × 3 Contingency Table
for Guest Satisfaction
Survey

	HOTEL			
CHOOSE HOTEL AGAIN?	**Golden Palm**	**Palm Royale**	**Palm Princess**	**Total**
Yes	128	199	186	513
No	88	33	66	187
Total	216	232	252	700

Because the null hypothesis states that there are no differences among the three hotels in the proportion of guests who would likely return again, you use Equation (12.3) to calculate an estimate of π, the population proportion of guests who would likely return again:

$$\bar{p} = \frac{X_1 + X_2 + \cdots + X_c}{n_1 + n_2 + \cdots + n_c} = \frac{X}{n}$$

$$= \frac{(128 + 199 + 186)}{(216 + 232 + 252)} = \frac{513}{700}$$

$$= 0.733$$

The estimated overall proportion of guests who would *not* be likely to return again is the complement, $(1 - \bar{p})$, or 0.267. Multiplying these two proportions by the sample size for each hotel yields the expected number of guests who would and would not likely return.

EXAMPLE 12.2

Computing the Expected Frequencies

Compute the expected frequencies for each of the six cells in Table 12.6.

SOLUTION

Yes—Golden Palm: $\bar{p} = 0.733$ and $n_1 = 216$, so $f_e = 158.30$

Yes—Palm Royale: $\bar{p} = 0.733$ and $n_2 = 232$, so $f_e = 170.02$

Yes—Palm Princess: $\bar{p} = 0.733$ and $n_3 = 252$, so $f_e = 184.68$

No—Golden Palm: $1 - \bar{p} = 0.267$ and $n_1 = 216$, so $f_e = 57.70$

No—Palm Royale: $1 - \bar{p} = 0.267$ and $n_2 = 232$, so $f_e = 61.98$

No—Palm Princess: $1 - \bar{p} = 0.267$ and $n_3 = 252$, so $f_e = 67.32$

Table 12.7 presents these expected frequencies.

TABLE 12.7

Contingency Table of Expected Frequencies from a Guest Satisfaction Survey of Three Hotels

	HOTEL			
CHOOSE HOTEL AGAIN?	**Golden Palm**	**Palm Royale**	**Palm Princess**	**Total**
Yes	158.30	170.02	184.68	513
No	57.70	61.98	67.32	187
Total	216.00	232.00	252.00	700

To test the null hypothesis that the proportions are equal:

$$H_0: \pi_1 = \pi_2 = \pi_3$$

against the alternative that not all three proportions are equal:

$$H_1: \text{Not all } \pi_j \text{ are equal (where } j = 1, 2, 3)$$

you use the observed frequencies from Table 12.6 and the expected frequencies from Table 12.7 to compute the χ^2_{STAT} test statistic [given by Equation (12.1) on page 425]. Table 12.8 presents the calculations.

TABLE 12.8

Computing the χ^2_{STAT} Test Statistic for the Guest Satisfaction Survey of Three Hotels

f_o	f_e	$(f_o - f_e)$	$(f_o - f_e)^2$	$(f_o - f_e)^2/f_e$
128	158.30	−30.30	918.09	5.80
199	170.02	28.98	839.84	4.94
186	184.68	1.32	1.74	0.01
88	57.70	30.30	918.09	15.91
33	61.98	−28.98	839.84	13.55
66	67.32	−1.32	1.74	0.02
				40.23

You use Table E.4 to find the critical value of the χ^2 test statistic. In the guest satisfaction survey, because there are three hotels, there are $(2 - 1)(3 - 1) = 2$ degrees of freedom. Using $\alpha = 0.05$, the χ^2 critical value with 2 degrees of freedom is 5.991 (see Figure 12.5). Because the computed χ^2_{STAT} test statistic is 40.23, which is greater than this critical value, you reject the null hypothesis. Figure 12.6 shows the worksheet solution for this problem. The worksheet results also report the p-value. Because the cell B26 p-value is (approximately) 0.0000, less than $\alpha = 0.05$, you reject the null hypothesis. Further, this p-value indicates that there is virtually no chance that there will be differences this large or larger among the three sample proportions, if the population proportions for the three hotels are equal. Thus, there is sufficient evidence to conclude that the hotel properties are different with respect to the proportion of guests who are likely to return.

FIGURE 12.5

Regions of rejection and nonrejection when testing for differences in three proportions at the 0.05 level of significance, with 2 degrees of freedom

FIGURE 12.6

Chi-square test worksheet for the Table 12.6 guest satisfaction data

Figure 12.6 displays the ChiSquare2x3 worksheet of the Chi-Square Worksheets workbook. Create this worksheet using the instructions in Section EG12.2. Read the In-Depth Excel instructions for this worksheet to learn about the formulas used in rows 4 through 15 (not shown in Figure 12.6).

	A	B	C	D	E	F	G	H	I
1	Chi-Square Test								
2									
3		**Observed Frequencies**							
4			Hotel					Calculations	
5	Choose Again?	Golden Palm	Palm Royale	Palm Princess	Total			fo -fe	
6	Yes	128	199	186	513		-30.2971	28.9771	1.32
7	No	88	33	66	187		30.2971	-28.9771	-1.32
8	Total	216	232	252	700				
9									
10		**Expected Frequencies**							
11			Hotel						
12	Choose Again?	Golden Palm	Palm Royale	Palm Princess	Total			(fo - fe)^2/fe	
13	Yes	158.2971	170.0229	184.68	513		5.7987	4.9386	0.0094
14	No	57.7029	61.9771	67.32	187		15.9077	13.5481	0.0259
15	Total	216	232	252	700				
16									
17	**Data**								
18	Level of Significance	0.05							
19	Number of Rows	2							
20	Number of Columns	3							
21	Degrees of Freedom	2	=(B19 - 1) * (B20 - 1)						
22									
23	**Results**								
24	Critical Value	5.9915	=CHIINV(B18, B21)						
25	Chi-Square Test Statistic	40.2284	=SUM(G13:I14)						
26	*p*-Value	0.0000	=CHIDIST(B25, B21)						
27	Reject the null hypothesis		=IF(B26 < B18, "Reject the null hypothesis",						
28			"Do not reject the null hypothesis")						
29	*Expected frequency assumption*								
30	*is met.*		=IF(OR(B13 < 1, C13 < 1, D13 < 1, B14 < 1, C14 < 1, D14 < 1), "						
			" is violated.", " is met.")						

For the χ^2 test to give accurate results when dealing with $2 \times c$ contingency tables, all expected frequencies must be large. The definition of "large" has led to research among statisticians. Some statisticians (see reference 5) have found that the test gives accurate results as long as all expected frequencies are at least 0.5. Other statisticians, more conservative in their approach, believe that no more than 20% of the cells should contain expected frequencies less than 5 and no cells should have expected frequencies less than 1 (see reference 3). As a reasonable compromise between these points of view, to assure the validity of the test, you should make sure that each expected frequency is at least 1. To do this, you may need to collapse two or more low-expected-frequency categories into one category in the contingency table before performing the test. If combining categories is undesirable, you can use one of the available alternative procedures (see references 1, 2, and 7).

The Marascuilo Procedure

Rejecting the null hypothesis in a χ^2 test of equality of proportions in a $2 \times c$ table only allows you to reach the conclusion that not all c population proportions are equal. But how do you determine *which* of the proportions differ? Because the result of the χ^2 test for equality of proportions does not specifically answer this question, you need to use a multiple comparisons procedure such as the Marascuilo procedure.

The **Marascuilo procedure** enables you to make comparisons between all pairs of groups. First, you compute the sample proportions. Then, you use Equation (12.4) to compute the critical ranges for the Marascuilo procedure. You need to compute a different critical range for each pairwise comparison of sample proportions.

CRITICAL RANGE FOR THE MARASCUILO PROCEDURE

$$\text{Critical range} = \sqrt{\chi_\alpha^2}\sqrt{\frac{p_j(1-p_j)}{n_j} + \frac{p_{j'}(1-p_{j'})}{n_{j'}}} \qquad (12.4)$$

In the final step, you compare each of the $c(c-1)/2$ pairs of sample proportions against its corresponding critical range. You declare a specific pair significantly different if the absolute difference in the sample proportions, $|p_j - p_{j'}|$, is greater than its critical range.

To apply the Marascuilo procedure, return to the guest satisfaction survey. Using the χ^2 test, you concluded that there was evidence of a significant difference among the population proportions. From Table 12.6 on page 432, the three sample proportions are

$$p_1 = \frac{X_1}{n_1} = \frac{128}{216} = 0.5926$$

$$p_2 = \frac{X_2}{n_2} = \frac{199}{232} = 0.8578$$

$$p_3 = \frac{X_3}{n_3} = \frac{186}{252} = 0.7381$$

Next, you compute the absolute differences in sample proportions and their corresponding critical ranges. Because there are three hotels, there are $(3)(3-1)/2 = 3$ pairwise comparisons. Using Table E.4 and an overall level of significance of 0.05, the upper-tail critical value for a chi-square distribution having $(c-1) = 2$ degrees of freedom is 5.991. Thus,

$$\sqrt{\chi_\alpha^2} = \sqrt{5.991} = 2.4477$$

Absolute Difference in Proportions   **Critical Range**

$$|p_j - p_{j'}| \qquad\qquad 2.4477\sqrt{\frac{p_j(1-p_j)}{n_j} + \frac{p_{j'}(1-p_{j'})}{n_{j'}}}$$

$$|p_1 - p_2| = |0.5926 - 0.8578| = 0.2652 \quad 2.4477\sqrt{\frac{(0.5926)(0.4074)}{216} + \frac{(0.8578)(0.1422)}{232}} = 0.0992$$

$$|p_1 - p_3| = |0.5926 - 0.7381| = 0.1455 \quad 2.4477\sqrt{\frac{(0.5926)(0.4074)}{216} + \frac{(0.7381)(0.2619)}{252}} = 0.1063$$

$$|p_2 - p_3| = |0.8578 - 0.7381| = 0.1197 \quad 2.4477\sqrt{\frac{(0.8578)(0.1422)}{232} + \frac{(0.7381)(0.2619)}{252}} = 0.0880$$

Figure 12.7 shows a worksheet solution for this example.

FIGURE 12.7

Marascuilo procedure worksheet for the guest satisfaction survey

Figure 12.7 displays the Marascuilo2x3 worksheet of the Chi-Square Worksheets workbook. Many formulas in this worksheet use values from the ChiSquare2x3 worksheet shown in Figure 12.6 on page 434. Create this worksheet using the instructions in Section EG12.2. Read the In-Depth Excel instructions for this worksheet to learn about the formulas used in rows 13 through 16 (not shown in Figure 12.7).

	A	B	C	D
1	Marascuilo Procedure for Guest Satisfaction Analysis			
2				
3	Level of Significance	0.05	=ChiSquare2x3!B18	
4	Square Root of Critical Value	2.4477	=SQRT(ChiSquare2x3!B24)	
5				
6	Group Sample Proportions			
7	1: Golden Palm	0.5926	=ChiSquare2x3!B6/ChiSquare2x3!B8	
8	2: Palm Royale	0.8578	=ChiSquare2x3!C6/ChiSquare2x3!C8	
9	3: Palm Princess	0.7381	=ChiSquare2x3!D6/ChiSquare2x3!D8	
10				
11	MARASCUILO TABLE			
12	Proportions	Absolute Differences	Critical Range	
13	| Group 1 - Group 2 |	0.2652	0.0992	Significant
14	| Group 1 - Group 3 |	0.1455	0.1063	Significant
15				
16	| Group 2 - Group 3 |	0.1197	0.0880	Significant

The final step is to compare the absolute differences to the critical ranges. If the absolute difference is greater than its critical range, the proportions are significantly different. At the 0.05 level of significance, you can conclude that guest satisfaction is higher at the Palm Royale ($p_2 = 0.858$) than at either the Golden Palm ($p_1 = 0.593$) or the Palm Princess ($p_3 = 0.738$) and that guest satisfaction is also higher at the Palm Princess than at the Golden Palm. These results clearly suggest that you investigate possible reasons for these differences. In particular, you should try to determine why satisfaction is significantly lower at the Golden Palm than at the other two hotels.

⊕ *Online Topic:* The Analysis of Proportions (ANOP)

The ANOP procedure provides a confidence interval approach that allows you to determine which, if any, of the c groups has a proportion significantly different from the overall mean of all the group proportions combined. To study this topic, read the **ANOP** online topic file that is available on this book's companion Web site. (See Appendix Section D.8 to learn how to access the online topic files.)

Problems for Section 12.2

LEARNING THE BASICS

12.11 Consider a contingency table with two rows and five columns.
a. How many degrees of freedom are there in the contingency table?.
b. Determine the critical value for $\alpha = 0.05$.
c. Determine the critical value for $\alpha = 0.01$.

12.12 Use the following contingency table:

	A	B	C	Total
1	10	30	50	90
2	40	45	50	135
Total	50	75	100	225

a. Compute the expected frequencies for each cell.
b. Compute χ^2_{STAT}. Is it significant at $\alpha = 0.05$?

12.13 Use the following contingency table:

	A	B	C	Total
1	20	30	25	75
2	30	20	25	75
Total	50	50	50	150

a. Compute the expected frequencies for each cell.
b. Compute χ^2_{STAT}. Is it significant at $\alpha = 0.05$?
c. If appropriate, use the Marascuilo procedure and $\alpha = 0.05$ to determine which groups are different.

APPLYING THE CONCEPTS

12.14 In a recent article in *Quality Progress*, the author argues that improving organizational performance (in schools, government, or business) can occur only after good approaches have been selected and implemented. Danville Community Schools in Indiana rated the faculty on their use of quality tools that will lead to improved performance. The results are recorded in the following contingency table:

| USE OF TOOLS | SCHOOL | | | |
	North Elementary	South Elementary	Middle School	High School
Low	24	5	18	32
High	7	21	4	12

Source: *Data extracted from S. Benjamin, "Keeping Score,"* Quality Progress, *April 2009, pp. 38–45.*

a. Is there evidence of a significance difference among the schools with respect to the proportion of teachers who have obtained a "High" rating? (Use $\alpha = 0.05$).
b. Determine the *p*-value in (a) and interpret its meaning.
c. If appropriate, use the Marascuilo procedure and $\alpha = 0.05$ to determine which schools are different.

12.15 The health-care industry and consumer advocacy groups are at odds over the sharing of a patient's medical records without the patient's consent. The health-care industry believes that no consent should be necessary to openly share data among doctors, hospitals, pharmacies, and insurance companies.

Suppose a study is conducted in which 600 patients are randomly assigned, 200 each, to three "organizational groupings"—insurance companies, pharmacies, and medical researchers. Each patient is given material to read about the advantages and disadvantages concerning the sharing of medical records within the assigned "organizational grouping." Each patient is then asked "would you object to the sharing of your medical records with...."; the results are recorded in the following contingency table:

| OBJECT TO SHARING INFORMATION | ORGANIZATIONAL GROUPING | | |
	Insurance	Pharmacies	Research
Yes	40	80	90
No	160	120	110

a. Is there evidence of a difference in objection to sharing information among the organizational groupings? (Use $\alpha = 0.05$.)
b. Compute the *p*-value and interpret its meaning.
c. If appropriate, use the Marascuilo procedure and $\alpha = 0.05$ to determine which groups are different.

SELF Test **12.16** More shoppers do the majority of their grocery shopping on Saturday than any other day of the week. However, is there a difference in the various age groups in the proportion of people who do the majority of their grocery shopping on Saturday? A study showed the results for the different age groups (data extracted from "Major Shopping by Day," *Progressive Grocer Annual Report*, April 30, 2002). The data were reported as percentages, and no sample sizes were given:

| MAJOR SHOPPING DAY | AGE | | |
	Under 35	35–54	Over 54
Saturday	24%	28%	12%
A day other than Saturday	76%	72%	88%

Assume that 200 shoppers for each age group were surveyed.
a. Is there evidence of a significant difference among the age groups with respect to major grocery shopping day? (Use $\alpha = 0.05$.)
b. Determine the *p*-value in (a) and interpret its meaning.
c. If appropriate, use the Marascuilo procedure and $\alpha = 0.05$ to determine which age groups are different.
d. Discuss the managerial implications of (a) and (c). How can grocery stores use this information to improve marketing and sales? Be specific.

12.17 Repeat (a) and (b) of Problem 12.16, assuming that only 50 shoppers for each age group were surveyed. Discuss the implications of sample size on the χ^2 test for differences among more than two populations.

12.18 More and more people are finding that they need to delay retirement for financial reasons (data extracted from T. Luhby, "When Retirement Is a Luxury You Can't Afford," *Newsday*, September 30, 2006, pp. B4, B5, B8). A study reported that 52% of men ages 62 to 64 were still working, 41% of women ages 62 to 64 were still working, 31% of men ages 65 to 69 were still working, and 23% of women ages 65 to 69 were still working. Suppose that the study was based on a sample size of 100 in each group.
a. Is there evidence of a significant difference among the groups with respect to the proportion who are still working? (Use $\alpha = 0.05$.)
b. Determine the *p*-value in (a) and interpret its meaning.
c. If appropriate, use the Marascuilo procedure and $\alpha = 0.05$. to determine which groups are different.

12.19 More and more people are paying with credit cards (data extracted from *USA Today Snapshots*, March 6, 2007, p. 1B). A study conducted in 1995 reported that 18% of the respondents paid for a specific type of purchase with plastic, whereas a similar study in 2005 indicated that 25% paid for a specific type of purchase with plastic. (No sample sizes were reported for either study.) Suppose that a new survey taken in 2007 indicated that 31% paid for a specific type of purchase with plastic. Suppose that all three studies used a sample size of 500.

a. Is there evidence of a significant difference among the three years in the proportion of respondents who paid for a specific type of purchase with plastic? (Use $\alpha = 0.05$.)

b. Determine the p-value in (a) and interpret its meaning.

c. If appropriate, use the Marascuilo procedure and $\alpha = 0.05$. to determine which years are different.

12.3 Chi-Square Test of Independence

In Sections 12.1 and 12.2, you used the χ^2 test to evaluate potential differences among population proportions. For a contingency table that has r rows and c columns, you can generalize the χ^2 test as a *test of independence* for two categorical variables.

For a test of independence, the null and alternative hypotheses follow:

H_0: The two categorical variables are independent (i.e., there is no relationship between them).

H_1: The two categorical variables are dependent (i.e., there is a relationship between them).

Once again, you use Equation (12.1) on page 425 to compute the test statistic:

$$\chi^2_{STAT} = \sum_{all\,cells} \frac{(f_o - f_e)^2}{f_e}$$

You reject the null hypothesis at the α level of significance if the computed value of the χ^2_{STAT} test statistic is greater than χ^2_α, the upper-tail critical value from a chi-square distribution with $(r - 1)(c - 1)$ degrees of freedom (see Figure 12.8). Thus, the decision rule is

Reject H_0 if $\chi^2_{STAT} > \chi^2_\alpha$;

otherwise, do not reject H_0.

FIGURE 12.8

Regions of rejection and nonrejection when testing for independence in an $r \times c$ contingency table, using the χ^2 test

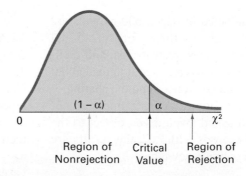

The χ^2 **test of independence** is similar to the χ^2 test for equality of proportions. The test statistics and the decision rules are the same, but the null and alternative hypotheses and conclusions are different. For example, in the guest satisfaction survey of Sections 12.1 and 12.2, there is evidence of a significant difference between the hotels with respect to the proportion of guests who would return. From a different viewpoint, you could conclude that there is a significant relationship between the hotels and the likelihood that a guest would return. However, the two types of tests differ in how the samples are selected.

In a test for equality of proportions, there is one factor of interest, with two or more levels. These levels represent samples drawn from independent populations. The categorical responses in each group or level are classified into two categories, such as *item of interest* and *not an item of interest*. The objective is to make comparisons and evaluate differences between the proportions of the *items of interest* among the various levels. However, in a test for independence, there are two factors of interest, each of which has two or more levels. You select one sample and tally the joint responses to the two categorical variables into the cells of a contingency table.

To illustrate the χ^2 test for independence, suppose that, in the survey on hotel guest satisfaction, respondents who stated they were not likely to return were asked what was the primary reason for their unwillingness to return to the hotel. Table 12.9 presents the resulting 4×3 contingency table.

TABLE 12.9

Contingency Table of Primary Reason for Not Returning and Hotel

PRIMARY REASON FOR NOT RETURNING	HOTEL			
	Golden Palm	Palm Royale	Palm Princess	Total
Price	23	7	37	67
Location	39	13	8	60
Room accommodation	13	5	13	31
Other	13	8	8	29
Total	88	33	66	187

In Table 12.9, observe that of the primary reasons for not planning to return to the hotel, 67 were due to price, 60 were due to location, 31 were due to room accommodation, and 29 were due to other reasons. As in Table 12.6 on page 432, there were 88 guests at the Golden Palm, 33 guests at the Palm Royale, and 66 guests at the Palm Princess who were not planning to return. The observed frequencies in the cells of the 4×3 contingency table represent the joint tallies of the sampled guests with respect to primary reason for not returning and the hotel they had stayed at.

The null and alternative hypotheses are

H_0: There is no relationship between the primary reason for not returning and the hotel.

H_1: There is a relationship between the primary reason for not returning and the hotel.

To test this null hypothesis of independence against the alternative that there is a relationship between the two categorical variables, you use Equation (12.1) on page 425 to compute the test statistic:

$$\chi^2_{STAT} = \sum_{all\ cells} \frac{(f_o - f_e)^2}{f_e}$$

where

f_o = observed frequency in a particular cell of the $r \times c$ contingency table

f_e = expected frequency in a particular cell if the null hypothesis of independence were true

To compute the expected frequency, f_e, in any cell, you use the multiplication rule for independent events discussed on page 146 [see Equation (4.7)]. For example, under the null hypothesis of independence, the probability of responses expected in the upper-left-corner cell representing primary reason of price for the Golden Palm is the product of the two separate probabilities $P(Price)$ and $P(Golden\ Palm)$. Here, the proportion of reasons that are due to price, $P(Price)$, is $67/187 = 0.3583$, and the proportion of all responses from the Golden Palm, $P(Golden\ Palm)$, is $88/187 = 0.4706$. If the null hypothesis is true, then the primary reason for not returning and the hotel are independent:

$$P(Price\ and\ Golden\ Palm) = P(Price) \times P(Golden\ Palm)$$

$$= (0.3583) \times (0.4706)$$

$$= 0.1686$$

The expected frequency is the product of the overall sample size, n, and this probability, $187 \times 0.1686 = 31.53$. The f_e values for the remaining cells are calculated in a similar manner (see Table 12.10).

Equation (12.5) presents a simpler way to compute the expected frequency.

COMPUTING THE EXPECTED FREQUENCY

The expected frequency in a cell is the product of its row total and column total, divided by the overall sample size.

$$f_e = \frac{\text{Row total} \times \text{Column total}}{n} \qquad \textbf{(12.5)}$$

where

$$\text{row total} = \text{sum of all the frequencies in the row}$$
$$\text{column total} = \text{sum of all the frequencies in the column}$$
$$n = \text{overall sample size}$$

For example, using Equation (12.5) for the upper-left-corner cell (price for the Golden Palm),

$$f_e = \frac{\text{Row total} \times \text{Column total}}{n} = \frac{(67)(88)}{187} = 31.53$$

and for the lower-right-corner cell (other reason for the Palm Princess),

$$f_e = \frac{\text{Row total} \times \text{Column total}}{n} = \frac{(29)(66)}{187} = 10.24$$

Table 12.10 lists the entire set of f_e values.

TABLE 12.10

Contingency Table of Expected Frequencies of Primary Reason for Not Returning with Hotel

PRIMARY REASON FOR NOT RETURNING	HOTEL			
	Golden Palm	Palm Royale	Palm Princess	Total
Price	31.53	11.82	23.65	67
Location	28.24	10.59	21.18	60
Room accommodation	14.59	5.47	10.94	31
Other	13.65	5.12	10.24	29
Total	88.00	33.00	66.00	187

To perform the test of independence, you use the χ^2_{STAT} test statistic shown in Equation (12.1) on page 425. The χ^2_{STAT} test statistic approximately follows a chi-square distribution, with degrees of freedom equal to the number of rows in the contingency table minus 1, multiplied by the number of columns in the table minus 1:

$$\text{Degrees of freedom} = (r - 1)(c - 1)$$
$$= (4 - 1)(3 - 1) = 6$$

Table 12.11 illustrates the computations for the χ^2_{STAT} test statistic.

TABLE 12.11

Computing the χ^2_{STAT} Test Statistic for the Test of Independence

Cell	f_o	f_e	$(f_o - f_e)$	$(f_o - f_e)^2$	$(f_o - f_e)^2/f_e$
Price/Golden Palm	23	31.53	−8.53	72.76	2.31
Price/Palm Royale	7	11.82	−4.82	23.23	1.97
Price/Palm Princess	37	23.65	13.35	178.22	7.54
Location/Golden Palm	39	28.24	10.76	115.78	4.10
Location/Palm Royale	13	10.59	2.41	5.81	0.55
Location/Palm Princess	8	21.18	−13.18	173.71	8.20
Room/Golden Palm	13	14.59	−1.59	2.53	0.17
Room/Palm Royale	5	5.47	−0.47	0.22	0.04
Room/Palm Princess	13	10.94	2.06	4.24	0.39
Other/Golden Palm	13	13.65	−0.65	0.42	0.03
Other/Palm Royale	8	5.12	2.88	8.29	1.62
Other/Palm Princess	8	10.24	−2.24	5.02	0.49
					27.41

Using the $\alpha = 0.05$ level of significance, the upper-tail critical value from the chi-square distribution with 6 degrees of freedom is 12.592 (see Table E.4). Because $\chi^2_{STAT} = 27.41 > 12.592$, you reject the null hypothesis of independence (see Figure 12.9).

FIGURE 12.9

Regions of rejection and nonrejection when testing for independence in the hotel guest satisfaction survey example at the 0.05 level of significance, with 6 degrees of freedom

The worksheet results for this test, shown in Figure 12.10, include the p-value, 0.0001. Using the p-value approach, you reject the null hypothesis of independence because the p-value $= 0.0001 < 0.05$. The p-value indicates that there is virtually no chance of having a relationship this strong or stronger in a sample between the hotel and the primary reasons for not returning, if the primary reasons for not returning are independent of the specific hotels in the entire population. Thus, there is strong evidence of a relationship between primary reason for not returning and the hotel.

FIGURE 12.10

Chi-square test worksheet for the Table 12.9 primary reason for not returning and hotel data

*Figure 12.10 displays the **ChiSquare4x3 worksheet** of the **Chi-Square Worksheets workbook**. Create this worksheet using the instructions in Section EG12.3. Read the In-Depth Excel instructions for this worksheet to learn about the formulas used in rows 4 through 19 (not shown in Figure 12.10).*

	A	B	C	D	E
1	Chi-Square Test of Independence				
2					
3		**Observed Frequencies**			
4			Hotel		
5	Reason for Not Returning	Golden Palm	Palm Royale	Palm Princess	Total
6	Price	23	7	37	67
7	Location	39	13	8	60
8	Room accommodation	13	5	13	31
9	Other	13	8	8	29
10	Total	88	33	66	187
11					
12		**Expected Frequencies**			
13			Hotel		
14	Reason for Not Returning	Golden Palm	Palm Royale	Palm Princess	Total
15	Price	31.5294	11.8235	23.6471	67
16	Location	28.2353	10.5882	21.1765	60
17	Room accommodation	14.5882	5.4706	10.9412	31
18	Other	13.6471	5.1176	10.2353	29
19	Total	88	33	66	187
20					
21		**Data**			
22	Level of Significance	0.05			
23	Number of Rows	4			
24	Number of Columns	3			
25	Degrees of Freedom	6	=(B23 - 1) * (B24 - 1)		
26					
27		**Results**			
28	Critical Value	12.5916	=CHIINV(B22, B25)		
29	Chi-Square Test Statistic	27.4104	=SUM(G15:I18)		
30	*p*-Value	0.0001	=CHIDIST(B29, B25)		
31	Reject the null hypothesis		=IF(B30 < B22, "Reject the null hypothesis",		
32			"Do not reject the null hypothesis")		
33	*Expected frequency assumption*				
34	*is met.*		=IF(OR(B15 < 1, C15 < 1, D15 < 1, B16 < 1, C16 < 1 ,D16 < 1,		
			B17 < 1, C17 < 1, D17 < 1, B18 < 1, C18 < 1, D18 < 1),			
			" is violated."," is met.")			

Examination of the observed and expected frequencies (see Table 12.11 on page 440) reveals that price is underrepresented as a reason for not returning to the Golden Palm (i.e., $f_o = 23$ and $f_e = 31.53$) but is overrepresented at the Palm Princess. Guests are more satisfied with the price at the Golden Palm than at the Palm Princess. Location is overrepresented as a reason for not returning to the Golden Palm but greatly underrepresented at the Palm Princess. Thus, guests are much more satisfied with the location of the Palm Princess than with that of the Golden Palm.

To ensure accurate results, all expected frequencies need to be large in order to use the χ^2 test when dealing with $r \times c$ contingency tables. As in the case of $2 \times c$ contingency tables in Section 12.2, all expected frequencies should be at least 1. For contingency tables in which one or more expected frequencies are less than 1, you can use the chi-square test after collapsing two or more low-frequency rows into one row (or collapsing two or more low-frequency columns into one column). Merging rows or columns usually results in expected frequencies sufficiently large to assure the accuracy of the χ^2 test.

Problems for Section 12.3

LEARNING THE BASICS

12.20 If a contingency table has three rows and four columns, how many degrees of freedom are there for the χ^2 test for independence?

12.21 When performing a χ^2 test for independence in a contingency table with r rows and c columns, determine the upper-tail critical value of the test statistic in each of the following circumstances:
a. $\alpha = 0.05, r = 4$ rows, $c = 5$ columns
b. $\alpha = 0.01, r = 4$ rows, $c = 5$ columns
c. $\alpha = 0.01, r = 4$ rows, $c = 6$ columns
d. $\alpha = 0.01, r = 3$ rows, $c = 6$ columns
e. $\alpha = 0.01, r = 6$ rows, $c = 3$ columns

APPLYING THE CONCEPTS

12.22 The Committee of 200 is an international not-for-profit association comprising preeminent businesswomen who collectively control over $100 billion annually in revenue. According to the association's Web site, **www.c200.org**, the purpose of the Committee of 200 "is to meet the needs of our membership in areas of business synergies, leadership advancement, education, mentoring, and recognition. Additionally, as an agent of change, we want to improve opportunities for women business leaders, be a source for governmental representation, and a source for research on issues relevant to women in business." The association sponsored a survey in which MBAs from top business schools were asked if executives were paid too much. The responses (in percentages, but without sample sizes) are shown in the following table (data extracted from "Snapshots: Are Execs Paid Too Much?" **www.usatoday.com**, January 15, 2007):

	Yes	No	Neutral
Women	61%	11%	28%
Men	49%	27%	24%

a. Do you think executives are paid too much?
b. Suppose that the survey was based on 100 males and 100 females. Using the 0.01 level of significance, perform a hypothesis test to see if there is a difference in attitude about executive pay between men and women.
c. Suppose that the survey was based on 200 males and 200 females. Using the 0.01 level of significance, perform a hypothesis test to see if there is a difference in attitude about executive pay between men and women.
d. Discuss the importance of sample size on reporting survey results.

12.23 *USA Today* reported on preferred types of office communication by different age groups ("Talking Face to Face vs. Group Meetings," *USA Today*, October 13, 2003, p. A1). Suppose the results were based on a survey of 500 respondents in each age group. The results are cross-classified in the following table:

	TYPE OF COMMUNICATION PREFERRED				
AGE GROUP	Group Meetings	Face-to-Face Meetings with Individuals	E-mails	Other	Total
Generation Y	180	260	50	10	500
Generation X	210	190	65	35	500
Boomer	205	195	65	35	500
Mature	200	195	50	55	500
Total	795	840	230	135	2,000

Source: *Data extracted from "Talking Face to Face vs. Group Meetings,"* USA Today, *October 13, 2003, p. A1.*

At the 0.05 level of significance, is there evidence of a relationship between age group and type of communication preferred?

 12.24 A large corporation is interested in determining whether a relationship exists between the commuting time of its employees and the level of stress-related problems observed on the job. A study of 116 workers reveals the following:

COMMUTING TIME	STRESS LEVEL			
	High	Moderate	Low	Total
Under 15 min.	9	5	18	32
15–45 min.	17	8	28	53
Over 45 min.	18	6	7	31
Total	44	19	53	116

a. At the 0.01 level of significance, is there evidence of a significant relationship between commuting time and stress level?
b. What is your answer to (a) if you use the 0.05 level of significance?

12.25 Where people turn for news is different for various age groups. A study indicated where different age groups primarily get their news:

MEDIA	AGE GROUP		
	Under 36	36–50	50+
Local TV	107	119	133
National TV	73	102	127
Radio	75	97	109
Local newspaper	52	79	107
Internet	95	83	76

At the 0.05 level of significance, is there evidence of a significant relationship between the age group and where people primarily get their news? If so, explain the relationship.

12.26 *USA Today* reported on when the decision of what to have for dinner is made. Suppose the results were based on a survey of 1,000 respondents and considered whether the household included any children under 18 years old. The results are cross-classified in the following table:

WHEN DECISION MADE	TYPE OF HOUSEHOLD		
	One Adult/No Children	Two or More Adults/ Children	Two or More Adults/ No Children
Just before eating	162	54	154
In the afternoon	73	38	69
In the morning	59	58	53
A few days before	21	64	45
The night before	15	50	45
Always eat the same thing on this night	2	16	2
Not sure	7	6	7

Source: *Data extracted from "What's for Dinner,"* **www.usatoday.com**, *January 10, 2000.*

At the 0.05 level of significance, is there evidence of a significant relationship between when the decision is made of what to have for dinner and the type of household?

12.4 McNemar Test for the Difference Between Two Proportions (Related Samples)

In Section 10.3, you used the Z test, and in Section 12.1, you used the chi-square test to examine whether there was a difference in the proportion of items of interest between two populations. These tests require that the samples selected from each population be independent. However, sometimes when you are testing differences between the proportion of items of interest between two populations, the data are collected from repeated measurements or matched samples. For example, in marketing, these situations can occur when you want to determine whether there has been a change in attitude, perception, or behavior from one time period to another. To test whether there is evidence of a difference between the proportions when the data have been collected from two related samples, you can use the **McNemar test**.

Table 12.12 presents the 2 × 2 table needed for the McNemar test.

TABLE 12.12
2 × 2 Contingency Table for the McNemar Test

CONDITION (GROUP) 1	CONDITION (GROUP) 2		
	Yes	No	Totals
Yes	A	B	A + B
No	C	D	C + D
Totals	A + C	B + D	n

where

A = number of respondents who answer yes to condition 1 and yes to condition 2
B = number of respondents who answer yes to condition 1 and no to condition 2
C = number of respondents who answer no to condition 1 and yes to condition 2
D = number of respondents who answer no to condition 1 and no to condition 2
n = number of respondents in the sample

The sample proportions are

$$p_1 = \frac{A + B}{n} = \text{proportion of respondents in the sample who answer yes to condition 1}$$

$$p_2 = \frac{A + C}{n} = \text{proportion of respondents in the sample who answer yes to condition 2}$$

The population proportions are

$$\pi_1 = \text{proportion in the population who would answer yes to condition 1}$$

$$\pi_2 = \text{proportion in the population who would answer yes to condition 2}$$

When testing differences between the proportions, you can perform a two-tail test or a one-tail test. In both cases, you use a test statistic that approximately follows the normal distribution. Equation (12.6) presents the McNemar test statistic used to test $H_0: \pi_1 = \pi_2$.

> ### McNEMAR TEST
>
> $$Z_{STAT} = \frac{B - C}{\sqrt{B + C}} \tag{12.6}$$
>
> where the Z_{STAT} test statistic is approximately normally distributed.

To illustrate the McNemar test, suppose that the business problem facing a cell phone provider was to determine the effect of a marketing campaign on the brand loyalty of cell phone customers. Data were collected from $n = 600$ participants. In the study, the participants were initially asked to state their preferences for two competing cell phone providers, Sprint and Verizon. Initially, 282 panelists said they preferred Sprint and 318 said they preferred Verizon. After exposing the set of participants to an intensive marketing campaign strategy for Verizon, the same 600 participants are again asked to state their preferences. Of the 282 panelists who previously preferred Sprint, 246 maintained their brand loyalty, but 36 switched their preference to Verizon. Of the 318 participants who initially preferred Verizon, 306 remained brand loyal, but 12 switched their preference to Sprint. These results are organized into the contingency table presented in Table 12.13.

TABLE 12.13
Brand Loyalty of Cell Phone Providers

BEFORE MARKETING CAMPAIGN	AFTER MARKETING CAMPAIGN		
	Sprint	Verizon	Total
Sprint	246	36	282
Verizon	12	306	318
Total	258	342	600

You use the McNemar test for these data because you have repeated measurements from the same set of panelists. Each participant gave a response about whether he or she preferred Sprint or Verizon before exposure to the intensive marketing campaign and then again after exposure to the campaign.

To determine whether the intensive marketing campaign was effective, you want to investigate whether there is a difference between the population proportion who favor Sprint before the campaign, π_r, versus the proportion who favor Sprint after the campaign, π_2. The null and alternative hypotheses are

$$H_0: \pi_1 = \pi_2$$
$$H_1: \pi_1 \neq \pi_2$$

Using a 0.05 level of significance, the critical values are -1.96 and $+1.96$ (see Figure 12.11), and the decision rule is

Reject H_0 if $Z_{STAT} < -1.96$ or if $Z_{STAT} > +1.96$;
otherwise, do not reject H_0.

FIGURE 12.11

Two-tail McNemar test at the 0.05 level of significance

For the data in Table 12.13,

$$A = 246 \quad B = 36 \quad C = 12 \quad D = 306$$

so that

$$p_1 = \frac{A + B}{n} = \frac{246 + 36}{600} = \frac{282}{600} = 0.47 \quad \text{and} \quad p_2 = \frac{A + C}{n} = \frac{246 + 12}{600} = \frac{258}{600} = 0.43$$

Using Equation (12.6),

$$Z = \frac{B - C}{\sqrt{B + C}} = \frac{36 - 12}{\sqrt{36 + 12}} = \frac{24}{\sqrt{48}} = 3.4641$$

Because $Z_{STAT} = 3.4641 > 1.96$, you reject H_0. Using the p-value approach (see Figure 12.12), the p-value is 0.0005. Because $0.0005 < 0.05$, you reject H_0. You can conclude that the population proportion who prefer Sprint before the intensive marketing campaign is different from the population proportion who prefer Sprint after exposure to the intensive Verizon marketing campaign. In fact, from Figure 12.12, observe that more panelists actually preferred Verizon over Sprint after exposure to the intensive marketing campaign.

FIGURE 12.12

McNemar test worksheet for brand loyalty of cell phone providers

Figure 12.12 displays the **COMPUTE worksheet** *of the* **McNemar workbook.** *Create this worksheet using the instructions in Section EG12.4.*

▲	A	B	C	D
1	McNemar Test			
2				
3	**Observed Frequencies**			
4		After Campaign		
5	Before Campaign	Sprint	Verizon	Total
6	Sprint	246	36	282
7	Verizon	12	306	318
8	Total	258	342	600
9				
10	**Data**			
11	Level of Significance	0.05		
12				
13	**Intermediate Calculations**			
14	Numerator	24	=C6 - B7	
15	Denominator	6.9282	=SQRT(C6 + B7)	
16	Z Test Statistic	3.4641	=B14/B15	
17				
18	**Two-Tail Test**			
19	Lower Critical Value	-1.9600	=NORMSINV(B11/2)	
20	Upper Critical Value	1.9600	=NORMSINV(1 - B11/2)	
21	*p*-Value	0.0005	=2 * (1 - NORMSDIST(ABS(B16)))	
22	Reject the null hypothesis		=IF(B21 < B11, "Reject the null hypothesis", "Do not reject the null hypothesis")	

Problems for Section 12.4

LEARNING THE BASICS

12.27 Given the following table for two related samples:

| | GROUP 2 | | |
GROUP 1	Yes	No	Total
Yes	46	25	71
No	16	59	75
Total	62	84	146

a. Compute the McNemar test statistic.
b. At the 0.05 level of significance, is there evidence of a difference between group 1 and group 2?

APPLYING THE CONCEPTS

✓ SELF Test **12.28** A market researcher wanted to determine whether the proportion of coffee drinkers who preferred Brand A increased as a result of an advertising campaign. A random sample of 200 coffee drinkers was selected. The results indicating preference for Brand A or Brand B prior to the beginning of the advertising campaign and after its completion are shown in the following table:

PREFERENCE PRIOR TO ADVERTISING CAMPAIGN	PREFERENCE AFTER COMPLETION OF ADVERTISING CAMPAIGN		
	Brand A	Brand B	Total
Brand A	101	9	110
Brand B	22	68	90
Total	123	77	200

a. At the 0.05 level of significance, is there evidence that the proportion of coffee drinkers who prefer Brand A is lower at the beginning of the advertising campaign than at the end of the advertising campaign?
b. Compute the p-value in (a) and interpret its meaning.

12.29 Two candidates for governor participated in a televised debate. A political pollster recorded the preferences of 500 registered voters in a random sample prior to and after the debate:

PREFERENCE PRIOR TO DEBATE	PREFERENCE AFTER DEBATE		
	Candidate A	Candidate B	Total
Candidate A	269	21	290
Candidate B	36	174	210
Total	305	195	500

a. At the 0.01 level of significance, is there evidence of a difference in the proportion of voters who favored Candidate A prior to and after the debate?
b. Compute the p-value in (a) and interpret its meaning.

12.30 A taste-testing experiment compared two brands of Chilean merlot wines. After the initial comparison, 60 preferred Brand A, and 40 preferred Brand B. The 100 respondents were then exposed to a very professional and powerful advertisement promoting Brand A. The 100 respondents were then asked to taste the two wines again and declare which brand they preferred. The results are shown in the following table:

PREFERENCE PRIOR TO ADVERTISING	PREFERENCE AFTER COMPLETION OF ADVERTISING		
	Brand A	Brand B	Total
Brand A	55	5	60
Brand B	15	25	40
Total	70	30	100

a. At the 0.05 level of significance, is there evidence that the proportion who preferred Brand A was lower before the advertising than after the advertising?
b. Compute the p-value in (a) and interpret its meaning.

12.31 The CEO of a large metropolitan health-care facility would like to assess the effects of the recent implementation of the Six Sigma management approach on customer satisfaction. A random sample of 100 patients is selected from a list of patients who were at the facility the past week and also a year ago:

SATISFIED LAST YEAR	SATISFIED NOW		
	Yes	No	Total
Yes	67	5	72
No	20	8	28
Total	87	13	100

a. At the 0.05 level of significance, is there evidence that satisfaction was lower last year, prior to introduction of Six Sigma management?
b. Compute the p-value in (a) and interpret its meaning.

12.32 The personnel director of a large department store wants to reduce absenteeism among sales associates. She decides to institute an incentive plan that provides financial rewards for sales associates who are absent fewer than five days in a given calendar year. A sample of 100 sales associates selected at the end of the second year reveals the following:

	YEAR 2		
YEAR 1	**<5 Days Absent**	**≥5 Days Absent**	**Total**
<5 days absent	32	4	36
≥5 days absent	25	39	64
Total	57	43	100

a. At the 0.05 level of significance, is there evidence that the proportion of employees absent fewer than 5 days was lower in year 1 than in year 2?

b. Compute the p-value in (a) and interpret its meaning.

12.5 Wilcoxon Rank Sum Test: Nonparametric Analysis for Two Independent Populations

"A nonparametric procedure is a statistical procedure that has (certain) desirable properties that hold under relatively mild assumptions regarding the underlying population(s) from which the data are obtained."

—Myles Hollander and Douglas A. Wolfe (reference 4, p. 1)

In Section 10.1, you used the t test for the difference between the means of two independent populations. If sample sizes are small and you cannot assume that the data in each sample are from normally distributed populations, you have two choices:

- Use the Wilcoxon rank sum test, which does not depend on the assumption of normality for the two populations.
- Use the pooled-variance t test, following some *normalizing transformation* on the data (see reference 9).

This section introduces the **Wilcoxon rank sum test** for testing whether there is a difference between two *medians*. The Wilcoxon rank sum test is almost as powerful as the pooled-variance and separate-variance t tests discussed in Section 10.1 under conditions appropriate to these tests and is likely to be more powerful when the assumptions of those t tests are not met. In addition, you can use the Wilcoxon rank sum test when you have only ordinal data, as often happens in consumer behavior and marketing research.

To perform the Wilcoxon rank sum test, you replace the values in the two samples of size n_1 and n_2 with their combined ranks (unless the data contained the ranks initially). You begin by defining $n = n_1 + n_2$ as the total sample size. Next, you assign the ranks so that rank 1 is given to the smallest of the n combined values, rank 2 is given to the second smallest, and so on, until rank n is given to the largest. If several values are tied, you assign each the average of the ranks that otherwise would have been assigned had there been no ties.

Whenever the two sample sizes are unequal, n_1 represents the smaller sample and n_2 the larger sample. The Wilcoxon rank sum test statistic, T_1, is defined as the sum of the ranks assigned to the n_1 values in the smaller sample. (For equal-sized samples, either sample may be used for determining T_1.) For any integer value n, the sum of the first n consecutive integers is $n(n + 1)/2$. Therefore, the test statistic T_1 plus T_2, the sum of the ranks assigned to the n_2 items in the second sample, must equal $n(n + 1)/2$. You can use Equation (12.7) to check the accuracy of your rankings.

CHECKING THE RANKINGS

$$T_1 + T_2 = \frac{n(n + 1)}{2} \qquad (12.7)$$

When n_1 and n_2 are both ≤ 10, you use Table E.6 to find the critical values of the test statistic T_1. For a two-tail test, you reject the null hypothesis (see Panel A of Figure 12.13) if the computed value of T_1 equals or is greater than the upper critical value, or if T_1 is less than or equal to the lower critical value. For one-tail tests having the alternative hypothesis $H_1: M_1 < M_2$ [i.e., the median of population 1 (M_1) is less than the median of population 2 (M_2)], you reject the null hypothesis if the observed value of T_1 is less than or equal to the lower critical value (see Panel B of Figure 12.13). For one-tail tests having the alternative hypothesis $H_1: M_1 > M_2$, you reject the null hypothesis if the observed value of T_1 equals or is greater than the upper critical value (see Panel C of Figure 12.13).

FIGURE 12.13

Regions of rejection and nonrejection using the Wilcoxon rank sum test

- Region of Rejection
- Region of Nonrejection

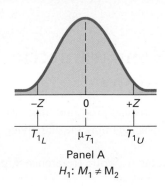

Panel A

$H_1: M_1 \neq M_2$

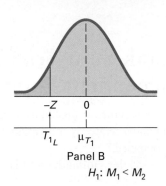

Panel B

$H_1: M_1 < M_2$

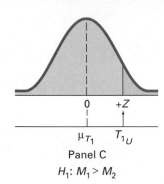

Panel C

$H_1: M_1 > M_2$

For large sample sizes, the test statistic T_1 is approximately normally distributed, with the mean, μ_{T_1}, equal to

$$\mu_{T_1} = \frac{n_1(n + 1)}{2}$$

and the standard deviation, σ_{T_1}, equal to

$$\sigma_{T_1} = \sqrt{\frac{n_1 n_2(n + 1)}{12}}$$

Therefore, Equation (12.8) defines the standardized Z test statistic.

LARGE SAMPLE WILCOXON RANK SUM TEST

$$Z_{STAT} = \frac{T_1 - \dfrac{n_1(n + 1)}{2}}{\sqrt{\dfrac{n_1 n_2(n + 1)}{12}}} \qquad (12.8)$$

where the test statistic Z_{STAT} approximately follows a standardized normal distribution.

You use Equation (12.8) for testing the null hypothesis when the sample sizes are outside the range of Table E.6. Based on α, the level of significance selected, you reject the null hypothesis if the Z_{STAT} test statistic falls in the rejection region.

To study an application of the Wilcoxon rank sum test, return to the Using Statistics scenario of Chapter 10 concerning sales of BLK Cola for the two locations: normal shelf display and end-aisle location (see page 335). If you cannot assume that the populations are normally distributed, you can use the Wilcoxon rank sum test for evaluating possible differences in the median sales for the two display locations.[2] The data (stored in Cola) and the combined ranks are shown in Table 12.14.

[2]To test for differences in the median sales between the two locations, you must assume that the distributions of sales in both populations are identical except for differences in location (i.e., the medians).

TABLE 12.14

Forming the Combined Rankings

Sales			
Normal Display $(n_1 = 10)$	**Combined Ranking**	**End-Aisle Display** $(n_2 = 10)$	**Combined Ranking**
22	1.0	52	5.5
34	3.0	71	14.0
52	5.5	76	15.0
62	10.0	54	7.0
30	2.0	67	13.0
40	4.0	83	17.0
64	11.0	66	12.0
84	18.5	90	20.0
56	8.0	77	16.0
59	9.0	84	18.5

Source: *Data are taken from Table 10.1 on page 337.*

Because you have not stated in advance which display location is likely to have a higher median, you use a two-tail test with the following null and alternative hypotheses:

$$H_0: M_1 = M_2 \text{ (the median sales are equal)}$$

$$H_1: M_1 \neq M_2 \text{ (the median sales are not equal)}$$

Now you need to compute T_1, the sum of the ranks assigned to the *smaller* sample. When the sample sizes are equal, as in this example, you can define either sample as the group from which to compute T_1. Choosing the normal display as the first sample,

$$T_1 = 1 + 3 + 5.5 + 10 + 2 + 4 + 11 + 18.5 + 8 + 9 = 72$$

As a check on the ranking procedure, you compute T_2 from

$$T_2 = 5.5 + 14 + 15 + 7 + 13 + 17 + 12 + 20 + 16 + 18.5 = 138$$

and then use Equation (12.7) on page 447 to show that the sum of the first $n = 20$ integers in the combined ranking is equal to $T_1 + T_2$:

$$T_1 + T_2 = \frac{n(n + 1)}{2}$$

$$72 + 138 = \frac{20(21)}{2} = 210$$

$$210 = 210$$

Next, you use Table E.6 to determine the lower- and upper-tail critical values for the test statistic T_1. From Table 12.15, a portion of Table E.6, observe that for a level of significance of 0.05, the critical values are 78 and 132. The decision rule is

Reject H_0 if $T_1 \leq 78$ or if $T_1 \geq 132$;

otherwise, do not reject H_0.

TABLE 12.15

Finding the Lower- and Upper-Tail Critical Values for the Wilcoxon Rank Sum Test Statistic, T_1, Where $n_1 = 10$, $n_2 = 10$, and $\alpha = 0.05$

α			n_1						
n_2	One-Tail	Two-Tail	4	5	6	7	8	9	10
					(Lower, Upper)				
9	.05	.10	16,40	24,51	33,63	43,76	54,90	66,105	
	.025	.05	14,42	22,53	31,65	40,79	51,93	62,109	
	.01	.02	13,43	20,55	28,68	37,82	47,97	59,112	
	.005	.01	11,45	18,57	26,70	35,84	45,99	56,115	
10	.05	.10	17,43	26,54	35,67	45,81	56,96	69,111	82,128
	.025	.05	15,45	23,57	32,70	42,84	53,99	65,115	78,132
	.01	.02	13,47	21,59	29,73	39,87	49,103	61,119	74,136
	.005	.01	12,48	19,61	27,75	37,89	47,105	58,122	71,139

Source: *Extracted from Table E.6.*

Because the test statistic $T_1 = 72 < 78$, you reject H_0. There is evidence of a significant difference in the median sales for the two display locations. Because the sum of the ranks is higher for the end-aisle display, you conclude that median sales are higher for the end-aisle display. From the Figure 12.14 worksheet solution, observe that the p-value is 0.0126, which is less than $\alpha = 0.05$. The p-value indicates that if the medians of the two populations are equal, the chance of finding a difference at least this large in the samples is only 0.0126.

FIGURE 12.14

Wilcoxon rank sum test worksheet for the BLK Cola sales example

Figure 12.14 displays the COMPUTE worksheet of the Wilcoxon workbook. The COMPUTE worksheet uses the sorted ranks of the SortedRanks worksheet to help compute the intermediate calculations. Create these worksheets using the instructions in Section EG12.5.

	A	B	
1	Wilcoxon Rank Sum Test		
2			
3	**Data**		
4	Level of Significance	0.05	
5			
6	**Population 1 Sample**		
7	Sample Size	10	=COUNTIF(SortedRanks!A2:A21,"Normal")
8	Sum of Ranks	72	=SUMIF(SortedRanks!A2:A21,"Normal",SortedRanks!C2:C21)
9	**Population 2 Sample**		
10	Sample Size	10	=COUNTIF(SortedRanks!A2:A21,"End-Aisle")
11	Sum of Ranks	138	=SUMIF(SortedRanks!A2:A21,"End-Aisle",SortedRanks!C2:C21)
12			
13	**Intermediate Calculations**		
14	Total Sample Size n	20	=B7 + B10
15	T1 Test Statistic	72	=IF(B7 <= B10, B8, B11)
16	T1 Mean	105	=IF(B7 <= B10, B7 * (B14 + 1)/2, B10 * (B14 + 1)/2)
17	Standard Error of T1	13.2288	=SQRT(B7 * B10 * (B14 + 1)/12)
18	Z Test Statistic	-2.4946	=(B15 - B16)/B17
19			
20	**Two-Tail Test**		
21	Lower Critical Value	-1.9600	=NORMSINV(B4/2)
22	Upper Critical Value	1.9600	=NORMSINV(1 - B4/2)
23	p -Value	0.0126	=2 * (1 - NORMSDIST(ABS(B18)))
24	Reject the null hypothesis		=IF(B23 < B4, "Reject the null hypothesis", "Do not reject the null hypothesis")

Table E.6 shows the lower and upper critical values of the Wilcoxon rank sum test statistic, T_1, but only for situations in which both n_1 and n_2 are less than or equal to 10. If either one or both of the sample sizes are greater than 10, you *must* use the large-sample Z approximation formula [Equation (12.8) on page 448]. However, you can also use this approximation formula for small sample sizes. To demonstrate the large-sample Z approximation formula, consider the BLK Cola sales data. Using Equation (12.8),

$$Z_{STAT} = \dfrac{T_1 - \dfrac{n_1(n + 1)}{2}}{\sqrt{\dfrac{n_1 n_2(n + 1)}{12}}}$$

$$= \dfrac{72 - \dfrac{(10)(21)}{2}}{\sqrt{\dfrac{(10)(10)(21)}{12}}}$$

$$= \dfrac{72 - 105}{13.2288} = -2.4946$$

Because $Z_{STAT} = -2.4946 < -1.96$, the critical value of Z at the 0.05 level of significance (or p-value $= 0.0126 < 0.05$), you reject H_0.

Problems for Section 12.5

LEARNING THE BASICS

12.33 Using Table E.6, determine the lower- and upper-tail critical values for the Wilcoxon rank sum test statistic, T_1, in each of the following two-tail tests:
a. $\alpha = 0.10, n_1 = 6, n_2 = 8$
b. $\alpha = 0.05, n_1 = 6, n_2 = 8$
c. $\alpha = 0.01, n_1 = 6, n_2 = 8$
d. Given your results in (a) through (c), what do you conclude regarding the width of the region of nonrejection as the selected level of significance, α, gets smaller?

12.34 Using Table E.6, determine the lower-tail critical value for the Wilcoxon rank sum test statistic, T_1, in each of the following one-tail tests:
a. $\alpha = 0.05, n_1 = 6, n_2 = 8$
b. $\alpha = 0.025, n_1 = 6, n_2 = 8$
c. $\alpha = 0.01, n_1 = 6, n_2 = 8$
d. $\alpha = 0.005, n_1 = 6, n_2 = 8$

12.35 The following information is available for two samples selected from independent populations:

Sample 1: $n_1 = 7$ Assigned ranks: 4 1 8 2 5 10 11

Sample 2: $n_2 = 9$ Assigned ranks: 7 16 12 9 3 14 13 6 15

What is the value of T_1 if you are testing the null hypothesis $H_0: M_1 = M_2$?

12.36 In Problem 12.35, what are the lower- and upper-tail critical values for the test statistic T_1 from Table E.6 if you use a 0.05 level of significance and the alternative hypothesis is $H_1: M_1 \neq M_2$?

12.37 In Problems 12.35 and 12.36, what is your statistical decision?

12.38 The following information is available for two samples selected from independent and similarly shaped right-skewed populations:

Sample 1: $n_1 = 5$ 1.1 2.3 2.9 3.6 14.7

Sample 2: $n_2 = 6$ 2.8 4.4 4.4 5.2   6.0 18.5

a. Replace the observed values with the corresponding ranks (where $1 =$ smallest value; $n = n_1 + n_2 = 11 =$ largest value) in the combined samples.
b. What is the value of the test statistic T_1?
c. Compute the value of T_2, the sum of the ranks in the larger sample.
d. To check the accuracy of your rankings, use Equation (12.7) on page 447 to demonstrate that

$$T_1 + T_2 = \dfrac{n(n + 1)}{2}$$

12.39 From Problem 12.38, at the 0.05 level of significance, determine the lower-tail critical value for the Wilcoxon rank sum test statistic, T_1, if you want to test the null hypothesis, $H_0: M_1 \geq M_2$, against the one-tail alternative, $H_1: M_1 < M_2$.

12.40 In Problems 12.38 and 12.39, what is your statistical decision?

APPLYING THE CONCEPTS

12.41 A vice president for marketing recruits 20 college graduates for management training. Each of the 20 individuals is randomly assigned, 10 each, to one of two groups. A "traditional" method of training (T) is used in one group, and an "experimental" method (E) is used in the other. After the graduates spend six months on the job, the vice president ranks them on the basis of their performance, from 1 (worst) to 20 (best), with the following results (stored in the file **TestRank**):

T: 1 2 3 5   9 10 12 13 14 15

E: 4 6 7 8 11 16 17 18 19 20

Is there evidence of a difference in the median performance between the two methods? (Use $\alpha = 0.05$.)

12.42 Wine experts Gaiter and Brecher use a six-category scale when rating wines: Yech, OK, Good, Very Good, Delicious, and Delicious! (data extracted from D. Gaiter and J. Brecher, "A Good U.S. Cabernet Is Hard to Find," *The Wall Street Journal*, May 19, 2006, p. W7). Suppose Gaiter and Brecher tested a random sample of eight inexpensive California Cabernets and a random sample of eight inexpensive Washington Cabernets. *Inexpensive* is defined as a suggested retail value in the United States of under $20. The data, stored in **Cabernet**, are as follows:

California—Good, Delicious, Yech, OK, OK, Very Good, Yech, OK

Washington—Very Good, OK, Delicious!, Very Good, Delicious, Good, Delicious, Delicious!

a. Are the data collected by rating wines using this scale nominal, ordinal, interval, or ratio?

b. Why is the two-sample *t* test defined in Section 10.1 inappropriate to test the mean rating of California Cabernets versus Washington Cabernets?

c. Is there evidence of a significance difference in the median rating of California Cabernets and Washington Cabernets? (Use $\alpha = 0.05$.)

12.43 In intaglio printing, a design or figure is carved beneath the surface of hard metal or stone. Suppose that an experiment is designed to compare differences in surface hardness of steel plates used in intaglio printing (measured in indentation numbers), based on two different surface conditions—untreated and treated by lightly polishing with emery paper. In the experiment, 40 steel plates are randomly assigned—20 that are untreated and 20 that are treated. The data are shown in the following table and stored in **Intaglio**:

Untreated		Treated	
164.368	177.135	158.239	150.226
159.018	163.903	138.216	155.620
153.871	167.802	168.006	151.233
165.096	160.818	149.654	158.653
157.184	167.433	145.456	151.204
154.496	163.538	168.178	150.869
160.920	164.525	154.321	161.657
164.917	171.230	162.763	157.016
169.091	174.964	161.020	156.670
175.276	166.311	167.706	147.920

a. Is there evidence of a difference in the median surface hardness between untreated and treated steel plates? (Use $\alpha = 0.05$.)

b. What assumptions must you make in (a)?

c. Compare the results of (a) with those of Problem 10.14(a) on page 345.

 12.44 The management of a hotel was concerned with increasing the return rate for hotel guests. One aspect of first impressions by guests relates to the time it takes to deliver a guest's luggage to the room after check-in to the hotel. A random sample of 20 deliveries on a particular day were selected in Wing A of the hotel, and a random sample of 20 deliveries were selected in Wing B. The results are stored in **Luggage**.

a. Is there evidence of a difference in the median delivery times in the two wings of the hotel? (Use $\alpha = 0.05$.)

b. Compare the results of (a) with those of Problem 10.67 on page 370.

12.45 The lengths of life (in hours) of a sample of 40 100-watt light bulbs produced by Manufacturer A and a sample of 40 100-watt light bulbs produced by Manufacturer B are stored in **Bulbs**.

a. Using a 0.05 level of significance, is there evidence of a difference in the median life of bulbs produced by the two manufacturers?

b. What assumptions must you make in (a)?

c. Compare the results of (a) with those of Problem 10.66 (a) on page 370. Discuss.

12.46 Nondestructive evaluation is used to measure the properties of components or materials without causing any permanent physical change to the components or materials. It includes the determination of properties of materials and the classification of flaws by size, shape, type, and location. Nondestructive evaluation is very effective for detecting surface flaws and characterizing surface properties of electrically conductive materials. Data were collected that classified each component as having a flaw or not, based on manual inspection and operator judgment, and also reported the size of the crack in the material. Do the components classified as unflawed have a smaller median crack size than components classified as flawed? The results in terms of crack size (in inches) are stored in **Crack** and shown below (data extracted from B. D. Olin and W. Q. Meeker, "Applications of Statistical Methods to Nondestructive Evaluation," *Technometrics*, 38, 1996, p. 101).

Unflawed

0.003 0.004 0.012 0.014 0.021 0.023 0.024 0.030 0.034
0.041 0.041 0.042 0.043 0.045 0.057 0.063 0.074 0.076

Flawed

0.022	0.026	0.026	0.030	0.031	0.034	0.042	0.043	0.044
0.046	0.046	0.052	0.055	0.058	0.060	0.060	0.070	0.071
0.073	0.073	0.078	0.079	0.079	0.083	0.090	0.095	0.095
0.096	0.100	0.102	0.103	0.105	0.114	0.119	0.120	0.130
0.160	0.306	0.328	0.440					

a. Using a 0.05 level of significance, is there evidence that the median crack size is less for unflawed components than for flawed components?
b. What assumptions must you make in (a)?
c. Compare the results of (a) with those of Problem 10.17 (a) on page 345. Discuss.

12.47 A bank with a branch located in a commercial district of a city has developed an improved process for serving customers during the noon-to-1 P.M. lunch period. The waiting time (defined as the time elapsed from when the customer enters the line until he or she reaches the teller window) needs to be shortened to increase customer satisfaction. A random sample of 15 customers is selected (and stored in Bank1); the results (in minutes) are as follows:

| 4.21 | 5.55 | 3.02 | 5.13 | 4.77 | 2.34 | 3.54 | 3.20 |
| 4.50 | 6.10 | 0.38 | 5.12 | 6.46 | 6.19 | 3.79 | |

Another branch, located in a residential area, is also concerned with the noon-to-1 P.M. lunch period. A random sample of 15 customers is selected (and stored in the file Bank2); the results (in minutes) are as follows:

| 9.66 | 5.90 | 8.02 | 5.79 | 8.73 | 3.82 | 8.01 | 8.35 |
| 10.49 | 6.68 | 5.64 | 4.08 | 6.17 | 9.91 | 5.47 | |

a. Is there evidence of a difference in the median waiting time between the two branches? (Use $\alpha = 0.05$.)
b. What assumptions must you make in (a)?
c. Compare the results (a) with those of Problem 10.12 (a) on page 344. Discuss.

12.48 Digital cameras have taken over the majority of the point-and-shoot camera market. One of the important features of a camera is the battery life, as measured by the number of shots taken until the battery needs to be recharged. The file DigitalCameras contains the battery life of 29 subcompact cameras and 16 compact cameras (data extracted from "Digital Cameras," *Consumer Reports*, July 2009, pp. 28–29).
a. Is there evidence of a difference in the median battery life between subcompact cameras and compact cameras? (Use $\alpha = 0.05$.)
b. What assumptions must you make in (a)?
c. Compare the results of (a) with those of Problem 10.11 (a) on page 344. Discuss.

12.6 Kruskal-Wallis Rank Test: Nonparametric Analysis for the One-Way ANOVA

If the normality assumption of the one-way ANOVA F test is violated, you can use the Kruskal-Wallis rank test. The Kruskal-Wallis rank test for differences among c medians (where $c > 2$) is an extension of the Wilcoxon rank sum test for two independent populations, discussed in Section 12.5. Thus, the Kruskal-Wallis test has the same power relative to the one-way ANOVA F test that the Wilcoxon rank sum test has relative to the t test.

You use the **Kruskal-Wallis rank test** to test whether c independent groups have equal medians. The null hypothesis is

$$H_0: M_1 = M_2 = \cdots = M_c$$

and the alternative hypothesis is

$$H_1: \text{Not all } M_j \text{ are equal (where } j = 1, 2, \ldots, c).$$

To use the Kruskal-Wallis rank test, you first replace the values in the c samples with their combined ranks (if necessary). Rank 1 is given to the smallest of the combined values and rank n to the largest of the combined values (where $n = n_1 + n_2 + \cdots + n_c$). If any values are tied, you assign them the mean of the ranks they would have otherwise been assigned if ties had not been present in the data.

The Kruskal-Wallis test is an alternative to the one-way ANOVA F test. Instead of comparing each of the c group means against the grand mean, the Kruskal-Wallis test compares the mean rank in each of the c groups against the overall mean rank, based on all n combined values. Equation (12.9) defines the Kruskal-Wallis test statistic, H.

KRUSKAL-WALLIS RANK TEST FOR DIFFERENCES AMONG c MEDIANS

$$H = \left[\frac{12}{n(n+1)} \sum_{j=1}^{c} \frac{T_j^2}{n_j} \right] - 3(n+1) \qquad \textbf{(12.9)}$$

where

n = total number of values over the combined samples

n_j = number of values in the jth sample ($j = 1, 2, \ldots, c$)

T_j = sum of the ranks assigned to the jth sample

T_j^2 = square of the sum of the ranks assigned to the jth sample

c = number of groups

If there is a significant difference among the c groups, the mean rank differs considerably from group to group. In the process of squaring these differences, the test statistic H becomes large. If there are no differences present, the test statistic H is small because the mean of the ranks assigned in each group should be very similar from group to group.

As the sample sizes in each group get large (i.e., greater than 5), you can approximate the test statistic, H, by the chi-square distribution with $c - 1$ degrees of freedom. Thus, you reject the null hypothesis if the computed value of H is greater than the upper-tail critical value (see Figure 12.15). Therefore, the decision rule is

$$\text{Reject } H_0 \text{ if } H > \chi_\alpha^2;$$

$$\text{otherwise, do not reject } H_0.$$

FIGURE 12.15

Determining the rejection region for the Kruskal-Wallis test

To illustrate the Kruskal-Wallis rank test for differences among c medians, return to the Using Statistics scenario from Chapter 11 on page 381, concerning the strength of parachutes. If you cannot assume that the tensile strength of the parachutes is normally distributed in all c groups, you can use the Kruskal-Wallis rank test.

The null hypothesis is that the median tensile strengths of parachutes for the four suppliers are equal. The alternative hypothesis is that at least one of the suppliers differs from the others:

$$H_0: M_1 = M_2 = M_3 = M_4$$

$$H_1: \text{Not all } M_j \text{ are equal (where } j = 1, 2, 3, 4).$$

Table 12.16 presents the data (stored in the file **Parachute**), along with the corresponding ranks.

TABLE 12.16

Tensile Strength and Ranks of Parachutes Woven from Synthetic Fibers from Four Suppliers

	Supplier							
	1		**2**		**3**		**4**	
Amount	**Rank**	**Amount**	**Rank**	**Amount**	**Rank**	**Amount**	**Rank**
18.5	4	26.3	20	20.6	8	25.4	19
24.0	13.5	25.3	18	25.2	17	19.9	5.5
17.2	1	24.0	13.5	20.8	9	22.6	11
19.9	5.5	21.2	10	24.7	16	17.5	2
18.0	3	24.5	15	22.9	12	20.4	7

In converting the 20 tensile strengths to ranks, observe in Table 12.16 that the third parachute for Supplier 1 has the lowest tensile strength, 17.2. It is assigned a rank of 1. The fourth value for Supplier 1 and the second value for Supplier 4 each have a value of 19.9. Because they are tied for ranks 5 and 6, they are assigned the rank 5.5. Finally, the first value for Supplier 2 is the largest value, 26.3, and is assigned a rank of 20.

After all the ranks are assigned, you compute the sum of the ranks for each group:

Rank sums: $T_1 = 27$ $T_2 = 76.5$ $T_3 = 62$ $T_4 = 44.5$

As a check on the rankings, recall from Equation (12.7) on page 447 that for any integer n, the sum of the first n consecutive integers is $n(n + 1)/2$. Therefore

$$T_1 + T_2 + T_3 + T_4 = \frac{n(n + 1)}{2}$$

$$27 + 76.5 + 62 + 44.5 = \frac{(20)(21)}{2}$$

$$210 = 210$$

To test the null hypothesis of equal population medians, you calculate the test statistic H using Equation (12.9) on page 454:

$$H = \left[\frac{12}{n(n + 1)}\sum_{j=1}^{c}\frac{T_j^2}{n_j}\right] - 3(n + 1)$$

$$= \left\{\frac{12}{(20)(21)}\left[\frac{(27)^2}{5} + \frac{(76.5)^2}{5} + \frac{(62)^2}{5} + \frac{(44.5)^2}{5}\right]\right\} - 3(21)$$

$$= \left(\frac{12}{420}\right)(2,481.1) - 63 = 7.8886$$

The test statistic H approximately follows a chi-square distribution with $c - 1$ degrees of freedom. Using a 0.05 level of significance, χ_α^2, the upper-tail critical value of the chi-square distribution with $c - 1 = 3$ degrees of freedom is 7.815 (see Table 12.17). Because the computed

TABLE 12.17

Finding χ_α^2, the Upper-Tail Critical Value for the Kruskal-Wallis Rank Test, at the 0.05 Level of Significance with 3 Degrees of Freedom

	Cumulative Area									
	.005	.01	.025	.05	.10	.25	.75	.90	.95	.975
	Upper-Tail Area									
Degrees of Freedom	.995	.99	.975	.95	.90	.75	.25	.10	.05	.025
1	—	—	0.001	0.004	0.016	0.102	1.323	2.706	3.841	5.024
2	0.010	0.020	0.051	0.103	0.211	0.575	2.773	4.605	5.991	7.378
3	0.072	0.115	0.216	0.352	0.584	1.213	4.108	6.251	7.815	9.348
4	0.207	0.297	0.484	0.711	1.064	1.923	5.385	7.779	9.488	11.143
5	0.412	0.554	0.831	1.145	1.610	2.675	6.626	9.236	11.071	12.833

Source: *Extracted from Table E.4.*

value of the test statistic $H = 7.8886$ is greater than the critical value, you reject the null hypothesis and conclude that the median tensile strength is not the same for all the suppliers. You reach the same conclusion by using the p-value approach, because, as shown in Figure 12.16, the p-value $= 0.0484 < 0.05$.

FIGURE 12.16

Kruskal-Wallis rank test worksheet for differences among the four medians in the parachute example

Figure 12.16 displays the KruskalWallis4 worksheet of the Kruskal-Wallis Worksheets workbook. Create this worksheet using the instructions in Section EG12.6.

	A	B	C	D	E	F	G
1	Kruskal-Wallis Rank Test						
2							
3	**Data**				**Calculations**		
4	Level of Significance	0.05		Group	Sample Size	Sum of Ranks	Mean Ranks
5				1	5	27	5.4
6	**Intermediate Calculations**			2	5	76.5	15.3
7	Sum of Squared Ranks/Sample Size	2481.1		3	5	62	12.4
8	Sum of Sample Sizes	20		4	5	44.5	8.9
9	Number of Groups	4					
10							
11	**Test Result**						
12	H Test Statistic	7.8886	=(12/(B8 * (B8 + 1))) * B7 - (3 * (B8 + 1))				
13	Critical Value	7.8147	=CHIINV(B4, B9 - 1)				
14	p -Value	0.0484	=CHIDIST(B12, B9 - 1)				
15	Reject the null hypothesis		=IF(B14 < B4, "Reject the null hypothesis", "Do not reject the null hypothesis")				

Also

Cell B7: $= (G5 * F5) + (G6 * F6) + (G7 * F7) + (G8 * F8)$

Cell B8: $=SUM(E5:E8)$

You reject the null hypothesis and conclude that there is evidence of a significant difference in median tensile strength among the suppliers. At this point, you could simultaneously compare all pairs of suppliers to determine which ones differ (see reference 2).

The following assumptions are needed to use the Kruskal-Wallis rank test:

- The c samples are randomly and independently selected from their respective populations.
- The underlying variable is continuous.
- The data provide at least a set of ranks, both within and among the c samples.
- The c populations have the same variability.
- The c populations have the same shape.

The Kruskal-Wallis procedure makes less stringent assumptions than does the F test. If you ignore the last two assumptions (variability and shape), you can still use the Kruskal-Wallis rank test to determine whether at least one of the populations differs from the other populations in some characteristic—such as central tendency, variation, or shape.

To use the F test, you must assume that the c samples are from normal populations that have equal variances. When the more stringent assumptions of the F test hold, you should use the F test instead of the Kruskal-Wallis test because it has slightly more power to detect significant differences among groups. However, if the assumptions of the F test do not hold, you should use the Kruskal-Wallis test.

Problems for Section 12.6

LEARNING THE BASICS

12.49 What is the upper-tail critical value from the chi-square distribution if you use the Kruskal-Wallis rank test for comparing the medians in six populations at the 0.01 level of significance?

12.50 For this problem, use the results of Problem 12.49.
a. State the decision rule for testing the null hypothesis that all six groups have equal population medians.

b. What is your statistical decision if the computed value of the test statistic H is 13.77?

APPLYING THE CONCEPTS

12.51 A pet food company is looking to expand its product line beyond its current kidney- and shrimp-based cat foods. The company developed two new products, one based on chicken livers and the other based on salmon. The company conducted an experiment to compare the two new products with its two existing ones as well as a generic beef-based product sold in a supermarket chain.

For the experiment, a sample of 50 cats from the population at a local animal shelter was selected. Ten cats were randomly assigned to each of the five products being tested. Each of the cats was then presented with 3 ounces of the selected food in a dish at feeding time. The researchers defined the variable to be measured as the number of ounces of food that the cat consumed within a 10-minute time interval that began when the filled dish was presented. The results for this experiment are summarized in the following table and stored in CatFood:

Kidney	Shrimp	Chicken Liver	Salmon	Beef
2.37	2.26	2.29	1.79	2.09
2.62	2.69	2.23	2.33	1.87
2.31	2.25	2.41	1.96	1.67
2.47	2.45	2.68	2.05	1.64
2.59	2.34	2.25	2.26	2.16
2.62	2.37	2.17	2.24	1.75
2.34	2.22	2.37	1.96	1.18
2.47	2.56	2.26	1.58	1.92
2.45	2.36	2.45	2.18	1.32
2.32	2.59	2.57	1.93	1.94

a. At the 0.05 level of significance, is there evidence of a significant difference in the median amount of food eaten among the various products?

b. Compare the results of (a) with those of Problem 11.13 (a) on page 395.

c. Which test is more appropriate for these data, the Kruskal-Wallis rank test or the one-way ANOVA *F* test? Explain.

✓ **SELF Test** **12.52** A hospital conducted a study of the waiting time in its emergency room. The hospital has a main campus, along with three satellite locations. Management had a business objective of reducing waiting time for emergency room cases that did not require immediate attention. To study this, a random sample of 15 emergency room cases at each location were selected on a particular day, and the waiting time (recorded from check-in to when the patient was called into the clinic area) was measured. The results are stored in ERWaiting.

a. At the 0.05 level of significance, is there evidence of a difference in the median waiting times in the four locations?

b. Compare the results of (a) with those of Problem 11.9 (a) on page 394.

12.53 The file SavingsRate contains the yields for a money market account, a one-year certificate of deposit (CD), and a five-year CD for 23 banks in the metropolitan New York area, as of May 28, 2009 (extracted from **www.bankrate.com**, May 28, 2009).

a. At the 0.05 level of significance, is there evidence of a difference in the median yields of the different accounts?

b. Compare the results of (a) with those of Problem 11.11 (a) on page 394.

12.54 An advertising agency has been hired by a manufacturer of pens to develop an advertising campaign for the upcoming holiday season. To prepare for this project, the research director decides to initiate a study of the effect of advertising on product perception. An experiment is designed to compare five different advertisements. Advertisement A greatly undersells the pen's characteristics. Advertisement B slightly undersells the pen's characteristics. Advertisement C slightly oversells the pen's characteristics. Advertisement D greatly oversells the pen's characteristics. Advertisement E attempts to correctly state the pen's characteristics. A sample of 30 adult respondents, taken from a larger focus group, is randomly assigned to the five advertisements (so that there are six respondents to each). After reading the advertisement and developing a sense of product expectation, all respondents unknowingly receive the same pen to evaluate. The respondents are permitted to test the pen and the plausibility of the advertising copy. The respondents are then asked to rate the pen from 1 to 7 on the product characteristic scales of appearance, durability, and writing performance. The *combined* scores of three ratings (appearance, durability, and writing performance) for the 30 respondents (stored in Pen) are as follows:

A	B	C	D	E
15	16	8	5	12
18	17	7	6	19
17	21	10	13	18
19	16	15	11	12
19	19	14	9	17
20	17	14	10	14

a. At the 0.05 level of significance, is there evidence of a difference in the median ratings of the five advertisements?

b. Compare the results of (a) with those of Problem 11.10 (a) on page 394.

c. Which test is more appropriate for these data, the Kruskal-Wallis rank test or the one-way ANOVA *F* test? Explain.

12.55 A sporting goods manufacturing company wanted to compare the distance traveled by golf balls produced using each of four different designs. Ten balls of each design were manufactured and brought to the local golf course for the club professional to test. The order in which the balls were hit with the same club from the first tee was randomized so that the pro did not know which type of ball was being hit. All 40 balls were hit in a short period of time, during which the environmental conditions were essentially the same. The results (distance traveled in yards) for the four designs are stored in Golfball:

a. At the 0.05 level of significance, is there evidence of a difference in the median distances traveled by the golf balls with different designs?

b. Compare the results of (a) with those of Problem 11.14 (a) on page 395.

12.56 Students in a business statistics course performed an experiment to test the strength of four brands of trash bags.

One-pound weights were placed into a bag, one at a time, until the bag broke. A total of 40 bags were used (10 for each brand). The file Trashbags gives the weight (in pounds) required to break the trash bags.

a. At the 0.05 level of significance, is there evidence of a difference in the median strength of the four brands of trash bags?

b. Compare the results in (a) to those in Problem 11.8 (a) on page 394.

12.7 🌐➤ *Online Topic:* Chi-Square Test for the Variance or Standard Deviation

When analyzing numerical data, sometimes you need to make conclusions about the population variance or standard deviation. To study this topic, read the **Section 12.7** online topic file that is available on this book's companion Web site. (See Appendix Section D.8 to learn how to access the online topic files.)

USING STATISTICS @ T.C. Resort Properties Revisited

I n the Using Statistics scenario, you were the manager of T.C. Resort Properties, a collection of five upscale hotels located on two tropical islands. To assess the quality of services being provided by your hotels, guests are encouraged to complete a satisfaction survey when they check out. You analyzed the data from these surveys to determine the overall satisfaction with the services provided, the likelihood that the guests will return to the hotel, and the reasons given by some guests for not wanting to return.

On one island, T.C. Resort Properties operates the Beachcomber and Windsurfer hotels. You performed a chi-square test for the difference in two proportions and concluded that a greater proportion of guests are willing to return to the Beachcomber Hotel than to the Windsurfer. On the other island, T.C. Resort Properties operates the Golden Palm, Palm Royale, and Palm Princess hotels. To see if guest satisfaction was the same among the three hotels, you performed a chi-square test for the differences among more than two proportions. The test confirmed that the three proportions are not equal, and guests are most likely to return to the Palm Royale and least likely to return to the Golden Palm.

In addition, you investigated whether the reasons given for not returning to the Golden Palm, Palm Royale, and Palm Princess were unique to a certain hotel or common to all three hotels. By performing a chi-square test of independence, you determined that the reasons given for wanting to return or not depended on which hotel they had been staying in. By examining the observed and expected frequencies, you concluded that guests are more satisfied with the price at the Golden Palm and were much more satisfied with the location of the Palm Princess. Guest satisfaction with room accommodations was not significantly different among the three hotels.

SUMMARY

Figure 12.17 presents a roadmap for this chapter. First, you used hypothesis testing for analyzing categorical response data from two independent samples and from more than two independent samples. In addition, the rules of probability from Section 4.2 were extended to the hypothesis of independence in the joint responses to two categorical variables.

You also used the McNemar test to study situations where the samples were not independent. In addition to these tests, you studied two nonparametric tests. You used the Wilcoxon rank sum test when the assumptions of the *t* test for two independent samples were violated and the Kruskal-Wallis test when the assumptions of the one-way ANOVA *F* test were violated.

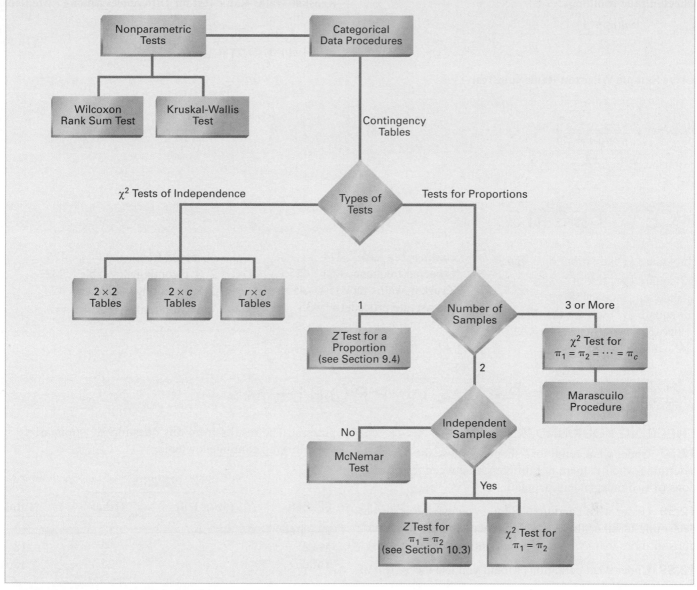

FIGURE 12.17   Roadmap of Chapter 12

KEY EQUATIONS

χ^2 Test Statistic

$$\chi^2_{STAT} = \sum_{all\ cells} \frac{(f_0 - f_e)^2}{f_e} \qquad (12.1)$$

Computing the Estimated Overall Proportion for Two Groups

$$\bar{p} = \frac{X_1 + X_2}{n_1 + n_2} = \frac{X}{n} \qquad (12.2)$$

Computing the Estimated Overall Proportion for c Groups

$$\bar{p} = \frac{X_1 + X_2 + \cdots + X_c}{n_1 + n_2 + \cdots + n_c} = \frac{X}{n} \qquad (12.3)$$

Critical Range for the Marascuilo Procedure

$$\text{Critical range} = \sqrt{\chi^2_\alpha}\sqrt{\frac{p_j(1 - p_j)}{n_j} + \frac{p_{j'}(1 - p_{j'})}{n_{j'}}} \qquad (12.4)$$

Computing the Expected Frequency

$$f_e = \frac{\text{row total} \times \text{column total}}{n} \qquad (12.5)$$

McNemar Test

$$Z_{STAT} = \frac{B - C}{\sqrt{B + C}} \qquad (12.6)$$

Checking the Rankings

$$T_1 + T_2 = \frac{n(n + 1)}{2} \qquad (12.7)$$

Large Sample Wilcoxon Rank Sum Test

$$Z_{STAT} = \frac{T_1 - \dfrac{n_1(n + 1)}{2}}{\sqrt{\dfrac{n_1 n_2(n + 1)}{12}}} \qquad (12.8)$$

Kruskal-Wallis Rank Test for Differences Among c Medians

$$H = \left[\frac{12}{n(n + 1)}\sum_{j=1}^{c}\frac{T_j^2}{n_j}\right] - 3(n + 1) \qquad (12.9)$$

KEY TERMS

chi-square (χ^2) distribution   426
chi-square (χ^2) test of
    independence   438
chi-square (χ^2) test for the difference
    between two proportions   425

contingency table   424
expected frequency (f_e)   425
Kruskal-Wallis rank test   453
Marascuilo procedure   435
McNemar test   443

observed frequency (f_o)   425
$2 \times c$ contingency table   432
2×2 contingency table   424
Wilcoxon rank sum test   447

CHAPTER REVIEW PROBLEMS

CHECKING YOUR UNDERSTANDING

12.57 Under what conditions should you use the χ^2 test to determine whether there is a difference between the proportions of two independent populations?

12.58 Under what conditions should you use the χ^2 test to determine whether there is a difference among the proportions of more than two independent populations?

12.59 Under what conditions should you use the χ^2 test of independence?

12.60 Under what conditions should you use the McNemar test?

12.61 What is a nonparametric procedure?

12.62 Under what conditions should you use the Wilcoxon rank sum test?

12.63 Under what conditions should you use the Kruskal-Wallis rank test?

APPLYING THE CONCEPTS

12.64 Undergraduate students at Miami University in Oxford, Ohio, were surveyed in order to evaluate the effect of gender and price on purchasing a pizza from Pizza Hut. Students were told to suppose that they were planning on having a large two-topping pizza delivered to their residence that evening. The students had to decide between ordering from Pizza Hut at a reduced price of $8.49 (the regular price for a large two-topping pizza from the Oxford Pizza Hut at this time was $11.49) and ordering a pizza from a different

pizzeria. The results from this question are summarized in the following contingency table:

GENDER	PIZZERIA Pizza Hut	Other	Total
Female	4	13	17
Male	6	12	18
Total	10	25	35

A subsequent survey evaluated purchase decisions at other prices. These results are summarized in the following contingency table:

PIZZERIA	PRICE $8.49	$11.49	$14.49	Total
Pizza Hut	10	5	2	17
Other	25	23	27	75
Total	35	28	29	92

a. Using a 0.05 level of significance and using the data in the first contingency table, is there evidence of a significant relationship between a student's gender and his or her pizzeria selection?

b. What is your answer to (a) if nine of the male students selected Pizza Hut and nine selected another pizzeria?

c. Using a 0.05 level of significance and using the data in the second contingency table, is there evidence of a difference in pizzeria selection based on price?

d. Determine the p-value in (c) and interpret its meaning.

12.65 Many companies are finding that customers are using various types of online content before purchasing products (data extracted from K. Spors, "How Are We Doing?" *The Wall Street Journal*, November 13, 2006, p. R9). The following results are the percentages of older adults (over age 45), younger adults (21–45), and youths (below 21) who use various sources of online content. Suppose the survey was based on 100 older adults, 100 younger adults, and 100 youths.

TYPE OF ONLINE CONTENT	USE ONLINE CONTENT		
	Older Adults	Younger Adults	Youth
Customer product ratings/reviews	71	78	81
For sale listings without seller ratings	58	60	65
Online classified ads	57	59	66
For sale listings with seller ratings	69	72	77
Message-board posts	57	65	71
Web logs (blogs)	55	61	67
Dating site profiles/personals	49	52	59
Peer-generated and peer-reference information	49	55	68
Peer-posted event listings	46	53	71

For *each type of online content*, is there a significant difference among the age groups in the proportion who use the type of online content? (Use $\alpha = 0.05$.)

12.66 A company is considering an organizational change involving the use of self-managed work teams. To assess the attitudes of employees of the company toward this change, a sample of 400 employees is selected and asked whether they favor the institution of self-managed work teams in the organization. Three responses are permitted: favor, neutral, or oppose. The results of the survey, cross-classified by type of job and attitude toward self-managed work teams, are summarized as follows:

TYPE OF JOB	SELF-MANAGED WORK TEAMS			
	Favor	Neutral	Oppose	Total
Hourly worker	108	46	71	225
Supervisor	18	12	30	60
Middle management	35	14	26	75
Upper management	24	7	9	40
Total	185	79	136	400

a. At the 0.05 level of significance, is there evidence of a relationship between attitude toward self-managed work teams and type of job?

The survey also asked respondents about their attitudes toward instituting a policy whereby an employee could take one additional vacation day per month without pay. The results, cross-classified by type of job, are as follows:

TYPE OF JOB	VACATION TIME WITHOUT PAY			
	Favor	Neutral	Oppose	Total
Hourly worker	135	23	67	225
Supervisor	39	7	14	60
Middle management	47	6	22	75
Upper management	26	6	8	40
Total	247	42	111	400

b. At the 0.05 level of significance, is there evidence of a relationship between attitude toward vacation time without pay and type of job?

12.67 A company that produces and markets continuing education programs on DVDs for the educational testing industry has traditionally mailed advertising to prospective customers. A market research study was undertaken to compare two approaches: mailing a sample DVD upon request that contained highlights of the full DVD and sending an e-mail containing a link to a Web site from which sample material could be downloaded. Of those who responded to either the mailing or the e-mail, the results were as follows in terms of purchase of the complete DVD:

PURCHASED	TYPE OF MEDIA USED		
	Mailing	E-mail	Total
Yes	26	11	37
No	227	247	474
Total	253	258	511

a. At the 0.05 level of significance, is there evidence of a difference in the proportion of DVDs purchased on the basis of the type of media used?
b. On the basis of the results of (a), which type of media should the company use in the future? Explain the rationale for your decision.

The company also wanted to determine which of three sales approaches should be used to generate sales among those who either requested the sample DVD by mail or downloaded the sample DVD but did not purchase the full DVD: (1) a sales-information e-mail, (2) a DVD that contained additional features, or (3) a telephone call to prospective customers. The 474 respondents who did not initially purchase the full DVD were randomly assigned to each of the three sales approaches. The results, in terms of purchases of the full-program DVD, are as follows:

| | SALES APPROACH | | | |
ACTION	Sales Information E-mail	More Complete DVD	Telephone Call	Total
Purchase	5	17	18	40
Don't purchase	153	141	140	434
Total	158	158	158	474

c. At the 0.05 level of significance, is there evidence of a difference in the proportion of DVDs purchased on the basis of the sales strategy used?

d. On the basis of the results of (c), which sales approach do you think the company should use in the future? Explain the rationale for your decision.

12.68 A market researcher investigated consumer preferences for Coca-Cola and Pepsi before a taste test and after a taste test. The following table summarizes the results from a sample of 200 consumers:

| PREFERENCE BEFORE TASTE TEST | PREFERENCE AFTER TASTE TEST | | |
	Coca-Cola	Pepsi	Total
Coca-Cola	104	6	110
Pepsi	14	76	90
Total	118	82	200

a. Is there evidence of a difference in the proportion of respondents who prefer Coca-Cola before and after the taste tests? (Use $\alpha = 0.10$.)

b. Compute the p-value and interpret its meaning.

c. Show how the following table was derived from the table above:

| PREFERENCE | SOFT DRINK | | |
	Coca-Cola	Pepsi	Total
Before taste test	110	90	200
After taste test	118	82	200
Total	228	172	400

d. Using the second table, is there evidence of a difference in preference for Coca-Cola before and after the taste test? (Use $\alpha = 0.05$.)

e. Determine the p-value and interpret its meaning.

f. Explain the difference in the results of (a) and (d). Which method of analyzing the data should you use? Why?

12.69 A market researcher was interested in studying the effect of advertisements on brand preference of new car buyers. Prospective purchasers of new cars were first asked whether they preferred Toyota or GM and then watched video advertisements of comparable models of the two manufacturers. After viewing the ads, the prospective customers again indicated their preferences. The results are summarized in the following table:

| PREFERENCE BEFORE ADS | PREFERENCE AFTER ADS | | |
	Toyota	GM	Total
Toyota	97	3	100
GM	11	89	100
Total	108	92	200

a. Is there evidence of a difference in the proportion of respondents who prefer Toyota before and after viewing the ads? (Use $\alpha = 0.05$.)

b. Compute the p-value and interpret its meaning.

c. Show how the following table was derived from the table above:

| PREFERENCE | MANUFACTURER | | |
	Toyota	GM	Total
Before ad	100	100	200
After ad	108	92	200
Total	208	192	400

d. Using the second table, is there evidence of a difference in preference for Toyota before and after viewing the ads? (Use $\alpha = 0.05$.)

e. Determine the p-value and interpret its meaning.

f. Explain the difference in the results of (a) and (d). Which method of analyzing the data should you use? Why?

12.70 Researchers studied the goals and outcomes of 349 work teams from various manufacturing companies in Ohio. In the first table, teams are categorized as to whether they had specified environmental improvements as a goal and also according to one of four types of manufacturing processes that best described their workplace. The second through fourth tables indicate different outcomes the teams accomplished, based on whether the team had specified cost cutting as one of the team goals.

| TYPE OF MANUFACTURING PROCESS | ENVIRONMENTAL GOAL | | |
	Yes	No	Total
Job shop or batch	2	42	44
Repetitive batch	4	57	61
Discrete process	15	147	162
Continuous process	17	65	82
Total	38	311	349

	COST-CUTTING GOAL		
OUTCOME	**Yes**	**No**	**Total**
Improved environmental			
performance	77	52	129
Environmental performance			
not improved	91	129	220
Total	168	181	349

	COST-CUTTING GOAL		
OUTCOME	**Yes**	**No**	**Total**
Improved profitability	70	68	138
Profitability not improved	98	113	211
Total	168	181	349

	COST-CUTTING GOAL		
OUTCOME	**Yes**	**No**	**Total**
Improved morale	67	55	122
Morale not improved	101	126	227
Total	168	181	349

Source: *Data extracted from M. Hanna, W. Newman, and P. Johnson, "Linking Operational and Environmental Improvement Through Employee Involvement,"* International Journal of Operations and Production Management, *2000, 20, pp. 148–165.*

a. At the 0.05 level of significance, determine whether there is evidence of a significant relationship between the presence of environmental goals and the type of manufacturing process.
b. Determine the *p*-value in (a) and interpret its meaning.
c. At the 0.05 level of significance, is there evidence of a difference in improved environmental performance for teams with and without a specified goal of cutting costs?
d. Determine the *p*-value in (c) and interpret its meaning.
e. At the 0.05 level of significance, is there evidence of a difference in improved profitability for teams with a specified goal of cutting costs?
f. Determine the *p*-value in (e) and interpret its meaning.
g. At the 0.05 level of significance, is there evidence of a difference in improved morale for teams with and without a specified goal of cutting costs?
h. Determine the *p*-value in (g) and interpret its meaning.

TEAM PROJECT

The file **Bond Funds** contains information regarding eight variables from a sample of 180 mutual funds:

Type—Type of bonds comprising the bond fund (Intermediate Government or short term corporate)
Assets—In millions of dollars

Fees—Sales charges (no or yes)
Expense ratio—Ratio of expenses to net assets in percentage
Return 2008—Twelve-month return in 2008
Three-year return—Annualized return, 2006–2008
Five-year return—Annualized return, 2004–2008
Risk—Risk-of-loss factor of the bond mutual fund (below average, average, or above average)

12.71 a. Construct a 2 × 2 contingency table, using fees as the row variable and type as the column variable.
b. At the 0.05 level of significance, is there evidence of a significant relationship between the type of mutual fund and whether there is a fee?
12.72 a. Construct a 2 × 3 contingency table, using fees as the row variable and risk as the column variable.
b. At the 0.05 level of significance, is there evidence of a significant relationship between the perceived risk of a mutual fund and whether there is a fee?
12.73 a. Construct a 3 × 2 contingency table, using risk as the row variable and category as the column variable.
b. At the 0.05 level of significance, is there evidence of a significant relationship between the category of a mutual fund and its perceived risk?

STUDENT SURVEY DATABASE

12.74 Problem 2.117 on page 65 describes a survey of 50 undergraduate students (stored in UndergradSurvey). For these data, construct contingency tables, using gender, major, plans to go to graduate school, and employment status. (You need to construct six tables, taking two variables at a time.) Analyze the data at the 0.05 level of significance to determine whether any significant relationships exist among these variables.

12.75 Problem 2.117 on page 65 describes a survey of 50 undergraduate students (stored in UndergradSurvey).
a. Select a sample of 50 undergraduate students at your school and conduct a similar survey for those students.
b. For the data collected in (a), repeat Problem 12.74.
c. Compare the results of (b) to those of Problem 12.74.

12.76 Problem 2.119 on page 65 describes a survey of 40 MBA students (see the file GradSurvey). For these data, construct contingency tables, using gender, undergraduate major, graduate major, and employment status. (You need to construct six tables, taking two variables at a time.) Analyze the data at the 0.05 level of significance to determine whether any significant relationships exist among these variables.

12.77 Problem 2.119 on page 65 describes a survey of 40 MBA students (stored in GradSurvey).
a. Select a sample of 40 graduate students in your MBA program and conduct a similar survey for those students.
b. For the data collected in (a), repeat Problem 12.76.
c. Compare the results of (b) to those of Problem 12.76.

MANAGING THE *SPRINGVILLE HERALD*

Phase 1

Reviewing the results of its research, the marketing department team concluded that a segment of Springville households might be interested in a discounted trial home subscription to the *Herald*. The team decided to test various discounts before determining the type of discount to offer during the trial period. It decided to conduct an experiment using three types of discounts plus a plan that offered no discount during the trial period:

1. No discount for the newspaper. Subscribers would pay $4.50 per week for the newspaper during the 90-day trial period.

2. Moderate discount for the newspaper. Subscribers would pay $4.00 per week for the newspaper during the 90-day trial period.

3. Substantial discount for the newspaper. Subscribers would pay $3.00 per week for the newspaper during the 90-day trial period.

4. Discount restaurant card. Subscribers would be given a card providing a discount of 15% at selected restaurants in Springville during the trial period.

Each participant in the experiment was randomly assigned to a discount plan. A random sample of 100 subscribers to each plan during the trial period was tracked to determine how many would continue to subscribe to the *Herald* after the trial period. Table SH12.1 summarizes the results.

TABLE SH12.1

Number of Subscribers Who Continue Subscriptions After Trial Period with Four Discount Plans

CONTINUE SUBSCRIPTIONS AFTER TRIAL PERIOD	DISCOUNT PLANS				
	No Discount	Moderate Discount	Substantial Discount	Restaurant Card	Total
Yes	34	37	38	61	170
No	66	63	62	39	230
Total	100	100	100	100	400

EXERCISE

SH12.1 Analyze the results of the experiment. Write a report to the team that includes your recommendation for which discount plan to use. Be prepared to discuss the limitations and assumptions of the experiment.

DO NOT CONTINUE UNTIL THE PHASE 1 EXERCISE HAS BEEN COMPLETED.

Phase 2

The marketing department team discussed the results of the survey presented in Chapter 8, on pages 289–290. The team realized that the evaluation of individual questions was providing only limited information. In order to further understand the market for home-delivery subscriptions, the data were organized in the following contingency tables:

	READ OTHER NEWSPAPER		
HOME DELIVERY	Yes	No	Total
Yes	61	75	136
No	77	139	216
Total	138	214	352

	RESTAURANT CARD		
HOME DELIVERY	Yes	No	Total
Yes	26	110	136
No	40	176	216
Total	66	286	352

INTEREST IN TRIAL SUBSCRIPTION	MONDAY–SATURDAY PURCHASE BEHAVIOR			
	Every Day	Most Days	Occasionally or Never	Total
Yes	29	14	3	46
No	49	81	40	170
Total	78	95	43	216

INTEREST IN TRIAL SUBSCRIPTION	SUNDAY PURCHASE BEHAVIOR			
	Every Sunday	2–3 Times a Month	No More Than Once a Month	Total
Yes	35	10	1	46
No	103	44	23	170
Total	138	54	24	216

WHERE PURCHASED	INTEREST IN TRIAL SUBSCRIPTION		
	Yes	No	Total
Convenience store	12	62	74
Newsstand/candy store	15	80	95
Vending machine	10	11	21
Supermarket	5	8	13
Other locations	4	9	13
Total	46	170	216

SUNDAY PURCHASE BEHAVIOR	MONDAY–SATURDAY PURCHASE BEHAVIOR			
	Every Day	Most Days	Occasionally or Never	Total
Every Sunday	55	65	18	138
2–3 times/month	19	23	12	54
Once/month	4	7	13	24
Total	78	95	43	216

EXERCISE

SH12.2 Analyze the results of the contingency tables. Write a report for the marketing department team and discuss the marketing implications of the results for the *Springville Herald*.

WEB CASE

Apply your knowledge of testing for the difference between two proportions in this Web Case, which extends the T.C. Resort Properties Using Statistics scenario of this chapter.

As T.C. Resort Properties seeks to improve its customer service, the company faces new competition from SunLow Resorts. SunLow has recently opened resort hotels on the islands where T.C. Resort Properties has its five hotels. SunLow is currently advertising that a random survey of 300 customers revealed that about 60% of the customers preferred its "Concierge Class" travel reward program over the T.C. Resorts "TCPass Plus" program.

Using a Web browser, open to the Web page for the Chapter 12 Web Case or open **SunLowHome.htm**, if you have downloaded the Web Case files, to visit the SunLow Web site and examine the survey data. Then answer the following questions:

1. Are the claims made by SunLow valid?
2. What analyses of the survey data would lead to a more favorable impression about T.C. Resort Properties?
3. Perform one of the analyses identified in your answer to step 2.
4. Review the data about the T.C. Resorts Properties customers presented in this chapter. Are there any other questions that you might include in a future survey of travel reward programs? Explain.

REFERENCES

1. Conover, W. J., *Practical Nonparametric Statistics*, 3rd ed. (New York: Wiley, 2000).
2. Daniel, W. W., *Applied Nonparametric Statistics*, 2nd ed. (Boston: PWS Kent, 1990).
3. Dixon, W. J., and F. J. Massey, Jr., *Introduction to Statistical Analysis*, 4th ed. (New York: McGraw-Hill, 1983).
4. Hollander, M., and D. A. Wolfe, *Nonparametric Statistical Methods* 2nd ed. (New York: Wiley, 1999).
5. Lewontin, R. C., and J. Felsenstein, "Robustness of Homogeneity Tests in 2 × n Tables," *Biometrics* 21 (March 1965): 19–33.
6. Marascuilo, L. A., "Large-Sample Multiple Comparisons," *Psychological Bulletin* 65 (1966): 280–290.
7. Marascuilo, L. A., and M. McSweeney, *Nonparametric and Distribution-Free Methods for the Social Sciences* (Monterey, CA: Brooks/Cole, 1977).
8. *Microsoft Excel 2007* (Redmond, WA: Microsoft Corp., 2007).
9. Winer, B. J., D. R. Brown, and K. M. Michels, *Statistical Principles in Experimental Design*, 3rd ed. (New York: McGraw-Hill, 1989).

EG12.1 CHI-SQUARE TEST for the DIFFERENCE BETWEEN TWO PROPORTIONS

PHStat2 Use the **Chi-Square Test for Differences in Two Proportions** procedure to perform this chi-square test. For example, to perform the Figure 12.3 test for the two-hotel guest satisfaction data (see page 428), select **PHStat → Two-Sample Tests (Summarized Data) → Chi-Square Test for Differences in Two Proportions**. In the procedure's dialog box, enter **0.05** as the **Level of Significance**, enter a **Title**, and click **OK**. In the new worksheet:

1. Read the yellow note about entering values and then press the **Delete** key to delete the note.
2. Enter **Hotel** in cell **B4** and **Choose Again?** in cell **A5**.
3. Enter **Beachcomber** in cell **B5** and **Windsurfer** in cell **C5**.
4. Enter **Yes** in cell **A6** and **No** in cell **A7**.
5. Enter **163**, **154**, **64**, and **108** in cells **B6**, **B7**, **C6**, and **C7**, respectively.

In-Depth Excel Use the **CHIINV** and **CHIDIST** functions to help perform the chi-square test for the difference between two proportions. Enter **CHIINV**(*level of significance, degrees of freedom*) to compute the critical value for the test and enter **CHIDIST**(*chi-square test statistic, degrees of freedom*) to compute the *p*-value.

Use the **COMPUTE worksheet** of the **Chi-Square workbook**, shown in Figure 12.3 on page 428, as a template for performing this test. The worksheet contains the Table 12.3 two-hotel guest satisfaction data. The formulas **=D6 * B8/D8** and **=D7 * B8/D8** in cells B13 and B14, and the formulas **=D6 * C8/D8** and **=D7 * C8/D8** in cells C13 and C14 compute the expected frequencies using totals found in row 8 and column D.

For other problems, change the **Observed Frequencies** cell counts and row and column labels in rows 4 through 7.

EG12.2 CHI-SQUARE TEST for DIFFERENCES AMONG MORE than TWO PROPORTIONS

PHStat2 Use the **Chi-Square Test procedure** to perform the test for the difference among more than two proportions. For example, to perform this chi-square test for the Table 12.6 guest satisfaction data (see Figure 12.6 on page 434), select **PHStat → Multiple-Sample Tests → Chi-Square Test**. In the procedure's dialog box (shown below):

1. Enter **0.05** as the **Level of Significance**.
2. Enter **2** as the **Number of Rows**.
3. Enter **3** as the **Number of Columns**.
4. Enter a **Title** and click **OK**.

In the new worksheet:

5. Read the yellow note about entering values and then press the **Delete** key to delete the note.
6. Enter the Table 12.6 data on page 432, including row and column labels, in rows 4 through 7.

In-Depth Excel Use the **CHIINV** and **CHIDIST** functions (described in the Section EG12.1 *In-Depth Excel* instructions) to help perform the chi-square test for differences among more than two populations.

Use the **ChiSquare2x3 worksheet** of the **Chi-Square Worksheets workbook**, shown in Figure 12.6 on page 434, as a model for this chi-square test. The worksheet contains the data for Table 12.6 guest satisfaction data (see page 432). The worksheet uses formulas to compute the expected frequencies and the intermediate results for the chi-square test statistic in much the same way as the COMPUTE worksheet of the Chi-Square workbook discussed in the Section EG12.1 *In-Depth Excel* instructions and shown in Figure 12.3 on page 428. (Open to the **ChiSquare2x3_FORMULAS worksheet** to examine all the formulas used in the worksheet.)

For other 2 × 3 problems, change the **Observed Frequencies** cell counts and row and column labels in rows 4 through 7. For 2 × 4 problems, use the **ChiSquare2x4 worksheet**. For 2 × 5 problems, use the **ChiSquare2x5 worksheet**. In either case, enter the contingency table

◢	B	C	D
11		**MARASCUILO TABLE**	
12	**Absolute Differences**	**Critical Range**	
13	=ABS(B7 - B8)	=B4 * SQRT(B7 * (1 - B7)/ChiSquare2x3!B8+B8 * (1 - B8)/ChiSquare2x3!C8)	=IF(B13 > C13, "Significant", "Not significant")
14	=ABS(B7 - B9)	=B4 * SQRT(B7 * (1 - B7)/ChiSquare2x3!B8+B9 * (1 - B9)/ChiSquare2x3!D8)	=IF(B14 > C14, "Significant", "Not significant")
15			
16	=ABS(B8 - B9)	=B4 * SQRT(B8 * (1 - B8)/ChiSquare2x3!C8+B9 * (1 - B9)/ChiSquare2x3!D8)	=IF(B16 > C16, "Significant", "Not significant")

FIGURE EG12.1   Marascuilo table area formulas for the Marascuilo 2×3 worksheet

data for the problem in the rows 4 through 7 Observed Frequencies area.

The Marascuilo Procedure

PHStat2 Modify the *PHStat2* instructions for the chi-square test to include the Marascuilo procedure to test for the difference among more than two proportions (see page 466). In step 4, enter a **Title**, check **Marascuilo Procedure**, and then click **OK**.

In-Depth Excel Use the Marascuilo worksheet linked to a particular chi-square $2 \times c$ worksheet in the **Chi-Square workbook** to perform the Marascuilo procedure.

For example, Figure 12.7 on page 436 shows the **Marascuilo2x3 worksheet**, which is linked to the **ChiSquare2x3 worksheet**. This Marascuilo worksheet uses values from the ChiSquare2x3 worksheet to compute group sample proportions in cells B7 through B9 (shown in Figure 12.7) and to compute the critical range in rows 13, 14, and 16 (shown in Figure EG12.1). In column D, the worksheet uses IF functions in the form **IF(*absolute difference > critical range, display "Significant" message, display "Not significant" message*)** to indicate which pairs of groups are significantly different. (Open to the **Marascuilo2x3_FORMULAS worksheet** to examine together all the formulas used in the worksheet.)

EG12.3 CHI-SQUARE TEST of INDEPENDENCE

PHStat2 Use the **Chi-Square Test procedure** to perform the chi-square test of independence. For example, to perform this chi-square test for the data in Table 12.9 on page 439 concerning the primary reason for not returning and hotel data guest satisfaction (see Figure 12.10 on page 441), select **PHStat → Multiple-Sample Tests → Chi-Square Test**. In the procedure's dialog box:

1. Enter **0.05** as the **Level of Significance**.
2. Enter **4** as the **Number of Rows**.
3. Enter **3** as the **Number of Columns**.
4. Enter a **Title** and click **OK**.

In the new worksheet:

5. Read the yellow note about entering values and then press the **Delete** key to delete the note.
6. Enter the Table 12.9 data, including row and column labels, in rows 4 through 9.

In-Depth Excel Use one of the $r \times c$ worksheets in the **Chi-Square worksheets workbook** to perform the chi-square test of independence.

For example, Figure 12.10 on page 441 shows the **ChiSquare4x3 worksheet** that contains the data for Table 12.9 which was the contingency table of primary reason for not returning and hotel (see page 439). The worksheet computes the expected frequencies and the intermediate results for the chi-square test statistic in much the same way as the COMPUTE worksheet of the Chi-Square workbook discussed in the Section EG12.1 *In-Depth Excel* instructions.

For other 4×3 problems, change the **Observed Frequencies** cell counts and row and column labels in rows 4 through 9. For 3×4 problems, use the **ChiSquare3x4 worksheet**. For 4×3 problems, use the **ChiSquare4x3 worksheet**. For 7×3 problems, use the **ChiSquare7x3 worksheet**. For 8×3 problems, use the **ChiSquare8x3 worksheet**. In each case, enter the contingency table data for the problem in the Observed Frequencies area.

EG12.4 McNEMAR TEST for the DIFFERENCE BETWEEN TWO PROPORTIONS (RELATED SAMPLES)

PHStat2 Use the **McNemar Test** procedure to perform this test. For example, to perform the Figure 12.12 test for the brand loyalty of cell phone providers (see page 445), select **PHStat → Two-Sample Tests (Summarized Data) → McNemar Test**. In the procedure's dialog box (shown at the top of page 468):

1. Enter **0.05** as the **Level of Significance**.
2. Click **Two-Tail Test**.
3. Enter a **Title** and click **OK**.

In the new worksheet:

4. Read the yellow note about entering values and then press the **Delete** key to delete the note.

5. Enter the Table 12.13 data (see page 444), including row and column labels, in rows 4 through 7.

In-Depth Excel Use the **NORMSINV** and **NORMSDIST** functions to help perform the McNemar test. Enter **NORMSINV((1 – *level of significance*)/2)** and **NORMSINV** (*level of significance*/2) to compute the upper and lower critical values. Enter the expression **2 * (1 – NORMSDIST** (*absolute value of the Z test statistic*) to compute the *p*-value.

Use the **COMPUTE worksheet** of the **McNemar workbook**, shown in Figure 12.12 on page 445, as a template for performing the McNemar test. The worksheet contains the data of Table 12.13 concerning the brand loyalty for cell phone providers (see page 444). To perform the McNemar two-tail test for other problems, change the row 4 through 7 entries in the **Observed Frequencies** area and enter the level of significance for the test in cell B11.

For one-tail tests, change the Observed Frequencies area and level of significance in the **COMPUTE_ALL worksheet** in the **McNemar workbook**. (Open to the **COMPUTE_ALL_FORMULAS worksheet** to examine the formulas used in the worksheet.)

EG12.5 WILCOXON RANK SUM TEST: NONPARAMETRIC ANALYSIS for TWO INDEPENDENT POPULATIONS

PHStat2 Use the **Wilcoxon Rank Sum Test** procedure to perform this test. For example, to perform the Figure 12.14 test for the BLK Cola sales example (see page 450), open to the **DATA worksheet** of the **Cola workbook**. Select **PHStat → Two-Sample Tests (Unsummarized Data) → Wilcoxon Rank Sum Test**. In the procedure's dialog box (shown at the top of the next column):

1. Enter **0.05** as the **Level of Significance**.

2. Enter **A1:A11** as the **Population 1 Sample Cell Range**.

3. Enter **B1:B11** as the **Population 2 Sample Cell Range**.

4. Check **First cells in both ranges contain label**.

5. Click **Two-Tail Test**.

6. Enter a **Title** and click **OK**.

The procedure creates a worksheet that contains sorted ranks as well as the worksheet shown in Figure 12.14. Both of these worksheets are explained in the following *In-Depth Excel* instructions.

In-Depth Excel Use the **NORMSINV** and **NORMSDIST** functions to help perform the Wilcoxon rank sum test. Enter **NORMSINV((1 – *level of significance*)/2)** and **NORMSINV** (*level of significance*/2) to compute the upper and lower critical values. Enter the expression **2 * (1 – NORMSDIST** (*absolute value of the Z test statistic*)) to compute the *p*-value.

Use the **COMPUTE worksheet** of the **Wilcoxon workbook**, shown in Figure 12.14 on page 450, as a template for performing the two-tail Wilcoxon rank sum test. The worksheet contains data and formulas to use the unsummarized data for the BLK Cola example. For other problems, use the COMPUTE worksheet with either unsummarized or summarized data. For summarized data, overwrite the formulas that compute the **Sample Size** and **Sum of Ranks** in cells B7, B8, B10, and B11, with the values for these statistics.

For unsummarized data, first enter the sorted values for both groups in stacked format in the **SortedRanks worksheet**. Use column A for the sample names and column B for the sorted values. Assign a rank for each value and enter the ranks in column C of the same worksheet. Then open to the COMPUTE worksheet (or the similar COMPUTE_ALL worksheet, if performing a one-tail test) and edit the formulas in cells B7, B8, B10, and B11. Enter **COUNTIF** functions in the form **COUNTIF(*cell range for all sample names, sample name to be matched*)** to compute the sample size for a sample. Enter **SUMIF** functions in the form **SUMIF(*cell range for all sample names, sample name to be matched, cell range in which to select cells for summing*)** to compute the sum of ranks for a sample.

For example, in the COMPUTE worksheet, the formula =COUNTIF(SortedRanks!A2:A21, "Normal") counts the number of occurrences of the sample name "**Normal**" in column A to compute the sample size of the **Population 1 Sample**. The formula =SUMIF(SortedRanks!A2:A21,

"Normal", C1:C21) computes the sum of ranks for the **Population 1 Sample** by summing the column C ranks for rows in which the column A value is **Normal**.

EG12.6 KRUSKAL-WALLIS RANK TEST: NONPARAMETRIC ANALYSIS for the ONE-WAY ANOVA

PHStat2 Use the **Kruskal-Wallis Rank Test** procedure to perform this test. For example, to perform the Figure 12.16 (see page 456). Kruskal-Wallis rank test for differences among the four medians in the parachute example, open to the **DATA worksheet** of the **Parachute workbook**. Select **PHStat → Multiple-Sample Tests → Kruskal-Wallis Rank Test**. In the procedure's dialog box (shown below):

1. Enter **0.05** as the **Level of Significance**.
2. Enter **A1:D6** as the **Sample Data Cell Range**.
3. Check **First cells contain label**.
4. Enter a **Title** and click **OK**.

The procedure creates a worksheet that contains sorted ranks as well as the worksheet shown in Figure 12.16. Both of these worksheets are explained in the following *In-Depth Excel* instructions.

In-Depth Excel Use the **CHIINV** and **CHIDIST** functions to help perform the Kruskal-Wallis rank test. Enter **CHIINV(*level of significance, number of groups* – 1)** to compute the critical value and **CHIDIST(*H test statistic, number of groups* – 1)** to compute the *p*-value.

Use the **KruskalWallis4 worksheet** of the **Kruskal-Wallis Worksheets workbook**, shown in Figure 12.16 on page 456, as a model for performing the Kruskal-Wallis rank test. The worksheet contains the data and formulas to use the unsummarized data for the Section 12.6 four-supplier parachute example. For other problems with four groups, use the KruskalWallis4 worksheet with either unsummarized or summarized data. For summarized data, overwrite the formulas that display the group names and compute the **Sample Size** and **Sum of Ranks** in columns D, E and F, shown in Figure EG12.2, with the values for these statistics.

For unsummarized data, first enter the sorted values for both groups in stacked format in the **SortedRanks worksheet**. Use column A for the sample names and column B for the sorted values. Assign ranks for each value and enter the ranks in column C of the same worksheet. Also paste your unsummarized stacked data in columns, starting with Column E. (The row 1 cells, starting with cell E1, are used to identify each group.) Then open to the KruskalWallis4 worksheet (or the similar **KruskalWallis3 worksheet**, if using three groups) and edit the formulas in columns E and F. Enter **COUNTIF** functions in the form **COUNTIF(*cell range for all group names, group name to be matched*)** to compute the sample size for a group. Enter **SUMIF** functions in the form **SUMIF(*cell range for all group names, group name to be matched, cell range in which to select cells for summing*)** to compute the sum of ranks for a group.

	D	E	F	G
3			Calculations	
4	Group	Sample Size	Sum of Ranks	Mean Ranks
5	=SortedRanks!E1	=COUNTIF(SortedRanks!A2:A21, D5)	=SUMIF(SortedRanks!A2:A21, D5, SortedRanks!C2:C21)	=F5/E5
6	=SortedRanks!F1	=COUNTIF(SortedRanks!A2:A21, D6)	=SUMIF(SortedRanks!A2:A21, D6, SortedRanks!C2:C21)	=F6/E6
7	=SortedRanks!G1	=COUNTIF(SortedRanks!A2:A21, D7)	=SUMIF(SortedRanks!A2:A21, D7, SortedRanks!C2:C21)	=F7/E7
8	=SortedRanks!H1	=COUNTIF(SortedRanks!A2:A21, D8)	=SUMIF(SortedRanks!A2:A21, D8, SortedRanks!C2:C21)	=F8/E8

FIGURE EG12.2 KruskalWallis4 worksheet formulas for columns D through G

13 Simple Linear Regression

Learning Objectives

In this chapter, you learn:

- To use regression analysis to predict the value of a dependent variable based on an independent variable
- The meaning of the regression coefficients b_0 and b_1
- To evaluate the assumptions of regression analysis and know what to do if the assumptions are violated
- To make inferences about the slope and correlation coefficient
- To estimate mean values and predict individual values

USING STATISTICS

@ Sunflowers Apparel

The sales for Sunflowers Apparel, a chain of upscale clothing stores for women, have increased during the past 12 years as the chain has expanded the number of stores. Until now, Sunflowers managers selected sites based on subjective factors, such as the availability of a good lease or the perception that a location seemed ideal for an apparel store. As the new director of planning, you need to develop a systematic approach that will lead to making better decisions during the site selection process. As a starting point, you believe that the size of the store significantly contributes to store sales, and you want to use this relationship in the decision-making process. How can you use statistics so that you can forecast the annual sales of a proposed store based on the size of that store?

I n this chapter and the next two chapters, you learn how **regression analysis** enables you to develop a model to predict the values of a numerical variable, based on the value of other variables.

In regression analysis, the variable you wish to predict is called the **dependent variable**. The variables used to make the prediction are called **independent variables**. In addition to predicting values of the dependent variable, regression analysis also allows you to identify the type of mathematical relationship that exists between a dependent variable and an independent variable, to quantify the effect that changes in the independent variable have on the dependent variable, and to identify unusual observations. For example, as the director of planning, you might want to predict sales for a Sunflowers store based on the size of the store. Other examples include predicting the monthly rent of an apartment based on its size and predicting the monthly sales of a product in a supermarket based on the amount of shelf space devoted to the product.

This chapter discusses **simple linear regression**, in which a *single* numerical independent variable, *X*, is used to predict the numerical dependent variable *Y*, such as using the size of a store to predict the annual sales of the store. Chapters 14 and 15 discuss *multiple regression models*, which use *several* independent variables to predict a numerical dependent variable, *Y*. For example, you could use the amount of advertising expenditures, price, and the amount of shelf space devoted to a product to predict its monthly sales.

13.1 Types of Regression Models

In Section 2.7, you used a **scatter plot** (also known as a **scatter diagram**) to examine the relationship between an *X* variable on the horizontal axis and a *Y* variable on the vertical axis. The nature of the relationship between two variables can take many forms, ranging from simple to extremely complicated mathematical functions. The simplest relationship consists of a straight-line relationship, or **linear relationship**. Figure 13.1 illustrates a straight-line relationship.

FIGURE 13.1

A straight-line relationship

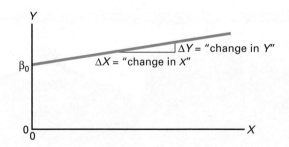

Equation (13.1) represents the straight-line (linear) model.

SIMPLE LINEAR REGRESSION MODEL

$$Y_i = \beta_0 + \beta_1 X_i + \varepsilon_i \qquad (13.1)$$

where

$\beta_0 = Y$ intercept for the population

$\beta_1 = $ slope for the population

$\varepsilon_i = $ random error in Y for observation i

$Y_i = $ dependent variable (sometimes referred to as the **response variable**) for observation i

$X_i = $ independent variable (sometimes referred to as the **explanatory variable**) for observation i

The $Y_i = \beta_0 + \beta_1 X_i$ portion of the simple linear regression model expressed in Equation (13.1) is a straight line. The **slope** of the line, β_1, represents the expected change in Y per unit change in X. It represents the mean amount that Y changes (either positively or negatively) for a one-unit change in X. The **Y intercept**, β_0, represents the mean value of Y when X equals 0. The last component of the model, ε_i, represents the random error in Y for each observation, i. In other words, ε_i is the vertical distance of the actual value of Y_i above or below the expected value of Y_i on the line.

The selection of the proper mathematical model depends on the distribution of the X and Y values on the scatter plot. Figure 13.2 illustrates six different types of relationships.

In Panel A, the values of Y are generally increasing linearly as X increases. This panel is similar to Figure 13.3 on page 474, which illustrates the positive relationship between the square footage of the store and the annual sales at branches of the Sunflowers Apparel women's clothing store chain.

Panel B is an example of a negative linear relationship. As X increases, the values of Y are generally decreasing. An example of this type of relationship might be the price of a particular product and the amount of sales.

The data in Panel C show a positive curvilinear relationship between X and Y. The values of Y increase as X increases, but this increase tapers off beyond certain values of X. An example of a positive curvilinear relationship might be the age and maintenance cost of a machine. As a machine gets older, the maintenance cost may rise rapidly at first but then level off beyond a certain number of years.

Panel D shows a U-shaped relationship between X and Y. As X increases, at first Y generally decreases; but as X continues to increase, Y not only stops decreasing but actually increases above its minimum value. An example of this type of relationship might be the number of errors per hour at a task and the number of hours worked. The number of errors per hour decreases as the individual becomes more proficient at the task, but then it increases beyond a certain point because of factors such as fatigue and boredom.

FIGURE 13.2

Six types of relationships found in scatter plots

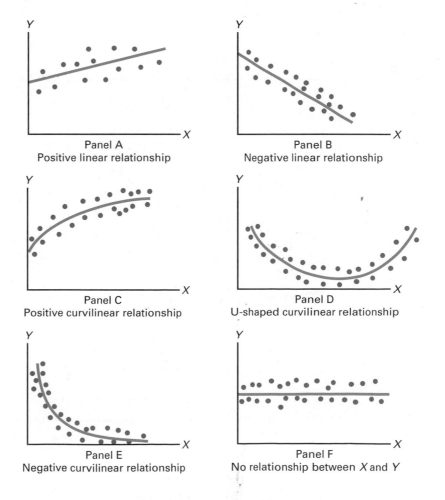

Panel A
Positive linear relationship

Panel B
Negative linear relationship

Panel C
Positive curvilinear relationship

Panel D
U-shaped curvilinear relationship

Panel E
Negative curvilinear relationship

Panel F
No relationship between X and Y

Panel E illustrates an exponential relationship between X and Y. In this case, Y decreases very rapidly as X first increases, but then it decreases much less rapidly as X increases further. An example of an exponential relationship could be the value of an automobile and its age. The value drops drastically from its original price in the first year, but it decreases much less rapidly in subsequent years.

Finally, Panel F shows a set of data in which there is very little or no relationship between X and Y. High and low values of Y appear at each value of X.

Although scatter plots are useful in visually displaying the mathematical form of a relationship, more sophisticated statistical procedures are available to determine the most appropriate model for a set of variables. The rest of this chapter discusses the model used when there is a *linear* relationship between variables.

13.2 Determining the Simple Linear Regression Equation

In the Sunflowers Apparel scenario on page 471, the business objective of the director of planning is to forecast annual sales for all new stores, based on store size. To examine the relationship between the store size in square feet and its annual sales, data were collected from a sample of 14 stores. Table 13.1 shows the organized data, which are stored in [Site].

Figure 13.3 displays the scatter plot for the data in Table 13.1. Observe the increasing relationship between square feet (X) and annual sales (Y). As the size of the store increases,

TABLE 13.1

Square Footage (in Thousands of Square Feet) and Annual Sales (in Millions of Dollars) for a Sample of 14 Branches of Sunflowers Apparel

Store	Square Feet (Thousands)	Annual Sales (in Millions of Dollars)	Store	Square Feet (Thousands)	Annual Sales (in Millions of Dollars)
1	1.7	3.7	8	1.1	2.7
2	1.6	3.9	9	3.2	5.5
3	2.8	6.7	10	1.5	2.9
4	5.6	9.5	11	5.2	10.7
5	1.3	3.4	12	4.6	7.6
6	2.2	5.6	13	5.8	11.8
7	1.3	3.7	14	3.0	4.1

FIGURE 13.3

Scatter plot for the Sunflowers Apparel data

Create scatter plots using the instructions in Section EG2.7.

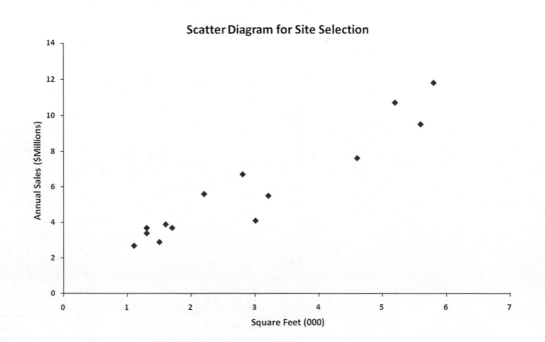

Scatter Diagram for Site Selection

annual sales increase approximately as a straight line. Thus, you can assume that a straight line provides a useful mathematical model of this relationship. Now you need to determine the specific straight line that is the *best* fit to these data.

The Least-Squares Method

In the preceding section, a statistical model is hypothesized to represent the relationship between two variables, square footage and sales, in the entire population of Sunflowers Apparel stores. However, as shown in Table 13.1, the data are from only a random sample of stores. If certain assumptions are valid (see Section 13.4), you can use the sample Y intercept, b_0, and the sample slope, b_1, as estimates of the respective population parameters, β_0 and β_1. Equation (13.2) uses these estimates to form the **simple linear regression equation**. This straight line is often referred to as the **prediction line**.

SIMPLE LINEAR REGRESSION EQUATION: THE PREDICTION LINE

The predicted value of Y equals the Y intercept plus the slope multiplied by the value of X.

$$\hat{Y}_i = b_0 + b_1 X_i \tag{13.2}$$

where

$\hat{Y}_i$ = predicted value of Y for observation i

X_i = value of X for observation i

b_0 = sample Y intercept

b_1 = sample slope

Equation (13.2) requires you to determine two **regression coefficients**—b_0 (the sample Y intercept) and b_1 (the sample slope). The most common approach to finding b_0 and b_1 is using the least-squares method. This method minimizes the sum of the squared differences between the actual values (Y_i) and the predicted values ($\hat{Y}_i$) using the simple linear regression equation [i.e., the prediction line; see Equation (13.2)]. This sum of squared differences is equal to

$$\sum_{i=1}^{n}(Y_i - \hat{Y}_i)^2$$

Because $\hat{Y}_i = b_0 + b_1 X_i$,

$$\sum_{i=1}^{n}(Y_i - \hat{Y}_i)^2 = \sum_{i=1}^{n}[Y_i - (b_0 + b_1 X_i)]^2$$

[1] The equations used to compute these results are shown in Examples 13.3 and 13.4 on pages 478–480 and 485–486. For large data sets, you should rely on software to do these computations for you, given the complex nature of the computations.

Because this equation has two unknowns, b_0 and b_1, the sum of squared differences depends on the sample Y intercept, b_0, and the sample slope, b_1. The **least-squares method** determines the values of b_0 and b_1 that minimize the sum of squared differences around the prediction line. Any values for b_0 and b_1 other than those determined by the least-squares method result in a greater sum of squared differences between the actual values (Y_i) and the predicted values ($\hat{Y}_i$). Figure 13.4[1] presents the worksheet results for the simple linear regression model of the Table 13.1 data.

FIGURE 13.4

Worksheet results for the
simple linear regression
model of the Table 13.1
Sunflowers Apparel data

Figure 13.4 displays the
COMPUTE worksheet of the
Simple Linear Regression
workbook. Create this
worksheet using the
instructions in Section
EG13.2. Read the In-Depth
Excel instructions for this
worksheet to learn about the
formulas used throughout this
worksheet, including the
Calculations area in columns
K through M (not shown in
Figure 13.4).

	A	B	C	D	E	F	G	H	I
1	Simple Linear Regression								
2									
3	Regression Statistics								
4	Multiple R	0.9509							
5	R Square	0.9042							
6	Adjusted R Square	0.8962							
7	Standard Error	0.9664							
8	Observations	14							
9									
10	ANOVA								
11		df	SS	MS	F	Significance F			
12	Regression	1	105.7476	105.7476	113.2335	0.0000			
13	Residual	12	11.2067	0.9339					
14	Total	13	116.9543						
15									
16		Coefficients	Standard Error	t Stat	P-value	Lower 95%	Upper 95%	Lower 95.0%	Upper 95.0%
17	Intercept	0.9645	0.5262	1.8329	0.0917	-0.1820	2.1110	-0.1820	2.11095
18	Square Feet	1.6699	0.1569	10.6411	0.0000	1.3280	2.0118	1.3280	2.01177

In Figure 13.4, observe that $b_0 = 0.9645$ and $b_1 = 1.6699$. Thus, the prediction line [see Equation (13.2) on page 475] for these data is

$$\hat{Y}_i = 0.9645 + 1.6699X_i$$

The slope, b_1, is $+1.6699$. This means that for each increase of 1 unit in X, the predicted value of Y is estimated to increase by 1.6699 units. In other words, for each increase of 1.0 thousand square feet in the size of the store, the predicted annual sales are estimated to increase by 1.6699 millions of dollars. Thus, the slope represents the portion of the annual sales that are estimated to vary according to the size of the store.

The Y intercept, b_0, is $+0.9645$. The Y intercept represents the predicted value of Y when X equals 0. Because the square footage of the store cannot be 0, this Y intercept has little or no practical interpretation. Also, the Y intercept for this example is outside the range of the observed values of the X variable, and therefore interpretations of the value of b_0 should be made cautiously. Figure 13.5 displays the actual observations and the prediction line. To illustrate a situation in which there is a direct interpretation for the Y intercept, b_0, see Example 13.1.

FIGURE 13.5

Scatter plot and prediction
line for Sunflowers Apparel
data

Add a prediction line and a
regression equation using
the instructions in Section
EG13.2.

Scatter Diagram for Site Selection

EXAMPLE 13.1

Interpreting the Y Intercept, b_0, and the Slope, b_1

A statistics professor wants to use the number of hours a student studies for a statistics final exam (X) to predict the final exam score (Y). A regression model was fit based on data collected from a class during the previous semester, with the following results:

$$\hat{Y}_i = 35.0 + 3X_i$$

What is the interpretation of the Y intercept, b_0, and the slope, b_1?

SOLUTION The Y intercept $b_0 = 35.0$ indicates that when the student does not study for the final exam, the predicted final exam score is 35.0. The slope $b_1 = 3$ indicates that for each increase of one hour in studying time, the predicted change in the final exam score is $+3.0$. In other words, the final exam score is predicted to increase by 3 points for each one-hour increase in studying time.

Return to the Sunflowers Apparel scenario on page 471. Example 13.2 illustrates how you use the prediction line to predict the annual sales.

EXAMPLE 13.2

Predicting Annual Sales Based on Square Footage

Use the prediction line to predict the annual sales for a store with 4,000 square feet.

SOLUTION You can determine the predicted value by substituting $X = 4$ (thousands of square feet) into the simple linear regression equation:

$$\hat{Y}_i = 0.9645 + 1.6699X_i$$
$$\hat{Y}_i = 0.9645 + 1.6699(4) = 7.644 \text{ or } \$7,644,000$$

Thus, a store with 4,000 square feet has predicted annual sales of $7,644,000.

Predictions in Regression Analysis: Interpolation Versus Extrapolation

When using a regression model for prediction purposes, you should consider only the **relevant range** of the independent variable in making predictions. This relevant range includes all values from the smallest to the largest X used in developing the regression model. Hence, when predicting Y for a given value of X, you can interpolate within this relevant range of the X values, but you should not extrapolate beyond the range of X values. When you use the square footage to predict annual sales, the square footage (in thousands of square feet) varies from 1.1 to 5.8 (see Table 13.1 on page 474). Therefore, you should predict annual sales *only* for stores whose size is between 1.1 and 5.8 thousands of square feet. Any prediction of annual sales for stores outside this range assumes that the observed relationship between sales and store size for store sizes from 1.1 to 5.8 thousand square feet is the same as for stores outside this range. For example, you cannot extrapolate the linear relationship beyond 5,800 square feet in Example 13.2. It would be improper to use the prediction line to forecast the sales for a new store containing 8,000 square feet because the relationship between sales and store size has a point of diminishing returns. If that is true, as square footage increases beyond 5,800 square feet, the effect on sales becomes smaller and smaller.

Computing the Y Intercept, b_0, and the Slope, b_1

For small data sets, you can use a hand calculator to compute the least-squares regression coefficients. Equations (13.3) and (13.4) give the values of b_0 and b_1, which minimize

$$\sum_{i=1}^{n}(Y_i - \hat{Y}_i)^2 = \sum_{i=1}^{n}[Y_i - (b_0 + b_1 X_i)]^2$$

COMPUTATIONAL FORMULA FOR THE SLOPE, b_1

$$b_1 = \frac{SSXY}{SSX} \tag{13.3}$$

where

$$SSXY = \sum_{i=1}^{n}(X_i - \bar{X})(Y_i - \bar{Y}) = \sum_{i=1}^{n}X_i Y_i - \frac{\left(\sum_{i=1}^{n}X_i\right)\left(\sum_{i=1}^{n}Y_i\right)}{n}$$

$$SSX = \sum_{i=1}^{n}(X_i - \bar{X})^2 = \sum_{i=1}^{n}X_i^2 - \frac{\left(\sum_{i=1}^{n}X_i\right)^2}{n}$$

COMPUTATIONAL FORMULA FOR THE Y INTERCEPT, b_0

$$b_0 = \bar{Y} - b_1 \bar{X} \tag{13.4}$$

where

$$\bar{Y} = \frac{\sum_{i=1}^{n}Y_i}{n}$$

$$\bar{X} = \frac{\sum_{i=1}^{n}X_i}{n}$$

EXAMPLE 13.3

Computing the Y Intercept, b_0, and the Slope, b_1

Compute the Y intercept, b_0, and the slope, b_1, for the Sunflowers Apparel data.

SOLUTION In Equations (13.3) and (13.4), five quantities need to be computed to determine b_1 and b_0. These are n, the sample size; $\sum_{i=1}^{n}X_i$, the sum of the X values; $\sum_{i=1}^{n}Y_i$, the sum of the Y values; $\sum_{i=1}^{n}X_i^2$, the sum of the squared X values; and $\sum_{i=1}^{n}X_i Y_i$, the sum of the product of X and Y. For the Sunflowers Apparel data, the number of square feet (X) is used to predict the annual sales (Y) in a store. Table 13.2 presents the computations of the sums needed for the site selection problem. The table also includes $\sum_{i=1}^{n}Y_i^2$, the sum of the squared Y values that will be used to compute SST in Section 13.3.

TABLE 13.2

Computations for the Sunflowers Apparel Data

Store	Square Feet (X)	Annual Sales (Y)	X^2	Y^2	XY
1	1.7	3.7	2.89	13.69	6.29
2	1.6	3.9	2.56	15.21	6.24
3	2.8	6.7	7.84	44.89	18.76
4	5.6	9.5	31.36	90.25	53.20
5	1.3	3.4	1.69	11.56	4.42
6	2.2	5.6	4.84	31.36	12.32
7	1.3	3.7	1.69	13.69	4.81
8	1.1	2.7	1.21	7.29	2.97
9	3.2	5.5	10.24	30.25	17.60
10	1.5	2.9	2.25	8.41	4.35
11	5.2	10.7	27.04	114.49	55.64
12	4.6	7.6	21.16	57.76	34.96
13	5.8	11.8	33.64	139.24	68.44
14	3.0	4.1	9.00	16.81	12.30
Totals	40.9	81.8	157.41	594.90	302.30

Using Equations (13.3) and (13.4), you can compute b_0 and b_1:

$$SSXY = \sum_{i=1}^{n}(X_i - \bar{X})(Y_i - \bar{Y}) = \sum_{i=1}^{n}X_iY_i - \frac{\left(\sum_{i=1}^{n}X_i\right)\left(\sum_{i=1}^{n}Y_i\right)}{n}$$

$$SSXY = 302.3 - \frac{(40.9)(81.8)}{14}$$

$$= 302.3 - 238.97285$$

$$= 63.32715$$

$$SSX = \sum_{i=1}^{n}(X_i - \bar{X})^2 = \sum_{i=1}^{n}X_i^2 - \frac{\left(\sum_{i=1}^{n}X_i\right)^2}{n}$$

$$= 157.41 - \frac{(40.9)^2}{14}$$

$$= 157.41 - 119.48642$$

$$= 37.92358$$

Therefore,

$$b_1 = \frac{SSXY}{SSX}$$

$$= \frac{63.32715}{37.92358}$$

$$= 1.6699$$

And,

$$\bar{Y} = \frac{\sum_{i=1}^{n}Y_i}{n} = \frac{81.8}{14} = 5.842857$$

$$\bar{X} = \frac{\sum_{i=1}^{n}X_i}{n} = \frac{40.9}{14} = 2.92143$$

Therefore,

$$b_0 = \overline{Y} - b_1 \overline{X}$$

$$= 5.842857 - (1.6699)(2.92143)$$

$$= 0.9645$$

VISUAL EXPLORATIONS   Exploring Simple Linear Regression Coefficients

Use the Visual Explorations Simple Linear Regression procedure to create a prediction line that is as close as possible to the prediction line defined by the least-squares solution. Open the **Visual Explorations** add-in workbook (see Appendix Section D.7) and:

1. In Excel 2007, select **Add-ins → VisualExplorations → Simple Linear Regression**. In Excel 2003, select **VisualExplorations → Simple Linear Regression**.

In the Simple Linear Regression dialog box (shown below):

2. Click for the spinner buttons for **b1 slope** (the slope of the prediction line), and **b0 intercept** (the Y intercept of the prediction line) to change the prediction line.

3. Using the visual feedback of the chart, try to create a prediction line that is as close as possible to the prediction line defined by the least-squares estimates. In other words, try to make the **Difference from Target**

SSE value as small as possible (see page 484 for an explanation of *SSE*).

At any time, click **Reset** to reset the b_1 and b_0 values or **Solution** to reveal the prediction line defined by the least-squares method. Click **Finish** when you are finished with this exercise.

Using Your Own Regression Data

Select **Simple Linear Regression with your worksheet data** from the **VisualExplorations** menu to explore the simple linear regression coefficients using data you supply from a worksheet. In the procedure's dialog box, enter the cell range of your Y variable as the **Y Variable Cell Range** and the cell range of your X variable as the **X Variable Cell Range**. Click **First cells in both ranges contain a label**, enter a **Title**, and click **OK**. After the scatter plot appears onscreen, continue with the step 2 and 3 instructions

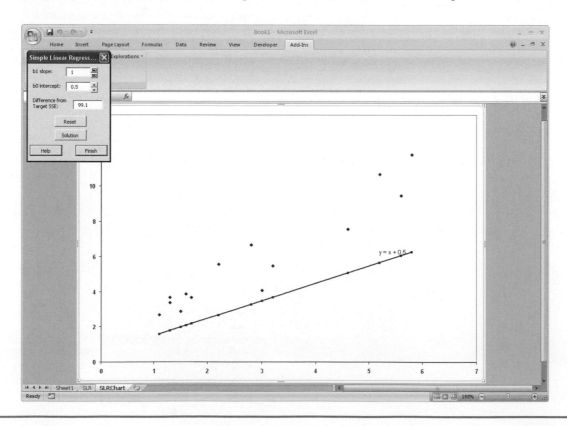

Problems for Section 13.2

LEARNING THE BASICS

13.1 Fitting a straight line to a set of data yields the following prediction line:

$$\hat{Y}_i = 2 + 5X_i$$

a. Interpret the meaning of the Y intercept, b_0.
b. Interpret the meaning of the slope, b_1.
c. Predict the value of Y for $X = 3$.

13.2 If the values of X in Problem 13.1 range from 2 to 25, should you use this model to predict the mean value of Y when X equals
a. 3?
b. −3?
c. 0?
d. 24?

13.3 Fitting a straight line to a set of data yields the following prediction line:

$$\hat{Y}_i = 16 - 0.5X_i$$

a. Interpret the meaning of the Y intercept, b_0.
b. Interpret the meaning of the slope, b_1.
c. Predict the value of Y for $X = 6$.

APPLYING THE CONCEPTS

SELF Test **13.4** The marketing manager of a large supermarket chain would like to use shelf space to predict the sales of pet food. A random sample of 12 equal-sized stores is selected, with the following results (stored in **Petfood**):

Store	Shelf Space (X) (Feet)	Weekly Sales (Y) ($)
1	5	160
2	5	220
3	5	140
4	10	190
5	10	240
6	10	260
7	15	230
8	15	270
9	15	280
10	20	260
11	20	290
12	20	310

a. Construct a scatter plot.
For these data, $b_0 = 145$ and $b_1 = 7.4$.
b. Interpret the meaning of the slope, b_1, in this problem.
c. Predict the weekly sales of pet food for stores with 8 feet of shelf space for pet food.

13.5 Circulation is the lifeblood of the publishing business. The larger the sales of a magazine, the more it can charge advertisers. However, a circulation gap has appeared between the publishers' reports of magazines' newsstand sales and subsequent audits by the Audit Bureau of Circulations. The file **Circulation** contains the reported and audited newsstand yearly sales (in thousands) for the following 10 magazines:

Magazine	Reported (X)	Audited (Y)
YM	621.0	299.6
CosmoGirl	359.7	207.7
Rosie	530.0	325.0
Playboy	492.1	336.3
Esquire	70.5	48.6
TeenPeople	567.0	400.3
More	125.5	91.2
Spin	50.6	39.1
Vogue	353.3	268.6
Elle	263.6	214.3

Source: *Data extracted from M. Rose, "In Fight for Ads, Publishers Often Overstate Their Sales,"* The Wall Street Journal, *August 6, 2003, pp. A1, A10.*

a. Construct a scatter plot.
For these data, $b_0 = 26.724$ and $b_1 = 0.5719$.
b. Interpret the meaning of the slope, b_1, in this problem.
c. Predict the audited newsstand sales for a magazine that reports newsstand sales of 400,000.

13.6 The owner of a moving company typically has his most experienced manager predict the total number of labor hours that will be required to complete an upcoming move. This approach has proved useful in the past, but the owner has the business objective of developing a more accurate method of predicting labor hours. In a preliminary effort to provide a more accurate method, the owner has decided to use the number of cubic feet moved as the independent variable and has collected data for 36 moves in which the origin and destination were within the borough of Manhattan in New York City and in which the travel time was an insignificant portion of the hours worked. The data are stored in **Moving**.
a. Construct a scatter plot.
b. Assuming a linear relationship, use the least-squares method to determine the regression coefficients b_0 and b_1.
c. Interpret the meaning of the slope, b_1, in this problem.
d. Predict the labor hours for moving 500 cubic feet.

13.7 A critically important aspect of customer service in a supermarket is the waiting time at the checkout (defined as the time the customer enters the line until he or she is served). Data were collected during time periods in which a constant

number of checkout counters were open. The total number of customers in the store and the waiting times (in minutes) were recorded. The results are stored in Supermarket.
a. Construct a scatter plot.
b. Assuming a linear relationship, use the least-squares method to determine the regression coefficients b_0 and b_1.
c. Interpret the meaning of the slope, b_1, in this problem.
d. Predict the waiting time when there are 20 customers in the store.

13.8 The value of a sports franchise is directly related to the amount of revenue that a franchise can generate. The file BBRevenue represents the value in 2009 (in millions of dollars) and the annual revenue (in millions of dollars) for the 30 major league baseball franchises. Suppose you want to develop a simple linear regression model to predict franchise value based on annual revenue generated.
a. Construct a scatter plot.
b. Use the least-squares method to determine the regression coefficients b_0 and b_1.
c. Interpret the meaning of b_0 and b_1 in this problem.
d. Predict the value of a baseball franchise that generates $200 million of annual revenue.

13.9 An agent for a residential real estate company in a large city would like to be able to predict the monthly rental cost for apartments, based on the size of an apartment, as defined by square footage. The agent selects a sample of 25 apartments in a particular residential neighborhood and gathers the data below (stored in Rent).

a. Construct a scatter plot.
b. Use the least-squares method to determine the regression coefficients b_0 and b_1.
c. Interpret the meaning of b_0 and b_1 in this problem.
d. Predict the monthly rent for an apartment that has 1,000 square feet.
e. Why would it not be appropriate to use the model to predict the monthly rent for apartments that have 500 square feet?
f. Your friends Jim and Jennifer are considering signing a lease for an apartment in this residential neighborhood. They are trying to decide between two apartments, one with 1,000 square feet for a monthly rent of $1,275 and the other with 1,200 square feet for a monthly rent of $1,425. Based on (a) through (d), which apartment do you think is a better deal?

13.10 A company that holds the DVD distribution rights to movies previously released only in theaters wants to estimate sales of DVDs based on box office success. The file Movie lists the box office gross (in $millions) for each of 30 movies and the number of DVDs sold (in thousands). For these data,
a. construct a scatter plot.
b. assuming a linear relationship, use the least-squares method to determine the regression coefficients b_0 and b_1.
c. interpret the meaning of the slope, b_1, in this problem.
d. predict the sales for a movie DVD that had a box office gross of $75 million.

Table for Problem 13.9

Apartment	Monthly Rent ($)	Size (Sq. Feet)	Apartment	Monthly Rent ($)	Size (Sq. Feet)
1	950	850	14	1,800	1,369
2	1,600	1,450	15	1,400	1,175
3	1,200	1,085	16	1,450	1,225
4	1,500	1,232	17	1,100	1,245
5	950	718	18	1,700	1,259
6	1,700	1,485	19	1,200	1,150
7	1,650	1,136	20	1,150	896
8	935	726	21	1,600	1,361
9	875	700	22	1,650	1,040
10	1,150	956	23	1,200	755
11	1,400	1,100	24	800	1,000
12	1,650	1,285	25	1,750	1,200
13	2,300	1,985			

13.3 Measures of Variation

When using the least-squares method to determine the regression coefficients for a set of data, you need to compute three measures of variation. The first measure, the **total sum of squares** **(SST)**, is a measure of variation of the Y_i values around their mean, $\bar{Y}$. The **total variation**, or total sum of squares, is subdivided into **explained variation** and **unexplained variation**. The explained variation, or **regression sum of squares (SSR)**, represents variation due to the relationship between X and Y, and the unexplained variation, or **error sum of squares (SSE)**, represents variation due to factors other than the relationship between X and Y. Figure 13.6 shows these different measures of variation.

FIGURE 13.6

Measures of variation

Computing the Sum of Squares

The regression sum of squares (SSR) is based on the difference between $\hat{Y}_i$ (the predicted value of Y from the prediction line) and $\overline{Y}$ (the mean value of Y). The error sum of squares (SSE) represents the part of the variation in Y that is not explained by the regression. It is based on the difference between Y_i and $\hat{Y}_i$ Equations (13.5), (13.6), (13.7), and (13.8) define these measures of variation.

MEASURES OF VARIATION IN REGRESSION

The total sum of squares is equal to the regression sum of squares (SSR) plus the error sum of squares (SSE).

$$SST = SSR + SSE \qquad \textbf{(13.5)}$$

TOTAL SUM OF SQUARES (SST)

The total sum of squares (SST) is equal to the sum of the squared differences between each observed value of Y and the mean value of Y.

$$SST = \text{Total sum of squares}$$

$$= \sum_{i=1}^{n}(Y_i - \overline{Y})^2 \qquad \textbf{(13.6)}$$

REGRESSION SUM OF SQUARES (SSR)

The regression sum of squares (SSR) is equal to the sum of the squared differences between each predicted value of Y and the mean value of Y.

$$SSR = \text{Explained variation or regression sum of squares}$$

$$= \sum_{i=1}^{n}(\hat{Y}_i - \overline{Y})^2 \qquad \textbf{(13.7)}$$

ERROR SUM OF SQUARES (*SSE*)

The error sum of squares (*SSE*) is equal to the sum of the squared differences between each observed value of Y and the predicted value of Y.

$$SSE = \text{Unexplained variation or error sum of squares}$$

$$= \sum_{i=1}^{n}(Y_i - \hat{Y}_i)^2 \tag{13.8}$$

Figure 13.7 shows the sum of squares portion of the worksheet for the Sunflowers Apparel data. The total variation, *SST*, is equal to 116.9543. This amount is subdivided into the sum of squares explained by the regression (*SSR*), equal to 105.7476, and the sum of squares unexplained by the regression (*SSE*), equal to 11.2067. From Equation (13.5) on page 483:

$$SST = SSR + SSE$$

$$116.9543 = 105.7476 + 11.2067$$

FIGURE 13.7

Sum of squares worksheet results for the Sunflowers Apparel data

In the worksheet, SSR is labeled **Regression SS** *cell (C12), and SSE is labeled* **Residual SS** *(C13).*

	A	B	C	D	E	F
10	ANOVA					
11		df	SS	MS	F	Significance F
12	Regression	1	105.7476	105.7476	113.2335	0.0000
13	Residual	12	11.2067	0.9339		
14	Total	13	116.9543			

The Coefficient of Determination

By themselves, *SSR*, *SSE*, and *SST* provide little information. However, the ratio of the regression sum of squares (*SSR*) to the total sum of squares (*SST*) measures the proportion of variation in Y that is explained by the independent variable X in the regression model. This ratio, called the coefficient of determination, r^2, is defined in Equation (13.9).

COEFFICIENT OF DETERMINATION

The coefficient of determination is equal to the regression sum of squares (i.e., explained variation) divided by the total sum of squares (i.e., total variation).

$$r^2 = \frac{\text{Regression sum of squares}}{\text{Total sum of squares}} = \frac{SSR}{SST} \tag{13.9}$$

The **coefficient of determination** measures the proportion of variation in Y that is explained by the independent variable X in the regression model.

For the Sunflowers Apparel data, with $SSR = 105.7476$, $SSE = 11.2067$, and $SST = 116.9543$,

$$r^2 = \frac{105.7476}{116.9543} = 0.9042$$

Therefore, 90.42% of the variation in annual sales is explained by the variability in the size of the store as measured by the square footage. This large r^2 indicates a strong linear relationship between these two variables because the use of a regression model has reduced the variability in predicting annual sales by 90.42%. Only 9.58% of the sample variability in annual sales is due to factors other than what is accounted for by the linear regression model that uses square footage.

Figure 13.8 presents the Regression Statistics table portion of the regression results worksheet for the Sunflowers Apparel data. This table contains the coefficient of determination in cell B5 (labeled R Square).

FIGURE 13.8

Regression Statistics portion of the worksheet results for the Sunflowers Apparel data

▲	A	B
3	**Regression Statistics**	
4	Multiple R	0.9509
5	R Square	0.9042
6	Adjusted R Square	0.8962
7	Standard Error	0.9664
8	Observations	14

EXAMPLE 13.4

Computing the Coefficient of Determination

Compute the coefficient of determination, r^2, for the Sunflowers Apparel data.

SOLUTION You can compute *SST*, *SSR*, and *SSE*, which are defined in Equations (13.6), (13.7), and (13.8) on pages 483 and 484, by using Equations (13.10), (13.11), and (13.12).

COMPUTATIONAL FORMULA FOR *SST*

$$SST = \sum_{i=1}^{n}(Y_i - \bar{Y})^2 = \sum_{i=1}^{n}Y_i^2 - \frac{\left(\sum_{i=1}^{n}Y_i\right)^2}{n} \qquad (13.10)$$

COMPUTATIONAL FORMULA FOR *SSR*

$$SSR = \sum_{i=1}^{n}(\hat{Y}_i - \bar{Y})^2$$

$$= b_0\sum_{i=1}^{n}Y_i + b_1\sum_{i=1}^{n}X_iY_i - \frac{\left(\sum_{i=1}^{n}Y_i\right)^2}{n} \qquad (13.11)$$

COMPUTATIONAL FORMULA FOR *SSE*

$$SSE = \sum_{i=1}^{n}(Y_i - \hat{Y}_i)^2 = \sum_{i=1}^{n}Y_i^2 - b_0\sum_{i=1}^{n}Y_i - b_1\sum_{i=1}^{n}X_iY_i \qquad (13.12)$$

Using the summary results from Table 13.2 on page 479,

$$SST = \sum_{i=1}^{n}(Y_i - \bar{Y})^2 = \sum_{i=1}^{n}Y_i^2 - \frac{\left(\sum_{i=1}^{n}Y_i\right)^2}{n}$$

$$= 594.9 - \frac{(81.8)^2}{14}$$

$$= 594.9 - 477.94571$$

$$= 116.95429$$

$$SSR = \sum_{i=1}^{n} (\hat{Y}_i - \bar{Y})^2$$

$$= b_0 \sum_{i=1}^{n} Y_i + b_1 \sum_{i=1}^{n} X_i Y_i - \frac{\left(\sum_{i=1}^{n} Y_i\right)^2}{n}$$

$$= (0.9645)(81.8) + (1.6699)(302.3) - \frac{(81.8)^2}{14}$$

$$= 105.74726$$

$$SSE = \sum_{i=1}^{n} (Y_i - \hat{Y}_i)^2$$

$$= \sum_{i=1}^{n} Y_i^2 - b_0 \sum_{i=1}^{n} Y_i - b_1 \sum_{i=1}^{n} X_i Y_i$$

$$= 594.9 - (0.9645)(81.8) - (1.6699)(302.3)$$

$$= 11.2067$$

Therefore,

$$r^2 = \frac{105.74726}{116.95429} = 0.9042$$

Standard Error of the Estimate

Although the least-squares method produces the line that fits the data with the minimum amount of error, unless all the observed data points fall on a straight line, the prediction line is not a perfect predictor. Just as all data values cannot be expected to be exactly equal to their mean, neither can all the values in a regression analysis be expected to fall exactly on the prediction line. Figure 13.5 on page 476 illustrates the variability around the prediction line for the Sunflowers Apparel data. Observe that many of the actual values of Y fall near the prediction line, but none of the values are exactly on the line.

The **standard error of the estimate** measures the variability of the actual Y values from the predicted Y values in the same way that the standard deviation in Chapter 3 measures the variability of each value around the sample mean. In other words, the standard error of the estimate is the standard deviation *around* the prediction line, whereas the standard deviation in Chapter 3 is the standard deviation *around* the sample mean. Equation (13.13) defines the standard error of the estimate, represented by the symbol S_{YX}.

STANDARD ERROR OF THE ESTIMATE

$$S_{YX} = \sqrt{\frac{SSE}{n-2}} = \sqrt{\frac{\sum_{i=1}^{n}(Y_i - \hat{Y}_i)^2}{n-2}} \tag{13.13}$$

where

Y_i = actual value of Y for a given X_i

$\hat{Y}_i$ = predicted value of Y for a given X_i

SSE = error sum of squares

From Equation (13.8) and Figure 13.4 or Figure 13.7 on pages 476 or 484, $SSE = 11.2067$. Thus,

$$S_{YX} = \sqrt{\frac{11.2067}{14-2}} = 0.9664$$

This standard error of the estimate, equal to 0.9664 millions of dollars (i.e., $966,400), is labeled Standard Error in the Figure 13.8 worksheet results. The standard error of the estimate represents a measure of the variation around the prediction line. It is measured in the same units as the dependent variable Y. The interpretation of the standard error of the estimate is similar to that of the standard deviation. Just as the standard deviation measures variability around the mean, the standard error of the estimate measures variability around the prediction line. For Sunflowers Apparel, the typical difference between actual annual sales at a store and the predicted annual sales using the regression equation is approximately $966,400.

Problems for Section 13.3

LEARNING THE BASICS

13.11 How do you interpret a coefficient of determination, r^2, equal to 0.80?

13.12 If $SSR = 36$ and $SSE = 4$, determine SST and then compute the coefficient of determination, r^2, and interpret its meaning.

13.13 If $SSR = 66$ and $SST = 88$, compute the coefficient of determination, r^2, and interpret its meaning.

13.14 If $SSE = 10$ and $SSR = 30$, compute the coefficient of determination, r^2, and interpret its meaning.

13.15 If $SSR = 120$, why is it impossible for SST to equal 110?

APPLYING THE CONCEPTS

✓SELF **13.16** In Problem 13.4 on page 481, the marketing manager used shelf space for pet food **Test** to predict weekly sales (stored in Petfood). For those data, $SSR = 20,535$ and $SST = 30,025$.
a. Determine the coefficient of determination, r^2, and interpret its meaning.
b. Determine the standard error of the estimate.
c. How useful do you think this regression model is for predicting sales?

13.17 In Problem 13.5 on page 481, you used reported magazine newsstand sales to predict audited sales (stored in Circulation). For those data, $SSR = 130,301.41$ and $SST = 144,538.64$.
a. Determine the coefficient of determination, r^2, and interpret its meaning.
b. Determine the standard error of the estimate.
c. How useful do you think this regression model is for predicting audited sales?

13.18 In Problem 13.6 on page 481, an owner of a moving company wanted to predict labor hours, based on the cubic feet moved (stored in Moving). Using the results of that problem,
a. determine the coefficient of determination, r^2, and interpret its meaning.
b. determine the standard error of the estimate.

c. How useful do you think this regression model is for predicting labor hours?

13.19 In Problem 13.7 on page 481, you used the number of customers to predict the waiting time at the checkout line in a supermarket (stored in Supermarket). Using the results of that problem,
a. determine the coefficient of determination, r^2, and interpret its meaning.
b. determine the standard error of the estimate.
c. How useful do you think this regression model is for predicting the waiting time at the checkout line in a supermarket?

13.20 In Problem 13.8 on page 482, you used annual revenues to predict the value of a baseball franchise (stored in BBRevenue). Using the results of that problem,
a. determine the coefficient of determination, r^2, and interpret its meaning.
b. determine the standard error of the estimate.
c. How useful do you think this regression model is for predicting the value of a baseball franchise?

13.21 In Problem 13.9 on page 482, an agent for a real estate company wanted to predict the monthly rent for apartments, based on the size of the apartment (stored in Rent). Using the results of that problem,
a. determine the coefficient of determination, r^2, and interpret its meaning.
b. determine the standard error of the estimate.
c. How useful do you think this regression model is for predicting the monthly rent?
d. Can you think of other variables that might explain the variation in monthly rent?

13.22 In Problem 13.10 on page 482, you used box office gross to predict sales of DVDs (stored in Movie). Using the results of that problem,
a. determine the coefficient of determination, r^2, and interpret its meaning.
b. determine the standard error of the estimate.
c. How useful do you think this regression model is for predicting sales of DVDs?
d. Can you think of other variables that might explain the variation in DVD sales?

13.4 Assumptions

When hypothesis testing and the analysis of variance were discussed in Chapters 9 through 12, the importance of the assumptions to the validity of any conclusions reached was emphasized. The assumptions necessary for regression are similar to those of the analysis of variance because both are part of the general category of *linear models* (reference 4).

The four **assumptions of regression** (known by the acronym LINE) are as follows:

- Linearity
- Independence of errors
- Normality of error
- Equal variance

The first assumption, **linearity**, states that the relationship between variables is linear. Relationships between variables that are not linear are discussed in Chapter 15.

The second assumption, **independence of errors**, requires that the errors (ε_i) are independent of one another. This assumption is particularly important when data are collected over a period of time. In such situations, the errors in a specific time period are sometimes correlated with those of the previous time period.

The third assumption, **normality**, requires that the errors (ε_i) are normally distributed at each value of X. Like the t test and the ANOVA F test, regression analysis is fairly robust against departures from the normality assumption. As long as the distribution of the errors at each level of X is not extremely different from a normal distribution, inferences about β_0 and β_1 are not seriously affected.

The fourth assumption, **equal variance**, or **homoscedasticity**, requires that the variance of the errors (ε_i) be constant for all values of X. In other words, the variability of Y values is the same when X is a low value as when X is a high value. The equal variance assumption is important when making inferences about β_0 and β_1. If there are serious departures from this assumption, you can use either data transformations or weighted least-squares methods (see reference 4).

13.5 Residual Analysis

Sections 13.2 and 13.3 developed a regression model using the least-squares approach for the Sunflowers Apparel data. Is this the correct model for these data? Are the assumptions presented in Section 13.4 valid? **Residual analysis** visually evaluates these assumptions and helps you to determine whether the regression model that has been selected is appropriate.

The **residual**, or estimated error value, e_i, is the difference between the observed (Y_i) and predicted ($\hat{Y}_i$) values of the dependent variable for a given value of X_i. A residual appears on a scatter plot as the vertical distance between an observed value of Y and the prediction line. Equation (13.14) defines the residual.

RESIDUAL

The residual is equal to the difference between the observed value of Y and the predicted value of Y.

$$e_i = Y_i - \hat{Y}_i \qquad\qquad \textbf{(13.14)}$$

Evaluating the Assumptions

Recall from Section 13.4 that the four assumptions of regression (known by the acronym LINE) are linearity, independence, normality, and equal variance.

Linearity   To evaluate linearity, you plot the residuals on the vertical axis against the corresponding X_i values of the independent variable on the horizontal axis. If the linear model is appropriate for the data, you will not see any apparent pattern in the plot. However, if the linear model is not appropriate, in the residual plot, there will be a relationship between the X_i values and the residuals, e_i.

You can see such a pattern in Figure 13.9. Panel A shows a situation in which, although there is an increasing trend in Y as X increases, the relationship seems curvilinear because the upward trend decreases for increasing values of X. This quadratic effect is highlighted in Panel B, where there is a clear relationship between X_i and e_i. By plotting the residuals, the linear trend of X with Y has been removed, thereby exposing the lack of fit in the simple linear model. Thus, a quadratic model is a better fit and should be used in place of the simple linear model. (See Section 15.1 for further discussion of fitting curvilinear models.)

FIGURE 13.9

Studying the appropriateness of the simple linear regression model

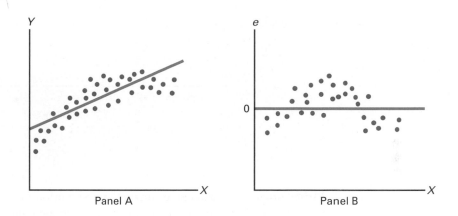

To determine whether the simple linear regression model is appropriate, return to the evaluation of the Sunflowers Apparel data. Figure 13.10 displays the predicted annual sales values and residuals.

FIGURE 13.10

Table of residuals for the Sunflowers Apparel data

Figure 13.10 displays the **RESIDUALS worksheet** *of the* **Simple Linear Regression workbook**. *Create this worksheet using the instructions in Section EG13.5. If you use the Analysis ToolPak Regression procedure, the residual table will not include the second and fourth columns and will appear in a RESIDUAL OUTPUT area of the main regression results worksheet.*

	A	B	C	D	E
1	Observation	Square Feet	Predicted Annual Sales	Annual Sales	Residuals
2	1	1.7	3.803239598	3.7	0.103239598
3	2	1.6	3.636253367	3.9	-0.263746633
4	3	2.8	5.640088147	6.7	-1.059911853
5	4	5.6	10.31570263	9.5	0.815702635
6	5	1.3	3.135294672	3.4	-0.264705328
7	6	2.2	4.638170757	5.6	-0.961829243
8	7	1.3	3.135294672	3.7	-0.564705328
9	8	1.1	2.801322208	2.7	0.101322208
10	9	3.2	6.308033074	5.5	0.808033074
11	10	1.5	3.469267135	2.9	0.569267135
12	11	5.2	9.647757708	10.7	-1.052242292
13	12	4.6	8.645840318	7.6	1.045840318
14	13	5.8	10.6496751	11.8	-1.150324902
15	14	3.0	5.974060611	4.1	1.874060611

To assess linearity, the residuals are plotted against the independent variable (store size, in thousands of square feet) in Figure 13.11. Although there is widespread scatter in the residual plot, there is no clear pattern or relationship between the residuals and X_i. The residuals appear to be evenly spread above and below 0 for different values of X. You can conclude that the linear model is appropriate for the Sunflowers Apparel data.

FIGURE 13.11

Plot of residuals against
the square footage of a
store for the Sunflowers
Apparel data

*Create residual plots using
the instructions in Section
EG13.5.*

Square Feet Residual Plot

Independence You can evaluate the assumption of independence of the errors by plotting the residuals in the order or sequence in which the data were collected. If the values of Y are part of a time series (see Section 2.7), one residual may sometimes be related to the previous residual. If this relationship exists between consecutive residuals (which violates the assumption of independence), the plot of the residuals versus the time in which the data were collected will often show a cyclical pattern. Because the Sunflowers Apparel data were collected during the same time period, you do not need to evaluate the independence assumption for these data.

Normality You can evaluate the assumption of normality in the errors by organizing the residuals into a frequency distribution as shown in Table 13.3. You cannot construct a meaningful histogram because the sample size is too small. And with such a small sample size ($n = 14$), it can be difficult to evaluate the normality assumption using a stem-and-leaf display (see Section 2.6), a boxplot (see Section 3.3) or a normal probability plot (see Section 6.3).

TABLE 13.3

Frequency Distribution
lof 14 Residual Values
for the Sunflowers
Apparel Data

Residuals	Frequency
-2.25 but less than -1.75	1
-1.75 but less than -1.25	0
-1.25 but less than -0.75	3
-0.75 but less than -0.25	1
-0.25 but less than $+0.25$	2
$+0.25$ but less than $+0.75$	3
$+0.75$ but less than $+1.25$	4
	14

That said, from the normal probability plot of the residuals in Figure 13.12, the data do not appear to depart substantially from a normal distribution. The robustness of regression analysis with modest departures from normality enables you to conclude that you should not be overly concerned about departures from this normality assumption in the Sunflowers Apparel data.

FIGURE 13.12

Normal probability plot of the residuals for the Sunflowers Apparel data

Create normal probability plots using the instructions in Section EG6.3.

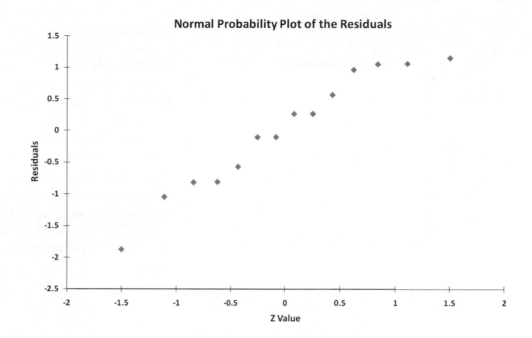

Normal Probability Plot of the Residuals

Equal Variance You can evaluate the assumption of equal variance from a plot of the residuals with X_i. For the Sunflowers Apparel data of Figure 13.11 on page 490, there do not appear to be major differences in the variability of the residuals for different X_i values. Thus, you can conclude that there is no apparent violation in the assumption of equal variance at each level of X.

To examine a case in which the equal variance assumption is violated, observe Figure 13.13, which is a plot of the residuals with X_i for a hypothetical set of data. In this plot, the variability of the residuals increases dramatically as X increases, demonstrating the lack of homogeneity in the variances of Y_i at each level of X. For these data, the equal variance assumption is invalid.

FIGURE 13.13

Violation of equal variance

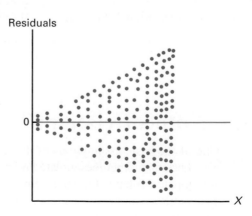

Problems for Section 13.5

LEARNING THE BASICS

13.23 The results below provide the X values, residuals, and a residual plot from a regression analysis:

Is there any evidence of a pattern in the residuals? Explain.

13.24 The results below show the X values, residuals, and a residual plot from a regression analysis:

Is there any evidence of a pattern in the residuals? Explain.

APPLYING THE CONCEPTS

13.25 In Problem 13.5 on page 481, you used reported magazine newsstand sales to predict audited sales. Perform a residual analysis for these data (stored in **Circulation**). Evaluate whether the assumptions of regression have been seriously violated.

✓ SELF Test 13.26 In Problem 13.4 on page 481, the marketing manager used shelf space for pet food to predict weekly sales. Perform a residual analysis for these data (stored in **Petfood**). Evaluate whether the assumptions of regression have been seriously violated.

13.27 In Problem 13.7 on page 481, you used the number of customers to predict the waiting time at a supermarket checkout. Perform a residual analysis for these data (stored in **Supermarket**). Based on these results, evaluate whether the assumptions of regression have been seriously violated.

13.28 In Problem 13.6 on page 481, the owner of a moving company wanted to predict labor hours based on the cubic feet moved. Perform a residual analysis for these data (stored in **Moving**). Based on these results, evaluate whether the assumptions of regression have been seriously violated.

13.29 In Problem 13.9 on page 482, an agent for a real estate company wanted to predict the monthly rent for apartments, based on the size of the apartments. Perform a residual analysis for these data (stored in **Rent**). Based on these results, evaluate whether the assumptions of regression have been seriously violated.

13.30 In Problem 13.8 on page 482, you used annual revenues to predict the value of a baseball franchise. Perform a residual analysis for these data (stored in **BBRevenue**). Based on these results, evaluate whether the assumptions of regression have been seriously violated.

13.31 In Problem 13.10 on page 482, you used box office gross to predict the sales of DVDs. Perform a residual analysis for these data (stored in **Movie**). Based on these results, evaluate whether the assumptions of regression have been seriously violated.

13.6 Measuring Autocorrelation: The Durbin-Watson Statistic

One of the basic assumptions of the regression model is the independence of the errors. This assumption is sometimes violated when data are collected over sequential time periods because a residual at any one time period may tend to be similar to residuals at adjacent time periods. This pattern in the residuals is called **autocorrelation**. When a set of data has substantial autocorrelation, the validity of a regression model is in serious doubt.

Residual Plots to Detect Autocorrelation

As mentioned in Section 13.5, one way to detect autocorrelation is to plot the residuals in time order. If a positive autocorrelation effect exists, there will be clusters of residuals with the same sign, and you will readily detect an apparent pattern. If negative autocorrelation exists, residuals will tend to jump back and forth from positive to negative to positive, and so on. This type of pattern is very rarely seen in regression analysis. Thus, the focus of this section is on positive autocorrelation. To illustrate positive autocorrelation, consider the following example.

The business problem faced by the manager of a package delivery store is to predict weekly sales. In approaching this problem, she has decided to develop a regression model to use the number of customers making purchases as an independent variable. Data are collected for a period of 15 weeks. Table 13.4 organizes the data (stored in **Custsale**).

TABLE 13.4

Customers and Sales for a Period of 15 Consecutive Weeks

Week	Customers	Sales (Thousands of Dollars)	Week	Customers	Sales (Thousands of Dollars)
1	794	9.33	9	880	12.07
2	799	8.26	10	905	12.55
3	837	7.48	11	886	11.92
4	855	9.08	12	843	10.27
5	845	9.83	13	904	11.80
6	844	10.09	14	950	12.15
7	863	11.01	15	841	9.64
8	875	11.49			

Because the data are collected over a period of 15 consecutive weeks at the same store, you need to determine whether autocorrelation is present. Figure 13.14 presents worksheet results for these data.

FIGURE 13.14

Regression results worksheet for the package delivery store data of Table 13.4

Create simple linear models using the instructions in Section EG13.2.

	A	B	C	D	E	F	G
1	Package Delivery Store Sales Analysis						
2							
3	*Regression Statistics*						
4	Multiple R	0.8108					
5	R Square	0.6574					
6	Adjusted R Square	0.6311					
7	Standard Error	0.9360					
8	Observations	15					
9							
10	ANOVA						
11		*df*	*SS*	*MS*	*F*	*Significance F*	
12	Regression	1	21.8604	21.8604	24.9501	0.0002	
13	Residual	13	11.3901	0.8762			
14	Total	14	33.2506				
15							
16		*Coefficients*	*Standard Error*	*t Stat*	*P-value*	*Lower 95%*	*Upper 95%*
17	Intercept	-16.0322	5.3102	-3.0192	0.0099	-27.5041	-4.5603
18	Customers	0.0308	0.0062	4.9950	0.0002	0.0175	0.0441

From Figure 13.14, observe that r^2 is 0.6574, indicating that 65.74% of the variation in sales is explained by variation in the number of customers. In addition, the Y intercept, b_0, is -16.0322, and the slope, b_1, is 0.0308. However, before using this model for prediction, you must perform a residual analysis. Because the data have been collected over a consecutive period of 15 weeks, in addition to checking the linearity, normality, and equal-variance assumptions, you must investigate the independence-of-errors assumption. To do this, you plot the residuals versus time in Figure 13.15 to help examine whether a pattern exists. In Figure 13.15, you can see that the residuals tend to fluctuate up and down in a cyclical pattern. This cyclical pattern provides strong cause for concern about the existence of autocorrelation in the residuals and, therefore, a violation of the independence-of-errors assumption.

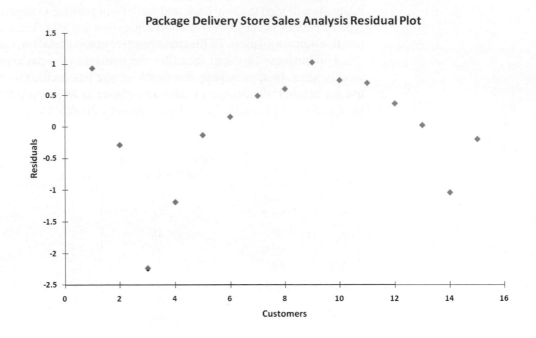

Package Delivery Store Sales Analysis Residual Plot

The Durbin-Watson Statistic

The **Durbin-Watson statistic** is used to measure autocorrelation. This statistic measures the correlation between each residual and the residual for the previous time period. Equation (13.15) defines the Durbin-Watson statistic.

DURBIN-WATSON STATISTIC

$$D = \frac{\sum_{i=2}^{n}(e_i - e_{i-1})^2}{\sum_{i=1}^{n}e_i^2}$$
(13.15)

where

$$e_i = \text{residual at the time period } i$$

To better understand the Durbin-Watson statistic, D, you can examine Equation (13.15). The numerator, $\sum_{i=2}^{n}(e_i - e_{i-1})^2$, represents the squared difference between two successive residuals, summed from the second value to the nth value. The denominator, $\sum_{i=1}^{n}e_i^2$, represents the sum of the squared residuals. When successive residuals are positively autocorrelated, the value of D approaches 0. If the residuals are not correlated, the value of D will be close to 2. (If there is negative autocorrelation, D will be greater than 2 and could even approach its maximum value of 4.) For the package delivery store data, the Figure 13.16 worksheet results show that the Durbin-Watson statistic, D, is 0.8830.

FIGURE 13.16

Durbin-Watson statistic worksheet for the package delivery store data

*Figure 13.16 displays a worksheet similar to the **DURBIN_WATSON** worksheet of the **Simple Linear Regression workbook**. Create worksheets that compute the Durbin-Watson statistic using the instructions in Section EG13.6.*

	A	B
1	Durbin-Watson Statistics	
2		
3	Sum of Squared Difference of Residuals	10.0575 =SUMXMY2(RESIDUALS!E3:E16,RESIDUALS!E2:E15)
4	Sum of Squared Residuals	11.3901 =SUMSQ(RESIDUALS!E2:E16)
5		
6	Durbin-Watson Statistic	0.8830 =B3/B4

You need to determine when the autocorrelation is large enough to conclude that there is significant positive autocorrelation. After computing D, you compare it to the critical values of the Durbin-Watson statistic found in Table E.8, a portion of which is presented in Table 13.5. The critical values depend on α, the significance level chosen, n, the sample size, and k, the number of independent variables in the model (in simple linear regression, $k = 1$).

TABLE 13.5

Finding Critical Values of the Durbin-Watson Statistic

						$\alpha = .05$					
		$k = 1$		$k = 2$		$k = 3$		$k = 4$		$k = 5$	
n		d_L	d_U	d_L	d_U	d_L	d_U	d_L	d_U	d_L	d_U
15		1.08	1.36	.95	1.54	.82	1.75	.69	1.97	.56	2.21
16		1.10	1.37	.98	1.54	.86	1.73	.74	1.93	.62	2.15
17		1.13	1.38	1.02	1.54	.90	1.71	.78	1.90	.67	2.10
18		1.16	1.39	1.05	1.53	.93	1.69	.82	1.87	.71	2.06

In Table 13.5, two values are shown for each combination of α (level of significance), n (sample size), and k (number of independent variables in the model). The first value, d_L, represents the lower critical value. If D is below d_L, you conclude that there is evidence of positive autocorrelation among the residuals. If this occurs, the least-squares method used in this chapter is inappropriate, and you should use alternative methods (see reference 4). The second value, d_U, represents the upper critical value of D, above which you would conclude that there is no evidence of positive autocorrelation among the residuals. If D is between d_L and d_U, you are unable to arrive at a definite conclusion.

For the package delivery store data, with one independent variable ($k = 1$) and 15 values ($n = 15$), $d_L = 1.08$ and $d_U = 1.36$. Because $D = 0.8830 < 1.08$, you conclude that there is positive autocorrelation among the residuals. The least-squares regression analysis of the data is inappropriate because of the presence of significant positive autocorrelation among the residuals. In other words, the independence-of-errors assumption is invalid. You need to use alternative approaches, discussed in reference 4.

Problems for Section 13.6

LEARNING THE BASICS

13.32 The residuals for 10 consecutive time periods are as follows:

Time Period	Residual	Time Period	Residual
1	−5	6	+1
2	−4	7	+2
3	−3	8	+3
4	−2	9	+4
5	−1	10	+5

a. Plot the residuals over time. What conclusion can you reach about the pattern of the residuals over time?
b. Based on (a), what conclusion can you reach about the autocorrelation of the residuals?

13.33 The residuals for 15 consecutive time periods are as follows:

Time Period	Residual	Time Period	Residual
1	+4	9	+6
2	−6	10	−3
3	−1	11	+1
4	−5	12	+3
5	+2	13	0
6	+5	14	−4
7	−2	15	−7
8	+7		

a. Plot the residuals over time. What conclusion can you reach about the pattern of the residuals over time?

b. Compute the Durbin-Watson statistic. At the 0.05 level of significance, is there evidence of positive autocorrelation among the residuals?

c. Based on (a) and (b), what conclusion can you reach about the autocorrelation of the residuals?

APPLYING THE CONCEPTS

13.34 In Problem 13.4 on page 481 concerning pet food sales, the marketing manager used shelf space for pet food to predict weekly sales.

a. Is it necessary to compute the Durbin-Watson statistic in this case? Explain.

b. Under what circumstances is it necessary to compute the Durbin-Watson statistic before proceeding with the least-squares method of regression analysis?

13.35 What is the relationship between the price of crude oil and the price you pay at the pump for gasoline? The file **Oil & Gas** contains the price for a barrel of crude oil and a gallon of gasoline for 100 weeks ending June 1, 2009 (data extracted from Energy Information Administration, U.S. Department of Energy, **www.eia.doe.gov**).

a. Construct a scatter plot with oil on the horizontal axis and gasoline on the vertical axis.

b. Use the least-squares method to develop a simple linear regression equation to predict the price of a gallon of gasoline using the price of a barrel of crude oil as the independent variable.

c. Interpret the meaning of the slope, b_1, in this problem.

d. Plot the residuals versus the time period.

e. Compute the Durbin-Watson statistic.

f. At the 0.05 level of significance, is there evidence of positive autocorrelation among the residuals?

g. Based on the results of (d) through (f), is there reason to question the validity of the model?

✓ SELF Test **13.36** A mail-order catalog business that sells personal computer supplies, software, and hardware maintains a centralized warehouse for the distribution of products ordered. Management is currently examining the process of distribution from the warehouse and is interested in studying the factors that affect warehouse distribution costs. Currently, a small handling fee is added to the order, regardless of the amount of the order. Data that indicate the warehouse distribution costs and the number of orders received have been collected over the past 24 months and stored in **Warecost**. The results are shown at the top of the next column.

a. Assuming a linear relationship, use the least-squares method to find the regression coefficients b_0 and b_1.

b. Predict the monthly warehouse distribution costs when the number of orders is 4,500.

c. Plot the residuals versus the time period.

d. Compute the Durbin-Watson statistic. At the 0.05 level of significance, is there evidence of positive autocorrelation among the residuals?

e. Based on the results of (c) and (d), is there reason to question the validity of the model?

Months	Distribution Cost (Thousands of Dollars)	Number of Orders
1	52.95	4,015
2	71.66	3,806
3	85.58	5,309
4	63.69	4,262
5	72.81	4,296
6	68.44	4,097
7	52.46	3,213
8	70.77	4,809
9	82.03	5,237
10	74.39	4,732
11	70.84	4,413
12	54.08	2,921
13	62.98	3,977
14	72.30	4,428
15	58.99	3,964
16	79.38	4,582
17	94.44	5,582
18	59.74	3,450
19	90.50	5,079
20	93.24	5,735
21	69.33	4,269
22	53.71	3,708
23	89.18	5,387
24	66.80	4,161

13.37 A freshly brewed shot of espresso has three distinct components: the heart, body, and crema. The separation of these three components typically lasts only 10 to 20 seconds. To use the espresso shot in making a latte, a cappuccino, or another drink, the shot must be poured into the beverage during the separation of the heart, body, and crema. If the shot is used after the separation occurs, the drink becomes excessively bitter and acidic, ruining the final drink. Thus, a longer separation time allows the drink-maker more time to pour the shot and ensure that the beverage will meet expectations. An employee at a coffee shop hypothesized that the harder the espresso grounds were tamped down into the portafilter before brewing, the longer the separation time would be. An experiment using 24 observations was conducted to test this relationship. The independent variable Tamp measures the distance, in inches, between the espresso grounds and the top of the portafilter (i.e., the harder the tamp, the larger the distance). The dependent variable Time is the number of seconds the heart, body, and crema are separated (i.e., the amount of time after the shot is poured before it must be used for the customer's beverage). The data are stored in **Espresso** and are shown on page 497:

a. Use the least-squares method to develop a simple regression equation with Time as the dependent variable and Tamp as the independent variable.

b. Predict the separation time for a Tamp distance of 0.50 inch.

c. Plot the residuals versus the time order of experimentation. Are there any noticeable patterns?

Shot	Tamp (Inches)	Time (Seconds)	Shot	Tamp (Inches)	Time (Seconds)
1	0.20	14	13	0.50	18
2	0.50	14	14	0.50	13
3	0.50	18	15	0.35	19
4	0.20	16	16	0.35	19
5	0.20	16	17	0.20	17
6	0.50	13	18	0.20	18
7	0.20	12	19	0.20	15
8	0.35	15	20	0.20	16
9	0.50	9	21	0.35	18
10	0.35	15	22	0.35	16
11	0.50	11	23	0.35	14
12	0.50	16	24	0.35	16

d. Compute the Durbin-Watson statistic. At the 0.05 level of significance, is there evidence of positive autocorrelation among the residuals?

e. Based on the results of (c) and (d), is there reason to question the validity of the model?

13.38 The owner of a chain of ice cream stores has the business objective of improving the forecast of daily sales so that staffing shortages can be minimized during the summer season. The owner has decided to begin by developing a simple linear regression model to predict daily sales based on atmospheric temperature. A sample of 21 consecutive days is selected, and the results are stored in IceCream.

(Hint: Determine which are the independent and dependent variables.)

a. Assuming a linear relationship, use the least-squares method to compute the regression coefficients b_0 and b_1.

b. Predict the sales for a day in which the temperature is 83°F.

c. Plot the residuals versus the time period.

d. Compute the Durbin-Watson statistic. At the 0.05 level of significance, is there evidence of positive autocorrelation among the residuals?

e. Based on the results of (c) and (d), is there reason to question the validity of the model?

13.7 Inferences About the Slope and Correlation Coefficient

In Sections 13.1 through 13.3, regression was used solely for descriptive purposes. You learned how the least-squares method determines the regression coefficients and how to predict Y for a given value of X. In addition, you learned how to compute and interpret the standard error of the estimate and the coefficient of determination.

When residual analysis, as discussed in Section 13.5, indicates that the assumptions of a least-squares regression model are not seriously violated and that the straight-line model is appropriate, you can make inferences about the linear relationship between the variables in the population.

t Test for the Slope

To determine the existence of a significant linear relationship between the X and Y variables, you test whether β_1 (the population slope) is equal to 0. The null and alternative hypotheses are as follows:

$$H_0: \beta_1 = 0 \text{ [There is no linear relationship (the slope is zero).]}$$

$$H_1: \beta_1 \neq 0 \text{ [There is a linear relationship (the slope is not zero).]}$$

If you reject the null hypothesis, you conclude that there is evidence of a linear relationship. Equation (13.16) defines the test statistic.

TESTING A HYPOTHESIS FOR A POPULATION SLOPE, β_1, USING THE t TEST

The t_{STAT} test statistic equals the difference between the sample slope and hypothesized value of the population slope divided by the standard error of the slope.

$$t_{STAT} = \frac{b_1 - \beta_1}{S_{b_1}}$$

(13.16)

where

$$S_{b_1} = \frac{S_{YX}}{\sqrt{SSX}}$$

$$SSX = \sum_{i=1}^{n} (X_i - \bar{X})^2$$

The t_{STAT} test statistic follows a t distribution with $n - 2$ degrees of freedom.

Return to the Sunflowers Apparel scenario on page 471. To test whether there is a significant linear relationship between the size of the store and the annual sales at the 0.05 level of significance, refer to the worksheet t test results shown in Figure 13.17.

FIGURE 13.17

Worksheet t test results for the slope for the Sunflowers Apparel data

In Figure 13.17, the t_{STAT} test statistic appears in cell D18 and is labeled t Stat.

	A	B	C	D	E	F	G	H	I
16		Coefficients	Standard Error	t Stat	P-value	Lower 95%	Upper 95%	Lower 95.0%	Upper 95.0%
17	Intercept	0.9645	0.5262	1.8329	0.0917	-0.1820	2.1110	-0.1820	2.11095
18	Square Feet	1.6699	0.1569	10.6411	0.0000	1.3280	2.0118	1.3280	2.01177

From Figure 13.17,

$$b_1 = +1.6699 \quad n = 14 \quad S_{b_1} = 0.1569$$

and

$$t_{STAT} = \frac{b_1 - \beta_1}{S_{b_1}}$$

$$= \frac{1.6699 - 0}{0.1569} = 10.6411$$

Using the 0.05 level of significance, the critical value of t with $n - 2 = 12$ degrees of freedom is 2.1788. Because $t_{STAT} = 10.6411 > 2.1788$ or because the p-value is approximately 0, which is less than, $\alpha = 0.05$, you reject H_0 (see Figure 13.18). Hence, you can conclude that there is a significant linear relationship between mean annual sales and the size of the store.

FIGURE 13.18

Testing a hypothesis about the population slope at the 0.05 level of significance, with 12 degrees of freedom

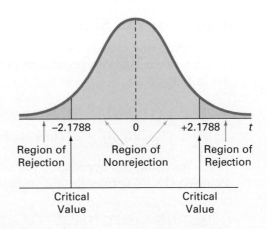

F Test for the Slope

As an alternative to the t test, you can use an F test to determine whether the slope in simple linear regression is statistically significant. In Section 10.4, you used the F distribution to test the ratio of two variances. Equation (13.17) defines the F test for the slope as the ratio of the variance that is due to the regression (MSR) divided by the error variance ($MSE = S_{YX}^2$).

TESTING A HYPOTHESIS FOR A POPULATION SLOPE, β_1, USING THE F TEST

The F_{STAT} test statistic is equal to the regression mean square (MSR) divided by the mean square error (MSE).

$$F_{STAT} = \frac{MSR}{MSE} \qquad\qquad (13.17)$$

where

$$MSR = \frac{SSR}{1} = SSR$$

$$MSE = \frac{SSE}{n-2}$$

The F_{STAT} test statistic follows an F distribution with 1 and $n-2$ degrees of freedom.

Using a level of significance α, the decision rule is

$$\text{Reject } H_0 \text{ if } F_{STAT} > F_\alpha;$$

otherwise, do not reject H_0.

Table 13.6 organizes the complete set of results into an analysis of variance (ANOVA) table.

TABLE 13.6
ANOVA Table for Testing the Significance of a Regression Coefficient

Source	df	Sum of Squares	Mean Square (Variance)	F
Regression	1	SSR	$MSR = \dfrac{SSR}{1} = SSR$	$F_{STAT} = \dfrac{MSR}{MSE}$
Error	$n-2$	SSE	$MSE = \dfrac{SSE}{n-2}$	
Total	$n-1$	SST		

Figure 13.19, a completed ANOVA table for the Sunflowers sales data, shows that the computed F_{STAT} test statistic is 113.2335 and the p-value is approximately 0.

FIGURE 13.19
Worksheet F-test results for the Sunflowers Apparel data

	A	B	C	D	E	F	G	H	I
10	**ANOVA**								
11		df	SS	MS	F	Significance F			
12	Regression	1	105.7476	105.7476	113.2335	0.0000			
13	Residual	12	11.2067	0.9339					
14	Total	13	116.9543						
15									
16		Coefficients	Standard Error	t Stat	P-value	Lower 95%	Upper 95%	Lower 95.0%	Upper 95.0%
17	Intercept	0.9645	0.5262	1.8329	0.0917	-0.1820	2.1110	-0.1820	2.11095
18	Square Feet	1.6699	0.1569	10.6411	0.0000	1.3280	2.0118	1.3280	2.01177

Using a level of significance of 0.05, from Table E.5, the critical value of the F distribution, with 1 and 12 degrees of freedom, is 4.75 (see Figure 13.20). Because $F_{STAT} = 113.2335 > 4.75$

FIGURE 13.20
Regions of rejection and nonrejection when testing for the significance of the slope at the 0.05 level of significance, with 1 and 12 degrees of freedom

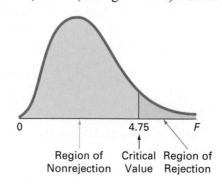

or because the p-value $= 0.0000 < 0.05$, you reject H_0 and conclude that the size of the store is significantly related to annual sales. Because the F test in Equation (13.17) on page 499 is equivalent to the t test in Equation (13.16) on page 497, you reach the same conclusion.

Confidence Interval Estimate for the Slope

As an alternative to testing for the existence of a linear relationship between the variables, you can construct a confidence interval estimate of β_1 using Equation (13.18).

> ### CONFIDENCE INTERVAL ESTIMATE OF THE SLOPE, β_1
>
> The confidence interval estimate for the population slope can be constructed by taking the sample slope, b_1, and adding and subtracting the critical t value multiplied by the standard error of the slope.
>
> $$b_1 \pm t_{\alpha/2}S_{b_1} \qquad\qquad (13.18)$$
>
> where
>
> > $t_{\alpha/2}$ is the critical value corresponding to an upper-tail probability of $\alpha/2$ from the t distribution with $n-2$ degrees of freedom (i.e., a cumulative area of $1 - \alpha/2$).

From the Figure 13.17 worksheet results on page 498,

$$b_1 = 1.6699 \quad n = 14 \quad S_{b_1} = 0.1569$$

To construct a 95% confidence interval estimate, $\alpha/2 = 0.025$, and from Table E.3, $t_{\alpha/2} = 2.1788$. Thus,

$$b_1 \pm t_{\alpha/2}S_{b_1} = 1.6699 \pm (2.1788)(0.1569)$$

$$= 1.6699 \pm 0.3419$$

$$1.3280 \le \beta_1 \le 2.0118$$

Therefore, you estimate with 95% confidence that the population slope is between 1.3280 and 2.0118. Because these values are both above 0, you conclude that there is a significant linear relationship between annual sales and the size of the store. Had the interval included 0, you would have concluded that no significant relationship exists between the variables. The confidence interval indicates that for each increase of 1,000 square feet, predicted annual sales are estimated to increase by at least $1,328,000 but no more than $2,011,800.

t Test for the Correlation Coefficient

In Section 3.5 on page 116, the strength of the relationship between two numerical variables was measured using the **correlation coefficient**, r. The values of the coefficient of correlation range from -1 for a perfect negative correlation to $+1$ for a perfect positive correlation. You can use the correlation coefficient to determine whether there is a statistically significant linear relationship between X and Y. To do so, you hypothesize that the population correlation coefficient, ρ, is 0. Thus, the null and alternative hypotheses are

$$H_0\!: \rho = 0 \text{ (no correlation)}$$

$$H_1\!: \rho \neq 0 \text{ (correlation)}$$

Equation (13.19) defines the test statistic for determining the existence of a significant correlation.

TESTING FOR THE EXISTENCE OF CORRELATION

$$t_{STAT} = \frac{r - \rho}{\sqrt{\dfrac{1 - r^2}{n - 2}}} \qquad \text{(13.19a)}$$

where

$$r = +\sqrt{r^2} \quad \text{if} \quad b_1 > 0$$
$$r = -\sqrt{r^2} \quad \text{if} \quad b_1 < 0$$

The t_{STAT} test statistic follows a t distribution with $n - 2$ degrees of freedom.

r is calculated as follows:

$$r = \frac{\text{cov}(X,Y)}{S_X S_Y} \qquad \text{(13.19b)}$$

where

$$\text{cov}(X, Y) = \frac{\displaystyle\sum_{i=1}^{n} (X_i - \bar{X})(Y_i - \bar{Y})}{n - 1}$$

$$S_X = \sqrt{\frac{\displaystyle\sum_{i=1}^{n} (X_i - \bar{X})^2}{n - 1}}$$

$$S_Y = \sqrt{\frac{\displaystyle\sum_{i=1}^{n} (Y_i - \bar{Y})^2}{n - 1}}$$

In the Sunflowers Apparel problem, $r^2 = 0.9042$ and $b_1 = +1.6699$ (see Figure 13.4 on page 476). Because $b_1 > 0$, the correlation coefficient for annual sales and store size is the positive square root of r^2, that is, $r = +\sqrt{0.9042} = +0.9509$. Using Equation (13.19a) to test the null hypothesis that there is no correlation between these two variables results in the following observed t statistic:

$$t_{STAT} = \frac{r - 0}{\sqrt{\dfrac{1 - r^2}{n - 2}}}$$

$$= \frac{0.9509 - 0}{\sqrt{\dfrac{1 - (0.9509)^2}{14 - 2}}} = 10.6411$$

Using the 0.05 level of significance, because $t_{STAT} = 10.6411 > 2.1788$, you reject the null hypothesis. You conclude that there is a significant association between annual sales and store size. This t_{STAT} test statistic is equivalent to the t_{STAT} test statistic found when testing whether the population slope, β_1, is equal to zero.

Problems for Section 13.7

LEARNING THE BASICS

13.39 You are testing the null hypothesis that there is no linear relationship between two variables, X and Y. From your sample of $n = 10$, you determine that $r = 0.80$.

a. What is the value of the t test statistic t_{STAT}?

b. At the $\alpha = 0.05$ level of significance, what are the critical values?

c. Based on your answers to (a) and (b), what statistical decision should you make?

13.40 You are testing the null hypothesis that there is no linear relationship between two variables, X and Y. From your sample of $n = 18$, you determine that $b_1 = +4.5$ and $S_{b_1} = 1.5$.

a. What is the value of t_{STAT}?

b. At the $\alpha = 0.05$ level of significance, what are the critical values?

c. Based on your answers to (a) and (b), what statistical decision should you make?

d. Construct a 95% confidence interval estimate of the population slope, β_1.

13.41 You are testing the null hypothesis that there is no linear relationship between two variables, X and Y. From your sample of $n = 20$, you determine that $SSR = 60$ and $SSE = 40$.

a. What is the value of F_{STAT}?

b. At the $\alpha = 0.05$ level of significance, what is the critical value?

c. Based on your answers to (a) and (b), what statistical decision should you make?

d. Compute the correlation coefficient by first computing r^2 and assuming that b_1 is negative.

e. At the 0.05 level of significance, is there a significant correlation between X and Y?

APPLYING THE CONCEPTS

✓ SELF Test **13.42** In Problem 13.4 on page 481, the marketing manager used shelf space for pet food to predict weekly sales. The data are stored in **Petfood**. From the results of that problem, $b_1 = 7.4$ and $S_{b_1} = 1.59$.

a. At the 0.05 level of significance, is there evidence of a linear relationship between shelf space and sales?

b. Construct a 95% confidence interval estimate of the population slope, β_1.

13.43 In Problem 13.5 on page 481, you used reported magazine newsstand sales to predict audited sales. The data are stored in **Circulation**. Using the results of that problem, $b_1 = 0.5719$ and $S_{b_1} = 0.0668$.

a. At the 0.05 level of significance, is there evidence of a linear relationship between reported sales and audited sales?

b. Construct a 95% confidence interval estimate of the population slope, β_1.

13.44 In Problem 13.6 on page 481, the owner of a moving company wanted to predict labor hours, based on the number of cubic feet moved. The data are stored in **Moving**. Using the results of that problem,

a. at the 0.05 level of significance, is there evidence of a linear relationship between the number of cubic feet moved and labor hours?

b. construct a 95% confidence interval estimate of the population slope, β_1.

13.45 In Problem 13.7 on page 481, you used the number of customers to predict the waiting time on the checkout line. The data are stored in **Supermarket**. Using the results of that problem,

a. at the 0.05 level of significance, is there evidence of a linear relationship between the number of customers and the waiting time on the checkout line?

b. construct a 95% confidence interval estimate of the population slope, β_1.

13.46 In Problem 13.8 on page 482, you used annual revenues to predict the value of a baseball franchise. The data are stored in **BBRevenue**. Using the results of that problem,

a. at the 0.05 level of significance, is there evidence of a linear relationship between annual revenue and franchise value?

b. construct a 95% confidence interval estimate of the population slope, β_1.

13.47 In Problem 13.9 on page 482, an agent for a real estate company wanted to predict the monthly rent for apartments, based on the size of the apartment. The data are stored in **Rent**. Using the results of that problem,

a. at the 0.05 level of significance, is there evidence of a linear relationship between the size of the apartment and the monthly rent?

b. construct a 95% confidence interval estimate of the population slope, β_1.

13.48 In Problem 13.10 on page 482, you used box office gross to predict the sales of DVDs. The data are stored in **Movie**. Using the results of that problem,

a. at the 0.05 level of significance, is there evidence of a linear relationship between box office gross and sales of DVDs?

b. construct a 95% confidence interval estimate of the population slope, β_1.

13.49 The volatility of a stock is often measured by its beta value. You can estimate the beta value of a stock by developing a simple linear regression model, using the percentage weekly change in the stock as the dependent variable and the percentage weekly change in a market index as the independent variable. The S&P 500 Index is a common index to use. For example, if you wanted to estimate the beta for Disney, you could use the following model, which is sometimes referred to as a *market model*:

$$(\% \text{ weekly change in Disney}) = \beta_0$$

$$+ \beta_1(\% \text{ weekly change in S\&P 500 index}) + \varepsilon$$

The least-squares regression estimate of the slope b_1 is the estimate of the beta value for Disney. A stock with a beta value of 1.0 tends to move the same as the overall market. A stock with a beta value of 1.5 tends to move 50% more than the overall market, and a stock with a beta value of 0.6 tends to move only 60% as much as the overall market. Stocks with negative beta values tend to move in a direction opposite that of the overall market. The following table gives some beta values for some widely held stocks, using a year's worth of data ending in May, 2009. Note that in the first 10 months of this time frame the S&P 500 lost approximately 40% of its value and then rebounded by about 10% in the last 2 months:

Company	Ticker Symbol	Beta
Procter & Gamble	PG	0.54
AT&T	T	0.73
Disney	DIS	1.10
Apple	AAPL	1.52
eBay	EBAY	1.69
Ford	F	2.86

Source: *Data extracted from* **finance.yahoo.com**, *May 27, 2009.*

a. For each of the six companies, interpret the beta value.
b. How can investors use the beta value as a guide for investing?

13.50 Index funds are mutual funds that try to mimic the movement of leading indexes, such as the S&P 500 or the Russell 2000. The beta values (as described in Problem 13.49) for these funds are therefore approximately 1.0, and the estimated market models for these funds are approximately

$$(\% \text{ weekly change in index fund}) =$$

$$0.0 + 1.0 \,(\% \text{ weekly change in the index})$$

Leveraged index funds are designed to magnify the movement of major indexes. Direxion Funds is a leading provider of leveraged index and other alternative-class mutual fund products for investment advisors and sophisticated investors. Two of the company's most popular funds are shown in the following table (extracted from **www.direxionfunds.com**, January 7, 2009).

Name	Ticker Symbol	Description
S&P 500 Bull 2.5× Fund	DXSLX	250% of the S&P 500 Index
China Bull 2× Fund	DXHLX	200% of the Xinhua China 25 Index

The estimated market models for these funds are approximately

(% weekly change in DXSLX) = 0.0 + 2.5
  (% weekly change in the S&P 500)
(% weekly change in DXHLX) = 0.0 + 2
  (% weekly change in the Xinhua China 25)

Thus, if the S&P 500 Index gains 10% over a period of time, the leveraged mutual fund DXSLX gains approximately 25%. On the downside, if the same index loses 20%, DXSLX loses approximately 50%.

a. The objective of the Direxion Funds Small Cap Bull 2.5× fund, DXRLX, is 250% of the performance of the Russell 2000 Index. What is its approximate market model?
b. If the Russell 2000 Index gains 10% in a year, what return do you expect DXRLX to have?
c. If the Russell 2000 Index loses 20% in a year, what return do you expect DXRLX to have?
d. What type of investors should be attracted to leveraged index funds? What type of investors should stay away from these funds?

13.51 The file CoffeeDrink represent the calories and fat (in grams) of 16-ounce iced coffee drinks at Dunkin' Donuts and Starbucks:

Product	Calories	Fat
Dunkin' Donuts Iced Mocha Swirl latte (whole milk)	240	8.0
Starbucks Coffee Frappuccino blended coffee	260	3.5
Dunkin' Donuts Coffee Coolatta (cream)	350	22.0
Starbucks Iced Coffee Mocha Espresso (whole milk and whipped cream)	350	20.0
Starbucks Mocha Frappuccino blended coffee (whipped cream)	420	16.0
Starbucks Chocolate Brownie Frappuccino blended coffee (whipped cream)	510	22.0
Starbucks Chocolate Frappuccino Blended Crème (whipped cream)	530	19.0

Source: *Data extracted from "Coffee as Candy at Dunkin' Donuts and Starbucks,"* Consumer Reports, *June 2004, p. 9.*

a. Compute and interpret the coefficient of correlation, r.
b. At the 0.05 level of significance, is there a significant linear relationship between calories and fat?

13.52 There are several methods for calculating fuel economy. The file Mileage (data shown on page 504) contains mileage as calculated by owners and by current government standards:
a. Compute and interpret the coefficient of correlation, r.
b. At the 0.05 level of significance, is there a significant linear relationship between the mileage as calculated by owners and by current government standards?

Vehicle	Owner	Government Standards
2005 Ford F-150	14.3	16.8
2005 Chevrolet Silverado	15.0	17.8
2002 Honda Accord LX	27.8	26.2
2002 Honda Civic	27.9	34.2
2004 Honda Civic Hybrid	48.8	47.6
2002 Ford Explorer	16.8	18.3
2005 Toyota Camry	23.7	28.5
2003 Toyota Corolla	32.8	33.1
2005 Toyota Prius	37.3	56.0

13.53 College basketball is big business, with coaches' salaries, revenues, and expenses in millions of dollars. The file **Colleges-Basketball** represent the coaches' salaries and revenues for college basketball at selected schools in a recent year (data extracted from R. Adams, "Pay for Playoffs," *The Wall Street Journal*, March 11–12, 2006, pp. P1, P8).

a. Compute and interpret the coefficient of correlation, *r*.
b. At the 0.05 level of significance, is there a significant linear relationship between a coach's salary and revenue?

13.54 College football players trying out for the NFL are given the Wonderlic standardized intelligence test. The file **Wonderlic** lists the average Wonderlic scores of football players trying out for the NFL and the graduation rates for football players at the schools they attended (data extracted from S. Walker, "The NFL's Smartest Team," *The Wall Street Journal*, September 30, 2005, pp. W1, W10).

a. Compute and interpret the coefficient of correlation, *r*.
b. At the 0.05 level of significance, is there a significant linear relationship between the average Wonderlic score of football players trying out for the NFL and the graduation rates for football players at selected schools?
c. What conclusions can you reach about the relationship between the average Wonderlic score of football players trying out for the NFL and the graduation rates for football players at selected schools?

13.8 Estimation of Mean Values and Prediction of Individual Values

This section presents methods of estimating the mean of *Y* and predicting individual values of *Y*.

The Confidence Interval Estimate

In Example 13.2 on page 477, you used the prediction line to predict the value of *Y* for a given *X*. The annual sales for stores with 4,000 square feet was predicted to be 7.644 millions of dollars ($7,644,000). This estimate, however, is a *point estimate* of the population mean. In Chapter 8, you studied the concept of the confidence interval estimate of the population mean. In a similar fashion, Equation (13.20) defines the **confidence interval estimate for the mean response** for a given *X*.

CONFIDENCE INTERVAL ESTIMATE FOR THE MEAN OF Y

$$\hat{Y}_i \pm t_{\alpha/2} S_{YX} \sqrt{h_i}$$

$$\hat{Y}_i - t_{\alpha/2} S_{YX} \sqrt{h_i} \leq \mu_{Y|X=X_i} \leq \hat{Y}_i + t_{\alpha/2} S_{YX} \sqrt{h_i} \qquad (13.20)$$

where

$$h_i = \frac{1}{n} + \frac{(X_i - \bar{X})^2}{SSX}$$

$\hat{Y}_i$ = predicted value of *Y*; $\hat{Y}_i = b_0 + b_1 X_i$

S_{YX} = standard error of the estimate

n = sample size

X_i = given value of *X*

$\mu_{Y|X=X_i}$ = mean value of *Y* when $X = X_i$

$$SSX = \sum_{i=1}^{n} (X_i - \bar{X})^2$$

$t_{\alpha/2}$ is the critical value corresponding to an upper-tail probability of $\alpha/2$ from the *t* distribution with $n - 2$ degrees of freedom (i.e., a cumulative area of $1 - \alpha/2$).

The width of the confidence interval in Equation (13.20) depends on several factors. Increased variation around the prediction line, as measured by the standard error of the estimate, results in a wider interval. As you would expect, increased sample size reduces the width of the interval. In addition, the width of the interval varies at different values of X. When you predict Y for values of X close to $\overline{X}$, the interval is narrower than for predictions for X values further away from $\overline{X}$.

In the Sunflowers Apparel example, suppose you want to construct a 95% confidence interval estimate of the mean annual sales for the entire population of stores that contain 4,000 square feet ($X = 4$). Using the simple linear regression equation,

$$\hat{Y}_i = 0.9645 + 1.6699X_i$$

$$= 0.9645 + 1.6699(4) = 7.6439 \text{ (millions of dollars)}$$

Also, given the following:

$$\overline{X} = 2.9214 \quad S_{YX} = 0.9664$$

$$SSX = \sum_{i=1}^{n}(X_i - \overline{X})^2 = 37.9236$$

From Table E.3, $t_{\alpha/2} = 2.1788$. Thus,

$$\hat{Y}_i \pm t_{\alpha/2}S_{YX}\sqrt{h_i}$$

where

$$h_i = \frac{1}{n} + \frac{(X_i - \overline{X})^2}{SSX}$$

so that

$$\hat{Y}_i \pm t_{\alpha/2}S_{YX}\sqrt{\frac{1}{n} + \frac{(X_i - \overline{X})^2}{SSX}}$$

$$= 7.6439 \pm (2.1788)(0.9664)\sqrt{\frac{1}{14} + \frac{(4 - 2.9214)^2}{37.9236}}$$

$$= 7.6439 \pm 0.6728$$

so

$$6.9711 \leq \mu_{Y|X=4} \leq 8.3167$$

Therefore, the 95% confidence interval estimate is that the mean annual sales are between $6,971,100 and $8,316,700 for the population of stores with 4,000 square feet.

The Prediction Interval

In addition to constructing a confidence interval for the mean value of Y, you can also construct a prediction interval for an individual value of Y. Although the form of this interval is similar to that of the confidence interval estimate of Equation (13.20), the prediction interval is predicting an individual value, not estimating a parameter. Equation (13.21) defines the **prediction interval for an individual response, Y**, at a particular value, X_i, denoted by $Y_{X=X_i}$.

PREDICTION INTERVAL FOR AN INDIVIDUAL RESPONSE, Y

$$\hat{Y}_i \pm t_{\alpha/2}S_{YX}\sqrt{1 + h_i} \qquad \textbf{(13.21)}$$

$$\hat{Y}_i - t_{\alpha/2}S_{YX}\sqrt{1 + h_i} \leq Y_{X=X_i} \leq \hat{Y}_i + t_{\alpha/2}S_{YX}\sqrt{1 + h_i}$$

where

h_i, $\hat{Y}_i$, S_{YX}, n, and X_i are defined as in Equation (13.20) on page 504 and $Y_{X=X_i}$ is a future value of Y when $X = X_i$.

$t_{\alpha/2}$ is the critical value corresponding to an upper-tail probability of $\alpha/2$ from the t distribution with $n - 2$ degrees of freedom (i.e., a cumulative area of $1 - \alpha/2$).

To construct a 95% prediction interval of the annual sales for an individual store that contains 4,000 square feet ($X = 4$), you first compute $\hat{Y}_i$. Using the prediction line:

$$\hat{Y}_i = 0.9645 + 1.6699X_i$$
$$= 0.9645 + 1.6699(4)$$
$$= 7.6439 \text{ (millions of dollars)}$$

Also, given the following:

$$\overline{X} = 2.9214 \quad S_{YX} = 0.9664$$

$$SSX = \sum_{i=1}^{n}(X_i - \overline{X})^2 = 37.9236$$

From Table E.3, $t_{\alpha/2} = 2.1788$. Thus,

$$\hat{Y}_i \pm t_{\alpha/2}S_{YX}\sqrt{1 + h_i}$$

where

$$h_i = \frac{1}{n} + \frac{(X_i - \overline{X})^2}{\sum_{i=1}^{n}(X_i - \overline{X})^2}$$

so that

$$\hat{Y}_i \pm t_{\alpha/2}S_{YX}\sqrt{1 + \frac{1}{n} + \frac{(X_i - \overline{X})^2}{SSX}}$$

$$= 7.6439 \pm (2.1788)(0.9664)\sqrt{1 + \frac{1}{14} + \frac{(4 - 2.9214)^2}{37.9236}}$$

$$= 7.6439 \pm 2.2104$$

so

$$5.4335 \le Y_{X=4} \le 9.8543$$

Therefore, with 95% confidence, you predict that the annual sales for an individual store with 4,000 square feet is between $5,433,500 and $9,854,300.

Figure 13.21 presents a worksheet that computes the confidence interval estimate and the prediction interval for the Sunflowers Apparel data. If you compare the results of the confidence interval estimate and the prediction interval, you see that the width of the prediction interval for an individual store is much wider than the confidence interval estimate for the mean. Remember that there is much more variation in predicting an individual value than in estimating a mean value.

FIGURE 13.21

Confidence interval
estimate and prediction
interval worksheet for the
Sunflowers Apparel data

Figure 13.21 displays the
CIEandPI worksheet *of the*
Simple Linear Regression
workbook*. Create this*
worksheet using the
instructions in Section
EG13.8.

	A	B
1	Confidence Interval Estimate and Prediction Interval	
2		
3	**Data**	
4	X Value	4
5	Confidence Level	95%
6		
7	**Intermediate Calculations**	
8	Sample Size	14 =COUNT(SLRData!A:A)
9	Degrees of Freedom	12 =B8 - 2
10	t Value	2.1788 =TINV(1 - B5, B9)
11	Sample Mean	2.9214 =AVERAGE(SLRData!A:A)
12	Sum of Squared Difference	37.9236 =DEVSQ(SLRData!A:A)
13	Standard Error of the Estimate	0.9664 =COMPUTE!B7
14	h Statistic	0.1021 =1/B8 + (B4 - B11)^2/B12
15	Predicted Y (YHat)	7.6439 =TREND(SLRData!B2:B15, SLRData!A2:A15, B4)
16		
17	**For Average Y**	
18	Interval Half Width	0.6728 =B10 * B13 * SQRT(B14)
19	Confidence Interval Lower Limit	6.9711 =B15 - B18
20	Confidence Interval Upper Limit	8.3167 =B15 + B18
21		
22	**For Individual Response Y**	
23	Interval Half Width	2.2104 =B10 * B13 * SQRT(1 + B14)
24	Prediction Interval Lower Limit	5.4335 =B15 - B23
25	Prediction Interval Upper Limit	9.8544 =B15 + B23

Problems for Section 13.8

LEARNING THE BASICS

13.55 Based on a sample of $n = 20$, the least-squares method was used to develop the following prediction line: $\hat{Y}_i = 5 + 3X_i$. In addition,

$$S_{YX} = 1.0 \quad \bar{X} = 2 \quad \sum_{i=1}^{n}(X_i - \bar{X})^2 = 20$$

a. Construct a 95% confidence interval estimate of the population mean response for $X = 2$.
b. Construct a 95% prediction interval of an individual response for $X = 2$.

13.56 Based on a sample of $n = 20$, the least-squares method was used to develop the following prediction line: $\hat{Y}_i = 5 + 3X_i$. In addition,

$$S_{YX} = 1.0 \quad \bar{X} = 2 \quad \sum_{i=1}^{n}(X_i - \bar{X})^2 = 20$$

a. Construct a 95% confidence interval estimate of the population mean response for $X = 4$.
b. Construct a 95% prediction interval of an individual response for $X = 4$.
c. Compare the results of (a) and (b) with those of Problem 13.55 (a) and (b). Which interval is wider? Why?

APPLYING THE CONCEPTS

13.57 In Problem 13.5 on page 481, you used reported sales to predict audited sales of magazines. The data are stored in **Circulation**. For these data $S_{YX} = 42.186$ and $h_i = 0.108$ when $X = 400$.
a. Construct a 95% confidence interval estimate of the mean audited sales for magazines that report newsstand sales of 400,000.
b. Construct a 95% prediction interval of the audited sales for an individual magazine that reports newsstand sales of 400,000.
c. Explain the difference in the results in (a) and (b).

✓ SELF Test **13.58** In Problem 13.4 on page 481, the marketing manager used shelf space for pet food to predict weekly sales. The data are stored in **Petfood**. For these data $S_{YX} = 30.81$ and $h_i = 0.1373$ when $X = 8$.
a. Construct a 95% confidence interval estimate of the mean weekly sales for all stores that have 8 feet of shelf space for pet food.
b. Construct a 95% prediction interval of the weekly sales of an individual store that has 8 feet of shelf space for pet food.
c. Explain the difference in the results in (a) and (b).

13.59 In Problem 13.7 on page 481, you used the total number of customers in the store to predict the waiting time at the checkout counter. The data are stored in Supermarket.

a. Construct a 95% confidence interval estimate of the mean waiting time for all customers when there are 20 customers in the store.

b. Construct a 95% prediction interval of the waiting time for an individual customer when there are 20 customers in the store.

c. Why is the interval in (a) narrower than the interval in (b)?

13.60 In Problem 13.6 on page 481, the owner of a moving company wanted to predict labor hours based on the number of cubic feet moved. The data are stored in Moving.

a. Construct a 95% confidence interval estimate of the mean labor hours for all moves of 500 cubic feet.

b. Construct a 95% prediction interval of the labor hours of an individual move that has 500 cubic feet.

c. Why is the interval in (a) narrower than the interval in (b)?

13.61 In Problem 13.9 on page 482, an agent for a real estate company wanted to predict the monthly rent for apartments, based on the size of an apartment. The data are stored in Rent.

a. Construct a 95% confidence interval estimate of the mean monthly rental for all apartments that are 1,000 square feet in size.

b. Construct a 95% prediction interval of the monthly rental of an individual apartment that is 1,000 square feet in size.

c. Explain the difference in the results in (a) and (b).

13.62 In Problem 13.8 on page 482, you predicted the value of a baseball franchise, based on current revenue. The data are stored in BBRevenue.

a. Construct a 95% confidence interval estimate of the mean value of all baseball franchises that generate $150 million of annual revenue.

b. Construct a 95% prediction interval of the value of an individual baseball franchise that generates $200 million of annual revenue.

c. Explain the difference in the results in (a) and (b).

13.63 In Problem 13.10 on page 482, you used box office gross to predict the number of DVDs sold. The data are stored in Movie. The company is about to release a movie on DVD that had a box office gross of $30 million.

a. What is the predicted number of DVDs that the company will sell?

b. Which interval is more useful here, the confidence interval estimate of the mean or the predicted interval for an individual response? Explain.

c. Construct and interpret the interval you selected in (b).

13.9 Pitfalls in Regression

Some of the pitfalls involved in using regression analysis are as follows:

- Lacking awareness of the assumptions of least-squares regression
- Not knowing how to evaluate the assumptions of least-squares regression
- Not knowing what the alternatives are to least-squares regression if a particular assumption is violated
- Using a regression model without knowledge of the subject matter
- Extrapolating outside the relevant range
- Concluding that a significant relationship identified in an observational study is due to a cause-and-effect relationship

The widespread availability of spreadsheet and statistical software has made regression analysis much more feasible. However, for many users, this enhanced availability of software has not been accompanied by an understanding of how to use regression analysis properly. Someone who is not familiar with either the assumptions of regression or how to evaluate the assumptions cannot be expected to know what the alternatives to least-squares regression are if a particular assumption is violated.

The data in Table 13.7 (stored in Anscombe) illustrate the importance of using scatter plots and residual analysis to go beyond the basic number crunching of computing the Y intercept, the slope, and r^2.

TABLE 13.7

Four Sets of Artificial Data

Data Set A		Data Set B		Data Set C		Data Set D	
X_i	Y_i	X_i	Y_i	X_i	Y_i	X_i	Y_i
10	8.04	10	9.14	10	7.46	8	6.58
14	9.96	14	8.10	14	8.84	8	5.76
5	5.68	5	4.74	5	5.73	8	7.71
8	6.95	8	8.14	8	6.77	8	8.84
9	8.81	9	8.77	9	7.11	8	8.47
12	10.84	12	9.13	12	8.15	8	7.04
4	4.26	4	3.10	4	5.39	8	5.25
7	4.82	7	7.26	7	6.42	19	12.50
11	8.33	11	9.26	11	7.81	8	5.56
13	7.58	13	8.74	13	12.74	8	7.91
6	7.24	6	6.13	6	6.08	8	6.89

Source: *Data extracted from F. J. Anscombe, "Graphs in Statistical Analysis,"* The American Statistician, *27 (1973), 17–21.*

Anscombe (reference 1) showed that all four data sets given in Table 13.7 have the following identical results:

$$\hat{Y}_i = 3.0 + 0.5X_i$$

$$S_{YX} = 1.237$$

$$S_{b_1} = 0.118$$

$$r^2 = 0.667$$

$$SSR = \text{Explained variation} = \sum_{i=1}^{n}(\hat{Y}_i - \bar{Y})^2 = 27.51$$

$$SSE = \text{Unexplained variation} = \sum_{i=1}^{n}(Y_i - \hat{Y}_i)^2 = 13.76$$

$$SST = \text{Total variation} = \sum_{i=1}^{n}(Y_i - \bar{Y})^2 = 41.27$$

If you stopped the analysis at this point, you would fail to observe the important differences among the four data sets.

From the scatter plots of Figure 13.22 and the residual plots of Figure 13.23 on page 510, you see how different the data sets are. Each has a different relationship between X and Y. The only data set that seems to approximately follow a straight line is data set A. The residual plot for data set A does not show any obvious patterns or outlying residuals. This is certainly not true for data sets B, C, and D. The scatter plot for data set B shows that a curvilinear regression model is more appropriate. This conclusion is reinforced by the residual plot for data set B. The scatter plot and the residual plot for data set C clearly show an outlying observation. In this case, one approach used is to remove the outlier and reestimate the regression model (see reference 4). The scatter plot for data set D represents a situation in which the model is heavily dependent on the outcome of a single data point ($X_8 = 19$ and $Y_8 = 12.50$). Any regression model with this characteristic should be used with caution.

In summary, scatter plots and residual plots are of vital importance to a complete regression analysis. The information they provide is so basic to a credible analysis that you should

FIGURE 13.22

Scatter plots for four data sets

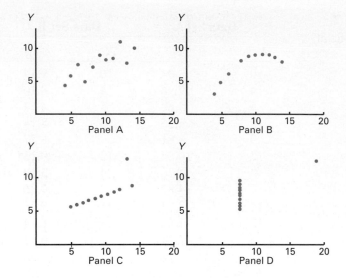

FIGURE 13.23

Residual plots for four data sets

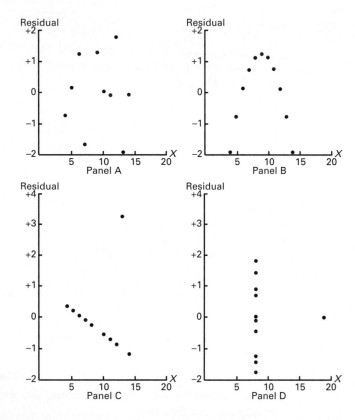

always include these graphical methods as part of a regression analysis. Thus, a strategy you can use to help avoid the pitfalls of regression is as follows:

1. Start with a scatter plot to observe the possible relationship between X and Y.
2. Check the assumptions of regression (**l**inearity, **i**ndependence, **n**ormality, **e**qual variance) by performing a residual analysis that includes the following:
   a. Plotting the residuals versus the independent variable to determine whether the linear model is appropriate and to check for equal variance.
   b. Constructing a histogram, stem-and-leaf display, boxplot, or normal probability plot of the residuals to check for normality.
   c. Plotting the residuals versus time to check for independence (this step is necessary only if the data are collected over time).
3. If there are violations of the assumptions, use alternative methods to least-squares regression or alternative least-squares models (see reference 4).

4. If there are no violations of the assumptions, carry out tests for the significance of the regression coefficients and develop confidence and prediction intervals.
5. Avoid making predictions and forecasts outside the relevant range of the independent variable.
6. Keep in mind that the relationships identified in observational studies may or may not be due to cause-and-effect relationships. Remember that, although causation implies correlation, correlation does not imply causation.

THINK ABOUT THIS   America's Top Models

Perhaps you are familiar with the TV competition produced by Tyra Banks to find "America's next top model." You may be less familiar with another set of top models that are emerging from the business world.

In a January 23, 2006, *BusinessWeek* article (S. Baker, "Why Math Will Rock Your World: More Math Geeks Are Calling the Shots in Business. Is Your Industry Next?" *BusinessWeek*, pp. 54–62), Stephen Baker talks about how "quants" turned finance upside down and are moving on to other business fields. The name *quants* derives from the "quantitative methods" that "math geeks" use to develop models and forecasts. These methods are built on the principles of regression analysis discussed in this chapter, although the actual models are much more complicated than the simple linear models discussed in this chapter. Another article (S. Lohr, "For Today's Graduate, Just One Word: Statistics." *The New York Times*, August 6, 2009, p. A1, A3) discusses how statistics is being used to "mine" large data sets to discover patterns (often using regression models).

Regression-based models have become the top models for many types of business analyses. Some examples include the following:

• **Advertising and marketing** Managers use econometric models (in other words, regression models) to determine the effect of an advertisement on sales, based on a set of factors. Also, managers use data mining to predict patterns of behavior of what customers will buy in the future, based on historic information about the consumer.

• **Finance** Any time you read about a financial "model," you should assume that some type of regression model is being used. For example, a *New York Times* article on June 18, 2006, titled "An Old Formula That Points to New Worry" by Mark Hulbert (p. BU8) discusses a market timing model that predicts the returns of stocks in the next three to five years, based on the dividend yield of the stock market and the interest rate of 90-day Treasury bills.

• **Food and beverage** Enologix, a California consulting company, has developed a "formula" (a regression model) that predicts a wine's quality index, based on a set of chemical compounds found in the wine (see D. Darlington, "The Chemistry of a 90+ Wine," *The New York Times Magazine*, August 7, 2005, pp. 36–39).

• **Publishing** A study of the effect of price changes on sales at Amazon.com and BN.com (again, regression analysis) found that a 1% price increase at BN.com pushed sales down 4%, but the same price increase at Amazon.com pushed sales down only 0.5% (see V. Postrel, "Economic Scene: When It Comes to Books, Internet Selling Has Not Led to Uniformly Low Prices," *The New York Times*, September 11, 2003, p. C2).

• **Transportation** Farecast.com uses data mining and predictive technologies to objectively predict airfare pricing (see D. Darlin, "Airfares Made Easy (Or Easier)," *The New York Times*, July 1, 2006, pp. C1, C6).

• **Real estate** Zillow.com uses information about the features contained in a home and its location to develop estimates about the market value of the home, using a "formula" built with a proprietary model.

In the *BusinessWeek* article, Baker states that statistics and probability will become core skills for businesspeople and consumers. Those who are successful will know how to use statistics, whether they are building financial models or making marketing plans. He also strongly endorses the need for people in business to know how to use Microsoft Excel to perform statistical analysis and create reports. In *The New York Times* article, Lohr quotes Hal Varian, chief economist at Google, as saying, "I keep saying that the sexy job in the next ten years will be statisticians."

USING STATISTICS   @ Sunflowers Apparel Revisited

In the Sunflowers Apparel scenario, you were the director of planning for a chain of upscale clothing stores for women. Until now, Sunflowers managers selected sites based on factors such as the availability of a good lease or a subjective opinion that a location seemed like a good place for a store. To make more objective decisions, you developed a regression model to analyze the relationship between the size of a store and its annual sales. The model indicated that about 90.4% of the variation in sales was explained by the size of the store. Furthermore, for each increase of 1,000 square feet, mean annual sales were estimated to increase by $1.67 million. You can now use your model to help make better decisions when selecting new sites for stores as well as to forecast sales for existing stores.

SUMMARY

As you can see from the chapter roadmap in Figure 13.24, this chapter develops the simple linear regression model and discusses the assumptions and how to evaluate them. Once you are assured that the model is appropriate, you can predict values by using the prediction line and test for the significance of the slope. In Chapter 14, regression analysis is extended to situations in which more than one independent variable is used to predict the value of a dependent variable.

FIGURE 13.24
Roadmap for simple
linear regression

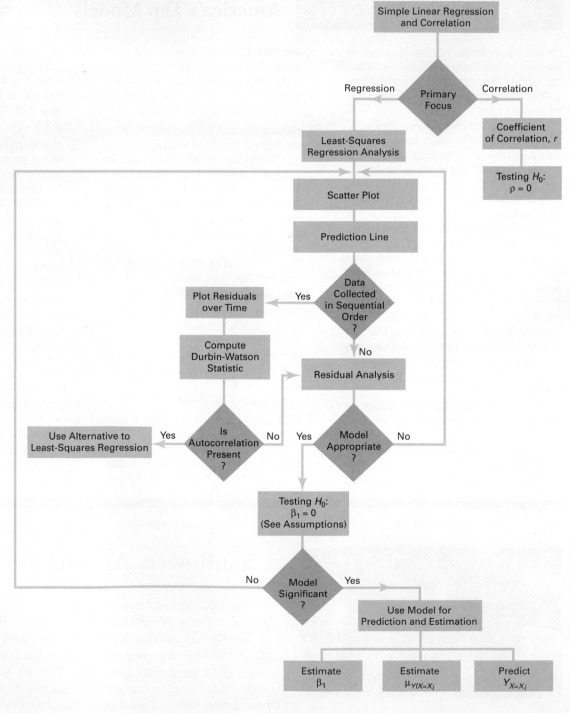

KEY EQUATIONS

Simple Linear Regression Model

$$Y_i = \beta_0 + \beta_1 X_i + \varepsilon_i \qquad (13.1)$$

Simple Linear Regression Equation: The Prediction Line

$$\hat{Y}_i = b_0 + b_1 X_i \qquad (13.2)$$

Computational Formula for the Slope, b_1

$$b_1 = \frac{SSXY}{SSX} \qquad (13.3)$$

Computational Formula for the Y Intercept, b_0

$$b_0 = \bar{Y} - b_1 \bar{X} \qquad (13.4)$$

Measures of Variation in Regression

$$SST = SSR + SSE \qquad (13.5)$$

Total Sum of Squares (SST)

$$SST = \text{Total sum of squares} = \sum_{i=1}^{n}(Y_i - \bar{Y})^2 \qquad (13.6)$$

Regression Sum of Squares (SSR)

$SSR = $ Explained variation or regression sum of squares

$$= \sum_{i=1}^{n}(\hat{Y}_i - \bar{Y})^2 \qquad (13.7)$$

Error Sum of Squares (SSE)

$SSE = $ Unexplained variation or error sum of squares

$$= \sum_{i=1}^{n}(Y_i - \hat{Y}_i)^2 \qquad (13.8)$$

Coefficient of Determination

$$r^2 = \frac{\text{Regression sum of squares}}{\text{Total sum of squares}} = \frac{SSR}{SST} \qquad (13.9)$$

Computational Formula for SST

$$SST = \sum_{i=1}^{n}(Y_i - \bar{Y})^2 = \sum_{i=1}^{n}Y_i^2 - \frac{\left(\sum_{i=1}^{n}Y_i\right)^2}{n} \qquad (13.10)$$

Computational Formula for SSR

$$SSR = \sum_{i=1}^{n}(\hat{Y}_i - \bar{Y})^2$$

$$= b_0\sum_{i=1}^{n}Y_i + b_1\sum_{i=1}^{n}X_iY_i - \frac{\left(\sum_{i=1}^{n}Y_i\right)^2}{n} \qquad (13.11)$$

Computational Formula for SSE

$$SSE = \sum_{i=1}^{n}(Y_i - \hat{Y}_i)^2 = \sum_{i=1}^{n}Y_i^2 - b_0\sum_{i=1}^{n}Y_i - b_1\sum_{i=1}^{n}X_iY_i \qquad (13.12)$$

Standard Error of the Estimate

$$S_{YX} = \sqrt{\frac{SSE}{n-2}} = \sqrt{\frac{\sum_{i=1}^{n}(Y_i - \hat{Y}_i)^2}{n-2}} \qquad (13.13)$$

Residual

$$e_i = Y_i - \hat{Y}_i \qquad (13.14)$$

Durbin-Watson Statistic

$$D = \frac{\sum_{i=2}^{n}(e_i - e_{i-1})^2}{\sum_{i=1}^{n}e_i^2} \qquad (13.15)$$

Testing a Hypothesis for a Population Slope, β_1, Using the t Test

$$t_{STAT} = \frac{b_1 - \beta_1}{S_{b_1}} \qquad (13.16)$$

Testing a Hypothesis for a Population Slope, β_1, Using the F Test

$$F_{STAT} = \frac{MSR}{MSE} \qquad (13.17)$$

Confidence Interval Estimate of the Slope, β_1

$$b_1 \pm t_{\alpha/2}S_{b_1}$$

$$b_1 - t_{\alpha/2}S_{b_1} \leq \beta_1 \leq b_1 + t_{\alpha/2}S_{b_1} \qquad (13.18)$$

Testing for the Existence of Correlation

$$t_{STAT} = \frac{r - \rho}{\sqrt{\dfrac{1 - r^2}{n - 2}}} \tag{13.19a}$$

$$r = \frac{cov(X,Y)}{S_X S_Y} \tag{13.19b}$$

Confidence Interval Estimate for the Mean of Y

$$\hat{Y}_i \pm t_{\alpha/2} S_{YX} \sqrt{h_i}$$

$$\hat{Y}_i - t_{\alpha/2} S_{YX} \sqrt{h_i} \le \mu_{Y|X=X_i} \le \hat{Y}_i + t_{\alpha/2} S_{YX} \sqrt{h_i} \tag{13.20}$$

Prediction Interval for an Individual Response, Y

$$\hat{Y}_i \pm t_{\alpha/2} S_{YX} \sqrt{1 + h_i}$$

$$\hat{Y}_i - t_{\alpha/2} S_{YX} \sqrt{1 + h_i} \le Y_{X=X_i} \le \hat{Y}_i + t_{\alpha/2} S_{YX} \sqrt{1 + h_i} \tag{13.21}$$

KEY TERMS

assumptions of regression 488
autocorrelation 492
coefficient of determination 484
confidence interval estimate for the
   mean response 504
correlation coefficient 500
dependent variable 472
Durbin-Watson statistic 494
equal variance 488
error sum of squares (SSE) 483
explained variation 482
explanatory variable 472
homoscedasticity 488
independence of errors 488

independent variable 472
least-squares method 475
linearity 488
linear relationship 472
normality 488
prediction interval for an individual
   response, Y 505
prediction line 475
regression analysis 472
regression coefficient 475
regression sum of squares (SSR)
   482
relevant range 477
residual 488

residual analysis 488
response variable 472
scatter diagram 472
scatter plot 472
simple linear regression 472
simple linear regression
   equation 475
slope 473
standard error of the estimate 486
total sum of squares (SST) 482
total variation 482
unexplained variation 482
Y intercept 473

CHAPTER REVIEW PROBLEMS

CHECKING YOUR UNDERSTANDING

13.64 What is the interpretation of the Y intercept and the slope in the simple linear regression equation?

13.65 What is the interpretation of the coefficient of determination?

13.66 When is the unexplained variation (i.e., error sum of squares) equal to 0?

13.67 When is the explained variation (i.e., regression sum of squares) equal to 0?

13.68 Why should you always carry out a residual analysis as part of a regression model?

13.69 What are the assumptions of regression analysis?

13.70 How do you evaluate the assumptions of regression analysis?

13.71 When and how do you use the Durbin-Watson statistic?

13.72 What is the difference between a confidence interval estimate of the mean response, $\mu_{Y|X=X_i}$, and a prediction interval of $Y_{X=X_i}$?

APPLYING THE CONCEPTS

13.73 Researchers from the Pace University Lubin School of Business conducted a study on Internet-supported courses. In one part of the study, four numerical variables were collected on 108 students in an introductory management course that met once a week for an entire semester. One variable collected was *hit consistency*. To measure hit consistency, the researchers did the following: If a student did not visit the Internet site between classes, the student was given a 0 for that time period. If a student visited the

Internet site one or more times between classes, the student was given a 1 for that time period. Because there were 13 time periods, a student's score on hit consistency could range from 0 to 13.

The other three variables included the student's course average, the student's cumulative grade point average (GPA), and the total number of hits the student had on the Internet site supporting the course. The following table gives the correlation coefficient for all pairs of variables. Note that correlations marked with an * are statistically significant, using $\alpha = 0.001$:

Variable	Correlation
Course Average, Cumulative GPA	0.72*
Course Average, Total Hits	0.08
Course Average, Hit Consistency	0.37*
Cumulative GPA, Total Hits	0.12
Cumulative GPA, Hit Consistency	0.32*
Total Hits & Hit Consistency	0.64*

Source: *Data extracted from D. Baugher, A. Varanelli, and E. Weisbord, "Student Hits in an Internet-Supported Course: How Can Instructors Use Them and What Do They Mean?" Decision Sciences Journal of Innovative Education, 1 (Fall 2003), 159–179.*

a. What conclusions can you reach from this correlation analysis?
b. Are you surprised by the results, or are they consistent with your own observations and experiences?

13.74 Management of a soft-drink bottling company has the business objective of developing a method for allocating delivery costs to customers. Although one cost clearly relates to travel time within a particular route, another variable cost reflects the time required to unload the cases of soft drink at the delivery point. To begin, management decided to develop a regression model to predict delivery time based on the number of cases delivered. A sample of 20 deliveries within a territory was selected. The delivery times and the number of cases delivered were organized in the following table (and stored in Delivery):

Customer	Number of Cases	Delivery Time (Minutes)	Customer	Number of Cases	Delivery Time (Minutes)
1	52	32.1	11	161	43.0
2	64	34.8	12	184	49.4
3	73	36.2	13	202	57.2
4	85	37.8	14	218	56.8
5	95	37.8	15	243	60.6
6	103	39.7	16	254	61.2
7	116	38.5	17	267	58.2
8	121	41.9	18	275	63.1
9	143	44.2	19	287	65.6
10	157	47.1	20	298	67.3

a. Use the least-squares method to compute the regression coefficients b_0 and b_1.
b. Interpret the meaning of b_0 and b_1 in this problem.
c. Predict the delivery time for 150 cases of soft drink.
d. Should you use the model to predict the delivery time for a customer who is receiving 500 cases of soft drink? Why or why not?
e. Determine the coefficient of determination, r^2, and explain its meaning in this problem.
f. Perform a residual analysis. Is there any evidence of a pattern in the residuals? Explain.
g. At the 0.05 level of significance, is there evidence of a linear relationship between delivery time and the number of cases delivered?
h. Construct a 95% confidence interval estimate of the mean delivery time for 150 cases of soft drink and a 95% prediction interval of the delivery time for a single delivery of 150 cases of soft drink.

13.75 Mixed costs are very common in business and consist of a fixed cost element and a variable cost element. Fixed costs are a recurring, constant cost that does not vary when business activity varies. Variable costs are added costs associated with each unit of business activity the organization experiences. The relationship can be characterized by the following equation:

$$\text{Total costs} = \text{Fixed cost} + (\text{Cost per unit})$$
$$\times (\text{Number of units of business activity})$$

In a leading managerial accounting textbook, the authors discuss a hospital's total maintenance costs and use regression analysis to estimate the fixed-cost element of maintenance and the variable cost associated with the number of patient-days. The hospital's total maintenance costs and number of patient-days for seven months are listed in the following table and stored in MixedCosts:

Total Maintenance Costs	Patient-Days
$7,900	5,600
$8,500	7,100
$7,400	5,000
$8,200	6,500
$9,100	7,300
$9,800	8,000
$7,800	6,200

Source: *Data extracted from P. C. Brewer, R. H. Garrison, and E. W. Noreen, Introduction to Managerial Accounting, 4th ed. (Boston: McGraw-Hill Irwin, 2008).*

a. Using total maintenance costs as the dependent variable and patient-days as the independent variable, use the least-squares method to find the regression coefficients b_0 and b_1.
b. Which regression coefficient represents fixed cost?

c. Which regression coefficient represents the variable cost per each patient-day?

d. Predict total maintenance costs for a month with 7,500 patient-days.

13.76 You want to develop a model to predict the selling price of homes based on assessed value. A sample of 30 recently sold single-family houses in a small city is selected to study the relationship between selling price (in thousands of dollars) and assessed value (in thousands of dollars). The houses in the city were reassessed at full value one year prior to the study. The results are in House1.

(Hint: First, determine which are the independent and dependent variables.)

a. Construct a scatter plot and, assuming a linear relationship, use the least-squares method to compute the regression coefficients b_0 and b_1.

b. Interpret the meaning of the Y intercept, b_0, and the slope, b_1, in this problem.

c. Use the prediction line developed in (a) to predict the selling price for a house whose assessed value is $170,000.

d. Determine the coefficient of determination, r^2, and interpret its meaning in this problem.

e. Perform a residual analysis on your results and evaluate the regression assumptions.

f. At the 0.05 level of significance, is there evidence of a linear relationship between selling price and assessed value?

g. Construct a 95% confidence interval estimate of the population slope.

13.77 You want to develop a model to predict the assessed value of houses, based on heating area. A sample of 15 single-family houses in a city is selected. The assessed value (in thousands of dollars) and the heating area of the houses (in thousands of square feet) are recorded; the results are stored in House2.

(Hint: First, determine which are the independent and dependent variables.)

a. Construct a scatter plot and, assuming a linear relationship, use the least-squares method to compute the regression coefficients b_0 and b_1.

b. Interpret the meaning of the Y intercept, b_0, and the slope, b_1, in this problem.

c. Use the prediction line developed in (a) to predict the assessed value for a house whose heating area is 1,750 square feet.

d. Determine the coefficient of determination, r^2, and interpret its meaning in this problem.

e. Perform a residual analysis on your results and evaluate the regression assumptions.

f. At the 0.05 level of significance, is there evidence of a linear relationship between assessed value and heating area?

13.78 The director of graduate studies at a large college of business would like to predict the grade point average (GPA) of students in an MBA program based on Graduate Management Admission Test (GMAT) score. A sample of 20 students who have completed two years in the program is selected. The results are stored in GPIGMAT.

(Hint: First, determine which are the independent and dependent variables.)

a. Construct a scatter plot and, assuming a linear relationship, use the least-squares method to compute the regression coefficients b_0 and b_1.

b. Interpret the meaning of the Y intercept, b_0, and the slope, b_1, in this problem.

c. Use the prediction line developed in (a) to predict the GPA for a student with a GMAT score of 600.

d. Determine the coefficient of determination, r^2, and interpret its meaning in this problem.

e. Perform a residual analysis on your results and evaluate the regression assumptions.

f. At the 0.05 level of significance, is there evidence of a linear relationship between GMAT score and GPA?

g. Construct a 95% confidence interval estimate of the mean GPA of students with a GMAT score of 600 and a 95% prediction interval of the GPA for a particular student with a GMAT score of 600.

h. Construct a 95% confidence interval estimate of the population slope.

13.79 An accountant for a large department store would like to develop a model to predict the amount of time it takes to process invoices. Data are collected from the past 32 working days, and the number of invoices processed and completion time (in hours) are stored in Invoice.

(Hint: First, determine which are the independent and dependent variables.)

a. Assuming a linear relationship, use the least-squares method to compute the regression coefficients b_0 and b_1.

b. Interpret the meaning of the Y intercept, b_0, and the slope, b_1, in this problem.

c. Use the prediction line developed in (a) to predict the amount of time it would take to process 150 invoices.

d. Determine the coefficient of determination, r^2, and interpret its meaning.

e. Plot the residuals against the number of invoices processed and also against time.

f. Based on the plots in (e), does the model seem appropriate?

g. Based on the results in (e) and (f), what conclusions can you make about the validity of the prediction made in (c)?

13.80 On January 28, 1986, the space shuttle *Challenger* exploded, and seven astronauts were killed. Prior to the launch, the predicted atmospheric temperature was for freezing weather at the launch site. Engineers for Morton Thiokol (the manufacturer of the rocket motor) prepared charts to make the case that the launch should not take place due to the cold weather. These arguments were rejected, and the launch tragically took place. Upon investigation after the tragedy, experts agreed that the disaster occurred because of leaky rubber O-rings that did not seal properly due to the cold temperature. Data indicating the atmospheric temperature at the time of 23 previous launches and the O-ring damage index are stored in `O-ring`).

Note: Data from flight 4 is omitted due to unknown O-ring condition.

Source: *Data extracted from* Report of the Presidential Commission on the Space Shuttle Challenger Accident, *Washington, DC, 1986, Vol. II (H1-H3) and Vol. IV (664), and* Post Challenger Evaluation of Space Shuttle Risk Assessment and Management, Washington, DC, 1988, pp. 135–136.

a. Construct a scatter plot for the seven flights in which there was O-ring damage (O-ring damage index $\neq 0$). What conclusions, if any, can you draw about the relationship between atmospheric temperature and O-ring damage?

b. Construct a scatter plot for all 23 flights.

c. Explain any differences in the interpretation of the relationship between atmospheric temperature and O-ring damage in (a) and (b).

d. Based on the scatter plot in (b), provide reasons why a prediction should not be made for an atmospheric temperature of 31°F, the temperature on the morning of the launch of the *Challenger*.

e. Although the assumption of a linear relationship may not be valid for the set of 23 flights, fit a simple linear regression model to predict O-ring damage, based on atmospheric temperature.

f. Include the prediction line found in (e) on the scatter plot developed in (b).

g. Based on the results in (f), do you think a linear model is appropriate for these data? Explain.

h. Perform a residual analysis. What conclusions do you reach?

13.81 Crazy Dave, a well-known baseball analyst, would like to study various team statistics for the 2008 baseball season to determine which variables might be useful in predicting the number of wins achieved by teams during the season. He has decided to begin by using a team's earned run average (ERA), a measure of pitching performance, to predict the number of wins. The data for the 30 Major League Baseball teams are stored in `BB2008`.

(Hint: First, determine which are the independent and dependent variables.)

a. Assuming a linear relationship, use the least-squares method to compute the regression coefficients b_0 and b_1.

b. Interpret the meaning of the Y intercept, b_0, and the slope, b_1, in this problem.

c. Use the prediction line developed in (a) to predict the number of wins for a team with an ERA of 4.50.

d. Compute the coefficient of determination, r^2, and interpret its meaning.

e. Perform a residual analysis on your results and determine the adequacy of the fit of the model.

f. At the 0.05 level of significance, is there evidence of a linear relationship between the number of wins and the ERA?

g. Construct a 95% confidence interval estimate of the mean number of wins expected for teams with an ERA of 4.50.

h. Construct a 95% prediction interval of the number of wins for an individual team that has an ERA of 4.50.

i. Construct a 95% confidence interval estimate of the population slope.

j. The 30 teams constitute a population. In order to use statistical inference, as in (f) through (i), the data must be assumed to represent a random sample. What "population" would this sample be drawing conclusions about?

k. What other independent variables might you consider for inclusion in the model?

13.82 Can you use the annual revenues generated by National Basketball Association (NBA) franchises to predict franchise values? Figure 2.18 on page 49 shows a scatter plot of revenue with franchise value, and Figure 3.9 on page 118, shows the correlation coefficient. Now, you want to develop a simple linear regression model to predict franchise values based on revenues. (Franchise values and revenues are stored in `NBAValues`.)

a. Assuming a linear relationship, use the least-squares method to compute the regression coefficients b_0 and b_1.

b. Interpret the meaning of the Y intercept, b_0, and the slope, b_1, in this problem.

c. Predict the value of an NBA franchise that generates $200 million of annual revenue.

d. Compute the coefficient of determination, r^2, and interpret its meaning.

e. Perform a residual analysis on your results and evaluate the regression assumptions.

f. At the 0.05 level of significance, is there evidence of a linear relationship between the annual revenues generated and the value of an NBA franchise?

g. Construct a 95% confidence interval estimate of the mean value of all NBA franchises that generate $150 million of annual revenue.

h. Construct a 95% prediction interval of the value of an individual NBA franchise that generates $150 million of annual revenue.

i. Compare the results of (a) through (h) to those of baseball franchises in Problems 13.8, 13.20, 13.30, 13.46, and 13.62 and National Football League franchises in Problem 13.83.

13.83 In Problem 13.82 you used annual revenue to develop a model to predict the franchise value of National Basketball Association (NBA) teams. Can you also use the annual revenues generated by National Football League (NFL) franchises to predict franchise values? (NFL franchise values and revenues are stored in NFLValues .)

a. Repeat Problem 13.82 (a) through (h) for the NFL franchises

b. Compare the results of (a) to those of baseball franchises in Problems 13.8, 13.20, 13.30, 13.46, and 13.62 and NBA franchises in Problem 13.82.

13.84 During the fall harvest season in the United States, pumpkins are sold in large quantities at farm stands. Often, instead of weighing the pumpkins prior to sale, the farm stand operator will just place the pumpkin in the appropriate circular cutout on the counter. When asked why this was done, one farmer replied, "I can tell the weight of the pumpkin from its circumference." To determine whether this was really true, a sample of 23 pumpkins were measured for circumference and weighed; the results are stored in Pumpkin.

a. Assuming a linear relationship, use the least-squares method to compute the regression coefficients b_0 and b_1.

b. Interpret the meaning of the slope, b_1, in this problem.

c. Predict the weight for a pumpkin that is 60 centimeters in circumference.

d. Do you think it is a good idea for the farmer to sell pumpkins by circumference instead of weight? Explain.

e. Determine the coefficient of determination, r^2, and interpret its meaning.

f. Perform a residual analysis for these data and evaluate the regression assumptions.

g. At the 0.05 level of significance, is there evidence of a linear relationship between the circumference and weight of a pumpkin?

h. Construct a 95% confidence interval estimate of the population slope, β_1.

13.85 Can demographic information be helpful in predicting sales at sporting goods stores? The file Sporting contains the monthly sales totals from a random sample of 38 stores in a large chain of nationwide sporting goods stores. All stores in the franchise, and thus within the sample, are approximately the same size and carry the same merchandise. The county or, in some cases, counties in which the store draws the majority of its customers is referred to here as the customer base. For each of the 38 stores, demographic information about the customer base is provided. The data are real, but the name of the franchise is not used, at the request of the company. The data set contains the following variables:

Sales—Latest one-month sales total (dollars)
Age—Median age of customer base (years)
HS—Percentage of customer base with a high school diploma
College—Percentage of customer base with a college diploma
Growth—Annual population growth rate of customer base over the past 10 years
Income—Median family income of customer base (dollars)

a. Construct a scatter plot, using sales as the dependent variable and median family income as the independent variable. Discuss the scatter plot.

b. Assuming a linear relationship, use the least-squares method to compute the regression coefficients b_0 and b_1.

c. Interpret the meaning of the Y intercept, b_0, and the slope, b_1, in this problem.

d. Compute the coefficient of determination, r^2, and interpret its meaning.

e. Perform a residual analysis on your results and determine the adequacy of the fit of the model.

f. At the 0.05 level of significance, is there evidence of a linear relationship between the independent variable and the dependent variable?

g. Construct a 95% confidence interval estimate of the population slope and interpret its meaning.

13.86 For the data of Problem 13.85, repeat (a) through (g), using median age as the independent variable.

13.87 For the data of Problem 13.85, repeat (a) through (g), using high school graduation rate as the independent variable.

13.88 For the data of Problem 13.85, repeat (a) through (g), using college graduation rate as the independent variable.

13.89 For the data of Problem 13.85, repeat (a) through (g), using population growth as the independent variable.

13.90 Zagat's publishes restaurant ratings for various locations in the United States. The file RestCost contains the Zagat rating for food, décor, service, and the cost per person for a sample of 100 restaurants located in New York City and in a suburb of New York City. Develop a regression model to predict the price per person, based on a variable that represents the sum of the ratings for food, décor, and service.

Source: *Extracted from* Zagat Survey 2008 New York City Restaurants *and* Zagat Survey 2007–2008, Long Island Restaurants.

a. Assuming a linear relationship, use the least-squares method to compute the regression coefficients b_0 and b_1.

b. Interpret the meaning of the Y intercept, b_0, and the slope, b_1, in this problem.

c. Use the prediction line developed in (a) to predict the price per person for a restaurant with a summated rating of 50.

d. Compute the coefficient of determination, r^2, and interpret its meaning.

e. Perform a residual analysis on your results and evaluate the regression assumptions.

f. At the 0.05 level of significance, is there evidence of a linear relationship between the price per person and the summated rating?

g. How useful do you think the summated rating is as a predictor of price? Explain.

13.91 Refer to the discussion of beta values and market models in Problem 13.49 on page 502. The S&P 500 Index tracks the overall movement of the stock market by considering the stock prices of 500 large corporations. The file `Stocks 2009` contains weekly data for the S&P 500 and three companies for 100 weeks ending June 1, 2009. The following variables are included:

WEEK—Week ending on date given

S&P—Weekly closing value for the S&P 500 Index

GE—Weekly closing stock price for General Electric

IBM—Weekly closing stock price for IBM

XOM—Weekly closing stock price for Exxon Mobil

Source: *Data extracted from* **finance.yahoo.com**, *June 3, 2009.*

a. Estimate the market model for GE. (Hint: Use the percentage change in the S&P 500 Index as the independent variable and the percentage change in GE's stock price as the dependent variable.)

b. Interpret the beta value for GE.

c. Repeat (a) and (b) for IBM.

d. Repeat (a) and (b) for Exxon Mobil.

e. Write a brief summary of your findings.

13.92 Do you think that bonuses and total compensation packages for CEOs of large companies are correlated with the stock performance of the companies? In 2009, the stocks included in the S&P 500 were down 38.5%, but how did the CEOs fare? The variables in the file `Compensation` include the following data on the 385 CEOs in the S&P 500 that filed their proxies between January 1 and April 20, 2009:

COMPANY—Names of a sample of 385 of the 500 companies listed on the S&P 500

STOCK—2009 stock performance (percentage increase or decrease)

BONUS—Bonuses paid to the CEOs in 2009

COMPENSATION—Total financial compensation (salary, bonuses, stock options, etc.) paid to the CEOs in 2009

Source: *Extracted from D. Jones and B. Hansen, "CEO Pay Dives in a Rough 2008,"* **usatoday.com**, *May 1, 2009.*

a. Calculate the coefficients of correlation for STOCK and BONUS, STOCK and COMPENSATION, and BONUS and COMPENSATION.

b. At the 0.05 level of significance, are any of the correlations statistically significant?

c. Write a short summary of your findings in (a) and (b). Do the results surprise you?

13.93 The file `Invest 2009` contains the daily closing price of gold, silver, the S&P 500, and the NASDAQ for the first 68 trading days of 2009 (data extracted from **finance.yahoo.com**, April 10, 2009).

a. Compute the coefficients of correlation among the four different investments. (There are six of them.)

b. At the 0.05 level of significance, are any of the correlations of the different investments statistically significant?

c. Write a short summary of your findings.

REPORT WRITING EXERCISES

13.94 In Problems 13.85 through 13.89 on page 518, you developed regression models to predict monthly sales at a sporting goods store. Now, write a report based on the models you developed. Append to your report all appropriate charts and statistical information.

MANAGING THE *SPRINGVILLE HERALD*

To ensure that as many trial subscriptions as possible are converted to regular subscriptions, the *Herald* marketing department works closely with the distribution department to accomplish a smooth initial delivery process for the trial subscription customers. To assist in this effort, the marketing department needs to accurately forecast the number of new regular subscriptions for the coming months.

A team consisting of managers from the marketing and distribution departments was convened to develop a better method of forecasting new subscriptions. Previously, after examining new subscription data for the prior three months, a group of three managers would develop a subjective forecast of the number of new subscriptions. Lauren Hall, who was recently hired by the company to provide expertise in quantitative forecasting methods, suggested that the department look for factors that might help in predicting new subscriptions.

Members of the team found that the forecasts in the past year had been particularly inaccurate because in some months, much more time was spent on telemarketing than in other months. In particular, in the past month, only 1,055 hours were completed because callers were busy during the first week of the month, attending training sessions on the personal but formal greeting style and a new standard presentation guide (see "Managing the *Springville Herald*" in Chapter 11). Lauren collected data (stored in `SH13`) for the number of new subscriptions and hours spent on telemarketing for each month for the past two years.

EXERCISES

SH13.1 What criticism can you make concerning the method of forecasting that involved taking the new subscriptions data for the prior three months as the basis for future projections?

SH13.2 What factors other than number of telemarketing hours spent might be useful in predicting the number of new subscriptions? Explain.

SH13.3 a. Analyze the data and develop a regression model to predict the number of new subscriptions for a month, based on the number of hours spent on telemarketing for new subscriptions.
   b. If you expect to spend 1,200 hours on telemarketing per month, estimate the number of new subscriptions for the month. Indicate the assumptions on which this prediction is based. Do you think these assumptions are valid? Explain.
   c. What would be the danger of predicting the number of new subscriptions for a month in which 2,000 hours were spent on telemarketing?

WEB CASE

Apply your knowledge of simple linear regression in this Web Case, which extends the Sunflowers Apparel Using Statistics scenario from this chapter.

Leasing agents from the Triangle Mall Management Corporation have suggested that Sunflowers consider several locations in some of Triangle's newly renovated lifestyle malls that cater to shoppers with higher-than-mean disposable income. Although the locations are smaller than the typical Sunflowers location, the leasing agents argue that higher-than-mean disposable income in the surrounding community is a better predictor than store size of higher sales. The leasing agents maintain that sample data from 14 Sunflowers stores prove that this is true.

Using a Web browser, open to the Web page for the Chapter 13 Web Case, or open **Triangle_Sunflower.htm**, if you have downloaded the Web Case files, to review the leasing agents' proposal and supporting documents. Then answer the following questions:

1. Should mean disposable income be used to predict sales based on the sample of 14 Sunflowers stores?

2. Should the management of Sunflowers accept the claims of Triangle's leasing agents? Why or why not?

3. Is it possible that the mean disposable income of the surrounding area is not an important factor in leasing new locations? Explain.

4. Are there any other factors not mentioned by the leasing agents that might be relevant to the store leasing decision?

REFERENCES

1. Anscombe, F. J., "Graphs in Statistical Analysis," *The American Statistician*, 27 (1973), 17–21.
2. Hoaglin, D. C., and R. Welsch, "The Hat Matrix in Regression and ANOVA," *The American Statistician* 32 (1978), 17–22.
3. Hocking, R. R., "Developments in Linear Regression Methodology: 1959–1982," *Technometrics* 25 (1983), 219–250.
4. Kutner, M. H., C. J. Nachtsheim, J. Neter, and W. Li, *Applied Linear Statistical Models*, 5th ed. (New York: McGraw-Hill/Irwin, 2005).
5. *Microsoft Excel 2007* (Redmond, WA: Microsoft Corp., 2007).

CHAPTER 13 EXCEL GUIDE

EG13.1 TYPES of REGRESSION MODELS

There are no Excel Guide instructions for this section.

EG13.2 DETERMINING the SIMPLE LINEAR REGRESSION EQUATION

PHStat2 Use the **Simple Linear Regression** procedure to perform a simple linear regression analysis. For example, to perform the analysis shown in Figure 13.4 on page 476 for the Table 13.1 Sunflowers Apparel data, open to the **DATA worksheet** of the **Site workbook**. Select **PHStat → Regression → Simple Linear Regression**, and in the procedure's dialog box (shown below):

1. Enter **C1:C15** as the **Y Variable Cell Range**.
2. Enter **B1:B15** as the **X Variable Cell Range**.
3. Check **First cells in both ranges contain label**.
4. Enter **95** as the **Confidence level for regression coefficients**.
5. Check **Regression Statistics Table** and **ANOVA and Coefficients Table**.
6. Enter a **Title** and click **OK**.

The procedure creates a worksheet that contains a copy of your data as well as the worksheet shown in Figure 13.4. For more information about these worksheets, read the following *In-Depth Excel* section.

In-Depth Excel Use the **LINEST** function to help perform a simple linear regression. Enter **LINEST(*cell range of Y variable, cell range of X variable*, True, True)** as part of an array formula placed into a 5-row-by-2-column cell range to compute the simple linear regression and various other statistics associated with the regression.

Use the **COMPUTE worksheet** of the **Simple Linear Regression workbook**, shown in Figure 13.4 on page 476, as a template for performing simple linear regression. Columns A through I of this worksheet duplicate the visual design of the Analysis ToolPak regression worksheet. The worksheet uses the regression data in the **SLRDATA worksheet** to perform the regression analysis for the Table 13.1 Sunflowers Apparel data.

Not shown in Figure 13.4 is the columns K through M Calculations area (see Figure EG13.1 on page 522). This area contains a LINEST array formula in the cell range L2:M6 and calculations for the t test of the slope (see Section 13.7 on page 498). The array formula computes the b_1 and b_0 coefficients in cells L2 and M2, the b_1 and b_0 standard errors in cells L3 and M3, r^2 and the standard error of the estimate in cells L4 and M4, the F test statistic and error df in cells L5 and M5, and SSR and SSE in cells L6 and M6. The cell L9 formula in the form =**TINV(1 − *confidence level, Error degrees of freedom*)** computes the critical value for the t test.

Open the **COMPUTE_FORMULAS worksheet** to examine all the formulas in the worksheet, some of which are discussed in later sections of this Excel Guide.

To perform simple linear regression for other data, paste the regression data into the SLRDATA worksheet. Paste the values for the X variable into column A and the values for the Y variable into column B. Open to the COMPUTE worksheet. First, enter the confidence level in cell L8. Then edit the array formula: Select the cell range L2:M6, edit the cell ranges in the formulas, and then, while holding down the **Control** and **Shift** keys (or the **Apple** key on a Mac), press the **Enter** key.

Analysis ToolPak Use the **Regression** procedure to perform simple linear regression. For example, to perform the Figure 13.4 analysis for the Table 13.1 Sunflowers Apparel data (see page 476), open to the **DATA worksheet** of the **Site workbook** and:

1. Select **Data → Data Analysis** (Excel 2007) or **Tools → Data Analysis** (Excel 2003).
2. In the Data Analysis dialog box, select **Regression** from the **Analysis Tools** list and then click **OK**.

	K	L	M
1		Calculations	
2	b1, b0 Coefficients	=LINEST(SLRData!B2:B15, SLRData!A2:A15, TRUE, TRUE)	=LINEST(SLRData!B2:B15, SLRData!A2:A15, TRUE, TRUE)
3	Standard Error	=LINEST(SLRData!B2:B15, SLRData!A2:A15, TRUE, TRUE)	=LINEST(SLRData!B2:B15, SLRData!A2:A15, TRUE, TRUE)
4	R Square, Standard Error	=LINEST(SLRData!B2:B15, SLRData!A2:A15, TRUE, TRUE)	=LINEST(SLRData!B2:B15, SLRData!A2:A15, TRUE, TRUE)
5	F, Residual df	=LINEST(SLRData!B2:B15, SLRData!A2:A15, TRUE, TRUE)	=LINEST(SLRData!B2:B15, SLRData!A2:A15, TRUE, TRUE)
6	Regression SS, Residual SS	=LINEST(SLRData!B2:B15, SLRData!A2:A15, TRUE, TRUE)	=LINEST(SLRData!B2:B15, SLRData!A2:A15, TRUE, TRUE)
7			
8	Confidence level	0.95	
9	t Critical Value	=TINV(1-L8, B13)	
10	Half Width b0	=L9*C17	
11	Half Width b1	=L9*C18	

FIGURE EG13.1 Calculations area of the simple linear regression worksheet (column N not shown)

In the Regression dialog box (see below):

3. Enter **C1:C15** as the **Input Y Range** and enter **B1:B15** as the **Input X Range**.

4. Check **Labels** and check **Confidence Level** and enter **95** in its box.

5. Click **New Worksheet Ply** and then click **OK**.

Adding a Prediction Line and Regression Equation to a Scatter Plot

PHStat2 Use the *PHStat2* instructions at the beginning of this section. Modify step 6 by checking the **Scatter Plot** output option before clicking **OK**.

In-Depth Excel Use the scatter plot instructions in Section EG2.7 to add a prediction line and regression equation to a scatter plot. For example, to create the Figure 13.5 scatter plot on page 476, open to the **DATA worksheet** of the **Site workbook** and use the Section EG2.7 instructions to create a scatter plot. Continue with either the *In-Depth Excel 2007* or *In-Depth Excel 2003* instructions.

In-Depth Excel 2007 *Continued from In-Depth Excel . . .* Open to the chart sheet containing that plot and:

1. Select **Layout → Trendline** and select **More Trendline Options** from the Trendline gallery.

In the Format Trendline dialog box (shown below):

2. Click **Trendline Options** in the left pane. In the Trendline Options pane on the right, click **Linear**, check **Display Equation on chart**, check **Display R-squared value on chart**, and then click **Close**.

For other scatter plots, if the *X* axis does not appear at the bottom of the plot, right-click the *Y* **axis** and click **Format Axis** from the shortcut menu. In the Format Axis dialog box, click **Axis Options** in the left pane. In the Axis Options pane on the right, click **Axis value** and in its box enter the value shown in the dimmed **Minimum** box at the top of the pane. Then click **Close**.

In-Depth Excel 2003 *Continued from In-Depth Excel . . .* Open to the chart sheet containing that plot and:

1. Select **Chart → Add Trendline**.

In the Add Trendline dialog box (shown below):

2. Click the **Type** tab. In the **Trend/Regression type** gallery, click **Linear**.
3. Click the **Options** tab. Click **Automatic**. Check **Display equation on chart** and **Display R-squared value on chart** and then click **OK**.

For other scatter plots, if the *X* axis does not appear at the bottom of the plot, right-click the **Y axis** and click **Format Axis** from the shortcut menu. In the Format Axis dialog box that appears, click the **Scale** tab and enter the

value found in the **Minimum** box as the **Value (X) axis Crosses at** value. Then click **OK**.

EG13.3 MEASURES of VARIATION

The measures of variation are computed as part of creating the simple linear regression worksheet using the instructions in Section EG13.2.

Figure EG13.2 shows the formulas used to compute these measures in the **COMPUTE worksheet** of the **Simple Linear Regression workbook**, created by using either the Section EG13.2 *PHStat2* or *In-Depth Excel* instructions. Formulas in cells B5, B7, B13, C12, C13, D12, and E12 copy values computed by the array formula in cell range L2:M6 that uses the **LINEST** function (see the Section EG13.2 *In-Depth Excel* instructions). The cell F12 formula, in the form **=FDIST(F test statistic, 1, error degrees of freedom)**, computes the *p*-value for the *F* test for the slope, discussed in Section 13.7.

EG13.4 ASSUMPTIONS

There are no Excel Guide instructions for this section.

EG13.5 RESIDUAL ANALYSIS

PHStat2 Use the Section EG13.2 *PHStat2* instructions. Modify step 5 by checking **Residuals Table** and **Residual Plot** in addition to checking **Regression Statistics Table** and **ANOVA and Coefficients Table**.

In-Depth Excel Create a worksheet that calculates residuals and then create a scatter plot of the original *X* variable and the residuals (plotted as the *Y* variable.)

Use the **RESIDUALS worksheet** of the **Simple Linear Regression workbook**, shown in Figure 13.10 on page 489, as a template for creating a residuals worksheet. The

	A	B	C	D	E	F	G
1	Simple Linear Regression						
2							
3		*Regression Statistics*					
4	Multiple R	=SQRT(C12/C14)					
5	R Square	=L4					
6	Adjusted R Square	=1-(B14/B13)*(C13/C14)					
7	Standard Error	=M4					
8	Observations	=COUNT(SLRData!A:A)					
9							
10	**ANOVA**						
11		*df*	*SS*	*MS*	*F*	*Significance F*	
12	Regression	1	=L6	=L6	=L5	=FDIST(E12, B12, B13)	
13	Residual	=M5	=M6	=C13/B13			
14	Total	=B12+B13	=C12+C13				
15							
16		*Coefficients*	*Standard Error*	*t Stat*	*P-value*	="Lower " & L8 * 100 & "%"	="Upper " & L8 * 100 & "%"
17	Intercept	=M2	=M3	=B17/C17	=TDIST(ABS(D17), B13, 2)	=B17-L10	=B17+L10
18	=SLRData!A1	=L2	=L3	=B18/C18	=TDIST(ABS(D18), B13, 2)	=B18-L11	=B18+L11

FIGURE EG13.2 COMPUTE worksheet formulas for columns A through G

	A	B	C	D	E
1	Observation	Square Feet	Predicted Annual Sales	Annual Sales	Residuals
2	1	1.7	=COMPUTE!$B$18 * B2 + COMPUTE!$B$17	3.7	=D2 - C2
3	2	1.6	=COMPUTE!$B$18 * B3 + COMPUTE!$B$17	3.9	=D3 - C3
4	3	2.8	=COMPUTE!$B$18 * B4 + COMPUTE!$B$17	6.7	=D4 - C4
13	12	4.6	=COMPUTE!$B$18 * B13 + COMPUTE!$B$17	7.6	=D13 - C13
14	13	5.8	=COMPUTE!$B$18 * B14 + COMPUTE!$B$17	11.8	=D14 - C14
15	14	3	=COMPUTE!$B$18 * B15 + COMPUTE!$B$17	4.1	=D15 - C15

FIGURE EG13.3 RESIDUALS worksheet formulas (showing only rows 1 through 4 and 13 through 15)

formulas in this worksheet (see Figure EG13.3) compute the residuals for the regression analysis for the Table 13.1 Sunflowers Apparel data by using the regression data in the **SLRDATA worksheet** in the same workbook.

In column C, the worksheet computes the predicted Y values (labeled Predicted Annual Sales in Figure EG13.3) by first multiplying the X values by the b_1 coefficient in cell B18 of the **COMPUTE worksheet** (see Figure EG13.2 on page 523) and then adding the b_0 coefficient (in cell B17 of COMPUTE). In column E, the worksheet computes residuals by subtracting the predicted Y values from the Y values.

For other problems, modify this worksheet by pasting the X values into column B and the Y values into column D. Then, for sample sizes smaller than 14, delete the extra rows. For sample sizes greater than 14, copy the column C and E formulas down through the row containing the last pair and X and Y values and add the new observation numbers in column A.

Analysis ToolPak Use the Section EG13.2 *Analysis ToolPak* instructions. Modify step 5 by checking **Residuals** and **Residual Plots** before clicking **New Worksheet Ply** and then **OK**.

EG13.6 MEASURING AUTOCORRELATION: The DURBIN-WATSON STATISTIC

PHStat2 Use the *PHStat2* instructions at the beginning of Section EG13.2. Modify step 6 by checking the **Durbin-Watson Statistic** output option before clicking **OK**.

In-Depth Excel Use the **SUMXMY2** and **SUMSQ** functions to help compute the Durbin-Watson statistic. Enter **SUMXMY2(***cell range of the second through last residual, cell range of the first through the second-to-last residual***)** to compute the sum of squared difference of the residuals (the numerator in Equation 13.15 on page 494). Enter **SUMSQ(***cell range of the residuals***)** to compute the sum of squared residuals.

Use the **DURBIN_WATSON worksheet** of the **Simple Linear Regression workbook**, similar to the worksheet shown in Figure 13.16 on page 495, as a template for computing the Durbin-Watson statistic. The worksheet computes the statistic for the package delivery simple linear regression model by dividing the value computed by the SUMXMY2 function in cell B3 by the value computed by the SUMSQ functions in cell B4.

To compute the Durbin-Watson statistic for other problems, first create the simple linear regression model and the RESIDUALS worksheet for the problem, using the instructions in Sections EG13.2 and EG13.5. Then open the DURBIN_WATSON worksheet and edit the formulas in cell B3 and B4 to point to the proper cell ranges of the new residuals.

EG13.7 INFERENCES ABOUT the SLOPE and CORRELATION COEFFICIENT

t Test for the Slope and F Test for the Slope

These tests are included in the worksheet created by using the Section EG13.2 instructions. The t test computations in the worksheets created by using the *PHStat2* and *In-Depth Excel* instructions are discussed in Section EG13.2. The F test computations are discussed in Section EG13.3.

EG13.8 ESTIMATION of MEAN VALUES AND PREDICTION of INDIVIDUAL VALUES

PHStat2 Use the Section EG13.2 *PHStat2* instructions but replace step 6 with the following new step 6 and 7 instructions:

6. Check **Confidence Int. Est. & Prediction Int. for X =** and enter **4** in its box. Enter **95** as the percentage for **Confidence level for intervals**.

7. Enter a **Title** and click **OK**.

The additional worksheet created is explained in the following *In-Depth Excel* passage.

In-Depth Excel Use the **TINV**, **TREND**, and **DEVSQ** functions to help compute a confidence interval estimate and determine the sample size needed for estimating the mean. Enter **TINV((1 – *confidence level, degrees of freedom*))** to compute the *t* value and enter **TREND(*Y variable cell range, X variable cell range, X value*)** to compute the predicted *Y* value for the *X* value. Enter **DEVSQ(*X variable cell range*)** to compute the *SSX* value that is used, in turn, to help compute the *h* statistic.

Use the **CIEandPI worksheet** of the **Simple Linear Regression workbook**, shown in Figure 13.21 on page 507, as a template for computing confidence interval estimates and prediction intervals. The worksheet contains the data and formulas for the Section 13.8 examples that use the Table 13.1 Sunflowers Apparel data shown on page 474. To compute a confidence interval estimate and prediction interval for other problems:

1. Paste the regression data into the **SLRData worksheet**. Use column A for the *X* variable data and column B for the *Y* variable data.

2. Open to the **CIEandPI worksheet**.

In the CIEandPI worksheet:

3. Change values for the **X Value** and **Confidence Level**, as is necessary.

4. Edit the cell ranges used in the cell B15 formula that uses the TREND function to refer to the new cell ranges for the *Y* and *X* variables.

14 Introduction to Multiple Regression

Learning Objectives

In this chapter, you learn:

- How to develop a multiple regression model
- How to interpret the regression coefficients
- How to determine which independent variables to include in the regression model
- How to determine which independent variables are most important in predicting a dependent variable
- How to use categorical independent variables in a regression model

USING STATISTICS

@ OmniFoods

You are the marketing manager for OmniFoods, a large food products company. The company is planning a nationwide introduction of OmniPower, a new high-energy bar. Originally marketed to runners, mountain climbers, and other athletes, high-energy bars are now popular with the general public. OmniFoods is anxious to capture a share of this thriving market. Because the marketplace already contains several successful energy bars, you need to develop an effective marketing strategy. In particular, you need to determine the effect that price and in-store promotions will have on sales of OmniPower. Before marketing the bar nationwide, you plan to conduct a test-market study of OmniPower sales, using a sample of 34 stores in a supermarket chain. How can you extend the linear regression methods discussed in Chapter 13 to incorporate the effects of price *and* promotion into the same model? How can you use this model to improve the success of the nationwide introduction of OmniPower?

Chapter 13 focused on simple linear regression models that use *one* numerical independent variable, X, to predict the value of a numerical dependent variable, Y. Often you can make better predictions by using *more than one* independent variable. This chapter introduces you to **multiple regression models** that use two or more independent variables to predict the value of a dependent variable.

14.1 Developing a Multiple Regression Model

The business objective facing the marketing manager at OmniFoods is to develop a model to predict monthly sales volume per store of OmniPower bars and to determine what variables influence sales. Two independent variables are considered here: the price of an OmniPower bar, as measured in cents (X_1), and the monthly budget for in-store promotional expenditures, measured in dollars (X_2). In-store promotional expenditures typically include signs and displays, in-store coupons, and free samples. The dependent variable Y is the number of OmniPower bars sold in a month. Data are collected from a sample of 34 stores in a supermarket chain selected for a test-market study of OmniPower. All the stores selected have approximately the same monthly sales volume. The data are organized and stored in `OmniPower` and presented in Table 14.1.

TABLE 14.1

Monthly OmniPower Sales, Price, and Promotional Expenditures

Store	Sales	Price	Promotion	Store	Sales	Price	Promotion
1	4,141	59	200	18	2,730	79	400
2	3,842	59	200	19	2,618	79	400
3	3,056	59	200	20	4,421	79	400
4	3,519	59	200	21	4,113	79	600
5	4,226	59	400	22	3,746	79	600
6	4,630	59	400	23	3,532	79	600
7	3,507	59	400	24	3,825	79	600
8	3,754	59	400	25	1,096	99	200
9	5,000	59	600	26	761	99	200
10	5,120	59	600	27	2,088	99	200
11	4,011	59	600	28	820	99	200
12	5,015	59	600	29	2,114	99	400
13	1,916	79	200	30	1,882	99	400
14	675	79	200	31	2,159	99	400
15	3,636	79	200	32	1,602	99	400
16	3,224	79	200	33	3,354	99	600
17	2,295	79	400	34	2,927	99	600

Interpreting the Regression Coefficients

When there are several independent variables, you can extend the simple linear regression model of Equation (13.1) on page 472 by assuming a linear relationship between each independent variable and the dependent variable. For example, with k independent variables, the multiple regression model is expressed in Equation (14.1).

MULTIPLE REGRESSION MODEL WITH k INDEPENDENT VARIABLES

$$Y_i = \beta_0 + \beta_1 X_{1i} + \beta_2 X_{2i} + \beta_3 X_{3i} + \cdots + \beta_k X_{ki} + \varepsilon_i \qquad \textbf{(14.1)}$$

where

$\beta_0 = Y$ intercept

$\beta_1 =$ slope of Y with variable X_1, holding variables $X_2, X_3, \ldots, X_k$ constant

$\beta_2 =$ slope of Y with variable X_2, holding variables $X_1, X_3, \ldots, X_k$ constant

$\beta_3 = $ slope of Y with variable X_3, holding variables $X_1, X_2, X_4, \ldots, X_k$ constant

$\vdots$

$\beta_k = $ slope of Y with variable X_k, holding variables $X_1, X_2, X_3, \ldots, X_{k-1}$ constant

$\varepsilon_i = $ random error in Y for observation i

Equation (14.2) defines the multiple regression model with two independent variables.

MULTIPLE REGRESSION MODEL WITH TWO INDEPENDENT VARIABLES

$$Y_i = \beta_0 + \beta_1 X_{1i} + \beta_2 X_{2i} + \varepsilon_i \qquad \textbf{(14.2)}$$

where

$\beta_0 = Y$ intercept

$\beta_1 = $ slope of Y with variable X_1, holding variable X_2 constant

$\beta_2 = $ slope of Y with variable X_2, holding variable X_1 constant

$\varepsilon_i = $ random error in Y for observation i

Compare the multiple regression model to the simple linear regression model [Equation (13.1) on page 472]:

$$Y_i = \beta_0 + \beta_1 X_i + \varepsilon_i$$

In the simple linear regression model, the slope, β_1, represents the change in the mean of Y per unit change in X and does not take into account any other variables. In the multiple regression model with two independent variables [Equation (14.2)], the slope, β_1, represents the change in the mean of Y per unit change in X_1, taking into account the effect of X_2.

As in the case of simple linear regression, you use the Least Squares method to compute sample regression coefficients (b_0, b_1, and b_2) as estimates of the population parameters (β_0, β_1, and β_2). Equation (14.3) defines the regression equation for a multiple regression model with two independent variables.

MULTIPLE REGRESSION EQUATION WITH TWO INDEPENDENT VARIABLES

$$\hat{Y}_i = b_0 + b_1 X_{1i} + b_2 X_{2i} \qquad \textbf{(14.3)}$$

Figure 14.1 on page 530 shows a regression results worksheet for the OmniPower sales data that contains the values for the three regression coefficients in cells B17 through B19.

From Figure 14.1, the computed values of the regression coefficients are

$$b_0 = 5{,}837.5208 \quad b_1 = -53.2173 \quad b_2 = 3.6131$$

Therefore, the multiple regression equation is

$$\hat{Y}_i = 5{,}837.5208 - 53.2173 X_{1i} + 3.6131 X_{2i}$$

where

$\hat{Y}_i = $ predicted monthly sales of OmniPower bars for store i

$X_{1i} = $ price of OmniPower bar (in cents) for store i

$X_{2i} = $ monthly in-store promotional expenditures (in dollars) for store i

FIGURE 14.1

Partial multiple regression results worksheet for the OmniPower sales data

Figure 14.1 displays the **COMPUTE worksheet** of the **Multiple Regression workbook**. Create this worksheet using the instructions in Section EG14.1. Read the In-Depth Excel instructions for this worksheet to learn about the formulas used throughout this worksheet, including the Calculations area in columns K through N (not shown in Figure 14.1).

	A	B	C	D	E	F	G	H	I
1	Multiple Regression								
2									
3	*Regression Statistics*								
4	Multiple R	0.8705							
5	R Square	0.7577							
6	Adjusted R Square	0.7421							
7	Standard Error	638.0653							
8	Observations	34							
9									
10	ANOVA								
11		*df*	*SS*	*MS*	*F*	*Significance F*			
12	Regression	2	39472730.7730	19736365.3865	48.4771	0.0000			
13	Residual	31	12620946.6682	407127.3119					
14	Total	33	52093677.4412						
15									
16		*Coefficients*	*Standard Error*	*t Stat*	*P-value*	*Lower 95%*	*Upper 95%*	*Lower 95.0%*	*Upper 95.0%*
17	Intercept	5837.5208	628.1502	9.2932	0.0000	4556.3999	7118.6416	4556.3999	7118.6416
18	Price	-53.2173	6.8522	-7.7664	0.0000	-67.1925	-39.2421	-67.1925	-39.2421
19	Promotion	3.6131	0.6852	5.2728	0.0000	2.2155	5.0106	2.2155	5.0106

The sample Y intercept ($b_0 = 5,837.5208$) estimates the number of OmniPower bars sold in a month if the price is $0.00 and the total amount spent on promotional expenditures is also $0.00. Because these values of price and promotion are outside the range of price and promotion used in the test-market study, and because they make no sense in the context of the problem, the value of b_0 has little or no practical interpretation.

The slope of price with OmniPower sales ($b_1 = -53.2173$) indicates that, for a given amount of monthly promotional expenditures, the predicted sales of OmniPower are estimated to decrease by 53.2173 bars per month for each 1-cent increase in the price. The slope of monthly promotional expenditures with OmniPower sales ($b_2 = 3.6131$) indicates that, for a given price, the estimated sales of OmniPower are predicted to increase by 3.6131 bars for each additional $1 spent on promotions. These estimates allow you to better understand the likely effect that price and promotion decisions will have in the marketplace. For example, a 10-cent decrease in price is predicted to increase sales by 532.173 bars, with a fixed amount of monthly promotional expenditures. A $100 increase in promotional expenditures is predicted to increase sales by 361.31 bars, for a given price.

Regression coefficients in multiple regression are called **net regression coefficients**; they estimate the predicted change in Y per unit change in a particular X, *holding constant the effect of the other X variables*. For example, in the study of OmniPower bar sales, for a store with a given amount of promotional expenditures, the estimated sales are predicted to decrease by 53.2173 bars per month for each 1-cent increase in the price of an OmniPower bar. Another way to interpret this "net effect" is to think of two stores with an equal amount of promotional expenditures. If the first store charges 1 cent more than the other store, the net effect of this difference is that the first store is predicted to sell 53.2173 fewer bars per month than the second store. To interpret the net effect of promotional expenditures, you can consider two stores that are charging the same price. If the first store spends $1 more on promotional expenditures, the net effect of this difference is that the first store is predicted to sell 3.6131 more bars per month than the second store.

Predicting the Dependent Variable Y

You can use the multiple regression equation computed by Microsoft Excel to predict values of the dependent variable. For example, what are the predicted sales for a store charging 79 cents during a month in which promotional expenditures are $400? Using the multiple regression equation,

$$\hat{Y}_i = 5,837.5208 - 53.2173X_{1i} + 3.6131X_{2i}$$

with $X_{1i} = 79$ and $X_{2i} = 400$,

$$\hat{Y}_i = 5{,}837.5208 - 53.2173(79) + 3.6131(400)$$
$$= 3{,}078.57$$

Thus, you predict that stores charging 79 cents and spending \$400 in promotional expenditures will sell 3,078.57 OmniPower bars per month.

After you have developed the regression equation, done a residual analysis (see Section 14.3), and determined the significance of the overall fitted model (see Section 14.2), you can construct a confidence interval estimate of the mean value and a prediction interval for an individual value. You should rely on software to do these computations for you, given the complex nature of the computations. Figure 14.2 presents a confidence interval estimate and a prediction interval worksheet for the OmniPower sales data.

FIGURE 14.2

Confidence interval estimate and prediction interval worksheet for the OmniPower sales data

*Figure 14.2 displays the **CIEandPI worksheet** of the **Multiple Regression workbook**. Create this worksheet using the instructions in Section EG14.4.*

	A	B	C	D
1	Confidence Interval Estimate and Prediction Interval			
2				
3	**Data**			
4	Confidence Level	95%		
5		1		
6	Price given value	79		
7	Promotion given value	400		
8				
9	X'X	34	2646	13200
10		2646	214674	1018800
11		13200	1018800	6000000
12				
13	Inverse of X'X	0.9692	-0.0094	-0.0005
14		-0.0094	0.0001	0.0000
15		-0.0005	0.0000	0.0000
16				
17	X'G times Inverse of X'X	0.0121	0.0001	0.0000
18				
19	[X'G times Inverse of X'X] times XG	0.0298	=MMULT(B17:D17, B5:B7)	
20	t Statistic	2.0395	=TINV(1 - B4, COMPUTE!B13)	
21	Predicted Y (YHat)	3078.57	{=MMULT(TRANSPOSE(B5:B7), COMPUTE!B17:B19)}	
22				
23	**For Average Predicted Y (YHat)**			
24	Interval Half Width	224.50	=B20 * SQRT(B19) * COMPUTE!B7	
25	Confidence Interval Lower Limit	2854.07	=B21 - B24	
26	Confidence Interval Upper Limit	3303.08	=B21 + B24	
27				
28	**For Individual Response Y**			
29	Interval Half Width	1320.57	=B20 * SQRT(1 + B19) * COMPUTE!B7	
30	Prediction Interval Lower Limit	1758.01	=B21 - B29	
31	Prediction Interval Upper Limit	4399.14	=B21 + B29	

Also:

Cell range B9:D11	=MMULT(TRANSPOSE(MRArray!A2:C35), MRArray!A2:C35)
Cell range B13:B15	=MINVERSE(B9:D11)
Cell range B17:D17	=MMULT(TRANSPOSE(B5:B7), B13:D15)

The 95% confidence interval estimate of the mean OmniPower sales for all stores charging 79 cents and spending \$400 in promotional expenditures is 2,854.07 to 3,303.08 bars. The prediction interval for an individual store is 1,758.01 to 4,399.14 bars.

Problems For Section 14.1

LEARNING THE BASICS

14.1 For this problem, use the following multiple regression equation:

$$\hat{Y}_i = 10 + 5X_{1i} + 3X_{2i}$$

a. Interpret the meaning of the slopes.
b. Interpret the meaning of the Y intercept.

14.2 For this problem, use the following multiple regression equation:

$$\hat{Y}_i = 50 - 2X_{1i} + 7X_{2i}$$

a. Interpret the meaning of the slopes.
b. Interpret the meaning of the Y intercept.

APPLYING THE CONCEPTS

14.3 A shoe manufacturer is considering the development of a new brand of running shoes. The business problem facing the marketing analyst is to determine which variables should be used to predict durability (i.e., the effect of long-term impact). Two independent variables under consideration are X_1 (FOREIMP), a measurement of the forefoot shock-absorbing capability, and X_2 (MIDSOLE), a measurement of the change in impact properties over time. The dependent variable Y is LTIMP, a measure of the shoe's durability after a repeated impact test. Data are collected from a random sample of 15 types of currently manufactured running shoes, with the following results:

Variable	Coefficients	Standard Error	t Statistic	p-Value
INTERCEPT	−0.02686	0.06905	−0.39	0.7034
FOREIMP	0.79116	0.06295	12.57	0.0000
MIDSOLE	0.60484	0.07174	8.43	0.0000

a. State the multiple regression equation.
b. Interpret the meaning of the slopes, b_1 and b_2, in this problem.

SELF Test **14.4** A mail-order catalog business selling personal computer supplies, software, and hardware maintains a centralized warehouse. Management is currently examining the process of distribution from the warehouse. The business problem facing management relates to the factors that affect warehouse distribution costs. Currently, a small handling fee is added to each order, regardless of the amount of the order. Data collected over the past 24 months (stored in WareCost) indicate the warehouse distribution costs (in thousands of dollars), the sales (in thousands of dollars), and the number of orders received.

a. State the multiple regression equation.
b. Interpret the meaning of the slopes, b_1 and b_2, in this problem.
c. Explain why the regression coefficient, b_0, has no practical meaning in the context of this problem.
d. Predict the monthly warehouse distribution cost when sales are $400,000 and the number of orders is 4,500.
e. Construct a 95% confidence interval estimate for the mean monthly warehouse distribution cost when sales are $400,000 and the number of orders is 4,500.
f. Construct a 95% prediction interval for the monthly warehouse distribution cost for a particular month when sales are $400,000 and the number of orders is 4,500.
g. Explain why the interval in (e) is narrower than the interval in (f).

14.5 A consumer organization wants to develop a regression model to predict mileage (as measured by miles per gallon) based on the horsepower of the car's engine and the weight of the car (in pounds). Data were collected from a sample of 50 recent car models, and the results are organized and stored in Auto.

a. State the multiple regression equation.
b. Interpret the meaning of the slopes, b_1 and b_2, in this problem.
c. Explain why the regression coefficient, b_0, has no practical meaning in the context of this problem.
d. Predict the miles per gallon for cars that have 60 horsepower and weigh 2,000 pounds.
e. Construct a 95% confidence interval estimate for the mean miles per gallon for cars that have 60 horsepower and weigh 2,000 pounds.
f. Construct a 95% prediction interval for the miles per gallon for an individual car that has 60 horsepower and weighs 2,000 pounds.

14.6 The business problem facing a consumer products company is to measure the effectiveness of different types of advertising media in the promotion of its products. Specifically, the company is interested in the effectiveness of radio advertising and newspaper advertising (including the cost of discount coupons). Data were collected from a sample of 22 cities with approximately equal populations selected for study during a test period of one month. Each city is allocated a specific expenditure level for radio advertising and for newspaper advertising. The sales of the product (in thousands of dollars) and also the levels of media expenditure (in thousands of dollars) during the test month are recorded, with the following results shown at the top of page 533 and stored in Advertise:

a. State the multiple regression equation.
b. Interpret the meaning of the slopes, b_1 and b_2, in this problem.
c. Interpret the meaning of the regression coefficient, b_0.
d. Which type of advertising is more effective? Explain.

City	Sales ($000)	Radio Adverting ($000)	Newspaper Advertising ($000)
1	973	0	40
2	1,119	0	40
3	875	25	25
4	625	25	25
5	910	30	30
6	971	30	30
7	931	35	35
8	1,177	35	35
9	882	40	25
10	982	40	25
11	1,628	45	45
12	1,577	45	45
13	1,044	50	0
14	914	50	0
15	1,329	55	25
16	1,330	55	25
17	1,405	60	30
18	1,436	60	30
19	1,521	65	35
20	1,741	65	35
21	1,866	70	40
22	1,717	70	40

14.7 The business problem facing the director of broadcasting operations for a television station was the issue of standby hours (i.e., hours in which unionized graphic artists at the station are paid but are not actually involved in any activity) and what factors were related to standby hours. The study included the following variables:

Standby hours (Y)—Total number of standby hours in a week

Total staff present (X_1)—Weekly total of people-days

Remote hours (X_2)—Total number of hours worked by employees at locations away from the central plant

Data were collected for 26 weeks; these data are organized and stored in Standby.

a. State the multiple regression equation.
b. Interpret the meaning of the slopes, b_1 and b_2, in this problem.
c. Explain why the regression coefficient, b_0, has no practical meaning in the context of this problem.
d. Predict the standby hours for a week in which the total staff present have 310 people-days and the remote hours are 400.
e. Construct a 95% confidence interval estimate for the mean standby hours for weeks in which the total staff present have 310 people-days and the remote hours are 400.
f. Construct a 95% prediction interval for the standby hours for a single week in which the total staff present have 310 people-days and the remote hours are 400.

14.8 Nassau County is located approximately 25 miles east of New York City. The data organized and stored in GlenCove include the appraised value, land area of the property in acres, and age, in years, for a sample of 30 single-family homes located in Glen Cove, a small city in Nassau County. Develop a multiple linear regression model to predict appraised value based on land area of the property and age, in years.

a. State the multiple regression equation.
b. Interpret the meaning of the slopes, b_1 and b_2, in this problem.
c. Explain why the regression coefficient, b_0, has no practical meaning in the context of this problem.
d. Predict the appraised value for a house that has a land area of 0.25 acres and is 45 years old.
e. Construct a 95% confidence interval estimate for the mean appraised value for houses that have a land area of 0.25 acres and are 45 years old.
f. Construct a 95% prediction interval estimate for the appraised value for an individual house that has a land area of 0.25 acres and is 45 years old.

14.2 r^2, Adjusted r^2, and the Overall F Test

This section discusses three methods you can use to evaluate the overall multiple regression model: the coefficient of multiple determination, r^2, the adjusted r^2, and the overall F test.

Coefficient of Multiple Determination

Recall from Section 13.3 that the coefficient of determination, r^2, measures the proportion of the variation in Y that is explained by the independent variable X in the simple linear regression model. In multiple regression, the **coefficient of multiple determination** represents the proportion of the variation in Y that is explained by the set of independent variables. Equation (14.4) defines the coefficient of multiple determination for a multiple regression model with two or more independent variables.

COEFFICIENT OF MULTIPLE DETERMINATION

The coefficient of multiple determination is equal to the regression sum of squares (SSR) divided by the total sum of squares (SST).

$$r^2 = \frac{\text{Regression sum of squares}}{\text{Total sum of squares}} = \frac{SSR}{SST} \qquad \textbf{(14.4)}$$

where

SSR = Regression sum of squares

SST = Total sum of squares

In the OmniPower example, from Figure 14.1 on page 530, $SSR = 39{,}472{,}730.77$ and $SST = 52{,}093{,}677.44$. Thus,

$$r^2 = \frac{SSR}{SST} = \frac{39{,}472{,}730.77}{52{,}093{,}677.44} = 0.7577$$

The coefficient of multiple determination ($r^2 = 0.7577$) indicates that 75.77% of the variation in sales is explained by the variation in the price and in the promotional expenditures. You can also find the coefficient of multiple determination directly from the Microsoft Excel results in Figure 14.1 on page 530, labeled R Square.

Adjusted r^2

When considering multiple regression models, some statisticians suggest that you should use the **adjusted r^2** to reflect both the number of independent variables in the model and the sample size. Reporting the adjusted r^2 is extremely important when you are comparing two or more regression models that predict the same dependent variable but have a different number of independent variables. Equation (14.5) defines the adjusted r^2.

ADJUSTED r^2

$$r^2_{\text{adj}} = 1 - \left[(1 - r^2) \frac{n - 1}{n - k - 1} \right] \qquad \textbf{(14.5)}$$

where k is the number of independent variables in the regression equation.

Thus, for the OmniPower data, because $r^2 = 0.7577, n = 34$, and $k = 2$,

$$r^2_{\text{adj}} = 1 - \left[(1 - 0.7577) \frac{34 - 1}{34 - 2 - 1} \right]$$

$$= 1 - \left[(0.2423) \frac{33}{31} \right]$$

$$= 1 - 0.2579$$

$$= 0.7421$$

Therefore, 74.21% of the variation in sales is explained by the multiple regression model—adjusted for number of independent variables and sample size. You can also find the adjusted r^2 directly from the worksheet results in Figure 14.1 on page 530, labeled Adjusted R Square.

Test for the Significance of the Overall Multiple Regression Model

You use the **overall F test** to determine whether there is a significant relationship between the dependent variable and the entire set of independent variables (the overall multiple regression model). Because there is more than one independent variable, you use the following null and alternative hypotheses:

H_0: $\beta_1 = \beta_2 = \cdots = \beta_k = 0$ (There is no linear relationship between the dependent variable and the independent variables.)

H_1: At least one $\beta_j \neq 0$, $j = 1, 2, \ldots, k$ (There is a linear relationship between the dependent variable and at least one of the independent variables.)

Equation (14.6) defines the statistic for the overall F test. Table 14.2 presents the ANOVA summary table.

OVERALL F TEST

The F_{STAT} test statistic is equal to the regression mean square (*MSR*) divided by the mean square error (*MSE*).

$$F_{STAT} = \frac{MSR}{MSE} \tag{14.6}$$

where

$$F_{STAT} = \text{test statistic from an } F \text{ distribution with } k \text{ and } n - k - 1 \text{ degrees of freedom}$$

$$k = \text{number of independent variables in the regression model}$$

TABLE 14.2

ANOVA Summary Table for the Overall F Test

Source	Degrees of Freedom	Sum of Squares	Mean Squares (Variance)	F
Regression	k	SSR	$MSR = \dfrac{SSR}{k}$	$F_{STAT} = \dfrac{MSR}{MSE}$
Error	$n - k - 1$	SSE	$MSE = \dfrac{SSE}{n - k - 1}$	
Total	$n - 1$	SST		

The decision rule is

Reject H_0 at the α level of significance if $F_{STAT} > F_\alpha$;

otherwise, do not reject H_0.

Using a 0.05 level of significance, the critical value of the F distribution with 2 and 31 degrees of freedom found from Table E.5 is approximately 3.32 (see Figure 14.3 below). From

FIGURE 14.3

Testing for the significance of a set of regression coefficients at the 0.05 level of significance, with 2 and 31 degrees of freedom

.95

.05

0   3.32   F

Region of Nonrejection   Region of Rejection

Critical Value

Figure 14.1 on page 530, the F_{STAT} test statistic given in the ANOVA summary table is 48.4771. Because 48.4771 > 3.32, or because the p-value = 0.000 < 0.05, you reject H_0 and conclude that at least one of the independent variables (price and/or promotional expenditures) is related to sales.

Problems for Section 14.2

LEARNING THE BASICS

14.9 The following ANOVA summary table is for a multiple regression model with two independent variables:

Source	Degrees of Freedom	Sum of Squares	Mean Squares	F
Regression	2	60		
Error	18	120		
Total	20	180		

a. Determine the regression mean square (MSR) and the mean square error (MSE).
b. Compute the overall F_{STAT} test statistic.
c. Determine whether there is a significant relationship between Y and the two independent variables at the 0.05 level of significance.
d. Compute the coefficient of multiple determination, r^2, and interpret its meaning.
e. Compute the adjusted r^2.

14.10 The following ANOVA summary table is for a multiple regression model with two independent variables:

Source	Degrees of Freedom	Sum of Squares	Mean Squares	F
Regression	2	30		
Error	10	120		
Total	12	150		

a. Determine the regression mean square (MSR) and the mean square error (MSE).
b. Compute the overall F_{STAT} test statistic.
c. Determine whether there is a significant relationship between Y and the two independent variables at the 0.05 level of significance.
d. Compute the coefficient of multiple determination, r^2, and interpret its meaning.
e. Compute the adjusted r^2.

APPLYING THE CONCEPTS

14.11 Eileen M. Van Aken and Brian M. Kleiner, professors at Virginia Polytechnic Institute and State University, investigated the factors that contribute to the effectiveness of teams [data extracted from "Determinants of Effectiveness for Cross-Functional Organizational Design Teams," *Quality Management Journal*, 4 (1997), 51–79]. The researchers

studied 34 independent variables, such as team skills, diversity, meeting frequency, and clarity in expectations. For each of the teams studied, each of the variables was given a value of 1 through 100, based on the results of interviews and survey data, where 100 represents the highest rating. The dependent variable, team performance, was also given a value of 1 through 100, with 100 representing the highest rating. Many different regression models were explored, including the following:

Model 1

$$\text{Team performance} = \beta_0 + \beta_1 (\text{Team skill}) + \varepsilon,$$
$$r_{adj}^2 = 0.68$$

Model 2

$$\text{Team performance} = \beta_0 + \beta_1 (\text{Clarity in expectations}) + \varepsilon,$$
$$r_{adj}^2 = 0.78$$

Model 3

$$\text{Team performance} = \beta_0 + \beta_1 (\text{Team skills})$$
$$+ \beta_2 (\text{Clarity in expectations}) + \varepsilon$$
$$r_{adj}^2 = 0.97$$

a. Interpret the adjusted r^2 for each of the three models.
b. Which of these three models do you think is the best predictor of team performance?

14.12 In Problem 14.3 on page 532, you predicted the durability of a brand of running shoe, based on the forefoot shock-absorbing capability and the change in impact properties over time. The regression analysis resulted in the following ANOVA summary table:

Source	Degrees of Freedom	Sum of Squares	Mean Squares	F	p-value
Regression	2	12.61020	6.30510	97.69	0.0001
Error	12	0.77453	0.06454		
Total	14	13.38473			

a. Determine whether there is a significant relationship between durability and the two independent variables at the 0.05 level of significance.
b. Interpret the meaning of the p-value.
c. Compute the coefficient of multiple determination, r^2, and interpret its meaning.
d. Compute the adjusted r^2.

14.13 In Problem 14.5 on page 532, you used horsepower and weight to predict mileage (stored in `Auto`). Using the results from that problem,
a. determine whether there is a significant relationship between mileage and the two independent variables (horsepower and weight) at the 0.05 level of significance.
b. interpret the meaning of the p-value.
c. compute the coefficient of multiple determination, r^2, and interpret its meaning.
d. compute the adjusted r^2.

SELF Test **14.14** In Problem 14.4 on page 532, you used sales and number of orders to predict distribution costs at a mail-order catalog business (stored in `Warecost`). Using the results from that problem,
a. determine whether there is a significant relationship between distribution costs and the two independent variables (sales and number of orders) at the 0.05 level of significance.
b. interpret the meaning of the p-value.
c. compute the coefficient of multiple determination, r^2, and interpret its meaning.
d. compute the adjusted r^2.

14.15 In Problem 14.7 on page 533, you used the total staff present and remote hours to predict standby hours (stored in `Standby`). Using the results from that problem,
a. determine whether there is a significant relationship between standby hours and the two independent variables (total staff present and remote hours) at the 0.05 level of significance.

b. interpret the meaning of the p-value.
c. compute the coefficient of multiple determination, r^2, and interpret its meaning.
d. compute the adjusted r^2.

14.16 In Problem 14.6 on page 532, you used radio advertising and newspaper advertising to predict sales (stored in `Advertise`). Using the results from that problem,
a. determine whether there is a significant relationship between sales and the two independent variables (radio advertising and newspaper advertising) at the 0.05 level of significance.
b. interpret the meaning of the p-value.
c. compute the coefficient of multiple determination, r^2, and interpret its meaning.
d. compute the adjusted r^2.

14.17 In Problem 14.8 on page 533, you used the land area of a property and the age of a house to predict appraised value (stored in `GlenCove`). Using the results from that problem,
a. determine whether there is a significant relationship between appraised value and the two independent variables (land area of a property and age of a house) at the 0.05 level of significance.
b. interpret the meaning of the p-value.
c. compute the coefficient of multiple determination, r^2, and interpret its meaning.
d. compute the adjusted r^2.

14.3 Residual Analysis for the Multiple Regression Model

In Section 13.5, you used residual analysis to evaluate the fit of the simple linear regression model. For the multiple regression model with two independent variables, you need to construct and analyze the following residual plots:

1. Residuals versus $\hat{Y}_i$
2. Residuals versus X_{1i}
3. Residuals versus X_{2i}
4. Residuals versus time

The first residual plot examines the pattern of residuals versus the predicted values of Y. If the residuals show a pattern for the predicted values of Y, there is evidence of a possible curvilinear effect (see Section 15.1) in at least one independent variable, a possible violation of the assumption of equal variance (see Figure 13.13 on page 491), and/or the need to transform the Y variable.

The second and third residual plots involve the independent variables. Patterns in the plot of the residuals versus an independent variable may indicate the existence of a curvilinear effect and, therefore, the need to add a curvilinear independent variable to the multiple regression model (see Section 15.1). The fourth plot is used to investigate patterns in the residuals in order to validate the independence assumption when the data are collected in time order. Associated with this residual plot, as in Section 13.6, you can compute the Durbin-Watson statistic to determine the existence of positive autocorrelation among the residuals.

Figure 14.4 presents the residual plots for the OmniPower sales example. There is very little or no pattern in the relationship between the residuals and the predicted value of Y, the

FIGURE 14.4

Residual plots for the
OmniPower sales data:
Panel A, residuals versus
predicted Y;
Panel B, residuals versus
price;
Panel C, residuals versus
promotional
expenditures

*Create residual plots using
the instructions in Section
EG13.5.*

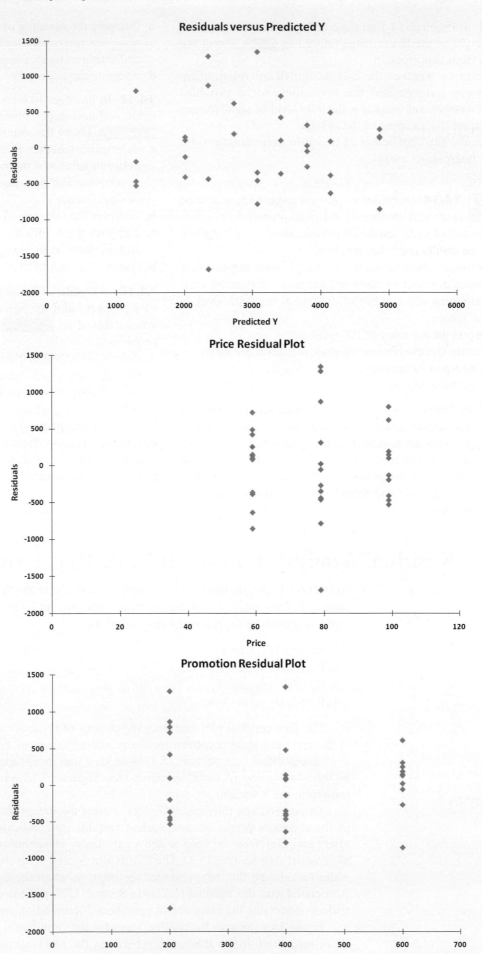

value of X_1 (price), or the value of X_2 (promotional expenditures). Thus, you can conclude that the multiple regression model is appropriate for predicting sales. There is no need to plot the residuals versus time because the data were not collected in time order.

Problems for Section 14.3

APPLYING THE CONCEPTS

14.18 In Problem 14.4 on page 532, you used sales and number of orders to predict distribution costs at a mail-order catalog business (stored in WareCost).
a. Plot the residuals versus $\hat{Y}_i$
b. Plot the residuals versus X_{1i}.
c. Plot the residuals versus X_{2i}.
d. Plot the residuals versus time.
e. In the residuals plots created in (a) through (d), is there any evidence of a violation of the regression assumptions? Explain.
f. Determine the Durbin-Watson statistic.
g. At the 0.05 level of significance, is there evidence of positive autocorrelation in the residuals?

14.19 In Problem 14.5 on page 532, you used horsepower and weight to predict mileage (stored in Auto).
a. Plot the residuals versus $\hat{Y}_i$
b. Plot the residuals versus X_{1i}.
c. Plot the residuals versus X_{2i}.
d. In the residuals plots created in (a) through (c), is there any evidence of a violation of the regression assumptions? Explain.
e. Should you compute the Durbin-Watson statistic for these data? Explain.

14.20 In Problem 14.6 on page 532, you used radio advertising and newspaper advertising to predict sales (stored in Advertise).
a. Perform a residual analysis on your results.
b. If appropriate, perform the Durbin-Watson test, using $\alpha = 0.05$.
c. Are the regression assumptions valid for these data?

14.21 In Problem 14.7 on page 533, you used the total staff present and remote hours to predict standby hours (stored in Standby).
a. Perform a residual analysis on your results.
b. If appropriate, perform the Durbin-Watson test, using $\alpha = 0.05$.
c. Are the regression assumptions valid for these data?

14.22 In Problem 14.8 on page 533, you used the land area of a property and the age of a house to predict appraised value (stored in GlenCove).
a. Perform a residual analysis on your results.
b. If appropriate, perform the Durbin-Watson test, using $\alpha = 0.05$.
c. Are the regression assumptions valid for these data?

14.4 Inferences Concerning the Population Regression Coefficients

In Section 13.7, you tested the slope in a simple linear regression model to determine the significance of the relationship between X and Y. In addition, you constructed a confidence interval estimate of the population slope. This section extends those procedures to multiple regression.

Tests of Hypothesis

In a simple linear regression model, to test a hypothesis concerning the population slope, β_1, you used Equation (13.16) on page 497:

$$t_{STAT} = \frac{b_1 - \beta_1}{S_{b_1}}$$

Equation (14.7) generalizes this equation for multiple regression.

TESTING FOR THE SLOPE IN MULTIPLE REGRESSION

$$t_{STAT} = \frac{b_j - \beta_j}{S_{b_j}}$$

(14.7)

where

$$b_j = \text{slope of variable } j \text{ with } Y, \text{ holding constant the effects of all other independent variables}$$

$$S_{b_j} = \text{standard error of the regression coefficient } b_j$$

$$t_{STAT} = \text{test statistic for a } t \text{ distribution with } n - k - 1 \text{ degrees of freedom}$$

$$k = \text{number of independent variables in the regression equation}$$

$$\beta_j = \text{hypothesized value of the population slope for variable } j, \text{ holding constant the effects of all other independent variables}$$

To determine whether variable X_2 (amount of promotional expenditures) has a significant effect on sales, taking into account the price of OmniPower bars, the null and alternative hypotheses are

$$H_0: \beta_2 = 0$$
$$H_1: \beta_2 \neq 0$$

From Equation (14.7) and Figure 14.1 on page 530,

$$t_{STAT} = \frac{b_2 - \beta_2}{S_{b_2}}$$

$$= \frac{3.6131 - 0}{0.6852} = 5.2728$$

If you select a level of significance of 0.05, the critical values of t for 31 degrees of freedom from Table E.3 are -2.0395 and $+2.0395$ (see Figure 14.5).

FIGURE 14.5

Testing for significance of a regression coefficient at the 0.05 level of significance, with 31 degrees of freedom

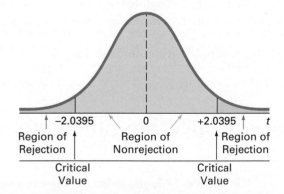

From Figure 14.1 on page 530, observe that the computed t_{STAT} test statistic is 5.2728. Because $t_{STAT} = 5.2728 > 2.0395$ or because the p-value is approximately zero, you reject H_0 and conclude that there is a significant relationship between the variable X_2 (promotional expenditures) and sales, taking into account the price, X_1. The extremely small p-value allows you to strongly reject the null hypothesis that there is no linear relationship between sales and promotional expenditures. Example 14.1 presents the test for the significance of β_1, the slope of sales with price.

EXAMPLE 14.1

Testing for the Significance of the Slope of Sales with Price

At the 0.05 level of significance, is there evidence that the slope of sales with price is different from zero?

SOLUTION From Figure 14.1 on page 530, $t_{STAT} = -7.7664 < -2.0395$ (the critical value for $\alpha = 0.05$) or the p-value $= 0.0000 < 0.05$. Thus, there is a significant relationship between price, X_1, and sales, taking into account the promotional expenditures, X_2.

As shown with these two independent variables, the test of significance for a specific regression coefficient in multiple regression is a test for the significance of adding that variable into a regression model, given that the other variable is included. In other words, the t test for the regression coefficient is actually a test for the contribution of each independent variable.

Confidence Interval Estimation

Instead of testing the significance of a population slope, you may want to estimate the value of a population slope. Equation (14.8) defines the confidence interval estimate for a population slope in multiple regression.

CONFIDENCE INTERVAL ESTIMATE FOR THE SLOPE

$$b_j \pm t_{\alpha/2} S_{b_j} \qquad \textbf{(14.8)}$$

where $t_{\alpha/2}$ is the critical value corresponding to an upper-tail probability of $\alpha/2$ from the t distribution with $n - k - 1$ degrees of freedom (i.e., a cumulative area of $1 - \alpha/2$), and k is the number of independent variables.

To construct a 95% confidence interval estimate of the population slope, β_1 (the effect of price, X_1, on sales, Y, holding constant the effect of promotional expenditures, X_2), the critical value of t at the 95% confidence level with 31 degrees of freedom is 2.0395 (see Table E.3). Then, using Equation (14.8) and Figure 14.1 on page 530,

$$b_1 \pm t_{\alpha/2} S_{b_1}$$

$$-53.2173 \pm (2.0395)(6.8522)$$

$$-53.2173 \pm 13.9752$$

$$-67.1925 \le \beta_1 \le -39.2421$$

Taking into account the effect of promotional expenditures, the estimated effect of a 1-cent increase in price is to reduce mean sales by approximately 39.2 to 67.2 bars. You have 95% confidence that this interval correctly estimates the relationship between these variables. From a hypothesis-testing viewpoint, because this confidence interval does not include 0, you conclude that the regression coefficient, β_1, has a significant effect.

Example 14.2 constructs and interprets a confidence interval estimate for the slope of sales with promotional expenditures.

EXAMPLE 14.2

Constructing a Confidence Interval Estimate for the Slope of Sales with Promotional Expenditures

Construct a 95% confidence interval estimate of the population slope of sales with promotional expenditures.

SOLUTION The critical value of t at the 95% confidence level, with 31 degrees of freedom, is 2.0395 (see Table E.3). Using Equation (14.8) and Figure 14.1 on page 530,

$$b_2 \pm t_{\alpha/2} S_{b_2}$$

$$3.6131 \pm (2.0395)(0.6852)$$

$$3.6131 \pm 1.3975$$

$$2.2156 \le \beta_2 \le 5.0106$$

Thus, taking into account the effect of price, the estimated effect of each additional dollar of promotional expenditures is to increase mean sales by approximately 2.22 to 5.01 bars. You have 95% confidence that this interval correctly estimates the relationship between these variables. From a hypothesis-testing viewpoint, because this confidence interval does not include 0, you can conclude that the regression coefficient, β_2, has a significant effect.

Problems for Section 14.4

LEARNING THE BASICS

14.23 Use the following information from a multiple regression analysis:

$$n = 25 \quad b_1 = 5 \quad b_2 = 10 \quad S_{b_1} = 2 \quad S_{b_2} = 8$$

a. Which variable has the largest slope, in units of a t statistic?
b. Construct a 95% confidence interval estimate of the population slope, β_1.
c. At the 0.05 level of significance, determine whether each independent variable makes a significant contribution to the regression model. On the basis of these results, indicate the independent variables to include in this model.

14.24 Use the following information from a multiple regression analysis:

$$n = 20 \quad b_1 = 4 \quad b_2 = 3 \quad S_{b_1} = 1.2 \quad S_{b_2} = 0.8$$

a. Which variable has the largest slope, in units of a t statistic?
b. Construct a 95% confidence interval estimate of the population slope, β_1.
c. At the 0.05 level of significance, determine whether each independent variable makes a significant contribution to the regression model. On the basis of these results, indicate the independent variables to include in this model.

APPLYING THE CONCEPTS

14.25 In Problem 14.3 on page 532, you predicted the durability of a brand of running shoe, based on the forefoot shock-absorbing capability (FOREIMP) and the change in impact properties over time (MIDSOLE) for a sample of 15 pairs of shoes. Use the following results:

Variable	Coefficient	Standard Error	t Statistic	p-Value
INTERCEPT	−0.02686	0.06905	−0.39	0.7034
FOREIMP	0.79116	0.06295	12.57	0.0000
MIDSOLE	0.60484	0.07174	8.43	0.0000

a. Construct a 95% confidence interval estimate of the population slope between durability and forefoot shock-absorbing capability.
b. At the 0.05 level of significance, determine whether each independent variable makes a significant contribution to the regression model. On the basis of these results, indicate the independent variables to include in this model.

 14.26 In Problem 14.4 on page 532, you used sales and number of orders to predict distribution costs at a mail-order catalog business (stored in **WareCost**). Using the results from that problem,
a. construct a 95% confidence interval estimate of the population slope between distribution cost and sales.
b. at the 0.05 level of significance, determine whether each independent variable makes a significant contribution to the regression model. On the basis of these results, indicate the independent variables to include in this model.

14.27 In Problem 14.5 on page 532, you used horsepower and weight to predict mileage (stored in **Auto**). Using the results from that problem,
a. construct a 95% confidence interval estimate of the population slope between mileage and horsepower.
b. at the 0.05 level of significance, determine whether each independent variable makes a significant contribution to the regression model. On the basis of these results, indicate the independent variables to include in this model.

14.28 In Problem 14.6 on page 532, you used radio advertising and newspaper advertising to predict sales (stored in **Advertise**). Using the results from that problem,
a. construct a 95% confidence interval estimate of the population slope between sales and radio advertising.
b. at the 0.05 level of significance, determine whether each independent variable makes a significant contribution to the regression model. On the basis of these results, indicate the independent variables to include in this model.

14.29 In Problem 14.7 on page 533, you used the total number of staff present and remote hours to predict standby hours (stored in **Standby**). Using the results from that problem,
a. construct a 95% confidence interval estimate of the population slope between standby hours and total number of staff present.
b. at the 0.05 level of significance, determine whether each independent variable makes a significant contribution to the regression model. On the basis of these results, indicate the independent variables to include in this model.

14.30 In Problem 14.8 on page 533, you used land area of a property and age of a house to predict appraised value (stored in **GlenCove**). Using the results from that problem,
a. construct a 95% confidence interval estimate of the population slope between appraised value and land area of a property.
b. at the 0.05 level of significance, determine whether each independent variable makes a significant contribution to the regression model. On the basis of these results, indicate the independent variables to include in this model.

14.5 Testing Portions of the Multiple Regression Model

In developing a multiple regression model, you want to use only those independent variables that significantly reduce the error in predicting the value of a dependent variable. If an independent variable does not improve the prediction, you can delete it from the multiple regression model and use a model with fewer independent variables.

The **partial F test** is an alternative method to the t test discussed in Section 14.4 for determining the contribution of an independent variable. Using this method, you determine the contribution to the regression sum of squares made by each independent variable after all the other independent variables have been included in the model. The new independent variable is included only if it significantly improves the model.

To conduct partial F tests for the OmniPower sales example, you need to evaluate the contribution of promotional expenditures (X_2) after price (X_1) has been included in the model, and also evaluate the contribution of price (X_1) after promotional expenditures (X_2) have been included in the model.

In general, if there are several independent variables, you determine the contribution of each independent variable by taking into account the regression sum of squares of a model that includes all independent variables except the one of interest, j. This regression sum of squares is denoted SSR (all Xs except j). Equation (14.9) determines the contribution of variable j, assuming that all other variables are already included.

DETERMINING THE CONTRIBUTION OF AN INDEPENDENT VARIABLE TO THE REGRESSION MODEL

$$SSR(X_j \mid \text{All } Xs \text{ except } j) = SSR\,(\text{All } Xs) - SSR\,(\text{All } Xs \text{ except } j) \quad \textbf{(14.9)}$$

If there are two independent variables, you use Equations (14.10a) and (14.10b) to determine the contribution of each.

CONTRIBUTION OF VARIABLE X_1, GIVEN THAT X_2 HAS BEEN INCLUDED

$$SSR(X_1 \mid X_2) = SSR(X_1 \text{ and } X_2) - SSR(X_2) \quad \textbf{(14.10a)}$$

CONTRIBUTION OF VARIABLE X_2, GIVEN THAT X_1 HAS BEEN INCLUDED

$$SSR(X_2 \mid X_1) = SSR(X_1 \text{ and } X_2) - SSR(X_1) \quad \textbf{(14.10b)}$$

The term $SSR\,(X_2)$ represents the sum of squares due to regression for a model that includes only the independent variable X_2 (promotional expenditures). Similarly, $SSR(X_1)$ represents the sum of squares due to regression for a model that includes only the independent variable X_1 (price). Figures 14.6 and 14.7 on page 544 present worksheet results for these two models.

From Figure 14.6, $SSR(X_2) = 14,915,814.10$ and from Figure 14.1 on page 530, $SSR\,(X_1$ and $X_2) = 39,472,730.77$. Then, using Equation (14.10a),

$$SSR(X_1 \mid X_2) = SSR(X_1 \text{ and } X_2) - SSR(X_2)$$
$$= 39,472,730.77 - 14,915,814.10$$
$$= 24,556,916.67$$

FIGURE 14.6

Regression results worksheet for a simple linear regression analysis for sales and promotional expenditures, $SSR(X_2)$

	A	B	C	D	E	F	G
1	Sales & Promotional Expenses Analysis						
2							
3	Regression Statistics						
4	Multiple R	0.5351					
5	R Square	0.2863					
6	Adjusted R Square	0.2640					
7	Standard Error	1077.8721					
8	Observations	34					
9							
10	ANOVA						
11		df	SS	MS	F	Significance F	
12	Regression	1	14915814.1025	14915814.1025	12.8384	0.0011	
13	Residual	32	37177863.3387	1161808.2293			
14	Total	33	52093677.4412				
15							
16		Coefficients	Standard Error	t Stat	P-value	Lower 95%	Upper 95%
17	Intercept	1496.0161	483.9789	3.0911	0.0041	510.1843	2481.8480
18	Promotion	4.1281	1.1521	3.5831	0.0011	1.7813	6.4748

FIGURE 14.7

Regression results worksheet for a simple linear regression model for sales and price, $SSR(X_1)$

Create the worksheets shown in Figure 14.6 and Figure 14.7 using the instructions in Section EG13.2.

	A	B	C	D	E	F	G
1	Sales & Price Analysis						
2							
3	Regression Statistics						
4	Multiple R	0.7351					
5	R Square	0.5404					
6	Adjusted R Square	0.5261					
7	Standard Error	864.9457					
8	Observations	34					
9							
10	ANOVA						
11		df	SS	MS	F	Significance F	
12	Regression	1	28153486.1482	28153486.1482	37.6318	0.0000	
13	Residual	32	23940191.2930	748130.9779			
14	Total	33	52093677.4412				
15							
16		Coefficients	Standard Error	t Stat	P-value	Lower 95%	Upper 95%
17	Intercept	7512.3480	734.6189	10.2262	0.0000	6015.9796	9008.7164
18	Price	-56.7138	9.2451	-6.1345	0.0000	-75.5455	-37.8822

To determine whether X_1 significantly improves the model after X_2 has been included, you divide the regression sum of squares into two component parts, as shown in Table 14.3.

TABLE 14.3

ANOVA Table Dividing the Regression Sum of Squares into Components to Determine the Contribution of Variable X_1

Source	Degrees of Freedom	Sum of Squares	Mean Square (Variance)	F
Regression	2	39,472,730.77	19,736,365.39	
$\left\{\begin{array}{c} X_2 \\ X_1 \mid X_2 \end{array}\right.$	$\left\{\begin{array}{c} 1 \\ 1 \end{array}\right.$	$\left\{\begin{array}{c} 14,915,814.10 \\ 24,556,916.67 \end{array}\right.$	24,556,916.67	60.32
Error	31	12,620,946.67	407,127.31	
Total	33	52,093,677.44		

The null and alternative hypotheses to test for the contribution of X_1 to the model are

H_0: Variable X_1 does not significantly improve the model after variable X_2 has been included.

H_1: Variable X_1 significantly improves the model after variable X_2 has been included.

Equation (14.11) defines the partial F test statistic for testing the contribution of an independent variable.

PARTIAL F TEST STATISTIC

$$F_{STAT} = \frac{SSR(X_j \mid \text{All } Xs \text{ } except \text{ } j)}{MSE}$$ (14.11)

The partial F test statistic follows an F distribution with 1 and $n - k - 1$ degrees of freedom.

From Table 14.3,

$$F_{STAT} = \frac{24,556,916.67}{407,127.31} = 60.32$$

The partial F_{STAT} test statistic has 1 and $n - k - 1 = 34 - 2 - 1 = 31$ degrees of freedom. Using a level of significance of 0.05, the critical value from Table E.5 is approximately 4.17 (see Figure 14.8).

FIGURE 14.8
Testing for the contribution of a regression coefficient to a multiple regression model at the 0.05 level of significance, with 1 and 31 degrees of freedom

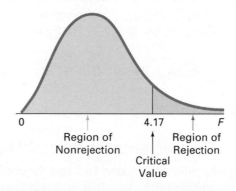

Because the computed partial F_{STAT} test statistic is greater than this critical F value (60.32 > 4.17), reject H_0. You can conclude that the addition of variable X_1 (price) significantly improves a regression model that already contains variable X_2 (promotional expenditures).

To evaluate the contribution of variable X_2 (promotional expenditures) to a model in which variable X_1 (price) has been included, you need to use Equation (14.10b). First, from Figure 14.7 on page 544, observe that $SSR(X_1) = 28,153,486.15$. Second, from Table 14.3, observe that $SSR(X_1 \text{ and } X_2) = 39,472,730.77$. Then, using Equation (14.10b) on page 543,

$$SSR(X_2 \mid X_1) = 39,472,730.77 - 28,153,486.15 = 11,319,244.62$$

To determine whether X_2 significantly improves a model after X_1 has been included, you can divide the regression sum of squares into two component parts, as shown in Table 14.4.

TABLE 14.4
ANOVA Table Dividing the Regression Sum of Squares into Components to Determine the Contribution of Variable X_2

Source	Degrees of Freedom	Sum of Squares	Mean Square (Variance)	F
Regression	2	39,472,730.77	19,736,365.39	
$\begin{Bmatrix} X_1 \\ X_2 \mid X_1 \end{Bmatrix}$	$\begin{Bmatrix} 1 \\ 1 \end{Bmatrix}$	$\begin{Bmatrix} 28,153,486.15 \\ 11,319,244.62 \end{Bmatrix}$	11,319,244.62	27.80
Error	31	12,620,946.67	407,127.31	
Total	33	52,093,677.44		

The null and alternative hypotheses to test for the contribution of X_2 to the model are

H_0: Variable X_2 does not significantly improve the model after variable X_1 has been included.

H_1: Variable X_2 significantly improves the model after variable X_1 has been included.

Using Equation (14.11) and Table 14.4,

$$F_{STAT} = \frac{11,319,244.62}{407,127.31} = 27.80$$

In Figure 14.8, you can see that, using a 0.05 level of significance, the critical value of F, with 1 and 31 degrees of freedom, is approximately 4.17. Because the computed partial F_{STAT} test statistic is greater than this critical value (27.80 > 4.17), reject H_0. You can conclude that the addition of variable X_2 (promotional expenditures) significantly improves the multiple regression model already containing X_1 (price).

Thus, by testing for the contribution of each independent variable after the other has been included in the model, you determine that each of the two independent variables significantly improves the model. Therefore, the multiple regression model should include both price, X_1, and promotional expenditures, X_2.

The partial F-test statistic developed in this section and the t-test statistic of Equation (14.7) on page 539 are both used to determine the contribution of an independent variable to a multiple regression model. The hypothesis tests associated with these two statistics always result in the same decision (i.e., the p-values are identical). The t_{STAT} test statistics for the OmniPower regression model are -7.7664 and $+5.2728$, and the corresponding F_{STAT} test statistics are 60.32 and 27.80. Equation (14.12) states this relationship between t and F.[1]

[1] This relationship holds only when the F_{STAT} statistic has 1 degree of freedom in the numerator.

RELATIONSHIP BETWEEN A t STATISTIC AND AN F STATISTIC

$$t_{STAT}^2 = F_{STAT} \tag{14.12}$$

Coefficients of Partial Determination

Recall from Section 14.2 that the coefficient of multiple determination, r^2, measures the proportion of the variation in Y that is explained by variation in the independent variables. The **coefficients of partial determination** ($r_{Y1.2}^2$ and $r_{Y2.1}^2$) measure the proportion of the variation in the dependent variable that is explained by each independent variable while controlling for, or holding constant, the other independent variable. Equation (14.13) defines the coefficients of partial determination for a multiple regression model with two independent variables.

COEFFICIENTS OF PARTIAL DETERMINATION FOR A MULTIPLE REGRESSION MODEL CONTAINING TWO INDEPENDENT VARIABLES

$$r_{Y1.2}^2 = \frac{SSR(X_1 \mid X_2)}{SST - SSR(X_1 \, and \, X_2) + SSR(X_1 \mid X_2)} \tag{14.13a}$$

and

$$r_{Y2.1}^2 = \frac{SSR(X_2 \mid X_1)}{SST - SSR(X_1 \, and \, X_2) + SSR(X_2 \mid X_1)} \tag{14.13b}$$

where

$SSR(X_1 \mid X_2) = $ sum of squares of the contribution of variable X_1 to the regression model, given that variable X_2 has been included in the model

$SST = $ total sum of squares for Y

$$SSR(X_1 \text{ and } X_2) = \text{regression sum of squares when variables } X_1 \text{ and } X_2 \text{ are both included in the multiple regression model}$$

$$SSR(X_2 \mid X_1) = \text{sum of squares of the contribution of variable } X_2 \text{ to the regression model, given that variable } X_1 \text{ has been included in the model}$$

For the OmniPower sales example,

$$r_{Y1.2}^2 = \frac{24{,}556{,}916.67}{52{,}093{,}677.44 - 39{,}472{,}730.77 + 24{,}556{,}916.67}$$

$$= 0.6605$$

$$r_{Y2.1}^2 = \frac{11{,}319{,}244.62}{52{,}093{,}677.44 - 39{,}472{,}730.77 + 11{,}319{,}244.62}$$

$$= 0.4728$$

The coefficient of partial determination, $r_{Y1.2}^2$, of variable Y with X_1 while holding X_2 constant is 0.6605. Thus, for a given (constant) amount of promotional expenditures, 66.05% of the variation in OmniPower sales is explained by the variation in the price. The coefficient of partial determination, $r_{Y2.1}^2$, of variable Y with X_2 while holding X_1 constant is 0.4728. Thus, for a given (constant) price, 47.28% of the variation in sales of OmniPower bars is explained by variation in the amount of promotional expenditures.

Equation (14.14) defines the coefficient of partial determination for the jth variable in a multiple regression model containing several (k) independent variables.

COEFFICIENT OF PARTIAL DETERMINATION FOR A MULTIPLE REGRESSION MODEL CONTAINING k INDEPENDENT VARIABLES

$$r_{Y_j.(\text{All variables } except\, j)}^2 = \frac{SSR(X_j \mid \text{All } Xs \; except\, j)}{SST - SSR(\text{All } Xs) + SSR(X_j \mid \text{All } Xs \; except\, j)} \quad \textbf{(14.14)}$$

Problems for Section 14.5

LEARNING THE BASICS

14.31 The following is the ANOVA summary table for a multiple regression model with two independent variables:

Source	Degrees of Freedom	Sum of Squares	Mean Squares	F
Regression	2	60		
Error	18	120		
Total	20	180		

If $SSR(X_1) = 45$ and $SSR(X_2) = 25$,
a. determine whether there is a significant relationship between Y and each independent variable at the 0.05 level of significance.
b. compute the coefficients of partial determination, $r_{Y1.2}^2$ and $r_{Y2.1}^2$, and interpret their meaning.

14.32 The following is the ANOVA summary table for a multiple regression model with two independent variables:

Source	Degrees of Freedom	Sum of Squares	Mean Squares	F
Regression	2	30		
Error	10	120		
Total	12	150		

If $SSR(X_1) = 20$ and $SSR(X_2) = 15$,
a. determine whether there is a significant relationship between Y and each independent variable at the 0.05 level of significance.
b. compute the coefficients of partial determination, $r_{Y1.2}^2$ and $r_{Y2.1}^2$, and interpret their meaning.

APPLYING THE CONCEPTS

14.33 In Problem 14.5 on page 532, you used horsepower and weight to predict mileage (stored in **Auto**). Using the results from that problem,
a. at the 0.05 level of significance, determine whether each independent variable makes a significant contribution to

the regression model. On the basis of these results, indicate the most appropriate regression model for this set of data.

b. compute the coefficients of partial determination, $r^2_{Y1.2}$ and $r^2_{Y2.1}$, and interpret their meaning.

SELF Test **14.34** In Problem 14.4 on page 532, you used sales and number of orders to predict distribution costs at a mail-order catalog business (stored in **WareCost**). Using the results from that problem,

a. at the 0.05 level of significance, determine whether each independent variable makes a significant contribution to the regression model. On the basis of these results, indicate the most appropriate regression model for this set of data.

b. compute the coefficients of partial determination, $r^2_{Y1.2}$ and $r^2_{Y2.1}$, and interpret their meaning.

14.35 In Problem 14.7 on page 533, you used the total staff present and remote hours to predict standby hours (stored in **Standby**). Using the results from that problem,

a. at the 0.05 level of significance, determine whether each independent variable makes a significant contribution to the regression model. On the basis of these results, indicate the most appropriate regression model for this set of data.

b. compute the coefficients of partial determination, $r^2_{Y1.2}$ and $r^2_{Y2.1}$, and interpret their meaning.

14.36 In Problem 14.6 on page 532, you used radio advertising and newspaper advertising to predict sales (stored in **Advertise**). Using the results from that problem,

a. at the 0.05 level of significance, determine whether each independent variable makes a significant contribution to the regression model. On the basis of these results, indicate the most appropriate regression model for this set of data.

b. compute the coefficients of partial determination, $r^2_{Y1.2}$ and $r^2_{Y2.1}$, and interpret their meaning.

14.37 In Problem 14.8 on page 533, you used land area of a property and age of a house to predict appraised value (stored in **GlenCove**). Using the results from that problem,

a. at the 0.05 level of significance, determine whether each independent variable makes a significant contribution to the regression model. On the basis of these results, indicate the most appropriate regression model for this set of data.

b. compute the coefficients of partial determination, $r^2_{Y1.2}$ and $r^2_{Y2.1}$, and interpret their meaning.

14.6 Using Dummy Variables and Interaction Terms in Regression Models

The multiple regression models discussed in Sections 14.1 through 14.5 assumed that each independent variable is numerical. For example, in Section 14.1, you used price and promotional expenditures, two numerical independent variables, to predict the monthly sales of OmniPower high-energy bars. However, for some models, you might want to include the effect of a categorical independent variable. For example, to predict the monthly sales of the OmniPower bars, you might want to include the categorical variable shelf location (not end-aisle or end-aisle) in the model.

To include a categorical independent variable in a regression model, use a **dummy variable**. A dummy variable recodes the categories of a categorical variable using the numeric values 0 and 1. If a given categorical independent variable has only two categories, such as shelf location in the previous example, then you can define one dummy variable, X_d, to represent the two categories as

$$X_d = 0 \text{ if the observation is in category 1 (not end-aisle in the example)}$$

$$X_d = 1 \text{ if the observation is in category 2 (end-aisle in the example)}$$

To illustrate using dummy variables in regression, consider a business problem that involves developing a model for predicting the assessed value of houses ($000), based on the size of the house (in thousands of square feet) and whether the house has a fireplace. To include the categorical variable for the presence of a fireplace, the dummy variable X_2 is defined as

$$X_2 = 0 \text{ if the house does not have a fireplace}$$

$$X_2 = 1 \text{ if the house has a fireplace}$$

Data collected from a sample of 15 houses are organized and stored in **House3**. Table 14.5 presents the data. In the last column of Table 14.5, you can see how the categorical data are converted to numerical values.

TABLE 14.5

Predicting Assessed Value, Based on Size of House and Presence of a Fireplace

Create dummy variable terms using the instructions in Section EG14.6.

Assessed Value	Size	Fireplace	Fireplace Coded
234.4	2.00	Yes	1
227.4	1.71	No	0
225.7	1.45	No	0
235.9	1.76	Yes	1
229.1	1.93	No	0
220.4	1.20	Yes	1
225.8	1.55	Yes	1
235.9	1.93	Yes	1
228.5	1.59	Yes	1
229.2	1.50	Yes	1
236.7	1.90	Yes	1
229.3	1.39	Yes	1
224.5	1.54	No	0
233.8	1.89	Yes	1
226.8	1.59	No	0

Assuming that the slope of assessed value with the size of the house is the same for houses that have and do not have a fireplace, the multiple regression model is

$$Y_i = \beta_0 + \beta_1 X_{1i} + \beta_2 X_{2i} + \varepsilon_i$$

where

Y_i = assessed value, in thousands of dollars, for house i

β_0 = Y intercept

X_{1i} = size of the house, in thousands of square feet, for house i

β_1 = slope of assessed value with size of the house, holding constant the presence or absence of a fireplace

X_{2i} = dummy variable representing the absence or presence of a fireplace for house i

β_2 = net effect of the presence of a fireplace on assessed value, holding constant the size of the house

ε_i = random error in Y for house i

Figure 14.9 presents the regression results worksheet for this model.

FIGURE 14.9

Regression results worksheet for the regression model that includes size of house and presence of fireplace

Create dummy variable terms using the instructions in Section EG14.6.

	A	B	C	D	E	F	G
1	Assessed Value Analysis						
2							
3	*Regression Statistics*						
4	Multiple R	0.9006					
5	R Square	0.8111					
6	Adjusted R Square	0.7796					
7	Standard Error	2.2626					
8	Observations	15					
9							
10	ANOVA						
11		*df*	*SS*	*MS*	*F*	*Significance F*	
12	Regression	2	263.7039	131.8520	25.7557	0.0000	
13	Residual	12	61.4321	5.1193			
14	Total	14	325.1360				
15							
16		*Coefficients*	*Standard Error*	*t Stat*	*P-value*	*Lower 95%*	*Upper 95%*
17	Intercept	200.0905	4.3517	45.9803	0.0000	190.6090	209.5719
18	Size	16.1858	2.5744	6.2871	0.0000	10.5766	21.7951
19	FireplaceCoded	3.8530	1.2412	3.1042	0.0091	1.1486	6.5574

From Figure 14.9, the regression equation is

$$\hat{Y}_i = 200.0905 + 16.1858X_{1i} + 3.8530X_{2i}$$

For houses without a fireplace, you substitute $X_2 = 0$ into the regression equation:

$$\hat{Y}_i = 200.0905 + 16.1858X_{1i} + 3.8530X_{2i}$$
$$= 200.0905 + 16.1858X_{1i} + 3.8530(0)$$
$$= 200.0905 + 16.1858X_{1i}$$

For houses with a fireplace, you substitute $X_2 = 1$ into the regression equation:

$$\hat{Y}_i = 200.0905 + 16.1858X_{1i} + 3.8530X_{2i}$$
$$= 200.0905 + 16.1858X_{1i} + 3.8530(1)$$
$$= 203.9435 + 16.1858X_{1i}$$

In this model, the regression coefficients are interpreted as follows:

1. Holding constant whether a house has a fireplace, for each increase of 1.0 thousand square feet in the size of the house, the predicted assessed value is estimated to increase by 16.1858 thousand dollars (i.e., $16,185.80).
2. Holding constant the size of the house, the presence of a fireplace is estimated to increase the predicted assessed value of the house by 3.8530 thousand dollars (i.e. $3,853).

In Figure 14.9, the t_{STAT} test statistic for the slope of the size of the house with assessed value is 6.2871, and the p-value is approximately 0.000; the t_{STAT} test statistic for presence of a fireplace is 3.1042, and the p-value is 0.0091. Thus, each of the two variables makes a significant contribution to the model at the 0.01 level of significance. In addition, the coefficient of multiple determination indicates that 81.11% of the variation in assessed value is explained by variation in the size of the house and whether the house has a fireplace.

EXAMPLE 14.3

Modeling a Three-Level Categorical Variable

Define a multiple regression model using sales as the dependent variable and package design and price as independent variables. Package design is a three-level categorical variable with designs A, B, or C.

SOLUTION To model the three-level categorical variable package design, two dummy variables, X_1 and X_2, are needed:

$$X_{1i} = 1 \text{ if package design } A \text{ is used in observation } i; 0 \text{ otherwise}$$

$$X_{2i} = 1 \text{ if package design } B \text{ is used in observation } i; 0 \text{ otherwise}$$

Thus, if observation i uses package design A, then $X_{1i} = 1$ and $X_{2i} = 0$; if observation i uses package design B, then $X_{1i} = 0$ and $X_{2i} = 1$; and if observation i uses package design C, then $X_{1i} = X_{2i} = 0$. A third independent variable is used for price:

$$X_{3i} = \text{price for observation } i$$

Thus, the regression model for this example is

$$Y_i = \beta_0 + \beta_1 X_{1i} + \beta_2 X_{2i} + \beta_3 X_{3i} + \varepsilon_i$$

where

$$Y_i = \text{sales for observation } i$$

$$\beta_0 = Y \text{ intercept}$$

$$\beta_1 = \text{difference between the predicted sales of design } A \text{ and the predicted sales of design } C, \text{ holding price constant}$$

$$\beta_2 = \text{difference between the predicted sales of design } B \text{ and the predicted sales of design } C, \text{ holding price constant}$$

$$\beta_3 = \text{slope of sales with price, holding the package design constant}$$

$$\varepsilon_i = \text{random error in } Y \text{ for observation } i$$

Interactions

In all the regression models discussed so far, the effect an independent variable has on the dependent variable has been assumed to be independent of the other independent variables in the model. An **interaction** occurs if the effect of an independent variable on the dependent variable changes according to the *value* of a second independent variable. For example, it is possible for advertising to have a large effect on the sales of a product when the price of a product is low. However, if the price of the product is too high, increases in advertising will not dramatically change sales. In this case, price and advertising are said to interact. In other words, you cannot make general statements about the effect of advertising on sales. The effect that advertising has on sales is *dependent* on the price. You use an **interaction term** (sometimes referred to as a **cross-product term**) to model an interaction effect in a regression model.

To illustrate the concept of interaction and use of an interaction term, return to the example concerning the assessed values of homes discussed on pages 548–550. In the regression model, you assumed that the effect the size of the home has on the assessed value is independent of whether the house has a fireplace. In other words, you assumed that the slope of assessed value with size is the same for houses with fireplaces as it is for houses without fireplaces. If these two slopes are different, an interaction exists between the size of the home and the fireplace.

To evaluate whether an interaction exists, you first define an interaction term that is the product of the independent variable X_1 (size of house) and the dummy variable X_2 (fireplace). You then test whether this interaction variable makes a significant contribution to the regression model. If the interaction is significant, you cannot use the original model for prediction. For the data of Table 14.5 on page 549, you define the following

$$X_3 = X_1 \times X_2$$

Figure 14.10 presents a regression results worksheet for this regression model, which includes the size of the house, X_1, the presence of a fireplace, X_2, and the interaction of X_1 and X_2 (defined as X_3).

FIGURE 14.10

Regression results worksheet for a regression model that includes size, presence of fireplace, and interaction of size and fireplace

Create interaction terms using the instructions in Section EG14.6.

	A	B	C	D	E	F	G
1	Assessed Value Analysis						
2							
3	*Regression Statistics*						
4	Multiple R	0.9179					
5	R Square	0.8426					
6	Adjusted R Square	0.7996					
7	Standard Error	2.1573					
8	Observations	15					
9							
10	ANOVA						
11		*df*	*SS*	*MS*	*F*	*Significance F*	
12	Regression	3	273.9441	91.3147	19.6215	0.0001	
13	Residual	11	51.1919	4.6538			
14	Total	14	325.1360				
15							
16		*Coefficients*	*Standard Error*	*t Stat*	*P-value*	*Lower 95%*	*Upper 95%*
17	Intercept	212.9522	9.6122	22.1544	0.0000	191.7959	234.1084
18	Size	8.3624	5.8173	1.4375	0.1784	-4.4414	21.1662
19	FireplaceCoded	-11.8404	10.6455	-1.1122	0.2898	-35.2710	11.5902
20	Size * FireplaceCoded	9.5180	6.4165	1.4834	0.1661	-4.6046	23.6406

To test for the existence of an interaction, you use the null hypothesis

$$H_0: \beta_3 = 0$$

versus the alternative hypothesis

$$H_1: \beta_3 \neq 0.$$

In Figure 14.10, the t_{STAT} test statistic for the interaction of size and fireplace is 1.4834. Because $t_{STAT} = 1.4834 < 2.201$ or the *p*-value $= 0.1661 > 0.05$, you do not reject the null hypothesis. Therefore, the interaction does not make a significant contribution to the model, given that size and presence of a fireplace are already included. You can conclude that the slope of assessed value with size is the same for houses with fireplaces and without fireplaces.

Regression models can have several numerical independent variables. Example 14.4 illustrates a regression model in which there are two numerical independent variables and a categorical independent variable.

EXAMPLE 14.4

Studying a Regression Model That Contains a Dummy Variable

The business problem facing a real estate developer involves predicting heating oil consumption in single-family houses. The independent variables considered are atmospheric temperature, X_1, and the amount of attic insulation, X_2. Data are collected from a sample of 15 single-family houses. Of the 15 houses selected, houses 1, 4, 6, 7, 8, 10, and 12 are ranch-style houses. The data are organized and stored in HtngOil . Develop and analyze an appropriate regression model, using these three independent variables X_1, X_2, and X_3 (where X_3 is the dummy variable for ranch-style houses).

SOLUTION Define X_3, a dummy variable for ranch-style house, as follows:

$$X_3 = 0 \text{ if the style is not ranch}$$

$$X_3 = 1 \text{ if the style is ranch}$$

Assuming that the slope between heating oil consumption and atmospheric temperature, X_1, and between heating oil consumption and the amount of attic insulation, X_2, is the same for both styles of houses, the regression model is

$$Y_i = \beta_0 + \beta_1 X_{1i} + \beta_2 X_{2i} + \beta_3 X_{3i} + \varepsilon_i$$

where
Y_i = monthly heating oil consumption, in gallons, for house i
β_0 = Y intercept
β_1 = slope of heating oil consumption with atmospheric temperature, holding constant the effect of attic insulation and the style of the house
β_2 = slope of heating oil consumption with attic insulation, holding constant the effect of atmospheric temperature and the style of the house
β_3 = incremental effect of the presence of a ranch-style house, holding constant the effect of atmospheric temperature and attic insulation
ε_i = random error in Y for house i

Figure 14.11 presents a regression results worksheet for this model.

FIGURE 14.11

Regression results worksheet for a regression model that includes temperature, insulation, and style for the heating oil data

	A	B	C	D	E	F	G
1	Heating Oil Consumption Analysis						
2							
3	*Regression Statistics*						
4	Multiple R	0.9942					
5	R Square	0.9884					
6	Adjusted R Square	0.9853					
7	Standard Error	15.7489					
8	Observations	15					
9							
10	ANOVA						
11		*df*	*SS*	*MS*	*F*	*Significance F*	
12	Regression	3	233406.9094	77802.3031	313.6822	0.0000	
13	Residual	11	2728.3200	248.0291			
14	Total	14	236135.2293				
15							
16		*Coefficients*	*Standard Error*	*t Stat*	*P-value*	*Lower 95%*	*Upper 95%*
17	Intercept	592.5401	14.3370	41.3295	0.0000	560.9846	624.0956
18	Temperature	-5.5251	0.2044	-27.0267	0.0000	-5.9751	-5.0752
19	Insulation	-21.3761	1.4480	-14.7623	0.0000	-24.5632	-18.1891
20	Ranch-style	-38.9727	8.3584	-4.6627	0.0007	-57.3695	-20.5759

From the results in Figure 14.11, the regression equation is

$$\hat{Y}_i = 592.5401 - 5.5251X_{1i} - 21.3761X_{2i} - 38.9727X_{3i}$$

For houses that are not ranch style, because $X_3 = 0$, the regression equation reduces to

$$\hat{Y}_i = 592.5401 - 5.5251X_{1i} - 21.3761X_{2i}$$

For houses that are ranch style, because $X_3 = 1$, the regression equation reduces to

$$\hat{Y}_i = 553.5674 - 5.5251X_{1i} - 21.3761X_{2i}$$

The regression coefficients are interpreted as follows:

1. Holding constant the attic insulation and the house style, for each additional 1°F increase in atmospheric temperature, you estimate that the predicted heating oil consumption decreases by 5.5251 gallons.
2. Holding constant the atmospheric temperature and the house style, for each additional 1-inch increase in attic insulation, you estimate that the predicted heating oil consumption decreases by 21.3761 gallons.
3. b_3 measures the effect on oil consumption of having a ranch-style house ($X_3 = 1$) compared with having a house that is not ranch style ($X_3 = 0$). Thus, with atmospheric temperature and attic insulation held constant, you estimate that the predicted heating oil consumption is 38.9727 gallons less for a ranch-style house than for a house that is not ranch style.

The three t_{STAT} test statistics representing the slopes for temperature, insulation, and ranch style are -27.0267, -14.7623, and -4.6627. Each of the corresponding p-values is extremely small (less than 0.001). Thus, each of the three variables makes a significant contribution to the model. In addition, the coefficient of multiple determination indicates that 98.84% of the variation in oil usage is explained by variation in temperature, insulation, and whether the house is ranch style.

Before you can use the model in Example 14.4, you need to determine whether the independent variables interact with each other. In Example 14.5, three interaction terms are added to the model.

EXAMPLE 14.5

Evaluating a Regression Model with Several Interactions

For the data of Example 14.4, determine whether adding the interaction terms make a significant contribution to the regression model.

SOLUTION To evaluate possible interactions between the independent variables, three interaction terms are constructed as follows: $X_4 = X_1 \times X_2$, $X_5 = X_1 \times X_3$, and $X_6 = X_2 \times X_3$. The regression model is now

$$Y_i = \beta_0 + \beta_1X_{1i} + \beta_2X_{2i} + \beta_3X_{3i} + \beta_4X_{4i} + \beta_5X_{5i} + \beta_6X_{6i} + \varepsilon_i$$

where X_1 is temperature, X_2 is insulation, X_3 is the dummy variable ranch style, X_4 is the interaction between temperature and insulation, X_5 is the interaction between temperature and ranch style, and X_6 is the interaction between insulation and ranch style. Figure 14.12 on page 554 presents a regression results worksheet for this model.

To test whether the three interactions significantly improve the regression model, you use the partial F test. The null and alternative hypotheses are

$$H_0\text{: } \beta_4 = \beta_5 = \beta_6 = 0 \text{ (There are no interactions among } X_1, X_2, \text{ and } X_3.)$$

$$H_1\text{: } \beta_4 \neq 0 \text{ and/or } \beta_5 \neq 0 \text{ and/or } \beta_6 \neq 0 \text{ (}X_1 \text{ interacts with } X_2,$$
$$\text{and/or } X_1 \text{ interacts with } X_3, \text{ and/or } X_2 \text{ interacts with } X_3.)$$

From Figure 14.12,

$$SSR(X_1, X_2, X_3, X_4, X_5, X_6) = 234{,}510.5818 \text{ with 6 degrees of freedom}$$

FIGURE 14.12

Regression results worksheet for a regression model that includes temperature, X_1; insulation, X_2; the dummy variable ranch style, X_3; the interaction of temperature and insulation, X_4; the interaction of temperature and ranch style, X_5; and the interaction of insulation and ranch style, X_6

	A	B	C	D	E	F	G
1	Heating Oil Consumption Analysis						
2							
3	**Regression Statistics**						
4	Multiple R	0.9966					
5	R Square	0.9931					
6	Adjusted R Square	0.9880					
7	Standard Error	14.2506					
8	Observations	15					
9							
10	ANOVA						
11		df	SS	MS	F	Significance F	
12	Regression	6	234510.5818	39085.0970	192.4607	0.0000	
13	Residual	8	1624.6475	203.0809			
14	Total	14	236135.2293				
15							
16		Coefficients	Standard Error	t Stat	P-value	Lower 95%	Upper 95%
17	Intercept	642.8867	26.7059	24.0728	0.0000	581.3027	704.4707
18	Temperature	-6.9263	0.7531	-9.1969	0.0000	-8.6629	-5.1896
19	Insulation	-27.8825	3.5801	-7.7882	0.0001	-36.1383	-19.6268
20	Style	-84.6088	29.9956	-2.8207	0.0225	-153.7788	-15.4389
21	Temperature * Insulation	0.1702	0.0886	1.9204	0.0911	-0.0342	0.3746
22	Temperature * Ranch-style	0.6596	0.4617	1.4286	0.1910	-0.4051	1.7242
23	Insulation * Ranch-style	4.9870	3.5137	1.4193	0.1936	-3.1156	13.0895

and from Figure 14.11 on page 552, $SSR (X_1, X_2, X_3) = 233,406.9094$ with 3 degrees of freedom. Thus, $SSR(X_1, X_2, X_3, X_4, X_5, X_6) - SSR(X_1, X_2, X_3) = 234,510.5818 - 233,406.9094 = 1,103.6724$. The difference in degrees of freedom is $6 - 3 = 3$.

To use the partial F test for the simultaneous contribution of three variables to a model, you use an extension of Equation (14.11) on page 545.[2] The partial F_{STAT} test statistic is

[2]In general, if a model has several independent variables and you want to test whether additional independent variables contribute to the model, the numerator of the F test is SSR(for all independent variables) minus SSR(for the initial set of variables) divided by the number of independent variables whose contribution is being tested.

$$F = \frac{[SSR(X_1, X_2, X_3, X_4, X_5, X_6) - SSR(X_1, X_2, X_3)]/3}{MSE(X_1, X_2, X_3, X_4, X_5, X_6)} = \frac{1,103.6724/3}{203.0809} = 1.8115$$

You compare the computed F_{STAT} test statistic to the critical F value for 3 and 8 degrees of freedom. Using a level of significance of 0.05, the critical F value from Table E.5 is 4.07. Because $F_{STAT} = 1.8115 < 4.07$, you conclude that the interactions do not make a significant contribution to the model, given that the model already includes temperature, X_1; insulation, X_2; and whether the house is ranch style, X_3. Therefore, the multiple regression model using X_1, X_2, and X_3 but no interaction terms is the better model. If you rejected this null hypothesis, you would then test the contribution of each interaction separately in order to determine which interaction terms to include in the model.

Problems for Section 14.6

LEARNING THE BASICS

14.38 Suppose X_1 is a numerical variable and X_2 is a dummy variable and the regression equation for a sample of $n = 20$ is

$$\hat{Y}_i = 6 + 4X_{1i} + 2X_{2i}$$

a. Interpret the regression coefficient associated with variable X_1.
b. Interpret the regression coefficient associated with variable X_2.

c. Suppose that the t_{STAT} test statistic for testing the contribution of variable X_2 is 3.27. At the 0.05 level of significance, is there evidence that variable X_2 makes a significant contribution to the model?

APPLYING THE CONCEPTS

14.39 The chair of the accounting department plans to develop a regression model to predict the grade point average in accounting for those students who are graduating and have completed the accounting major, based on the student's SAT

score and whether the student received a grade of B or higher in the introductory statistics course (0 = no and 1 = yes).
a. Explain the steps involved in developing a regression model for these data. Be sure to indicate the particular models you need to evaluate and compare.
b. Suppose the regression coefficient for the variable whether the student received a grade of B or higher in the introductory statistics course is +0.30. How do you interpret this result?

14.40 A real estate association in a suburban community would like to study the relationship between the size of a single-family house (as measured by the number of rooms) and the selling price of the house (in thousands of dollars). Two different neighborhoods are included in the study, one on the east side of the community (=0) and the other on the west side (=1). A random sample of 20 houses was selected, with the results stored in Neighbor. For (a) through (k), do not include an interaction term.
a. State the multiple regression equation that predicts the selling price, based on the number of rooms and the neighborhood.
b. Interpret the regression coefficients in (a).
c. Predict the selling price for a house with nine rooms that is located in an east-side neighborhood. Construct a 95% confidence interval estimate and a 95% prediction interval.
d. Perform a residual analysis on the results and determine whether the regression assumptions are valid.
e. Is there a significant relationship between selling price and the two independent variables (rooms and neighborhood) at the 0.05 level of significance?
f. At the 0.05 level of significance, determine whether each independent variable makes a contribution to the regression model. Indicate the most appropriate regression model for this set of data.
g. Construct and interpret a 95% confidence interval estimate of the population slope for the relationship between selling price and number of rooms.
h. Construct and interpret a 95% confidence interval estimate of the population slope for the relationship between selling price and neighborhood.
i. Compute and interpret the adjusted r^2.
j. Compute the coefficients of partial determination and interpret their meaning.
k. What assumption do you need to make about the slope of selling price with number of rooms?
l. Add an interaction term to the model and, at the 0.05 level of significance, determine whether it makes a significant contribution to the model.
m. On the basis of the results of (f) and (l), which model is most appropriate? Explain.

14.41 The marketing manager of a large supermarket chain faced the business problem of determining the effect on the sales of pet food of shelf space and whether the product was placed at the front (=1) or back (=0) of the aisle. Data are collected from a random sample of 12 equal-sized

stores. The results are shown in the following table (and organized and stored in Petfood):

Store	Shelf Space (Feet)	Location	Weekly Sales (Dollars)
1	5	Back	160
2	5	Front	220
3	5	Back	140
4	10	Back	190
5	10	Back	240
6	10	Front	260
7	15	Back	230
8	15	Back	270
9	15	Front	280
10	20	Back	260
11	20	Back	290
12	20	Front	310

For (a) through (m), do not include an interaction term.
a. State the multiple regression equation that predicts sales based on shelf space and location.
b. Interpret the regression coefficients in (a).
c. Predict the weekly sales of pet food for a store with 8 feet of shelf space situated at the back of the aisle. Construct a 95% confidence interval estimate and a 95% prediction interval.
d. Perform a residual analysis on the results and determine whether the regression assumptions are valid.
e. Is there a significant relationship between sales and the two independent variables (shelf space and aisle position) at the 0.05 level of significance?
f. At the 0.05 level of significance, determine whether each independent variable makes a contribution to the regression model. Indicate the most appropriate regression model for this set of data.
g. Construct and interpret 95% confidence interval estimates of the population slope for the relationship between sales and shelf space and between sales and aisle location.
h. Compare the slope in (b) with the slope for the simple linear regression model of Problem 13.4 on page 481. Explain the difference in the results.
i. Compute and interpret the meaning of the coefficient of multiple determination, r^2.
j. Compute and interpret the adjusted r^2.
k. Compare r^2 with the r^2 value computed in Problem 13.16(a) on page 487.
l. Compute the coefficients of partial determination and interpret their meaning.
m. What assumption about the slope of shelf space with sales do you need to make in this problem?
n. Add an interaction term to the model and, at the 0.05 level of significance, determine whether it makes a significant contribution to the model.
o. On the basis of the results of (f) and (n), which model is most appropriate? Explain.

14.42 In mining engineering, holes are often drilled through rock, using drill bits. As a drill hole gets deeper, additional rods are added to the drill bit to enable additional drilling to take place. It is expected that drilling time increases with depth. This increased drilling time could be caused by several factors, including the mass of the drill rods that are strung together. The business problem relates to whether drilling is faster using dry drilling holes or wet drilling holes. Using dry drilling holes involves forcing compressed air down the drill rods to flush the cuttings and drive the hammer. Using wet drilling holes involves forcing water rather than air down the hole. Data have been collected from a sample of 50 drill holes that contains measurements of the time to drill each additional 5 feet (in minutes), the depth (in feet), and whether the hole was a dry drilling hole or a wet drilling hole. The data are organized and stored in Drill. Develop a model to predict additional drilling time, based on depth and type of drilling hole (dry or wet). For (a) through (k) do not include an interaction term.

Source: *Data extracted from R. Penner and D. G. Watts, "Mining Information," The American Statistician, 45, 1991, pp. 4–9.*

a. State the multiple regression equation.
b. Interpret the regression coefficients in (a).
c. Predict the additional drilling time for a dry drilling hole at a depth of 100 feet. Construct a 95% confidence interval estimate and a 95% prediction interval.
d. Perform a residual analysis on the results and determine whether the regression assumptions are valid.
e. Is there a significant relationship between additional drilling time and the two independent variables (depth and type of drilling hole) at the 0.05 level of significance?
f. At the 0.05 level of significance, determine whether each independent variable makes a contribution to the regression model. Indicate the most appropriate regression model for this set of data.
g. Construct a 95% confidence interval estimate of the population slope for the relationship between additional drilling time and depth.
h. Construct a 95% confidence interval estimate of the population slope for the relationship between additional drilling time and the type of hole drilled.
i. Compute and interpret the adjusted r^2.
j. Compute the coefficients of partial determination and interpret their meaning.
k. What assumption do you need to make about the slope of additional drilling time with depth?
l. Add an interaction term to the model and, at the 0.05 level of significance, determine whether it makes a significant contribution to the model.
m. On the basis of the results of (f) and (l), which model is most appropriate? Explain.

14.43 The owner of a moving company typically has his most experienced manager predict the total number of labor hours that will be required to complete an upcoming move. This approach has proved useful in the past, but the owner has the business objective of developing a more accurate method of predicting labor hours. In a preliminary effort to provide a more accurate method, the owner has decided to use the number of cubic feet moved and whether there is an elevator in the apartment building as the independent variables and has collected data for 36 moves in which the origin and destination were within the borough of Manhattan in New York City and the travel time was an insignificant portion of the hours worked. The data are organized and stored in Moving. For (a) through (k), do not include an interaction term.

a. State the multiple regression equation for predicting labor hours, using the number of cubic feet moved and whether there is an elevator.
b. Interpret the regression coefficients in (a).
c. Predict the labor hours for moving 500 cubic feet in an apartment building that has an elevator and construct a 95% confidence interval estimate and a 95% prediction interval.
d. Perform a residual analysis on the results and determine whether the regression assumptions are valid.
e. Is there a significant relationship between labor hours and the two independent variables (cubic feet moved and whether there is an elevator in the apartment building) at the 0.05 level of significance?
f. At the 0.05 level of significance, determine whether each independent variable makes a contribution to the regression model. Indicate the most appropriate regression model for this set of data.
g. Construct a 95% confidence interval estimate of the population slope for the relationship between labor hours and cubic feet moved.
h. Construct a 95% confidence interval estimate for the relationship between labor hours and the presence of an elevator.
i. Compute and interpret the adjusted r^2.
j. Compute the coefficients of partial determination and interpret their meaning.
k. What assumption do you need to make about the slope of labor hours with cubic feet moved?
l. Add an interaction term to the model and, at the 0.05 level of significance, determine whether it makes a significant contribution to the model.
m. On the basis of the results of (f) and (l), which model is most appropriate? Explain.

14.44 In Problem 14.4 on page 532, you used sales and orders to predict distribution cost (stored in WareCost). Develop a regression model to predict distribution cost that includes sales, orders, and the interaction of sales and orders.

a. At the 0.05 level of significance, is there evidence that the interaction term makes a significant contribution to the model?
b. Which regression model is more appropriate, the one used in (a) or the one used in Problem 14.4? Explain.

14.45 Zagat's publishes restaurant ratings for various locations in the United States. The file RestCost contains the Zagat rating for food, décor, service, and cost per person for a sample of 50 restaurants located in a city and 50 restaurants located in a suburb. Develop a regression model to predict the cost per person, based on a variable that represents the sum of the ratings for food, décor, and service and a dummy variable concerning location (city vs. suburban). For (a) through (m), do not include an interaction term.

Source: *Extracted from* Zagat Survey 2008 New York City Restaurants *and* Zagat Survey 2007–2008 Long Island Restaurants.

a. State the multiple regression equation.
b. Interpret the regression coefficients in (a).
c. Predict the cost for a restaurant with a summated rating of 60 that is located in a city and construct a 95% confidence interval estimate and a 95% prediction interval.
d. Perform a residual analysis on the results and determine whether the regression assumptions are satisfied.
e. Is there a significant relationship between price and the two independent variables (summated rating and location) at the 0.05 level of significance?
f. At the 0.05 level of significance, determine whether each independent variable makes a contribution to the regression model. Indicate the most appropriate regression model for this set of data.
g. Construct a 95% confidence interval estimate of the population slope for the relationship between cost and summated rating.
h. Compare the slope in (b) with the slope for the simple linear regression model of Problem 13.90 on page 518. Explain the difference in the results.
i. Compute and interpret the meaning of the coefficient of multiple determination.
j. Compute and interpret the adjusted r^2.
k. Compare r^2 with the r^2 value computed in Problem 13.90 (d) on page 518.
l. Compute the coefficients of partial determination and interpret their meaning.
m. What assumption about the slope of cost with summated rating do you need to make in this problem?
n. Add an interaction term to the model and, at the 0.05 level of significance, determine whether it makes a significant contribution to the model.
o. On the basis of the results of (f) and (n), which model is most appropriate? Explain.

14.46 In Problem 14.6 on page 532, you used radio advertising and newspaper advertising to predict sales (stored in Advertise). Develop a regression model to predict sales that includes radio advertising, newspaper advertising, and the interaction of radio advertising and newspaper advertising.
a. At the 0.05 level of significance, is there evidence that the interaction term makes a significant contribution to the model?
b. Which regression model is more appropriate, the one used in this problem or the one used in Problem 14.6? Explain.

14.47 In Problem 14.5 on page 532, horsepower and weight were used to predict miles per gallon (stored in Auto). Develop a regression model that includes horsepower, weight, and the interaction of horsepower and weight to predict miles per gallon.
a. At the 0.05 level of significance, is there evidence that the interaction term makes a significant contribution to the model?
b. Which regression model is more appropriate, the one used in this problem or the one used in Problem 14.5? Explain.

14.48 In Problem 14.7 on page 533, you used total staff present and remote hours to predict standby hours (stored in Standby). Develop a regression model to predict standby hours that includes total staff present, remote hours, and the interaction of total staff present and remote hours.
a. At the 0.05 level of significance, is there evidence that the interaction term makes a significant contribution to the model?
b. Which regression model is more appropriate, the one used in this problem or the one used in Problem 14.7? Explain.

14.49 The director of a training program for a large insurance company has the business objective of determining which training method is best for training underwriters. The three methods to be evaluated are traditional, CD-ROM based, and Web based. The 30 trainees are divided into three randomly assigned groups of 10. Before the start of the training, each trainee is given a proficiency exam that measures mathematics and computer skills. At the end of the training, all students take the same end-of-training exam. The results are organized and stored in Underwriting.

Develop a multiple regression model to predict the score on the end-of-training exam, based on the score on the proficiency exam and the method of training used. For (a) through (k), do not include an interaction term.
a. State the multiple regression equation.
b. Interpret the regression coefficients in (a).
c. Predict the end-of-training exam score for a student with a proficiency exam score of 100 who had Web-based training.
d. Perform a residual analysis on your results and determine whether the regression assumptions are valid.
e. Is there a significant relationship between the end-of-training exam score and the independent variables (proficiency score and training method) at the 0.05 level of significance?
f. At the 0.05 level of significance, determine whether each independent variable makes a contribution to the regression model. Indicate the most appropriate regression model for this set of data.
g. Construct and interpret 95% confidence interval estimate of the population slope for the relationship between end-of-training exam score and proficiency exam.
h. Construct and interpret 95% confidence interval estimates of the population slope for the relationship between end-of-training exam score and type of training method.

i. Compute and interpret the adjusted r^2.
j. Compute the coefficients of partial determination and interpret their meaning.
k. What assumption about the slope of proficiency score with end-of-training exam score do you need to make in this problem?

l. Add interaction terms to the model and, at the 0.05 level of significance, determine whether any interaction terms make a significant contribution to the model.
m. On the basis of the results of (f) and (l), which model is most appropriate? Explain.

USING STATISTICS @ OmniFoods Revisited

I n the Using Statistics scenario, you were the marketing manager for OmniFoods, a large food products company planning a nationwide introduction of a new high-energy bar, OmniPower. You needed to determine the effect that price and in-store promotions would have on sales of OmniPower in order to develop an effective marketing strategy. A sample of 34 stores in a supermarket chain was selected for a test-market study. The stores charged between 59 and 99 cents per bar and were given an in-store promotion budget between $200 and $600.

At the end of the one-month test-market study, you performed a multiple regression analysis on the data. Two independent variables were considered: the price of an OmniPower bar and the monthly budget for in-store promotional expenditures. The dependent variable was the number of OmniPower bars sold in a month. The coefficient of determination indicated that 75.8% of the variation in sales was explained by knowing the price charged and the amount spent on in-store promotions. The model indicated that the predicted sales of OmniPower are estimated to decrease by 532 bars per month for each 10-cent increase in the price, and the predicted sales are estimated to increase by 361 bars for each additional $100 spent on promotions.

After studying the relative effects of price and promotion, OmniFoods needs to set price and promotion standards for a nationwide introduction (obviously, lower prices and higher promotion budgets lead to more sales, but they do so at a lower profit margin). You determined that if stores spend $400 a month in in-store promotions and charge 79 cents, the 95% confidence interval estimate of the mean monthly sales is 2,854 to 3,303 bars. OmniFoods can multiply the lower and upper bounds of this confidence interval by the number of stores included in the nationwide introduction to estimate total monthly sales. For example, if 1,000 stores are in the nationwide introduction, then total monthly sales should be between 2.854 million and 3.308 million bars.

SUMMARY

In this chapter, you learned how multiple regression models allow you to use two or more independent variables to predict the value of a dependent variable. You also learned how to include categorical independent variables and interaction terms in regression models. Figure 14.13 presents a roadmap of the chapter.

FIGURE 14.13
Roadmap for multiple regression

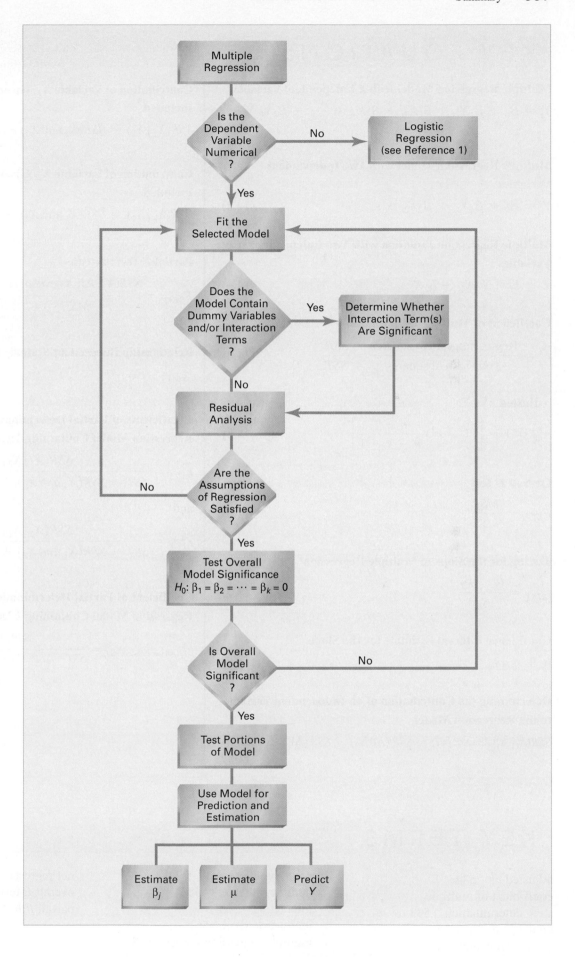

KEY EQUATIONS

Multiple Regression Model with k Independent Variables

$$Y_i = \beta_0 + \beta_1 X_{1i} + \beta_2 X_{2i} + \beta_3 X_{3i} + \cdots + \beta_k X_{ki} + \varepsilon_i \tag{14.1}$$

Multiple Regression Model with Two Independent Variables

$$Y_i = \beta_0 + \beta_1 X_{1i} + \beta_2 X_{2i} + \varepsilon_i \tag{14.2}$$

Multiple Regression Equation with Two Independent Variables

$$\hat{Y}_i = b_0 + b_1 X_{1i} + b_2 X_{2i} \tag{14.3}$$

Coefficient of Multiple Determination

$$r^2 = \frac{\text{Regression sum of squares}}{\text{Total sum of squares}} = \frac{SSR}{SST} \tag{14.4}$$

Adjusted r^2

$$r^2_{\text{adj}} = 1 - \left[(1 - r^2) \frac{n-1}{n-k-1} \right] \tag{14.5}$$

Overall F Test

$$F_{STAT} = \frac{MSR}{MSE} \tag{14.6}$$

Testing for the Slope in Multiple Regression

$$t_{STAT} = \frac{b_j - \beta_j}{S_{b_j}} \tag{14.7}$$

Confidence Interval Estimate for the Slope

$$b_j \pm t_{\alpha/2} S_{b_j} \tag{14.8}$$

Determining the Contribution of an Independent Variable to the Regression Model

$$SSR(X_j \mid \text{All } Xs \text{ except } j) = SSR (\text{All } Xs) - SSR (\text{All } Xs \text{ except } j) \tag{14.9}$$

Contribution of Variable X_1, Given That X_2 Has Been Included

$$SSR(X_1 \mid X_2) = SSR(X_1 \text{ and } X_2) - SSR(X_2) \tag{14.10a}$$

Contribution of Variable X_2, Given That X_1 Has Been Included

$$SSR(X_2 \mid X_1) = SSR(X_1 \text{ and } X_2) - SSR(X_1) \tag{14.10b}$$

Partial F Test Statistic

$$F_{STAT} = \frac{SSR(X_j \mid \text{All } Xs \text{ except } j)}{MSE} \tag{14.11}$$

Relationship Between a t Statistic and an F Statistic

$$t^2_{STAT} = F_{STAT} \tag{14.12}$$

Coefficients of Partial Determination for a Multiple Regression Model Containing Two Independent Variables

$$r^2_{Y1.2} = \frac{SSR(X_1 \mid X_2)}{SST - SSR(X_1 \text{ and } X_2) + SSR(X_1 \mid X_2)} \tag{14.13a}$$

and

$$r^2_{Y2.1} = \frac{SSR(X_2 \mid X_1)}{SST - SSR(X_1 \text{ and } X_2) + SSR(X_2 \mid X_1)} \tag{14.13b}$$

Coefficient of Partial Determination for a Multiple Regression Model Containing k Independent Variables

$$r^2_{Y_j.(\text{All variables } except\, j)} = \frac{SSR(X_j \mid \text{All } Xs \text{ except } j)}{SST - SSR(\text{All } Xs) + SSR(X_j \mid \text{All } Xs \text{ except } j)} \tag{14.14}$$

KEY TERMS

CHAPTER REVIEW PROBLEMS

CHECKING YOUR UNDERSTANDING

14.50 How does the interpretation of the regression coefficients differ in multiple regression and simple linear regression?

14.51 How does testing the significance of the entire multiple regression model differ from testing the contribution of each independent variable?

14.52 How do the coefficients of partial determination differ from the coefficient of multiple determination?

14.53 Why and how do you use dummy variables?

14.54 How can you evaluate whether the slope of the dependent variable with an independent variable is the same for each level of the dummy variable?

14.55 Under what circumstances do you include an interaction term in a regression model?

14.56 When a dummy variable is included in a regression model that has one numerical independent variable, what assumption do you need to make concerning the slope between the dependent variable, Y, and the numerical independent variable, X?

APPLYING THE CONCEPTS

14.57 Increasing customer satisfaction typically results in increased purchase behavior. For many products, there is more than one measure of customer satisfaction. In many of these instances, purchase behavior can increase dramatically with an increase in any one of the customer satisfaction measures, not necessarily all of them at the same time. Gunst and Barry ("One Way to Moderate Ceiling Effects," *Quality Progress*, October 2003, pp. 83–85) consider a product with two satisfaction measures, X_1 and X_2, that range from the lowest level of satisfaction, 1, to the highest level of satisfaction, 7. The dependent variable, Y, is a measure of purchase behavior, with the highest value generating the most sales. The following regression equation is presented:

$$\hat{Y}_i = -3.888 + 1.449 X_{1i} + 1.462 X_{2i} - 0.190 X_{1i} X_{2i}$$

Suppose that X_1 is the perceived quality of the product and X_2 is the perceived value of the product. (Note: If the customer thinks the product is overpriced, he or she perceives it to be of low value and vice versa.)

a. What is the predicted purchase behavior when $X_1 = 2$ and $X_2 = 2$?

b. What is the predicted purchase behavior when $X_1 = 2$ and $X_2 = 7$?

c. What is the predicted purchase behavior when $X_1 = 7$ and $X_2 = 2$?

d. What is the predicted purchase behavior when $X_1 = 7$ and $X_2 = 7$?

e. What is the regression equation when $X_2 = 2$? What is the slope for X_1 now?

f. What is the regression equation when $X_2 = 7$? What is the slope for X_1 now?

g. What is the regression equation when $X_1 = 2$? What is the slope for X_2 now?

h. What is the regression equation when $X_1 = 7$? What is the slope for X_2 now?

i. Discuss the implications of (a) through (h) within the context of increasing sales for this product with two customer satisfaction measures.

14.58 The owner of a moving company typically has his most experienced manager predict the total number of labor hours that will be required to complete an upcoming move. This approach has proved useful in the past, but the owner has the business objective of developing a more accurate method of predicting labor hours. In a preliminary effort to provide a more accurate method, the owner has decided to use the number of cubic feet moved and the number of pieces of large furniture as the independent variables and has collected data for 36 moves in which the origin and destination were within the borough of Manhattan in New York City and the travel time was an insignificant portion of the hours worked. The data are organized and stored in Moving .

a. State the multiple regression equation.

b. Interpret the meaning of the slopes in this equation.

c. Predict the labor hours for moving 500 cubic feet with two large pieces of furniture.

d. Perform a residual analysis on your results and determine whether the regression assumptions are valid.

e. Determine whether there is a significant relationship between labor hours and the two independent variables (the number of cubic feet moved and the number of pieces of large furniture) at the 0.05 level of significance.

f. Determine the p-value in (e) and interpret its meaning.

g. Interpret the meaning of the coefficient of multiple determination in this problem.

h. Determine the adjusted r^2.

i. At the 0.05 level of significance, determine whether each independent variable makes a significant contribution to the regression model. Indicate the most appropriate regression model for this set of data.

j. Determine the p-values in (i) and interpret their meaning.

k. Construct a 95% confidence interval estimate of the population slope between labor hours and the number of cubic feet moved. How does the interpretation of the slope here differ from that in Problem 13.44 on page 502?

l. Compute and interpret the coefficients of partial determination.

14.59 Professional basketball has truly become a sport that generates interest among fans around the world. More and more players come from outside the United States to play in the National Basketball Association (NBA). You want to develop a regression model to predict the number of wins achieved by each NBA team, based on field goal (shots made) percentage for the team and for the opponent. The data are stored in NBA2009.

a. State the multiple regression equation.
b. Interpret the meaning of the slopes in this equation.
c. Predict the number of wins for a team that has a field goal percentage of 45% and an opponent field goal percentage of 44%.
d. Perform a residual analysis on your results and determine whether the regression assumptions are valid.
e. Is there a significant relationship between number of wins and the two independent variables (field goal percentage for the team and for the opponent) at the 0.05 level of significance?
f. Determine the p-value in (e) and interpret its meaning.
g. Interpret the meaning of the coefficient of multiple determination in this problem.
h. Determine the adjusted r^2.
i. At the 0.05 level of significance, determine whether each independent variable makes a significant contribution to the regression model. Indicate the most appropriate regression model for this set of data.
j. Determine the p-values in (i) and interpret their meaning.
k. Compute and interpret the coefficients of partial determination.

14.60 A sample of 30 recently sold single-family houses in a small city is selected. Develop a model to predict the selling price (in thousands of dollars), using the assessed value (in thousands of dollars) as well as time period (in months since reassessment). The houses in the city had been reassessed at full value one year prior to the study. The results are stored in House1.

a. State the multiple regression equation.
b. Interpret the meaning of the slopes in this equation.
c. Predict the selling price for a house that has an assessed value of $170,000 and was sold in time period 12.
d. Perform a residual analysis on your results and determine whether the regression assumptions are valid.
e. Determine whether there is a significant relationship between selling price and the two independent variables (assessed value and time period) at the 0.05 level of significance.
f. Determine the p-value in (e) and interpret its meaning.
g. Interpret the meaning of the coefficient of multiple determination in this problem.
h. Determine the adjusted r^2.
i. At the 0.05 level of significance, determine whether each independent variable makes a significant contribu-

tion to the regression model. Indicate the most appropriate regression model for this set of data.
j. Determine the p-values in (i) and interpret their meaning.
k. Construct a 95% confidence interval estimate of the population slope between selling price and assessed value. How does the interpretation of the slope here differ from that in Problem 13.76 on page 516?
l. Compute and interpret the coefficients of partial determination.

14.61 Measuring the height of a California redwood tree is very difficult because these trees grow to heights over 300 feet. People familiar with these trees understand that the height of a California redwood tree is related to other characteristics of the tree, including the diameter of the tree at the breast height of a person and the thickness of the bark of the tree. The file Redwood contains the height, diameter at breast height of a person, and bark thickness for a sample of 21 California redwood trees.

a. State the multiple regression equation that predicts the height of a tree, based on the tree's diameter at breast height and the thickness of the bark.
b. Interpret the meaning of the slopes in this equation.
c. Predict the height for a tree that has a breast diameter of 25 inches and a bark thickness of 2 inches.
d. Interpret the meaning of the coefficient of multiple determination in this problem.
e. Perform a residual analysis on the results and determine whether the regression assumptions are valid.
f. Determine whether there is a significant relationship between the height of redwood trees and the two independent variables (breast-height diameter and bark thickness) at the 0.05 level of significance.
g. Construct a 95% confidence interval estimate of the population slope between the height of redwood trees and breast-height diameter and between the height of redwood trees and the bark thickness.
h. At the 0.05 level of significance, determine whether each independent variable makes a significant contribution to the regression model. Indicate the independent variables to include in this model.
i. Construct a 95% confidence interval estimate of the mean height for trees that have a breast-height diameter of 25 inches and a bark thickness of 2 inches, along with a prediction interval for an individual tree.
j. Compute and interpret the coefficients of partial determination.

14.62 Develop a model to predict the assessed value (in thousands of dollars), using the size of the houses (in thousands of square feet) and the age of the houses (in years) from the table at the top of page 563 (stored in House2):

a. State the multiple regression equation.
b. Interpret the meaning of the slopes in this equation.

House	Assessed Value ($000)	Size of House (Thousands of Square Feet)	Age (Years)
1	184.4	2.00	3.42
2	177.4	1.71	11.50
3	175.7	1.45	8.33
4	185.9	1.76	0.00
5	179.1	1.93	7.42
6	170.4	1.20	32.00
7	175.8	1.55	16.00
8	185.9	1.93	2.00
9	178.5	1.59	1.75
10	179.2	1.50	2.75
11	186.7	1.90	0.00
12	179.3	1.39	0.00
13	174.5	1.54	12.58
14	183.8	1.89	2.75
15	176.8	1.59	7.17

c. Predict the assessed value for a house that has a size of 1,750 square feet and is 10 years old.

d. Perform a residual analysis on the results and determine whether the regression assumptions are valid.

e. Determine whether there is a significant relationship between assessed value and the two independent variables (size and age) at the 0.05 level of significance.

f. Determine the p-value in (e) and interpret its meaning.

g. Interpret the meaning of the coefficient of multiple determination in this problem.

h. Determine the adjusted r^2.

i. At the 0.05 level of significance, determine whether each independent variable makes a significant contribution to the regression model. Indicate the most appropriate regression model for this set of data.

j. Determine the p-values in (i) and interpret their meaning.

k. Construct a 95% confidence interval estimate of the population slope between assessed value and size. How does the interpretation of the slope here differ from that of Problem 13.77 on page 516?

l. Compute and interpret the coefficients of partial determination.

m. The real estate assessor's office has been publicly quoted as saying that the age of a house has no bearing on its assessed value. Based on your answers to (a) through (l), do you agree with this statement? Explain.

14.63 Crazy Dave, a well-known baseball analyst, wants to determine which variables are important in predicting a team's wins in a given season. He has collected data related to wins, earned run average (ERA), and runs scored for the 2008 season (stored in BB2008). Develop a model to predict the number of wins based on ERA and runs scored.

a. State the multiple regression equation.

b. Interpret the meaning of the slopes in this equation.

c. Predict the number of wins for a team that has an ERA of 4.50 and has scored 750 runs.

d. Perform a residual analysis on the results and determine whether the regression assumptions are valid.

e. Is there a significant relationship between number of wins and the two independent variables (ERA and runs scored) at the 0.05 level of significance?

f. Determine the p-value in (e) and interpret its meaning.

g. Interpret the meaning of the coefficient of multiple determination in this problem.

h. Determine the adjusted r^2.

i. At the 0.05 level of significance, determine whether each independent variable makes a significant contribution to the regression model. Indicate the most appropriate regression model for this set of data.

j. Determine the p-values in (i) and interpret their meaning.

k. Construct a 95% confidence interval estimate of the population slope between wins and ERA.

l. Compute and interpret the coefficients of partial determination.

m. Which is more important in predicting wins—pitching, as measured by ERA, or offense, as measured by runs scored? Explain.

14.64 Referring to Problem 14.63, suppose that in addition to using ERA to predict the number of wins, Crazy Dave wants to include the league (American vs. National) as an independent variable. Develop a model to predict wins based on ERA and league. For (a) through (k), do not include an interaction term.

a. State the multiple regression equation.

b. Interpret the slopes in (a).

c. Predict the number of wins for a team with an ERA of 4.50 in the American League. Construct a 95% confidence interval estimate for all teams and a 95% prediction interval for an individual team.

d. Perform a residual analysis on the results and determine whether the regression assumptions are valid.

e. Is there a significant relationship between wins and the two independent variables (ERA and league) at the 0.05 level of significance?

f. At the 0.05 level of significance, determine whether each independent variable makes a contribution to the regression model. Indicate the most appropriate regression model for this set of data.

g. Construct a 95% confidence interval estimate of the population slope for the relationship between wins and ERA.

h. Construct a 95% confidence interval estimate of the population slope for the relationship between wins and league.

i. Compute and interpret the adjusted r^2.

j. Compute and interpret the coefficients of partial determination.

k. What assumption do you have to make about the slope of wins with ERA?

l. Add an interaction term to the model and, at the 0.05 level of significance, determine whether it makes a significant contribution to the model.

m. On the basis of the results of (f) and (l), which model is most appropriate? Explain.

14.65 You are a real estate broker who wants to compare property values in Glen Cove and Roslyn (which are located approximately 8 miles apart). In order to do so, you will analyze the data in GCRoslyn, a file that includes samples of houses from Glen Cove and Roslyn. Making sure to include the dummy variable for location (Glen Cove or Roslyn), develop a regression model to predict appraised value, based on the land area of a property, the age of a house, and location. Be sure to determine whether any interaction terms need to be included in the model.

14.66 A recent article discussed a metal deposition process in which a piece of metal is placed in an acid bath and an alloy is layered on top of it. The business objective of engineers working on the process was to reduce variation in the thickness of the alloy layer. To begin, the temperature and the pressure in the tank holding the acid bath are to be studied as independent variables. Data are collected from 50 samples. The results are organized and stored in Thickness (data extracted from J. Conklin, "It's a Marathon, Not a Sprint," *Quality Progress*, June 2009, pp. 46–49).

Develop a multiple regression model that uses temperature and the pressure in the tank holding the acid bath to predict the thickness of the alloy layer. Be sure to perform a thorough residual analysis. The article suggests that there is a significant interaction between the pressure and the temperature in the tank. Do you agree?

MANAGING THE *SPRINGVILLE HERALD*

In its continuing study of the home-delivery subscription solicitation process, a marketing department team wants to test the effects of two types of structured sales presentations (personal formal and personal informal) and the number of hours spent on telemarketing on the number of new subscriptions. The staff has recorded these data in the file SH14 for the past 24 weeks.

Analyze these data and develop a multiple regression model to predict the number of new subscriptions for a week, based on the number of hours spent on telemarketing and the sales presentation type. Write a report, giving detailed findings concerning the regression model used.

WEB CASE

Apply your knowledge of multiple regression models in this Web Case, which extends the OmniFoods Using Statistics scenario from this chapter.

To ensure a successful test marketing of its OmniPower energy bars, the OmniFoods marketing department has contracted with In-Store Placements Group (ISPG), a merchandising consultancy. ISPG will work with the grocery store chain that is conducting the test-market study. Using the same 34-store sample used in the test-market study, ISPG claims that the choice of shelf location and the presence of in-store OmniPower coupon dispensers both increase sales of the energy bars.

Using a Web browser, open to the Web page for the Chapter 14 Web Case, or open **Omni_ISPGMemo.htm**, if

you have downloaded the Web Case files, to review the ISPG claims and supporting data. Then answer the following questions:

1. Are the supporting data consistent with ISPG's claims? Perform an appropriate statistical analysis to confirm (or discredit) the stated relationship between sales and the two independent variables of product shelf location and the presence of in-store OmniPower coupon dispensers.

2. If you were advising OmniFoods, would you recommend using a specific shelf location and in-store coupon dispensers to sell OmniPower bars?

3. What additional data would you advise collecting in order to determine the effectiveness of the sales promotion techniques used by ISPG?

REFERENCES

1. Hosmer, D. W., and S. Lemeshow, *Applied Logistic Regression*, 2nd ed. (New York: Wiley, 2001).
2. Kutner, M., C. Nachtsheim, J. Neter, and W. Li, *Applied Linear Statistical Models*, 5th ed. (New York: McGraw-Hill/Irwin, 2005).
3. *Microsoft Excel 2007* (Redmond, WA: Microsoft Corp., 2007).

EG14.1 DEVELOPING a MULTIPLE REGRESSION MODEL

Interpreting the Regression Coefficients

PHStat2 Use the **Multiple Regression** procedure to perform a multiple regression analysis. For example, to perform the Figure 14.1 analysis for the Table 14.1 OmniPower sales data (on page 528), open to the **DATA worksheet** of the **OmniPower workbook**. Select **PHStat → Regression → Multiple Regression**, and in the procedure's dialog box (shown below):

1. Enter **A1:A35** as the **Y Variable Cell Range**.
2. Enter **B1:C35** as the **X Variables Cell Range**.
3. Check **First cells in both ranges contain label**.
4. Enter **95** as the **Confidence level for regression coefficients**.
5. Check **Regression Statistics Table** and **ANOVA and Coefficients Table**.
6. Enter a **Title** and click **OK**.

The procedure creates a worksheet that contains a copy of your data in addition to the regression results worksheet shown in Figure 14.1. For more information about these worksheets, read the following *In-Depth Excel* section.

In-Depth Excel Use the **LINEST** function to help perform a multiple regression. Enter **LINEST**(*cell range of Y variable, cell range of X variable,* **True, True**) as part of an array formula placed into a 5-row-by-k-column cell range, where k is the number of independent variables, to compute the statistics associated with the multiple regression analysis.

Use the **COMPUTE worksheet** of the **Multiple Regression workbook**, shown in Figure 14.1 on page 530, as a template for performing multiple regression. Columns A through I of this worksheet duplicate the visual design of the Analysis ToolPak regression worksheet. The worksheet uses the regression data in the **MRDATA worksheet** to perform the regression analysis for the Table 14.1 OmniPower sales data.

Figure 14.1 does not show the columns K through N Calculations area (see Figure EG14.1 below). This area contains a LINEST array formula in the cell range L2:N6 and calculations for the *t* test of the slope (see Section 13.7 on page 497). The array formula computes the b_2, b_1, and b_0 coefficients in cells L2, M2, and N2; the b_2, b_1, and b_0 standard error in cells L3, M3, and N3; r^2 and the standard error of the estimate in cells L4 and M4; the *F* test statistic and error *df* in cells L5 and M5; and *SSR* and *SSE* in cells L6 and M6. (The rest of the cell range, N4, N5, and N6, displays the **#N/A** message. This is not an error.)

Open to the **COMPUTE_FORMULAS worksheet** to examine all the formulas in the worksheet, some of which are discussed in the *In-Depth Excel* passages of the Chapter 13 Excel Guide. The cell L9 formula, in the form =**TINV(1** − *confidence level, Error degrees of freedom*), computes the critical value for the *t* test.

	K	L	M
1			*Calculations*
2	*b2, b1, b0* intercepts	=LINEST(MRDATA!A2:A35, MRDATA!B2:C35, TRUE, TRUE)	=LINEST(MRDATA!A2:A35, MRDATA!B2:C35, TRUE, TRUE)
3	*b1, b0* Standard Error	=LINEST(MRDATA!A2:A35, MRDATA!B2:C35, TRUE, TRUE)	=LINEST(MRDATA!A2:A35, MRDATA!B2:C35, TRUE, TRUE)
4	R Square, Standard Error	=LINEST(MRDATA!A2:A35, MRDATA!B2:C35, TRUE, TRUE)	=LINEST(MRDATA!A2:A35, MRDATA!B2:C35, TRUE, TRUE)
5	F, Residual *df*	=LINEST(MRDATA!A2:A35, MRDATA!B2:C35, TRUE, TRUE)	=LINEST(MRDATA!A2:A35, MRDATA!B2:C35, TRUE, TRUE)
6	Regression SS, Residual SS	=LINEST(MRDATA!A2:A35, MRDATA!B2:C35, TRUE, TRUE)	=LINEST(MRDATA!A2:A35, MRDATA!B2:C35, TRUE, TRUE)
7			
8	Confidence level	0.95	
9	*t* Critical Value	=TINV(1-L8, B13)	
10	Half Width *b0*	=L9 * C17	
11	Half Width *b1*	=L9 * C18	
12	Half Width *b2*	=L9 * C19	

FIGURE EG14.1 Calculations area of the multiple regression worksheet (columns N and O not shown)

To perform multiple regression for other data, paste the regression data into the MRDATA worksheet. Paste the values for the *Y* variable into column A. (This is the opposite of the simple linear regression paste discussed in Section EG13.2.) Paste the values for the *X* variables into consecutive columns, starting with column B. Open to the COMPUTE worksheet. First, enter the confidence level in cell L8. Then, edit the correct 5-row-by–*k*-column array that starts with cell L2. Edit the cell ranges in the array formula, and then, while holding down the **Control** and **Shift** keys (or the **Apple** key on a Mac), press the **Enter** key.

To match the worksheet the Analysis ToolPak Regression procedure creates, the COMPUTE worksheet (unnecessarily) duplicates the values for the confidence intervals in columns H and I. These duplicated values are not shown in the chapter figures.

Analysis ToolPak Use the **Regression** procedure to perform a multiple regression analysis. For example, to perform the Figure 14.1 analysis (on page 530) for the Table 14.1 OmniPower sales data (on page 528), open to the **DATA worksheet** of the **OmniPower workbook** and:

1. Select **Data → Data Analysis** (Excel 2007) or **Tools → Data Analysis** (Excel 2003).
2. In the Data Analysis dialog box, select **Regression** from the **Analysis Tools** list and then click **OK**.

In the Regression dialog box (see top of next column):

3. Enter **A1:A35** as the **Input Y Range** and enter **B1:C35** as the **Input X Range**.
4. Check **Labels** and check **Confidence Level** and enter **95** in its box.
5. Click **New Worksheet Ply**.
6. Click **OK**.

Predicting the Dependent Variable *Y*

PHStat2 Use the Section EG14.1 "Interpreting the Regression Coefficients" *PHStat2* instructions but replace step 6 with the following new step 6 and 7 instructions:

6. Check **Confidence Interval Estimate & Prediction Interval** and enter **95** as the percentage for **Confidence level for intervals**.
7. Enter a **Title** and click **OK**.

The additional worksheet created is explained in the following *In-Depth Excel* passage.

In-Depth Excel Use the **TINV**, **MMULT**, and **MINVERSE** functions to help compute a confidence interval estimate and a prediction interval. Enter **TINV((1 −** *confidence level, Error degrees of freedom*)) to compute the *t* test statistic.

Examine the **CIEandPI worksheet** of the **Multiple Regression workbook**, shown in Figure 14.2 on page 531, as a model for computing confidence interval estimates and

prediction intervals. In an array formula, MMULT computes the matrix product X′X by treating the specially prepared **MRArray worksheet** as a matrix. In another array formula, MINVERSE computes the inverse of the X′X matrix created by MMULT. Other uses of MMULT compute X′G multiplied by the inverse of X′X and [X′G multiplied by the inverse of X′X] multiplied by XG.

The worksheet contains the data and formulas for the Table 14.1 OmniPower sales data (on page 528). Modifying this worksheet (and the MRArray worksheet) for other problems requires knowledge that is beyond the scope of this book.

EG14.2 r^2, ADJUSTED r^2, and the OVERALL *F* TEST

The three topics discussed in Section EG14.2 are computed in the multiple regression worksheet created using the "Interpreting the Regression Coefficients" instructions of Section EG14.1.

Figure EG14.2 on page 568 shows the formulas used to compute the coefficient of multiple determination, r^2, the adjusted r^2, and the overall *F* test in the **COMPUTE worksheet** of the **Multiple Regression workbook**, created when using either the Section EG14.1 *PHStat2* or *In-Depth Excel* instructions. Formulas in cells B5, B7, B13, C12, C13, D12, and E12 copy values computed by the array formula in cell range L2:N6 that uses the **LINEST** function. (See the Section EG14.1 *In-Depth Excel* instructions for further information.) The cell F12 formula, in the form =**FDIST(***F test statistic***, 1,** *error degrees of* **freedom)**, computes the *p*-value for the *F* test for the slope, discussed in Section 13.7.

EG14.3 RESIDUAL ANALYSIS for the MULTIPLE REGRESSION MODEL

PHStat2 Use the Section EG14.1 "Interpreting the Regression Coefficients" *PHStat2* instructions. Modify step 5 by checking **Residuals Table** and **Residual Plots** in addition to checking **Regression Statistics Table** and **ANOVA and Coefficients Table**.

	A	B	C	D	E	F
1	Multiple Regression					
2						
3	*Regression Statistics*					
4	Multiple R	=SQRT(C12/C14)				
5	R Square	=L4				
6	Adjusted R Square	=1 - (B14/B13) * (C13/C14)				
7	Standard Error	=M4				
8	Observations	=COUNT(MRDATA!A:A)				
9						
10	ANOVA					
11		*df*	*SS*	*MS*	*F*	*Significance F*
12	Regression	=B14 - B13	=L6	=C12/B12	=L5	=FDIST(E12, B12, B13)
13	Residual	=M5	=M6	=C13/B13		
14	Total	=B8 - 1	=C12 + C13			

FIGURE EG14.2 Formulas for the cell range A1:F14 of the multiple regression results worksheet

In-Depth Excel Create a worksheet that calculates residuals and then create a scatter plot of the original X variable and the residuals (plotted as the Y variable).

Use the **RESIDUALS worksheet** of the **Multiple Regression workbook**, shown in Figure EG14.3, as a template for creating a residuals worksheet. The formulas in this worksheet compute the residuals for the regression analysis for the Table 14.1 OmniPower sales data (on page 528) by using the regression data in the **MRDATA worksheet** in the same workbook.

In column D, the worksheet computes the predicted Y values (labeled Predicted Bars in Figure EG14.3) by multiplying the X_1 values by the b_1 coefficient and the X_2 values by the b_2 coefficient and adding these products to the b_0 coefficient. In column F, the worksheet computes residuals by subtracting the predicted Y values from the Y values. For other problems, modify this worksheet as follows:

1. If the number of independent variables is greater than 2, select column D, right-click, and click **Insert** from the shortcut menu. Repeat this step as many times as necessary to create the additional columns to hold all the X variables.

2. Paste the data for the X variables into columns, starting with column B.

3. Paste Y values in column E (or in the second-to-last column if there are more than two X variables).

4. For sample sizes smaller than 34, delete the extra rows. For sample sizes greater than 34, copy the predicted Y and residuals formulas (columns D and F in Figure EG14.3) down through the row containing the last pair of X and Y values. Also, add the new observation numbers in column A.

To create residual plots, use copy-and-paste special values (see Appendix Section C.12) to paste data values on a new worksheet in the proper order before applying the Section EG2.7 scatter plot instructions.

Analysis ToolPak Use the Section EG14.1 *Analysis ToolPak* instructions. Modify step 5 by checking **Residuals** and **Residual Plots** before clicking **New Worksheet Ply** and then **OK**. (Note that the **Residuals Plots** option creates residual plots only for each independent variable.)

EG14.4 INFERENCES CONCERNING the POPULATION REGRESSION COEFFICIENTS

The regression results worksheets created by using the EG14.1 instructions include the information needed to make the inferences discussed in Section 14.4.

	A	B	C	D	E	F
1	*Observation*	*Price*	*Promotion*	*Predicted Bars*	*Bars*	*Residuals*
2	1	59	200	=COMPUTE!B18 * B2 + COMPUTE!B19 * C2 + COMPUTE!B17	4141	=E2-D2
3	2	59	200	=COMPUTE!B18 * B3 + COMPUTE!B19 * C3 + COMPUTE!B17	3842	=E3-D3
4	3	59	200	=COMPUTE!B18 * B4 + COMPUTE!B19 * C4 + COMPUTE!B17	3056	=E4-D4
32	31	99	400	=CO...		=32-D...
33	32	99	400	=COMPUTE!B18 * B33 + COMPUTE!B19 * C33 + COMPUTE!B17	1602	=E33-D33
34	33	99	600	=COMPUTE!B18 * B34 + COMPUTE!B19 * C34 + COMPUTE!B17	3354	=E34-D34
35	34	99	600	=COMPUTE!B18 * B35 + COMPUTE!B19 * C35 + COMPUTE!B17	2927	=E35-D35

FIGURE EG14.3 Residuals worksheet formulas (showing only rows 1 through 4 and 33 through 35)

EG14.5 TESTING PORTIONS of the MULTIPLE REGRESSION MODEL

Coefficients of Partial Determination

PHStat2 Use the Section EG14.1 "Interpreting the Regression Coefficients" *PHStat2* instructions but modify step 6 by checking **Coefficients of Partial Determination** before you click **OK**.

In-Depth Excel You compute the coefficients of partial determination by using a two-step process. You first use the Section EG14.1 *In-Depth Excel* instructions to create all possible regression results worksheets in a copy of the **Multiple Regression workbook**. For example, if you have two independent variables, you perform three regression analyses: Y with X_1 and X_2, Y with X_1, and Y with X_2 to create three regression results worksheets. Then open to the **CPD worksheet** for the number of independent variables (**CPD_2, CPD_3**, and **CPD_4 worksheets** are included) and follow the italicized instructions to copy and paste special values from the regression results worksheets. The **CPD_2 worksheet** contains the data to compute the coefficients of partial determination for the OmniPower regression model used as an example in Section 14.5.

EG14.6 USING DUMMY VARIABLES and INTERACTION TERMS in REGRESSION MODELS

Creating Dummy Variables

To create dummy variables, add new columns to the worksheet that contains your regression data.

For the case of a categorical variable that contains two levels, open to the regression data worksheet. Copy and paste into a new column the values of the two-level categorical variable. Select all of the newly pasted values and then press **Crtl+H**, the keyboard shortcut for **Find and Replace**. In the Find and Replace dialog box:

1. Enter the first categorical value in the **Find what** box.
2. Enter the dummy value (**1** or **0**) that will represent that categorical value in the **Replace with** box.
3. Click **Replace All**. If a message box to confirm the replacement appears, click **OK** to continue.

Repeat the find and replace for the other categorical value and enter the other dummy value in the **Replace with** box. Then click **Close**.

Categorical variables that have more than two levels require the use of formulas in multiple columns. For example, to create the dummy variables for Example 14.3 on page 550, two columns are needed. Assume that the three-level categorical variable mentioned in the example is in Column D of the opened worksheet. A first new column that contains formulas in the form **=IF(*column D cell = first level*, 1, 0)** and a second new column that contains formulas in the form **=IF (*column D cell = second level*, 1, 0)** would properly create the two dummy variables that the example requires.

Creating Interactions

To create an interaction, add a column of formulas that multiply one independent variable by another. For example, if the first independent variable appeared in column B and the second independent variable appeared in column C, enter the formula **=B2 * C2** in the row 2 cell of an empty new column and then copy the formula down through all rows of data to create the interaction.

15 Multiple Regression Model Building

Learning Objectives

In this chapter, you learn:

- To use quadratic terms in a regression model
- To use transformed variables in a regression model
- To measure the correlation among independent variables
- To build a regression model, using either the stepwise or best-subsets approach
- To avoid the pitfalls involved in developing a multiple regression model

USING STATISTICS

@ WTT-TV

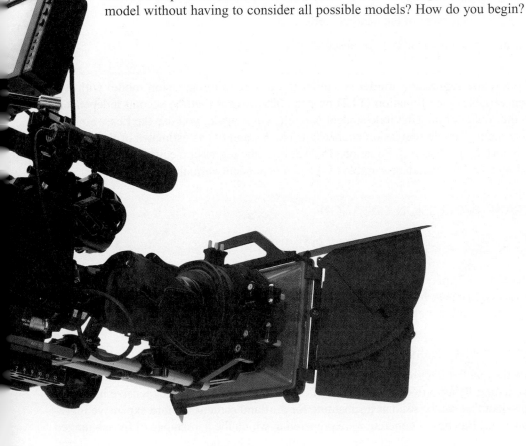

As part of your job as the operations manager at WTT-TV, you look for ways to reduce labor expenses. Currently, the unionized graphic artists at the station receive hourly pay for a significant number of hours during which they are idle. These hours are called standby hours. You have collected data concerning standby hours and four factors that you suspect are related to the excessive number of standby hours the station is currently experiencing: the total number of staff present, remote hours, Dubner hours, and total labor hours.

You plan to build a multiple regression model to help determine which factors most heavily affect standby hours. You believe that an appropriate model will help you to predict the number of future standby hours, identify the root causes of excessive numbers of standby hours, and allow you to reduce the total number of future standby hours. How do you build the model with the most appropriate mix of independent variables? Are there statistical techniques that can help you identify a "best" model without having to consider all possible models? How do you begin?

Chapter 14 discussed multiple regression models with two independent variables. This chapter extends regression analysis to models containing more than two independent variables. The chapter introduces you to various topics related to model building to help you learn to develop the best model when confronted with a large set of data (such as the one described in the WTT-TV scenario). These topics include quadratic independent variables, transformations of either the dependent or independent variables, stepwise regression, and best-subsets regression.

15.1 The Quadratic Regression Model

The simple regression model discussed in Chapter 13 and the multiple regression model discussed in Chapter 14 assumed that the relationship between Y and each independent variable is linear. However, in Section 13.1, several different types of nonlinear relationships between variables were introduced. One of the most common nonlinear relationships is a quadratic or curvilinear relationship between two variables in which Y increases (or decreases) at a changing rate for various values of X (see Figure 13.2, Panels C–E, on page 473). You can use the quadratic regression model defined in Equation (15.1) to analyze this type of relationship between X and Y.

QUADRATIC REGRESSION MODEL

$$Y_i = \beta_0 + \beta_1 X_{1i} + \beta_2 X_{1i}^2 + \varepsilon_i \qquad (15.1)$$

where

$\beta_0 = Y$ intercept

$\beta_1 = $ coefficient of the linear effect on Y

$\beta_2 = $ coefficient of the quadratic effect on Y

$\varepsilon_i = $ random error in Y for observation i

This **quadratic regression model** is similar to the multiple regression model with two independent variables [see Equation (14.2) on page 529] except that the second independent variable is the square of the first independent variable. Once again, you use the Least Squares method to compute sample regression coefficients (b_0, b_1, and b_2) as estimates of the population parameters (β_0, β_1, and β_2). Equation (15.2) defines the regression equation for the quadratic model with one independent variable (X_1) and a dependent variable (Y).

QUADRATIC REGRESSION EQUATION

$$\hat{Y}_i = b_0 + b_1 X_{1i} + b_2 X_{1i}^2 \qquad (15.2)$$

In Equation (15.2), the first regression coefficient, b_0, represents the Y intercept; the second regression coefficient, b_1, represents the linear effect; and the third regression coefficient, b_2, represents the quadratic effect.

Finding the Regression Coefficients and Predicting Y

To illustrate the quadratic regression model, consider a study that examined the business problem of how adding fly ash affects the strength of concrete. (Fly ash is an inexpensive industrial waste by-product that can be used as a substitute for Portland cement, a more expensive ingredient of concrete.) Batches of concrete were prepared in which the percentage of fly ash ranged from 0% to 60%. Data were collected from a sample of 18 batches and organized and stored in Flyash. Table 15.1 summarizes the results.

TABLE 15.1

Fly Ash Percentage and
Strength of 18 Batches of
28-Day-Old Concrete

Fly Ash %	Strength (psi)	Fly Ash %	Strength (psi)
0	4,779	40	5,995
0	4,706	40	5,628
0	4,350	40	5,897
20	5,189	50	5,746
20	5,140	50	5,719
20	4,976	50	5,782
30	5,110	60	4,895
30	5,685	60	5,030
30	5,618	60	4,648

By creating the scatter plot in Figure 15.1 to visualize these data, you will be better able to select the proper model for expressing the relationship between fly ash percentage and strength.

FIGURE 15.1

Scatter plot of fly ash
percentage (X) and
strength (Y)

*Create scatter plots using the
instructions in Section EG2.7.*

Figure 15.1 indicates an initial increase in the strength of the concrete as the percentage of fly ash increases. The strength appears to level off and then drop after achieving maximum strength at about 40% fly ash. Strength for 50% fly ash is slightly below strength at 40%, but strength at 60% is substantially below strength at 50%. Therefore, you should choose a quadratic model, not a linear model, to estimate strength based on fly ash percentage.

Figure 15.2 on page 574 shows a regression results worksheet for these data.

From Figure 15.2 on page 574,

$$b_0 = 4{,}486.3611 \quad b_1 = 63.0052 \quad b_2 = -0.8765$$

Therefore, the quadratic regression equation is

$$\hat{Y}_i = 4{,}486.3611 + 63.0052X_{1i} - 0.8765X_{1i}^2$$

where

$\hat{Y}_i$ = predicted strength for sample i

X_{1i} = percentage of fly ash for sample i

	A	B	C	D	E	F	G
1	Concrete Strength Analysis						
2							
3	*Regression Statistics*						
4	Multiple R	0.8053					
5	R Square	0.6485					
6	Adjusted R Square	0.6016					
7	Standard Error	312.1129					
8	Observations	18					
9							
10	ANOVA						
11		*df*	*SS*	*MS*	*F*	*Significance F*	
12	Regression	2	2695473.4897	1347736.745	13.8351	0.0004	
13	Residual	15	1461217.0103	97414.4674			
14	Total	17	4156690.5000				
15							
16		*Coefficients*	*Standard Error*	*t Stat*	*P-value*	*Lower 95%*	*Upper 95%*
17	Intercept	4486.3611	174.7531	25.6726	0.0000	4113.8834	4858.8389
18	Fly Ash%	63.0052	12.3725	5.0923	0.0001	36.6338	89.3767
19	Fly Ash% ^2	-0.8765	0.1966	-4.4578	0.0005	-1.2955	-0.4574

Figure 15.3 is a scatter plot of this quadratic regression equation that shows the fit of the quadratic regression model to the original data.

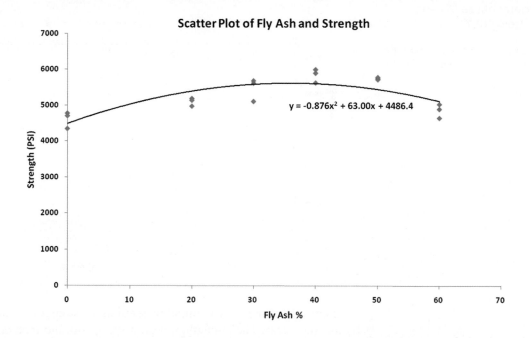

From the quadratic regression equation and Figure 15.3, the Y intercept ($b_0 = 4,486.3611$) is the predicted strength when the percentage of fly ash is 0. To interpret the coefficients b_1 and b_2, observe that after an initial increase, strength decreases as fly ash percentage increases. This nonlinear relationship is further demonstrated by predicting the strength for fly ash percentages of 20, 40, and 60. Using the quadratic regression equation,

$$\hat{Y}_i = 4,486.3611 + 63.0052X_{1i} - 0.8765X_{1i}^2$$

for $X_{1i} = 20$,

$$\hat{Y}_i = 4,486.3611 + 63.0052(20) - 0.8765(20)^2 = 5,395.865$$

for $X_{1i} = 40$,

$$\hat{Y}_i = 4,486.3611 + 63.0052(40) - 0.8765(40)^2 = 5,604.169$$

and for $X_{1i} = 60$,

$$\hat{Y}_i = 4,486.3611 + 63.0052(60) - 0.8765(60)^2 = 5,111.273$$

Thus, the predicted concrete strength for 40% fly ash is 208.304 psi above the predicted strength for 20% fly ash, but the predicted strength for 60% fly ash is 492.896 psi below the predicted strength for 40% fly ash.

Testing for the Significance of the Quadratic Model

After you calculate the quadratic regression equation, you can test whether there is a significant overall relationship between strength, Y, and fly ash percentage, X_1. The null and alternative hypotheses are as follows:

$$H_0: \beta_1 = \beta_2 = 0 \text{ (There is no overall relationship between } X_1 \text{ and } Y.)$$

$$H_1: \beta_1 \text{ and/or } \beta_2 \neq 0 \text{ (There is an overall relationship between } X_1 \text{ and } Y.)$$

Equation (14.6) on page 535 defines the overall F_{STAT} test statistic used for this test:

$$F_{STAT} = \frac{MSR}{MSE}$$

From the Figure 15.2 results on page 574,

$$F_{STAT} = \frac{MSR}{MSE} = \frac{1,347,736.745}{97,414.4674} = 13.8351$$

If you choose a level of significance of 0.05, from Table E.5, the critical value of the F distribution, with 2 and 15 degrees of freedom, is 3.68 (see Figure 15.4). Because $F_{STAT} = 13.8351 > 3.68$, or because the p-value $= 0.0004 < 0.05$, you reject the null hypothesis (H_0) and conclude that there is a significant overall relationship between strength and fly ash percentage.

FIGURE 15.4

Testing for the existence of the overall relationship at the 0.05 level of significance, with 2 and 15 degrees of freedom

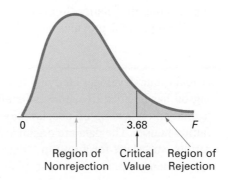

0   3.68   F

Region of   Critical   Region of
Nonrejection   Value   Rejection

Testing the Quadratic Effect

In using a regression model to examine a relationship between two variables, you want to find not only the most accurate model but also the simplest model that expresses that relationship. Therefore, you need to examine whether there is a significant difference between the quadratic model:

$$Y_i = \beta_0 + \beta_1 X_{1i} + \beta_2 X_{1i}^2 + \varepsilon_i$$

and the linear model:

$$Y_i = \beta_0 + \beta_1 X_{1i} + \varepsilon_i$$

In Section 14.4, you used the t test to determine whether each independent variable makes a significant contribution to the regression model. To test the significance of the contribution of the quadratic effect, you use the following null and alternative hypotheses:

H_0: Including the quadratic effect does not significantly improve the model ($\beta_2 = 0$).

H_1: Including the quadratic effect significantly improves the model ($\beta_2 \neq 0$).

The standard error of each regression coefficient and its corresponding t_{STAT} test statistic are part of the regression results worksheet (see Figure 15.2 on page 574). Equation (14.7) on page 539 defines the t_{STAT} test statistic:

$$t_{STAT} = \frac{b_2 - \beta_2}{S_{b_2}}$$

$$= \frac{-0.8765 - 0}{0.1966} = -4.4578$$

If you select the 0.05 level of significance, then from Table E.3, the critical values for the t distribution with 15 degrees of freedom are -2.1315 and $+2.1315$ (see Figure 15.5).

FIGURE 15.5

Testing for the contribution of the quadratic effect to a regression model at the 0.05 level of significance, with 15 degrees of freedom

Because $t_{STAT} = -4.4578 < -2.1315$ or because the p-value $= 0.0005 < 0.05$, you reject H_0 and conclude that the quadratic model is significantly better than the linear model for representing the relationship between strength and fly ash percentage.

Example 15.1 provides an additional illustration of a possible quadratic effect.

EXAMPLE 15.1

Studying the Quadratic Effect in a Multiple Regression Model

A real estate developer studying the business problem of estimating the consumption of heating oil has decided to examine the effect of atmospheric temperature and the amount of attic insulation on heating oil consumption. Data are collected from a random sample of 15 single-family houses. The data are organized and stored in HtngOil. Figure 15.6 shows the regression results worksheet for a multiple regression model using the two independent variables atmospheric temperature and attic insulation.

FIGURE 15.6

Regression results worksheet for the multiple linear regression model predicting monthly consumption of heating oil

Create multiple regression result worksheets using the instructions in Section EG14.1.

	A	B	C	D	E	F	G
1	Heating Oil Consumption Analysis						
2							
3	*Regression Statistics*						
4	Multiple R	0.9827					
5	R Square	0.9656					
6	Adjusted R Square	0.9599					
7	Standard Error	26.0138					
8	Observations	15					
9							
10	ANOVA						
11		*df*	*SS*	*MS*	*F*	*Significance F*	
12	Regression	2	228014.6263	114007.3132	168.4712	0.0000	
13	Residual	12	8120.6030	676.7169			
14	Total	14	236135.2293				
15							
16		*Coefficients*	*Standard Error*	*t Stat*	*P-value*	*Lower 95%*	*Upper 95%*
17	Intercept	562.1510	21.0931	26.6509	0.0000	516.1931	608.1089
18	Temperature	-5.4366	0.3362	-16.1699	0.0000	-6.1691	-4.7040
19	Insulation	-20.0123	2.3425	-8.5431	0.0000	-25.1162	-14.9084

The residual plot for attic insulation (not shown here) contained some evidence of a quadratic effect. Thus, the real estate developer reanalyzed the data by adding a quadratic term for attic insulation to the multiple regression model. At the 0.05 level of significance, is there evidence of a significant quadratic effect for attic insulation?

SOLUTION Figure 15.7 shows the worksheet results for this regression model.

FIGURE 15.7

Worksheet for the multiple regression model with a quadratic term for attic insulation

Create multiple regression result worksheets using the instructions in Section EG14.1. Create a quadratic term using the instructions in Section EG15.1.

	A	B	C	D	E	F	G
1	Quadratic Effect for Insulation Variable?						
2							
3	Regression Statistics						
4	Multiple R	0.9862					
5	R Square	0.9725					
6	Adjusted R Square	0.9650					
7	Standard Error	24.2938					
8	Observations	15					
9							
10	ANOVA						
11		df	SS	MS	F	Significance F	
12	Regression	3	229643.1645	76547.7215	129.7006	0.0000	
13	Residual	11	6492.0649	590.1877			
14	Total	14	236135.2293				
15							
16		Coefficients	Standard Error	t Stat	P-value	Lower 95%	Upper 95%
17	Intercept	624.5864	42.4352	14.7186	0.0000	531.1872	717.9856
18	Temperature	-5.3626	0.3171	-16.9099	0.0000	-6.0606	-4.6646
19	Insulation	-44.5868	14.9547	-2.9815	0.0125	-77.5019	-11.6717
20	Insulation ^2	1.8667	1.1238	1.6611	0.1249	-0.6067	4.3401

The multiple regression equation is

$$\hat{Y}_i = 624.5864 - 5.3626X_{1i} - 44.5868X_{2i} + 1.8667X_{2i}^2$$

To test for the significance of the quadratic effect,

H_0: Including the quadratic effect does not significantly improve the model ($\beta_3 = 0$).

H_1: Including the quadratic effect significantly improves the model ($\beta_3 \neq 0$).

From Figure 15.7 and Table E.3, $-2.2010 < t_{STAT} = 1.6611 < 2.2010$ (or the p-value = $0.1249 > 0.05$). Therefore, you do not reject the null hypothesis. You conclude that there is insufficient evidence that the quadratic effect for attic insulation is different from zero. In the interest of keeping the model as simple as possible, you should use the multiple regression equation shown in Figure 15.6:

$$\hat{Y}_i = 562.1510 - 5.4366X_{1i} - 20.0123X_{2i}$$

The Coefficient of Multiple Determination

In the multiple regression model, the coefficient of multiple determination, r^2 (see Section 14.2), represents the proportion of variation in Y that is explained by variation in the independent variables. Consider the quadratic regression model you used to predict the strength of concrete using fly ash and fly ash squared. You compute r^2 by using Equation (14.4) on page 534:

$$r^2 = \frac{SSR}{SST}$$

From Figure 15.2 on page 574,

$$SSR = 2,695,473.897 \quad SST = 4,156,690.5$$

Thus,

$$r^2 = \frac{SSR}{SST} = \frac{2,695,473.897}{4,156,690.5} = 0.6485$$

This coefficient of multiple determination indicates that 64.85% of the variation in strength is explained by the quadratic relationship between strength and the percentage of fly ash. You should also compute r_{adj}^2 to account for the number of independent variables and the sample size. In the quadratic regression model, $k = 2$ because there are two independent variables, X_1 and X_1^2. Thus, using Equation (14.5) on page 534,

$$r_{adj}^2 = 1 - \left[(1 - r^2)\frac{(n - 1)}{(n - k - 1)}\right]$$

$$= 1 - \left[(1 - 0.6485)\frac{17}{15}\right]$$

$$= 1 - 0.3984$$

$$= 0.6016$$

Problems for Section 15.1

LEARNING THE BASICS

15.1 The following quadratic regression equation is for a sample of $n = 25$:

$$\hat{Y}_i = 5 + 3X_{1i} + 1.5X_{1i}^2$$

a. Predict Y for $X_1 = 2$.
b. Suppose that the computed t_{STAT} test statistic for the quadratic regression coefficient is 2.35. At the 0.05 level of significance, is there evidence that the quadratic model is better than the linear model?
c. Suppose that the computed t_{STAT} test statistic for the quadratic regression coefficient is 1.17. At the 0.05 level of significance, is there evidence that the quadratic model is better than the linear model?
d. Suppose the regression coefficient for the linear effect is -3.0. Predict Y for $X_1 = 2$.

APPLYING THE CONCEPTS

15.2 Businesses actively recruit business students with well-developed higher-order cognitive skills (HOCS) such as problem identification, analytical reasoning, and content integration skills. Researchers conducted a study to see if improvement in students' HOCS was related to the students' GPA (data extracted from R. V. Bradley, C. S. Sankar, H. R. Clayton, V. W. Mbarika, and P. K. Raju, "A Study on the Impact of GPA on Perceived Improvement of Higher-Order Cognitive Skills," *Decision Sciences Journal of Innovative Education*, January 2007, 5(1), pp 151–168). The researchers conducted a study in which business students were taught using the case study method. Using data collected from 300 business students, the following quadratic regression equation was derived:

$$HOCS = -3.48 + 4.53(GPA) - 0.68(GPA)^2$$

where the dependent variable HOCS measured the improvement in higher-order cognitive skills, with 1 being the lowest

improvement in HOCS and 5 being the highest improvement in HOCS.
a. Construct a table of predicted HOCS, using GPA equal to $2.0, 2.1, 2.2, \ldots, 4.0$.
b. Plot the values in the table constructed in (a), with GPA on the horizontal axis and predicted HOCS on the vertical axis.
c. Discuss the curvilinear relationship between students' GPA and their predicted improvement in HOCS.
d. The researchers reported that the model had an r^2 of 0.07 and an adjusted r^2 of 0.06. What does this tell you about the scatter of individual HOCS scores around the curvilinear relationship plotted in (b) and discussed in (c)?

15.3 The following market research study was conducted by a national chain of consumer electronics stores. To promote sales, the chain relies heavily on local newspaper advertising to support its modest exposure in nationwide television commercials. A sample of 20 cities with similar populations and monthly sales totals were assigned different newspaper advertising budgets for one month. The following table (stored in Advertising) summarizes the sales (in $millions) and the newspaper advertising budgets (in $000) observed during the study:

Sales	Newspaper Advertising	Sales	Newspaper Advertising
6.14	5	6.84	15
6.04	5	6.66	15
6.21	5	6.95	20
6.32	5	6.65	20
6.42	10	6.83	20
6.56	10	6.81	20
6.67	10	7.03	25
6.35	10	6.88	25
6.76	15	6.84	25
6.79	15	6.99	25

a. Construct a scatter plot for advertising and sales.
b. Fit a quadratic regression model and state the quadratic regression equation.
c. Predict the monthly sales for a city with newspaper advertising of $20,000.
d. Perform a residual analysis on the results and determine whether the regression assumptions are valid.
e. At the 0.05 level of significance, is there a significant quadratic relationship between monthly sales and newspaper advertising?
f. At the 0.05 level of significance, determine whether the quadratic model is a better fit than the linear model.
g. Interpret the meaning of the coefficient of multiple determination.
h. Compute the adjusted r^2.

15.4 Is the number of calories in a beer related to the number of carbohydrates and/or the percentage of alcohol in the beer? Data concerning 128 of the best-selling domestic beers in the United States are stored in DomesticBeer. The values for three variables are included: the number of calories per 12 ounces, the alcohol percentage, and the number of carbohydrates (in grams) per 12 ounces (data extracted from **www.Beer100.com**, May 4, 2007).
a. Perform a multiple linear regression analysis, using calories as the dependent variable and percentage alcohol and number of carbohydrates as the independent variable.
b. Add quadratic terms for alcohol percentage and the number of carbohydrates.
c. Which model is better, the one in (a) or (b)?
d. Write a short summary concerning the relationship between the number of calories in a beer and the alcohol percentage and number of carbohydrates.

15.5 The marketing department of a large supermarket chain wants to study the effect of price on the sales of packages of disposable razors. Data are collected from a sample of 15 stores with equivalent store traffic and product placement (i.e., at the checkout counter). Five stores are randomly assigned to each of three price levels (79, 99, and 119 cents) for the package of razors. The number of packages sold over a full week and the price at each store are in the following table (and stored in DispRazor):

Sales	Price (Cents)	Sales	Price (Cents)
142	79	115	99
151	79	126	99
163	79	77	119
168	79	86	119
176	79	95	119
91	99	100	119
100	99	106	119
107	99		

a. Construct a scatter plot for price and sales.
b. Fit a quadratic regression model and state the quadratic regression equation.
c. Predict the weekly sales for a price per package of 79 cents.
d. Perform a residual analysis on the results and determine whether the regression model is valid.
e. At the 0.05 level of significance, is there a significant quadratic relationship between weekly sales and price?
f. At the 0.05 level of significance, determine whether the quadratic model is a better fit than the linear model.
g. Interpret the meaning of the coefficient of multiple determination.
h. Compute the adjusted r^2.

✓ SELF Test **15.6** An agronomist designed a study in which tomatoes were grown using six different amounts of fertilizer: 0, 20, 40, 60, 80, and 100 pounds per 1,000 square feet. These fertilizer application rates were then randomly assigned to plots of land. The results including the yield of tomatoes (in pounds) were as follows (stored in Tomato):

Plot	Fertilizer Application Rate	Yield	Plot	Fertilizer Application Rate	Yield
1	0	6	7	60	46
2	0	9	8	60	50
3	20	19	9	80	48
4	20	24	10	80	54
5	40	32	11	100	52
6	40	38	12	100	58

a. Construct a scatter plot for fertilizer application rate and yield.
b. Fit a quadratic regression model and state the quadratic regression equation.
c. Predict the yield for a plot of land fertilized with 70 pounds per 1,000 square feet.
d. Perform a residual analysis on the results and determine whether the regression model is valid.
e. At the 0.05 level of significance, is there a significant overall relationship between the fertilizer application rate and tomato yield?
f. What is the p-value in (e)? Interpret its meaning.
g. At the 0.05 level of significance, determine whether there is a significant quadratic effect.
h. What is the p-value in (g)? Interpret its meaning.
i. Interpret the meaning of the coefficient of multiple determination.
j. Compute the adjusted r^2.

15.7 An auditor for a county government would like to develop a model to predict county taxes, based on the age of single-family houses. She selects a random sample of 19 single-family houses, and the results are stored in Taxes.

a. Construct a scatter plot of age and county taxes.

b. Fit a quadratic regression model and state the quadratic regression equation.

c. Predict the county taxes for a house that is 20 years old.

d. Perform a residual analysis on the results and determine whether the regression model is valid.

e. At the 0.05 level of significance, is there a significant overall relationship between age and county taxes?

f. What is the p-value in (e)? Interpret its meaning.

g. At the 0.05 level of significance, determine whether the quadratic model is superior to the linear model.

h. What is the p-value in (g)? Interpret its meaning.

i. Interpret the meaning of the coefficient of multiple determination.

j. Compute the adjusted r^2.

15.2 Using Transformations in Regression Models

This section introduces regression models in which the independent variable, the dependent variable, or both are transformed in order to either overcome violations of the assumptions of regression or to make the form of a model linear. Among the many transformations available (see reference 1) are the square-root transformation and transformations involving the common logarithm (base 10) and the natural logarithm (base e).[1]

[1]For more information on logarithms, see Section A.3 in Appendix A.

The Square-Root Transformation

The **square-root transformation** is often used to overcome violations of the equal-variance assumption as well as to transform a model that is not linear in form into one that is linear. Equation (15.3) shows a regression model that uses a square-root transformation of the independent variable.

> REGRESSION MODEL WITH A SQUARE-ROOT TRANSFORMATION
> $$Y_i = \beta_0 + \beta_1 \sqrt{X_{1i}} + \varepsilon_i \qquad (15.3)$$

Example 15.2 illustrates the use of a square-root transformation.

EXAMPLE 15.2

Using the Square-Root Transformation

Given the following values for Y and X, use a square-root transformation for the X variable:

Y	X	Y	X
42.7	1	100.4	3
50.4	1	104.7	4
69.1	2	112.3	4
79.8	2	113.6	5
90.0	3	123.9	5

Construct a scatter plot for X and Y and for the square root of X and Y.

SOLUTION Figure 15.8, Panel A, displays the scatter plot of X and Y; Panel B shows the square root of X versus Y.

FIGURE 15.8

Panel A: Scatter plot
of X and Y; Panel B:
Scatter plot of the
square root of X and Y

*Create scatter plots using
the instructions in Section
EG2.7.*

You can see that the square-root transformation has transformed a nonlinear relationship into a linear relationship.

The Log Transformation

The **logarithmic transformation** is often used to overcome violations to the equal-variance assumption. You can also use the logarithmic transformation to change a nonlinear model into a linear model. Equation (15.4) shows a multiplicative model.

ORIGINAL MULTIPLICATIVE MODEL

$$Y_i = \beta_0 X_{1i}^{\beta_1} X_{2i}^{\beta_2} \varepsilon_i \qquad \qquad (15.4)$$

By taking base 10 logarithms of both the dependent and independent variables, you can transform Equation (15.4) to the model shown in Equation (15.5).

TRANSFORMED MULTIPLICATIVE MODEL

$$\log Y_i = \log(\beta_0 X_{1i}^{\beta_1} X_{2i}^{\beta_2} \varepsilon_i) \tag{15.5}$$

$$= \log\beta_0 + \log(X_{1i}^{\beta_1}) + \log(X_{2i}^{\beta_2}) + \log \varepsilon_i$$

$$= \log\beta_0 + \beta_1 \log X_{1i} + \beta_2 \log X_{2i} + \log \varepsilon_i$$

Thus, Equation (15.5) is linear in the logarithms. Similarly, you can transform the exponential model shown in Equation (15.6) to linear form by taking the natural logarithm of both sides of the equation. Equation (15.7) is the transformed model.

ORIGINAL EXPONENTIAL MODEL

$$Y_i = e^{\beta_0 + \beta_1 X_{1i} + \beta_2 X_{2i}} \varepsilon_i \tag{15.6}$$

TRANSFORMED EXPONENTIAL MODEL

$$\ln Y_i = \ln\left(e^{\beta_0 + \beta_1 X_{1i} + \beta_2 X_{2i}} \varepsilon_i\right) \tag{15.7}$$

$$= \ln\left(e^{\beta_0 + \beta_1 X_{1i} + \beta_2 X_{2i}}\right) + \ln \varepsilon_i$$

$$= \beta_0 + \beta_1 X_{1i} + \beta_2 X_{2i} + \ln \varepsilon_i$$

Example 15.3 illustrates the use of a natural log transformation.

EXAMPLE 15.3

Using the Natural Log Transformation

Given the following values for Y and X, use a natural logarithm transformation for the Y variable:

Y	X	Y	X
0.7	1	4.8	3
0.5	1	12.9	4
1.6	2	11.5	4
1.8	2	32.1	5
4.2	3	33.9	5

Construct a scatter plot for X and Y and for X and the natural logarithm of Y.

SOLUTION As shown in Figure 15.9, the natural logarithm transformation has transformed a nonlinear relationship into a linear relationship.

FIGURE 15.9

Panel A: Scatter plot of X and Y; Panel B: Scatter plot of X and the natural logarithm of Y

Create scatter plots using the instructions in Section EG2.7.

Scatter Plot of X and Y

Scatter Plot of X and the Natural Logarithm of Y

Problems for Section 15.2

LEARNING THE BASICS

15.8 Consider the following regression equation:

$$\log \hat{Y}_i = \log 3.07 + 0.9 \log X_{1i} + 1.41 \log X_{2i}$$

a. Predict the value of Y when $X_1 = 8.5$ and $X_2 = 5.2$.
b. Interpret the meaning of the regression coefficients b_0, b_1, and b_2.

15.9 Consider the following regression equation:

$$\ln \hat{Y}_i = 4.62 + 0.5X_{1i} + 0.7X_{2i}$$

a. Predict the value of Y when $X_1 = 8.5$ and $X_2 = 5.2$.
b. Interpret the meaning of the regression coefficients b_0, b_1, and b_2.

APPLYING THE CONCEPTS

SELF Test **15.10** Using the data of Problem 15.4 on page 579, stored in **DomesticBeer**, perform a square-root transformation on each of the independent variables (percentage alcohol and number of carbohydrates). Using calories as the dependent variable and the transformed independent variables, perform a multiple regression analysis.

a. State the regression equation.

b. Perform a residual analysis of the results and determine whether the regression model is valid.

c. At the 0.05 level of significance, is there a significant relationship between calories and the square root of the percentage of alcohol and the square root of the number of carbohydrates?

d. Interpret the meaning of the coefficient of determination, r^2, in this problem.

e. Compute the adjusted r^2.

f. Compare your results with those in Problem 15.4. Which model is better? Why?

15.11 Using the data of Problem 15.4 on page 579, stored in DomesticBeer , perform a natural logarithmic transformation of the dependent variable (calories). Using the transformed dependent variable and the percentage of alcohol and the number of carbohydrates as the independent variables, perform a multiple regression analysis.

a. State the regression equation.

b. Perform a residual analysis of the results and determine whether the regression assumptions are valid.

c. At the 0.05 level of significance, is there a significant relationship between the natural logarithm of calories and the percentage of alcohol and the number of carbohydrates?

d. Interpret the meaning of the coefficient of determination, r^2, in this problem.

e. Compute the adjusted r^2.

f. Compare your results with those in Problems 15.4 and 15.10. Which model is best? Why?

15.12 Using the data of Problem 15.6 on page 579, stored in Tomato , perform a natural logarithm transformation of the dependent variable (yield). Using the transformed dependent variable and the fertilizer application rate as the independent variable, perform a regression analysis.

a. State the regression equation.

b. Predict the yield when 55 pounds of fertilizer is applied per 1,000 square feet.

c. Perform a residual analysis of the results and determine whether the regression assumptions are valid.

d. At the 0.05 level of significance, is there a significant relationship between the natural logarithm of yield and the fertilizer application rate?

e. Interpret the meaning of the coefficient of determination, r^2, in this problem.

f. Compute the adjusted r^2.

g. Compare your results with those in Problem 15.6. Which model is better? Why?

15.13 Using the data of Problem 15.6 on page 579, stored in Tomato , perform a square-root transformation of the independent variable (fertilizer application rate). Using yield as the dependent variable and the transformed independent variable, perform a regression analysis.

a. State the regression equation.

b. Predict the yield when 55 pounds of fertilizer is applied per 1,000 square feet.

c. Perform a residual analysis of the results and determine whether the regression model is valid.

d. At the 0.05 level of significance, is there a significant relationship between yield and the square root of the fertilizer application rate?

e. Interpret the meaning of the coefficient of determination, r^2, in this problem.

f. Compute the adjusted r^2.

g. Compare your results with those of Problems 15.6 and 15.12. Which model is best? Why?

h. How much fertilizer should you apply in order to grow the most tomatoes?

15.3 Collinearity

One important problem in the application of multiple regression analysis involves the possible **collinearity** of the independent variables. This condition refers to situations in which two or more of the independent variables are highly correlated with each other. In such situations, collinear variables do not provide unique information, and it becomes difficult to separate the effects of such variables on the dependent variable. When collinearity exists, the values of the regression coefficients for the correlated variables may fluctuate drastically, depending on which independent variables are included in the model.

One method of measuring collinearity is the **variance inflationary factor (VIF)** for each independent variable. Equation (15.8) defines VIF_j, the variance inflationary factor for variable j.

VARIANCE INFLATIONARY FACTOR

$$VIF_j = \frac{1}{1 - R_j^2}$$ (15.8)

where

R_j^2 is the coefficient of multiple determination for a regression model using variable X_j as the dependent variable and all other X variables as independent variables.

If there are only two independent variables, R_1^2 is the coefficient of determination between X_1 and X_2. It is identical to R_2^2, which is the coefficient of determination between X_2 and X_1. If there are three independent variables, then R_1^2 is the coefficient of multiple determination of X_1 with X_2 and X_3; R_2^2 is the coefficient of multiple determination of X_2 with X_1 and X_3; and R_3^2 is the coefficient of multiple determination of X_3 with X_1 and X_2.

If a set of independent variables is uncorrelated, each VIF_j is equal to 1. If the set is highly correlated, then a VIF_j might even exceed 10. Marquardt (see reference 2) suggests that if VIF_j is greater than 10, there is too much correlation between the variable X_j and the other independent variables. However, other statisticians suggest a more conservative criterion. Snee (see reference 4) recommends using alternatives to least-squares regression if the maximum VIF_j exceeds 5.

You need to proceed with extreme caution when using a multiple regression model that has one or more large VIF values. You can use the model to predict values of the dependent variable *only* in the case where the values of the independent variables used in the prediction are in the relevant range of the values in the data set. However, you cannot extrapolate to values of the independent variables not observed in the sample data. And because the independent variables contain overlapping information, you should always avoid interpreting the regression coefficient estimates separately because there is no way to accurately estimate the individual effects of the independent variables. One solution to the problem is to delete the variable with the largest VIF value. The reduced model (i.e., the model with the independent variable with the largest VIF value deleted) is often free of collinearity problems. If you determine that all the independent variables are needed in the model, you can use methods discussed in reference 1.

In the OmniPower sales data (see Section 14.1), the correlation between the two independent variables, price and promotional expenditure, is -0.0968. Because there are only two independent variables in the model, from Equation (15.8) on page 584:

$$VIF_1 = VIF_2 = \frac{1}{1 - (-0.0968)^2}$$
$$= 1.009$$

Thus, you can conclude that there is no problem with collinearity for the OmniPower sales data.

In models containing quadratic and interaction terms, collinearity is usually present. The linear and quadratic terms of an independent variable are usually highly correlated with each other, and an interaction term is often correlated with one or both of the independent variables making up the interaction. Thus, you cannot interpret individual parameter estimates separately. You need to interpret the linear and quadratic parameter estimates together in order to understand the nonlinear relationship. Likewise, you need to interpret an interaction parameter estimate in conjunction with the two parameter estimates associated with the variables comprising the interaction. In summary, large VIFs in quadratic or interaction models do not necessarily mean that the model is a poor one. They do, however, require you to carefully interpret the parameter estimates.

Problems for Section 15.3

LEARNING THE BASICS

15.14 If the coefficient of determination between two independent variables is 0.20, what is the VIF?

15.15 If the coefficient of determination between two independent variables is 0.50, what is the VIF?

APPLYING THE CONCEPTS

SELF Test **15.16** Refer to Problem 14.4 on page 532. Perform a multiple regression analysis using the data in WareCost and determine the VIF for each independent variable in the model. Is there reason to suspect the existence of collinearity?

15.17 Refer to Problem 14.5 on page 532. Perform a multiple regression analysis using the data in Auto and determine the *VIF* for each independent variable in the model. Is there reason to suspect the existence of collinearity?

15.18 Refer to Problem 14.6 on page 532. Perform a multiple regression analysis using the data in Advertise and determine the *VIF* for each independent variable in the model. Is there reason to suspect the existence of collinearity?

15.19 Refer to Problem 14.7 on page 533. Perform a multiple regression analysis using the data in Standby and determine the *VIF* for each independent variable in the model. Is there reason to suspect the existence of collinearity?

15.20 Refer to Problem 14.8 on page 533. Perform a multiple regression analysis using the data in GlenCove and determine the *VIF* for each independent variable in the model. Is there reason to suspect the existence of collinearity?

15.4 Model Building

This chapter and Chapter 14 have introduced you to many different topics in regression analysis, including quadratic terms, dummy variables, and interaction terms. In this section, you learn a structured approach to building the most appropriate regression model. As you will see, successful model building incorporates many of the topics you have studied so far.

To begin, refer to the WTT-TV scenario introduced on page 571, in which four independent variables (total staff present, remote hours, Dubner hours, and total labor hours) are considered in the business problem that involves developing a regression model to predict standby hours of unionized graphic artists. Data are collected over a period of 26 weeks and organized and stored in Standby. Table 15.2 summarizes the data.

TABLE 15.2

Predicting Standby Hours Based on Total Staff Present, Remote Hours, Dubner Hours, and Total Labor Hours

Week	Standby Hours	Total Staff Present	Remote Hours	Dubner Hours	Total Labor Hours
1	245	338	414	323	2,001
2	177	333	598	340	2,030
3	271	358	656	340	2,226
4	211	372	631	352	2,154
5	196	339	528	380	2,078
6	135	289	409	339	2,080
7	195	334	382	331	2,073
8	118	293	399	311	1,758
9	116	325	343	328	1,624
10	147	311	338	353	1,889
11	154	304	353	518	1,988
12	146	312	289	440	2,049
13	115	283	388	276	1,796
14	161	307	402	207	1,720
15	274	322	151	287	2,056
16	245	335	228	290	1,890
17	201	350	271	355	2,187
18	183	339	440	300	2,032
19	237	327	475	284	1,856
20	175	328	347	337	2,068
21	152	319	449	279	1,813
22	188	325	336	244	1,808
23	188	322	267	253	1,834
24	197	317	235	272	1,973
25	261	315	164	223	1,839
26	232	331	270	272	1,935

To develop a model to predict the dependent variable, standby hours in the WTT-TV scenario, you need to be guided by a general problem-solving strategy or *heuristic*. One heuristic appropriate for building regression models uses the principle of parsimony.

Parsimony guides you to select the regression model with the fewest independent variables that can predict the dependent variable adequately. Regression models with fewer independent variables are easier to interpret, particularly because they are less likely to be affected by collinearity problems (described in Section 15.3).

The selection of an appropriate model when many independent variables are under consideration involves complexities that are not present with a model that has only two independent variables. The evaluation of all possible regression models is more computationally complex. And, although you can quantitatively evaluate competing models, there may not be a *uniquely* best model but several *equally appropriate* models.

To begin analyzing the standby-hours data, you compute the variance inflationary factors [see Equation (15.8) on page 584] to measure the amount of collinearity among the independent variables. Panel A of Figure 15.10 shows a worksheet that summarizes the *VIF* computations. Panel B of Figure 15.10 shows the regression results worksheet for the model that uses the four independent variables and also shows a Durbin-Watson statistic worksheet for this model (inset).

FIGURE 15.10

Panel A:
VIF computational summary worksheet

Compute VIFs using the instructions in Section EG15.3.

Panel B:
Regression results worksheet for predicting standby hours based on four independent variables (with Durbin-Watson computation inset)

Create these worksheets using the instructions in Sections EG14.1 and EG13.6.

Observe that all the *VIF* values are relatively small, ranging from a high of 1.999 for the total labor hours to a low of 1.233 for remote hours. Thus, on the basis of the criteria developed by Snee that all *VIF* values should be less than 5.0 (see reference 4), there is little evidence of collinearity among the set of independent variables.

The Stepwise Regression Approach to Model Building

You continue your analysis of the standby-hours data by attempting to determine whether a subset of all independent variables yields an adequate and appropriate model. The first approach described here is **stepwise regression**, which attempts to find the "best" regression model without examining all possible models.

The first step of stepwise regression is to find the best model that uses one independent variable. The next step is to find the best of the remaining independent variables to add to the model selected in the first step. An important feature of the stepwise approach is that an independent variable that has entered into the model at an early stage may subsequently be removed after other independent variables are considered. Thus, in stepwise regression, variables are either added to or deleted from the regression model at each step of the model-building process. The t test for the slope (see Section 14.4) or the partial F_{STAT} test statistic (see Section 14.5) is used to determine whether variables are added or deleted. The stepwise procedure terminates with the selection of a best-fitting model when no additional variables can be added to or deleted from the last model evaluated. Figure 15.11 shows the stepwise regression results worksheet created by using PHStat2 for the standby-hours data.

FIGURE 15.11

Stepwise regression results worksheet for the standby-hours data

*Figure 15.11 displays a worksheet created by the PHStat2 **Stepwise Regression** procedure. Although the task of creating a stepwise results worksheet is not impossible to do manually, the decision-making inherent in adding and deleting variables and the need to cut-and-paste or delete partial regression results such as Figure 15.11 makes this task impractical by any other means in Excel.*

Create this worksheet using the PHStat2 instructions in Section EG15.4.

		df	SS	MS	F	Significance F	
Stepwise Analysis for Standby Hours							
Table of Results for General Stepwise							
Total Staff entered.							
		df	SS	MS	F	Significance F	
Regression		1	20667.3980	20667.3980	13.8563	0.0011	
Residual		24	35797.2174	1491.5507			
Total		25	56464.6154				
		Coefficients	Standard Error	t Stat	P-value	Lower 95%	Upper 95%
Intercept		-272.3816	124.2402	-2.1924	0.0383	-528.8008	-15.9625
Total Staff		1.4241	0.3826	3.7224	0.0011	0.6345	2.2136
Remote entered.							
		df	SS	MS	F	Significance F	
Regression		2	27662.5429	13831.2714	11.0450	0.0004	
Residual		23	28802.0725	1252.2640			
Total		25	56464.6154				
		Coefficients	Standard Error	t Stat	P-value	Lower 95%	Upper 95%
Intercept		-330.6748	116.4802	-2.8389	0.0093	-571.6322	-89.7175
Total Staff		1.7649	0.3790	4.6562	0.0001	0.9808	2.5490
Remote		-0.1390	0.0588	-2.3635	0.0269	-0.2606	-0.0173
No other variables could be entered into the model. Stepwise ends.							

For this example, a significance level of 0.05 is used to enter a variable into the model or to delete a variable from the model. The first variable entered into the model is total staff, the variable that correlates most highly with the dependent variable standby hours. Because the p-value of 0.0011 is less than 0.05, total staff is included in the regression model.

The next step involves selecting a second independent variable for the model. The second variable chosen is one that makes the largest contribution to the model, given that the first variable has been selected. For this model, the second variable is remote hours. Because the p-value of 0.0269 for remote hours is less than 0.05, remote hours is included in the regression model.

After the remote hours variable is entered into the model, the stepwise procedure determines whether total staff is still an important contributing variable or whether it can be eliminated from the model. Because the *p*-value of 0.0001 for total staff is less than 0.05, total staff remains in the regression model.

The next step involves selecting a third independent variable for the model. Because none of the other variables meets the 0.05 criterion for entry into the model, the stepwise procedure terminates with a model that includes total staff present and the number of remote hours.

This stepwise regression approach to model building was originally developed more than four decades ago, when regression computations on computers were time-consuming and costly. Although stepwise regression limited the evaluation of alternative models, the method was deemed a good tradeoff of evaluation and cost.

Given the ability of today's computers to perform regression computations at very low cost and high speed, stepwise regression has been superseded to some extent with the best-subsets approach, discussed next, which evaluates a larger set of alternative models. Stepwise regression is not obsolete, however. Today, many businesses use stepwise regression as part of the research technique called **data mining**, which tries to identify significant statistical relationships in very large data sets that contain extremely large numbers of variables.

The Best-Subsets Approach to Model Building

The **best-subsets approach** evaluates all possible regression models for a given set of independent variables. Figure 15.12 presents a best-subsets regression result worksheet of all possible regression models for the standby-hours data.

FIGURE 15.12

Best-subsets regression results worksheet for the standby-hours data

Figure 15.12 displays a worksheet created by the PHStat2 **Best Subsets** procedure. Although the task of creating a best-subsets results worksheet is not impossible to do manually, the need to create regression results worksheets for every possible combination of variables and the need to report results to a worksheet such as Figure 15.12, makes this task impractical by any other means in Excel.

Create this worksheet using the PHStat2 instructions in Section EG15.4.

	A	B	C	D	E	F
1	Best Subsets Analysis for Standby Hours					
2						
3	Intermediate Calculations					
4	R2T	0.6231				
5	1 - R2T	0.3769				
6	n	26				
7	T	5				
8	n - T	21				
9						
10	Model	Cp	k+1	R Square	Adj. R Square	Std. Error
11	X1	13.3215	2	0.3660	0.3396	38.6206
12	X1X2	8.4193	3	0.4899	0.4456	35.3873
13	X1X2X3	7.8418	4	0.5362	0.4729	34.5029
14	X1X2X3X4	5.0000	5	0.6231	0.5513	31.8350
15	X1X2X4	9.3449	4	0.5092	0.4423	35.4921
16	X1X3	10.6486	3	0.4499	0.4021	36.7490
17	X1X3X4	7.7517	4	0.5378	0.4748	34.4426
18	X1X4	14.7982	3	0.3754	0.3211	39.1579
19	X2	33.2078	2	0.0091	-0.0322	48.2836
20	X2X3	32.3067	3	0.0612	-0.0205	48.0087
21	X2X3X4	12.1381	4	0.4591	0.3853	37.2608
22	X2X4	23.2481	3	0.2238	0.1563	43.6540
23	X3	30.3884	2	0.0597	0.0205	47.0345
24	X3X4	11.8231	3	0.4288	0.3791	37.4466
25	X4	24.1846	2	0.1710	0.1365	44.1619

A criterion often used in model building is the adjusted r^2, which adjusts the r^2 of each model to account for the number of independent variables in the model as well as for the sample size (see Section 14.2). Because model building requires you to compare models with different numbers of independent variables, the adjusted r^2 is more appropriate than r^2.

Referring to Figure 15.12, you see that the adjusted r^2 reaches a maximum value of 0.5513 when all four independent variables plus the intercept term (for a total of five estimated parameters) are included in the model.

A second criterion often used in the evaluation of competing models is the C_p statistic developed by Mallows (see reference 1). The **C_p statistic**, defined in Equation (15.9), measures the differences between a fitted regression model and a *true* model, along with random error.

C_p STATISTIC

$$C_p = \frac{(1 - R_k^2)(n - T)}{1 - R_T^2} - [n - 2(k + 1)] \tag{15.9}$$

where

k = number of independent variables included in a regression model

T = total number of parameters (including the intercept) to be estimated in the full regression model

R_k^2 = coefficient of multiple determination for a regression model that has k independent variables

R_T^2 = coefficient of multiple determination for a full regression model that contains all T estimated parameters

Using Equation (15.9) to compute C_p for the model containing total staff and remote hours,

$$n = 26 \quad k = 2 \quad T = 4 + 1 = 5 \quad R_k^2 = 0.4899 \quad R_T^2 = 0.6231$$

so that

$$C_p = \frac{(1 - 0.4899)(26 - 5)}{1 - 0.6231} - [26 - 2(2 + 1)]$$

$$= 8.4193$$

When a regression model with k independent variables contains only random differences from a *true* model, the mean value of C_p is $k + 1$, the number of parameters. Thus, in evaluating many alternative regression models, the goal is to find models whose C_p is close to or less than $k + 1$. In Figure 15.12 on page 589, you see that only the model with all four independent variables considered contains a C_p value close to or below $k + 1$. Therefore, using the C_p criterion, you should choose that model.

Although it was not the case here, the C_p statistic often provides several alternative models for you to evaluate in greater depth. Moreover, the best model or models using the C_p criterion might differ from the model selected using the adjusted r^2 and/or the model selected using the stepwise procedure. (Note here that the model selected using stepwise regression has a C_p value of 8.4193, which is substantially above the suggested criterion of $k + 1 = 3$ for that model.) Remember that there may not be a uniquely best model, but there may be several equally appropriate models. Final model selection often involves using subjective criteria, such as parsimony, interpretability, and departure from model assumptions (as evaluated by residual analysis).

When you have finished selecting the independent variables to include in the model, you should perform a residual analysis to evaluate the regression assumptions, and because the data were collected in time order, you also need to compute the Durbin-Watson statistic to determine whether there is autocorrelation in the residuals (see Section 13.6). From Panel *B* of Figure 15.10 on page 587, you see that the Durbin-Watson statistic, *D*, is 2.2197. Because *D* is greater than 2.0, there is no indication of positive correlation in the residuals. Figure 15.13 (on pages 591 and 592) presents the residual plots used in the residual analysis.

None of the residual plots versus the total staff, the remote hours, the Dubner hours, and the total labor hours reveal apparent patterns. In addition, a histogram of the residuals (not shown here) indicates only moderate departure from normality, and a plot of the residuals versus the predicted values of Y (also not shown here) does not show evidence of unequal variance. Thus, from Figure 15.10 on page 587, the regression equation is

$$\hat{Y}_i = -330.8318 + 1.2456X_{1i} - 0.1184X_{2i} - 0.2971X_{3i} + 0.1305X_{4i}$$

Example 15.4 on page 592 presents a situation in which there are several alternative models in which the C_p statistic is close to or less than $k + 1$.

FIGURE 15.13

Residual plots for the standby-hours data

Create residual plots using the instructions in Section EG13.5.

FIGURE 15.13
(Continued)

Dubner Residual Plot

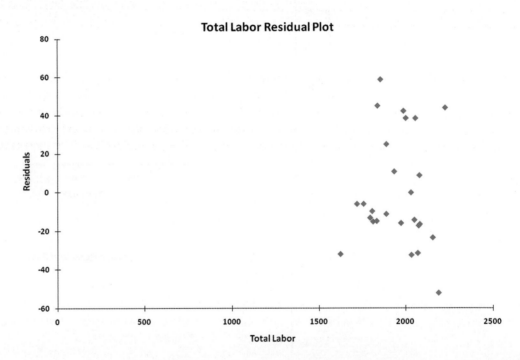

Total Labor Residual Plot

EXAMPLE 15.4

Choosing Among Alternative Regression Models

Table 15.3 on page 592 shows results from a best-subsets regression analysis of a regression model with seven independent variables. Determine which regression model you would choose as the *best* model.

SOLUTION From Table 15.3, you need to determine which models have C_p values that are less than or close to $k + 1$. Two models meet this criterion. The model with six independent variables $(X_1, X_2, X_3, X_4, X_5, X_6)$ has a C_p value of 6.8, which is less than $k + 1 = 6 + 1 = 7$, and the full model with seven independent variables $(X_1, X_2, X_3, X_4, X_5, X_6, X_7)$ has a C_p value of 8.0. One way you can choose among the two models is to select the model with the largest adjusted r^2—that is, the model with six independent variables. Another way to select a final model is to determine whether the models contain a subset of variables that are common. Then you test whether the contribution of the additional variables is significant. In this case,

TABLE 15.3

Partial Results from Best-Subsets Regression

Number of Variables	r^2	Adjusted r^2	C_p	Variables Included
1	0.121	0.119	113.9	X_4
1	0.093	0.090	130.4	X_1
1	0.083	0.080	136.2	X_3
2	0.214	0.210	62.1	X_3, X_4
2	0.191	0.186	75.6	X_1, X_3
2	0.181	0.177	81.0	X_1, X_4
3	0.285	0.280	22.6	X_1, X_3, X_4
3	0.268	0.263	32.4	X_3, X_4, X_5
3	0.240	0.234	49.0	X_2, X_3, X_4
4	0.308	0.301	11.3	X_1, X_2, X_3, X_4
4	0.304	0.297	14.0	X_1, X_3, X_4, X_6
4	0.296	0.289	18.3	X_1, X_3, X_4, X_5
5	0.317	0.308	8.2	X_1, X_2, X_3, X_4, X_5
5	0.315	0.306	9.6	X_1, X_2, X_3, X_4, X_6
5	0.313	0.304	10.7	X_1, X_3, X_4, X_5, X_6
6	0.323	0.313	6.8	$X_1, X_2, X_3, X_4, X_5, X_6$
6	0.319	0.309	9.0	$X_1, X_2, X_3, X_4, X_5, X_7$
6	0.317	0.306	10.4	$X_1, X_2, X_3, X_4, X_6, X_7$
7	0.324	0.312	8.0	$X_1, X_2, X_3, X_4, X_5, X_6, X_7$

because the models differ only by the inclusion of variable X_7 in the full model, you test whether variable X_7 makes a significant contribution to the regression model, given that the variables X_1, X_2, X_3, X_4, X_5, and X_6 are already included in the model. If the contribution is statistically significant, then you should include variable X_7 in the regression model. If variable X_7 does not make a statistically significant contribution, you should not include it in the model.

Exhibit 15.1 summarizes the steps involved in model building.

EXHIBIT 15.1

Steps Involved in Model Building

1. Compile a list of all independent variables under consideration.
2. Fit a regression model that includes all the independent variables under consideration and determine the *VIF* for each independent variable. Three possible results can occur:
   a. None of the independent variables has a *VIF* > 5; in this case, proceed to step 3.
   b. One of the independent variables has a *VIF* > 5; in this case, eliminate that independent variable and proceed to step 3.
   c. More than one of the independent variables has a *VIF* > 5; in this case, eliminate the independent variable that has the highest *VIF* and repeat step 2.
3. Perform a best-subsets regression with the remaining independent variables and determine the C_p statistic and/or the adjusted r^2 for each model.
4. List all models that have C_p close to or less than $k + 1$ and/or a high adjusted r^2.
5. From the models listed in step 4, choose a best model.
6. Perform a complete analysis of the model chosen, including a residual analysis.
7. Depending on the results of the residual analysis, add quadratic and/or interaction terms, transform variables, and reanalyze the data.
8. Use the selected model for prediction and inference.

Figure 15.14 represents a roadmap for the steps involved in model building.

FIGURE 15.14
Roadmap for model building

Model Validation

The final step in the model-building process is to validate the selected regression model. This step involves checking the model against data that were not part of the sample analyzed. The following are several ways of validating a regression model:

- Collect new data and compare the results.
- Compare the results of the regression model to previous results.
- If the data set is large, split the data into two parts and cross-validate the results.

Perhaps the best way of validating a regression model is by collecting new data. If the results with new data are consistent with the selected regression model, you have strong reason to believe that the fitted regression model is applicable in a wide set of circumstances.

If it is not possible to collect new data, you can use one of the two other approaches. In one approach, you compare your regression coefficients and predictions to previous results. If the data set is large, you can use **cross-validation**. First, you split the data into two parts. Then you use the first part of the data to develop the regression model. You then use the second part of the data to evaluate the predictive ability of the regression model.

Problems for Section 15.4

LEARNING THE BASICS

15.21 You are considering four independent variables for inclusion in a regression model. You select a sample of 30 observations, with the following results:
1. The model that includes independent variables A and B has a C_p value equal to 4.6.
2. The model that includes independent variables A and C has a C_p value equal to 2.4.
3. The model that includes independent variables A, B, and C has a C_p value equal to 2.7.
   a. Which models meet the criterion for further consideration? Explain.
   b. How would you compare the model that contains independent variables A, B, and C to the model that contains independent variables A and B? Explain.

15.22 You are considering six independent variables for inclusion in a regression model. You select a sample of 40 observations, with the following results:

$$n = 40 \quad k = 2 \quad T = 6 + 1 = 7 \quad R_k^2 = 0.274 \quad R_T^2 = 0.653$$

a. Compute the C_p value for this two-independent-variable model.
b. Based on your answer to (a), does this model meet the criterion for further consideration as the best model? Explain.

APPLYING THE CONCEPTS

15.23 In Problems 13.85–13.89 on page 518, you constructed simple linear regression models to investigate the relationship between demographic information and monthly sales for a chain of sporting goods stores using the data in Sporting. Develop the most appropriate multiple regression model to predict a store's monthly sales. Be sure to include a thorough residual analysis. In addition, provide a detailed explanation of the results, including a comparison of the most appropriate multiple regression model to the best simple linear regression model.

15.24 You need to develop a model to predict the selling price of houses in a small city, based on assessed value, time period in which a house is sold, and whether the house is new (0 = no; 1 = yes). A sample of 30 recently sold single-family houses that were reassessed at full value one year prior to the study is selected and the results are stored in House1. Develop the most appropriate multiple regression model to predict selling price. Be sure to perform a thorough residual analysis. In addition, provide a detailed explanation of the results.

15.25 The human resources (HR) director for a large company that produces highly technical industrial instrumentation devices has the business objective of improving recruiting decisions concerning sales managers. The company has 45 sales regions, each headed by a sales manager. Many of the sales managers have degrees in electrical engineering and, due to the technical nature of the product line, several company officials believe that only applicants with degrees in electrical engineering should be considered. At the time of their application, candidates are asked to take the Strong-Campbell Interest Inventory Test and the Wonderlic Personnel Test. Due to the time and money involved with the testing, some discussion has taken place about dropping one or both of the tests. To start, the HR director gathered information on each of the 45 current sales managers, including years of selling experience, electrical engineering background, and the scores from both the Wonderlic and Strong-Campbell tests. The HR director has decided to use regression modeling to predict a dependent variable of "sales index" score, which is the ratio of the regions' actual sales divided by the target sales. The target values are constructed each year by upper management, in consultation with the sales managers, and are based on past performance and market potential within each region. The file Managers contains information on the 45 current sales managers. The following variables are included:

Sales—Ratio of yearly sales divided by the target sales value for that region. The target values were mutually agreed-upon "realistic expectations."
Wonder—Score from the Wonderlic Personnel Test. The higher the score, the higher the applicant's perceived ability to manage.
SC—Score on the Strong-Campbell Interest Inventory Test. The higher the score, the higher the applicant's perceived interest in sales.
Experience—Number of years of selling experience prior to becoming a sales manager.
Engineer—Dummy variable that equals 1 if the sales manager has a degree in electrical engineering and 0 otherwise.

a. Develop the most appropriate regression model to predict sales.

b. Do you think that the company should continue administering both the Wonderlic and Strong-Campbell tests? Explain.

c. Do the data support the argument that electrical engineers outperform the other sales managers? Would you support the idea to hire only electrical engineers? Explain.

d. How important is prior selling experience in this case? Explain.

e. Discuss in detail how the HR director should incorporate the regression model you developed into the recruiting process.

15.5 Pitfalls in Multiple Regression and Ethical Issues

Pitfalls in Multiple Regression

Model building is an art as well as a science. Different individuals may not always agree on the best multiple regression model. To try to find a best regression model, you should use the process described in Exhibit 15.1 on page 593. In doing so, you must avoid certain pitfalls that can interfere with the development of a useful model. Section 13.9 discussed pitfalls in simple linear regression and strategies for avoiding them. Now that you have studied a variety of multiple regression models, you need to take some additional precautions. To avoid pitfalls in multiple regression, you also need to

- Interpret the regression coefficient for a particular independent variable from a perspective in which the values of all other independent variables are held constant.
- Evaluate residual plots for each independent variable.
- Evaluate interaction and quadratic terms.
- Compute the *VIF* for each independent variable before determining which independent variables to include in the model.
- Examine several alternative models, using best-subsets regression.
- Validate the model before implementing it.

Ethical Issues

Ethical issues arise when a user who wants to make predictions manipulates the development process of the multiple regression model. The key here is intent. In addition to the situations discussed in Section 13.9, unethical behavior occurs when someone uses multiple regression analysis and *willfully fails* to remove from consideration variables that exhibit a high collinearity with other independent variables or *willfully fails* to use methods other than least-squares regression when the assumptions necessary for least-squares regression are seriously violated.

USING STATISTICS @ WTT-TV Revisited

In the Using Statistics scenario, you were the operations manager of WTT-TV, looking for ways to reduce labor expenses. You needed to determine which variables have an effect on standby hours, the time during which unionized graphic artists are idle but are getting paid. You have collected data concerning standby hours and the total number of staff present, remote hours, Dubner hours, and total labor hours over a period of 26 weeks.

You performed a multiple regression analysis on the data. The coefficient of multiple determination indicated that 62.31% of the variation in standby hours can be explained by variation in the total number of staff present, remote hours, Dubner hours, and total labor hours. The model indicated that standby hours are estimated to increase by 1.2456 hours for each additional staff hour holding constant the other independent variables; to decrease by 0.1184 hour for each additional remote hour holding constant the other independent variables; to decrease by 0.2974 hour for each additional Dubner hour holding constant the other independent variables; and to increase by 0.1305 hour for each additional labor hour holding constant the other independent variables. Each of the four independent variables had a significant effect on standby hours holding constant the other independent variables. This regression model enables you to predict standby hours based on the total number of staff present, remote hours, Dubner hours, and total labor hours. It also enables you to investigate how changing each of these four independent variables could affect standby hours.

SUMMARY

In this chapter, various multiple regression topics were considered (see Figure 15.15), including quadratic regression models, transformations, collinearity, and model building.

FIGURE 15.15

Roadmap for multiple regression

KEY EQUATIONS

Quadratic Regression Model

$$Y_i = \beta_0 + \beta_1 X_{1i} + \beta_2 X_{1i}^2 + \varepsilon_i \tag{15.1}$$

Quadratic Regression Equation

$$\hat{Y}_i = b_0 + b_1 X_{1i} + b_2 X_{1i}^2 \tag{15.2}$$

Regression Model with a Square-Root Transformation

$$Y_i = \beta_0 + \beta_1 \sqrt{X_{1i}} + \varepsilon_i \tag{15.3}$$

Original Multiplicative Model

$$Y_i = \beta_0 X_{1i}^{\beta_1} X_{2i}^{\beta_2} \varepsilon_i \tag{15.4}$$

Transformed Multiplicative Model

$$\log Y_i = \log(\beta_0 X_{1i}^{\beta_1} X_{2i}^{\beta_2} \varepsilon_i) \tag{15.5}$$
$$= \log \beta_0 + \log(X_{1i}^{\beta_1}) + \log(X_{2i}^{\beta_2}) + \log \varepsilon_i$$
$$= \log \beta_0 + \beta_1 \log X_{1i} + \beta_2 \log X_{2i} + \log \varepsilon_i$$

Original Exponential Model

$$Y_i = e^{\beta_0 + \beta_1 X_{1i} + \beta_2 X_{2i}} \varepsilon_i \tag{15.6}$$

Transformed Exponential Model

$$\ln Y_i = \ln(e^{\beta_0 + \beta_1 X_{1i} + \beta_2 X_{2i}} \varepsilon_i) \tag{15.7}$$
$$= \ln(e^{\beta_0 + \beta_1 X_{1i} + \beta_2 X_{2i}}) + \ln \varepsilon_i$$
$$= \beta_0 + \beta_1 X_{1i} + \beta_2 X_{2i} + \ln \varepsilon_i$$

Variance Inflationary Factor

$$VIF_j = \frac{1}{1 - R_j^2} \tag{15.8}$$

C_p Statistic

$$C_p = \frac{(1 - R_k^2)(n - T)}{1 - R_T^2} - [n - 2(k + 1)] \tag{15.9}$$

KEY TERMS

best-subsets approach 589
C_p statistic 590
collinearity 584
cross-validation 595

data mining 589
logarithmic transformation 581
parsimony 587
quadratic regression model 572

square-root transformation 580
stepwise regression 588
variance inflationary
    factor (*VIF*) 584

CHAPTER REVIEW PROBLEMS

CHECKING YOUR UNDERSTANDING

15.26 How can you evaluate whether collinearity exists in a multiple regression model?

15.27 What is the difference between stepwise regression and best-subsets regression?

15.28 How do you choose among models according to the C_p statistic in best-subsets regression?

APPLYING THE CONCEPTS

15.29 Crazy Dave has expanded his analysis, presented in Problem 14.63 on page 563, of which variables are important

in predicting a team's wins in a given baseball season. He has collected data in BB2008 related to wins, ERA, saves, runs scored, hits allowed, walks allowed, and errors for the 2008 season.

a. Develop the most appropriate multiple regression model to predict a team's wins. Be sure to include a thorough residual analysis. In addition, provide a detailed explanation of the results.

b. Develop the most appropriate multiple regression model to predict a team's ERA on the basis of hits allowed, walks allowed, errors, and saves. Be sure to include a thorough residual analysis. In addition, provide a detailed explanation of the results.

15.30 Professional basketball has truly become a sport that generates interest among fans around the world. More and more players come from outside the United States to play in the National Basketball Association (NBA). Many factors could impact the number of wins achieved by each NBA team. In addition to the number of wins, the file NBA2009 contains team statistics for points per game (for team, opponent, and the difference between team and opponent), field goal (shots made) percentage (for team, opponent, and the difference between team and opponent), turnovers (losing the ball before a shot is taken) per game (for team, opponent, and the difference between team and opponent), offensive rebound percentage, and defensive rebound percentage.
a. Consider team points per game, opponent points per game, team field goal percentage, opponent field goal percentage, difference in team and opponent turnovers, offensive rebound percentage, and defensive rebound percentage as independent variables for possible inclusion in the multiple regression model. Develop the most appropriate multiple regression model to predict the number of wins.
b. Consider the difference between team points and opponent points per game, the difference between team field goal percentage and opponent field goal percentage, the difference in team and opponent turnovers, offensive rebound percentage, and defensive rebound percentage as independent variables for possible inclusion in the multiple regression model. Develop the most appropriate multiple regression model to predict the number of wins.
c. Compare the results of (a) and (b). Which model is better for predicting the number of wins? Explain.

15.31 Hemlock Farms is a community located in the Pocono Mountains area of eastern Pennsylvania. The file HemlockFarms contains information on homes that were for sale as of July 4, 2006. The variables included were

List Price—Asking price of the house
Hot Tub—Whether the house has a hot tub, with 0 = No and 1 = Yes
Lake View—Whether the house has a lake view, with 0 = No and 1 = Yes
Bathrooms—Number of bathrooms
Bedrooms—Number of bedrooms
Loft/Den—Whether the house has a loft or den, with 0 = No and 1 = Yes
Finished basement—Whether the house has a finished basement, with 0 = No and 1 = Yes
Acres—Number of acres for the property

Develop the most appropriate multiple regression model to predict the asking price. Be sure to perform a thorough residual analysis. In addition, provide a detailed explanation of your results.

15.32 Nassau County is located approximately 25 miles east of New York City. Data in GlenCove are from a sample of 30 single-family homes located in Glen Cove. Variables included are the appraised value, land area of the property (acres), interior size of the house (square feet), age (years), number of rooms, number of bathrooms, and number of cars that can be parked in the garage.
a. Develop the most appropriate multiple regression model to predict appraised value.
b. Compare the results in (a) with those of Problems 15.33 (a) and 15.34 (a).

15.33 Data similar to those in Problem 15.32 are available for homes located in Roslyn and are stored in Roslyn.
a. Perform an analysis similar to that of Problem 15.32.
b. Compare the results in (a) with those of Problems 15.32 (a) and 15.34 (a).

15.34 Data similar to Problem 15.32 are available for homes located in Freeport and are stored in Freeport.
a. Perform an analysis similar to that of Problem 15.32.
b. Compare the results in (a) with those of Problems 15.32 (a) and 15.33 (a).

15.35 You are a real estate broker who wants to compare property values in Glen Cove and Roslyn (which are located approximately 8 miles apart). Use the data in GCRoslyn. Make sure to include the dummy variable for location (Glen Cove or Roslyn) in the regression model.
a. Develop the most appropriate multiple regression model to predict appraised value.
b. What conclusions can you reach concerning the differences in appraised value between Glen Cove and Roslyn?

15.36 You are a real estate broker who wants to compare property values in Glen Cove, Freeport, and Roslyn. Use the data in GCFreeRoslyn.
a. Develop the most appropriate multiple regression model to predict appraised value.
b. What conclusions can you reach concerning the differences in appraised value between Glen Cove, Freeport, and Roslyn?

15.37 Over the past 30 years, public awareness and concern about air pollution have escalated dramatically. Venturi scrubbers are used for the removal of submicron particulate matter from smoke stacks. An experiment was conducted to determine the effect of air flow rate, water flow rate (liters/minute), recirculating water flow rate (liters/minute), and orifice size (mm) in the air side of the pneumatic nozzle on the performance of the scrubber, as measured by the number of transfer units. The results are stored in Scrubber.
Develop the most appropriate multiple regression model to predict the number of transfer units. Be sure to perform a thorough residual analysis. In addition, provide a detailed explanation of your results.

Source: *Data extracted from D. A. Marshall, R. J. Sumner, and C. A. Shook, "Removal of SiO$_2$ Particles with an Ejector Venturi Scrubber,"* Environmental Progress, *14 (1995), 28–32.*

15.38 A recent article (data extracted from J. Conklin, "It's a Marathon, Not a Sprint," *Quality Progress*, June 2009, pp. 46–49) discussed a metal deposition process in which a piece of metal is placed in an acid bath and an alloy is layered on top of it. The key quality characteristic is the thickness of the alloy layer. The file Thickness contains the following variables:

Thickness—Thickness of the alloy layer
Catalyst—Catalyst concentration in the acid bath
pH—pH level of the acid bath
Pressure—Pressure in the tank holding the acid bath
Temp—Temperature in the tank holding the acid bath
Voltage—Voltage applied to the tank holding the acid bath

Develop the most appropriate multiple regression model to predict the thickness of the alloy layer. Be sure to perform a thorough residual analysis. The article suggests that there is a significant interaction between the pressure and the temperature in the tank. Do you agree?

15.39 A headline on page 1 of *The New York Times* on March 4, 1990, read: "Wine equation puts some noses out of joint." The article explained that Professor Orley Ashenfelter, a Princeton University economist, had developed a multiple regression model to predict the quality of French Bordeaux, based on the amount of winter rain, the average temperature during the growing season, and the harvest rain. The multiple regression equation is

$$Q = -12.145 + 0.00117WR + 0.6164TMP - 0.00386HR$$

where

Q = logarithmic index of quality

WR = winter rain (October through March), in millimeters

TMP = average temperature during the growing season (April through September), in degrees Celsius

HR = harvest rain (August to September), in millimeters

You are at a cocktail party, sipping a glass of wine, when one of your friends mentions to you that she has read the article. She asks you to explain the meaning of the coefficients in the equation and also asks you about analyses that might have been done and were not included in the article. What is your reply?

REPORT WRITING EXERCISES

15.40 In Problem 15.23 on page 595, you developed a multiple regression model to predict monthly sales at sporting goods stores for the data stored in Sporting. Now write a report based on the model you developed. Append all appropriate charts and statistical information to your report.

TEAM PROJECT

15.41 The file Bond Funds contains information regarding eight variables from a sample of 180 mutual funds:

Type—Type of bonds comprising the bond fund (intermediate government or short-term corporate)
Assets—In millions of dollars
Fees—Sales charges (no or yes)
Expense ratio—Ratio of expenses to net assets in percentage
Return 2008—Twelve-month return in 2008
Three-year return—Annualized return, 2006–2008
Five-year return—Annualized return, 2004–2008
Risk—Risk-of-loss factor of the mutual fund (below average, average, or above average)

Develop regression models to predict the 2008 return, the three-year return, and the five-year return, based on fees, expense ratio, type, and risk. (For the purpose of this analysis, combine below-average risk and average risk into one category.) Be sure to perform a thorough residual analysis. In addition, provide a detailed explanation of your results. Append all appropriate charts and statistical information to your report.

THE MOUNTAIN STATES POTATO COMPANY

Mountain States Potato Company sells a by-product of its potato-processing operation, called a filter cake, to area feedlots as cattle feed. The business problem faced by the feedlot owners is that the cattle are not gaining weight as quickly as they once were. The feedlot owners believe that the root cause of the problem is that the percentage of solids in the filter cake is too low.

Historically, the percentage of solids in the filter cakes ran slightly above 12%. Lately, however, the solids are running in the 11% range. What is actually affecting the solids is a mystery, but something has to be done quickly. Individuals involved in the process were asked to identify variables that might affect the percentage of solids. This review turned up the six variables (in addition to the percentage of solids) listed in the table on page 601. Data collected by monitoring the process several times daily for 20 days are stored in Potato.

Variable	Comments
SOLIDS	Percentage solids in the filter cake.
PH	Acidity. This measure of acidity indicates bacterial action in the clarifier and is controlled by the amount of downtime in the system. As bacterial action progresses, organic acids are produced that can be measured using pH.
LOWER	Pressure of the vacuum line below the fluid line on the rotating drum.
UPPER	Pressure of the vacuum line above the fluid line on the rotating drum.
THICK	Filter cake thickness, measured on the drum.
VARIDRIV	Setting used to control the drum speed. May differ from DRUMSPD due to mechanical inefficiencies.
DRUMSPD	Speed at which the drum is rotating when collecting the filter cake. Measured with a stopwatch.

1. Thoroughly analyze the data and develop a regression model to predict the percentage of solids.
2. Write an executive summary concerning your findings to the president of the Mountain States Potato Company.

Include specific recommendations on how to get the percentage of solids back above 12%.

WEB CASE

Apply your knowledge of multiple regression model building in this Web Case, which extends the Chapter 14 OmniFoods Using Statistics scenario.

Still concerned about ensuring a successful test marketing of its OmniPower energy bars, the marketing department of OmniFoods has contacted Connect2Coupons (C2C), another merchandising consultancy. C2C suggests that earlier analysis done by In-Store Placements Group (ISPG) was faulty because it did not use the correct type of data. C2C claims that its Internet-based viral marketing will have an even greater effect on OmniPower energy bar sales, as new data from the same 34-store sample will show. In response, ISPG says its earlier claims are valid and has reported to the OmniFoods marketing department that it can discern no simple relationship between C2C's viral marketing and increased OmniPower sales.

Using a Web browser, open to the Web page for the Chapter 15 Web Case (or open **Omni_OmniPowerMB.htm** if you have downloaded the Web Case files) to review all these claims on the message board at the OmniFoods internal Web site. Then answer the following:

1. Which of the claims are true? False? True but misleading? Support your answer by performing an appropriate statistical analysis.
2. If the grocery store chain allowed OmniFoods to use an unlimited number of sales techniques, which techniques should it use? Explain.
3. If the grocery store chain allowed OmniFoods to use only one sales technique, which technique should it use? Explain.

REFERENCES

1. Kutner, M., C. Nachtsheim, J. Neter, and W. Li, *Applied Linear Statistical Models*, 5th ed. (New York: McGraw-Hill/Irwin, 2005).
2. Marquardt, D. W., "You Should Standardize the Predictor Variables in Your Regression Models," discussion of "A Critique of Some Ridge Regression Methods," by G. Smith and F. Campbell, *Journal of the American Statistical Association*, 75 (1980), 87–91.
3. *Microsoft Excel 2007* (Redmond, WA: Microsoft Corp., 2007).
4. Snee, R. D., "Some Aspects of Nonorthogonal Data Analysis, Part I. Developing Prediction Equations," *Journal of Quality Technology*, 5 (1973), 67–79.

CHAPTER 15 EXCEL GUIDE

EG15.1 The QUADRATIC REGRESSION MODEL

Creating a Quadratic Term

To create a quadratic term, to the worksheet that contains your regression data, add a new column of formulas that compute the square of one of the independent variables.

For example, to create a quadratic term for the Section 15.1 fly ash example, open to the **DATA worksheet** of the **FlyAsh workbook**. That worksheet contains the independent variable **FlyAsh%** in column A and the dependent variable **Strength** in column B. While the quadratic term **FlyAsh%^2** could be created in any column, a good practice is to place independent variables in contiguous columns. (This is mandatory if you are using the Analysis ToolPak Regression procedure). To do so, first select column B (**Strength**), right-click, and click **Insert** from the shortcut menu to add a new column B. (Strength becomes column C.) Enter the label **FlyAsh%^2** in cell B1 and then enter the formula $=A2^2$ in cell **B2**. Copy this formula down the column through all the data rows.

EG15.2 USING TRANSFORMATIONS in REGRESSION MODELS

The Square-Root Transformation

To create a square-root transformation, to the worksheet that contains your regression data, add a new column of formulas that compute the square root of one of the independent variables. For example, to create a square root transformation in a blank column D for an independent variable in a column C, enter the formula $=\mathbf{SQRT(C2)}$ in cell D2 of that worksheet and copy the formula down through all data rows. If the rightmost column in the worksheet contains the dependent variable, first select that column, right-click, and click **Insert** from the shortcut menu and place the transformation in that new column.

The Log Transformation

To create a log transformation, to the worksheet that contains your regression data, add a new column of formulas that compute the common (base 10) logarithm or natural logarithm of one of the independent variables. For example, to create a common logarithm transformation in a blank column D for an independent variable in a column C, enter the formula $=\mathbf{LOG(C2)}$ in cell D2 of that worksheet and copy the

formula down through all data rows. To create a natural logarithm transformation in a blank column D for an independent variable in a column C, enter the formula $=\mathbf{LN(C2)}$ in cell D2 of that worksheet and copy the formula down through all data rows.

If the rightmost column in the worksheet contains the dependent variable, first select that column, right-click, and click **Insert** from the shortcut menu and place the transformation in that new column.

EG15.3 COLLINEARITY

PHStat2 Use the Section EG14.1 "Interpreting the Regression Coefficients" *PHStat2* instructions on page 566 but modify step 6 by checking **Variance Inflationary Factor** (*VIF*) before you click **OK**. The *VIF* will appear in cell B9 of the regression results worksheets, immediately following the Regression Statistics area.

In-Depth Excel To compute the variance inflationary factor, first use the Section EG14.1 "Interpreting the Regression Coefficients" *In-Depth Excel* instructions on page 566 to create regression results worksheets for every combination of independent variables in which one serves as the dependent variable. Then, in each of the regression results worksheets, enter the label *VIF* in cell **A9** and enter the formula $=1/(1-\mathbf{B5})$ in cell **B9** to compute the *VIF*.

EG15.4 MODEL BUILDING

The Stepwise Regression Approach to Model Building

PHStat2 Use the **Stepwise Regression** procedure to use a stepwise regression approach to model building. For example, to use the stepwise approach with the Table 15.2 hourly data for unionized graphic artists on page 586, open to the **DATA worksheet** of the **Standby workbook**. Select **PHStat → Regression → Stepwise Regression**. In the procedure's dialog box (on page 603):

1. Enter **A1:A27** as the **Y Variable Cell Range**.
2. Enter **B1:E27** as the **X Variables Cell Range**.
3. Check **First cells in both ranges contain label**.
4. Enter **95** as the **Confidence level for regression coefficients**.
5. Click **p values** as the **Stepwise Criteria**.

6. Click **General Stepwise** and keep the pair of **.05** values as the **p value to enter** and the **p value to remove**.

7. Enter a **Title** and click **OK**.

This procedure creates and deletes many regression results worksheets (seen as a flickering in the Excel windows) as it searches for variables to add to and delete from the model. The procedure finishes when the statement "Stepwise ends" (seen in row 29 in Figure 15.11 on page 588) is added to the stepwise regression results worksheet.

The Best-Subsets Approach to Model Building

PHStat2 Use the **Best Subsets** procedure to use a best-subsets approach to model building. For example, to use the best-subsets approach with the Table 15.2 hourly data for unionized graphic artists on page 586, open to the **DATA worksheet** of the **Standby workbook**. Select **PHStat → Regression → Best Subsets**. In the procedure's dialog box (shown below) and:

1. Enter **A1:A27** as the **Y Variable Cell Range**.

2. Enter **B1:E27** as the **X Variables Cell Range**.

3. Check **First cells in each range contains label**.

4. Enter **95** as the **Confidence level for regression coefficients**.

5. Enter a **Title** and click **OK**.

This procedure creates many regression results worksheets (seen as a flickering in the Excel windows) as it evaluates each subset of independent variables.

16 Time-Series Forecasting

Learning Objectives

In this chapter, you learn:

- About different time-series forecasting models: moving averages, exponential smoothing, the linear trend, the quadratic trend, the exponential trend, and the autoregressive models, and least-squares models for seasonal data
- To choose the most appropriate time-series forecasting model

@ The Principled

Y ou are a financial analyst for The Principled, a large financial services company. You need to forecast revenues for three companies in order to better evaluate investment opportunities for your clients. To assist in the forecasting, you have collected time-series data on three companies: Cabot Corporation, The Coca-Cola Company, and Wal-Mart Stores, Inc. Each time series has unique characteristics due to the different types of business activities and growth patterns experienced by the three companies. You understand that you can use several different types of forecasting models. How do you decide which type of forecasting model is best for each company? How do you use the information gained from the forecasting models to evaluate investment opportunities for your clients?

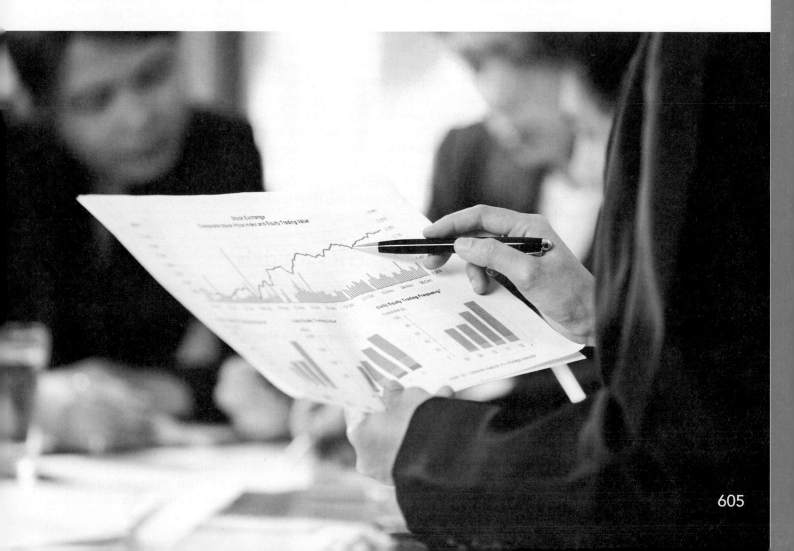

In Chapters 13 through 15, you used regression analysis as a tool for model building and prediction. In this chapter, regression analysis and other statistical methodologies are applied to time-series data. A **time series** is a set of numerical data collected over time. Due to differences in the features of data for various companies such as the three companies described in the Using Statistics scenario, you need to consider several different approaches to forecasting time-series data.

This chapter begins with an introduction to the importance of business forecasting (see Section 16.1) and a description of the components of time-series models (see Section 16.2). The coverage of forecasting models begins with annual time-series data. Section 16.3 presents moving averages and exponential smoothing methods for smoothing a series. This is followed by least-squares trend fitting and forecasting in Section 16.4 and autoregressive modeling in Section 16.5. Section 16.6 discusses how to choose among alternative forecasting models. Section 16.7 develops models for monthly and quarterly time series.

16.1 The Importance of Business Forecasting

Forecasting is done by monitoring changes that occur over time and projecting into the future. Forecasting is commonly used in both the for-profit and not-for-profit sectors of the economy. For example, marketing executives of a retailing corporation forecast product demand, sales revenues, consumer preferences, inventory, and so on in order to make decisions regarding product promotions and strategic planning. Government officials forecast unemployment, inflation, industrial production, and revenues from income taxes in order to formulate policies. And the administrators of a college or university forecast student enrollment in order to plan for the construction of dormitories and academic facilities, plan for student and faculty recruitment, and make assessments of other needs.

There are two common approaches to forecasting: *qualitative* and *quantitative*. **Qualitative forecasting methods** are especially important when historical data are unavailable. Qualitative forecasting methods are considered to be highly subjective and judgmental.

Quantitative forecasting methods make use of historical data. The goal of these methods is to use past data to predict future values. Quantitative forecasting methods are subdivided into two types: *time series* and *causal*. **Time-series forecasting methods** involve forecasting future values based entirely on the past and present values of a variable. For example, the daily closing prices of a particular stock on the New York Stock Exchange constitute a time series. Other examples of economic or business time series are the consumer price index (CPI), the quarterly gross domestic product (GDP), and the annual sales revenues of a particular company.

Causal forecasting methods involve the determination of factors that relate to the variable you are trying to forecast. These include multiple regression analysis with lagged variables, econometric modeling, leading indicator analysis, diffusion indexes, and other economic barometers that are beyond the scope of this text (see references 2–4). The primary emphasis in this chapter is on time-series forecasting methods.

16.2 Component Factors of Time-Series Models

Time-series forecasting assumes that the factors that have influenced activities in the past and present will continue to do so in approximately the same way in the future. Time-series forecasting seeks to identify and isolate these component factors in order to make predictions. Typically, the following four factors are examined in time-series models:

- Trend
- Cyclical effect
- Irregular or random effect
- Seasonal effect

A **trend** is an overall long-term upward or downward movement in a time series. Trend is not the only component factor that can influence data in a time series. The **cyclical effect** depicts the up-and-down swings or movements through the series. Cyclical movements vary in length, usually lasting from 2 to 10 years. They differ in intensity and are often correlated with a business cycle. In some time periods, the values are higher than would be predicted by a trend line (i.e., they are at or near the peak of a cycle). In other time periods, the values are lower than would be predicted by a trend line (i.e., they are at or near the bottom of a cycle). Any data that do not follow the trend modified by the cyclical component are considered part of the **irregular** or **random effect**. When you have monthly or quarterly data, an additional component, the **seasonal effect**, is considered, along with the trend, cyclical, and irregular effects.

Your first step in a time-series analysis is to plot the data and observe any patterns that occur over time. You must determine whether there is a long-term upward or downward movement in the series (i.e., a trend). If there is no obvious long-term upward or downward trend, then you can use moving averages or exponential smoothing to smooth the series and provide an overall long-term impression (see Section 16.3). If a trend is present, you can consider several time-series forecasting methods. (See Sections 16.4 and 16.5 for forecasting annual data and Section 16.7 for forecasting monthly or quarterly time series.)

16.3 Smoothing an Annual Time Series

One of the companies of interest in The Principled scenario is the Cabot Corporation. The Cabot Corporation is a Boston-based global specialty chemicals company. The company operates 39 manufacturing facilities and 8 research and development facilities in 19 countries, and its stock is traded on the New York Stock Exchange with the ticker symbol CBT. Revenues in fiscal 2008 were approximately $3.2 billion. Table 16.1 gives the total revenues, in millions of dollars, for 1982 to 2008 (stored in Cabot). Figure 16.1 presents the time-series plot.

TABLE 16.1

Revenues (in Millions of Dollars) for the Cabot Corporation from 1982 to 2008

Year	Revenue	Year	Revenue	Year	Revenue
1982	1,588	1991	1,488	2000	1,698
1983	1,558	1992	1,562	2001	1,523
1984	1,753	1993	1,619	2002	1,557
1985	1,408	1994	1,687	2003	1,795
1986	1,310	1995	1,841	2004	1,934
1987	1,424	1996	1,865	2005	2,125
1988	1,677	1997	1,637	2006	2,543
1989	1,937	1998	1,653	2007	2,616
1990	1,685	1999	1,699	2008	3,191

Source: *Data extracted from* Moody's Handbook of Common Stocks, *1992*; Mergent's Handbook of Common Stocks, *2008; and **www.cabot-corp.com***.

FIGURE 16.1

Plot of revenues (in millions of dollars) for the Cabot Corporation (1982–2008)

Create this chart sheet using the instructions in Section EG2.7.

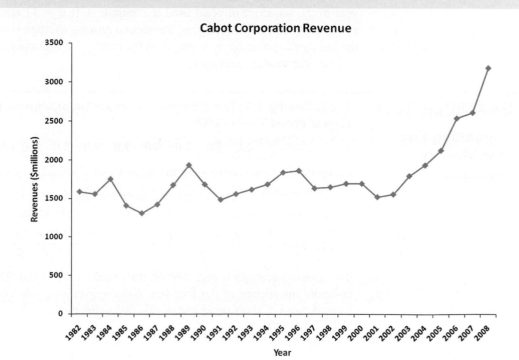

Cabot Corporation Revenue

When you examine annual data, your visual impression of the long-term trend in the series is sometimes obscured by the amount of variation from year to year. Often, you cannot judge whether any long-term upward or downward trend exists in the series. To get a better overall impression of the pattern of movement in the data over time, you can use the methods of *moving averages* or *exponential smoothing*.

Moving Averages

Compute moving averages using the instructions in Section EG16.3.

Moving averages for a chosen period of length L consist of a series of means, each computed over time for a sequence of L observed values. Moving averages, represented by the symbol $MA(L)$, can be greatly affected by the value chosen for L, which should be an integer value that corresponds to, or is a multiple of, the estimated average length of a cycle in the time series.

To illustrate, suppose you want to compute five-year moving averages from a series that has $n = 11$ years. Because $L = 5$, the five-year moving averages consist of a series of means computed by averaging consecutive sequences of five values. You compute the first five-year moving average by summing the values for the first five years in the series and dividing by 5:

$$MA(5) = \frac{Y_1 + Y_2 + Y_3 + Y_4 + Y_5}{5}$$

You compute the second five-year moving average by summing the values of years 2 through 6 in the series and then dividing by 5:

$$MA(5) = \frac{Y_2 + Y_3 + Y_4 + Y_5 + Y_6}{5}$$

You continue this process until you have computed the last of these five-year moving averages by summing the values of the last 5 years in the series (i.e., years 7 through 11) and then dividing by 5:

$$MA(5) = \frac{Y_7 + Y_8 + Y_9 + Y_{10} + Y_{11}}{5}$$

When you are dealing with annual time-series data, L should be an *odd* number of years. By following this rule, you are unable to compute any moving averages for the first $(L - 1)/2$ years or the last $(L - 1)/2$ years of the series. Thus, for a five-year moving average, you cannot make computations for the first two years or the last two years of the series.

When plotting moving averages, you plot each of the computed values against the middle year of the sequence of years used to compute it. If $n = 11$ and $L = 5$, the first moving average is centered on the third year, the second moving average is centered on the fourth year, and the last moving average is centered on the ninth year. Example 16.1 illustrates the computation of five-year moving averages.

EXAMPLE 16.1

Computing Five-Year Moving Averages

The following data represent total revenues (in $millions) for a fast-food store over the 11-year period 1999 to 2009:

4.0   5.0   7.0   6.0   8.0   9.0   5.0   2.0   3.5   5.5   6.5

Compute the five-year moving averages for this annual time series.

SOLUTION To compute the five-year moving averages, you first compute the five-year moving total and then divide this total by 5. The first of the five-year moving averages is

$$MA(5) = \frac{Y_1 + Y_2 + Y_3 + Y_4 + Y_5}{5} = \frac{4.0 + 5.0 + 7.0 + 6.0 + 8.0}{5} = \frac{30.0}{5} = 6.0$$

The moving average is centered on the middle value—the third year of this time series. To compute the second of the five-year moving averages, you compute the moving total of the second through sixth years and divide this value by 5:

$$MA(5) = \frac{Y_2 + Y_3 + Y_4 + Y_5 + Y_6}{5} = \frac{5.0 + 7.0 + 6.0 + 8.0 + 9.0}{5} = \frac{35.0}{5} = 7.0$$

This moving average is centered on the new middle value—the fourth year of the time series. The remaining moving averages are

$$MA(5) = \frac{Y_3 + Y_4 + Y_5 + Y_6 + Y_7}{5} = \frac{7.0 + 6.0 + 8.0 + 9.0 + 5.0}{5} = \frac{35.0}{5} = 7.0$$

$$MA(5) = \frac{Y_4 + Y_5 + Y_6 + Y_7 + Y_8}{5} = \frac{6.0 + 8.0 + 9.0 + 5.0 + 2.0}{5} = \frac{30.0}{5} = 6.0$$

$$MA(5) = \frac{Y_5 + Y_6 + Y_7 + Y_8 + Y_9}{5} = \frac{8.0 + 9.0 + 5.0 + 2.0 + 3.5}{5} = \frac{27.5}{5} = 5.5$$

$$MA(5) = \frac{Y_6 + Y_7 + Y_8 + Y_9 + Y_{10}}{5} = \frac{9.0 + 5.0 + 2.0 + 3.5 + 5.5}{5} = \frac{25.0}{5} = 5.0$$

$$MA(5) = \frac{Y_7 + Y_8 + Y_9 + Y_{10} + Y_{11}}{5} = \frac{5.0 + 2.0 + 3.5 + 5.5 + 6.5}{5} = \frac{22.5}{5} = 4.5$$

These moving averages are centered on their respective middle values—the fifth, sixth, seventh, eighth, and ninth years in the time series. By using the five-year moving averages, you are unable to compute a moving average for the first two or last two values in the time series.

In practice, you can avoid the tedious computations by using worksheet formulas that use the **AVERAGE** function to compute moving averages. Figure 16.2 presents the annual Cabot Corporation revenue data for the 27-year period from 1982 through 2008, the computations for 3- and 7-year moving averages, and a plot of the original data and the moving averages.

FIGURE 16.2

Worksheet with superimposed chart for the three-year and seven-year moving averages for Cabot Corporation revenues

Create this worksheet and superimposed chart using the instructions in Section EG16.3.

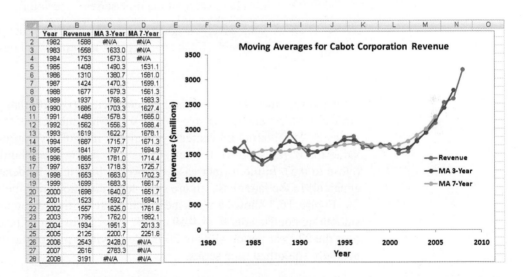

In Figure 16.2, there is no three-year moving average for the first year and the last year and there is no seven-year moving average for the first three years and last three years. The seven-year moving averages smoothes the series more than the three-year moving averages because the period is longer. Unfortunately, the longer the period, the smaller the number of moving averages you can compute. Therefore, selecting moving averages that are longer than seven years is usually undesirable because too many moving average values are missing at the beginning and end of the series. This makes it more difficult to get an overall impression of the entire series.

The selection of L, the length of the period used for constructing the averages, is highly subjective. If cyclical fluctuations are present in the data, choose an integer value of L that corresponds to (or is a multiple of) the estimated length of a cycle in the series. For annual time-series data that has no obvious cyclical fluctuations, most people choose either 3 years, 5 years, or 7 years as the value of L, depending on the amount of smoothing desired and the amount of data available.

Exponential Smoothing

Compute exponentially-smoothed values using the instructions in Section EG16.3.

Exponential smoothing consists of a series of *exponentially weighted* moving averages. The weights assigned to the values change so that the most recent value receives the highest weight, the previous value receives the second-highest weight, and so on, with the first value receiving the lowest weight. Throughout the series, each exponentially smoothed value depends on all previous values, which is an advantage of exponential smoothing over the method of moving averages. Exponential smoothing also allows you to compute short-term (one period into the future) forecasts when the presence and type of long-term trend in a time series is difficult to determine.

The equation developed for exponentially smoothing a series in any time period, i, is based on only three terms—the current value in the time series, Y_i; the previously computed exponentially smoothed value, E_{i-1}; and an assigned weight or smoothing coefficient, W. You use Equation (16.1) to exponentially smooth a time series.

COMPUTING AN EXPONENTIALLY SMOOTHED VALUE IN TIME PERIOD i

$$E_1 = Y_1 \tag{16.1}$$

$$E_i = WY_i + (1 - W)E_{i-1} \quad i = 2, 3, 4, \ldots$$

where

E_i = value of the exponentially smoothed series being computed in time period i

E_{i-1} = value of the exponentially smoothed series already computed in time period $i - 1$

Y_i = observed value of the time series in period i

W = subjectively assigned weight or smoothing coefficient (where $0 < W < 1$). Although W can approach 1.0, in virtually all business applications, $W \le 0.5$.

Choosing the weight or smoothing coefficient (i.e., W) that you assign to the time series is critical. Unfortunately, this selection is somewhat subjective. If your goal is only to smooth a series by eliminating unwanted cyclical and irregular variations, you should select a small value for W (close to 0). If your goal is forecasting, you should choose a large value for W (close to 0.5). In the former case, the overall long-term tendencies of the series will be more apparent; in the latter case, future short-term directions may be more adequately predicted.

Figure 16.3 shows a worksheet that presents the exponentially smoothed values (with smoothing coefficients $W = 0.50$ and $W = 0.25$) for annual revenue of the Cabot Corporation over the 27-year period 1982 to 2008, along with a plot of the original data and the two exponentially smoothed time series.

FIGURE 16.3

Worksheet with super-imposed chart for the exponentially smoothed series ($W = 0.50$ and $W = 0.25$) of the Cabot Corporation revenues

Create this worksheet and superimposed chart using the instructions in Section EG16.3.

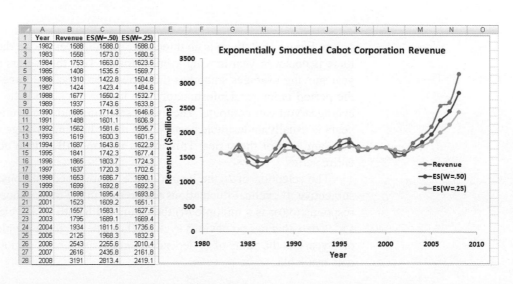

	Year	Revenue	ES(W=.50)	ES(W=.25)
2	1982	1588	1588.0	1588.0
3	1983	1558	1573.0	1580.5
4	1984	1753	1663.0	1623.6
5	1985	1408	1535.5	1569.7
6	1986	1310	1422.8	1504.8
7	1987	1424	1423.4	1484.6
8	1988	1677	1550.2	1532.7
9	1989	1937	1743.6	1633.8
10	1990	1685	1714.3	1646.6
11	1991	1488	1601.1	1606.9
12	1992	1562	1581.6	1595.7
13	1993	1619	1600.3	1601.5
14	1994	1687	1643.6	1622.9
15	1995	1841	1742.3	1677.4
16	1996	1865	1803.7	1724.3
17	1997	1637	1720.3	1702.5
18	1998	1653	1686.7	1690.1
19	1999	1699	1692.8	1692.3
20	2000	1698	1695.4	1693.8
21	2001	1523	1609.2	1651.1
22	2002	1557	1583.1	1627.5
23	2003	1795	1689.1	1669.4
24	2004	1934	1811.5	1735.6
25	2005	2125	1968.3	1832.9
26	2006	2543	2255.6	2010.4
27	2007	2616	2435.8	2161.8
28	2008	3191	2813.4	2419.1

Exponentially Smoothed Cabot Corporation Revenue

To illustrate these exponential smoothing computations for a smoothing coefficient of $W = 0.25$, you begin with the initial value $Y_{1982} = 1,588$ as the first smoothed value ($E_{1982} = 1,588$). Then, using the value of the time series for 1983 ($Y_{1983} = 1,558$), you smooth the series for 1983 by computing

$$E_{1983} = WY_{1983} + (1 - W)E_{1982}$$
$$= (0.25)(1,558) + (0.75)(1,588) = 1,580.5$$

To smooth the series for 1984:

$$E_{1984} = WY_{1984} + (1 - W)E_{1983}$$
$$= (0.25)(1,753) + (0.75)(1,580.5) = 1,623.6$$

To smooth the series for 1985:

$$E_{1985} = WY_{1985} + (1 - W)E_{1984}$$
$$= (0.25)(1,408) + (0.75)(1,623.6) = 1,569.7$$

You continue this process until you have computed the exponentially smoothed values for all 27 years in the series, as shown in Figure 16.3.

To use exponential smoothing for forecasting, you use the smoothed value in the current time period as the forecast of the value in the following period ($\hat{Y}_{i+1}$).

FORECASTING TIME PERIOD $i + 1$

$$\hat{Y}_{i+1} = E_i \tag{16.2}$$

To forecast the revenue of Cabot Corporation during 2009, using a smoothing coefficient of $W = 0.25$, you use the smoothed value for 2008 as its estimate. Figure 16.3 shows that this value is $2,419.1 million. (How close is this forecast? Look up Cabot Corporation's revenue at **www.cabot-corp.com** to find out.) When the value for 2009 becomes available, you can use Equation (16.1) to make a forecast for 2010 by computing the smoothed value for 2009, as follows:

$$\text{Current smoothed value} = (W)(\text{Current value}) + (1 - W)(\text{previous smoothest value})$$
$$E_{2009} = WY_{2009} + (1 - W)E_{2008}$$

Or, in terms of forecasting, you compute the following:

$$\text{New forecast} = (W)(\text{Current value}) + (1 - W)(\text{Current forecast})$$
$$\hat{Y}_{2010} = WY_{2009} + (1 - W)\hat{Y}_{2009}$$

Problems for Section 16.3

LEARNING THE BASICS

16.1 If you are using exponential smoothing for forecasting an annual time series of revenues, what is your forecast for next year if the smoothed value for this year is $32.4 million?

16.2 Consider a nine-year moving average used to smooth a time series that was first recorded in 1955.
a. Which year serves as the first centered value in the smoothed series?

b. How many years of values in the series are lost when computing all the nine-year moving averages?

16.3 You are using exponential smoothing on an annual time series concerning total revenues (in millions of dollars). You decide to use a smoothing coefficient of $W = 0.20$, and the exponentially smoothed value for 2009 is $E_{2009} = (0.20)(12.1) + (0.80)(9.4)$.
a. What is the smoothed value of this series in 2009?
b. What is the smoothed value of this series in 2010 if the value of the series in that year is $11.5 million?

APPLYING THE CONCEPTS

SELF Test **16.4** The following data (stored in **Movie Attendance**) represent the yearly movie attendance (in billions) from 2001 to 2008:

Year	Attendance
2001	1.44
2002	1.60
2003	1.52
2004	1.48
2005	1.38
2006	1.40
2007	1.40
2008	1.36

Source: *Data extracted from Movie Picture Association of America, www.mpaa.org.*

a. Plot the time series.
b. Fit a three-year moving average to the data and plot the results.
c. Using a smoothing coefficient of $W = 0.50$, exponentially smooth the series and plot the results.
d. Repeat (c), using $W = 0.25$.
e. Compare the results of (c) and (d).

16.5 The following data, stored in **NASCAR**, provide the number of accidents in the NASCAR Sprint Cup series from 2001 to 2008.

Year	Accidents
2001	200
2002	186
2003	235
2004	204
2005	253
2006	237
2007	240
2008	211

Source: *Data extracted from C. Graves, "On-Track Incidents Decrease in Sprint Cup," USA Today, December 16, 2008, p. 1C.*

a. Plot the time series.
b. Fit a three-year moving average to the data and plot the results.
c. Using a smoothing coefficient of $W = 0.50$, exponentially smooth the series and plot the results.
d. Repeat (c), using $W = 0.25$.
e. Compare the results of (c) and (d).

16.6 The NASDAQ stock market includes small- and medium-sized companies, many of which are in high-tech industries. Because of the nature of these companies, the NASDAQ tends to be more volatile than the Dow Jones Industrial Average or the S&P 500. The daily closing values for the NASDAQ index during the first 70 trading days

in 2009 are stored in **Daily Nasdaq** (data extracted from finance.yahoo.com):
a. Plot the time series.
b. Fit a three-period moving average to the data and plot the results.
c. Using a smoothing coefficient of $W = 0.50$, exponentially smooth the series and plot the results.
d. Repeat (c), using $W = 0.25$.
e. What conclusions can you reach concerning the presence or absence of trends during the first 70 trading days in 2009?

16.7 The following data (stored in **Treasury**) represent the three-month Treasury bill rates in the United States from 1991 to 2008:

Year	Rate	Year	Rate
1991	5.38	2000	5.82
1992	3.43	2001	3.40
1993	3.00	2002	1.61
1994	4.25	2003	1.01
1995	5.49	2004	1.37
1996	5.01	2005	3.15
1997	5.06	2006	4.73
1998	4.78	2007	4.36
1999	4.64	2008	1.37

Source: *Board of Governors of the Federal Reserve System, www.federalreserve.gov.*

a. Plot the data.
b. Fit a three-year moving average to the data and plot the results.
c. Using a smoothing coefficient of $W = 0.50$, exponentially smooth the series and plot the results.
d. What is your exponentially smoothed forecast for 2009?
e. Repeat (c) and (d), using a smoothing coefficient of $W = 0.25$.
f. Compare the results of (d) and (e).

16.8 The following data (stored in **Electricity**) represent the average residential prices of electricity, in cost per kilowatt hour, in the October–March winter months from 1994–1995 to 2008–2009.

Year	Cost	Year	Cost
1994–1995	8.16	2002–2003	8.20
1995–1996	8.10	2003–2004	8.49
1996–1997	8.17	2004–2005	8.78
1997–1998	8.12	2005–2006	9.67
1998–1999	7.94	2006–2007	10.14
1999–2000	7.98	2007–2008	10.49
2000–2001	8.11	2008–2009	11.32
2001–2002	8.37		

Source: *Energy Information Administration, Department of Energy, www.eia.doe.gov.*

a. Plot the data.
b. Fit a three-year moving average to the data and plot the results.
c. Using a smoothing coefficient of $W = 0.50$, exponentially smooth the series and plot the results.

d. What is your exponentially smoothed forecast for 2009–2010?
e. Repeat (c) and (d), using a smoothing coefficient of $W = 0.25$.
f. Compare the results of (d) and (e).

16.4 Least-Squares Trend Fitting and Forecasting

Trend is the component factor of a time series most often used to make intermediate and long-range forecasts. To get a visual impression of the overall long-term movements in a time series, you construct a time-series plot. If a straight-line trend adequately fits the data, you can use a linear trend model [see Equation (16.3) and Section 13.2]. If the time-series data indicate some long-run downward or upward quadratic movement, you can use a quadratic trend model [see Equation (16.4) and Section 15.1]. When the time-series data increase at a rate such that the percentage difference from value to value is constant, you can use an exponential trend model [see Equation (16.5)].

The Linear Trend Model

The **linear trend model**:

$$Y_i = \beta_0 + \beta_1 X_i + \varepsilon_i$$

is the simplest forecasting model. Equation (16.3) defines the linear trend forecasting equation.

LINEAR TREND FORECASTING EQUATION

$$\hat{Y}_i = b_0 + b_1 X_i \tag{16.3}$$

Recall that in linear regression analysis, you use the method of least squares to compute the sample slope, b_1, and the sample Y intercept, b_0. You then substitute the values for X into Equation (16.3) to predict Y.

When using the least-squares method for fitting trends in a time series, you first simplify the interpretation of the coefficients by assigning coded values to the X (time) variable. You assign consecutively numbered integers, starting with 0, as the coded values for the time periods. For example, in time-series data that have been recorded annually for 14 years, you assign the coded value 0 to the first year, the coded value 1 to the second year, the coded value 2 to the third year, and so on, concluding by assigning 13 to the fourteenth year.

In The Principled scenario on page 605, one of the companies of interest is The Coca-Cola Company. Founded in 1886 and headquartered in Atlanta, Georgia, Coca-Cola manufactures, distributes, and markets nonalcoholic beverages and syrups worldwide. The company markets its nonalcoholic beverages under the Coca-Cola, Diet Coke, Sprite, Fanta, and Diet Sprite brand names. Revenues in 2008 topped $31.9 billion (The Coca-Cola Company, **www.coca-cola.com**).

Table 16.2 lists the gross revenues (in billions of dollars) from 1995 to 2008 (stored in Coca-Cola).

TABLE 16.2

Revenues (in Billions of Dollars) for The Coca-Cola Company (1995–2008)

Year	Revenue	Year	Revenue
1995	18.0	2002	19.6
1996	18.5	2003	21.0
1997	18.9	2004	21.9
1998	18.8	2005	23.1
1999	19.8	2006	24.1
2000	20.5	2007	28.9
2001	20.1	2008	31.9

Source: *Data extracted from* Mergent's Handbook of Common Stocks, *2006; and **www.coca-cola.com**.*

Figure 16.4 presents the regression results worksheet for the simple linear regression that uses the consecutive coded values 0 through 13 as the X (coded year) variable. These results produce the following linear trend forecasting equation:

$$\hat{Y}_i = 16.3143 + 0.8429X_i$$

where $X_1 = 0$ represents 1995.

FIGURE 16.4

Regression results worksheet for a linear trend model to forecast revenues (in billions of dollars) for The Coca-Cola Company

Create this worksheet using the instructions in Sections EG13.2 and EG16.4.

	A	B	C	D	E	F	G
1	Linear Trend Model for Coca-Cola Company Revenue						
2							
3	*Regression Statistics*						
4	Multiple R	0.8646					
5	R Square	0.7475					
6	Adjusted R Square	0.7265					
7	Standard Error	2.1329					
8	Observations	14					
9							
10	ANOVA						
11		*df*	*SS*	*MS*	*F*	*Significance F*	
12	Regression	1	161.6179	161.6179	35.5260	0.0001	
13	Residual	12	54.5914	4.5493			
14	Total	13	216.2093				
15							
16		*Coefficients*	*Standard Error*	*t Stat*	*P-value*	*Lower 95%*	*Upper 95%*
17	Intercept	16.3143	1.0816	15.0837	0.0000	13.9577	18.6708
18	Coded Year	0.8429	0.1414	5.9604	0.0001	0.5348	1.1510

You interpret the regression coefficients as follows:

- The Y intercept, $b_0 = 16.3143$, is the predicted revenues (in billions of dollars) at The Coca-Cola Company during the origin or base year, 1995.
- The slope, $b_1 = 0.8429$, indicates that revenues are predicted to increase by 0.8429 billion dollars per year.

To project the trend in the revenues at Coca-Cola to 2009, you substitute $X_{15} = 14$, the code for 2009, into the linear trend forecasting equation:

$$\hat{Y}_i = 16.3143 + 0.8429(14) = 28.1149 \text{ billions of dollars}$$

The trend line is plotted in Figure 16.5, along with the observed values of the time series. There is a strong upward linear trend, and the adjusted r^2 is 0.7265, indicating that more than

FIGURE 16.5

Plot of the linear trend forecasting equation for The Coca-Cola Company revenues data

Create this chart sheet using the "Adding a Prediction Line and Regression Equation to a Scatter Plot" instructions in Section EG13.2.

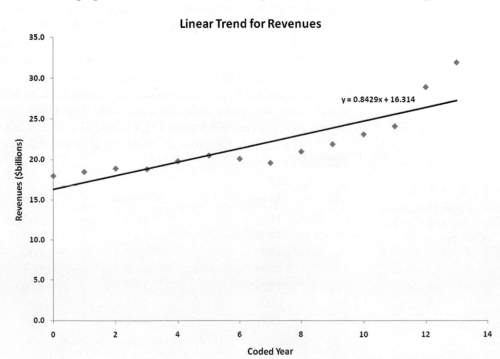

72% of the variation in revenues is explained by the linear trend over the time series. To investigate whether a different trend model might provide an even better fit, a *quadratic* trend model and an *exponential* trend model are fitted next.

The Quadratic Trend Model

A **quadratic trend model**:

$$\hat{Y}_i = \beta_0 + \beta_1 X_i + \beta_2 X_i^2 + \varepsilon_i$$

is the simplest nonlinear model. Using the least-squares method described in Section 15.1, you can develop a quadratic trend forecasting equation, as presented in Equation (16.4).

QUADRATIC TREND FORECASTING EQUATION

$$\hat{Y}_i = b_0 + b_1 X_i + b_2 X_i^2 \qquad\qquad (16.4)$$

where

b_0 = estimated Y intercept

b_1 = estimated *linear* effect on Y

b_2 = estimated *quadratic* effect on Y

Figure 16.6 presents the regression results worksheet for the quadratic trend model used to forecast revenues at The Coca-Cola Company.

FIGURE 16.6

Regression results worksheet for the quadratic trend model to forecast revenues for The Coca-Cola Company

Create this worksheet using the instructions in Section EG16.4, along with the instructions in Sections EG15.1 and EG14.1.

	A	B	C	D	E	F	G
1	Quadratic Trend Model for Coca-Cola Company Revenue						
2							
3	*Regression Statistics*						
4	Multiple R	0.9606					
5	R Square	0.9228					
6	Adjusted R Square	0.9087					
7	Standard Error	1.2319					
8	Observations	14					
9							
10	ANOVA						
11		*df*	*SS*	*MS*	*F*	*Significance F*	
12	Regression	2	199.5151	99.7576	65.7316	0.0000	
13	Residual	11	16.6942	1.5177			
14	Total	13	216.2093				
15							
16		*Coefficients*	*Standard Error*	*t Stat*	*P-value*	*Lower 95%*	*Upper 95%*
17	Intercept	19.2804	0.8617	22.3742	0.0000	17.0794	21.4813
18	Coded Year	-0.6402	0.3078	-2.0798	0.0617	-2.5368	1.2565
19	Coded Year Squared	0.1141	0.0228	4.9971	0.0004	-0.5634	0.7916

In Figure 16.6,

$$\hat{Y}_i = 19.2804 - 0.6402 X_i + 0.1141 X_i^2$$

where the year coded 0 is 1995.

To compute a forecast using the quadratic trend equation, you substitute the appropriate coded X value into this equation. For example, to forecast the trend in revenues for 2009 (i.e., $X = 14$),

$$\hat{Y}_i = 19.2804 - 0.6402(14) + 0.1141(14)^2 = 32.6812$$

Figure 16.7 plots the quadratic trend forecasting equation along with the time series for the actual data. This quadratic trend model provides a better fit (adjusted $r^2 = 0.9087$) to the time

FIGURE 16.7

Plot of the quadratic trend forecasting equation for the Coca-Cola Company revenues data

Create this chart sheet using the instructions in Sections EG13.2 and EG16.4.

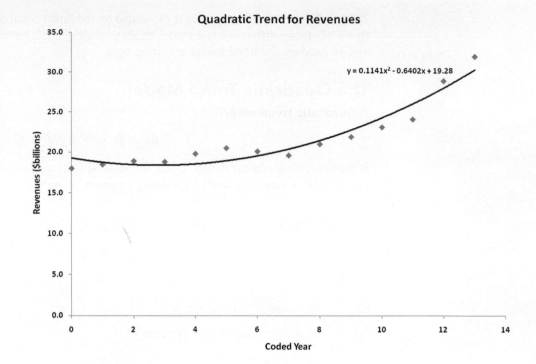

Quadratic Trend for Revenues

$y = 0.1141x^2 - 0.6402x + 19.28$

series than does the linear trend model. The t_{STAT} test statistic for the contribution of the quadratic term to the model is 4.9971 (p-value $= 0.0004$).

The Exponential Trend Model

When a time series increases at a rate such that the percentage difference from value to value is constant, an exponential trend is present. Equation (16.5) defines the **exponential trend model**.

EXPONENTIAL TREND MODEL

$$Y_i = \beta_0 \beta_1^{X_i} \varepsilon_i \qquad (16.5)$$

where

$\beta_0 = Y$ intercept

$(\beta_1 - 1) \times 100\%$ is the annual compound growth rate (in %)

The model in Equation (16.5) is not in the form of a linear regression model. To transform this nonlinear model to a linear model, you use a base 10 logarithm transformation.[1] Taking the logarithm of each side of Equation (16.5) results in Equation (16.6).

[1] Alternatively, you can use base e logarithms. For more information on logarithms, see Section A.3 in Appendix A.

TRANSFORMED EXPONENTIAL TREND MODEL

$$\log(Y_i) = \log(\beta_0 \beta_1^{X_i} \varepsilon_i) \qquad (16.6)$$

$$= \log(\beta_0) + \log(\beta_1^{X_i}) + \log(\varepsilon_i)$$

$$= \log(\beta_0) + X_i \log(\beta_1) + \log(\varepsilon_i)$$

Equation (16.6) is a linear model you can estimate using the least-squares method, with $\log(Y_i)$ as the dependent variable and X_i as the independent variable. This results in Equation (16.7).

EXPONENTIAL TREND FORECASTING EQUATION

$$\log(\hat{Y}_i) = b_0 + b_1X_i \tag{16.7a}$$

where

$$b_0 = \text{estimate of } \log(\beta_0) \text{ and thus } 10^{b_0} = \hat{\beta}_0$$
$$b_1 = \text{estimate of } \log(\beta_1) \text{ and thus } 10^{b_1} = \hat{\beta}_1$$

therefore,

$$\hat{Y}_i = \hat{\beta}_0\hat{\beta}_1^{X_i} \tag{16.7b}$$

where

$(\hat{\beta}_1 - 1) \times 100\%$ is the estimated annual compound growth rate (in %)

Figure 16.8 shows a regression results worksheet for an exponential trend model of revenues at The Coca-Cola Company.

FIGURE 16.8

Regression results worksheet for an exponential model to forecast revenues for The Coca-Cola Company

Create this worksheet using the instructions in Sections EG13.2, EG13.5, EG15.2, and EG16.4.

	A	B	C	D	E	F	G
1	Exponential Trend Model for Coca-Cola Company Revenue						
2							
3	*Regression Statistics*						
4	Multiple R	0.8968					
5	R Square	0.8043					
6	Adjusted R Square	0.7880					
7	Standard Error	0.0339					
8	Observations	14					
9							
10	ANOVA						
11		*df*	*SS*	*MS*	*F*	*Significance F*	
12	Regression	1	0.0566	0.0566	49.3150	0.0000	
13	Residual	12	0.0138	0.0011			
14	Total	13	0.0704				
15							
16		*Coefficients*	*Standard Error*	*t Stat*	*P-value*	*Lower 95%*	*Upper 95%*
17	Intercept	1.2296	0.0172	71.5699	0.0000	1.1922	1.2670
18	Coded Year	0.0158	0.0022	7.0225	0.0000	0.0109	0.0207

Using Equation (16.7a) and the results from Figure 16.8,

$$\log(\hat{Y}_i) = 1.2296 + 0.0158X_i$$

where the year coded 0 is 1995.

You compute the values for $\hat{\beta}_0$ and $\hat{\beta}_1$ by taking the antilog of the regression coefficients (b_0 and b_1):

$$\hat{\beta}_0 = \text{antilog}(b_0) = \text{antilog}(1.2296) = 10^{1.2296} = 16.9668$$
$$\hat{\beta}_1 = \text{antilog}(b_1) = \text{antilog}(0.0158) = 10^{0.0158} = 1.0371$$

Thus, using Equation (16.7b), the exponential trend forecasting equation is

$$\hat{Y}_i = (16.9668)(1.0371)^{X_i}$$

where the year coded 0 is 1995.

The Y intercept, $\hat{\beta}_0 = 16.9668$ billions of dollars, is the revenue forecast for the base year 1995. The value $(\hat{\beta}_1 - 1) \times 100\% = 3.71\%$ is the annual compound growth rate in revenues at The Coca-Cola Company.

For forecasting purposes, you substitute the appropriate coded X values into either Equation (16.7a) or Equation (16.7b). For example, to forecast revenues for 2009 (i.e., $X = 14$) using Equation (16.7a),

$$\log(\hat{Y}_i) = 1.2296 + 0.0158(14) = 1.4508$$

$$\hat{Y}_i = \text{antilog}(1.4508) = 10^{1.4508} = 28.2358 \text{ billions of dollars}$$

Figure 16.9 plots the exponential trend forecasting equation, along with the time-series data. The adjusted r^2 for the exponential trend model (0.7880) is greater than the adjusted r^2 for the linear trend model (0.7265) but less than the quadratic model (0.9087).

FIGURE 16.9

Plot of the exponential trend forecasting equation for The Coca-Cola Company revenues

Create this chart sheet using the instructions in Section EG16.4.

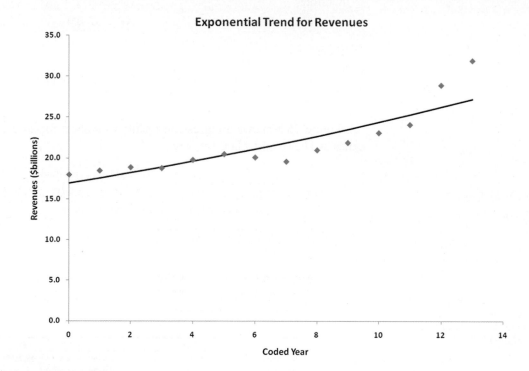

Model Selection Using First, Second, and Percentage Differences

You have used the linear, quadratic, and exponential models to forecast revenues for The Coca-Cola Company. How can you determine which of these models is the most appropriate model? In addition to visually inspecting time-series plots and comparing adjusted r^2 values, you can compute and examine first, second, and percentage differences. The identifying features of linear, quadratic, and exponential trend models are as follows:

- If a linear trend model provides a perfect fit to a time series, then the first differences are constant. Thus,

$$(Y_2 - Y_1) = (Y_3 - Y_2) = \dots = (Y_n - Y_{n-1})$$

- If a quadratic trend model provides a perfect fit to a time series, then the second differences are constant. Thus,

$$[(Y_3 - Y_2) - (Y_2 - Y_1)] = [(Y_4 - Y_3) - (Y_3 - Y_2)] = \dots = [(Y_n - Y_{n-1}) - (Y_{n-1} - Y_{n-2})]$$

- If an exponential trend model provides a perfect fit to a time series, then the percentage differences between consecutive values are constant. Thus,

$$\frac{Y_2 - Y_1}{Y_1} \times 100\% = \frac{Y_3 - Y_2}{Y_2} \times 100\% = \dots = \frac{Y_n - Y_{n-1}}{Y_{n-1}} \times 100\%$$

Although you should not expect a perfectly fitting model for any particular set of time-series data, you can consider the first differences, second differences, and percentage differences for a given series as guides in choosing an appropriate model. Examples 16.2, 16.3, and 16.4 illustrate linear, quadratic, and exponential trend models that have perfect (or nearly perfect) fits to their respective data sets.

EXAMPLE 16.2

A Linear Trend Model with a Perfect Fit

The following time series represents the number of passengers per year (in millions) on ABC Airlines:

	Year									
	2000	**2001**	**2002**	**2003**	**2004**	**2005**	**2006**	**2007**	**2008**	**2009**
Passengers	30.0	33.0	36.0	39.0	42.0	45.0	48.0	51.0	54.0	57.0

Using first differences, show that the linear trend model provides a perfect fit to these data.

SOLUTION The following table shows the solution:

	Year									
	2000	**2001**	**2002**	**2003**	**2004**	**2005**	**2006**	**2007**	**2008**	**2009**
Passengers	30.0	33.0	36.0	39.0	42.0	45.0	48.0	51.0	54.0	57.0
First differences		3.0	3.0	3.0	3.0	3.0	3.0	3.0	3.0	3.0

The differences between consecutive values in the series are the same throughout. Thus, ABC Airlines shows a linear growth pattern. The number of passengers increases by 3 million per year.

EXAMPLE 16.3

A Quadratic Trend Model with a Perfect Fit

The following time series represents the number of passengers per year (in millions) on XYZ Airlines:

	Year									
	2000	**2001**	**2002**	**2003**	**2004**	**2005**	**2006**	**2007**	**2008**	**2009**
Passengers	30.0	31.0	33.5	37.5	43.0	50.0	58.5	68.5	80.0	93.0

Using second differences, show that the quadratic trend model provides a perfect fit to these data.

SOLUTION The following table shows the solution:

	Year									
	2000	**2001**	**2002**	**2003**	**2004**	**2005**	**2006**	**2007**	**2008**	**2009**
Passengers	30.0	31.0	33.5	37.5	43.0	50.0	58.5	68.5	80.0	93.0
First differences		1.0	2.5	4.0	5.5	7.0	8.5	10.0	11.5	13.0
Second differences			1.5	1.5	1.5	1.5	1.5	1.5	1.5	1.5

The second differences between consecutive pairs of values in the series are the same throughout. Thus, XYZ Airlines shows a quadratic growth pattern. Its rate of growth is accelerating over time.

EXAMPLE 16.4

An Exponential Trend Model with a Perfect Fit

The following time series represents the number of passengers per year (in millions) for EXP Airlines:

	Year									
	2000	2001	2002	2003	2004	2005	2006	2007	2008	2009
Passengers	30.0	31.5	33.1	34.8	36.5	38.3	40.2	42.2	44.3	46.5

Using percentage differences, show that the exponential trend model provides almost a perfect fit to these data.

SOLUTION The following table shows the solution:

	Year									
	2000	2001	2002	2003	2004	2005	2006	2007	2008	2009
Passengers	30.0	31.5	33.1	34.8	36.5	38.3	40.2	42.2	44.3	46.5
First differences		1.5	1.6	1.7	1.7	1.8	1.9	2.0	2.1	2.2
Percentage differences		5.0	5.1	5.1	4.9	4.9	5.0	5.0	5.0	5.0

The percentage differences between consecutive values in the series are approximately the same throughout. Thus, EXP Airlines shows an exponential growth pattern. Its rate of growth is approximately 5% per year.

Figure 16.10 shows a worksheet that compares the first, second, and percentage differences for the revenues data at The Coca-Cola Company. Neither the first differences, second differences, nor percentage differences are constant across the series. Therefore, other models (including those considered in Section 16.5) may be more appropriate.

FIGURE 16.10

Worksheet that compares first, second, and percentage differences in revenues (in billions of dollars) for The Coca-Cola Company

Create this worksheet using the instructions in Section EG16.4.

	A	B	C	D	E
1	Year	Revenue	First Difference	Second Difference	Percentage Difference
2	1995	18.0	#N/A	#N/A	#N/A
3	1996	18.5	0.5	#N/A	2.78%
4	1997	18.9	0.4	-0.1	2.16%
5	1998	18.8	-0.1	-0.5	-0.53%
6	1999	19.8	1.0	1.1	5.32%
7	2000	20.5	0.7	-0.3	3.54%
8	2001	20.1	-0.4	-1.1	-1.95%
9	2002	19.6	-0.5	-0.1	-2.49%
10	2003	21.0	1.4	1.9	7.14%
11	2004	21.9	0.9	-0.5	4.29%
12	2005	23.1	1.2	0.3	5.48%
13	2006	24.1	1.0	-0.2	4.33%
14	2007	28.9	4.8	3.8	19.92%
15	2008	31.9	3.0	-1.8	10.38%

Problems for Section 16.4

LEARNING THE BASICS

16.9 If you are using the method of least squares for fitting trends in an annual time series containing 25 consecutive yearly values,

a. what coded value do you assign to X for the first year in the series?

b. what coded value do you assign to X for the fifth year in the series?

c. what coded value do you assign to X for the most recent recorded year in the series?

d. what coded value do you assign to X if you want to project the trend and make a forecast five years beyond the last observed value?

16.10 The linear trend forecasting equation for an annual time series containing 22 values (from 1988 to 2009) on total revenues (in millions of dollars) is

$$\hat{Y}_i = 4.0 + 1.5X_i$$

a. Interpret the Y intercept, b_0.
b. Interpret the slope, b_1.
c. What is the fitted trend value for the fifth year?
d. What is the fitted trend value for the most recent year?
e. What is the projected trend forecast three years after the last value?

16.11 The linear trend forecasting equation for an annual time series containing 42 values (from 1968 to 2009) on net sales (in billions of dollars) is

$$\hat{Y}_i = 1.2 + 0.5X_i$$

a. Interpret the Y intercept, b_0.
b. Interpret the slope, b_1.
c. What is the fitted trend value for the tenth year?
d. What is the fitted trend value for the most recent year?
e. What is the projected trend forecast two years after the last value?

APPLYING THE CONCEPTS

✓SELF Test **16.12** Bed Bath & Beyond Inc. is a nationwide chain of retail stores that sell a wide assortment of merchandise, principally including domestics merchandise and home furnishings, as well as food, giftware, and health and beauty care items. The following data (stored in **Bed & Bath**) show the number of stores open at the end of the fiscal year from 1993 to 2009:

Year	Stores Open	Year	Stores Open
1993	38	2002	396
1994	45	2003	519
1995	61	2004	629
1996	80	2005	721
1997	108	2006	809
1998	141	2007	888
1999	186	2008	971
2000	241	2009	1,037
2001	311		

Source: *Data extracted from Bed Bath & Beyond Annual Report, 2005, 2007, 2009.*

a. Plot the data.
b. Compute a linear trend forecasting equation and plot the results.
c. Compute a quadratic trend forecasting equation and plot the results.

d. Compute an exponential trend forecasting equation and plot the results.
e. Using the forecasting equations in (b) through (d), what are your annual forecasts of the number of stores open for 2010 and 2011?
f. How can you explain the differences in the three forecasts in (e)? What forecast do you think you should use? Why?

16.13 Gross domestic product (GDP) is a major indicator of a nation's overall economic activity. It consists of personal consumption expenditures, gross domestic investment, net exports of goods and services, and government consumption expenditures. The GDP (in billions of current dollars) for the United States from 1980 to 2008 is stored in **GDP**.

Source: *Data extracted from Bureau of Economic Analysis, U.S. Department of Commerce, www.bea.gov.*

a. Plot the data.
b. Compute a linear trend forecasting equation and plot the trend line.
c. What are your forecasts for 2009 and 2010?
d. What conclusions can you reach concerning the trend in GDP?

16.14 The data in **FedReceipt** represent federal receipts from 1978 through 2008, in billions of current dollars, from individual and corporate income tax, social insurance, excise tax, estate and gift tax, customs duties, and federal reserve deposits.

Source: *Data extracted from Tax Policy Center, www.taxpolicycenter.org.*

a. Plot the series of data.
b. Compute a linear trend forecasting equation and plot the trend line.
c. What are your forecasts of the federal receipts for 2009 and 2010?
d. What conclusions can you reach concerning the trend in federal receipts?

16.15 The data in **Strategic** represent the amount of oil, in billions of barrels, held in the U.S. strategic oil reserve, from 1981 through 2008.

Source: *Data extracted from Energy Information Administration, U.S. Department of Energy, www.eia.doe.gov.*

a. Plot the data.
b. Compute a linear trend forecasting equation and plot the trend line.
c. Compute a quadratic trend forecasting equation and plot the results.
d. Compute an exponential trend forecasting equation and plot the results.
e. Which model is the most appropriate?
f. Using the most appropriate model, forecast the number of barrels, in billions, for 2009. Check how accurate your forecast is by locating the true value for 2009 on the Internet or in your library.

16.16 The data shown in the following table (and stored in Solar Power) represent the yearly amount of solar power installed (in megawatts) in the United States from 2000 through 2008:

Year	Amount of Solar Power Installed
2000	18
2001	27
2002	44
2003	68
2004	83
2005	100
2006	140
2007	210
2008	250

Source: Data extracted from P. Davidson, "Glut of Rooftop Solar Systems Sinks Price," USA Today, January 13, 2009, p. 1B.

a. Plot the data.
b. Compute a linear trend forecasting equation and plot the trend line.
c. Compute a quadratic trend forecasting equation and plot the results.
d. Compute an exponential trend forecasting equation and plot the results.
e. Using the models in (b) through (d), what are your annual trend forecasts of yearly amount of solar power installed (in megawatts) in the United States in 2009 and 2010?

16.17 The data in the following table represent the closing values of the Dow Jones Industrial Average (DJIA) from 1979 through 2007 (see DJIA):

Year	DJIA	Year	DJIA	Year	DJIA
1979	838.7	1989	2,753.2	1999	11,497.1
1980	964.0	1990	2,633.7	2000	10,788.0
1981	875.0	1991	3,168.8	2001	10,021.5
1982	1,046.5	1992	3,301.1	2002	8,341.6
1983	1,258.6	1993	3,754.1	2003	10,453.9
1984	1,211.6	1994	3,834.4	2004	10,788.0
1985	1,546.7	1995	5,117.1	2005	10,717.5
1986	1,896.0	1996	6,448.3	2006	12,463.2
1987	1,938.8	1997	7,908.3	2007	13,264.8
1988	2,168.6	1998	9,181.4		

Source: Data extracted from finance.yahoo.com.

a. Plot the data.
b. Compute a linear trend forecasting equation and plot the trend line.
c. Compute a quadratic trend forecasting equation and plot the results.
d. Compute an exponential trend forecasting equation and plot the results.
e. Which model is the most appropriate?

f. Using the most appropriate model, forecast the closing value for the DJIA in 2008. The actual value was 8,776.4. How accurate was your forecast? If it was not very accurate, what happened?
g. Add the 2008 value to the data set and redo (a) through (e).
h. Using the most appropriate model in (g), forecast the closing values for 2009 and 2010.

16.18 General Electric (GE) is one of the world's largest companies; it develops, manufactures, and markets a wide range of products, including medical diagnostic imaging devices, jet engines, lighting products, and chemicals. Through its affiliate NBC Universal, GE produces and delivers network television and motion pictures. The data in GE represent the January 1 stock prices for the 22-year period from 1987 to 2008.

Source: Data extracted from finance.yahoo.com.

a. Plot the data.
b. Compute a linear trend forecasting equation and plot the trend line.
c. Compute a quadratic trend forecasting equation and plot the results.
d. Compute an exponential trend forecasting equation and plot the results.
e. Which model is the most appropriate?
f. Using the most appropriate model, forecast the stock price for January 1, 2009. The actual value was $16.58. How accurate was your forecast? If it was not very accurate, what happened?
g. Add the 2009 value to the data set and redo (a) through (e).
h. Using the most appropriate model in (g), forecast the stock price for January 1, 2010, and January 1, 2011.

16.19 Although you should not expect a perfectly fitting model for any time-series data, you can consider the first differences, second differences, and percentage differences for a given series as guides in choosing an appropriate model. For this problem, use each of the time series presented in the following table and stored in Tsmodel1:

	1999	2000	2001	2002	2003
Time series I	10.0	15.1	24.0	36.7	53.8
Time series II	30.0	33.1	36.4	39.9	43.9
Time series III	60.0	67.9	76.1	84.0	92.2

	2004	2005	2006	2007	2008
Time series I	74.8	100.0	129.2	162.4	199.0
Time series II	48.2	53.2	58.2	64.5	70.7
Time series III	100.0	108.0	115.8	124.1	132.0

a. Determine the most appropriate model.
b. Compute the forecasting equation.
c. Forecast the value for 2009.

16.20 A time-series plot often helps you determine the appropriate model to use. For this problem, use each of the time series presented in the following table and stored in TsModel2 .

	Year				
	1999	**2000**	**2001**	**2002**	**2003**
Time series I	100.0	115.2	130.1	144.9	160.0
Time series II	100.0	115.2	131.7	150.8	174.1

	Year				
	2004	**2005**	**2006**	**2007**	**2008**
Time series I	175.0	189.8	204.9	219.8	235.0
Time series II	200.0	230.8	266.1	305.5	351.8

a. Plot the observed data (Y) over time (X) and plot the logarithm of the observed data (log Y) over time (X) to determine whether a linear trend model or an exponential trend model is more appropriate. (Hint: If the plot of log Y vs. X appears to be linear, an exponential trend model provides an appropriate fit.)
b. Compute the appropriate forecasting equation.
c. Forecast the value for 2009.

16.21 The following data, stored in Hotels , provide the average hotel room rates from 1996 to 2006:

Year	Rate ($)	Year	Rate ($)
1996	70.63	2002	83.54
1997	75.31	2003	82.52
1998	78.62	2004	86.23
1999	81.33	2005	90.88
2000	85.89	2006	97.78
2001	88.27		

Source: *Data extracted from* USA Today *Snapshots, February 13, 2008, p. 1A.*

a. Compare the first differences, second differences, and percentage differences to determine the most appropriate model.
b. Compute the appropriate forecasting equation.
c. Forecast the average hotel room rates for 2007 and 2008.

16.22 The data in CPI-U reflect the annual values of the Consumer Price Index (CPI) in the United States over the 44-year period 1965 through 2008, using 1982 through 1984 as the base period. This index measures the average change in prices over time in a fixed "market basket" of goods and services purchased by all urban consumers, including urban wage earners (i.e., clerical, professional, managerial, and technical workers; self-employed individuals; and short-term workers), unemployed individuals, and retirees.
Source: *Data extracted from Bureau of Labor Statistics, U.S. Department of Labor,* **www.bls.gov**.

a. Plot the data.
b. Describe the movement in this time series over the 44-year period.
c. Compute a linear trend forecasting equation and plot the trend line.
d. Compute a quadratic trend forecasting equation and plot the results.
e. Compute an exponential trend forecasting equation and plot the results.
f. Which model is the most appropriate?
g. Using the most appropriate model, forecast the CPI for 2009 and 2010.

16.5 Autoregressive Modeling for Trend Fitting and Forecasting

[2]The exponential smoothing model described in Section 16.3 and the autoregressive models described in this section are special cases of autoregressive integrated moving average (ARIMA) models developed by Box and Jenkins (reference 2).

Frequently, the values of a time series are highly correlated with the values that precede and succeed them. This type of correlation is called *autocorrelation*. **Autoregressive modeling**[2] is a technique used to forecast time series with autocorrelation. A **first-order autocorrelation** refers to the association between consecutive values in a time series. A **second-order autocorrelation** refers to the relationship between values that are two periods apart. A ***p*th-order autocorrelation** refers to the correlation between values in a time series that are p periods apart. You can take into account the autocorrelation in data by using autoregressive modeling methods.

Equations (16.8), (16.9), and (16.10) define first-order, second-order, and pth-order autoregressive models.

FIRST-ORDER AUTOREGRESSIVE MODEL

$$Y_i = A_0 + A_1 Y_{i-1} + \delta_i \qquad \textbf{(16.8)}$$

SECOND-ORDER AUTOREGRESSIVE MODEL

$$Y_i = A_0 + A_1 Y_{i-1} + A_2 Y_{i-2} + \delta_i \qquad \textbf{(16.9)}$$

pTH-ORDER AUTOREGRESSIVE MODELS

$$Y_i = A_0 + A_1 Y_{i-1} + A_2 Y_{i-2} + \cdots + A_p Y_{i-p} + \delta_i \qquad \textbf{(16.10)}$$

where

Y_i = the observed value of the series at time i

Y_{i-1} = the observed value of the series at time $i - 1$

Y_{i-2} = the observed value of the series at time $i - 2$

Y_{i-p} = the observed value of the series at time $i - p$

$A_0, A_1, A_2, \ldots, A_p$ = autoregression parameters to be estimated from least-squares regression analysis

δ_i = a nonautocorrelated random error component (with mean = 0 and constant variance)

The **first-order autoregressive model** [Equation (16.8)] is similar in form to the simple linear regression model [Equation (13.1) on page 472]. The **second-order autoregressive model** [Equation (16.9)] is similar to the multiple regression model with two independent variables [Equation (14.2) on page 529]. The **pth-order autoregressive model** [Equation (16.10)] is similar to the multiple regression model [Equation (14.1) on page 528]. In the regression models, the regression parameters are given by the symbols $\beta_0, \beta_1, \ldots, \beta_k$, with corresponding estimates denoted by $b_0, b_1, \ldots, b_k$. In the autoregressive models, the parameters are given by the symbols $A_0, A_1, \ldots, A_p$, with corresponding estimates denoted by $a_0, a_1, \ldots, a_p$.

Selecting an appropriate autoregressive model can be complicated. You must weigh the advantages that are due to simplicity against the concern of failing to take into account important autocorrelation in the data. You also must be concerned with selecting a higher-order model requiring the estimation of numerous unnecessary parameters—especially if n, the number of values in the series, is small. The reason for this concern is that when computing an estimate of A_p, you lose p out of the n data values when comparing each data value with the data value p periods earlier.

Examples 16.5 and 16.6 illustrate this loss of data values.

EXAMPLE 16.5

Comparison Schema for a First-Order Autoregressive Model

Consider the following series of $n = 7$ consecutive annual values:

| | \multicolumn{7}{c}{**Year**} |
	1	**2**	**3**	**4**	**5**	**6**	**7**
Series	31	34	37	35	36	43	40

Show the comparisons needed for a first-order autoregressive model.

Year	First-Order Autoregressive Model
i	$(Y_i$ vs. $Y_{i-1})$
1	$31 \leftrightarrow \ldots$
2	$34 \leftrightarrow 31$
3	$37 \leftrightarrow 34$
4	$35 \leftrightarrow 37$
5	$36 \leftrightarrow 35$
6	$43 \leftrightarrow 36$
7	$40 \leftrightarrow 43$

SOLUTION Because there is no value recorded prior to Y_1, this value is lost for regression analysis. Therefore, the first-order autoregressive model is based on six pairs of values.

EXAMPLE 16.6

Comparison Schema for a Second-Order Autoregressive Model

Consider the following series of $n = 7$ consecutive annual values:

	Year						
	1	2	3	4	5	6	7
Series	31	34	37	35	36	43	40

Show the comparisons needed for a second-order autoregressive model.

Year	Second-Order Autoregressive Model
i	$(Y_i$ vs. Y_{i-1} and Y_i vs. $Y_{i-2})$
1	$31 \leftrightarrow \ldots$ and $31 \leftrightarrow \ldots$
2	$34 \leftrightarrow 31$ and $34 \leftrightarrow \ldots$
3	$37 \leftrightarrow 34$ and $37 \leftrightarrow 31$
4	$35 \leftrightarrow 37$ and $35 \leftrightarrow 34$
5	$36 \leftrightarrow 35$ and $36 \leftrightarrow 37$
6	$43 \leftrightarrow 36$ and $43 \leftrightarrow 35$
7	$40 \leftrightarrow 43$ and $40 \leftrightarrow 36$

SOLUTION Because there is no value recorded prior to Y_1, two values are lost when performing regression analysis. Therefore, the second-order autoregressive model is based on five pairs of values.

After selecting a model and using the least-squares method to compute estimates of the parameters, you need to determine the appropriateness of the model. Either you can select a particular pth-order autoregressive model based on previous experiences with similar data or, as a starting point, you can choose a model with several parameters and then eliminate the higher-order parameters that do not significantly contribute to the model. In this latter approach, you use a t test for the significance of A_p, the highest-order autoregressive parameter in the current model under consideration. The null and alternative hypotheses are

$$H_0: A_p = 0$$
$$H_1: A_p \neq 0$$

Equation (16.11) defines the test statistic.

t TEST FOR SIGNIFICANCE OF THE HIGHEST-ORDER AUTOREGRESSIVE PARAMETER, A_p

$$t_{STAT} = \frac{a_p - A_p}{S_{a_p}}$$ (16.11)

where

A_p = hypothesized value of the highest-order parameter, A_p, in the autoregressive model

a_p = estimate of the highest-order parameter, A_p, in the autoregressive model

S_{a_p} = standard deviation of a_p

The t_{STAT} test statistic follows a t distribution with $n - 2p - 1$ degrees of freedom.[3]

[3] In addition to the degrees of freedom lost for each of the p population parameters you are estimating, p additional degrees of freedom are lost because there are p fewer comparisons to be made out of the original n values in the time series.

For a given level of significance, α, you reject the null hypothesis if the t_{STAT} test statistic is greater than the upper-tail critical value from the t distribution or if the t_{STAT} test statistic is less than the lower-tail critical value from the t distribution. Thus, the decision rule is

Reject H_0 if $t_{STAT} < -t_{\alpha/2}$ or if $t_{STAT} > t_{\alpha/2}$;

otherwise, do not reject H_0.

Figure 16.11 illustrates the decision rule and regions of rejection and nonrejection.

FIGURE 16.11

Rejection regions for a two-tail test for the significance of the highest-order autoregressive parameter, A_p

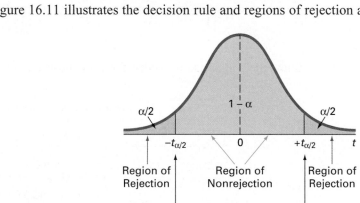

If you do not reject the null hypothesis that $A_p = 0$, you conclude that the selected model contains too many estimated parameters. You then discard the highest-order term and estimate an autoregressive model of order $p - 1$, using the least-squares method. You then repeat the test of the hypothesis that the new highest-order parameter is 0. This testing and modeling continues until you reject H_0. When this occurs, you can conclude that the remaining highest-order parameter is significant, and you can use that model for forecasting purposes.

Equation (16.12) defines the fitted pth-order autoregressive equation.

FITTED pTH-ORDER AUTOREGRESSIVE EQUATION

$$\hat{Y}_i = a_0 + a_1 Y_{i-1} + a_2 Y_{i-2} + \cdots + a_p Y_{i-p}$$ (16.12)

where

$\hat{Y}_i$ = fitted values of the series at time i

Y_{i-1} = observed value of the series at time $i - 1$

Y_{i-2} = observed value of the series at time $i - 2$

Y_{i-p} = observed value of the series at time $i - p$

$a_0, a_1, a_2, \ldots, a_p$ = regression estimates of the parameters $A_0, A_1, A_2, \ldots, A_p$

You use Equation (16.13) to forecast j years into the future from the current nth time period.

pTH-ORDER AUTOREGRESSIVE FORECASTING EQUATION

$$\hat{Y}_{n+j} = a_0 + a_1\hat{Y}_{n+j-1} + a_2\hat{Y}_{n+j-2} + \cdots + a_p\hat{Y}_{n+j-p} \qquad (16.13)$$

where

$$a_0, a_1, a_2, \ldots, a_p = \text{regression estimates of the parameters } A_0, A_1, A_2, \ldots, A_p$$

$$j = \text{number of years into the future}$$

$$\hat{Y}_{n+j-p} = \text{forecast of } Y_{n+j-p} \text{ from the current time period for } j - p > 0$$

$$\hat{Y}_{n+j-p} = \text{observed value for } Y_{n+j-p} \text{ for } j - p \leq 0$$

Thus, to make forecasts j years into the future, using a third-order autoregressive model, you need only the most recent $p = 3$ values (Y_n, Y_{n-1}, and Y_{n-2}) and the regression estimates a_0, a_1, a_2, and a_3.

To forecast one year ahead, Equation (16.13) becomes

$$\hat{Y}_{n+1} = a_0 + a_1 Y_n + a_2 Y_{n-1} + a_3 Y_{n-2}$$

To forecast two years ahead, Equation (16.13) becomes

$$\hat{Y}_{n+2} = a_0 + a_1\hat{Y}_{n+1} + a_2 Y_n + a_3 Y_{n-1}$$

To forecast three years ahead, Equation (16.13) becomes

$$\hat{Y}_{n+3} = a_0 + a_1\hat{Y}_{n+2} + a_2\hat{Y}_{n+1} + a_3 Y_n$$

and so on.

Autoregressive modeling is a powerful forecasting technique for time series that have autocorrelation. Although slightly more complicated than other methods, the following step-by-step approach guides you through the analysis:

1. Choose a value for p, the highest-order parameter in the autoregressive model to be evaluated, realizing that the t test for significance is based on $n - 2p - 1$ degrees of freedom.
2. Create a set of p "lagged predictor" variables such that the first lagged predictor variable lags by one time period, the second variable lags by two time periods, and so on and the last predictor variable lags by p time periods (see Figure 16.12).
3. Perform a least-squares analysis of the multiple regression model containing all p lagged predictor variables (using Excel).
4. Test for the significance of A_p, the highest-order autoregressive parameter in the model.
    a. If you do not reject the null hypothesis, discard the pth variable and repeat steps 3 and 4. The test for the significance of the new highest-order parameter is based on a t distribution whose degrees of freedom are revised to correspond with the new number of predictors.
    b. If you reject the null hypothesis, select the autoregressive model with all p predictors for fitting [see Equation (16.12)] and forecasting [see Equation (16.13)].

To demonstrate the autoregressive modeling approach, return to the time series concerning the revenues for The Coca-Cola Company over the 14-year period 1995 through 2008. Figure 16.12 displays a worksheet that organizes the data for the first-order, second-order, and third-order autoregressive models. The worksheet contains the lagged predictor variables Lag1, Lag2, and Lag3 in columns C, D, and E. Use all three lagged predictors to fit the third-order autoregressive model. Use only Lag1 and Lag2 to fit the second-order autoregressive model, and use only Lag1 to fit the first-order autoregressive models. Thus, out of $n = 14$ values, $p = 1, 2,$ or 3 values out of $n = 14$ are lost in the comparisons needed for developing the first-order, second-order, and third-order autoregressive models.

FIGURE 16.12

Worksheet data for developing first-order, second-order, and third-order autoregressive models on revenues for The Coca-Cola Company (1995–2008)

Create this worksheet using the instructions in Section EG16.5.

	A	B	C	D	E
1	Year	Revenue	Lag1	Lag2	Lag3
2	1995	18.0	#N/A	#N/A	#N/A
3	1996	18.5	18.0	#N/A	#N/A
4	1997	18.9	18.5	18.0	#N/A
5	1998	18.8	18.9	18.5	18.0
6	1999	19.8	18.8	18.9	18.5
7	2000	20.5	19.8	18.8	18.9
8	2001	20.1	20.5	19.8	18.8
9	2002	19.6	20.1	20.5	19.8
10	2003	21.0	19.6	20.1	20.5
11	2004	21.9	21.0	19.6	20.1
12	2005	23.1	21.9	21.0	19.6
13	2006	24.1	23.1	21.9	21.0
14	2007	28.9	24.1	23.1	21.9
15	2008	31.9	28.9	24.1	23.1

Selecting an autoregressive model that best fits the annual time series begins with the third-order autoregressive model shown in Figure 16.13.

FIGURE 16.13

Regression results worksheet for the third-order autoregressive model for The Coca-Cola Company revenues

Create this worksheet using the instructions in Section EG16.5.

	A	B	C	D	E	F	G
1	Third-Order Autoregressive Model						
2							
3	*Regression Statistics*						
4	Multiple R	0.9714					
5	R Square	0.9437					
6	Adjusted R Square	0.9196					
7	Standard Error	1.1814					
8	Observations	11					
9							
10	ANOVA						
11		*df*	*SS*	*MS*	*F*	*Significance F*	
12	Regression	3	163.7904	54.5968	39.1192	0.0001	
13	Residual	7	9.7696	1.3957			
14	Total	10	173.5600				
15							
16		*Coefficients*	*Standard Error*	*t Stat*	*P-value*	*Lower 95%*	*Upper 95%*
17	Intercept	-15.1024	6.3920	-2.3627	0.0501	-30.2171	0.0123
18	X Variable 1	0.8849	0.3571	2.4778	0.0423	0.0404	1.7293
19	X Variable 2	0.3294	0.7476	0.4406	0.6728	-1.4384	2.0973
20	X Variable 3	0.5987	0.7187	0.8330	0.4324	-1.1008	2.2982

From Figure 16.13, the fitted third-order autoregressive equation is

$$\hat{Y}_i = -15.1024 + 0.8849Y_{i-1} + 0.3294Y_{i-2} + 0.5987Y_{i-3}$$

where the first year in the series is 1998.

Next, you test for the significance of A_3, the highest-order parameter. The highest-order parameter estimate, a_3, for the fitted third-order autoregressive model is 0.5987, with a standard error of 0.7187.

To test the null hypothesis:

$$H_0: A_3 = 0$$

against the alternative hypothesis:

$$H_1: A_3 \neq 0$$

using Equation (16.11) on page 626 and the worksheet results given in Figure 16.13,

$$t_{STAT} = \frac{a_3 - A_3}{S_{a_3}} = \frac{0.5987 - 0}{0.7187} = 0.833$$

Using a 0.05 level of significance, the two-tail t test with 7 degrees of freedom has critical values of ±2.3646. Because $-2.3646 < t_{STAT} = 0.833 < +2.3646$ or because the p-value $= 0.4324 > 0.05$, you do not reject H_0. You conclude that the third-order parameter of the autoregressive model is not significant and can be deleted.

Next, you fit a second-order autoregressive model (see Figure 16.14).

FIGURE 16.14

Regression results worksheet for the second-order autoregressive model for The Coca-Cola Company revenues data

Create this worksheet using the instructions in Section EG16.5.

	A	B	C	D	E	F	G
1	Second-Order Autoregressive Model						
2							
3	*Regression Statistics*						
4	Multiple R	0.9692					
5	R Square	0.9394					
6	Adjusted R Square	0.9259					
7	Standard Error	1.1218					
8	Observations	12					
9							
10	ANOVA						
11		df	SS	MS	F	Significance F	
12	Regression	2	175.4704	87.7352	69.7153	0.0000	
13	Residual	9	11.3263	1.2585			
14	Total	11	186.7967				
15							
16		Coefficients	Standard Error	t Stat	P-value	Lower 95%	Upper 95%
17	Intercept	-10.7579	4.6459	-2.3156	0.0458	-13.0201	-8.4958
18	X Variable 1	0.9903	0.3246	3.0505	0.0138	-9.5193	11.5000
19	X Variable 2	0.5934	0.5112	1.1607	0.2756	-0.1410	1.3278

The fitted second-order autoregressive equation is

$$\hat{Y}_i = -10.7579 + 0.9903\,Y_{i-1} + 0.5934\,Y_{i-2}$$

where the first year of the series is 1997.

From Figure 16.14, the highest-order parameter estimate is $a_2 = 0.5934$, with a standard error of 0.5112.

To test the null hypothesis:

$$H_0: A_2 = 0$$

against the alternative hypothesis:

$$H_1: A_2 \neq 0$$

using Equation (16.11) on page 626,

$$t_{STAT} = \frac{a_2 - A_2}{S_{a_2}} = \frac{0.5934 - 0}{0.5112} = 1.1607$$

Using the 0.05 level of significance, the two-tail t test with 9 degrees of freedom has critical values of ±2.2622. Because $-2.2622 < t_{STAT} = 1.1607 < 2.2622$ or because the p-value $= 0.2756 > 0.05$, you do not reject H_0. You conclude that the second-order parameter of the autoregressive model is not significant and should be deleted from the model. You then fit a first-order autoregressive model (see Figure 16.15).

FIGURE 16.15

Regression results worksheet for the first-order autoregressive model for the Coca-Cola Company revenues data

Create this worksheet using the instructions in Section EG16.5.

	A	B	C	D	E	F	G
1	First-Order Autoregressive Model						
2							
3	*Regression Statistics*						
4	Multiple R	0.9665					
5	R Square	0.9341					
6	Adjusted R Square	0.9281					
7	Standard Error	1.0969					
8	Observations	14					
9							
10	ANOVA						
11		*df*	*SS*	*MS*	*F*	*Significance F*	
12	Regression	1	187.4826	187.4826	155.8307	0.0000	
13	Residual	11	13.2343	1.2031			
14	Total	12	200.7169				
15							
16		*Coefficients*	*Standard Error*	*t Stat*	*P-value*	*Lower 95%*	*Upper 95%*
17	Intercept	-5.8384	2.2574	-2.5863	0.0253	-10.8070	-0.8698
18	Coded Year	1.3287	0.1064	12.4832	0.0000	1.0944	1.5630

From Figure 16.15, the fitted first-order autoregressive equation is

$$\hat{Y}_i = -5.8384 + 1.3287 Y_{i-1}$$

where the first year of the series is 1996.

From Figure 16.15, the highest-order parameter estimate is $a_1 = 1.3287$, with a standard error of 0.1064.

To test the null hypothesis:

$$H_0: A_1 = 0$$

against the alternative hypothesis:

$$H_1: A_1 \neq 0$$

using Equation (16.11) on page 626,

$$t_{STAT} = \frac{a_1 - A_1}{S_{a_1}} = \frac{1.3287 - 0}{0.1064} = 12.4832$$

Using the 0.05 level of significance, the two-tail t test with 11 degrees of freedom has critical values of ± 2.201. Because $t_{STAT} = 12.4832 > 2.201$ or because the p-value = 0.0000 < 0.05, you reject H_0. You conclude that the first-order parameter of the autoregressive model is significant and should remain in the model.

The model-building approach has led to the selection of the first-order autoregressive model as the most appropriate for the given data. Using the estimates $a_0 = -5.8384$, and $a_1 = 1.3287$, as well as the most recent data value $Y_{14} = 31.9$, the forecasts of revenues at The Coca-Cola Company for 2009 and 2010 from Equation (16.13) on page 627 are

$$\hat{Y}_{n+j} = -5.8384 + 1.3287 \hat{Y}_{n+j-1}$$

Therefore,

2009: 1 year ahead, $\hat{Y}_{15} = -5.8384 + 1.3287(31.9) = 36.5471$ billions of dollars

2010: 2 years ahead, $\hat{Y}_{16} = -5.8384 + 1.3287(36.5471) = 42.7217$ billions of dollars

Figure 16.16 displays the actual and predicted Y values from the first-order autoregressive model.

FIGURE 16.16

Plot of actual and predicted revenues from a first-order autoregressive model at The Coca-Cola Company

Create this worksheet using the instructions in Section EG2.7.

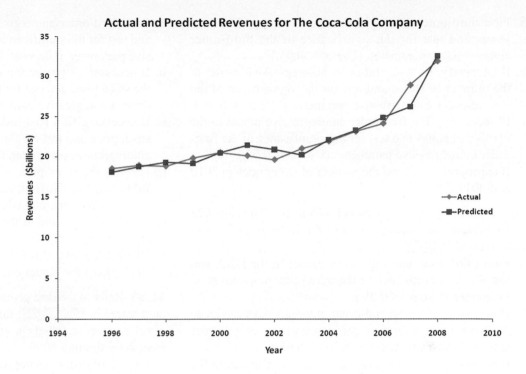

Actual and Predicted Revenues for The Coca-Cola Company

Problems for Section 16.5

LEARNING THE BASICS

16.23 You are given an annual time series with 40 consecutive values and asked to fit a fifth-order autoregressive model.
a. How many comparisons are lost in the development of the autoregressive model?
b. How many parameters do you need to estimate?
c. Which of the original 40 values do you need for forecasting?
d. State the fifth-order autoregressive model.
e. Write an equation to indicate how you would forecast j years into the future.

16.24 A third-order autoregressive model is fitted to an annual time series with 17 values and has the following estimated parameters and standard errors:

$$a_0 = 4.50 \quad a_1 = 1.80 \quad a_2 = 0.80 \quad a_3 = 0.24$$
$$S_{a_1} = 0.50 \quad S_{a_2} = 0.30 \quad S_{a_3} = 0.10$$

At the 0.05 level of significance, test the appropriateness of the fitted model.

16.25 Refer to Problem 16.24. The three most recent values are

$$Y_{15} = 23 \quad Y_{16} = 28 \quad Y_{17} = 34$$

Forecast the values for the next year and the following year.

16.26 Refer to Problem 16.24. Suppose, when testing for the appropriateness of the fitted model, the standard errors are

$$S_{a_1} = 0.45 \quad S_{a_2} = 0.35 \quad S_{a_3} = 0.15$$

a. What conclusions can you make?
b. Discuss how to proceed if forecasting is still your main objective.

APPLYING THE CONCEPTS

16.27 Refer to the data given in Problem 16.15 on page 621 that represent the amount of oil (in billions of barrels) held in the U.S. strategic reserve from 1981 through 2008 (stored in Strategic).
a. Fit a third-order autoregressive model to the amount of oil and test for the significance of the third-order autoregressive parameter. (Use $\alpha = 0.05$.)
b. If necessary, fit a second-order autoregressive model to the amount of oil and test for the significance of the second-order autoregressive parameter. (Use $\alpha = 0.05$.)
c. If necessary, fit a first-order autoregressive model to the amount of oil and test for the significance of the first-order autoregressive parameter. (Use $\alpha = 0.05$.)
d. If appropriate, forecast the barrels held in 2009.

16.28 Refer to the data given in Problem 16.12 on page 621 that represent the number of stores open for Bed Bath & Beyond from 1993 through 2009 (stored in Bed & Bath).

a. Fit a third-order autoregressive model to the number of stores and test for the significance of the third-order autoregressive parameter. (Use $\alpha = 0.05$.)

b. If necessary, fit a second-order autoregressive model to the number of stores and test for the significance of the second-order autoregressive parameter. (Use $\alpha = 0.05$.)

c. If necessary, fit a first-order autoregressive model to the number of stores and test for the significance of the first-order autoregressive parameter. (Use $\alpha = 0.05$.)

d. If appropriate, forecast the number of stores open in 2010 and 2011.

16.29 Refer to the data given in Problem 16.17 on page 622 that represent the closing values of the DJIA from 1979 to 2007 (stored in DJIA).

a. Fit a third-order autoregressive model to the DJIA and test for the significance of the third-order autoregressive parameter. (Use $\alpha = 0.05$.)

b. If necessary, fit a second-order autoregressive model to the DJIA and test for the significance of the second-order autoregressive parameter. (Use $\alpha = 0.05$.)

c. If necessary, fit a first-order autoregressive model to the DJIA and test for the significance of the first-order autoregressive parameter. (Use $\alpha = 0.05$.)

d. Forecast the DJIA for 2008. The actual value was 8,776.4. How accurate was your forecast? If it was not very accurate, what happened?

e. Add the 2008 value to the data set and redo (a) through (c).

f. Using the most appropriate model in (e), forecast the closing values for 2009 and 2010.

16.30 Refer to the data given in Problem 16.18 on page 622 (stored in GE) that represent the stock prices for GE from 1987 through 2008.

a. Fit a third-order autoregressive model to the stock price and test for the significance of the third-order autoregressive parameter. (Use $\alpha = 0.05$.)

b. If necessary, fit a second-order autoregressive model to the stock price and test for the significance of the second-order autoregressive parameter. (Use $\alpha = 0.05$.)

c. If necessary, fit a first-order autoregressive model to the stock price and test for the significance of the first-order autoregressive parameter. (Use $\alpha = 0.05$.)

d. Forecast the stock price for January 1, 2009. The actual value was $16.58. How accurate was your forecast? If it was not very accurate, what happened?

e. Add the 2008 value to the data set and redo (a) through (c).

f. Using the most appropriate model in (e), forecast the stock prices for January 1, 2010, and January 1, 2011.

16.31 Refer to the data given in Problem 16.16 on page 622 (and stored in SolarPower) that represent the yearly amount of solar power installed (in megawatts) in the United States from 2000 through 2008.

a. Fit a third-order autoregressive model to the amount of solar power and test for the significance of the third-order autoregressive parameter. (Use $\alpha = 0.05$.)

b. If necessary, fit a second-order autoregressive model to the amount of solar power and test for the significance of the second-order autoregressive parameter. (Use $\alpha = 0.05$.)

c. If necessary, fit a first-order autoregressive model to the amount of solar power and test for the significance of the first-order autoregressive parameter. (Use $\alpha = 0.05$.)

d. Forecast the yearly amount of solar power installed (in megawatts) in the United States in 2009 and 2010.

16.6 Choosing an Appropriate Forecasting Model

In Sections 16.4 and 16.5, you studied six time-series methods for short-term, intermediate term, and long-term forecasting: the linear trend model, the quadratic trend model, and the exponential trend model in Section 16.4; and the first-order, second-order, and pth-order autoregressive models in Section 16.5. Is there a *best* model? Among these models, which one should you select for forecasting? The following guidelines are provided for determining the adequacy of a particular forecasting model. These guidelines are based on a judgment of how well the model fits the data and assume that future movements in the time series can be projected by a study of the past data:

- Perform a residual analysis.
- Measure the magnitude of the residuals through squared differences.
- Measure the magnitude of the residuals through absolute differences.
- Use the principle of parsimony.

A discussion of these guidelines follows.

Performing a Residual Analysis

Recall from Sections 13.5 and 14.3 that residuals are the differences between observed and predicted values. After fitting a particular model to a time series, you plot the residuals over the n time periods. As shown in Figure 16.17 Panel A, if the particular model fits adequately, the residuals represent the irregular component of the time series. Therefore, they should be randomly distributed throughout the series. However, as illustrated in the three remaining panels of Figure 16.17, if the particular model does not fit adequately, the residuals may show a systematic pattern, such as a failure to account for trend (Panel B), a failure to account for cyclical variation (Panel C), or, with monthly or quarterly data, a failure to account for seasonal variation (Panel D).

FIGURE 16.17
Residual analysis for studying error patterns

Panel A
Randomly distributed forecast errors

Panel B
Trend not accounted for

Panel C
Cyclical effects not accounted for

Panel D
Seasonal effects not accounted for

Measuring the Magnitude of the Residuals Through Squared or Absolute Differences

If, after performing a residual analysis, you still believe that two or more models appear to fit the data adequately, you can use additional methods for model selection. Numerous measures based on the residuals are available (see references 1 and 4).

Based on the principle of least squares, one measure that you have already used in regression analysis (see Section 13.3) is the standard error of the estimate (S_{YX}). For a particular model, this measure is based on the sum of squared differences between the actual and predicted values in a time series. If a model fits the time-series data perfectly, then the standard error of the estimate is zero. If a model fits the time-series data poorly, then S_{YX} is large. Thus, when comparing the adequacy of two or more forecasting models, you can select the model with the minimum S_{YX} as most appropriate.

However, a major drawback to using S_{YX} when comparing forecasting models is that whenever there is a large difference between even a single Y_i and $\hat{Y}_i$, the value of S_{YX} becomes inflated through the squaring process. For this reason, many statisticians prefer the **mean absolute deviation (MAD)**. Equation (16.14) defines the *MAD* as the mean of the absolute differences between the actual and predicted values in a time series.

Compute the mean absolute deviation (MAD) using the instructions in Section EG16.6.

MEAN ABSOLUTE DEVIATION

$$MAD = \frac{\sum_{i=1}^{n} |Y_i - \hat{Y}_i|}{n} \qquad (16.14)$$

If a model fits the time-series data perfectly, the *MAD* is zero. If a model fits the time-series data poorly, the *MAD* is large. When comparing two or more forecasting models, you can select the one with the minimum *MAD* as the most appropriate model.

Using the Principle of Parsimony

If, after performing a residual analysis and comparing the S_{YX} and MAD measures, you still believe that two or more models appear to adequately fit the data, then you can use the principle of parsimony for model selection. As first explained in Section 15.4, **parsimony** guides you to select the regression model with the fewest independent variables that can predict the dependent variable adequately. In a more general sense, the principle of parsimony guides you to select the least complex regression model. Among the six forecasting models studied in this chapter, most statisticians consider the least-squares linear and quadratic models and the first-order autoregressive model as simpler than the second- and pth-order autoregressive models and the least-squares exponential model.

A Comparison of Four Forecasting Methods

Consider once again The Coca-Cola Company's revenue data. To illustrate the model selection process, you can compare four of the forecasting models used in Sections 16.4 and 16.5: the linear model, the quadratic model, the exponential model, and the first-order autoregressive model. (There is no need to further study the second-order or third-order autoregressive model for this time series because these models did not significantly improve the fit compared to the first-order autoregressive model.)

Figure 16.18 displays the residual plots for the four models. In reaching conclusions from these residual plots, you must use caution because there are only 14 values.

FIGURE 16.18

Residual plots for four forecasting methods

Create residual plots for the four forecasting methods using the instructions in Section EG16.6.

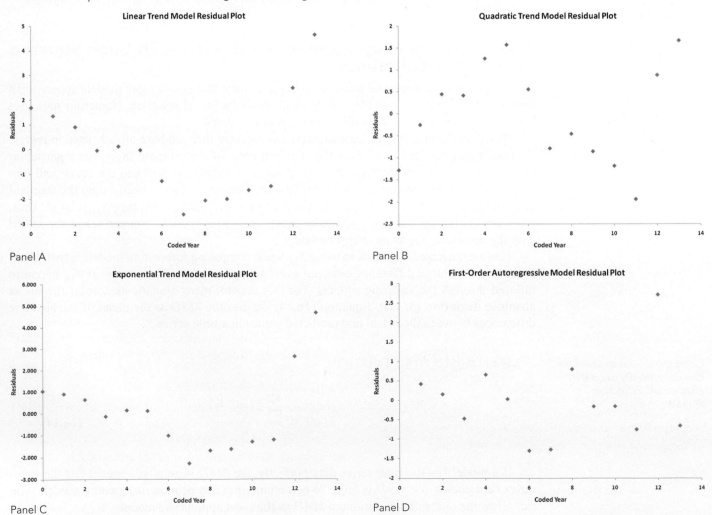

Panel A

Panel B

Panel C

Panel D

In Figure 16.18, observe the systematic structure of the residuals in the linear model (Panel A), quadratic model (Panel B), and exponential model (Panel C). For the autoregressive model (Panel D), the residuals appear more random.

To summarize, on the basis of the residual analysis of all four forecasting models, it appears that the first-order autoregressive model is the most appropriate, and the linear, quadratic, and exponential models are less appropriate. For further verification, you can compare the four models with respect to the magnitude of their residuals. Figure 16.19 shows the actual values (Y_i) along with the predicted values $\hat{Y}_i$ the residuals (e_i), the error sum of squares (SSE), the standard error of the estimate (S_{YX}), and the mean absolute deviation (MAD) for each of the four models.

FIGURE 16.19

Worksheet that summarizes and compares four forecasting methods, using S_{YX} and MAD

	A	B	C	D	E	F	G	H	I	J	K	L	M	N
1				Linear			Quadratic			Exponential			First-Order Autoregressive	
2	Year	Revenue		Predicted	Residual		Predicted	Residual		Predicted	Residual		Predicted	Residual
3	1995	18.0		16.3143	1.6857		19.2804	-1.2804		16.9670	1.0330		#N/A	#N/A
4	1996	18.5		17.1571	1.3429		18.7543	-0.2543		17.5946	0.9054		18.0781	0.4219
5	1997	18.9		18.0000	0.9000		18.4563	0.4437		18.2454	0.6546		18.7424	0.1576
6	1998	18.8		18.8429	-0.0429		18.3865	0.4135		18.9203	-0.1203		19.2739	-0.4739
7	1999	19.8		19.6857	0.1143		18.5449	1.2551		19.6201	0.1799		19.1411	0.6589
8	2000	20.5		20.5286	-0.0286		18.9315	1.5685		20.3458	0.1542		20.4697	0.0303
9	2001	20.1		21.3714	-1.2714		19.5462	0.5538		21.0984	-0.9984		21.3998	-1.2998
10	2002	19.6		22.2143	-2.6143		20.3890	-0.7890		21.8788	-2.2788		20.8684	-1.2684
11	2003	21.0		23.0571	-2.0571		21.4600	-0.4600		22.6881	-1.6881		20.2040	0.7960
12	2004	21.9		23.9000	-2.0000		22.7592	-0.8592		23.5273	-1.6273		22.0642	-0.1642
13	2005	23.1		24.7429	-1.6429		24.2865	-1.1865		24.3976	-1.2976		23.2600	-0.1600
14	2006	24.1		25.5857	-1.4857		26.0420	-1.9420		25.3000	-1.2000		24.8544	-0.7544
15	2007	28.9		26.4286	2.4714		28.0257	0.8743		26.2358	2.6642		26.1831	2.7169
16	2008	31.9		27.2714	4.6286		30.2375	1.6625		27.2063	4.6937		32.5608	-0.6608
17				SSE	54.5914		SSE	16.6942		SSE	46.326		SSE	13.2343
18				S_{YX}	2.1329		S_{YX}	1.2319		S_{YX}	1.965		S_{YX}	1.0969
19				MAD	1.592		MAD	0.967		MAD	1.393		MAD	0.762

For this time series, S_{YX} and MAD provide similar results. A comparison of the S_{YX} and MAD clearly indicates that the linear model provides the poorest fit. The first-order autoregressive model provides the best fit. Considering the results of the residual analysis and S_{YX} and MAD, the choice for the best model is the first-order autoregressive model.

After you select a particular forecasting model, you need to continually monitor your forecasts. If large errors occur between forecasted and actual values, the underlying structure of the time series may have changed. Remember that the forecasting methods presented in this chapter assume that the patterns inherent in the past will continue into the future. Large forecasting errors are an indication that an assumption is no longer true.

Problems for Section 16.6

LEARNING THE BASICS

16.32 The following residuals are from a linear trend model used to forecast sales:

2.0 −0.5 1.5 1.0 0.0 1.0 −3.0 1.5 −4.5 2.0 0.0 −1.0

a. Compute S_{YX} and interpret your findings.
b. Compute the MAD and interpret your findings.

16.33 Refer to Problem 16.32. Suppose the first residual is 12.0 (instead of 2.0) and the last residual is −11.0 (instead of −1.0).

a. Compute S_{YX} and interpret your findings
b. Compute the MAD and interpret your findings.

APPLYING THE CONCEPTS

16.34 Refer to the results in Problem 16.13 on page 621 (see GDP).
a. Perform a residual analysis.
b. Compute the standard error of the estimate (S_{YX}).
c. Compute the MAD.
d. On the basis of (a) through (c), are you satisfied with your linear trend forecasts in Problem 16.13? Discuss.

16.35 Refer to the results in Problem 16.15 on page 621 and Problem 16.27 on page 631 concerning the number of barrels of oil in the U.S. strategic oil reserve (stored in `Strategic`).
a. Perform a residual analysis for each model.
b. Compute the standard error of the estimate (S_{YX}) for each model.
c. Compute the *MAD* for each model.
d. On the basis of (a) through (c) and the principle of parsimony, which forecasting model would you select? Discuss.

SELF Test ✓ **16.36** Refer to the results in Problem 16.12 on page 621 and Problem 16.28 on page 631 concerning the number of Bed Bath & Beyond stores open (stored in `Bed & Bath`).
a. Perform a residual analysis for each model.
b. Compute the standard error of the estimate (S_{YX}) for each model.
c. Compute the *MAD* for each model.
d. On the basis of (a) through (c) and the principle of parsimony, which forecasting model would you select? Discuss.

16.37 Refer to the results in Problem 16.17 on page 622 and Problem 16.29 on page 632 concerning the DJIA (stored in `DJIA`).
a. Perform a residual analysis for each model.

b. Compute the standard error of the estimate (S_{YX}) for each model.
c. Compute the *MAD* for each model.
d. On the basis of (a) through (c) and the principle of parsimony, which forecasting model would you select? Discuss.

16.38 Refer to the results in Problem 16.18 on page 622 and Problem 16.30 on page 632 concerning the price per share for GE stock (stored in `GE`).
a. Perform a residual analysis for each model.
b. Compute the standard error of the estimate (S_{YX}) for each model.
c. Compute the *MAD* for each model.
d. On the basis of (a) through (c) and the principle of parsimony, which forecasting model would you select? Discuss.

16.39 Refer to the results in Problem 16.16 on page 622 and Problem 16.31 on page 632 concerning the yearly amount of solar power installed (in megawatts) in the United States from 2000 through 2008 (and stored in `SolarPower`).
a. Perform a residual analysis for each model.
b. Compute the standard error of the estimate (S_{YX}) for each model.
c. Compute the *MAD* for each model.
d. On the basis of (a) through (c) and the principle of parsimony, which forecasting model would you select? Discuss.

16.7 Time-Series Forecasting of Seasonal Data

So far, this chapter has focused on forecasting annual data. However, many time series are collected quarterly or monthly, and others are collected weekly, daily, and even hourly. When a time series is collected quarterly or monthly, you must consider the impact of seasonal effects. In this section, regression model building is used to forecast monthly or quarterly data.

One of the companies of interest in the Using Statistics scenario is Wal-Mart Stores, Inc. In 2009, Wal-Mart Stores, Inc., operated more than 8,000 retail units in 15 countries and had revenues that exceeded $400 billion (Wal-Mart Stores, Inc., **investor.walmartstores.com**). Wal-Mart revenues are highly seasonal, and therefore you need to analyze quarterly revenues. The fiscal year for the company ends January 31. Thus, the fourth quarter of 2009 includes November and December 2008 and January 2009. Table 16.3 lists the quarterly revenues, in billions of dollars, from 2004 to 2009 (stored in `WalMart`). Figure 16.20 displays the time series.

TABLE 16.3

Quarterly Revenues for Wal-Mart Stores, Inc., in Billions of Dollars (2004–2009)

| Quarter | Year | | | | | |
	2004	2005	2006	2007	2008	2009
1	56.7	64.8	71.6	79.6	86.4	95.3
2	62.6	69.7	76.8	84.5	93.0	102.7
3	62.4	68.5	75.4	83.5	91.9	98.6
4	74.5	82.2	88.6	98.1	107.3	109.1

Source: *Data extracted from Wal-Mart Stores, Inc.,* **investor.walmartstores.com**.

FIGURE 16.20

FIGURE 16.20

Plot of quarterly
revenues for Wal-Mart
Stores, Inc., in billions of
dollars (2004–2009)

*Create this worksheet using
the instructions in Section
EG2.7.*

Least-Squares Forecasting with Monthly or Quarterly Data

To develop a least-squares regression model that includes a seasonal component, the least-squares exponential trend fitting method used in Section 16.4 is combined with dummy variables (see Section 14.6) to model the seasonal component.

Equation (16.15) defines the exponential trend model for quarterly data.

EXPONENTIAL MODEL WITH QUARTERLY DATA

$$Y_i = \beta_0 \beta_1^{X_i} \beta_2^{Q_1} \beta_3^{Q_2} \beta_4^{Q_3} \varepsilon_i \qquad (16.15)$$

where

$$X_i = \text{coded quarterly value, } i = 0, 1, 2, \ldots$$

$$Q_1 = 1 \text{ if first quarter, 0 if not first quarter}$$

$$Q_2 = 1 \text{ if second quarter, 0 if not second quarter}$$

$$Q_3 = 1 \text{ if third quarter, 0 if not third quarter}$$

$$\beta_0 = Y \text{ intercept}$$

$$(\beta_1 - 1) \times 100\% = \text{quarterly compound growth rate (in \%)}$$

$$\beta_2 = \text{multiplier for first quarter relative to fourth quarter}$$

$$\beta_3 = \text{multiplier for second quarter relative to fourth quarter}$$

$$\beta_4 = \text{multiplier for third quarter relative to fourth quarter}$$

$$\varepsilon_i = \text{value of the irregular component for time period } i$$

---

[4]Alternatively, you can use base e logarithms. For more information on logarithms, see Section A.3 in Appendix A.

The model in Equation (16.15) is not in the form of a linear regression model. To transform this nonlinear model to a linear model, you use a base 10 logarithmic transformation.[4] Taking the logarithm of each side of Equation (16.15) results in Equation (16.16).

TRANSFORMED EXPONENTIAL MODEL WITH QUARTERLY DATA

$$\log(Y_i) = \log(\beta_0 \beta_1^{X_i} \beta_2^{Q_1} \beta_3^{Q_2} \beta_4^{Q_3} \varepsilon_i) \qquad \textbf{(16.16)}$$

$$= \log(\beta_0) + \log(\beta_1^{X_i}) + \log(\beta_2^{Q_1}) + \log(\beta_3^{Q_2}) + \log(\beta_4^{Q_3}) + \log(\varepsilon_i)$$

$$= \log(\beta_0) + X_i \log(\beta_1) + Q_1 \log(\beta_2) + Q_2 \log(\beta_3) + Q_3 \log(\beta_4) + \log(\varepsilon_i)$$

Equation (16.16) is a linear model that you can estimate using least-squares regression. Performing the regression analysis using $\log(Y_i)$ as the dependent variable and X_i, Q_1, Q_2, and Q_3 as the independent variables results in Equation (16.17).

EXPONENTIAL GROWTH WITH QUARTERLY DATA FORECASTING EQUATION

$$\log(\hat{Y}_i) = b_0 + b_1 X_i + b_2 Q_1 + b_3 Q_2 + b_4 Q_3 \qquad \textbf{(16.17)}$$

where

b_0 = estimate of $\log(\beta_0)$ and thus $10^{b_0} = \hat{\beta}_0$

b_1 = estimate of $\log(\beta_1)$ and thus $10^{b_1} = \hat{\beta}_1$

b_2 = estimate of $\log(\beta_2)$ and thus $10^{b_2} = \hat{\beta}_2$

b_3 = estimate of $\log(\beta_3)$ and thus $10^{b_3} = \hat{\beta}_3$

b_4 = estimate of $\log(\beta_4)$ and thus $10^{b_4} = \hat{\beta}_4$

Equation (16.18) is used for monthly data.

EXPONENTIAL MODEL WITH MONTHLY DATA

$$Y_i = \beta_0 \beta_1^{X_i} \beta_2^{M_1} \beta_3^{M_2} \beta_4^{M_3} \beta_5^{M_4} \beta_6^{M_5} \beta_7^{M_6} \beta_8^{M_7} \beta_9^{M_8} \beta_{10}^{M_9} \beta_{11}^{M_{10}} \beta_{12}^{M_{11}} \varepsilon_i \qquad \textbf{(16.18)}$$

where

X_i = coded monthly value, $i = 0, 1, 2, \ldots$

M_1 = 1 if January, 0 if not January

M_2 = 1 if February, 0 if not February

M_3 = 1 if March, 0 if not March

$\vdots$

M_{11} = 1 if November, 0 if not November

β_0 = Y intercept

$(\beta_1 - 1) \times 100\%$ = monthly compound growth rate (in %)

β_2 = multiplier for January relative to December

β_3 = multiplier for February relative to December

β_4 = multiplier for March relative to December

$\vdots$

β_{12} = multiplier for November relative to December

ε_i = value of the irregular component for time period i

The model in Equation (16.18) is not in the form of a linear regression model. To transform this nonlinear model to a linear model, you can use a base 10 logarithm transformation. Taking the logarithm of each side of Equation (16.18) results in Equation (16.19).

TRANSFORMED EXPONENTIAL MODEL WITH MONTHLY DATA

$$\log(Y_i) = \log(\beta_0 \beta_1^{X_i} \beta_2^{M_1} \beta_3^{M_2} \beta_4^{M_3} \beta_5^{M_4} \beta_6^{M_5} \beta_7^{M_6} \beta_8^{M_7} \beta_9^{M_8} \beta_{10}^{M_9} \beta_{11}^{M_{10}} \beta_{12}^{M_{11}} \varepsilon_i) \quad (16.19)$$

$$= \log(\beta_0) + X_i \log(\beta_1) + M_1 \log(\beta_2) + M_2 \log(\beta_3)$$
$$+ M_3 \log(\beta_4) + M_4 \log(\beta_5) + M_5 \log(\beta_6) + M_6 \log(\beta_7)$$
$$+ M_7 \log(\beta_8) + M_8 \log(\beta_9) + M_9 \log(\beta_{10}) + M_{10} \log(\beta_{11})$$
$$+ M_{11} \log(\beta_{12}) + \log(\varepsilon_i)$$

Equation (16.19) is a linear model that you can estimate using the least-squares method. Performing the regression analysis using $\log(Y_i)$ as the dependent variable and $X_i, M_1, M_2, \ldots,$ and M_{11} as the independent variables results in Equation (16.20).

EXPONENTIAL GROWTH WITH MONTHLY DATA FORECASTING EQUATION

$$\log(\hat{Y}_i) = b_0 + b_1 X_i + b_2 M_1 + b_3 M_2 + b_4 M_3 + b_5 M_4 + b_6 M_5 + b_7 M_6$$
$$+ b_8 M_7 + b_9 M_8 + b_{10} M_9 + b_{11} M_{10} + b_{12} M_{11} \quad (16.20)$$

where

$$b_0 = \text{estimate of } \log(\beta_0) \text{ and thus } 10^{b_0} = \hat{\beta}_0$$
$$b_1 = \text{estimate of } \log(\beta_1) \text{ and thus } 10^{b_1} = \hat{\beta}_1$$
$$b_2 = \text{estimate of } \log(\beta_2) \text{ and thus } 10^{b_2} = \hat{\beta}_2$$
$$b_3 = \text{estimate of } \log(\beta_3) \text{ and thus } 10^{b_3} = \hat{\beta}_3$$
$$\vdots$$
$$b_{12} = \text{estimate of } \log(\beta_{12}) \text{ and thus } 10^{b_{12}} = \hat{\beta}_{12}$$

$Q_1, Q_2,$ and Q_3 are the three dummy variables needed to represent the four quarter periods in a quarterly time series. $M_1, M_2, M_3, \ldots, M_{11}$ are the 11 dummy variables needed to represent the 12 months in a monthly time series. In building the model, you use $\log(Y_i)$ instead of Y_i values and then find the regression coefficients by taking the antilog of the regression coefficients developed from Equations (16.17) and (16.20).

Although at first glance these regression models look imposing, when fitting or forecasting in any one time period, the values of all or all but one of the dummy variables in the model are set equal to zero, and the equations simplify dramatically. In establishing the dummy variables for quarterly time-series data, the fourth quarter is the base period and has a coded value of zero for each dummy variable. With a quarterly time series, Equation (16.17) reduces as follows:

For any first quarter: $\log(\hat{Y}_i) = b_0 + b_1 X_i + b_2$
For any second quarter: $\log(\hat{Y}_i) = b_0 + b_1 X_i + b_3$
For any third quarter: $\log(\hat{Y}_i) = b_0 + b_1 X_i + b_4$
For any fourth quarter: $\log(\hat{Y}_i) = b_0 + b_1 X_i$

When establishing the dummy variables for each month, December serves as the base period and has a coded value of 0 for each dummy variable. For example, with a monthly time series, Equation (16.20) reduces as follows:

For any January: $\log(\hat{Y}_i) = b_0 + b_1X_i + b_2$
For any February: $\log(\hat{Y}_i) = b_0 + b_1X_i + b_3$

$$\vdots$$

For any November: $\log(\hat{Y}_i) = b_0 + b_1X_i + b_{12}$
For any December: $\log(\hat{Y}_i) = b_0 + b_1X_i$

To demonstrate the process of model building and least-squares forecasting with a quarterly time series, return to the Wal-Mart Stores, Inc., revenue data (in billions of dollars) originally displayed in Table 16.3 on page 636. The data are from each quarter from the first quarter of 2004 through the last quarter of 2009. Figure 16.21 shows the regression results worksheet for the quarterly exponential trend model.

FIGURE 16.21

Regression results worksheet for fitting and forecasting with the quarterly revenue data for Wal-Mart Stores, Inc.

Create this worksheet using the instructions in Section EG14.1.

	A	B	C	D	E	F	G
1	Quarterly Revenues Regression Model for Wal-Mart Stores						
2							
3	*Regression Statistics*						
4	Multiple R	0.9943					
5	R Square	0.9887					
6	Adjusted R Square	0.9863					
7	Standard Error	0.0093					
8	Observations	24					
9							
10	ANOVA						
11		*df*	*SS*	*MS*	*F*	*Significance F*	
12	Regression	4	0.1432	0.0358	414.6073	0.0000	
13	Residual	19	0.0016	0.0001			
14	Total	23	0.1449				
15							
16		*Coefficients*	*Standard Error*	*t Stat*	*P-value*	*Lower 95%*	*Upper 95%*
17	Intercept	1.8339	0.0052	350.1573	0.0000	1.8229	1.8448
18	Coded Quarter	0.0101	0.0003	36.5301	0.0000	0.0096	0.0107
19	Q1	-0.0626	0.0054	-11.5210	0.0000	-0.0739	-0.0512
20	Q2	-0.0401	0.0054	-7.4379	0.0000	-0.0514	-0.0288
21	Q3	-0.0578	0.0054	-10.7502	0.0000	-0.0690	-0.0465

From Figure 16.21, the model fits the data extremely well. The coefficient of determination $r^2 = 0.9887$ and the adjusted $r^2 = 0.9863$, and the overall F test results in an F_{STAT} test statistic of 414.6073 (p-value $= 0.000$). Looking further, at the 0.05 level of significance, each regression coefficient is highly statistically significant and contributes to the model. Taking the antilogs of all the regression coefficients, you have the following summary:

Regression Coefficient	$b_i = \log \hat{\beta}_i$	$\hat{\beta}_i = \text{antilog } (b_i) = 10^{b_i}$
b_0: Y intercept	1.8339	68.2182
b_1: coded quarter	0.0101	1.0235
b_2: first quarter	-0.0626	0.8658
b_3: second quarter	-0.0401	0.9118
b_4: third quarter	-0.0578	0.8754

The interpretations for $\hat{\beta}_0, \hat{\beta}_1, \hat{\beta}_2, \hat{\beta}_3,$ and $\hat{\beta}_4$ are as follows:

- The Y intercept, $\hat{\beta}_0 = 68.2182$ (in billions of dollars), is the *unadjusted* forecast for quarterly revenues in the first quarter of 2004, the initial quarter in the time series. *Unadjusted* means that the seasonal component is not incorporated in the forecast.
- The value $(\hat{\beta}_1 - 1) \times 100\% = 0.0235$, or 2.35%, is the estimated *quarterly compound growth rate* in revenues, after adjusting for the seasonal component.
- $\hat{\beta}_2 = 0.8658$ is the seasonal multiplier for the first quarter relative to the fourth quarter; it indicates that there is 13.42% less revenue for the first quarter as compared with the fourth quarter.
- $\hat{\beta}_3 = 0.9118$ is the seasonal multiplier for the second quarter relative to the fourth quarter; it indicates that there is 8.82% less revenue for the second quarter as compared with the fourth quarter.
- $\hat{\beta}_4 = 0.8754$ is the seasonal multiplier for the third quarter relative to the fourth quarter; it indicates that there is 12.46% less revenue for the third quarter than the fourth quarter. Thus, the fourth quarter, which includes the holiday shopping season, has the strongest sales.

Using the regression coefficients $b_0, b_1, b_2, b_3, b_4,$ and Equation (16.17) on page 638, you can make forecasts for selected quarters. As an example, to predict revenues for the fourth quarter of 2009 ($X_i = 23$):

$$\log(\hat{Y}_i) = b_0 + b_1 X_i$$

$$= 1.8339 + (0.0101)(23)$$

$$= 2.0662$$

Thus,

$$\log(\hat{Y}_i) = 10^{2.0662} = 116.4662$$

The predicted revenue for the fourth quarter of fiscal 2009 is $116.4662 billion. To make a forecast for a future time period, such as the first quarter of fiscal 2010 ($X_i = 24, Q_1 = 1$):

$$\log(\hat{Y}_i) = b_0 + b_1 X_i + b_2 Q_1$$

$$= 1.8339 + (0.0101)(24) + (-0.0626)(1)$$

$$= 2.0137$$

Thus,

$$\hat{Y}_i = 10^{2.0137} = 103.2048$$

The predicted revenue for the first quarter of fiscal 2010 is $103.2048 billion.

Problems for Section 16.7

LEARNING THE BASICS

16.40 In forecasting a monthly time series over a five-year period from January 2005 to December 2009, the exponential trend forecasting equation for January is

$$\log \hat{Y}_i = 2.0 + 0.01X_i + 0.10 \text{ (January)}$$

Take the antilog of the appropriate coefficient from this equation and interpret the
a. Y intercept, $\hat{b}_0$.
b. monthly compound growth rate.
c. January multiplier.

16.41 In forecasting daily time-series data, how many dummy variables are needed to account for the seasonal component day of the week?

16.42 In forecasting a quarterly time series over the five-year period from the first quarter of 2005 through the fourth quarter of 2009, the exponential trend forecasting equation is given by

$$\log \hat{Y}_i = 3.0 + 0.10X_i - 0.25Q_1 + 0.20Q_2 + 0.15Q_3$$

where quarter zero is the first quarter of 2005. Take the antilog of the appropriate coefficient from this equation and interpret the
a. Y intercept, $\hat{b}_0$.
b. quarterly compound growth rate.
c. second-quarter multiplier.

16.43 Refer to the exponential model given in Problem 16.42.

a. What is the fitted value of the series in the fourth quarter of 2007?
b. What is the fitted value of the series in the first quarter of 2007?
c. What is the forecast in the fourth quarter of 2009?
d. What is the forecast in the first quarter of 2010?

APPLYING THE CONCEPTS

✓ SELF Test **16.44** The data in `Toys R Us` are quarterly revenues (in millions of dollars) for Toys R Us from 1996 through 2008.

Source: *Data extracted from* Standard & Poor's Stock Reports, *November 1995, November 1998, and April 2002, New York: McGraw-Hill, Inc.; and Toys R Us, Inc.,* **www.toysrus.com**.

a. Do you think that the revenues for Toys R Us are subject to seasonal variation? Explain.
b. Plot the data. Does this chart support your answer in (a)?
c. Develop an exponential trend forecasting equation with quarterly components.
d. Interpret the quarterly compound growth rate.
e. Interpret the quarterly multipliers.
f. What are the forecasts for all four quarters of 2009?

16.45 Are gasoline prices higher during the height of the summer vacation season? The data in `Unleaded` gives the mean monthly prices (in dollars per gallon) for unleaded gasoline in the United States from January 2003 to February 2009.

Source: *Data extracted from Energy Information Administration, U.S. Department of Energy,* **www.eia.doe.gov**.

a. Construct a time-series plot.
b. Develop an exponential trend forecasting equation for monthly data.
c. Interpret the monthly compound growth rate.
d. Interpret the monthly multipliers.
e. Write a short summary of your findings.

16.46 The U.S. Bureau of Labor Statistics compiles data on a wide variety of workforce issues. The data in `Unemployment2` give the monthly seasonally adjusted civilian unemployment rates for the United States from January 2002 to April 2009.

Source: *Data extracted from Bureau of Labor Statistics, U.S. Department of Labor,* **www.bls.gov**.

a. Plot the time-series data.
b. Develop an exponential trend forecasting equation with monthly components.
c. What is the fitted value in April 2009?
d. What are the forecasts for the last eight months of 2009?
e. Interpret the monthly compound growth rate.
f. Interpret the July multiplier.
g. Go to your library or the Internet and locate the actual unemployment rates for the last eight months of 2009. Discuss.

16.47 The following data (stored in `Credit`) are monthly credit card charges (in millions of dollars) for a popular credit card issued by a large bank (the name of which is not disclosed at its request):

	Year		
Month	**2007**	**2008**	**2009**
January	31.9	39.4	45.0
February	27.0	36.2	39.6
March	31.3	40.5	
April	31.0	44.6	
May	39.4	46.8	
June	40.7	44.7	
July	42.3	52.2	
August	49.5	54.0	
September	45.0	48.8	
October	50.0	55.8	
November	50.9	58.7	
December	58.5	63.4	

a. Construct the time-series plot.
b. Describe the monthly pattern that is evident in the data.
c. In general, would you say that the overall dollar amounts charged on the bank's credit cards is increasing or decreasing? Explain.
d. Note that December 2008 charges were more than $63 million, but those for February 2009 were less than $40 million. Was February's total close to what you would have expected?
e. Develop an exponential trend forecasting equation with monthly components.
f. Interpret the monthly compound growth rate.
g. Interpret the January multiplier.
h. What is the predicted value for March 2009?
i. What is the predicted value for April 2009?
j. How can this type of time-series forecasting benefit the bank?

16.48 The data in `S&P Index` represent the S&P Composite Stock Price Index recorded at the end of each quarter from 1998 through the first quarter of 2009.

Source: *Data extracted from* **finance.yahoo.com**.

a. Plot the data.
b. Develop an exponential trend forecasting equation with quarterly components.
c. Interpret the quarterly compound growth rate.
d. Interpret the first quarter multiplier.
e. What is the fitted value for the first quarter of 2009?
f. What are the forecasts for the remaining three quarters of 2009?
g. Were the forecasts in (f) accurate? Explain.

16.49 The data in `Ford` are quarterly revenues (in millions of dollars) for the Ford Motor Company, from 1996 through 2008.

Source: *Data extracted from* Standard & Poor's Stock Reports, *November 2000 and April 2002, New York: McGraw-Hill, Inc.; and Ford Motor Company,* **www.ford.com**.

a. Do you think that the revenues for the Ford Motor Company are subject to seasonal variation? Explain.

b. Plot the data. Does this chart support your answer to (a)?

c. Develop an exponential trend forecasting equation with quarterly components.

d. Interpret the quarterly compound growth rate.

e. Interpret the quarterly multipliers.

f. What are the forecasts for all four quarters of 2009?

16.8 *Online Topic:* Index Numbers

Index numbers measure the value of an item (or group of items) at a particular point in time as a percentage of the value of an item (or group of items) at another point in time. To study this topic, read the **Section 16.8** online topic file that is available on this book's companion Web site. (See Appendix Section D.8 to learn how to access the online topic files.)

THINK ABOUT THIS | Let the Model User Beware

When you use a model, you must always review the assumptions built into the model and must always reflect how novel or changing circumstances may render the model less useful. No model can completely remove the risk involved in making a decision.

Implicit in the time-series models developed in this chapter is that past data can be used to help predict the future. While using past data in this way is a legitimate application of time-series models, every so often, a crisis in financial markets illustrates that using models that rely on the past to predict the future is not without risk.

For example, during August 2007, many hedge funds suffered unprecedented losses.

Apparently, many hedge fund managers used models that based their investment strategy on trading patterns over long time periods. These models did not—and could not—reflect trading patterns contrary to historical patterns (G. Morgenson, "A Week When Risk Came Home to Roost," *The New York Times*, August 12, 2007, pp. B1, B7). When fund managers in early August 2007 needed to sell stocks due to losses in their fixed income portfolios, stocks that were previously stronger became weaker, and weaker ones became stronger—the reverse of what the models expected. Making matters worse was the fact that many fund managers were using similar models and rigidly

made investment decisions solely based on what those models said. These similar actions multiplied the effect of the selling pressure, an effect that the models had not considered and that therefore could not be seen in the models' results.

This example illustrates that using models does not absolve you of the responsibility of being a thoughtful decision maker. Do go ahead and use models—when appropriately used, they will enhance your decision making—but don't use them mindlessly, for, in the words of a famous public service announcement, "a mind is a terrible thing to waste".

USING STATISTICS | @ The Principled Revisited

In the Using Statistics scenario, you were the financial analyst for The Principled, a large financial services company. You needed to forecast revenues for the Cabot Corporation, Coca-Cola, and Wal-Mart to better evaluate investment opportunities for your clients.

For the Cabot Corporation you used moving averages and exponential smoothing methods to develop forecasts. You predicted that the revenue of Cabot Corporation during 2009 would be $2,419.1 million.

For The Coca-Cola Company, you used least-squares linear, quadratic, and exponential models and autoregressive models to develop forecasts. You evaluated these alternative models and determined that the first-order autoregressive model gave the best forecast according to several criteria. You predicted that the revenue of The Coca-Cola Company would be $36.5471 billion in 2009 and $42.7217 billion in 2010.

For Wal-Mart Stores, Inc., you used a least-squares regression model with seasonal components to develop forecasts. You predicted that Wal-Mart Stores would have revenues of $103.2048 billion in the first quarter of fiscal 2010.

Given these forecasts for these three companies, you now need to determine whether your clients should invest, and if so, how much should they invest in these companies.

SUMMARY

In this chapter, you used time-series methods to develop forecasts for Cabot Corporation, The Coca-Cola Company, and Wal-Mart Stores, Inc. You studied smoothing techniques, least-squares trend fitting, autoregressive models, and forecasting of seasonal data. Figure 16.22 provides a summary chart for the time-series methods discussed in this chapter.

When using time-series forecasting, you need to plot the time series and answer the following question: Is there a trend in the data? If there is a trend, then you can use the autoregressive model or the linear, quadratic, or exponential trend models. If there is no obvious trend in the time-series plot, then you should use moving averages or exponential smoothing to smooth out the effect of random effects and possible cyclical effects. After smoothing the data, if a trend is still not present, then you can use exponential smoothing to forecast future values. If smoothing the data reveals a trend, then you can use the autoregressive model, or the linear, quadratic, or exponential trend models.

FIGURE 16.22

Summary chart of time-series forecasting methods

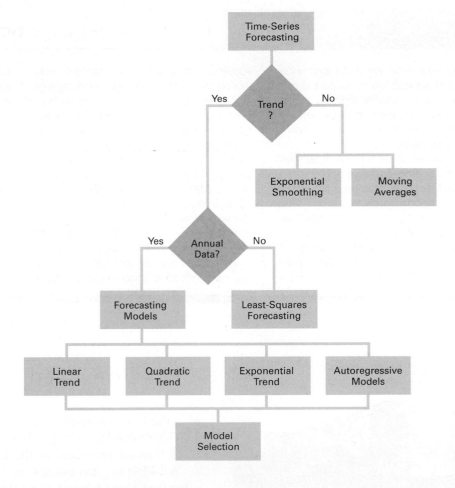

KEY EQUATIONS

Computing an Exponentially Smoothed Value in Time Period i

$$E_1 = Y_1 \tag{16.1}$$

$$E_i = WY_i + (1 - W)E_{i-1} \quad i = 2, 3, 4, \ldots$$

Forecasting Time Period $i + 1$

$$\hat{Y}_{i+1} = E_i \tag{16.2}$$

Linear Trend Forecasting Equation

$$\hat{Y}_i = b_0 + b_1 X_i \tag{16.3}$$

Quadratic Trend Forecasting Equation

$$\hat{Y}_i = b_0 + b_1 X_i + b_2 X_i^2 \tag{16.4}$$

Exponential Trend Model

$$Y_i = \beta_0 \beta_1^{X_i} \varepsilon_i \tag{16.5}$$

Transformed Exponential Trend Model

$$\begin{aligned}\log(Y_i) &= \log(\beta_0 \beta_1^{X_i} \varepsilon_i) & \textbf{(16.6)}\\ &= \log(\beta_0) + \log(\beta_1^{X_i}) + \log(\varepsilon_i)\\ &= \log(\beta_0) + X_i \log(\beta_1) + \log(\varepsilon_i)\end{aligned}$$

Exponential Trend Forecasting Equation

$$\log(\hat{Y}_i) = b_0 + b_1 X_i \qquad \textbf{(16.7a)}$$

$$\hat{Y}_i = \hat{\beta}_0 \, \hat{\beta}_1^{X_i} \qquad \textbf{(16.7b)}$$

First-Order Autoregressive Model

$$Y_i = A_0 + A_1 Y_{i-1} + \delta_i \qquad \textbf{(16.8)}$$

Second-Order Autoregressive Model

$$Y_i = A_0 + A_1 Y_{i-1} + A_2 Y_{i-2} + \delta_i \qquad \textbf{(16.9)}$$

***p*th-Order Autoregressive Models**

$$Y_i = A_0 + A_1 Y_{i-1} + A_2 Y_{i-2} + \cdots + A_p Y_{i-p} + \delta_i \quad \textbf{(16.10)}$$

***t* Test for Significance of the Highest-Order Autoregressive Parameter, A_p**

$$t_{STAT} = \frac{a_p - A_p}{S_{a_p}} \qquad \textbf{(16.11)}$$

Fitted *p*th-Order Autoregressive Equation

$$\hat{Y}_i = a_0 + a_1 Y_{i-1} + a_2 Y_{i-2} + \cdots + a_p Y_{i-p} \qquad \textbf{(16.12)}$$

***p*th-Order Autoregressive Forecasting Equation**

$$\hat{Y}_{n+j} = a_0 + a_1 \hat{Y}_{n+j-1} + a_2 \hat{Y}_{n+j-2} + \cdots + a_p \hat{Y}_{n+j-p} \quad \textbf{(16.13)}$$

Mean Absolute Deviation

$$MAD = \frac{\sum_{i=1}^{n} |Y_i - \hat{Y}_i|}{n} \qquad \textbf{(16.14)}$$

Exponential Model with Quarterly Data

$$Y_i = \beta_0 \beta_1^{X_i} \beta_2^{Q_1} \beta_3^{Q_2} \beta_4^{Q_3} \varepsilon_i \qquad \textbf{(16.15)}$$

Transformed Exponential Model with Quarterly Data

$$\begin{aligned}\log(Y_i) &= \log(\beta_0 \beta_1^{X_i} \beta_2^{Q_1} \beta_3^{Q_2} \beta_4^{Q_3} \varepsilon_i)\\ &= \log(\beta_0) + \log(\beta_1^{X_i}) + \log(\beta_2^{Q_1}) + \log(\beta_3^{Q_2})\\ &\quad + \log(\beta_4^{Q_3}) + \log(\varepsilon_i)\\ &= \log(\beta_0) + X_i \log(\beta_1) + Q_1 \log(\beta_2)\\ &\quad + Q_2 \log(\beta_3) + Q_3 \log(\beta_4) + \log(\varepsilon_i) \quad \textbf{(16.16)}\end{aligned}$$

Exponential Growth with Quarterly Data Forecasting Equation

$$\log(\hat{Y}_i) = b_0 + b_1 X_i + b_2 Q_1 + b_3 Q_2 + b_4 Q_3 \qquad \textbf{(16.17)}$$

Exponential Model with Monthly Data

$$Y_i = \beta_0 \beta_1^{X_i} \beta_2^{M_1} \beta_3^{M_2} \beta_4^{M_3} \beta_5^{M_4} \beta_6^{M_5} \beta_7^{M_6} \beta_8^{M_7} \beta_9^{M_8} \beta_{10}^{M_9} \beta_{11}^{M_{10}} \beta_{12}^{M_{11}} \varepsilon_i \qquad \textbf{(16.18)}$$

Transformed Exponential Model with Monthly Data

$$\begin{aligned}\log(Y_i) &= \log(\beta_0 \beta_1^{X_i} \beta_2^{M_1} \beta_3^{M_2} \beta_4^{M_3} \beta_5^{M_4} \beta_6^{M_5} \beta_7^{M_6} \beta_8^{M_7} \beta_9^{M_8} \beta_{10}^{M_9} \beta_{11}^{M_{10}} \beta_{12}^{M_{11}} \varepsilon_i)\\ &= \log(\beta_0) + X_i \log(\beta_1) + M_1 \log(\beta_2) + M_2 \log(\beta_3)\\ &\quad + M_3 \log(\beta_4) + M_4 \log(\beta_5) + M_5 \log(\beta_6) + M_6 \log(\beta_7)\\ &\quad + M_7 \log(\beta_8) + M_8 \log(\beta_9) + M_9 \log(\beta_{10})\\ &\quad + M_{10} \log(\beta_{11}) + M_{11} \log(\beta_{12}) + \log(\varepsilon_i) \quad \textbf{(16.19)}\end{aligned}$$

Exponential Growth with Monthly Data Forecasting Equation

$$\begin{aligned}\log(\hat{Y}_i) &= b_0 + b_1 X_i + b_2 M_1 + b_3 M_2 + b_4 M_3 + b_5 M_4 + b_6 M_5\\ &\quad + b_7 M_6 + b_8 M_7 + b_9 M_8 + b_{10} M_9 + b_{11} M_{10} + b_{12} M_{11} \quad \textbf{(16.20)}\end{aligned}$$

KEY TERMS

CHAPTER REVIEW PROBLEMS

CHECKING YOUR UNDERSTANDING

16.50 What is a time series?

16.51 What are the different components of a time-series model?

16.52 What is the difference between moving averages and exponential smoothing?

16.53 Under what circumstances is the exponential trend model most appropriate?

16.54 How does the least-squares linear trend forecasting model developed in this chapter differ from the least-squares linear regression model considered in Chapter 13?

16.55 How does autoregressive modeling differ from the other approaches to forecasting?

16.56 What are the different approaches to choosing an appropriate forecasting model?

16.57 What is the major difference between using S_{YX} and MAD for evaluating how well a particular model fits the data?

16.58 How does forecasting for monthly or quarterly data differ from forecasting for annual data?

APPLYING THE CONCEPTS

16.59 The following table (stored in Polio) represents the annual incidence rates (per 100,000 persons) of reported acute poliomyelitis recorded over five-year periods from 1915 to 1955:

Year	1915	1920	1925	1930	1935	1940	1945	1950	1955
Rate	3.1	2.2	5.3	7.5	8.5	7.4	10.3	22.1	17.6

Source: *Data extracted from B. Wattenberg, ed., The Statistical History of the United States: From Colonial Times to the Present, ser. B303 (New York: Basic Books, 1976).*

a. Plot the data.
b. Compute the linear trend forecasting equation and plot the trend line.
c. What are your forecasts for 1960, 1965, and 1970?
d. Using a library or the Internet, find the actually reported incidence rates of acute poliomyelitis for 1960, 1965, and 1970. Record your results.
e. Why are the forecasts you made in (c) not useful? Discuss.

16.60 The U.S. Department of Labor gathers and publishes statistics concerning the labor market. The file Workforce contains the U.S. civilian noninstitutional population of people 16 years and over (in thousands) and the U.S. civilian noninstitutional workforce of people 16 years and over (in thousands) for 1984–2008. The workforce variable reports

the number of people in the population who have a job or are actively looking for a job.

Source: *Data extracted from Bureau of Labor Statistics, U.S. Department of Labor,* **www.bls.gov**.

a. Plot the time series for the U.S. civilian noninstitutional population of people 16 years and older.
b. Compute the linear trend forecasting equation.
c. Forecast the U.S. civilian noninstitutional population of people 16 years and older for 2009 and 2010.
d. Repeat (a) through (c) for the U.S. civilian noninstitutional workforce of people 16 years and older.

16.61 The quarterly price for natural gas (dollars per 40 therms) in the United States from 1994 through 2008 is stored in Natural Gas.

Source: *Data extracted from Energy Information Administration, U.S. Department of Energy,* **www.eia.gov**.

a. Do you think the price for natural gas has a seasonal component?
b. Plot the time series. Does this chart support your answer in (a)?
c. Compute an exponential trend forecasting equation for quarterly data.
d. Interpret the quarterly compound growth rate.
e. Interpret the quarter multipliers. Do the multipliers support your answers in (a) and (b)?

16.62 The data in the following table (stored in McDonalds) represent the gross revenues (in billions of current dollars) of McDonald's Corporation from 1975 through 2008:

Year	Revenues	Year	Revenues	Year	Revenues
1975	1.0	1987	4.9	1999	13.3
1976	1.2	1988	5.6	2000	14.2
1977	1.4	1989	6.1	2001	14.8
1978	1.7	1990	6.8	2002	15.2
1979	1.9	1991	6.7	2003	16.8
1980	2.2	1992	7.1	2004	18.6
1981	2.5	1993	7.4	2005	19.8
1982	2.8	1994	8.3	2006	20.9
1983	3.1	1995	9.8	2007	22.8
1984	3.4	1996	10.7	2008	23.5
1985	3.8	1997	11.4		
1986	4.2	1998	12.4		

Source: *Data extracted from Moody's Handbook of Common Stocks, 1980, 1989, and 1999; Mergent's Handbook of Common Stocks, Spring 2002; and* **www.mcdonalds.com**.

a. Plot the data.
b. Compute the linear trend forecasting equation.
c. Compute the quadratic trend forecasting equation.
d. Compute the exponential trend forecasting equation.
e. Find the best-fitting autoregressive model, using $\alpha = 0.05$.

f. Perform a residual analysis for each of the models in (b) through (e).

g. Compute the standard error of the estimate (S_{YX}) and the *MAD* for each corresponding model in (f).

h. On the basis of your results in (f) and (g), along with a consideration of the principle of parsimony, which model would you select for purposes of forecasting? Discuss.

i. Using the selected model in (h), forecast gross revenues for 2009.

16.63 The U.S. Census Bureau tracks the number of new houses for which construction is begun each quarter. This metric of economic activity is often referred to as "housing starts." The file `Housing` contains quarterly data from 2000 to 2008.

a. Do you think new housing construction is seasonal? Why or why not?

b. Plot the data.

c. Does your graph in (b) support your answer in (a)?

d. Develop an exponential trend forecasting equation with quarterly data.

e. Based on (d), which quarter has the most housing starts? The smallest number of housing starts?

f. Is there a long-term trend from 2000 to 2008 in the number of new houses being built?

16.64 Teachers' Retirement System of the City of New York offers several types of investments for its members. Among the choices are investments with fixed and variable rates of return. There are currently two categories of variable-return investments. Variable *A* consists of investments that are primarily made in stocks, and Variable *B* consists of investments in corporate bonds and other types of lower-risk instruments. The data (stored in TRSNYC) represent the value of a unit of each type of variable-return investment at the beginning of each year from 1984 to 2009.

Source: *Data extracted from Teachers' Retirement System of the City of New York,* **www.trs.nyc.ny.us**.

For each of the two time series,

a. plot the data.

b. compute the linear trend forecasting equation.

c. compute the quadratic trend forecasting equation.

d. compute the exponential trend forecasting equation.

e. find the best-fitting autoregressive model, using $\alpha = 0.05$.

f. Perform a residual analysis for each of the models in (b) through (e).

g. Compute the standard error of the estimate (S_{YX}) and the *MAD* for each corresponding model in (f).

h. On the basis of your results in (f) and (g), along with a consideration of the principle of parsimony, which model would you select for purposes of forecasting? Discuss.

i. Using the selected model in (h), forecast the unit values for 2010.

j. Based on the results of (a) through (i), what investment strategy would you recommend for a member of the Teachers' Retirement System of the City of New York? Explain.

REPORT WRITING EXERCISES

16.65 As a consultant to an investment company trading in various currencies, you have been assigned the task of studying long-term trends in the exchange rates of the Canadian dollar, the Japanese yen, and the English pound. Data from 1980 to 2008 are stored in `Currency`, where the Canadian dollar, the Japanese yen, and the English pound are expressed in units per U.S. dollar.

Develop a forecasting model for the exchange rate of each of these three currencies and provide forecasts for 2009 and 2010 for each currency. Write an executive summary for a presentation to be given to the investment company. Append to this executive summary a discussion regarding possible limitations that may exist in these models.

MANAGING THE *SPRINGVILLE HERALD*

As part of the continuing strategic initiative to increase home-delivery subscriptions, the circulation department is closely monitoring the number of such subscriptions. The circulation department wants to forecast future home-delivery subscriptions. To accomplish this task, the circulation department compiled the number of home-delivery subscriptions for the most recent 24-month period and stored the data in `SH16`.

EXERCISES

SH16.1 a. Analyze these data and develop a model to forecast home-delivery subscriptions. Present your findings in a report that includes the assump-

tions of the model and its limitations. Forecast home-delivery subscriptions for the next four months.

b. Would you be willing to use the model developed to forecast home-delivery subscriptions one year into the future? Explain.

c. Compare the trend in home-delivery subscriptions to the number of new subscriptions per month stored in `SH13`. What explanation can you provide for any differences?

WEB CASE

Apply your knowledge about time-series forecasting in this Web Case, which extends the running "Managing the Springville Herald" case that appears in selected chapters of this book.

The *Springville Herald* competes for readers in the Tri-Cities area with the newer *Oxford Glen Journal* (*OGJ*). Recently, the circulation staff at the *OGJ* claimed that their newspaper's circulation and subscription base is growing faster than that of the *Herald* and that local advertisers would do better if they transferred their advertisements from the *Herald* to the *OGJ*. The circulation department of the *Herald* has complained to the Springville Chamber of Commerce about *OGJ*'s claims and has asked the chamber to investigate, a request that was welcomed by *OGJ*'s circulation staff.

Using a Web browser, open to the Web page for the Chapter 16 Web Case (or open **SCC_CirculationDispute.htm** if you have downloaded the Web Case files) to review the circulation dispute information collected by the Springville Chamber of Commerce. Then answer the following:

1. Which newspaper would you say has the right to claim the fastest-growing circulation and subscription base? Support your answer by performing and summarizing an appropriate statistical analysis.

2. What is the single most positive fact about the *Herald*'s circulation and subscription base? What is the single most positive fact about the *OGJ*'s circulation and subscription base? Explain your answers.

3. What additional data would be helpful in investigating the circulation claims made by the staffs of each newspaper?

REFERENCES

1. Bowerman, B. L., R. T. O'Connell, and A. Koehler, *Forecasting, Time Series, and Regression*, 4th ed. (Belmont, CA: Duxbury Press, 2005).
2. Box, G. E. P., G. M. Jenkins, and G. C. Reinsel, *Time Series Analysis: Forecasting and Control*, 3rd ed. (Upper Saddle River, NJ: Prentice Hall, 1994).
3. Frees, E. W., *Data Analysis Using Regression Models: The Business Perspective* (Upper Saddle River, NJ: Prentice Hall, 1996).
4. Hanke, J. E., D. W. Wichern, and A. G. Reitsch, *Business Forecasting*, 7th ed. (Upper Saddle River, NJ: Prentice Hall, 2001).
5. *Microsoft Excel 2007* (Redmond, WA: Microsoft Corp., 2007).

CHAPTER 16 EXCEL GUIDE

EG16.1 The IMPORTANCE of BUSINESS FORECASTING

There are no Excel Guide instructions for this section.

EG16.2 COMPONENT FACTORS of TIME-SERIES MODELS

There are no Excel Guide instructions for this section.

EG16.3 SMOOTHING an ANNUAL TIME SERIES

Moving Averages

In-Depth Excel Use the **AVERAGE** function in a series of formulas to compute moving averages for time-series data. Enter the function as **AVERAGE***(cell range that contains a sequence of L observed values)*. For time periods in which no moving average can be computed, use the special worksheet value **#N/A** (not available). For example, for a three-year moving average, enter the #N/A value for the first and last time periods; for a seven-year moving average, enter the #N/A value for the first three and the last three time periods.

Use the **COMPUTE worksheet** of the **Moving Averages workbook**, shown in Figure 16.2 on page 609, as a template for creating moving averages. For other problems, paste the time-series data into columns A and B and adjust the moving average entries in columns C and D. The COMPUTE worksheet also contains a superimposed chart, an exception to the general rule in this book that places each chart on its own chart sheet. To use this chart for other problems, double-click the chart titles and labels to change them to appropriate values. (The plot of points changes automatically when you change the data.) To create the chart from scratch on its own chart sheet, keep the COMPUTE worksheet open. Select the cell range **A1:D28**, the cell range of the time-series data and the moving averages. Continue with either the *In-Depth Excel 2007* or *In-Depth Excel 2003* instructions.

In-Depth Excel 2007 *Continued from In-Depth Excel...*
Select **Insert → Scatter** and select the second **Scatter** gallery choice in the second row of choices (**Scatter with Straight Lines and Markers**). Relocate the chart to a chart sheet and adjust the chart formatting by using the instructions in Appendix Section C.7 on page 726, ignoring the instruction to select **None** from the **Legend** gallery.

In-Depth Excel 2003 *Continued from In-Depth Excel...*
Select **Insert → Chart** and:
In the Chart Wizard Step 1 dialog box:
1. Click the **Standard Types** tab. Click **XY (Scatter)** as the **Chart type** and then click the first **Chart sub-type** choice in the third row, labeled **Scatter with data points connected by lines** when selected.
2. Click **Next**.
In the Chart Wizard Step 2 dialog box:
3. Click **Next**.
In the Chart Wizard Step 3 dialog box:
4. Click the **Titles** tab. Enter a **Chart title**, **Year** as the **Value (X) axis** title, and **Revenues ($millions)** as the **Value (Y) axis** title. Use the formatting settings discussed in Appendix Section C.8 on page 727 for the **Axes**, **Gridlines**, **Data Labels**, and **Data Table** tabs.
In the Chart Wizard Step 4 dialog box:
5. Click **As new sheet** and then click **Finish** to complete the chart.

Exponential Smoothing

In-Depth Excel Use a series of formulas to compute exponential smoothed values. Enter formulas for the second through last time periods in the form =(*W * time period value* + (1 − *W*)* *previous row's smoothed value*). For the first time period, enter the formula in the form =(*time period value*).

Use the **COMPUTE worksheet** of the **Exponential Smoothing workbook**, shown in Figure 16.3 on page 610, as a template for creating exponentially smoothed values. In this worksheet, cells C2 and D2 contain the formula **=B2**, cell **C3** contains the formula **=0.5*B3 + 0.5*C2**, and cell **D3** contains the formula **=0.25*B3 + 0.75*D2**. The other formulas in columns C and D are the result of copying the C3 and D3 formulas down the columns. (Note that in the C3 and D3 formulas, the expression 1 − *W* has been simplified to the values 0.5 and 0.75, respectively.)

For other problems with fewer than 27 time periods, delete the excess rows. For problems with more than 27 time periods, select row 28, right-click, and click **Insert** in the shortcut menu. Repeat as many times as there are new rows. Then select cell range **C27:D27** and copy their contents down through the new table rows.

The COMPUTE worksheet also contains a superimposed chart, an exception to the general rule in this book that places each chart on its own chart sheet. To use this chart for other problems, double-click the chart titles and labels to change them to appropriate values. (The plot of points changes automatically when you change the data.) To create the chart from scratch on its own chart sheet, keep the COMPUTE worksheet open. Select the cell range **A1:D28**, the cell range of the time-series data and the moving averages. Continue with either the *In-Depth Excel 2007* or *In-Depth Excel 2003* instructions that are presented as part of the "Moving Averages": *In-Depth Excel* instructions on page 651.

Analysis ToolPak   Use the **Exponential Smoothing** procedure to create exponentially smoothed values. For example, to create the column C exponentially smoothed Cabot Corporation revenue values (smoothing coefficient $W = 0.50$) in Figure 16.3 on page 610, open to the **DATA worksheet** of the **Cabot workbook** and:

1. Select **Data → Data Analysis** (Excel 2007) or **Tools → Data Analysis** (Excel 2003).

2. In the Data Analysis dialog box, select **Exponential Smoothing** from the **Analysis Tools** list and then click **OK**.

In the Exponential Smoothing dialog box (shown below):

3. Enter **B1:B28** as the **Input Range**.

4. Enter **0.5** as the **Damping factor**. (The damping factor is equal to $1 - W$.)

5. Check **Labels**, enter **C1** as the **Output Range**, and click **OK**.

In the new column C:

6. Copy the last formula in cell **C27** to cell **C28**.

7. Enter the column heading **ES(W = .50)** in cell **D1**, replacing the #N/A value.

For other problems, to create exponentially smoothed values using a smoothing coefficient of $W = 0.25$, enter **0.75** as the damping factor in step 4. (The damping factor is equal to $1 - W$.)

EG16.4 LEAST-SQUARES TREND FITTING and FORECASTING

Creating Coded Values   Create coded values (see page 613) for an X (time) variable by adding a new column in a time-series data worksheet that contains consecutive

integers starting with 0. Use the Fill Series command to create the entries in this cell. For example, to created coded values for the Year column for The Coca-Cola Company revenues shown in Table 16.2 on page 613, open to the **DATA worksheet** of the **Coca-Cola workbook**. Select column B, right-click, and click **Insert** from the shortcut menu to insert a new blank column B. Enter the label **Coded Year** in cell **B1** as the column heading. Enter **0** in cell **B2**. (Re)select cell **B2** and then select **Home → Fill** (in the Editing group) → **Series** (Excel 2007) or **Edit → Fill → Series** (Excel 2003). In the Series dialog box (shown below), click **Columns** and **Linear**, enter **1** as the **Step value** and **13** as the **Stop value**, and click **OK**.

The Linear Trend Model   Modify the Section EG13.2 instructions (see page 521) to create a linear trend model. Use the cell range of the coded variable as the X variable cell range (called the **X Variable Cell Range** in the *PHStat2* instructions, called the *cell range of X variable* in the *In-Depth Excel* instructions, and called the **Input X Range** in the *Analysis ToolPak* instructions).

The Quadratic Trend Model   Modify the Section EG15.1 instructions (see page 602) to create a quadratic trend model. Use the cell range of the coded variable and the squared coded variable as the X variables cell range (called the **X Variables Cell Range** in the *PHStat2* instructions, called the *cell range of X variables* in the *In-Depth Excel* instructions, and called the **Input X Range** in the *Analysis ToolPak* instructions). Use the Section EG15.1 instructions to create the squared coded variable.

To plot the quadratic trend, modify the "Adding a Prediction Line and Regression Equation to a Scatter Plot" instructions in Section EG13.2 (see page 521). Choose the polynomial type (not linear) by clicking **Polynomial** in step 2 of the instructions for either *In-Depth Excel 2007* or *In-Depth Excel 2003*.

The Exponential Trend Model   Due to the limitations of Excel, creating an exponential trend model requires more work than creating the other trend models. First, modify the Section EG13.5 and EG13.2 instructions (see pages 523 and 521) to use the cell range of the log Y values as the

Y variable cell range and the cell range of the coded variable as the *X* variable cell range. (The *Y* variable cell range and the *X* variable cell range are called the **Y Variable Cell Range** and **X Variable Cell Range** in the *PHStat2* instructions, the *cell range of Y variable* and *cell range of X variable* in the *In-Depth Excel* instructions, and the **Input Y Range** and **Input X Range** in the *Analysis ToolPak* instructions). Use the Section EG15.2 instructions to create the log *Y* values.

Using the modified instructions will create a regression results worksheet for a simple linear regression model and create additional columns for the logs of the residuals and the logs of the predicted *Y* values, in a residual worksheet, if using the *PHStat2* or *In-Depth Excel* instructions, or in the RESIDUAL OUTPUT area in the regression results worksheet, if using the *Analysis ToolPak* instructions. (If using the *Analysis ToolPak* instructions, note that the additional column for the logs of the residuals has the misleading label **Residuals**—and not the label **LOG(Residuals),** as one would expect.)

To these results, you must add a column that contains the original (untransformed) *Y* values, and a column of formulas that use the **POWER** function to transform the logs of the predicted *Y* values to the predicted *Y* values. To do so, first copy the original *Y* values to the empty column in the residuals worksheet (if using *PHStat2* or *In-Depth Excel*) or a column to the right of RESIDUALS OUTPUT area (if using the *Analysis ToolPak* instructions). Then create a new column that contains formulas in the form =**POWER(10,** *log of predicted value***)** to compute the predicted *Y* values.

Use columns F and G of the **RESIDUALS worksheet** of the **Exponential Trend workbook** as a model for creating the two additional columns. This worksheet contains the values needed to create the Figure 16.9 plot that fits an exponential trend forecasting equation for The Coca-Cola Company revenues (see page 618). (In this worksheet, the formula =**POWER(10, C2)** was entered in cell G2 and copied down through row 15.)

With the original *X* (time) variable column, the original *Y* variable column, and the predicted *Y* variable column, in that order, create and modify a scatter plot using the *In-Depth Excel* instructions given below. (Use these instructions even if you originally used PHStat2 or the Analysis ToolPak to create the data for this plot.)

For example, to create an exponential trend plot for The Coca-Cola Company revenue, open to the **RESIDUALS worksheet** of the **Exponential Trend workbook**. Select cell range **B1:B15** and while holding down the **Ctrl** key, select the cell range **F1:G15**. With columns B, F, and G selected, continue with either the *In-Depth Excel 2007* or *In-Depth Excel 2003* instructions.

In-Depth Excel 2007 *Continued from In-Depth Excel . . .*
Select **Insert → Scatter** and select the **first Scatter gallery** choice **(Scatter with only Markers)**. Right-click

one of the predicted revenues data points (typically a reddish square) and select **Format Data Series** from the shortcut menu. Click **Marker Options** in the left pane and in the **Marker Options** right pane click **None**. Back in the left pane, click **Line Style** and in the **Line Style** right pane enter **2** as the **Width**. Click **OK**.

Relocate the chart to a chart sheet and adjust the chart formatting by using the instructions in Appendix Section C.7 on page 726.

In-Depth Excel 2003 *Continued from In-Depth Excel . . .*
Select **Insert → Chart** and:

In the Chart Wizard Step 1 dialog box:

1. Click the **Standard Types** tab and then click **XY (Scatter)** as the **Chart type**. Click the first **Chart subtype**, labeled **Scatter**.
2. Click **Next**.

In the Chart Wizard Step 2 dialog box:

3. Click **Next**. (Entries and selections in this dialog box are correct as is.)

In the Chart Wizard Step 3 dialog box:

4. Click the **Titles** tab. Enter a **Chart title**, **Coded Year** as the **Value (X) axis** title, and **Revenues ($millions)** as the **Value (Y) axis** title. Adjust the chart formatting by using the instructions in Appendix Section C.8 on page 727 for the **Axes**, **Gridlines**, and **Data Labels** tabs.
5. Click **Next**.

In the Chart Wizard Step 4 dialog box:

6. Click **As new sheet** and then click **Finish** to create the chart.

In the newly created chart sheet:

7. Right-click one of the predicted revenues data points (typically a reddish square) and select **Format Data Series** from the shortcut menu.
8. In the Format Data Series dialog box, click the **Patterns** tab and then click **Automatic** in the **Line group** and click **None** in the **Marker group** and then click **OK**.
9. Right-click the chart legend and click **Clear** from the shortcut menu to eliminate the unnecessary legend.

Model Selection Using First, Second, and Percentage Differences

Use simple formulas to compute the first, second, and percentage differences. Use simple division formulas to compute the percentage differences and use simple subtraction formulas to compute the first and second differences. Use the **COMPUTE worksheet** of the **Differences workbook**, shown in Figure 16.10 on page 620 as a model for developing a differences worksheet.

EG16.5 AUTOREGRESSIVE MODELING for TREND FITTING and FORECASTING

Creating Lagged Predictor Variables

Create lagged predictor variables by creating a column of formulas that refer to a previous row's (previous time period's) Y value. Enter the special worksheet value **#N/A** (not available) for the cells in the column to which lagged values do not apply.

Use the **COMPUTE worksheet** of the **Lagged Predictors workbook**, shown in Figure 16.12 on page 628 as a model for developing lagged predictor variables for the first-order, second-order, and third-order autoregressive models.

When using lagged predictor variables, you select or refer to only those rows that contain lagged values. Unlike the general case in this book, you do not include rows that contain **#N/A**, nor do you include the row 1 column heading.

Modify the Section EG14.1 instructions (see page 566) to create a third-order or second-order autoregressive model. Use the cell range of the first-order, second-order, and third-order lagged predictor variables as the X variables cell range for the third-order model. Use the cell range of the first-order and second-order lagged predictor variables as the X variables cell range for the second-order model (The X variables cell range is the **X Variables Cell Range** in the *PHStat2* instructions, called the *cell range of X variables* in the *In-Depth Excel* instructions and called the **Input X Range** in the *Analysis ToolPak* instructions). If using the *PHStat2* instructions, omit step 3 (do *not* check **First cells in both ranges contain label**). If using the *Analysis ToolPak* instructions, do not check **Labels** in step 4.

Modify the Section EG13.2 instructions (see page 521) to create a first-order autoregressive model. Use the cell range of the first-order lagged predictor variable as the X variable cell range (called the **X Variable Cell Range** in the *PHStat2* instructions, called the *cell range of X variable* in the *In-Depth Excel* instructions, and called the **Input X Range** in the *Analysis ToolPak* instructions). If using the *PHStat2* instructions, omit step 3 (do *not* check **First cells in both ranges contain label**). If using the *Analysis ToolPak* instructions, do not check **Labels** in step 4.

EG16.6 CHOOSING an APPROPRIATE FORECASTING MODEL

Measuring the Magnitude of the Residuals Through Squared or Absolute Differences

Use a two-part process to compute the mean absolute deviation (*MAD*). First, perform the appropriate residuals analysis using either the Section EG13.5 or Section EG14.3 instructions (see pages 523 and 567). Then, add a column

(or columns) of formulas to compute the mean absolute deviation (*MAD*) to the table that includes the residuals (in a residuals worksheet if using the *PHStat2* or *In-Depth Excel* instructions, or as part of a regression results worksheet, if using the *Analysis ToolPak* instructions).

For a linear, quadratic, or autoregressive model, add a column of formulas in the form **=ABS(*residual cell*)**, to compute the absolute value of the residuals and then add the single formula in the form **=AVERAGE(*cell range of the absolute values of the residuals*)** to compute the *MAD*.

For an exponential model, you must first create the additional columns for the logs of the residuals and the logs of the "predicted Y" values as is first explained in "The Exponential Trend Model" instructions of Section EG16.4 on page 650. (As explained in that section, use columns F and G of the **RESIDUALS worksheet** of the **Exponential Trend workbook** as a model for creating the two additional columns.)

To these two columns, add a third column of formulas in the form **=ABS(*original Y value cell − predicted Y value cell*)** to calculate the absolute value of the residuals. At the end of this column, add a single formula in the form **=AVERAGE(*cell range of residual absolute values*)** to compute the *MAD*. Use column H of the **RESIDUALS worksheet** of the **Exponential Trend workbook** as a model for creating this third column. In this worksheet, the formula **=ABS(F2 − G2)** was entered in cell **H2** and copied down through row 15 and the single formula **=AVERAGE(H2:H15)** was entered in cell **H16**.

A Comparison of Four Forecasting Methods

When you compare the four forecasting models, you use residual analysis to examine the models. Use the instructions in Section EG13.5 to create residual plots for the linear trend model or first-order autoregressive models. Use the instructions in Section EG14.3 to create residual plots for the quadratic trend model.

As is the case in other instructions in this Excel Guide, creating residual plots for the exponential trend model requires additional work. First create the additional columns for the logs of the residuals and the logs of the predicted Y values as is first explained in "The Exponential Trend Model" instructions of Section EG16.4 on page 650. (As explained in that section, use columns F and G of the **RESIDUALS worksheet** of the **Exponential Trend workbook** as a model for creating the two additional columns.)

To these two columns, add a third column of formulas in the form **=*original Y value cell − predicted Y value cell*** to calculate the residuals. Use column I of the **RESIDUALS worksheet** of the **Exponential Trend workbook** as a model for creating this third column. Then select the original X (time) variable column and the new column of computed residuals, in that order, and use the Section EG2.7 instructions for creating a scatter plot to create the exponential trend residual plot.

EG16.7 TIME-SERIES FORECASTING of SEASONAL DATA

Least-Squares Forecasting with Monthly or Quarterly Data

To develop a least-squares regression model for monthly or quarterly data, add columns of formulas that use the **IF** function to create dummy variables for the quarterly or monthly data. Enter all formulas in the form =**IF** (*comparison*, **1, 0**).

Figure EG16.1 shows the first four rows of columns F through K of a data worksheet that contains dummy variables. Columns F, G, and H contain the quarterly dummy variables Q1, Q2, and Q3 that are based on column B coded quarter values (not shown). Columns J and K contain the two monthly variables M1 and M6 that are based on column C month values (also not shown).

	F	G	H	I	J	K
1	Q1	Q2	Q3		M1	M6
2	=IF(B2 = 1, 1, 0)	=IF(B2 = 2, 1, 0)	=IF(B2 = 3, 1, 0)		=IF(C2 ="January", 1, 0)	=IF(C2 = "June", 1, 0)
3	=IF(B3 = 1, 1, 0)	=IF(B3 = 2, 1, 0)	=IF(B3 = 3, 1, 0)		=IF(C3 ="January", 1, 0)	=IF(C3 = "June", 1, 0)
4	=IF(B4 = 1, 1, 0)	=IF(B4 = 2, 1, 0)	=IF(B4 = 3, 1, 0)		=IF(C4 ="January", 1, 0)	=IF(C4 = "June", 1, 0)
5	=IF(B5 = 1, 1, 0)	=IF(B5 = 2, 1, 0)	=IF(B5 = 3, 1, 0)		=IF(C5 ="January", 1, 0)	=IF(C5 = "June", 1, 0)

FIGURE EG16.1 Dummy variables for quarterly and monthly data

17

Statistical Applications in Quality Management

Learning Objectives

In this chapter, you learn:

- How to construct various control charts
- Which control chart to use for a particular type of data
- The basic themes of total quality management and Deming's 14 points
- The basic aspects of Six Sigma

@ Beachcomber Hotel

You find yourself managing the Beachcomber Hotel, one of the resorts owned by T.C. Resort Properties (see Chapter 12). Your business objective is to continually improve the quality of service that your guests receive so that overall guest satisfaction increases. To help you achieve this improvement, T.C. Resort Properties has provided its managers with training in Six Sigma. In order to meet the business objective of increasing the return rate of guests at your hotel, you have decided to focus on the critical first impressions of the service that your hotel provides. Is the assigned hotel room ready when a guest checks in? Are all expected amenities, such as extra towels and a complimentary guest basket, in the room when the guest first walks in? Are the video-entertainment center and high-speed Internet access working properly? And do guests receive their luggage in a reasonable amount of time?

To study these guest satisfaction issues, you have embarked on an improvement project that focuses on the readiness of the room and the time it takes to deliver luggage. You would like to learn the following:

- Are the proportion of rooms ready and the time required to deliver luggage to the rooms acceptable?
- Are the proportion of rooms ready and the luggage delivery time consistent from day to day, or are they increasing or decreasing?
- On the days when the proportion of rooms that are not ready or the time to deliver luggage is greater than normal, are these fluctuations due to a chance occurrence, or are there fundamental flaws in the processes used to make rooms ready and to deliver luggage?

All companies, whether they manufacture products or provide services, as T.C. Resort Properties does in the Beachcomber Hotel scenario, understand that quality is essential for survival in the global economy. Quality has an impact on our everyday work and personal lives in many ways: in the design, production, and reliability of our automobiles; in the services provided by hotels, banks, schools, retailing operations, and mail-order companies; in the continuous improvement in integrated circuits that makes for more capable consumer electronics and computers; and in the availability of new technology and equipment that has led to improved diagnosis of illnesses and improved delivery of health care services.

In this chapter you will learn how to develop and analyze control charts, a statistical tool that is widely used for quality improvement. You will then learn how businesses and organizations around the world are using control charts as part of two important quality improvement approaches: total quality management (TQM) and Six Sigma.

17.1 The Theory of Control Charts

A **process** is the value-added transformation of inputs to outputs. The inputs and outputs of a process can involve machines, materials, methods, measurement, people, and the environment. Each of the inputs is a source of variability. Variability in the output can result in poor service and poor product quality, both of which often decrease customer satisfaction.

Control charts, developed by Walter Shewhart in the 1920s (see reference 16), are commonly used statistical tools for monitoring and improving processes. A **control chart** analyzes a process in which data are collected sequentially over time. You use a control chart to study past performance, to evaluate present conditions, or to predict future outcomes. You use control charts at the beginning of quality improvement efforts to study an existing process (such charts are called Phase 1 control charts). Information gained from analyzing Phase 1 control charts forms the basis for process improvement. After improvements to the process are implemented, you then use control charts to monitor the processes to ensure that the improvements continue (these charts are called Phase 2 control charts).

Different types of control charts allow you to analyze different types of critical-to-quality (*CTQ* in Six Sigma lingo—see Section 17.8) variables—for categorical variables, such as the proportion of hotel rooms that are nonconforming in terms of the availability of amenities and the working order of all appliances in the room; for discrete variables such as the number of hotel guests registering complaints in a week; and for continuous variables, such as the length of time required for delivering luggage to the room.

In addition to providing a visual display of data representing a process, a principal focus of a control chart is the attempt to separate special causes of variation from common causes of variation.

> ### THE TWO TYPES OF CAUSES OF VARIATION
>
> **Special causes of variation** represent large fluctuations or patterns in data that are not part of a process. These fluctuations are often caused by unusual events and represent either problems to correct or opportunities to exploit. Some organizations refer to special causes of variation as **assignable causes of variation**.
>
> **Common causes of variation** represent the inherent variability that exists in a process. These fluctuations consist of the numerous small causes of variability that operate randomly or by chance. Some organizations refer to common causes of variation as **chance causes of variation**.

Walter Shewhart (see reference 16) developed an experiment that illustrates the distinction between common and special causes of variation. The experiment asks you to repeatedly write the letter A in a horizontal line across a piece of paper:

AAAAAAAAAAAAAAAAAA

When you do this, you immediately notice that the A's are all similar but not exactly the same. In addition, you may notice some difference in the size of the A's from letter to letter. This difference is due to common cause variation. Nothing special happened that caused the differences in the size of the A. You probably would have a hard time trying to explain why the largest A is bigger than the smallest A. These types of differences almost certainly represent common cause variation.

However, if you did the experiment over again but wrote half of the A's with your right hand and the other half of the A's with your left hand, you would almost certainly see a very big difference in the A's written with each hand. In this case, which hand was used to write the A's is the source of the special cause variation.

The distinction between the two causes of variation is crucial because special causes of variation are not part of a process and are correctable or exploitable without changing the process. Common causes of variation, however, can be reduced only by changing the process. Such systemic changes are the responsibility of management.

Control charts allow you to monitor a process and identify the presence or absence of special causes. By doing so, control charts help prevent two types of errors. The first type of error involves the belief that an observed value represents special cause variation when it is due to the common cause variation of the process. Treating common cause variation as special cause variation often results in overadjusting a process. This overadjustment, known as **tampering**, increases the variation in the process. The second type of error involves treating special cause variation as common cause variation. This error results in not taking immediate corrective action when necessary. Although both of these types of errors can occur even when using a control chart, they are far less likely.

To construct a control chart, you collect samples from the output of a process over time. The samples used for constructing control charts are known as **subgroups**. For each subgroup (i.e., sample), you calculate a sample statistic. Commonly used statistics include the sample proportion for a categorical variable (see Section 17.2), the number of nonconformities (see Section 17.4), and the mean and range of a numerical variable (see Section 17.5). You then plot the values over time and add control limits around the center line of the chart. The most typical form of a control chart sets control limits that are within ± 3 standard deviations[1] of the statistical measure of interest. Equation (17.1) defines, in general, the upper and lower control limits for control charts.

[1]Recall from Section 6.2 that in the normal distribution, $\mu \pm 3\sigma$ includes almost all (99.73%) of the values in the population.

CONSTRUCTING CONTROL LIMITS

$$\text{Process mean} \pm 3 \text{ standard deviations} \qquad \textbf{(17.1)}$$

so that

upper control limit(UCL) = process mean $+3$ standard deviations

lower control limit(LCL) = process mean -3 standard deviations

When these control limits are set, you evaluate the control chart by trying to find any pattern that might exist in the values over time and by determining whether any points fall outside the control limits. Figure 17.1 illustrates three different patterns.

FIGURE 17.1

Three control chart patterns

In Panel A of Figure 17.1, there is no apparent pattern in the values over time, and there are no points that fall outside the 3 standard deviation control limits. The process appears stable and contains only common cause variation. Panel B, on the contrary, contains two points that fall outside the 3 standard deviation control limits. You should investigate these points to try to determine the special causes that led to their occurrence. Although Panel C does not have any points outside the control limits, it has a series of consecutive points above the mean value (the center line) as well as a series of consecutive points below the mean value. In addition, a long-term overall downward trend is clearly visible. You should investigate the situation to try to determine what may have caused this pattern.

Detecting a pattern is not always so easy. The following simple rule (see references 9, 13, and 18) can help you to detect a trend or a shift in the mean level of a process:

> Eight or more *consecutive* points that lie above the center line or eight or more *consecutive* points that lie below the center line[2]

A process whose control chart indicates an out-of-control condition (i.e., a point outside the control limits or a series of points that exhibits a pattern) is said to be out of control. An **out-of-control process** contains both common causes of variation and special causes of variation. Because special causes of variation are not part of the process design, an out-of-control process is unpredictable. When you determine that a process is out of control, you must identify the special causes of variation that are producing the out-of-control conditions. If the special causes are detrimental to the quality of the product or service, you need to implement plans to eliminate this source of variation. When a special cause increases quality, you should change the process so that the special cause is incorporated into the process design. Thus, this beneficial special cause now becomes a common cause source of variation, and the process is improved.

A process whose control chart does not indicate any out-of-control conditions is said to be in control. An **in-control process** contains only common causes of variation. Because these sources of variation are inherent to the process itself, an in-control process is predictable. In-control processes are sometimes said to be in a **state of statistical control**. When a process is in control, you must determine whether the amount of common cause variation in the process is small enough to satisfy the customers of the products or services. If the common cause variation is small enough to consistently satisfy the customer, you then use control charts to monitor the process on a continuing basis to make sure the process remains in control. If the common cause variation is too large, you need to alter the process itself.

[2]This rule is often referred to as the *runs rule*. A similar rule used by some companies is called the *trend rule*: eight or more consecutive points that increase in value or eight or more consecutive points that decrease in value. Some statisticians (see reference 5) have criticized the trend rule. It should be used only with extreme caution.

17.2 Control Chart for the Proportion: The *p* Chart

Various types of control charts are used to monitor processes and determine whether special cause variation is present in a process. **Attribute control charts** are used for categorical or discrete variables. This section introduces the ***p* chart**, which is used for categorical variables. The *p* chart gets its name from the fact that you plot the *proportion* of items in a sample that are in a category of interest. For example, sampled items are often classified according to whether they conform or do not conform to operationally defined requirements. Thus, the *p* chart is frequently used to monitor and analyze the proportion of nonconforming items in repeated samples (i.e., subgroups) selected from a process.

To begin the discussion of *p* charts, recall that you studied proportions and the binomial distribution in Section 5.3. Then, in Equation (7.6) on page 241, the sample proportion is defined as $p = X/n$, and the standard deviation of the sample proportion is defined as

$$\sigma_p = \sqrt{\frac{\pi(1 - \pi)}{n}}$$

[3]In this chapter, and in quality management, the phrase "proportion of nonconforming items" is often used, although the *p* chart can be used to monitor any proportion of interest. Recall that in the earlier discussions of the binomial distribution, the phrase "proportion of items of interest" was used.

Using Equation (17.1) on page 657, control limits for the proportion of nonconforming[3] items from the sample data are established in Equation (17.2).

CONTROL LIMITS FOR THE *p* CHART

$$\bar{p} \pm 3\sqrt{\frac{\bar{p}(1-\bar{p})}{\bar{n}}}$$

$$\text{UCL} = \bar{p} + 3\sqrt{\frac{\bar{p}(1-\bar{p})}{\bar{n}}}$$

$$\text{LCL} = \bar{p} - 3\sqrt{\frac{\bar{p}(1-\bar{p})}{\bar{n}}} \qquad (17.2)$$

For equal n_i,

$$\bar{n} = n_i \text{ and } \bar{p} = \frac{\sum_{i=1}^{k} p_i}{k}$$

or in general,

$$\bar{n} = \frac{\sum_{i=1}^{k} n_i}{k} \text{ and } \bar{p} = \frac{\sum_{i=1}^{k} X_i}{\sum_{i=1}^{k} n_i}$$

where

X_i = number of nonconforming items in subgroup i

n_i = sample (or subgroup) size for subgroup i

$p_i = \dfrac{X_i}{n_i}$ = proportion of nonconforming items in subgroup i

k = number of subgroups selected

$\bar{n}$ = mean subgroup size

$\bar{p}$ = proportion of nonconforming items in the k subgroups combined

Any negative value for the LCL means that the LCL does not exist.

To show the application of the *p* chart, return to the Beachcomber Hotel scenario on page 655. During the process improvement effort in the *Measure* phase of Six Sigma (see Section 17.8), a nonconforming room was operationally defined as the absence of an amenity or an appliance not in working order upon check-in. During the *Analyze* phase of Six Sigma, data on the nonconformances were collected daily from a sample of 200 rooms (stored in Hotel1). Table 17.1 on page 660 lists the number and proportion of nonconforming rooms for each day in the four-week period.

For these data, $k = 28$, $\sum_{i=1}^{k} p_i = 2.315$ and, because the n_i are equal, $n_i = \bar{n} = 200$. Thus,

$$\bar{p} = \frac{\sum_{i=1}^{k} p_i}{k} = \frac{2.315}{28} = 0.0827$$

TABLE 17.1

Nonconforming Hotel Rooms at Check-in over a 28-Day Period

Day (i)	Rooms Studied (n_i)	Rooms Not Ready (X_i)	Proportion (p_i)	Day (i)	Rooms Studied (n_i)	Rooms Not Ready (X_i)	Proportion (p_i)
1	200	16	0.080	15	200	18	0.090
2	200	7	0.035	16	200	13	0.065
3	200	21	0.105	17	200	15	0.075
4	200	17	0.085	18	200	10	0.050
5	200	25	0.125	19	200	14	0.070
6	200	19	0.095	20	200	25	0.125
7	200	16	0.080	21	200	19	0.095
8	200	15	0.075	22	200	12	0.060
9	200	11	0.055	23	200	6	0.030
10	200	12	0.060	24	200	12	0.060
11	200	22	0.110	25	200	18	0.090
12	200	20	0.100	26	200	15	0.075
13	200	17	0.085	27	200	20	0.100
14	200	26	0.130	28	200	22	0.110

Using Equation (17.2),

$$0.0827 \pm 3\sqrt{\frac{(0.0827)(0.9173)}{200}}$$

so that

$$UCL = 0.0827 + 0.0584 = 0.1411$$

and

$$LCL = 0.0827 - 0.0584 = 0.0243$$

Figure 17.2 displays a p chart for the data of Table 17.1. Figure 17.2 shows a process in a state of statistical control, with the individual points distributed around $\bar{p}$ without any pattern and all the points within the control limits. Thus, any improvement in the process of making rooms ready for guests must come from the reduction of common cause variation. Such reductions require changes in the process. These changes are the responsibility of management. Remember that improvements in quality cannot occur until changes to the process itself are successfully implemented.

FIGURE 17.2

p chart for the nonconforming hotel rooms

Create this chart sheet using the instructions in Section EG17.2.

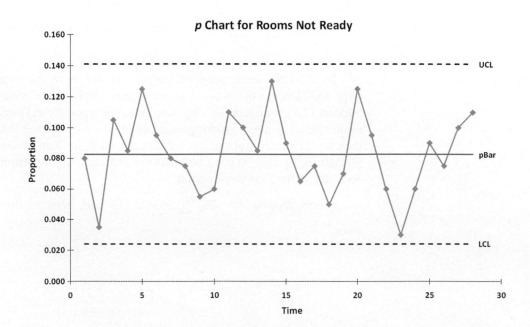

This example illustrates a situation in which the subgroup size does not vary. As a general rule, as long as none of the subgroup sizes, n_i, differ from the mean subgroup size, $\bar{n}$, by more than $\pm 25\%$ of $\bar{n}$ (see reference 9), you can use Equation (17.2) on page 659 to compute the control limits for the *p* chart. If any subgroup size differs by more than $\pm 25\%$ of $\bar{n}$, you use alternative formulas for calculating the control limits (see references 9 and 13). To illustrate the use of the *p* chart when the subgroup sizes are unequal, Example 17.1 studies the production of medical sponges.

EXAMPLE 17.1

Using the *p* Chart for Unequal Subgroup Sizes

TABLE 17.2

Medical Sponges Produced and Number Nonconforming over a 32-Day Period

Table 17.2 indicates the number of medical sponges produced daily and the number that are nonconforming for a period of 32 days (stored in Sponge). Construct a control chart for these data.

Day (*i*)	Sponges Produced (*n_i*)	Nonconforming Sponges (*X_i*)	Proportion (*p_i*)	Day (*i*)	Sponges Produced (*n_i*)	Nonconforming Sponges (*X_i*)	Proportion (*p_i*)
1	690	21	0.030	17	575	20	0.035
2	580	22	0.038	18	610	16	0.026
3	685	20	0.029	19	596	15	0.025
4	595	21	0.035	20	630	24	0.038
5	665	23	0.035	21	625	25	0.040
6	596	19	0.032	22	615	21	0.034
7	600	18	0.030	23	575	23	0.040
8	620	24	0.039	24	572	20	0.035
9	610	20	0.033	25	645	24	0.037
10	595	22	0.037	26	651	39	0.060
11	645	19	0.029	27	660	21	0.032
12	675	23	0.034	28	685	19	0.028
13	670	22	0.033	29	671	17	0.025
14	590	26	0.044	30	660	22	0.033
15	585	17	0.029	31	595	24	0.040
16	560	16	0.029	32	600	16	0.027

SOLUTION For these data,

$$k = 32, \sum_{i=1}^{k} n_i = 19{,}926$$

$$\sum_{i=1}^{k} X_i = 679$$

Thus, using Equation (17.2) on page 659,

$$\bar{n} = \frac{19{,}926}{32} = 622.69$$

$$\bar{p} = \frac{679}{19{,}926} = 0.034$$

so that

$$0.034 \pm 3\sqrt{\frac{(0.034)(1 - 0.034)}{622.69}}$$

$$= 0.034 \pm 0.022$$

Thus,

$$UCL = 0.034 + 0.022 = 0.056$$

$$LCL = 0.034 - 0.022 = 0.012$$

Figure 17.3 displays the control chart for the sponge data. From Figure 17.3, you can see that day 26, on which there were 39 nonconforming sponges produced out of 651 sampled, is above the UCL. Management needs to determine the reason (i.e., root cause) for this special cause variation and take corrective action. Once actions are taken, you can remove the data from day 26 and then construct and analyze a new control chart.

FIGURE 17.3

p chart for the proportion of nonconforming medical sponges

Create this worksheet using the instructions in Section EG17.2.

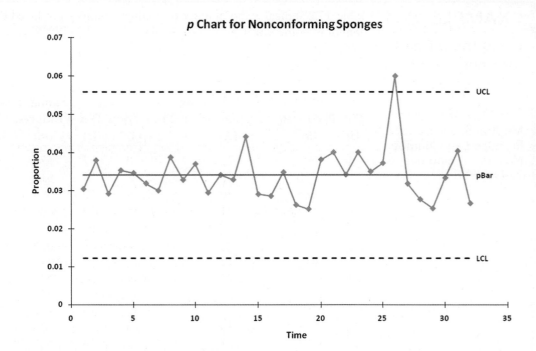

Problems for Section 17.2

LEARNING THE BASICS

17.1 The following data were collected on nonconformances for a period of 10 days:

Day	Sample Size	Nonconformances
1	100	12
2	100	14
3	100	10
4	100	18
5	100	22
6	100	14
7	100	15
8	100	13
9	100	14
10	100	16

a. On what day is the proportion of nonconformances largest? Smallest?

b. What are the LCL and UCL?

c. Are there any special causes of variation?

17.2 The following data were collected on nonconformances for a period of 10 days:

Day	Sample Size	Nonconformances
1	111	12
2	93	14
3	105	10
4	92	18
5	117	22
6	88	14
7	117	15
8	87	13
9	119	14
10	107	16

a. On what day is the proportion of nonconformances largest? Smallest?
b. What are the LCL and UCL?
c. Are there any special causes of variation?

APPLYING THE CONCEPTS

17.3 A medical transcription service enters medical data on patient files for hospitals. The service has the business objective of improving the turnaround time (defined as the time between sending data and the time the client receives completed files). After studying the process, it was determined that turnaround time was increased by transmission errors. A transmission error was defined as data transmitted that did not go through as planned and needed to be retransmitted. For a period of 31 days, a sample of 125 transmissions were randomly selected and evaluated for errors and stored in Transmit. The following table presents the number and proportion of transmissions with errors:

Day (i)	Number of Errors (X_i)	Proportion of Errors (p_i)	Day (i)	Number of Errors (X_i)	Proportion of Errors (p_i)
1	6	0.048	17	4	0.032
2	3	0.024	18	6	0.048
3	4	0.032	19	3	0.024
4	4	0.032	20	5	0.040
5	9	0.072	21	1	0.008
6	0	0.000	22	3	0.024
7	0	0.000	23	14	0.112
8	8	0.064	24	6	0.048
9	4	0.032	25	7	0.056
10	3	0.024	26	3	0.024
11	4	0.032	27	10	0.080
12	1	0.008	28	7	0.056
13	10	0.080	29	5	0.040
14	9	0.072	30	0	0.000
15	3	0.024	31	3	0.024
16	1	0.008			

a. Construct a *p* chart.
b. Is the process in a state of statistical control? Why?

✓ SELF Test **17.4** The data at the top of the next column (stored in Canister) represent the findings from a study conducted at a factory that manufactures film canisters. For 32 days, 500 film canisters were sampled and inspected. The following table lists the number of defective film canisters (the nonconforming items) for each day (the subgroup):
a. Construct a *p* chart.
b. Is the process in a state of statistical control? Why?

Day	Number Nonconforming	Day	Number Nonconforming
1	26	17	23
2	25	18	19
3	23	19	18
4	24	20	27
5	26	21	28
6	20	22	24
7	21	23	26
8	27	24	23
9	23	25	27
10	25	26	28
11	22	27	24
12	26	28	22
13	25	29	20
14	29	30	25
15	20	31	27
16	19	32	19

17.5 A hospital administrator has the business objective of reducing the time to process patients' medical records after discharge. She determined that all records should be processed within 5 days of discharge. Thus, any record not processed within 5 days of a patient's discharge is nonconforming. The administrator recorded the number of patients discharged and the number of records not processed within the 5-day standard for a 30-day period and stored in MedRec.
a. Construct a *p* chart for these data.
b. Does the process give an out-of-control signal? Explain.
c. If the process is out of control, assume that special causes were subsequently identified and corrective action was taken to keep them from happening again. Then eliminate the data causing the out-of-control signals and recalculate the control limits.

17.6 The bottling division of Sweet Suzy's Sugarless Cola maintains daily records of the occurrences of unacceptable cans flowing from the filling and sealing machine. The data in Colaspc lists the number of cans filled and the number of nonconforming cans for one month (based on a five-day workweek).
a. Construct a *p* chart for the proportion of unacceptable cans for the month. Does the process give an out-of-control signal?
b. If you want to develop a process for reducing the proportion of unacceptable cans, how should you proceed?

17.7 The manager of the accounting office of a large hospital has the business objective of reducing the number of incorrect account numbers entered into the computer system. A subgroup of 200 account numbers is selected from each day's output, and each account number is inspected to determine whether it is a nonconforming item. The results for a period of 39 days are stored in Errorspc.

a. Construct a p chart for the proportion of nonconforming items. Does the process give an out-of-control signal?

b. Based on your answer in (a), if you were the manager of the accounting office, what would you do to improve the process of account number entry?

17.8 A regional manager of a telephone company is responsible for processing requests concerning additions, changes, or deletions of telephone service. She forms a service improvement team to look at the corrections to the orders in terms of central office equipment and facilities required to process the orders that are issued to service requests. Data collected over a period of 30 days are stored in Telespc .

a. Construct a p chart for the proportion of corrections. Does the process give an out-of-control signal?

b. What should the regional manager do to improve the processing of requests for changes in telephone service?

17.3 The Red Bead Experiment: Understanding Process Variability

[4]For information on how to purchase such a bowl, contact Lightning Calculator at **www.qualitytng.com** or call 248-641-7030.

This chapter began with a discussion of common cause variation and special cause variation. Now that you have studied the p chart, this section presents a famous parable, the **red bead experiment**, to enhance your understanding of common cause and special cause variation. The red bead experiment involves the selection of beads from a bowl that contains 4,000 beads.[4] Unknown to the participants in the experiment, 3,200 (80%) of the beads are white and 800 (20%) are red. You can use several different scenarios for conducting the experiment. The one used here begins with a facilitator (who will play the role of company supervisor) asking members of the audience to volunteer for the jobs of workers (at least four are needed), inspectors (two are needed), chief inspector (one is needed), and recorder (one is needed). A worker's job consists of using a paddle that has five rows of 10 bead-size holes to select 50 beads from the bowl of beads.

When the participants have been selected, the supervisor explains the jobs to them. The job of the workers is to produce white beads because red beads are unacceptable to the customers. Strict procedures are to be followed. Work standards call for the daily production of exactly 50 beads by each worker (a strict quota system). Management has established a standard that no more than 2 red beads (4%) per worker are to be produced on any given day.

Each worker dips the paddle into the box of beads so that when it is removed, each of the 50 holes contains a bead. The worker carries the paddle to the two inspectors, who independently record the count of red beads. The chief inspector compares their counts and announces the results to the audience. The recorder writes down the number and percentage of red beads next to the name of the worker.

When all the people know their jobs, "production" can begin. Suppose that on the first "day," the number of red beads "produced" by the four workers (call them Alyson, David, Peter, and Sharyn) was 9, 12, 13, and 7, respectively. How should management react to the day's production when the standard says that no more than 2 red beads per worker should be produced? Should all the workers be reprimanded, or should only David and Peter be warned that they will be fired if they don't improve?

Suppose that production continues for an additional two days. Table 17.3 summarizes the results for all three days.

TABLE 17.3

Red Bead Experiment Results for Four Workers over Three Days

WORKER	DAY 1	DAY 2	DAY 3	All Three Days
Alyson	9 (18%)	11 (22%)	6 (12%)	26 (17.33%)
David	12 (24%)	12 (24%)	8 (16%)	32 (21.33%)
Peter	13 (26%)	6 (12%)	12 (24%)	31 (20.67%)
Sharyn	7 (14%)	9 (18%)	8 (16%)	24 (16.0%)
All four workers	41	38	34	113
Mean	10.25	9.5	8.5	9.42
Percentage	20.5%	19%	17%	18.83%

From Table 17.3, on each day, some of the workers were above the mean and some below the mean. On Day 1, Sharyn did best, but on Day 2, Peter (who had the worst record on Day 1) was best, and on Day 3, Alyson was best. How can you explain all this variation? Using Equation (17.2) on page 659 to develop a p chart for these data,

$$k = 4 \text{ workers} \times 3 \text{ days} = 12, n = 50, \sum_{i=1}^{k} X_i = 113, \text{ and } \sum_{i=1}^{k} n_i = 600$$

Thus,

$$\bar{p} = \frac{113}{600} = 0.1883$$

so that

$$\bar{p} \pm 3\sqrt{\frac{\bar{p}(1 - \bar{p})}{n}}$$

$$= 0.1883 \pm 3\sqrt{\frac{0.1883(1 - 0.1883)}{50}}$$

$$= 0.1883 \pm 0.1659$$

Thus,

$$\text{UCL} = 0.1883 + 0.1659 = 0.3542$$

$$\text{LCL} = 0.1883 - 0.1659 = 0.0224$$

Figure 17.4 represents the p chart for the data of Table 17.3. In Figure 17.4, all the points are within the control limits, and there are no patterns in the results. The differences between the workers merely represent common cause variation inherent in an in-control process.

FIGURE 17.4

p chart for the red bead experiment

Four morals to the parable of the red beads are

- Variation is an inherent part of any process.
- Workers work within a process over which they have little control. It is the process that primarily determines their performance.
- Only management can change the process.
- There will always be some workers above the mean and some workers below the mean.

Problems for Section 17.3

APPLYING THE CONCEPTS

17.9 In the red bead experiment, how do you think many managers would have reacted after Day 1? Day 2? Day 3?

17.10 (Class Project) Obtain a version of the red bead experiment for your class.

a. Conduct the experiment in the same way as described in this section.

b. Remove 400 red beads from the bead bowl before beginning the experiment. How do your results differ from those in (a)? What does this tell you about the effect of the process on the results?

17.4 Control Chart for an Area of Opportunity: The *c* Chart

Recall that you use a *p* chart for monitoring and analyzing the proportion of nonconforming items. Nonconformities are defects or flaws in a product or service. To monitor and analyze the number of nonconformities in an area of opportunity, you use a ***c* chart**. An **area of opportunity** is an individual unit of a product or service, or a unit of time, space, or area. Examples of "the number of nonconformities in an area of opportunity" would be the number of flaws in a square foot of carpet, the number of typographical errors on a printed page, and the number of hotel customers filing complaints in a given week.

Counting the number of nonconformities in an area of opportunity is unlike the process used to prepare a *p* chart in which you *classify* each unit as conforming or nonconforming. The *c* chart process fits the assumptions of a Poisson distribution (see Section 5.4). For the Poisson distribution, the standard deviation of the number of nonconformities is the square root of the mean number of nonconformities (λ). Assuming that the size of each area of opportunity remains constant,[5] you can compute the control limits for the number of nonconformities per area of opportunity using the observed mean number of nonconformities as an estimate of λ. Equation (17.3) defines the control limits for the *c* chart, which you use to monitor and analyze the number of nonconformities per area of opportunity.

[5] If the size of the unit varies, you should use a *u* chart instead of a *c* chart (see references 9, 13, and 18).

CONTROL LIMITS FOR THE *c* CHART

$$\bar{c} \pm 3\sqrt{\bar{c}}$$

$$\text{UCL} = \bar{c} + 3\sqrt{\bar{c}}$$

$$\text{LCL} = \bar{c} - 3\sqrt{\bar{c}} \tag{17.3}$$

where

$$\bar{c} = \frac{\sum_{i=1}^{k} c_i}{k}$$

k = number of units sampled

c_i = number of nonconformities in unit i

To help study the hotel service quality in the Beachcomber Hotel scenario on page 655, you can use a *c* chart to monitor the number of customer complaints filed with the hotel. If guests of the hotel are dissatisfied with any part of their stay, they are asked to file a customer complaint form. At the end of each week, the number of complaints filed is recorded. In this example, a complaint is a nonconformity, and the area of opportunity is one week. Table 17.4 lists the number of complaints from the past 50 weeks (stored in **Complaints**).

Week	Number of Complaints	Week	Number of Complaints	Week	Number of Complaints
1	8	18	7	35	3
2	10	19	10	36	5
3	6	20	11	37	2
4	7	21	8	38	4
5	5	22	7	39	3
6	7	23	8	40	3
7	9	24	6	41	4
8	8	25	7	42	2
9	7	26	7	43	4
10	9	27	5	44	5
11	10	28	8	45	5
12	7	29	6	46	3
13	8	30	7	47	2
14	11	31	5	48	5
15	10	32	5	49	4
16	9	33	4	50	4
17	8	34	4		

For these data,

$$k = 50 \text{ and } \sum_{i=1}^{k} c_i = 312$$

Thus,

$$\bar{c} = \frac{312}{50} = 6.24$$

so that using Equation (17.3) on page 666,

$$\bar{c} \pm 3\sqrt{\bar{c}}$$

$$= 6.24 \pm 3\sqrt{6.24}$$

$$= 6.24 \pm 7.494$$

Thus,

$$\text{UCL} = 6.24 + 7.494 = 13.734$$

$$\text{LCL} = 6.24 - 7.494 < 0$$

Therefore, the LCL does not exist.

Figure 17.5 displays the control chart for the complaint data of Table 17.4. The *c* chart does not indicate any points outside the control limits. However, because there are eight or more consecutive points that lie above the center line and there are also eight or more consecutive points that lie below the center line, the process is out of control. There is a clear pattern to the number of customer complaints over time. During the first half of the sequence, the number of complaints for almost all the weeks is greater than the mean number of complaints, and the number of complaints for almost all the weeks in the second half are less than the mean number of complaints. This change, which is an improvement, is due to a special cause of variation. The next step is to investigate the process and determine the special cause that produced this pattern. When identified, you then need to ensure that this becomes a permanent improvement, not a temporary phenomenon. In other words, the source of the special cause of variation must become part of the permanent ongoing process in order for the number of customer complaints not to slip back to the high levels experienced in the first twenty-five weeks.

FIGURE 17.5

c chart for hotel complaints

Create this worksheet using the instructions in Section EG17.4.

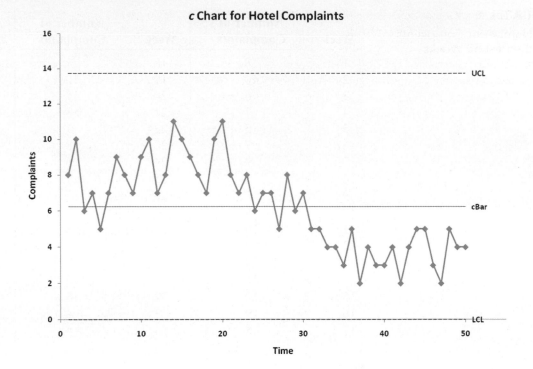

c Chart for Hotel Complaints

Problems for Section 17.4

LEARNING THE BASICS

17.11 The following data were collected on the number of nonconformities per unit for 10 time periods:

Time	Nonconformities per Unit	Time	Nonconformities per Unit
1	7	6	5
2	3	7	3
3	6	8	5
4	3	9	2
5	4	10	0

a. Construct the appropriate control chart and determine the LCL and UCL.
b. Are there any special causes of variation?

17.12 The following data were collected on the number of nonconformities per unit for 10 time periods:

Time	Nonconformities per Unit	Time	Nonconformities per Unit
1	25	6	15
2	11	7	12
3	10	8	10
4	11	9	9
5	6	10	6

a. Construct the appropriate control chart and determine the LCL and UCL.
b. Are there any special causes of variation?

APPLYING THE CONCEPTS

17.13 To improve service quality, the owner of a dry-cleaning business has the business objective of reducing the number of dry-cleaned items that are returned for rework per day. Records were kept for a four-week period (the store is open Monday through Saturday), with the results given in the following table and in the file **Dryclean**.

Day	Items Returned for Rework	Day	Items Returned for Rework
1	4	13	5
2	6	14	8
3	3	15	3
4	7	16	4
5	6	17	10
6	8	18	9
7	6	19	6
8	4	20	5
9	8	21	8
10	6	22	6
11	5	23	7
12	12	24	9

a. Construct a *c* chart for the number of items per day that are returned for rework. Do you think that the process is in a state of statistical control?

b. Should the owner of the dry-cleaning store take action to investigate why 12 items were returned for rework on Day 12? Explain. Would your answer change if 20 items were returned for rework on Day 12?

c. On the basis of the results in (a), what should the owner of the dry-cleaning store do to reduce the number of items per day that are returned for rework?

SELF Test **17.14** The branch manager of a savings bank has recorded the number of errors of a particular type that each of 12 tellers has made during the past year. The results (stored in **Teller**) were as follows:

Teller	Number of Errors	Teller	Number of Errors
Alice	4	Mitchell	6
Carl	7	Nora	3
Gina	12	Paul	5
Jane	6	Salvador	4
Livia	2	Tripp	7
Marla	5	Vera	5

a. Do you think the bank manager will single out Gina for any disciplinary action regarding her performance in the past year?

b. Construct a *c* chart for the number of errors committed by the 12 tellers. Is the number of errors in a state of statistical control?

c. Based on the *c* chart developed in (b), do you now think that Gina should be singled out for disciplinary action regarding her performance? Does your conclusion now agree with what you expected the manager to do?

d. On the basis of the results in (b), what should the branch manager do to reduce the number of errors?

17.15 Falls are one source of preventable hospital injury. Although most patients who fall are not hurt, a risk of serious injury is involved. The data in **PtFalls** represent the number of patient falls per month over a 28-month period in a 19-bed AIDS unit at a major metropolitan hospital.

a. Construct a *c* chart for the number of patient falls per month. Is the process of patient falls per month in a state of statistical control?

b. What effect would it have on your conclusions if you knew that the AIDS unit was started only one month prior to the beginning of data collection?

c. Compile a list of factors that might produce special cause variation in this problem?

17.16 A member of the volunteer fire department for Trenton, Ohio, decided to apply the control chart methodology he learned in his business statistics class to data col-

lected by the fire department. He was interested in determining whether weeks containing more than the mean number of fire runs were due to inherent, chance-cause variation, or if there were special causes of variation such as increased arson, severe drought, or holiday-related activities. The file **FireRuns** contains the number of fire runs made per week (Sunday through Saturday) during a recent year.

Source: *Data extracted from* The City of Trenton 2001 Annual Report, *Trenton, Ohio, February 21, 2002.*

a. What is the mean number of fire runs made per week?

b. Construct a *c* chart for the number of fire runs per week.

c. Is the process in a state of statistical control?

d. Weeks 15 and 41 experienced seven fire runs each. Are these large values explainable by common causes, or does it appear that special causes of variation occurred in these weeks?

e. Explain how the fire department can use these data to chart and monitor future weeks in real-time (i.e., on a week-to-week basis)?

17.17 Rochester-Electro-Medical Inc. is a manufacturing company based in Tampa, Florida, that produces medical products. Management had the business objective of improving the safety of the workplace and began a safety sampling study. The following data (stored in **Safety**) represent the number of unsafe acts observed by the company safety director over an initial time period in which he made 20 tours of the plant.

Tour	Number of Unsafe Acts	Tour	Number of Unsafe Acts
1	10	11	2
2	6	12	8
3	6	13	7
4	10	14	6
5	8	15	6
6	12	16	11
7	2	17	13
8	1	18	9
9	23	19	6
10	3	20	9

Source: *Data extracted from H. Gitlow, A. R. Berkins, and M. He, "Safety Sampling: A Case Study,"* Quality Engineering, *14 (2002), 405–419.*

a. Construct a *c* chart for the number of unsafe acts.

b. Based on the results of (a), is the process in a state of statistical control?

c. What should management do next to improve the process?

17.5 Control Charts for the Range and the Mean

You use **variables control charts** to monitor and analyze a process when you have numerically measured data. Common numerical variables include time, money, and weight. Because numerical variables provide more information than categorical data, such as the proportion of nonconforming items, variables control charts are more sensitive than the p chart in detecting special cause variation. Variables charts are typically used in pairs, with one chart monitoring the variability in a process and the other monitoring the process mean. You must examine the chart that monitors variability first because if it indicates the presence of out-of-control conditions, the interpretation of the chart for the mean will be misleading. Although businesses currently use several alternative pairs of charts (see references 9, 13, and 18), this book considers only the control charts for the range and the mean.

The R Chart

You can use several different types of control charts to monitor the variability in a numerically measured characteristic of interest. The simplest and most common is the control chart for the range, the **R chart**. You use the range chart only when the sample size or subgroup is 10 or less. If the sample size is greater than 10, a standard deviation chart is preferable (see references 9, 13, and 18). Because sample sizes of 5 or less are typically used in many applications, the standard deviation chart is not illustrated in this book. An R chart enables you to determine whether the variability in a process is in control or whether changes in the amount of variability are occurring over time. If the process range is in control, then the amount of variation in the process is consistent over time, and you can use the results of the R chart to develop the control limits for the mean.

To develop control limits for the range, you need an estimate of the mean range and the standard deviation of the range. As shown in Equation (17.4), these control limits depend on two constants, the **d_2 factor**, which represents the relationship between the standard deviation and the range for varying sample sizes, and the **d_3 factor**, which represents the relationship between the standard deviation and the standard error of the range for varying sample sizes. Table E.9 contains values for these factors. Equation (17.4) defines the control limits for the R chart.

CONTROL LIMITS FOR THE RANGE

$$\bar{R} \pm 3\bar{R}\frac{d_3}{d_2}$$

$$\text{UCL} = \bar{R} + 3\bar{R}\frac{d_3}{d_2}$$

$$\text{LCL} = \bar{R} - 3\bar{R}\frac{d_3}{d_2} \tag{17.4}$$

where

$$\bar{R} = \frac{\sum\limits_{i=1}^{k} R_i}{k}$$

k = number of subgroups selected

You can simplify the computations in Equation (17.4) by using the **D_3 factor**, equal to $1 - 3(d_3/d_2)$, and the **D_4 factor**, equal to $1 + 3(d_3/d_2)$, to express the control limits (see Table E.9), as shown in Equations (17.5a) and (17.5b).

COMPUTING CONTROL LIMITS FOR THE RANGE

$$UCL = D_4\bar{R} \qquad\qquad (17.5a)$$

$$LCL = D_3\bar{R} \qquad\qquad (17.5b)$$

To illustrate the R chart, return to the Beachcomber Hotel scenario on page 655. As part of the *Measure* phase of a Six Sigma project (see Section 17.8), the amount of time to deliver luggage was operationally defined as the time from when the guest completes check-in procedures to the time the luggage arrives in the guest's room. During the *Analyze* phase of the Six Sigma project, data were recorded over a four-week period (see the file Hotel2). Subgroups of five deliveries were selected from the evening shift on each day. Table 17.5 summarizes the results for all 28 days.

TABLE 17.5

Luggage Delivery Times and Subgroup Mean and Range for 28 Days

Day	Luggage Delivery Times (in minutes)					Mean	Range
1	6.7	11.7	9.7	7.5	7.8	8.68	5.0
2	7.6	11.4	9.0	8.4	9.2	9.12	3.8
3	9.5	8.9	9.9	8.7	10.7	9.54	2.0
4	9.8	13.2	6.9	9.3	9.4	9.72	6.3
5	11.0	9.9	11.3	11.6	8.5	10.46	3.1
6	8.3	8.4	9.7	9.8	7.1	8.66	2.7
7	9.4	9.3	8.2	7.1	6.1	8.02	3.3
8	11.2	9.8	10.5	9.0	9.7	10.04	2.2
9	10.0	10.7	9.0	8.2	11.0	9.78	2.8
10	8.6	5.8	8.7	9.5	11.4	8.80	5.6
11	10.7	8.6	9.1	10.9	8.6	9.58	2.3
12	10.8	8.3	10.6	10.3	10.0	10.00	2.5
13	9.5	10.5	7.0	8.6	10.1	9.14	3.5
14	12.9	8.9	8.1	9.0	7.6	9.30	5.3
15	7.8	9.0	12.2	9.1	11.7	9.96	4.4
16	11.1	9.9	8.8	5.5	9.5	8.96	5.6
17	9.2	9.7	12.3	8.1	8.5	9.56	4.2
18	9.0	8.1	10.2	9.7	8.4	9.08	2.1
19	9.9	10.1	8.9	9.6	7.1	9.12	3.0
20	10.7	9.8	10.2	8.0	10.2	9.78	2.7
21	9.0	10.0	9.6	10.6	9.0	9.64	1.6
22	10.7	9.8	9.4	7.0	8.9	9.16	3.7
23	10.2	10.5	9.5	12.2	9.1	10.30	3.1
24	10.0	11.1	9.5	8.8	9.9	9.86	2.3
25	9.6	8.8	11.4	12.2	9.3	10.26	3.4
26	8.2	7.9	8.4	9.5	9.2	8.64	1.6
27	7.1	11.1	10.8	11.0	10.2	10.04	4.0
28	11.1	6.6	12.0	11.5	9.7	10.18	5.4
					Sums:	265.38	97.5

For the data in Table 17.5,

$$k = 28, \ \sum_{i=1}^{k} R_i = 97.5, \ \bar{R} = \frac{\sum_{i=1}^{k} R_i}{k} = \frac{97.5}{28} = 3.482$$

For $n = 5$, from Table E.9, $D_3 = 0$ and $D_4 = 2.114$. Then, using Equation (17.5),

$$UCL = D_4\bar{R} = (2.114)(3.482) = 7.36$$

and the LCL does not exist.

Figure 17.6 displays the R chart for the luggage delivery times. Figure 17.6 does not indicate any individual ranges outside the control limits or any obvious patterns.

FIGURE 17.6

R chart for the luggage delivery times

Create this worksheet using the instructions in Section EG17.5.

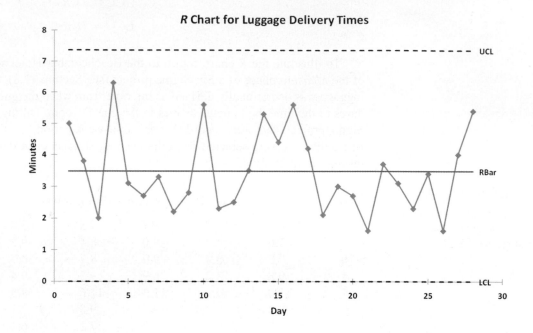

R Chart for Luggage Delivery Times

The $\bar{X}$ Chart

When you have determined from the R chart that the range is in control, you examine the control chart for the process mean, the $\bar{X}$ **chart**.

The control chart for $\bar{X}$ uses k subgroups collected in k consecutive periods of time. Each subgroup contains n items. You calculate an $\bar{X}$ for each subgroup and plot these $\bar{X}$ values on the control chart. To compute control limits for the mean, you need to compute the mean of the subgroup means (called $\bar{X}$ double bar and denoted $\bar{\bar{X}}$ and the estimate of the standard error of the mean (denoted $\bar{R}/(d_2\sqrt{n})$). The estimate of the standard error of the mean is a function of the d_2 factor, which represents the relationship between the standard deviation and the range for varying sample sizes.[6] Equations (17.6) and (17.7) define the control limits for the $\bar{X}$ chart.

[6] $\bar{R}/d_2$ is used to estimate the standard deviation of the individual items in the population, and $\bar{R}/d_2\sqrt{n}$ is used to estimate the standard error of the mean.

CONTROL LIMITS FOR THE $\bar{X}$ CHART

$$\bar{\bar{X}} \pm 3\frac{\bar{R}}{d_2\sqrt{n}}$$

$$\text{UCL} = \bar{\bar{X}} + 3\frac{\bar{R}}{d_2\sqrt{n}}$$

$$\text{LCL} = \bar{\bar{X}} - 3\frac{\bar{R}}{d_2\sqrt{n}} \qquad (17.6)$$

where

$$\bar{\bar{X}} = \frac{\sum_{i=1}^{k}\bar{X}_i}{k}, \quad \bar{R} = \frac{\sum_{i=1}^{k}R_i}{k}$$

$\bar{X}_i$ = sample mean of n observations at time i

R_i = range of n observations at time i

k = number of subgroups

You can simplify the computations in Equation (17.6) by utilizing the A_2 **factor** given in Table E.9, equal to $3/d_2\sqrt{n}$. Equations (17.7a) and (17.7b) show the simplified control limits.

COMPUTING CONTROL LIMITS FOR THE MEAN, USING THE A_2 FACTOR

$$UCL = \overline{\overline{X}} + A_2\overline{R} \tag{17.7a}$$

$$LCL = \overline{\overline{X}} - A_2\overline{R} \tag{17.7b}$$

From Table 17.5 on page 671,

$$k = 28, \quad \sum_{i=1}^{k} \overline{X}_i = 265.38, \quad \sum_{i=1}^{k} R_i = 97.5$$

so that

$$\overline{\overline{X}} = \frac{\sum_{i=1}^{k} \overline{X}_i}{k} = \frac{265.38}{28} = 9.478$$

$$\overline{R} = \frac{\sum_{i=1}^{k} R_i}{k} = \frac{97.5}{28} = 3.482$$

Using Equations (17.7a) and (17.7b), since $n = 5$, from Table E.9, $A_2 = 0.577$, so that

$$UCL = 9.478 + (0.577)(3.482) = 9.478 + 2.009 = 11.487$$

$$LCL = 9.478 - (0.577)(3.482) = 9.478 - 2.009 = 7.469$$

Figure 17.7 displays the $\overline{X}$ chart for the luggage delivery time data.

FIGURE 17.7

$\overline{X}$ chart for the luggage delivery times

Create this worksheet using the instructions in Section EG17.5.

Figure 17.7 does not reveal any points outside the control limits, and there are no obvious patterns in either chart. Although there is a considerable amount of variability among the 28 subgroup means, because both the R chart and the $\overline{X}$ chart are in control, you know that the luggage delivery process is in a state of statistical control. If you want to reduce the variation or lower the mean delivery time, you need to change the process.

Problems for Section 17.5

LEARNING THE BASICS

17.18 For subgroups of $n = 4$, what is the value of
a. the d_2 factor?
b. the d_3 factor?
c. the D_3 factor?
d. the D_4 factor?
e. the A_2 factor?

17.19 For subgroups of $n = 3$, what is the value of
a. the d_2 factor?
b. the d_3 factor?
c. the D_3 factor?
d. the D_4 factor?
e. the A_2 factor?

17.20 The following summary of data is for subgroups of $n = 3$ for a 10-day period:

Day	Mean	Range	Day	Mean	Range
1	48.03	0.29	6	48.07	0.22
2	48.08	0.43	7	47.99	0.16
3	47.90	0.16	8	48.04	0.15
4	48.03	0.13	9	47.99	0.46
5	47.81	0.32	10	48.04	0.15

a. Compute control limits for the range.
b. Is there evidence of special cause variation in (a)?
c. Compute control limits for the mean.
d. Is there evidence of special cause variation in (c)?

17.21 The following summary of data is for subgroups of $n = 4$ for a 10-day period:

Day	Mean	Range	Day	Mean	Range
1	13.6	3.5	6	12.9	4.8
2	14.3	4.1	7	17.3	4.5
3	15.3	5.0	8	13.9	2.9
4	12.6	2.8	9	12.6	3.8
5	11.8	3.7	10	15.2	4.6

a. Compute control limits for the range.
b. Is there evidence of special cause variation in (a)?
c. Compute control limits for the mean.
d. Is there evidence of special cause variation in (c)?

APPLYING THE CONCEPTS

✓ SELF Test **17.22** The manager of a branch of a local bank wants to study waiting times of customers for teller service during the 12:00 noon-to-1:00 P.M. lunch hour. A subgroup of four customers is selected (one at each 15-minute interval during the hour), and the time, in minutes, is measured from the point each customer enters the line to when he or she reaches the teller window. The results over a four-week period, stored in **Banktime**, are as follows:

Day	Time in Minutes			
1	7.2	8.4	7.9	4.9
2	5.6	8.7	3.3	4.2
3	5.5	7.3	3.2	6.0
4	4.4	8.0	5.4	7.4
5	9.7	4.6	4.8	5.8
6	8.3	8.9	9.1	6.2
7	4.7	6.6	5.3	5.8
8	8.8	5.5	8.4	6.9
9	5.7	4.7	4.1	4.6
10	3.7	4.0	3.0	5.2
11	2.6	3.9	5.2	4.8
12	4.6	2.7	6.3	3.4
13	4.9	6.2	7.8	8.7
14	7.1	6.3	8.2	5.5
15	7.1	5.8	6.9	7.0
16	6.7	6.9	7.0	9.4
17	5.5	6.3	3.2	4.9
18	4.9	5.1	3.2	7.6
19	7.2	8.0	4.1	5.9
20	6.1	3.4	7.2	5.9

a. Construct control charts for the range and the mean.
b. Is the process in control?

17.23 The manager of a warehouse for a telephone company is involved in a process that receives expensive circuit boards and returns them to central stock so that they can be reused at a later date. Speedy processing of these circuit boards is critical in providing good service to customers and reducing capital expenditures. The data in **Warehse** represent the number of circuit boards processed per day by a subgroup of five employees over a 30-day period.
a. Construct control charts for the range and the mean.
b. Is the process in control?

17.24 An article in the *Mid-American Journal of Business* presents an analysis for a spring water bottling operation. One of the characteristics of interest is the amount of magnesium, measured in parts per million (ppm), in the water. The data in the table on page 675 (stored in **SpWater**) represent the magnesium levels from 30 subgroups of four bottles collected over a 30-hour period:
a. Construct a control chart for the range.
b. Construct a control chart for the mean.
c. Is the process in control?

Hour	1	2	3	4
1	19.91	19.62	19.15	19.85
2	20.46	20.44	20.34	19.61
3	20.25	19.73	19.98	20.32
4	20.39	19.43	20.36	19.85
5	20.02	20.02	20.13	20.34
6	19.89	19.77	20.92	20.09
7	19.89	20.45	19.44	19.95
8	20.08	20.13	20.11	19.32
9	20.30	20.42	20.68	19.60
10	20.19	20.00	20.23	20.59
11	19.66	21.24	20.35	20.34
12	20.30	20.11	19.64	20.29
13	19.83	19.75	20.62	20.60
14	20.27	20.88	20.62	20.40
15	19.98	19.02	20.34	20.34
16	20.46	19.97	20.32	20.83
17	19.74	21.02	19.62	19.90
18	19.85	19.26	19.88	20.20
19	20.77	20.58	19.73	19.48
20	20.21	20.82	20.01	19.93
21	20.30	20.09	20.03	20.13
22	20.48	21.06	20.13	20.42
23	20.60	19.74	20.52	19.42
24	20.20	20.08	20.32	19.51
25	19.66	19.67	20.26	20.41
26	20.72	20.58	20.71	19.99
27	19.77	19.40	20.49	19.83
28	19.99	19.65	19.41	19.58
29	19.44	20.15	20.17	20.76
30	20.03	19.96	19.86	19.91

Source: *Data extracted from Susan K. Humphrey and Timothy C. Krehbiel, "Managing Process Capability,"* The Mid-American Journal of Business, *14 (Fall 1999), 7–12.*

17.25 The data in Tensile are the tensile strengths of bolts of cloth. The data were collected in subgroups of three bolts of cloth over a 25-hour period:

a. Construct a control chart for the range.
b. Construct a control chart for the mean.
c. Is the process in control?

17.26 The director of radiology at a large metropolitan hospital has the business objective of improving the scheduling in the radiology facilities. On a typical day, 250 patients are transported to the radiology department for treatment or diagnostic procedures. If patients do not reach the radiology unit at their scheduled times, backups occur, and other patients experience delays. The time it takes to transport patients to the radiology unit is operationally defined as the time between when the transporter is assigned to the patient and when the patient arrives at the radiology unit. A sample of $n = 4$ patients was selected each day for 20 days, and the time to transport each patient (in minutes) was determined, with the results stored in Transport.
a. Construct control charts for the range and the mean.
b. Is the process in control?

17.27 A filling machine for a tea bag manufacturer produces approximately 170 tea bags per minute. The process manager monitors the weight of the tea placed in individual bags. A subgroup of $n = 4$ tea bags is taken every 15 minutes for 25 consecutive time periods. The results are stored in Tea3.
a. What are some of the sources of common cause variation that might be present in this process?
b. What problems might occur that would result in special causes of variation?
c. Construct control charts for the range and the mean.
d. Is the process in control?

17.28 A manufacturing company makes brackets for bookshelves. The brackets provide critical structural support and must have a 90-degree bend ±1 degree. Measurements of the bend of the brackets were taken at 18 different times. Five brackets were sampled at each time. The data are stored in Angle.
a. Construct control charts for the range and the mean.
b. Is the process in control?

17.6 Process Capability

Often, it is necessary to analyze the amount of common cause variation present in an in-control process. Is the common cause variation small enough to satisfy customers with the product or service? Or is the common cause variation so large that there are too many dissatisfied customers, and a process change is needed?

Analyzing the capability of a process is a way to answer these questions. **Process capability** is the ability of a process to consistently meet specified customer-driven requirements. There are many methods available for analyzing and reporting process capability (see reference 3). This section begins with a method for estimating the percentage of products or services that will satisfy the customer. Later in the section, capability indices are introduced.

Customer Satisfaction and Specification Limits

Quality is defined by the customer. A customer who believes that a product or service has met or exceeded his or her expectations will be satisfied. The management of a company must listen to the customer and translate the customer's needs and expectations into easily measured critical-to-quality (CTQ) variables. Management then sets specification limits for these CTQ variables.

Specification limits are technical requirements set by management in response to customers' needs and expectations. The **upper specification limit (USL)** is the largest value a CTQ variable can have and still conform to customer expectations. Likewise, the **lower specification limit (LSL)** is the smallest value a CTQ variable can have and still conform to customer expectations.

For example, a soap manufacturer understands that customers expect their soap to produce a certain amount of lather. The customer can become dissatisfied if the soap produces too much or too little lather. Product engineers know that the level of free fatty acids in the soap controls the amount of lather. Thus, the process manager, with input from the product engineers, sets both a USL and a LSL for the amount of free fatty acids in the soap.

As an example of a case in which only a single specification limit is involved, consider the Beachcomber Hotel scenario on page 655. Because customers want their bags delivered as quickly as possible, hotel management sets a USL for the time required for delivery. In this case, there is no LSL. As you can see in both the luggage delivery time and soap examples, specification limits are customer-driven requirements placed on a product or a service. If a process consistently meets these requirements, the process is capable of satisfying the customer.

One way to analyze the capability of a process is to estimate the percentage of products or services that are within specifications. To do this, you must have an in-control process because an out-of-control process does not allow you to predict its capability. If you are dealing with an out-of-control process, you must first identify and eliminate the special causes of variation before performing a capability analysis. Out-of-control processes are unpredictable, and, therefore, you cannot conclude that such processes are capable of meeting specifications or satisfying customer expectations in the future. In order to estimate the percentage of product or service within specifications, first you must estimate the mean and standard deviation of the population of all X values, the CTQ variable of interest for the product or service. The estimate for the mean of the population is $\bar{\bar{X}}$, the mean of all the sample means [see Equation (17.6) on page 672]. The estimate of the standard deviation of the population is $\bar{R}$ divided by d_2. You can use the $\bar{\bar{X}}$ and $\bar{R}$ from in-control $\bar{X}$ and R charts, respectively. You need to find the appropriate d_2 value in Table E.9.

Assuming that the process is in control and X is approximately normally distributed, you can use Equation (17.8) to estimate the probability that a process outcome is within specifications. (If your data are not approximately normally distributed, see reference 3 for an alternative approach.)

ESTIMATING THE CAPABILITY OF A PROCESS

For a CTQ variable with an LSL and a USL:

$$P(\text{An outcome will be within specifications}) = P(\text{LSL} < X < \text{USL}) \qquad \textbf{(17.8a)}$$

$$= P\left(\frac{\text{LSL} - \bar{\bar{X}}}{\bar{R}/d_2} < Z < \frac{\text{USL} - \bar{\bar{X}}}{\bar{R}/d_2}\right)$$

For a CTQ variable with only a USL:

$$P(\text{An outcome will be within specifications}) = P(X < \text{USL}) \qquad \textbf{(17.8b)}$$

$$= P\left(Z < \frac{\text{USL} - \bar{\bar{X}}}{\bar{R}/d_2}\right)$$

For a CTQ variable with only an LSL:

$$P(\text{An outcome will be within specifications}) = P(\text{LSL} < X) \qquad \textbf{(17.8c)}$$

$$= P\left(\frac{\text{LSL} - \bar{\bar{X}}}{\bar{R}/d_2} < Z\right)$$

where Z is a standardized normal random variable

In Section 17.5, you determined that the luggage delivery process was in control. Suppose that the hotel management has instituted a policy that 99% of all luggage deliveries must be completed in 14 minutes or less. From the summary computations on page 673:

$$n = 5 \qquad \overline{\overline{X}} = 9.478 \qquad \overline{R} = 3.482$$

and from Table E.9,

$$d_2 = 2.326$$

Using Equation (17.8b),

$$P(\text{Delivery is made within specifications}) = P(X < 14)$$

$$= P\left(Z < \frac{14 - 9.478}{3.482/2.326}\right)$$

$$= P(Z < 3.02)$$

Using Table E.2,

$$P(Z < 3.02) = 0.99874$$

Thus, you estimate that 99.874% of the luggage deliveries will be made within the specified time. The process is capable of meeting the 99% goal set by the hotel management.

Capability Indices

A common approach in business is to use capability indices to report the capability of a process. A **capability index** is an aggregate measure of a process's ability to meet specification limits. The larger the value of a capability index, the more capable the process is of meeting customer requirements. Equation (17.9) defines C_p, the most commonly used index.

> The **COMPUTE worksheet** of the **Capability workbook** computes this index as well as the other indices discussed in this section.

THE C_p INDEX

$$C_p = \frac{\text{USL} - \text{LSL}}{6(\overline{R}/d_2)} \qquad \qquad \textbf{(17.9)}$$

$$= \frac{\text{Specification spread}}{\text{Process spread}}$$

The numerator in Equation (17.9) represents the distance between the upper and lower specification limits, referred to as the *specification spread*. The denominator, $6(\overline{R}/d_2)$, represents a 6 standard deviation spread in the data (the mean ± 3 standard deviations), referred to as the *process spread*. (Recall from Chapter 6 that approximately 99.73% of the values from a normal distribution fall in the interval from the mean ± 3 standard deviations.) You want the process spread to be small in comparison to the specification spread in order for the vast majority of the process output to fall within the specification limits. Therefore, the larger the value of C_p, the better the capability of the process.

C_p is a measure of process potential, not of actual performance, because it does not consider the current process mean. A C_p value of 1 indicates that if the process mean could be centered (i.e., equal to the halfway point between the USL and LSL), approximately 99.73% of the values would be inside the specification limits. A C_p value greater than 1 indicates that a process has the potential of having more than 99.73% of its outcomes within specifications. A C_p value less than 1 indicates that the process is not very capable of meeting customer requirements, for even if the process is perfectly centered, fewer than 99.73% of the process outcomes will be within specifications. Historically, many companies required a C_p greater than or equal to 1. Now that the global economy has become more quality conscious, many companies are requiring a C_p as large as 1.33, 1.5, or, for companies adopting Six Sigma management, 2.0.

To illustrate the calculation and interpretation of the C_p index, suppose a soft-drink producer bottles its beverage into 12-ounce bottles. The LSL is 11.82 ounces, and the USL is 12.18 ounces. Each hour, four bottles are selected, and the range and the mean are plotted on control charts. At the end of 24 hours, the capability of the process is studied. Suppose that the control charts indicate that the process is in control and the following summary calculations were recorded on the control charts:

$$n = 4 \qquad \overline{\overline{X}} = 12.02 \qquad \overline{R} = 0.10$$

To calculate the C_p index, assuming that the data are normally distributed, from Table E.9, $d_2 = 2.059$ for $n = 4$. Using Equation (17.9),

$$C_p = \frac{\text{USL} - \text{LSL}}{6(\overline{R}/d_2)}$$

$$= \frac{12.18 - 11.82}{6(0.10/2.059)} = 1.24$$

Because the C_p index is greater than 1, the bottling process has the potential to fill more than 99.73% of the bottles within the specification limits.

In summary, the C_p index is an aggregate measure of process potential. The larger the value of C_p, the more potential the process has of satisfying the customer. In other words, a large C_p indicates that the current amount of common cause variation is small enough to consistently produce items within specifications. For a process to reach its full potential, the process mean needs to be at or near the center of the specification limits. Capability indices that measure actual process performance are considered next.

CPL, CPU, and C_{pk}

To measure the capability of a process in terms of actual process performance, the most common indices are *CPL*, *CPU*, and C_{pk}. Equation (17.10) defines *CPL* and *CPU*.

CPL AND CPU

$$CPL = \frac{\overline{\overline{X}} - \text{LSL}}{3(\overline{R}/d_2)} \qquad \qquad \textbf{(17.10a)}$$

$$CPU = \frac{\text{USL} - \overline{\overline{X}}}{3(\overline{R}/d_2)} \qquad \qquad \textbf{(17.10b)}$$

Because the process mean is used in the calculation of *CPL* and *CPU*, these indices measure process performance—unlike C_p, which measures only potential. A value of *CPL* (or *CPU*) equal to 1.0 indicates that the process mean is 3 standard deviations away from the LSL (or USL). For CTQ variables with only an LSL, the *CPL* measures the process performance. For CTQ variables with only a USL, the *CPU* measures the process performance. In either case, the larger the value of the index, the greater the capability of the process.

In the Beachcomber Hotel scenario, the hotel management has a policy that luggage deliveries are to be made in 14 minutes or less. Thus, the CTQ variable delivery time has a USL of 14, and there is no LSL. Because you previously determined that the luggage delivery process was in control, you can now compute the *CPU*. From the summary computations on page 673,

$$\overline{\overline{X}} = 9.478 \qquad \overline{R} = 3.482$$

And, from Table E.9, $d_2 = 2.326$. Then, using Equation (17.10b),

$$CPU = \frac{\text{USL} - \overline{\overline{X}}}{3(\overline{R}/d_2)} = \frac{14 - 9.478}{3(3.482/2.326)} = 1.01$$

The capability index for the luggage delivery CTQ variable is 1.01. Because this value is slightly more than 1, the USL is slightly more than 3 standard deviations above the mean. To increase *CPU* even farther above 1.00 and therefore increase customer satisfaction, you need to investigate changes in the luggage delivery process. To study a process that has a *CPL* and a *CPU*, see the bottling process scenario in Example 17.2.

| **EXAMPLE 17.2**

Computing *CPL* and *CPU* for the Bottling Process | In the soft-drink bottle-filling process described on page 678, the following information was provided:

$n = 4$ $\bar{\bar{X}} = 12.02$ $\bar{R} = 0.10$ LSL $= 11.82$ USL $= 12.18$ $d_2 = 2.059$

Compute the *CPL* and *CPU* for these data.

SOLUTION You compute the capability indices *CPL* and *CPU* by using Equations (17.10a) and (17.10b):

$$CPL = \frac{\bar{\bar{X}} - \text{LSL}}{3(\bar{R}/d_2)}$$

$$= \frac{12.02 - 11.82}{3(0.10/2.059)} = 1.37$$

$$CPU = \frac{\text{USL} - \bar{\bar{X}}}{3(\bar{R}/d_2)}$$

$$= \frac{12.18 - 12.02}{3(0.10/2.059)} = 1.10$$

Both the *CPL* and *CPU* are greater than 1, indicating that the process mean is more than 3 standard deviations away from both the LSL and USL. Because the *CPU* is less than the *CPL*, you know that the mean is closer to the USL than to the LSL. |

The capability index, C_{pk} [shown in Equation (17.11)], measures actual process performance for quality characteristics with two-sided specification limits. C_{pk} is equal to the value of either the *CPL* or *CPU*, whichever is smaller.

C_{pk}

$$C_{pk} = \text{MIN}[CPL, CPU] \qquad \textbf{(17.11)}$$

A value of 1 for C_{pk} indicates that the process mean is 3 standard deviations away from the closest specification limit. If the characteristic is normally distributed, then a value of 1 indicates that at least 99.73% of the current output is within specifications. As with all other capability indices, the larger the value of C_{pk}, the better. Example 17.3 illustrates the use of the C_{pk} index.

| **EXAMPLE 17.3**

Computing C_{pk} for the Bottling Process | The soft-drink producer in Example 17.2 requires the bottle filling process to have a C_{pk} greater than or equal to 1. Calculate the C_{pk} index.

SOLUTION In Example 17.2, *CPL* = 1.37 and *CPU* = 1.10. Using Equation (17.11):

$$C_{pk} = \text{MIN}[CPL, CPU]$$
$$= \text{MIN}[1.37, 1.10] = 1.10$$

The C_{pk} index is greater than 1, indicating that the actual process performance exceeds the company's requirement. More than 99.73% of the bottles contain between 11.82 and 12.18 ounces. |

Problems for Section 17.6

LEARNING THE BASICS

17.29 For an in-control process with subgroup data $n = 4$, $\bar{\bar{X}} = 20$, and $\bar{R} = 2$, find the estimate of
a. the population mean of all X values.
b. the population standard deviation of all X values.

17.30 For an in-control process with subgroup data $n = 3$, $\bar{\bar{X}} = 100$, and $\bar{R} = 3.386$, compute the percentage of outcomes within specifications if
a. LSL = 98 and USL = 102.
b. LSL = 93 and USL = 107.5.
c. LSL = 93.8 and there is no USL.
d. USL = 110 and there is no LSL.

17.31 For an in-control process with subgroup data $n = 3$, $\bar{\bar{X}} = 100$, and $\bar{R} = 3.386$, compute the C_p, CPL, CPU, and C_{pk} if
a. LSL = 98 and USL = 102.
b. LSL = 93 and USL = 107.5.

APPLYING THE CONCEPTS

✓**SELF** **17.32** Referring to the data of Problem 17.24 on
Test page 674, stored in **SpWater**, the researchers stated, "Some of the benefits of a capable process are increased customer satisfaction, increased operating efficiencies, and reduced costs." To illustrate this point, the authors presented a capability analysis for a spring water bottling operation. One of the CTQ variables is the amount of magnesium, measured in parts per million (ppm), in the water. The LSL and USL for the level of magnesium in a bottle are 18 ppm and 22 ppm, respectively.
a. Estimate the percentage of bottles that are within specifications.
b. Compute the C_p, CPL, CPU, and C_{pk}.

17.33 Refer to the data in Problem 17.25 on page 675 concerning the tensile strengths of bolts of cloth (stored in

Tensile). There is no USL for tensile strength, and the LSL is 13.
a. Estimate the percentage of bolts that are within specifications.
b. Calculate the C_p and CPL.

17.34 Refer to Problem 17.27 on page 675 concerning a filling machine for a tea bag manufacturer (data stored in **Tea3**). In that problem, you should have concluded that the process is in control. The label weight for this product is 5.5 grams, the LSL is 5.2 grams, and the USL is 5.8 grams. Company policy states that at least 99% of the tea bags produced must be inside the specifications in order for the process to be considered capable.
a. Estimate the percentage of the tea bags that are inside the specification limits. Is the process capable of meeting the company policy?
b. If management implemented a new policy stating that 99.7% of all tea bags are required to be within the specifications, is this process capable of reaching that goal? Explain.

17.35 Refer to Problem 17.22 on page 674 concerning waiting time for customers at a bank (data stored in **BankTime**). Suppose management has set a USL of 5 minutes on waiting time and specified that at least 99% of the waiting times must be less than 5 minutes in order for the process to be considered capable.
a. Estimate the percentage of the waiting times that are inside the specification limits. Is the process capable of meeting the company policy?
b. If management implemented a new policy, stating that 99.7% of all waiting times are required to be within specifications, is this process capable of reaching that goal? Explain.

17.7 Total Quality Management

An increased interest in improving the quality of products and services in the United States occurred as a reaction to improvements of Japanese industry that began as early as 1950. Individuals such as W. Edwards Deming, Joseph Juran, and Kaoru Ishikawa developed an approach that focuses on continuous improvement of products and services through an increased emphasis on statistics, process improvement, and optimization of the total system. This approach, widely known as **total quality management (TQM)**, is characterized by these themes:

- The primary focus is on process improvement.
- Most of the variation in a process is due to the system and not the individual.
- Teamwork is an integral part of a quality management organization.
- Customer satisfaction is a primary organizational goal.
- Organizational transformation must occur in order to implement quality management.
- Fear must be removed from organizations.
- Higher quality costs less, not more, but requires an investment in training.

In the 1980s, the federal government of the United States increased its efforts to encourage the improvement of quality in American business. Congress passed the Malcolm Baldrige National Improvement Act of 1987 and began awarding the Malcolm Baldrige Award to companies making the greatest strides in improving quality and customer satisfaction. Deming became a prominent consultant to many Fortune 500 companies, including Ford and Procter & Gamble. Many companies adopted some or all the basic themes of TQM.

Today, many quality improvement systems are in place in organizations worldwide. Although most organizations no longer use the name TQM, the underlying philosophy and statistical methods used in today's quality improvement systems are consistent with TQM and the work of Deming. This holistic approach to quality is captured in **Deming's 14 points for management** listed here:

1. Create constancy of purpose for improvement of product and service.
2. Adopt the new philosophy.
3. Cease dependence on inspection to achieve quality.
4. End the practice of awarding business on the basis of price tag alone. Instead, minimize total cost by working with a single supplier.
5. Improve constantly and forever every process for planning, production, and service.
6. Institute training on the job.
7. Adopt and institute leadership.
8. Drive out fear.
9. Break down barriers between staff areas.
10. Eliminate slogans, exhortations, and targets for the workforce.
11. Eliminate numerical quotas for the workforce and numerical goals for management.
12. Remove barriers that rob people of pride of workmanship. Eliminate the annual rating or merit system.
13. Institute a vigorous program of education and self-improvement for everyone.
14. Put everyone in the company to work to accomplish the transformation.

Points 1, 2, 5, 7, and 14 focus on the need for organizational transformation and the responsibility of top management to assert leadership in committing to the transformation. Without this commitment, any improvements obtained will be limited.

One aspect of the improvement process is illustrated by the **Shewhart-Deming cycle**, shown in Figure 17.8. The Shewhart-Deming cycle represents a continuous cycle of "plan, do, study, and act." The first step, planning, represents the initial design phase for planning a change in a manufacturing or service process. This step involves teamwork among individuals from different areas within an organization. The second step, doing, involves implementing the change, preferably on a small scale. The third step, studying, involves analyzing the results, using statistical methods to determine what was learned. The fourth step, acting, involves the acceptance of the change, its abandonment, or further study of the change under different conditions.

FIGURE 17.8
Shewhart-Deming cycle

Point 3, cease dependence on inspection to achieve quality, implies that any inspection whose purpose is to improve quality is too late because the quality is already built into the product. It is better to focus on making it right the first time. Among the difficulties involved in inspection (besides high costs) are the failure of inspectors to agree on the operational definitions for nonconforming items and the problem of separating good and bad items. The following example illustrates the difficulties inspectors face.

Suppose your job involves proofreading the sentence in Figure 17.9, with the objective of counting the number of occurrences of the letter F. Perform this task and record the number of occurrences of the letter F that you discover.

FINISHED FILES ARE THE RESULT OF YEARS OF SCIENTIFIC STUDY COMBINED WITH THE EXPERIENCE OF MANY YEARS

People usually see either three F's or six F's. The correct number is six F's. The number you see depends on the method you use to examine the sentence. You are likely to find three F's if you read the sentence phonetically and six F's if you count the number of F's carefully. If such a simple process as counting F's leads to inconsistency of inspectors' results, what will happen when a much more complicated process fails to provide clear operational definitions?

Point 4, end the practice of awarding business on the basis of price tag alone, focuses on the idea that there is no real long-term meaning to price without knowledge of the quality of the product. In addition, minimizing the number of entities in the supply chain will reduce the variation involved.

Points 6 and 13 refer to training and reflect the needs of all employees. Continuous learning is critical for quality improvement within an organization. In particular, management needs to understand the differences between special causes and common causes of variation so that proper action is taken in each circumstance.

Points 8 through 12 relate to the evaluation of employee performance. Deming believed that an emphasis on targets and exhortations places an improper burden on the workforce. Workers cannot produce beyond what the system allows (as illustrated in the red bead experiment in Section 17.3). It is management's job to *improve* the system, not to raise the expectations on workers beyond the system's capability.

Although Deming's points are thought provoking, some have criticized his approach for lacking a formal, objective accountability (see reference 12). Many managers of large organizations, used to seeing financial analyses of policy changes, need a more prescriptive approach.

17.8 Six Sigma

Six Sigma is a quality improvement system originally developed by Motorola in the mid-1980s. After seeing the huge financial successes at Motorola, GE, and other early adopters of Six Sigma, many companies worldwide have now instituted Six Sigma to improve efficiency, cut costs, eliminate defects, and reduce product variation (see references 1, 4, 11, and 17). Six Sigma offers a more prescriptive and systematic approach to process improvement than TQM. It is also distinguished from other quality improvement systems by its clear focus on achieving bottom-line results in a relatively short three- to six-month period of time.

The name Six Sigma comes from the fact that it is a managerial approach designed to create processes that result in no more than 3.4 defects per million. The Six Sigma approach assumes that processes are designed so that the upper and lower specification limits are six standard deviations away from the mean. Then, if the processes are monitored correctly with control charts, the worst possible scenario is for the mean to shift to within 4.5 standard deviations from the nearest specification limit. The area under the normal curve less than 4.5 standard deviations below the mean is approximately 3.4 out of 1 million. (Table E.2 reports this probability as 0.000003398.)

The DMAIC Model

To guide managers in their task of improving short- and long-term results, Six Sigma uses a five-step process known as the **DMAIC model**—named for the five steps in the process:

- **Define** The problem is defined, along with the costs, the benefits, and the impact on the customer.
- **Measure** Important characteristics related to the quality of the service or product are identified and discussed. Variables measuring these characteristics are defined and

called **critical-to-quality (CTQ)** variables. Operational definitions for all the CTQ variables are then developed. In addition, the measurement procedure is verified so that it is consistent over repeated measurements.

- **Analyze** The root causes of *why* defects occur are determined, and variables in the process causing the defects are identified. Data are collected to determine benchmark values for each process variable. This analysis often uses control charts (discussed in Sections 17.2–17.5).
- **Improve** The importance of each process variable on the CTQ variable is studied using designed experiments (see Chapter 11 and references 9, 10, and 13). The objective is to determine the best level for each variable.
- **Control** The objective is to maintain the benefits for the long term by avoiding potential problems that can occur when a process is changed.

The *Define* phase of a Six Sigma project consists of the development of a project charter, performing a SIPOC analysis, and identifying the customers for the output of the process. The development of a project charter involves forming a table of business objectives and indicators for all potential Six Sigma projects. Importance ratings are assigned by top management, projects are prioritized, and the most important project is selected. A **SIPOC analysis** is used to identify the **S**uppliers to the process, list the **I**nputs provided by the suppliers, flowchart the **P**rocess, list the process **O**utputs, and identify the **C**ustomers of the process. This is followed by a Voice of the Customer analysis that involves market segmentation in which different types of users of the process are identified and the circumstances of their use of the process are identified. Statistical methods used in the *Define* phase include tables and charts, descriptive statistics, and control charts.

In the *Measure* phase of a Six Sigma project, members of a team identify the CTQ variables that measure important quality characteristics. Next, operational definitions (see Section 1.3) of each CTQ variable are developed so that everyone will have a firm understanding of the CTQ. Then studies are undertaken to ensure that there is a valid measurement system for the CTQ that is consistent across measurements. Finally, baseline data are collected to determine the capability and stability of the current process. Statistical methods used in the *Measure* phase include tables and charts, descriptive statistics, the normal distribution, the Analysis of Variance, and control charts.

The *Analyze* phase of a Six Sigma project focuses on the factors that affect the central tendency, variation, and shape of each CTQ variable. Factors are identified, and the relationships between the factors and the CTQs are analyzed. Statistical methods used in the *Analyze* phase include tables and charts, descriptive statistics, the Analysis of Variance, regression analysis, and control charts.

In the *Improve* phase of a Six Sigma project, team members carry out designed experiments to actively intervene in a process. The objective of the experiments is to determine the settings of the factors that will optimize the central tendency, variation, and shape of each CTQ variable. Statistical methods used in the *Improve* phase include tables and charts, descriptive statistics, regression analysis, hypothesis testing, the Analysis of Variance, and designed experiments.

The *Control* phase of a Six Sigma project focuses on the maintenance of improvements that have been made in the *Improve* phase. A risk abatement plan is developed to identify elements that can cause damage to a process. Statistical methods used in the *Control* phase include tables and charts, descriptive statistics, and control charts.

Roles in a Six Sigma Organization

Six Sigma requires that the employees of an organization have well-defined roles. The roles senior executive (CEO or president), executive committee, champion, process owner, master black belt, black belt, and green belt are critical to Six Sigma. More importantly, everyone must be properly trained in order to successfully fulfill their roles' tasks and responsibilities.

The role of the **senior executive** is critical for Six Sigma's ultimate success. The most successful, highly publicized Six Sigma efforts have all had unwavering, clear, and committed leadership from top management. Although Six Sigma concepts and processes can be initiated at lower levels, high-level success cannot be achieved without the leadership of the senior executive.

The members of the **executive committee** consist of the top management of an organization. They need to operate at the same level of commitment to Six Sigma as the senior executive.

Champions take a strong sponsorship and leadership role in conducting and implementing Six Sigma projects. They work closely with the executive committee, the black belt assigned to their project, and the master black belt overseeing their project. A champion should be a member of the executive committee, or at least someone who reports directly to a member of the executive committee. He or she should have enough influence to remove obstacles or provide resources without having to go higher in the organization.

A **process owner** is the manager of a process. He or she has responsibility for the process and has the authority to change the process on her or his signature. The process owner should be identified and involved immediately in all Six Sigma projects related to his or her own area.

A **master black belt** takes on a leadership role in the implementation of the Six Sigma process and as an advisor to senior executives. The master black belt must use his or her skills while working on projects that are led by black belts and green belts. A master black belt has successfully led many teams through complex Six Sigma projects. He or she is a proven change agent, leader, facilitator, and technical expert in Six Sigma.

A **black belt** works full time on Six Sigma projects. A black belt is mentored by a master black belt but may report to a manager for his or her tour of duty as a black belt. Ideally, a black belt works well in a team format, can manage meetings, is familiar with statistics and systems theory, and has a focus on the customer.

A **green belt** is an individual who works on Six Sigma projects part time (approximately 25%), either as a team member for complex projects or as a project leader for simpler projects. Most managers in a mature Six Sigma organization are green belts. Green belt certification is a critical prerequisite for advancement into upper management in a Six Sigma organization.

Recent research (see reference 4) indicates that more than 80% of the top 100 publicly traded companies in the United States use Six Sigma. So, you do need to be aware of the distinction between master black belt, black belt, and green belt if you are to function effectively in a Six Sigma organization.

In a Six Sigma organization, 25% to 50% of the organization will be green belts, only 6% to 12% of the organization need to be black belts, and only 1% of the organization needs to be master black belts (reference 9). Individual companies, professional organizations such as the American Society for Quality, and universities such as the University of Miami offer certification programs for green belt, black belt, and master black belt. For more information on certification and other aspects of Six Sigma, see references 9, 10, and 13.

USING STATISTICS @ Beachcomber Hotel Revisited

In the Using Statistics scenario, you were the manager of the Beachcomber Hotel. After being trained in Six Sigma, you decided to focus on two critical first impressions: Is the room ready when a guest checks in? And, do guests receive their luggage in a reasonable amount of time?

You constructed a p chart on the proportion of rooms not ready at check-in. The p chart indicated that the check-in process was in control and that, on average, the proportion of rooms not ready was approximately 0.08 (i.e., 8%). You then constructed $\overline{X}$ and R charts for the amount of time required to deliver luggage. Although there was a considerable amount of variability around the overall mean of approximately 9.5 minutes, you determined that the luggage delivery process was also in control.

You have learned that an in-control process contains common causes but no special causes of variation. Improvements in the outcomes of in-control processes must come from changes in the actual processes. Thus, if you want to reduce the proportion of rooms not ready at check-in and/or lower the mean luggage delivery time, you will need to change the check-in process and/or the luggage delivery process. From your knowledge of Six Sigma and statistics, you know that during the *Improve* phase of the DMAIC model, you will be able to perform and analyze experiments using different process designs. Hopefully you will discover better process designs that will lead to a higher percentage of rooms being ready on time and/or quicker luggage delivery times. These improvements should ultimately lead to greater guest satisfaction.

SUMMARY

In this chapter you have learned how to use control charts to distinguish between common causes and special causes of variation. For categorical variables, you learned how to construct and analyze p charts. For discrete variables involving a count of nonconformances, you learned how to construct and analyze c charts. For numerically measured variables, you learned how to construct and analyze $\bar{X}$ and R charts. The chapter also discussed managerial approaches used such as TQM and Six Sigma that improve the quality of products and services.

KEY EQUATIONS

Constructing Control Limits

Process mean ±3 standard deviations

Upper control limit (UCL) = process mean
                              $+3$ standard deviations

Lower control limit (LCL) = process mean
                              -3 standard deviations **(17.1)**

Control Limits for the p Chart

$$\bar{p} \pm 3\sqrt{\frac{\bar{p}(1-\bar{p})}{\bar{n}}}$$

$$\text{UCL} = \bar{p} + 3\sqrt{\frac{\bar{p}(1-\bar{p})}{\bar{n}}}$$

$$\text{LCL} = \bar{p} - 3\sqrt{\frac{\bar{p}(1-\bar{p})}{\bar{n}}} \qquad \textbf{(17.2)}$$

Control Limits for the c Chart

$$\bar{c} \pm 3\sqrt{\bar{c}}$$

$$\text{UCL} = \bar{c} + 3\sqrt{\bar{c}}$$

$$\text{LCL} = \bar{c} - 3\sqrt{\bar{c}} \qquad \textbf{(17.3)}$$

Control Limits for the Range

$$\bar{R} \pm 3\bar{R}\frac{d_3}{d_2}$$

$$\text{UCL} = \bar{R} + 3\bar{R}\frac{d_3}{d_2}$$

$$\text{LCL} = \bar{R} - 3\bar{R}\frac{d_3}{d_2} \qquad \textbf{(17.4)}$$

Computing Control Limits for the Range

$$\text{UCL} = D_4\bar{R} \qquad \textbf{(17.5a)}$$

$$\text{LCL} = D_3\bar{R} \qquad \textbf{(17.5b)}$$

Control Limits for the $\bar{X}$ Chart

$$\bar{\bar{X}} \pm 3\frac{\bar{R}}{d_2\sqrt{n}}$$

$$\text{UCL} = \bar{\bar{X}} + 3\frac{\bar{R}}{d_2\sqrt{n}}$$

$$\text{LCL} = \bar{\bar{X}} - 3\frac{\bar{R}}{d_2\sqrt{n}} \qquad \textbf{(17.6)}$$

Computing Control Limits for the Mean, Using the A_2 Factor

$$\text{UCL} = \bar{\bar{X}} + A_2\bar{R} \qquad \textbf{(17.7a)}$$

$$\text{LCL} = \bar{\bar{X}} - A_2\bar{R} \qquad \textbf{(17.7b)}$$

Estimating the Capability of a Process

For a CTQ variable with an LSL and a USL:

$$P\binom{\text{An outcome will be}}{\text{within specification}} = P(\text{LSL} < X < \text{USL})$$

$$= P\left(\frac{\text{LSL} - \bar{\bar{X}}}{\bar{R}/d_2} < Z < \frac{\text{USL} - \bar{\bar{X}}}{\bar{R}/d_2}\right) \qquad \textbf{(17.8a)}$$

For a CTQ variable with only a USL:

$$P\binom{\text{An outcome will be}}{\text{within specification}} = P(X < \text{USL})$$

$$= P\left(Z < \frac{\text{USL} - \bar{\bar{X}}}{\bar{R}/d_2}\right) \qquad \textbf{(17.8b)}$$

For a CTQ variable with only an LSL:

$$P\left(\begin{array}{c}\text{An outcome will be} \\ \text{within specification}\end{array}\right) = P(\text{LSL} < X)$$

$$= P\left(\frac{\text{LSL} - \bar{\bar{X}}}{\bar{R}/d_2} < Z\right) \qquad \textbf{(17.8c)}$$

The C_p Index

$$C_p = \frac{\text{USL} - \text{LSL}}{6(\bar{R}/d_2)}$$

$$= \frac{\text{Specification spread}}{\text{Process spread}} \qquad \textbf{(17.9)}$$

CPL and CPU

$$CPL = \frac{\bar{\bar{X}} - \text{LSL}}{3(\bar{R}/d_2)} \qquad \textbf{(17.10a)}$$

$$CPU = \frac{\text{USL} - \bar{\bar{X}}}{3(\bar{R}/d_2)} \qquad \textbf{(17.10b)}$$

C_{pk}

$$C_{pk} = MIN[CPL, CPU] \qquad \textbf{(17.11)}$$

KEY TERMS

CHAPTER REVIEW PROBLEMS

CHECKING YOUR UNDERSTANDING

17.36 What is the difference between common cause variation and special cause variation?

17.37 What should you do to improve a process when special causes of variation are present?

17.38 What should you do to improve a process when only common causes of variation are present?

17.39 Under what circumstances do you use a p chart?

17.40 What is the difference between attribute control charts and variables control charts?

17.41 Why are $\bar{X}$ and R charts used together?

17.42 What principles did you learn from the red bead experiment?

17.43 What is the difference between process potential and process performance?

17.44 A company requires a C_{pk} value of 1 or larger. If a process has $C_p = 1.5$ and $C_{pk} = 0.8$, what changes should you make to the process?

17.45 Why is a capability analysis *not* performed on out-of-control processes?

APPLYING THE CONCEPTS

17.46 According to the American Society for Quality, customers in the United States consistently rate service quality lower than product quality (American Society for Quality, *The Quarterly Quality Report*, **www.asq.org**, May 16, 2006). For example, products in the beverage, personal care, and cleaning industries, as well as the major appliance sector all received very high customer satisfaction ratings. At the other extreme, services provided by airlines, banks, and insurance companies all received low customer satisfaction ratings.

a. Why do you think service quality consistently rates lower than product quality?

b. What are the similarities and differences between measuring service quality and product quality?

c. Do Deming's 14 points apply to both products and services?

d. Can Six Sigma be used for both products and services?

17.47 Six Flags Amusement Parks lost $133 million on revenue of $1.09 billion in 2005. To turn things around, Six Flags CEO Mark Shapiro is focusing on big problems (e.g., cutting long-term debt) and small details (e.g., cleaner restrooms and grounds). His attention to providing clean parks is part of his overall strategy to get entire families to enjoy their day in the park so much that they want to return (data extracted from L. Petrecca, "Six Flags CEO Waves the Signal Flag for Families," **www.usatoday.com**, June 13, 2006). Suppose that you have been hired as a summer intern at a large amusement park. Every day, your task is to conduct 200 exit interviews in the parking lot when customers leave. You need to construct questions to address the cleanliness of the park and the customers' intent to return. When you begin to construct a short questionnaire, you remember the control chart material you learned in a statistics course, and you decide to write questions that will provide you with data to graph on control charts. After collecting data for 30 days, you plan to construct the control charts.

a. Write a question that will allow you to develop a control chart of customers' perceptions of cleanliness of the park.

b. Give examples of common cause variation and special cause variation for the control chart.

c. If the control chart is in control, what does that indicate, and what do you do next?

d. If the control chart is out of control, what does that indicate, and what do you do next?

e. Repeat (a) through (d), this time addressing the customers' intent to return to the park.

f. After the initial 30 days, assuming that the charts indicate in-control processes or that the root sources of special cause variation have been corrected, explain how the charts can be used on a daily basis to monitor and improve the quality in the park.

17.48 Researchers at Miami University in Oxford, Ohio, investigated the use of p charts to monitor the market share of a product and to document the effectiveness of marketing promotions. Market share is defined as the company's proportion of the total number of products sold in a category. If a p chart based on a company's market share indicates an in-control process, then the company's share in the marketplace is deemed to be stable and consistent over time. In the example given in the article, the RudyBird Disk Company collected daily sales data from a nationwide retail audit service. The first 30 days of data in the accompanying table (stored in RudyBird) indicate the total number of cases of

computer disks sold and the number of RudyBird disks sold. The final 7 days of data were taken after RudyBird launched a major in-store promotion. A control chart was used to see if the in-store promotion would result in special cause variation in the marketplace.

Cases Sold Before the Promotion

Day	Total	RudyBird	Day	Total	RudyBird
1	154	35	16	177	56
2	153	43	17	143	43
3	200	44	18	200	69
4	197	56	19	134	38
5	194	54	20	192	47
6	172	38	21	155	45
7	190	43	22	135	36
8	209	62	23	189	55
9	173	53	24	184	44
10	171	39	25	170	47
11	173	44	26	178	48
12	168	37	27	167	42
13	184	45	28	204	71
14	211	58	29	183	64
15	179	35	30	169	43

Cases Sold After the Promotion

Day	Total	RudyBird
31	201	92
32	177	76
33	205	85
34	199	90
35	187	77
36	168	79
37	198	97

Source: *Data extracted from C. T. Crespy, T. C. Krehbiel, and J. M. Stearns, "Integrating Analytic Methods into Marketing Research Education: Statistical Control Charts as an Example,"* Marketing Education Review, 5 (Spring 1995), 11–23.

a. Construct a p chart using data from the first 30 days (prior to the promotion) to monitor the market share for RudyBird disks.

b. Is the market share for RudyBird in control before the start of the in-store promotion?

c. On your control chart, extend the control limits generated in (b) and plot the proportions for days 31 through 37. What effect, if any, did the in-store promotion have on RudyBird's market share?

17.49 The manufacturer of Boston and Vermont asphalt shingles constructed control charts and analyzed several quality characteristics. One characteristic of interest is the strength of the sealant on the shingle. During each day of production, three shingles are tested for their sealant strength. (Thus, a subgroup is operationally defined as one day of production, and the sample size for each subgroup is 3.) Separate pieces are cut from the upper and lower portions of a shingle and then reassembled to simulate shingles on a roof. A timed heating process is used to simulate the sealing process. The sealed shingle pieces are pulled apart, and the amount of force (in pounds) required to break the sealant bond is measured and recorded. This variable is called the *sealant strength*. The file **Sealant** contains sealant strength measurements on 25 days of production for Boston shingles and 19 days for Vermont shingles.

For the 25 days of production for Boston shingles,
a. construct a control chart for the range.
b. construct a control chart for the mean.
c. is the process in control?
d. Repeat (a) through (c), using the 19 production days for Vermont shingles.

17.50 A professional basketball player has embarked on a program to study his ability to shoot foul shots. On each day in which a game is not scheduled, he intends to shoot 100 foul shots. He maintains records over a period of 40 days of practice, with the results stored in **Foulspc**:
a. Construct a *p* chart for the proportion of successful foul shots. Do you think that the player's foul-shooting process is in statistical control? If not, why not?
b. What if you were told that the player used a different method of shooting foul shots for the last 20 days? How might this information change your conclusions in (a)?
c. If you knew the information in (b) prior to doing (a), how might you do the analysis differently?

17.51 The funds-transfer department of a bank is concerned with turnaround time for investigations of funds-transfer payments. A payment may involve the bank as a remitter of funds, a beneficiary of funds, or an intermediary in the payment. An investigation is initiated by a payment inquiry or a query by a party involved in the payment or any department affected by the flow of funds. When a query is received, an investigator reconstructs the transaction trail of the payment and verifies that the information is correct and that the proper payment is transmitted. The investigator then reports the results of the investigation, and the transaction is considered closed. It is important that investigations are closed rapidly, preferably within the same day. The number of new investigations and the number and proportion closed on the same day that the inquiry was made are stored in **FundTran**.
a. Construct a control chart for these data.
b. Is the process in a state of statistical control? Explain.
c. Based on the results of (a) and (b), what should management do next to improve the process?

17.52 A branch manager of a brokerage company is concerned with the number of undesirable trades made by her sales staff. A trade is considered undesirable if there is an error on the trade ticket. Trades with errors are canceled and resubmitted. The cost of correcting errors is billed to the brokerage company. The branch manager wants to know whether the proportion of undesirable trades is in a state of statistical control so she can plan the next step in a quality improvement process. Data were collected for a 30-day period and stored in **Trade**.
a. Construct a control chart for these data.
b. Is the process in control? Explain.
c. Based on the results of (a) and (b), what should the manager do next to improve the process?

17.53 As chief operating officer of a local community hospital, you have just returned from a three-day seminar on quality and productivity. It is your intention to implement many of the ideas that you learned at the seminar. You have decided to construct control charts for the upcoming month for the proportion of rework in the laboratory (based on 1,000 daily samples), the number of daily admissions, and time (in hours) between receipt of a specimen at the laboratory and completion of the work (based on a subgroup of 10 specimens per day). The data collected are summarized and stored in **HospAdm**. You are to make a presentation to the chief executive officer of the hospital and the board of directors. Prepare a report that summarizes the conclusions drawn from analyzing control charts for these variables. In addition, recommend additional variables to measure and monitor by using control charts.

17.54 A team working at a cat food company had the business objective of reducing nonconformance in the cat food canning process. As the team members began to investigate the current process, they found that, in some instances, production needed expensive overtime costs to meet the requirements requested by the market forecasting team. They also realized that no data were available about the stability and magnitude of the rate of nonconformance and the production volume throughout the day. Their previous study of the process indicated that output could be nonconforming for a variety of reasons. The reasons broke down into two categories: quality characteristics due to the can and characteristics concerning the fill weight of the container. Because these nonconformities stemmed from different sets of underlying causes, they decided to study them separately. The group assigned to study and reduce the nonconformities due to the can decided that at 15-minute intervals during each shift, a sample of 100 cans would be selected, and the number of nonconforming cans would be determined. In addition, the total number of cans produced during this time period would be recorded. The results for a single day's production of kidney cat food and a single day's production of shrimp cat food are stored in **CatFood3**. You want to study the process of producing cans of cat food for the two shifts and the two types of food. Completely analyze the data.

17.55 Refer to Problem 17.54. The production team at the cat food company investigating nonconformities due to the weight of the cans determined that at 15-minute intervals during each shift, a subgroup of five cans would be selected, and the contents of the selected cans would be weighed. The results for a single day's production of kidney cat food and a single day's production of shrimp cat food are stored in `CatFood4`. You want to study the process of producing cans of cat food for the two shifts and the two types of food. Completely analyze the data.

17.56 For a period of four weeks, record your pulse rate (in beats per minute) just after you get out of bed in the morning and also before you go to sleep at night. Construct $\bar{X}$ and R charts and determine whether your pulse rate is in a state of statistical control. Discuss.

17.57 (Class Project) Use the table of random numbers (Table E.1) to simulate the selection of different-colored balls from an urn, as follows:

1. Start in the row corresponding to the day of the month in which you were born plus the last two digits of the year in which you were born. For example, if you were born October 3, 1986, you would start in row $3 + 86 = 89$. If your total exceeds 100, subtract 100 from the total.
2. Select two-digit random numbers.
3. If you select a random number from 00 to 94, consider the ball to be white; if the random number is from 95 to 99, consider the ball to be red.

Each student is to select 100 such two-digit random numbers and report the number of "red balls" in the sample. Construct a control chart for the proportion of red balls. What conclusions can you draw about the system of selecting red balls? Are all the students part of the system? Is anyone outside the system? If so, what explanation can you give for someone who has too many red balls? If a bonus were paid to the top 10% of the students (the 10% with the fewest red balls), what effect would that have on the rest of the students? Discuss.

THE HARNSWELL SEWING MACHINE COMPANY CASE

PHASE 1

For more than 40 years, the Harnswell Sewing Machine Company has manufactured industrial sewing machines. The company specializes in automated machines called pattern tackers that sew repetitive patterns on such mass-produced products as shoes, garments, and seat belts. Aside from the sales of machines, the company sells machine parts. Because the company's products have a reputation for being superior, Harnswell is able to command a price premium for its product line.

Recently, the operations manager, Natalie York, purchased several books related to quality at a local bookstore. After reading them, she considered the feasibility of beginning a quality program at the company. At the current time, the company has no formal quality program. Parts are 100% inspected at the time of shipping to a customer or installation in a machine, yet Natalie has always wondered why inventory of certain parts (in particular, the half-inch cam rollers) invariably falls short before a full year lapses, even though 7,000 pieces have been produced for a demand of 5,000 pieces per year.

After a great deal of reflection and with some apprehension, Natalie has decided that she will approach John Harnswell, the owner of the company, about the possibility of beginning a program to improve quality in the company, starting with a trial project in the machine parts area. As she is walking to Mr. Harnswell's office for the meeting, she has second thoughts about whether this is such a good idea. After all, just last month, Mr. Harnswell told her, "Why do you need to go to graduate school for your master's degree in business? That is a waste of your time and will not be of any value to the Harnswell Company. All those professors are just up in their ivory towers and don't know a thing about running a business, like I do."

As she enters his office, Mr. Harnswell, ever courteous to her, invites Natalie to sit down across from him. "Well, what do you have on your mind this morning?" Mr. Harnswell asks her in an inquisitive tone. She begins by starting to talk about the books that she has just completed reading and about how she has some interesting ideas for making production even better than it is now and improving profits. Before she can finish, Mr. Harnswell has started to answer. "Look, everything has been fine since I started this company in 1968. I have built this company up from nothing to one that employs more than 100 people. Why do you want to make waves? Remember, if it ain't broke, don't fix it." With that, he ushers her from his office with the admonishment of, "What am I going to do with you if you keep coming up with these ridiculous ideas?"

EXERCISES

HS17.1 Based on what you have read, which of Deming's 14 points of management are most lacking in the Harnswell Sewing Machine Company? Explain.

HS17.2 What changes, if any, do you think that Natalie York might be able to institute in the company? Explain.

DO NOT CONTINUE UNTIL YOU HAVE COMPLETED THE PHASE 1 EXERCISES.

PHASE 2

Natalie slowly walks down the hall after leaving Mr. Harnswell's office, feeling rather downcast. He just won't listen to anyone, she thinks. As she walks, Jim Murante, the shop foreman, comes up beside her. "So," he says, "did you really think that he would listen to you? I've been here more than 25 years. The only way he listens is if he is shown something that worked after it has already been done. Let's see what we can plan together."

Natalie and Jim decide to begin by investigating the production of the cam rollers, which are precision-ground parts. The last part of the production process involves the grinding of the outer diameter. After grinding, the part mates with the cam groove of the particular sewing pattern. The half-inch rollers technically have an engineering specification for the outer diameter of the roller of 0.5075 inch (the specifications are actually metric, but in factory floor jargon, they are referred to as half-inch), plus a tolerable error of 0.0003 inch on the lower side. Thus, the outer diameter is allowed to be between 0.5072 and 0.5075 inch. Anything larger is reclassified into a different and less costly category, and anything smaller is unusable for anything other than scrap.

TABLE HS17.1

Diameter of Cam Rollers (in Inches)

Batch	Cam Roller				
	1	2	3	4	5
1	.5076	.5076	.5075	.5077	.5075
2	.5075	.5077	.5076	.5076	.5075
3	.5075	.5075	.5075	.5075	.5076
4	.5075	.5076	.5074	.5076	.5073
5	.5075	.5074	.5076	.5073	.5076
6	.5076	.5075	.5076	.5075	.5075
7	.5076	.5076	.5076	.5075	.5075
8	.5075	.5076	.5076	.5075	.5074
9	.5074	.5076	.5075	.5075	.5076
10	.5076	.5077	.5075	.5075	.5075
11	.5075	.5075	.5075	.5076	.5075
12	.5075	.5076	.5075	.5077	.5075
13	.5076	.5076	.5073	.5076	.5074
14	.5075	.5076	.5074	.5076	.5075
15	.5075	.5075	.5076	.5074	.5073
16	.5075	.5074	.5076	.5075	.5075
17	.5075	.5074	.5075	.5074	.5072
18	.5075	.5075	.5076	.5075	.5076
19	.5076	.5076	.5075	.5075	.5076
20	.5075	.5074	.5077	.5076	.5074
21	.5075	.5074	.5075	.5075	.5075
22	.5076	.5076	.5075	.5076	.5074
23	.5076	.5076	.5075	.5075	.5076
24	.5075	.5076	.5075	.5076	.5075
25	.5075	.5075	.5075	.5075	.5074
26	.5077	.5076	.5076	.5074	.5075
27	.5075	.5075	.5074	.5076	.5075
28	.5077	.5076	.5075	.5075	.5076
29	.5075	.5075	.5074	.5075	.5075
30	.5076	.5075	.5075	.5076	.5075

The grinding of the cam roller is done on a single machine with a single tool setup and no change in the grinding wheel after initial setup. The operation is done by Dave Martin, the head machinist, who has 30 years of experience in the trade and specific experience producing the cam roller part. Because production occurs in batches, Natalie and Jim sample five parts produced from each batch. Table HS17.1 presents data collected over 30 batches (stored in Harnswell).

EXERCISE

HS17.3 a. Is the process in control? Why?

b. What recommendations do you have for improving the process?

DO NOT CONTINUE UNTIL YOU HAVE COMPLETED THE PHASE 2 EXERCISE.

PHASE 3

Natalie examines the $\overline{X}$ and R charts developed from the data presented in Table HS17.1. The R chart indicates that the process is in control, but the $\overline{X}$ chart reveals that the mean for batch 17 is outside the LCL. This immediately gives her cause for concern because low values for the roller diameter could mean that parts have to be scrapped. Natalie goes to see Jim Murante, the shop foreman, to try to find out what had happened to batch 17. Jim looks up the production records to determine when this batch was produced. "Aha!" he exclaims. "I think I've got the answer! This batch was produced on that really cold morning we had last month. I've been after Mr. Harnswell for a long time to let us install an automatic thermostat here in the shop so that the place doesn't feel so cold when we get here in the morning. All he ever tells me is that people aren't as tough as they used to be."

Natalie is almost in shock. She realizes that what happened is that, rather than standing idle until the environment and the equipment warmed to acceptable temperatures, the machinist opted to manufacture parts that might have to be scrapped. In fact, Natalie recalls that a major problem occurred on that same day, when several other expensive parts had to be scrapped. Natalie says to Jim, "We just have to do something. We can't let this go on now that we know what problems it is potentially causing." Natalie and Jim decide to take enough money out of petty cash to get the thermostat without having to fill out a requisition requiring Mr. Harnswell's signature. They install the thermostat and set the heating control so that the heat turns on a half hour before the shop opens each morning.

EXERCISES

HS17.4 What should Natalie do now concerning the cam roller data? Explain.

HS17.5 Explain how the actions of Natalie and Jim to avoid this particular problem in the future have resulted in quality improvement.

DO NOT CONTINUE UNTIL YOU HAVE COMPLETED THE PHASE 3 EXERCISES.

PHASE 4

Because corrective action was taken to eliminate the special cause of variation, Natalie removes the data for batch 17 from the analysis. The control charts for the remaining days indicate a stable system, with only common causes of variation operating on the system. Then, Natalie and Jim sit down with Dave Martin and several other machinists to try to determine all the possible causes for the existence of oversized and scrapped rollers. Natalie is still troubled by the data. After all, she wants to find out whether the process is giving oversizes (which are downgraded) and undersizes (which are scrapped). She thinks about which tables and charts might be most helpful.

EXERCISE

HS17.6 a. Construct a frequency distribution and a stem-and-leaf display of the cam roller diameters. Which one do you prefer?

b. Based on your results in (a), construct all appropriate charts of the cam roller diameters.

c. Write a report, expressing your conclusions concerning the cam roller diameters. Be sure to discuss the diameters as they relate to the specifications.

DO NOT CONTINUE UNTIL YOU HAVE COMPLETED THE PHASE 4 EXERCISE.

PHASE 5

Natalie notices immediately that the overall mean diameter with batch 17 eliminated is 0.507527, which is higher than the specification value. Thus, the mean diameter of the rollers produced is so high that they will be downgraded in value. In fact, 55 of the 150 rollers sampled (36.67%) are above the specification value. If this percentage is extrapolated to the full year's production, 36.67% of the 7,000 pieces manufactured, or 2,567, could not be sold as half-inch rollers, leaving only 4,433 available for sale. "No wonder we often have shortages that require costly emergency runs," she thinks. She also notes that not one diameter is below the lower specification of 0.5072, so not one of the rollers had to be scrapped.

Natalie realizes that there has to be a reason for all this. Along with Jim Murante, she decides to show the results to Dave Martin, the head machinist. Dave says that the results don't surprise him that much. "You know," he says, "there is only 0.0003 inch in diameter that I'm allowed in variation. If I aim for exactly halfway between 0.5072 and 0.5075, I'm afraid that I'll make a lot of short pieces that will have to be scrapped. I know from way back when I first started here that Mr. Harnswell and everybody else will come down on my head if they start seeing too many of those scraps. I figure that if I aim at 0.5075, the worst thing that will happen will be a bunch of downgrades, but I won't make any pieces that have to be scrapped."

EXERCISES

HS17.7 What approach do you think the machinist should take in terms of the diameter he should aim for? Explain.

HS17.8 What do you think that Natalie should do next? Explain.

MANAGING THE *SPRINGVILLE HERALD*

PHASE 1

An advertising production team is charged with reducing the number and dollar amount of the advertising errors, with initial focus on the ran-in-error category. The team collects data, including the number of ads with errors, on a Monday-to-Saturday basis. Table SH17.1 includes the total number of ads and the number containing errors for a period of one month (stored in SH17-1). (Sundays are excluded because a special type of production is used for that day.)

EXERCISES

SH17.1 What is the first thing that the team from the advertising production department should do to reduce the number of errors? Explain.

SH17.2 a. Construct the appropriate control chart for these data.

b. Is the process in a state of statistical control? Explain.

c. What should the team recommend as the next step to improve the process?

TABLE SH17.1

Number of Ads with Errors and Daily Number of Display Ads

Day	Number of Ads with Errors	Total Number of Ads	Day	Number of Ads with Errors	Total Number of Ads
1	4	228	14	5	245
2	6	273	15	7	266
3	5	239	16	2	197
4	3	197	17	4	228
5	6	259	18	5	236
6	7	203	19	4	208
7	8	289	20	3	214
8	14	241	21	8	258
9	9	263	22	10	267
10	5	199	23	4	217
11	6	275	24	9	277
12	4	212	25	7	258
13	3	207			

DO NOT CONTINUE UNTIL YOU HAVE COMPLETED THE PHASE 1 EXERCISES.

PHASE 2

The advertising production team examines the *p* chart developed from the data of Table SH17.1. Using the rules for determining out-of-control points, the team members observe that day 8 is above the UCL. Upon investigation, they determine that on that day, there was an employee from another work area assigned to the processing of the ads because several employees were out ill. The group brainstorms ways of avoiding the problem in the future and recommends that a team of people from other work areas receive training on the work done by this area. Members of this team can then cover the processing of the ads by rotating in one- or two-hour shifts.

EXERCISES

SH17.3 What should the advertising production team now do concerning the data in Table SH17.1? Explain.

SH17.4 Explain how the actions of the team to avoid this particular problem in the future have resulted in quality improvement.

SH17.5 In addition to the number of ads with errors, what other information concerning errors on a daily basis should the team collect?

DO NOT CONTINUE UNTIL YOU HAVE COMPLETED THE PHASE 2 EXERCISES.

PHASE 3

A print production team also is charged with improving the quality of the *Herald*. The team has chosen the blackness of the print of the newspaper as its first project. Blackness is measured on a device that records the results on a standard scale, where the blacker the spot, the higher the blackness measure. The blackness of the print should be approximately 1.0. The lower and upper specifications for blackness are 0.8 and 1.2, respectively. Five spots on the first newspaper printed each day are randomly selected, and the blackness of each spot is measured. Table SH17.2 presents the results for 25 days (stored in SH17-2).

TABLE SH17.2
Newsprint Blackness for 25 Consecutive Days

Day	1	2	3	4	5
1	0.96	1.01	1.12	1.07	0.97
2	1.06	1.00	1.02	1.16	0.96
3	1.00	0.90	0.98	1.18	0.96
4	0.92	0.89	1.01	1.16	0.90
5	1.02	1.16	1.03	0.89	1.00
6	0.88	0.92	1.03	1.16	0.91
7	1.05	1.13	1.01	0.93	1.03
8	0.95	0.86	1.14	0.90	0.95
9	0.99	0.89	1.00	1.15	0.92
10	0.89	1.18	1.03	0.96	1.04
11	0.97	1.13	0.95	0.86	1.06
12	1.00	0.87	1.02	0.98	1.13
13	0.96	0.79	1.17	0.97	0.95
14	1.03	0.89	1.03	1.12	1.03
15	0.96	1.12	0.95	0.88	0.99
16	1.01	0.87	0.99	1.04	1.16
17	0.98	0.85	0.99	1.04	1.16
18	1.03	0.82	1.21	0.98	1.08
19	1.02	0.84	1.15	0.94	1.08
20	0.90	1.02	1.10	1.04	1.08
21	0.96	1.05	1.01	0.93	1.01
22	0.89	1.04	0.97	0.99	0.95
23	0.96	1.00	0.97	1.04	0.95
24	1.01	0.98	1.04	1.01	0.92
25	1.01	1.00	0.92	0.90	1.11

EXERCISE

SH17.6 a. Construct the appropriate control charts for these data.

b. Is the process in a state of statistical control? Explain.

c. What should the team recommend as the next step to improve the process?

REFERENCES

1. Arndt, M., "Quality Isn't Just for Widgets," *BusinessWeek*, July 22, 2002, pp. 72–73.
2. Automotive Industry Action Group (AIAG), *Statistical Process Control Reference Manual* (Chrysler, Ford, and General Motors Quality and Supplier Assessment Staff, 1995).
3. Bothe, D. R., *Measuring Process Capability* (New York: McGraw-Hill, 1997).
4. Cyger, M., "The Last Word—Riding the Bandwagon," *iSixSigma Magazine*, November/December 2006.
5. Davis, R. B., and T. C. Krehbiel, "Shewhart and Zone Control Charts Under Linear Trend," *Communications*

in Statistics: Simulation and Computation, 31 (2002), 91–96.

6. Deming, W. E., *The New Economics for Business, Industry, and Government* (Cambridge, MA: MIT Center for Advanced Engineering Study, 1993).

7. Deming, W. E., *Out of the Crisis* (Cambridge, MA: MIT Center for Advanced Engineering Study, 1986).

8. Gabor, A., *The Man Who Discovered Quality* (New York: Time Books, 1990).

9. Gitlow, H., and D. Levine, *Six Sigma for Green Belts and Champions* (Upper Saddle River, NJ: Financial Times/Prentice Hall, 2005).

10. Gitlow, H., D. Levine, and E. Popovich, *Design for Six Sigma for Green Belts and Champions* (Upper Saddle River, NJ: Financial Times/Prentice Hall, 2006).

11. Hahn, G. J., N. Doganaksoy, and R. Hoerl, "The Evolution of Six Sigma," *Quality Engineering*, 12 (2000), 317–326.

12. Lemak, D. L. , N. P. Mero, and R. Reed, "When Quality Works: A Premature Post-Mortem on TQM," *Journal of Business and Management*, 8 (2002), 391–407.

13. Levine, D. M., *Statistics for Six Sigma for Green Belts with Minitab and JMP* (Upper Saddle River, NJ: Financial Times/Prentice Hall, 2006).

14. *Microsoft Excel 2007* (Redmond, WA: Microsoft Corp., 2007).

15. Scherkenbach, W. W., *The Deming Route to Quality and Productivity: Road Maps and Roadblocks* (Washington, DC: CEEP Press, 1987).

16. Shewhart, W. A., *Economic Control of the Quality of Manufactured Product* (New York: Van Nostrand-Reinhard, 1931, reprinted by the American Society for Quality Control, Milwaukee, 1980).

17. Snee, R. D., "Impact of Six Sigma on Quality," *Quality Engineering*, 12 (2000), ix–xiv.

18. Vardeman, S. B., and J. M. Jobe, *Statistical Methods for Quality Assurance: Basics, Measurement, Control, Capability and Improvement* (New York: Springer-Verlag, 2009).

19. Walton, M., *The Deming Management Method* (New York: Perigee Books, 1986).

EG17.1 The THEORY of CONTROL CHARTS

There are no Excel Guide instructions for this section.

EG17.2 CONTROL CHART for the PROPORTION: THE *p* CHART

PHStat2 Use the **p Chart** procedure to create a *p* chart and supporting worksheets that compute the control limits and plot points. For example, to create the Figure 17.2 *p* chart for the Table 17.1 nonconforming hotel room data (see page 660), open to the **DATA worksheet** of the **Hotel1 workbook**. Select **PHStat → Control Charts → p Chart** and in the procedure's dialog box (shown below):

1. Enter **C1:C29** as the **Nonconformances Cell Range.**
2. Check **First cell contains label.**
3. Click **Size does not vary** and enter **200** as the **Sample/Subgroup Size.**
4. Enter a **Title** and click **OK.**

The procedure creates a *p* chart on its own chart sheet and two supporting worksheets: one that computes the control limits and one that computes the values to be plotted. For more information about these two worksheets, read the following *In-Depth Excel* instructions.

For other problems in which the sample/subgroup sizes vary, replace step 3 with this step: Click **Size varies**, enter the cell range that contains the sample/subgroup sizes as the **Sample/Subgroup Cell Range**, and click **First cell contain label**.

In-Depth Excel Create a *p* chart from worksheets that use arithmetic formulas to compute control limits and plot points.

Use the **pCHARTDATA** and **COMPUTE worksheets** of the **p Chart workbook**, shown in Figure EG17.1 and Figure EG17.2, as a template for computing control limits and plot points. The pCHARTDATA worksheet contains the Table 17.1 nonconforming hotel room data (see page 660) in columns A through D, using formulas in column D that divide the column C value by the column B value to compute the proportion (p_i). Formulas in columns E through G display the values for the LCL, $\bar{p}$, and UCL that are computed in cells B12 through B14 of the COMPUTE worksheet (see Figure EG17.1).

In turn, the **COMPUTE** worksheet uses the subgroup sizes and the proportion values (p_i) found in pCHARTDATA to compute the control limits (see Figure EG17.2).

Computing control limits and plotting points for other problems requires changes to the pCHARTDATA worksheet. First, paste the time period, subgroup/sample size, and number of nonconformances data into columns A through C of the pCHARTDATA worksheet. If there are more than 28 time periods, select cell range **D29:G29** and copy the range down through all the rows. If there are fewer than 28 time periods, delete the extra rows from the bottom up, starting with row 29.

Use the pCHARTDATA worksheet as the basis for creating a *p* chart. For example, to create the Figure 17.2 *p* chart for the Table 17.1 nonconforming hotel room data (see page 660), open to the pCHARTDATA worksheet. Select the cell range **A1:A29** and while holding down the

	A	B	C	D	E	F	G
1	Time Period	Subgroup/ Sample Size	Number of Nonconformances	p	LCL	Center	UCL
2	1	200	16	=C2/B2	=COMPUTE!$B$12	=COMPUTE!$B$13	=COMPUTE!$B$14
3	2	200	7	=C3/B3	=COMPUTE!$B$12	=COMPUTE!$B$13	=COMPUTE!$B$14
4	3	200	21	=C4/B4	=COMPUTE!$B$12	=COMPUTE!$B$13	=COMPUTE!$B$14
		200	17	=C5/B5	=COMPUTE!$B$12	=COMPUTE!$B$13	=COMPUTE!$B$14
26	25	200	18	=C26/B26	=COMPUTE!$B$12	=COMPUTE!$B$13	=COMPUTE!$B$14
27	26	200	15	=C27/B27	=COMPUTE!$B$12	=COMPUTE!$B$13	=COMPUTE!$B$14
28	27	200	20	=C28/B28	=COMPUTE!$B$12	=COMPUTE!$B$13	=COMPUTE!$B$14
29	28	200	22	=C29/B29	=COMPUTE!$B$12	=COMPUTE!$B$13	=COMPUTE!$B$14

FIGURE EG17.1 pCHARTDATA worksheet of the p Chart workbook

	A	B	
1	p Chart Summary		
2			
3	Intermediate Calculations		
4	Sum of Subgroup Sizes	5600	=SUM(pCHARTDATA!B:B)
5	Number of Subgroups Taken	28	=COUNT(pCHARTDATA!B:B)
6	Average Sample/Subgroup Size	200	=B4/B5
7	Average Proportion of Nonconforming Items	0.0827	=SUM(pCHARTDATA!C:C)/B4
8	Three Standard Deviations	0.0584	=3 * SQRT(B7 * (1 - B7)/B6)
9	Preliminary Lower Control Limit	0.0243	=B7 - B8
10			
11	p Chart Control Limits		
12	Lower Control Limit	0.0243	=IF(B9 > 0, B9, 0)
13	Center	0.0827	=B7
14	Upper Control Limit	0.1411	=B7 + B8

FIGURE EG17.2 COMPUTE worksheet of the **p Chart workbook**

Ctrl key, select the cell range **D1:G29**. (This operation selects the cell range **A1:A29, D1:G29**.) Continue with either the following *In-Depth Excel 2007* or *In-Depth Excel 2003* instructions.

In-Depth Excel 2007 *Continued from In-Depth Excel . . .*
Select **Insert → Scatter** and select the fourth choice from the **Scatter** gallery **(Scatter with Straight Lines and Markers)**. Relocate the chart to a chart sheet and adjust chart formatting by using the instructions in Appendix Section C.7 on page 726.

At this point, a recognizable chart begins to take shape, but the control limit and center lines are improperly formatted and are not properly labeled. Use the following three sets of instructions to correct these formatting errors:

To reformat each control limit line:

1. Right-click the control limit line and select **Format Data Series** from the shortcut menu.
2. In the Format Data Series dialog box left pane, click **Marker Options** and in the **Marker Options** right panel, click **None**.
3. In the left pane, click **Line Style** and in the **Line Style** right panel, select the sixth choice (a dashed line) from the **Dash type** drop-down gallery list.
4. In the left pane, click **Line Color** and in the **Line Color** right panel, select the black color from the **Color** drop-down gallery list.
5. Click **Close**.

To reformat the center line:

1. Right-click the center line and select **Format Data Series** from the shortcut menu.
2. In the Format Data Series dialog box left pane, click **Marker Options** and in the **Marker Options** right panel, click **None**.
3. In the left pane, click **Line Color** and in the **Line Color** right panel, click **Solid line** and then select a red color from the **Color** drop-down gallery.
4. Click **Close**.

To properly label a control limit or center line:

1. Select **Layout → Text Box** (in Insert group) and starting slightly above and to the right of the line, drag the special cursor diagonally to form a new text box.
2. Enter the line label in the text box and then click on the chart background.

In-Depth Excel 2003 *Continued from In-Depth Excel . . .*
Select **Insert → Chart** and:

In the Chart Wizard Step 1 dialog box:

1. Click the **Standard Types** tab and then click **XY (Scatter)** as the **Chart type**. Click the fourth **Chart sub-type**, labeled **Scatter with data points connected by lines**.
2. Click **Next**.

In the Chart Wizard Step 2 dialog box:

3. Click **Next**. (Entries and selections in this dialog box are correct as is.)

In the Chart Wizard Step 3 dialog box:

4. Click the **Titles** tab. Enter a **Chart title**, as well as a **Value (X) axis** title and a **Value (Y) axis** title. Adjust chart formatting by using the instructions in Appendix Section C.8 on page 727 for the **Axes**, **Gridlines**, **Legend**, and **Data Labels** tabs.
5. Click **Next**.

In the Chart Wizard Step 4 dialog box:

6. Click **As new sheet** and then click **Finish** to create the chart.

At this point, a recognizable chart begins to take shape, but the control limit and center lines are improperly formatted and are not properly labeled. Use the following three sets of instructions to correct these formatting errors.

To reformat each control limit line:

1. Right-click the control limit line and select **Format Data Series** from the shortcut menu.
2. In the Format Data Series dialog box, click the **Patterns** tab. In the **Line** group, select the first dashed line choice

from the **Style drop-down** list and select the black color from the **Color** drop-down list. In the **Marker** group, click **None**. Click **OK**.

To reformat the center line:

1. Right-click the center line and select **Format Data Series** from the shortcut menu.
2. In the Format Data Series dialog box, click the **Patterns** tab. In the **Line** group, select a red color from the **Color** drop-down list. In the **Marker** group, click **None**. Click **OK**.

To properly label a control limit or center line:

1. Select **View → Toolbars → Drawing** the Drawing toolbar.
2. Click the **Text Box** icon (see Figure EG17.3).
3. Starting slightly above and to the right of the line, drag the special cursor diagonally to form a new text box.
4. Enter the line label in the text box and then click on the chart background.

FIGURE EG17.3 Drawing toolbar with Text Box icon highlighted

EG17.3 The RED BEAD EXPERIMENT: UNDERSTANDING PROCESS VARIABILITY

There are no Excel Guide instructions for this section

EG17.4 CONTROL CHART for an AREA of OPPORTUNITY: The *c* CHART

PHStat2 Use the **c Chart** procedure to create a *c* chart and supporting worksheets that compute the control limits and plot points. For example, to create the Figure 17.5 *c* chart for the Table 17.4 hotel complaint data (see page 667), open to the **DATA worksheet** of the **Complaints workbook**. Select

PHStat → Control Charts → c Chart and in the procedure's dialog box (shown below):

1. Enter **B1:B51** as the **Nonconformances Cell Range**.
2. Check **First cell contains label**.
3. Enter a **Title** and click **OK**.

The procedure creates a *c* chart on its own chart sheet and two supporting worksheets: one that computes the control limits and one that computes the values to be plotted. For more information about these two worksheets, read the following *In-Depth Excel* instructions.

In-Depth Excel Create a *c* chart from worksheets that use arithmetic formulas to compute control limits and plot points.

Use the **cCHARTDATA** and **COMPUTE worksheets** of the **c Chart workbook**, shown in Figure EG17.4 and EG17.5, as a template for computing control limits and plot points. The cCHARTDATA worksheet contains the Table 17.4 hotel complaint data (see page 667) in columns A and B. Formulas in columns C through E display the values for the LCL, cBar, and UCL that are computed in cells B10 through B12 of the COMPUTE worksheet (see Figure EG17.4).

In turn, the COMPUTE worksheet computes sums and counts of the number of nonconformities found in the cCHARTDATA worksheet to help compute the control limits (see Figure EG17.5 on page 697).

Computing control limits and plotting points for other problems requires changes to the cCHARTDATA worksheet. First, paste the time period and number of nonconformances

	A	B	C	D	E
1	Time Period	Number of Nonconformances	LCL	Center Line	UCL
2	1	8	=COMPUTE!$B$10	=COMPUTE!$B$11	=COMPUTE!$B$12
3	2	10	=COMPUTE!$B$10	=COMPUTE!$B$11	=COMPUTE!$B$12
4	3	6	=COMPUTE!$B$10	=COMPUTE!$B$11	=COMPUTE!$B$12
		7	=COMPUTE!$B$10	=COMP...	...MPUTE!$B$12
48	47		=COMPUTE!B...	...PUTE!$B$11	=COM... $12
49	48	5	=COMPUTE!$B$10	=COMPUTE!$B$11	=COMPUTE!$B$12
50	49	4	=COMPUTE!$B$10	=COMPUTE!$B$11	=COMPUTE!$B$12
51	50	4	=COMPUTE!$B$10	=COMPUTE!$B$11	=COMPUTE!$B$12

FIGURE EG17.4 cCHARTDATA worksheet of the c Chart workbook

	A	B	
1	c Chart Summary		
2			
3	Intermediate Calculations		
4	Sum of NonConformities	312	=SUM(cCHARTDATA!B:B)
5	Number of Units Sampled	50	=COUNT(cCHARTDATA!B:B)
6	CBar	6.24	=B4/B5
7	Preliminary Lower Control Limit	-1.2540	=B6 - 3 * SQRT(B6)
8			
9	c Chart Control Limits		
10	Lower Control Limit	0.0000	=IF(B7 > 0, B7, 0)
11	Center	6.2400	=B6
12	Upper Control Limit	13.7340	=B6 + 3 * SQRT(B6)

F I G U R E   E G 1 7 . 5   **COMPUTE worksheet** of the **c Chart** workbook

data into columns A and B of the cCHARTDATA worksheet. If there are more than 50 time periods, select cell range **C51:E51** and copy the range down through all the rows. If there are fewer than 50 time periods, delete the extra rows from the bottom up, starting with row 51.

Use the cCHARTDATA worksheet as the basis for creating a c chart. For example, to create the Figure 17.5 c chart for the Table 17.4 hotel complaint data (see page 667), open to the cCHARTDATA worksheet and select the cell range **B1:E51**. Continue with either the following *In-Depth Excel 2007* or *In-Depth Excel 2003* instructions.

In-Depth Excel 2007   *Continued from In-Depth Excel . . .*
Select **Insert → Scatter** and select the fourth choice from the **Scatter** gallery **(Scatter with Straight Lines and Markers)**. Relocate the chart to a chart sheet and adjust the chart formatting by using the instructions in Appendix Section C.7 on page 726.

At this point, a recognizable chart begins to take shape, but the control limit and center lines are improperly formatted and are not properly labeled. To correct these formatting errors, use the three sets of instructions given in the Section EG17.2 *In-Depth Excel 2007* instructions.

In-Depth Excel 2003   *Continued from In-Depth Excel . . .*
Select **Insert → Chart** and:

In the Chart Wizard Step 1 dialog box:

1. Click the **Standard Types** tab and then click **XY (Scatter)** as the **Chart type**. Click the fourth **Chart sub-type**, labeled **Scatter with data points connected by lines**.

2. Click **Next**.

In the Chart Wizard Step 2 dialog box:

3. Click **Next**. (Entries and selections in this dialog box are correct as is.)

In the Chart Wizard Step 3 dialog box:

4. Click the **Titles** tab. Enter a **Chart title**, as well as a **Value (X) axis** title and a **Value (Y) axis** title. Adjust the chart formatting by using the instructions in Appendix

Section C.8 on page 727 for the **Axes**, **Gridlines**, **Legend**, and **Data Labels** tabs.

5. Click Next.

In the Chart Wizard Step 4 dialog box:

6. Click **As new sheet** and then click **Finish** to create the chart.

At this point, a recognizable chart begins to take shape, but the control limit and center lines are improperly formatted and are not properly labeled. To correct these formatting errors, use the three sets of instructions given in the Section EG17.2 *In-Depth Excel 2003* instructions.

EG17.5   CONTROL CHARTS for the RANGE and the MEAN

The *R* Chart and the $\overline{X}$ Chart

PHStat2 Use the **R and XBar Charts** procedure to create *R* and $\overline{X}$ charts and supporting worksheets that compute the control limits and plot points. For example, to create the Figure 17.6 *R* chart and the Figure 17.7 $\overline{X}$ chart for the Table 17.5 luggage delivery times (see page 671), open to the **DATA worksheet** of the **Hotel2 workbook**. Because the PHStat2 procedure requires means or ranges as the data, first add two columns that compute the mean and ranges on this worksheet. Enter the column heading **Mean** in cell **G1** and the heading **Range** in cell **H1**. Enter the formula =**AVERAGE(B2:F2)** in cell **G2** and the formula =**MAX(B2:F2)** − **MIN(B2:F2)** in cell **H2**. Select the cell range **G2:H2** and copy the range down through row 29.

Select **PHStat → Control Charts → R and XBar Chart**, and in the procedure's dialog box (shown below):

1. Enter **5** as the **Subgroup/Sample Size**.

2. Enter **H1:H29** as the **Subgroup Ranges Cell Range**.

3. Check **First cell contains label**.

4. Click **R and XBar Charts**. Enter **G1:G29** as the **Subgroup Means Cell Range** and check **First cell contains label**.

5. Enter a **Title** and click **OK**.

The procedure creates the two charts on separate chart sheets and two supporting worksheets: one that computes the control limits and one that computes the values to be plotted. For more information about these two worksheets, read the following *In-Depth Excel* section.

In-Depth Excel Create R and $\overline{X}$ charts from worksheets that use arithmetic formulas to compute control limits and plot points.

Use the **RXCHARTDATA, DATA**, and **COMPUTE worksheets** of the **R and XBar Chart workbook** as a template for computing control limits and plotting points. The RXCHARTDATA worksheet (see Figure EG17.6, Panels A and B) contains formulas in columns B and C to compute the mean and range values (Panel A) based on the Table 17.5 luggage delivery times (on page 671) stored in the DATA worksheet (not shown). Formulas in columns D through I (Panel B) display the values for the control limit and center lines, using values that are computed in the COMPUTE worksheet (shown in Figure EG17.7).

Columns D and G of the RXCHARTDATA worksheet contain IF functions that omit the lower control limit if the LCL value is computed to be less than 0.

The COMPUTE worksheet uses the computed means and ranges to compute $\overline{R}$ and $\overline{\overline{X}}$, the mean of the subgroup means. Unlike the COMPUTE worksheets for other control charts, you must manually enter the **Sample/Subgroup Size** in cell **B4** (**5** in Figure EG17.7) in addition to the $D3$, $D4$, and $A2$ factors in cells **B8**, **B9**, and **B18** (**0**, **2.114**, and **0.577** in Figure EG17.7). Use Table E.9 on page 750 to lookup the values for the three factors.

Computing control limits and plotting points for other problems requires changes to the RXCHARTDATA or the DATA worksheet, depending on whether means and ranges have been previously computed.

	A	B	
1	R and XBar Chart Summary		
2			
3	Data		
4	Sample/Subgroup Size	5	
5			
6	R Chart Intermediate Calculations		
7	RBar	3.4821	=AVERAGE(RXCHARTDATA!C:C)
8	D_3 Factor	0	
9	D_4 Factor	2.114	
10			
11	R Chart Control Limits		
12	Lower Control Limit	0.0000	=B8 * B7
13	Center	3.4821	=B7
14	Upper Control Limit	7.3613	=B9 * B7
15			
16	XBar Chart Intemediate Calculations		
17	Average of Subgroup Averages	9.4779	=AVERAGE(RXCHARTDATA!B:B)
18	A_2 Factor	0.577	
19	A_2 Factor * RBar	2.0092	=B18 * B7
20			
21	XBar Chart Control Limits		
22	Lower Control Limit	7.4687	=B17- B19
23	Center	9.4779	=B17
24	Upper Control Limit	11.4871	=B17 + B19

FIGURE EG17.7 COMPUTE worksheet of the R and XBar Chart workbook

If the means and ranges have been previously computed, paste these values into column B and C of the RXCHART-DATA worksheet. If there are more than 28 time periods, select cell range **D29:I29** and copy the range down through all the rows. If there are fewer than 28 time periods, delete the extra rows from the bottom up, starting with row 29.

If the means and ranges have not been previously computed, changes must be made to the DATA worksheet. First, determine the subgroup size. If the subgroup size is less than 5, delete the extra columns, right-to-left, starting with column F. If the subgroup size is greater than 5, select column F, right-click, and click **Insert** from the short-cut menu. (Repeat as many times as necessary.) With the DATA worksheet so adjusted, paste the time and subgroup data into the worksheet, starting with cell A1. Then open to the RXCHARTDATA worksheet, and if the number of time periods is not equal to 28, adjust the number of rows using the instructions of the previous paragraph.

Use the RXCHARTDATA worksheet as the basis for creating R and $\overline{X}$ charts. For example, to create the Figure 17.6 R chart for the Table 17.5 luggage delivery times data (see page 671), open to the RXCHARTDATA worksheet. Select the cell range **C1:F29**. Continue with either the following *In-Depth*

	B	C
1	XBar	Range
2	=AVERAGE(DATA!B2:F2)	=MAX(DATA!B2:F2)-MIN(DATA!B2:F2)
3	=AVERAGE(DATA!B3:F3)	=MAX(DATA!B3:F3)-MIN(DATA!B3:F3)
4	=AVERAGE(DATA!B4:F4)	=MAX(DATA!B4:F4)-MIN(DATA!B4:F4)
26	=AVERAGE(DATA!B5:F5)	=MAX(DATA!B5:F5)-MIN(DATA!B26:F26)
27	=AVERAGE(DATA!B27:F27)	=MAX(DATA!B27:F27)-MIN(DATA!B27:F27)
28	=AVERAGE(DATA!B28:F28)	=MAX(DATA!B28:F28)-MIN(DATA!B28:F28)
29	=AVERAGE(DATA!B29:F29)	=MAX(DATA!B29:F29)-MIN(DATA!B29:F29)

Panel A: Worksheet columns B and C

	D	E	F	G	H	I
1	LCL-R	Center-R	UCL-R	LCL-X	Center-X	UCL-X
2	=IF(COMPUTE!$B$12<0,"",COMPUTE!$B$12)	=COMPUTE!$B$13	=COMPUTE!$B$14	=IF(COMPUTE!$B$22<0,"",COMPUTE!$B$22)	=COMPUTE!$B$23	=COMPUTE!$B$24
3	=IF(COMPUTE!$B$12<0,"",COMPUTE!$B$12)	=COMPUTE!$B$13	=COMPUTE!$B$14	=IF(COMPUTE!$B$22<0,"",COMPUTE!$B$22)	=COMPUTE!$B$23	=COMPUTE!$B$24
4	=IF(COMPUTE!$B$12<0,"",COMPUTE!$B$12)	=COMPUTE!$B$13	=COMPUTE!$B$14	=IF(COMPUTE!$B$22<0,"",COMPUTE!$B$22)	=COMPUTE!$B$23	=COMPUTE!$B$24
26	=IF(COMPUTE!$B$12<0,"",COMPUTE!$B$12)	=COMPUTE!$B$13	=COMPUTE!$B$14	=IF(COMPUTE!$B$22<0,"",COMPUTE!$B$22)	=COMPUTE!$B$23	=COMPUTE!$B$24
27	=IF(COMPUTE!$B$12<0,"",COMPUTE!$B$12)	=COMPUTE!$B$13	=COMPUTE!$B$14	=IF(COMPUTE!$B$22<0,"",COMPUTE!$B$22)	=COMPUTE!$B$23	=COMPUTE!$B$24
28	=IF(COMPUTE!$B$12<0,"",COMPUTE!$B$12)	=COMPUTE!$B$13	=COMPUTE!$B$14	=IF(COMPUTE!$B$22<0,"",COMPUTE!$B$22)	=COMPUTE!$B$23	=COMPUTE!$B$24
29	=IF(COMPUTE!$B$12<0,"",COMPUTE!$B$12)	=COMPUTE!$B$13	=COMPUTE!$B$14	=IF(COMPUTE!$B$22<0,"",COMPUTE!$B$22)	=COMPUTE!$B$23	=COMPUTE!$B$24

Panel B: Worksheet columns D through I

FIGURE EG17.6 RXCHARTDATA worksheet of the R and XBar Chart workbook

Excel 2007 or *In-Depth Excel 2003* instructions. To create the Figure 17.7 $\bar{X}$ chart on page 673, select the cell range **B1:B29 G1:I29**, (while holding down the **Ctrl key**, select the cell range **B1:B29** and then the cell range **G1:I29**). Continue with either the following *In-Depth* Excel 2007 or *In-Depth* Excel 2003 instructions.)

In-Depth Excel 2007 *Continued from In-Depth Excel . . .*
Select **Insert → Scatter** and select the fourth choice from the **Scatter** gallery **(Scatter with Straight Lines and Markers)**. Relocate the chart to a chart sheet and adjust the chart formatting by using the instructions in Appendix Section C.7 on page 726.

At this point, a recognizable chart begins to take shape, but the control limit and center lines are improperly formatted and are not properly labeled. To correct these formatting errors, use the three sets of instructions given in the Section EG17.2 *In-Depth Excel 2007* instructions.

In-Depth Excel 2003 *Continued from In-Depth Excel . . .*
Select **Insert → Chart** and:

In the Chart Wizard Step 1 dialog box:

1. Click the **Standard Types** tab and then click **XY (Scatter)** as the **Chart type**. Click the fourth **Chart sub-type**, labeled **Scatter with data points connected by lines**.
2. Click **Next**.

In the Chart Wizard Step 2 dialog box:

3. Click **Next**. (Entries and selections in this dialog box are correct as is.)

In the Chart Wizard Step 3 dialog box:

4. Click the **Titles** tab. Enter a **Chart title**, as well as a **Value (X) axis** title and a **Value (Y) axis** title. Adjust the chart formatting by using the instructions in Appendix Section C.8 on page 727 for the **Axes**, **Gridlines**, **Legend**, and **Data Labels** tabs.
5. Click **Next**.

In the Chart Wizard Step 4 dialog box:

6. Click **As new sheet** and then click **Finish** to create the chart.

At this point, a recognizable chart begins to take shape, but the control limit and center lines are improperly formatted and are not properly labeled. To correct these formatting errors, use the three sets of instructions given in the Section EG17.2 *In-Depth Excel 2003* instructions.

EG17.6 PROCESS CAPABILITY

Use the **COMPUTE worksheet** of the **CAPABILITY workbook** as a template for computing the process capability indices discussed in Section 17.6.

EG17.7 TOTAL QUALITY MANAGEMENT

There are no Excel Guide instructions for this section.

EG17.8 SIX SIGMA

There are no Excel Guide instructions for this section.

18 Data Analysis Overview

Learning Objectives

In this chapter, you learn:

- The steps involved in choosing what statistical methods to use to conduct a data analysis

USING STATISTICS *IN* YOUR LIFE

A s a student who is completing an introductory business statistics course, you find yourself needing to analyze data in other courses and in new business situations. Analyzing data is the last part of the **D**efine, **C**ollect, **O**rganize, **V**isualize, **A**nalyze (DCOVA) approach to which you were introduced in Chapter 2. Determining what methods to use to analyze data may have seemed straightforward when doing homework problems in various chapters in this book, but in real-life situations it is much more difficult; after all, when doing a problem in the multiple regression chapter, you "knew" that methods of multiple regression would be used somewhere in your analysis. In your new situation, you might wonder if you should use multiple regression—or whether using simple linear regression would be better—or even if any type of regression would be appropriate. You also might wonder if you should use several methods from more than one chapter to do your analysis. The question for you becomes: How can you apply the statistics you have learned to future situations that require you to analyze data?

logical starting point is to review and summarize what you have learned from this book. Table 18.1 presents a summary of the contents of this book, arranged by data analysis task.

TABLE 18.1

Commonly Used Data Analysis Tasks Discussed in This Book

DESCRIBING A GROUP OR SEVERAL GROUPS

For Numerical Variables:
Ordered array, stem-and-leaf display, frequency distribution, relative frequency distribution, percentage distribution, cumulative percentage distribution, histogram, polygon, cumulative percentage polygon **(Sections 2.4 and 2.6)**
Boxplot **(Section 3.3)**
Normal probability plot **(Section 6.3)**
Mean, median, mode, quartiles, geometric mean, range, interquartile range, standard deviation, variance, coefficient of variation **(Sections 3.1, 3.2, and 3.3)**
Index numbers **(*Online Topic* Section 16.8)**

For Categorical Variables:
Summary table, bar chart, pie chart, Pareto chart **(Sections 2.3 and 2.5)**
Contingency tables and PivotTables **(Sections 2.3 and 2.8)**

MAKING INFERENCES ABOUT ONE GROUP

For Numerical Variables:
Confidence interval estimate of the mean **(Sections 8.1 and 8.2)**
t test for the mean **(Section 9.2)**
Chi-square test for a variance or standard deviation **(*Online Topic* Section 12.7)**

For Categorical Variables:
Confidence interval estimate of the proportion **(Section 8.3)**
Z test for the proportion **(Section 9.4)**

COMPARING TWO GROUPS

For Numerical Variables:
Tests for the difference in the means of two independent populations **(Section 10.1)**
Wilcoxon rank sum test **(Section 12.5)**
Paired t test **(Section 10.2)**
F test for the difference between two variances **(Section 10.4)**

For Categorical Variables:
Z test for the difference between two proportions **(Section 10.3)**
Chi-square test for the difference between two proportions **(Section 12.1)**
McNemar test for two related samples **(Section 12.4)**

COMPARING MORE THAN TWO GROUPS

For Numerical Variables:
One-way analysis of variance **(Section 11.1)**
Kruskal-Wallis test **(Section 12.6)**
Two-way analysis of variance **(Section 11.2)**
Randomized block design **(*Online Topic* Section 11.3)**

For Categorical Variables:
Chi-square test for differences among more than two proportions **(Section 12.2)**

ANALYZING THE RELATIONSHIP BETWEEN TWO VARIABLES

For Numerical Variables:
Scatter plot, time-series plot **(Section 2.7)**
Covariance, coefficient of correlation, t test of correlation **(Sections 3.5 and 13.7)**
Simple linear regression **(Chapter 13)**
Time-series forecasting **(Chapter 16)**

TABLE 18.1
(continued)

For Categorical Variables:
Contingency table, side-by-side bar chart **(Sections 2.3 and 2.5)**
Chi-square test of independence **(Section 12.3)**

ANALYZING THE RELATIONSHIP BETWEEN TWO OR MORE VARIABLES

For Numerical Dependent Variables:
Multiple regression **(Chapters 14 and 15)**
For Categorical Dependent Variables:
Logistic regression **(see reference 1 in Chapter 14)**

ANALYZING PROCESS DATA

For Numerical Variables:
$\overline{X}$ and R control charts **(Section 17.5)**
For Categorical Variables:
p chart **(Section 17.2)**
For Counts of Nonconformities:
c chart **(Section 17.4)**

As Table 18.1 reflects, the first step in applying statistics is to determine the type of variable—numerical or categorical—you are analyzing. Remember that *numerical variables* have values that represent quantities. *Categorical variables* have values that can only be placed into categories, such as yes and no.

Once you know the variable type, you can select the statistical methods that are appropriate for that variable type. Doing so helps you avoid some serious errors such as taking the arithmetic mean of a categorical variable.

Even though knowing which methods belong with which type of variable is helpful, a list such as Table 18.1 does not help you get started in applying your statistical knowledge to a specific data analysis task. Use the rest of this chapter to learn the questions that will help guide you and allow you to constructively apply what you have learned in this book. Not surprisingly, the chapter contains separate sections for numerical and categorical variables.

18.1 Analyzing Numerical Variables

When you analyze numerical variables, there are a number of data analysis tasks you can undertake. These tasks can be summarized by the list of questions in Exhibit 18.1. Each question is independent of the others, and you can ask as many or as few questions as is appropriate for your analysis. How to go about answering these questions follows Exhibit 18.1.

EXHIBIT 18.1 Questions to Ask When Analyzing Numerical Variables
When analyzing numerical variables, ask yourself, do you want to

- Describe the characteristics of the variable (possibly broken down into several groups)?
- Reach conclusions about the mean and standard deviation of the variable in a population?
- Determine whether the mean and standard deviation of the variable differs depending on the group?
- Determine which factors affect the value of a variable?
- Predict the value of the variable based on the value of other variables?
- Determine whether the values of the variable are stable over time?

How to Describe the Characteristics of a Numerical Variable

You develop tables and charts and compute descriptive statistics to describe characteristics. Specifically, you can create a stem-and-leaf display, percentage distribution, histogram, polygon, boxplot, and normal probability plot (see Sections 2.4, 2.6, 3.3, and 6.3), and you can compute statistics such as the mean, median, mode, quartiles, range, interquartile range, standard deviation, variance, and coefficient of variation (see Sections 3.1, 3.2, and 3.3).

How to Draw Conclusions About the Population Mean or Standard Deviation

You have several different choices, and you can use any combination of these choices. To estimate the mean value of the variable in a population, you construct a confidence interval estimate of the mean (see Section 8.2). To determine whether the population mean is equal to a specific value, you conduct a t test of hypothesis for the mean (see Section 9.2). To determine whether the population standard deviation or variance is equal to a specific value, you conduct a χ^2 test of hypothesis for the standard deviation or variance (see *Online Topic* Section 12.7).

How to Determine Whether the Mean or Standard Deviation Differs Depending on the Group

When examining differences between groups, you first need to establish which categorical variable divides your data into groups. You then need to know whether this grouping variable divides your data in two groups, as a gender variable would divide your data into male and female groups, or whether the variable divides your data into more than two groups (such as the four parachute suppliers discussed in Section 11.1). Finally, you must ask whether your data set contains independent groups or whether your data set contains matched or repeated measurements.

If the Grouping Variable Defines Two Independent Groups and You Are Interested in Central Tendency Which hypothesis tests you use depends on the assumptions you make about your data.

If you assume that your numerical variable is normally distributed and that the variances are equal, you conduct a pooled t test for the difference between the means (see Section 10.1). To evaluate the assumption of normality that this test includes, you can construct boxplots and normal probability plots for each group.

If you cannot assume that the variances are equal, you conduct a separate-variance t test for the difference between the means (see Section 10.1). To test whether the variances are equal, assuming that the populations are normally distributed, you can conduct an F test for the differences between the variances.

In either case, if you believe that your numerical variables are not normally distributed, you can perform a Wilcoxon rank sum test (see Section 12.5) and compare its results to those of the t test.

If the Grouping Variable Defines Two Groups of Matched Samples or Repeated Measurements If you can assume that the paired differences are normally distributed, you conduct a paired t test (see Section 10.2).

If the Grouping Variable Defines Two Independent Groups and You Are Interested in Variability If you can assume that your numerical variable is normally distributed, you conduct an F test for the difference between two variances (see Section 10.4).

If the Grouping Variable Defines More Than Two Independent Groups If you can assume that the values of the numerical variable are normally distributed, you conduct a one-way analysis of variance (see Section 11.1); otherwise, you conduct a Kruskal-Wallis test (see Section 12.6).

If the Grouping Variable Defines More Than Two Groups of Matched Samples or Repeated Measurements You have a design where the rows represent the blocks and the columns represent the levels of a factor. If you can assume that the values of the numerical variable are normally distributed, you conduct a randomized block design F test (see *Online Topic* Section 11.3)

How to Determine Which Factors Affect the Value of a Variable

If there are two factors to be examined to determine their effect on the values of a variable, you develop a two-factor factorial design (see Section 11.2).

How to Predict the Value of a Variable Based on the Value of Other Variables

You conduct least-squares regression analysis. If you have values over a period of time and you want to forecast the variable for future time periods, you can use moving averages, exponential smoothing, least-squares forecasting, and autoregressive modeling (see Chapter 16).

When predicting the values of a numerical dependent variable, which least-squares regression model you develop depends on the number of independent variables in your model. If there is only one independent variable being used to predict the numerical dependent variable of interest, you develop a simple linear regression model (see Chapter 13); otherwise, you develop a multiple regression model (see Chapters 14 and 15).

How to Determine Whether the Values of a Variable Are Stable over Time

If you are studying a process and have collected data on the values of a numerical variable over a time period, you construct R and $\overline{X}$ charts (see Section 17.5). If you have collected data in which the values are counts of the number of nonconformities, you construct a c chart (see Section 17.4).

18.2 Analyzing Categorical Variables

When you analyze categorical variables, there are also several data analysis tasks you can undertake. These tasks can be summarized according to the list of questions in Exhibit 18.2. Each question is independent of the others, and you can ask as many or as few questions as is appropriate for your analysis. How to go about answering these questions follows Exhibit 18.2.

EXHIBIT 18.2 QUESTIONS TO ASK WHEN ANALYZING CATEGORICAL VARIABLES

When analyzing categorical variables, ask yourself, do you want to

- Describe the proportion of items of interest in each category (possibly broken down into several groups)?
- Draw conclusions about the proportion of items of interest in a population?
- Determine whether the proportion of items of interest differs depending on the group?
- Predict the proportion of items of interest based on the value of other variables?
- Determine whether the proportion of items of interest is stable over time?

How to Describe the Proportion of Items of Interest in Each Category

You create summary tables and use these charts: bar chart, pie chart, Pareto chart, or side-by-side bar chart (see Sections 2.3 and 2.5).

How to Draw Conclusions About the Proportion of Items of Interest

You have two different choices. You can estimate the proportion of items of interest in a population by constructing a confidence interval estimate of the proportion (see Section 8.3). Or, you can determine whether the population proportion is equal to a specific value by conducting a Z test of hypothesis for the proportion (see Section 9.4).

How to Determine Whether the Proportion of Items of Interest Differs Depending on the Group

When examining this difference, you first need to establish the number of categories associated with your categorical variable and the number of groups in your analysis. If your data contain two groups, you must also ask if your data contain independent groups or if your data contain matched samples or repeated measurements.

For Two Categories and Two Independent Groups You conduct either the Z test for the difference between two proportions (see Section 10.3) or the χ^2 test for the difference between two proportions (see Section 12.1).

For Two Categories and Two Groups of Matched or Repeated Measurements You conduct the McNemar test (see Section 12.4).

For Two Categories and More Than Two Independent Groups You conduct a χ^2 test for the difference among several proportions (see Section 12.2).

For More Than Two Categories and More Than Two Groups You develop contingency tables and use PivotTables to drill down to examine relationships among two or more categorical variables (Sections 2.3 and 2.8). When you have two categorical variables, you conduct a χ^2 test of independence (see Section 12.3).

How to Predict the Proportion of Items of Interest Based on the Value of Other Variables

You develop a logistic regression model (see reference 1 in Chapter 14).

How to Determine Whether the Proportion of Items of Interest Is Stable over Time

If you are studying a process and have collected data over a time period, you can create the appropriate control chart. If you have collected the proportion of items of interest over a time period, you develop a p chart (see Section 17.2).

USING STATISTICS *IN* YOUR LIFE REVISITED

This chapter summarized all the methods discussed in the first 17 chapters of this book. The entire set of data analysis methods discussed in the book are organized in Table 18.1 according to whether the method is used for describing a group or several groups, for making inferences about one group or comparing two or more groups, or for analyzing relationships between two or more variables. Then, sets of questions are listed in Exhibits 18.1 and 18.2 to assist you in determining what method to use to analyze your data.

CHAPTER REVIEW PROBLEMS

18.1 In many manufacturing processes, the term *work-in-process* (often abbreviated WIP) is used. At the BLK Publishing book manufacturing plants, WIP represents the time it takes for sheets from a press to be folded, gathered, sewn, tipped on end sheets, and bound together to form a book, and the book placed in a packing carton. The operational definition of the variable of interest, processing time, is the number of days (measured in hundredths) from when the sheets come off the press to when the book is placed in a packing carton. The company has the business objective of determining whether there are differences in the WIP between plants. Data have been collected from samples of 20 books at each of two production plants. The data, stored in **WIP**, are as follows:

Plant A

5.62	5.29	16.25	10.92	11.46	21.62	8.45	8.58	5.41	11.42
11.62	7.29	7.50	7.96	4.42	10.50	7.58	9.29	7.54	8.92

Plant B

9.54	11.46	16.62	12.62	25.75	15.41	14.29	13.13	13.71	10.04
5.75	12.46	9.17	13.21	6.00	2.33	14.25	5.37	6.25	9.71

Completely analyze the data.

18.2 Many factors determine the attendance at Major League Baseball games. These factors can include when the game is played, the weather, the opponent, whether the team is having a good season, and whether a marketing promotion is held. Popular promotions during a recent season included the traditional hat days and poster days and the new craze, bobble-heads of star players (extracted from T. C. Boyd and T. C. Krehbiel, "An Analysis of the Effects of Specific Promotion Types on Attendance at Major League Baseball Games," *Mid-American Journal of Business*, 2006, 21, pp. 21–32). The file **Baseball** includes the following variables for a recent Major League Baseball season:

TEAM—Kansas City Royals, Philadelphia Phillies, Chicago Cubs, or Cincinnati Reds
ATTENDANCE—Paid attendance for the game
TEMP—High temperature for the day
WIN%—Team's winning percentage at the time of the game
OPWIN%—Opponent team's winning percentage at the time of the game
WEEKEND—1 if game played on Friday, Saturday, or Sunday; 0 otherwise
PROMOTION—1 if a promotion was held; 0 if no promotion was held

You want to predict attendance and determine the factors that influence attendance. Completely analyze the data for the Kansas City Royals.

18.3 Repeat Problem 18.2 for the Philadelphia Phillies.

18.4 Repeat Problem 18.2 for the Chicago Cubs.

18.5 Repeat Problem 18.3 for the Cincinnati Reds.

18.6 The economics of baseball has caused a great deal of controversy, with owners arguing that they are losing money, players arguing that owners are making money, and fans complaining about how expensive it is to attend a game and watch games on cable television. In addition to data related to team performance statistics, including the number of wins, the file **BB2001** contains ticket prices, the fan cost index, regular-season gate receipts, local television, radio, and cable receipts, all other operating revenue, player compensation and benefits, national and other local expenses, and income from baseball operations.

You want to examine each of the non-team performance statistics and also be able to predict the number of wins. Write a report that summarizes your results.

18.7 The file **Homes** contains information on all the single-family houses sold in a small city in the midwestern United States for one year. The following variables are included:

Price—Selling price of home, in dollars
Location—Rating of the location from 1 to 5, with 1 the worst and 5 the best
Condition—Rating of the condition of the home from 1 to 5, with 1 the worst and 5 the best
Bedrooms—Number of bedrooms in the home
Bathrooms—Number of bathrooms in the home
Other Rooms—Number of rooms in the home other than bedrooms and bathrooms

You want to be able to predict the selling price of the homes. Completely analyze the data.

18.8 Zagat's publishes restaurant ratings for various locations in the United States. The file **Restaurants** contains the Zagat rating for food, decor, service, and price per person for a sample of 50 restaurants located in New York City and 50 restaurants located in suburban areas outside New York City.

You want to study differences in the cost of a meal between restaurants in New York City and suburban areas and also want to be able to predict the cost of a meal. Completely analyze the data.

Source: *Data extracted from* Zagat Survey 2009 New York City Restaurants *and* Zagat Survey 2009–2010 Long Island Restaurants.

18.9 The data in **Auto2008** represent different characteristics of 171 2008 automobiles. The variables included are make/model, length (in.), width (in.), height (in.), wheelbase (in.), weight (lbs.), maximum cargo load (lbs.), cargo volume (cu. ft.), front shoulder room (in), front leg room (in), front head room (in), horsepower, miles per gallon, acceleration (in sec.) from 0 to 60 miles per hour, braking distance in feet from 60 miles per hour (dry), braking distance in feet from 60 miles per hour (wet), turning circle (in ft.), country of origin (Asia, Europe, United States), vehicle type (4 door SUV, Sedan, 4 Door Hatchback, Coupe, Minivan, Wagon) transmission type (auto 4, auto 5, auto 6, auto 7, CVT, manual 5, manual 6).

You want to describe each of these variables in this sample of 2008 automobiles. In addition, you would like to predict the miles per gallon and dry braking distance and determine which variables are important in predicting these variables. Analyze the data.

Source: *Data extracted from "Vehicle Ratings,"* Consumer Reports, *April 2008, pp. 31–75.*

18.10 The data in UsedAutos represent different characteristics of used automobiles advertised for sale in a recent year. The variables included are car, model, year of model (2000 = 0), asking price (in $000), miles driven by the car (in 000s), age in years, and type (Coupe, Minivan, Pickup truck, Sedan, Sedan wagon, Sports car, SUV, Van, Wagon).

You want to describe each of these variables, and you would like to predict the asking price of used autos. Analyze the data.

Source: *Data extracted from* The Newark Star Ledger, *January 3, 2009, pp. 35–38.*

18.11 The data in Credit Unions consist of different characteristics of 7,903 credit unions in the United States. The variables included are name, city, state, zip code, region, total assets ($), total investments ($), net income ($), total net worth ($), total amount of delinquent loans and leases ($), number of credit union members, number of potential members, number of full-time credit union employees, and number of credit union employees.

Your job is to present a report that summarizes descriptive characteristics of credit unions and highlight factors that differ among the credit unions. Analyze the data.

Source: *www.ncua.gov, January 29, 2009.*

18.12 The data in Loans and Leases consist of the different characteristics of 382 banks in the Tri-State New York City area as of June 30, 2008. The variables included are name, state, zip code, number of domestic and foreign offices, ownership type, regulator, Federal Reserve district, total deposits ($000), gross loans and leases ($000), real estate loans ($000), construction and development loans ($000), all real estate loans ($000), commercial real estate loans ($000), multifamily real estate loans ($000), 1–4 family real estate loans ($000), farmland loans ($000), commercial and industrial loans ($000), credit card loans ($000), related plans ($000), other loans to individuals ($000), and all other loans and leases ($000).

Your job is to present a report that summarizes descriptive characteristics of banks in the Tri-State New York City area and highlight factors that differ among the banks. Analyze the data.

Source: *www.fdic.gov.*

Appendices

APPENDIX A | Basic Math Concepts and Symbols

A.1 Rules for Arithmetic Operations

RULE	EXAMPLE
1. $a + b = c$ and $b + a = c$	$2 + 1 = 3$ and $1 + 2 = 3$
2. $a + (b + c) = (a + b) + c$	$5 + (7 + 4) = (5 + 7) + 4 = 16$
3. $a - b = c$ but $b - a \neq c$	$9 - 7 = 2$ but $7 - 9 \neq 2$
4. $(a)(b) = (b)(a)$	$(7)(6) = (6)(7) = 42$
5. $(a)(b + c) = ab + ac$	$(2)(3 + 5) = (2)(3) + (2)(5) = 16$
6. $a \div b \neq b \div a$	$12 \div 3 \neq 3 \div 12$
7. $\dfrac{a + b}{c} = \dfrac{a}{c} + \dfrac{b}{c}$	$\dfrac{7 + 3}{2} = \dfrac{7}{2} + \dfrac{3}{2} = 5$
8. $\dfrac{a}{b + c} \neq \dfrac{a}{b} + \dfrac{a}{c}$	$\dfrac{3}{4 + 5} \neq \dfrac{3}{4} + \dfrac{3}{5}$
9. $\dfrac{1}{a} + \dfrac{1}{b} = \dfrac{b + a}{ab}$	$\dfrac{1}{3} + \dfrac{1}{5} = \dfrac{5 + 3}{(3)(5)} = \dfrac{8}{15}$
10. $\left(\dfrac{a}{b}\right)\left(\dfrac{c}{d}\right) = \left(\dfrac{ac}{bd}\right)$	$\left(\dfrac{2}{3}\right)\left(\dfrac{6}{7}\right) = \left(\dfrac{(2)(6)}{(3)(7)}\right) = \dfrac{12}{21}$
11. $\dfrac{a}{b} \div \dfrac{c}{d} = \dfrac{ad}{bc}$	$\dfrac{5}{8} \div \dfrac{3}{7} = \left(\dfrac{(5)(7)}{(8)(3)}\right) = \dfrac{35}{24}$

A.2 Rules for Algebra: Exponents and Square Roots

RULE	EXAMPLE
1. $(X^a)(X^b) = X^{a+b}$	$(4^2)(4^3) = 4^5$
2. $(X^a)^b = X^{ab}$	$(2^2)^3 = 2^6$
3. $(X^a/X^b) = X^{a-b}$	$\dfrac{3^5}{3^3} = 3^2$
4. $\dfrac{X^a}{X^a} = X^0 = 1$	$\dfrac{3^4}{3^4} = 3^0 = 1$
5. $\sqrt{XY} = \sqrt{X}\sqrt{Y}$	$\sqrt{(25)(4)} = \sqrt{25}\sqrt{4} = 10$
6. $\sqrt{\dfrac{X}{Y}} = \dfrac{\sqrt{X}}{\sqrt{Y}}$	$\sqrt{\dfrac{16}{100}} = \dfrac{\sqrt{16}}{\sqrt{100}} = 0.40$

A.3 Rules for Logarithms

Base 10

Log is the symbol used for base-10 logarithms:

RULE	EXAMPLE
1. $\log(10^a) = a$	$\log(100) = \log(10^2) = 2$
2. If $\log(a) = b$, then $a = 10^b$	If $\log(a) = 2$, then $a = 10^2 = 100$
3. $\log(ab) = \log(a) + \log(b)$	$\log(100) = \log[(10)(10)] = \log(10) + \log(10)$
	$= 1 + 1 = 2$
4. $\log(a^b) = (b)\log(a)$	$\log(1{,}000) = \log(10^3) = (3)\log(10) = (3)(1) = 3$
5. $\log(a/b) = \log(a) - \log(b)$	$\log(100) = \log(1{,}000/10) = \log(1{,}000) - \log(10)$
	$= 3 - 1 = 2$

EXAMPLE

Take the base-10 logarithm of each side of the following equation:

$$Y = \beta_0 \beta_1^X \varepsilon$$

SOLUTION: Apply rules 3 and 4:

$$\log(Y) = \log(\beta_0 \beta_1^X \varepsilon)$$
$$= \log(\beta_0) + \log(\beta_1^X) + \log(\varepsilon)$$
$$= \log(\beta_0) + X\log(\beta_1) + \log(\varepsilon)$$

Base e

ln is the symbol used for base e logarithms, commonly referred to as natural logarithms. e is Euler's number, and $e \cong 2.718282$:

RULE	EXAMPLE
1. $\ln(e^a) = a$	$\ln(7.389056) = \ln(e^2) = 2$
2. If $\ln(a) = b$, then $a = e^b$	If $\ln(a) = 2$, then $a = e^2 = 7.389056$
3. $\ln(ab) = \ln(a) + \ln(b)$	$\ln(100) = \ln[(10)(10)]$
	$= \ln(10) + \ln(10) = 2.302585 + 2.302585 = 4.605170$
4. $\ln(a^b) = (b)\ln(a)$	$\ln(1{,}000) = \ln(10^3) = 3\ln(10) = 3(2.302585) = 6.907755$
5. $\ln(a/b) = \ln(a) - \ln(b)$	$\ln(100) = \ln(1{,}000/10) = \ln(1{,}000) - \ln(10)$
	$= 6.907755 - 2.302585 = 4.605170$

EXAMPLE

Take the base e logarithm of each side of the following equation:

$$Y = \beta_0 \beta_1^X \varepsilon$$

SOLUTION: Apply rules 3 and 4:

$$\ln(Y) = \ln(\beta_0 \beta_1^X \varepsilon)$$
$$= \ln(\beta_0) + \ln(\beta_1^X) + \ln(\varepsilon)$$
$$= \ln(\beta_0) + X\ln(\beta_1) + \ln(\varepsilon)$$

A.4 Summation Notation

The symbol Σ, the Greek capital letter sigma, represents "taking the sum of." Consider a set of n values for variable X. The expression $\sum_{i=1}^{n} X_i$ means to take the sum of the n values for variable X. Thus:

$$\sum_{i=1}^{n} X_i = X_1 + X_2 + X_3 + \cdots + X_n$$

The following problem illustrates the use of the symbol Σ. Consider five values of a variable X: $X_1 = 2, X_2 = 0, X_3 = -1, X_4 = 5$, and $X_5 = 7$. Thus:

$$\sum_{i=1}^{5} X_i = X_1 + X_2 + X_3 + X_4 + X_5 = 2 + 0 + (-1) + 5 + 7 = 13$$

In statistics, the squared values of a variable are often summed. Thus:

$$\sum_{i=1}^{n} X_i^2 = X_1^2 + X_2^2 + X_3^2 + \cdots + X_n^2$$

and, in the example above:

$$\sum_{i=1}^{5} X_i^2 = X_1^2 + X_2^2 + X_3^2 + X_4^2 + X_5^2$$

$$= 2^2 + 0^2 + (-1)^2 + 5^2 + 7^2$$

$$= 4 + 0 + 1 + 25 + 49$$

$$= 79$$

$\sum_{i=1}^{n} X_i^2$, the summation of the squares, is *not* the same as $\left(\sum_{i=1}^{n} X_i \right)^2$, the square of the sum:

$$\sum_{i=1}^{n} X_i^2 \neq \left(\sum_{i=1}^{n} X_i \right)^2$$

In the example given earlier, the summation of squares is equal to 79. This is not equal to the square of the sum, which is $13^2 = 169$.

Another frequently used operation involves the summation of the product. Consider two variables, X and Y, each having n values. Then:

$$\sum_{i=1}^{n} X_i Y_i = X_1 Y_1 + X_2 Y_2 + X_3 Y_3 + \cdots + X_n Y_n$$

Continuing with the previous example, suppose there is a second variable, Y, whose five values are $Y_1 = 1, Y_2 = 3, Y_3 = -2, Y_4 = 4$, and $Y_5 = 3$. Then,

$$\sum_{i=1}^{n} X_i Y_i = X_1 Y_1 + X_2 Y_2 + X_3 Y_3 + X_4 Y_4 + X_5 Y_5$$

$$= (2)(1) + (0)(3) + (-1)(-2) + (5)(4) + (7)(3)$$

$$= 2 + 0 + 2 + 20 + 21$$

$$= 45$$

In computing $\sum_{i=1}^{n} X_i Y_i$, you need to realize that the first value of X is multiplied by the first value of Y, the second value of X is multiplied by the second value of Y, and so on. These products are then summed in order to compute the desired result. However, the summation of products is *not* equal to the product of the individual sums:

$$\sum_{i=1}^{n} X_i Y_i \neq \left(\sum_{i=1}^{n} X_i \right)\left(\sum_{i=1}^{n} Y_i \right)$$

In this example,

$$\sum_{i=1}^{5} X_i = 13$$

and

$$\sum_{i=1}^{5} Y_i = 1 + 3 + (-2) + 4 + 3 = 9$$

so that

$$\left(\sum_{i=1}^{5} X_i \right)\left(\sum_{i=1}^{5} Y_i \right) = (13)(9) = 117$$

However,

$$\sum_{i=1}^{5} X_i Y_i = 45$$

The following table summarizes these results:

VALUE	X_i	Y_i	$X_i Y_i$
1	2	1	2
2	0	3	0
3	−1	−2	2
4	5	4	20
5	7	3	21
	$\sum_{i=1}^{5} X_i = 13$	$\sum_{i=1}^{5} Y_i = 9$	$\sum_{i=1}^{5} X_i Y_i = 45$

Rule 1   The summation of the values of two variables is equal to the sum of the values of each summed variable:

$$\sum_{i=1}^{n} (X_i + Y_i) = \sum_{i=1}^{n} X_i + \sum_{i=1}^{n} Y_i$$

Thus,

$$\sum_{i=1}^{5} (X_i + Y_i) = (2 + 1) + (0 + 3) + (-1 + (-2)) + (5 + 4) + (7 + 3)$$

$$= 3 + 3 + (-3) + 9 + 10$$

$$= 22$$

$$\sum_{i=1}^{5} X_i + \sum_{i=1}^{5} Y_i = 13 + 9 = 22$$

Rule 2   The summation of a difference between the values of two variables is equal to the difference between the summed values of the variables:

$$\sum_{i=1}^{n}(X_i - Y_i) = \sum_{i=1}^{n}X_i - \sum_{i=1}^{n}Y_i$$

Thus,

$$\sum_{i=1}^{5}(X_i - Y_i) = (2 - 1) + (0 - 3) + (-1 - (-2)) + (5 - 4) + (7 - 3)$$

$$= 1 + (-3) + 1 + 1 + 4$$

$$= 4$$

$$\sum_{i=1}^{5}X_i - \sum_{i=1}^{5}Y_i = 13 - 9 = 4$$

Rule 3   The sum of a constant times a variable is equal to that constant times the sum of the values of the variable:

$$\sum_{i=1}^{n}cX_i = c\sum_{i=1}^{n}X_i$$

where c is a constant. Thus, if $c = 2$,

$$\sum_{i=1}^{5}cX_i = \sum_{i=1}^{5}2X_i = (2)(2) + (2)(0) + (2)(-1) + (2)(5) + (2)(7)$$

$$= 4 + 0 + (-2) + 10 + 14$$

$$= 26$$

$$c\sum_{i=1}^{5}X_i = 2\sum_{i=1}^{5}X_i = (2)(13) = 26$$

Rule 4   A constant summed n times will be equal to n times the value of the constant.

$$\sum_{i=1}^{n}c = nc$$

where c is a constant. Thus, if the constant $c = 2$ is summed 5 times,

$$\sum_{i=1}^{5}c = 2 + 2 + 2 + 2 + 2 = 10$$

$$nc = (5)(2) = 10$$

EXAMPLE

Suppose there are six values for the variables X and Y, such that $X_1 = 2, X_2 = 1, X_3 = 5, X_4 = -3, X_5 = 1, X_6 = -2$ and $Y_1 = 4, Y_2 = 0, Y_3 = -1, Y_4 = 2, Y_5 = 7$, and $Y_6 = -3$. Compute each of the following:

(a) $\sum_{i=1}^{6}X_i$

(b) $\sum_{i=1}^{6}Y_i$

(c) $\sum_{i=1}^{6}X_i^2$

(d) $\sum_{i=1}^{6}Y_i^2$

(e) $\sum_{i=1}^{6}X_iY_i$

(f) $\sum_{i=1}^{6}(X_i + Y_i)$

(g) $\sum_{i=1}^{6}(X_i - Y_i)$ (i) $\sum_{i=1}^{6}(cX_i)$, where $c = -1$

(h) $\sum_{i=1}^{6}(X_i - 3Y_i + 2X_i^2)$ (j) $\sum_{i=1}^{6}(X_i - 3Y_i + c)$, where $c = +3$

Answers

(a) 4 (b) 9 (c) 44 (d) 79 (e) 10 (f) 13 (g) −5 (h) 65 (i) −4 (j) −5

References

1. Bashaw, W. L., *Mathematics for Statistics* (New York: Wiley, 1969).
2. Lanzer, P., *Basic Math: Fractions, Decimals, Percents* (Hicksville, NY: Video Aided Instruction, 2006).
3. Levine, D., *The MBA Primer: Business Statistics* (Cincinnati, OH: South-Western Publishing, 2000).
4. Levine, D., *Statistics* (Hicksville, NY: Video Aided Instruction, 2006).
5. Shane, H., *Algebra 1* (Hicksville, NY: Video Aided Instruction, 2006).

A.5 Statistical Symbols

+ add   × multiply
− subtract   ÷ divide
= equal to   ≠ not equal to
≅ approximately equal to   < less than
> greater than   ≤ less than or equal to
≥ greater than or equal to

A.6 Greek Alphabet

GREEK LETTER		LETTER NAME	ENGLISH EQUIVALENT	GREEK LETTER		LETTER NAME	ENGLISH EQUIVALENT
A	α	Alpha	a	N	ν	Nu	n
B	β	Beta	b	Ξ	ξ	Xi	x
Γ	γ	Gamma	g	O	o	Omicron	ŏ
Δ	δ	Delta	d	Π	π	Pi	p
E	ε	Epsilon	ĕ	P	ρ	Rho	r
Z	ζ	Zeta	z	Σ	σ	Sigma	s
H	η	Eta	ē	T	τ	Tau	t
Θ	θ	Theta	th	Y	υ	Upsilon	u
I	ι	Iota	i	Φ	ϕ	Phi	ph
K	κ	Kappa	k	X	χ	Chi	ch
Λ	λ	Lambda	l	Ψ	ψ	Psi	ps
M	μ	Mu	m	Ω	ω	Omega	ō

B.1 Purpose of This Appendix

To use Microsoft Excel successfully, you need to know fundamental computing operations, as well as the terms and concepts for the objects and actions you find in Excel. This appendix defines the minimum set of prerequisite knowledge you need in order to make sense of the sets of instructions found in the end-of-chapter Excel Guides.

B.2 Fundamental Computing Operations

Before learning the specifics of Excel, you need to know the names and functions of objects you see onscreen and how you use a mouse (or equivalent pointing device) to interact with those objects.

Figure B.1 displays and Table B.1 defines the objects you will commonly encounter when Excel opens in its own application window. As you use a program, the program will communicate to you by displaying **dialog boxes**, pop-up windows that contain messages or ask you to make entries or selections. Figure B.2 on page 718 shows two examples of dialog boxes and the elements commonly found in all dialog boxes and explained in Table B.2.

FIGURE B.1

Excel 2003 (top, partially obscured) and Excel 2007 application windows. In both windows, the **Book1 workbook** is opened to the **Sheet1 worksheet**.

To interact with the objects defined in Table B.1 as well as the dialog box elements defined in Table B.2, you use one of seven mouse operations. Mouse operations assume a mouse with two buttons, one designated as the primary button (typically the left button) and the other button designated as the secondary button (typically the right button).

Click, **select**, **check**, and **clear** are operations in which you move the mouse pointer over an object and press the primary button. **Click** is used when pressing the primary button completes an action, as in "click (the) **OK** (button)." **Select** is used when pressing the primary button to choose or highlight one choice from a list of choices. **Check** is used when pressing the primary button places a checkmark in the dialog box's check box. (**Clear** reverses this action, removing the checkmark.)

TABLE B.1
Program Window
Elements

Element	Function
Title bar	Displays the name of the program and contains the Minimize, Resize, and Close buttons for the program window. You drag and drop the title bar to reposition a program window onscreen.
Minimize, Resize, and Close buttons	Changes the display of the program window. **Minimize** hides the window without closing the program, **Resize** permits you to change the size of the window, and **Close** removes the window from the screen and closes the program. A second set of these buttons that appear below the first set perform the three actions for the currently active workbook.
Menu Bar	The horizontal list of words, where each word represents either a command operation or leads to another list of choices.
Toolbars	Sets of commands represented by graphical icons that serve as shortcuts to other ways of selecting a command operation.
Task Pane	A floating window area that lists shortcuts to a subset of command operations (seen only in Excel 2003).
Ribbon	A selectable area that combines the functions of a menu bar, a task pane, and toolbars. In the Ribbon, functions are grouped into **tabs**, and tabs are further divided into **groups.** Some groups contain **launcher buttons** that display additional choices presented in a dialog box or as a **gallery**, a set of pictorial choices (seen in Excel 2007 and Excel 2010).
Office Button	The circular logo in the upper left of the window that displays a menu of basic computing commands when clicked. Seen in Excel 2007, the Office Button functions much like the File menu in Excel 2003 and other programs and the File Tab in Excel 2010.
Quick Access Toolbar	A set of graphical icons that define shortcuts to commonly used commands. (The Quick Access Toolbar is not used in any set of Excel instructions in this book.)
Workbook area	Displays the currently open workbook or workbooks. In typical use, this area displays the currently active worksheet in the workbook and shows the other worksheets as **sheet tabs** near the bottom of the workbook area.
Scroll bar	Allows you to move through a worksheet vertically or horizontally to reveal rows and columns that cannot otherwise be seen.

Double-click is an operation in which two clicks are made in rapid succession. Most double-click operations enable an object for following use, such as double-clicking a chart in order to make changes to the chart. **Right-click** is an operation in which you move the mouse pointer over an object and press the *secondary* button. In the Excel Guide instructions, you will often right-click an object in order to display a pop-up **shortcut menu** of context-sensitive command operations.

Drag is an operation in which you hold down the primary button over an object and then move the mouse. (The drag operation ends when you release the mouse button.) Dragging is done to select multiple objects, such as selecting all the cells in a cell range, as well as to physically move an object to another part of the screen. The related **drag-and-drop** operation permits you to move one object over another to trigger an action. You drag the first object across the screen, and when the first object is over the second object, you release the primary mouse button. (In most cases, releasing the primary button causes the first object to reappear in its original position onscreen.)

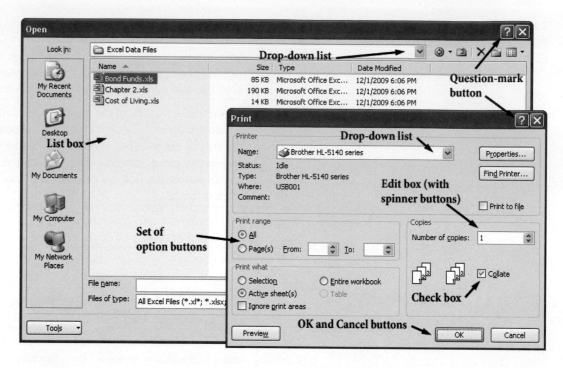

TABLE B.2
Dialog Box Elements

Element	Function
Command button	A clickable area that tells a program to take some action. For example, a dialog box **OK button** causes a program to take an action using the current entries and selections of the dialog box. A dialog box **Cancel button** closes a dialog box and cancels the pending operation associated with the entries and selections in the dialog box.
List box	A box that displays a list of clickable choices. If a list exceeds the dimensions of a list box, list boxes display **scroll buttons** or **sliders** (not shown in Figure B.2) that can be clicked to reveal choices not currently displayed.
Drop-down list	A special button that, when clicked, displays a list of choices.
Edit box	An area into which entries can be typed. Some edit boxes also contain drop-down lists or **spinner buttons** that can be used to make entries. A cell range edit box typically contains a clickable button that allows you to drag the mouse over a cell range as an alternative to typing the cell range.
Set of option buttons	A set of buttons that represent a set of mutually exclusive choices. Clicking one option button clears all the other option buttons in the set.
Check box	A clickable area that represents an optional action. A check box displays either a checkmark or nothing, depending on whether the optional action has been selected. Unlike with option buttons, clicking a check box does not affect the status of other check boxes, and more than one check box can be checked at a time. Clicking a check box that already contains a checkmark *clears* the check box. (To distinguish between the two states, instructions in this book use the verbs *check* and *clear*.)
Question-mark button	A special type of button that causes the display of help messages that are related to a dialog box. Dialog boxes that do not contain a question-mark button may contain the **Help** command button that performs the same function.

B.3 Worksheets and Workbooks

In Excel, you work with data that have been entered into **worksheets**. Worksheets are tabular arrangements of data in which the intersections of rows and columns form **cells**, boxes into which you make entries. By convention, you place the data for a variable in a column and enter a variable name or column heading into the first row's cell of that column. (The instructions in this book always assume this standard practice.)

Collections of worksheets and **chart sheets**, each of which displays a single chart, form a **workbook**. Workbooks are the objects that you open and save in Microsoft Excel. Workbooks are the objects to which people refer when they say informally that they are using "an Excel file." (You can download the Excel files, or workbooks, mentioned in this book from this book's companion Web site. See Section D.2 in Appendix D for more information.)

Excel assigns worksheet names in the form **Sheet1**, **Sheet2**, and so on. Because sheet names are used so frequently, you should change these default names to names that are more meaningful, such as **DATA** or **COMPUTE** or **RESULTS**. To change the name of a sheet, double-click the sheet tab for the worksheet, type the new name, and then press **Enter**.

B.4 Worksheet Entries

When you open to a specific worksheet in a workbook, you use the cursor keys or your pointing device to move a **cell pointer** through the worksheet to select a specific cell for entry. As you type an entry, it appears in the formula bar, and you place that entry into the cell by either pressing the **Tab** key or **Enter** key or clicking the checkmark button in the formula bar.

In worksheets that you use for intermediate calculations or results, you might enter **formulas**, instructions to perform a calculation or some other task, in addition to the numeric and text entries you otherwise make in cells. Formulas typically use values found in other cells to compute a result that is displayed in the cell that stores the formula. With formulas, the displayed result automatically changes as the dependent values in the other cell change. This process, called **recalculation**, was the original novel feature of spreadsheet programs and led to these programs being widely used in accounting.

Worksheets that contain formulas are sometimes called "live" worksheets to distinguish them from "dead" worksheets, worksheets without any formulas (and therefore not capable of recalculation).

B.5 Cell References

To refer to a cell in a formula, you use a **cell reference** in the form *SheetName!ColumnRow*. For example, **DATA!A2** refers to the cell that is in column A and row 2 of the **DATA worksheet**. You can also use just the *ColumnRow* portion of a full address (for example, **A2**) if you are referring to a cell on the same worksheet as the one into which you are entering a formla. If the sheet name contains spaces or special characters (for example, **CITY DATA** or **FIGURE_1.2**), you must enclose the sheet name in a pair of single quotes, as in **'CITY DATA'!A2** or **'FIGURE_1.2'!A2**.

When you want to refer to a group of cells (for example, to the cells of a column that store the data for a particular variable), you use a **cell range**. A cell range names the upper-leftmost cell and the lower-rightmost cell of the group, using the form *SheetName!Upper LeftCell:LowerRightCell*. For example, the cell range **DATA!A1:A11** identifies the first 11 cells in the first column of the **DATA worksheet**. Cell ranges can extend over multiple columns; the cell range **DATA!A1:D11** would refer to the first 11 cells in the first 4 columns of the worksheet.

As with a single cell reference, you can skip the *SheetName!* part of the reference if you are referring to a cell range on the current worksheet, and you must use a pair of single quotes if a sheet name contains spaces or special characters. However, in some dialog boxes or other situations, you must include the sheet name in a cell reference in order to get the proper results. In such cases, the instructions in this book include the sheet name; otherwise, they do not.

Although not used in this book, cell references can include a workbook name in the form **'[*WorkbookName*]*SheetName*'!*ColumnRow*** or **'[*WorkbookName*]*SheetName*'!*UpperLeftCell: LowerRightCell***. You may discover such references if you inadvertently copy certain types of worksheets or chart sheets from one workbook to another.

B.6 Entering Formulas into Worksheets

You enter formulas by typing the equal sign (=) and then a combination of mathematical or other data-processing operations. For simple formulas, you use the symbols +, −, *, /, and ∧ for the operations addition, subtraction, multiplication, division, and exponentiation (raising a number to a power), respectively. For example, the formula **=DATA!B2 + DATA!B3 + DATA!B4** adds the contents of the cells B2, B3, and B4 of the DATA worksheet and displays the sum as the value in the cell containing the formula.

You can also use **worksheet functions** in formulas to simplify computations or perform advanced statistical methods. To use a worksheet function in a formula, either type the function as shown for a particular instruction in this book or use the Insert Function feature of Excel. To use this feature, select **Formulas → Insert Function** (Excel 2007) or **Insert → Function** (Excel 2003). In the Insert Function dialog box, double-click the function you want to use. Then, in the Function Arguments dialog box, complete the function entry and click **OK.**

B.7 Absolute and Relative Cell References

Many worksheets contain columns (or rows) of similar-looking formulas. For example, column C in a worksheet might contain formulas that sum the contents of the column A and column B rows. The formula for cell C2 would be **=A2 + B2**, the formula for cell C3 would be **=A3 + B3**, for cell C4, **=A4 + B4**, and so on down column C. To avoid the drudgery of typing many similar formulas, you can copy a formula and then paste it into all of the cells in a selected cell range. For example, to copy a formula that has been entered in cell C2 down the column through row 12:

1. Right-click cell **C2** and click **Copy** from the shortcut menu. A movie marquee–like highlight appears around cell C2.
2. Select the cell range **C3:C12**. (Use the drag operation discussed in Section B.2 to select the cell range).
3. With the cell range highlighted, right-click over the cell range and click **Copy** from the shortcut menu.

When you perform this copy-and-paste operation, Excel adjusts these **relative cell references** in formulas, so that copying the formula **=A2 + B2** from cell C2 to cell C3 results in the formula **=A3 + B3** being pasted into cell C3, the formula **=A4 + B4** being pasted into cell C4, and so on.

There are circumstances in which you do not want Excel to adjust all or part of a formula. For example, if you were copying the cell C2 formula **=(A2 + B2)/B15**, and cell B15 contained the divisor to be used in all formulas, you would not want to see pasted into cell C3 the formula **=(A3 + B3)/B16**. To prevent Excel from adjusting a cell reference, you use an **absolute cell reference** by inserting dollar signs ($) before the column and row references. For example, the absolute cell reference **$B$15** in the copied cell C2 formula **=(A2 + B2)/$B$15** would cause Excel to paste **=(A3 + B3)/$B$15** into cell C3.[1]

Do not confuse the use of the U.S. dollar symbol in an absolute reference with the formatting operation that displays numbers as U.S. currency values. To format a cell for U.S. currency display, see Section C.5 in Appendix C on page 723.

[1] For ease of reading, formulas shown with the worksheet illustrations in this book always use relative cell references

C.1 Opening and Saving Workbooks

In Excel you open and save workbooks, collections of worksheets, and chart sheets. To open a workbook, click the **Office Button** and then select **Open** (Excel 2007) or select **File → Open**. In the Open dialog box (shown in Figure B.2 on page 718), select the folder in which to open the workbook from the **Look-in** drop-down list, select the workbook to be opened from the file list, and click **Open**. To open to a particular worksheet in a just-opened workbook, click the sheet tab for the worksheet.

To save a workbook, use the **Save As** command and use the older **.xls** workbook format to maximize compatibility across all Excel versions. In Excel 2007, click the **Office button** and then move the mouse pointer over (do not click) **Save As** and, in the Save As gallery, click **Excel 97-2003 Workbook** (see Figure C.1, left panel, below). In Excel 2003, select **File → Save As**. In both Excel versions, Excel displays a Save As dialog box (right panel in Figure C.1) in which you select the folder in which to open the workbook from the **Save in** drop-down list, accept or edit the workbook name in the **File name** box, and click **Save**. Give your workbooks self-defining names, and if you opened one of the workbooks downloaded for this book, be sure to edit the name in the **File name** box to preserve the contents of the downloaded workbook.

FIGURE C.1

Save As gallery (Excel 2007 only) and Save As dialog box

To save your file for later use with another program that cannot open Excel workbooks, select either **Text (Tab delimited) (*.txt)** or **CSV (Comma delimited) (*.csv)** in the **Save as type** drop-down list of the Save As dialog box before clicking **Save**.

Although both Excel versions contain a **Save** command, you should avoid this choice until you gain experience. Using Save makes it too easy to inadvertently overwrite your work, and, in Excel 2007, may save your workbook in the newer **.xlsx** workbook format that, while optimized for Excel 2007, offers reduced compatibility across Excel versions. Also, the Save command cannot be used for any opened workbook that Excel has marked as read-only (use Save As to save such workbooks).

C.2 Creating New Workbooks and Worksheets

To create a new workbook in Excel 2007, select **Office Button → New** and in the New Workbook dialog box, click **Blank workbook** and then **Create**. To create a new workbook in Excel 2003, select **File → New** and then click **Blank workbook** in the New Workbook task pane.

New workbooks are created with a fixed number of worksheets. You can delete extra worksheets or insert more sheets by right-clicking a sheet tab and clicking either **Delete** or **Insert**.

C.3 Printing Worksheets

To print a worksheet (or a chart sheet), first open to the worksheet by clicking its sheet tab. In Excel 2007, click **Office Button**, move the mouse pointer over (do not click) **Print**, and, in the Preview and Print gallery, click **Print Preview**. In Excel 2003, select **File → Print Preview**. In both Excel versions, Excel displays a Print Preview window (see Figure C.2). Figure C.2 shows a partial window for Excel 2003 (bottom) and Excel 2007 (top).

FIGURE C.2

Partial Print Preview display for Excel 2007 (top) and Excel 2003 (bottom)

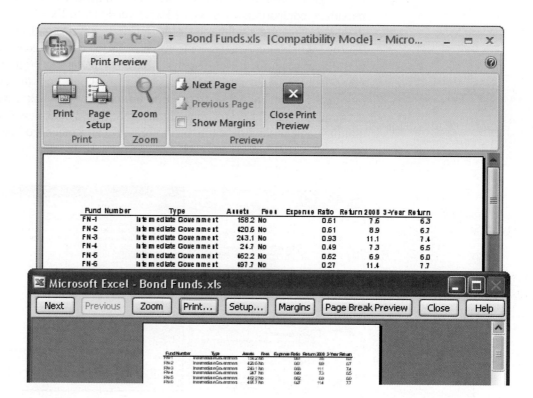

If the preview contains errors or displays the worksheet in an undesirable manner, click **Close Print Preview** (Excel 2007) or **Close** (Excel 2003), make the necessary changes, and reselect the print preview. If necessary, adjust your printout by clicking **Page Setup** (or **Setup**) and make changes in the Page Setup dialog box. For example, to print your worksheet with gridlines and numbered row and lettered column headings (similar to the appearance of the worksheet onscreen), click the **Sheet** tab in the Page Setup dialog box, check **Gridlines** and **Row and column headings**, and click **OK** (see Figure C.3 on page 723).

After completing all corrections and adjustments, click **Print** in the Print Preview window to display the Print dialog box (shown in Figure B.2 on page 718). Select the printer to be used from the **Name** drop-down list, click **All** and **Active sheet(s)**, adjust the **Number of copies**, and click **OK.**

Although the Print dialog box contains the **Entire workbook** "Print what" option, **printing** each worksheet separately will create the best results if you need to print all of the contents of a workbook.

FIGURE C.3

Excel 2007 Page Setup dialog box. (The Excel 2003 version of this dialog box is similar.)

C.4 Verifying Formulas and Worksheets

If you use formulas in your worksheets, you should review and verify formulas before you use their results. To view the formulas in a worksheet, press **Ctrl+`** (grave accent key). To restore the original view, the results of the formulas, press **Ctrl+`** a second time.

As you create and use more complicated worksheets, you might want to visually examine the relationships among a formula and the cells it uses (called the *precedents*) and the cells that use the results of the formula (the *dependents*). In Excel 2007, select **Formulas → Trace Precedents** (or **Trace Dependents**). In Excel 2003, select **Tools → Formula Auditing → Trace Precedents** (or **Trace Dependents**). When you are finished, clear all trace arrows by selecting **Formulas → Remove Arrows** (Excel 2007) or **Tools → Formula Auditing → Remove All Arrows** (Excel 2003).

C.5 Enhancing Workbook Presentation

Enhance workbook presentation by using common formatting commands and rearranging the order of the worksheets and chart sheets in a workbook.

Table C.1 presents the shortcuts for worksheet formatting operations used to create the Excel Guide workbooks and the results shown throughout this book. These shortcuts are available on the Excel 2007 Home tab and the Excel 2003 Formatting toolbar (both shown in Figure C.4).

Use the **Move or Copy** command to rearrange the order of the worksheets and chart sheets in a workbook. To move or copy a worksheet, right-click the sheet tab of the worksheet and click **Move or Copy** from the shortcut menu. In the Move or Copy dialog box, select the destination workbook from the **To book** drop-down list—select **(new book)** to place the worksheet in a new workbook—and select a position for the worksheet in the **Before sheet** list. If making a copy, also check **Create a copy**. Click **OK** to complete the move or copy operation.

FIGURE C.4

Excel 2007 Home tab and the Excel 2003 Formatting toolbar. (See Table C.1 for explanations of the numbered objects.)

TABLE C.1

Shortcuts to Common
Formatting Operations

Number	Operation Name	Use
❶	**Font Face** and **Font Size**	Changes the text font face and size for cell entries and chart labels. Worksheets shown in this book have been formatted as **Calibri 11**. Many DATA worksheets have been formatted as **Arial 10**.
❷	**Boldface**	Toggles on (or off) boldface text style for the currently selected object.
❸	**Italic**	Toggles on (or off) italic text style for the currently selected object.
❹	**Borders**	Displays a gallery of choices that permit drawing lines (borders) around a cell or cell range.
❺	**Fill Color**	Displays a gallery of choices for the background color of a cell. Immediately to the right of **Fill Color** is the related **Font Color** (not used in any example in this book).
❻	**Align Text**	Aligns the display of the contents of a worksheet cell. Three buttons are available: **Align Text Left**, **Center**, and **Align Text Right**.
❼	**Merge & Center**	Merges (combines) adjacent cells into one cell and centers the display of the contents of that cell. In Excel 2007, this button is also a drop-down list that offers additional **Merge** and **Unmerge** choices.
❽	**Percent**	Formats the display of a number value in a cell as a percentage. The value 1 displays as 100%, the value 0.01 displays as 1%. To the immediate left of **Percent** is **Currency**, which formats values as dollars and cents. Do not confuse **Currency** formatting with the symbol used to identify absolute cell references (see Section B.7 in Appendix B on page 720).
❾	**Increase Decimal** and **Decrease Decimal**	Adjusts the number of decimal places to display for a number value in a cell.
❿	**Format** (Excel 2007)	Displays a gallery of choices that affect the row height and column width of a cell. The most common usage is to select a column and then select **Format → AutoFit Column Width**. (In Excel 2003, the equivalent operation is **Format → Column → AutoFit Selection**.)

FIGURE C.5

Excel 2007 Format Cells dialog box (The Excel 2003 version of this dialog box is similar.)

Worksheet cell formatting can also be done through the **Format Cells** command. In many of the Excel Guide instructions, you are instructed to right-click a cell and click **Format Cells** from the shortcut menu. This operation displays the Format Cells dialog box (shown in Figure C.5), in which you can perform all the formatting operations discussed in Table C.1 and more.

C.6 Useful Keyboard Shortcuts

In Excel, certain keys or keystroke combinations (one or more keys held down as you press another key) are keyboard shortcuts that act as alternate means of executing common operations. Table C.2 presents some common shortcuts that represent some of the common Excel

TABLE C.2

Useful Keyboard Shortcuts

Key	Operation
Backspace	Erases typed characters to the left of the current position, one character at a time.
Delete	Erases characters to the right of the cursor, one character at a time.
Enter or Tab	Finalizes an entry typed into a worksheet cell. Implied by the use of the verb *enter* in the Excel Guides.
Esc	Cancels an action or a dialog box. Equivalent to the dialog box **Cancel** button.
F1	Displays the Excel help system.
Ctrl+C	Copies the currently selected worksheet entry or chart label.
Ctrl+V	Pastes the currently copied object into the currently selected worksheet cell or chart label.
Ctrl+X	Cuts the currently selected worksheet entry or chart label. You cut, and not delete, something in order to paste it somewhere else.
Ctrl+B	Toggles on (or off) boldface text style for the currently selected object.
Ctrl+I	Toggles on (or off) italic text style for the currently selected object.
Ctrl+F	Finds a **Find what** value.
Ctrl+H	Replaces a **Find what** value with the **Replace with** value.
Ctrl+Z	Undoes the last operation.
Ctrl+Y	Redoes the last operation.
Ctrl+`	Toggles on (or off) formulas view of worksheet.
Ctrl+Shift+Enter	Enters an array formula.

Note: Using the copy-and-paste keyboard shortcut, **Ctrl+C** and **Ctrl+V**, to copy formulas from one worksheet cell to another is subject to the same type of adjustment as discussed in Section B.7.

operations described in this book. (Keystroke combinations are shown using a plus sign, as in **Ctrl+C**, which means "while holding down the **Ctrl** key, press the **C** key.")

C.7 Chart Formatting (Excel 2007)

Excel incorrectly formats the charts created by the *In-Depth Excel 2007* instructions. Use the formatting adjustments in Table C.3 to properly format charts you create. Before applying these adjustments, relocate a chart to its own chart sheet. To do so, right-click the chart background and click **Move Chart** from the shortcut menu. In the Move Chart dialog box, click **New Sheet**, enter a name for the new chart sheet, and click **OK.**

Use all of the adjustments in Table C.3, unless a particular set of charting instructions tells you otherwise. To apply the adjustments, you must be open to the chart sheet that contains the chart to be adjusted. All adjustments are made by first selecting the **Layout** tab (under the Chart Tools heading). If a Layout tab selection cannot be made, the adjustment does not apply to the type of chart being adjusted. (Excel hides or disables chart formatting choices that do not apply to a particular chart type.)

Occasionally, when you open to a chart sheet, the chart is either too large to be fully seen or too small, surrounded by a chart frame mat that is too large. Click the **Zoom Out** or **Zoom In** buttons, located in the lower-right portion of the Excel window frame, to adjust the display.

TABLE C.3
Excel 2007 Chart
Formatting Adjustments

Layout Tab Selection	Notes
Chart Title → Above Chart	In the box that is added to the chart, double-click **Chart Title** and enter an appropriate title.
Axes Titles → Primary Horizontal Axis Title → Title Below Axis	In the box that is added to the chart, double-click **Axis Title** and enter an appropriate title.
Axes Titles → Primary Vertical Axis Title → Rotated Title	In the box that is added to the chart, double-click **Axis Title** and enter an appropriate title.
Axes Titles → Secondary Horizontal → Axis Title → None and **Axes Titles → Secondary Vertical Axis Title → Rotated Title**	Only for charts that contain secondary axes.
Legend → None	Turns off the chart legend.
Data Labels → None	Turns off the display of values at plotted points or bars in the charts.
Data Table → None	Turns off the display of a summary table on the chart sheet.
Axes → Primary Horizontal Axis → Show Left to Right Axis (or **Show Default Axis,** if listed)	Turns on the display of the X axis.
Axes → Primary Vertical Axis → Show Default Axis	Turns on the display of the Y axis.
Gridlines → Primary Horizontal Gridlines → None	Turns off the improper horizontal gridlines.
Gridlines → Primary Vertical Gridlines → None	Turns off the improper vertical gridlines.

C.8 Chart Formatting (Excel 2003)

Excel incorrectly formats the charts created by the *In-Depth Excel 2003* instructions. Use the formatting adjustments in Table C.4 to properly format charts you create. Before applying these adjustments, relocate the chart to its own chart sheet. To do so, right-click the chart background and click **Location** from the shortcut menu. In the Chart Location dialog box, click **As new sheet**, enter a name for the new chart sheet, and click **OK**.

Use all of the adjustments in Table C.4, unless a particular set of charting instructions tells you otherwise. To apply the adjustments, you must be open to the chart sheet containing the chart to be adjusted. Excel hides or disables chart formatting choices that do not apply to a particular chart type.

Occasionally, when you open to a chart sheet, the chart is either too large to be fully seen or too small, surrounded by a chart frame mat that is too large. To adjust the size of the chart, select **View → Zoom** and in the Zoom dialog box click **Fit selection** and then click **OK**.

TABLE C.4

Excel 2003 Chart
Formatting Adjustments

Adjustment	Notes
Remove chart background	Right-click the chart background and click **Format Plot Area** in the shortcut menu. In the dialog box that appears, click **None** in the **Area** group and click **OK**.
Add chart and axis titles	Right-click the chart background and click **Chart Options** in the shortcut menu. In the Chart Options dialog box, click the **Titles** tab and enter a **Chart title** and titles for the axes. Click **OK** to finish.
Format axes and gridlines	Right-click the chart background and click **Chart Options** in the shortcut menu. In the Chart Options dialog box, click the **Axes** tab, check the check boxes for both the **(X) axis** and **(Y) axis** and click **Automatic** under the (X) axis check box. Then, click the **Gridlines** tab and clear all check boxes. Click **OK** to finish.
Turn off the chart legend, data labels, and data table	Right-click the chart background and click **Chart Options** in the shortcut menu. In the Chart Options dialog box, click the **Legend** tab and clear **Show legend**. Then click the **Data Labels** tab and clear all check boxes. Then click the **Data Table** tab and clear all check boxes. Click **OK** to finish.

C.9 Creating Histograms for Discrete Probability Distributions (Excel 2007)

You can create a histogram for a discrete probability distribution based on a discrete probabilities table. For example, to create a histogram based on the Figure 5.2 binomial probabilities worksheet on page 174, open to the **COMPUTE worksheet** of the **Binomial workbook**. Select the cell range **B14: B18**, the probabilities in the Binomial Probabilities Table, and:

1. Select **Insert → Column** and select the first **2-D Column** gallery choice **(Clustered Column)**.

2. Right-click the chart background and click **Select Data**.

In the Select Data Source dialog box:

3. Click **Edit** under the **Horizontal (Categories) Axis Labels** heading.

4. In the Axis Labels dialog box, enter **=COMPUTE!A14:A18**, the cell range of the X axis values. (This cell range must be entered as a formula in the form *=SheetName! CellRange*.) Then, click OK to return to the Select Data Source dialog box.

5. Click **OK**.

In the chart:

6. Right-click inside a bar and click **Format Data Series** in the shortcut menu.

In the Format Data Series dialog box:

7. Click **Series Options** in the left pane. In the Series Options right pane, change the **Gap Width** slider to **Large Gap**. Click **Close**.

Relocate the chart to a chart sheet and adjust the chart formatting by using the instructions in Appendix Section C.7 on page 726.

C.10 Creating Histograms for Discrete Probability Distributions (Excel 2003)

You can create a histogram for a discrete probability distribution based on a discrete probabilities table. For example, to create a histogram based on the Figure 5.2 binomial probabilities worksheet on page 174, open to the **COMPUTE worksheet** of the **Binomial workbook**. Select the cell range **B14: B18**, the probabilities in the Binomial Probabilities Table, and:

1. Select **Insert → Chart**.

In the Chart Wizard Step 1 dialog box:

2. Click the **Standard Types** tab and then click **Column** as the **Chart type.** Click the first **Chart sub-type** choice, labeled **Clustered Column**.

3. Click **Next**.

In the Chart Wizard Step 2 dialog box:

4. Click the **Series tab**. Enter **=COMPUTE!A14:A18** as the **Category (X) axis labels**. (This cell range must be entered as a formula, in the form =*SheetName!CellRange*.)

5. Click **Next**.

In the Chart Wizard Step 3 dialog box:

6. Click the **Titles** tab. Enter a **Chart title**, **X** as the **Category (X) axis** title, and **P(X)** as the **Value (Y) axis** title. Adjust the chart formatting by using the instructions in Section C.8 on page 727 for the **Axes**, **Gridlines**, **Legend**, **Data Labels**, and **Data Table** tabs.

In the Chart Wizard Step 4 dialog box:

7. Click **As new sheet** and then click **Finish** to create a chart.

In the chart, right-click inside a bar and select **Format Data Series** in the shortcut menu. In the Format Data Series dialog box, click the **Options tab**, set the **Gap width** to **0**, and click **OK**.

C.11 Formula "Tricks" of the ANOVA Workbooks

The **COMPUTE worksheets** of both the **One-Way ANOVA workbook** and **Two-Way ANOVA workbook** use the **COUNTA** function in a tricky way to determine the number of levels for a factor. Unlike the **COUNT** function, which counts the number of numeric values in a range, **COUNTA** counts the number of cells that contain any value. In the One-Way ANOVA workbook, COUNTA determines the number of levels by counting the number of column headings in row 1 of the **ASFDATA worksheet**.

The COMPUTE worksheet in the Two-Way ANOVA workbook additionally uses the **COUNTIF**(*cell range, value to count*) and **INT** functions to help compute $r - 1$, the number of levels of factor A minus 1. COUNTIF is similar to COUNT, but it counts those cells whose value matches the *value to count*. INT rounds a number down to the nearest integer to force a whole number as a result.

These formulas are combined in the cell C25 formula, **=INT(COUNTA (TWAData!A:A)/COUNTIF(TWAData!A:A, TWAData!A2)) − 1**. In this formula, **COUNTA(TWAData!A:A)** counts the number of factor A level labels in column A of the

TWADATA worksheet. COUNTIF(TWAData!A:A, TWAData!A2) counts the number of times the first factor A level label occurs in column A. Dividing this count computes r, a "tricky" way of getting the value needed for cell C25.

C.12 Pasting with Paste Special

Pasting data from one worksheet to another can sometimes lead to unexpected side effects. When the two worksheets are in different workbooks, a simple paste creates an external link to the original workbook. This can lead to errors later if the first workbook is unavailable when the second one is being used. Even pasting between worksheets in the same workbook can lead to problems if what is being pasted is a cell range of formulas.

To avoid such side effects, use **Paste Special** in these special situations. To use this operation, copy the original cell range as you would do normally and select the cell or cell range to be the target of the paste. Right-click the target and click **Paste Special** from the shortcut menu. In the Paste Special dialog box (shown in Figure C.6, below), click **Values** and then click **OK**. For the first case, Paste Special Values pastes the current values of the cells in the first workbook and not formulas that use cell references to the first workbook. For the second case, Paste Special Values pastes the current evaluation of the formulas copied and not the formulas themselves.

If you use PHStat2 and have data for a procedure in the form of formulas, use Paste Special Values to create columns of equivalent values before using the procedure. (PHStat2 will not work properly if data for a procedure are in the form of formulas.)

As Figure C.6 illustrates, Paste Special can paste other types of information, including cell formatting information. For a full discussion of Paste Special, see the Excel help system.

FIGURE C.6

Excel 2007 Paste Special dialog box. (The Excel 2003 version of this dialog box is similar.)

D.1 Visiting the Companion Website for This Book

The Companion Web site for this book contains study resources, Excel workbook files, the free PHStat2 add-in, and the optional online topics. To visit this site, open a Web browser and go to **www.pearsonhighered.com/levine**. On that Web page, click the **Companion Website** link for this book. (Be careful; the Web page lists several books, each with its own **Companion Website** link.)

The link takes you to the home page of the Companion Web site. On the home page, there are links for downloading the files for this book (see Section D.2), any updates or corrections to this book, and a horizontal menu of chapter numbers that you can use to display the companion materials for an individual chapter.

D.2 Downloading the Files for This Book

The home page for the Companion Web site (see Section D.1) provides links that will allow you to download the following sets of files:

- **Excel Data Workbooks** Workbooks that contain the data used in chapter examples or named in problems. These workbooks are stored in the **.xls** format, compatible with all Excel versions. See Section F.1 in Appendix F on page 752 for a complete list of these workbooks.
- **Excel Guide Workbooks** Workbooks that contain model solutions that can also be reused as templates for solving other problems.
- **Case Files** A mix of data and document files, including facsimiles of Web pages, that support the "Managing the *Springville Herald*" running case and the end-of-chapter Web Cases.
- **Visual Explorations Files** The files needed to use the Visual Explorations add-in workbook, the interactive Excel add-in that illustrates selected statistical concepts. (Requires Microsoft Windows–based Excel or Mac Excel 2004.)
- **Online Topics** A set of files in Adobe PDF format that contain the optional online topics for this book.
- **PHStat2 Readme File and PHStat2 Setup Program** Files that allow you to set up and install the free PHStat2 add-in (see Section D.4 in Appendix D on page 731 and see Appendix G on page 759). (Requires Microsoft Windows–based Excel.)

To download a set of files, right-click its download link and click the "save as" choice from the shortcut menu (**Save Target As** in Internet Explorer, **Save Link As** in Mozilla Firefox). Other than PHStat2, each set is downloaded as a self-extracting archive of compressed files, which you extract and store in the folder of your choice.

D.3 Checking for and Applying Excel Updates

To check for and apply Excel (and related Microsoft Office) updates, your system must be connected to the Internet. You can check and apply updates using one of two methods. If Internet Explorer is set as the default Web browser on your system, an easy way to check for and apply updates is to use the "check for updates" feature in Excel. In Excel 2007, click the **Office Button** and then **Excel Options** (at the bottom of the Office Button menu window). In the Excel options dialog box, click **Resources** in the left pane and then in the right pane click **Check for Updates**. In the Web browser that opens, follow the Web page instructions displayed to complete a Microsoft Update. In Excel 2003, select **Help → Check for Updates** to trigger the display of the same Web page.

If the first method fails for any reason, you can manually download Excel and Microsoft Office updates by opening a Web browser and going to **office.microsoft.com/officeupdate**. On the Web page that is displayed, you can find download links arranged by popularity as well as by product version. If you use this second method, you need to know the exact version and

about Microsoft Office Excel 2007

FIGURE D.1

Detailed information about Excel 2007. (This information varies from one copy of Excel to another and is subject to change when updates are applied to Excel or Microsoft Office.)

about Microsoft Office Excel 2007

Microsoft® Office Excel® 2007 (12.0.6504.5001) SP2 MSO (12.0.6425.1000)

status of your copy of Excel. In Excel 2007, click the **Office Button** and then **Excel Options**. In the Excel options dialog box, click **Resources** in the left pane and then in the right pane note the detail line under the heading "about Microsoft Office Excel 2007," shown in Figure D.1. In Excel 2003, select **Help → About Microsoft Office Excel** to display a dialog box with similar information about Excel 2003.

The numbers and codes that follow the words "Microsoft Office Excel" indicate the version number and updates already applied. In particular, look for codes that begin with SP (SP2 in Figure D.1), which indicates the latest service pack that has been applied. (*Service pack* is Microsoft's name for a significant and large update.) By knowing the latest service pack applied, you can avoid unnecessarily downloading earlier, lower-numbered service packs.

Special Notes About Updates

If you use a Microsoft Windows–based system and have previously turned on the Windows Update service, your system has not necessarily downloaded and applied Excel and Microsoft Office updates. If you use Windows Update, you can upgrade for free to the Microsoft Update services that searches for and downloads updates for all Microsoft products, including Excel and Office. (Learn more about this service by visiting **www.microsoft.com/security/updates/mu.aspx**.)

If you plan to use PHStat2, you must, as discussed in Section D.4 and elsewhere, first apply all outstanding updates to Excel, including all service packs.

If you use Mac Excel, select **Help → Check for Updates** to begin Microsoft AutoUpdate for Mac, similar to Microsoft Update, described above, for checking and applying updates.

D.4 Concise Instructions for Installing PHStat2

If your system can run the Microsoft Windows-based Excel 2003, Excel 2007, or Excel 2010, and has 15 MB of storage space free, you will be able to install and use PHStat2. To install PHStat2, first check for and apply all Excel updates by using the instructions in Section D.3. Next, download the PHStat2 readme file (see Section D.2) and review the detailed technical requirements presented in that document as well as any updates to the information presented in this appendix.

After reviewing the readme file, download the PHStat2 setup program (see Section D.2) and save the file to the folder of your choice. The PHStat2 setup program copies the PHStat2 files to your system and adds entries in the Windows registry file on your system. Run the setup program only after first logging on to Windows using a user account that has administrator privileges. (Running the setup program with a Windows user account that does not include these privileges will prevent the setup program from properly installing PHStat2.)

If your system runs Windows Vista, Windows 7, or certain third-party security programs, you may see messages asking you to "permit" or "allow" specific system operations as the setup program executes. If you do not give the setup program the necessary permissions, PHStat2 will *not* be properly installed on your computer.

After the setup completes, check the installation by opening PHStat2. If the installation ran properly, Excel will display a PHStat menu in the Add-Ins tab (Excel 2007 or Excel 2010) or the menu bar (Excel 2003). If you have skipped checking for and applying necessary Excel updates, or if some of the updates were unable to be applied, when you first attempt to use PHStat2, you may see a "Compile Error" message that talks about a "hidden module." If this occurs, repeat the process of checking for and applying updates to Excel. (If the bandwidth of the Internet connection is limited, you may need to use another connection.)

As you use PHStat2, check the PHStat2 Web site, **www.prenhall.com/phstat** on a regular basis to see if any free updates are available for your version. For more information about PHStat2 without going online, read Section G.1 in Appendix G on page 759.

D.5 Configuring Excel for PHStat2 Usage

Configuring Excel for PHStat2 usage is a two-step process. In the first step, you configure Excel security settings before you attempt to open or use PHStat2. In the second step, you click **Enable Macros** in a security dialog box (see Figure D.2) as you attempt to open and use PHStat2.

FIGURE D.2

Excel 2007 (top) and Excel 2003 (bottom) security dialog boxes

To configure Excel 2007 security settings for PHStat2 usage, do the following:

1. Click the **Office Button** and then click **Excel Options** (at the bottom of the Office Button menu window).

In the Excel Options dialog box:

2. Click **Trust Center** in the left pane and then click **Trust Center Settings** in the right pane (see the top of Figure D.3).

In the Trust Center dialog box:

3. Click **Add-ins** in the next left pane, and in the Add-ins right pane clear all of the check-boxes (see the bottom left of Figure D.3).

4. Click **Macro Settings** in the left pane, and in the Macro Settings right pane click **Disable all macros with notification** (see the bottom right of Figure D.3).

5. Click **OK** to close the Trust Center dialog box.

Back in the Excel Options dialog box:

6. Click **OK** to finish.

On some systems that have stringent security settings, you might need to modify step 5. For such systems, in step 5, click **Trusted Locations** in the left pane and then, in the Trusted

FIGURE D.3

Configuring Excel 2007
security settings

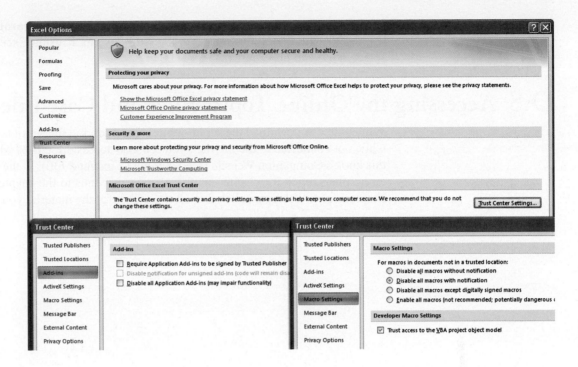

Locations right pane, click **Add new location** to add the folder path to the PHStat2 add-in (typically C:\Program Files\PHStat2) and then click **OK**.

To configure Excel 2003 security settings for PHStat2 usage, select **Tools → Macro → Security**. In the Security dialog box, click the **Security Level** tab, then click **Medium**, and then click **OK**. (If you set the Security Level to **Very High** or **High** you will prevent PHStat2 from opening. Do not set the Security Level to **Low**, which creates a security vulnerability in your copy of Excel.)

D.6 Checking for the Presence of the Analysis ToolPak

Checking for the presence of the Analysis ToolPak requires reviewing the list of active Excel add-ins.

To do this in Excel 2007, click the **Office Button** and then click **Excel Options** (at bottom of the Office Button menu window). In the Excel Options dialog box, click **Add-Ins** in the left pane and look for an entry **Analysis ToolPak** in the right pane, under **Active Application Add-ins**. If this entry does not appear or appears in the **Inactive Application Add-ins** list, click **Go**. In the Add-Ins dialog box, check **Analysis ToolPak** in the **Add-Ins available** list and click **OK**. If Analysis ToolPak does not appear in the list, rerun the Microsoft Office setup program to install this component.

To check for the presence of the Analysis ToolPak in Excel 2003, select **Tools → Add-Ins**, and in the Add-Ins dialog box that appears, check **Analysis ToolPak** in the **Add-Ins available** list and click **OK**. If Analysis ToolPak does not appear in the list, rerun the Microsoft Office setup program to install this component.

Note that the Analysis ToolPak add-in is not available in Mac Excel 2008 but does exist for the older Mac Excel 2004.

D.7 Using the Visual Explorations Add-in Workbook

To use the Visual Explorations add-in workbook, first download the set of three files that comprise Visual Explorations from this book's companion Website (see Section D.2). Place the three files together in a folder of your choosing. Next, use the Section D.5 instructions for configuring Excel for PHStat2 usage. Then open the **Visual Explorations.xla** file in Excel and use the VisualExplorations menu (in the **Add-Ins** tab, if using Excel 2007 or Excel 2010) to select individual procedures.

D.8 Accessing the Online Topics Files and Case Files Online

While you can download the set of online topic files and the set of case files for your own use while not connected to the Internet, you can also access these files while online. To do so, visit this book's Companion Website (see Section D.2 on page 730). In the horizontal menu of chapter numbers, click the chapter number that corresponds to the chapter you want. Then, in that chapter's own Web page, click the left menu link for the material you want to use online.

TABLE E.1
Table of Random Numbers

	Column							
Row	00000 12345	00001 67890	11111 12345	11112 67890	22222 12345	22223 67890	33333 12345	33334 67890
01	49280	88924	35779	00283	81163	07275	89863	02348
02	61870	41657	07468	08612	98083	97349	20775	45091
03	43898	65923	25078	86129	78496	97653	91550	08078
04	62993	93912	30454	84598	56095	20664	12872	64647
05	33850	58555	51438	85507	71865	79488	76783	31708
06	97340	03364	88472	04334	63919	36394	11095	92470
07	70543	29776	10087	10072	55980	64688	68239	20461
08	89382	93809	00796	95945	34101	81277	66090	88872
09	37818	72142	67140	50785	22380	16703	53362	44940
10	60430	22834	14130	96593	23298	56203	92671	15925
11	82975	66158	84731	19436	55790	69229	28661	13675
12	30987	71938	40355	54324	08401	26299	49420	59208
13	55700	24586	93247	32596	11865	63397	44251	43189
14	14756	23997	78643	75912	83832	32768	18928	57070
15	32166	53251	70654	92827	63491	04233	33825	69662
16	23236	73751	31888	81718	06546	83246	47651	04877
17	45794	26926	15130	82455	78305	55058	52551	47182
18	09893	20505	14225	68514	47427	56788	96297	78822
19	54382	74598	91499	14523	68479	27686	46162	83554
20	94750	89923	37089	20048	80336	94598	26940	36858
21	70297	34135	53140	33340	42050	82341	44104	82949
22	85157	47954	32979	26575	57600	40881	12250	73742
23	11100	02340	12860	74697	96644	89439	28707	25815
24	36871	50775	30592	57143	17381	68856	25853	35041
25	23913	48357	63308	16090	51690	54607	72407	55538
26	79348	36085	27973	65157	07456	22255	25626	57054
27	92074	54641	53673	54421	18130	60103	69593	49464
28	06873	21440	75593	41373	49502	17972	82578	16364
29	12478	37622	99659	31065	83613	69889	58869	29571
30	57175	55564	65411	42547	70457	03426	72937	83792
31	91616	11075	80103	07831	59309	13276	26710	73000
32	78025	73539	14621	39044	47450	03197	12787	47709
33	27587	67228	80145	10175	12822	86687	65530	49325
34	16690	20427	04251	64477	73709	73945	92396	68263
35	70183	58065	65489	31833	82093	16747	10386	59293
36	90730	35385	15679	99742	50866	78028	75573	67257
37	10934	93242	13431	24590	02770	48582	00906	58595
38	82462	30166	79613	47416	13389	80268	05085	96666
39	27463	10433	07606	16285	93699	60912	94532	95632
40	02979	52997	09079	92709	90110	47506	53693	49892
41	46888	69929	75233	52507	32097	37594	10067	67327
42	53638	83161	08289	12639	08141	12640	28437	09268
43	82433	61427	17239	89160	19666	08814	37841	12847
44	35766	31672	50082	22795	66948	65581	84393	15890
45	10853	42581	08792	13257	61973	24450	52351	16602
46	20341	27398	72906	63955	17276	10646	74692	48438
47	54458	90542	77563	51839	52901	53355	83281	19177
48	26337	66530	16687	35179	46560	00123	44546	79896
49	34314	23729	85264	05575	96855	23820	11091	79821
50	28603	10708	68933	34189	92166	15181	66628	58599
51	66194	28926	99547	16625	45515	67953	12108	57846
52	78240	43195	24837	32511	70880	22070	52622	61881
53	00833	88000	67299	68215	11274	55624	32991	17436
54	12111	86683	61270	58036	64192	90611	15145	01748
55	47189	99951	05755	03834	43782	90599	40282	51417
56	76396	72486	62423	27618	84184	78922	73561	52818
57	46409	17469	32483	09083	76175	19985	26309	91536

TABLE E.1
Table of Random
Numbers (continued)

	Column							
Row	**00000** **12345**	**00001** **67890**	**11111** **12345**	**11112** **67890**	**22222** **12345**	**22223** **67890**	**33333** **12345**	**33334** **67890**
58	74626	22111	87286	46772	42243	68046	44250	42439
59	34450	81974	93723	49023	58432	67083	36876	93391
60	36327	72135	33005	28701	34710	49359	50693	89311
61	74185	77536	84825	09934	99103	09325	67389	45869
62	12296	41623	62873	37943	25584	09609	63360	47270
63	90822	60280	88925	99610	42772	60561	76873	04117
64	72121	79152	96591	90305	10189	79778	68016	13747
65	95268	41377	25684	08151	61816	58555	54305	86189
66	92603	09091	75884	93424	72586	88903	30061	14457
67	18813	90291	05275	01223	79607	95426	34900	09778
68	38840	26903	28624	67157	51986	42865	14508	49315
69	05959	33836	53758	16562	41081	38012	41230	20528
70	85141	21155	99212	32685	51403	31926	69813	58781
71	75047	59643	31074	38172	03718	32119	69506	67143
72	30752	95260	68032	62871	58781	34143	68790	69766
73	22986	82575	42187	62295	84295	30634	66562	31442
74	99439	86692	90348	66036	48399	73451	26698	39437
75	20389	93029	11881	71685	65452	89047	63669	02656
76	39249	05173	68256	36359	20250	68686	05947	09335
77	96777	33605	29481	20063	09398	01843	35139	61344
78	04860	32918	10798	50492	52655	33359	94713	28393
79	41613	42375	00403	03656	77580	87772	86877	57085
80	17930	00794	53836	53692	67135	98102	61912	11246
81	24649	31845	25736	75231	83808	98917	93829	99430
82	79899	34061	54308	59358	56462	58166	97302	86828
83	76801	49594	81002	30397	52728	15101	72070	33706
84	36239	63636	38140	65731	39788	06872	38971	53363
85	07392	64449	17886	63632	53995	17574	22247	62607
86	67133	04181	33874	98835	67453	59734	76381	63455
87	77759	31504	32832	70861	15152	29733	75371	39174
88	85992	72268	42920	20810	29361	51423	90306	73574
89	79553	75952	54116	65553	47139	60579	09165	85490
90	41101	17336	48951	53674	17880	45260	08575	49321
91	36191	17095	32123	91576	84221	78902	82010	30847
92	62329	63898	23268	74283	26091	68409	69704	82267
93	14751	13151	93115	01437	56945	89661	67680	79790
94	48462	59278	44185	29616	76537	19589	83139	28454
95	29435	88105	59651	44391	74588	55114	80834	85686
96	28340	29285	12965	14821	80425	16602	44653	70467
97	02167	58940	27149	80242	10587	79786	34959	75339
98	17864	00991	39557	54981	23588	81914	37609	13128
99	79675	80605	60059	35862	00254	36546	21545	78179
100	72335	82037	92003	34100	29879	46613	89720	13274

Source: *Partially extracted from the Rand Corporation,* A Million Random Digits with 100,000 Normal Deviates *(Glencoe, IL, The Free Press, 1955).*

TABLE E.2
The Cumulative Standardized Normal Distribution

Entry represents area under the cumulative standardized
normal distribution from $-\infty$ to Z

					Cumulative Probabilities					
Z	0.00	0.01	0.02	0.03	0.04	0.05	0.06	0.07	0.08	0.09
−6.0	0.000000001									
−5.5	0.000000019									
−5.0	0.000000287									
−4.5	0.000003398									
−4.0	0.000031671									
−3.9	0.00005	0.00005	0.00004	0.00004	0.00004	0.00004	0.00004	0.00004	0.00003	0.00003
−3.8	0.00007	0.00007	0.00007	0.00006	0.00006	0.00006	0.00006	0.00005	0.00005	0.00005
−3.7	0.00011	0.00010	0.00010	0.00010	0.00009	0.00009	0.00008	0.00008	0.00008	0.00008
−3.6	0.00016	0.00015	0.00015	0.00014	0.00014	0.00013	0.00013	0.00012	0.00012	0.00011
−3.5	0.00023	0.00022	0.00022	0.00021	0.00020	0.00019	0.00019	0.00018	0.00017	0.00017
−3.4	0.00034	0.00032	0.00031	0.00030	0.00029	0.00028	0.00027	0.00026	0.00025	0.00024
−3.3	0.00048	0.00047	0.00045	0.00043	0.00042	0.00040	0.00039	0.00038	0.00036	0.00035
−3.2	0.00069	0.00066	0.00064	0.00062	0.00060	0.00058	0.00056	0.00054	0.00052	0.00050
−3.1	0.00097	0.00094	0.00090	0.00087	0.00084	0.00082	0.00079	0.00076	0.00074	0.00071
−3.0	0.00135	0.00131	0.00126	0.00122	0.00118	0.00114	0.00111	0.00107	0.00103	0.00100
−2.9	0.0019	0.0018	0.0018	0.0017	0.0016	0.0016	0.0015	0.0015	0.0014	0.0014
−2.8	0.0026	0.0025	0.0024	0.0023	0.0023	0.0022	0.0021	0.0021	0.0020	0.0019
−2.7	0.0035	0.0034	0.0033	0.0032	0.0031	0.0030	0.0029	0.0028	0.0027	0.0026
−2.6	0.0047	0.0045	0.0044	0.0043	0.0041	0.0040	0.0039	0.0038	0.0037	0.0036
−2.5	0.0062	0.0060	0.0059	0.0057	0.0055	0.0054	0.0052	0.0051	0.0049	0.0048
−2.4	0.0082	0.0080	0.0078	0.0075	0.0073	0.0071	0.0069	0.0068	0.0066	0.0064
−2.3	0.0107	0.0104	0.0102	0.0099	0.0096	0.0094	0.0091	0.0089	0.0087	0.0084
−2.2	0.0139	0.0136	0.0132	0.0129	0.0125	0.0122	0.0119	0.0116	0.0113	0.0110
−2.1	0.0179	0.0174	0.0170	0.0166	0.0162	0.0158	0.0154	0.0150	0.0146	0.0143
−2.0	0.0228	0.0222	0.0217	0.0212	0.0207	0.0202	0.0197	0.0192	0.0188	0.0183
−1.9	0.0287	0.0281	0.0274	0.0268	0.0262	0.0256	0.0250	0.0244	0.0239	0.0233
−1.8	0.0359	0.0351	0.0344	0.0336	0.0329	0.0322	0.0314	0.0307	0.0301	0.0294
−1.7	0.0446	0.0436	0.0427	0.0418	0.0409	0.0401	0.0392	0.0384	0.0375	0.0367
−1.6	0.0548	0.0537	0.0526	0.0516	0.0505	0.0495	0.0485	0.0475	0.0465	0.0455
−1.5	0.0668	0.0655	0.0643	0.0630	0.0618	0.0606	0.0594	0.0582	0.0571	0.0559
−1.4	0.0808	0.0793	0.0778	0.0764	0.0749	0.0735	0.0721	0.0708	0.0694	0.0681
−1.3	0.0968	0.0951	0.0934	0.0918	0.0901	0.0885	0.0869	0.0853	0.0838	0.0823
−1.2	0.1151	0.1131	0.1112	0.1093	0.1075	0.1056	0.1038	0.1020	0.1003	0.0985
−1.1	0.1357	0.1335	0.1314	0.1292	0.1271	0.1251	0.1230	0.1210	0.1190	0.1170
−1.0	0.1587	0.1562	0.1539	0.1515	0.1492	0.1469	0.1446	0.1423	0.1401	0.1379
−0.9	0.1841	0.1814	0.1788	0.1762	0.1736	0.1711	0.1685	0.1660	0.1635	0.1611
−0.8	0.2119	0.2090	0.2061	0.2033	0.2005	0.1977	0.1949	0.1922	0.1894	0.1867
−0.7	0.2420	0.2388	0.2358	0.2327	0.2296	0.2266	0.2236	0.2206	0.2177	0.2148
−0.6	0.2743	0.2709	0.2676	0.2643	0.2611	0.2578	0.2546	0.2514	0.2482	0.2451
−0.5	0.3085	0.3050	0.3015	0.2981	0.2946	0.2912	0.2877	0.2843	0.2810	0.2776
−0.4	0.3446	0.3409	0.3372	0.3336	0.3300	0.3264	0.3228	0.3192	0.3156	0.3121
−0.3	0.3821	0.3783	0.3745	0.3707	0.3669	0.3632	0.3594	0.3557	0.3520	0.3483
−0.2	0.4207	0.4168	0.4129	0.4090	0.4052	0.4013	0.3974	0.3936	0.3897	0.3859
−0.1	0.4602	0.4562	0.4522	0.4483	0.4443	0.4404	0.4364	0.4325	0.4286	0.4247
−0.0	0.5000	0.4960	0.4920	0.4880	0.4840	0.4801	0.4761	0.4721	0.4681	0.4641

TABLE E.2
The Cumulative Standardized Normal Distribution (*continued*)

Entry represents area under the cumulative standardized
normal distribution from $-\infty$ to Z

	Cumulative Probabilities									
Z	0.00	0.01	0.02	0.03	0.04	0.05	0.06	0.07	0.08	0.09
0.0	0.5000	0.5040	0.5080	0.5120	0.5160	0.5199	0.5239	0.5279	0.5319	0.5359
0.1	0.5398	0.5438	0.5478	0.5517	0.5557	0.5596	0.5636	0.5675	0.5714	0.5753
0.2	0.5793	0.5832	0.5871	0.5910	0.5948	0.5987	0.6026	0.6064	0.6103	0.6141
0.3	0.6179	0.6217	0.6255	0.6293	0.6331	0.6368	0.6406	0.6443	0.6480	0.6517
0.4	0.6554	0.6591	0.6628	0.6664	0.6700	0.6736	0.6772	0.6808	0.6844	0.6879
0.5	0.6915	0.6950	0.6985	0.7019	0.7054	0.7088	0.7123	0.7157	0.7190	0.7224
0.6	0.7257	0.7291	0.7324	0.7357	0.7389	0.7422	0.7454	0.7486	0.7518	0.7549
0.7	0.7580	0.7612	0.7642	0.7673	0.7704	0.7734	0.7764	0.7794	0.7823	0.7852
0.8	0.7881	0.7910	0.7939	0.7967	0.7995	0.8023	0.8051	0.8078	0.8106	0.8133
0.9	0.8159	0.8186	0.8212	0.8238	0.8264	0.8289	0.8315	0.8340	0.8365	0.8389
1.0	0.8413	0.8438	0.8461	0.8485	0.8508	0.8531	0.8554	0.8577	0.8599	0.8621
1.1	0.8643	0.8665	0.8686	0.8708	0.8729	0.8749	0.8770	0.8790	0.8810	0.8830
1.2	0.8849	0.8869	0.8888	0.8907	0.8925	0.8944	0.8962	0.8980	0.8997	0.9015
1.3	0.9032	0.9049	0.9066	0.9082	0.9099	0.9115	0.9131	0.9147	0.9162	0.9177
1.4	0.9192	0.9207	0.9222	0.9236	0.9251	0.9265	0.9279	0.9292	0.9306	0.9319
1.5	0.9332	0.9345	0.9357	0.9370	0.9382	0.9394	0.9406	0.9418	0.9429	0.9441
1.6	0.9452	0.9463	0.9474	0.9484	0.9495	0.9505	0.9515	0.9525	0.9535	0.9545
1.7	0.9554	0.9564	0.9573	0.9582	0.9591	0.9599	0.9608	0.9616	0.9625	0.9633
1.8	0.9641	0.9649	0.9656	0.9664	0.9671	0.9678	0.9686	0.9693	0.9699	0.9706
1.9	0.9713	0.9719	0.9726	0.9732	0.9738	0.9744	0.9750	0.9756	0.9761	0.9767
2.0	0.9772	0.9778	0.9783	0.9788	0.9793	0.9798	0.9803	0.9808	0.9812	0.9817
2.1	0.9821	0.9826	0.9830	0.9834	0.9838	0.9842	0.9846	0.9850	0.9854	0.9857
2.2	0.9861	0.9864	0.9868	0.9871	0.9875	0.9878	0.9881	0.9884	0.9887	0.9890
2.3	0.9893	0.9896	0.9898	0.9901	0.9904	0.9906	0.9909	0.9911	0.9913	0.9916
2.4	0.9918	0.9920	0.9922	0.9925	0.9927	0.9929	0.9931	0.9932	0.9934	0.9936
2.5	0.9938	0.9940	0.9941	0.9943	0.9945	0.9946	0.9948	0.9949	0.9951	0.9952
2.6	0.9953	0.9955	0.9956	0.9957	0.9959	0.9960	0.9961	0.9962	0.9963	0.9964
2.7	0.9965	0.9966	0.9967	0.9968	0.9969	0.9970	0.9971	0.9972	0.9973	0.9974
2.8	0.9974	0.9975	0.9976	0.9977	0.9977	0.9978	0.9979	0.9979	0.9980	0.9981
2.9	0.9981	0.9982	0.9982	0.9983	0.9984	0.9984	0.9985	0.9985	0.9986	0.9986
3.0	0.99865	0.99869	0.99874	0.99878	0.99882	0.99886	0.99889	0.99893	0.99897	0.99900
3.1	0.99903	0.99906	0.99910	0.99913	0.99916	0.99918	0.99921	0.99924	0.99926	0.99929
3.2	0.99931	0.99934	0.99936	0.99938	0.99940	0.99942	0.99944	0.99946	0.99948	0.99950
3.3	0.99952	0.99953	0.99955	0.99957	0.99958	0.99960	0.99961	0.99962	0.99964	0.99965
3.4	0.99966	0.99968	0.99969	0.99970	0.99971	0.99972	0.99973	0.99974	0.99975	0.99976
3.5	0.99977	0.99978	0.99978	0.99979	0.99980	0.99981	0.99981	0.99982	0.99983	0.99983
3.6	0.99984	0.99985	0.99985	0.99986	0.99986	0.99987	0.99987	0.99988	0.99988	0.99989
3.7	0.99989	0.99990	0.99990	0.99990	0.99991	0.99991	0.99992	0.99992	0.99992	0.99992
3.8	0.99993	0.99993	0.99993	0.99994	0.99994	0.99994	0.99994	0.99995	0.99995	0.99995
3.9	0.99995	0.99995	0.99996	0.99996	0.99996	0.99996	0.99996	0.99996	0.99997	0.99997
4.0	0.999968329									
4.5	0.999996602									
5.0	0.999999713									
5.5	0.999999981									
6.0	0.999999999									

TABLE E.3
Critical Values of t

For a particular number of degrees of freedom, entry represents the critical value of t corresponding to the cumulative probability $(1 - \alpha)$ and a specified upper-tail area (α).

Degrees of Freedom	Cumulative Probabilities					
	0.75	0.90	0.95	0.975	0.99	0.995
	Upper-Tail Areas					
	0.25	0.10	0.05	0.025	0.01	0.005
1	1.0000	3.0777	6.3138	12.7062	31.8207	63.6574
2	0.8165	1.8856	2.9200	4.3027	6.9646	9.9248
3	0.7649	1.6377	2.3534	3.1824	4.5407	5.8409
4	0.7407	1.5332	2.1318	2.7764	3.7469	4.6041
5	0.7267	1.4759	2.0150	2.5706	3.3649	4.0322
6	0.7176	1.4398	1.9432	2.4469	3.1427	3.7074
7	0.7111	1.4149	1.8946	2.3646	2.9980	3.4995
8	0.7064	1.3968	1.8595	2.3060	2.8965	3.3554
9	0.7027	1.3830	1.8331	2.2622	2.8214	3.2498
10	0.6998	1.3722	1.8125	2.2281	2.7638	3.1693
11	0.6974	1.3634	1.7959	2.2010	2.7181	3.1058
12	0.6955	1.3562	1.7823	2.1788	2.6810	3.0545
13	0.6938	1.3502	1.7709	2.1604	2.6503	3.0123
14	0.6924	1.3450	1.7613	2.1448	2.6245	2.9768
15	0.6912	1.3406	1.7531	2.1315	2.6025	2.9467
16	0.6901	1.3368	1.7459	2.1199	2.5835	2.9208
17	0.6892	1.3334	1.7396	2.1098	2.5669	2.8982
18	0.6884	1.3304	1.7341	2.1009	2.5524	2.8784
19	0.6876	1.3277	1.7291	2.0930	2.5395	2.8609
20	0.6870	1.3253	1.7247	2.0860	2.5280	2.8453
21	0.6864	1.3232	1.7207	2.0796	2.5177	2.8314
22	0.6858	1.3212	1.7171	2.0739	2.5083	2.8188
23	0.6853	1.3195	1.7139	2.0687	2.4999	2.8073
24	0.6848	1.3178	1.7109	2.0639	2.4922	2.7969
25	0.6844	1.3163	1.7081	2.0595	2.4851	2.7874
26	0.6840	1.3150	1.7056	2.0555	2.4786	2.7787
27	0.6837	1.3137	1.7033	2.0518	2.4727	2.7707
28	0.6834	1.3125	1.7011	2.0484	2.4671	2.7633
29	0.6830	1.3114	1.6991	2.0452	2.4620	2.7564
30	0.6828	1.3104	1.6973	2.0423	2.4573	2.7500
31	0.6825	1.3095	1.6955	2.0395	2.4528	2.7440
32	0.6822	1.3086	1.6939	2.0369	2.4487	2.7385
33	0.6820	1.3077	1.6924	2.0345	2.4448	2.7333
34	0.6818	1.3070	1.6909	2.0322	2.4411	2.7284
35	0.6816	1.3062	1.6896	2.0301	2.4377	2.7238
36	0.6814	1.3055	1.6883	2.0281	2.4345	2.7195
37	0.6812	1.3049	1.6871	2.0262	2.4314	2.7154
38	0.6810	1.3042	1.6860	2.0244	2.4286	2.7116
39	0.6808	1.3036	1.6849	2.0227	2.4258	2.7079
40	0.6807	1.3031	1.6839	2.0211	2.4233	2.7045
41	0.6805	1.3025	1.6829	2.0195	2.4208	2.7012
42	0.6804	1.3020	1.6820	2.0181	2.4185	2.6981
43	0.6802	1.3016	1.6811	2.0167	2.4163	2.6951
44	0.6801	1.3011	1.6802	2.0154	2.4141	2.6923
45	0.6800	1.3006	1.6794	2.0141	2.4121	2.6896
46	0.6799	1.3002	1.6787	2.0129	2.4102	2.6870
47	0.6797	1.2998	1.6779	2.0117	2.4083	2.6846
48	0.6796	1.2994	1.6772	2.0106	2.4066	2.6822

Degrees of Freedom	Cumulative Probabilities					
	0.75	0.90	0.95	0.975	0.99	0.995
	Upper-Tail Areas					
	0.25	0.10	0.05	0.025	0.01	0.005
49	0.6795	1.2991	1.6766	2.0096	2.4049	2.6800
50	0.6794	1.2987	1.6759	2.0086	2.4033	2.6778
51	0.6793	1.2984	1.6753	2.0076	2.4017	2.6757
52	0.6792	1.2980	1.6747	2.0066	2.4002	2.6737
53	0.6791	1.2977	1.6741	2.0057	2.3988	2.6718
54	0.6791	1.2974	1.6736	2.0049	2.3974	2.6700
55	0.6790	1.2971	1.6730	2.0040	2.3961	2.6682
56	0.6789	1.2969	1.6725	2.0032	2.3948	2.6665
57	0.6788	1.2966	1.6720	2.0025	2.3936	2.6649
58	0.6787	1.2963	1.6716	2.0017	2.3924	2.6633
59	0.6787	1.2961	1.6711	2.0010	2.3912	2.6618
60	0.6786	1.2958	1.6706	2.0003	2.3901	2.6603
61	0.6785	1.2956	1.6702	1.9996	2.3890	2.6589
62	0.6785	1.2954	1.6698	1.9990	2.3880	2.6575
63	0.6784	1.2951	1.6694	1.9983	2.3870	2.6561
64	0.6783	1.2949	1.6690	1.9977	2.3860	2.6549
65	0.6783	1.2947	1.6686	1.9971	2.3851	2.6536
66	0.6782	1.2945	1.6683	1.9966	2.3842	2.6524
67	0.6782	1.2943	1.6679	1.9960	2.3833	2.6512
68	0.6781	1.2941	1.6676	1.9955	2.3824	2.6501
69	0.6781	1.2939	1.6672	1.9949	2.3816	2.6490
70	0.6780	1.2938	1.6669	1.9944	2.3808	2.6479
71	0.6780	1.2936	1.6666	1.9939	2.3800	2.6469
72	0.6779	1.2934	1.6663	1.9935	2.3793	2.6459
73	0.6779	1.2933	1.6660	1.9930	2.3785	2.6449
74	0.6778	1.2931	1.6657	1.9925	2.3778	2.6439
75	0.6778	1.2929	1.6654	1.9921	2.3771	2.6430
76	0.6777	1.2928	1.6652	1.9917	2.3764	2.6421
77	0.6777	1.2926	1.6649	1.9913	2.3758	2.6412
78	0.6776	1.2925	1.6646	1.9908	2.3751	2.6403
79	0.6776	1.2924	1.6644	1.9905	2.3745	2.6395
80	0.6776	1.2922	1.6641	1.9901	2.3739	2.6387
81	0.6775	1.2921	1.6639	1.9897	2.3733	2.6379
82	0.6775	1.2920	1.6636	1.9893	2.3727	2.6371
83	0.6775	1.2918	1.6634	1.9890	2.3721	2.6364
84	0.6774	1.2917	1.6632	1.9886	2.3716	2.6356
85	0.6774	1.2916	1.6630	1.9883	2.3710	2.6349
86	0.6774	1.2915	1.6628	1.9879	2.3705	2.6342
87	0.6773	1.2914	1.6626	1.9876	2.3700	2.6335
88	0.6773	1.2912	1.6624	1.9873	2.3695	2.6329
89	0.6773	1.2911	1.6622	1.9870	2.3690	2.6322
90	0.6772	1.2910	1.6620	1.9867	2.3685	2.6316
91	0.6772	1.2909	1.6618	1.9864	2.3680	2.6309
92	0.6772	1.2908	1.6616	1.9861	2.3676	2.6303
93	0.6771	1.2907	1.6614	1.9858	2.3671	2.6297
94	0.6771	1.2906	1.6612	1.9855	2.3667	2.6291
95	0.6771	1.2905	1.6611	1.9853	2.3662	2.6286
96	0.6771	1.2904	1.6609	1.9850	2.3658	2.6280
97	0.6770	1.2903	1.6607	1.9847	2.3654	2.6275
98	0.6770	1.2902	1.6606	1.9845	2.3650	2.6269
99	0.6770	1.2902	1.6604	1.9842	2.3646	2.6264
100	0.6770	1.2901	1.6602	1.9840	2.3642	2.6259
110	0.6767	1.2893	1.6588	1.9818	2.3607	2.6213
120	0.6765	1.2886	1.6577	1.9799	2.3578	2.6174
∞	0.6745	1.2816	1.6449	1.9600	2.3263	2.5758

TABLE E.4

Critical Values of χ^2

For a particular number of degrees of freedom, entry represents the critical value of χ^2 corresponding to the cumulative probability $(1 - \alpha)$ and a specified upper-tail area (α).

Degrees of Freedom	**Cumulative Probabilities**											
	0.005	0.01	0.025	0.05	0.10	0.25	0.75	0.90	0.95	0.975	0.99	0.995
	Upper-Tail Areas (α)											
	0.995	0.99	0.975	0.95	0.90	0.75	0.25	0.10	0.05	0.025	0.01	0.005
1			0.001	0.004	0.016	0.102	1.323	2.706	3.841	5.024	6.635	7.879
2	0.010	0.020	0.051	0.103	0.211	0.575	2.773	4.605	5.991	7.378	9.210	10.597
3	0.072	0.115	0.216	0.352	0.584	1.213	4.108	6.251	7.815	9.348	11.345	12.838
4	0.207	0.297	0.484	0.711	1.064	1.923	5.385	7.779	9.488	11.143	13.277	14.860
5	0.412	0.554	0.831	1.145	1.610	2.675	6.626	9.236	11.071	12.833	15.086	16.750
6	0.676	0.872	1.237	1.635	2.204	3.455	7.841	10.645	12.592	14.449	16.812	18.548
7	0.989	1.239	1.690	2.167	2.833	4.255	9.037	12.017	14.067	16.013	18.475	20.278
8	1.344	1.646	2.180	2.733	3.490	5.071	10.219	13.362	15.507	17.535	20.090	21.955
9	1.735	2.088	2.700	3.325	4.168	5.899	11.389	14.684	16.919	19.023	21.666	23.589
10	2.156	2.558	3.247	3.940	4.865	6.737	12.549	15.987	18.307	20.483	23.209	25.188
11	2.603	3.053	3.816	4.575	5.578	7.584	13.701	17.275	19.675	21.920	24.725	26.757
12	3.074	3.571	4.404	5.226	6.304	8.438	14.845	18.549	21.026	23.337	26.217	28.299
13	3.565	4.107	5.009	5.892	7.042	9.299	15.984	19.812	22.362	24.736	27.688	29.819
14	4.075	4.660	5.629	6.571	7.790	10.165	17.117	21.064	23.685	26.119	29.141	31.319
15	4.601	5.229	6.262	7.261	8.547	11.037	18.245	22.307	24.996	27.488	30.578	32.801
16	5.142	5.812	6.908	7.962	9.312	11.912	19.369	23.542	26.296	28.845	32.000	34.267
17	5.697	6.408	7.564	8.672	10.085	12.792	20.489	24.769	27.587	30.191	33.409	35.718
18	6.265	7.015	8.231	9.390	10.865	13.675	21.605	25.989	28.869	31.526	34.805	37.156
19	6.844	7.633	8.907	10.117	11.651	14.562	22.718	27.204	30.144	32.852	36.191	38.582
20	7.434	8.260	9.591	10.851	12.443	15.452	23.828	28.412	31.410	34.170	37.566	39.997
21	8.034	8.897	10.283	11.591	13.240	16.344	24.935	29.615	32.671	35.479	38.932	41.401
22	8.643	9.542	10.982	12.338	14.042	17.240	26.039	30.813	33.924	36.781	40.289	42.796
23	9.260	10.196	11.689	13.091	14.848	18.137	27.141	32.007	35.172	38.076	41.638	44.181
24	9.886	10.856	12.401	13.848	15.659	19.037	28.241	33.196	36.415	39.364	42.980	45.559
25	10.520	11.524	13.120	14.611	16.473	19.939	29.339	34.382	37.652	40.646	44.314	46.928
26	11.160	12.198	13.844	15.379	17.292	20.843	30.435	35.563	38.885	41.923	45.642	48.290
27	11.808	12.879	14.573	16.151	18.114	21.749	31.528	36.741	40.113	43.194	46.963	49.645
28	12.461	13.565	15.308	16.928	18.939	22.657	32.620	37.916	41.337	44.461	48.278	50.993
29	13.121	14.257	16.047	17.708	19.768	23.567	33.711	39.087	42.557	45.722	49.588	52.336
30	13.787	14.954	16.791	18.493	20.599	24.478	34.800	40.256	43.773	46.979	50.892	53.672

For larger values of degrees of freedom (df) the expression $Z = \sqrt{2\chi^2} - \sqrt{2(df) - 1}$ may be used and the resulting upper-tail area can be found from the cumulative standardized normal distribution (Table E.2).

α = 0.05

TABLE E.5

Critical Values of F

For a particular combination of numerator and denominator degrees of freedom, entry represents the critical values of F corresponding to the cumulative probability $(1 - \alpha)$ and a specified upper-tail area (α).

Cumulative Probabilities = 0.95

Upper-Tail Areas = 0.05

Numerator, df_1

Denominator, df_2	1	2	3	4	5	6	7	8	9	10	12	15	20	24	30	40	60	120	∞
1	161.40	199.50	215.70	224.60	230.20	234.00	236.80	238.90	240.50	241.90	243.90	245.90	248.00	249.10	250.10	251.10	252.20	253.30	254.30
2	18.51	19.00	19.16	19.25	19.30	19.33	19.35	19.37	19.38	19.40	19.41	19.43	19.45	19.45	19.46	19.47	19.48	19.49	19.50
3	10.13	9.55	9.28	9.12	9.01	8.94	8.89	8.85	8.81	8.79	8.74	8.70	8.66	8.64	8.62	8.59	8.57	8.55	8.53
4	7.71	6.94	6.59	6.39	6.26	6.16	6.09	6.04	6.00	5.96	5.91	5.86	5.80	5.77	5.75	5.72	5.69	5.66	5.63
5	6.61	5.79	5.41	5.19	5.05	4.95	4.88	4.82	4.77	4.74	4.68	4.62	4.56	4.53	4.50	4.46	4.43	4.40	4.36
6	5.99	5.14	4.76	4.53	4.39	4.28	4.21	4.15	4.10	4.06	4.00	3.94	3.87	3.84	3.81	3.77	3.74	3.70	3.67
7	5.59	4.74	4.35	4.12	3.97	3.87	3.79	3.73	3.68	3.64	3.57	3.51	3.44	3.41	3.38	3.34	3.30	3.27	3.23
8	5.32	4.46	4.07	3.84	3.69	3.58	3.50	3.44	3.39	3.35	3.28	3.22	3.15	3.12	3.08	3.04	3.01	2.97	2.93
9	5.12	4.26	3.86	3.63	3.48	3.37	3.29	3.23	3.18	3.14	3.07	3.01	2.94	2.90	2.86	2.83	2.79	2.75	2.71
10	4.96	4.10	3.71	3.48	3.33	3.22	3.14	3.07	3.02	2.98	2.91	2.85	2.77	2.74	2.70	2.66	2.62	2.58	2.54
11	4.84	3.98	3.59	3.36	3.20	3.09	3.01	2.95	2.90	2.85	2.79	2.72	2.65	2.61	2.57	2.53	2.49	2.45	2.40
12	4.75	3.89	3.49	3.26	3.11	3.00	2.91	2.85	2.80	2.75	2.69	2.62	2.54	2.51	2.47	2.43	2.38	2.34	2.30
13	4.67	3.81	3.41	3.18	3.03	2.92	2.83	2.77	2.71	2.67	2.60	2.53	2.46	2.42	2.38	2.34	2.30	2.25	2.21
14	4.60	3.74	3.34	3.11	2.96	2.85	2.76	2.70	2.65	2.60	2.53	2.46	2.39	2.35	2.31	2.27	2.22	2.18	2.13
15	4.54	3.68	3.29	3.06	2.90	2.79	2.71	2.64	2.59	2.54	2.48	2.40	2.33	2.29	2.25	2.20	2.16	2.11	2.07
16	4.49	3.63	3.24	3.01	2.85	2.74	2.66	2.59	2.54	2.49	2.42	2.35	2.28	2.24	2.19	2.15	2.11	2.06	2.01
17	4.45	3.59	3.20	2.96	2.81	2.70	2.61	2.55	2.49	2.45	2.38	2.31	2.23	2.19	2.15	2.10	2.06	2.01	1.96
18	4.41	3.55	3.16	2.93	2.77	2.66	2.58	2.51	2.46	2.41	2.34	2.27	2.19	2.15	2.11	2.06	2.02	1.97	1.92
19	4.38	3.52	3.13	2.90	2.74	2.63	2.54	2.48	2.42	2.38	2.31	2.23	2.16	2.11	2.07	2.03	1.98	1.93	1.83
20	4.35	3.49	3.10	2.87	2.71	2.60	2.51	2.45	2.39	2.35	2.28	2.20	2.12	2.08	2.04	1.99	1.95	1.90	1.84
21	4.32	3.47	3.07	2.84	2.68	2.57	2.49	2.42	2.37	2.32	2.25	2.18	2.10	2.05	2.01	1.96	1.92	1.87	1.81
22	4.30	3.44	3.05	2.82	2.66	2.55	2.46	2.40	2.34	2.30	2.23	2.15	2.07	2.03	1.98	1.91	1.89	1.84	1.78
23	4.28	3.42	3.03	2.80	2.64	2.53	2.44	2.37	2.32	2.27	2.20	2.13	2.05	2.01	1.96	1.91	1.86	1.81	1.76
24	4.26	3.40	3.01	2.78	2.62	2.51	2.42	2.36	2.30	2.25	2.18	2.11	2.03	1.98	1.94	1.89	1.84	1.79	1.73
25	4.24	3.39	2.99	2.76	2.60	2.49	2.40	2.34	2.28	2.24	2.16	2.09	2.01	1.96	1.92	1.87	1.82	1.77	1.71
26	4.23	3.37	2.98	2.74	2.59	2.47	2.39	2.32	2.27	2.22	2.15	2.07	1.99	1.95	1.90	1.85	1.80	1.75	1.69
27	4.21	3.35	2.96	2.73	2.57	2.46	2.37	2.31	2.25	2.20	2.13	2.06	1.97	1.93	1.88	1.84	1.79	1.73	1.67
28	4.20	3.34	2.95	2.71	2.56	2.45	2.36	2.29	2.24	2.19	2.12	2.04	1.96	1.91	1.87	1.82	1.77	1.71	1.65
29	4.18	3.33	2.93	2.70	2.55	2.43	2.35	2.28	2.22	2.18	2.10	2.03	1.94	1.90	1.85	1.81	1.75	1.70	1.64
30	4.17	3.32	2.92	2.69	2.53	2.42	2.33	2.27	2.21	2.16	2.09	2.01	1.93	1.89	1.84	1.79	1.74	1.68	1.62
40	4.08	3.23	2.84	2.61	2.45	2.34	2.25	2.18	2.12	2.08	2.00	1.92	1.84	1.79	1.74	1.69	1.64	1.58	1.51
60	4.00	3.15	2.76	2.53	2.37	2.25	2.17	2.10	2.04	1.99	1.92	1.84	1.75	1.70	1.65	1.59	1.53	1.47	1.39
120	3.92	3.07	2.68	2.45	2.29	2.17	2.09	2.02	1.96	1.91	1.83	1.75	1.66	1.61	1.55	1.50	1.43	1.35	1.25
∞	3.84	3.00	2.60	2.37	2.21	2.10	2.01	1.94	1.88	1.83	1.75	1.67	1.57	1.52	1.46	1.39	1.32	1.22	1.00

$\alpha = 0.025$

Upper-Tail Areas = 0.025

Denominator, df_2	Numerator, df_1																		
	1	2	3	4	5	6	7	8	9	10	12	15	20	24	30	40	60	120	∞
1	647.80	799.50	864.20	899.60	921.80	937.10	948.20	956.70	963.30	968.60	976.70	984.90	993.10	997.20	1,001.00	1,006.00	1,010.00	1,014.00	1,018.00
2	38.51	39.00	39.17	39.25	39.30	39.33	39.36	39.39	39.39	39.40	39.41	39.43	39.45	39.46	39.46	39.47	39.48	39.49	39.50
3	17.44	16.04	15.44	15.10	14.88	14.73	14.62	14.54	14.47	14.42	14.34	14.25	14.17	14.12	14.08	14.04	13.99	13.95	13.90
4	12.22	10.65	9.98	9.60	9.36	9.20	9.07	8.98	8.90	8.84	8.75	8.66	8.56	8.51	8.46	8.41	8.36	8.31	8.26
5	10.01	8.43	7.76	7.39	7.15	6.98	6.85	6.76	6.68	6.62	6.52	6.43	6.33	6.28	6.23	6.18	6.12	6.07	6.02
6	8.81	7.26	6.60	6.23	5.99	5.82	5.70	5.60	5.52	5.46	5.37	5.27	5.17	5.12	5.07	5.01	4.96	4.90	4.85
7	8.07	6.54	5.89	5.52	5.29	5.12	4.99	4.90	4.82	4.76	4.67	4.57	4.47	4.42	4.36	4.31	4.25	4.20	4.14
8	7.57	6.06	5.42	5.05	4.82	4.65	4.53	4.43	4.36	4.30	4.20	4.10	4.00	3.95	3.89	3.84	3.78	3.73	3.67
9	7.21	5.71	5.08	4.72	4.48	4.32	4.20	4.10	4.03	3.96	3.87	3.77	3.67	3.61	3.56	3.51	3.45	3.39	3.33
10	6.94	5.46	4.83	4.47	4.24	4.07	3.95	3.85	3.78	3.72	3.62	3.52	3.42	3.37	3.31	3.26	3.20	3.14	3.08
11	6.72	5.26	4.63	4.28	4.04	3.88	3.76	3.66	3.59	3.53	3.43	3.33	3.23	3.17	3.12	3.06	3.00	2.94	2.88
12	6.55	5.10	4.47	4.12	3.89	3.73	3.61	3.51	3.44	3.37	3.28	3.18	3.07	3.02	2.96	2.91	2.85	2.79	2.72
13	6.41	4.97	4.35	4.00	3.77	3.60	3.48	3.39	3.31	3.25	3.15	3.05	2.95	2.89	2.84	2.78	2.72	2.66	2.60
14	6.30	4.86	4.24	3.89	3.66	3.50	3.38	3.29	3.21	3.15	3.05	2.95	2.84	2.79	2.73	2.67	2.61	2.55	2.49
15	6.20	4.77	4.15	3.80	3.58	3.41	3.29	3.20	3.12	3.06	2.96	2.86	2.76	2.70	2.64	2.59	2.52	2.46	2.40
16	6.12	4.69	4.08	3.73	3.50	3.34	3.22	3.12	3.05	2.99	2.89	2.79	2.68	2.63	2.57	2.51	2.45	2.38	2.32
17	6.04	4.62	4.01	3.66	3.44	3.28	3.16	3.06	2.98	2.92	2.82	2.72	2.62	2.56	2.50	2.44	2.38	2.32	2.25
18	5.98	4.56	3.95	3.61	3.38	3.22	3.10	3.01	2.93	2.87	2.77	2.67	2.56	2.50	2.44	2.38	2.32	2.26	2.19
19	5.92	4.51	3.90	3.56	3.33	3.17	3.05	2.96	2.88	2.82	2.72	2.62	2.51	2.45	2.39	2.33	2.27	2.20	2.13
20	5.87	4.46	3.86	3.51	3.29	3.13	3.01	2.91	2.84	2.77	2.68	2.57	2.46	2.41	2.35	2.29	2.22	2.16	2.09
21	5.83	4.42	3.82	3.48	3.25	3.09	2.97	2.87	2.80	2.73	2.64	2.53	2.42	2.37	2.31	2.25	2.18	2.11	2.04
22	5.79	4.38	3.78	3.44	3.22	3.05	2.93	2.84	2.76	2.70	2.60	2.50	2.39	2.33	2.27	2.21	2.14	2.08	2.00
23	5.75	4.35	3.75	3.41	3.18	3.02	2.90	2.81	2.73	2.67	2.57	2.47	2.36	2.30	2.24	2.18	2.11	2.04	1.97
24	5.72	4.32	3.72	3.38	3.15	2.99	2.87	2.78	2.70	2.64	2.54	2.44	2.33	2.27	2.21	2.15	2.08	2.01	1.94
25	5.69	4.29	3.69	3.35	3.13	2.97	2.85	2.75	2.68	2.61	2.51	2.41	2.30	2.24	2.18	2.12	2.05	1.98	1.91
26	5.66	4.27	3.67	3.33	3.10	2.94	2.82	2.73	2.65	2.59	2.49	2.39	2.28	2.22	2.16	2.09	2.03	1.95	1.88
27	5.63	4.24	3.65	3.31	3.08	2.92	2.80	2.71	2.63	2.57	2.47	2.36	2.25	2.19	2.13	2.07	2.00	1.93	1.85
28	5.61	4.22	3.63	3.29	3.06	2.90	2.78	2.69	2.61	2.55	2.45	2.34	2.23	2.17	2.11	2.05	1.98	1.91	1.83
29	5.59	4.20	3.61	3.27	3.04	2.88	2.76	2.67	2.59	2.53	2.43	2.32	2.21	2.15	2.09	2.03	1.96	1.89	1.81
30	5.57	4.18	3.59	3.25	3.03	2.87	2.75	2.65	2.57	2.51	2.41	2.31	2.20	2.14	2.07	2.01	1.94	1.87	1.79
40	5.42	4.05	3.46	3.13	2.90	2.74	2.62	2.53	2.45	2.39	2.29	2.18	2.07	2.01	1.94	1.88	1.80	1.72	1.64
60	5.29	3.93	3.34	3.01	2.79	2.63	2.51	2.41	2.33	2.27	2.17	2.06	1.94	1.88	1.82	1.74	1.67	1.58	1.48
120	5.15	3.80	3.23	2.89	2.67	2.52	2.39	2.30	2.22	2.16	2.05	1.94	1.82	1.76	1.69	1.61	1.53	1.43	1.31
∞	5.02	3.69	3.12	2.79	2.57	2.41	2.29	2.19	2.11	2.05	1.94	1.83	1.71	1.64	1.57	1.48	1.39	1.27	1.00

continued

TABLE E.5
Critical Values of F (continued)

Cumulative Probabilities = 0.99

Upper-Tail Areas = 0.01

Denominator, df_2	Numerator, df_1																		
	1	2	3	4	5	6	7	8	9	10	12	15	20	24	30	40	60	120	∞
1	4,052.00	4,999.50	5,403.00	5,625.00	5,764.00	5,859.00	5,928.00	5,982.00	6,022.00	6,056.00	6,106.00	6,157.00	6,209.00	6,235.00	6,261.00	6,287.00	6,313.00	6,339.00	6,366.00
2	98.50	99.00	99.17	99.25	99.30	99.33	99.36	99.37	99.39	99.40	99.42	99.43	44.45	99.46	99.47	99.47	99.48	99.49	99.50
3	34.12	30.82	29.46	28.71	28.24	27.91	27.67	27.49	27.35	27.23	27.05	26.87	26.69	26.60	26.50	26.41	26.32	26.22	26.13
4	21.20	18.00	16.69	15.98	15.52	15.21	14.98	14.80	14.66	14.55	14.37	14.20	14.02	13.93	13.84	13.75	13.65	13.56	13.46
5	16.26	13.27	12.06	11.39	10.97	10.67	10.46	10.29	10.16	10.05	9.89	9.72	9.55	9.47	9.38	9.29	9.20	9.11	9.02
6	13.75	10.92	9.78	9.15	8.75	8.47	8.26	8.10	7.98	7.87	7.72	7.56	7.40	7.31	7.23	7.14	7.06	6.97	6.88
7	12.25	9.55	8.45	7.85	7.46	7.19	6.99	6.84	6.72	6.62	6.47	6.31	6.16	6.07	5.99	5.91	5.82	5.74	5.65
8	11.26	8.65	7.59	7.01	6.63	6.37	6.18	6.03	5.91	5.81	5.67	5.52	5.36	5.28	5.20	5.12	5.03	4.95	4.86
9	10.56	8.02	6.99	6.42	6.06	5.80	5.61	5.47	5.35	5.26	5.11	4.96	4.81	4.73	4.65	4.57	4.48	4.40	4.31
10	10.04	7.56	6.55	5.99	5.64	5.39	5.20	5.06	4.94	4.85	4.71	4.56	4.41	4.33	4.25	4.17	4.08	4.00	3.91
11	9.65	7.21	6.22	5.67	5.32	5.07	4.89	4.74	4.63	4.54	4.40	4.25	4.10	4.02	3.94	3.86	3.78	3.69	3.60
12	9.33	6.93	5.95	5.41	5.06	4.82	4.64	4.50	4.39	4.30	4.16	4.01	3.86	3.78	3.70	3.62	3.54	3.45	3.36
13	9.07	6.70	5.74	5.21	4.86	4.62	4.44	4.30	4.19	4.10	3.96	3.82	3.66	3.59	3.51	3.43	3.34	3.25	3.17
14	8.86	6.51	5.56	5.04	4.69	4.46	4.28	4.14	4.03	3.94	3.80	3.66	3.51	3.43	3.35	3.27	3.18	3.09	3.00
15	8.68	6.36	5.42	4.89	4.56	4.32	4.14	4.00	3.89	3.80	3.67	3.52	3.37	3.29	3.21	3.13	3.05	2.96	2.87
16	8.53	6.23	5.29	4.77	4.44	4.20	4.03	3.89	3.78	3.69	3.55	3.41	3.26	3.18	3.10	3.02	2.93	2.81	2.75
17	8.40	6.11	5.18	4.67	4.34	4.10	3.93	3.79	3.68	3.59	3.46	3.31	3.16	3.08	3.00	2.92	2.83	2.75	2.65
18	8.29	6.01	5.09	4.58	4.25	4.01	3.84	3.71	3.60	3.51	3.37	3.23	3.08	3.00	2.92	2.84	2.75	2.66	2.57
19	8.18	5.93	5.01	4.50	4.17	3.94	3.77	3.63	3.52	3.43	3.30	3.15	3.00	2.92	2.84	2.76	2.67	2.58	2.49
20	8.10	5.85	4.94	4.43	4.10	3.87	3.70	3.56	3.46	3.37	3.23	3.09	2.94	2.86	2.78	2.69	2.61	2.52	2.42
21	8.02	5.78	4.87	4.37	4.04	3.81	3.64	3.51	3.40	3.31	3.17	3.03	2.88	2.80	2.72	2.64	2.55	2.46	2.36
22	7.95	5.72	4.82	4.31	3.99	3.76	3.59	3.45	3.35	3.26	3.12	2.98	2.83	2.75	2.67	2.58	2.50	2.40	2.31
23	7.88	5.66	4.76	4.26	3.94	3.71	3.54	3.41	3.30	3.21	3.07	2.93	2.78	2.70	2.62	2.54	2.45	2.35	2.26
24	7.82	5.61	4.72	4.22	3.90	3.67	3.50	3.36	3.26	3.17	3.03	2.89	2.74	2.66	2.58	2.49	2.40	2.31	2.21
25	7.77	5.57	4.68	4.18	3.85	3.63	3.46	3.32	3.22	3.13	2.99	2.85	2.70	2.62	2.54	2.45	2.36	2.27	2.17
26	7.72	5.53	4.64	4.14	3.82	3.59	3.42	3.29	3.18	3.09	2.96	2.81	2.66	2.58	2.50	2.42	2.33	2.23	2.13
27	7.68	5.49	4.60	4.11	3.78	3.56	3.39	3.26	3.15	3.06	2.93	2.78	2.63	2.55	2.47	2.38	2.29	2.20	2.10
28	7.64	5.45	4.57	4.07	3.75	3.53	3.36	3.23	3.12	3.03	2.90	2.75	2.60	2.52	2.44	2.35	2.26	2.17	2.06
29	7.60	5.42	4.54	4.04	3.73	3.50	3.33	3.20	3.09	3.00	2.87	2.73	2.57	2.49	2.41	2.33	2.23	2.14	2.03
30	7.56	5.39	4.51	4.02	3.70	3.47	3.30	3.17	3.07	2.98	2.84	2.70	2.55	2.47	2.39	2.30	2.21	2.11	2.01
40	7.31	5.18	4.31	3.83	3.51	3.29	3.12	2.99	2.89	2.80	2.66	2.52	2.37	2.29	2.20	2.11	2.02	1.92	1.80
60	7.08	4.98	4.13	3.65	3.34	3.12	2.95	2.82	2.72	2.63	2.50	2.35	2.20	2.12	2.03	1.94	1.84	1.73	1.60
120	6.85	4.79	3.95	3.48	3.17	2.96	2.79	2.66	2.56	2.47	2.34	2.19	2.03	1.95	1.86	1.76	1.66	1.53	1.38
∞	6.63	4.61	3.78	3.32	3.02	2.80	2.64	2.51	2.41	2.32	2.18	2.04	1.88	1.79	1.70	1.59	1.47	1.32	1.00

$\alpha = 0.01$

Cumulative Probabilities = 0.995

Upper-Tail Areas = 0.005

Denominator, df_2	\multicolumn{19}{c}{Numerator, df_1}

df_2	1	2	3	4	5	6	7	8	9	10	12	15	20	24	30	40	60	120	∞
1	16,211.00	20,000.00	21,615.00	22,500.00	23,056.00	23,437.00	23,715.00	23,925.00	24,091.00	24,224.00	24,426.00	24,630.00	24,836.00	24,910.00	25,044.00	25,148.00	25,253.00	25,359.00	25,465.00
2	198.50	199.00	199.20	199.20	199.30	199.30	199.40	199.40	199.40	199.40	199.40	199.40	199.40	199.50	199.50	199.50	199.50	199.50	199.50
3	55.55	49.80	47.47	46.19	45.39	44.84	44.43	44.13	43.88	43.69	43.39	43.08	42.78	42.62	42.47	42.31	42.15	41.99	41.83
4	31.33	26.28	24.26	23.15	22.46	21.97	21.62	21.35	21.14	20.97	20.70	20.44	20.17	20.03	19.89	19.75	19.61	19.47	19.32
5	22.78	18.31	16.53	15.56	14.94	14.51	14.20	13.96	13.77	13.62	13.38	13.15	12.90	12.78	12.66	12.53	12.40	12.27	12.11
6	18.63	14.54	12.92	12.03	11.46	11.07	10.79	10.57	10.39	10.25	10.03	9.81	9.59	9.47	9.36	9.24	9.12	9.00	8.88
7	16.24	12.40	10.88	10.05	9.52	9.16	8.89	8.68	8.51	8.38	8.18	7.97	7.75	7.65	7.53	7.42	7.31	7.19	7.08
8	14.69	11.04	9.60	8.81	8.30	7.95	7.69	7.50	7.34	7.21	7.01	6.81	6.61	6.50	6.40	6.29	6.18	6.06	5.95
9	13.61	10.11	8.72	7.96	7.47	7.13	6.88	6.69	6.54	6.42	6.23	6.03	5.83	5.73	5.62	5.52	5.41	5.30	5.19
10	12.83	9.43	8.08	7.34	6.87	6.54	6.30	6.12	5.97	5.85	5.66	5.47	5.27	5.17	5.07	4.97	4.86	4.75	4.61
11	12.23	8.91	7.60	6.88	6.42	6.10	5.86	5.68	5.54	5.42	5.24	5.05	4.86	4.75	4.65	4.55	4.44	4.34	4.23
12	11.75	8.51	7.23	6.52	6.07	5.76	5.52	5.35	5.20	5.09	4.91	4.72	4.53	4.43	4.33	4.23	4.12	4.01	3.90
13	11.37	8.19	6.93	6.23	5.79	5.48	5.25	5.08	4.94	4.82	4.64	4.46	4.27	4.17	4.07	3.97	3.87	3.76	3.65
14	11.06	7.92	6.68	6.00	5.56	5.26	5.03	4.86	4.72	4.60	4.43	4.25	4.06	3.96	3.86	3.76	3.66	3.55	3.41
15	10.80	7.70	6.48	5.80	5.37	5.07	4.85	4.67	4.54	4.42	4.25	4.07	3.88	3.79	3.69	3.58	3.48	3.37	3.26
16	10.58	7.51	6.30	5.64	5.21	4.91	4.69	4.52	4.38	4.27	4.10	3.92	3.73	3.64	3.54	3.44	3.33	3.22	3.11
17	10.38	7.35	6.16	5.50	5.07	4.78	4.56	4.39	4.25	4.14	3.97	3.79	3.61	3.51	3.41	3.31	3.21	3.10	2.98
18	10.22	7.21	6.03	5.37	4.96	4.66	4.44	4.28	4.14	4.03	3.86	3.68	3.50	3.40	3.30	3.20	3.10	2.99	2.87
19	10.07	7.09	5.92	5.27	4.85	4.56	4.34	4.18	4.04	3.93	3.76	3.59	3.40	3.31	3.21	3.11	3.00	2.89	2.78
20	9.94	6.99	5.82	5.17	4.76	4.47	4.26	4.09	3.96	3.85	3.68	3.50	3.32	3.22	3.12	3.02	2.92	2.81	2.69
21	9.83	6.89	5.73	5.09	4.68	4.39	4.18	4.02	3.88	3.77	3.60	3.43	3.24	3.15	3.05	2.95	2.84	2.73	2.61
22	9.73	6.81	5.65	5.02	4.61	4.32	4.11	3.94	3.81	3.70	3.54	3.36	3.18	3.08	2.98	2.88	2.77	2.66	2.55
23	9.63	6.73	5.58	4.95	4.54	4.26	4.05	3.88	3.75	3.64	3.47	3.30	3.12	3.02	2.92	2.82	2.71	2.60	2.48
24	9.55	6.66	5.52	4.89	4.49	4.20	3.99	3.83	3.69	3.59	3.42	3.25	3.06	2.97	2.87	2.77	2.66	2.55	2.43
25	9.48	6.60	5.46	4.84	4.43	4.15	3.94	3.78	3.64	3.54	3.37	3.20	3.01	2.92	2.82	2.72	2.61	2.50	2.38
26	9.41	6.54	5.41	4.79	4.38	4.10	3.89	3.73	3.60	3.49	3.33	3.15	2.97	2.87	2.77	2.67	2.56	2.45	2.33
27	9.34	6.49	5.36	4.74	4.34	4.06	3.85	3.69	3.56	3.45	3.28	3.11	2.93	2.83	2.73	2.63	2.52	2.41	2.29
28	9.28	6.44	5.32	4.70	4.30	4.02	3.81	3.65	3.52	3.41	3.25	3.07	2.89	2.79	2.69	2.59	2.48	2.37	2.25
29	9.23	6.40	5.28	4.66	4.26	3.98	3.77	3.61	3.48	3.38	3.21	3.04	2.86	2.76	2.66	2.56	2.45	2.33	2.21
30	9.18	6.35	5.24	4.62	4.23	3.95	3.74	3.58	3.45	3.34	3.18	3.01	2.82	2.73	2.63	2.52	2.42	2.30	2.18
40	8.83	6.07	4.98	4.37	3.99	3.71	3.51	3.35	3.22	3.12	2.95	2.78	2.60	2.50	2.40	2.30	2.18	2.06	1.93
60	8.49	5.79	4.73	4.14	3.76	3.49	3.29	3.13	3.01	2.90	2.74	2.57	2.39	2.29	2.19	2.08	1.96	1.83	1.69
120	8.18	5.54	4.50	3.92	3.55	3.28	3.09	2.93	2.81	2.71	2.54	2.37	2.19	2.09	1.98	1.87	1.75	1.61	1.43
∞	7.88	5.30	4.28	3.72	3.35	3.09	2.90	2.74	2.62	2.52	2.36	2.19	2.00	1.90	1.79	1.67	1.53	1.36	1.00

Source: *Reprinted from E. S. Pearson and H. O. Hartley, eds., Biometrika Tables for Statisticians, 3rd ed., 1966, by permission of the Biometrika Trustees.*

TABLE E.6
Lower and Upper Critical Values, T_1, of the Wilcoxon Rank Sum Test

n_2	α One-tail	Two-tail	n_1 4	5	6	7	8	9	10
4	0.05	0.10	11,25						
	0.025	0.05	10,26						
	0.01	0.02	—,—						
	0.005	0.01	—,—						
5	0.05	0.10	12,28	19,36					
	0.025	0.05	11,29	17,38					
	0.01	0.02	10,30	16,39					
	0.005	0.01	—,—	15,40					
6	0.05	0.10	13,31	20,40	28,50				
	0.025	0.05	12,32	18,42	26,52				
	0.01	0.02	11,33	17,43	24,54				
	0.005	0.01	10,34	16,44	23,55				
7	0.05	0.10	14,34	21,44	29,55	39,66			
	0.025	0.05	13,35	20,45	27,57	36,69			
	0.01	0.02	11,37	18,47	25,59	34,71			
	0.005	0.01	10,38	16,49	24,60	32,73			
8	0.05	0.10	15,37	23,47	31,59	41,71	51,85		
	0.025	0.05	14,38	21,49	29,61	38,74	49,87		
	0.01	0.02	12,40	19,51	27,63	35,77	45,91		
	0.005	0.01	11,41	17,53	25,65	34,78	43,93		
9	0.05	0.10	16,40	24,51	33,63	43,76	54,90	66,105	
	0.025	0.05	14,42	22,53	31,65	40,79	51,93	62,109	
	0.01	0.02	13,43	20,55	28,68	37,82	47,97	59,112	
	0.005	0.01	11,45	18,57	26,70	35,84	45,99	56,115	
10	0.05	0.10	17,43	26,54	35,67	45,81	56,96	69,111	82,128
	0.025	0.05	15,45	23,57	32,70	42,84	53,99	65,115	78,132
	0.01	0.02	13,47	21,59	29,73	39,87	49,103	61,119	74,136
	0.005	0.01	12,48	19,61	27,75	37,89	47,105	58,122	71,139

Source: *Adapted from Table 1 of F. Wilcoxon and R. A. Wilcox,* Some Rapid Approximate Statistical Procedures *(Pearl River, NY: Lederle Laboratories, 1964), with permission of the American Cyanamid Company.*

TABLE E.7

Critical Values of the Studentized Range, Q

Upper 5% Points ($\alpha = 0.05$)

Denominator, df	Numerator, df																		
	2	3	4	5	6	7	8	9	10	11	12	13	14	15	16	17	18	19	20
1	18.00	27.00	32.80	37.10	40.40	43.10	45.40	47.40	49.10	50.60	52.00	53.20	54.30	55.40	56.30	57.20	58.00	58.80	59.60
2	6.09	8.30	9.80	10.90	11.70	12.40	13.00	13.50	14.00	14.40	14.70	15.10	15.40	15.70	15.90	16.10	16.40	16.60	16.80
3	4.50	5.91	6.82	7.50	8.04	8.48	8.85	9.18	9.46	9.72	9.95	10.15	10.35	10.52	10.69	10.84	10.98	11.11	11.24
4	3.93	5.04	5.76	6.29	6.71	7.05	7.35	7.60	7.83	8.03	8.21	8.37	8.52	8.66	8.79	8.91	9.03	9.13	9.23
5	3.64	4.60	5.22	5.67	6.03	6.33	6.58	6.80	6.99	7.17	7.32	7.47	7.60	7.72	7.83	7.93	8.03	8.12	8.21
6	3.46	4.34	4.90	5.31	5.63	5.89	6.12	6.32	6.49	6.65	6.79	6.92	7.03	7.14	7.24	7.34	7.43	7.51	7.59
7	3.34	4.16	4.68	5.06	5.36	5.61	5.82	6.00	6.16	6.30	6.43	6.55	6.66	6.76	6.85	6.94	7.02	7.09	7.17
8	3.26	4.04	4.53	4.89	5.17	5.40	5.60	5.77	5.92	6.05	6.18	6.29	6.39	6.48	6.57	6.65	6.73	6.80	6.87
9	3.20	3.95	4.42	4.76	5.02	5.24	5.43	5.60	5.74	5.87	5.98	6.09	6.19	6.28	6.36	6.44	6.51	6.58	6.64
10	3.15	3.88	4.33	4.65	4.91	5.12	5.30	5.46	5.60	5.72	5.83	5.93	6.03	6.11	6.20	6.27	6.34	6.40	6.47
11	3.11	3.82	4.26	4.57	4.82	5.03	5.20	5.35	5.49	5.61	5.71	5.81	5.90	5.99	6.06	6.14	6.20	6.26	6.33
12	3.08	3.77	4.20	4.51	4.75	4.95	5.12	5.27	5.40	5.51	5.62	5.71	5.80	5.88	5.95	6.03	6.09	6.15	6.21
13	3.06	3.73	4.15	4.45	4.69	4.88	5.05	5.19	5.32	5.43	5.53	5.63	5.71	5.79	5.86	5.93	6.00	6.05	6.11
14	3.03	3.70	4.11	4.41	4.64	4.83	4.99	5.13	5.25	5.36	5.46	5.55	5.64	5.72	5.79	5.85	5.92	5.97	6.03
15	3.01	3.67	4.08	4.37	4.60	4.78	4.94	5.08	5.20	5.31	5.40	5.49	5.58	5.65	5.72	5.79	5.85	5.90	5.96
16	3.00	3.65	4.05	4.33	4.56	4.74	4.90	5.03	5.15	5.26	5.35	5.44	5.52	5.59	5.66	5.72	5.79	5.84	5.90
17	2.98	3.63	4.02	4.30	4.52	4.71	4.86	4.99	5.11	5.21	5.31	5.39	5.47	5.55	5.61	5.68	5.74	5.79	5.84
18	2.97	3.61	4.00	4.28	4.49	4.67	4.82	4.96	5.07	5.17	5.27	5.35	5.43	5.50	5.57	5.63	5.69	5.74	5.79
19	2.96	3.59	3.98	4.25	4.47	4.65	4.79	4.92	5.04	5.14	5.23	5.32	5.39	5.46	5.53	5.59	5.65	5.70	5.75
20	2.95	3.58	3.96	4.23	4.45	4.62	4.77	4.90	5.01	5.11	5.20	5.28	5.36	5.43	5.49	5.55	5.61	5.66	5.71
24	2.92	3.53	3.90	4.17	4.37	4.54	4.68	4.81	4.92	5.01	5.10	5.18	5.25	5.32	5.38	5.44	5.50	5.54	5.59
30	2.89	3.49	3.84	4.10	4.30	4.46	4.60	4.72	4.83	4.92	5.00	5.08	5.15	5.21	5.27	5.33	5.38	5.43	5.48
40	2.86	3.44	3.79	4.04	4.23	4.39	4.52	4.63	4.74	4.82	4.91	4.98	5.05	5.11	5.16	5.22	5.27	5.31	5.36
60	2.83	3.40	3.74	3.98	4.16	4.31	4.44	4.55	4.65	4.73	4.81	4.88	4.94	5.00	5.06	5.11	5.16	5.20	5.24
120	2.80	3.36	3.69	3.92	4.10	4.24	4.36	4.48	4.56	4.64	4.72	4.78	4.84	4.90	4.95	5.00	5.05	5.09	5.13
∞	2.77	3.31	3.63	3.86	4.03	4.17	4.29	4.39	4.47	4.55	4.62	4.68	4.74	4.80	4.85	4.89	4.93	4.97	5.01

continued

TABLE E.7
Critical Values of the Studentized Range, Q (continued)

Upper 1% Points ($\alpha = 0.01$)

Denominator, df	\multicolumn{19}{c}{Numerator, df}
	2	3	4	5	6	7	8	9	10	11	12	13	14	15	16	17	18	19	20
1	90.00	135.00	164.00	186.00	202.00	216.00	227.00	237.00	246.00	253.00	260.00	266.00	272.00	277.00	282.00	286.00	290.00	294.00	298.00
2	14.00	19.00	22.30	24.70	26.60	28.20	29.50	30.70	31.70	32.60	33.40	34.10	34.80	35.40	36.00	36.50	37.00	37.50	37.90
3	8.26	10.60	12.20	13.30	14.20	15.00	15.60	16.20	16.70	17.10	17.50	17.90	18.20	18.50	18.80	19.10	19.30	19.50	19.80
4	6.51	8.12	9.17	9.96	10.60	11.10	11.50	11.90	12.30	12.60	12.80	13.10	13.30	13.50	13.70	13.90	14.10	14.20	14.40
5	5.70	6.97	7.80	8.42	8.91	9.32	9.67	9.97	10.24	10.48	10.70	10.89	11.08	11.24	11.40	11.55	11.68	11.81	11.93
6	5.24	6.33	7.03	7.56	7.97	8.32	8.61	8.87	9.10	9.30	9.49	9.65	9.81	9.95	10.08	10.21	10.32	10.43	10.54
7	4.95	5.92	6.54	7.01	7.37	7.68	7.94	8.17	8.37	8.55	8.71	8.86	9.00	9.12	9.24	9.35	9.46	9.55	9.65
8	4.74	5.63	6.20	6.63	6.96	7.24	7.47	7.68	7.87	8.03	8.18	8.31	8.44	8.55	8.66	8.76	8.85	8.94	9.03
9	4.60	5.43	5.96	6.35	6.66	6.91	7.13	7.32	7.49	7.65	7.78	7.91	8.03	8.13	8.23	8.32	8.41	8.49	8.57
10	4.48	5.27	5.77	6.14	6.43	6.67	6.87	7.05	7.21	7.36	7.48	7.60	7.71	7.81	7.91	7.99	8.07	8.15	8.22
11	4.39	5.14	5.62	5.97	6.26	6.48	6.67	6.84	6.99	7.13	7.25	7.36	7.46	7.56	7.65	7.73	7.81	7.88	7.95
12	4.32	5.04	5.50	5.84	6.10	6.32	6.51	6.67	6.81	6.94	7.06	7.17	7.26	7.36	7.44	7.52	7.59	7.66	7.73
13	4.26	4.96	5.40	5.73	5.98	6.19	6.37	6.53	6.67	6.79	6.90	7.01	7.10	7.19	7.27	7.34	7.42	7.48	7.55
14	4.21	4.89	5.32	5.63	5.88	6.08	6.26	6.41	6.54	6.66	6.77	6.87	6.96	7.05	7.12	7.20	7.27	7.33	7.39
15	4.17	4.83	5.25	5.56	5.80	5.99	6.16	6.31	6.44	6.55	6.66	6.76	6.84	6.93	7.00	7.07	7.14	7.20	7.26
16	4.13	4.78	5.19	5.49	5.72	5.92	6.08	6.22	6.35	6.46	6.56	6.66	6.74	6.82	6.90	6.97	7.03	7.09	7.15
17	4.10	4.74	5.14	5.43	5.66	5.85	6.01	6.15	6.27	6.38	6.48	6.57	6.66	6.73	6.80	6.87	6.94	7.00	7.05
18	4.07	4.70	5.09	5.38	5.60	5.79	5.94	6.08	6.20	6.31	6.41	6.50	6.58	6.65	6.72	6.79	6.85	6.91	6.96
19	4.05	4.67	5.05	5.33	5.55	5.73	5.89	6.02	6.14	6.25	6.34	6.43	6.51	6.58	6.65	6.72	6.78	6.84	6.89
20	4.02	4.64	5.02	5.29	5.51	5.69	5.84	5.97	6.09	6.19	6.29	6.37	6.45	6.52	6.59	6.65	6.71	6.76	6.82
24	3.96	4.54	4.91	5.17	5.37	5.54	5.69	5.81	5.92	6.02	6.11	6.19	6.26	6.33	6.39	6.45	6.51	6.56	6.61
30	3.89	4.45	4.80	5.05	5.24	5.40	5.54	5.65	5.76	5.85	5.93	6.01	6.08	6.14	6.20	6.26	6.31	6.36	6.41
40	3.82	4.37	4.70	4.93	5.11	5.27	5.39	5.50	5.60	5.69	5.77	5.84	5.90	5.96	6.02	6.07	6.12	6.17	6.21
60	3.76	4.28	4.60	4.82	4.99	5.13	5.25	5.36	5.45	5.53	5.60	5.67	5.73	5.79	5.84	5.89	5.93	5.98	6.02
120	3.70	4.20	4.50	4.71	4.87	5.01	5.12	5.21	5.30	5.38	5.44	5.51	5.56	5.61	5.66	5.71	5.75	5.79	5.83
∞	3.64	4.12	4.40	4.60	4.76	4.88	4.99	5.08	5.16	5.23	5.29	5.35	5.40	5.45	5.49	5.54	5.57	5.61	5.65

Source: Reprinted from E. S. Pearson and H. O. Hartley, eds., Table 29 of Biometrika Tables for Statisticians, Vol. 1, 3rd ed., 1966, by permission of the Biometrika Trustees, London.

TABLE E.8

Critical Values, d_L and d_U, of the Durbin-Watson Statistic, D (Critical Values Are One-Sided)[a]

| | $\alpha = 0.05$ | | | | | | | | | | $\alpha = 0.01$ | | | | | | | | | |
| | $k=1$ | | $k=2$ | | $k=3$ | | $k=4$ | | $k=5$ | | $k=1$ | | $k=2$ | | $k=3$ | | $k=4$ | | $k=5$ | |
n	d_L	d_U	d_L	d_U	d_L	d_U	d_L	d_U	d_L	d_U	d_L	d_U	d_L	d_U	d_L	d_U	d_L	d_U	d_L	d_U
15	1.08	1.36	.95	1.54	.82	1.75	.69	1.97	.56	2.21	.81	1.07	.70	1.25	.59	1.46	.49	1.70	.39	1.96
16	1.10	1.37	.98	1.54	.86	1.73	.74	1.93	.62	2.15	.84	1.09	.74	1.25	.63	1.44	.53	1.66	.44	1.90
17	1.13	1.38	1.02	1.54	.90	1.71	.78	1.90	.67	2.10	.87	1.10	.77	1.25	.67	1.43	.57	1.63	.48	1.85
18	1.16	1.39	1.05	1.53	.93	1.69	.82	1.87	.71	2.06	.90	1.12	.80	1.26	.71	1.42	.61	1.60	.52	1.80
19	1.18	1.40	1.08	1.53	.97	1.68	.86	1.85	.75	2.02	.93	1.13	.83	1.26	.74	1.41	.65	1.58	.56	1.77
20	1.20	1.41	1.10	1.54	1.00	1.68	.90	1.83	.79	1.99	.95	1.15	.86	1.27	.77	1.41	.68	1.57	.60	1.74
21	1.22	1.42	1.13	1.54	1.03	1.67	.93	1.81	.83	1.96	.97	1.16	.89	1.27	.80	1.41	.72	1.55	.63	1.71
22	1.24	1.43	1.15	1.54	1.05	1.66	.96	1.80	.86	1.94	1.00	1.17	.91	1.28	.83	1.40	.75	1.54	.66	1.69
23	1.26	1.44	1.17	1.54	1.08	1.66	.99	1.79	.90	1.92	1.02	1.19	.94	1.29	.86	1.40	.77	1.53	.70	1.67
24	1.27	1.45	1.19	1.55	1.10	1.66	1.01	1.78	.93	1.90	1.04	1.20	.96	1.30	.88	1.41	.80	1.53	.72	1.66
25	1.29	1.45	1.21	1.55	1.12	1.66	1.04	1.77	.95	1.89	1.05	1.21	.98	1.30	.90	1.41	.83	1.52	.75	1.65
26	1.30	1.46	1.22	1.55	1.14	1.65	1.06	1.76	.98	1.88	1.07	1.22	1.00	1.31	.93	1.41	.85	1.52	.78	1.64
27	1.32	1.47	1.24	1.56	1.16	1.65	1.08	1.76	1.01	1.86	1.09	1.23	1.02	1.32	.95	1.41	.88	1.51	.81	1.63
28	1.33	1.48	1.26	1.56	1.18	1.65	1.10	1.75	1.03	1.85	1.10	1.24	1.04	1.32	.97	1.41	.90	1.51	.83	1.62
29	1.34	1.48	1.27	1.56	1.20	1.65	1.12	1.74	1.05	1.84	1.12	1.25	1.05	1.33	.99	1.42	.92	1.51	.85	1.61
30	1.35	1.49	1.28	1.57	1.21	1.65	1.14	1.74	1.07	1.83	1.13	1.26	1.07	1.34	1.01	1.42	.94	1.51	.88	1.61
31	1.36	1.50	1.30	1.57	1.23	1.65	1.16	1.74	1.09	1.83	1.15	1.27	1.08	1.34	1.02	1.42	.96	1.51	.90	1.60
32	1.37	1.50	1.31	1.57	1.24	1.65	1.18	1.73	1.11	1.82	1.16	1.28	1.10	1.35	1.04	1.43	.98	1.51	.92	1.60
33	1.38	1.51	1.32	1.58	1.26	1.65	1.19	1.73	1.13	1.81	1.17	1.29	1.11	1.36	1.05	1.43	1.00	1.51	.94	1.59
34	1.39	1.51	1.33	1.58	1.27	1.65	1.21	1.73	1.15	1.81	1.18	1.30	1.13	1.36	1.07	1.43	1.01	1.51	.95	1.59
35	1.40	1.52	1.34	1.58	1.28	1.65	1.22	1.73	1.16	1.80	1.19	1.31	1.14	1.37	1.08	1.44	1.03	1.51	.97	1.59
36	1.41	1.52	1.35	1.59	1.29	1.65	1.24	1.73	1.18	1.80	1.21	1.32	1.15	1.38	1.10	1.44	1.04	1.51	.99	1.59
37	1.42	1.53	1.36	1.59	1.31	1.66	1.25	1.72	1.19	1.80	1.22	1.32	1.16	1.38	1.11	1.45	1.06	1.51	1.00	1.59
38	1.43	1.54	1.37	1.59	1.32	1.66	1.26	1.72	1.21	1.79	1.23	1.33	1.18	1.39	1.12	1.45	1.07	1.52	1.02	1.58
39	1.43	1.54	1.38	1.60	1.33	1.66	1.27	1.72	1.22	1.79	1.24	1.34	1.19	1.39	1.14	1.45	1.09	1.52	1.03	1.58
40	1.44	1.54	1.39	1.60	1.34	1.66	1.29	1.72	1.23	1.79	1.25	1.34	1.20	1.40	1.15	1.46	1.10	1.52	1.05	1.58
45	1.48	1.57	1.43	1.62	1.38	1.67	1.34	1.72	1.29	1.78	1.29	1.38	1.24	1.42	1.20	1.48	1.16	1.53	1.11	1.58
50	1.50	1.59	1.46	1.63	1.42	1.67	1.38	1.72	1.34	1.77	1.32	1.40	1.28	1.45	1.24	1.49	1.20	1.54	1.16	1.59
55	1.53	1.60	1.49	1.64	1.45	1.68	1.41	1.72	1.38	1.77	1.36	1.43	1.32	1.47	1.28	1.51	1.25	1.55	1.21	1.59
60	1.55	1.62	1.51	1.65	1.48	1.69	1.44	1.73	1.41	1.77	1.38	1.45	1.35	1.48	1.32	1.52	1.28	1.56	1.25	1.60
65	1.57	1.63	1.54	1.66	1.50	1.70	1.47	1.73	1.44	1.77	1.41	1.47	1.38	1.50	1.35	1.53	1.31	1.57	1.28	1.61
70	1.58	1.64	1.55	1.67	1.52	1.70	1.49	1.74	1.46	1.77	1.43	1.49	1.40	1.52	1.37	1.55	1.34	1.58	1.31	1.61
75	1.60	1.65	1.57	1.68	1.54	1.71	1.51	1.74	1.49	1.77	1.45	1.50	1.42	1.53	1.39	1.56	1.37	1.59	1.34	1.62
80	1.61	1.66	1.59	1.69	1.56	1.72	1.53	1.74	1.51	1.77	1.47	1.52	1.44	1.54	1.42	1.57	1.39	1.60	1.36	1.62
85	1.62	1.67	1.60	1.70	1.57	1.72	1.55	1.75	1.52	1.77	1.48	1.53	1.46	1.55	1.43	1.58	1.41	1.60	1.39	1.63
90	1.63	1.68	1.61	1.70	1.59	1.73	1.57	1.75	1.54	1.78	1.50	1.54	1.47	1.56	1.45	1.59	1.43	1.61	1.41	1.64
95	1.64	1.69	1.62	1.71	1.60	1.73	1.58	1.75	1.56	1.78	1.51	1.55	1.49	1.57	1.47	1.60	1.45	1.62	1.42	1.64
100	1.65	1.69	1.63	1.72	1.61	1.74	1.59	1.76	1.57	1.78	1.52	1.56	1.50	1.58	1.48	1.60	1.46	1.63	1.44	1.65

[a] n = *number of observations*; k = *number of independent variables.*

Source: *This table is reproduced from Biometrika, 41 (1951): pp. 173 and 175, with the permission of the Biometrika Trustees.*

TABLE E.9
Control Chart Factors

Number of Observations in Sample/Subgroup (n)	d_2	d_3	D_3	D_4	A_2
2	1.128	0.853	0	3.267	1.880
3	1.693	0.888	0	2.575	1.023
4	2.059	0.880	0	2.282	0.729
5	2.326	0.864	0	2.114	0.577
6	2.534	0.848	0	2.004	0.483
7	2.704	0.833	0.076	1.924	0.419
8	2.847	0.820	0.136	1.864	0.373
9	2.970	0.808	0.184	1.816	0.337
10	3.078	0.797	0.223	1.777	0.308
11	3.173	0.787	0.256	1.744	0.285
12	3.258	0.778	0.283	1.717	0.266
13	3.336	0.770	0.307	1.693	0.249
14	3.407	0.763	0.328	1.672	0.235
15	3.472	0.756	0.347	1.653	0.223
16	3.532	0.750	0.363	1.637	0.212
17	3.588	0.744	0.378	1.622	0.203
18	3.640	0.739	0.391	1.609	0.194
19	3.689	0.733	0.404	1.596	0.187
20	3.735	0.729	0.415	1.585	0.180
21	3.778	0.724	0.425	1.575	0.173
22	3.819	0.720	0.435	1.565	0.167
23	3.858	0.716	0.443	1.557	0.162
24	3.895	0.712	0.452	1.548	0.157
25	3.931	0.708	0.459	1.541	0.153

Source: *Reprinted from ASTM-STP 15D by kind permission of the American Society for Testing and Materials.*

TABLE E.10

The Standardized Normal Distribution

Entry represents area under the standardized normal
distribution from the mean to Z

Z	.00	.01	.02	.03	.04	.05	.06	.07	.08	.09
0.0	.0000	.0040	.0080	.0120	.0160	.0199	.0239	.0279	.0319	.0359
0.1	.0398	.0438	.0478	.0517	.0557	.0596	.0636	.0675	.0714	.0753
0.2	.0793	.0832	.0871	.0910	.0948	.0987	.1026	.1064	.1103	.1141
0.3	.1179	.1217	.1255	.1293	.1331	.1368	.1406	.1443	.1480	.1517
0.4	.1554	.1591	.1628	.1664	.1700	.1736	.1772	.1808	.1844	.1879
0.5	.1915	.1950	.1985	.2019	.2054	.2088	.2123	.2157	.2190	.2224
0.6	.2257	.2291	.2324	.2357	.2389	.2422	.2454	.2486	.2518	.2549
0.7	.2580	.2612	.2642	.2673	.2704	.2734	.2764	.2794	.2823	.2852
0.8	.2881	.2910	.2939	.2967	.2995	.3023	.3051	.3078	.3106	.3133
0.9	.3159	.3186	.3212	.3238	.3264	.3289	.3315	.3340	.3365	.3389
1.0	.3413	.3438	.3461	.3485	.3508	.3531	.3554	.3577	.3599	.3621
1.1	.3643	.3665	.3686	.3708	.3729	.3749	.3770	.3790	.3810	.3830
1.2	.3849	.3869	.3888	.3907	.3925	.3944	.3962	.3980	.3997	.4015
1.3	.4032	.4049	.4066	.4082	.4099	.4115	.4131	.4147	.4162	.4177
1.4	.4192	.4207	.4222	.4236	.4251	.4265	.4279	.4292	.4306	.4319
1.5	.4332	.4345	.4357	.4370	.4382	.4394	.4406	.4418	.4429	.4441
1.6	.4452	.4463	.4474	.4484	.4495	.4505	.4515	.4525	.4535	.4545
1.7	.4554	.4564	.4573	.4582	.4591	.4599	.4608	.4616	.4625	.4633
1.8	.4641	.4649	.4656	.4664	.4671	.4678	.4686	.4693	.4699	.4706
1.9	.4713	.4719	.4726	.4732	.4738	.4744	.4750	.4756	.4761	.4767
2.0	.4772	.4778	.4783	.4788	.4793	.4798	.4803	.4808	.4812	.4817
2.1	.4821	.4826	.4830	.4834	.4838	.4842	.4846	.4850	.4854	.4857
2.2	.4861	.4864	.4868	.4871	.4875	.4878	.4881	.4884	.4887	.4890
2.3	.4893	.4896	.4898	.4901	.4904	.4906	.4909	.4911	.4913	.4916
2.4	.4918	.4920	.4922	.4925	.4927	.4929	.4931	.4932	.4934	.4936
2.5	.4938	.4940	.4941	.4943	.4945	.4946	.4948	.4949	.4951	.4952
2.6	.4953	.4955	.4956	.4957	.4959	.4960	.4961	.4962	.4963	.4964
2.7	.4965	.4966	.4967	.4968	.4969	.4970	.4971	.4972	.4973	.4974
2.8	.4974	.4975	.4976	.4977	.4977	.4978	.4979	.4979	.4980	.4981
2.9	.4981	.4982	.4982	.4983	.4984	.4984	.4985	.4985	.4986	.4986
3.0	.49865	.49869	.49874	.49878	.49882	.49886	.49889	.49893	.49897	.49900
3.1	.49903	.49906	.49910	.49913	.49916	.49918	.49921	.49924	.49926	.49929
3.2	.49931	.49934	.49936	.49938	.49940	.49942	.49944	.49946	.49948	.49950
3.3	.49952	.49953	.49955	.49957	.49958	.49960	.49961	.49962	.49964	.49965
3.4	.49966	.49968	.49969	.49970	.49971	.49972	.49973	.49974	.49975	.49976
3.5	.49977	.49978	.49978	.49979	.49980	.49981	.49981	.49982	.49983	.49983
3.6	.49984	.49985	.49985	.49986	.49986	.49987	.49987	.49988	.49988	.49989
3.7	.49989	.49990	.49990	.49990	.49991	.49991	.49992	.49992	.49992	.49992
3.8	.49993	.49993	.49993	.49994	.49994	.49994	.49994	.49995	.49995	.49995
3.9	.49995	.49995	.49996	.49996	.49996	.49996	.49996	.49996	.49997	.49997

F.1 Downloadable Excel Data Workbooks

As discussed in Section D.2 in Appendix D on page 730, the Excel data workbooks are the set of downloadable workbooks that contain the data used in chapter examples and problems. Throughout this book, the names of Excel data workbooks appear in a special typeface—for example, **Bond Funds**.

All of these workbooks are stored in the **.xls** format, compatible with all Excel versions, and each contains a **DATA worksheet** that organizes the data for each variable by column, using the rules discussed in Section EG1.3. In the following alphabetical list, the variables for each workbook are presented in the order of their appearance in the DATA worksheet of the workbook.

AAAMILEAGE Vehicle Model, Owner, gasoline mileage from AAA members and Government, combined city/highway driving gasoline mileage, according to current government standards (Chapter 10)

ACCESS Buffer size, small file access read times (in msec.), medium file access read times, and large file access read times (Chapter 11)

ACT Method, ACT scores for condensed course, ACT scores for regular course (Chapter 11)

ACT-ONEWAY Group 1 ACT scores, Group 2 ACT scores, Group 3 ACT scores, Group 4 ACT scores (Chapter 11)

AD PAGES Magazine name, Magazine ad pages in 2008, and Magazine ad pages in 2006 (Chapter 10)

ADVERTISE Sales (in thousands of dollars), radio ads (in thousands of dollars), and newspaper ads (in thousands of dollars) for 22 cities (Chapters 14 and 15)

ADVERTISING Sales (in millions of dollars) and newspaper ads (in thousands of dollars) (Chapter 15)

ANGLE Subgroup number and angle (Chapter 17)

ANSCOMBE Data sets A, B, C, and D—each with 11 pairs of X and Y values (Chapter 13)

ATM TRANSACTIONS Cause, frequency, and percentage (Chapter 2)

AUTO Miles per gallon, horsepower, and weight for a sample of 50 car models (Chapters 14 and 15)

AUTO2008 Length (in.), width (in.), height (in.), wheelbase (in.), weight (lb.), maximum cargo load (lb.), cargo volume (cu. ft.), front shoulder room (in.), front leg room (in.), front head room (in.), horsepower, miles per gallon, acceleration from 0 to 60 mph (in sec.), braking from 60 mph dry (in sec.), braking from 60 mph wet (in sec.), AM max

speed (in mph), turning circle (ft.), region of origin, vehicle type, and transmission type (Chapter 18)

BANK1 Waiting time (in minutes) spent by a sample of 15 customers at a bank located in a commercial district (Chapters 3, 9, 10, and 12)

BANK2 Waiting time (in minutes) spent by a sample of 15 customers at a bank located in a residential area (Chapters 3, 10, and 12)

BANKTIME Day, waiting times of four bank customers (A, B, C, and D) (Chapter 17)

BANKYIELD Yield for money market account and yield for five-year CD (Chapters 3 and 10)

BASEBALL Team; attendance; high temperature on game day; winning percentage of home team; opponent's winning percentage; game played on Friday, Saturday, or Sunday (0 = no, 1 = yes); promotion held (0 = no, 1 = yes) (Chapter 18)

BB2001 Team; league (0 = American, 1 = National); wins; earned run average; runs scored; hits allowed; walks allowed; saves; errors; average ticket price; fan cost index; regular season gate receipts; local television, radio, and cable revenues; other local operating revenues; player compensation and benefits; national and other local expenses; and income from baseball operations (Chapter 18)

BB2008 Team, league (0 = American, 1 = National), wins, earned run average, runs scored, hits allowed, walks allowed, saves, and errors (Chapters 13, 14, and 15)

BBCOST Team and fan cost index (Chapters 2 and 6)

BBREVENUE Team, value, and revenue (Chapter 13)

BED & BATH Year, coded year, and number of stores open (Chapter 16)

BESTREST State, city, restaurant, hotel, cost (estimated price of dinner, including one drink and tip), and rating (1 to 100, with 1 the top-rated restaurant) (Chapter 3)

BILL PAYMENT Form of payment and percentage (Chapter 2)

BOND FUNDS Fund number, type, assets, fees, expense ratio, 2008 return, three-year return, five-year return, risk, bins, and midpoints (Chapters 2, 3, 4, 6, 8, 10, 11, 12, and 15)

BOOK PRICES Textbook, book store price, and Amazon.com price (Chapter 10)

BREAKFAST Menu choice, delivery time difference for early time period, and delivery time difference for late time period (Chapter 11)

BREAKFAST2 Menu choice, delivery time difference for early time period, and delivery time difference for late time period (Chapter 11)

BREAKSTW Operator, breaking strength for machines I, II, and III (Chapter 11)

BULBS Manufacturer (1 = A, 2 = B), length of life of 40 light bulbs from manufacturer (Chapters 2, 10, 12)

CABERNET California and Washington ratings and California and Washington rankings (Chapter 12)

CABOT Year and revenue for Cabot Corporation (Chapter 16)

CANISTER Day and number of nonconformances (Chapter 17)

CATFOOD Ounces eaten of kidney, shrimp, chicken liver, salmon, and beef cat food (Chapters 11 and 12)

CATFOOD2 Piece size (F = fine, C = chunky), coded weight for low fill height, coded weight for current fill height (Chapter 11)

CATFOOD3 Type (1 = kidney, 2 = shrimp), shift, time interval, nonconformances, and volume (Chapter 17)

CATFOOD4 Type (1 = kidney, 2 = shrimp), shift, time interval, and weight (Chapter 17)

CELLPHONES Year and cell phones collected (in millions) Chapter 2)

CELLRATING City and ratings for Verizon, AT&T, T-Mobile, and Sprint (Chapter 11)

CEO Number in S&P 500, company, and total compensation of CEO (Chapter 8)

CHOCOLATECHIP Cost (cents) of chocolate chip cookies (Chapter 3)

CIGARETTETAX State and cigarette tax ($) (Chapters 2 and 3)

CIRCUITS Batch, thickness of semiconductor wafers by position (Chapter 11)

CIRCULATION Magazine, reported newsstand sales, and audited newsstand sales (Chapter 13)

COCA-COLA Year, coded year, and operating revenues (in billions of dollars) at The Coca-Cola Company (Chapter 16)

COFFEE Expert, Rating of coffees, by brand A, B, C, and D (Chapters 10 and 11)

COFFEEDRINK Coffee drink product, calories, and fat (Chapters 3 and 13)

COFFEE PRICES Year and price per pound of coffee in the United States (Chapter 16)

COLA Sales for normal and end-aisle locations (Chapters 10 and 12)

COLASPC Day, total number of cans filled, and number of unacceptable cans (over a 22-day period) (Chapter 17)

COLLEGES-BASKETBALL School, coach's salary for 2005–2006, expenses for 2004–2005, revenues for 2004–2005 (in millions of dollars), and winning percentage in 2005–2006 (Chapters 2, 3, and 13)

COMPENSATION Company, bonus ($), compensation ($), and stock price change in percentage (Chapters 2, 3, and 13)

COMPLAINTS Day and number of complaints (Chapter 17)

CONCRETE1 Sample number, compressive strength after two days and seven days (Chapter 10)

CONCRETE2 Sample number, compressive strength after 2 days, 7 days, and 28 days (Chapter 11)

COST OF LIVING City; overall cost rating; apartment rent; and costs for a cup of coffee, a hamburger, dry cleaning a men's suit, toothpaste, and movie tickets (Chapters 2 and 3)

CPI-U Year, coded year, and value of CPI-U (the Consumer Price Index) (Chapter 16)

CRACK Type of crack and crack size (Chapters 10, 12)

CREDIT Month, coded month, and credit charges (Chapter 16)

CREDIT UNIONS Name, city, state, zip code, region, total assets ($), total investments ($), net income ($), total amount of delinquent loans and leases ($), number of current members, number of potential members, number of full-time credit union employees, and number of branches (Chapter 18)

CURRENCY Year, coded year, and mean annual exchange rates (against the U.S. dollar) for the Canadian dollar, Japanese yen, and English pound (Chapter 16)

CUSTSALE Week number, number of customers, and sales (in thousands of dollars) over a period of 15 consecutive weeks (Chapter 13)

DAILY NASDAQ Date and NASDAQ value (Chapter 16)

DARKCHOCOLATE Cost ($) per ounce of dark chocolate bars (Chapters 2, 3, and 8)

DELIVERY Customer number, number of cases, and delivery time (Chapter 13)

DENTAL Annual family dental expenses for 10 employees (Chapter 8)

DIFFTEST Differences in the sales invoices and actual amounts from a sample of 50 vouchers (Chapter 8)

DIGITALCAMERAS Battery life (in shots) for subcompact cameras and compact cameras (Chapters 10, 12)

DINNER Time to prepare and cook dinner (in minutes) (Chapter 9)

DISCOUNT Amount of discount not taken from 13 invoices (Chapter 8)

DISPRAZOR Price, price squared, and sales of disposable razors in 15 stores (Chapter 15)

DJIA Year, coded year, and Dow Jones Industrial Average at the end of the year (Chapter 16)

DOMESTICBEER Brand, alcohol percentage, calories, and carbohydrates in U.S. domestic beers (Chapters 2, 3, 6, 15)

DOWMARKETCAP Company and market capitalization, in billions of dollars (Chapter 3)

DRILL Depth, time to drill additional 5 feet, and type of hole (Chapter 14)

DRINK Amount of soft drink filled in a subgroup of 50 consecutive 2-liter bottles (Chapters 2, 9)

DRYCLEAN Days and number of items returned (Chapter 17)

ELECTRICITY Year and cost of electricity (Chapter 16)

ENERGY State and per capita kilowatt hour use (Chapter 3)

ENERGY PRICES Year, price of electricity, natural gas, and fuel oil (Chapter 16)

ERRORSPC Number of nonconforming items and number of accounts processed over 39 days (Chapter 17)

ERWAITING Emergency room waiting time (in minutes) at the main facility and at satellite 1, satellite 2, and satellite 3 (Chapters 11 and 12)

ESPRESSO Tamp (the distance in inches between the espresso grounds and the top of the portafilter) and time (the number of seconds the heart, body, and crema are separated) (Chapter 13)

FEDRECEIPT Year, coded year, and federal receipts (in billions of current dollars) (Chapter 16)

FFCHAIN Rater and ratings for restaurants A, B, C, and D (Chapter 11)

FIFO Historical cost (in dollars) and audited value (in dollars) for a sample of 120 inventory items (Chapter 8)

FIRERUNS Week and number of fire runs (Chapter 17)

FLYASH Fly ash percentage and strength (Chapter 15)

FORCE Force required to break an insulator (Chapters 2, 3, 8, and 9)

FORD Quarter, coded quarter, revenue, and three dummy variables for quarters (Chapter 16)

FOULSPC Number of foul shots made and number taken over 40 days (Chapter 17)

FREEPORT Address, appraised value, property size (acres), house size, age, number of rooms, number of bathrooms, and number of cars that can be parked in the garage located in Freeport, New York (Chapter 15)

FRUIT Fruit and year, price, and quantity (Chapter 16)

FUNDTRAN Day, number of new investigations, and number of investigations closed over a 30-day period (Chapter 17)

FURNITURE Days between receipt and resolution of a sample of 50 complaints regarding purchased furniture (Chapters 2, 3, 8, and 9)

GASOLINE Year, gasoline price, 1980 price index, and 1995 price index (Chapter 16)

GAS PRICES Week and price per gallon (cents) (Chapter 2)

GCFREEROSLYN Address, appraised value, location, property size (acres), house size, age, number of rooms, number of bathrooms, and number of cars that can be parked in the garage in Glen Cove, Freeport, and Roslyn, New York (Chapter 15)

GCROSLYN Address, appraised value, location, property size (acres), house size, age, number of rooms, number of bathrooms, and number of cars that can be parked in the garage in Glen Cove and Roslyn, New York (Chapters 14 and 15)

GDP Year and real Gross Domestic Product (Chapter 16)

GE Year, coded year, and stock price (Chapter 16)

GEAR Tooth size and gear distortion at low positioning, gear distortion at high positioning (Chapter 11)

GLENCOVE Address, appraised value, property size (acres), house size, age, number of rooms, number of bathrooms, and number of cars that can be parked in the garage in Glen Cove, New York (Chapters 14 and 15)

GOLFBALL Distance for designs 1, 2, 3, and 4 (Chapters 11 and 12)

GPIGMAT GMAT scores and GPI for 20 students (Chapter 13)

GRADSURVEY ID number, gender, age (as of last birthday), height (in inches), major (A = accounting, EF = economics and finance, IB = international business, IS = information systems, M = management, MR = marketing, UN = undecided), current cumulative grade point average, undergraduate area of specialization, undergraduate cumulative grade point average, GMAT score, current employment status, number of different full-time jobs held in the past 10 years, expected salary upon completion of MBA (in thousands of dollars), anticipated salary after 5 years of experience after MBA (in thousands of dollars), satisfaction with student advising services on campus, and amount spent for books and supplies this semester (Chapters 2, 3, 4, 6, 8, 10, 11, and 12)

GRANULE Granule loss in Boston and Vermont shingles (Chapters 3, 8, 9, and 10)

HARNSWELL Day and diameter of cam rollers (in inches) for samples of five parts produced in each of 30 batches (Chapter 17)

HEMLOCKFARMS Asking price, hot tub, rooms, lake view, bathrooms, bedrooms, loft/den, finished basement, and number of acres (Chapter 15)

HOMES Price, location, condition, bedrooms, bathrooms, and other rooms (Chapter 18)

HOSPADM Day, number of admissions, mean processing time (in hours), range of processing times, and proportion of laboratory rework (over a 30-day period) (Chapter 17)

HOTEL1 Day, number of rooms studied, number of nonconforming rooms per day over a 28-day period, and proportion of nonconforming items (Chapter 17)

HOTEL2 Day and delivery time for subgroups of five luggage deliveries per day over a 28-day period (Chapter 17)

HOTELS Year and average room rate (Chapters 2 and 16)

HOUSE1 Selling price (in thousands of dollars), assessed value (in thousands of dollars), type (new = 0, old = 1), and time period of sale for 30 houses (Chapters 13, 14, and 15)

HOUSE2 Assessed value (in thousands of dollars), size of heating area (in thousands of square feet), and age (in years) for 15 houses (Chapters 13 and 14)

HOUSE3 Assessed value (in thousands of dollars), size (in thousands of square feet), and presence of a fireplace for 15 houses (Chapter 14)

HOUSING Quarter and units (Chapter 16)

HTNGOIL Monthly consumption of heating oil (in gallons), temperature (in degrees Fahrenheit), attic insulation (in inches), and style (0 = not ranch, 1 = ranch) (Chapters 14, 15)

ICECREAM Daily temperature (in degrees Fahrenheit) and sales (in thousands of dollars) for 21 days (Chapter 13)

INDICES Year and total rate of return (in percentage) for the Dow Jones Industrial Average (DJIA), the Standards & Poor's 500 (S&P 500), and the technology-heavy NASDAQ Composite (NASDAQ) (Chapter 3)

INSURANCE Processing time for insurance policies (Chapters 3, 8, and 9)

INTAGLIO Surface hardness of untreated and treated steel plates (Chapters 10 and 12)

INVEST 2009 Date, value of gold ($), value of silver ($), S&P 500, and NASDAQ (Chapter 13)

INVOICE Number of invoices processed and amount of time (in hours) for 30 days (Chapter 13)

INVOICES Amount recorded (in dollars) from a sample of 12 sales invoices (Chapter 9)

ITEMERR Amount of error (in dollars) from a sample of 200 items (Chapter 8)

LARGESTBONDS One-year return of bond funds (Chapter 3)

LAUNDRY Detergent brand and dirt (in pounds) removed for cycle times of 18, 20, 22, and 24 (Chapter 11)

LOANS AND LEASES Name of bank, state, zip code, number of domestic and foreign offices, ownership type, regulator, Federal Reserve district, total deposits ($000), gross loans and leases ($000), all real estate loans ($000), construction and development loans ($000), commercial real estate ($000), multifamily residential real estate ($000), 1–4 family residential loans, ($000), farmland loans ($000), credit card loans ($000), related plans ($000), other loans to individuals ($000), and all other loans and leases ($000) (Chapter 18)

LUGGAGE Delivery time (in minutes) for luggage in Wing A and Wing B of a hotel (Chapters 10 and 12)

MANAGERS Sales (ratio of yearly sales divided by the target sales value for that region), score from the Wonderlic Personnel Test, score on the Strong-Campbell Interest Inventory Test, number of years of selling experience prior to becoming a sales manager, and whether the sales manager has a degree in electrical engineering (0 = no, 1 = yes) (Chapter 15)

MCDONALDS Year, coded year, and annual total revenues (in billions of dollars) at McDonald's Corporation (Chapter 16)

MEASUREMENT Sample, in-line measurement, and analytical lab measurement (Chapter 10)

MEDICARE Difference in amount reimbursed and amount that should have been reimbursed for office visits (Chapter 8)

MEDREC Day, number of discharged patients, and number of records not processed for a 30-day period (Chapter 17)

METALS Year and the total rate of return (in percentage) for platinum, gold, and silver (Chapter 3)

MILEAGE Vehicle, mileage of autos calculated by owner currently and forecasted according to government plans (Chapters 2, 3, 13)

MIXEDCOSTS Costs and days (Chapter 13)

MOISTURE Moisture content of Boston shingles and Vermont shingles (Chapter 9)

MOVIE Box office gross (in $millions) and video sales (in thousands) (Chapter 13)

MOVIE ATTENDANCE Year and movie attendance (Chapter 16)

MOVIEPRICES Movie chain and prices (Chapters 3, 8, and 9)

MOVING Labor hours, cubic feet, number of large pieces of furniture, and availability of an elevator (Chapters 13 and 14)

MUSICONLINE Album/artist and prices at iTunes, Wal-Mart, MusicNow, Musicmatch, and Napster (Chapter 11)

MUTUAL FUNDS Category, objective, assets, fees, expense ratio, 2006 return, three-year return, five-year return, risk (Chapters 2 and 3)

MYELOMA Patient, measurement before transplant, and measurement after transplant (Chapter 10)

NASCAR year and number of accidents (Chapter 16)

NATURAL GAS Coded quarter, price, and three dummy variables for quarters (Chapter 16)

NBA2009 Team, number of wins, points per game (for team, opponent, and the difference between team and opponent), field goal (shots made), percentage (for team, opponent, and the difference between team and opponent), turnovers (losing the ball before a shot is taken) per game (for team, opponent, and the difference between team and opponent), offensive rebound percentage, and defensive rebound percentage (Chapters 14 and 15)

NBAVALUES Team, value ($millions) and annual revenue ($millions) for NBA franchises (Chapters 2, 3, and 13)

NEIGHBOR Selling price ($000), number of rooms, and neighborhood location (0 = east, 1 = west) for 20 houses (Chapter 14)

NEW HOME PRICES Month, median price ($000), and mean price ($000) (Chapter 2)

NFL VALUES Team, value ($millions) and annual revenue ($millions) for NFL franchises (Chapter 13)

OIL & GAS Week, price of oil per barrel, and price of a gallon of gasoline (cents) (Chapter 13)

OMNIPOWER Bars sold, price, and promotion expenses (Chapter 14)

ORDER Time in minutes to fill orders for a population of 200 (Chapter 8)

O-RING Flight number, temperature, and O-ring damage index (Chapter 13)

PAINRELIEF Temperature and dissolve times for Equate, Kroger, and Alka-Seltzer tablets (Chapter 11)

PALLET Weight of Boston shingles and weight of Vermont shingles (Chapters 2, 8, 9, and 10)

PARACHUTE Tensile strength of parachutes from suppliers 1, 2, 3, and 4; the sample means and the sample standard deviations for the four suppliers in rows 8 and 9 (Chapters 11 and 12)

PARACHUTE2 Loom and tensile strength of parachutes from suppliers 1, 2, 3, and 4 (Chapter 11)

PASTA Type of pasta (A = American, I = Italian), weight for 4-minute cooking time, and weight for 8-minute cooking time (Chapter 11)

PEN Gender, ad, and product rating (Chapters 11 and 12)

PERFORM Performance rating before and after motivational training (Chapter 10)

PETFOOD Shelf space (in feet), weekly sales (in dollars), and aisle location (0 = back, 1 = front) (Chapters 13 and 14)

PHONE Time (in minutes) to clear telephone line problems and location (1 = I and 2 = II) for samples of 20 customer problems reported to each of the two office locations (Chapter 10)

PHOTO Developer strength, density at 10 minutes, and density at 14 minutes (Chapter 11)

PIZZATIME Time period, delivery time for local restaurant, delivery time for national chain (Chapter 10)

PLUMBINV Difference (in dollars) between actual amounts recorded on sales invoices and amounts entered into the accounting system (Chapter 8)

POLIO Year and incidence rates per 100,000 persons of reported poliomyelitis (Chapter 16)

POTATO Percentage of solids content in filter cake, acidity (in pH), lower pressure, upper pressure, cake thickness, varidrive speed, and drum speed setting for 54 measurements (Chapter 15)

PROPERTYTAXES State and property taxes per capita (Chapters 2, 3, and 6)

PROTEIN Type of food, calories (in grams), protein, percentage of calories from fat, percentage of calories from saturated fat, and cholesterol (in mg) for 25 popular protein foods (Chapters 2, 3)

PTFALLS Month and patient falls (Chapter 17)

PUMPKIN Circumference and weight of pumpkins (Chapter 13)

REDWOOD Height, diameter, and bark thickness (Chapter 14)

RENT Monthly rental cost (in dollars) and apartment size (in square footage) for a sample of 25 apartments (Chapter 13)

RESTAURANTS Location, food rating, decor rating, service rating, summated rating, coded location (0 = urban, 1 = suburban), and cost of a meal (Chapter 18)

RESTCOST Location, food rating, decor rating, service rating, summated rating, coded location (0 = city, 1 = suburban), and cost of a meal (Chapters 2, 10, 13, and 14)

ROSLYN Address, appraised value, property size (acres), house size, age, number of rooms, number of bathrooms, and number of cars that can be parked in the garage in Roslyn, New York (Chapter 15)

RUDYBIRD Day, total cases sold, and cases of Rudybird sold (Chapter 17)

S&P INDEX Coded quarters, end-of-quarter values of the quarterly Standard & Poor's Composite Stock Price Index, and three quarterly dummy variables (Chapter 16)

SAFETY Tour and number of unsafe acts (Chapter 17)

SAVINGSRATE Rate for a money market account, one-year CD, and five-year CD (Chapters 2, 3, 6, 11, and 12)

SCRUBBER Airflow, water flow, recirculating water flow, orifice diameter, and NTU (Chapter 15)

SEALANT Sample number, sealant strength for Boston shingles, and sealant strength for Vermont shingles (Chapter 17)

SEDANS Miles per gallon for 2009 sedans priced under $20,000 (Chapters 3 and 8)

SH2 Day and number of calls received at the help desk (Chapters 2 and 3)

SH8 Amount ($) willing to pay for the newspaper (Chapter 8)

SH9 Blackness of newsprint (Chapter 9)

SH10 Length of early calls (in seconds) and length of late calls (in seconds) (Chapter 10)

SH11-1 Call, presentation plan (1 = structured, 2 = semi-structured, 3 = unstructured), and length of call (in seconds) (Chapter 11)

SH11-2 Gender of caller, personal but formal length of call, personal but informal length of call, and impersonal length of call (Chapter 11)

SH13 Hours per month spent telemarketing and number of new subscriptions per month over a 24-month period (Chapter 13)

SH14 Week number, number of new subscriptions, hours per week spent telemarketing, and type of presentation (Chapter 14)

SH16 Month and number of home-delivery subscriptions over the most recent 24-month period (Chapter 16)

SH17-1 Day, number of ads with errors, and number of ads (Chapter 17)

SH17-2 Day and newsprint blackness measures for each of five spots made over 25 consecutive weekdays (Chapter 17)

SITE Store number, square footage (in thousands of square feet), and sales ($millions) in 14 Sunflowers Apparel stores (Chapter 13)

SOLAR POWER Year and amount of solar power installed (in megawatts) (Chapters 2 and 16)

SPONGE Day, number of sponges produced, number of nonconforming sponges, and proportion of nonconforming sponges (Chapter 17)

SPORTING Sales ($), age, annual population growth, income ($), percentage with high school diploma, and percentage with college diploma (Chapters 13 and 15)

SPWATER Sample number and amount of magnesium (Chapter 17)

STANDBY Standby hours, total staff present, remote hours, Dubner hours, and labor hours for 26 weeks (Chapters 14 and 15)

STEEL Error in actual length and specified length (Chapters 2, 6, 8, and 9)

STOCK PRICES Week, closing S&P 500 Index, and closing weekly stock price for GE, IBM, and Apple (Chapter 2)

STOCKS 2009 Week, closing S&P 500 Index, and closing weekly stock price for GE, IBM, and Exxon Mobil (Chapter 13)

STRATEGIC Year and number of barrels in U.S. strategic oil reserve (Chapter 16)

STUDYTIME Gender and study time (Chapter 10)

SUPERMARKET Day, number of customers, and checkout time (Chapter 13)

SUV Miles per gallon for 2009 small SUVs priced under $30,000 (Chapters 3, 6, and 8)

TAX Quarterly sales tax receipts ($000) for 50 business establishments (Chapter 3)

TAXES County taxes ($) and age of house (in years) for 19 single-family houses (Chapter 15)

TEA3 Sample number and weight of tea bags (Chapter 17)

TEABAGS Weight of tea bags (Chapters 3, 8, and 9)

TELESPC Number of orders and number of corrections over 30 days (Chapter 17)

TELLER Number of errors by tellers (Chapter 17)

TENSILE Sample number and strength (Chapter 17)

TESTRANK Rank scores and training method used (0 = traditional, 1 = experimental) for 10 people (Chapter 12)

THEMEPARKS Name of location and admission price for one-day tickets (Chapter 3)

THICKNESS Thickness, catalyst, pH, pressure, temperature, and voltage (Chapters 14 and 15)

TIMES Times to get ready (Chapter 3)

TOMATO Fertilizer and yield (Chapter 15)

TOMATO PRICE Year and price per pound in the United States (Chapter 16)

TOYS R US Quarter, coded quarter, revenue, and three dummy variables for quarters (Chapter 16)

TRADE Days, number of undesirable trades, and number of total trades made over a 30-day period (Chapter 17)

TRANSMIT Day and number of errors in transmission (Chapter 17)

TRANSPORT Days and patient transport times (in minutes) for samples of four patients per day over a 30-day period (Chapter 17)

TRASHBAGS Weight required to break four brands of trash bags (Chapters 11 and 12)

TREASURY Year and interest rate (Chapter 16)

TROUGH Width of trough (Chapters 2, 3, 8, and 9)

TRSNYC Year, unit value of variable A, and unit value of variable B (Chapter 16)

TSMODEL1 Year, coded year, and three time series (I, II, and III) (Chapter 16)

TSMODEL2 Year, coded year, and two time series (I and II) (Chapter 16)

UNDERGRADSURVEY ID number, gender, age (as of last birthday), height (in inches), class designation, major (A = accounting, EF = economics and finance, IB = international business, IS = information systems, M = management, MR = marketing, O = other, UN = undecided) graduate school intention (Y = yes, N = no, UN = undecided), cumulative grade point average, expected starting salary (in thousands of dollars), anticipated salary after five years of experience (in thousands of dollars), current employment status, number of campus club/group/organization/team affiliations, satisfaction with student advisement services on campus, and amount spent on books and supplies this semester (Chapters 2, 3, 4, 6, 8, 10, 11, and 12)

UNDERWRITING Score on proficiency exam, score on end of training exam, and training method (Chapter 14)

UNEMPLOYMENT Year, month, and monthly unemployment rates (Chapter 2)

UNEMPLOYMENT2 Year, month, and monthly unemployment rates (Chapter 16)

UNLEADED Year, month, and price (Chapter 16)

USEDAUTOS Car, model, year (2000 = 0), asking price in ($000), mileage (in thousands), age (in years), vehicle type, and region of origin (Chapter 18)

UTILITY Utilities charges for 50 one-bedroom apartments (Chapters 2 and 6)

VB Time (in minutes) for nine students to write and run a Visual Basic program (Chapter 10)

VEGGIEBURGER Calories and fat in veggie burgers (Chapters 2 and 3)

WAIT Waiting times and seating times (in minutes) in a restaurant (Chapter 6)

WALMART Quarter and quarterly revenues (Chapter 16)

WARECOST Distribution cost ($000), sales ($000), and number of orders for 24 months (Chapters 13, 14, and 15)

WAREHSE Day, Number of units handled per day by employee A, B, C, D, and E (Chapter 17)

WHOLEFOODS Item, price at Whole Foods, price at Gristede's, price at Fairway, and price at Stop & Shop (Chapter 11)

WIP Processing times at each of two plants (1 = A, 2 = B) (Chapter 18)

WONDERLIC School, average Wonderlic score of football players trying out for the NFL, and graduation rate (Chapters 2, 3, and 13)

WORKFORCE Year, population, and size of the workforce (Chapter 16)

YARN Side-by-side aspect and breaking strength scores for 30 psi, 40 psi, and 50 psi (Chapter 11)

YIELD Cleansing step, new etching step yield, and standard etching step yield (Chapter 11)

YIELD-ONEWAY Yield for new method 1, new method 2, and standard (Chapter 11)

F.2 Downloadable Excel Guide Workbooks

As discussed in Section D.2 in Appendix D on page 730, the Excel Guide workbooks contain model solutions that can be reused as templates for solving other problems. The workbooks are featured in the *In-Depth Excel* instructions of the Excel Guides and also serve to document the worksheets created by many PHStat2 procedures and provide many of the illustrations of Excel results throughout this book.

All of these workbooks are stored in the **.xls** format, compatible with all Excel versions. Most contain a **COMPUTE worksheet** (often shown in this book) that presents results as well as a **COMPUTE_FORMULAS worksheet** that presents the COMPUTE worksheet in formulas view, which allows for the easy inspection of all worksheet formulas used in the worksheet.

The Excel Guide workbooks for this book are:

Bayes	**Moving Averages**
Binomial	**Multiple Regression**
Boxplot	**Normal**
Capability	**NPP**
Chapter 2	**One-Way ANOVA**
***c* Chart**	**p Chart**
Chi-Square	**Paired T**
Chi-Square Variance	**PivotTable Examples**
Chi-Square Worksheets	**Poisson**
CIE Proportion	**Pooled-Variance T**
CIE sigma known	**Portfolio**
CIE sigma unknown	**Probabilities**
CIE Total Difference	**Quartiles**
CIE Total	**R and XBar Chart**
Correlation	**Random**
Covariance	**Randomized Block**
Differences	**Sample Size Mean**
Discrete Random Variable	**Sample Size Proportion**
Expected Monetary Value	**SDS**
Exponential Smoothing	**Separate-Variance T**
Exponential Trend	**Simple Linear Regression**
Exponential	**StackedAndUnstacked**
F Two Variances	**T Mean**
Hypergeometric	**Two-Way ANOVA**
Index Numbers	**Wilcoxon**
Kruskal-Wallis Worksheets	**Z Mean**
Lagged Predictors	**Z Proportion**
Levene	**Z Two Proportions**
McNemar	

F.3 Downloadable Online Topics

As discussed in Section D.2 of Appendix D on page 730, the optional online topics are files stored in Adobe PDF format that contain the optional topics for this book. These files can be opened and read in many Web browsers or Adobe Reader, the free program supplied by Adobe Systems and available for download at **get.adobe.com/reader/**.

The downloadable online topics for this book are:

Binomial	**Section 8.7**	**Chapter 19**
Poisson	**Section 9.6**	**ANOM**
Section 4.5	**Section 11.3**	**ANOP**
Section 6.6	**Section 12.7**	
Section 7.6	**Section 16.8**	

F.4 Other Downloadable Files

As discussed in Section D.2 of Appendix D on page 730, the set of case files and Visual Explorations files, as well as the files required to setup PHStat2, can also be downloaded from this book's companion Web site.

The case files are the set of files that support the "Managing the *Springville Herald*" running case and the end-of-chapter Web Cases; they come packaged as a self-extracting archive file. When this archive is expanded and extracted to the folder you choose, you will notice that some supporting files have been placed in one of three subfolders that the self-extraction process creates.

The Visual Explorations files are a set of three files also packaged as a self-extracting archive file. The three files can be extracted to any folder you choose, and all three must be present together in the same folder for the add-in workbook to function properly.

If you plan to install PHStat2, first review Section G.1 of Appendix G for answers to frequently asked questions about PHStat2. Then download and read the PHStat2 readme file for the latest and most detailed instructions for installing PHStat2 and review Section D.4 on page 731. The PHStat2 setup program will install several files in the **C:\Program Files\PHStat2** folder (or a folder that you choose) and make entries in the Windows registry file.

G.1 PHStat2 FAQs

What is PHStat2?

PHStat2 is software that makes operating Windows-based Microsoft Excel as distraction free as possible. As a student studying statistics, you can focus mainly on learning statistics and not worry about having to fully master Excel first. PHStat2 contains just about all the statistical methods taught in an introductory statistics course that can be illustrated using Excel.

How much storage space does PHStat2 require?

PHStat2 requires about 3MB of storage space, although the PHStat2 setup program that you run to install PHStat2 (see Section D.4 in Appendix D) requires about 15MB of storage space.

Are updates to PHStat2 available?

Yes, free minor updates to resolve issues or enhance functionality may be available for download from the PHStat2 Web site (**www.prenhall.com/phstat**).

Where can I find the latest and most complete technical information for setting up PHStat2?

Download and read the PHStat2 readme file (see Appendix Section D.2) for the latest and most complete technical information for setting up PHStat2. The readme file expands on the concise installation and configuration instructions presented in Appendix Sections D.4 and D.5. Also check the PHStat2 Web site (**www.prenhall.com/phstat**) for any technical issues created by Microsoft-supplied Excel updates distributed after the publication of this book.

Where can I get help setting up PHStat2?

If you need help in setting up PHStat2, first review the "Troubleshooting PHStat2" section of the downloadable PHStat2 readme file. If your problem is still unresolved, visit the PHStat2 frequently asked questions Web page and the Web page for your version at the PHStat2 Web site (**www.prenhall.com/phstat**) to see if your problem is addressed. If you need further assistance, click the **Contact Pearson Technical Support** on either Web page for free technical support. (Pearson Technical Support cannot answer questions about the statistical applications of PHStat2 or questions about specific PHStat2 procedures.)

How can I identify which PHStat2 version I have?

Open Microsoft Excel with PHStat2 and select **PHStat → Help for PHStat**. In the dialog box that appears, note the XLA and DLL version numbers. If you downloaded and installed the PHStat2 version designed for this book, both of these numbers will not be lower than 2.9.0.

Where can I find tips for using PHStat2?

While your classmates and instructor can be the best sources of tips, you can check for any tips that may be posted on the third-party PHStat2 community Web site **phstatcommunity.org**.

G.2 Microsoft Excel FAQs

In Excel 2007, how can I specify the custom settings that you recommend?

Click the **Office Button** and then click **Excel Options**. In the Excel Options dialog box, click **Formulas** in the left pane, and in the **Formulas** right pane, click **Automatic** under Workbook Calculation and verify that all check boxes are checked except **Enable iterative calculation**, **R1C1 reference style**, and **Formulas referring to empty cells**.

In Excel 2003, how can I specify the custom settings that you recommend?

First, select **Tools → Customize**. In the Customize dialog box, click the **Options** tab, check **Always show full menus** and then click **Close**. Next, select **Tools → Options**. In the Options dialog box, click the **Calculation** tab and click **Automatic**. Click the **Edit** tab and verify that all check boxes except **Fixed decimal**, **Provide feedback with Animation**, and **Enable automatic percent entry** have been checked. Still in the Options dialog box, click the **General** tab. Clear **R1C1 reference style**, enter **3** as the number of **Sheets in new workbook**, select **Arial** and **10** (or **Calibri** and **11**) from the **Standard font** and **Size** dropdown lists. Click **OK** to finish.

What Microsoft Excel security settings will allow the PHStat2 or Visual Explorations add-in to function properly?

Use the instructions in Section D.5 in Appendix D for configuring Excel for PHStat2 for both add-ins.

How can I install the Analysis ToolPak?

Close Microsoft Excel and rerun the Microsoft Office or Microsoft Excel setup program. When the setup program runs, choose the option that allows you to add components. This option is variously described as **Change** and **Add or Remove Features**. (If using Excel 2003, you will need to check **Choose advanced customization of applications** in the Custom Setup screen.) In the Installation Options screen (Excel 2007) or Advanced Customization screen (Excel 2003), double-click **Microsoft Office Excel** and then double-click **Add-ins.** Click the **Analysis**

ToolPak drop-down list button and select **Run from My Computer**. You may need access to the original Microsoft Office/Excel setup CD-ROMs or DVDs to complete this task.

G.3 FAQs for New Microsoft Excel 2007 or 2010 Users

I do not see the menu for an add-in workbook that I opened. Where is it?
Unlike earlier versions of Excel that allowed add-ins to add menus to the menu bar, Excel 2007 and Excel 2010 places all add-in menus under the Add-ins tab. In order to see the menu, click **Add-ins** and then click the name of the add-in menu.

What does "Compatibility Mode" in the title bar mean?
Excel displays "Compatibility Mode" when the workbook you are currently using has been previously stored using the **.xls** file format that is compatible with all Excel versions. Compatibility Mode does not affect Excel functionality but will cause Excel to review your workbook for exclusive-to-Excel-2007/2010 formatting properties and Excel objects the next time you save the workbook. (To preserve exclusive features, save the workbook in the newer **.xlsx** file format. In Excel 2007, click the **Office Button**, move the mouse pointer over **Save As**, and in the Save As gallery, click **Excel Workbook** to save the workbook in the Excel 2007 **.xlsx** file format. In Excel 2010, click the **File tab**, click the large **Convert** button and then click **Yes** in the subsequent dialog box.)

If you open any of the Excel data or Excel Guide workbooks for this book, you will see "Compatibility Mode," as all workbooks for this book have been stored using the **.xls** format.

G.4 FAQs for New Microsoft Excel 2010 Users

Can I use the Excel instructions in this book with Excel 2010?
Yes, by downloading the **Using Excel 2010 Guide** (in PDF format) from this book's companion Web site (see Appendix Section D.2), you can use the Excel instructions in this book with Excel 2010. (In most cases, instructions for using Excel 2010 will be identical to the instructions for Excel 2007.)

Why are there no *In-Depth Excel 2010* sections in this book?
This book was published before Microsoft finalized Excel 2010. The downloadable **Using Excel 2010 Guide** reflects the finalized details of Excel 2010 that were not available at publication time.

Will the version of PHStat2 distributed for this book work with Excel 2010?
Yes.

I read that Excel 2010 has new names for statistical functions. Does that mean I have to edit and rename each statistical function that appears in this book or in the Excel Guide Workbooks?
No, while Excel 2010 introduces a new naming scheme for its statistical functions, the function names used in earlier Excel versions (names that are used throughout this book) will work as is. There is no need, for example, to change every occurrence of **FDIST** to **F.DIST**, the new name for the FDIST function.

What is PowerPivot? Does it replace the PivotTable feature of earlier Excel versions?
PowerPivot is a Microsoft-supplied add-in that enables you to use PivotTable technology to explore and summarize very large sets of data that contain *millions* of rows of data. PowerPivot can be considered an example of a *business intelligence tool* and allows Excel to be used in conjunction with analytic techniques such as data mining (see page 589).

PowerPivot supplements, not replaces PivotTables, and uses similar concepts. The Section 2.8 discussion about using PivotTables to explore multidimensional data (see page 52) also serves as an orientation for using PowerPivot (which is discussed in the **Using Excel 2010 Guide** that is available on this book's companion Web site).

I cannot find the Office Button that was introduced in Excel 2007. Where is it?
In Excel/Office 2010, the Office Button has been replaced with a File tab that when clicked displays the **Backstage View**. The Backstage View contains a menu of commands, similar to the Excel 2003 File menu and a pane that displays information and buttons that represent possible actions for the opened workbook (such as the Convert button discussed in the second Section G.3 question).

In the Backstage View, click **Help** to display the exact version of your copy of Excel (see related Section D.2 on page 730). Click **Options** to display an Excel Options dialog box that is similar to one for Excel 2007 that is discussed in Section D.5 on page 732. For more information about the Backstage View, see the online **Using Excel 2010 Guide**.

Self-Test Solutions and Answers to Selected Even-Numbered Problems

The following represent worked-out solutions to Self-Test Problems and brief answers to most of the even-numbered problems in the text. For more detailed solutions, including explanations, interpretations, and Excel output, see the *Student Solutions Manual*.

CHAPTER 1

1.6 (a) All 3,727 full-time first-year students at the university. **(b)** The 2,821 students who responded to the survey. **(c)** The proportion of all 3,727 students who studied with other students. **(d)** The proportion of the sample of 2,821 responding students who studied with other students.

1.8 (a) Adults living in the United States, aged 18 and older. **(b)** The 1,012 adults living in the United States, aged 18 and older, who were selected in the sample. **(c)** Because the 80% is based on the sample, it is a statistic.

CHAPTER 2

2.2 Small, medium, and large sizes imply order but do not specify how much more soft drink is added at increasing levels.

2.4 (a) The number of telephones is a numerical variable that is discrete because the outcome is a count. It is ratio scaled because it has a true zero point. **(b)** The length of the longest long-distance call is a numerical variable that is continuous because any value within a range of values can occur. It is ratio scaled because it has a true zero point. **(c)** Whether there is a cell phone in the household is a categorical variable because the answer can be only yes or no. This also makes it a nominal-scaled variable. **(d)** Same answer as in **(c)**.

2.6 (a) Categorical, nominal scale. **(b)** Numerical, continuous, ratio scale. **(c)** Numerical, discrete, ratio scale. **(d)** Numerical, discrete, ratio scale.

2.8 (a) Numerical, continuous, ratio scale. **(b)** Numerical, discrete, ratio scale. **(c)** Numerical, continuous, ratio scale. **(d)** Categorical, nominal scale.

2.10 The underlying variable, ability of the students, may be continuous, but the measuring device, the test, does not have enough precision to distinguish between the two students.

2.12 (a) Categorical, categorical, numerical discrete, categorical.

2.20 (a) Table of frequencies for all student responses:

GENDER	STUDENT MAJOR CATEGORIES			
	A	C	M	Totals
Male	14	9	2	25
Female	6	6	3	15
Totals	20	15	5	40

(b) Table of percentages based on overall student responses:

GENDER	STUDENT MAJOR CATEGORIES			
	A	C	M	Totals
Male	35.0%	22.5%	5.0%	62.5%
Female	15.0	15.0	7.5	37.5
Totals	50.0	37.5	12.5	100.0

(c) Table based on row percentages:

GENDER	STUDENT MAJOR CATEGORIES			
	A	C	M	Totals
Male	56.0%	36.0%	8.0%	100.0%
Female	40.0	40.0	20.0	100.0
Totals	50.0	37.5	12.5	100.0

(d) Table based on column percentages:

GENDER	STUDENT MAJOR CATEGORIES			
	A	C	M	Totals
Male	70.0%	60.0%	40.0%	62.5%
Female	30.0	40.0	60.0	37.5
Totals	100.0	100.0	100.0	100.0

2.22 (a) The percentages are 48.52, 6.04, 21.33, 19.61, and 4.49. **(b)** Almost half the electricity is generated from coal. About 20% of the electricity is generated from natural gas, and about 20% is generated from nuclear power.

2.24 (a) Table of row percentages:

ENJOY SHOPPING FOR CLOTHING	GENDER		
	Male	Female	Total
Yes	38%	62%	100%
No	74	26	100
Total	48	52	100

Table of column percentages:

ENJOY SHOPPING FOR CLOTHING	GENDER		
	Male	Female	Total
Yes	57%	86%	72%
No	43	14	28
Total	100	100	100

Table of total percentages:

ENJOY SHOPPING FOR CLOTHING	GENDER		
	Male	Female	Total
Yes	27%	45%	72%
No	21	7	28
Total	48	52	100

(b) A higher percentage of females enjoy shopping for clothing.

2.26 (b) The percentage of MBA and undergraduate students who choose the lowest-cost fund and the second-lowest-cost fund is about the same. A higher percentage of MBA students chose the third-lowest-cost fund, whereas a higher percentage of undergraduate students chose the highest-cost fund.

2.28 73   78   78   78   85   88   91.

2.30 (a) 10 but less than 20, 20 but less than 30, 30 but less than 40, 40 but less than 50, 50 but less than 60, 60 but less than 70, 70 but less than 80, 80 but less than 90, 90 but less than 100. **(b)** 10. **(c)** 15, 25, 35, 45, 55, 65, 75, 85, 95.

2.32 (a)

Electricity Costs	Frequency	Percentage
$80 up to $99	4	8%
$100 up to $119	7	14
$120 up to $139	9	18
$140 up to $159	13	26
$160 up to $179	9	18
$180 up to $199	5	10
$200 up to $219	3	6

(b)

Electricity Costs	Frequency	Percentage	Cumulative %
$ 99	4	8.00%	8.00%
$119	7	14.00	22.00
$139	9	18.00	40.00
$159	13	26.00	66.00
$179	9	18.00	84.00
$199	5	10.00	94.00
$219	3	6.00	100.00

(c) The majority of utility charges are clustered between $120 and $180.

2.34 (a)

Width	Frequency	Percentage
8.310–8.329	3	6.12%
8.330–8.349	2	4.08
8.350–8.369	1	2.04
8.370–8.389	4	8.16
8.390–8.409	5	10.20
8.410–8.429	16	32.65
8.430–8.449	5	10.20
8.450–8.469	5	10.20
8.470–8.489	6	12.24
8.490–8.509	2	4.08

(b)

Width	Percentage Less Than
8.310	0
8.330	6.12
8.350	10.20
8.370	12.24
8.390	20.40
8.410	30.60
8.430	63.25
8.450	73.45
8.470	83.65
8.490	95.89
8.51	100.00

(c) All the troughs will meet the company's requirements of between 8.31 and 8.61 inches wide.

2.36 (a)

Bulb Life (hrs)	Percentage, Mfgr A	Percentage, Mfgr B
650–749	7.5%	0.0%
750–849	12.5	5.0
850–949	50.0	20.0
950–1,049	22.5	40.0
1,050–1,149	7.5	22.5
1,150–1,249	0.0	12.5

(b)

% Less Than	Percentage Less Than, Mfgr A	Percentage Less Than, Mfgr B
750	7.5%	0.0%
850	20.0	5.0
950	70.0	25.0
1,050	92.5	65.0
1,150	100.0	87.5
1,250	100.0	100.0

(c) Manufacturer B produces bulbs with longer lives than Manufacturer A. The cumulative percentage for Manufacturer B shows that 65% of its bulbs lasted less than 1,050 hours, contrasted with 70% of Manufacturer A's bulbs, which lasted less than 950 hours. None of Manufacturer A's bulbs lasted more than 1,149 hours, but 12.5% of Manufacturer B's bulbs lasted between 1,150 and 1,249 hours. At the same time, 7.5% of Manufacturer A's bulbs lasted less than 750 hours, whereas all of Manufacturer B's bulbs lasted at least 750 hours.

2.38 (b) The Pareto chart is best for portraying these data because it not only sorts the frequencies in descending order but also provides the cumulative line on the same scale. **(c)** You can conclude that friends/family account for the largest percentage, 45%. When other, news media, and online user reviews are added to friends/family, this accounts for 83%.

2.40 (b) 89.46%. **(d)** The Pareto chart allows you to see which sources account for most of the electricity.

2.42 (b) Because a large percentage of students are from Asia, the Pareto chart allows you to focus on this dominant group. Almost 60% are from Asia. Including Asia, Europe, and Latin America represents 83% of all the foreign students.

2.44 (b) A higher percentage of females enjoy shopping for clothing.

2.46 (b) The number of MBA and undergraduate students who choose the lowest-cost fund and the second-lowest-cost fund is about the same. More MBA students chose the third-lowest-cost fund, whereas more undergraduate students chose the highest-cost fund.

2.48 50   74   74   76   81   89   92.

2.50 (a)

Stem unit:	10	Stem unit:	10	Stem unit:	10
11	4	22	0 2 3 4	33	
12		23		34	
13	5	24		35	
14	1 5 6	25	9	36	
15	1 8	26		37	
16	1 2 4 5 6	27		38	
17	0 0 2	28		39	
18	0 5 7	29		40	
19		30	5	41	1
20	5	31			
21	0 5 6	32	6		

(b) The results are concentrated between $160 and $225.

2.52 (c) The majority of utility charges are clustered between $120 and $180.

2.54 The property taxes per capita appear to be right-skewed, with approximately 90% falling between $399 and $1,700 and the remaining 10% falling between $1,700 and $2,100. The center is at about $1,000.

2.56 (d) All the troughs will meet the company's requirements of between 8.31 and 8.61 inches wide.

2.58 (c) Manufacturer B produces bulbs with longer lives than Manufacturer A.

2.60 (b) Yes, there is a strong positive relationship between X and Y. As X increases, so does Y.

2.62 (b) There is a positive relationship between owner mileage and current government standard mileage.

2.64 (c) There appears to be a positive relationship between the coaches' salary and revenue. Yes, this is borne out by the data.

2.66 (b) The unemployment rate trended upward and leveled off at around 6% by December 2001. Around October 2003, it started to trend downward and reached about 4.5% by December 2006 before staying between 4.5% and 5% in 2007. It then trended upward and reached 7.2% in December 2008.

2.68 (b) There is an obvious increasing trend from 2004 to 2008, with a sharp increase in 2008. **(c)** You would predict about 6.5 to 7 million in 2009.

2.70 (a)

Objective Risk

Count of Risk Category	Growth			Growth Total	Value			Value Total	Grand Total
	Average	High	Low		Average	High	Low		
Large cap	97	116	18	231	77	11	131	219	450
Mid cap	32	76	3	111	23	10	30	63	174
Small cap	11	110	1	122	71	32	19	122	244
Grand Total	140	302	22	464	171	53	180	404	868

(b) Large-cap growth funds are very likely to be high risk, while large-cap value funds are very likely to be low risk. Mid-cap growth funds are very likely to be high risk, while mid-cap value funds are very likely to be average or low risk. Small-cap growth funds are very likely to be high risk, while small-cap value funds are likely to be high or average risk.

2.72 (a)

Fees Risk

Count of Risk Category	No			No Total	Yes			Yes Total	Grand Total
	Average	High	Low		Average	High	Low		
Large cap	95	76	80	251	79	51	69	199	450
Mid cap	33	41	23	97	22	45	10	77	174
Small cap	52	84	16	152	30	58	4	92	244
Grand Total	180	201	119	500	131	154	83	368	868

(b) Large-cap funds without fees are fairly evenly spread in risk, while large-cap funds with fees are more likely to have average or low risk. Mid-cap and small-cap funds, regardless of fees, are more likely to have average or high risk.

2.92 (c) The publisher gets the largest portion (64.8%) of the revenue. About half (32.3%) of the revenue received by the publisher covers manufacturing costs. The publisher's marketing and promotion account for the next largest share of the revenue, at 15.4%. Author, bookstore employee salaries and benefits, and publisher administrative costs and taxes each account for around 10% of the revenue, whereas the publisher after-tax profit, bookstore operations, bookstore pretax profit, and freight constitute the "trivial few" allocations of the revenue. Yes, the bookstore gets twice the revenue of the authors.

2.94 (b) The Pareto plot is most appropriate because it not only sorts the frequencies in descending order, it also provides the cumulative polygon on the same scale. **(d)** The Pareto plot is most appropriate because it not only sorts the frequencies in descending order but also provides the cumulative polygon on the same scale. **(e)** "Paid search" constitutes the largest category on U.S. online ad spending, at 43%. Excluding the generic keyword "sneakers," searches using the keywords "sneaker pimps" and "Jordan sneaker" make up the majority of the searches for sneakers on specific brands.

2.96 (a)

DESSERT ORDERED	GENDER		
	Male	Female	Total
Yes	71%	29%	100%
No	48	52	100
Total	53	47	100

DESSERT ORDERED	GENDER		
	Male	Female	Total
Yes	30%	14%	23%
No	70	86	77
Total	100	100	100

DESSERT ORDERED	GENDER		
	Male	Female	Total
Yes	16%	7%	23%
No	37	40	77
Total	53	47	100

DESSERT ORDERED	BEEF ENTRÉE		
	Yes	No	Total
Yes	52%	48%	100%
No	25	75	100
Total	31	69	100

DESSERT ORDERED	BEEF ENTRÉE		
	Yes	No	Total
Yes	38%	16%	23%
No	62	84	77
Total	100	100	100

DESSERT ORDERED	BEEF ENTRÉE		
	Yes	No	Total
Yes	12%	11%	23%
No	19	58	77
Total	31	69	100

(b) If the owner is interested in finding out the percentage of males and females who order dessert or the percentage of those who order a beef entrée and a dessert among all patrons, the table of total percentages is most informative. If the owner is interested in the effect of gender on ordering of dessert or the effect of ordering a beef entrée on the ordering of dessert, the table of column percentages will be most informative. Because dessert is usually ordered after the main entrée, and the owner has no direct control over the gender of patrons, the table of row percentages is not very useful here. **(c)** 30% of the men ordered desserts, compared to 14% of the women; men are more than twice as likely to order dessert as women. Almost 38% of the patrons ordering a beef entrée ordered dessert, compared to 16% of patrons ordering all other entrées. Patrons ordering beef are more than 2.3 times as likely to order dessert as patrons ordering any other entrée.

2.98 (a) 23575R15 accounts for over 80% of the warranty claims. **(b)** 91.82% of the warranty claims are from the ATX model. **(c)** Tread separation accounts for 73.23% of the warranty claims among the ATX model. **(d)** The number of claims is evenly distributed among the three incidents; other/unknown incidents account for almost 40% of the claims, tread separation accounts for about 35% of the claims, and blowout accounts for about 25% of the claims.

2.100 The alcohol percentage is concentrated between 4% and 6%, with more between 4% and 5%. The calories are concentrated between 140 and 160. The carbohydrates are concentrated between 12 and 15. There are outliers in the percentage of alcohol in both tails. The outlier in the lower tail is due to the non-alcoholic beer O'Doul's, with only a 0.4% alcohol content. There are a few beers with alcohol content as high as around 10.5%. There are a few beers with calorie contents as high as around 302.5 and carbohydrates as high as 31.5.

There is a strong positive relationship between percentage alcohol and calories, there is a strong positive relationship between calories and carbohydrates, and there is a moderately positive relationship between percentage alcohol and carbohydrates.

2.102 The money market yield is concentrated between 0.2 and 0.3. The one-year CD is concentrated between 1 and 2.1. The five-year CD yield is concentrated between 1.7 and 1.8 and 3.0 and 3.4. In general, the five-year CD has the highest yield, followed by the one-year CD and then the money market.

There appears to be a positive relationship between the yield of the one-year CD and the five-year CD, but no obvious relationship exists between the yield of the money market and the one-year CD and between the money market and the five-year CD.

2.104 (a)

Frequencies (Boston)		
Weight (Boston)	Frequency	Percentage
3,015 but less than 3,050	2	0.54%
3,050 but less than 3,085	44	11.96
3,085 but less than 3,120	122	33.15
3,120 but less than 3,155	131	35.60
3,155 but less than 3,190	58	15.76
3,190 but less than 3,225	7	1.90
3,225 but less than 3,260	3	0.82
3,260 but less than 3,295	1	0.27

(b)

Frequencies (Vermont)		
Weight (Vermont)	Frequency	Percentage
3,550 but less than 3,600	4	1.21%
3,600 but less than 3,650	31	9.39
3,650 but less than 3,700	115	34.85
3,700 but less than 3,750	131	39.70
3,750 but less than 3,800	36	10.91
3,800 but less than 3,850	12	3.64
3,850 but less than 3,900	1	0.30

(d) 0.54% of the Boston shingles pallets are underweight, whereas 0.27% are overweight. 1.21% of the Vermont shingles pallets are underweight, whereas 3.94% are overweight.

2.106 (a), (c)

Calories	Frequency	Percentage	Limit	Percentage Less Than
50 but less than 100	3	12%	100	12%
100 but less than 150	3	12	150	24
150 but less than 200	9	36	200	60
200 but less than 250	6	24	250	84
250 but less than 300	3	12	300	96
300 but less than 350	0	0	350	96
350 but less than 400	1	4	400	100

Cholesterol	Frequency	Percentage	Limit	Percentage Less Than
0 but less than 50	2	8%	50	8%
50 but less than 100	17	68	100	76
100 but less than 150	4	16	150	92
150 but less than 200	1	4	200	96
200 but less than 250	0	0	250	96
250 but less than 300	0	0	300	96
300 but less than 350	0	0	350	96
350 but less than 400	0	0	400	96
400 but less than 450	0	0	450	96
450 but less than 500	1	4	500	100

(d) The sampled fresh red meats, poultry, and fish vary from 98 to 397 calories per serving, with the highest concentration between 150 to 200 calories. One protein source, spareribs, with 397 calories, is more than 100 calories above the next-highest-caloric food. The protein content of the sampled foods varies from 16 to 33 grams, with 68% of the data values falling between 24 and 32 grams. Spareribs and fried liver are both very different from other foods sampled—the former on calories and the latter on cholesterol content.

2.108 (b) There is a downward trend in the amount filled. **(c)** The amount filled in the next bottle will most likely be below 1.894 liter. **(d)** The scatter plot of the amount of soft drink filled against time reveals the trend of the data, whereas a histogram only provides information on the distribution of the data.

CHAPTER 3

3.2 (a) Mean = 7, median = 7, mode = 7. **(b)** Range = 9, S^2 = 10.8, S = 3.286, CV = 46.948%. **(c)** Z scores: 0, −0.913, 0.609, 0, −1.217, 1.522. None of the Z scores are larger than 3.0 or smaller than −3.0. There is no outlier. **(d)** Symmetric because mean = median.

3.4 (a) Mean $= 2$, median $= 7$, mode $= 7$. **(b)** Range $= 17$, $S^2 = 62$ $S = 7.874$, $CV = 393.7\%$. **(d)** Left-skewed because mean $<$ median.

3.6 -0.085.

3.8 (a)

	Grade X	Grade Y
Mean	575	575.4
Median	575	575
Standard deviation	6.40	2.07

(b) If quality is measured by central tendency, Grade X tires provide slightly better quality because X's mean and median are both equal to the expected value, 575 mm. If, however, quality is measured by consistency, Grade Y provides better quality because, even though Y's mean is only slightly larger than the mean for Grade X, Y's standard deviation is much smaller. The range in values for Grade Y is 5 mm compared to the range in values for Grade X, which is 16 mm.

(c)

	Grade X	Grade Y, Altered
Mean	575	577.4
Median	575	575
Standard deviation	6.40	6.11

When the fifth Y tire measures 588 mm rather than 578 mm, Y's mean inner diameter becomes 577.4 mm, which is larger than X's mean inner diameter, and Y's standard deviation increases from 2.07 mm to 6.11 mm. In this case, X's tires are providing better quality in terms of the mean inner diameter, with only slightly more variation among the tires than Y's.

3.10 (a) Mean $= \dfrac{219.2}{6} = 36.53$,

median $= 3.5$ ranked value $= \dfrac{35.05 + 36.15}{2} = 35.6$.

Variance $= (36.15 - 36.53)^2 + (31.00 - 36.53)^2 + (35.05 - 36.53)^2$
$\qquad + (40.25 - 36.53)^2 + (33.75 - 36.53)^2 + (43.00 - 36.53)^2$
$\qquad = \dfrac{96.3433}{6 - 1} = 19.269$,

standard deviation $= \sqrt{19.269} = 4.39$, range $= 43 - 31 = 12$,

coefficient of variation $= \dfrac{4.39}{36.53} \times 100\% = 12.02\%$

(c) The mean is only slightly larger than the median, so the data are only slightly right-skewed. **(d)** The mean cost is $36.53, and the median cost is $35.60. The average scatter of cost around the mean is $4.39. The difference between the highest cost and the lowest cost is $12.

3.12 (a) Mean $= 19.9565$, median $= 21$, mode $= 22$. **(b)** $S^2 = 5.0435$, $S = 2.2458$, range $= 8$, coefficient of variation $= 11.25\%$, and Z scores are 1.80, 1.36, 0.91, 0.46, 0.91, 0.91, -0.87, -0.43, -0.43, -0.43, 0.46, 0.46, 0.46, -0.87, -0.43, 0.46, -1.32, 0.91, -0.87, -0.87, 0.91, -1.76, and -1.76. **(c)** Because the mean is less than the median, the data are left-skewed. **(d)** The distributions of MPG of the sedans is symmetric, while the MPG of the SUVs is left skewed. The mean MPG of sedans is 7.48 higher than that of SUVs. The average scatter of the MPG of sedans is slightly higher than that for SUVs. The range of sedans is the same as SUVs.

3.14 (a) Mean $= \$0.9257$, median $= \$0.88$. **(b)** Variance $= 0.1071$, standard deviation $= \$0.3273$, range $= \$0.96$, $CV = 35.36\%$. There is no outlier because none of the Z scores has an absolute value that is greater than 3.0.

(c) The data appear to be right skewed because the mean is greater than the median.

3.16 (a) Mean $= 46.8$, median $= 42.5$. **(b)** Range $= 34$, variance $= 123.29$, standard deviation $= 11.10$ **(c)** The admission price for one-day tickets is slightly right skewed because the mean is slightly greater than the median. **(d) (a)** Mean $= 50.8$, median $= 42.5$ **(b)** Range $= 69$, variance $= 382.84$, standard deviation $= 19.57$ **(c)** The admission price for one-day tickets is right skewed because the mean is much greater than the median due to the much higher price of the first observation, at $98.

3.18 (a) Mean $= 7.11$, median $= 6.68$. **(b)** Variance $= 4.336$, standard deviation $= 2.082$, range $= 6.67$, $CV = 29.27\%$ **(c)** Because the mean is greater than the median, the distribution is right-skewed. **(d)** The mean and median are both greater than 5 minutes. The distribution is right-skewed, meaning that there are some unusually high values. Further, 13 of the 15 bank customers sampled (or 86.7%) had waiting times greater than 5 minutes. So the customer is likely to experience a waiting time in excess of 5 minutes. The manager overstated the bank's service record in responding that the customer would "almost certainly" not wait longer than 5 minutes for service.

3.20 (a) $[(1 + 0.8909) \times (1 - 0.6331)]^{1/2} - 1 = 0.8329 - 1 = -16.71\%$. **(b)** $693.72. **(c)** The result for Taser was better than the result for GE, which was worth $472.93.

3.22 (a) Platinum $= -2.34\%$, gold $= 19.23\%$, silver $= 6.9\%$. **(b)** Gold had a much higher return than either platinum or silver. **(c)** Gold and silver had positive returns, whereas the three stock indices all had negative returns.

3.24 (a) 4, 9, 5. **(b)** 3, 4, 7, 9, 12. **(c)** The distances between the median and the extremes are close, 4 and 5, but the differences in the tails are different (1 on the left and 3 on the right), so this distribution is slightly right-skewed. **(d)** In Problem 3.2 (d), because mean $=$ median, the distribution is symmetric. The box part of the graph is symmetric, but the tails show right-skewness.

3.26 (a) -6.5, 8, 14.5. **(b)** -8, -6.5, 7, 8, 9. **(c)** The shape is left-skewed. **(d)** This is consistent with the answer in Problem 3.4 (d).

3.28 (a) $Q_1 = \dfrac{14 + 1}{4} = 3.75$ ranked value $= 4$th ranked value $= \$0.68$,

$Q_3 = \dfrac{3(14 + 1)}{4} = \dfrac{45}{4} = 11.25$ ranked value $= 11$th ranked value $= \$1.14$,

Interquartile range $= 1.14 - 0.68 = \$0.46$. **(b)** Five-number summary: 0.55 0.68 0.88 1.14 1.51. **(c)** The distribution is right-skewed.

3.30 (a) $Q_1 = 18$, $Q_3 = 22$, interquartile range $= 4$. **(b)** Five-number summary: 16 18 21 22 24. **(c)** The MPG of SUVs is left-skewed.

3.32 (a) Commercial district five-number summary: 0.38 3.2 4.5 5.55 6.46. Residential area five-number summary: 3.82 5.64 6.68 8.73 10.49. **(b)** Commercial district: The distribution is left skewed. Residential area: The distribution is slightly right skewed. **(c)** The central tendency of the waiting times for the bank branch located in the commercial district of a city is lower than that of the branch located in the residential area. There are a few long waiting times for the branch located in the residential area, whereas there are a few exceptionally short waiting times for the branch located in the commercial area.

3.34 (a)

Average of 3-Year Return	Risk			
Category	Average	High	Low	Grand Total
Large Cap	9.7000	6.6251	12.2403	9.6733
Mid Cap	13.2782	10.7488	15.5424	12.4575
Small Cap	14.8329	10.5887	15.0700	12.3824
Grand Total	11.6862	9.2096	13.0599	10.9930

(b)

StdDev of 3-Year Return	Risk			
Category	Average	High	Low	Grand Total
Large Cap	3.0090	3.7220	2.4975	3.7745
Mid Cap	2.8689	3.0296	2.1528	3.3787
Small Cap	2.7130	4.2092	2.7475	4.2220
Grand Total	3.7003	4.2340	2.8207	4.0657

(c) Among the average-risk funds, small cap has the highest average three-year return but the lowest standard deviation. Mid cap has the highest average three-year return and the lowest standard deviation among the high-risk funds and the low-risk funds.

3.36 (a)

Average of Return 2006		Risk			
Category	Objective	Average	High	Low	Grand Total
• Large Cap	Growth	8.3041	5.3863	10.9333	7.0437
	Value	16.7104	16.1455	18.0198	17.4653
Large Cap Total		12.0241	6.3181	17.1638	12.1156
• Mid Cap	Growth	10.1375	8.4487	12.9000	9.0559
	Value	15.5391	12.0300	16.7233	15.5460
Mid Cap Total		12.3964	8.8651	16.3758	11.4057
• Small Cap	Growth	13.9636	11.1563	28.5000	11.5516
	Value	16.4845	17.1844	15.5842	16.5279
Small Cap Total		16.1463	12.5148	16.2300	14.0398
Grand Total		13.1768	9.4138	16.9426	12.5142

(b)

StdDev of Return 2006		Risk			
Category	Objective	Average	High	Low	Grand Total
• Large Cap	Growth	4.1607	4.8464	4.7636	4.8874
	Value	3.1941	3.0608	2.9439	3.1030
Large Cap Total		5.6233	5.6046	3.9482	6.6411
• Mid Cap	Growth	4.8667	4.7452	5.6000	4.8575
	Value	3.2932	3.3659	3.3215	3.6493
Mid Cap Total		5.0245	4.7330	3.6337	5.4370
• Small Cap	Growth	4.8929	5.4631	—	5.6488
	Value	5.0358	5.8491	4.158426	5.1248
Small Cap Total		5.0615	6.0813	4.9722	5.9315
Grand Total		5.6502	6.2175	4.0071	6.2916

(c) Small cap has the highest average 2006 return and the highest standard deviation among the average-risk and growth funds, the high-risk and growth funds, and the high-risk and value funds. Small cap also has the highest average 2006 return but the lowest standard deviation among the low-risk and growth funds. The large cap has the highest average 2006 return but the lowest standard deviation among the low-risk and value funds and among the average risk and value funds.

3.38 (a) Population mean, $\mu = 6$. **(b)** Population standard deviation, $\sigma = 1.673$, population variance, $\sigma^2 = 2.8$.

3.40 (a) 68%. **(b)** 95%. **(c)** Not calculable, 75%, 88.89%. **(d)** $\mu - 4\sigma$ to $\mu + 4\sigma$ or -2.8 to 19.2.

3.42 (a) Mean $= \dfrac{662,960}{51} = 12,999.22$, variance $= \dfrac{762,944,726.6}{51} = 14,959,700.52$, standard deviation $= \sqrt{14,959,700.52} = 3,867.78$. **(b)** 64.71%, 98.04%, and 100% of these states have mean per-capita energy consumption within 1, 2, and 3 standard deviations of the mean, respectively. **(c)** This is consistent with 68%, 95%, and 99.7%, according to the empirical rule. **(d)(a)** Mean $= \dfrac{642,887}{50} = 12,857.74$, variance $= \dfrac{711,905,533.6}{50} = 14,238,110.67$, standard deviation $= \sqrt{14,238,110.67} = 3,773.34$. **(b)** 66%, 98%, and 100% of these states have a mean per-capita energy consumption within 1, 2, and 3 standard deviations of the mean, respectively. **(c)** This is consistent with 68%, 95%, and 99.7%, according to the empirical rule.

3.44 Covariance $= 65.2909, r = +1.0$.

3.46 (a) $\text{cov}(X, Y) = \dfrac{\displaystyle\sum_{i=1}^{n}(X_i - \overline{X})(Y_i - \overline{Y})}{n-1} = \dfrac{3550}{6} = 591.6667$.

(b) $r = \dfrac{\text{cov}(X, Y)}{S_X S_Y} = \dfrac{591.6667}{(113.1371)(7.2678)} = 0.7196$.

(c) The correlation coefficient is more valuable for expressing the relationship between calories and fat because it does not depend on the units used to measure calories and fat. **(d)** There is a strong positive linear relationship between calories and fat.

3.48 (a) Covariance $= 1.2132$. **(b)** $r = 0.6092$. **(c)** There is a moderate positive linear relationship between the coaches' salary and revenue.

3.62 (a) Mean $= 43.89$, median $= 45$, 1st quartile $= 18$, 3rd quartile $= 63$. **(b)** Range $= 76$, interquartile range $= 45$, variance $= 639.2564$, standard deviation $= 25.28, CV = 57.61\%$. **(c)** The distribution is right skewed because there are a few policies that require an exceptionally long period to be approved. **(d)** The mean approval process takes 43.89 days, with 50% of the policies being approved in less than 45 days. 50% of the applications are approved between 18 and 63 days. About 67% of the applications are approved between 18.6 and 69.2 days.

3.64 (a) Mean $= 8.421$, median $= 8.42$, range $= 0.186, S = 0.0461$. The mean and median width are both 8.42 inches. The range of the widths is 0.186 inch, and the average scatter around the mean is 0.0461 inch. **(b)** 8.312, 8.404, 8.42, 8.459, 8.498. **(c)** Even though mean $=$ median, the left tail is slightly longer, so the distribution is slightly left-skewed. **(d)** All the troughs in this sample meet the specifications.

3.66 (a), (b)

	Calories	Fat
Mean	108.3333	3.375
Median	110	3.25
Standard deviation	19.46247	1.759713
Sample variance	378.7879	3.096591
Range	70	5.5
First quartile	90	1.5
Third quartile	120	5
Interquartile range	30	3.5
Coefficient of variation	17.97%	52.14%

(c) The distribution of calories and total fat are symmetrical.

(d) $r = \dfrac{\text{cov}(X, Y)}{S_X S_Y} = 0.6969$.

(e) The number of calories of the veggie burgers centers around 110, and its distribution is symmetrical. The amount of fat centers around 3.3 grams per serving, and its distribution is symmetrical. There is a positive linear relationship between calories and fat.

3.68 (a) Boston: 0.04, 0.17, 0.23, 0.32, 0.98; Vermont: 0.02, 0.13, 0.20, 0.28, 0.83. **(b)** Both distributions are right-skewed. **(c)** Both sets of shingles did quite well in achieving a granule loss of 0.8 gram or less. The Boston shingles had only two data points greater than 0.8 gram. The next highest to these was 0.6 gram. These two data points can be considered outliers. Only 1.176% of the shingles failed the specification. In the Vermont shingles, only one data point was greater than 0.8 gram. The next highest was 0.58 gram. Thus, only 0.714% of the shingles failed to meet the specification.

3.70 (a) The correlation between calories and protein is 0.4644. **(b)** The correlation between calories and cholesterol is 0.1777. **(c)** The correlation between protein and cholesterol is 0.1417. **(d)** There is a weak positive linear relationship between calories and protein, with a correlation coefficient of 0.46. The positive linear relationships between calories and cholesterol and between protein and cholesterol are very weak.

3.72 (a), (b)

Property Taxes per Capita ($)

Mean	1,040.863
Median	981
Standard deviation	428.5385
Sample variance	183645.2
Range	1732
First quartile	713
Third quartile	1306
Interquartile range	593
Coefficient of variation	41.17%

(c), (d) The distribution of the property taxes per capita is right-skewed, with a mean value of $1,040.83, a median of $981, and an average spread around the mean of $428.54. There is an outlier in the right tail at $2,099, while the standard deviation is about 41.17% of the mean. 25% of the states have property tax that falls below $713 per capita, and 25% have property taxes that are higher than $1,306 per capita.

CHAPTER 4

4.2 (a) Simple events include selecting a red ball. **(b)** Selecting a white ball.

4.4 (a) $60/100 = 3/5 = 0.6$. **(b)** $10/100 = 1/10 = 0.1$. **(c)** $35/100 = 7/20 = 0.35$. **(d)** $9/10 = 0.9$.

4.6 (a) Mutually exclusive, not collectively exhaustive. **(b)** Not mutually exclusive, not collectively exhaustive. **(c)** Mutually exclusive, not collectively exhaustive. **(d)** Mutually exclusive, collectively exhaustive.

4.8 (a) "Makes less than $50,000." **(b)** "Makes less than $50,000 and tax code is unfair." **(c)** The complement of "tax code is fair" is "tax code is unfair." **(d)** "Tax code is fair and makes less than $50,000" is a joint event because it consists of two characteristics.

4.10 (a) A respondent who answers quickly. **(b)** A respondent who answers quickly who is over 70 years old. **(c)** A respondent who does not answer quickly. **(d)** A respondent who answers quickly and is over 70 years old is a joint event because it consists of two characteristics, answering quickly and being over 70 years old.

4.12 (a) $796/3,790 = 0.21$. **(b)** $1,895/3,790 = 0.50$. **(c)** $796/3,790 + 1,895/3,790 - 550/3,790 = 2,141/3790 = 0.5649$. **(d)** The probability of "is engaged with their workplace *or* is a U.S. worker" includes the

probability of "is engaged with their workplace" plus the probability of "is a U.S. worker" minus the joint probability of "is engaged with their workplace *and* is a U.S. worker."

4.14 (a) $360/500 = 18/25 = 0.72$. **(b)** $224/500 = 56/125 = 0.448$. **(c)** $396/500 = 99/125 = 0.792$. **(d)** $500/500 = 1.00$.

4.16 (a) $10/30 = 1/3 = 0.33$. **(b)** $20/60 = 1/3 = 0.33$. **(c)** $40/60 = 2/3 = 0.67$. **(d)** Because $P(A/B) = P(A) = 1/3$, events A and B are independent.

4.18 $\frac{1}{2} = 0.5$.

4.20 Because $P(A \text{ and } B) = 0.20$ and $P(A)P(B) = 0.12$, events A and B are not independent.

4.22 (a) $536/1,000 = 0.536$. **(b)** $707/1,000 = 0.707$. **(c)** $P(\text{Answers quickly}) = 1,243/2,000 = 0.6215$ which is not equal to $P(\text{Answers quickly}/\text{between 12 and 50}) = 0.536$. Therefore, answers quickly and age are not independent.

4.24 (a) $550/1,895 = 0.2902$. **(b)** $1,345/1,895 = 0.7098$. **(c)** $246/1,895 = 0.1298$. **(d)** $1,649,895 = 0.8702$.

4.26 (a) $0.025/0.6 = 0.0417$. **(b)** $0.015/0.4 = 0.0375$. **(c)** Because $P(\text{Needs warranty repair} \mid \text{Manufacturer based in U.S.}) = 0.0417$ and $P(\text{Needs warranty repair}) = 0.04$, the two events are not independent.

4.28 (a) 0.0045. **(b)** 0.012. **(c)** 0.0059. **(d)** 0.0483.

4.30 0.095.

4.32 (a) 0.736. **(b)** 0.997.

4.34 (a) $P(B' \mid O) = \dfrac{(0.5)(0.3)}{(0.5)(0.3) + (0.25)(0.7)} = 0.4615$.

(b) $P(O) = 0.175 + 0.15 = 0.325$.

4.36 (a) $P(\text{Huge success} \mid \text{Favorable review}) = 0.099/0.459 = 0.2157$; $P(\text{Moderate success} \mid \text{Favorable review}) = 0.14/0.459 = 0.3050$; $P(\text{Break even} \mid \text{Favorable review}) = 0.16/0.459 = 0.3486$; $P(\text{Loser} \mid \text{Favorable review}) = 0.06/0.459 = 0.1307$. **(b)** $P(\text{Favorable review}) = 0.459$.

4.46 (a)

Goals	18–25	26–40	Total
Getting Rich	405	310	715
Other	95	190	285
Total	500	500	1,000

(Age heading spans 18–25 and 26–40 columns.)

(b) Simple event: "Has a goal of getting rich." Joint event: "Has a goal of getting rich and is between 18–25 years old." **(c)** $P(\text{Has a goal of getting rich}) = 715/1,000 = 0.715$. **(d)** $P(\text{Has a goal of getting rich and is in the 26–40-year-old group}) = 310/1000 = 0.31$. **(e)** Not independent.

4.48 (a) $P(\text{selected the lowest- or second-lowest-cost fund}) = (19 + 19 + 37 + 40)/200 = 0.575$. **(b)** $P(\text{selected the lowest-cost fund and is an undergraduate}) = 19/200 = 0.095$. **(c)** $P(\text{selected the lowest-cost fund or is an undergraduate}) = (38 + 100 - 19)/200 = 0.595$. **(d)** $P(\text{selected the highest-cost fund} \mid \text{undergraduate}) = 27/100 = 0.27$. **(e)** Because $P(\text{selected the highest-cost fund}) = (27 + 18)/200 = 0.225$ is not equal to $P(\text{selected the highest-cost fund} \mid \text{undergraduate}) = 0.27$, selected the highest-cost fund and undergraduate are not statistically independent. The same result holds for having selected any other type of funds. Hence, what type of fund is selected by a student is not independent of whether a student is an undergraduate or a graduate student. Therefore, undergraduate students and graduate students differ in their fund selection.

4.50 (a) 0.4712. **(b)** Because the probability that a fatality involved a rollover, given that the fatality involved an SUV, a van, or a pickup is 0.4712, which is almost twice the probability that a fatality involved a rollover with any vehicle type, at 0.24, SUVs, vans, and pickups are generally more prone to rollover accidents.

CHAPTER 5

5.2 (a) $\mu = 0(0.10) + 1(0.20) + 2(0.45) + 3(0.15) + 4(0.05) + 5(0.05) = 2.0.$

(b) $\sigma = \sqrt{\begin{array}{c}(0 - 2)^2(0.10) + (1 - 2)^2(0.20) + (2 - 2)^2(0.45) + \\ (3 - 2)^2(0.15) + (4 - 2)^2(0.05) + (5 - 2)^2(0.05)\end{array}}$

$= 1.183.$

5.4 (a)

X	P(X)
$ - 1	21/36
$ + 1	15/36

(b)

X	P(X)
$ - 1	21/36
$ + 1	15/36

(c)

X	P(X)
$ - 1	30/36
$ + 4	6/36

(d) $ - 0.167 for each method of play.

5.6 (a) 2.105769. **(b)** 1.467063.

5.8 (a) 90; 30. **(b)** 126.10, 10.95. **(c)** $-1,300$. **(d)** 120.

5.10 (a) 9.5 minutes. **(b)** 1.9209 minutes.

5.12

X*P(X)	Y*P(Y)	$(X - \mu_X)^{2*}$ $P(X)$	$(Y - \mu_Y)^{2*}$ $P(Y)$	$(X - \mu_X)(Y - \mu_Y)^*$ $P(XY)$
-10	5	2,528.1	129.6	-572.4
0	45	1,044.3	5,548.8	$-2,407.2$
24	-6	132.3	346.8	-214.2
45	-30	2,484.3	3,898.8	$-3,112.2$

(a) $E(X) = \mu_X = \sum_{i-1}^{N} X_i P(X_i) = 59, E(Y) = \mu_Y = \sum_{i-1}^{N} Y_i P(Y_i) = 14.$

(b) $\sigma_X = \sqrt{\sum_{i=1}^{N}[X_i - E(X)]^2 P(X_i)} = 78.6702$

$\sigma_Y = \sqrt{\sum_{i=1}^{N}[Y_i - E(Y)]^2 P(Y_i)} = 99.62.$

(c) $\sigma_{XY} = \sum_{i=1}^{N}[X_i - E(X)][Y_i - E(Y)]P(X_iY_i) = -6,306.$

(d) Stock X gives the investor a lower standard deviation while yielding a higher expected return, so the investor should select stock X.

5.14 (a) \$71; \$97. **(b)** 61.88; 84.27. **(c)** 5,113. **(d)** Risk-averse investors would invest in stock X, whereas risk takers would invest in stock Y.

5.16 (a) $E(X) = \$67.50; E(Y) = \$70.$ **(b)** $\sigma_X = \$52.43; \sigma_Y = \$167.63.$ **(c)** $\sigma_{XY} = \$8,425.$ **(d)** The common stock fund gives the investor a slightly higher expected return than the corporate bond fund but also has a standard deviation more than three times higher than that for the corporate bond fund. An investor should carefully weigh the increased risk.

5.18 (a) 0.0768 **(b)** 0.9130 **(c)** 0.3370 **(d)** 0.6630

5.20 (a) 0.40, 0.60. **(b)** 1.60, 0.98. **(c)** 4.0, 0.894. **(d)** 1.50, 0.866.

5.22 (a) $P(X = 0) = 0.7351.$ **(b)** If the probabilities of the six events are not all equal, then you would calculate the probability in (a) by multiplying together the probability of no failure in each of the six events.

5.24 (a) 0.0834. **(b)** 0.2351. **(c)** 0.6169. **(d)** 0.3831.

5.26 Given $\pi = 0.84$ and $n = 3,$

(a) $P(X = 3) = \dfrac{n!}{X!(n - x)!}\pi^X(1 - \pi)^{n-x} = \dfrac{3!}{3!0!}(0.84)^3(0.16)^0 = 0.5927.$

(b) $P(X = 0) = \dfrac{n!}{X!(n - x)!}\pi^X(1 - \pi)^{n-x} = \dfrac{3!}{0!3!}(0.84)^0(0.16)^3 = 0.0041.$

(c) $P(X \geq 2) = P(X = 2) + P(X = 3)$

$= \dfrac{3!}{2!1!}(0.84)^2(0.16)^1 + \dfrac{3!}{3!0!}(0.84)^3(0.16)^0 = 0.9314.$

(d) $E(X) = n\pi = 3(0.84) = 2.52 \; \sigma_X = \sqrt{n\pi(1 - \pi)}$

$= \sqrt{3(0.84)(0.16)} = 0.6350.$

5.28 (a) 0.2565. **(b)** 0.1396. **(c)** 0.3033. **(d)** 0.0247.

5.30 (a) 0.0337. **(b)** 0.0067. **(c)** 0.9596. **(d)** 0.0404.

5.32 (a) $P(X < 5) = P(X = 0) + P(X = 1) + P(X = 2) + P(X = 3) + P(X = 4)$

$= \dfrac{e^{-6}(6)^0}{0!} + \dfrac{e^{-6}(6)^1}{1!} + \dfrac{e^{-6}(6)^2}{2!} + \dfrac{e^{-6}(6)^3}{3!} + \dfrac{e^{-6}(6)^4}{4!}$

$= 0.002479 + 0.014873 + 0.044618 + 0.089235 + 0.133853$

$= 0.2851.$

(b) $P(X = 5) = \dfrac{e^{-6}(6)^5}{5!} = 0.1606.$

(c) $P(X \geq 5) = 1 - P(X < 5) = 1 - 0.2851 = 0.7149.$

(d) $P(X = 4 \text{ or } X = 5) = P(X = 4) + P(X = 5) = \dfrac{e^{-6}(6)^4}{4!} + \dfrac{e^{-6}(6)^5}{5!}$

$= 0.2945.$

5.34 (a) $P(X = 0) = 0.0009.$ **(b)** $P(X \geq 1) = 0.9991.$ **(c)** $P(X \geq 2) = 0.9927.$

5.36 (a) 0.0176. **(b)** 0.9093. **(c)** 0.9220.

5.38 (a) 0.2618. **(b)** 0.8478. **(c)** Because Ford had a lower mean rate of problems per car in 2009 compared to Dodge, the probability of a randomly selected Ford having zero problems and the probability of no more than 2 problems are both higher than their values for Dodge.

5.40 (a) 0.2441. **(b)** 0.8311. **(c)** Because Dodge had a lower mean rate of problems per car in 2009 compared to 2008, the probability of a randomly selected Dodge having zero problems and the probability of no more than 2 problems are both lower in 2009 than their values in 2008.

5.42 (a) 0.238. **(b)** 0.2. **(c)** 0.1591. **(d)** 0.0083.

5.44 (a) If $n = 6, A = 25,$ and $N = 100,$

$P(X \geq 2) = 1 - [P(X = 0) + P(X = 1)]$

$= 1 - \left[\dfrac{\dbinom{25}{0}\dbinom{100 - 25}{6 - 0}}{\dbinom{100}{6}} + \dfrac{\dbinom{25}{1}\dbinom{100 - 25}{6 - 1}}{\dbinom{100}{6}}\right].$

$= 1 - [0.1689 + 0.3620] = 0.4691$

(b) If $n = 6, A = 30$, and $N = 100$,

$$P(X \geq 2) = 1 - [P(X = 0) + P(X = 1)]$$

$$= 1 - \left[\frac{\binom{30}{0}\binom{100-30}{6-0}}{\binom{100}{6}} + \frac{\binom{30}{1}\binom{100-30}{6-1}}{\binom{100}{6}} \right].$$

$$= 1 - [0.1100 + 0.3046] = 0.5854$$

(c) If $n = 6, A = 5$, and $N = 100$,

$$P(X \geq 2) = 1 - [P(X = 0) + P(X = 1)]$$

$$= 1 - \left[\frac{\binom{5}{0}\binom{100-5}{6-0}}{\binom{100}{6}} + \frac{\binom{5}{1}\binom{100-5}{6-1}}{\binom{100}{6}} \right].$$

$$= 1 - [0.7291 + 0.2430] = 0.0279$$

(d) If $n = 6, A = 10$, and $N = 100$,

$$P(X \geq 2) = 1 - [P(X = 0) + P(X = 1)]$$

$$= 1 - \left[\frac{\binom{10}{0}\binom{100-10}{6-0}}{\binom{100}{6}} + \frac{\binom{10}{1}\binom{100-10}{6-1}}{\binom{100}{6}} \right].$$

$$= 1 - [0.5223 + 0.3687] = 0.1090$$

(e) The probability that the entire group will be audited is very sensitive to the true number of improper returns in the population. If the true number is very low ($A = 5$), the probability is very low (0.0279). When the true number is increased by a factor of 6 ($A = 30$), the probability the group will be audited increases by a factor of almost 21 (0.5854).

5.46 (a) $P(X = 4) = 0.00003649$. **(b)** $P(X = 0) = 0.5455$. **(c)** $P(X \geq 1) = 0.4545$. **(d)** $X = 6$. **(a)** $P(X = 4) = 0.0005$. **(b)** $P(X = 0) = 0.3877$. **(c)** $P(X \geq 1) = 0.6123$.

5.48 (a) $P(X = 1) = 0.4835$. **(b)** $P(X \geq 1) = 0.6374$. **(c)** $P(X \leq 2) = 0.9912$. **(d)** $\mu = n \times (A/N) = 0.8$.

5.54 (a) 0.74. **(b)** 0.74. **(c)** 0.3898. **(d)** 0.0012. **(e)** The assumption of independence may not be true.

5.56 (a) If $\pi = 0.50$ and $n = 12, P(X \geq 9) = 0.0730$. **(b)** If $\pi = 0.75$ and $n = 12, P(X \geq 9) = 0.6488$.

5.58 (a) 0.1074. **(b)** 0.2684. **(c)** 0.6242. **(d)** Mean $= 2.0$, standard deviation $= 1.2649$.

5.60 (a) $\mu = n\pi = 13.6$. **(b)** $\sigma = \sqrt{n\pi(1 - \pi)} = 2.0861$. **(c)** $P(X = 15) = 0.1599$. **(d)** $P(X \leq 10) = 0.0719$. **(e)** $P(X \geq 10) = 0.9721$

5.62 (a) If $\pi = 0.50$ and $n = 38, P(X \geq 32) = 0.00001$. **(b)** If $\pi = 0.70$ and $n = 38, P(X \geq 32) = 0.03595$. **(c)** If $\pi = 0.90$ and $n = 38, P(X \geq 32) = 0.92005$. **(d)** Based on the results in (a)–(c), the probability that the Standard & Poor's 500 Index will increase if there is an early gain in the first five trading days of the year is very likely to be close to 0.90 because that yields a probability of 92% that at least 32 of the 38 years the Standard & Poor's 500 Index will increase the entire year.

5.64 (a) The assumptions needed are (i) the probability that a golfer loses a golf ball in a given interval is constant, (ii) the probability that a golfer loses more than one golf ball approaches 0 as the interval gets smaller, and (iii) the probability that a golfer loses a golf ball is independent from interval to interval. **(b)** 0.0111. **(c)** 0.70293. **(d)** 0.29707.

5.66 (a) Virtually 0. **(b)** 0.00000037737. **(c)** 0.00000173886. **(d)** 0.000168669. **(e)** 0.0011998. **(f)** 0.00407937. **(g)** 0.006598978. **(h)** 0.0113502. **(i)** 0.976601.

CHAPTER 6

6.2 (a) 0.9089. **(b)** 0.0911. **(c)** $+1.96$. **(d)** -1.00 and $+1.00$.

6.4 (a) 0.1401. **(b)** 0.4168. **(c)** 0.3918. **(d)** $+1.00$.

6.6 (a) 0.9599. **(b)** 0.0228. **(c)** 43.42. **(d)** 46.64 and 53.36.

6.8 (a) $P(34 < X < 50) = P(-1.33 < Z < 0) = 0.4082$. **(b)** $P(X < 30) + P(X > 60) = P(Z < -1.67) + P(Z > 0.83) = 0.0475 + (1.0 - 0.7967) = 0.2508$. **(c)** $P(Z < -0.84) \cong 0.20, Z = -0.84 = \dfrac{X - 50}{12}, X = 50 - 0.84(12) = 39.92$ thousand miles, or 39,920 miles. **(d)** The smaller standard deviation makes the Z values larger. **(a)** $P(34 < X < 50) = P(-1.60 < Z < 0) = 0.4452$. **(b)** $P(X < 30) + P(X > 60) = P(Z < -2.00) + P(Z > 1.00) = 0.0228 + (1.0 - 0.8413) = 0.1815$. **(c)** $X = 50 - 0.84(10) = 41.6$ thousand miles, or 41,600 miles.

6.10 (a) 0.9878. **(b)** 0.8185. **(c)** 86.16%. **(d)** Option 1: Because your score of 81% on this exam represents a Z score of 1.00, which is below the minimum Z score of 1.28, you will not earn an A grade on the exam under this grading option. Option 2: Because your score of 68% on this exam represents a Z score of 2.00, which is well above the minimum Z score of 1.28, you will earn an A grade on the exam under this grading option. You should prefer Option 2.

6.12 (a) 0.1123. **(b)** 0.4539. **(c)** 0.0741.

6.14 With 39 values, the smallest of the standard normal quantile values covers an area under the normal curve of 0.025. The corresponding Z value is -1.96. The middle (20th) value has a cumulative area of 0.50 and a corresponding Z value of 0.0. The largest of the standard normal quantile values covers an area under the normal curve of 0.975, and its corresponding Z value is $+1.96$.

6.16 (a) Mean $= 19.9565$, median $= 21, S = 2.2458$, range $= 8$, $6S = 6(2.2458) = 13.4748$, interquartile range $= 4, 1.33(2.2458) = 2.9869$. The mean is less than the median. The range is much less than $6S$, and the interquartile range is more than $1.33S$. **(b)** The normal probability plot does not appear to be skewed. The data may be symmetrical but not normally distributed.

6.18 (a) Mean $= 1,040.863$, median $= 981$, range $= 1732$, $6(S) = 2,571.2310$, interquartile range $= 593, 1.33 (S) = 569.9562$. There are 62.75%, 78.43%, and 94.12% of the observations that fall within 1, 1.28, and 2 standard deviations of the mean, respectively, as compared to the approximate theoretical 66.67%, 80%, and 95%. Because the mean is slightly larger than the median, the interquartile range is slightly larger than 1.33 times the standard deviation, and the range is much smaller than 6 times the standard deviation, the data appear to deviate slightly from the normal distribution. **(b)** The normal probability plot suggests that the data appear to be slightly right-skewed.

6.20 (a) Interquartile range $= 0.0025, S = 0.0017$, range $= 0.008, 1.33(S) = 0.0023, 6(S) = 0.0102$. Because the interquartile range is close to $1.33S$ and the range is also close to $6S$, the data appear to be approximately normally distributed. **(b)** The normal probability plot suggests that the data appear to be approximately normally distributed.

6.22 (a) Five-number summary: 82 127 148.5 168 213; mean $= 147.06$, mode $= 130$, range $= 131$, interquartile range $= 41$, standard deviation $= 31.69$. The mean is very close to the median. The five-number summary suggests that the distribution is approximately symmetrical around the median. The interquartile range is very close to

1.33*S*. The range is about $50 below 6*S*. In general, the distribution of the data appears to closely resemble a normal distribution. **(b)** The normal probability plot confirms that the data appear to be approximately normally distributed.

6.24 (a) $(20 - 0)/120 = 0.1667$. **(b)** $(30 - 10)/120 = 0.1667$. **(c)** $(120 - 35)/120 = 0.7083$. **(d)** Mean $= 60$, standard deviation $= 34.641$.

6.26 (a) 0.1. **(b)** 0.3333. **(c)** 0.3333. **(d)** Mean $= 4.5$, standard deviation $= 0.8660$.

6.28 (a) 0.6321. **(b)** 0.3679. **(c)** 0.2326. **(d)** 0.7674.

6.30 (a) 0.7769. **(b)** 0.2231. **(c)** 0.1410. **(d)** 0.8590.

6.32 (a) For $\lambda = 2, P(X \le 1) = 0.864665$. **(b)** For $\lambda = 2, P(X \le 5) = 0.99996$. **(c)** For $\lambda = 1, P(X \le 1) = 0.6321$, for $\lambda = 1, P(X \le 5) = 0.9933$.

6.34 (a) 0.6321. **(b)** 0.3935. **(c)** 0.0952.

6.36 (a) 0.8647. **(b)** 0.3297. **(c)(a)** 0.9765. **(b)** 0.5276.

6.46 (a) 0.4772. **(b)** 0.9544. **(c)** 0.0456. **(d)** 1.8835. **(e)** 1.8710 and 2.1290.

6.48 (a) 0.2734. **(b)** 0.2038. **(c)** 4.404 ounces. **(d)** 4.188 ounces and 5.212 ounces.

6.50 (a) Waiting time will more closely resemble an exponential distribution. **(b)** Seating time will more closely resemble a normal distribution. **(c)** Both the histogram and normal probability plot suggest that waiting time more closely resembles an exponential distribution. **(d)** Both the histogram and normal probability plot suggest that seating time more closely resembles a normal distribution.

6.52 (a) 0.8413. **(b)** 0.9330. **(c)** 0.9332. **(d)** 0.3347. **(e)** 0.4080 and 1.1920.

CHAPTER 7

7.2 Sample without replacement: Read from left to right in three-digit sequences and continue unfinished sequences from the end of the row to the beginning of the next row:

Row 05: 338 505 855 551 438 855 077 186 579 488 767 833 170
Rows 05–06: 897
Row 06: 340 033 648 847 204 334 639 193 639 411 095 924
Rows 06–07: 707
Row 07: 054 329 776 100 871 007 255 980 646 886 823 920 461
Row 08: 893 829 380 900 796 959 453 410 181 277 660 908 887
Rows 08–09: 237
Row 09: 818 721 426 714 050 785 223 801 670 353 362 449
Rows 09–10: 406
Note: All sequences above 902 and duplicates are discarded.

7.4 A simple random sample would be less practical for personal interviews because of travel costs (unless interviewees are paid to go to a central interviewing location).

7.6 Here all members of the population are equally likely to be selected, and the sample selection mechanism is based on chance. But selection of two elements is not independent; for example, if *A* is in the sample, we know that *B* is also and that *C* and *D* are not.

7.8 (a)

Row 16: 2323 6737 5131 8888 1718 0654 6832 4647 6510 4877
Row 17: 4579 4269 2615 1308 2455 7830 5550 5852 5514 7182
Row 18: 0989 3205 0514 2256 8514 4642 7567 8896 2977 8822
Row 19: 5438 2745 9891 4991 4523 6847 9276 8646 1628 3554
Row 20: 9475 0899 2337 0892 0048 8033 6945 9826 9403 6858
Row 21: 7029 7341 3553 1403 3340 4205 0823 4144 1048 2949
Row 22: 8515 7479 5432 9792 6575 5760 0408 8112 2507 3742
Row 23: 1110 0023 4012 8607 4697 9664 4894 3928 7072 5815
Row 24: 3687 1507 7530 5925 7143 1738 1688 5625 8533 5041
Row 25: 2391 3483 5763 3081 6090 5169 0546
Note: All sequences above 5,000 are discarded. There were no repeating sequences.

(b) 089 189 289 389 489 589 689 789 889 989 1089 1189 1289 1389 1489 1589 1689 1789 1889 1989 2089 2189 2289 2389 2489 2589 2689 2789 2889 2989 3089 3189 3289 3389 3489 3589 3689 3789 3889 3989 4089 4189 4289 4389 4489 4589 4689 4789 4889 4989

(c) With the single exception of invoice 0989, the invoices selected in the simple random sample are not the same as those selected in the systematic sample. It would be highly unlikely that a simple random sample would select the same units as a systematic sample.

7.10 Before accepting the results of a survey of college students, you might want to know, for example:

Who funded the survey? Why was it conducted? What was the population from which the sample was selected? What sampling design was used? What mode of response was used: a personal interview, a telephone interview, or a mail survey? Were interviewers trained? Were survey questions field-tested? What questions were asked? Were the questions clear, accurate, unbiased, and valid? What operational definition of "vast majority" was used? What was the response rate? What was the sample size?

7.12 (a) The four types of survey errors are coverage error, nonresponse error, sampling error, and measurement error. **(b)** When people who answer the survey tell you what they think you want to hear, rather than what they really believe, this is the halo effect, which is a source of measurement error. Also, every survey will have sampling error that reflects the chance differences from sample to sample, based on the probability of particular individuals being selected in the particular sample.

7.14 Before accepting the results of the survey, you might want to know, for example: Who funded the study? Why was it conducted? What was the population from which the sample was selected? What sampling design was used? What mode of response was used: a personal interview, a telephone interview, or a mail survey? Were interviewers trained? Were survey questions field-tested? What other questions were asked? Were the questions clear, accurate, unbiased, and valid? What was the response rate? What was the margin of error? What was the sample size? What the frame was used?

7.16 (a) Virtually 0. **(b)** 0.1587. **(c)** 0.0139. **(d)** 50.195.

7.18 (a) Both means are equal to 6. This property is called unbiasedness. **(c)** The distribution for $n = 3$ has less variability. The larger sample size has resulted in sample means being closer to μ.

7.20 (a) When $n = 2$, because the mean is larger than the median, the distribution of the sales price of new houses is skewed to the right, and so is the sampling distribution of $\bar{X}$ although it will be less skewed than the population. **(b)** If you select samples of $n = 100$, the shape of the sampling distribution of the sample mean will be very close to a normal distribution, with a mean of \$274,300 and a standard deviation of \$9,000. **(c)** 0.9979. **(d)** 0.4285.

7.22 (a) $P(\overline{X} > 3) = P(Z > -1.00) = 1.0 - 0.1587 = 0.8413$. **(b)** $P(Z < 1.04) = 0.85; \overline{X} = 3.10 + 1.04(0.1) = 3.204$. **(c)** To be able to use the standardized normal distribution as an approximation for the area under the curve, you must assume that the population is approximately symmetrical. **(d)** $P(Z < 1.04) = 0.85; \overline{X} = 3.10 + 1.04(0.05) = 3.152$.

7.24 (a) 0.30. **(b)** 0.0693.

7.26 (a) $\pi = 0.501, \sigma_P = \sqrt{\dfrac{\pi(1 - \pi)}{n}} = \sqrt{\dfrac{0.501(1 - 0.501)}{100}} = 0.05$

$P(p > 0.55) = P(Z > 0.98) = 1.0 - 0.8365 = 0.1635$.

(b) $\pi = 0.60, \sigma_P = \sqrt{\dfrac{\pi(1 - \pi)}{n}} = \sqrt{\dfrac{0.6(1 - 0.6)}{100}} = 0.04899$

$P(p > 0.55) = P(Z > -1.021) = 1.0 - 0.1539 = 0.8461$.

(c) $\pi = 0.49, \sigma_P = \sqrt{\dfrac{\pi(1 - \pi)}{n}} = \sqrt{\dfrac{0.49(1 - 0.49)}{100}} = 0.05$

$P(p > 0.55) = P(Z > 1.20) = 1.0 - 0.8849 = 0.1151$.

(d) Increasing the sample size by a factor of 4 decreases the standard error by a factor of 2.

(a) $P(p > 0.55) = P(Z > 1.96) = 1.0 - 0.9750 = 0.0250$.
(b) $P(p > 0.55) = P(Z > -2.04) = 1.0 - 0.0207 = 0.9793$.
(c) $P(p > 0.55) = P(Z > 2.40) = 1.0 - 0.9918 = 0.0082$.

7.28 (a) 0.9298. **(b)** 0.8596. **(c)** 0.9865. **(d) (a)** 0.7695. **(b)** 0.5390. **(c)** 0.8656.

7.30 (a) .6065 **(b)** $P(A < \pi < B) = P(-1.6449 < Z < 1.6449) = 0.90$. The probability is 90% that the sample percentage will be contained within 5.79% (0.4021 to 0.5179) symmetrically around the population percentage. **(c)** The probability is 95% that the sample percentage will be contained within 6.9% (0.391 to 0.529) symmetrically around the population percentage.

7.32 (a) 0.1134. **(b)** 0.0034. **(c)** Increasing the sample size by a factor of 5 decreases the standard error by a factor of $\sqrt{5}$. The sampling distribution of the proportion becomes more concentrated around the true proportion of 0.56 and, hence, the probability in (b) becomes smaller than that in (a).

7.44 (a) 0.4999. **(b)** 0.00009. **(c)** 0. **(d)** 0. **(e)** 0.7518.

7.46 (a) 0.8944. **(b)** 4.617; 4.783. **(c)** 4.641.

7.48 (a) 0.9999 **(b)** 0.0001. **(c)** 0.0137.

7.50 Even though Internet polling is less expensive and faster and offers higher response rates than telephone surveys, it is a self-selection response method. Because respondents who choose to participate in the survey may not represent the view of the public, the data collected may not be appropriate for making inferences about the general population.

7.52 (a) Before accepting the results of this survey, you would like to know (i) how big is the sample size, (ii) what is the purpose of the survey, (iii) what sampling method is being used, (iv) what is the frame being used, (v) what is the response rate, and (vi) how the questions are being phrased. **(b)** The population will be all the AOL users. The frame can be compiled from the list of the AOL subscribers. Because there are two natural strata in the population, adults and teens, a stratified sampling method should be used to better represent the population.

CHAPTER 8

8.2 $114.68 \le \mu \le 135.32$.

8.4 Yes, it is true because 5% of intervals will not include the population mean.

8.6 (a) You would compute the mean first because you need the mean to compute the standard deviation. If you had a sample, you would compute the sample mean. If you had the population mean, you would compute the population standard deviation. **(b)** If you have a sample, you are computing the sample standard deviation, not the population standard deviation needed in Equation (8.1). If you have a population and have computed the population mean and population standard deviation, you don't need a confidence interval estimate of the population mean because you already know the mean.

8.8 Equation (8.1) assumes that you know the population standard deviation. Because you are selecting a sample of 100 from the population, you are computing a sample standard deviation, not the population standard deviation.

8.10 (a) $\overline{X} \pm Z \cdot \dfrac{\sigma}{\sqrt{n}} = 350 \pm 1.96 \cdot \dfrac{100}{\sqrt{64}}; 325.50 \le \mu \le 374.50$. **(b)** No, the manufacturer cannot support a claim that the bulbs have a mean of 400 hours. Based on the data from the sample, a mean of 400 hours would represent a distance of 4 standard deviations above the sample mean of 350 hours. **(c)** No. Because σ is known and $n = 64$, from the Central Limit Theorem, you know that the sampling distribution of $\overline{X}$ is approximately normal. **(d)** The confidence interval is narrower, based on a population standard deviation of 80 hours rather than the original standard deviation of 100 hours. $\overline{X} \pm Z \cdot \dfrac{\sigma}{\sqrt{n}} = 350 \pm 1.96 \cdot \dfrac{80}{\sqrt{64}}, 330.4 \le \mu \le 369.6$. Based on the smaller standard deviation, a mean of 400 hours would represent a distance of 5 standard deviations above the sample mean of 350 hours. No, the manufacturer cannot support a claim that the bulbs have a mean life of 400 hours.

8.12 (a) 2.2622. **(b)** 3.2498. **(c)** 2.0395. **(d)** 1.9977. **(e)** 1.7531.

8.14 $-0.12 \le \mu \le 11.84, 2.00 \le \mu \le 6.00$. The presence of the outlier increases the sample mean and greatly inflates the sample standard deviation.

8.16 (a) $32 \pm (2.0096)(9)/\sqrt{50}; 29.44 \le \mu \le 34.56$ **(b)** The quality improvement team can be 95% confident that the population mean turnaround time is between 29.44 hours and 34.56 hours. **(c)** The project was a success because the initial turnaround time of 68 hours does not fall within the interval.

8.18 (a) $31.9267 \le \mu \le 41.1399$. **(b)** You can be 95% confident that the population mean price for two tickets with online service charges, large popcorn, and two medium soft drinks is somewhere between \$31.93 and \$41.14.

8.20 (a) $18.99 \le \mu \le 20.93$. **(b)** You can be 95% confident that the population mean miles per gallon of 2009 SUVs priced under \$30,000 is between 18.99 and 20.93. **(c)** Because the 95% confidence interval for population mean miles per gallon of 2009 SUVs priced under \$30,000 does not overlap with that for the population mean miles per gallon of 2009 sedans priced under \$20,000, you are 95% confident that the population mean miles per gallon of 2009 SUVs is lower than that of 2009 sedans.

8.22 (a) $31.12 \le \mu \le 54.96$. **(b)** The number of days is approximately normally distributed. **(c)** No, the outliers skew the data. **(d)** Because the sample size is fairly large, at $n = 50$, the use of the t distribution is appropriate.

8.24 (a) $\$0.7367 \leq \mu \leq \$1.1147$. **(b)** The population distribution needs to be normally distributed. **(c)** Both the normal probability plot and the boxplot show that the distribution of the cost of dark chocolate bars is right-skewed.

8.26 $0.19 \leq \pi \leq 0.31$.

8.28 (a) $p = \dfrac{X}{n} = \dfrac{135}{500} = 0.27, p \pm Z\sqrt{\dfrac{p(1-p)}{n}} = 0.27 \pm$

$2.58\sqrt{\dfrac{0.27(0.73)}{500}} \; 0.2189 \leq \pi \leq 0.3211$. **(b)** The manager in charge of promotional programs concerning residential customers can infer that the proportion of households that would purchase an additional telephone line if it were made available at a substantially reduced installation cost is somewhere between 0.22 and 0.32, with 99% confidence.

8.30 (a) $0.4762 \leq \pi \leq 0.5638$. **(b)** No, you cannot, because the interval estimate includes 0.50 (50%). **(c)** $0.5062 \leq \pi \leq 0.5338$. Yes, you can, because the interval is above 0.50 (50%). **(d)** The larger the sample size, the narrower the confidence interval, holding everything else constant.

8.32 (a) $0.784 \leq \pi \leq 0.816$. **(b)** $0.5099 \leq \pi \leq 0.5498$. **(c)** Many more people think that e-mail messages are easier to misinterpret.

8.34 $n = 35$.

8.36 $n = 1{,}041$.

8.38 (a) $n = \dfrac{Z^2\sigma^2}{e^2} = \dfrac{(1.96)^2(400)^2}{50^2} = 245.86$. Use $n = 246$.

(b) $n = \dfrac{Z^2\sigma^2}{e^2} = \dfrac{(1.96)^2(400)^2}{25^2} = 983.41$. Use $n = 984$.

8.40 $n = 97$.

8.42 (a) $n = 167$. **(b)** $n = 97$.

8.44 (a) $n = 246$. **(b)** $n = 385$. **(c)** $n = 554$. **(d)** When there is more variability in the population, a larger sample is needed to accurately estimate the mean.

8.46 (a) $p = 0.28; 0.2522 \leq \pi \leq 0.3078$. **(b)** $p = 0.19; 0.1657 \leq \pi \leq 0.2143$. **(c)** $p = 0.07; 0.0542 \leq \pi \leq 0.0858$. **(d) (a)** $n = 1{,}937$. **(b)** $n = 1{,}479$. **(c)** $n = 626$.

8.48 (a) If you conducted a follow-up study to estimate the population proportion of individuals who view oil companies favorably, you would use $\pi = 0.84$ in the sample size formula because it is based on past information on the proportion. **(b)** $n = 574$.

8.50 $\$10{,}721.53 \leq$ Total $\leq \$14{,}978.47$.

8.52 (a) 0.054. **(b)** 0.0586. **(c)** 0.066.

8.54 $(3{,}000)(\$261.40) \pm (3{,}000)(1.8331)\dfrac{(138.8046)}{\sqrt{10}}\sqrt{\dfrac{3{,}000 - 10}{3{,}000 - 1}}$.

$\$543{,}176.96 \leq$ Total $\leq \$1{,}025{,}224.04$.

8.56 $\$5{,}443 \leq$ Total difference $\leq \$54{,}229$.

8.58 (a) 0.0542. **(b)** Because the upper bound is higher than the tolerable exception rate of 0.04, the auditor should request a larger sample.

8.66 $940.50 \leq \mu \leq 1007.50$. Based on the evidence gathered from the sample of 34 stores, the 95% confidence interval for the mean per-store count in all of the franchise's stores is from 940.50 to 1,007.50. With a 95% level of confidence, the franchise can conclude that the mean per-store count in all its stores is somewhere between 940.50 and 1,007.50, which is larger than the original average of 900 mean per-store count before the price reduction. Hence, reducing coffee prices is a good strategy to increase the mean customer count.

8.68 (a) $14.085 \leq \mu \leq 16.515$. **(b)** $0.530 \leq \pi \leq 0.820$. **(c)** $n = 25$. **(d)** $n = 784$. **(e)** If a single sample were to be selected for both purposes, the larger of the two sample sizes ($n = 784$) should be used.

8.70 (a) $8.049 \leq \mu \leq 11.351$. **(b)** $0.284 \leq \pi \leq 0.676$. **(c)** $n = 35$. **(d)** $n = 121$. **(e)** If a single sample were to be selected for both purposes, the larger of the two sample sizes ($n = 121$) should be used.

8.72 (a) $\$25.80 \leq \mu \leq \$31.24$. **(b)** $0.3037 \leq \pi \leq 0.4963$. **(c)** $n = 97$. **(d)** $n = 423$. **(e)** If a single sample were to be selected for both purposes, the larger of the two sample sizes ($n = 423$) should be used.

8.74 (a) $\$36.66 \leq \mu \leq \$40.42$. **(b)** $0.2027 \leq \pi \leq 0.3973$. **(c)** $n = 110$. **(d)** $n = 423$. **(e)** If a single sample were to be selected for both purposes, the larger of the two sample sizes ($n = 423$) should be used.

8.76 (a) $\pi \leq 0.2013$. **(b)** Because the upper bound is higher than the tolerable exception rate of 0.15, the auditor should request a larger sample.

8.78 (a) $n = 27$. **(b)** $\$402{,}652.53 \leq$ Population total $\leq \$450{,}950.79$.

8.80 (a) $8.41 \leq \mu \leq 8.43$. **(b)** With 95% confidence, the population mean width of troughs is somewhere between 8.41 and 8.43 inches. **(c)** The assumption is valid as the width of the troughs is approximately normally distributed.

8.82 (a) $0.2425 \leq \mu \leq 0.2856$. **(b)** $0.1975 \leq \mu \leq 0.2385$. **(c)** The amounts of granule loss for both brands are skewed to the right, but the sample sizes are large enough. **(d)** Because the two confidence intervals do not overlap, you can conclude that the mean granule loss of Boston shingles is higher than that of Vermont shingles.

CHAPTER 9

9.2 Because $Z_{STAT} = +2.21 > 1.96$, reject H_0.

9.4 Reject H_0 if $Z_{STAT} < -2.58$ or if $Z_{STAT} > 2.58$.

9.6 p-value $= 0.0456$.

9.8 p-value $= 0.1676$.

9.10 H_0: Defendant is guilty; H_1: Defendant is innocent. A Type I error would be not convicting a guilty person. A Type II error would be convicting an innocent person.

9.12 $H_0: \mu = 20$ minutes. 20 minutes is adequate travel time between classes. $H_1: \mu \neq 20$ minutes. 20 minutes is not adequate travel time between classes.

9.14 (a) $Z_{Stat} = \dfrac{350 - 375}{\dfrac{100}{\sqrt{64}}} = -2.0$. Because $Z_{Stat} = -2.00 < -1.96$, reject H_0. **(b)** p-value $= 0.0456$. **(c)** $325.5 \leq \mu \leq 374.5$. **(d)** The conclusions are the same.

9.16 $t_{STAT} = 2.00$.

9.18 (a) ± 2.1315.

9.20 No, you should not use a t test because the original population is left-skewed, and the sample size is not large enough for the t test to be valid.

9.22 (a) $t_{STAT} = (3.57 - 3.70)/0.8\sqrt{64} = -1.30$. Because $-1.9983 < t_{STAT} = -1.30 < 1.9983$ and p-value $= 0.1984 > 0.05$. There is no evidence that the population mean waiting time is different from 3.7 minutes. **(b)** Because $n = 64$, the central limit theorem should ensure that the sampling distribution of the mean is approximately normal. In general, the t test is appropriate for this sample size except for the case where the population is extremely skewed or bimodal.

9.24 (a) $-1.9842 < t_{STAT} = -1.7094 < 1.9842$. There is no evidence that the population mean waiting time is different from 36.5 hours. **(b)** p-value $= 0.0905 > 0.05$. The probability of getting a t_{STAT} statistic greater than $+1.7094$ or less than -1.7094, given that the null hypothesis is true, is 0.0905.

9.26 (a) Because $-2.5706 < t_{STAT} = 0.8556 < 2.5706$, do not reject H_0. There is not enough evidence to conclude that the mean price for two tickets, with online service charges, large popcorn, and two medium soft drinks, is different from \$35. **(b)** The p-value is 0.4313. If the population mean is \$35, the probability of observing a sample of six theater chains that will result in a sample mean farther away from the hypothesized value than this sample is 0.4313. **(c)** The distribution of prices is normally distributed. **(d)** With a small sample size, it is difficult to evaluate the assumption of normality. However, the distribution may be symmetric because the mean and the median are close in value.

9.28 (a) Because $-2.0096 < t_{STAT} = 0.114 < 2.0096$, do not reject H_0. There is no evidence that the mean amount is different from 2 liters. **(b)** p-value $= 0.9095$. **(c)**, **(d)** Yes, the data appear to have met the normality assumption. **(e)** The amount of fill is decreasing over time. Therefore, the t test is invalid.

9.30 (a) Because $t_{STAT} = -5.9355 < -2.0106$, reject H_0. There is enough evidence to conclude that mean widths of the troughs is different from 8.46 inches. **(b)** The population distribution is normal. **(c)** Although the distribution of the widths is left-skewed, the large sample size means that the validity of the t test is not seriously affected.

9.32 (a) Because $-2.68 < t_{STAT} = 0.094 < 2.68$, do not reject H_0. There is no evidence that the mean amount is different from 5.5 grams **(b)** $5.462 \leq \mu \leq 5.542$. **(c)** The conclusions are the same.

9.34 p-value $= 0.0228$.

9.36 p-value $= 0.0838$.

9.38 p-value $= 0.9162$.

9.40 $t_{STAT} = 2.7638$.

9.42 $t_{STAT} = -2.5280$.

9.44 (a) $t_{STAT} = -1.7094 < -1.6604$. There is evidence that the population mean waiting time is less than 36.5 hours. **(b)** p-value $= 0.0453 < 0.05$. The probability of getting a t_{Stat} statistic less than -1.7094, given that the null hypothesis is true, is 0.0453. **(c)** The results are different because in this problem you have conducted a one-tail test with the entire rejection region in the lower tail.

9.46 (a) $t_{STAT} = (2.73 - 2.80)/0.2/\sqrt{25} = -1.75$. Because $t_{STAT} = -1.75 < -1.7109$, reject H_0. **(b)** p-value $= 0.0464 < 0.05$, reject H_0. **(c)** The probability of getting a sample mean of 2.73 feet or less if the population mean is 2.8 feet is 0.0464. **(d)** They are the same.

9.48 (a) $H_0: \mu \leq 5; H_1: \mu > 5$. **(b)** A Type I error occurs when you conclude that children take a mean of more than five trips a week to the store when in fact they take a mean of no more than five trips a week to the store. A Type II error occurs when you conclude that children take a mean of no more than five trips a week to the store when in fact they take a mean of more than five trips a week to the store. **(c)** Because $t_{STAT} = 2.9375 > 2.3646$ or p-value $= 0.0021 < 0.01$, reject H_0. There is enough evidence to conclude the population mean number of trips to the store is greater than five per week. **(d)** The probability that the sample mean is 5.47 trips or more when the null hypothesis is true is 0.0021.

9.50 $p = 0.22$.

9.52 Do not reject H_0.

9.54 (a) $Z_{STAT} = 9.61, p$-value $= 0.0000$. Because $Z_{STAT} = 9.61 > 1.645$ or $0.0000 < 0.05$, reject H_0. There is evidence to show that more than half the readers of online magazines have linked to an advertiser's Web site. **(b)** $Z_{STAT} = 1.20 \, p$-value $= 0.115$. Because $Z_{STAT} = 1.20 < 1.645$, do not reject H_0. There is insufficient evidence to show that more than half of the readers of online magazines have linked to an advertiser's Web site. **(c)** The sample size had a major effect on being able to reject the null hypothesis. **(d)** You would be very unlikely to reject the null hypothesis with a sample of 20.

9.56 (a) $H_1: \pi = 0.6; H_1: \pi \neq 0.6$. Decision rule: If $Z_{STAT} > 1.96$ or $Z_{STAT} < -1.96$, reject H_0.

$$p = \frac{650}{1,000} = 0.65$$

Test statistic:

$$Z_{STAT} = \frac{p - \pi}{\sqrt{\dfrac{\pi(1 - \pi)}{n}}} = \frac{0.65 - 0.60}{\sqrt{\dfrac{0.6(1 - 0.6)}{1,000}}} = 3.2275$$

Because $Z_{STAT} = 3.2275 > 1.96$ or p-value $= 0.0012 < 0.05$, reject H_0 and conclude that there is evidence that the percentage of young job seekers who prefer to look for a job in a place they want to reside is different from 60%.

9.58 (a) $H_0: \pi \leq 0.08$. No more than 8% of students at your school are omnivores. $H_1: \pi > 0.08$. More than 8% of students at your school are omnivores. **(b)** $Z_{STAT} = 3.6490, p$-value $= 0.0001316$. Because $Z_{STAT} = 3.6490 > 1.96$ or p-value $= 0.0001316 < 0.05$, reject H_0. There is enough evidence to show that the percentage of omnivores at your school is greater than 8%.

9.68 (a) Buying a site that is not profitable. **(b)** Not buying a profitable site. **(c)** Type I. **(d)** If the executives adopt a less stringent rejection criterion by buying sites for which the computer model predicts moderate or large profit, the probability of committing a Type I error will increase. Many more of the sites the computer model predicts that will generate moderate profit may end up not being profitable at all. On the other hand, the less stringent rejection criterion will lower the probability of committing a Type II error because more potentially profitable sites will be purchased.

9.70 (a) Because $t_{STAT} = 3.248 > 2.0010$, reject H_0. **(b)** p-value $= 0.0019$. **(c)** Because $Z_{STAT} = -0.32 > -1.645$, do not reject H_0. **(d)** Because $-2.0010 < t_{STAT} = 0.75 < 2.0010$, do not reject H_0. **(e)** Because $Z_{STAT} = -1.61 > -1.645$, do not reject H_0.

9.72 (a) Because $t_{STAT} = -1.69 > -1.7613$, do not reject H_0. **(b)** The data are from a population that is normally distributed. **(c)**, **(d)** With the exception of one extreme point, the data are approximately normally distributed. **(e)** There is insufficient evidence to state that the waiting time is less than five minutes.

9.74 (a) Because $t_{STAT} = -1.47 > -1.6896$, do not reject H_0. **(b)** p-value $= 0.0748$. If the null hypothesis is true, the probability of obtaining a t_{STAT} of -1.47 or more extreme is 0.0748. **(c)** Because $t_{STAT} = -3.10 < -1.6973$, reject H_0. **(d)** p-value $= 0.0021$. If the null hypothesis is true, the probability of obtaining a t_{STAT} of -3.10 or more extreme is 0.0021. **(e)** The data in the population are assumed to be normally distributed. **(f)** Both boxplots suggest that the data are skewed slightly to the right, more so for the Boston shingles. However, the very large sample sizes mean that the results of the t test are relatively insensitive to the departure from normality.

9.76 (a) $t_{STAT} = -21.61$, reject H_0. **(b)** p-value $= 0.0000$. **(c)** $t_{STAT} = -27.19$, reject H_0. **(d)** p-value $= 0.0000$. **(e)** Because of the large sample sizes, you do not need to be concerned with the normality assumption.

CHAPTER 10

10.2 (a) $t = 3.8959$. **(b)** $df = 21$. **(c)** 2.5177. **(d)** Because $t_{STAT} = 3.8959 > 2.5177$, reject H_0.

10.4 $3.73 \leq \mu_1 - \mu_2 \leq 12.27$.

10.6 Because $t_{STAT} = 2.6762 < 2.9979$ or p-value $= 0.0158 > 0.01$, do not reject H_0. There is no evidence of a difference in the means of the two populations.

10.8 (a) Because $t_{STAT} = 5.7883 > 1.6581$ or p-value $= 0.0000 < 0.05$, reject H_0. There is evidence that the mean amount of Goldfish crackers eaten by children is higher for those who watched food ads than for those who did not watch food ads. **(b)** $5.79 \leq \mu_1 - \mu_2 \leq 11.81$. **(c)** The results cannot be compared because (a) is a one-tail test and (b) is a confidence interval that is comparable only to the results of a two-tail test.

10.10 (a) $H_0: \mu_1 = \mu_2$, where Populations: $1 = $ Males, $2 = $ Females. $H_1: \mu_1 \neq \mu_2$. Decision rule: $df = 170$. If $t_{STAT} < -1.974$ or $t_{STAT} > 1.974$, reject H_0.
Test statistic:

$$S_p^2 = \frac{(n_1 - 1)(S_1^2) + (n_2 - 1)(S_2^2)}{(n_1 - 1) + (n_2 - 1)}$$

$$= \frac{(99)(13.35^2) + (71)(9.42^2)}{99 + 71} = 140.8489$$

$$t_{STAT} = \frac{(\overline{X}_1 - \overline{X}_2) - (\mu_1 - \mu_2)}{\sqrt{S_p^2\left(\frac{1}{n_1} + \frac{1}{n_2}\right)}}$$

$$= \frac{(40.26 - 36.85) - 0}{\sqrt{140.8489\left(\frac{1}{100} + \frac{1}{72}\right)}} = 1.859.$$

Decision: Because $-1.974 < t_{STAT} = 1.859 < 1.974$, do not reject H_0. There is not enough evidence to conclude that the mean computer anxiety experienced by males and females is different. **(b)** p-value $= 0.0648$. **(c)** In order to use the pooled-variance t test, you need to assume that the populations are normally distributed with equal variances.

10.12 (a) Because $t_{STAT} = -4.1343 < -2.0484$, reject H_0. **(b)** p-value $= 0.0003$ **(c)** The original populations of waiting times are approximately normally distributed. **(d)** $-4.2292 \leq \mu_1 - \mu_2 \leq -1.4268$.

10.14 (a) Because $t_{STAT} = 4.10 > 2.024$, reject H_0. There is evidence of a difference in the mean surface hardness between untreated and treated steel plates. **(b)** p-value $= 0.0002$. The probability that two samples have a mean difference of 9.3634 or more is 0.02% if there is no difference in the mean surface hardness between untreated and treated steel plates. **(c)** You need to assume that the population distribution of hardness of both untreated and treated steel plates is normally distributed. **(d)** $4.7447 \leq \mu_1 - \mu_2 \leq 13.9821$.

10.16 (a) Because $t_{STAT} = -7.8124 < -1.9845$ or p-value $= 0.0000 < 0.05$, reject H_0. There is evidence that the mean number of calls is less for cell phone users under age 12 than for cell phone users who are between 13 and 17 years of age. **(b)** You must assume that each of the two independent populations is normally distributed.

10.18 $df = 19$.

10.20 (a) $t_{STAT} = (-1.5566)/(1.424)/\sqrt{9} = -3.2772$. Because $t_{STAT} = -3.2772 < -2.306$ or p-value $= 0.0112 < 0.05$, reject H_0. There is enough evidence of a difference in the mean summated ratings between the two brands. **(b)** You must assume that the distribution of the differences between the two ratings is approximately normal. **(c)** p-value $= 0.0112$. The probability of obtaining a mean difference in ratings that gives rise to a test statistic that deviates from 0 by 3.2772 or more in either direction is 0.0112 if there is no difference in the mean summated ratings between the two brands. **(d)** $-2.6501 \leq \mu_D \leq -0.4610$. You are 95% confident that the mean difference in summated ratings between brand A and brand B is somewhere between -2.6501 and -0.4610.

10.22 (a) Because $t_{STAT} = 5.2445 > 2.8784$ or p-value $= 0.0000 < 0.01$, reject H_0. There is evidence to conclude that there is a difference between the mean price of textbooks at the local bookstore and Amazon.com. **(b)** You must assume that the distribution of the differences between the measurements is approximately normal. **(c)** $\$7.25 \leq \mu_D \leq \$24.89$. You are 99% confident that the mean difference between the price of textbooks at the local bookstore and Amazon.com is somewhere between $\$7.25$ and $\$24.89$. **(d)** The results in (a) and (c) are the same. The hypothesized value of 0 for the difference in the price of textbooks between the local bookstore and Amazon.com is outside the 99% confidence interval.

10.24 (a) Because $t_{STAT} = 1.8425 < 1.943$, do not reject H_0. There is not enough evidence to conclude that the mean bone marrow microvessel density is higher before the stem cell transplant than after the stem cell transplant. **(b)** p-value $= 0.0575$. The probability that the t statistic for the mean difference in density is 1.8425 or more is 5.75% if the mean density is not higher before the stem cell transplant than after the stem cell transplant. **(c)** $-28.26 \leq \mu_D \leq 200.55$. You are 95% confident that the mean difference in bone marrow microvessel density before and after the stem cell transplant is somewhere between -28.26 and 200.55.

10.26 (a) Because $t_{STAT} = -9.3721 < -2.4258$, reject H_0. There is evidence that the mean strength is lower at two days than at seven days. **(b)** The population of differences in strength is approximately normally distributed. **(c)** $p = 0.000$.

10.28 (a) Because $-2.58 \leq Z_{STAT} = -0.58 \leq 2.58$, do not reject H_0. **(b)** $-0.273 \leq \pi_1 - \pi_2 \leq 0.173$.

10.30 (a) $H_0: \pi_1 \leq \pi_2$. $H_1: \pi_1 > \pi_2$. Populations: $1 = $ expensive pill, $2 = $ cheap pill. **(b)** Because $Z_{STAT} = 2.4924 > 1.6449$ or p-value $= 0.0064 < 0.05$, reject H_0. There is sufficient evidence to conclude that the population proportion of people who think the expensive pill works better is greater than the population proportion of people who think the cheap pill works better. **(c)** Yes, the result in (b) makes it appropriate to claim that people think the expensive pill works better.

10.32 (a) $H_0: \pi_1 = \pi_2$. $H_1: \pi_1 \neq \pi_2$. Decision rule: If $|Z_{STAT}| > 2.58$, reject H_0.

Test statistic: $\overline{p} = \frac{X_1 + X_2}{n_1 + n_2} = \frac{707 + 536}{1,000 + 1,000} = 0.6215$

$$Z_{STAT} = \frac{(p_1 - p_2) - (\pi_2 - \pi_2)}{\sqrt{\overline{p}(1 - \overline{p})\left(\frac{1}{n_1} + \frac{1}{n_2}\right)}} = \frac{(0.707 - 0.536) - 0}{\sqrt{0.6215(1 - 0.6215)\left(\frac{1}{1,000} + \frac{1}{1,000}\right)}}.$$

$Z_{STAT} = 7.8837 > 2.58$, reject H_0. There is evidence of a difference in the proportion who believe that e-mail messages should be answered quickly between the two age groups. **(b)** p-value $= 0.0000$. The probability of obtaining a difference in proportions that gives rise to a test statistic that deviates from 0 by 7.8837 or more in either direction is 0.0000 if there is no difference in the proportion of people in the two age groups who believe that e-mail messages should be answered quickly.

10.34 (a) Because $-1.96 < Z_{STAT} = 1.5240 < 1.96$, do not reject H_0. There is insufficient evidence of a difference between undergraduate and MBA students in the proportion who selected the highest-cost fund.

(b) p-value $= 0.1275$. The probability of obtaining a difference in proportions that gives rise to a test statistic that deviates from 0 by 1.5240 or more in either direction is 0.1275 if there is no difference between undergraduate and MBA students in the proportion who selected the highest-cost fund.

10.36 (a) 2.20. **(b)** 2.57. **(c)** 3.50.

10.38 (a) Population B. $S^2 = 25$. **(b)** 1.5625.

10.40 $df_{numerator} = 24$, $df_{denominator} = 24$.

10.42 Because $F_{STAT} = 1.2109 < 2.27$, do not reject H_0.

10.44 (a) Because $F_{STAT} = 1.2995 < 3.18$, do not reject H_0. **(b)** Because $F_{STAT} = 1.2995 < 2.62$, do not reject H_0.

10.46 (a) $H_0: \sigma_1^2 = \sigma_2^2. H_1: \sigma_1^2 \neq \sigma_2^2$.

Decision rule: If $F_{STAT} > 1.556$, reject H_0.

Test statistic: $F_{STAT} = \dfrac{S_1^2}{S_2^2} = \dfrac{(13.35)^2}{(9.42)^2} = 2.008$.

Decision: Because $F_{STAT} = 2.008 > 1.556$, reject H_0. There is evidence to conclude that the two population variances are different. **(b)** p-value $= 0.0022$. **(c)** The test assumes that each of the two populations is normally distributed. **(d)** Based on (a) and (b), a separate-variance t test should be used.

10.48 (a) Because $F_{STAT} = 5.1802 > 2.34$ or p-value $= 0.0002 < 0.05$, reject H_0. There is evidence of a difference in the variability of the battery life between the two types of digital cameras. **(b)** p-value $= 0.0002$. The probability of obtaining a sample that yields a test statistic more extreme than 5.1802 is 0.0002 if there is no difference in the two population variances. **(c)** The test assumes that the two populations are both normally distributed. **(d)** Based on (a) and (b), a separate-variance t test should be used.

10.50 Because $F_{STAT} = 1.1452 < 9.60$, or p-value $= 0.8986 > 0.05$, do not reject H_0. There is not enough evidence of a difference in the variance of the yield between money market accounts and five-year CDs.

10.58 (a) $H_0: \sigma_1^2 \geq \sigma_2^2$ and $H_0: \sigma_1^2 < \sigma_2^2$. **(b)** Type I error: Rejecting the null hypothesis that the price variance on the Internet is no lower than the price variance in the brick-and-mortar market when the price variance on the Internet is no lower than the price variance in the brick-and-mortar market. Type II error: Failing to reject the null hypothesis that price variance on the Internet is lower than the price variance in the brick-and-mortar market when the price variance on the Internet is lower than the price variance in the brick-and-mortar market. **(c)** An F test for differences in two variances can be used. **(d)** You need to assume that each of the two populations is normally distributed. **(e) (a)** $H_0: \mu_1 \geq \mu_2$ and $H_1: \mu_1 < \mu_2$. **(b)** Type I error: Rejecting the null hypothesis that the mean price in the electronic market is no lower than the mean price in the physical market when the mean price in the electronic market is no lower than the mean price in the physical market. Type II error: Failing to reject the null hypothesis that the mean price in the electronic market is no lower than the mean price in the physical market when the mean price in the electronic market is lower than the mean price in the physical market. **(c)** A pooled t test or a separate-variance t test for the difference in the means can be used. **(d)** You must assume that the distribution of the prices in the electronic market and in the physical market are approximately normally distributed.

10.60 (a) Because $F_{STAT} = 1.0529 < 1.2643$, or p-value $= 0.6539 > 0.05$, do not reject H_0. There is not enough evidence of a difference in the variance of the salary of managers and Black Belts. **(b)** The pooled-

variance t test. **(c)** Because $t_{STAT} = -12.9605 < -1.96$ or p-value $= 0.0000 < 0.05$, reject H_0. There is evidence that the mean salary of managers is less than the mean salary of Black Belts.

10.62 (a) Because $F_{STAT} = 22.7067 > F_\alpha = 1.6275$, reject H_0. There is enough evidence to conclude that there is a difference between the variances in age of students at the Western school and at the Eastern school. **(b)** Because there is a difference between the variances in the age of students at the Western school and at the Eastern school, schools should take that into account when designing their curriculum to accommodate the larger variance in age of students in the state university in the Western United States. **(c)** It is more appropriate to use a separate-variance t test. **(d)** Because $F_{STAT} = 1.3061 < 1.6275$, do not reject H_0. There is not enough evidence to conclude that there is a difference between the variances in years of spreadsheet usage of students at the Western school and at the Eastern school. **(e)** Using the pooled-variance t test, because $t_{STAT} = -4.6650 < -2.5978$, reject H_0. There is enough evidence of a difference in the mean years of spreadsheet usage of students at the Western school and at the Eastern school.

10.64 (a) Because $t_{STAT} = 3.3282 > 1.8595$, reject H_0. There is enough evidence to conclude that the introductory computer students required more than a mean of 10 minutes to write and run a program in Visual Basic. **(b)** Because $t_{STAT} = 1.3636 < 1.8595$, do not reject H_0. There is not enough evidence to conclude that the introductory computer students required more than a mean of 10 minutes to write and run a program in Visual Basic. **(c)** Although the mean time necessary to complete the assignment increased from 12 to 16 minutes as a result of the increase in one data value, the standard deviation went from 1.8 to 13.2, which reduced the t value. **(d)** Because $F_{STAT} = 1.2308 < 3.8549$, do not reject H_0. There is not enough evidence to conclude that the population variances are different for the Introduction to Computers students and computer majors. Hence, the pooled-variance t test is a valid test to determine whether computer majors can write a Visual Basic program in less time than introductory students, assuming that the distributions of the time needed to write a Visual Basic program for both the Introduction to Computers students and the computer majors are approximately normally distributed. Because $t_{STAT} = 4.0666 > 1.7341$, reject H_0. There is enough evidence that the mean time is higher for Introduction to Computers students than for computer majors. **(e)** p-value $= 0.000362$. If the true population mean amount of time needed for Introduction to Computer students to write a Visual Basic program is no more than 10 minutes, the probability of observing a sample mean greater than the 12 minutes in the current sample is 0.0362%. Hence, at a 5% level of significance, you can conclude that the population mean amount of time needed for Introduction to Computer students to write a Visual Basic program is more than 10 minutes. As illustrated in part (d), in which there is not enough evidence to conclude that the population variances are different for the Introduction to Computers students and computer majors, the pooled-variance t test performed is a valid test to determine whether computer majors can write a Visual Basic program in less time than introductory students, assuming that the distribution of the time needed to write a Visual Basic program for both the Introduction to Computers students and the computer majors are approximately normally distributed.

10.66 From the boxplot and the summary statistics, both distributions are approximately normally distributed. $F_{STAT} = 1.056 < 1.89$. There is insufficient evidence to conclude that the two population variances are significantly different at the 5% level of significance. $t_{STAT} = -5.084 < -1.99$. At the 5% level of significance, there is sufficient evidence to reject the null hypothesis of no difference in the mean life of the bulbs between the two manufacturers. You can conclude that there is a significant difference in the mean life of the bulbs between the two manufacturers.

10.68 Spending cutbacks: Because $-1.96 < Z_{STAT} = -1.8497 < 1.96$ and p-value $= 0.0644 > 0.05$, do not reject H_0. There is not enough evidence that there is a difference between men and women in the proportion who spend less on entertainment and eating out. Because $-1.96 < Z_{STAT} = -1.1334 < 1.96$ and p-value $= 0.2570 > 0.05$, do not reject H_0. There is not enough evidence that there is a difference between men and women in the proportion who have reduced their credit card spending. Because $Z_{STAT} = -3.8186 < -1.96$ and p-value $= 0.0001 < 0.05$, reject H_0. There is evidence that there is a difference between men and women in the proportion who plan to cut down on holiday spending. Because $-1.96 < Z_{STAT} = -0.1446 < 1.96$ and p-value $= 0.8850 > 0.05$, do not reject H_0. There is not enough evidence that there is a difference between men and women in the proportion who put more money into savings. Because $Z_{STAT} = -2.5287 < -1.96$ and p-value $= 0.0114 < 0.05$, reject H_0. There is enough evidence that there is a difference between men and women in the proportion who would postpone a home improvement project. Because $Z_{STAT} = -2.2834 < -1.96$ and p-value $= 0.0224 < 0.05$, reject H_0. There is evidence that there is a difference between men and women in the proportion who put off a big home purchase. Because $-1.96 < Z_{STAT} = -1.37 < 1.96$ and p-value $= 0.1707 > 0.05$, do not reject H_0. There is not enough evidence that there is a difference between men and women in the proportion who cancelled or postponed a vacation. Because $-1.96 < Z_{STAT} = -1.0751 < 1.96$ and p-value $= 0.2823 > 0.05$, do not reject H_0. There is not enough evidence that there is a difference between men and women in the proportion who put off buying a new car. Because $-1.96 < Z_{STAT} = -1.1674 < 1.96$ and p-value $= 0.2431 > 0.05$, do not reject H_0. There is not enough evidence that there is a difference between men and women in the proportion who put off a doctor visit or a medical procedure.

10.70 The normal probability plots suggest that the two populations are not normally distributed. An F test is inappropriate for testing the difference in two variances. The sample variances for Boston and Vermont shingles are 0.0203 and 0.015, respectively. Because $t_{STAT} = 3.015 > 1.967$ or p-value $= 0.0028 < \alpha = 0.05$, reject H_0. There is sufficient evidence to conclude that there is a difference in the mean granule loss of Boston and Vermont shingles.

CHAPTER 11

11.2 (a) $SSW = 150$. (b) $MSA = 15$. (c) $MSW = 5$. (d) $F_{STAT} = 3$.

11.4 (a) 2. (b) 18. (c) 20.

11.6 (a) Reject H_0 if $F_{STAT} > 2.95$; otherwise, do not reject H_0.
(b) Because $F_{STAT} = 4 > 2.95$, reject H_0. (c) The table does not have 28 degrees of freedom in the denominator, so use the next larger critical value, $Q_\alpha = 3.90$. (d) Critical range $= 6.166$.

11.8 (a) $H_0: \mu_A = \mu_B = \mu_C = \mu_D$ and H_1: At least one mean is different.

$$MSA = \frac{SSA}{c-1} = \frac{1986.475}{3} = 662.1583.$$

$$MSW = \frac{SSW}{n-c} = \frac{495.5}{36} = 13.76389.$$

$$F_{STAT} = \frac{MSA}{MSW} = \frac{662.1583}{13.76389} = 48.1084.$$

$$F_{0.05,3,36} = 2.8663.$$

Because the p-value is approximately 0 and $F_{STAT} = 48.1084 > 2.8663$, reject H_0. There is sufficient evidence of a difference in the mean strength of the four brands of trash bags.

(b) Critical range $= Q_\alpha \sqrt{\frac{MSW}{2}\left(\frac{1}{n_j} + \frac{1}{n_{j'}}\right)} = 3.79\sqrt{\frac{13.7639}{2}\left(\frac{1}{10} + \frac{1}{10}\right)}$

$= 4.446$.

From the Tukey-Kramer procedure, there is a difference in mean strength between Kroger and Tuffstuff, Glad and Tuffstuff, and Hefty and Tuffstuff. **(c)** ANOVA output for Levene's test for homogeneity of variance:

$$MSA = \frac{SSA}{c-1} = \frac{24.075}{3} = 8.025.$$

$$MSW = \frac{SSW}{n-c} = \frac{198.2}{36} = 5.5056.$$

$$F_{STAT} = \frac{MSA}{MSW} = \frac{8.025}{5.5056} = 1.4576.$$

$$F_{0.05,3,36} = 2.8663.$$

Because p-value $= 0.2423 > 0.05$ and $F_{STAT} = 1.458 < 2.866$, do not reject H_0. There is insufficient evidence to conclude that the variances in strength among the four brands of trash bags are different. **(d)** From the results in (a) and (b), Tuffstuff has the lowest mean strength and should be avoided.

11.10 (a) Because $F_{STAT} = 12.56 > 2.76$, reject H_0. (b) Critical range $= 4.67$. Advertisements A and B are different from Advertisements C and D. Advertisement E is only different from Advertisement D. (c) Because $F_{STAT} = 1.927 < 2.76$, do not reject H_0. There is no evidence of a significant difference in the variation in the ratings among the five advertisements. (d) The advertisements underselling the pen's characteristics had the highest mean ratings, and the advertisements overselling the pen's characteristics had the lowest mean ratings. Therefore, use an advertisement that undersells the pen's characteristics and avoid advertisements that oversell the pen's characteristics.

11.12 (a) Because the p-value for this test, 0.922, is greater than the level of significance, $\alpha = 0.05$ (or the computed F test statistic, 0.0817, is less than the critical value $F = 3.6823$), you cannot reject the null hypothesis. You conclude that there is insufficient evidence of a difference in the mean yield between the three methods used in the cleansing step. **(b)** Because there is no evidence of a difference between the methods, you should not develop any multiple comparisons. **(c)** Because the p-value for this test, 0.8429, is greater than the level of significance, $\alpha = 0.05$ (or the computed F test statistic, 0.1728, is less than the critical value, $F = 3.6823$), you cannot reject the null hypothesis. You conclude that there is insufficient evidence of a difference in the variation in the yield between the three methods used in the cleansing step. **(d)** Because there is no evidence of a difference in the variation between the methods, the validity of the conclusion reached in (a) is not affected.

11.14 (a) Because $F_{STAT} = 53.03 > F_{0.05,3,30} = 2.92$, reject H_0. **(b)** Critical range $= 5.27$ (using 30 degrees of freedom). Designs 3 and 4 are different from Designs 1 and 2. Designs 1 and 2 are different from each other. **(c)** The assumptions are that the samples are randomly and independently selected (or randomly assigned), the original populations of distances are approximately normally distributed, and the variances are equal. **(d)** Because $F_{STAT} = 2.093 < 2.92$, do not reject H_0. There is no evidence of a significant difference in the variation in the distance among the four designs. **(e)** The manager should choose Design 3 or 4.

11.16 (a) 40. (b) 60 and 55. (c) 10. (d) 10.

11.18 (a) Because $F_{STAT} = 6.00 > 3.35$, reject H_0. (b) Because $F_{STAT} = 5.50 > F = 3.35$, reject H_0. (c) Because $F_{STAT} = 1.00 < F = 2.73$, do not reject H_0.

11.20 df B = 4, df total = 44, $SSA = 160$, $SSAB = 80$, $SSE = 150$, $SST = 610$, $MSB = 55$, $MSE = 5$. For A: $F_{STAT} = 16$. For AB: $F_{STAT} = 2$.

11.22 (a) Because $F_{STAT} = 1.37 < 4.75$, do not reject H_0. **(b)** Because $F_{STAT} = 23.58 > 4.75$, reject H_0. **(c)** Because $F_{STAT} = 0.70 < 4.75$, do not reject H_0. **(e)** Developer strength has a significant effect on density, but development time does not.

11.24 (a) H_0: There is no interaction between brand and water temperature. H_1: There is an interaction between brand and water temperature. Because $F_{STAT} = \dfrac{253.1552}{12.2199} = 20.7167 > 3.555$ or the p-value $= 0.0000214 < 0.05$, reject H_0. There is evidence of interaction between brand of pain reliever and temperature of the water. **(b)** Because there is an interaction between brand and the temperature of the water, it is inappropriate to analyze the main effect due to brand. **(c)** Because there is an interaction between brand and the temperature of the water, it is inappropriate to analyze the main effect due to water temperature. **(e)** The difference in the mean time a tablet took to dissolve in cold and hot water depends on the brand, with Alka-Seltzer having the largest difference and Equate with the smallest difference.

11.26 (a) Because $F_{STAT} = 0.43 < 4.20$, do not reject H_0. **(b)** Because $F_{STAT} = 0.02 < 4.20$, do not reject H_0. **(c)** Because $F_{STAT} = 45.47 > 4.20$, reject H_0. **(e)** Only part positioning has a significant effect on distortion.

11.36 (a) Because $F_{STAT} = 1.485 < 2.54$, do not reject H_0. **(b)** Because $F_{STAT} = 0.79 < 3.24$, do not reject H_0. **(c)** Because $F_{STAT} = 52.07 > 3.24$, reject H_0. **(e)** Critical range $= 0.0189$. Washing cycles for 22 and 24 minutes are not different with respect to dirt removal, but they are both different from 18- and 20-minute cycles. **(f)** 22 minutes. (24 minutes was not different, but 22 does just as well and would use less energy.) **(g)** The results are the same.

11.38 (a) Because $F_{STAT} = 0.075 < 3.68$, do not reject H_0. **(b)** Because $F_{STAT} = 4.09 > 3.68$, reject H_0. **(c)** Critical range $= 1.489$. Breaking strength is significantly different between 30 and 50 psi.

11.40 (a) Because $F_{STAT} = 0.1899 < 4.1132$, do not reject H_0. There is insufficient evidence to conclude that there is any interaction between type of breakfast and desired time. **(b)** Because $F_{STAT} = 30.4434 > 4.1132$, reject H_0. There is sufficient evidence to conclude that there is an effect that is due to type of breakfast. **(c)** Because $F_{STAT} = 12.4441 > 4.1132$, reject H_0. There is sufficient evidence to conclude that there is an effect that is due to desired time. **(e)** At the 5% level of significance, both the type of breakfast ordered and the desired time have an effect on delivery time difference. There is no interaction between the type of breakfast ordered and the desired time.

11.42 (a) $F_{STAT} = 4.5764 > 3.4668$ or p-value $= 0.0224 < 0.05$, reject H_0. There is sufficient evidence to conclude that there is a difference in the variance of the access read time for the different file sizes. **(b)** Assuming that the F test is robust to the difference in the variances between the file sizes, $F_{STAT} = 2.60 < 3.47$ or p-value $= 0.098 > 0.05$, don't reject H_0. There is insufficient evidence of a difference in the mean access times for the three file sizes. **(c)** The Tukey-Kramer procedure should not be used because there is no evidence of a difference in the file sizes.

11.44 Interaction: $F_{STAT} = 0.2169 < 3.9668$ or p-value $= 0.6428 > 0.05$. There is insufficient evidence of an interaction between piece size and fill height. Piece size: $F_{STAT} = 842.2242 > 3.9668$ or p-value $= 0.0000 < 0.05$. There is evidence of an effect due to piece size. The fine piece size has a lower difference in coded weight. Fill height: $F_{STAT} = 217.0816 > 3.9668$ or p-value $= 0.0000 < 0.05$. There is evidence of an effect due to fill height. The low fill height has a lower difference in coded weight.

CHAPTER 12

12.2 (a) For $df = 1$ and $\alpha = 0.05$, $\chi_\alpha^2 = 3.841$. **(b)** For $df = 1$ and $\alpha = 0.025$, $\chi^2 = 5.024$. **(c)** For $df = 1$ and $\alpha = 0.01$, $\chi^2 = 6.635$.

12.4 (a) All $f_e = 25$. **(b)** Because $\chi_{STAT}^2 = 4.00 > 3.841$, reject H_0.

12.6 (a) Because $\chi_{STAT}^2 = 6.212 > 3.841$, reject H_0. There is enough evidence to conclude that there is a significant difference between the proportion of people who think the expensive pill works better to reduce pain and the proportion of people who think an inexpensive pill works better to reduce pain. **(b)** p-value $= 0.0127$. The probability of obtaining a test statistic of 6.212 or larger when the null hypothesis is true is 0.0127. **(c)** You should not compare the results in (a) to those of Problem 10.30 (b) because that was a one-tail test.

12.8 (a) H_0: $\pi_1 = \pi_2$. H_1: $\pi_1 \neq \pi_2$. Because $\chi_{STAT}^2 = (536 - 621.5)^2/621.5 + (464 - 378.5)^2/378.5 + (707 - 621.5)^2/621.5 + (293 - 378.5)^2/378.5 = 62.152 > 6.635$, reject H_0. There is evidence of a difference in the proportion who believe that e-mail messages should be answered quickly between the two age groups. **(b)** p-value $= 0.0000$. The probability of obtaining a difference in proportions that gives rise to a test statistic greater than 62.152 is 0.0000 if there is no difference in the proportion of people in the two age groups who believe that e-mail messages should be answered quickly. **(c)** The results of (a) and (b) are exactly the same as those of Problem 10.32. The χ^2 in (a) and the Z in Problem 10.32 (a) satisfy the relationship that $\chi^2 = 62.152 = Z^2 = (7.8837)^2$, and the p-value in (b) is exactly the same as the p-value obtained in Problem 10.32 (b).

12.10 (a) Since $\chi_{STAT}^2 = 2.3226 < 3.841$, do not reject H_0. There is not enough evidence to conclude that there is a significant difference between undergraduate and MBA students in the proportion who selected the highest-cost fund. **(b)** p-value $= 0.1275$. The probability of obtaining a test statistic of 2.3226 or larger when the null hypothesis is true is 0.1275. **(c)** The results of (a) and (b) are exactly the same as those of Problem 10.34. The χ^2 in (a) and the Z in Problem 10.34 (a) satisfy the relationship that $\chi_{STAT}^2 = 2.3226 = (Z_{Stat})^2 = (1.5240)^2$, and the p-value in Problem 10.34 (b) is exactly the same as the p-value obtained in (b).

12.12 (a) The expected frequencies for the first row are 20, 30, and 40. The expected frequencies for the second row are 30, 45, and 60. **(b)** Because $\chi_{STAT}^2 = 12.5 > 5.991$, reject H_0.

12.14 (a) Because the calculated test statistic $\chi_{STAT}^2 = 29.6066 > 7.815$, reject H_0 and conclude that there is a difference in the proportion making use of quality tools between the schools. **(b)** The p-value is virtually 0. The probability of a test statistic greater than 29.6066 or more is approximately 0 if there is no difference between the schools in the proportion using quality tools. **(c)** South elementary school is different from the other three schools. It has a much higher proportion of high ratings in the use of quality tools.

12.16 (a) H_0: $\pi_1 = \pi_2 = \pi_3$. H_1: At least one proportion differs.

f_0	f_e	$(f_0 - f_e)$	$(f_0 - f_e)^2/f_e$
48	42.667	5.333	0.667
152	157.333	−5.333	0.181
56	42.667	13.333	4.166
144	157.333	−13.333	1.130
24	42.667	−18.667	8.167
176	157.333	18.667	2.215
			16.526

Decision rule: $df = (c - 1) = (3 - 1) = 2$. If $\chi^2_{STAT} > 5.9915$, reject H_0.

Test statistic: $\chi^2_{STAT} = \sum_{\text{all cells}} \frac{(f_0 - f_e)^2}{f_e} = 16.526$.

Decision: Because $\chi^2_{STAT} = 16.526 > 5.9915$, reject H_0. There is a significant difference in the age groups with respect to major grocery shopping day. **(b)** p-value $= 0.0003$. The probability that the test statistic is greater than or equal to 16.526 is 0.03%, if the null hypothesis is true.

(c)	Pairwise Comparisons	Critical Range	$\lvert p_j - p_{j'} \rvert$
	1 to 2	0.1073	0.04
	2 to 3	0.0959	0.16*
	1 to 3	0.0929	0.12*

There is a significant difference between the 35–54 and over-54 groups and between the under-35 and over-54 groups. **(d)** The stores can use this information to target their marketing to the specific groups of shoppers on Saturday and the days other than Saturday.

12.18 (a) Because $\chi^2_{STAT} = 20.3383 > 7.815$, reject H_0. There is evidence of a difference in the percentage working among the groups. **(b)** p-value $= 0.0001$. **(c)** Men 62–64 vs. women 62–64: $0.11 < 0.196$; there is no significant difference. Men 62–64 vs. men 65–69: $0.21 > 0.1903$; there is a significant difference. Men 62–64 vs. women 65–69: $0.29 > 0.1826$; there is a significant difference. Women 62–64 vs. men 65–69: $0.10 < 0.1887$; there is no significant difference. Women 62–64 vs. women 65–69: $0.18 < 0.181$; there is no significant difference. Men 65–69 vs. women 65–69: $0.08 < 0.174$; there is no significant difference.

12.20 $df = (r - 1)(c - 1) = (3 - 1)(4 - 1) = 6$.

12.22 (b) $\chi^2_{STAT} = 8.3536 < 9.2103$, do not reject H_0 and conclude that there is not enough evidence that men and women feel differently about executive pay. **(c)** $\chi^2_{STAT} = 16.7073 > 9.2103$, reject H_0 and conclude that there is enough evidence that men and women feel differently about executive pay. **(d)** As you can see from the results in (b) and (c), the same proportions will result in a different test statistic and, hence, potentially different decisions.

12.24 (a) H_0: There is no relationship between the commuting time of company employees and the level of stress-related problems observed on the job. H_1: There is a relationship between the commuting time of company employees and the level of stress-related problems observed on the job.

f_0	f_e	$(f_0 - f_e)$	$(f_0 - f_e)^2/f_e$
9	12.1379	−3.1379	0.8112
17	20.1034	−3.1034	0.4791
18	11.7586	6.2414	3.3129
5	5.2414	−0.2414	0.0111
8	8.6810	−0.6810	0.0534
6	5.0776	0.9224	0.1676
18	14.6207	3.3793	0.7811
28	24.2155	3.7845	0.5915
7	14.1638	−7.1638	3.6233
			9.8311

Decision rule: If $\chi^2_{STAT} > 13.277$, reject H_0.

Test statistic: $\chi^2_{STAT} = \sum_{\text{all cells}} \frac{(f_0 - f_e)^2}{f_e} = 9.8311$.

Decision: Because $\chi^2_{STAT} = 9.8311 < 13.277$, do not reject H_0. There is not enough evidence to conclude that there is a relationship between the commuting time of company employees and the level of stress-related problems observed on the job. **(b)** Because $\chi^2_{STAT} = 9.831 > 9.488$, reject H_0. There is enough evidence at the 0.05 level to conclude that there is a relationship.

12.26 Because $\chi^2_{STAT} = 129.520 > 21.026$, reject H_0. There is a relationship between when the decision is made of what to have for dinner and the type of household.

12.28 (a) H_0: $\pi_1 \geq \pi_2$ and H_1: $\pi_1 < \pi_2$, where $1 =$ beginning, $2 =$ end. Decision rule: If $Z < -1.645$, reject H_0.

Test statistic: $Z_{STAT} = \dfrac{B - C}{\sqrt{B + C}} = \dfrac{9 - 22}{\sqrt{9 + 22}} = -2.3349$.

Decision: Because $Z_{STAT} = -2.3349 < -1.645$, reject H_0. There is evidence that the proportion of coffee drinkers who prefer Brand A is lower at the beginning of the advertising campaign than at the end of the advertising campaign. **(b)** p-value $= 0.0098$. The probability of a test statistic smaller than -2.3349 is 0.98% if the proportion of coffee drinkers who prefer Brand A is not lower at the beginning of the advertising campaign than at the end of the advertising campaign.

12.30 (a) Because $Z_{STAT} = -2.2361 < -1.645$, reject H_0. There is evidence that the proportion who prefer Brand A is lower before the advertising than after the advertising. **(b)** p-value $= 0.0127$. The probability of a test statistic less than -2.2361 is 1.27% if the proportion who prefer Brand A is not lower before the advertising than after the advertising.

12.32 (a) Because $Z_{STAT} = -3.8996 < -1.645$, reject H_0. There is evidence that the proportion of employees absent fewer than five days was lower in Year 1 than in Year 2. **(b)** The p-value is virtually 0. The probability of a test statistic smaller than -3.8996 is essentially 0 if the proportion of employees absent fewer than five days was not lower in Year 1 than in Year 2.

12.34 (a) 31. **(b)** 29. **(c)** 27. **(d)** 25.

12.36 40 and 79.

12.38 (a) The ranks for Sample 1 are 1, 2, 4, 5, and 10. The ranks for Sample 2 are 3, 6.5, 6.5, 8, 9, and 11. **(b)** 22. **(c)** 44.

12.40 Because $T_1 = 22 > 20$, do not reject H_0.

12.42 (a) The data are ordinal. **(b)** The two-sample t test is inappropriate because the data can only be placed in ranked order. **(c)** Because $Z_{STAT} = -2.2054 < -1.96$, reject H_0. There is evidence of a significance difference in the median rating of California Cabernets and Washington Cabernets.

12.44 (a) H_0: $M_1 = M_2$, where Populations: $1 =$ Wing A, $2 =$ Wing B. H_1: $M_1 \neq M_2$.

Population 1 Sample: Sample Size	20 Sum of Ranks	561
Population 2 Sample: Sample Size	20 Sum of Ranks	259

$$\mu_{T_1} = \frac{n_1(n + 1)}{2} = \frac{20(40 + 1)}{2} = 410$$

$$\sigma_{T_1} = \sqrt{\frac{n_1 n_2(n + 1)}{12}} = \sqrt{\frac{20(20)(40 + 1)}{12}} = 36.9685$$

$$Z_{STAT} = \frac{T_1 - \mu_{T_1}}{\sigma_{T_1}} = \frac{561 - 410}{36.9685} = 4.0846$$

Decision: Because $Z_{STAT} = 4.0846 > 1.96$ (or p-value $= 0.0000 < 0.05$), reject H_0. There is sufficient evidence of a difference in the median delivery time in the two wings of the hotel. **(b)** The results of (a) are consistent with the results of Problem 10.67.

12.46 (a) Because $Z_{STAT} = -4.118 < -1.645$, reject H_0. There is enough evidence to conclude that the median crack size is less for the unflawed sample than for the flawed sample. **(b)** You must assume approximately equal variability in the two populations. **(c)** Using both the pooled-variance t test and the separate-variance t test allowed you to reject the null hypothesis and conclude in Problem 10.17 that the mean crack size is less for the unflawed sample than for the flawed sample. In this test, using the Wilcoxon rank sum test with large-sample Z approximation also allowed you to reject the null hypothesis and conclude that the median crack size is less for the unflawed sample than for the flawed sample.

12.48 (a) Because $-1.96 < Z_{STAT} = 1.956 < 1.96$ (or the p-value $= 0.0504 > 0.05$), do not reject H_0. There is not enough evidence to conclude that there is a difference in the median battery life between subcompact cameras and compact cameras. **(b)** You must assume approximately equal variability in the two populations. **(c)** Using the pooled-variance t-test, you reject the null hypothesis ($t = 2.8498 > 2.0167$; p-value $= 0.0067 < 0.05$) and conclude that there is evidence of a difference in the mean battery life between the two types of digital cameras in Problem 10.11 (a). However, in Problem 10.48, the F test for the ratio of two variances shows a significant difference between the variances in the battery life. Therefore, the pooled-variance t test is not valid for these data. The separate-variance t test, however, also shows evidence of a difference in the mean battery life between the two types of digital cameras ($t = 2.3248 > 2.1009$; p-value $= 0.0320 < 0.05$). The difference in results can be explained by the violation of the equal-variance assumption needed for the Wilcoxon rank sum test. Thus, the Wilcoxon rank sum test in this case is a test of differences in the two populations, not a test of difference in the medians.

12.50 (a) Decision rule: If $H > \chi_U^2 = 15.086$, reject H_0. **(b)** Because $H = 13.77 < 15.086$, do not reject H_0.

12.52 (a) $H = 13.517 > 7.815$, p-value $= 0.0036 < 0.05$, reject H_0. There is sufficient evidence of a difference in the median waiting time in the four locations. **(b)** The results are consistent with those of Problem 11.9.

12.54 (a) $H = 19.3269 > 9.488$, reject H_0. There is evidence of a difference in the median ratings of the ads. **(b)** The results are consistent with those of Problem 11.10. **(c)** Because the combined scores are not true continuous variables, the nonparametric Kruskal-Wallis rank test is more appropriate because it does not require that the scores be normally distributed.

12.56 (a) Because $H = 22.26 > 7.815$ or the p-value is approximately 0, reject H_0. There is sufficient evidence of a difference in the median strength of the four brands of trash bags. **(b)** The results are the same.

12.64 (a) Because $\chi_{STAT}^2 = 0.412 < 3.841$, do not reject H_0. There is not enough evidence to conclude that there is a relationship between a student's gender and pizzeria selection. **(b)** Because $\chi_{STAT}^2 = 2.624 < 3.841$, do not reject H_0. There is not enough evidence to conclude that there is a relationship between a student's gender and pizzeria selection. **(c)** Because $\chi_{STAT}^2 = 4.956 < 5.991$, do not reject H_0. There is not enough evidence to conclude that there is a relationship between price and pizzeria selection. **(d)** p-value $= 0.0839$. The probability of a sample that gives a test statistic equal to or greater than 4.956 is 8.39% if the null hypothesis of no relationship between price and pizzeria selection is true.

12.66 (a) Because $\chi_{STAT}^2 = 11.895 < 12.592$, do not reject H_0. There is not enough evidence to conclude that there is a relationship between the attitudes of employees toward the use of self-managed work teams and employee job classification. **(b)** Because $\chi_{STAT}^2 = 3.294 < 12.592$, do not reject H_0. There is not enough evidence to conclude that there is a relationship between the attitudes of employees toward vacation time without pay and employee job classification.

12.68 (a) Because $Z_{STAT} = -1.7889 < -1.645$, reject H_0. There is enough evidence of a difference in the proportion of respondents who prefer Coca-Cola before and after viewing the ads. **(b)** p-value $= 0.0736$. The probability of a test statistic that differs from 0 by 1.7889 or more in either direction is 7.36% if there is not difference in the proportion of respondents who prefer Coca-Cola before and after viewing the ads. **(c)** The frequencies in the second table are computed from the row and column totals of the first table. **(d)** Because the calculated test statistic $\chi_{STAT}^2 = 0.6528 < 3.8415$, do not reject H_0 and conclude that there is not a significant difference in preference for Coca-Cola before and after viewing the ads. **(e)** p-value $= 0.4191$. The probability of a test statistic larger than 0.6528 is 41.91% if there is not a significant difference in preference for Coca-Cola before and after viewing the ads. **(f)** The McNemar test performed using the information in the first table takes into consideration the fact that the same set of respondents is surveyed before and after viewing the ads while the chi-square test performed using the information in the second table ignores this fact. The McNemar test should be used because of the related samples (before–after comparison).

12.70 (a) Because $\chi_{STAT}^2 = 11.635 > 7.815$, reject H_0. There is enough evidence to conclude that there is a relationship between the presence of environmental goals and the type of manufacturing process. **(b)** p-value $= 0.00874$. The probability of obtaining a data set that gives rise to a test statistic of 11.635 or more is 0.00874 if there is no relationship between the presence of environmental goals and the type of manufacturing process. **(c)** Because $\chi_{STAT}^2 = 10.94 > 3.841$, reject H_0. There is enough evidence to conclude that there is a difference in improved environmental performance for teams with a specified goal of cutting costs. **(d)** p-value $= 0.000941$. The probability of obtaining a data set that gives rise to a test statistic of 10.94 or more is 0.000941 if there is no difference in improved environmental performance for teams with a specified goal of cutting costs. **(e)** Because $\chi_{STAT}^2 = 0.612 < 3.841$, do not reject H_0. There is not enough evidence to conclude that there is a difference in improved profitability for teams with a specified goal of cutting costs. **(f)** p-value $= 0.4341$. The probability of obtaining a data set that gives rise to a test statistic of 0.612 or more is 0.4341 if there is no difference in improved profitability for teams with a specified goal of cutting costs. **(g)** $\chi_{STAT}^2 = 3.454 < 3.841$, do not reject H_0. There is not enough evidence to conclude that there is a difference in improved morale for teams with a specified goal of cutting costs. **(h)** p-value $= 0.063$. The probability of obtaining a data set that gives rise to a test statistic of 3.454 or more is 0.063 if there is no difference in improved morale for teams with a specified goal of cutting costs.

CHAPTER 13

13.2 (a) Yes. **(b)** No. **(c)** No. **(d)** Yes.

13.4 (a) The scatter plot shows a positive linear relationship. **(b)** For each increase in shelf space of an additional foot, weekly sales are estimated to increase by \$7.40. **(c)** $\hat{Y} = 145 + 7.4X = 145 + 7.4(8) = 204.2$, or \$204.20.

13.6 (b) $b_0 = -2.37$, $b_1 = 0.0501$. **(c)** For every cubic foot increase in the amount moved, labor hours are estimated to increase by 0.0501. **(d)** 22.67 labor hours.

13.8 (b) $b_0 = -533.7995$, $b_1 = 5.2039$. **(c)** For each additional million-dollar increase in revenue, the annual value will increase by an estimated \$5.2039 million. Literal interpretation of b_0 is not meaningful because an operating franchise cannot have zero revenue. **(d)** \$506.977 million.

13.10 (b) $b_0 = -140.1203$, $b_1 = 4.3331$ $\hat{Y} = b_0 + b_1X$. $\hat{Y} = -140.1203 + 4.3331X$ **(c)** For each increase of one additional million dollars of box office gross, the estimated DVDs sold will increase by 4.3331 thousands. **(d)** $\hat{Y} = b_0 + b_1X$. $\hat{Y} = -140.1203 + 4.3331(75) = 184.86285$ thousands.

13.12 $r^2 = 0.90$. 90% of the variation in the dependent variable can be explained by the variation in the independent variable.

13.14 $r^2 = 0.75$. 75% of the variation in the dependent variable can be explained by the variation in the independent variable.

13.16 (a) $r^2 = \dfrac{SSR}{SST} = \dfrac{20{,}535}{30{,}025} = 0.684$. 68.4% of the variation in sales can be explained by the variation in shelf space.

(b) $S_{YX} = \sqrt{\dfrac{SSE}{n-2}} = \dfrac{\sqrt{\sum_{i=1}^{n}(Y_i - \hat{Y}_i)^2}}{n-2} = \sqrt{\dfrac{9{,}490}{10}} = 30.8058$.

(c) Based on (a) and (b), the model should be useful for predicting sales.

13.18 (a) $r^2 = 0.8892$. 88.92% of the variation in labor hours can be explained by the variation in cubic feet moved. **(b)** $S_{YX} = 5.0314$. **(c)** Based on (a) and (b), the model should be very useful for predicting the labor hours.

13.20 (a) $r^2 = 0.939$. 93.9% of the variation in the value of a baseball franchise can be explained by the variation in its annual revenue. **(b)** $S_{YX} = 63.0753$. **(c)** Based on (a) and (b), the model should be very useful for predicting the value of a baseball franchise.

13.22 (a) $r^2 = 0.7278$. 72.78% of the variation in DVDs sold can be explained by the variation in box office gross. **(b)** $S_{YX} = 47.8668$. The variation of DVDs sold around the prediction line is 47.8668 thousands. The typical difference between actual DVDs sold and the predicted DVDs sold using the regression equation is approximately 47.8668 thousands. **(c)** Based on (a) and (b), the model is useful for predicting DVDs sold. **(d)** Other variables that might explain the variation in DVDs sold could be the amount spent on advertising, the timing of the release of the DVDs, and the distribution channels of the DVDs.

13.24 A residual analysis of the data indicates a pattern, with sizable clusters of consecutive residuals that are either all positive or all negative. This pattern indicates a violation of the assumption of linearity. A curvilinear model should be investigated.

13.26 There does not appear to be a pattern in the residual plot. The assumptions of regression do not appear to be seriously violated.

13.28 Based on the residual plot, there does not appear to be a curvilinear pattern in the residuals. The assumptions of normality and equal variance do not appear to be seriously violated.

13.30 Based on the residual plot, there appears to be a nonlinear pattern in the residuals. A curvilinear model should be investigated. There is some right-skewness in the residuals, and there is some violation of the equal-variance assumption.

13.32 (a) An increasing linear relationship exists. **(b)** There is evidence of a strong positive autocorrelation among the residuals.

13.34 (a) No, because the data were not collected over time. **(b)** If a single store had been selected and studied over a period of time, you would compute the Durbin-Watson statistic.

13.36 (a)

$$b_1 = \frac{SSXY}{SSX} = \frac{201399.05}{12495626} = 0.0161$$

$$b_0 = \bar{Y} - b_1\bar{X} = 71.2621 - 0.0161(4393) = 0.458$$

(b) $\hat{Y} = 0.458 + 0.0161X = 0.458 + 0.0161(4500) = 72.908$, or \$72,908. **(c)** There is no evidence of a pattern in the residuals over time.

(d) $D = \dfrac{\sum_{i=2}^{n}(e_i - e_{i-1})^2}{\sum_{i=1}^{n}e_i^2} = \dfrac{1243.2244}{599.0683} = 2.08 > 1.45$. There is no evidence of positive autocorrelation among the residuals. **(e)** Based on a residual analysis, the model appears to be adequate.

13.38 (a) $b_0 = -2.535$, $b_1 = .06073$. **(b)** \$2,505.40. **(d)** $D = 1.64 > d_U = 1.42$, so there is no evidence of positive autocorrelation among the residuals. **(e)** The plot shows some nonlinear pattern, suggesting that a nonlinear model might be better. Otherwise, the model appears to be adequate.

13.40 (a) 3.00. **(b)** ± 2.1199. **(c)** Reject H_0. There is evidence that the fitted linear regression model is useful. **(d)** $1.32 \le \beta_1 \le 7.68$.

13.42 (a) $t_{STAT} = \dfrac{b_1 - \beta_1}{S_{b_1}} = \dfrac{7.4}{1.59} = 4.65 > 2.2281$. Reject H_0. There is evidence of a linear relationship between shelf space and sales. **(b)** $b_1 \pm t_{\alpha/2}S_{b_1} = 7.4 \pm 2.2281(1.59)\ 3.86 \le \beta_1 \le 10.94$.

13.44 (a) $t_{STAT} = 16.52 > 2.0322$; reject H_0. There is evidence of a linear relationship between the number of cubic feet moved and labor hours. **(b)** $0.0439 \le \beta_1 \le 0.0562$.

13.46 (a) $t_{STAT} = 20.7528 > 2.0484$ or because the p-value is approximately 0, reject H_0 at the 5% level of significance. There is evidence of a linear relationship between annual revenue and franchise value. **(b)** $4.6902 \le \beta_1 \le 5.7175$.

13.48 (a) $t_{STAT} = 8.65 > 2.0484$ or because the p-value is virtually $0 < 0.05$; reject H_0. There is evidence of a linear relationship between box office gross and sales of DVDs. **(b)** $3.3072 \le \beta_1 \le 5.3590$.

13.50 (a) (% daily change in DXRLX) $= b_0 + 2.50$ (% daily change in Russell 2000 index). **(b)** If the Russell 2000 gains 10% in a year, DXRLX is expected to gain an estimated 25%. **(c)** If the Russell 2000 loses 20% in a year, DXRLX is expected to lose an estimated 50%. **(d)** Risk takers will be attracted to leveraged funds, and risk-averse investors will stay away.

13.52 (a) $r = 0.8935$. There appears to be a strong positive linear relationship between the mileage as calculated by owners and by current government standards. **(b)** $t_{STAT} = 5.2639 > 2.3646$, p-value $= 0.0012 < 0.05$. Reject H_0. At the 0.05 level of significance, there is a significant linear relationship between the mileage as calculated by owners and by current government standards.

13.54 (a) $r = 0.5497$. There appears to be a moderate positive linear relationship between the average Wonderlic score of football players trying out for the NFL and the graduation rate for football players at selected schools. **(b)** $t_{STAT} = 3.9485$, p-value $= 0.0004 < 0.05$. Reject H_0. At the 0.05 level of significance, there is a significant linear relationship between the average Wonderlic score of football players trying out for the NFL and the graduation rate for football players at selected schools. **(c)** There is a significant linear relationship between the average Wonderlic score of football players trying out for the NFL and the graduation rate for football players at selected schools, but the positive linear relationship is only moderate.

13.56 (a) $15.95 \leq \mu_{Y|X=4} \leq 18.05$. **(b)** $14.651 \leq Y_{X=4} \leq 19.349$.

13.58 (a) $\hat{Y} = 145 + 7.4(8) = 204.2$ $\hat{Y} \pm t_{\alpha/2}S_{YX}\sqrt{h_i}$

$$= 204.2 \pm 2.2281(30.81)\sqrt{0.1373}$$

$$178.76 \leq \mu_{Y|X=8} \leq 229.64.$$

(b) $\hat{Y} \pm t_{\alpha/2}S_{YX}\sqrt{1 + h_i}$

$$= 204.2 \pm 2.2281(30.81)\sqrt{1 + 0.1373}$$

$$131.00 \leq Y_{X=8} \leq 277.40.$$

(c) Part (b) provides a prediction interval for the individual response given a specific value of the independent variable, and part (a) provides an interval estimate for the mean value, given a specific value of the independent variable. Because there is much more variation in predicting an individual value than in estimating a mean value, a prediction interval is wider than a confidence interval estimate.

13.60 (a) $20.799 \leq \mu_{Y|X=500} \leq 24.542$. **(b)** $12.276 \leq Y_{X=500} \leq 33.065$. **(c)** You can estimate a mean more precisely than you can predict a single observation.

13.62 (a) $214.1497 \leq \mu_{Y|X=200} \leq 279.416$. **(b)** $375.5999 \leq Y_{X=200} \leq 638.3541$. **(c)** Part (b) provides a prediction interval for an individual response given a specific value of X, and part (a) provides a confidence interval estimate for the mean value, given a specific value of X. Because there is much more variation in predicting an individual value than in estimating a mean, the prediction interval is wider than the confidence interval.

13.74 (a) $b_0 = 24.84, b_1 = 0.14$. **(b)** For each additional case, the predicted delivery time is estimated to increase by 0.14 minutes. **(c)** 45.84. **(d)** No, 500 is outside the relevant range of the data used to fit the regression equation. **(e)** $r^2 = 0.972$. **(f)** There is no obvious pattern in the residuals, so the assumptions of regression are met. The model appears to be adequate. **(g)** $t_{STAT} = 24.88 > 2.1009$; reject H_0. **(h)** $44.88 \leq \mu_{Y|X=150} \leq 46.80$. $41.56 \leq Y_{X=150} \leq 50.12$.

13.76 (a) $b_0 = -122.3439, b_1 = 1.7817$. **(b)** For each additional thousand dollars in assessed value, the estimated selling price of a house increases by $1.7817 thousand. The estimated selling price of a house with a 0 assessed value is -122.3439 thousand. However, this interpretation is not meaningful in the current setting because the assessed value cannot be below 0. **(c)** $\hat{Y} = -122.3439 + 1.78171X = -122.3439 + 1.78171(170) = 180.5475$ thousand dollars. **(d)** $r^2 = 0.9256$. So 92.56% of the variation in selling price can be explained by the variation in assessed value. **(e)** Neither the residual plot nor the normal probability plot reveals any potential violation of the linearity, equal variance, and normality assumptions. **(f)** $t_{STAT} = 18.6648 > 2.0484$, p-value is virtually 0. Because p-value < 0.05, reject H_0. There is evidence of a linear relationship between selling price and assessed value. **(g)** $1.5862 \leq \beta_1 \leq 1.9773$.

13.78 (a) $b_0 = 0.30, b_1 = 0.00487$. **(b)** For each additional point on the GMAT score, the predicted GPA is estimated to increase by 0.00487. Because a GMAT score of 0 is not possible, the Y intercept does not have a practical interpretation. **(c)** 3.222. **(d)** $r^2 = 0.798$. **(e)** There is no obvious pattern in the residuals, so the assumptions of regression are met. The model appears to be adequate. **(f)** $t_{STAT} = 8.43 > 2.1009$; reject H_0. **(g)** $3.144 \leq \mu_{Y|X=600} \leq 3.301, 2.886 \leq Y_{X=600} \leq 3.559$. **(h)** $.00366 \leq \beta_1 \leq .00608$.

13.80 (a) There is no clear relationship shown on the scatter plot. **(c)** Looking at all 23 flights, when the temperature is lower, there is likely to be some O-ring damage, particularly if the temperature is below 60 degrees. **(d)** 31 degrees is outside the relevant range, so a prediction should not be made. **(e)** Predicted $Y = 18.036 - 0.240X$, where $X =$ temperature

and $Y =$ O-ring damage. **(g)** A nonlinear model would be more appropriate. **(h)** The appearance on the residual plot of a nonlinear pattern indicates that a nonlinear model would be better. It also appears that the normality assumption is invalid.

13.82 (a) $b_0 = 16.022, b_1 = 2.896$. **(b)** For each additional million-dollar increase in revenue, the franchise value will increase by an estimated $2.896 million. Literal interpretation of b_0 is not meaningful because an operating franchise cannot have zero revenue. **(c)** $595.2167 million. **(d)** $r^2 = 0.9718$. 97.18% of the variation in the value of an NBA franchise can be explained by the variation in its annual revenue. **(e)** There does not appear to be a pattern in the residual plot. The assumptions of regression do not appear to be seriously violated. **(f)** $t_{STAT} = 31.0863 > 2.0484$ or because the p-value is approximately 0, reject H_0 at the 5% level of significance. There is evidence of a linear relationship between annual revenue and franchise value. **(g)** $442.9125 \leq \mu_{Y|X=200} \leq 457.9236$. **(h)** $417.394 \leq Y_{X=200} \leq 483.442$. **(i)** The strength of the relationship between revenue and value is much stronger for baseball and NBA franchises than for NFL franchises. However, the value for NFL franchises is much higher, as is the predicted value for a given revenue.

13.84 (a) $b_0 = -2,629.222, b_1 = 82.472$. **(b)** For each additional centimeter in circumference, the weight is estimated to increase by 82.472 grams. **(c)** 2,319.08 grams. **(e)** $r^2 = 0.937$. **(f)** There appears to be a nonlinear relationship between circumference and weight. **(g)** p-value is virtually $0 < 0.05$; reject H_0. **(h)** $72.7875 \leq \beta_1 \leq 92.156$.

13.86 (b) $\hat{Y} = 931,626.16 + 21,782.76X$. **(c)** $b_1 = 21,782.76$ For each increase of the median age of the customer base by one year, the latest one-month sales total is estimated to increase by $21,782.76. **(d)** $r^2 = 0.0017$. Only 0.17% of the total variation in the franchise's latest one-month sales total can be explained by using the median age of the customer base. **(e)** The residuals are very evenly spread out across different ranges of median age. **(f)** Because $-2.4926 < t_{STAT} = 0.2482 < 2.4926$, do not reject H_0. There is not enough evidence to conclude that there is a linear relationship between the one-month sales total and the median age of the customer base. **(g)** $-156,181.50 \leq \beta_1 \leq 199,747.02$.

13.88 (a) There is a positive linear relationship between total sales and the percentage of the customer base with a college diploma. **(b)** $\hat{Y} = 789,847.38 + 35,854.15X$. **(c)** $b_1 = 35,854.15$ For each increase of 1% of the customer base having received a college diploma, the latest one-month mean sales total is estimated to increase by $35,854.15. **(d)** $r^2 = 0.1036$. 10.36% of the total variation in the franchise's latest one-month sales total can be explained by the percentage of the customer base with a college diploma. **(e)** The residuals are evenly spread out around zero. **(f)** Because $t_{STAT} = 2.0392 > 2.0281$, reject H_0. There is enough evidence to conclude that there is a linear relationship between one-month sales total and percentage of customer base with a college diploma. **(g)** $b_1 \pm t_{\alpha/2}, S_{b_1} = 35,854.15 \pm 2.0281(17,582.269)$, $195.75 \leq \beta_1 \leq 71,512.60$.

13.90 (a) $b_0 = -30.2524, b_1 = 1.2267$. **(b)** For each additional unit increase in summated rating, the cost per person is estimated to increase by $1.2267. Because no restaurant will receive a summated rating of 0, it is inappropriate to interpret the Y intercept. **(c)** $31.08. **(d)** $r^2 = 0.5452$. 54.52% of the variation in cost per person can be explained by the variation in the summated rating. **(e)** There is no obvious pattern in the residuals, so the assumptions of regression are met. The model appears to be adequate. **(f)** $t_{STAT} = 10.8387$, the p-value is virtually $0 < 0.05$; reject H_0. There is enough evidence to conclude that there is a linear relationship between price per person and summated rating. **(g)** The linear regression model appears to have provided an adequate fit and shown a significant linear relationship between price per person and summated rating. Because 54.52% of the variation in the cost per person can be explained by the variation in summated rating, summated rating is moderately useful in predicting the cost per person.

13.92 (a) The correlation between bonus and compensation is 0.5870, between compensation and stock performance is 0.0464, and between bonus and stock performance -0.0273. **(b)** The t_{STAT} values are 14.1167, 0.9038, and -0.5317. The correlation between bonus and compensation is significant. **(c)** The lack of correlation between bonus and compensation and stock performance was surprising.

CHAPTER 14

14.2 (a) For each one-unit increase in X_1, you estimate that Y will decrease 2 units, holding X_2 constant. For each one-unit increase in X_2, you estimate that Y will increase 7 units, holding X_1 constant. **(b)** The Y intercept equal to 50 estimates the value of Y when both X_1 and X_2 are 0.

14.4 (a) $\hat{Y} = -2.72825 + 0.047114X_1 + 0.011947X_2$. **(b)** For a given number of orders, for each increase of $1,000 in sales, the distribution cost is estimated to increase by $47.114. For a given amount of sales, for each increase of one order, the distribution cost is estimated to increase by $11.95. **(c)** The interpretation of b_0 has no practical meaning here because it would represent the estimated distribution cost when there were no sales and no orders. **(d)** $\hat{Y} = -2.72825 + 0.047114(400) + 0.011947(4500) = 69.878$, or $69,878. **(e)** $66,419.93 \le \mu_{Y|X} \le$ $73,337.01$. **(f)** $59,380.61 \le Y_X \le 80,376.33$. **(g)** The interval in (e) is narrower because it is estimating the mean value, not an individual value.

14.6 (a) $\hat{Y} = 156.4 + 13.081X_1 + 16.795X_2$. **(b)** For a given amount of newspaper advertising, each increase by $1,000 in radio advertising is estimated to result in an increase in sales of $13,081. For a given amount of radio advertising, each increase by $1,000 in newspaper advertising is estimated to result in an increase in sales of $16,795. **(c)** When there is no money spent on radio advertising and newspaper advertising, the estimated mean sales is $156,430.44. **(d)** Holding the other independent variable constant, newspaper advertising seems to be more effective because its slope is greater.

14.8 (a) $\hat{Y} = 400.8057 + 456.4485X_1 - 2.4708X_2$, where $X_1 =$ land, $X_2 =$ age. **(b)** For a given age, each increase by one acre in land area is estimated to result in an increase in appraised value by $456.45 thousands. For a given acreage, each increase of one year in age is estimated to result in a decrease in appraised value by $2.47 thousands. **(c)** The interpretation of b_0 has no practical meaning here because it would represent the estimated appraised value of a new house that has no land area. **(d)** $\hat{Y} = 400.8057 + 456.4485(0.25) - 2.4708(45) = $403.73 thousands. **(e)** $372.7370 \le \mu_{Y|X} \le 434.7243$. **(f)** $235.1964 \le Y_X \le 572.2649$.

14.10 (a) $MSR = 15, MSE = 12$. **(b)** 1.25. **(c)** $F_{STAT} = 1.25 < 4.10$; do not reject H_0. **(d)** 0.20. **(e)** 0.04.

14.12 (a) $F_{STAT} = 97.69 > F_\alpha = 3.89$ with 2 and $15 - 2 - 1 = 12$ degrees of freedom. Reject H_0. There is evidence of a significant linear relationship with at least one of the independent variables. **(b)** p-value $= 0.0001$. **(c)** $r^2 = 0.9421$. 94.21% of the variation in the long-term ability to absorb shock can be explained by variation in forefoot absorbing capability and variation in midsole impact. **(d)** $r^2_{adj} = 0.93245$.

14.14 (a) $F_{STAT} = 74.13 > 3.467$; reject H_0. **(b)** p-value $= 0$. **(c)** $r^2 = 0.8759$. 87.59% of the variation in distribution cost can be explained by variation in sales and variation in number of orders. **(d)** $r^2_{adj} = 0.8641$.

14.16 (a) $F_{STAT} = 40.16 > F_\alpha = 3.522$ with 2 and $22 - 2 - 1 = 19$ degrees of freedom. Reject H_0. There is evidence of a significant linear

relationship. **(b)** p-value < 0.001. **(c)** $r^2 = 0.8087$. 80.87% of the variation in sales can be explained by variation in radio advertising and variation in newspaper advertising. **(d)** $r^2_{adj} = 0.7886$.

14.18 (a)–(e) Based on a residual analysis, there is no evidence of a violation in the assumptions of regression.

14.20 (a) There appears to be a quadratic relationship in the plot of the residuals against both radio and newspaper advertising. **(c)** Curvilinear terms for both of these explanatory variables should be considered for inclusion in the model.

14.22 (a) The residual analysis reveals no patterns. **(b)** There are no apparent violations in the assumptions.

14.24 (a) Variable X_2 has a larger slope in terms of the t statistic of 3.75 than variable X_1, which has a smaller slope in terms of the t statistic of 3.33. **(b)** $1.46824 \le \beta_1 \le 6.53176$. **(c)** For X_1: $t_{STAT} = 4/1.2 = 3.33 >$ 2.1098, with 17 degrees of freedom for $\alpha = 0.05$. Reject H_0. There is evidence that X_1 contributes to a model already containing X_2. For X_2: $t_{STAT} = 3/0.8 = 3.75 > 2.1098$, with 17 degrees of freedom for $\alpha = 0.05$. Reject H_0. There is evidence that X_2 contributes to a model already containing X_1. Both X_1 and X_2 should be included in the model.

14.26 (a) 95% confidence interval on β_1: $b_1 \pm tS_{b_1}$, 0.0471 ± 2.0796 (0.0203), $0.00488 \le \beta_1 \le 0.08932$. **(b)** For X_1: $t_{STAT} = b_1/S_{b_1} =$ $0.0471/0.0203 = 2.32 > 2.0796$. Reject H_0. There is evidence that X_1 contributes to a model already containing X_2. For X_2: $t_{STAT} = b_1/S_{b_1} =$ $0.01195/0.00225 = 5.31 > 2.0796$. Reject H_0. There is evidence that X_2 contributes to a model already containing X_1. Both X_1 (sales) and X_2 (orders) should be included in the model.

14.28 (a) $9.398 \le \beta_1 \le 16.763$. **(b)** For X_1: $t_{STAT} = 7.43 > 2.093$. Reject H_0. There is evidence that X_1 contributes to a model already containing X_2. For X_2: $t_{STAT} = 5.67 > 2.093$. Reject H_0. There is evidence that X_2 contributes to a model already containing X_1. Both X_1 (radio advertising) and X_2 (newspaper advertising) should be included in the model.

14.30 (a) $227.5865 \le \beta_1 \le 685.3104$. **(b)** For X_1: $t_{STAT} = 4.0922$ and p-value $= 0.0003$. Because p-value < 0.05, reject H_0. There is evidence that X_1 contributes to a model already containing X_2. For X_2: $t_{STAT} = -3.6295$ and p-value $= 0.0012$. Because p-value < 0.05, reject H_0. There is evidence that X_2 contributes to a model already containing X_1. Both X_1 (land area) and X_2 (age) should be included in the model.

14.32 (a) For X_1: $F_{STAT} = 1.25 < 4.96$; do not reject H_0. For X_2: $F_{STAT} = 0.833 < 4.96$; do not reject H_0. **(b)** 0.1111, 0.0769.

14.34 (a) For X_1: $SSR(X_1 | X_2) = SSR(X_1 \text{ and } X_2) - SSR(X_2) =$

$$3,368.087 - 3,246.062 = 122.025, F_{STAT} = \frac{SSR(X_2 | X_1)}{MSE} =$$

$$\frac{122.025}{477.043/21} = 5.37 > 4.325. \text{ Reject } H_0. \text{ There is evidence that } X_1$$

contributes to a model already containing X_2. For X_2: $SSR(X_2 | X_1) =$ $SSR(X_1 \text{ and } X_2) - SSR(X_1) = 3,368.087 - 2,726.822 = 641.265$,

$$F_{STAT} = \frac{SSR(X_2 | X_1)}{MSE} = \frac{641.265}{477.043/21} = 28.23 > 4.325. \text{ Reject } H_0.$$

There is evidence that X_2 contributes to a model already containing X_1. Because both X_1 and X_2 make a significant contribution to the model in the presence of the other variable, both variables should be included in the model.

(b) $r^2_{Y1.2} = \dfrac{SSR(X_1 | X_2)}{SST - SSR(X_1 \text{ and } X_2) + SSR(X_1 | X_2)}$

$$= \frac{122.025}{3,845.13 - 3,368.087 + 122.025} = 0.2037.$$

Holding constant the effect of the number of orders, 20.37% of the variation in distribution cost can be explained by the variation in sales.

$$r^2_{Y2.1} = \frac{SSR(X_2 \mid X_1)}{SST - SSR(X_1 \text{ and } X_2) + SSR(X_2 \mid X_1)}$$

$$= \frac{641.265}{3,845.13 - 3,368.087 + 641.265} = 0.5734$$

Holding constant the effect of sales, 57.34% of the variation in distribution cost can be explained by the variation in the number of orders.

14.36 (a) For X_1: $F_{STAT} = 55.28 > 4.381$. There is evidence that X_1 contributes to a model containing X_2. For X_2: $F_{STAT} = 32.12 > 4.381$. Reject H_0. There is evidence that X_2 contributes to a model already containing X_1. Because both X_1 and X_2 make a significant contribution to the model in the presence of the other variable, both variables should be included in the model. **(b)** $r^2_{Y1.2} = 0.7442$. Holding constant the effect of newspaper advertising, 74.42% of the variation in sales can be explained by the variation in radio advertising. $r^2_{Y2.1} = 0.6283$. Holding constant the effect of radio advertising, 62.83% of the variation in sales can be explained by the variation in newspaper advertising.

14.38 (a) Holding constant the effect of X_2, for each increase of one unit of X_1, Y increases by 4 units. **(b)** Holding constant the effect of X_1, for each increase of one unit of X_2, Y increases by 2 units. **(c)** Because $t_{STAT} = 3.27 > 2.1098$, reject H_0. Variable X_2 makes a significant contribution to the model.

14.40 (a) $\hat{Y} = 243.7371 + 9.2189X_1 + 12.6967X_2$, where X_1 = number of rooms and X_2 = neighborhood (east = 0). **(b)** Holding constant the effect of neighborhood, for each additional room, the selling price is estimated to increase by 9.2189 thousands of dollars, or \$9218.9. For a given number of rooms, a west neighborhood is estimated to increase the selling price over an east neighborhood by 12.6967 thousands of dollars, or \$12,696.7. **(c)** $\hat{Y} = 243.7371 + 9.2189(9) + 12.6967(0) = 326.7076$, or \$326,707.6. $309,560.04 \le Y_X \le \$343,855.1$. $\$321,471.44 \le \mu_{Y|X} \le \$331,943.71$. **(d)** Based on a residual analysis, the model appears to be adequate. **(e)** $F_{STAT} = 55.39$, the p-value is virtually 0. Because p-value < 0.05, reject H_0. There is evidence of a significant relationship between selling price and the two independent variables (rooms and neighborhood). **(f)** For X_1: $t_{STAT} = 8.9537$, the p-value is virtually 0. Reject H_0. Number of rooms makes a significant contribution and should be included in the model. For X_2: $t_{STAT} = 3.5913$, p-value $= 0.0023 < 0.05$. Reject H_0. Neighborhood makes a significant contribution and should be included in the model. Based on these results, the regression model with the two independent variables should be used. **(g)** $7.0466 \le \beta_1 \le 11.3913$. **(h)** $5.2378 \le \beta_2 \le 20.1557$. **(i)** $r^2_{adj} = 0.851$. **(j)** $r^2_{Y1.2} = 0.825$. Holding constant the effect of neighborhood, 82.5% of the variation in selling price can be explained by variation in number of rooms. $r^2_{Y2.1} = 0.431$. Holding constant the effect of number of rooms, 43.1% of the variation in selling price can be explained by variation in neighborhood. **(k)** The slope of selling price with number of rooms is the same, regardless of whether the house is located in an east or west neighborhood. **(l)** $\hat{Y} = 253.95 + 8.032X_1 - 5.90X_2 + 2.089X_1X_2$. For X_1X_2, p-value $= 0.330$. Do not reject H_0. There is no evidence that the interaction term makes a contribution to the model. **(m)** The model in (a) should be used.

14.42 (a) Predicted time $= 8.01 + 0.00523$ Depth $- 2.105$ Dry. **(b)** Holding constant the effect of type of drilling, for each foot increase in depth of the hole, the drilling time is estimated to increase by 0.00523 minutes. For a given depth, a dry drilling hole is estimated to reduce the drilling time over wet drilling by 2.1052 minutes. **(c)** 6.428 minutes, $6.210 \le \mu_{Y|X} \le 6.646$, $4.923 \le Y_X \le 7.932$. **(d)** The model appears to be adequate. **(e)** $F_{STAT} = 111.11 > 3.09$; reject H_0. **(f)** $t_{STAT} = 5.03 > 1.9847$; reject H_0. $t_{STAT} = -14.03 < -1.9847$; reject H_0. Include both

variables. **(g)** $0.0032 \le \beta_1 \le 0.0073$. **(h)** $-2.403 \le \beta_2 \le -1.808$. **(i)** 69.0%. **(j)** 0.207, 0.670. **(k)** The slope of the additional drilling time with the depth of the hole is the same, regardless of the type of drilling method used. **(l)** The p-value of the interaction term $= 0.462 > 0.05$, so the term is not significant and should not be included in the model. **(m)** The model in part (a) should be used.

14.44 (a) $\hat{Y} = 31.5594 + 0.0296X_1 + 0.0041X_2 + 0.000017159X_1X_2$, where X_1 = sales, X_2 = orders, p-value $= 0.3249 > 0.05$. Do not reject H_0. There is not enough evidence that the interaction term makes a contribution to the model. **(b)** Because there is not enough evidence of any interaction effect between sales and orders, the model in Problem 14.4 should be used.

14.46 (a) The p-value of the interaction term $= 0.002 < 0.05$, so the term is significant and should be included in the model. **(b)** Use the model developed in this problem.

14.48 (a) For X_1X_2, p-value $= 0.2353 > 0.05$. Do not reject H_0. There is not enough evidence that the interaction term makes a contribution to the model. **(b)** Because there is not enough evidence of an interaction effect between total staff present and remote hours, the model in Problem 14.7 should be used.

14.58 (a) $\hat{Y} = -3.9152 + 0.0319X_1 + 4.2228X_2$, where X_1 = number of cubic feet moved and X_2 = number of pieces of large furniture. **(b)** Holding constant the number of pieces of large furniture, for each additional cubic foot moved, the labor hours are estimated to increase by 0.0319. Holding constant the amount of cubic feet moved, for each additional piece of large furniture, the labor hours are estimated to increase by 4.2228. **(c)** $\hat{Y} = -3.9152 + 0.0319(500) + 4.2228(2) = 20.4926$. **(d)** Based on a residual analysis, the errors appear to be normally distributed. The equal-variance assumption might be violated because the variances appear to be larger around the center region of both independent variables. There might also be violation of the linearity assumption. A model with quadratic terms for both independent variables might be fitted. **(e)** $F_{STAT} = 228.80$, p-value is virtually 0. Because p-value < 0.05, reject H_0. There is evidence of a significant relationship between labor hours and the two independent variables (the amount of cubic feet moved and the number of pieces of large furniture). **(f)** The p-value is virtually 0. The probability of obtaining a test statistic of 228.80 or greater is virtually 0 if there is no significant relationship between labor hours and the two independent variables (the amount of cubic feet moved and the number of pieces of large furniture). **(g)** $r^2 = 0.9327$. 93.27% of the variation in labor hours can be explained by variation in the number of cubic feet moved and the number of pieces of large furniture. **(h)** $r^2_{adj} = 0.9287$. **(i)** For X_1: $t_{STAT} = 6.9339$, the p-value is virtually 0. Reject H_0. The number of cubic feet moved makes a significant contribution and should be included in the model. For X_2: $t_{STAT} = 4.6192$, the p-value is virtually 0. Reject H_0. The number of pieces of large furniture makes a significant contribution and should be included in the model. Based on these results, the regression model with the two independent variables should be used. **(j)** For X_1: $t_{STAT} = 6.9339$, the p-value is virtually 0. The probability of obtaining a sample that will yield a test statistic farther away than 6.9339 is virtually 0 if the number of cubic feet moved does not make a significant contribution, holding the effect of the number of pieces of large furniture constant. For X_2: $t_{STAT} = 4.6192$, the p-value is virtually 0. The probability of obtaining a sample that will yield a test statistic farther away than 4.6192 is virtually 0 if the number of pieces of large furniture does not make a significant contribution, holding the effect of the amount of cubic feet moved constant. **(k)** $0.0226 \le \beta_1 \le 0.0413$. You are 95% confident that the mean labor hours will increase by between 0.0226 and 0.0413 for each additional cubic foot moved, holding constant the number of pieces of large furniture. In Problem 13.44, you are 95% confident that the labor hours will increase by between 0.0439 and 0.0562 for each additional cubic foot moved, regardless of the number of pieces of large furniture. **(l)** $r^2_{Y1.2} = 0.5930$. Holding constant the effect of the number of pieces of large furniture, 59.3% of the variation in labor hours can be explained by variation in the amount of cubic feet moved. $r^2_{Y2.1} = 0.3927$. Holding constant the effect of the number of cubic feet moved, 39.27% of the variation in labor hours can be explained by variation in the number of pieces of large furniture.

14.60 (a) $\hat{Y} = -120.0483 + 1.7506X_1 + 0.3680X_2$, where $X_1 = $ assessed value and $X_2 = $ time period. **(b)** Holding constant the time period, for each additional thousand dollars of assessed value, the selling price is estimated to increase by 1.7507 thousand dollars. Holding constant the assessed value, for each additional month since assessment, the selling price is estimated to increase by 0.3680 thousand dollars. **(c)** $\hat{Y} = -120.0483 + 1.7506(170) + 0.3680(12) = 181.9692$ thousand dollars. **(d)** Based on a residual analysis, the model appears to be adequate. **(e)** $F_{STAT} = 223.46$, the p-value is virtually 0. Because p-value < 0.05, reject H_0. There is evidence of a significant relationship between selling price and the two independent variables (assessed value and time period). **(f)** The p-value is virtually 0. The probability of obtaining a test statistic of 223.46 or greater is virtually 0 if there is no significant relationship between selling price and the two independent variables (assessed value and time period). **(g)** $r^2 = 0.9430$. 94.30% of the variation in selling price can be explained by variation in assessed value and time period. **(h)** $r^2_{adj} = 0.9388$. **(i)** For X_1: $t_{STAT} = 20.4137$, the p-value is virtually 0. Reject H_0. The assessed value makes a significant contribution and should be included in the model. For X_2: $t_{STAT} = 2.8734$, p-value $= 0.0078 < 0.05$. Reject H_0. The time period makes a significant contribution and should be included in the model. Based on these results, the regression model with the two independent variables should be used. **(j)** For X_1: $t_{STAT} = 20.4137$, the p-value is virtually 0. The probability of obtaining a sample that will yield a test statistic farther away than 20.4137 is virtually 0 if the assessed value does not make a significant contribution, holding time period constant. For X_2: $t_{STAT} = 2.8734$, the p-value is virtually 0. The probability of obtaining a sample that will yield a test statistic farther away than 2.8734 is virtually 0 if the time period does not make a significant contribution holding the effect of the assessed value constant. **(k)** $1.5746 \le \beta_1 \le 1.9266$. You are 95% confident that the selling price will increase by an amount somewhere between \$1.5746 thousand and \$1.9266 thousand for each additional thousand-dollar increase in assessed value, holding constant the time period. In Problem 13.76, you are 95% confident that the selling price will increase by an amount somewhere between \$1.5862 thousand and \$1.9773 thousand for each additional thousand-dollar increase in assessed value, regardless of the time period. **(l)** $r^2_{Y1.2} = 0.9392$. Holding constant the effect of the time period, 93.92% of the variation in selling price can be explained by variation in the assessed value. $r^2_{Y2.1} = 0.2342$. Holding constant the effect of the assessed value, 23.42% of the variation in selling price can be explained by variation in the time period.

14.62 (a) $\hat{Y} = 163.7751 + 10.7252X_1 - 0.2843X_2$, where $X_1 = $ size and $X_2 = $ age. **(b)** Holding age constant, for each additional thousand square feet, the assessed value is estimated to increase by \$10.7252 thousand. Holding size constant, for each additional year, the assessed value is estimated to decrease by \$0.2843 thousand. **(c)** $\hat{Y} = 163.7751 + 10.7252(1.75) - 0.2843(10) = 179.7017$ thousand dollars. **(d)** Based on a residual analysis, the errors appear to be normally distributed. The equal-variance assumption appears to be valid. There might be a violation of the linearity assumption for age. You might want to include in the model a quadratic term for age. **(e)** $F_{STAT} = 28.58$, p-value $= 0.0000272776$. Because p-value $= 0.0000 < 0.05$, reject H_0. There is evidence of a significant relationship between assessed value and the two independent variables (size and age). **(f)** p-value $= 0.0000272776$. The probability of obtaining an F_{STAT} test statistic of 28.58 or greater is virtually 0 if there is no significant relationship between assessed value

and the two independent variables (size and age). **(g)** $r^2 = 0.8265$. 82.65% of the variation in assessed value can be explained by variation in size and age. **(h)** $r^2_{adj} = 0.7976$. **(i)** For X_1: $t_{STAT} = 3.5581$, p-value $= 0.0039 < 0.05$. Reject H_0. The size of a house makes a significant contribution and should be included in the model. For X_2: $t_{STAT} = -3.4002$, p-value $= 0.0053 < 0.05$. Reject H_0. The age of a house makes a significant contribution and should be included in the model. Based on these results, the regression model with the two independent variables should be used. **(j)** For X_1: p-value $= 0.0039$. The probability of obtaining a sample that will yield a test statistic farther away than 3.5581 is 0.0039 if the size of a house does not make a significant contribution, holding age constant. For X_2: p-value $= 0.0053$. The probability of obtaining a sample that will yield a test statistic farther away than -3.4002 is 0.0053 if the age of a house does not make a significant contribution, holding the effect of the size constant. **(k)** $4.1572 \le \beta_1 \le 17.2928$. You are 95% confident that the mean assessed value will increase by an amount somewhere between \$4.1575 thousand and \$17.2928 thousand for each additional thousand-square-foot increase in the size of a house, holding constant the age. In Problem 13.77, you are 95% confident that the mean assessed value will increase by an amount somewhere between \$9.4695 thousand and \$23.7972 thousand for each additional thousand-square-foot increase in heating area, regardless of the age. **(l)** $r^2_{Y1.2} = 0.5134$. Holding constant the effect of age, 51.34% of the variation in assessed value can be explained by variation in the size. $r^2_{Y2.1} = 0.4907$. Holding constant the effect of the size, 49.07% of the variation in assessed value can be explained by variation in the age. **(m)** Based on your answers to (a) through (l), the age of a house does have an effect on its assessed value.

14.64 (a) $\hat{Y} = 156.1205 - 16.8995X_1 - 4.2052X_2$, where $X_1 = $ ERA and $X_2 = $ league (American $= 0$). **(b)** Holding constant the effect of the league, for each additional ERA, the number of wins is estimated to decrease by 16.8995. For a given ERA, a team in the National League is estimated to have 4.2052 fewer wins than a team in the American League. **(c)** 81.8611 wins. **(d)** Based on a residual analysis, the errors appear to be normally distributed. There is no apparent violation of other assumptions. **(e)** $F_{STAT} = 12.8582 > 3.35$, p-value $= 0.0001$. Because p-value < 0.05, reject H_0. There is evidence of a significant relationship between wins and the two independent variables (ERA and league). **(f)** For X_1: $t_{STAT} = -4.9626 < -2.0518$, the p-value is virtually 0. Reject H_0. ERA makes a significant contribution and should be included in the model. For X_2: $t_{STAT} = -1.3969 > -2.0518$, p-value $= 0.1738 > 0.05$. Do not reject H_0. The league does not make a significant contribution and should not be included in the model. Based on these results, the regression model with only the ERA as the independent variable should be used. **(g)** $-23.8868 \le \beta_1 \le -9.9122$. **(h)** $-10.3820 \le \beta_1 \le 1.9715$. **(i)** $r^2_{adj} = 0.4499$. 44.99% of the variation in wins can be explained by the variation in ERA and league after adjusting for number of independent variables and sample size. **(j)** $r^2_{Y1.2} = 0.4770$. Holding constant the effect of league, 47.70% of the variation in number of wins can be explained by the variation in ERA. $r^2_{Y2.1} = 0.0674$. Holding constant the effect of ERA, 6.74% of the variation in number of wins can be explained by the variation in league. **(k)** The slope of the number of wins with ERA is the same, regardless of whether the team belongs to the American League or the National League. **(l)** For X_1X_2: $t_{STAT} = -1.1057 > -2.0555$ the p-value is 0.2790. Do not reject H_0. There is no evidence that the interaction term makes a contribution to the model. **(m)** The model with one independent variable (ERA) should be used.

14.66 The r^2 of the multiple regression is very low, at 0.0645. Only 6.45% of the variation in thickness can be explained by the variation of pressure and temperature. The F test statistic for the combined significant of pressure and temperature is 1.621, with p-value $= 0.2085$. Hence, at a 5% level of significance, there is not enough evidence to conclude that both pressure and temperature affect thickness. The p-value of the t test for the significance of pressure is $0.8307 > 0.05$. Hence, there is insufficient evidence to conclude that pressure affects thickness, holding constant the effect of temperature. The p-value of the t test for the significance of temperature is 0.0820, which is also > 0.05. There is not enough evidence to conclude that temperature affects thickness at the 5% level of significance, holding constant the effect of pressure. Hence, neither pressure nor temperature affects thickness individually.

The normal probability plot does not suggest any potential violation of the normality assumption. The residual plots do not indicate potential violation of the equal variance assumption. The temperature residual plot, however, suggests that there might be a nonlinear relationship between temperature and thickness.

The r^2 of the multiple regression is very low, at 0.0734. Only 7.34% of the variation in thickness can be explained by the variation of pressure, temperature, and the interaction of the two. The F test statistic for the combined significant of pressure and temperature is 1.214, with a p-value of 0.3153. Hence, at a 5% level of significance, there is not enough evidence to conclude that pressure, temperature, and the interaction of the two affect thickness. The p-value of the t test for the significance of pressure, temperature, and the interaction term are 0.5074, 0.4053, and 0.5111, respectively, which are all greater than 5%. Hence, there is insufficient evidence to conclude that pressure, temperature, or the interaction individually affects thickness, holding constant the effect of the other variables.

The pattern in the normal probability plot and residual plots is similar to that in the regression without the interaction term. Hence the article's suggestion that there is a significant interaction between pressure and the temperature in the tank cannot be validated.

CHAPTER 15

15.2 (a) Predicted HOCS is 2.8600, 3.0342, 3.1948, 3.3418, 3.4752, 3.5950, 3.7012, 3.7938, 3.8728, 3.9382, 3.99, 4.0282, 4.0528, 4.0638, 4.0612, 4.045, 4.0152, 3.9718, 3.9148, 3.8442, and 3.76. **(c)** The curvilinear relationship suggests that HOCS increases at a decreasing rate. It reaches its maximum value of 4.0638 at GPA = 3.3 and declines after that as GPA continues to increase. **(d)** An r^2 of 0.07 and an adjusted r^2 of 0.06 tell you that GPA has very low explanatory power in identifying the variation in HOCS. You can tell that the individual HOCS scores are scattered widely around the curvilinear relationship.

15.4 (a) $\hat{Y} = -5.1001 + 21.2942X_1 + 3.9841X_2$, where $X_1 =$ alcohol % and $X_2 =$ carbohydrates. **(b)** $\hat{Y} = 14.1296 + 13.7273X_1 + 4.3922X_2 + 0.6206X_1^2 - 0.0156X_2^2$, where $X_1 =$ alcohol % and $X_2 =$ carbohydrates. **(c)** $F_{STAT} = 8.2152$, with 2 and 123 degrees of freedom. p-value $= 0.0004 < 0.05$, so reject H_0. At the 5% level of significance, the quadratic terms are significant together. Hence, the model in (b) is better. $t_{STAT} = 4.0426$, and the p-value is virtually 0. Reject H_0. There is enough evidence that the quadratic term for alcohol % is significant at the 5% level of significance. $t_{STAT} = -1.1010$, p-value $= 0.2730$. Do not reject H_0. There is not enough evidence that the quadratic term for carbohydrates is significant at the 5% level of significance. The normal probability plot suggests some left-skewness in the errors. However, because of the large sample size, the validity of the results is not seriously impacted. The residual plots of the alcohol percentage and carbohydrates in the quadratic model do not reveal any remaining nonlinearity. **(d)** The number of calories in a beer depends quadratically on the alcohol percentage but linearly on the number of carbohydrates. The alcohol percentage and number of carbohydrates explain about 97.68% of the variation in the number of calories in a beer.

15.6 (b) Predicted yield $= 6.643 + 0.895$ AmtFert $- 0.00411$ AmtFert^2. **(c)** Predicted yield $= 6.643 + 0.895(70) - 0.00411(70)^2 = 49.168$

pounds. **(d)** The model appears to be adequate. **(e)** $F_{STAT} = 157.32 > 4.26$; reject H_0. **(f)** p-value $= 0.0000 < 0.05$, so the model is significant. **(g)** $t_{STAT} = -4.27 < -2.2622$; reject H_0. There is a significant quadratic effect. **(h)** p-value $= 0.002 < 0.05$, so the quadratic term is significant. **(i)** 97.2% of the variation in yield can be explained by the quadratic model. **(j)** 96.6%.

15.8 (a) 215.37. **(b)** For each additional unit of the logarithm of X_1, the logarithm of Y is estimated to increase by 0.9 units, holding all other variables constant. For each additional unit of the logarithm of X_2, the logarithm of Y is estimated to increase by 1.41 units, holding all other variables constant.

15.10 (a) $\hat{Y} = -12.9347 - 15.4674\sqrt{X_1} + 4.8815\sqrt{X_2}$, where $X_1 =$ alcohol % and $X_2 =$ carbohydrates. **(b)** The normal probability plot suggests that the errors are quite normally distributed. The residual plots of the square-root transformation of alcohol percentage and carbohydrates do not reveal any remaining nonlinearity. **(c)** $F_{STAT} = 479.5259$. Because the p-value is virtually 0, reject H_0 at the 5% level of significance. There is evidence of a significant linear relationship between calories and the square root of the percentage of alcohol and the square root of the number of carbohydrates. **(d)** $r^2 = 0.8847$. So 88.47% of the variation in calories can be explained by the variation in the square root of the percentage of alcohol and the square root of the number of carbohydrates. **(e)** Adjusted $r^2 = 0.8828$. **(f)** The model in Problem 15.4 is better because it has a higher r^2.

15.12 (a) Predicted ln(Yield) $= 2.475 + 0.0185$ AmtFert. **(b)** 32.95 pounds. **(c)** A quadratic pattern exists, so the model is not adequate. **(d)** $t_{STAT} = 6.11 > 2.2281$; reject H_0. **(e)** 78.9%. **(f)** 76.8%. **(g)** Choose the model from Problem 15.6. That model has a much higher adjusted r^2 of 96.6%.

15.14 1.25.

15.16 $R_1^2 = 0.64$, $VIF_1 = \dfrac{1}{1 - 0.64} = 2.778$, $R_2^2 = 0.64$, $VIF_2 = \dfrac{1}{1 - 0.64} - 2.778$. There is no evidence of collinearity.

15.18 $VIF = 1.0 < 5$. There is no evidence of collinearity.

15.20 $VIF = 1.0428$. There is no evidence of collinearity.

15.22 (a) 35.04. **(b)** $C_p > 3$. This does not meet the criterion for consideration of a good model.

15.24 Let $Y =$ selling price, $X_1 =$ assessed value, $X_2 =$ time period, and $X_3 =$ whether house was new (0 = no, 1 = yes). Based on a full regression model involving all of the variables, all the VIF values (1.32, 1.04, and 1.31, respectively) are less than 5. There is no reason to suspect the existence of collinearity. Based on a best-subsets regression and examination of the resulting C_p values, the best models appear to be a model with variables X_1 and X_2, which has $C_p = 2.84$, and the full regression model, which has $C_p = 4.0$. Based on a regression analysis with all the original variables, variable X_3 fails to make a significant contribution to the model at the 0.05 level. Thus, the best model is the model using the assessed value (X_1) and time (X_2) as the independent variables. A residual analysis shows no strong patterns. The final model is $\hat{Y} = -120.0483 + 1.7506X_1 + 0.3680X_2$, $r^2 = 0.9430$, $r_{adj}^2 = 0.9388$. Overall significance of the model: $F_{STAT} = 223.4575$, $p < 0.001$. Each independent variable is significant at the 0.05 level.

15.30 (a) An analysis of the linear regression model using PHStat2 with all of the seven possible independent variables reveals that the variable points allowed has $VIF = 5.31 > 5.0$. Based on the procedure recommended in the text, this variable should be deleted from the model. An analysis of the linear regression model with the remaining independent variables indicates that none of the remaining variables have a *VIF* value that is 5.0 or larger. A best-subsets regression produces only one model that has C_p values less than or equal to $k + 1$. That model includes variables X_1, X_2, X_3, X_4, X_5, and X_6. where X_1 = points scored, X_2 = field goal %, X_3 = field goal % allowed, X_4 = turnover difference, X_5 = offensive rebound %, and X_6 = defensive rebound %. Looking at the *p*-values of the *t* statistics for each slope coefficient of the model that includes X_1 through X_6 reveals that offensive rebound % is not significant at the 5% level of significance. The multiple regression model with offensive rebound % deleted shows that all coefficients are significant individually at the 5% level of significance. The best linear model is determined to be

$$\hat{Y} = -16.9427 + 0.7178X_1 + 305.05X_2 - 624.64X_3 - 1.6405X_4 + 181.02X_6.$$

The overall model has $F = 41.5480$ (5 and 24 degrees of freedom) with a *p*-value that is virtually 0. $r^2 = 0.8964$, $r^2_{adj} = 0.8749$. A residual analysis does not reveal any strong patterns. The distribution of the errors appears to be slightly left-skewed. **(b)** An analysis of the linear regression model using PHStat2 with all of the five possible independent variables reveals that none of the variables have *VIF* values in excess of 5.0. A best-subsets regression reveals that the regression models that have C_p values less than or equal to $k + 1$ are X_1, X_2, X_3, and X_5 and X_1, X_2, X_3, X_4, and X_5, where X_1 = point difference, X_2 = field goal % difference, X_3 = turnover difference, X_4 = offensive rebound %, X_5 = defensive rebound %. Analysis of the *p*-value of the slope coefficients for the model that include X_1 through X_5 indicates that turnover difference and offensive rebound % are not significant at the 5% level of significance. Dropping offensive rebound %, which has the highest *p*-value, the new regression again indicates that turnover difference is not significant at the 5% level of significance. Dropping turnover difference, the new regression indicates that defensive rebound is not significant at the 5% level of significance. Dropping defensive rebound, the new regression indicates that all the remaining variables are significant at the 5% level of significance. The best linear model is determined to be

$$\hat{Y} = 40.6289 + 1.9674X_1 + 259.16X_2.$$

$r^2 = 0.9208, r^2_{adj} = 0.9149$. The normal probability plot reveals some left-skewness in the residuals. The residual plot does not reveal any strong patterns. **(c)** The model in (b) with a higher adjusted r^2 of 0.9149 is better than that in (a) in predicting the number of wins.

15.32 (a) Best model: predicted appraised value = 136.794 + 276.0876 land + 0.1288 house size (sq ft) − 1.3989 age.

15.34 (a) Predicted appraised value = 110.27 + 0.0821 house size (sq ft).

15.36 Let Y = appraised value, X_1 = land area, X_2 = interior size, X_3 = age, X_4 = number of rooms, X_5 = number of bathrooms, X_6 = garage size, X_7 = 1 if Glen Cove and 0 otherwise, and X_8 = 1 if Roslyn and 0 otherwise. **(a)** All *VIFs* are less than 5 in a full regression model involving all the variables: There is no reason to suspect collinearity between any pair of variables. The following is the multiple regression model that has the smallest C_p (9.0) and the highest adjusted r^2 (0.891):

Appraised Value = 49.4 + 343 Land (acres) + 0.115 House Size (sq ft) − 0.585 Age − 8.24 Rooms + 26.9 Baths + 5.0 Garage + 56.4 Glen Cove + 210 Roslyn

The individual *t* test for the significance of each independent variable at the 5% level of significance concludes that only X_1, X_2, X_5, X_7, and X_8 are significant individually. This subset, however, is not chosen when the C_p

criterion is used. The following is the multiple regression result for the model chosen by stepwise regression:

Appraised Value = 23.4 + 347 Land (acres) + 0.106 House Size (sq ft) − 0.792 Age + 26.4 Baths + 57.7 Glen Cove + 213 Roslyn

This model has a C_p value of 7.7 and an adjusted r^2 of 89.0. All the variables are significant individually at the 5% level of significance. Combining the stepwise regression and the best-subsets regression results along with the individual *t*-test results, the most appropriate multiple regression model for predicting the appraised value is

$$\hat{Y} = 23.40 + 347.02X_1 + 0.10614X_2 - 0.7921X_3 + 26.38X_5 + 57.74X_7 + 213.46X_8$$

(b) The estimated appraised value in Glen Cove is 57.74 thousand dollars above Freeport for two otherwise identical properties. The estimated appraised value in Roslyn is 213.46 thousand dollars above Freeport for two otherwise identical properties.

15.38 In the multiple regression model with catalyst, pH, pressure, temperature, and voltage as independent variables, none of the variables has a *VIF* value of 5 or larger. The best-subsets approach showed that only the model containing X_1, X_2, X_3, X_4, and X_5 should be considered, where X_1 = catalyst, X_2 = pH, X_3 = pressure, X_4 = temp, and X_5 = voltage. Looking at the *p*-values of the *t* statistics for each slope coefficient of the model that includes X_1 through X_5 reveals that pH level is not significant at the 5% level of significance (*p*-value = 0.2862). The multiple regression model with pH level deleted shows that all coefficients are significant individually at the 5% level of significance. The best linear model is determined to be $\hat{Y} = 3.6833 + 0.1548X_1 - 0.04197X_3 - 0.4036X_4 + 0.4288X_5$. The overall model has $F = 77.0793$ (4 and 45 degrees of freedom), with a *p*-value that is virtually 0. $r^2 = 0.8726$, $r^2_{adj} = 0.8613$. The normal probability plot does not suggest possible violation of the normality assumption. A residual analysis reveals a potential nonlinear relationship in temperature. The *p*-value of the squared term for temperature (0.1273) in the following quadratic transformation of temperature does not support the need for a quadratic transformation at the 5% level of significance. The *p*-value of the interaction term between pressure and temperature (0.0780) indicates that there is not enough evidence of an interaction at the 5% level of significance. The best model is the one that includes catalyst, pressure, temperature, and voltage which explains 87.26% of the variation in thickness.

CHAPTER 16

16.2 (a) 1959. **(b)** The first four years and the last four years.

16.4 (b)–(d)

Year	Attendance	MA(3)	ES(W = 0.5)	ES(W = 0.25)
2001	1.44		1.4400	1.4400
2002	1.60	1.5200	1.5200	1.4800
2003	1.52	1.5333	1.5200	1.4900
2004	1.48	1.4600	1.5000	1.4875
2005	1.38	1.4200	1.4400	1.4606
2006	1.40	1.3933	1.4200	1.4455
2007	1.40	1.3867	1.4100	1.4341
2008	1.36		1.3850	1.4156

(e) A smoothing coefficient of $W = 0.25$ smoothes out the attendance more than $W = 0.50$. The exponential smoothing with $W = 0.50$ assigns more weight to the more recent values and is better for forecasting, while the exponential smoothing with $W = 0.25$, which assigns more weight to more distant values, is better suited for eliminating unwanted cyclical and irregular variations.

16.6 (e) There is no obvious trend during the first 70 trading days in 2009.

16.8 (d) $W = 0.5$: $\hat{Y}_{2009-2010} = E_{2008-2009} = 10.69$ **(e)** $W = 0.25$: $\hat{Y}_{2009-2010} = E_{2009-2010} = 9.89$ **(f)** The exponentially smoothed forecast for 2009–2010 with $W = 0.5$ is higher than that with $W = 0.25$. The exponential smoothing with $W = 0.5$ assigns more weight to the more recent values and is better for forecasting, while the exponential smoothing with $W = 0.25$, which assigns more weight to more distance values, is better suited for eliminating unwanted cyclical and irregular variations.

16.10 (a) The Y intercept $b_0 = 4.0$ is the fitted trend value reflecting the real total revenues (in millions of dollars) during the origin, or base year, 1988. **(b)** The slope $b_1 = 1.5$ indicates that the real total revenues are increasing at an estimated rate of $1.5 million per year. **(c)** Year is 1992, $X = 1992 - 1988 = 4$, $\hat{Y}_5 = 4.0 + 1.5(4) = 10.0$ million dollars. **(d)** Year is 2009, $X = 2009 - 1988 = 21$, $\hat{Y}_{20} = 4.0 + 1.5(21) = 35.5$ million dollars. **(e)** Year is 2012, $X = 2012 - 1988 = 24$, $\hat{Y}_{23} = 4.0 + 1.5(24) = 40$ million dollars.

16.12 (b) Linear trend: $\hat{Y} = -123.0392 + 68.1814X$, where X is relative to 1993. **(c)** Quadratic trend: $\hat{Y} = 12.56450 + 13.9399X + 3.3901X^2$, where X is relative to 1993. **(d)** Exponential trend: $\log_{10}\hat{Y} = 1.6480 + 0.0960X$, where X is relative to 1993. **(e)** Linear trend: $\hat{Y}_{2010} = -123.0392 + 68.1814(17) = 1036.0441 = 1,036$, $\hat{Y}_{2011} = -123.0392 + 68.1814(18) = 1104.2255 = 1,104$. Quadratic trend: $\hat{Y}_{2010} = 12.56450 + 13.9399(17) + 3.3901(17)^2 = 1,229.2794 = 1,229$, $\hat{Y}_{2011} = 12.56450 + 13.9399(18) + 3.3901(18)^2 = 1,361.8725 = 1,362$. Exponential trend: $\hat{Y}_{2010} = 10^{1.6480+0.0960(17)} = 1,908.1609 = 1,908$, $\hat{Y}_{2011} = 10^{1.6480+0.0960(18)} = 2380.3982 = 2,380$. **(f)** The quadratic trend model fits the data better and, hence, its forecast should be used.

16.14 (b) $\hat{Y} = 264.3260 + 70.1970X$, where $X = $ years relative to 1978. **(c)** $X = 2009 - 1978 = 31$, $\hat{Y} = 264.3260 + 70.1970(31) = \$2,440.4323$ billion, $X = 2010 - 1978 = 32$, $\hat{Y} = 264.3260 + 70.1970(32) = \$2,510.6292$ billion. **(d)** There is an upward trend in federal receipts between 1978 and 2008. The trend appears to be nonlinear. A quadratic trend or an exponential trend model could be explored.

16.16 (b) Linear trend: $\hat{Y} = -8.9556 + 28.35X$, where X is relative to 2000. **(c)** Quadratic trend: $\hat{Y} = 23.1152 + 0.8608X + 3.4361X^2$, where X is relative to 2000. **(d)** Exponential trend: $\log_{10}\hat{Y} = 1.3220 + 0.1403X$, where X is relative to 2000. **(e)** Linear trend: $\hat{Y}_{2009} = -8.9556 + 28.35(9) = 246.1944$ megawatts, $\hat{Y}_{2010} = -8.9556 + 28.35(10) = 274.5444$ megawatts. Quadratic trend: $\hat{Y}_{2009} = 23.1152 + 0.8608(9) + 3.4361(9)^2 = 309.1905$ megawatts, $\hat{Y}_{2010} = 23.1152 + 0.8608(10) + 3.4361(10)^2 = 375.3381$ megawatts. Exponential trend: $\hat{Y}_{2009} = 10^{1.3220+0.1403(9)} = 384.1023$ megawatts, $\hat{Y}_{2010} = 10^{1.3220+0.1403(10)} = 530.5360$ megawatts.

16.18 (b) Linear trend: $\hat{Y} = -2.2696 + 2.0685X$, where X is relative to 1987. **(c)** Quadratic trend: $\hat{Y} = -4.0741 + 2.6099X - 0.0258X^2$, where X is relative to 1987. **(d)** Exponential trend: $\log_{10}\hat{Y} = 0.3799 + 0.0679X$, where X is relative to 1987. **(e)** Investigating the first, second, and percentage differences suggests that the linear and quadratic trend models have about the same fit, while the exponential trend model seems to fit the early years' data better. **(f)** Using the exponential trend model, $\hat{Y}_{2009} = 0.3799 + 0.0679(22) = 74.6031$. Using the linear trend model, $\hat{Y}_{2009} = -2.2696 + 2.0685(22) = 43.2382$. Using the quadraatic trend model, $\hat{Y}_{2009} = -4.0741 + 2.6099(22) - 0.0258(22)^2 = 40.8666$. The exponential trend fits the data in the earlier years better than the linear or

quadratic model. However, the economy went into a recession in 2009, and the exponential trend was no longer able to forecast the stock price accurately in 2009. If the trend of the latter years continues, the linear and quadratic models appear to be able to forecast the stock price more accurately in 2009. **(g) (b)** Linear trend: $\hat{Y} = -0.2413 + 1.7788X$, where X is relative to 1987. **(c)** Quadratic trend: $\hat{Y} = -6.2916 + 3.5074X - 0.0786X^2$, where X is relative to 1987. **(d)** Exponential trend: $\log_{10}\hat{Y} = 0.4296 + 0.0608X$, where X is relative to 1987. **(e)** Investigating the first, second, and percentage differences suggests that the linear and quadratic trend models have about the same fit while the exponential trend model seems to fit the early years' data better, while the linear and quadratic trend fit the more recent years' data better. **(h)** For 2010: $X = 2010 - 1987 = 23$. For 2011: $X = 2011 - 1987 = 24$. Using the linear trend model, $\hat{Y}_{2010} = -0.2413 + 1.7788(23) = \$40.67$, $\hat{Y}_{2011} = -0.2413 + 1.7788(24) = \$42.45$. Using the quadratic trend model, $\hat{Y}_{2010} = -6.2916 + 3.5074(23) - 0.0786(23)^2 = \$32.81$, $\hat{Y}_{2011} = -6.2916 + 3.5074(24) - 0.0786(24)^2 = \$32.63$.

16.20 (a) For Time Series I, the graph of Y vs. X appears to be more linear than the graph of $\log Y$ vs. X, so a linear model appears to be more appropriate. For Time Series II, the graph of $\log Y$ vs. X appears to be more linear than the graph of Y vs. X, so an exponential model appears to be more appropriate. **(b)** Time Series I: $\hat{Y} = 100.082 + 14.9752X$, where $X = $ years relative to 1999. Time Series II: $\hat{Y} = 99.704(1.1501)^X$, where $X = $ years relative to 1999. **(c)** Forecasts for 2009: Time Series I: 249.834; Time Series II: 403.709.

16.22 (b) There has been an upward trend in the CPI in the United States over the 44-year period. The rate of increase became faster in the late 1970s but tapered off in the early 1980s. **(c)** Linear trend: $\hat{Y} = 16.4924 + 4.4760X$. **(d)** Quadratic trend: $\hat{Y} = 20.3043 + 3.9315X + 0.0127X^2$. **(e)** Exponential trend: $\log_{10}\hat{Y} = 1.5436 + 0.02036X$. **(f)** The quadratic trend appears to be a better model, according to the narrow spread of the second difference. **(g)** Quadratic trend: For 2009: $\hat{Y}_{2009} = 20.3043 + 3.9315(44) + 0.0127(44)^2 = 217.8072$. For 2010: $\hat{Y}_{2009} = 20.3043 + 3.9315(45) + 0.0127(45)^2 = 222.8658$.

16.24 $t_{STAT} = 2.40 > 2.2281$; reject H_0.

16.26 (a) $t_{STAT} = 1.60 < 2.2281$; do not reject H_0.

16.28 (a) Because p-value $= 0.8778 > 0.05$ level of significance, the third-order term can be dropped **(b)** Because the p-value is virtually 0 and is less than the 0.05 level of significance, the second-order term cannot be dropped. **(c)** It is not necessary to fit a first-order regression. **(d)** The most appropriate model for forecasting is the second-order autoregressive model: $\hat{Y}_{2010} = 13.7690 + 1.9832Y_{2009} - 1.0087Y_{2008} = 1,090.9094 = 1,091$ stores. $\hat{Y}_{2011} = 13.7690 + 1.9832Y_{2010} - 1.0087\hat{Y}_{2009} = 1,131.2491 = 1,131$ stores.

16.30 (a) Because p-value $= 0.5954 > 0.05$ level of significance, the third-order term can be dropped. **(b)** Because p-value $= 0.1386 > 0.05$ level of significance, the second-order term can be dropped. **(c)** Because the p-value is virtually 0, the first-order term cannot be dropped. **(d)** The most appropriate model for forecasting is the first-order autoregressive model: $\hat{Y}_{2009} = 3.0339 + 0.9186Y_{2008} = \$34.16$. The forecast was not very accurate. GE's stock price experienced a big drop in 2008. The autoregressive model is not very good at forecasting such dramatic deviation from the usual trend. **(e) (a)** Because p-value $= 0.6139 > 0.05$ level of significance, the third-order term can be dropped. **(b)** Because p-value $= 0.0691 > 0.05$ level of significance, the second-order term can be dropped. **(c)** Because the p-value is virtually 0, the first-order term cannot be dropped. **(f)** The most appropriate model for forecasting is the first-order autoregressive model: $\hat{Y}_{2010} = 3.2378 + 0.8670Y_{2009} = \$17.61$ $\hat{Y}_{2011} = 3.2378 + 0.8670\hat{Y}_{2010} = \$18.51$.

16.32 (a) 2.121. **(b)** 1.515.

16.34 (a) The residuals in the linear trend model show strings of consecutive positive and negative values. **(b)** $S_{YX} = 519.2116$. **(c)** $MAD = 427.4790$. **(d)** The residuals in the linear trend model show strings of consecutive positive and negative values. The linear trend model is inadequate in capturing the nonlinear trend.

16.36 (b), (c)

	Linear	Quadratic	Exponential	Second-Order Aotoregressive
SSE	107,418.6961	18,327.0552	362,244.4713	2,094.3191
S_{YX}	84.6241	36.1811	155.4015	13.2109
MAD	68.1315	28.1827	82.2738	8.4443

(d) The residuals in the three trend models show strings of consecutive positive and negative values. The autoregressive model performs well for the historical data and has a fairly random pattern of residuals. The autoregressive model also has the smallest values in MAD and S_{YX}. Based on the principle of parsimony, the autoregressive model would be the best model for forecasting.

16.38 (b), (c)

	Linear	Quadratic	Exponential	First-Order Aotoregressive
SSE	1,130.3499	1,111.5207	2,971.8765	642.6098
S_{YX}	7.5178	7.64860	12.1899	5.8156
MAD	5.3475	5.4482	7.4636	4.0881

(d) The residuals in the linear, quadratic, and exponential trend models show strings of consecutive positive and negative values. The autoregressive model performs well for the historical data and has a fairly random pattern of residuals. The autoregressive model also has the smallest values in MAD and S_{YX}. Based on the principle of parsimony, the autoregressive model would be the best model for forecasting.

16.40 (a) $\log \hat{\beta}_0 = 2$, $\hat{\beta}_0 = 10^2 = 100$. This is the fitted value for January 2005 prior to adjustment with the January multiplier. **(b)** $\log \hat{\beta}_1 = 0.01$, $\hat{\beta}_1 = 10^{0.01} = 1.0233$. The estimated monthly compound growth rate is 2.33%. **(c)** $\log \hat{\beta}_2 = 0.1$, $\hat{\beta}_2 = 10^{0.1} = 1.2589$. The January values in the time series are estimated to have a mean 25.89% higher than the December values.

16.42 (a) $\log \hat{\beta}_0 = 3.0$, $\hat{\beta}_0 = 10^{3.0} = 1,000$. This is the fitted value for the first quarter of 2005 prior to adjustment by the quarterly multiplier. **(b)** $\log \hat{\beta}_1 = 0.1$, $\hat{\beta}_1 = 10^{0.1} = 1.2589$. The estimated quarterly compound growth rate is $(\hat{\beta}_1 - 1)100\% = 25.89\%$. **(c)** $\log \hat{\beta}_3 = 0.2$, $\hat{\beta}_3 = 10^{0.2} = 1.5849$.

16.44 (a) The retail industry is heavily subject to seasonal variation due to the holiday season, and so are the revenues for Toys R Us. **(b)** There is an obvious seasonal effect in the time series. **(c)** $\log_{10} \hat{Y} = 3.6210 + 0.0030X - 0.3669Q_1 - 0.3715Q_2 - 0.3445Q_3$. **(d)** $\log_{10} \hat{\beta}_1 = 0.0030$. $\hat{\beta}_1 = 10^{0.0030} = 1.0069$. The estimated quarterly compound growth rate is $(\hat{\beta}_1 - 1)100\% = 0.69\%$. **(e)** $\log_{10} \hat{\beta}_2 = -0.3669$. $\hat{\beta}_2 = 10^{-0.3669} = 0.4296$. $(\hat{\beta}_2 - 1)100\% = -57.0391\%$. The first-quarter values in the time series are estimated to be 57.04% below the fourth-quarter values. $\log_{10}\hat{\beta}_3 = -0.3715$. $\hat{\beta}_3 = 10^{-0.3715} = 0.4251$. $(\hat{\beta}_3 - 1)100\% = 57.49\%$. The second-quarter values in the time series are estimated to be 57.49% below the fourth-quarter values. $\log_{10}\hat{\beta}_4 = -0.3445$. $\hat{\beta} = 10^{-0.3445} = 0.4523$. $(\hat{\beta}_4 - 1)100\% = 54.77\%$. The third-quarter

values in the time series are estimated to be 54.77% below the fourth-quarter values. **(f)** Forecasts for 2009: $\hat{Y}_{53} = \$2,560.7240$ millions; $\hat{Y}_{54} = \$2,551.4693$ millions; $\hat{Y}_{55} = \$2,733.2744$ millions; $\hat{Y}_{56} = \$6,084.0383$ millions.

16.46 (b) $\log \hat{Y} = 0.745429583 - 0.000184347$ coded month $- 0.000556223$ M1 $+ 0.003933405$ M2 $+ 005520611$ M3 $+ 0.00919183$ M4 $- 0.015077279$ M5 $- 0.011638476$ M6 $- 0.007412815$ M7 $- 0.008876687$ M8 $- 0.007544616$ M9 $- 0.008440585$ M10 $- 0.00396577$ M11. **(c)** $\hat{Y}_{88} = 5.4775\%$. **(d)** Forecasts for the last eight months of 2009 are May: 5.1776, June: 5.2166, July: 5.2653, August: 5.2454, September: 5.2593, October: 5.2462, November: 5.2983, and December: 5.3446. **(e)** $\log_{10}\hat{\beta}_1 = -0.0001843$; $\hat{\beta}_1 = 10^{-0.0001843} = 0.9996$. The estimated monthly compound growth rate is $(\hat{\beta}_1 - 1)100\% = -0.0424$. **(f)** $\log_{10}\hat{\beta}_8 = -0.007413$; $\hat{\beta}_8 = 10^{-0.007413} = 0.9831$. $(\hat{\beta}_8 - 1)100\% = -1.6924\%$. The July values in the time series are estimated to be 1.69% below the December values.

16.48 (b) $\log \hat{Y} = 3.078946516 + 0.0000538372$ coded quarter $- 0.014136971$ Q1 $+ 0.006152678$ Q2 $- 0.015395325$ Q3. **(c)** $\log_{10} \hat{\beta}_1 = 5.38372(10)^{-05}$; $\hat{\beta}_1 = 10^{5.38372(10)^{-05}} = 1.0001240$; $(\hat{\beta}_1 - 1)100\% = 0.01240\%$ The estimated *quarterly* compound growth rate in the S&P Composite Stock Price Index is 0.0124%, after adjusting for the seasonal component. **(d)** $\log_{10}\hat{\beta}_2 = -0.01414$, $\hat{\beta}_2 = 10^{-0.01414} = 0.9680$, $(\hat{\beta}_2 - 1)100\% = 0.032027$. The first-quarter values in the time series are estimated to be 3.2027% below the fourth-quarter values. **(e)** First quarter, 2009: $\hat{Y}_{44} = 1167.2890$. **(f)** 2009: Second quarter: 1,223.2687, third quarter: 1,164.2003, fourth quarter: 1,206.3598. **(g)** The forecasts in (f) were not accurate because the S&P Index experienced a drastic decline in 2009, and the exponential trend model was not very good at picking up this drastic decline.

16.60 (b) Linear trend: $\hat{Y} = 174,246.8308 + 2,408.3608X$, where X is relative to 1984.

(c)

2009: $\hat{Y}_{2009} = 174,246.8308 + 2,408.3608(25) = 234,455.85$ *thousands*

2010: $\hat{Y}_{2010} = 174246.8308 + 2408.3608(26) = 236,864.2108$ *thousands*

(d) Linear trend: $\hat{Y} = 114542.0985 + 1673.7185X$, where X is relative to 1984.

(c)

2009: $\hat{Y}_{2009} = 114,542.0985 + 1,673.7185(25) = 156,385.06$ thousands

2010: $\hat{Y}_{2010} = 114,542.0985 + 1,673.7185(26) = 158,058.7785$ thousands

16.62 (b) Linear trend: $\hat{Y} = -1.9255 + 0.6627X$, where X is relative to 1975. **(c)** Quadratic trend: $\hat{Y} = 1.4309 + 0.0334X + 0.0191X^2$, where X is relative to 1975. **(d)** Exponential trend: $\log_{10}\hat{Y} = 0.1474 + 0.0397X$, where X is relative to 1975. **(e)** AR(3): $\hat{Y}_i = 0.2624 + 1.1371Y_{i-1} - 0.3443Y_{i-2} + 0.2704Y_{i-3}$ Test of A_3: p-value $= 0.2489 > 0.05$. Do not reject H_0 that $A_3 = 0$. Third-order term can be deleted. AR(2): $\hat{Y}_i = 0.2178 + 1.0990Y_{i-1} - 0.0483Y_{i-2}$ Test of A_2: p-value $= 0.8265 > 0.05$. Do not reject H_0 that $A_2 = 0$. Second-order term can be deleted. AR(1): $\hat{Y}_i = 0.2179 + 1.0541Y_{i-1}$ Test of A_1: p-value is virtually 0. Reject H_0 that $A_1 = 0$. A first-order autoregressive model is appropriate.

(g)

	Linear	Quadratic	Exponential	First-Order Aotoregressive
SSE	96.3067	4.9008	69.3350	3.8091
S_{YX}	1.7348	0.3976	1.4720	0.3505
MAD	1.4253	0.2851	0.9226	0.2336

(h) The residuals in the first three models show strings of consecutive positive and negative values. The autoregressive model performs well for the historical data and has a fairly random pattern of residuals. It also has the smallest values in the standard error of the estimate, MAD, and SSE. Based on the principle of parsimony, the autoregressive model would probably be the best model for forecasting. **(i)** $\hat{Y}_{2009} = 0.2179 + 1.0541Y_{2008} = 24.9901$ billions.

16.64 (b) Variable A: $\hat{Y} = 12.0615 + 2.3581X$, where X = years relative to 1984. Variable B: $\hat{Y} = 12.2201 + 0.3676X$, where X = years relative to 1984. **(c)** Variable A: $\hat{Y} = 4.9605 + 4.1334X - 0.0710X^2$, where X = years relative to 1984. Variable B: $\hat{Y} = 10.2300 + 0.8651X - 0.01990X^2$, where X = years relative to 1984. **(d)** Variable A: $\log_{10}\hat{Y} = 1.1911 + 0.02931X$, where X = years relative to 1984. Variable B: $\log_{10}\hat{Y} = 1.0901 + 0.01025X$, where X = years relative to 1984. **(e)** Variable A: AR(3): Test of A_3: p-value = 0.5202 > 0.05. Do not reject H_0 that $A_3 = 0$. Third-order term can be deleted. AR(2): Test of A_2: p-value = 0.2195 > 0.05. Do not reject H_0 that $A_2 = 0$. Second-order term can be deleted. AR(1): Test of A_1: p-value is virtually 0. Reject H_0 that $A_1 = 0$. A first-order autoregressive model is appropriate. Variable B: AR(3): Test of A_3: p-value = 0.0779 > 0.05. Do not reject H_0 that $A_3 = 0$. Third-order term can be deleted. AR(2): Test of A_2: p-value is virtually 0. Reject H_0 that $A_2 = 0$. A second-order autoregressive model is appropriate. **(f)–(h)** Variable A:

	Linear	Quadratic	Exponential	First-Order Autoregressive
SSE	2408.2830	2077.8978	3999.1056	1655.6040
S_{YX}	10.0172	9.5049	12.9085	8.4843
MAD	6.2165	7.0157	7.7257	6.0903

Variable B:

	Linear	Quadratic	Exponential	Second-Order Autoregressive
SSE	26.3216	0.3734	40.8356	0.1500
S_{YX}	1.0472	0.1274	1.3044	0.0845
MAD	0.8848	0.0941	1.0893	0.0648

Variable A: The residuals in three trend models show strings of consecutive positive and negative values. There is no apparent pattern in the residuals of the autoregressive AR(1) model. The autoregressive model has the smallest values in the standard error of the estimate and MAD. Based on the principle of parsimony, the autoregressive model would probably be the best model for forecasting. Variable B: The residuals in the linear and exponential trend models show strings of consecutive positive and negative values. There is no apparent pattern in the residuals of the quadratic trend and autoregressive AR(2) model. The autoregressive model AR(2) has the smallest values in the standard error of the estimate and MAD. Based on the principle of parsimony, the autoregressive model would probably be the best model for forecasting. **(i)** Variable A: $\hat{Y}_{2009} = 6.4186 + 0.8737Y_{2008} = 43.5428$. Variable B: $\hat{Y}_{2009} = 0.6718 + 1.6354Y_{2008} - 0.6694Y_{2007} = 19.5081$. **(j)** You would recommend Variable A, which consists of investments that are primarily made in stocks, for a member of Teachers' Retirement System of New York City because it had a higher return than Variable B over the past 24-year period.

CHAPTER 17

17.2 (a) Day 4, Day 3. **(b)** LCL = 0.0397, UCL = 0.2460. **(c)** No, proportions are within control limits.

17.4 (a) $n = 500, \bar{p} = 761/16,000 = 0.0476$.

$$UCL = \bar{p} + 3\sqrt{\frac{\bar{p}(1 - \bar{p})}{n}}$$

$$= 0.0476 + 3\sqrt{\frac{0.0476(1 - 0.0476)}{500}} = 0.0761$$

$$LCL = \bar{p} - 3\sqrt{\frac{\bar{p}(1 - \bar{p})}{n}}$$

$$= 0.0476 - 3\sqrt{\frac{0.0476(1 - 0.0476)}{500}} = 0.0190$$

(b) Because the individual points are distributed around $\bar{p}$ without any pattern and all the points are within the control limits, the process is in a state of statistical control.

17.6 (a) UCL = 0.0176, LCL = 0.0082. The proportion of unacceptable cans is below the LCL on Day 4. There is evidence of a pattern over time because the last eight points are all above the mean, and most of the earlier points are below the mean. Therefore, this process is out of control.

17.8 (a) UCL = 0.1431, LCL = 0.0752. Days 9, 26, and 30 are above the UCL. Therefore, this process is out of control.

17.12 (a) UCL = 21.6735, LCL = 1.3265. **(b)** Yes, time 1 is above the UCL.

17.14 (a) The 12 errors committed by Gina appear to be much higher than all others, and Gina would need to explain her performance. **(b)** $\bar{c} = 66/12 = 5.5$, UCL = 12.5356, LCL does not exist. The number of errors is in a state of statistical control because none of the tellers is outside the UCL. **(c)** Because Gina is within the control limits, she is operating within the system and should not be singled out for further scrutiny. **(d)** The process needs to be studied and potentially changed, using principles of Six Sigma and/or total quality management.

17.16 (a) $\bar{c} = 3.0566$. **(b)** LCL does not exist, UCL = 8.3015. **(c)** There are no weeks outside the control limits. Therefore, this process is in control. Note, however that the first eight weeks are below the mean. **(d)** Because these weeks are within the control limits, the results are explainable by common cause variation.

17.18 (a) $d_2 = 2.059$. **(b)** $d_3 = 0.880$. **(c)** $D_3 = 0$. **(d)** $D_4 = 2.282$. **(e)** $A_2 = 0.729$.

17.20 (a) $\bar{R} = 0.247$, R chart: UCL = 0.636; LCL does not exist. **(b)** According to the R chart, the process appears to be in control, with all points lying inside the control limits, without any pattern and no evidence of special cause variation. **(c)** $\bar{\bar{X}} = 47.998$, $\bar{X}$ chart: UCL = 48.2507; LCL = 47.7453. **(d)** According to the $\bar{X}$ chart, the process appears to be in control, with all points lying inside the control limits, without any pattern and no evidence of special cause variation.

17.22 (a) $\bar{R} = \dfrac{\sum_{i=1}^{k} R_i}{k} = 3.275, \bar{\bar{X}} = \dfrac{\sum_{i=1}^{k} \bar{X}_i}{k} = 5.941$. R chart: $UCL = D_4\bar{R} = 2.282(3.275) = 7.4736$. LCL does not exist. $\bar{X}$ chart: $UCL = \bar{\bar{X}} + A_2\bar{R} = 5.9413 + 0.729(3.275) = 8.3287$. $LCL = \bar{\bar{X}} - A_2\bar{R} = 5.9413 - 0.729(3.275) = 3.5538$. **(b)** The process appears to be in control because there are no points outside the control limits, there is no evidence of a pattern in the range chart, there are no points outside the control limits, and there is no evidence of a pattern in the $\bar{X}$ chart.

17.24 (a) $\bar{R} = 0.8794$, LCL does not exist, UCL = 2.0068. **(b)** $\bar{\bar{X}} = 20.1065$, LCL = 19.4654, UCL = 20.7475. **(c)** The process is in control.

17.26 (a) $\bar{R} = 8.145$, LCL does not exist, UCL = 18.5869; $\bar{\bar{X}} = 18.12$, UCL = 24.0577, LCL = 12.1823. **(b)** There are no sample ranges outside the control limits, and there does not appear to be a pattern in the range chart. The mean is above the UCL on Day 15 and below the LCL on Day 16. Therefore, the process is not in control.

17.28 (a) $\bar{R} = 0.3022$, LCL does not exist, UCL $= 0.6389$; $\bar{\bar{X}} = 90.1312$, UCL $= 90.3060$, LCL $= 89.9573$. **(b)** On Days 5 and 6, the sample ranges were above the UCL. The mean chart may be erroneous because the range is out of control. The process is out of control.

17.30 (a) $P(98 < X < 102) = P(-1 < Z < 1) = 0.6826$. **(b)** $P(93 < X < 107.5) = P(-3.5 < Z < 3.75) = 0.99968$. **(c)** $P(X > 93.8) = P(Z > -3.1) = 0.99903$. **(d)** $P(X < 110) = P(Z < 5) = 0.999999713$.

17.32 (a) $P(18 < X < 22)$

$$= P\left(\frac{18 - 20.1065}{0.8794/2.059} < Z < \frac{22 - 20.1065}{0.8794/2.059}\right)$$

$$= P(-4.932 < Z < 4.4335) = 0.9999$$

(b)

$$C_p = \frac{(USL - LSL)}{6(\bar{R}/d_2)} = \frac{(22 - 18)}{6(0.8794/2.059)}$$

$$= 1.56$$

$$CPL = \frac{(\bar{\bar{X}} - LSL)}{3(\bar{R}/d_2)} = \frac{(20.1065 - 18)}{3(0.8794/2.059)}$$

$$= 1.644$$

$$CPU = \frac{(USL - \bar{\bar{X}})}{3(\bar{R}/d_2)} = \frac{22 - 20.1065}{3(0.8794/2.059)}$$

$$= 1.477$$

$$C_{pk} = \min(CPL, CPU) = 1.477$$

17.34 $\bar{R} = 0.2248$, $\bar{\bar{X}} = 5.509$, $n = 4$, $d_2 = 2.059$. **(a)** $P(5.2 < X < 5.8) = P(-2.83 < Z < 2.67) = 0.9962 - 0.0023 = 0.9939$. **(b)** Because only 99.39% of the tea bags are within the specification limits, this process is not capable of meeting the goal of 99.7%.

17.46 (a) The main reason that service quality is lower than product quality is because the former involves human interaction, which is prone to variation. Also, the most critical aspects of a service are often timeliness and professionalism, and customers can always perceive that the service could be done more quickly and with greater professionalism. For products, customers often cannot perceive a better or more ideal

product than the one they are getting. For example, a new laptop is better and contains more interesting features than any laptop the owner has ever imagined. **(b)** Both services and products are the results of processes. However, measuring services is often harder because of the dynamic variation due to the human interaction between the service provider and the customer. Product quality is often a straightforward measurement of a static physical characteristic such as the amount of sugar in a can of soda. Categorical data are also more common in service quality. **(c)** Yes. **(d)** Yes.

17.48 (a) $\bar{p} = 0.2702$, LCL $= 0.1700$, UCL $= 0.3703$. **(b)** Yes, RudyBird's market share is in control before the in-store promotion. **(c)** All seven days of the in-store promotion are above the UCL. The promotion increased market share.

17.50 (a) $\bar{p} = 0.75175$, LCL $= 0.62215$, UCL $= 0.88135$. Although none of the points are outside the control limits, there is a clear pattern over time, with the last 13 points above the center line. Therefore, this process is not in control. **(b)** Because the increasing trend begins around Day 20, this change in method would be the assignable cause. **(c)** The control chart would have been developed using the first 20 days, and then a different control chart would be used for the final 20 points because they represent a different process.

17.52 (a) $\bar{p} = 0.1198$, LCL $= 0.0205$, UCL $= 0.2191$. **(b)** Day 24 is below the LCL; therefore, the process is out of control. **(c)** Special causes of variation should be investigated to improve the process. Next, the process should be improved to decrease the proportion of undesirable trades.

17.54 Separate p charts should be developed for each food for each shift:

Kidney—Shift 1: $\bar{p} = 0.01395$, UCL $= 0.02678$, LCL $= 0.00112$. Although there are no points outside the control limits, there is a strong increasing trend in nonconformances over time.

Kidney—Shift 2: $\bar{p} = 0.01829$, UCL $= 0.03329$, LCL $= 0.00329$. Although there are no points outside the control limits, there is a strong increasing trend in nonconformances over time.

Shrimp—Shift 1: $\bar{p} = 0.006995$, UCL $= 0.01569$, LCL $= 0$. There are no points outside the control limits, and there is no pattern over time.

Shrimp—Shift 2: $\bar{p} = 0.01023$, UCL $= 0.021$, LCL $= 0$. There are no points outside the control limits, and there is no pattern over time.

The team needs to determine the reasons for the increase in nonconformances for the kidney product. The production volume for kidney is clearly decreasing for both shifts. This can be observed from a plot of the production volume over time. The team needs to investigate the reasons for this.

Index